ETHICS IN THE WORKPLACE
SELECTED READINGS IN BUSINESS ETHICS

Robert A. Larmer
University of New Brunswick

West Publishing Company
Minneapolis/St. Paul   New York   Los Angeles   San Francisco

Cover Image: Stephen Simpson/FPG International

Composition: Carlisle Communications, Ltd.

WEST'S COMMITMENT TO THE ENVIRONMENT

In 1906, West Publishing Company began recycling materials left
over from the production of books. This began a tradition of
efficient and responsible use of resources. Today, 100% of our
legal bound volumes are printed on acid-free, recycled paper consisting
of 50% new paper pulp and 50% paper than has undergone a de-inking
process. We also use vegetable-based inks to print all of our
books. West recycles nearly 27,700,000 pounds of scrap paper
annually—the equivalent of 229,300 trees. Since the 1960s, West
has devised ways to capture and recycle waste inks, solvents, oils,
and vapors created in the printing process. We also recycle plastics
of all kinds, wood, glass, corrugated carboard, and batteries, and
have eliminated the use of polystyrene book packaging. We at West are
proud of the longevity and the scope of our commitment to the environment.

West pocket parts and advance sheets are printed on recyclable paper and
can be collected and recycled with newspapers. Staples do not have to be
removed. Bound volumes can be recycled after removing the cover.

Production, Prepress, Printing and Binding by West Publishing Company.

 TEXT IS PRINTED ON 10% POST CONSUMER RECYCLED PAPER

 Printed with **Printwise** Environmentally Advanced Water Washable Ink

British Library Cataloguing-in-Publication Data. A catalogue
record for this book is available from the British Library.

COPYRIGHT © 1996   By WEST PUBLISHING COMPANY
                     610 Opperman Drive
                     P.O. Box 64526
                     St. Paul, MN 55164-0526

Printed in the United States of America

03 02 01 00 99 98 97 96   8 7 6 5 4 3 2 1 0

Library of Congress Cataloging-in-Publication Data

Ethics in the workplace : selected readings in business ethics /
   [compiled by] Robert A. Larmer.
       p.   cm.
   Includes bibliographical references.
   ISBN 0-314-06802-3 (pbk. : alk. paper)
   1. Business ethics.   I. Larmer, Robert A. H., 1954
HF5387.E848 1996
174'.4--dc20
                                                    95-45562
                                                        CIP

To my father, J. Robert Larmer,
with whom I have worked many happy hours.

CONTENTS

Chapter Fifteen
Business and the Family   473

Chapter Sixteen
Business and the Community   510

Chapter Seventeen
Business and the International Community   536

Chapter Eighteen
Business and the Environment   573

PREFACE

Ethics in the Workplace is intended to provide an introduction to the field of business ethics for both upper- and lower-division undergraduate students. It aims to present, through a series of readings, a reasonably comprehensive examination of the major ethical issues associated with business and the professions.

Organizationally, I begin by demonstrating the relevance of moral theory to business and then structure the practical discussions so that they lead to widening spheres of moral relevance. A major goal in organizing the text in this manner is to help students realize that ethical problems typically intertwine and must be dealt with at both individual and societal levels. Part I explores the relation of morality to business and introduces the major ethical theories. Part II examines the ethical issues arising from the employer/employee relationship. Part III focuses on the relationship between business and the consumer and Part IV examines the relationship between business and society.

Throughout the text I have attempted to present articles that are readily accessible to the non-specialist, yet reflect the increasing philosophical sophistication of work in this area. In recognition of the fact that students using this text will often have little or no acquaintance with philosophy, I have sought to make the acquisition of the tools of the trade a little easier by providing brief introductions to the articles found within each chapter. I have also included case studies, review questions, and suggestions for further reading at the end of each chapter. In addition, I have included appendices providing sample summaries, advice on writing article summaries and critical essays and an explanation of Latin terms commonly used in philosophical discussions.

An instructor's manual is also available. In it I have provided sample summaries for each chapter of the text and the outcomes of the legal cases discussed. I have also included further cases to supplement those given at the end of each chapter.

Several expressions of gratitude are appropriate. David Tonen from West Publishing encouraged me to propose a text in the area of business ethics and Clark Baxter, Linda Poirier, and Deb Meyer at West have provided valuable editorial guidance. Further thanks are due to the following reviewers who read earlier drafts and provided a great deal of constructive criticism: Gary Cox, SUNY/Geneseo; David B. Fletcher, Wheaton College; Norris Frederick, Queens College; Geoffrey P. Lantos, Stonehill College; Richard N. Lee, University of Arkansas; Anne M. McCarthy, Indiana University; Marcia A. McKelligan, DePauw University; Peter J. Mehl, University of Central Arkansas; Steven K. Paulson, University of North Florida; Lena B. Prewitt, University of Alabama; Doran Smolkin, Kansas State University; Peter K. Steinfeld, Buena Vista College. I would also like to thank Ann Pugh of the University of New Brunswick Philosophy Department for her willingness to provide secretarial services above and beyond the call of duty. Most of all I would like to thank my wife Lorena Henry for her love and support.

My hope is that the enjoyment and intellectual challenge I have found in selecting and preparing these readings will be shared by students and instructors and that the material I have chosen will prove useful to those endeavoring to act ethically in the workplace.

Robert A. Larmer

Introduction: Philosophy, Ethics and Business

Why study ethics?

In writing this introduction, I have been reminded of the old joke about the millipede who was asked to describe the process of walking. After giving the question considerable thought, the millipede was unable to ever walk again. The point is that it is one thing to engage in an activity and quite another to give an accurate description of it. Plato long ago reminded his readers that a courageous person may give an inadequate account of what courage is. Similarly, there are many people who are highly ethical, but have little acquaintance with moral theory. It is also true that it is far better actually to be ethical than simply to be able to give an account of morality.

Nevertheless, it is important to reflect on what it means to be ethical. Unlike the millipede's walking, which demands no theoretical knowledge on the part of the millipede, attempts to be ethical pose practical problems that can only be addressed by appealing to ethical theory. A person may hold an ethical theory consciously, or, as is often the case, subconsciously, but it influences decision making. The person who claims that it would have been morally permissible to assassinate Hitler if that would have shortened the World War II and saved many lives, may not realize that she is appealing to what ethicists call the Principle of Utility, but it is nonetheless a theoretical belief that influences her ethical practice. The advantage of making implicit theoretical beliefs explicit is that we can then examine them in order to determine how they fit with other beliefs we hold and whether we should modify or abandon them altogether.

Making ethical theory explicit is valuable insofar as it helps persons who want to act morally to evaluate their experience and to assess situations they find ethically perplexing. Ethical theory does not by itself, however, produce moral individuals. Understanding this enables us to avoid the easy assumption that taking a course in ethical theory will develop moral character. Aristotle long ago warned that people often

> take refuge in theory and think they are being philosophers and will become good in this way, behaving . . . like patients who listen attentively to their doctors, but do none of the things they are ordered to do. As the latter will not be made well in body by such a course of treatment, the former will not be made well in soul by such a course of philosophy.[1]

In popular slang, his point could be put as "You can't just talk the talk, you gotta walk the walk."

A Brief Introduction To Philosophy

It is impossible to discuss ethical theory in any kind of systematic way without at least a nodding acquaintance with philosophy. Unfortunately, those who have never studied philosophy often think of it as a somewhat mysterious discipline. There is a tendency on the part of many to think of philosophy as especially profound or especially silly, or sometimes both. We have a curious respect for philosophers, but we often also picture them as rather strange individuals who have trouble dealing with the practical realities of life. Nor is this a particularly recent view. Thales, a Greek who lived in the sixth century B.C. and is generally given the title of being the first philosopher, was said to have fallen down a well while trying to observe the stars. Although the story is probably not true, it does illustrate the long history of this view of philosophers.

No doubt part of this ambivalence toward philosophy results from the fact that philosophers study important questions, but what they say in response to these questions is sometimes disturbing. We respect them for inquiring into difficult issues, but we sometimes fear that we may not be entirely comfortable with what they might tell us. Add to this the sneaking suspicion that, although a lot of intellectual horsepower is being expended, it is not easy or sometimes even possible to connect the abstractions of philosophers to the workaday world, and it becomes understandable why many people have mixed feelings towards philosophy.

It must be emphasized, however, that philosophy is not unique in these respects. All disciplines have implications for the important issues of our lives and it is possible in all disciplines for intelligent persons to expend a lot of time and energy, yet reach incorrect conclusions. Nor is philosophy unique in the sense that it can lose touch with the practicalities of everyday life. It is true that philosophical discussions can become quite esoteric, but then so can a good number of scientific discussions. It may be no easy matter to follow a philosophical discussion of the morality of whistleblowing, but I suspect it is less difficult to understand than a scientific discussion of "quaternary history of upwelling, paleoproductivity and the oxygen minimum on the Oman margin."[2] At the very least, it is less clear that this particular scientific discussion is more relevant to the practicalities of life than a philosophic discussion of whistleblowing.

Many people might grant the point I have just made, namely that disciplines other than philosophy run the risk of becoming so abstract as to lose touch with reality, but they would suggest that philosophy is more apt to fall into this trap than most. The view that the sciences are much more tough-minded than the humanities, that the standards of what constitute good science are clear and concrete, whereas the standards in the arts and especially in philosophy are obscure and soft, is a common one even among academics.

Space does not permit a lengthy discussion but I think this view can be shown to be badly mistaken. In the present context, it is enough to observe that many of the specialized disciplines we now distinguish from philosophy were in the past considered to be part of it. Psychology, political science, physics, chemistry, and biology were all at one time included in the discipline of philosophy. These disciplines are no longer considered part of philosophy, not because philosophers have no interest in these areas or that philosophical questions are not relevant to them, but because the accumulation of knowledge and the development of sophisticated and specialized techniques for studying their subject matter has made it necessary for them to develop into independent areas of study. For these disciplines to be contemptuous of philosophy is like someone insulting the sexual morality and childrearing practices of his parents; it does not reflect well on one's own origin and history.[3]

With regard to gaining an initial understanding of what philosophy is and what philosophers do, we can begin by noting that the word "philosophy" comes from two Greek words *philo* and *sophia*, meaning love and wisdom respectively. Philosophy, then, means love of wisdom, and a philosopher is presumably, a lover of wisdom. It is noteworthy in the context of our present discussion, that for the ancient Greeks who began western philosophy, wisdom was understood not only to include knowledge, but the practice of virtue.

Philosophers are typically interested in four inter-related areas of study. These are:

1. logic, the study of correct methods of reasoning,
2. metaphysics, the study of what it is that exists,
3. epistemology, the study of how that which exists is known, and
4. axiology, which includes ethics, the study of what is good, and aesthetics, the study of what is beautiful.

That these four areas cover, in one way or another, all of reality reveals that philosophy is what we might call an interdisciplinary discipline. Not only do various disciplines such as history, biology, sociology, and business administration, to name only a few, raise particular issues that are of importance for the pursuit of wisdom and hence philosophy, but they have foundations that are, in the final analysis, philosophical.

Ethical Theory and Its Application to Business

At its most general level, ethical inquiry is an attempt to comprehend the foundations of value and to systematize the principles of correct moral reasoning. Built into the ethical endeavor of determining what is of value is the view that people ought to pursue that which is valuable. Although for purposes of convenience we often treat ethical questions independently of questions of logic, metaphysics, and epistemology, it is clear that in the long run these questions are intricately interwoven. Questions of what is of value can scarcely be answered independently of answering logical questions concerning what constitutes correct reasoning, metaphysical questions concerning what is real, and epistemological questions concerning how we come to know. All inquiry must begin somewhere, however, and it would be a mistake to insist that we cannot begin to study ethics until we have studied logic, metaphysics, and epistemology. Nevertheless, if we are wise we will realize that the more we study any branch of philosophy the more its interconnectedness with other branches of philosophy will emerge.

Business ethics involves the practical application of ethical theory. We are familiar with the idea that an engineer wanting to build a bridge must know the principles of physics and chemistry and then creatively apply them to the situation at hand. We are also familiar with the fact that although there may be many different ways of applying these principles so as to produce a satisfactory bridge, it is not the case that

"anything goes." One cannot ignore the principles governing the design of bridges and expect a good result. Similarly, if one wishes to create an ethical company one must know the principles of ethics and creatively apply them to the situation at hand. There may be many different ways of applying these principles to produce an ethical company, but, as in bridge-building, it is emphatically not the case that "anything goes." One can no more ignore ethical principles and expect a moral company than one can ignore the principles of physics and expect a safe bridge.

I have been developing an analogy between engineering and the application of ethical principles in business. An important difference is that whereas very few of us have to design bridges, most of us are involved with business in one form or another; whether it be as worker, owner, or consumer. As individuals we can often safely ignore the proper principles of design for bridges because we will probably never need to build one. We cannot, however, safety ignore the principles of ethics, since we are all faced with ethical decisions not only in the business environment, but in many other areas of our lives. With this in mind, let us procede.

Notes

1. Aristotle, *Nicomachean Ethics*, Bk. 2, Ch. 4, Lines 13–18, transl. W.D. Ross in *The Basic Works of Aristotle*, ed. Richard McKeon (New York: Random House, 1941)
2. I am indebted to John Thorp's excellent article "The Emperor's Clothes," *The Canadian Federation for the Humanities Bulletin*, Vol. 13, No. 1, Winter 1990, pp. 1–4, for this example.
3. It is revealing in this regard that it is far easier to get a scholarly article published in a science journal than in a humanities journal. Recent surveys indicate that the typical science journal accepts for publication 65-70% of the manuscripts submitted, whereas the typical humanities journal accepts only 20-30% of the submissions it receives. One Canadian journal in philosophy accepts only 5% of the manuscripts it receives. (See *Bulletin of the Canadian Federation for the Humanities*, Vol. 13, No. 1, Winter 1990, p. 4) It seems difficult to hold, therefore, that other disciplines, especially the sciences, are inherently more tough-minded than philosophy and have higher standards of objectivity.

Part I

Business and Morality

Chapter One

THE RELEVANCE OF MORALITY TO BUSINESS

Introduction

Many people feel that the words *business* and *ethics* do not really go together. We are probably all familiar with the comment that *business ethics,* like *square triangle* or *married bachelor,* is a contradiction in terms. Underlying such comments is the perception that either in theory or in practice there exists tension between the requirements of business and the dictates of morality. Sometimes all that is meant is that in actual practise business people often act unethically. Sometimes, however, what is meant is that it is in principle impossible to engage in business and act morally. Implied in this latter claim is the view that, since it is impossible to be in business and act ethically, we cannot blame those in business for failing to fulfil the requirements of morality.

The view that business people often act unethically cannot be taken to support the assertion that *business ethics* is a contradiction in terms. Ethical claims describe not how in fact people act, but rather prescribe how people should act. They indicate not how individuals necessarily behave, but rather how they should behave. When, for example, I claim that people should not steal, I am not claiming that people do not as a matter of fact steal things, but that they ought not to.

Our aim is that ultimately people will come to act in the way that they should and that our descriptions of how people in fact act will come to coincide with our prescriptive claims about how they should act. To say that business people frequently act unethically in no way demonstrates that ethics is irrelevant to business. On the contrary, if such a claim is true it indicates that special efforts are needed to bring business practice into line with the requirements of morality.

The view that it is impossible to engage in business and yet act ethically seems a stronger proposal if one wishes to support the idea that *business ethics* is a contradiction in terms. The problem with this view is that it seems clearly false. Not only do many successful business people take ethics very seriously, but it is hard to see how business could occur in the absence of a moral environment. To provide only one of many possible examples, unless those in business recognize the obligation to keep promises and honor contracts, business could not exist. This is not to suggest that business people never break contracts, but if such behavior ever became general, business would be impossible. Just as telling a lie is advantageous only if most people generally tell the truth, shady business practices are advantageous only if most business people recognize the existence of moral obligations. Immorality in business is essentially parasitic because it tends to destroy the moral environment which makes its very existence possible.

Generally, those who claim that it is impossible to act morally and engage in business do not mean to suggest that morality is entirely irrelevant to business, but rather that being morally responsible is quite different in business than in other areas of life. As for the claim that *business ethics* is a contradiction in terms, this can be understood in two ways. It might be taken as suggesting that an individual may have obligations and duties as a private citizen that he or she does not have as a business person. It could also be taken as making the more radical claim that fundamentally different principles of morality apply to business than to other areas of life; thus, what constitutes ethical behavior in business is completely different from what constitutes ethical behavior in other activities.

The suggestion that we have obligations and duties as private citizens that we do not have as business persons does not imply that there are no basic principles of morality that apply

to all spheres of life. I may have duties and obligations to my wife that I do not have to my secretary, but this scarcely implies that I have no common duties to both. The importance of respect for persons generate duties that cross the boundaries of life-activities. I should, for example, no more break a promise to my secretary than I should to my wife.

The more ambitious claim that radically different principles of morality apply to business would justify the conclusion that what constitutes ethical behavior in business cannot be judged by the standards we employ in other areas of life. The problem for someone who wishes to hold this position is to make clear what these other principles are and what justifies employing them in business, but not elsewhere. This is no easy matter, if for no other reason than there are no watertight divisions between business and other areas of life. How we conduct ourselves in the workplace affects how we conduct ourselves in other environments and vice versa. Attempts to argue that completely different moral principles govern the workplace seem in danger of falling victim to moral schizophrenia.

The selections in Chapter One illustrate that it is impossible to separate business from ethical issues. Albert Carr's well-known article "Is Business Bluffing Ethical" was an early attempt to make clear the relationship between business and morality. Carr has often been interpreted as suggesting that ethical considerations have no place in business, but this is not what he really says. His claim is not that ethics has no place in business, but that radically different standards of right and wrong apply. What would be clearly immoral in private life is not, and should not be considered immoral in business. Carr would not deny that business people should behave ethically and do indeed have moral obligations, but he would insist that we not measure these obligations by the standards of morality relative to private life, but rather by those relative to business.

Carr's view—that the principles of morality are in no sense absolute, but rather relative to different contexts—is a variation of a theory of morality known as *moral relativism*. Although many people find it initially attractive, deeper inspection reveals that it has grave flaws as an account of morality. The difficulties inherent in moral relativism are explored both in the subsequent article, "Is There 'No Such Thing as Business Ethics'?" by Eric Beversluis and in the Mary Midgley's "Trying Out One's New Sword," in Chapter Two.

The suggestion that business is in some sense a game and that, like a game, it must be judged by completely different moral standards than those governing other areas of life is central to Carr's argument. Beversluis asks us to examine this analogy between business and games more closely. He suggests that when we do, two things emerge. The first is that although some of the constraints of ordinary morality do not apply to games, many do. It is, therefore, a mistake to think that the gamelike quality of business justifies us in thinking it should be judged by completely different standards of morality.

The second is that there are important ways in which business is unlike a game. The suspension of the constraints of ordinary morality in games is usually justified on the basis that participation in a game is voluntary. Beversluis argues that this is not the case in business and it is therefore far from clear that we can easily justify adopting radically different standards of morality for business than for other areas of life.

Our final selection in this chapter is Michael Davis' "Explaining Wrongdoing." Davis focuses on a phenomenon he calls *microscopic vision* and the role it plays as a contributing cause of immoral actions. He does not deny that immoral actions may arise from a variety of other causes such as ignorance, weak will, self-deception or even outright wickedness, but he does not feel that they, by themselves, provide a full explanation.

Microscopic vision is essentially a narrowing of what one looks at, in order to see what remains in greater detail. It is essential in one form or another to virtually every human activity. Its danger is that it can easily lead to ignoring things which should not be ignored. In many instances, microscopic vision may result in perspectives that either lack ethical considerations or, if ethical considerations are present, lack the relevant facts and information required to implement them. The issue, as Davis points out, is not whether we should dispense with microscopic vision, but how it should be properly implemented.

Albert Z. Carr

Is Business Bluffing Ethical?

A respected businessman with whom I discussed the theme of this article remarked with some heat, "You mean to say you're going to

From Albert Z. Carr, "Is Business Bluffing Ethical?" *Harvard Business Review,* Vol. 46, No. 1, 1968. Reprinted by permission of *Harvard Business Review.* Copyright © 1968 by the President and Fellows of Harvard College; all rights reserved.

encourage men to bluff? Why, bluffing is nothing more than a form of lying! You're advising them to lie!"

I agreed that the basis of private morality is a respect for truth and that the closer a businessman comes to the truth, the more he deserves respect. At the same time, I suggested that most bluffing in business might be regarded simply as game strategy—much like bluffing in poker, which does not reflect on the morality of the bluffer. . . .

I reminded my friend that millions of businessmen feel constrained every day to say *yes* to their bosses when they secretly believe *no* and that this is generally accepted as permissible strategy when the alternative might be the loss of a job. The essential point, I said, is that the ethics of business are game ethics, different from the ethics of religion.

He remained unconvinced. Referring to the company of which he is president, he declared: "Maybe that's good enough for some businessmen, but I can tell you that we pride ourselves on our ethics. In 30 years not one customer has ever questioned my word or asked to check our figures. We're loyal to our customers and fair to our suppliers. I regard my handshake on a deal as a contract. I've never entered into price-fixing schemes with my competitors. I've never allowed my salesmen to spread injurious rumors about other companies. Our union contract is the best in our industry. And, if I do say so myself, our ethical standards are of the highest!"

He really was saying, without realizing it, that he was living up to the ethical standards of the business game—which are a far cry from those of private life. Like a gentlemanly poker player, he did not play in cahoots with others at the table, try to smear their reputations, or hold back chips he owed them.

But this same fine man, at that very time, was allowing one of his products to be advertised in a way that made it sound a great deal better than it actually was. Another item in his product line was notorious among dealers for its "built-in obsolescence." He was holding back from the market a much-improved product because he did not want it to interfere with sales of the inferior item it would have replaced. He had joined with certain of his competitors in hiring a lobbyist to push a state legislature, by methods that he preferred not to know too much about, into amending a bill then being enacted.

In his view these things had nothing to do with ethics; they were merely normal business practice. He himself undoubtedly avoided outright falsehoods—never lied in so many words. But the entire organization that he ruled was deeply involved in numerous strategies of deception.

PRESSURE TO DECEIVE

Most executives from time to time are almost compelled, in the interests of their companies or themselves, to practice some form of deception when negotiating with customers, dealers, labor unions, government officials, or even other departments of their companies. By conscious misstatements, concealment of pertinent facts, or exaggeration—in short, by bluffing—they seek to persuade others to agree with them. I think it is fair to say that if the individual executive refuses to bluff from time to time—if he feels obligated to tell the truth, the whole truth, and nothing but the truth—he is ignoring opportunities permitted under the rules and is at a heavy disadvantage in his business dealings.

But here and there a businessman is unable to reconcile himself to the bluff in which he plays a part. His conscience, perhaps spurred by religious idealism, troubles him. Before any executive can make profitable use of the strategy of the bluff, he needs to make sure that in bluffing he will not lose self-respect or become emotionally disturbed. If he is to reconcile personal integrity and high standards of honesty with the practical requirements of business, he must feel that his bluffs are ethically justified. The justification rests on the fact that business, as practiced by individuals as well as by corporations, has the impersonal character of a game—a game that demands both special strategy and an understanding of its special ethics.

The game is played at all levels of corporate life, from the highest to the lowest. At the very instant that a man decides to enter business, he may be forced into a game situation, as is shown by the recent experience of a Cornell honor graduate who applied for a job with a large company:

This applicant was given a psychological test which included the statement, "Of the following magazines, check any that you have read either regularly or from time to time, and double-check those which interest you most. *Reader's Digest, Time, Fortune, Saturday Evening Post, The New Republic, Life, Look, Ramparts, Newsweek, Business Week, U.S. News & World Report, The Nation, Playboy, Esquire, Harper's, Sports Illustrated.*"

His tastes in reading were broad, and at one time or another he had read almost all of these magazines. He was a subscriber to *The New Republic*, an enthusiast for *Ramparts*, and an avid student of the pictures in *Playboy*. He was not sure whether his interest in *Playboy* would be held against him, but he had a shrewd suspicion that if he confessed to an interest in

Ramparts and *The New Republic*, he would be thought a liberal, a radical, or at least an intellectual, and his chances of getting the job, which he needed, would greatly diminish. He therefore checked five of the more conservative magazines. Apparently it was a sound decision, for he got the job.

He had made a game player's decision, consistent with business ethics.

A similar case is that of a magazine space salesman who, owing to a merger, suddenly found himself out of a job:

This man was 58, and, in spite of a good record, his chance of getting a job elsewhere in a business where youth is favored in hiring practice was not good. He was a vigorous, healthy man, and only a considerable amount of gray in his hair suggested his age. Before beginning his job search he touched up his hair with a black dye to confine the gray to his temples. He knew that the truth about his age might well come out in time, but he calculated that he could deal with that situation when it arose. He and his wife decided that he could easily pass for 45, and he so stated his age on his résumé.

This was a lie; yet within the accepted rules of the business game, no moral culpability attaches to it.

THE POKER ANALOGY

We can learn a good deal about the nature of business by comparing it with poker. While both have a large element of chance, in the long run the winner is the man who plays with steady skill. In both games ultimate victory requires intimate knowledge of the rules, insight into the psychology of the other players, a bold front, a considerable amount of self-discipline, and the ability to respond swiftly and effectively to opportunities provided by chance.

No one expects poker to be played on the ethical principles preached in churches. In poker it is right and proper to bluff a friend out of the rewards of being dealt a good hand. A player feels no more than a slight twinge of sympathy, if that, when—with nothing better than a single ace in his hand—he strips a heavy loser, who holds a pair, of the rest of his chips. It was up to the other fellow to protect himself. In the words of an excellent poker player, former President Harry Truman, "If you can't stand the heat, stay out of the kitchen." If one shows mercy to a loser in poker, it is a personal gesture, divorced from the rules of the game.

Poker has its special ethics, and here I am not referring to rules against cheating. The man who keeps an ace up his sleeve or who marks the cards is more than unethical; he is a crook, and can be punished as such—kicked out of the game or, in the Old West, shot.

In contrast to the cheat, the unethical poker player is one who, while abiding by the letter of the rules, finds ways to put the other players at an unfair disadvantage. Perhaps he unnerves them with loud talk. Or he tries to get them drunk. Or he plays in cahoots with someone else at the table. Ethical poker players frown on such tactics.

Poker's own brand of ethics is different from the ethical ideals of civilized human relationships. The game calls for distrust of the other fellow. It ignores the claim of friendship. Cunning deception and concealment of one's strength and intentions, not kindness and open-heartedness, are vital in poker. No one thinks any the worse of poker on that account. And no one should think any the worse of the game of business because its standards of right and wrong differ from the prevailing traditions of morality in our society.

DISCARD THE GOLDEN RULE

This view of business is especially worrisome to people without much business experience. A minister of my acquaintance once protested that business cannot possibly function in our society unless it is based on the Judeo-Christian system of ethics. He told me:

I know some businessmen have supplied call girls to customers, but there are always a few rotten apples in every barrel. That doesn't mean the rest of the fruit isn't sound. Surely the vast majority of businessmen are ethical. I myself am acquainted with many who adhere to strict codes of ethics based fundamentally on religious teachings. They contribute to good causes. They participate in community activities. They cooperate with other companies to improve working conditions in their industries. Certainly they are not indifferent to ethics.

That most businessmen are not indifferent to ethics in their private lives, everyone will agree. My point is that in their office lives they cease to be private citizens; they become game players who must be guided by a somewhat different set of ethical standards.

The point was forcefully made to me by a Midwestern executive who has given a good deal of thought to the question:

So long as a businessman complies with the laws of the land and avoids telling malicious lies, he's ethical. If the law as written gives a man a wide-open chance to make a killing, he'd be a fool not to take advantage of it. If he doesn't, somebody else will. There's no obligation on him to stop and consider who is going to get hurt. If the law says he can do it, that's all the justification he needs. There's nothing unethical about that. It's just plain business sense.

This executive (call him Robbins) took the stand that even industrial espionage, which is frowned on by some businessmen, ought not to be considered unethical. He recalled a recent meeting of the National Industrial Conference Board where an authority on marketing made a speech in which he deplored the employment of spies by business organizations. More and more companies, he pointed out, find it cheaper to penetrate the secrets of competitors with concealed cameras and microphones or by bribing employees than to set up costly research and design departments of their own. A whole branch of the electronics industry has grown up with this trend, he continued, providing equipment to make industrial espionage easier.

Disturbing? The marketing expert found it so. But when it came to a remedy, he could only appeal to "respect for the golden rule." Robbins thought this a confession of defeat, believing that the golden rule, for all its value as an ideal for society, is simply not feasible as a guide for business. A good part of the time the businessman is trying to do unto others as he hopes others will *not* do unto him.[1] Robbins continued:

Espionage of one kind or another has become so common in business that it's like taking a drink during Prohibition—it's not considered sinful. And we don't even have Prohibition where espionage is concerned; the law is very tolerant in this area. There's no more shame for a business that uses secret agents than there is for a nation. Bear in mind that there already is at least one large corporation—you can buy its stock over the counter—that makes millions by providing counterespionage service to industrial firms. Espionage in business is not an ethical problem; it's an established technique of business competition.

"We Don't Make the Laws"

Wherever we turn in business, we can perceive the sharp distinction between its ethical standards and those of the churches. Newspapers abound with sensational stories growing out of this distinction:

1. We read one day that Senator Philip A. Hart of Michigan has attacked food processors for deceptive packaging of numerous products.[2]
2. The next day there is a Congressional to-do over Ralph Nader's book, *Unsafe At Any Speed,* which demonstrates that automobile companies for years have neglected the safety of car-owning families.[3]
3. Then another Senator, Lee Metcalf of Montana, and journalist Vic Reinemer show in their book, *Overcharge,* the methods by which utility companies elude regulating government bodies to extract unduly large payments from users of electricity.[4]

These are merely dramatic instances of a prevailing condition; there is hardly a major industry at which a similar attack could not be aimed. Critics of business regard such behavior as unethical, but the companies concerned know that they are merely playing the business game.

Among the most respected of our business institutions are the insurance companies. A group of insurance executives meeting recently in New England was startled when their guest speaker, social critic Daniel Patrick Moynihan, roundly berated them for "unethical" practices. They had been guilty, Moynihan alleged, of using outdated actuarial tables to obtain unfairly high premiums. They habitually delayed the hearings of lawsuits against them in order to tire out the plaintiffs and win cheap settlements. In their employment policies they used ingenious devices to discriminate against certain minority groups.[5]

It was difficult for the audience to deny the validity of these charges. But these men were business game players. Their reaction to Moynihan's attack was much the same as that of the automobile manufacturers to Nader, of the utilities to Senator Metcalf, and of the food processors to Senator Hart. If the laws governing their businesses change, or if public opinion becomes clamorous, they will make the necessary adjustments. But morally they have in their view done nothing wrong. As long as they comply with the letter of the law, they are within their rights to operate their businesses as they see fit. . . .

Violations of the ethical ideals of society are common in business, but they are not necessarily violations of business principles. Each year the Federal Trade Commission orders hundreds of companies, many of them of the first magnitude, to "cease and desist" from practices which, judged by ordinary standards, are of questionable morality but which are stoutly defended by the companies concerned.

In one case, a firm manufacturing a well-known mouthwash was accused of using a cheap form of alcohol possibly deleterious to health. The company's chief executive, after testifying in Washington, made this comment privately:

We broke no law. We're in a highly competitive industry. If we're going to stay in business, we have to look for profit wherever the law permits. We don't make the laws. We obey them. Then why do we have to put up with this "holier than thou" talk about ethics? It's sheer hypocrisy. We're not in business to promote ethics. Look at the cigarette companies, for God's sake! If the ethics aren't embodied in the laws by the men who made them, you can't expect businessmen to fill the lack. Why, a sudden submission to Christian ethics by businessmen would bring about the greatest economic upheaval in history!

It may be noted that the government failed to prove its case against him.

Cast Illusions Aside

Talk about ethics by businessmen is often a thin decorative coating over the hard realities of the game:

Once I listened to a speech by a young executive who pointed to a new industry code as proof that his company and its competitors were deeply aware of their responsibilities to society. It was a code of ethics, he said. The industry was going to police itself, to dissuade constituent companies from wrongdoing. His eyes shone with conviction and enthusiasm.

The same day there was a meeting in a hotel room where the industry's top executives met with the "czar" who was to administer the new code, a man of high repute. No one who was present could doubt their common attitude. In their eyes the code was designed primarily to forestall a move by the federal government to impose stern restrictions on the industry. They felt that the code would hamper them a good deal less than new federal laws would. It was, in other words, conceived as a protection for the industry, not for the public.

The young executive accepted the surface explanation of the code; these leaders, all experienced game players, did not deceive themselves for a moment about its purpose.

The illusion that business can afford to be guided by ethics as conceived in private life is often fostered by speeches and articles containing such phrases as, "It pays to be ethical," or, "Sound ethics is good business." Actually this is not an ethical position at all; it is a self-serving calculation in disguise. The speaker is really saying that in the long run a company can make more money if it does not antagonize competitors, suppliers, employees, and customers by squeezing them too hard. He is saying that oversharp policies reduce ultimate gains. That is true, but it has nothing to do with ethics. The underlying attitude is much like that in the familiar story of the shopkeeper who finds an extra $20 bill in the cash register, debates with himself the ethical problem—should he tell his partner?—and finally decides to share the money because the gesture will give him an edge over the s.o.b. the next time they quarrel.

I think it is fair to sum up the prevailing attitude of businessmen on ethics as follows:

We live in what is probably the most competitive of the world's civilized societies. Our customs encourage a high degree of aggression in the individual's striving for success. Business is our main area of competition, and it has been ritualized into a game of strategy. The basic rules of the game have been set by the government, which attempts to detect and punish business frauds. But as long as a company does not transgress the rules of the game set by law, it has the legal right to shape its strategy without reference to anything but its profits. If it takes a long-term view of its profits, it will preserve amicable relations, so far as possible, with those with whom it deals. A wise businessman will not seek advantage to the point where he generates dangerous hostility among employees, competitors, customers, government, or the public at large. But decisions in this area are, in the final test, decisions of strategy, not of ethics.

THE INDIVIDUAL & THE GAME

An individual within a company often finds it difficult to adjust to the requirements of the business game. He tries to preserve his private ethical standards in situations that call for game strategy. When he is obliged to carry out company policies that challenge his conception of himself as an ethical man, he suffers. . . .

If an executive allows himself to be torn between a decision based on business considerations and one based on his private ethical code, he exposes himself to a grave psychological strain.

This is not to say that sound business strategy necessarily runs counter to ethical ideals. They may frequently coincide; and when they do, everyone is gratified. But the major tests of every move in business, as in all games of strategy, are legality and profit. A man who intends to be a winner in the business game must have a game player's attitude.

The business strategist's decisions must be as impersonal as those of a surgeon performing an operation—concentrating on objective and technique, and subordinating personal feelings. . . .

All sensible businessmen prefer to be truthful, but they seldom feel inclined to tell the *whole* truth. In the business game truth-telling usually has to be kept within narrow limits if trouble is to be avoided. The point was neatly made a long time ago (in 1888) by one of John D. Rockefeller's associates, Paul Babcock, to Standard Oil Company executives who were about to testify before a government investigat-

ing committee: "Parry every question with answers which, while perfectly truthful, are evasive of *bottom* facts."[6] This was, is, and probably always will be regarded as wise and permissible business strategy.

For Office Use Only

An executive's family life can easily be dislocated if he fails to make a sharp distinction between the ethical systems of the home and the office—or if his wife does not grasp that distinction. Many a businessman who has remarked to his wife, "I had to let Jones go today" or "I had to admit to the boss that Jim has been goofing off lately," has been met with an indignant protest. "How could you do a thing like that? You know Jones is over 50 and will have a lot of trouble getting another job." Or, "You did that to Jim? With his wife ill and all the worry she's been having with the kids?"

If the executive insists that he had no choice because the profits of the company and his own security were involved, he may see a certain cool and ominous reappraisal in his wife's eyes. Many wives are not prepared to accept the fact that business operates with a special code of ethics. An illuminating illustration of this comes from a Southern sales executive who related a conversation he had had with his wife at a time when a hotly contested political campaign was being waged in their state:

I made the mistake of telling her that I had had lunch with Colby, who gives me about half my business. Colby mentioned that his company had a stake in the election. Then he said, "By the way, I'm treasurer of the citizens' committee for Lang. I'm collecting contributions. Can I count on you for a hundred dollars?"

Well, there I was. I was opposed to Lang, but I knew Colby. If he withdrew his business I could be in a bad spot. So I just smiled and wrote out a check then and there. He thanked me, and we started to talk about his next order. Maybe he thought I shared his political views. If so, I wasn't going to lose any sleep over it.

I should have had sense enough not to tell Mary about it. She hit the ceiling. She said she was disappointed in me. She said I hadn't acted like a man, that I should have stood up to Colby.

I said, "Look, it was an either-or situation. I had to do it or risk losing the business."

She came back at me with, "I don't believe it. You could have been honest with him. You could have said that you didn't feel you ought to contribute to a campaign for a man you weren't going to vote for. I'm sure he would have understood."

I said, "Mary, you're a wonderful woman, but you're way off the track. Do you know what would have happened if I had said that? Colby would have smiled and said, 'Oh, I didn't realize. Forget it.' But in his eyes from that moment I would be an oddball, maybe a bit of a radical. He would have listened to me talk about his order and would have promised to give it consideration. After that I wouldn't hear from him for a week. Then I would telephone and learn from his secretary that he wasn't yet ready to place the order. And in about a month I would hear through the grapevine that he was giving his business to another company. A month after that I'd be out of a job."

She was silent for a while. Then she said, "Tom, something is wrong with business when a man is forced to choose between his family's security and his moral obligation to himself. It's easy for me to say you should have stood up to him—but if you had, you might have felt you were betraying me and the kids. I'm sorry that you did it, Tom, but I can't blame you. Something is wrong with business!"

This wife saw the problem in terms of moral obligation as conceived in private life; her husband saw it as a matter of game strategy. As a player in a weak position, he felt that he could not afford to indulge an ethical sentiment that might have cost him his seat at the table. [This article was written in 1968. It reflects an attitude towards women that has been deservedly criticized in recent thinking.]

Playing to Win

Some men might challenge the Colbys of business—might accept serious setbacks to their business careers rather than risk a feeling of moral cowardice. They merit our respect— but as private individuals, not businessmen. When the skillful player of the business game is compelled to submit to unfair pressure, he does not castigate himself for moral weakness. Instead, he strives to put himself into a strong position where he can defend himself against such pressures in the future without loss.

If a man plans to take a seat in the business game, he owes it to himself to master the principles by which the game is played, including its special ethical outlook. He can then hardly fail to recognize that an occasional bluff may well be justified in terms of the game's ethics and warranted in terms of economic necessity. Once he clears his mind on this point, he is in a good position to match his strategy against that of the other players. He can then determine objectively whether a bluff in a given situation has a good chance of succeeding and can decide when and how to bluff, without a feeling of ethical transgression.

To be a winner, a man must play to win. This does not mean that he must be ruthless, cruel, harsh, or treacherous. On the contrary, the better his reputation for integrity, honesty, and decency, the better his chances of victory will be in the long run. But from time to time every businessman, like every poker player, is offered a choice between certain loss or bluffing within the legal rules of the game. If he is not resigned to losing, if he wants to rise in his company and industry, then in such a crisis he will bluff—and bluff hard. . . .

Notes

1. See Bruce D. Henderson, "Brinkmanship in Business," HBR March-April 1967, p. 49.
2. *The New York Times*, November 21, 1966.
3. New York, Grossman Publishers, Inc., 1965.
4. New York, David McKay Company, Inc., 1967.
5. *The New York Times*, January 17, 1967.
6. Babcock in a memorandum to Rockefeller (Rockefeller Archives).

Eric H. Beversluis

Is There "No Such Thing as Business Ethics"?

INTRODUCTION

Business ethics has become quite popular lately as an area of study and of research.

It is not unusual, however, to hear "practical people" say things like, "There is no such thing as business ethics." What kind of thinking might lie behind such a scepticism, and how can one deal with it? In this paper I address some of the arguments that could lead to scepticism regarding business ethics. Then I offer the sceptic a brief explanation of what business ethics is.

BUSINESS IS A GAME

Sometimes when the sceptic denies there is such a thing as business ethics she appeals to the idea that business is, after all, a game. Let us construct the kind of thinking (argument) that might be implicit in this claim. The reasoning might go something like this:

1. Business relationships are a very special sub-set of human relationships, governed by their own rules. In a market society, the important rules involve competition, profit maximization, and principles like *caveat emptor,* let the buyer beware.
2. Thus business can be considered a "game" people play, analogous in important respects to competitive games like basketball or boxing.

From Eric H. Beversluis, "Is There 'No Such Thing as Business Ethics,'" *Journal of Business Ethics,* Vol. 6, 1987. Reprinted by permission of Kluwer Academic Publishers.

3. But clearly ordinary morality does not hold in basketball or boxing. What if the basketball player "did unto others as he would have them do unto him"? What if the boxer decided that it was wrong to attempt to injure another person? Clearly in these games the rules change; ordinary *ethical* rules do not apply.
4. Likewise, then, in the game of business, ordinary ethical rules do not apply—there is "no such thing as business ethics."

What can we make of this argument? We must, I suggest, look more closely at what makes an activity a game. A key feature is that the activity is *rule-governed.* The essence of sport, even boxing, is that it is not a case of Hobbesian [*Thomas Hobbes* was a seventeenth century English philosopher. In his main work, *Leviathan,* he argued that, in the absence of establishing moral conventions, the natural state of humans is constant war with one another.] "war of all against all," in which everyone, by right of nature, can claim whatever he can get. The rules governing sport may be special rules; they may permit forms of human interaction which are not permitted outside the game (preventing the other from reaching her objective; attempting to knock the other out; violently grabbing the other and throwing him to the ground); but all of these activities are constrained by rules. We distinguish fair play from foul play. We insist on boxing gloves and helmets to prevent serious injury. We do not accept the view that "Winning's not the most important thing—it's the only thing." Thus there clearly are moral constraints on human interaction, even in games. They are, however, special constraints that arise from the nature and purpose of the game.

So if we are viewing business as a game, then by analogy with other games it is a rule-governed game. It is not an "anything goes" Hobbesian war. The game analogy cuts both ways. While it *may* provide a basis for saying that some of the ordinary constraints of morality do not apply, it also establishes that there must indeed be *some* constraints that apply. One way to think of business ethics, then, is as the effort to make clear which rules should apply in the game of business. (These rules may be legal rules, but need not be. In this essay I focus on *moral rules,* what I call, later in this paper, normative principles.)

But business is in an important way unlike other games. Most games are essentially voluntary. If I do not want to box with you, you may not force me to. This voluntariness is essential to the "teleological suspension of the ethical" in games. Only because one can withdraw from the game at any point is the suspension of some ordinary ethical restraints morally acceptable.

But this element of voluntary participation, which is crucial to the suspension of normal constraints of morality in games, is absent in business. In a real sense, no one has an option between being in business or not. Everyone, insofar as she must earn a living or purchase goods, is of necessity a participant in the "game" of business. Another way to put this is that no one is economically self-sufficient, and so no one can choose to withdraw from the game of business. While there is a distinction between "business" and "economic activity," it is important to see that business is not a game that is carried on apart from the necessity which faces all of us of being involved in economic activity. Thus the necessity of economic activity means (in a market economy, anyway) the necessity of participation in the "game" of business. So one of the crucial conditions justifying the suspension of normal moral constraints in the case of competitive games is missing from the game of business. Since one *must* participate in the "game" of business, it follows that business ethics must not only make clear what rules do and should apply in the "game" of business, but it must develop rules that are appropriate to the *nonvoluntary* character of participation in the game. The game of business differs in this significant way from other competitive games.

There is one final point concerning the game of business that we must touch on. This is that the models of a perfectly competitive economy that are developed in lower level economics courses do not provide a morally relevant description of reality. In the ideal world of these models (featuring no monopolies, no externalities, complete knowledge of products and pricing, etc.), there might well be no moral problem with everyone's concerning himself only with his own well-being; *caveat emptor* might well be a perfectly adequate policy; government regulation, codes of ethics, and the like might well be perfectly gratuitous. Unfortunately we live in a different world. ... How practical is it for you to quit your job when the firm across the street or two hundred miles away pays a higher wage (assuming you can even find out what the wages are)? How can you as an individual or group of individuals force the local industry (who may well be the chief employer in town, as well as being your employer) to stop polluting the air? Some of these problems the market can at least partially handle; but the "market solution" to many of these problems is not morally acceptable. Thus even if we view business ethics as the search for "rules of the game" to govern interpersonal relations in a competitive market economy, we must fit the rules to the economy as it is and not make believe that the models of the economists, even if they are useful for the economists' purpose of prediction and explanation, capture the *morally* relevant features of the game as it is actually played.

I have argued that it may well be quite appropriate to look at business (economic) relationships as being part of a game. But the game analogy does not imply that there is no such thing as business ethics. On the contrary, analysis of the game of business indicates (a) that as in any game there are moral constraints on the participants' behavior; (b) that unlike many games, the players participate of necessity—they cannot opt out; and (c) that the rules for the game of business must fit the game as it is really played, not as it is ideally modelled in the economists' abstractions. We turn now to a second argument of the sceptic.

ONE CANNOT SURVIVE IN BUSINESS IF ONE IS TOO "ETHICAL"

On this construction of the sceptic's position, the argument might look like the following:

1. We all have a right to economic survival, i.e., a right to survive in business.
2. This right implies that we have no obligation to do anything that is incompatible with surviving in business.
3. One cannot survive in business if one is ethical, i.e., if one takes everyday senses of honesty, law-abidingness, fair-play, etc. into one's business dealings; one has to "play the game."
4. Therefore if by "business ethics" we mean taking everyday senses of honesty, law-abidingness, fair-play, etc., into our business dealings, we have no obligation to do so, and hence there is "no such thing as business ethics."

This argument, like the first, draws too strong a conclusion. Premise 1 we can grant, at least for the sake of argument. But beware a possible equivocation. [Premise 1] is true in the sense that we have a right to the scarce (economic) resources necessary to survive. It is not true, however, that we have a right to survive in this or that particular job, or that we have a right to be successful in this or that particular business venture. It is fallacious to argue that I must pay this bribe or ignore that unsafe feature of the brake my company is designing because otherwise I will not survive in business. I may lose this job or I may be unable to make this particular enterprise go, without losing all opportunity to survive economically.

Notice, by the way, that with Premise 1 we are in a real sense "doing" business ethics. For what is a "right"? If one puts forward the claim to have certain moral rights (as opposed to legal rights), one is willy-nilly engaged in the activity of business ethics (as I will explain below), and one ought to be able to say what it is to have rights. That is, at this point the argument has moved on to substantive issues of business ethics, and we are no longer discussing whether there is such a thing as business ethics.

Premise 2 really raises the question whether there are circumstances in which one has the moral obligation not only to forego this or that particular advantage because of some duty to others, but to sacrifice one's entire existence or minimal well-being for another. That is, it raises what we might call question of "lifeboat ethics."

Let us bypass that set of problems and agree that, normally speaking (when there is "enough to go around"), the right to economic survival means that complete self-sacrifice cannot be an obligation.

Premise 3 raises a factual (empirical) issue: Is it true that one cannot survive in business if one is ethical? We have already noted that whether or not one can survive in a particular job or a particular venture is not the issue. While we do not have choice concerning participation in the economy, we do often have some choice concerning jobs and enterprises. It seems to me that [Premise 3] is clearly false. One can (normally) survive economically without selling one's soul. One may not become rich but the argument turns on survival, not riches.

For those many cases (e.g., American society today) in which [Premise 3] is false, the argument we have constructed for [Premise 4] fails and with it the second leg of our sceptic's case against business ethics.

But the sceptic may shift his ground and argue like this: Surely I have a right to more than economic survival. Surely I have a right to do as well as I can for myself and my family. Surely if everyone else in society is thriving by following a certain set of rules, I have the right to do so as well.

This argument involves an implied premise that everyone else in society is thriving by following a certain set of supposedly immoral or nonmoral rules. But, if everyone is thriving, what makes the rule immoral? As I shall suggest below, morality involves limitations on our right to benefit at the expense of another. If this set of "immoral" rules really protects everyone, allowing them to thrive, then morality can say nothing against it. But do lying, bribery, marketing of unsafe products, paying of exploitative wages really protect the rights of everyone? If one wants to justify such practices, then one's task as a morally responsible agent is to show that such a set of rules does protect the rights of everyone. If "everyone else in society is thriving by following a certain set of rules," then perhaps one does have the right to do so as well. The problem is, of course, that while some may thrive on "immoral" rules, it is not clear that everyone does.

In this section we have seen that a "right to economic survival" does not rule out business ethics. Now we turn from responding to the sceptic's arguments to explaining for the sceptic what business ethics is.

THE NATURE AND TASK OF BUSINESS ETHICS

In general, ethics is concerned with answering the question "What should one do?" Thus understood, it is an unavoidable activity. Each of us must decide what we will do. The only issue is how carefully and how seriously we will concern ourselves with the problem of responsible decision making. By extension, then, *business* ethics is the effort to answer the question, "What should one do in one's business relationships?" Thus defined it is trivially true that there is such a thing as business ethics, since everyone has business (i.e., economic) relationships, and everyone must decide how to behave in those relationships. The important question is not whether there *is* business ethics but how to go about answering the question (what should one do in one's business relationships?) in a responsible manner.

It is useful at this point to draw a distinction between three senses of the term "business ethics." "Business ethics" can mean, first, an activity, the process of reflecting and deciding what it is that one should do. Second, the term can be used to refer to the results or object of such reflection, to the set of principles which state what one should do. And third, it can refer to behavior—someone might mean by the claim "There is no such thing as business ethics" that business people do not in fact behave ethically. Let us keep the senses clear by retaining the term "business ethics" for the reflective activity. Thus "business ethics" will refer to a certain way of answering the question about what one should do. (Briefly, answering it philosophically or Socratically—see below). The results of that activity or, better, the true propositions we try to discover through that intellectual activity called business ethics we will refer to as moral or normative principles. Moral principles then are propositions that state what one should do.

(They can be either general or particular, both with regard to the individuals involved and the situations involved.) Thus consider the proposition "A salesperson should try to hide the faults of the car she is selling." This statement is normative principle (general in regard to the individual referred to; fairly particular with regard to the situation involved). The effort to decide whether it is true or false is "business ethics." Finally, we will use the term "ethical behavior" to capture the third possible sense of "business ethics."

We can now deal with another way in which there might be no such thing as business ethics. For in denying that there is any such thing as business ethics, some might mean that there are no true normative principles—that expressions such as "A salesperson should always try to hide the faults of the car she is selling" are not propositions at all since they are neither true nor false. This view is called "ethical noncognitivism." To answer this objection fully is beyond the scope of this paper; let it suffice here to indicate that there is at least as much burden of proof on one who would deny the existence of such true propositions as on one who would affirm it. Further, most of us believe that there are at least some such true propositions. Would anyone seriously deny the truth of the proposition that it is wrong for me to take out a gun and, arbitrarily picking someone from a crowd, blow off his head? Again would anyone seriously deny the truth of the proposition that, in a business situation where a blind man comes to the counter and orders a Coke, it is wrong for me to give him an appropriately perfumed glass of gasoline? There may well be philosophical problems with what it means to say that there are true normative statements, just as there are philosophical problems with what it means to say that there are physical objects. Yet we do not actually doubt the existence of either physical objects or of at least some true normative statements. What remains is to examine the normative propositions that present themselves as candidates and to try, as best we can, to discern which are true. Thus we return to business ethics as reflective activity.

The model of moral philosophy (including business ethics) that I would like to propose is that of the Socratic examined life. Socrates [*Socrates* was a fifth century B.C. Greek philosopher. He was the first western philosopher to take as central to his philosophy the ethical question "How should I act?".] proposed that we should not act just out of habit, or just on the basic principles we have absorbed from our environment, or just in a manner dictated by some authority figure. Nor should we simply follow our desires or be given direction by mass opinion. It is our responsibility, he urged, to *examine* our normative beliefs, to become *aware* of them, to become aware of *conflicting* and *competing* normative beliefs that others may hold, and to *evaluate* as best we can the grounds or reasons that can be offered in support of these various principles.

If reflection and awareness characterize the process of the examined life, the result of these processes is affirmation of and commitment to normative principles. We affirm in what we say and what we do that certain normative principles are true. But for someone living in the Socratic manner the commitment and affirmation can never be *dogmatic*. Our conclusions must be subject to review and possible revision. The approach can be termed *fallibilism*—recognition of one's fallibility. It is a half-way position between dogmatism, which recognizes no possibility that one is mistaken, and scepticism, which refuses even to make a decision, on the grounds that we cannot ever know the truth. Fallibilism is the position that any one of my beliefs may be mistaken. Thus while I believe that some statement p (e.g., that I should always tell the truth) is true, I recognize that I may be mistaken. This does not mean that when it is convenient not to tell the truth I let myself off the hook. Rather, it means that the Socratic examination is continuously ongoing. While I must adopt certain principles in order to make the decisions facing me now, I am also always alert to new evidence, new considerations which might show me that I am mistaken and ought to change my principles.

As we will see below, normative principles come in varying degrees of generality. Presumably, extremely general and fundamental principles will not very often be changed. (If they are one must suspect superficiality in one's

examination in the first place.) But less general and fundamental principles (applications to situations) may well change. For example, our understanding of the facts of the situation may change. Thus, e.g., new evidence may indicate that my plant's pollution not only engenders aesthetic costs (ugliness) but also seriously impairs people's health. So while yesterday I may have resisted clearing up the pollution (believing that the aesthetic costs did not impair the rights of others), today I believe myself obligated to work to end the pollution. The underlying principle has not changed but the belief concerning the specific normative principle has, because of changed beliefs concerning the facts.

Reference to the role of "factual beliefs" in our practical deliberations, our efforts to determine what we should do, brings us to a second aspect of the activity of business ethics: the structure of the reasoning process involved. The point here is that in deciding what to do in any given situation we must apply relatively general normative principles to particular situations. Clearly, the same principle can have different implications in different situations. And just as clearly a lot of "moral disagreement" arises from disagreement concerning the facts or the interpretations of the facts. Suppose you and your partner are arguing about whether you should continue to market your "chlinks." In the past year you have sold about a thousand of them and you have discovered that eighty of the people who purchased them have since died of pneumonia. As nearly as you can tell, the group who purchased the chlinks are fairly representative of the entire population; but normally, let us assume, there are only about three or four out of 100 who die from pneumonia in a given year. Your partner says that this indicates that chlinks are causing the additional deaths and should be discontinued. You do not think that they should be discontinued, since there is no direct proof that they are in any way contributing to the deaths. Clearly you differ on the moral conclusion:

C: We (morally) *should* discontinue the sale of chlinks.

Most likely you agree on one of the premises, the normative premise:

P_1: We should discontinue sale of any products which contribute to or cause death.

We will assume you do. The point is that both C and P_1 are normative principles, one rather general, the other quite specific. You disagree about C, a normative principle, but yours is not really a normative disagreement. It is a disagreement about the facts. If you could agree about whether the chlinks caused the deaths (P_2) you would agree about what you should do. Thus a crucial aspect of "business ethics" is discovering the facts. Many (but of course far from all) disputes in business ethics really pertain to the "facts." It is important to be clear when this is and when it is not the case.

Determining the facts is often not easy. Sometimes it cannot be done satisfactorily. But business people have plenty of training and experience in "discovering the facts." More useful here is to consider more closely the normative elements in moral reasoning.

We have already said a lot about ethical theory. Thus we have been assuming that ethics has to do with rules or principles that govern (or that should govern) interactions between persons. Furthermore, it should be quite clear that the interactions with which we are primarily concerned involve conflicts, particularly conflicts of interest. Thus, barring such possibilities as product liability suits, it is in your interest to continue selling the chlinks (profit and return on investment). But, if they cause death, it is clearly not in the customers' interest for you to do so. It is conflicts of interest such as this that are at least one of the major concerns of moral philosophy. . . .

Most people, I think, recognize that morality essentially involves a constraint on individuals' pursuit of their well-being. While few go so far as to deny that one has a right to one's well-being, they say that insofar as one has that right, everyone else has a *similar right* to his or her well-being. Thus *my* right is constrained by the equal rights of others. This approach leads to a view of morality in which the moral person is the one who recognizes that her concern with her well-being must be limited by her respect for the equal right of others to their well-being. Games maintain their morality by respecting this principle. People participate voluntarily and the rules see to it that one person's success is not at the expense of the other's absolute well-being. (A "moral" game is a win-win situation— even the "loser" wins. That's why he voluntarily plays.) We have seen that in the game of business we cannot count on an invisible hand to ensure that our unbridled pursuit of self-interest will be compatible with respect for the rights of the next person. . . .

CONCLUSION

Is there no such thing as business ethics? We have seen that scepticism about business ethics seems to reflect a number of questionable assumptions about games, invisible hands, and survival rights. We have further seen that, if we define business ethics as the effort to decide how one should act, there necessarily is such a thing as business ethics. Finally, we have looked at the nature of a Socratically conceived activity of business ethics and have seen that the task of business ethics is to investigate what it means, in the business context, to "So act as to treat humanity, whether in thine own person or in that of any other, in every case as an end withal, and never as a means only" (Kant).

Finally, perhaps the sceptic who says "There is no such thing as business ethics" means that nobody in the business world bothers to do what they should do. ("When in Rome do as the Romans" or, "It's foolish to be moral when no one is being moral.") But here again we have not avoided business ethics. For (1) we are admitting that there is such a thing as right and wrong behavior in business, and (2) we raise the important ethical question whether there are times when the moral structure of society so breaks down that individuals are no longer bound by morality.

Michael Davis

Explaining Wrongdoing

How often is a man, looking back at his past actions, astonished at finding himself dishonest!
Cesare Beccaria, On Crimes and Punishments,
Ch. 39

What first interested me in professional ethics were the social questions: the problems faced by those trying to act as members of a profession, the options available, the reasons relevant to deciding between those options, and the methods of assessing those reasons. I thought of myself as advising decision-makers within a complex institution. I could, it seemed to me, contribute to right action in the professions simply by applying skills developed in political and legal philosophy to this new domain. But, like many others who began to do applied ethics in this way, I soon learned that matters are not that simple.

Part of studying professional ethics is reading the newspaper accounts, congressional testimony, and court cases that wrongdoing in the professions generates. I read such documents to identify new problems. But, in the course of reading so much about wrongdoing, I began to wonder how much use my advice could be. Though the wrongdoers were usually well-educated and otherwise decent, much of what they did seemed obviously wrong. Surely, they did not need a philosopher to tell them so. I also began to wonder at how little the wrongdoers themselves had to say about why they did what they did. They seemed far less articulate about that than many an illiterate criminal.[1]

From Michael Davis, "Explaining Wrongdoing," *Journal of Social Philosophy,* Vol. 20, Nos. 1-2 (Spring-Fall 1989). Reprinted by permission of the *Journal of Social Philosophy.*

Having begun to wonder about the motivation of the wrongdoers I was studying, I turned to the philosophical literature explaining wrongdoing. I was surprised at how little there was—and at how unhelpful. My wrongdoers did not seem to have done what they did simply because they were weak-willed, self-deceiving, evil-willed, ignorant, or morally immature—or even because they combined several of these failings. At most, those failings seemed to have played a subsidiary part in what my wrongdoers did. Yet the philosophical literature offered no sustained discussion of anything else. Only when I turned to the more practical literature of organization analysis did I find more. And, even there, I did not find enough. I still did not have a satisfactory explanation of the wrongdoing I was studying. I concluded that we lack an adequate psychology of wrongdoing.

This paper has three objectives: first, to provide some evidence for the claim that evil will, weakness of will, self-deception, ignorance, and moral immaturity, even together, will not explain much wrongdoing of concern to students of professional (or business) ethics; second, to add one interesting alternative to the explanations now available; and third, to suggest the practical importance of that alternative. Ultimately, though, this paper has only one objective: to invite others to pick up where I leave off. We need a better psychology of wrongdoing.

THREE EXAMPLES OF WRONGDOING

Let's begin with the testimony of a minor figure in the General Electric price-fixing scandal of the 1950s. No longer facing criminal or civil charges, he described how he got into trouble in this way: "I got into it. . .when I was young. I probably was impressed by the manager of marketing asking me to go to a meeting with him [where price-fixing discussions took place]. I probably was naive."[2]

This explanation of our price fixer's wrongdoing is more interesting for what is missing than for what is actually there. We hear nothing about greed, temptation, fooling oneself, or anything else we tend to associate with those destined to do wrong. What we do hear about is *ordinary* socialization. Having worked nine years at GE as an engineer, our price fixer (at age 32) was promoted to "trainee in sales." His superior then showed him how things were done. Yet, something is wrong. Our witness twice indicates that this is only "probably" what happened. Though the acts in question are his, he talks about them like a scholar analyzing someone else's. A screen has come down between him and the person he was only a few years before.

An inability to understand their own past wrongdoing is, I think, not uncommon in wrongdoers like our witness. But I can give only one more example here, just enough to show that he is not unique. *The Wall Street Journal* recently carried a follow-up on the fifty people convicted of inside trading over the last ten years. Here is a part of what we learn from one of them: "When it all started, I didn't even know what inside information was." But around 1979, he says, he began reading about people being arrested for inside trading—yet he continued trading even though he knew it was illegal. It's a decision he wouldn't repeat. "In the long run," he says, "you are going to get caught."[3]

This testimony comes from a small investor, not a broker, analyst, arbitrageur, or the like. Unlike our price fixer, this inside trader was never really inside the relevant organization. He simply received information from inside that he had no right to. Yet, for our purposes, that doesn't matter. What matters is that he knew early on that he was doing something illegal and stood a fair chance of being arrested. He went on trading nonetheless. Why? He doesn't say and, more important, he doesn't seem to know. He does not report greed, temptation, or evil will. What he reports is that he would not have done it if he had known *then* what he knows *now*. What has changed? What does he know now that he did not know then? It cannot be what he says, that is, "In the long run, you are going to get caught." He has no way to know that every inside trader will get caught in the long run. Statistics on the occurrence of illegal inside trading do not exist; but, if inside trading

is like other crimes, a substantial percentage of those engaged in it will never be caught.

Our witness's overstatement of the risks of being caught is, I think, better understood as a way of calling attention to *what* he risked and would not risk again. He now regrets doing what he did because he now appreciates what was at stake in a way he did not at the time. He does not so much have new information as a new perspective on the information he had all along. It is this new perspective that makes it hard for him to understand how he could have done what he did. The person we are listening to differs in an important way from the person who engaged in inside trading a few years before, even if he does not know anything he did not know before. It is as if he sees the world with new eyes.

These two wrongdoers are minor figures in major scandals. One may therefore wonder whether the major figures differ in some significant way. I don't think they do. Consider the now familiar events on the night before the *Challenger* exploded:

The Space Center was counting down for a launch the next morning. Robert Lund, vice president for engineering at Morton Thiokol, had earlier presided at a meeting of engineers that unanimously recommended *against* the launch. He had concurred and informed his boss, Jerald Mason. Mason informed the Space Center. Lund had expected the flight to be postponed. The Center's safety record was good. It was good because the Center would not allow a launch unless the technical people approved.

Lund had not approved. He had not approved because the temperature at the launch site would be close to freezing at lift-off. The Space Center was worried about the ice already forming here and there on the boosters, but Lund's worry was the "O-rings" that sealed the booster's segments. Data from previous flights indicated that they tended to erode in flight, with the worst erosion occurring on the coldest preceding lift-off. Experimental evidence was sketchy but ominous. Erosion seemed to increase as the rings lost their resiliency and resiliency decreased with temperature. At some temperature, the rings could lose so much resiliency that one would fail to seal properly. If a ring failed in flight, the shuttle could explode.

Unfortunately, almost no testing had been done below 40°F and no lift-off had occurred after a night as cold as this one. The engineers had had to extrapolate. But, with the lives of seven astronauts at stake, the decision seemed clear enough: Safety first.

Or so it had seemed earlier in the day. Now Lund was not so sure. The Space Center had been "appalled" by the sketchy evidence on which the no-launch recommendation had been based. They wanted to launch. They didn't say why, but the reasons were obvious. Previous delays had put them well behind schedule already. The State of the Union message was only a day away. Everyone supposed the President was anxious to announce the first teacher in space. If the Space Center did not launch tonight, they would have to wait at least a month.

The Space Center wanted to launch, but they would not launch without Thiokol's approval. They urged Mason to reconsider. He reexamined the evidence and decided the O-rings should hold at the expected temperature. Joseph Kilminster, Thiokol's vice president for shuttle programs, was ready to sign a launch approval, but only if Lund approved. Lund was now all that stood in the way of launching.

Lund's first response was to repeat his objections. Nothing had happened to change his no-launch recommendation. Then Mason had drawn the managers to one side of the meeting room and said something that made Lund think again. Mason had urged Lund to "take off [your] engineering hat and put on [your] management hat." Lund did and changed his mind. The next morning the shuttle exploded during lift-off, killing all aboard. An O-ring had failed.[4]

EXPLAINING LUND'S DECISION

The story of the *Challenger* resembles many cases discussed in professional (and business) ethics. While no one broke the law, as many did in the General Electric price-fixing scandal, there was wrongdoing. And, in retrospect, everyone recognized that—or at least sensed it. Mason quickly took early retirement. Kilminster and Lund were moved to new offices, told they would be "reassigned," and left to read the handwriting on the wall. Morton Thiokol didn't treat them as if their errors were merely technical; nor did it defend their decision in the way we would expect a company to defend a decision it believes in. Thiokol's defense consisted largely of lame excuses, attempts to suppress embarrassing information, and similar self-convicting maneuvers.

What had gone wrong? Well, from the perspective of engineering ethics, it seems obvious. Lund, an engineer who held his position in part because he was an engineer, had a professional duty to act like an engineer. He was not free to take off his engineering hat (though he could wear other hats in addition). For an engineer, safety is the paramount consideration. The engineers could not say the launch would be safe. So, Lund should have delayed the launch. Seven people died, in part at least, because he did not do what, as an engineer, he was supposed to do.[5]

One of the features of the *Challenger* disaster that made it an instant classic is that it has what seems to be a clear clash of legitimate perspectives. Lund was not just an engineer. He was also a manager. Managers are *not*, by definition, evil doers in the way that even price fixers or inside traders are. Government openly supports institutions to train managers. Most of us want people to wear "management hats" now and then. Very few would want to forbid managers to practice their trade. As a vice president of Morton Thiokol, part of Lund's job was to wear a management hat. What then was wrong with his giving approval after putting on that hat?

The answer must be that, in the decision procedure he was part of, his job was to stand up for engineering. He was supposed to represent engineering judgment in management decision. He was vice president *for* engineering. When he took off his engineering hat, he simply became another manager. He ceased to perform the job he was needed for. That, in retrospect, is why, even from management's perspective, he had done something wrong.

Why then did he take off his engineering hat that night? Lund's explanation for deciding as he did was, and remains, that he had "no choice" given the Space Center's demand. Self-interest will not explain what he means by "no choice." To approve the launch was in effect to bet his career that the *Challenger* would not explode, to bet it against the best technical advice he could get. Had he refused to approve the launch, he would *at worst* have been eased out of his position to make way for someone less risk averse. He would have had no disaster on his record and a good chance for another good job either within Thiokol or outside. Self-interest would seem to support Lund's decision not to launch.

What about moral immaturity?[6] This is a possibility, but only that. The records we have tell nothing about anyone's moral development. Participants said nothing about social pressure, law, ordinary morality, or professional ethics. They spoke entirely in the bland technical language engineers and managers use to communicate with one another. Whatever we say about Lund's moral development as of that night would be mere speculation. Something similar is true of the hypothesis that Lund acted with evil intent. By all reports, Lund was too decent a person for that.

What about carelessness, ignorance, or incompetence?[7] I think none of these explanations will do. Too much time went into the decision to dismiss it as simply careless. Since Lund had the same training as his engineers and all the information they had, we can hardly suppose him to be ignorant in any obvious sense. Nor can we declare him to be incompetent. Too many experienced people—both at Thiokol and at NASA—concurred in Lund's decision for it to be incompetent. Lund may well have been operating at the limit of his ability or beyond. But that is not necessarily incompetence. We generally speak of "incompetence" only when we have competent alternatives. Here we have no reason to believe that anyone who could have occupied Lund's place that night would have done better.

Can we then explain Lund's decision by weakness of will?[8] Did he know better but yield to temptation, give in to pressure, or otherwise knowingly do what he considered wrong because he lacked the will to do better? The evidence seems against this explanation too. Mason's advice, "Take off [your] engineering hat and put on [your] management hat,"

does not sound like tempting Lund to act against his better judgment. It sounds much more like an appeal *to* his better judgment, an appeal from engineering instinct to management rationality.

Lund did, of course, give in to pressure. But to say that is not to explain his decision, only to describe it on the model of a physical process (for example, the collapse of a beer can when we stamp on it). We still need to explain why the appeal to management rationality was so convincing when nothing else was. (We need something like the physical theory that allows us to understand why the beer can collapses under our weight but not under the weight of, say, a cat.) Well, you will say, that's easy enough. The appeal to management rationality allowed Lund to fool himself into thinking he was doing the right thing.

Explaining Lund's decision in this way, that is, as a result of self-deception, is, I think, much closer to the mark. Mike Martin, coauthor of a good text in engineering ethics, recently published a book on self-deception. Among his many examples of self-deceivers are participants in the GE price-fixing scandal. So, I have no doubt that he could find some self-deception in Lund as well.[9]

Yet, if we can, we should avoid explaining what Lund did by self-deception. Self-deception, though common, is an abnormal process. It is something you *do*, not simply something that happens to you. You must knowingly fail to think about a question in the way you believe most likely to give the right answer. You must then not think about the unreliability of the answer you get even, or especially, when you must act on it. In its extreme form, self-deception may involve believing something while being aware that the evidence decisively supports the opposite belief. Self-deception is, as such, a conscious flight from reality.[10]

We should, I think, not explain the conduct of responsible people in this way unless the evidence requires it. The evidence hardly requires it in Lund's case. We can explain why Lund did what he did by a process which, though similar to self-deception, is normal, familiar, and at least as probable on the evidence we have as any of the explanations we have considered so far. For lack of a better name, let's call the process "microscopic vision."[11]

MICROSCOPIC VISION EXAMINED

What is microscopic vision? Perhaps the first thing to say about it is that it is *not* "tunnel vision." Tunnel vision is a narrowing of one's field of vision without any compensating advantage. Tunnel vision is literally a defect in vision and figuratively a defect in our ability to use the information we have available. Tunnel vision is often associated with self-deception. Microscopic vision resembles tunnel vision only insofar as both involve a narrowing of our field of vision. But, whereas tunnel vision reduces the information we have available below what we could effectively use, microscopic vision does not. Microscopic vision narrows our field of vision only because that is necessary to increase what we can see in what remains. Microscopic vision is enhanced vision, a giving up of information not likely to be useful under the circumstances for information more likely to be useful. If tunnel vision is like looking through a long tunnel to a point of light at the other end, microscopic vision is like looking into a microscope at things otherwise too small to see. Hence, my name for this mental process.

Microscopic vision is also not nearsightedness or myopia. A nearsighted person has lost the ability to see things far off. His acuity close up is what it always was. But when he looks into the distance, he sees only a blur. Like tunnel vision, myopia is partial blindness; microscopic vision is, in contrast, a kind of insight. The nearsighted person needs glasses or some other aid to regain normal vision. A person with microscopic vision need only cease using his special powers to see what others see. He need only look up from the microscope.

Every skill involves microscopic vision of some sort. A shoemaker, for example, can tell more about a shoe in a few seconds than I could tell if I had a week to examine it. He can see that the shoe is well or poorly made, that the materials are good or bad, and so on. I can't see any of that. But the shoemaker's insight has its price. While he is paying attention to people's shoes,

he may be missing what the people in them are saying or doing. Microscopic vision is a power, not a handicap, but even power has its price. You cannot both look into the microscope and see what you would see if you did not.

Though every skill involves what I am calling microscopic vision, the professions provide the most dramatic examples. In part, the professions provide these because the insight they give is relatively general. The microscopic vision of a lawyer, engineer, doctor, minister, or accountant concerns central features of social life as the microscopic vision of a shoemaker does not. In part, though, professions provide the most dramatic examples of microscopic vision because both the long training required to become a professional and the long hours characteristic of professional work make the professional's microscopic vision more central to his life. A profession is a way of life in a way shoemaking is not (or, at least, is not anymore).

Consider, for example, the stereotypes we have of professionals—the pushy lawyer, the comforting doctor, the quiet accountant, and so on. We do not, I think, have similar stereotypes of the shoemaker, the carpenter, or the personnel director. These skills don't seem to shape character as much. We joke about professional myopia—for example, the surgeon who thinks the operation a success even though the patient died. Behind the joke is an appreciation of the power a profession has to shape, and therefore, to misshape, the consciousness of its members. Real professional myopia is probably rare. Few professionals seem to lose altogether the ability to see the world as ordinary people do. Common, however, is a tendency not to look up from the microscope, a tendency unthinkingly to extend the profession's perspective to every aspect of life.

Managers are not professionals in the strict sense. Though managing now has schools like those of the professions, managers lack two features essential to professionals strictly so called: first, a formal commitment to public service; *and* second, a common code of ethics. Indeed, managers seem to me to lack even a clear sense of themselves as *managers,* that is, as *custodians* of other people's wealth, organization, and reputation. I am surprised by the number of managers who think of themselves as entrepreneurs or capitalists, that is to say, business people who risk their own money, not someone else's.

Nonetheless, managing does today have many of the characteristics of a profession, including distinctive skills and a corresponding perspective, but—most important—a way of life that can make their microscopic vision seem all that matters. We have the stereotype of the manager who can't see the toxic wastes beyond the end of his budget. Behind that stereotype is a certain reality. Managers, especially senior managers, work almost entirely with other managers. Their days are spent "in the office" doing the things that managers do. Often, those days are quite long, not 9 to 5 but 8 to 7 or even 7 to 8. They read management magazines and go to management meetings. They come to see the world from the perspective of a manager.

There is a natural process by which people are made into managers. But most companies are not satisfied with "normal acculturation." They have special programs to train managers in a certain style of management. Roger Boisjoly, one of the engineers who tried to get Lund to stick to his no-launch recommendation, was himself briefly a manager. He went back to being an engineer because he wanted to be closer to work on the shuttle. Though he has mocked the programs Thiokol had for managers as "charm schools," he has also pointed out that they helped to make the managers at Thiokol a cohesive team. They helped to give the engineer-turned-manager a clear sense of the priority of the manager's way of looking at things.[12]

What is the difference between the way an engineer might look at a decision and the way a manager might? For our purposes, what is important is the way engineers and managers approach risk. I think engineers and managers differ in at least two ways:

First, engineers would not normally include in their calculations certain risks, for example, the risk of losing the shuttle contract if the launch schedule was not kept. Such risks are not their professional concern. But such risks are properly a manager's normal concern.

Second, engineers are trained to be conservative in their assessment of permissible risk.

Often they work from tables approved by the appropriate professional association or other standard-setting agency. When they do not have such tables, they try not to go substantially beyond what experience has shown to be safe. Engineers do not, in general, balance risk against benefit. They reduce risk to permissible levels and only then proceed. Managers, on the other hand, generally do balance risk against benefit. That is one of the things they are trained to do.

We have then two perspectives that might be brought to the same problem, the engineer's and the manager's. Which is better? The answer is: Neither. The engineer's perspective is generally better for making engineering decisions while the manager's perspective is generally better for making management decisions. Either perspective has a tendency to yield a bad result only if applied to the wrong kind of decision. Indeed, that is nearly a tautology. If, for example, we thought a certain decision better made by managers than engineers, we would describe it as (properly) a management, rather than an engineering, decision.

If that is so, it's not too hard to understand why Lund changed his mind the night before the *Challenger* exploded (and why he might still claim that he had "no choice"). Once he began thinking about the launch as an ordinary management decision, he could rationally conclude that the risk of explosion was small enough to tolerate given the demands of NASA and how much was at stake for Morton Thiokol. But why *would* Lund think about the launch like a manager rather than an engineer?

As I described the difference between the engineer's perspective and the manager's, the two approaches to risk are inconsistent. Lund had to choose. In a way, Mason's plea to Lund to take off his engineering hat and put on his management hat accurately stated the choice Lund faced. In another way, however, it did not. Mason's plea assumed that the decision to launch was an ordinary management decision. This would be just what any manager would normally assume, especially a manager who had himself been an engineer. For an engineer to be made a manager is a promotion, an opening of new horizons. Managers are in charge of engineers. They regularly receive engineering recommendations and then act on them, taking into account more than the engineers did. Engineers generally defer to managers. Anyone who thought of relations between engineers and managers in this way would, I think, have succumbed to Mason's plea—*unless* he had a clear understanding of what made him different from other managers.

Lund seems to have had no such understanding. Indeed, Mason's plea probably shows that no one in the senior management at Morton Thiokol did. Mason could hardly have urged Lund to take off his engineering hat in front of so many managers if it had been common knowledge that Lund had a duty to keep his engineering hat on. Perhaps those who originally organized the decision procedure at Thiokol understood things better. If so, they failed to institutionalize their understanding. Without some way to preserve that understanding, ordinary management understanding would eventually take over. The *Challenger* explosion was the natural outcome of ordinary management.

My purpose here is not to defend Lund's decision but simply to understand how he might have made it without being careless, ignorant, incompetent, evil-willed, weak-willed, morally immature, or self-deceiving. I have explained his decision as rational from a particular perspective, that of an ordinary manager, and then explained why that perspective might seem the right one at the decisive moment. Earlier, I pointed out that, in retrospect, everyone seemed to see not only that Lund made an unfortunate decision but that the decision he made was wrong. I have now explained why. Lund was not an ordinary manager; he was supposed to be an engineer among managers.

I should now like to generalize what we have learned from Lund. We have a tendency to suppose that doing the right thing is normal, that doing the wrong thing is abnormal, and that when something goes wrong the cause must be something abnormal, usually a moral failing in the wrongdoer. What the analysis so far suggests is that sometimes at least the wrong may be the result of normal processes.

The analysis also suggests something more. Managers sometimes say of obeying the law, of doing what's morally right, or of maintaining professional standards, "That should go without saying"—or, in other words, that the importance of such things is so obvious that pointing it out is unnecessary. The truth, I think, is almost the reverse. I shall come back to this point later.

PRICE FIXING AND INSIDE TRADING

Lund may be taken to represent one category of wrongdoer, those whose conduct was merely unprofessional. There is another, those whose wrongdoing is illegal. Could what I said of Lund apply to this other category as well? Let's try to answer that question by briefly examining the two lawbreakers with whom we began. We are, I think, now ready to understand how they might have done what they did.

First, the price fixer at General Electric. Arriving at his new job eager to learn, he found that much he had learned as an engineer did not quite fit. Everyday was a struggle to get "up to speed," as they say. One day his superior invited him to go to a meeting. He went. The meeting consisted of sales managers from the other two major turbine manufacturers, clearly respectable people and clearly engaged in fixing market prices. There was no question that the meeting was secret. But what conclusion should he have drawn from that? A company like GE has many secrets. The meeting did not take long and soon our future price fixer was doing other things. After a few more meetings like this, he would be allowed to go without his superior. Soon the meetings would be routine.

He may initially have had qualms about the meetings. We often have qualms about a practice with which we are unfamiliar. But we have learned to suspend judgment for a decent interval. Often the qualms disappear as understanding increases. Of course, our price fixer may have had more than the usual reasons for qualms. He may have received in the mail a copy of a GE policy that forbad what he was doing ("policy 20.5"). But the policy would have come from the law department, not from anyone in his chain of command. Nothing would have made that mailing seem more important than other mailings from law or other nonline departments managers routinely ignore. What filled our price fixer's time, his field of vision, as we might say, was learning to be a manager. He had little time to think about matters that seemed to matter to no one with whom he dealt. Eventually, he would stop thinking about the price-fixing as price-fixing at all.[13]

I have now told the price fixer's story in terms appropriate to microscopic vision. I have described him as developing in a normal way a sense for what matters and what does not matter in a certain environment. The process is similar to the "desensitizing" that a surgeon must undergo before she can calmly cut off a human limb or put a knife into a still-beating heart. Though the process I have described does *not* require learning to block anything out, only failing to use some information because one is busy using other information, it does share at least one important feature with self-deception (something ordinary desensitizing does not). The price fixer was misled. The process nonetheless differs from self-deception in at least two ways:

First, while self-deception presupposes in the self-deceiver some sense for the unreliability of the procedure he is using to learn about the world, the process I have described presupposes no such thing. Our price fixer might well have believed his procedure would yield an accurate, albeit incomplete, picture of the world in which he worked.

Second, while self-deception presupposes that the procedure used is in fact generally unreliable, we need not presuppose that either. The procedure I have described might well be *generally* reliable. The problem is that the price-fixer's procedure was not "designed" to distinguish legal from illegal management. That design may well have made sense in the 1950s. Who then would have thought that the managers of a company like GE would have engaged in extensive illegal conduct? The discovery must have astonished many people, including our price fixer.

Now consider our inside trader. He did get warnings of a sort our price fixer did not. He actually read about indictments of people for inside trading. Yet, he continued to trade on inside information. Why? Perhaps he deceived himself about the chances of being caught. A more interesting possibility, though, is that he never thought about being caught. Consider: He began inside trading with a clear conscience. He read of its illegality only after he had grown used to inside trading. Perhaps those with whom he cooperated showed no fear. Busy with many things beside inside trading, normal prudence would have told him that, if he feared everything the newspapers invited him to fear, he would live with numberless terrors. We must use the judgment developed in daily life to put newspaper stories in perspective. His immediate environment seemed as safe as ever. So, why should he worry about what he read in the newspaper? Again, we have a normal process leading to an abnormal result.

I do not, of course, claim that this is how it was. What is important here is not that I have the story of these two right, but that what I say about them seems a plausible description of many of those who engage in wrongdoing of the sort that concerns us, even if it happens not to be true of these two. I am suggesting a hypothesis, not demonstrating it.

Though that is all I claim for these two stories, I should, I think, point out one piece of evidence suggesting that I have got both at least partly right. Remember that neither of these wrongdoers seemed to understand how he came to do what he did. That is what we should expect if my version of their stories is more or less right. As I have told their stories, each did wrong in part at least because he did not use certain facts—policy 20.5 in one case, arrests of inside traders in the other—in a way that would have led him to a true understanding of what he was doing or to the conduct such an understanding would normally lead to. The facts did not trigger the fear of punishment or concern about having done wrong that seems normal outside the environment in which they were working. The facts seemed to have been pushed from consciousness by other facts, as most of the world is pushed aside when we look into a microscope.

Once our two wrongdoers were pulled from the microscope, they would cease to see the world as they had. They would not, however, have that sense of having "known it all along" so characteristic of coming out of self-deception (since they could not have known it until they looked at the world somewhat differently). They would instead be aware of seeing something that—on the evidence now before them—*must* have been there all along. Microscopic vision is a metaphor for a mental process, a "mind set" or "cognitive map." Because the mechanics of such mental processes are no more visible to the person whose mind it is than it is to an outside observer, our two wrongdoers need not have been aware of what made them attend to other things until now. They could honestly be perplexed about how they could have missed for so long what is now as plain as day.

Some Practical Lessons

What I have tried to do so far is describe wrongdoing as the outcome of a social process the literature on wrongdoing seems to have overlooked. I have tried to avoid assuming such serious moral failings as weakness of will or self-deception. I have, of course, not described my wrongdoers as paragons of rationality or virtue. The price fixer and inside trader were certainly naive, that is, lacking enough insight into the way the world works to recognize signs of trouble a more experienced person would have. Lund, however, seems no more naive than the rest of us. I can imagine myself doing what he did. I assume many of you can too.

If the process I have described in fact explains much wrongdoing in large organizations, we may draw some interesting conclusions about how to prevent wrongdoing. The most obvious, perhaps, is that screening out potential wrongdoers of the sort we have been discussing is probably impractical. Who would be let in by a procedure that would screen out the wrongdoers we have been discussing? We must instead consider how to prevent wrongdoing by the relatively decent people an organization must employ.

The problem as I have described it is that normal processes can lead to important information going unused at a decisive moment. Lund's training as a manager would not prepare him to see how special his role was. The future price-fixer's way of learning his job would not alert him to the risks of illegality, much less to any moral objections to fixing prices. The inside-trader's experience would make him discount the warning signs in the newspaper. Though microscopic vision is not a flight from reality, it does involve a sacrifice of one part of reality for another. Usually, the sacrifice is worth it. Sometimes it is not. When it is not, we need to change the microscopic vision of those working in the environment in question or change the environment. Sometimes we need to change both. Often, changing one changes the other too.

How might we change the environment? One way is simply to talk openly and often about what we want to have people notice. Lund would, for example, probably have refused to do as Mason suggested if the people back at Morton Thiokol's headquarters in Chicago had regularly reminded him that he was no ordinary manager. "We are counting on you to stand up for engineering considerations whatever anyone else does." Indeed, had *Mason* heard headquarters say that to Lund even a few times, he could hardly have said what he did say. He might well have deferred to Lund's judgment, even though NASA was pressuring him. "Sorry," he could have said, "my hands are tied."

Business professors especially, but ordinary managers as well, often decline to talk about what they call "ethics" because, as they say, they do not want to "sermonize." Sermons, they say, cannot lead people to do the right thing. If adults haven't learned to be ethical by now, or don't want to, what can a sermon do?

These professors and managers seem to use the word "ethics" as a catch-all for whatever "value" considerations seem so obvious to them that they would be embarrassed to raise the matter. I must admit to some doubts about their consistency here. These same people regularly sermonize about profit. They do not seem to find mention of "profit" embarrassing though we might suppose that, for them, profit would be the most obvious value consideration of all.

Still, whatever doubts I have about their consistency, I can easily respond to their concern about the ineffectiveness of sermonizing. However obvious the sermon's content, the sermon itself can help to keep legal, moral, and professional considerations in an organization's collective field of vision. That, I think, is why both business professors and ordinary managers talk so much about profit. That is how they keep profit a primary concern. So, doing the same for ethical considerations should, by itself, be a significant contribution to getting decent people to do the right thing.

Sermons are, of course, hardly the best way to do that. Better than sermons are such familiar devices as a code of ethics, ethics audits, ethics seminars for managers, discussion of ethics in the course of ordinary decision-making, and reward of those who go out of their way to do the right thing ("reward" including not only praise but also the other valuables that normally go to those who serve their employer well, especially, money and promotion). But, whatever the merits of these particular devices in themselves, they all have this important characteristic in common. They help to keep employees alert to wrongdoing. They help to maintain a certain way of seeing the world.

Now, about teaching. Part of teaching is getting people used to thinking in a certain way. What academics call "disciplines" are in fact forms of "microscopic vision." We should, therefore, pay as much attention to what we don't teach as to what we do teach. If we limit ourselves to teaching technical aspects of a discipline, those we teach will tend to develop a perspective including *only* those technical aspects. They will not automatically include what we do not teach. Indeed, they would have to be quite unusual students even to see how to include such extras. If, then, we teach engineering without teaching engineering ethics, our graduates will begin work thinking about the technical aspects of engineering without thinking of the ethical aspects. They will not dismiss the ethical aspects. They will not even see them.

The same is true of business ethics. Business professors who limit themselves to technical matters do not simply fail to do good. However unintentionally, they *actively* contribute to the wrong their students do, if they eventually do wrong. They help to blind their students to something they might otherwise see.

Of course, we can teach what we should and still do little good. Good conduct in business or a profession presupposes a suitable social context. If a morally sensitive graduate goes to work in a company where ethics is ignored, he will, if he stays, slowly lose his sense of the ethical dimension of what he does. His field of vision will narrow. Eventually, he may be as blind as if we had taught him nothing. This is—I should stress—not a claim about moral development (as that term is now commonly understood). Our graduate may well score no worse on a Kohlberg test than he did before. He will simply have ceased to think of a certain range of decisions as raising questions to which moral categories are important. The questions will seem "merely technical," "an ordinary business decision," or in some other respect "merely routine."

That organizations can in this way make the teaching of ethics ineffective is, I think, no reason not to teach ethics. But it is good reason to conceive ethics teaching as part of a larger process; and good reason too, to try to transmit that conception to our students. Caroline Whitbeck of MIT has, I think, provided a good example of what I have in mind. As part of a course in Engineering Design, she has her students contact companies in the Boston area to find out how an engineer in the company could raise an issue of professional ethics related to design. Her students thus learn to think of their future employers as in part "ethics environments." But that is not all her students do. Their inquiries make it more likely that their future employers will think about how an engineer could raise an ethics issue. So, Professor Whitbeck may also be helping to improve the ethics environment in which her students will some day work.[14]

Notes

An early version of this paper was read at the Center for the Study of Ethics in Society, Western Michigan University, Kalamazoo, 27 October 1988, under the title "Keeping Good Apples from Going Bad." A later version, under the present title, was read at the Philosophy Colloquium, Illinois Institute of Technology, 30 March 1989. I [Michael Davis] should like to thank those present at these two events for their encouragement and criticism. I should also like to thank Paul Gomberg for his careful reading of the penultimate draft and Fay Sawyer for helping me to see microscopic vision for the first time.

1. My wrongdoers, for example, are not much like the "hard men" in Jack Katz, *Seductions of Crime: Moral and Sensual Attractions of Doing Evil* (New York: Basic Books, 1988). Katz's criminals do indeed seem to will evil.

2. "Price Fixing and Bid Rigging in the Electrical Manufacturing Industry," *Administered Prices*, Hearings Before the Subcommittee on Antitrust and Monopoly of the Committee on the Judiciary, United States Senate, Part 27, 1961: p. 16652.

3. "After the Fall: Fates are Disparate for Those Charged with Inside Trading," *Wall Street Journal* 210 (November 18, 1987): 22.

4. This description is derived from *The Presidential Commission on the Space Shuttle Challenger Disaster* (Washington, DC: June 6, 1986), esp. v. I, pp. 82–103. The quotation is on p. 93.

5. For the full defense of this claim, see Heinz Luegenbiehl and Michael Davis, *Engineering Codes of Ethics: Analysis and Applications,* forthcoming. For a shorter version, see "Why Engineers Should Support their Profession's Code" (Chicago: Center for the Study of Ethics in the Professions, 1987).

6. Compare Lawrence Kohlberg, *Essays on Moral Development* (San Francisco: Harper and Row, 1981).

7. Compare Chester A. Barnes, *The Functions of the Executive* (Cambridge, Mass.: Harvard University Press, 1938), p. 276: "It is apparent that executives frequently fail. This failure may be ascribed in most cases, I believe, to inadequate abilities as a first cause, usually resulting in the destruction of responsibility. But in many cases it may be inferred that the conditions impose a moral complexity and a moral conflict not soluble. Some actions which may within reason appear to be dictated by the good of the organization as a whole will obviously be counter to nearly all other codes, personal or official."

8. See, for example, Jan Elster, *Ulysses and the Sirens,* Revised Edition (New York: Cambridge University Press, 1984) for a good treatment of weakness of will.

9. Mike W. Martin, *Self-Deception and Morality* (Lawrence, Kansas: University Press of Kansas, 1986).

10. For a convenient survey of the literature on self-deception that brings out the range of mental state that might be included within that capacious term, see Alfred Mele, "Recent Work on Self-Deception," *American Philosophical Quarterly* Vol. 24 (January 1987): 1–17. For discussion of the related phenomenon of shifting responsibility, see Stanley Milgram, *Obedience to Authority: An Experimental View* (New York: Harper and Row, 1974). I have not discussed the hypothesis Milgram's work might suggest because, as far as I can see, no one ever offered to take responsibility for what Lund did. Lund's claim that he had "no choice" is not an appeal to the authority of others—though it is something equally troubling. After all, what can be more obvious than that Lund had a choice? He could simply have said "no" and taken the consequences.

11. I should like to thank Vivian Weil and Michael Pritchard for very helpful criticism of one or another earlier version of the explanation of microscopic vision below. They are, however, not responsible for any errors that remain.

12. I derive this information from a video of Boisjoly's appearance before Caroline Whitbeck's engineering design course, "Company Loyalty and Whistleblowing: Ethical Decisions and the Space Shuttle Disaster" (7 January 1987), especially his answers to student questions.

13. In fact, our price fixer has no memory of ever seeing the policy. "Price Fixing," p. 16152. For a somewhat different version of this story (including the claim that he must have seen the policy), see James A. Waters' excellent "Catch 20.5: Corporate Morality as an Organizational Phenomenon," *Organizational Dynamics* Vol. 6 (Spring, 1978): 3–19. Waters emphasizes "organizational blocks" to proper conduct rather than the normal processes that concern me. But I believe nothing I have said is inconsistent with what he says. Wrongdoing in a complex organization is likely to have many contributing causes. Waters and I differ only in being interested in different contributing causes. It is, of course, an empirical question whether either of us is even partly right (though one very hard decisively to test with the information we have or are likely to get).

14. Caroline Whitbeck, unpublished paper, "The Engineer's Responsibility for Safety: Integrating Ethics Teaching into Courses in Engineering Design."

QUESTIONS

1. How good is Carr's poker analogy? Does it show what Carr thinks it shows?

2. Does complying with the law guarantee that an action is moral? Explain.

3. Beversluis claims that ethical disagreements are frequently not over normative principles, but over facts? What does he mean and do you agree?

4. What does Beversluis mean when he suggests "that the rules for the game of business must fit the game as it is really played, not as it is ideally modelled in the economists' abstractions."?

5. What is microscopic vision and should one be blamed for wrongdoing that results from it?

6. Is wrongdoing ever solely due to microscopic vision? Defend your view.

John has recently been asked by his boss to deal with the disposal of a manufacturing by-product. Until several months ago, it had been legal to dispose of it in state landfills, but new legislation has made it illegal to do so. The new legislation is based on research that suggests serious health risks are associated with the by-product. So far as John can determine, there is no reason to doubt the validity of the research, although it is still in its early stages.

The technology exists to neutralize the by-product, but it is expensive both in its start-up costs and day-to-day operation. Neighboring states have not yet enacted legislation to forbid its disposal in their landfills and it seems clear that they will not do so in the immediate future. The cost of shipping the waste to neighboring landfills is much less than the cost of implementing the technology for neutralizing the by-product.

Two colleagues, Brian and Marjorie, give John quite different advice. Brian suggests that, since it is legal and much cheaper to ship the wastes to neighbouring land-fills, this is obviously the correct decision. Given the legality of shipping the waste, questions of morality do not arise.

Marjorie argues that in light of the health risks associated with the by-product, it is immoral to dispose of it in landfills. Her position is that the morality of different methods of waste disposal should be decided not on the basis of legality or cost, but on whether they pose a health hazard. She claims that given there is no reason to doubt the scientific research suggesting the by-product poses a health hazard, it would be immoral to dispose of it in neighboring landfills, even though it might be legal to do so.

John is sympathetic to Marjorie's view. He is concerned, however, that adopting the neutralizing technology will leave the company at a competitive disadvantage. He wishes to do what is morally right, but he doesn't want the company or his future prospects to suffer. Brian points out that the welfare of many employees may rest on his decision and that the scientific evidence, although suggestive, is not yet conclusive. Marjorie comments that the welfare of the employees should not take precedence over the public good and that it should not be assumed that the scientific evidence will be overturned.

John resolves to think about the issue further; knowing that he must make a decision in the next week.

CASE STUDY QUESTIONS

1. Is Marjorie correct when she asserts that John should not put the welfare of fellow employees above the public good?
2. Should the fact that he may jeopardize his career if he makes an unpopular decision affect John's decision-making?

FOR FURTHER READING

1.   Sir Adrian Cadbury, "Ethical Managers Make Their Own Rules" in *Ethics in Practice*, ed. Kenneth R. Andrews (Boston, Mass.: Harvard Business School Press, 1989) pp. 70–76.

2.   Joanne B. Ciulla, "Business Ethics as Moral Imagination" in *Business Ethics: The State of the Art*, ed. R. Edward Freeman (Oxford University Press, 1991) pp. 212–220.

3.   Scott Cook, "The Ethics of Bootstrapping," *Inc. Magazine*, September 1992, pp. 87, 90, 95.

4.   Laura L. Nash, "Ethics Without the Sermon" in *Ethics in Practice*, ed. Kenneth R. Andrews (Boston, Mass.: Harvard Business School Press, 1989) pp. 243–257.

5.   Barbara Ley Toffler, *Tough Choices: Managers Talk Ethics*, (New York: John Wiley & Sons, 1986).

Chapter Two

A Brief Introduction to Ethical Theory

Introduction

We have seen that moral concerns are inherent in business. Questions of how we ought to act towards others and how they ought to act towards us can no more be avoided in business than in other areas of life. Our goal in this text is to say something useful concerning various practical ethical issues arising from business activities. It is important, however, before proceeding directly to the problems we wish to discuss, to spend a little time examining ethical theory. Just as one cannot successfully build a piece of furniture without at least an elementary understanding of principles of design, it is impossible to resolve practical ethical issues without some understanding of the principles upon which ethical decisions should be made.

Cultural Relativism   The selections in this chapter illustrate diverse theoretical approaches to questions of morality. Mary Midgley's "Trying Out One's New Sword," describes and criticizes the theory of moral isolationism, i.e. what we have called cultural relativism. This is the view that the truth or falsity of moral claims is determined solely on the basis of what society one lives in. Midgley is especially concerned to assess whether this theory provides a basis for respecting and tolerating the views of other cultures. Her conclusion is that contrary to what is frequently assumed, it does not.

Ethical Egoism   W. D. Glasgow's article, "The Contradiction in Ethical Egoism" is a response to the theory of ethical egoism, which holds that what is morally correct is determined by whether it is in one's self interest or not. Glasgow focuses on one of the central difficulties associated with ethical egoism; the problem of recommending not only that what is ethically correct is what is in my self-interest, but recommending to other individuals that what is ethically correct is what is in their self-interest. If I am an ethical egoist, how can I recognize what someone else does in his or her self-interest as ethically correct if it thwarts what is in my self-interest?

The problem is that ethical egoism seems to imply subjectivism; an even more extreme version of relativism than cultural relativism. Whereas cultural relativism makes the truth of moral claims relative to the culture, subjectivism makes their truth relative to the individual. In cultural relativism it is impossible to make cross-cultural moral claims. In subjectivism it is impossible to make inter-personal moral claims. Given that morality is intimately associated with interaction between persons, subjectivism seems fatally flawed. If then, it can be shown that ethical egoism implies subjectivism, this would be a good reason to regard ethical egoism as inadequate.

Aristotle's Ethical Theory   Our next reading comes from Aristotle's (384-322 B.C.) chief ethical work the *Nicomachaen Ethics*. Aristotle's ethical theory is important not only in its own right, but in its influence both on medieval natural law theories and contemporary virtue ethics. Whereas Kant (Kantianism) and Mill (Utilitarianism) focus on the rightness or wrongness of specific actions done by a moral agent, Aristotle focuses on the qualities and dispositions of the agent. He emphasizes not the action produced, but the moral character of the agent by which it is produced.

Also characteristic of Aristotle is his emphasis that the good person can be defined as the person who acts according to human nature. For Aristotle, to be virtuous is to fulfil your proper function. The function of a knife is to cut, so a virtuous knife is a knife that cuts well. It should come as no surprise, then, to learn that much of the *Nicomachaen Ethics* is devoted to developing a theory of human nature. Whatever the difficulties in defining human nature, and these prove to be many, Aristotle would insist that we can have no idea of what it is to be morally good if we do not first have some idea of the proper function of humans.

Natural law theories are sometimes caricatured as suggesting rigid guidelines concerning every detail of human conduct. Although it is true that proponents of natural law such as Aristotle and the medieval philosopher Thomas Aquinas (1224-1274) think that the fundamental principles underlying proper human behavior are nonnegotiable, they are generally careful to acknowledge that there is room for flexibility and a certain amount of disagreement over how these principles are to be applied in particular situations. What is clear is that, for these thinkers, what is moral coincides with what will most truly fulfil human nature.

Kantianism   Immanuel Kant (1724-1804) emphasizes the idea that morality is essentially an outworking of applied or practical reason. Kant thinks that the only thing that is inherently good is a good will; a good will being defined as one which acts from duty. To act from duty, according to Kant, means to act in accordance with universal law, as determined by reason. If, therefore, one wishes to determine whether a proposed action is truly moral, one should ask oneself whether the principle according to which one is acting can be applied universally. If it can, then one's proposed action is morally justified, but if it cannot, then the action is immoral.

Kant suggests a litmus test by which we may determine the rightness or wrongness of our actions. Our actions are to be judged moral or immoral not on the basis of whether they fulfil some fundamental aspect of human nature or on the basis of their consequence, but on the basis of whether the principles underlying them can be universalized. Kant called this test the categorical imperative; formulating it in the following words, "Act only according to that maxim [principle] by which you can at the same time will that it should become a universal law of nature." It is this principle which provides the lynch-pin of Kant's extensive and complicated ethical system.

Utilitarianism   John Stuart Mill, (1806-1873) along with Jeremy Bentham, (1748-1832) is generally regarded as the founder of utilitarianism. Utilitarianism takes its name from its appeal to what Mill called the Principle of Utility or the Greatest Happiness Principle. Whereas for Kant the test of the morality of an action lies in whether the principle motivating it can universalized, for Mill the test of whether an action is moral lies in whether it promotes happiness. To the degree that an action tends to increase the sum total of happiness in the world it is to be judged moral; to the degree that it tends to decrease the sum total of happiness in the world it is to be judged immoral. Actions are not intrinsically right or wrong, but rather are judged right or wrong by virtue of their consequences.

As is evident in the selection I have chosen, Mill insisted that the quality of pleasure is as relevant as the quantity of pleasure. Later utilitarians have tended to concentrate simply on the question of quantity. I suspect that the reason for this is that not only does introducing the notion of higher and lower pleasures complicate the notoriously difficult task of quantifying happiness, but any non-arbitrary attempt to distinguish between higher and lower pleasures must make at least an implicit appeal to the notion of what is properly human, i.e., a theory of human nature. To do so seems to open the door to a natural law theory of ethics. Mill may have been right to distinguish between higher and lower pleasures, but it is not clear that his theory will permit such a distinction.

Virtue Ethics   As with the theory of natural law, virtue ethics has philosophic roots in Aristotle. Like both Aristotle and Aquinas, proponents of virtue ethics wish to focus on the qualities of the moral agent, rather than on particular actions. They emphasize not the rules and principles to guide specific actions, but rather the characteristic long-term patterns of behavior from which actions arise. Where

they tend to part company certainly with Aquinas, and to a degree with Aristotle, is their willingness to forego grounding the virtues in a metaphysical theory of human nature. Whether or not it is possible to reap the fruits of earlier traditions emphasizing the virtues without also following their lead in linking metaphysics and ethics remains to be made clear. In the selection I have chosen to illustrate this theory, David Norton argues that virtue ethics provides a far deeper and more adequate account of the moral life than do theories such as utilitarianism and Kantianism.

Feminist Ethics   The view that there is a distinctively feminist approach to ethics has become increasingly popular. Many feminists claim that not only have traditional moral theories been biased in their application, but they are inherently flawed and must be replaced by a feminist ethic. It is, however, no easy matter to describe or define such an ethic. In the reading I have selected, Alison Jaggar, a leading feminist, begins by saying that feminist ethics are distinguished by their explicit commitment to rethinking ethics with a view to correcting male bias. She ends with the observation that feminist ethics, far from being a rigid orthodoxy, is a ferment of ideas and controversy, many of them echoing and deepening debates in nonfeminist ethics.

That male bias has, in many instances skewed the application of moral theory and that feminists have been instrumental in exposing such bias, is evident. Whether this implies that not only is there a distinctively feminist approach to ethics, i.e. uncovering male bias in the application of moral theory, but a distinctively feminist ethical theory, is another matter. It is one thing to detect bias in the application of a theory, it is another to suggest the theory is so deeply flawed that it must be replaced with something fundamentally different. Many thinkers would admit the existence of moral bias, yet deny that this necessitates the wholesale rejection of traditional moral theory. All that can safely be said in the context of our present discussion is that Jaggar seems correct in her observation concerning the ferment of ideas and controversy and that, although a number of important feminist thinkers believe in the possibility and necessity of developing a distinctively feminist ethic and are actively working on this project, such an ethic has yet to be articulated and evaluated in detail.

Even so brief a glance at moral theory as we are taking, reveals deep disagreement. To many this seems a pessimistic conclusion. How, in the midst of such disagreement, can we hope to develop guideposts for determining what is ethically correct?

One way of approaching this question is to note that a theory may contain a good deal of truth and yet fail as a complete or total account of what needs to be explained. This opens up the possibility of a theory subsuming what is true in alternative theories, yet rejecting their claims to completeness. As you read these selections on various moral theories, keep in mind that it is possible to find truth in a theory without thereby accepting it completely. We do not, for example, have to accept Kantianism in its entirety, to accept the claim that the notion of duty plays an important role in the moral life. Neither do we have to accept utilitarianism in its entirety to accept that the morality of actions is often evaluated with regard to their consequences. Similar points could be made with respect to most of the theories we are examining. The issue, therefore, is not whether a particular ethical theory contains truth, but whether it gives a complete and comprehensive account of what it is to act morally. Remembering this will help in appreciating the merits of theories that must nevertheless be rejected as comprehensive accounts of morality.

Mary Midgley

Trying Out One's New Sword

All of us are, more or less, in trouble today about trying to understand cultures strange to us. We hear constantly of alien customs. We see changes in our lifetime which would have astonished our parents. I want to discuss here one very short way of dealing with this difficulty, a drastic way which many people now theoretically favour. It consists in simply denying that we can ever understand any culture except our own well enough to make judgements about it. Those who recommend this hold that the world is sharply divided into separate societies, sealed units, each with its own system of thought.

They feel that the respect and tolerance due from one system to another forbids us ever to take up a critical position to any other culture. Moral judgement, they suggest, is a kind of coinage valid only in its country of origin.

I shall call this position "moral isolationism." I shall suggest that it is certainly not forced upon us, and indeed that it makes no sense at all. People usually take it up because they think it is a respectful attitude to other cultures. In fact, however, it is not respectful. Nobody can respect what is entirely unintelligible to them. To respect someone, we have to know enough about him to make a *favourable* judgement, however general and tentative. And we do understand people in other cultures to this extent. Otherwise a great mass of our most valuable thinking would be paralysed.

To show this, I shall take a remote example, because we shall probably find it easier to think calmly about it than we should with a contemporary one, such as female circumcision in Africa or the Chinese Cultural Revolution. The principles involved will still be the same. My example is this. There is, it seems, a verb in classical Japanese which means "to try out one's new sword on a chance wayfarer." (The word is *tsujigiri,* literally "crossroads-cut.") A samurai sword had to be tried out because, if it was to work properly, it had to slice through someone at a single blow, from the shoulder to the opposite flank. Otherwise, the warrior bungled his stroke. This could injure his honour, offend his ancestors, and even let down his emperor. So tests were needed, and wayfarers had to be expended. Any wayfarer would do—provided, of course, that he was not another Samurai. Scientists will recognize a familiar problem about the rights of experimental subjects.

Now when we hear of a custom like this, we may well reflect that we simply do not understand it; and therefore are not qualified to criticize it at all, because we are not members of that culture. But we are not members of any other culture either, except our own. So we extend the principle to cover all extraneous cultures, and we seem therefore to be moral isolationists. But this is, as we shall see, an impossible position. Let us ask what it would involve.

We must ask first: Does the isolating barrier work both ways? Are people in other cultures equally unable to criticize *us?* This question struck me sharply when I read a remark in *The Guardian* by an anthropologist about a South American Indian who had been taken into a Brazilian town for an operation, which saved his life. When he came back to his village, he made several highly critical remarks about the white Brazilians' way of life. They may very well have been justified. But the interesting point was that the anthropologist called these remarks "a damning indictment of Western civilization." Now the Indian had been in that town about two weeks. Was he in a position to deliver a damning indictment? Would we ourselves be qualified to deliver such an indictment on the Samurai, provided we could spend two weeks in ancient Japan? What do we really think about this?

My own impression is that we believe that outsiders can, in principle, deliver perfectly good indictments—only, it usually takes more than two weeks to make them damning. Understanding has degrees. It is not a slapdash yes-or-no matter. Intelligent outsiders can

progress in it, and in some ways will be at an advantage over the locals. But if this is so, it must clearly apply to ourselves as much as anybody else.

Our next question is this: Does the isolating barrier between cultures block praise as well as blame? If I want to say that the Samurai culture has many virtues, or to praise the South American Indians, am I prevented from doing *that* by my outside status? Now, we certainly do need to praise other societies in this way. But it is hardly possible that we could praise them effectively if we could not, in principle, criticize them. Our praise would be worthless if it rested on no definite grounds, if it did not flow from some understanding. Certainly we may need to praise things which we do not *fully* understand. We say "there's something very good here, but I can't quite make out what it is yet." This happens when we want to learn from strangers. And we can learn from strangers. But to do this we have to distinguish between those strangers who are worth learning from and those who are not. Can we then judge which is which?

This brings us to our third question: What is involved in judging? Now plainly there is no question here of sitting on a bench in a red robe and sentencing people. Judging simply means forming an opinion, and expressing it if it is called for. Is there anything wrong about this? Naturally, we ought to avoid forming—and expressing—*crude* opinions, like that of a simple-minded missionary, who might dismiss the whole Samurai culture as entirely bad, because non-Christian. But this is a different objection. The trouble with crude opinions is that they are crude, whoever forms them, not that they are formed by the wrong people. Anthropologists, after all, are outsiders quite as much as missionaries. Moral isolationism forbids us to form *any* opinions on these matters. Its ground for doing so is that we don't understand them. But there is much that we don't understand in our own culture too. This brings us to our last question: If we can't judge other cultures, can we really judge our own? Our efforts to do so will be much damaged if we are really deprived of our opinions about other societies, because these provide the range of comparison, the spectrum of alternatives against which we set what we want to understand. We would have to stop using the mirror which anthropology so helpfully holds up to us.

In short, moral isolationism would lay down a general ban on moral reasoning. Essentially, this is the programme of immoralism, and it carries a distressing logical difficulty. Immoralists like Nietzsche [*Nietzsche* (1844-1900) was a German philosopher who attacked what he called *herd morality*, i.e. conventional, morality and urged that the individual must move beyond good and evil to create his or her own value.] are actually just a rather specialized sect of moralists. They can no more afford to put moralizing out of business than smugglers can afford to abolish customs regulations. The power of moral judgement is, in fact, not a luxury, not a perverse indulgence of the self-righteous. It is a necessity. When we judge something to be bad or good, better or worse than something else, we are taking it as an example to aim at or avoid. Without opinions of this sort, we would have no framework of comparison for our own policy, no chance of profiting by other people's insights or mistakes. In this vacuum, we could form no judgements on our own actions.

Now it would be odd if Homo sapiens had really got himself into a position as bad as this—a position where his main evolutionary asset, his brain, was so little use to him. None of us is going to accept this sceptical diagnosis. We cannot do so, because our involvement in moral isolationism does not flow from apathy, but from a rather acute concern about human hypocrisy and other forms of wickedness. But we polarize that concern around a few selected moral truths. We are rightly angry with those who despise, oppress or steamroll other cultures. We think that doing these things is actually *wrong*. But this is itself a moral judgement. We could not condemn oppression and insolence if we thought that all our condemnations were just a trivial local quirk of our own culture. We could still less do it if we tried to stop judging altogether.

Real moral scepticism, in fact, could lead only to inaction, to our losing all interest in moral questions, most of all in those which concern other societies. When we discuss these things, it becomes instantly clear how far we are from

doing this. Suppose, for instance, that I criticize the bisecting Samurai, that I say his behaviour is brutal. What will usually happen next is that someone will protest, will say that I have no right to make criticisms like that of another culture. But it is most unlikely that he will use this move to end the discussion of the subject. Instead, he will justify the Samurai. He will try to fill in the background, to make me understand the custom, by explaining the exalted ideals of discipline and devotion which produced it. He will probably talk of the lower value which the ancient Japanese placed on individual life generally. He may well suggest that this is a healthier attitude than our own obsession with security. He may add, too, that the wayfarers did not seriously mind being bisected, that in principle they accepted the whole arrangement.

Now an objector who talks like this is implying that it *is* possible to understand alien customs. That is just what he is trying to make me do. And he implies, too, that if I do succeed in understanding them, I shall do something better than giving up judging them. He expects me to change my present judgement to a truer one—namely, one that is favourable. And the standards I must use to do this cannot just be Samurai standards. They have to be ones current in my own culture. Ideals like discipline and devotion will not move anybody unless he himself accepts them. As it happens, neither discipline nor devotion is very popular in the West at present. Anyone who appeals to them may well have to do some more arguing to make *them* acceptable, before he can use them to explain the Samurai. But if he does succeed here, he will have persuaded us, not just that there was something to be said for them in ancient Japan, but that there would be here as well.

Isolating barriers simply cannot arise here. If we accept something as a serious moral truth about one culture, we can't refuse to apply it—in however different an outward form—to other cultures as well, wherever circumstance admit it. If we refuse to do this, we just are not taking the other culture seriously. This becomes clear if we look at the last argument used by my objector—that of justification by consent of the victim. It is suggested that sudden bisection is quite in order, *provided* that it takes place between consenting adults. I cannot now discuss how conclusive this justification is. What I am pointing out is simply that it can only work if we believe that *consent* can make such a transaction respectable—and this is a thoroughly modern and Western idea. It would probably never occur to a Samurai; if it did, it would surprise him very much. It is *our* standard. In applying it, too, we are likely to make another typically Western demand. We shall ask for good factual evidence that the wayfarers actually do have this rather surprising taste—that they are really willing to be bisected. In applying Western standards in this way, we are not being confused or irrelevant. We are asking the questions which arise *from where we stand,* questions which we can see the sense of. We do this because asking questions which you can't see the sense of is humbug. Certainly we can extend our questioning by imaginative effort. We can come to understand other societies better. By doing so, we may make their questions our own, or we may see that they are really forms of the questions which we are asking already. This is not impossible. It is just very hard work. The obstacles which often prevent it are simply those of ordinary ignorance, laziness and prejudice.

If there were really an isolating barrier, of course, our own culture could never have been formed. It is no sealed box,but a fertile jungle of different influences—Greek, Jewish, Roman, Norse, Celtic and so forth, into which further influences are still pouring—American, Indian, Japanese, Jamaican, you name it. The moral isolationist's picture of separate, unmixable cultures is quite unreal. People who talk about British history usually stress the value of this fertilizing mix, no doubt rightly. But this is not just an odd fact about Britain. Except for the very smallest and most remote, all cultures are formed out of many streams. All have the problem of digesting and assimilating things which, at the start, they do not understand. All have the choice of learning something from this challenge, or, alternatively, of refusing to learn, and fighting it mindlessly instead.

This universal predicament has been obscured by the fact that anthropologists used to concentrate largely on very small and remote cultures, which did not seem to have this problem. These tiny societies, which had often forgotten their own history, made neat, self-contained subjects for study. No doubt it was valuable to emphasize their remoteness, their extreme strangeness, their independence of our cultural tradition. This emphasis was, I think, the root of moral isolationism. But, as the tribal studies themselves showed, even there the anthropologists were able to interpret what they saw and make judgements—often favourable—about the tribesmen. And the tribesmen, too, were quite equal to making judgements about the anthropologists—and about the tourists and Coca-Cola salesmen who followed them. Both sets of judgements, no doubt, were somewhat hasty, both have been refined in the light of further experience. A similar transaction between us and the Samurai might take even longer. But that is no reason at all for deeming it impossible. Morally as well as physically, there is only one world, and we all have to live in it.

W. D. Glasgow

The Contradiction in Ethical Egoism

Ethical egoism is the doctrine that the agent has but one duty, viz., to produce for himself the greatest balance of good over evil. Such a theory is quite compatible with what is ordinarily regarded as the highest standards of human conduct. It is possible . . . for the egoist to be considerate and benevolent to others, . . . if he considers it to be in his own best interest to be so. In this paper I wish to point out what I consider to be the basic defect of this theory. . . .

The [ethical] egoist argues that Tom, Dick, Harry, in fact everyone, *ought* to look after his own interest. To say this is to grant at least that there are other human beings who are autonomous. By an autonomous individual is meant an individual who has the ability to consider the possibilities of actions that are open to him in a particular situation, who can deliberate upon each of these possibilities, in the sense that he can weigh up the reasons for and against actualizing any given possibility, and who can come to a decision which he has the ability to carry out. But it is quite possible for the individual to be autonomous in this sense, and yet deliberate, decide, and act within the confines of his own wants. Such would be the characterization of the prudent man. He would accept others, whom he could regard as autonomous in the sense outlined above, only insofar as they promote or impede his own interest. Their value to him would be instrumental not intrinsic. . . .

Yet the ethical egoist . . . does not seem to accept this position. He agrees that there are other autonomous individuals, in the sense that there are individuals who can deliberate, decide,

and act as the prudent man deliberates, decides, and acts. But he wants to say more than this. In stressing the normative character of his principle . . . he is recognizing that the judgments and actions of other individuals can be rationally justified, just as he himself can justify his own judgments and actions. In emphasizing that everyone must look after "his own interest" he is acknowledging that the wants of others can provide reasons for action for them, just as his own wants can provide reasons for action for him. So in believing that *every* rational agent ought to behave in a certain way, viz., look after his own interest, he implies that he, as a rational agent, is willing to consider seriously, and sometimes accept, the judgments, and the resultant actions, of other rational individuals. That is, he accepts the view that the possession of rationality confers upon him the ability to regard acceptable reasons for others as being also acceptable reasons for him.

There is, however, a problem here that is peculiar to the ethical egoist. In what way are such reasons "acceptable" to the egoist if they support a judgment and resultant action that is against the egoist's best interest? In such a case he may "accept" the reasonableness of the judgment: he may be willing to say, for example, that Tom ought to do X, even though to do X is against his own best interest. He cannot, however, advise Tom to do X, since to do so would be to encourage Tom to do something which from the egoist's point of view would be immoral. In fact, it is his duty to encourage Tom *not* to do X. So he finds himself in the position of *recognizing* that Tom ought to do X, but *advising* Tom that he ought not to do X. But if the egoist recognizes that Tom ought to do X, then he implies that he would approve of Tom's doing X. This, however, he cannot do, since he would be approving of something not in his own best interest—a position logically intolerable for the ethical egoist. The egoist, therefore, cannot really accept in any full-blooded sense that in a case of conflict of interests, Tom ought to do X. . . . Respect for the autonomy of Tom is not consistent with ethical egoism. There is . . .

From W. D. Glasgow, "The Contradiction in Ethical Egoism," *Philosophical Studies*, Vol. 19, No. 6 (Dec. 1968). Reprinted by permission of Kluwer Academic Pubishers.

for the egoist but one autonomous individual (himself) who is also an end in himself. To respect the autonomy of other individuals is to give up this position. . . .

It now becomes apparent where the inconsistency of . . . [ethical egoism] lies. To the nonegoist, who interprets ethical egoism in terms of ordinary moral concepts, it seems that in the statement of his doctrine, the ethical egoist implies that all autonomous (or potentially autonomous) individuals are ends in themselves. But it is also basic to his position to deny this, in making out that, apart from himself, there are no autonomous individuals who are also ends in themselves.

Aristotle

Selection from the *Nicomachean Ethics*

Every art and every inquiry, and similarly every action and pursuit, is thought to aim at some good; and for this reason the good has rightly been declared to be that at which all things aim. . . . If, then, there is some end [i.e. goal or purpose] of the things we do, which we desire for its own sake (everything else being desired for the sake of this), and if we do not choose everything for the sake of something else (for at that rate the process would go on to infinity, so that our desire would be empty and vain), clearly this must be the good and the chief good. Will not the knowledge of it, then, have a great influence on life? Shall we not, like archers who have a mark to aim at, be more likely to hit upon what is right? If so, we must try, in outline at least to determine what it is. . . .

Since there are evidently more than one end, and we choose some of these . . . for the sake of something else, clearly not all ends are final ends; but the chief good is evidently something final. Therefore, if there is only one final end, this will be what we are seeking, and if there are more than one, the most final of these will be what we are seeking. Now we call that which is in itself worthy of pursuit more final than that which is worthy of pursuit for the sake of something else, and that which is never desirable for the sake of something else more final than the things that are desirable both in themselves and for the sake of that other thing, and therefore we call final without qualification that which is always desirable in itself and never for the sake of something else.

Now such a thing happiness, above all else, is held to be; for this we choose always for itself and never for the sake of something else, but honour, pleasure, reason, and every virtue we choose indeed for themselves (for if nothing resulted from them we should still choose each of them), but we choose them also for the sake of happiness, judging that by means of them we shall be happy. Happiness, on the other hand, no one chooses for the sake of these, nor, in general, for anything other than itself.

From the point of view of self-sufficiency the same result seems to follow; for the final good is thought to be self-sufficient. Now by self-sufficient we do not mean that which is sufficient for a man by himself, for one who lives a solitary life, but also for parents, children, wife, and in general for his friends and fellow citizens, since man is born for citizenship. [T]he self-sufficient we . . . define as that which when isolated makes life desirable and lacking in nothing; and such we think happiness to be; and further we think it most desirable of all things, without being counted as one good thing among others - if it were so counted it would clearly be made more desirable by the addition of even the least of goods; for that which is added becomes an excess of goods, and

Reprinted from Aristotle's *Nicomachean Ethics* translated by W. D. Ross (1925) by permission of Oxford University Press.

of goods the greater is always more desirable. Happiness, then is something final and self-sufficient, and is the end of action.

. . . [T]o say that happiness is the chief good seems a platitude, and a clearer account of what it is is still desired. This might perhaps be given, if we could first ascertain the function of man. For just as for a flute-player, a sculptor, or any artist, and, in general, for all things that have a function or activity, the good and the "well" is thought to reside in the function, so would it seem to be for man if he has a function. Have the carpenter, then, and the tanner certain functions or activities, and has man none? Is he born without a function? Or as eye, hand, foot, and in general each of the parts evidently has a function, may one lay it down that man similarly has a function apart from all these? What then can this be? Life seems to be common even to plants, but we are seeking what is peculiar to man. . . . [H]uman good turns out to be activity of soul in accordance with virtue, and if there are more than one virtue, in accordance with the best and most complete.

But we must add "in a complete life." For one swallow does not make a summer, nor does one day; and so too one day, or a short time does not make a man blessed and happy.

. . . [N]o function of man has so much permanence as virtuous activities and of these the most valuable are more durable because those who are happy spend their life most readily and most continuously in these; for this seems to be the reason why we do not forget them. The happy man will be happy throughout his life; for always, or by preference to everything else, he will be engaged in virtuous action and contemplation, and he will bear the chances of life most nobly and altogether decorously, if he is "truly good" and "foursquare beyond reproach."

. . . Since happiness is an activity of soul in accordance with perfect virtue, we must consider the nature of virtue; for perhaps we shall thus see better the nature of happiness. . . .

Neither by nature . . . nor contrary to nature do the virtues arise in us; rather we are adapted by nature to receive them, and are made perfect by habit.

. . . [T]he virtues we get by first exercising them, as also happens in the case of the arts as well. For the things we have to learn before we can do them, we learn by doing them, e.g. men become builders by building and lyre-players by playing the lyre; so too we become just by doing just acts, temperate by doing temperate acts, brave by doing brave acts.

. . . [B]y doing the acts that we do in our transactions with other men we become just or unjust and by doing the acts that we do in the presence of danger, and being habituated to feel fear or confidence, we become brave or cowardly. The same is true of appetites and feelings of anger; some men become temperate and good-tempered, others self-indulgent and irascible [i.e. irritable], by behaving in one way or the other in the appropriate circumstances. Thus, in one word, states of character arise out of like activities. This is why the activities we exhibit must be of a certain kind; it is because the states of character correspond to the differences between these. It makes no small difference, then, whether we form habits of one kind or of another from our very youth; it makes a very great difference, or rather *all* the difference.

. . . The question might be asked, what we mean by saying that we must become just by doing just acts, and temperate by doing temperate acts; for if men do just and temperate acts, they are already just and temperate. . . .

Actions . . . are called just and temperate when they are such as the just or the temperate man would do; but it is not the man who does these that is just and temperate, but the man who also does them *as* just and temperate men do them. It is well said, then, that it is by doing just acts that the just man is produced, and by doing temperate acts the temperate man; without doing these no one would have even a prospect of becoming good.

. . . [W]e must consider what virtue is. Since things that are found in the soul are of three kinds—passions, faculties, states of character, virtue must be one of these. By passions I mean appetite, anger, fear, confidence, envy, joy, friendly feeling, hatred, longing, emulation, pity, and in general the feelings that are accompanied by pleasure or pain; by faculties the things in virtue of which we are said to be capable of feeling these, e.g. of becoming angry or being pained or feeling pity; by states of character the things in virtue of which we stand well or badly with reference to the passions, e.g. with reference to anger we stand badly if we feel it violently or too weakly, and well if we feel it moderately; and similarly with reference to the other passions.

Now neither the virtues nor the vices are *passions,* because we are not called good or bad on the ground of our passions, but are so called on the ground of our virtues and our vices, and because we are neither praised nor blamed for our passions (for the man who feels fear or anger is not praised, nor is the man who simply feels anger blamed, but the man who feels it in a certain way), but for our virtues and our vices we are praised or blamed.

Again, we feel anger and fear without choice, but the virtues are modes of choice or involve choice. Further, in respect of the passions we are said to be moved, but in respect of the virtues and the vices we are said not to be moved but to be disposed in a particular way.

For these reasons also they are not *faculties;* for we are neither called good nor bad, nor praised nor blamed, for the simple capacity of feeling the passions; again, we have the faculties by nature, but we are not made good or bad by nature . . . .

If, then, the virtues are neither passions nor faculties, all that remains is that they should be *states of character.* . . .

We must, however, not only describe virtue as a state of character, but also say what sort of state it is. . . .

[Moral] virtue must have the quality of aiming at the intermediate. . . . [I]t . . . is concerned with passions and actions, and in these there is excess, defect, and the intermediate. For instance, both fear and confidence and appetite and anger and pity and in general pleasure and pain may be felt both too much and too little, and in both cases not well; but to feel them at the right times, with reference to the right objects, towards the right people, with the right motive, and in the right way, is what is both intermediate and best, and this is characteristic of virtue. Similarly with regard to actions also there is excess, defect and the intermediate. Now virtue is concerned with passions and actions, in which excess is a form of failure, and so is defect, while the intermediate is praised and is a form of success; and being praised and being successful are both characteristics of virtue. Therefore virtue is a kind of mean, since, as we have seen, it aims at what is intermediate. . . .

Virtue, then, is a state of character concerned with choice, lying in a mean, i.e. the mean relative to us, this being determined by a rational principle, and by that principle by which the man of practical wisdom would determine it. Now it is a mean between two vices, that which depends on excess and that which depends on defect; and again it is a mean because the vices respectively fall short of or exceed what is right in both passions and actions, while virtue both finds and chooses that which is intermediate. Hence in respect of its substance and the definition which states its essence virtue is a mean, with regard to what is best and right an extreme.

Immanuel Kant

Grounding for the Metaphysics of Morals

There is no possibility of thinking of anything at all in the world, or even out of it, which can be regarded as good without qualification, except a *good will*. Intelligence, wit, judgment, and whatever talents of the mind one might want to name are doubtless in many respects good and desirable, as are such qualities of temperament as courage, resolution, perseverance. But they can also become extremely bad and harmful if the will, which is to make use of these gifts of nature and which in its special constitution is called character, is not good. The same holds with gifts of fortune; power, riches, honor, even health, and that complete well-being and contentment with one's condition which is called happiness make for pride and often hereby even arrogance, unless there is a good will to correct their influence on the mind and herewith also to rectify the whole principle of action and make it universally conformable to its end. The sight of a being who is not graced by any touch of a pure and good will but who yet enjoys an uninterrupted prosperity can never delight a rational and impartial spectator. Thus a good will seems to constitute the indispensable condition of being even worthy of happiness.

Some qualities are even conducive to this good will itself and can facilitate its work. Nevertheless, they have no intrinsic unconditional worth; but they always presuppose, rather, a good will, which restricts the high esteem in which they are otherwise rightly held, and does not permit them to be regarded as absolutely good. Moderation in emotions and

From Immanuel Kant, *Grounding for the Metaphysics of Morals*, 3rd Edition, 1993, translated by James W. Ellington, pp. 7–15, pp. 34-37 (edited).

passions, self-control, and calm deliberation are not only good in many respects but even seem to constitute part of the intrinsic worth of a person. But they are far from being rightly called good without qualification (however unconditionally they were commended by the ancients). For without the principles of a good will, they can become extremely bad; the coolness of a villain makes him not only much more dangerous but also immediately more abominable in our eyes than he would have been regarded by us without it.

A good will is good not because of what it effects or accomplishes; . . . it is good only through its willing, i.e., it is good in itself. . . .

The concept of a will estimable in itself and good without regard to any further end must now be developed. . . . Therefore, we shall take up the concept of *duty*. . . .

I here omit all actions already recognized as contrary to duty, even though they may be useful for this or that end; for in the case of these the question does not arise at all as to whether they might be done from duty, since they even conflict with duty. I also set aside those actions which are really in accordance with duty, yet to which men have no immediate inclination, but perform them because they are impelled thereto by some other inclination. For in this [second] case to decide whether the action which is in accord with duty has been done from duty or from some selfish purpose is easy. This difference is far more difficult to note in the [third] case where the action accords with duty and the subject has in addition an immediate inclination to do the action. For example,[1] that a dealer should not overcharge an inexperienced purchaser certainly accords with duty; and where there is much commerce, the prudent merchant does not overcharge but keeps to a fixed price for everyone in general, so that a child may buy from him just as well as everyone else may. Thus customers are honestly served, but this is not nearly enough for making us believe that the merchant has acted this way from duty and from principles of honesty; his own advantage required him to do it. He cannot, however, be assumed to have in addition [as in the third case] an immediate inclination toward his buyers, causing him, as it were, out of love to give no one as far as price is concerned any advantage over another. Hence the action was done neither from duty nor from immediate inclination, but merely for a selfish purpose. . . .

To be beneficent where one can is a duty; and besides this, there are many persons who are so sympathetically constituted that, without any further motive of vanity or self-interest, they find an inner pleasure in spreading joy around them and can rejoice in the satisfaction of others as their own work. But I maintain that in such a case an action of this kind, however dutiful and amiable it may be, has nevertheless no true moral worth.[2] It is on a level with such actions as arise from other inclinations, e.g., the inclination for honor, which if fortunately directed to what is in fact beneficial and accords with duty and is thus honorable, deserves praise and encouragement, but not esteem; for its maxim lacks the moral content of an action done not from inclination but from duty. Suppose then the mind of this friend of mankind to be clouded over with his own sorrow so that all sympathy with the lot of others is extinguished, and suppose him still to have the power to benefit others in distress, even though he is not touched by their trouble because he is sufficiently absorbed with his own; and now suppose that, even though no inclination moves him any longer, he nevertheless tears himself from this deadly insensibility and performs the action without any inclination at all, but solely from duty—then for the first time his action has genuine moral worth.[3] . . .

An action done from duty has its moral worth, not in the purpose that is to be attained by it, but in the maxim according to which the action is determined. The moral worth depends, therefore, not on the realization of the object of the action, but merely on the principle of volition according to which, without regard to any objects of the faculty of desire, the action has been done. From what has gone before it is clear that the purposes which we may have in our actions, as well as their effects regarded as ends

and incentives of the will, cannot give to actions any unconditioned and moral worth. Where, then, can this worth lie if it is not to be found in the will's relation to the expected effect? Nowhere but in the principle of the will, with no regard to the ends that can be brought about through such action. . . .

An action done from duty must altogether exclude the influence of inclination and therewith every object of the will. Hence there is nothing left which can determine the will except objectively the law and subjectively pure respect for this practical law, i.e., the will can be subjectively determined by the maxim[4] that I should follow such a law even if all my inclinations are thereby thwarted.

Thus the moral worth of an action does not lie in the effect expected from it nor in any principle of action that needs to borrow its motive from this expected effect. For all these effects (agreeableness of one's condition and even the furtherance of other people's happiness) could have been brought about also through other causes and would not have required the will of a rational being, in which the highest and unconditioned good can alone be found. Therefore, the pre-eminent good which is called moral can consist in nothing but the representation of the law in itself. . . .

But what sort of law can that be the thought of which must determine the will without reference to any expected effect, so that the will can be called absolutely good without qualification? Since I have deprived the will of every impulse that might arise for it from obeying any particular law, there is nothing left to serve the will as principle except the universal conformity of its actions to law as such, i.e., I should never act except in such a way that I can also will that my maxim should become a universal law.[5] Here mere conformity to law as such (without having as its basis any law determining particular actions) serves the will as principle and must so serve it if duty is not to be a vain delusion and a chimerical concept. The ordinary reason of mankind in its practical judgments agrees completely with this, and always has in view the aforementioned principle.

For example, take this question. When I am in distress, may I make a promise with the intention of not keeping it? I readily distinguish here the two meanings which the question may have; whether making a false promise conforms with prudence or with duty. Doubtless the former can often be the case. Indeed I clearly see that escape from some present difficulty by means of such a promise is not enough. In addition I must carefully consider whether from this lie there may later arise far greater inconvenience for me than from what I now try to escape. Furthermore, the consequences of my false promise are not easy to forsee, even with all my supposed cunning; loss of confidence in me might prove to be far more disadvantageous than the misfortune which I now try to avoid. The more prudent way might be to act according to a universal maxim and to make it a habit not to promise anything without intending to keep it. But that such a maxim is, nevertheless, always based on nothing but a fear of consequences becomes clear to me at once. To be truthful from duty is, however, quite different from being truthful from fear of disadvantageous consequences; in the first case the concept of the action itself contains a law for me, while in the second I must first look around elsewhere to see what are the results for me that might be connected with the action. For to deviate from the principle of duty is quite certainly bad; but to abandon my maxim of prudence can often be very advantageous for me, though to abide by it is certainly safer. The most direct and infallible way, however, to answer the question as to whether a lying promise accords with duty is to ask myself whether I would really be content if my maxim (of extricating myself from difficulty by means of a false promise) were to hold as a universal law for myself as well as for others, and could I really say to myself that everyone may promise falsely when he finds himself in a difficulty from which he can find no other way to extricate himself. Then I immediately become aware that I can indeed will the lie but can not at all will a universal law to lie. For by such a law there would really be no promises at all, since in vain would my willing future actions be professed to other people who would not believe what I professed, or if they over-hastily did believe, then they would pay me back in like coin.

Therefore, my maxim would necessarily destroy itself just as soon as it was made a universal law.[6]

Therefore, I need no far-reaching acuteness to discern what I have to do in order that my will may be morally good. Inexperienced in the course of the world and incapable of being prepared for all its contingencies, I only ask myself whether I can also will that my maxim should become a universal law. If not, then the maxim must be rejected, not because of any disadvantage accruing to me or even to others, but because it cannot be fitting as a principle in a possible legislation of universal law, and reason exacts from me immediate respect for such legislation. . . .

[S]uppose that there were something whose existence has in itself an absolute worth, something which as an end in itself could be a ground of determinate laws. In it, and in it alone, would there be the ground of a possible categorical imperative, i.e., of a practical law.

Now I say that man, and in general every rational being, exists as an end in himself and not merely as a means to be arbitrarily used by this or that will. He must in all his actions, whether directed to himself or to other rational beings, always be regarded at the same time as an end. . . . Rational beings are called persons inasmuch as their nature already marks them out as ends in themselves, i.e., as something which is not to be used merely as means and hence there is imposed thereby a limit on all arbitrary use of such beings, which are thus objects of respect. Persons are, therefore, not merely subjective ends, whose existence as an effect of our actions has a value for us; but such beings are objective ends, i.e., exist as ends in themselves. Such an end is one for which there can be substituted no other end to which such beings should serve merely as means. . . .

If then there is to be a supreme practical principle and, as far as the human will is concerned, a categorical imperative, then it must be such that from the conception of what is necessarily an end for everyone because this end is an end in itself it constitutes an objective principle of the will and can hence serve as a practical law. The ground of such a principle is this: rational nature exists as an end in itself. In this way man necessarily thinks of his own existence; thus far is it a subjective principle of human actions. But in this way also does every other rational being think of his existence on the same rational ground that holds also for me;[7] hence it is at the same time an objective principle, from which, as a supreme practical ground, all laws of the will must be able to be derived. The practical imperative will therefore be the following: Act in such a way that you treat humanity, whether in your own person or in the person of another, always at the same time as an end and never simply as a means.[8] . . .

Notes

1. [The ensuing example provides an illustration of the second case.]
2. [This is an example of case 3.]
3. [This is an example of case 4.]
4. A maxim is the subjective principle of volition. The objective principle (i.e., one which would serve all rational beings also subjectively as a practical principle if reason had full control over the faculty of desire) is the practical law.
5. [This is the first time in the *Grounding* that the categorical imperative is stated.]
6. [This means that when you tell a lie, you merely take exception to the general rule that says everyone should always tell the truth and believe that what you are saying is true. When you lie, you do not thereby will that everyone else lie and not believe that what you are saying is true, because in such a case your lie would never work to get you what you want.]
7. This proposition I here put forward as a postulate. The grounds for it will be found in the last section. [See below Ak. 446–63.]
8. [This oft-quoted version of the categorical imperative is usually referred to as the formula of the end in itself.]

John Stuart Mill

Utilitarianism

The creed which accepts as the foundation of morals, Utility, or the Greatest Happiness Principle, holds that actions are right in proportion as they tend to promote happiness, wrong as they tend to produce the reverse of happiness. By happiness is intended pleasure, and the absence of pain; by unhappiness, pain, and the privation of pleasure. To give a clear view of the moral standard set up by the theory, much more requires to be said; in particular, what things it includes in the ideas of pain and pleasure; and to what extent this is left an open question. But these supplementary explanations do not affect the theory of life on which this theory of morality is grounded—namely, that pleasure,

From John Stuart Mill, *Collected Works of John Stuart Mill, Vol. 10, Essays on Ethics, Religion and Society,* ed. J. M. Robson. Toronto: University of Toronto Press, © 1969. Reprinted by permission.

and freedom from pain, are the only things desirable as ends; and that all desirable things . . . are desirable either for the pleasure inherent in themselves, or as means to the promotion of pleasure and the prevention of pain.

Now, such a theory of life excites in many minds . . . inveterate [i.e. long-standing obstinate] dislike. To suppose that life has . . . no higher end than pleasure—no better and nobler object of desire and pursuit—they designate as utterly mean and grovelling; as a doctrine worthy only of swine, to whom the followers of Epicurus were, at a very early period, contemptuously likened; and modern holders of the doctrine are occasionally made the subject of equally polite comparisons . . . [Epicurus was an early Greek philosopher (341-270 B.C) who founded a system of ethics which held that the chief ethical goal was to live a pleasurable life.]

When thus attacked, the Epicureans have always answered, that it is not they, but their accusers, who represent human nature in a degrading light; since the accusation supposes human beings to be capable of no pleasures except those of which swine are capable. If this supposition were true, the charge could not be gainsaid, but would then be no longer an imputation; for if the sources of pleasure were precisely the same to human beings and to swine, the rule of life which is good enough for the one would be good enough for the other. The comparison of the Epicurean life to that of beasts is felt as degrading, precisely because a beast's pleasures do not satisfy a human being's conceptions of happiness. Human beings have faculties more elevated than the animal appetites, and when once made conscious of them, do not regard anything as happiness which does not include their gratification. ... It is quite compatible with the principle of utility to recognise the fact, that some *kinds* of pleasure are more desirable and more valuable than others. It would be absurd that while, in estimating all other things, quality is considered as well as quantity, the estimation of pleasures should be supposed to depend on quantity alone.

If I am asked, what I mean by difference of quality in pleasures, or what makes one pleasure more valuable than another, merely as a pleasure, except its being greater in amount, there is but one possible answer. Of two pleasures, if there be one to which all or almost all who have experience of both give a decided preference, irrespective of any feeling of moral obligation to prefer it, that is the more desirable pleasure. If one of the two is, by those who are competently acquainted with both, placed so far above the other that they prefer it, even though knowing it to be attended with a greater amount of discontent, and would not resign it for any quantity of the other pleasure which their nature is capable of, we are justified in ascribing to the preferred enjoyment a superiority in quality, so far outweighing quantity as to render it, in comparison, of small account.

Now it is an unquestionable fact that those who are equally acquainted with, and equally capable of appreciating and enjoying, both, do give a most marked preference to the manner of existence which employs their higher faculties. Few human creatures would consent to be changed into any of the lower animals, for a promise of the fullest allowance of a beast's pleasures; no intelligent human being would consent to be a fool, no instructed person would be an ignoramus, no person of feeling and conscience would be selfish and base, even though they should be persuaded that the fool, the dunce, or the rascal is better satisfied with his lot than they with theirs. ... A being of higher faculties requires more to make him happy, is capable probably of more acute suffering, and is certainly accessible to it at more points, than one of an inferior type; but in spite of these liabilities, he can never really wish to sink into what he feels to be a lower grade of existence. ... It is better to be a human being dissatisfied than a pig satisfied; better to be Socrates dissatisfied than a fool satisfied. And if the fool, or the pig, is of a different opinion, it is because they only know their own side of the question. The other party to the comparison knows both sides.

... I have dwelt on this point, as being a necessary part of a perfectly just conception of Utility or Happiness, considered as the directive rule of human conduct. But it is by no means an indispensable condition to the acceptance of the utilitarian standard; for that standard is not the agent's own greatest happiness, but the greatest amount of happiness altogether; and if it may possibly be doubted whether a noble character is always the happier for it nobleness, there can be no doubt that it makes other people happier, and that the world in general is immensely a gainer by it. ...

According to the Greatest Happiness Principle ... the ultimate end, with reference to and for the sake of which all other things are desirable (whether we are considering our own good or that of other people), is an existence exempt as far as possible from pain, and as rich as possible in enjoyments, both in point of quantity and quality; the test of quality, and the rule for measuring it against quantity, being the preference felt by those who, in their opportunities of experience, to which must be added their habits of self-consciousness and self-observation, are best furnished with the means of comparison. This, being, according to the utilitarian opinion, the end of human action, is necessarily also the standard of morality; which may accordingly be defined, the rules and precepts for human conduct, by the observance of which an existence such as has been described might be, to the greatest extent possible, secured to all mankind; and not to them only, but, so far as the nature of things admits, to the whole sentient creation.

Against this doctrine, however, arises another class of objectors, who say that happiness, in any form, cannot be the rational purpose of human life and action; because in the first place, it is unattainable [and in the second] ... men can do *without* happiness; that ... human beings ... could not have become noble but by learning the lesson of ... renunciation; which lesson, thoroughly learnt and submitted to ... [is] the beginning and necessary condition of all virtue.

The first of these objections would go to the root of the matter were it well founded; for if no happiness is to be had at all by human beings, the attainment of it cannot be the end of morality, or of any rational conduct. Though, even in that case, something might still be said for the utilitarian theory; since utility includes not solely the pursuit of happiness, but the prevention or mitigation of unhappiness; and if the former aim be chimerical, there will be all the greater scope and more imperative need for the latter ... When, however, it is thus positively asserted to be impossible that human life should be happy, the assertion, if not something like a verbal quibble, is at least an exaggeration. If by happiness be meant a continuity of highly pleasurable excitement, it is evident enough that this is impossible. A state of exalted pleasure lasts only moments, or in some cases, and with some intermissions, hours or days, and is the occasional brilliant flash of enjoyment, not its permanent and steady flame. Of this the philosophers who have taught that happiness is the end of life were as fully aware as those who taunt them. The happiness which they meant was not a life of rapture; but moments of such, in an existence made up of few and transitory pains, many and various pleasures, with a decided predominance of the active over the passive, and having as the foundation of the whole, not to expect more from life than it is capable of bestowing. A life thus composed, to those who have been fortunate enough to obtain it, has always appeared worthy of the name of happiness. And such an existence is even now the lot of many, during some considerable portion of their lives. The present wretched education, and wretched social arrangements, are the only real hindrance to its being attainable by almost all.

... In a world in which there is so much to interest, so much to enjoy, and so much also to correct and improve, every one who has ... [a] moderate amount of moral and intellectual requisites is capable of an existence which may be called enviable; and unless such a person, through bad laws, or subjection to the will of others, is denied the liberty to use the sources of happiness within his reach, he will not fail to find this enviable existence, if he escape the positive evils of life, the great sources of physical and mental suffering—such as indigence, disease, and the unkindness, worthlessness, or premature loss of objects of affection. The main stress of the problem lies, therefore, in the contest with these calamities, from which it is a rare good fortune entirely to escape; which, as things now are, cannot be obviated, and often cannot be in any material degree mitigated. Yet no one whose opinion deserves a moment's consideration can doubt that most of the great positive evils of the world are in themselves removable, and will, if human affairs continue to improve, be in the end reduced within narrow limits. Poverty, in any sense implying suffering, may be completely extinguished by the wisdom of society, combined with the good sense and providence of individuals. Even that most intractable of enemies, disease, may be indefinitely reduced in dimensions by good physical and moral education, and proper control of noxious influences; while the progress of science holds out a promise for the future of still more direct conquests over this detestable foe. And every advance in that direction relieves us from some, not only of the chances which cut short our own lives, but, what concerns us still more, which deprive us of those in whom our happiness is wrapt up. As for vicissitudes of fortune, and other disappointments connected with worldly circumstances, these are principally the effect either of gross imprudence, of ill-regulated desires, or of bad or imperfect social institutions. All the grand sources, in short, of human suffering are in a great degree, many of them almost entirely, conquerable by human care and effort. ...

And this leads to the true estimation of what is said by the objectors concerning the possibility, and the obligation, of learning to do without happiness. Unquestionably it is possible to do without happiness; it is done involuntarily by nineteen-twentieths of mankind, even in those parts of our present world which are least deep in barbarism; and it often has to be done voluntarily by the hero or the martyr, for the sake of something which he prizes more than his individual happiness. But this something, what is it, unless the happiness of others, or some of the requisites of happiness? It is noble to be capable of resigning entirely one's own portion of happiness, or chances of it: but, after all, this self-sacrifice must be for some end; it is not its own end; and if we are told that its end is not happiness, but virtue, which is better than happiness, I ask, would the sacrifice be made if the hero or martyr did not believe that it would earn for others immunity from similar sacrifices? Would it be made, if he thought that his renunciation of happiness for himself would produce no fruit for any of his fellow creature, but to make their lot like his, and place them also in the condition of persons who have renounced happiness? All honour to those who can abnegate for themselves the personal enjoyment of life, when by such renunciation they contribute worthily to increase the amount of happiness in the world; but he who does it, or professes to do it, for any other purpose, is no more deserving of admiration than the ascetic mounted on his pillar. He may be an inspiriting proof of what men *can* do, but assuredly not an example of what they *should*.

. . . The utilitarian morality does recognise in human beings the power of sacrificing their own greatest good for the good of others. It only refuses to admit that the sacrifice is itself a good. A sacrifice which does not increase, or tend to increase, the sum total of happiness, it considers as wasted. The only self-renunciation which it applauds, is devotion to the happiness, or to some of the means of happiness, of others; either of mankind collectively, or of individuals within the limits imposed by the collective interests of mankind.

I must again repeat, what the assailants of utilitarianism seldom have the justice to acknowledge, that the happiness which forms the utilitarian standard of what is right in conduct, is not the agent's own happiness, but that of all concerned. As between his own happiness and that of others, utilitarianism requires him to be as strictly impartial as a disinterested and benevolent spectator. In the golden rule of Jesus of Nazareth, we read the complete spirit of the ethics of utility. To do as one would be done by, and to love one's neighbour as oneself, constitute the ideal perfection of utilitarian morality. . . . If the impugners of the utilitarian morality represented it to their own minds in this its true character, I know not what recommendation possessed by any other morality they could possibly affirm to be wanting to it; what more beautiful or more exalted developments of human nature any other ethical system can be supposed to foster, or what springs of action, not accessible to the utilitarian, such systems rely on for giving effect to their mandates.

David L. Norton

Moral Minimalism and the Development of Moral Character

Three recent books in ethics—Alasdair MacIntyre's *After Virtue*, Richard Taylor's *Ethics, Faith, and Reason*, and Edmund L. Pincoffs's *Quandaries and Virtues*[1]—have, each in its own way, contrasted modern ethics and classical ethics as very disparate modes of ethical theorizing, and each has offered arguments for the superiority of the classical mode. It is my intent in what follows to contribute to their theses, both of the radical disparity of the two modes, and of the superiority of the classical mode in important respects. Specifically I will argue that modern ethics is typically minimalist (a) with respect to the kinds of situations and choices that count as moral, and (b) in its conception of moral character, and that its minimalism in these respects removes from moral consideration factors that cannot be disregarded without the dilution of moral thought and moral life. I will begin by attempting my own characterizations of modern and classical ethics.

MacIntyre calls the modern mode of moral thought "Nietzschean,"[Nietzsche (1844-1900) was a German philosopher who attacked what he called *herd morality*, i.e. conventional, morality, and urged that the individual must move beyond good and evil to create his or her own value.] and the classical mode "Aristotelian"; Richard Taylor contrasts the modern "ethics of duty" with the classical "ethics of aspiration"; and Edmund Pincoffs characterizes modern "quandary ethics" against classical "ethics of

From *Midwest Studies in Philosophy, Volume XIII: Ethical Theory* (French, Uehling, Wettstein, eds.) © 1988 by the University of Notre Dame Press. Reprinted by permission of the publisher.

virtue." Each of these pairings has indicative force, but the contrast I want to highlight can best be represented under the headings,"ethics of rules" and "ethics of character." By "ethics of rules" I refer to what I suggest has been the dominant mode of ethical theorizing since Thomas Hobbes. By "ethics of character" I intend to refer in general to ethical theory in classical Greece and Rome, whose fullest and soundest formulation I take to be the eudaimonism of Socrates, Plato, and Aristotle. [*Eudaimonism* is the view that the goal of the moral life is to achieve a happy life. Note that thinkers such as Socrates, Plato and Aristotle held that the happy life included far more than sensual pleasures.]

My attempted characterizations must be prefaced by a caveat. As for MacIntyre, Taylor, and Pincoffs, so for me, the modern-classical dichotomy must be understood not as "hard" but as "soft," and in two senses. In the first place the modern and the classical modes do not stand with respect to each other as mutually exclusive, but rather as a transformative difference in emphasis. Thus modern "rules morality" is not devoid of the concern for the development of moral character but gives remarkably less attention to it, and attends to it in the light in which it appears when rules are the paramount concern. Conversely, "character morality" does not altogether neglect rules, but subordinates them to the development of moral character and views them instrumentally with reference to that end. Secondly, the dichotomy is "soft" in the sense that historical exceptions are to be recognized: there are "character" ethicists in modernity (notable among them Nietzsche, Emerson, Henry Thoreau, and the Scottish "moral sense" school—e.g., Hutcheson, Hume, Adam Smith—and including brilliant flashes from John Stuart Mill), but they are a distinct minority and relatively lacking in influence; and "rules" ethics was by no means unknown in the ancient world, but was, so to speak, the moribund residue of ethics of character.

We will begin the study in contrast by observing that "rules ethics" and "character ethics" start with different primary questions. For modern moral philosophy the primary question is: "What is the right thing to do in particular (moral) situations?" and it is answered by finding the rule that applies to the given situation and acting in accordance with it. Thus if I am driving my car and collide with another vehicle, I am obligated by law to describe the event, and morality (here backed by law) holds me to the rule, "always tell the truth." Within this framework what we refer to as "contemporary moral problems"—e.g., abortion, euthanasia, compensatory preferential hiring—are problems for which the covering rule(s) is unsettled and in dispute. The point, however, is the unquestioned assumption that such problems are to be solved by arriving at the covering rule.

The accepted agenda of modern ethics is to formulate (discover; devise and contractually agree upon) a supreme and universally applicable moral principle—Hobbes's natural right of self-preservation, Kant's categorical imperative, Bentham's "greatest happiness of the greatest number," and Rawls's two principles of justice are famous examples—together with criteria for distinguishing moral from non-moral situations, criteria for recognizing relevantly different kinds of moral situations, and, as far as practicable, a complete list of rules representing the application of the supreme principle to all possible types of moral situations, or a set of rules for applying the supreme principle to particular situations. Then moral conduct is the conduct that best accords with the applicable rules in given moral situations. What is meant by a "prima facie duty" is a duty to obey a rule that is held to prevail in appropriate moral situations unless contravened by a higher rule.

By contrast, classical morality begins with the question, "What is a good life for a human being?" (Socrates: "But we ought to consider more carefully, for this is no light matter: it is the question, what is the right way to live?"[2]) It leads directly to the problem of the development of moral character, because any adequate description of a good human life will necessarily include attributes that are not manifest in persons in the beginning of their lives, but are developmental outcomes. The attributes on which classical ethics focuses are the moral virtues, and here it is enough to name the

famous four of Plato's *Republic*—wisdom, courage, temperance, and justice—to recognize that none of them can be expected of children, but only of persons in later life, and only in the later life of persons in whom the requisite moral development occurs.

In the classical understanding the virtues are excellences of character that are objective goods, of worth to others as well as to the virtues-bearer (for example, the courage of our friend enhances the assistance he or she renders to us, just as it strengthens his or her pursuit of independent ends). Second, the manifestation of a virtue is understood to be the actualization of what was theretofore not totally absent in the person, but present in the form of a potentiality.[3] In other words, to be a human being is to be capable of manifesting virtues, and the problem of moral development is the problem of discovering the conditions for the actualization of qualities that are originally within persons as potentialities.

Classical ethics endeavors to answer the question, "What is a good life for a human being?" but to deepen our understanding it is important to consider first the prior question, "What sort of a being is it to which the question of the good life is posed?" The eudaimonistic answer is famously expressed by Plato in his image of the human soul as chariot, charioteer, and two contrary-minded horses (*Phaedrus*): distinctively, human being is problematic being; to be a human is in the deepest sense to be a problem to oneself, specifically an identity problem. It is the problem of deciding what to become and endeavoring to become it. The problem of deciding what to become is the problem of learning to recognize ideal goods and choosing among them which good to aim at as the goal of one's self-fulfilling and objectively worthy life. The problem of endeavoring to become the person one chooses to become is the problem of acquiring the resourcefulness and force of character to overcome external and internal obstacles. In the eudaimonistic view, human freedom has its ground in the absence in human beings of the metaphysical necessity that characterizes all other kinds of being, and in virtue of which they cannot be other than they are. But the absence of metaphysical necessity in the individual human being must be compensated for if his or her chosen end is to be achievable, and the compensatory necessity, because it must itself be chosen, is termed moral necessity. . . . Persons in whom moral necessity is lacking are described by Thoreau as "thrown off the track by every nutshell and mosquito's wing that falls on the rails."[4] Moral necessity is the "I must" of the dedicated and resourceful person. As against "I wish to," "I hope to," and even "I will," it bespeaks the strength of character to overcome the inevitable obstacles in the world, as well as vagrant impulses and ordinary apprehensions within the self.

Deciding what to become requires knowledge of the good, which is wisdom, and endeavoring to become it requires moral necessity. Connecting these two sides of the problem that every person is to him- or herself is the virtue of integrity, consisting in integration of the separable and initially disordered aspects of the self-faculties, desires, interests, roles—such that they complement rather than contradict one another, and each contributes to the realization of the chosen good.

It will be evident that the classical themes briefly touched upon above have taken us a good distance into the development of moral character, for alike, moral necessity, wisdom, and integrity are developmental outcomes, possessed *ab initio* by persons not as manifest capacities but as unactualized potentialities. What now requires to be noticed is that modern ethics, in its dominant mode that I have termed "rule" ethics, is notable for its relative disregard of the problems pertaining to the development of moral character. This is an important respect in which modern morality is "minimalist" in comparison to classical morality—it makes minimal demands upon the intelligence and developed moral character of moral agents, requiring little or nothing of them in the way of wisdom, courage, or integrity. It is also minimalist in a second sense, namely that it delimits the arena of moral choice to but a small sector of human experience. We shall say something about each of these instances of minimalism, beginning with the delimitation of moral choice.

It has often been observed that modern ethical theory typically works with a threefold classification of actions from the standpoint of moral meaning—right actions, wrong actions, and morally indifferent actions. This classification is coupled with a distinction between moral and non-moral situations, which accounts for the restrictive stipulation in what we earlier offered as the foundational question of modern ethics, "What is the right thing to do in particular *moral situations*." The restriction is not to be found in classical ethics because the distinction does not exist. For classical ethics nothing in human experience is without moral meaning, and "the moral situation" is the life of each person in its entirety. If these contentions appear extreme, support for them will be offered shortly. Meanwhile it can readily be recognized that some situations typically adjudged non-moral in modern terms are importantly moral in classical terms.

An example of a situation that is generally understood to be non-moral by modern standards is the situation of vocational choice. Suppose, for instance, that my supreme moral principle is Kant's categorical imperative, and I decide to become a chemical engineer. I obviously cannot will that everyone in my situation, i.e., the situation of vocational choice, decide to become a chemical engineer, yet it is entirely conceivable that this choice is the right choice for me. This problem might be handled in a number of ways, but modern ethics is typified by the simple expedient of agreeing to regard the situation of vocational choice as normally a non-moral situation. Then to say that my choice is the "right" choice for me is to use the word "right" in one of its non-moral senses.

The same categorial distinction expels from the domain of the moral countless other types of choice that human beings characteristically make, e.g., of what friends to cultivate, what avocations to pursue, what books to read. Indeed, John Stuart Mill, in his utilitarian voice, says that "ninety-nine hundredths of all our actions are done from other [than moral] motives, and rightly so done if the rule of duty does not condemn them."[5] He is obliged to thus delimit the workings of the utilitarian principle in order to preserve any vestige of individual autonomy under utilitarianism. Were we at all times obliged to seek to produce the greatest happiness of the greatest number (with its correlative rule on diminishing pain), we would be morally culpable in reading a book, writing a poem, or attending to the needs of our children, for in these cases there are many things we might do instead that would better serve to alleviate human misery in the world. . . .

The distinction of moral from non-moral situations affords to persons, institutions, and practices the opportunity to pitch their tents on non-moral turf, and it is difficult to find arguments or incentives that will induce them to move to moral ground. One class of arguments to this end is conspicuously circular, resting on premises that the outlander is under no obligation to accept, while another, by offering non-moral incentives to moral conduct (e.g., prudence, happiness), appears to "degrade and prostitute virtue,"[6] setting it in the service of non-moral ends.

Two such non-moral campouts that have decisively shaped modern history are science and business management. Modern science gained its immunity on the ground of the supposed gulf between facts and values, description and prescription; its devotion to facts was thus at the same time its claim to be "value-free." And for approximately the past hundred years, business management has sought to claim for itself the status of applied social science on the bridge of economics, availing itself of moral exemption (except with respect to the "my station and its duties" type of code that no practice can be without) on the fact-value distinction. The prevailing spirit of management theory and practice is succinctly captured by management scholar Neil W. Chamberlain: "Employees are being paid to produce, not to make themselves into better people. Corporations are purchasing employee time to make a return on it, not investing in employees to enrich their lives. Employees are human capital, and when capital is hired or leased, the objective is not to embellish it for its own sake but to use it for financial advantage."[7]

The proliferation of non-moral domains of refuge from morality comes home to roost when the so-called private sector, which Mill (in his eudaimonistic voice) fought for as a sanctuary for the self-development of moral character, becomes regarded instead as an arena for the gratification of desires that are relieved of any obligation to answer for their worth. Self-development is arduous (albeit deeply rewarding) work, and private life has become, for many, the playground for mindless diversions from the public workplace. The modern rise to predominance of both science and business appears to be accounted for on the basis of powerful a priori human incentives—the love of truth on one side, and the desire for material gain on the other. But to this I believe the following consideration should be added. On any viable conception of human nature, *aspiration* is a definitive human characteristic. (I mean nothing heroic by this, but only that in order to understand any human being's present conduct, we must know the sought-for future toward which present conduct is meant to be contributory.) The effect of modern moral minimalism is to afford to moral life little space for aspiration; it is a small room with a low ceiling and not much of a view. In particular, it calls for little in the way of developed moral character—our second sense of modernity's moral minimalism. I believe an important consequence of this has been to redirect human aspirations away from the confines of morality and toward the apparently limitless horizons afforded by the laboratory and the market.

By contrast to modern ethics, classical ethics gives a central place to ideals, and it is characteristic of ideals that they are capable of enlisting the full measure of human aspiration. The function of ideals in classical ethical theory and moral life is to guide moral development, transforming random change in the lives of individuals and societies into the directed change that deserves to be called moral growth. Central to the development of moral character that constitutes moral growth is the achievement of integrity, by which all of an individual's faculties, desires, choices, dispositions, courses of conduct, and roles are alike expressive of him or her, and contribute to the chosen end. It is a common misconception of modern ethics that ideals are inappropriate *res gestae* of moral obligations because they make extravagant demands that the average person is unable and/or unwilling to accept. The partial truth that this misconception rests upon is the fact that ideals, by their very nature (as perfections) can never be fully actualized, hence the very best human conduct falls short of its ideal. The reason it is nevertheless a misconception is that under the guidance of an ideal, what counts *now* is the next step. The fact that each next step invokes another, and thus no step can be final, does not bespeak the impracticability of ideals per se, for next steps are always possible for a human being, which is to say that for a human being moral growth is always possible. Another modern misconception of the place of ideals in moral life has engendered discomfort over the supposed likeness of the moral idealist and the fanatic. It is true, as Hare observes,[8] that a moral idealist may cleave to his ideals at the expense of his present interests, but to understand this as "fanaticism" is to condemn an important way by which "interests" are moralized. (The ex-alcoholic's personal ideal of sobriety must override what for a considerable time is his immediate desire to have a drink.) With respect to the moral idealist's stance toward others, it may be true that some seek to impose their ideals upon others,[9] but that some moral idealists do not so conduct themselves is evidence of the contingency of such conduct. Eudaimonism's insistence on the autonomy of moral agents as the basis of respect is the requirement for consent by whomever an ideal affects, and condemns the imposition of the ideals of one person, or community, or party, or nation, upon resistant or unwitting others.

It will be immediately obvious that choices which were earlier cited as typically non-moral in the modern understanding of morality are moral choices in the classical understanding. This is because choices of vocation, of avocations, of friends to cultivate and books to read (our previous examples), have a direct bearing on the development of moral character. In the matter of vocation, for example: if it is the fundamental moral responsibility of every person to discover his or her innate potential worth and progressively actualize it in the world, then vocational choice is clearly one of the important means for such actualization, and *vocation* has thematic moral meaning beneath the periodic "moral situations" that arise in it. This is why

Socrates, Plato, and Aristotle refused to categorially divorce vocational skills from moral virtues (and not, as some modern commentators have hastily assumed, because they failed analytically to recognize the difference). Indeed, classical thought integrates the vocation and the life of the individual by the understanding that the true work of each person is his or her life, to which vocation and all other dimensions should be contributory. Were it possible here to pursue the implications of vocation as moral choice, I would argue for vocation as a foundational form of generosity, for by identifying with, and investing themselves in their vocations, persons are endeavoring to give the best of themselves to others in the products of their work, including their own developed traits of character.

Similarly friendship is inseparable from the moral work of self-discovery and self-actualization, and the long section given to it by Aristotle in the *Nicomachean Ethics* is not, as many modern moral philosophers have supposed, a diversionary ramble. According to Socrates in the *Lysis* and Aristotle in the *Nicomachean Ethics,* true friends, willing the best for one another, furnish reciprocal aid toward worthy living. Socrates says that friends, to be of such use to one another, must be alike in pursuing the good, but different and complementary in the kind of good that each pursues, each contributing something of worth to the other that the other cannot self-supply. Though I cannot develop the point, it is worth noting that Socrates is here working out a conception of individual autonomy that is compatible with interdependence, rather than implying a total self-sufficiency that would belie the social nature of humankind.

We have cited key instances of choices that are typically non-moral by modern parameters but moral in classical understanding. However our earlier contention that for classical ethics nothing in human experience is without moral meaning requires that we go further. Specifically we must speak to the trivial desires, choices, and acts which fill a considerable portion of our days. The answer, however, is the same: even our trivial desires, choices, and acts have moral meaning because they have some effect—no matter how small—on the person we are in process of becoming. To modern moral theory they appear to be devoid of moral meaning because they have no direct effect upon others, but classical morality is concerned with their effect upon the self, and quite clearly the kind of person one is in process of becoming has its effects upon others. But suppose that it did not and could not affect others? An individual marooned upon a desert island with no prospect of rescue would be relieved of all moral responsibility under the sort of theory that restricts moral meaning to the effects of a person's conduct on others. By contrast, under eudaimonistic theory such an individual would be nonetheless responsible for doing the utmost that circumstances allowed to manifest his or her potential worth. Because this worth is objective it is meant to be appreciated and utilized by (some) others, but the fact that in the desert island situation this is impossible is a contingency that does not abolish the moral responsibility to (as far as possible) actualize one's potential worth.

It is common in modern theory to distinguish prudential conduct from moral conduct (Kant is a notable example), but eudaimonism recognizes prudence as a necessary condition of worthy living and therefore a moral responsibility.

Returning to our trivial desires, choices, and acts—the virtue of integrity represents the integration of all dimensions of the self, such that each complements all others, and all contribute to the end of the worthy life that is one's own to live. It is an inclusive virtue, leaving nothing out, and an extraneous desire, choice, or act, however minor, is an inner disorder and in some degree (however small) an impediment. Granted, integrity as thus described is an ideal that, as such, cannot be fully realized. Granted also, our very finitude obliges us to adopt measures of economy, included among which is the measure of disregarding truly minor desires, choices, and acts in order to attend to larger ones (as, if asked to describe the features of the room in which I now sit, I would confine myself to conspicuous ones while recognizing that description in infinite detail literally could not be concluded in a lifetime). But notice that this policy of economy is but a plea *de minimus,* ignoring moral meaning that it acknowledges to exist.

If morality is coterminous with human life and unrestrictedly pervasive within it, then individuals are afforded no non-moral domain of refuge, and no human institution, practice, or discipline can claim exemption from morality's ultimate concern—the good life for human beings. Plato expresses this for state government when he says (*The Republic*), "Can anything be better for a commonwealth than to produce in it men and women of the best type?"[10] Mill is a modern spokesman for this view when he says, "The most important point of excellence which any form of government can possess is to promote the virtue and intelligence of the people themselves."[11] And John Dewey puts the same principle by saying, "Democracy has many meanings, but if it has a moral meaning, it is found in resolving that the supreme test of all political institutions and industrial arrangements shall be the contribution they make to the all-around growth of every member of society."[12]

By classical principles the physical sciences, the social sciences, business, and indeed all disciplines, institutions, and practices are ultimately to be judged by their contribution to the good life for humankind. It will perhaps be objected that this understanding would put an end to the so-called "pure research" that constitutes the leading edge of the physical and the social sciences. But "pure research" (presuming for purposes of argument that it exists or is possible) is not precluded by the classical moral picture. It can be sustained by arguments to show that the inalienable responsibility for improving the quality of human life is furthered by pure research. What *is* disallowed is the claim by entire disciplines (e.g., the "pure" sciences, business management) to be exempt from moral demands.

The other "minimalist" delimitation of modern morality that we have identified is the limited demands it makes upon developed moral character. The reason for this delimitation is that modern morality is built upon what Edmund Pincoffs terms the "Hobbesian truism"[13] that in the absence of recognized rules and generally rule-abiding conduct, the lives of persons would be unbearable. On this foundation morality is paired with law in the interest of the preservation of social order. This interest requires the observance by (almost) everyone of rules that are understood and acknowledged as authoritative by (almost) everyone. For this to be the case, the rules must be very simple and straightforward, and acting in accordance with them must require very little in the way of developed moral character. This accounts for the tendency of modern modes of normative ethics—contractarianism, deontology, utilitarianism, intuitionism, ideal observer theory, agent theory—to devolve (from their ultimate and far from simple principles) upon simple rules of the sort as, "Do not lie," "Do not steal," "Keep your promises," "Do not commit murder," etc., and to introduce exceptions and complications with great reluctance.

One consequence of directing morality to the preservation of social order is that morality becomes very difficult to distinguish from law; moral requirements are framed as rules, moral rules serve the same basic purpose as civil and criminal statutes, and moral judgments are modeled on judicial decisions in terms of impartiality and impersonality. Impartiality and impersonality mean that rightly made moral judgments will be made identically by whomever is called upon to judge, and will be applied identically to different persons in relevantly similar circumstances. We say of such judgments that they are "universalizable," typically meaning that what is right for any person in given circumstances is right for every person in relevantly similar circumstances. But there is an internal disparity here, for of the two principal factors in the formula—circumstances and persons—only the former is qualified by "relevantly similar."[14] The reason that differences among persons typically are disregarded or disallowed is that universalizability is intended to thwart the inherent propensity of individuals to regard themselves as the exception to any rule. The effect of this disregard is to preclude recognition of differences among persons in respect to levels of the development of moral character, and this in turn means that only such moral rules can be recognized as make no demands upon moral capacities that (almost) everyone cannot be expected to possess. In sum, the universalizability criterion, by the internal disparity just noted, is obliged to confine its demands upon moral character to the barest minimum. . . .

To be sure, this bare minimum is not nothing; it includes the ability to understand simple moral rules and recognize the situations to which they apply, together with the ability to act in accordance with them and the will to do so. . . . Nevertheless what is required remains characterizable under "conscientiousness" or "rule responsibility," which, as the single virtue (or closely interrelated set of virtues) implicated by the modern mode of ethical theorizing, neglects most of the developed moral capacities recognized as moral virtues in classical thought. This prompts Pincoffs's comment that "The attempt to reduce moral character to any given trait by philosophical fiat is open to suspicion."[15]

The question of what "rule responsibility" requires in the way of developed moral character has not often been addressed by modern ethical theorists, . . . What makes an attempt at adequate description unnecessary for our purposes is that by assigning responsibility for preserving social order to morality, modern ethics (as noted earlier) has been obliged to make minimal demands on developed moral character, whatever the precise description of the requisite character may prove to be. . . .

To summarize what has here been said about modernity's moral minimalism in the second of the two respects we have identified: modern ethics either disregards, or treats inadequately, "good" or "right" acts that make large demands upon developed moral character in individuals.

It may be supposed that Mill and Kant, as dominant figures in modern ethical theory, furnish decisive counterexamples to our thesis that modern ethics makes minimal demands upon developed moral character, and I will speak briefly to each case. It is true that Mill gives great importance to the "sympathetic feelings" in chapter 3 of *Utilitarianism*, and calls for their deliberate cultivation by the "influences of education." But his reason for this is that it is through sympathetic feelings that human beings are induced to act on the principle of "the greatest happiness of the greatest number." This is to say that character development is here conceived by Mill as instrumental to rule-adherence, which subsumes it under Pincoffs's "conscientiousness," and fits our description of "rules morality" offered at the outset.

Similarly Kant's preoccupation with "the good will," which is dutiful solely for duty's sake, is a "conscientiousness" that considers character development only insofar as it procures "rule responsibility." Otherwise he treats moral virtues, not as developed traits of character, but as "a matter of temperament," and of no moral importance. Kant does indeed (in his monograph *Education*) treat "moral culture" as the part of education intended to develop moral character, but for Kant moral character is the "readiness to act in accord with 'maxims' " which precisely subsumes it under Pincoffs's "conscientiousness."[16]

In the matter of conduct that makes large demands upon developed moral character we can effectively contrast the modern and classical perspectives by means of Urmson's "Saints and Heroes," which calls attention to the deficiency of modern moral theory in this respect, but then tries to rectify it in a distinctly modern—and, I believe, unsatisfactory—manner.

Urmson criticizes the three-part classification of actions by most ethical theorists—acts that are morally obligatory, acts that are morally forbidden, and acts that are morally indifferent—for its inability to handle supererogation, understood as the class of acts that are good to do but not wrong not to do. Using "saintly" and "heroic" acts as his paradigms, he says "It would be absurd to suggest that moral philosophers have hitherto been unaware of the existence of saints and heroes and have never even alluded to them in their work. But it does seem that these facts have been neglected in their general, systematic accounts of morality."[17] He thinks it possible to revise the theories he specifically considers (Kantianism, utilitarianism, and intuitionism) "to accommodate the facts," but adds that "until so modified successfully they must surely be treated as unacceptable, and the modifications required might well detract from their plausibility."[18]

A saint acts for the good in contexts in which inclination, desire, or self-interest would prevent most people from so-acting; a hero acts for the good in contexts in which terror, fear, or a drive to self-preservation would prevent such action by most people. Both the saint and the hero act "far beyond the limits of [their] duty,"[19] but Urmson indicates that the class of acts that ethical theory must be rectified to include begins with acts that exceed the limits of duty in the least measure, e.g., acts that are even "a little more generous, forebearing, helpful, or forgiving than fair dealing demands," and all cases of "going the second mile."[20] Because "basic duties" are uniformly obligatory for everyone they must make minimal demands on developed moral character, and Urmson (as we have seen in a previous citation) argues for retention of their minimalist character. The case he makes is for the revision of ethical theory to include the category of supererogation as "higher flights of morality [to be] regarded as more positive contributions that go beyond what is universally to be exacted." He says of these "higher flights" that while they are not to be "exacted publicly," they are "clearly equally pressing *in foro interno* on those who are not content merely to avoid the intolerable."[21]

The problems in Urmson's position to which I want to call attention are two. In the first place he has acknowledged a continuum of what might be called "degrees of difficulty" between basic duties and the "higher flights" of morality, which means that wherever the line is drawn between basic duties and acts that exceed basic duties (acts of supererogation), it will be prone to the appearance of arbitrariness. Second, Urmson acknowledges that saints and heroes regard their saintly and heroic deeds as their duty ("There is indeed no degree of saintliness that a suitable person may not come to consider it to be his duty to achieve"[22]),yet Urmson is in the position of contending that their deeds are in truth "far beyond the limits of [their] duty," and it is unclear by what authority Urmson contradicts the saint or hero.

At bottom, Urmson is beset by the same dilemma that is responsible for the deficiency he calls attention to in the ethical theories he cites. If impartiality precludes consideration of relevant differences among persons, then either moral heroism is obligatory for everyone, or moral duties are confined to what Urmson terms the "rock-bottom" minimum, and moral conduct that exceeds the minimum is the duty of no one. In the latter case there will be nothing *admirable* in moral conduct; ("the admirable" is what deserves to be "looked up to," whereas minimal moral demands are ground-level); in the former case everyone will be morally responsible for conduct that lies beyond the developed capacities of most, and which it is therefore unreasonable to expect of them. To avoid this consequence, Urmson opts for restriction of duties to "rock-bottom" minimum, to which he adds the category of supererogation. The supererogatory is what is morally good to do but not morally obligatory. The problem here is that by his fidelity to impartiality and universality, Urmson is obliged to conclude that whatever is supererogatory, i.e., whatever is in the least beyond minimum "rock-bottom" duties, is not morally obligatory for anyone. But he acknowledges that heroes perceive their heroic conduct as their duty.

Urmson's key mistake, I think, lies in minimizing the significance of the hero's or saint's own conception of his or her moral duty. Noting that only the saint or hero can thus identify his or her duty, and that he or she characteristically attributes this duty to no one else, Urmson says it is *not* "a piece of objective reporting."[23] This propensity to minimize the saint's or hero's own sense of moral responsibility is widespread in modern ethics. Thus Michael W. Jackson says it is "modesty" or "genuine confusion" when Dr. Bernard Rieux, in Albert Camus's *The Plague,* or Cornielle's El Cid, refer to their heroic conduct as their duty.[24] But on the contrary, I think that both Camus and Cornielle are astute in the matter of the psychology of heroism, and that this psychology accurately reflects the facts. The seeming warrant of Urmson's denial of objectivity to the hero's self-judgment is the equation of objective human responsibilities with universally distributed human responsibilities, but this ignores the objective fact of moral development—a morally developed individual possesses greater capabilities than does an individual of lesser development, as a skilled swimmer can accomplish a deep-water rescue that would be beyond the capabilities of a novice swimmer. The recognition that the moral life of individuals is a development is the recognition that moral demands continually increase, and this is corroborated by the testimony of "heroes" (Cornielle's, Camus's, Urmson's) that they demand more of themselves than they expect of most persons, and more than they expected of themselves at prior levels of development. Drawing upon eudaimonistic ethical theory, what we must add to this is the inalienable moral responsibility of every human being for continuous moral development. This cuts off the populist resort of contending that a handful of persons are "born heroes," while nothing but moral mediocrity is to be expected of the rest of us.

In sum, eudaimonism's thesis is that some of what is obligatory at later stages of moral development is supererogatory with respect to prior stages of moral development. This is a continuity-thesis concerning what exceeds or is included within the moral obligations of persons at given times. But the distinction between duty and supererogation is not arbitrary—it is grounded in the objective fact of moral development.

We have referred to the "Hobbesian truism" that for life to be tolerable (almost) everyone must conform to basic moral rules, which entails that demands upon developed moral character must be minimal. To this I will counterpose what I will term the "Socratic truism." It is the proposition that any person may in the course of his or her life encounter one or more ultimate tests in which to pursue the course of life that he or she has chosen to live is at the risk of life or well-being (Socrates, *Apology*: "This is the truth of the matter, gentlemen of the jury: wherever a man has taken a position that he believes to be best, or has been placed by his commander, there he must I think remain and face danger, without a thought for death or anything else, rather than disgrace."). My leave to call this a truism rests in well-recognized cases, for example, when citizens are called upon to risk their lives in defense of their country; or again, when a parent is called upon to risk his or her life to save his or her child. Similarly we recognize, I think, that were we residents of a Nazi-occupied country in WW II, our humanitarian principles would demand of us that we attempt to shelter Jews from Nazi genocide. In general, we know that we cannot live lives that are worthy in our own estimation if we abandon our commitments at the first sign of trouble. Our supreme test may or may not come, but because it may, we must prepare ourselves for it. The Hobbesian truism tells us that minimally acceptable conduct is required of everyone; the Socratic truism tells us that moral heroism may be required of anyone. The demands implicit in the Socratic truism are universalizable because the opportunity of moral growth is in principle universalizable. On the question of universality this is to say that eudaimonism holds the demand for moral growth in individuals to be universal, but holds that morally obligatory conduct in "relevantly similar" situations will differ among persons by virtue of differences in the levels of moral development that they have achieved.

Urmson is surely correct in holding as a paramount criterion of normative ethical philosophy that "our morality must be one that will work,"[25] (this follows from the definition of normative ethics as "practical reason") but modern ethical philosophy is mistaken in supposing this to entail moral minimalism. Large moral demands are practicable when they are proportional to moral development, and when moral development of individuals is a social undertaking. And until morality is understood to include the higher reaches of moral development (as represented by the classical virtues), it is so impoverished as to be unable to enlist human aspiration. The following, by mountaineer Reinhold Messner, will do metaphoric service here: "Striding along, my body becomes so highly-charged it would be quite impossible for me to stop. It feels as if something wants to break free, to burst from my breast. It is a surge of longing that carries me forward as if I were possessed."[26] It is a reflection recorded by Messner during his ascent of K-2 in the Karakoram Himalaya, and would not be likely to have visited him in the flatlands. Moral thought and moral life require their upper reaches if they are to enlist human aspiration lifelong, and ethical theory is bound to accommodate them. But we must recognize that, like the mountain, the upper reaches of moral character can only be attained by starting from where one is, and ascending in steps, and for this one must know how to climb. . . .

But how can it be other than futile to present a mountaineering demand to flatlands-dwellers without reckoning with the problem that they are devoid of climbing skills? It is precisely in its recognition that learning to climb must come first that the classical mode of ethical theorizing demonstrates its superiority to prevailing modern modes. . . . To distill the thesis of the present essay, it is by giving priority not to one contemporary moral ill or another, but to the neglected problem of the development of moral character, that we gain prospect of generalizing the dedication of persons in substantial numbers to the realization of moral ends.

Notes

For critical comments on earlier drafts of this essay, I am grateful to John Kekes, Edmund L. Pincoffs, William G. Scott, and Mary K. Norton. This should not be understood to imply their unqualified or qualified endorsement of the present version.

1. Alasdair MacIntyre, *After Virtue: A Study in Moral Theory* (Notre Dame, Ind., 1981); Richard Taylor, *Ethics, Faith, and Reason* (Englewood Cliffs, N.J., 1985); Edmund L. Pincoffs, *Quandaries and Virtues: Against Reductivism in Ethics* (Lawrence, Kans., 1986). My *Personal Destinies* (Princeton, 1976) attempted to outfit classical eudaimonism for current service. Bernard Williams shows some favor for the classical model of ethical theorizing in *Ethics and the Limits of Philosophy* (Cambridge, 1985). In addition it will be recognized that interest in "the virtues" has been mounting rapidly among ethical theorists for a decade or more, e.g., Philippa Foot, *Virtues and Vices* (Berkeley, 1978); James D. Wallace, *Virtues and Vices* (Ithaca, N.Y., 1978). First-rate work on virtues, coupled with the recognition that this emphasis is at home in the classical mode of ethical theorizing, is to be found in essays by Lester H. Hunt, John Kekes, Lawrence C. Becker, and R. W. Hepburn.
2. Plato, *Republic,* translated by F. M. Cornford (New York, 1945), 37.
3. A recent and thorough consideration of the concept of potentiality is Israel Scheffler, *Of Human Potential* (Boston, 1985).
4. Henry D. Thoreau, *Walden,* edited by J. Lyndon Shanley (Princeton, 1971), 97.
5. John Stuart Mill, *Utilitarianism* (Indianapolis, 1957), 23.
6. F. H. Bradley, *Ethical Studies,* cited in Peter Singer, *Practical Ethics* (Cambridge, 1979), 209.
7. Neil W. Chamberlain, *The Limits of Corporate Responsibility* (New York, 1973), 92. I am indebted to Prof. David K. Hart for this reference.
8. See R. M. Hare, *Freedom and Reason* (Oxford, 1965), 176. In his subsequent *Moral Thinking,* Hare believes he solves the problem that fanaticism poses to his

universal prescriptivism, but he retains the definition of the fanatic that is offered in *Freedom and Reason,* and it is the definition I am questioning.

9. This criticism is one of several directed against moralities consisting in "the self-conscious pursuit of moral ideals" by Michael Oakeshott in "The Tower of Babel," *Rationalism in Politics* (Totowa, N.J., 1977), 59–79.
10. Plato, *Republic,* 154.
11. John Stuart Mill, *Considerations on Representative Government* (Indianapolis, 1958), 25.
12. John Dewey, *Reconstruction in Philosophy* (Boston, 1957), 186.
13. Pincoffs, *Quandaries and Virtues,* 58.
14. See David Norton, "On an Internal Disparity in Universalizability-Criterion Formulations," *Review of Metaphysics* vol. 33, no. 3 (1980): 519–26.
15. Pincoffs, *Quandaries and Virtues,* 31–32.

16. For a fuller development of Kant's thinking on this point, see Lester H. Hunt, "Character and Thought," *American Philosophical Quarterly* vol. 15, no. 3, (1978): 180–81.
17. Urmson, "Saints and Heroes," 518.
18. Ibid., 519.
19. Ibid., 516.
20. Ibid., 518.
21. Ibid., 522.
22. Ibid., 517.
23. Ibid.
24. Michael W. Jackson, *Matters of Justice* (London, 1986), 126, 122.
25. Urmson, "Saints and Heroes," 520.
26. Reinhold Messner and Alessandro Gogna, *K-2, Mountain of Mountains* (New York, 1980), 78.

Alison M. Jaggar

Feminist Ethics: Some Issues for the Nineties

Feminist approaches to ethics are distinguished by their explicit commitment to rethinking ethics with a view to correcting whatever forms of male bias it may contain.[1] Feminist ethics, as these approaches are often called collectively, seeks to identify and challenge all those ways, overt but more often and more perniciously covert, in which western ethics has excluded women or rationalized their subordination. Its goal is to offer both practical guides to action and theoretical understandings of the nature of morality that do not, overtly or covertly, subordinate the interests of any woman or group of women to the interests of any other individual or group.

While those who practice feminist ethics are united by a shared project, they diverge widely

in their views as to how this project may be accomplished. These divergences result from a variety of philosophical differences, including differing conceptions of feminism itself, a perennially contested concept. The inevitability of such disagreement means that feminist ethics cannot be identified in terms of a specific range of topics, methods or orthodoxies. For example, it is a mistake, though one to which even some feminists occasionally have succumbed, to identify feminist ethics with any of the following: putting women's interests first; focusing exclusively on so-called women's issues; accepting women (or feminists) as moral experts or authorities; substituting "female" (or "feminine") for "male" (or "masculine") values; or extrapolating directly from women's experience.

Even though my initial characterization of feminist ethics is quite loose, it does suggest certain minimum conditions of adequacy for any approach to ethics that purports to be feminist.

Within the present social context, in which women remain systematically subordinated, a feminist approach to ethics must offer a guide to action that will tend to subvert rather than reinforce this subordination. Thus, such an approach must be practical, transitional and nonutopian, an extension of politics rather than a retreat from it. It must be sensitive, for instance,

From Alison M. Jaggar, "Feminist Ethics; Some Issues for the Nineties," *Journal of Social Philosophy,* vol. 20, Nos. 1–2 (Spring-Fall 1989). Reprinted by permission of the *Journal of Social Philosophy.*

to the symbolic meanings as well as the practical consequences of any actions that we take as gendered subjects in a male dominated society, and it must also provide the conceptual resources for identifying and evaluating the varieties of resistance and struggle in which women, particularly, have tended to engage. It must recognize the often unnoticed ways in which women and other members of the underclass have refused co-operation and opposed domination, while acknowledging the inevitability of collusion and the impossibility of totally clean hands [Ringelheim 1985; King 1989].

Since so much of women's struggle has been in the kitchen and the bedroom, as well as in the parliamentary chamber and on the factory floor, a second requirement for feminist ethics is that it should be equipped to handle moral issues in both the so-called public and private domains. It must be able to provide guidance on issues of intimate relations, such as affection and sexuality, which, until quite recently, were largely ignored by modern moral theory. In so doing, it cannot assume that moral concepts developed originally for application to the public realm, concepts such as impartiality or exploitation, are automatically applicable to the private realm. Similarly, an approach to ethics that is adequate for feminism must also provide appropriate guidance for activity in the public realm, for dealing with large numbers of people, including strangers.

Finally, feminist ethics must take the moral experience of all women seriously, though not, of course, uncritically. Though what is *feminist* will often turn out to be very different from what is *feminine,* a basic respect for women's moral experience is necessary to acknowledging women's capacities as moralists and to countering traditional stereotypes of women as less than full moral agents, as childlike or "natural." Furthermore, as Okin [1987], among others, has argued, empirical claims about differences in the moral experience of women and men make it impossible to assume that any approach to ethics will be unanimously accepted if it fails to consult the moral experience of women. Additionally, it seems plausible to suppose that women's distinctive social experience may make them especially perceptive regarding the impli-cations of domination, especially gender domination, and especially well equipped to detect the male bias that has been shown to pervade so much of male-authored western moral theory.

On the surface, at least, these conditions of adequacy for feminist ethics are quite minimal—although I believe that fulfilling them would have radical consequences for ethics. I think most feminist, and perhaps even many nonfeminist,[2] philosophers would be likely to find the general statement of these conditions relatively uncontroversial, but that inevitably there will be sharp disagreement over when the conditions have been met. Even feminists are likely to differ over, for instance, just what are women's interests and when they have been neglected, what is resistance to domination and which aspects of which women's moral experience are worth developing and in which directions.

I shall now go on to outline some of these differences as they have arisen in feminist discussions of five ethical and meta-ethical issues. These five certainly are not the only issues to confront feminist ethics; on the contrary, the domain of feminist ethics is identical with that of nonfeminist ethics—it is the whole domain of morality and moral theory. I have selected these five issues both because I believe they are especially pressing in the context of contemporary philosophical debate, and because I myself find them especially interesting. As will shortly become evident, the issues that I have selected are not independent of each other; they are unified at least by recurrent concern about questions of universality and particularity. Nevertheless, I shall separate the issues for purposes of exposition.

EQUALITY AND DIFFERENCE

The central insight of contemporary feminism without doubt has been the recognition of gender as a sometimes contradictory but always pervasive system of social norms that regulates the activity of individuals according to their biological sex. Thus individuals whose sex is male are expected to conform to prevailing norms of masculinity, while female individuals are expected to conform to prevailing norms of femininity. In 1970, Shulamith Firestone began her classic *The Dialectic of Sex* with the words "Sex class is so deep as to be invisible" and, for the first decade of the contemporary women's movement, feminists devoted themselves to rendering "sex-class" or gender visible; to exploring (and denouncing) the depth and extent of gender regulation in the life of every individual. Norms of gender were shown to influence not only dress, occupation and sexuality, but also bodily comportment, patterns of speech, eating habits and intellectual, emotional, moral and even physical development—mostly in ways that, practically and/or symbolically, reinforced the domination of men over women.

The conceptual distinction between sex and gender enabled feminists to articulate a variety of important insights. These included recognizing that the superficially nondiscriminatory acceptance of exceptional, i.e., "masculine," women is not only compatible with but actually presupposes a devaluation of "the feminine." The sex/gender distinction also enabled feminists to separate critical reflection on cultural norms of masculinity from antagonism towards actual men [Plumwood 1989].

Useful as the concept of gender has been to feminism, however, more recent feminist reflection has shown that it is neither as simple nor as unproblematic as it seemed when feminists first articulated it. Some feminists have challenged the initially sharp distinction between sex and gender, noting that, just as sex differences have influenced (though not ineluctably determined) the development of gender norms, so gender arrangements may well have influenced the biological evolution of certain secondary sexual characteristics and even of that defining criterion of sex, procreation itself [Jaggar 1983]. Other feminists have challenged the distinction between gender and other social categories such as race and class. Recognizing that feminist claims about "women" often had generalized illicitly from the experience of a relatively small group of middle-class white women, feminists in the last ten years have emphasized that gender is a variable rather than a constant, since norms of gender vary not only between but also within cultures, along dimensions such as class, race, age, marital status, sexual preference and

so on. Moreover, since every woman is a woman of some determinate age, race, class and marital status, gender is not even an independent variable; there is no concept of pure or abstract gender that can be isolated theoretically and studied independently of class, race, age or marital status [Spelman, 1989]. Neither, of course, can these other social categories be understood independently of gender.

Their increasingly sophisticated understandings of gender have complicated feminists' discussions of many moral and social issues. One of these is sexual equality. At the beginning of the contemporary women's movement, in the late 1960s, this seemed to be a relatively straightforward issue. The nineteenth century feminist preference for "separate spheres" for men and women [Freedman 1979] had been replaced by demands for identity of legal rights for men and women or, as it came to be called, equality before the law. By the end of the 1960s, most feminists in the United States had come to believe that the legal system should be sex-blind, that it should not differentiate in any way between women and men. This belief was expressed in the struggle for an Equal Rights Amendment to the U.S. Constitution, an amendment that, had it passed, would have made any sex-specific law unconstitutional.

By the late 1970s and early 1980s, however, it was becoming apparent that the assimilationist goal of strict equality before the law does not always benefit women, at least in the short term. One notorious example was "no fault" divorce settlements that divided family property equally between husband and wife but invariably left wives in a far worse economic situation than they did husbands. In one study, for instance, ex-husbands' standard of living was found to have risen by 42% a year after divorce, whereas ex-wives' standard of living declined by 73% [Weitzman 1985]. This huge discrepancy in the outcome of divorce resulted from a variety of factors, including the fact that women and men typically are differently situated in the job market, with women usually having much lower job qualifications and less work experience. In this sort of case, equality (construed as identity) in the treatment of the sexes appears to produce an outcome in which sexual inequality is increased.

The obvious alternative of seeking equality by providing women with special legal protection continues, however, to be as fraught with dangers for women as it was earlier in the century when the existence of protective legislation was used as an excuse for excluding women from many of the more prestigious and better paid occupations [Williams 1984-5]. For instance, mandating special leaves for disability on account of pregnancy or childbirth promotes the perception that women are less reliable workers than men; recognizing "pre-menstrual syndrome" or post-partum depression as periodically disabling conditions encourages the perception that women are less responsible than men; while attempts to protect women's sexuality through legislation restricting pornography or excluding women from employment in male institutions such as prisons, perpetuate the dangerous stereotype that women are by nature the sexual prey of men. This cultural myth serves as an implicit legitimation for the prostitution, sexual harassment and rape of women, because it implies that such activities are in some sense natural. In all these cases, attempts to achieve equality between the sexes by responding to perceived differences between men and women seem likely to reinforce rather than reduce existing differences, even differences that are acknowledged to be social rather than biological in origin.

Furthermore, a "sex-responsive," as opposed to "sex-blind," conception of equality ignores differences *between* women, separating all women into a single homogenous category and possibly penalizing one group of women by forcing them to accept protection that another group genuinely may need.

Sooner or later, most feminist attempts to formulate an adequate conception of sexual equality run up against the recognition that the baseline for discussions of equality typically has been a male standard. In Catharine MacKinnon's inimitable words:

Men's physiology defines most sports, their needs define auto and health insurance coverage, their socially designed biographies define workplace expectations and successful career patterns, their perspectives and concerns define quality in scholarship, their experiences and obsessions define merit, their objectification of life defines art, their military service defines citizenship, their presence defines family, their inability to get along with each other—their wars and rulerships—defines history, their image defines god, and their genitals define sex [MacKinnon 1987:36].

Having once reached this recognition, some feminist theorists have turned away from debating the pros and cons of what MacKinnon calls the "single" versus the "double standard" and begun speculating about the kinds of far-reaching social transformation that would make sex differences "costless" [Littleton 1986]. In discussions elaborating such notions as that of "equality as acceptance," feminists seem to be moving towards a radical construal of equality as similarity of individual outcome, equality of condition or effect, a conception quite at odds with traditional liberal understandings of equality as equality of procedure or opportunity.[3]

While some feminists struggle to formulate a conception of sexual equality that is adequate for feminism, others have suggested that the enterprise is hopeless. For them, equality is an integral part of an "ethic of justice" that is characteristically masculine insofar as it obscures human difference by abstracting from the particularity and uniqueness of concrete people in their specific situations and seeks to resolve conflicting interests by applying an abstract rule rather than by responding directly to needs that are immediately perceived. Such feminists suggest that a discourse of responsibility [Finley 1986] or care [Krieger 1987] may offer a more appropriate model for feminist ethics—even including feminist jurisprudence. Both of these suggestions remain to be worked out in detail.

The tangled debate over equality and difference provides an excellent illustration of one characteristic feature of contemporary feminist ethics, namely, its insistence that gender is often, if not invariably, a morally relevant difference between individuals. Given this insistence, the starting point of much feminist ethics may be different from that of modern moral theory: instead of assuming that all individuals should be treated alike until morally relevant grounds for difference in treatment can be identified, feminist theorists may shift the traditional burden of moral proof by assuming, until shown otherwise, that contemporary men and women are rarely "similarly situated." This leads into a related and equally crucial question for feminist ethics in the nineties, namely, how to characterize and evaluate impartiality.

IMPARTIALITY

In the modern western tradition, impartiality typically has been recognized as a fundamental value, perhaps even a defining characteristic of morality, distinguishing true morality from tribalism [Baier 1958]. Impartiality is said to require weighing the interests of each individual equally, permitting differentiation only on the basis of differences that can be shown to be morally relevant. Impartiality thus is linked conceptually with equality and also with rationality and objectivity, insofar as bias often has been defined as the absence of impartiality.

In the last few years, the preeminence traditionally ascribed to impartiality has been challenged both by feminist and nonfeminist philosophers. Nonfeminists have charged that an insistence on impartiality disregards our particular identities, constituted by reference to our particular projects and our unchosen relationships with others; and that it substitutes abstract "variables" for real human agents and patients. Williams [1973,1981], for instance, has argued that the requirement of impartiality may undermine our personal integrity because it may require us to abandon projects that are central to our identity, and he also suggests that acting from duty may sometimes be less valuable than acting from an immediate emotional response to a particular other. MacIntyre [1981] and Sommers [1986] have argued that impartiality fails to respect tradition, customary expectations and unchosen encumbrances, and may require behavior that is morally repugnant.

While some of the moral intuitions that motivate the nonfeminist critics of impartiality certainly are shared by many feminists, other intuitions most likely are not. It is implausible to suppose, for instance, that most feminists would join Williams in applauding Gaugin's abandonment of his family in order to pursue his art, or that they would join Sommers in accepting without question the claims of customary morality on issues such as women's responsibilities. Instead, the feminist criticisms of impartiality tend to be both less individualistic and less conventionalist. They are quite varied in character.

Nell Noddings [1984] is one of the most extreme opponents of impartiality and her work has been influential with a number of feminists, even though the sub-title of her book makes it clear that she takes herself to be elaborating a feminine rather than a feminist approach to ethics. Noddings views the emotion of caring as the natural basis of morality, a view that would require impartiality to be expressed in universal caring. Noddings claims, however, that we are psychologically able to care only for particular others with whom we are in actual relationships, i.e., relationships that can be "completed" by the cared-for's acknowledgement of our caring. She concludes that pretensions to care for humanity at large are not only hypocritical but self-defeating, undermining true caring for those with whom we are in actual relationship. Noddings' arguments, if valid, of course would apply indifferently to caring practised either by men or by women, and so the distinctively feminist interest of Noddings' work might seem to reside solely in her obviously debatable claim that women are "better equipped for caring than men" (97) and therefore less likely to be impartial. As we have noted already, however, feminist ethics is not committed to reproducing the moral practice even of most women and so feminist (and nonfeminist) moral theorists need to evaluate critically all of Noddings' arguments against impartiality, independently of whether her claims about "feminine" morality can be empirically confirmed.

A different criticism of impartiality has been made by those feminist philosophers who assert that, while impartiality is associated historically with individualism, it paradoxically undermines respect for individuality because it treats individuals as morally interchangeable [Code 1988; Sherwin 1987]. Many, though certainly not all, feminists claim that women are less likely than men to commit this alleged moral error because they are more likely to appreciate the special characteristics of particular individuals; again, however, feminist estimates of the soundness or otherwise of Code's and Sherwin's argument must be independent of this empirical claim.

Finally, at least one feminist has extended the claim that women need special protection in the law by recommending that feminist ethics should promote a double standard of morality, limiting moral communities on the basis of gender or perhaps gender solidarity. Susan Sherwin writes that feminists feel a special responsibility to reduce the suffering of women in particular; thus, "(b)y acknowledging the relevance of differences among people as a basis for a difference in sympathy and concern, feminism denies the legitimacy of a central premise of traditional moral theories, namely that all persons should be seen as morally equivalent by us" [Sherwin 1987:26. Cf. also Fisk 1980, Fraser 1986 and Hoagland 1989]. However, since women and even feminists are not homogenous groups, as we have seen, this kind of reasoning seems to push the suggested double standard towards becoming a multiple moral standard—which Enlightenment theorists might well interpret as the total abandonment of impartiality and thus of morality itself.

A variety of responses seems to be available to the foregoing criticisms of impartiality. One alternative is to argue that the criticisms are unwarranted, depending on misrepresentation, misunderstanding and caricature of the impartialist position [Herman 1983; Adler 1990]. If this response can be sustained, it may be possible to show that there is no real conflict between "masculine" impartialism and "feminine" particularism, "masculine" justice and "feminine" care. Another alternative is to bite the bullet of direct moral confrontation, providing arguments to challenge the intuitions of those who criticize impartiality as requiring courses of action that are morally repugnant or politically dangerous. Yet a third alternative may be to reconceive the concept of impartiality and the considerations appropriate for determining our responsibilities toward various individuals and groups. Feminist ethics must find a way of choosing between those or other options and evaluating the proper place of impartiality in ethics for the nineties.

MORAL SUBJECTIVITY

Related to the foregoing questions about impartiality are questions about how to conceptualize individuals, the subjects of moral theory. Feminists and nonfeminists alike have criticized the neo-Cartesian model of the moral self, a disembodied, separate, autonomous, unified, rational being, essentially similar to all other moral selves. Marx challenged the ahistoricism of this model; Freud challenged its claims to rationality; contemporary communitarians, such as Sandel and MacIntyre, challenge the assumption that individuals are "unencumbered," arguing instead that we are all members of communities from which we may be able to distance ourselves to some extent but which nevertheless are deeply constitutive of our identities; postmodernists have deconstructed the model to reveal fractured rather than unitary identities.

The gender bias alleged to contaminate each of the traditions mentioned above means that feminists cannot appropriate uncritically existing critiques of the neo-Cartesian moral self. Nevertheless, in developing their own challenges to this model of the self, feminist theorists often have paralleled and/or built on some nonfeminist work. For instance, feminist investigations into the social imposition of gender have drawn on neo-Freudian object relations theory in demonstrating how this central feature of our identity is socially constructed rather than given [e.g. Chodorow 1978]. Code's and Sherwin's previously mentioned accusations that modern moral theory recognizes individuals only as abstract variables, representatives of social types, is reminiscent of communitarian discussions of the encumbered self. And further connections with communitarianism, as well as phenomenology and Marxism, may be seen in the growing philosophical interest among feminists in embodiment and the ways in which it is constitutive of our identity [e.g., Spelman 1982; Young 1990]. All these theorists offer distinctively feminist grounds for resisting the universalism, essential-ism and ahistoricity of the Cartesian model and for refocusing on the need to recognize particularity and difference in conceptualizing the self.

Other feminist critiques of the neo-Cartesian subject concentrate on the common modern construal of rationality as egoism, which "overlooks the fact that millions of people (most of them women) have spent millions of hours for hundreds of years giving their utmost to millions of others" [Miller, 1976]. Others have challenged the frequent modern assumption, (explicit, for instance, in utilitarian revealed preference theory), that expressed or even felt desires and needs can be taken at face value, as givens in moral theory, pointing to the need for feminist ethics to offer an account of the social construction of desire and to suggest a way of conceptualizing the distinction between what the Marxist tradition has called "true" and "false" needs [Jaggar 1983]. Feminist explorations of the power of ideology over the unconscious and the revelation of conflicts within the self have challenged the Cartesian assumption of the unity of the self, as well as the assumption that the self is essentially rational [Grimshaw 1988]. Finally, descriptions of women's supposed "morality of caring" [Gilligan 1982] have challenged the assumption of the ontological separateness of the self and reinforced the importance, perhaps even the moral or epistemological priority, of the self as part of a moral and epistemic community.

Given this burgeoning literature, it is evident that a central concern for feminist ethics in the nineties must be to develop ways of thinking about moral subjects that are sensitive *both* to their concreteness, inevitable particularity and unique specificity, expressed in part through their relations with specific historical communities, *and* to their intrinsic and common value, the ideal expressed in Enlightenment claims about common humanity, equality and impartiality [Benhabib, 1986].

AUTONOMY

One aspect of this task is the rethinking of autonomy which, like impartiality, (to which it is often conceptually connected), has been a continuing ideal of modern moral theory. (In addition, a closely related concept of autonomy has played a central role in the Cartesian epistemological tradition, which envisions the search for knowledge as a project of the solitary knower.) The core intuition of autonomy is that of independence or self legislation, the self as the ultimate authority in matters of morality or truth. In the Kantian tradition, where the ideal of autonomy is particularly prominent, moral autonomy has been elaborated in terms of disinterest, detachment from particular attachments and interests, and freedom from prejudice and self-deception [Hill, 1987].

Contemporary feminists have had a mixed response to the modern ideal of moral autonomy. On the one hand, they have insisted that women are as autonomous in the moral and intellectual senses as men—as rational, as capable of a sense of justice, and so on; and they have also demanded political, social and economic autonomy for women through political representation, the abolition of sex discrimination and respect for women's choices on issues such as abortion. On the other hand, however, some feminists have questioned traditional interpretations of autonomy as masculine fantasies. For instance, they have explored some of the ways in which "choice" is socialized and "consent" manipulated [MacKinnon 1987; Meyers 1987]. In addition, they have questioned the possibility of separating ourselves from particular attachments and still retaining our personal identity, and they have suggested that freeing ourselves from particular attachments might result in a cold, rigid, moralistic rather than a truly moral response [Noddings 1984]. Rather than guaranteeing a response that is purely moral, freeing ourselves from particular attachments might instead make us *incapable* of morality if an ineliminable part of morality consists in responding emotionally to particular others.

Feminist ethics in the nineties must find ways of conceptualizing moral agency, choice and consent that are compatible with the feminist recognition of the gradual process of moral development, the gendered social construction of the psyche, and the historical constraints on our options. This is one area in which some promising work by feminists exists already [Holmstrom 1977; Gibson 1985; Meyers 1987].

Moral Epistemology and Anti-epistemology

Enlightenment moral theory characteristically assumed that morality was universal—that, if moral claims held, they were valid at all times and in all places. However, the modern abandonment of belief in a teleological and sacred universe rendered the justification of such claims constantly problematic, and much moral theory for the last three centuries has consisted in attempts to provide a rational grounding for morality. At the present time, both the continental European tradition, especially but not only in the form of post-modernism, and the Anglo-American tradition, especially but not only in the form of communitarianism, have developed powerful challenges to the very possibility of the view that morality consists in universally valid rules grounded in universal reason. The inevitable result of these sceptical challenges has been to reinforce normative and meta-ethical relativism.

Feminists are ambivalent about these challenges. On the one hand, many of the feminist criticisms of modern moral theory parallel the criticisms made by communitarianism and post-modernism. On the other hand, however, feminists are understandably concerned that their critique of male dominance should not be dismissed as just one point of view. It is therefore crucial for feminist ethics to develop some way of justifying feminist moral claims. However, moral epistemology is an area in which feminists' critiques are better developed than their alternatives.

Feminist discussions of moral epistemology may be divided into two categories, each distinguished by a somewhat different view of the nature of morality. Feminists in the first category do not explicitly challenge the modern conception of morality as consisting primarily in an impartial system of rationally justified rules or principles, though few feminists would assert that it is possible to identify rules that are substantive, specific and hold in all circumstances. Those in the second category, by contrast, deny that morality is reducible to rules and emphasize the impossibility of justifying the claims of ethics by appeal to a universal, impartial reason. The contrast between these two groups of feminists is not as sharp as this initial characterization might suggest: for instance, both share several criticisms of existing decision procedures in ethics. But feminists in the former group are more hopeful of repairing those procedures, while feminists in the latter group seem ready to abandon them entirely.

Feminists in the latter group frequently claim to be reflecting on a moral experience that is distinctively feminine and for this reason they are often—incorrectly—taken to represent a feminist orthodoxy. They include authors such as Gilligan [1982], Noddings [1984], Baier [1987], Blum [1987], Ruddick [1989] and Walker [1989]. While there is considerable variation in the views of these authors, they all reject the view attributed to modern moral theorists that the right course of action can be discovered by consulting a list of moral rules, charging that undue emphasis on the epistemological importance of rules obscures the crucial role of moral insight, virtue and character in determining what should be done. A feminist twist is given to this essentially Aristotelian criticism when claims are made that excessive reliance on rules reflects a juridical-administrative interest that is characteristic of modern masculinity [Blum 1982] while contemporary women, by contrast, are alleged to be more likely to disregard conventionally accepted moral rules because such rules are insensitive to the specificities of particular situations [Gilligan 1982; Noddings 1984]. A morality of rule, therefore is alleged to devalue the moral wisdom of women, as well as to give insufficient weight to such supposedly feminine virtues as kindness, generosity, helpfulness and sympathy.

Some feminists have claimed that "feminine" approaches to morality contrast with supposedly masculine rule-governed approaches in that they characteristically consist in immediate responses to particular others, responses based on supposedly natural feelings of empathy, care and compassion [Gilligan 1982; Noddings 1984] or loving attention [Murdoch 1970; Ruddick 1989]. However, apart from the difficulties of establishing that such a "particularist" approach to morality [Blum 1987] indeed is characteristically feminine, let alone feminist, attempts to develop a moral epistemology based on such responses face a variety of problems. First, they confront the familiar, though perhaps not insuperable, problems common to all moral epistemologies that take emotion as a guide to right action, namely, the frequent inconsistency, unavailability or plain inappropriateness of emotions [Lind 1989]. In other words, they face the danger of degenerating into a "do what feels good" kind of subjective relativism. In addition, it is not clear that even our emotional responses to others are not responses to them under some universal description and so in this sense general rather than particular—or, if indeed particular and therefore nonconceptual, then perhaps closer to animal than to distinctively human responses. It is further uncertain how these sorts of particular responses can guide our actions towards large numbers of people, most of whom we shall never meet. Finally, the feminist emphasis on the need for "contextual" reasoning opens up the obvious dangers of *ad hoc*ism, special pleading and partiality.

Not all feminists, of course, are committed to a particularist moral epistemology. Even some of those who take emotions as a proper guide to morality emphasize the intentionality of emotions and discuss the need for their moral education. Additionally, while most feminists criticize certain aspects of the decision procedures developed by modern moral theory,[4] some believe it may be possible to revise and reappropriate some of these procedures. The main candidates for such revision are the methods developed by Rawls and Habermas, each of whom believes that an idealized situation of dialogue (which each describes differently) will both generate and justify morally valid principles.

Rawls' decision procedure has been the target of a number of feminist criticisms. Okin, for instance, as noted earlier, has argued that Rawls' procedure will not generate moral consensus unless the considered judgements of men and women coincide, a coincidence she believes quite unlikely in any society that continues to be structured by gender. She has also attacked Rawls' assumption that the parties in the original position will be heads of households, correctly noting that this precludes them from considering the justice of household arrangements [1987]. Benhabib [1986] has argued that those who reason behind Rawls' veil of ignorance are so ignorant of their own circumstances that they have lost the specific identities characteristic of human agents. She takes this to mean that "there is no real *plurality* of perspectives in the Rawlsian original position, but only a *definitional identity*" [413, italics in original]. Benhabib criticizes what she calls this "monological" model of moral reasoning on the grounds that, by restricting itself to "the standpoint of the generalized other" and ignoring the "standpoint of the concrete other," it deprives itself of much morally relevant information necessary to adequately utilize the Kantian moral tests of reversibility and universalizability. In spite of these criticisms, Okin [1989] believes that Rawls' hypothetical contract procedure can be revised in such a way as to incorporate feminist concerns about justice within the household, about empathy and care and about difference.

Benhabib [1986] suggests that a "communicative ethic of need interpretations," based on Habermas' account of an ideal dialogue, is capable of overcoming what she perceives as Rawlsian monologism. It does this by acknowledging the differences of concrete others in ways compatible with the contextualist concerns that Gilligan attributes to women who utilize the ethic of care. Other feminists, such as Fraser [1986] and Young [1986], also seem attracted to such a method, although Young criticizes Habermasian descriptions of ideal dialogue for failing to take account of the affective and bodily dimensions of meaning [395]. In order to genuinely acknowledge the specific situations of concrete others, however, an *actual* rather than hypothetical dialogue seems to be required, albeit a dialogue under carefully specified conditions. But it is hard to imagine how actual dialogue could even approximate fairness in a world of unequal power, unequal access to the "socio-cultural means of interpretation and communication" [Fraser 1986] and even unequal availability of time for moral reflection and debate.

One possible alternative both to an unwelcome relativism and to what many feminists see as the pretensions of moral rationalism may be the development of a moral standpoint that is distinctively feminist. Sara Ruddick claims that such a standpoint can be found in maternal thinking [1989] but her work has been criticized by some feminists as ethnocentric [Lugones 1988] and overvaluing motherhood [Hoagland 1989]. Even if the feminist standpoint were differently identified, however, problems would remain. Standpoint epistemology derives from Marx and, at least in its Lukacian version, it seems to require an objectivist distinction between appearance and reality that is quite alien to the social constructionist tendencies in much contemporary feminism.

The controversy in feminist moral epistemology currently is so sharp that Held [1984] has suggested abandoning the search for a "unified field theory" covering all domains of life activity. However, other authors have pointed to the danger that, if a supposedly feminine "ethic of care" were limited to the realm of personal life, as Kohlberg, for instance has suggested, it would be perceived as subordinate to the supposedly masculine "ethic of justice," just as, in contemporary society, the private is subordinate to the public.

Conclusion

Even such a limited survey as this should make it evident that feminist ethics, far from being a rigid orthodoxy, instead is a ferment of ideas and controversy, many of them echoing and deepening debates in nonfeminist ethics. The centrality of the issues and the liveliness of the on-going discussions suggest that the nineties will be a fruitful period for feminist ethics—and thus for ethics generally.

Notes

1. Many of the ideas in this paper have been developed in the course of long-term discussions with Marcia Lind. This paper has benefitted tremendously from her insistent questioning and from her insightful responses to earlier drafts. Pamela Grath also made a number of helpful comments

2. "Nonfeminist" here refers to philosophers who do not make their feminist concerns explicit in their philosophical work; it is not intended to imply that such philosophers do not demonstrate feminist concern in other ways.

3. Feminists moving in this direction seem to be paralleling Marx's move, in his *Critique of the Gotha Programme*, towards a society where an emphasis on equality of rights has been abandoned, since the differences between individuals result in its producing inequalities of outcome, and where the principle of social organization is: "From each according to his (sic) ability, to each according to his (sic) needs."

4. Most feminists, for instance, perceive traditional formulations of social contract theory to be male biased in various ways [Jaggar 1983; Held 1987; Pateman 1988].

References

Adler, Jonathan, "Particularity, Gilligan and the Two-levels View: A Reply," *Ethics* 100:1 (October 1990).

Baier, Annette, "The Need for More Than Justice," *Science, Morality and Feminist Theory*, ed. Marsha Hanen and Kai Nielsen, Calgary: University of Calgary Press, 1987.

Baier, Kurt, *The Moral Point of View: A Rational Basis of Ethics*, New York: Random House, 1958.

Benhabib, Seyla, "The Generalized and the Concrete Other: The Kohlberg-Gilligan Controversy and Feminist Theory," *Praxis International* 5:4 (January 1986).

Blum, Lawrence, "Kant's and Hegel's Moral Rationalism: A Feminist Perspective," *Canadian Journal of Philosophy* 12:2 (June 1982).

Blum, Lawrence, "Particularity and Responsiveness," *The Emergence of Morality in Young Children*, eds. Jerome Kagan and Sharon Lamb, Chicago: University of Chicago Press, 1987.

Chodorow, Nancy, *The Reproduction of Mothering: Psychoanalysis and the Sociology of Gender*, Berkeley: University of California Press, 1987.

Code, Lorraine, "Experience, Knowledge and Responsibility," *Feminist Perspectives in Philosophy*, edited by Morwenna Griffiths and Margaret Whitford, Bloomington & Indianapolis: Indiana University Press, 1988.

Finley, Lucinda M., "Transcending Equality Theory: A Way Out of the Maternity and the Workplace Debate," *Columbia Law Review* 86:6 (October, 1986).

Fisk, Milton, *Ethics and Society: A Marxist Interpretation of Value*, New York: New York University Press, 1980.

Fraser, Nancy, "Toward a Discourse Ethic of Solidarity," *Praxis International* 5:4 (January, 1986).

Freedman, Estelle, "Separatism as Strategy: Female Institution Building and American Feminism 1870-1930," *Feminist Studies* 5:3 (1979).

Gibson, Mary, "Consent and Autonomy," *To Breathe Freely: Risk, Consent and Air*, Totowa, NJ: Rowman & Allanheld, 1985.

Gilligan, Carol, *In a Different Voice: Psychological Theory and Women's Development*, Cambridge, MA: Harvard University Press, 1982.

Grimshaw, Jean, "Autonomy and Identity in Feminist Thinking," *Feminist Perspectives in Philosophy*, eds. Morwenna Griffiths and Margaret Whitford, Bloomington and Indianapolis: Indiana University Press, 1988.

Held, Virginia, *Rights and Goods*, New York: The Free Press, 1984.

Held, Virginia, "Non-Contractual Society," *Science, Morality and Feminist Theory*, eds. Marsha Hanen and Kai Nielsen, Calgary: University of Calgary Press, 1987.

Herman, Barbara, "Integrity and Impartiality," *The Monist* 66:2 (April 1983).

Hill, Thomas E., Jr., "The Importance of Autonomy," *Women and Moral Theory*, eds. Eva Feder Kittay and Diana T. Meyers, Totowa, NJ: Rowman and Littlefield, 1987.

Hoagland, Sara Lucia, *Lesbian Ethics: Toward New Value*, Palo Alto, CA: Institute of Lesbian Studies, 1989.

Holmstrom, Nancy, "Firming Up Soft Determinism," *The Personalist* 58:1 (1977).

Jaggar, Alison M., *Feminist Politics and Human Nature*, Totowa, NJ: Rowman and Allanheld, 1983.

King, Ynestra, "Afterword," *Rocking the Ship of State: Toward a Feminist Peace Politics*, ed. Adrienne Harris and Ynestra King, Boulder CO: Westview Press, 1989.

Krieger, Linda J., "Through a Glass Darkly: Paradigms of Equality and the Search for a Woman's Jurisprudence," *Hypatia: A Journal of Feminist Philosophy* 2:1 (1987).

Lind, Marcia, "Hume and Feminist Moral Theory," paper read at conference on *Explorations in Feminist Ethics: Theory and Practice*, University of Minnesota-Duluth, October 7-8, 1988.

Lugones, Maria, "The Logic of Pluralism," paper read at the annual meeting of the American Philosophical Association (Eastern Division), Washington, D.C., December 1988.

MacIntyre, Alasdair, *After Virtue: A Study in Moral Theory*, London: Duckworth, 1981.

MacKinnon, Catharine A., *Feminism Unmodified: Discourses on Life and Law*, Cambridge, MA: Harvard University Press, 1987.

Meyers, Diana T., "Personal Autonomy and the Paradox of Feminine Socialization," *Journal of Philosophy* LXXXIV:11 (November, 1987).

Meyers, Diana T., "The Socialized Individual and Individual Autonomy: An Intersection between Philosophy and Psychology," *Women and Moral Theory*, ed. Eva Feder Kittay and Diana T. Meyers, Totowa, NJ: Rowman & Allanheld, 1987.

Miller, Jean Baker, *Toward a New Psychology of Women*, Boston: Beacon, 1976.

Murdoch, Iris, *The Sovereignty of Good*, London: Routledge & Kegan Paul, 1970.

Noddings, Nel, *Caring: A Feminine Approach to Ethics and Moral Education*, Berkeley: University of California Press, 1984.

Okin, Susan Moller, "Justice and Gender," *Philosophy and Public Affairs* 16:1, (Winter 1987).

Okin, Susan Moller, "Reason and Feeling in Thinking about Justice," *Ethics* 99:2 (January 1989).

Plumwood, Val, "Do We Need a Sex/Gender Distinction?" *Radical Philosophy* 51 (Spring 1989).

Ringelheim, Joan, "Women and the Holocaust: A Reconsideration of Research," *Signs* 10:4 (Summer 1985).

Ruddick, Sara, "Maternal Thinking," *Feminist Studies* 6:2 (Summer 1980).

Ruddick, Sara, "Preservative Love and Military Destruction: Some Reflections on Mothering and Peace," *Mothering: Essays in Feminist Theory*, ed. Joyce Trebilcot, Totowa, NJ: Rowman and Allanheld, 1984.

Ruddick, Sara, *Maternal Thinking: Toward a Politics of Peace*, Boston: Beacon Press, 1989.

Sherwin, Susan, "A Feminist Approach to Ethics," *Resources for Feminist Research* 16:3, 1987. (Special issue on Women and Philosophy").

Somers, Christina Hoff, "Filial Morality," *The Journal of Philosophy* 83:8 (August 1986).

Spelman, Elizabeth V., *Inessential Woman: Problems of Exclusion in Feminist Thought*, Boston: Beacon, 1989.

Walker, Margaret, "Moral Understandings: Alternative 'Epistemology' for a Feminist Ethics," *Hypatia: A Journal of Feminist Philosophy* 4:2 (Summer 1989).

Weitzman, Lenore J., *The Divorce Revolution*, New York: The Free Press, 1985

Williams, B., "A Critique of Utilitarianism," *Utilitarianim: For and Against*, Cambridge: Cambridge University Press, 1973.

Williams, B., "Morality and the Emotions," *Problems of the Self*, Cambridge: Cambridge University Press, 1973.

Williams, B., "Morality and the Emotions," *Problems of the Self*, Cambridge: Cambridge University Press, 1973.

Williams, B., "Persons, Character and Morality," "Moral Luck," and "Utilitarianism and Moral Selfindulgence," *Moral Luck*, Cambridge: Cambridge University Press, 1981.

Williams, Wendy W., "Equality's Riddle: Pregnancy and the Equal Treatment/Special Treatment Debate, *New York University Review of Law and Social Change* XIII:2 (1984-5).

Young, Iris Marion, "Impartiality and the Civic Public," *Praxis International* 5:4 (January 1986).

Young, Iris Marion, "Throwing Like a Girl: A Phenomenology of Feminine Body Comportment, Motility and Spatiality," "Pregnant Embodiment: Subjectivity and Alienation," "Breast as Experience: The Look and the Feeling," *Stretching Out: Essays in Feminist Social Theory and Female Body Experience*, Bloomington: Indiana University Press, 1990.

QUESTIONS

1. If we accept the claim that cultural relativism is true, does it follow that whether or not we should believe it depends on what society we live in?

2. Are people capable of acting unselfishly? If they are not, does it make any sense for the ethical egoist to suggest that people ought to act selfishly? If people are capable of acting unselfishly would this cast any doubt on the theory of ethical egoism?

3. Is there such a thing as human nature? Assuming there is, how would you go about determining what it is?

4. Are all moral actions universalizable?

5. Is it always more moral to act out of duty than out of some other motive, e.g., sympathy for one's fellow humans?

6. Utilitarianism judges actions moral or immoral solely on the basis of their consequences. Is this true of any other moral theory. If so, how does it differ from utilitarianism?

7. It seems possible that what is considered virtuous might vary from society to society. Would this imply that virtue ethics is a form of relativism?

8. Jaggar says that "feminist approaches to ethics are distinguished by their explicit commitment to rethinking ethics with a view to correcting whatever forms of male bias it may contain." Could a nonfeminist also have an explicit commitment to purifying ethics of male bias?

9. Jaggar suggests "that feminist ethics, far from being a rigid orthodoxy, . . . is a ferment of ideas and controversy, many of them echoing and deepening debates in nonfeminist ethics." Does this in any way diminish the possibility of distinguishing a distinctively feminist theory of ethics?

CASE STUDY 2:1 THE LIFE BOAT[1]

On July 5, 1884, the crew of an English yacht, Thomas Dudley, Edward Stephens, Richard Parker and another sailor surnamed Brooks, were forced to abandon ship 1600 miles from the Cape of Good Hope during a severe storm. Richard Parker was between seventeen and eighteen years of age, the others were mature adults.

The crew floated in an open lifeboat with no supply of food except for two one pound tins of turnips and no source of fresh water apart from any rain they could catch in their oilskin capes. For three days they had nothing to eat except for the turnips. On the fourth day they caught a small turtle. By the twelfth day the turtle had been entirely consumed and they were unable to catch any further food. They continued to drift on the open ocean roughly 1000 miles from land.

On the eighteenth day, July 23, after seven days without food and five without water, Dudley and Stephens approached Brooks suggesting that someone, this being understood to be Parker, should be sacrificed to save the rest. Brooks disagreed and Parker was not consulted.

On the nineteenth day, July 24, Dudley suggested to Stephens and Brooks that lots should be cast to determine who should be sacrificed to save the rest. Brooks again refused to consent and Parker was again not consulted. No drawing of lots took place. Later in the day Dudley and Stephens spoke of their families and suggested it would be better to kill Parker who had no dependents. Dudley proposed that if no help had arrived by the following morning Parker should be killed.

No help arrived the following day. Dudley told Brooks to take a sleep and made signs to Stephens and Brooks that Parker would be killed. Stephens agreed to the act, but Brooks again disagreed. Parker, who at no time had agreed to being killed, was lying at the bottom of the boat, helpless and greatly weakened by hunger and drinking sea water.

Dudley offered a prayer asking forgiveness for them all if either of them should be tempted to commit a rash act, and that their souls might be saved. Subsequently, Dudley, with the consent of Stephens, went to the boy, and, telling him that his time had come, cut his throat. The three man fed upon Parker's body and blood for four days. On the fourth day they were picked up by a passing vessel. It is clear that if the men had not fed upon Parker they would not have survived to be rescued. It also seems clear that Parker, being in a much weaker condition, was likely to have died before them.

CASE STUDY QUESTIONS

1. What are the implications of the various theories of morality concerning the morality of what occurred?

2. Was Brooks guilty of any wrongdoing?

3. If it was clear that Parker was going to die no matter what would this affect the morality of what occurred?

Notes

1. Selected from *The Queen v. Dudley and Stephens*, 1884, 14 *Law Reports Queen's Bench Division* 273.

FOR FURTHER READING

1. Jonathan Harrison (editor) *Challenges to Morality* (New York: Macmillan, 1993).

2. Kenneth F. Rogerson (editor) *Introduction to Ethical Theory* (Toronto: Holt, Rinehart & Winston, 1991).

3. James Sterba (editor) *Contemporary Ethics* (New Jersey: Prentice-Hall, 1989).

Part II

Business and the Employee

Chapter Three

Bargaining and Due Process

Introduction

Freedom of speech and conscience are highly valued in western society, as is the right to due process. However, this emphasis on civil liberty has not typically extended to the workplace. Although the right to collective bargaining has become firmly established, there are many who defend the doctrine of employment-at-will; namely the presumed right of an employer to hire, fire, promote, or demote employees without cause or notice. The issue of whether restrictions customarily placed on employees in the workplace are consistent with the emphasis placed on due process and individual freedom in other areas of life is an important one and has begun to receive a great deal of attention.

Many thinkers ground freedom of speech in the fact that it seems a necessary condition of human autonomy. They argue that the dignity and independence of an individual cannot be respected unless the importance of allowing him or her to speak freely is acknowledged. A consequence of this view is that an individual's freedom of speech is not absolute. For example, freedom of speech does not permit a person to yell "Fire" in a crowded theatre. Given that freedom of speech is only justified insofar as it promotes human autonomy, instances where speaking in a certain way clearly interferes with anther individual's ability to order his or her life cannot be justified by appealing to one's right to speak freely.

The question then, is not whether limits should be put on free speech; it is evident there must be limits if the autonomy of more than one individual is to be recognized and valued. The question rather, is how to balance the apparently competing interests of autonomous individuals? How to balance the legitimate interests of the employee, conceived as an autonomous agent worthy of dignity and respect, with those of the employer, conceived as an autonomous agent equally worth of dignity and respect? Clearly, employee free speech cannot be conceived of in such a way that it allows selling valuable confidential information to a competitor, thus undermining the employer's ability to act autonomously. Nor should an employer's freedom to use or dispose of his or her property be conceived of in such a way that it undermines any possibility of employees acting autonomously.

Respecting the autonomy of both employer and employee depends very largely on particular circumstances. In general, employees need to beware of emphasizing freedom of speech to a degree that it does not respect the legitimate interests of employers. Similarly, employers need to beware of discouraging the freedom of speech that is a condition of employee autonomy.

In his article "Speech, Conscience and Work," Richard Lippke explores the concept of a right to freedom of speech and its implications for how the workplace should be structured. Following the Kantian tradition, Lippke grounds freedom of speech in human autonomy. Freedom of speech is necessary if individuals are to pursue rationality and right conduct.

Recognizing that freedom of speech is not an indefeasible right, Lippke examines three arguments that attempt to justify the denial of free speech in the workplace:

1. the view that freedom of speech cannot be applied to private organizations,
2. the view that issues raised in the production of goods and services are primarily technical rather than moral, and hence that the issue of free speech does not arise, and
3. the view that in signing a contract an employee voluntarily relinquishes the right to free speech in return for wages and benefits.

Lippke finds none of these proposed justifications convincing, and argues that there should exist institutionalized protection of employee free speech. He is careful to note, however, that the proper exercise of free speech implies respect for others and hence could not be used to justify the selling of trade secrets or the malicious libelling of one's employer. Any institutionalization of free speech ought to include formal mechanisms by which an employer may appeal instances where employees appear to have gone beyond the bounds of free speech.

In "Employee Rights and the Doctrine of At Will Employment," David Hiley examines the traditional view that an employer has an unrestricted right to terminate employees. He argues that although this view has a long history in law, it is ethically suspect and the burden of proof rests on those trying to defend it on moral grounds. He examines three arguments that have been employed to support employment-at-will:

1. that it is well grounded in common-law tradition,
2. that it is implied by considerations of contract mutuality between employee and employer, and
3. that it is an extension of an employer's property rights.

Of these three, he finds the third most convincing, but even in this case, he does not feel that it will support the right of an employer to dismiss an employee arbitrarily.

In our third selection, "Collaborative Collective Bargaining: Toward an Ethically Defensible Approach to Labor Negotiations," Frederick Post addresses the issue of employee/employer antagonism that so often influences not only the collective bargaining process, but the day-to-day working environment. He argues that present methods of collective bargaining are based on an adversarial model which fosters resentment and immoral tactics of bargaining. In its place, he proposes a model of what he calls "collaborative collective bargaining," which fosters a non-adversarial environment and encourages truth and candor in the negotiation process.

Richard Lippke

Speech, Conscience, and Work

Several of the largest wine companies in the United States market fortified wines the alcohol content of which ranges from 18% to 21%, about twice the alcohol content of the ordinary table wines sold by these companies. These fortified wines are bought primarily by alcoholics in search of a cheap and swift drunk. While evidence suggests that the sale of these wines is highly profitable, the wine companies involved attempt to distance themselves from what some have labeled the "misery market."[1] None of the companies have their names printed on the bottle labels, and most routinely deny that they aim their products at the down-and-out in society.

Cynthia Rose, a fictional mid-level manager at one of these companies, has long been troubled by the actions of her company in selling these products. She learns that the company is planning to increase the alcohol content of its fortified wines in an attempt to gain a larger share of the market. She decides that she cannot remain silent any longer and approaches her immediate superiors to express her concerns about the company's actions. To her surprise, she is quickly and decisively rebuffed. She then seeks out individuals higher in the corporate hierarchy, believing she will eventually find someone who will at least take her concerns seriously. She is repeatedly disappointed. At last, out of frustration, she writes a letter to one of the major newspapers in her area where she clearly and carefully states her objections to the company's actions.

From Richard Lippke, "Speech, Conscience, and Work," *Social Theory and Practice*, Vol. 18, No. 3 (Fall 1992). Reprinted with modifications by permission of *Social Theory and Practice*.

If Cynthia was a real and not a fictional employee, chances are that her career with the company would be placed in jeopardy by her acts. In the United States, freedom of speech and conscience are rights central to the prevailing political morality. Yet, as numerous writers have noted, there is one area where such rights, as matters of social and political practice, are conspicuously absent. Workplace speech and conscience are rarely afforded legal or social protection.[2] Many if not most employees who engage in "work-related" speech, or who refuse to follow orders based on the dictates of their consciences, are subject to employer-imposed sanctions. By "work-related" speech I mean not only speech that occurs within the workplace, but also speech which is sufficiently about work so that though it occurs outside the workplace, it is subject to employer sanction. Admittedly, there is no sharp line between work-related and work-unrelated speech according to this definition. This imprecision in the definition mirrors social reality since employees are likely to be uncertain about whether what they say, even outside the workplace, is liable to incur their employers' displeasure. The important point here is that, historically, it is not simply employee speech inside the workplace that has been oppressed.

Like other recent writers on the subject, I doubt that the denial of such rights can be justified by reasoned moral argument. Where I differ with these theorists is over how to defend the claim that respect for basic moral rights requires work-related freedom of speech and conscience. For instance, David Ewing's argument holds that we should simply (and obviously) transfer civil rights of speech and conscience to the economic sphere.[3] Yet, this ignores the complications and objections such a straightforward transfer must address. Others, such as Thomas Donaldson, Patricia Werhane, and Richard DeGeorge, while urging respect for such rights, tend to narrowly construe them as rights to blow the whistle on employer wrongdoing or to express one's political and moral views outside the workplace.[4] However, as the preceding case illustrates, employees may form and wish to express judgments about work-related matters within the workplace. Also, their concerns need not be about illegal or even obviously immoral conduct. Their concerns may be "idiosyncratic," in the sense that they are based on beliefs that are not widely enough shared to be reflected in the law or in recognized codes of ethics. I suspect that such cases are not uncommon. An adequate treatment of employee speech and conscience must account for them. It must also clearly explain what interest individuals have in freedom of speech and conscience.

I begin with an analysis of the rights of freedom of speech and conscience. I then show how the analysis extends to the economic sphere, arguing that employees are entitled to institutionalized protection of work-related speech and conscience. While I concede that employee speech and conscience may legitimately be limited in order to protect other equally weighty interests, I argue against the view that employees have an obligation to first register their dissent internally. I also consider and attempt to defuse a variety of objections to work-related freedom of speech and conscience.

Let me note several limitations to my discussion. First, my concern is with the typical employee who works in a privately owned economic enterprise. Certain kinds of employees (for example, those who occupy special fiduciary roles) raise problems for my analysis that I will not pursue here. Second, my analysis focuses on the broad contours of institutional structures. I say little about the problems employees face in determining how to responsibly exercise their moral rights. Third, though I urge institutionalized protection for such rights, and indicate briefly what such protection would entail, I do not discuss the details of such protection nor the complications it is likely to engender. Finally, while I argue for a strong version of employee rights in these areas, I distinguish them from a full-fledged right to participation in work-related decisions. The latter, on my view, goes beyond speech in requiring employees to have an institutionalized say in workplace decisions. It is possible both analytically and practically to separate these rights.

Whether it is reasonable to do so, all things considered, is a question I will return to.

1

Most who have written about employee free speech and freedom of conscience have neglected to provide an analysis of the interests at stake in protecting these rights. A good place to begin such an analysis is by examining the writings of political and moral theorists on speech and conscience as moral rights in the civil (or political) realm. Unfortunately, there is no single agreed-upon theory for the justification of such rights. Familiar divisions among moral and political theorists are reflected in discussions of these matters. Instead of delving into these difficulties, my approach will be to simply stipulate what I think is the most plausible theory of these rights.[5]

My approach is squarely within the Kantian-contractarian tradition and focuses on the justification and limits of state interference in the lives of individuals. Fundamentally, the state must respect the capacity of persons to exercise their moral powers in two areas: the "rational" and the "reasonable." On the one hand, persons are beings who can formulate, critically reflect on, revise, and attempt to pursue a conception of the good. Part of respecting them is to act in ways consistent with the development and flourishing of this capacity—their rationality. On the other hand, persons can formulate, critically reflect on, revise, and attempt to act on conceptions of right conduct which, importantly, constrain their pursuit of the good. By doing so, they exhibit their reasonableness, their developed capacity to deliberate about what are the fair terms of cooperation and conflict resolution within a political community founded on mutual respect for persons. Failure by the state to act in ways consistent with either of these twin moral powers constitutes an affront to the dignity of persons.

One right in particular must be understood to have priority: the inalienable right of conscience. Its priority derives from the fact that the moral independence it secures is what enables persons to interpret the meaning and weigh the importance of other goods. State actions such as the imposition of an official religion, or the persecution of religion, are illegitimate on this view because they fail to respect this highest-order interest of persons. For the contractarian, respecting the moral independence of persons, and so their capacity to give free and rational consent, is what preserves "the ultimate sovereignty of persons both over themselves and their political community."[6] For the state to attempt to impose beliefs in such matters is to usurp the moral sovereignty of persons over their fundamental beliefs and life-choices.

Free speech is "a further elaboration of the equal respect that grounds the inalienable right of conscience."[7] It is through speech and other forms of communication that our capacities for rationality and reasonable-ness are developed, exercised, and expressed: "Both practical and epistemic rationality are expressed through speech and writing, which makes possible reflection about our ends, reasoning about our beliefs, and, in general, the imaginative constructions of reality that in art, science, and religion, are literally our ways of world- making."[8]

State attempts to judge the worth of communications imperils persons' twin moral powers. Decisions about whether, with whom, and about what to communicate, must remain in the hands of individuals. The scope of protected speech is as broad "as the range of facts and values that bear upon the independent exercise of our moral powers. . . ."[9]

We must recognize the need for limits on the exercise of our communicative capacities. The normative conception of the person this theory rests on contains the grounds for legitimate limitations of speech. First, the state may enact restrictions on speech aimed strictly at ensuring that audiences have the capacity to fairly and responsibly consider communications, so that their reflective moral powers are engaged rather than bypassed or run roughshod over. Widely-recognized forms of either deliberative incapacity or unfair manipulation may be proscribed: coercion, fraud, immediate provocation, mass hysteria, and so forth.[10] Second, there should be no objection, in principle, to those state regulations of time, manner, and place of speech "not aimed at the substance of what is said, but at the fair and neutral regulation of all communications."[11]

Third, from a contractarian perspective, there are general goods, goods persons want whatever else they want, which may appropriately qualify the scope of free speech. These goods include privacy and reputational integrity.[12]

I will discuss some of these limitations in greater detail when we turn to workplace speech. It is worth emphasizing the point that even in the civil realm, free speech is not to be conceived as an unlimited or unconstrained right. Its limits must be derived from a consideration of the conditions that must exist if social institutions are to nurture the twin moral powers of persons.

2

Even if we accept this theory of the grounds for freedom of speech and conscience as political rights, some might doubt that theory's relevance to the workplace. After all, it is about the limits of state power. If private businesses in advanced capitalist societies act in ways that deny employees these rights, perhaps that is a wholly different matter. Some might argue that private economic organizations can legitimately do what the state cannot.[13]

There may be reasons, some of which we will examine, why private organizations may permissibly do things that the state cannot. Yet, the mere fact that they are private does not, by itself, establish that organizations can ignore individual's moral rights. Most theorists who argue that individuals have moral rights that governments must respect do not see the role of government as limited to noninterference with or provision for such rights. They also regard government as responsible for securing such rights against violations by other individuals (and, incidentally, other governments). Little is gained if governments, while not themselves abrogating citizens' fundamental rights, stand idly by while other individuals do so. Moreover, governments in advanced capitalist societies maintain the conditions under which businesses can operate, by protecting private property and securing the conditions for market exchanges. Hence, they could hardly be viewed as free of complicity if they permit businesses to violate fundamental rights.

A second initial objection to the extension of this analysis to the workplace might be based on the claim that questions about the rational and reasonable do not arise in or with regard to the workplace. Some might argue that the social production of goods and services raises issues that are primarily technical in nature, and so better addressed by professionally trained managers, engineers, marketing specialists, and the like. Workers on the assembly line or engaged in the delivery of goods and services are, according to this argument, not deprived by generally authoritarian working conditions of speech or thought about matters which concern their moral powers. These powers, it will be argued, are best exercised over non-workplace matters which do not require specialized technical knowledge.

This argument contains, at best, a small grain of truth. The social production of goods and services is laden with decisions that presuppose substantive and controversial views about the rational and the reasonable. Decisions about what products to produce and why, what methods and resources to use in producing them, how to respond to the effects of their production on the environment, the organization of work, fair wages and adequate benefits, marketing methods, the treatment of women and minorities, the political activities of corporations, and so forth, all have significant moral dimensions.[14] While there may be aspects of social production that do require specialized knowledge, where experts should be deferred to, the sorts of matters just mentioned are not ones we have reason to believe business professionals have any special expertise about. Also, the value or usefulness of technical information and advice are matters about which non-experts often have to make decisions.

A third initial objection to extending rights of free speech and conscience to work-related matters rests on the notion that the wage-labor agreement represents a voluntary relinquishment by employees of these rights in exchange for wages and benefits.[15] It might be argued that most individuals surely realize that employers do not tolerate or appreciate employee dissent, and that employers expect employees to follow reasonable orders. Assuming wage-labor agreements are voluntary, the argument concludes that employees agree to silence their consciences and stifle their speech as conditions of employment.

Even if, for the moment, we leave aside questions about the voluntariness of wage-labor agreements, this argument is problematic. As stated, it rules out whistle-blowing by employees in cases where the business is acting in an illegal fashion (or where it is acting contrary to widely-accepted ethical standards). Also the argument makes it legitimate for employers to penalize employees who conscientiously refuse to follow orders requiring them to perform illegal or unethical acts. Surely it is unreasonable to hold that employees have waived or relinquished their rights to this extent.

A less extreme position would be that the relinquishment in question is a qualified one, where employees forgo rights of speech in cases other than those of legitimate whistle-blowing and conscience in cases other than those involving refusals to follow illegal or unethical orders. Yet, even this more moderate position seems gravely defective. Whether we regard an agreement to relinquish something as voluntary or not depends, among other things, on the surrounding social conditions and on the importance of what is alleged to have been relinquished.[16] It is widely recognized that most prospective employees in advanced capitalist systems lack feasible alternatives to the acceptance of work under conditions that deny them the exercise of their moral powers. It is simply not the case that there are work options readily available that respect these powers and ones that do not, and most workers freely choose the latter.

Moreover, employers, many of them large and influential corporations, engage in political activities that arguably help to maintain the sorts of social conditions that diminish the feasible options available to employees. For instance, employers are likely to resist measures that would provide employees with more generous and enduring unemployment compensation. Or, to take another example, they are likely to resist union activities that would place employees in a more equal bargaining position with their employers. These actions by businesses (and their owners, acting with the proceeds of ownership) go some way towards establishing conditions under which wage-labor tenders by employers are what David Zimmerman calls "coercive offers."[17] Coercive offers are offers where the recipient not only lacks reasonable options to acceptance of the offer, but lacks them because the party making the offer has taken steps to ensure that the recipient lacks them. While some may resist the claim that wage-labor tenders are coercive in this sense, the surrounding social conditions are such as to cast doubt on the proposition that employees have voluntarily relinquished their rights.

To the preceding we must add that what is alleged to have been relinquished is enormously important. If we accept my analysis, the rights in question are integral to the development and exercise of interests fundamental to persons. Indeed, freedom of conscience is inalienable.[18] In a similar vein, it can be argued that moral autonomy, the capacity of persons to exercise critical moral reflection over their decisions and actions is inalienable.[19] There is arguably a link between freedom of conscience, freedom of speech, and such critical moral reflection. The sorts of skills and motivations the latter requires seem more likely to be developed and maintained under conditions where individuals are permitted, or better, encouraged to exercise their moral powers. Thus, if moral autonomy is inalienable, and the denial of workplace speech and freedom of conscience would diminish it, we have further reason for declining to see such rights as relinquished to any extent.

Proponents of the moderate view might respond that employees' moral autonomy will be sustained so long as they are protected from employer sanction when they engage in legitimate whistle- blowing or refuse to follow illegal or unethical orders. Also, nothing in the moderate view would prevent employees from fully exercising their moral powers with regard to matters unrelated to work. Outside of work, the employee retains full-fledged rights of speech and conscience.

This response does not address the problems with voluntariness raised earlier. It remains unclear how we can reasonably regard employees as having relinquished the exercise of their moral powers to any extent. Further, the response suggests that it will be possible for employees to retain a lively sense of moral responsibility in the workplace, to be exercised on certain infrequent occasions, while facing employer disinterest or hostility to the exercise of their moral powers most of the time. What seems equally, if not more likely, is that employees will simply avoid morally evaluating their work, its conditions, and its consequences. Hence, they will lack the skills and motivation to exercise their moral powers on those occasions when (according to the moderate view) they might legitimately do so. If there are employees who secretly persevere in the active exercise of their moral powers though they know their views are not to be expressed, the emotional costs to them are likely to be significant. Suppose Cynthia Rose elected silence rather than expose herself to her supervisors' disapproval. She would in that case have to censor her own speech, ignore, deny, or conceal her "disloyal" thoughts, and endure the anger and frustration at having to do so. She may also have to accept the loss of self-respect that follows on the heels of failures to express her doubts, disagreements, or constructive criticisms. In the final analysis, it is not clear how the moderate position can avoid the charge that it requires employees to engage in deception and concealment, with possible grave consequences to their moral selves.

3

The failure of the relinquishment argument means that we have no reason to doubt that employees have fundamental rights of freedom of conscience and speech on work-related matters. My view is that these rights ought to be protected from employer interference by the state. This protection might take numerous forms, from some type of institutionalized due process to the establishment of special courts or arbitrators to which employees can appeal. Since, as we shall see, such rights are not unlimited ones, employers should be able to defend penalization of employees under certain conditions. However, it is vital that any institutionalized scheme place the burden of proof that employees have overstepped the bounds of their rights on employers. Since no scheme is likely to fully protect employees from employers hostile to employee exercises of these rights, the least we can do is make it more difficult for employers to justify penalization.

At this point, some might argue that employees ought to at least be required to exercise their rights in ways that are not disruptive to the businesses they are employed by. Many business people, and many who write abut employee rights, argue that employees ought to first voice their concerns internally, to their supervisors or, perhaps, co-workers. Admittedly, internal expressions of concern might be ineffective, or might enable wrongdoers to destroy damning evidence, or might expose the employee to unjust retaliation. Hence, the obligation to go internal first might be only *prima facie*. Still, it is argued that employees owe their employers at least the chance to respond to employee concerns prior to their concerns becoming public. Public dissent, including but not limited to whistle-blowing, does cause harm to businesses in myriad ways. One way to shield businesses from such harm would be to allow employers to defend penalization (in a due process hearing) if they can establish that employees have made no reasonable effort to first express their concerns internally.

What is the basis of this prima facie obligation on the part of employees? Richard DeGeorge, who has written extensively about whistle-blowing, suggests both that it is a duty of loyalty based on gratitude and that it is a duty of obedience. The former basis is problematic, as DeGeorge seems to recognize, because it implies that employers have done employees a favor by employing them. This does not quite square with the fact that the employment agreement involves the exchange of labor for wages and so is not unidirectional in the conferral of benefits. DeGeorge modifies his argument to say that because workers have "a stake" in the firm for which they work, this ought to translate into "positive concern" for the firm.[20] Yet, while employees have a stake in firms continuing to operate and employ them, it is not clear how this, by itself, establishes any moral obligation

on the part of employees to the firm to first air their concerns internally. Do employees have such an obligation regardless of the ways in which employers treat them, including whether they encourage or even tolerate internal exercises of employees' moral powers? Put another way, if employers do not show "positive concern" for the moral powers of their employees, is it reasonable to regard employees as obligated to show it for their employers?

Subsequently, DeGeorge argues that employees have a duty of obedience to firms and "disobedience typically requires justification if it is to be considered moral. . . ."[21] Unfortunately, DeGeorge relies too much on the dubious argument that employees have such a duty because most people think they do. He also compares disobedience to one's employer with civil disobedience and with a child's disobedience to his or her parents, both of which he argues, require justification. But, the latter case hardly seems germaine and the former is, at best, problematic. As the history of modern political theory attests, the conditions under which citizens have a duty of obedience to the state is a matter of great controversy. Perhaps citizens have such a duty under certain conditions, but DeGeorge offers no evidence that analogous conditions are satisfied by employees in relation to their employers.

Businesses vary a great deal with regard to how they treat and regard employee exercises of their moral powers. This alone casts doubt on the proposition that there is any sort of *prima facie* obligation on the part of all employees to first express their concerns internally. These variations are likely to remain even if some form of institutionalized protection for employees is adopted. As Patricia Werhane notes, businesses cannot be forced by laws to adopt moral attitudes towards their employees.[22] Some will no doubt obey laws protecting employee speech and conscience only grudgingly. There are numerous subtle ways in which businesses might try to penalize employees who exercise their moral powers, even where they do so internally. If we allow all employers to defend penalization on the grounds that employees have not used internal channels to express their concerns, this will create additional barriers to the exercise of employees' moral powers. Indeed, perhaps the single most effective way to make employers take employee speech and conscience seriously is to deny employers the means by which they can attempt to keep dissent "in house."

Still, my view about the normative contours of an institutionalized scheme of employee rights to speech and conscience is consistent with acknowledging the moral and practical problems many employees must face when it comes to the exercise of such rights. Though, on my view, employees will be acting within their rights if they express their work-related concerns publicly, there will often be compelling reasons for them to first seek out supervisors or co-workers to discuss their concerns. First, employees ought to acknowledge their own fallibility. They may be mistaken about empirical matters that bear on their concerns, or they may have only heard some of the facts. Second, individuals ought to realize that there is room for reasonable disagreement over the good and the right. Especially when employees' concerns are idiosyncratic, they might want to seek out others whose judgments diverge from theirs just to hear another side to things. In this way, employees affirm the moral powers of their supervisors or co-workers.[23] Third, as a practical matter, sometimes the most effective way to alter employer actions or practices will be to go through internal channels. If employees can effect changes through internal channels without exposing themselves to employer disfavor, this should weigh heavily in their deliberations about how to proceed.

Perhaps the most controversial feature of my view has to do with protecting external idiosyncratic speech on work-related matters. It is important to note that such external speech need not prevent employees from carrying out their assigned tasks in the workplace. I distinguish such cases from ones where employees conscientiously refuse to follow orders or perform assigned tasks on idiosyncratic grounds. I concede that such refusals constitute grounds for employers acting to demote or remove employees—assuming that the employees' reasons for refusal are indeed idiosyncratic.[24] Yet, where employees continue to perform their assigned tasks while engaging in external dissent, I maintain that such speech ought to be pro-

tected. Two things need to be emphasized about such speech. First, it will be legitimate for employers to publicly respond to such dissent. They can attempt to show that it is mistaken, unbalanced, or simply contentious. At least within certain limits, businesses ought to be able to defend themselves in public forums.[25] Second, it is a mistake to think of idiosyncratic speech as generally worthless or weird speech. Many reforms in business conduct that we today regard as required or exemplary were, when first suggested, idiosyncratic in the sense defined earlier. Idiosyncratic speech might eventually lead businesses to alter their conduct, or it might lead the public to demand different conduct from businesses through social pressure, laws, or regulations. In this way, business institutions are brought by such speech to more fully reflect and embody the moral powers of all persons.

Still, what if the external speech is careless, discloses trade secrets, or unfairly damages the business's reputation? Or, what if an employee continually disrupts work with tirades against management and co-workers? Here we run up against the limits on speech mentioned earlier. As with speech in the civil sphere, there must be limits on what employees can say in or with regard to the workplace. Employers who wish to encourage exercises of employees' moral powers within the workplace should establish special forums or venues to enable employees to express their concerns in ways that do not needlessly disrupt the workplace. Employers should be able to penalize employees who, without good reason, refuse to use available channels. These limits on work-related speech are analogous to the time, manner, and place restrictions Richards discusses with regard to civil speech. In addition, some types of external employee speech seem, in most cases, to be undeserving of immunity from employer sanction: external speech that carelessly or maliciously libels the business; external speech that divulges private information about employees or other individuals the business has information about; and external speech that discloses trade secrets.[26] All of these are cases where we might say that the employee who engages in such speech is not exercising her moral powers in ways that show respect for the moral powers of others. I agree that businesses ought to be able to justify demotion or discharge if they can establish, in a formal hearing, that the employee speech violated these limits.[27]

More difficult are cases of external employee speech that, even if only indirectly, reveal future plans of the business that management desires to keep secret. Suppose an employee, on idiosyncratic grounds, disagrees strongly with a planned new product, marketing procedure, lay-off, or move, and goes public with his concerns. Assuming his speech reveals no trade secrets, is not demonstrably false, and divulges no private information about individuals, should such speech be immune from employer sanction?

Some might argue that businesses, especially corporations, have moral rights to privacy much like natural persons. In that case, it might be claimed that the employee has violated the corporation's right to privacy in matters related to its future plans, and so has transgressed an important limit on speech.

I am skeptical of the claim that corporations themselves have moral rights, but let me try to say something about the present case without getting side-tracked on the question of the moral status of corporations. It seems that the interest individuals have in their privacy is different than the interest corporations—or more correctly, I think, their top-level managers and owners—have in privacy. Richards suggests that privacy is important to individuals because it enables them to shield themselves from "homogenizing and hostile public scrutiny."[28] In other words, if individuals were to find every aspect of their lives subject to the cold and sometimes cruel light of public scrutiny, it is unlikely that they would regard themselves as autonomous creatures, capable of and entitled to control their own lives.[29] Individuals are, as a rule, simply too vulnerable in the face of such scrutiny, and so are likely to surrender to its real or perceived demands.

For the sorts of large corporations common to advanced capitalism systems, the interest in privacy is primarily an economic interest in increased profits or market share. Greater public scrutiny of their activities is unlikely to affect the more personal privacy interests of their top-level managers and major shareholders. Also, one might plausibly argue that large corporations are in need of greater public scrutiny. Because of the enormous impact of their activities, it could be argued that their future plans really ought to be matters for public discussion and debate. This is precisely what external idiosyncratic speech about future plans is likely to foster. If it is argued that such disclosures will reveal future ventures to competing firms, thereby depriving firms whose employees make such disclosures of a competitive edge, two responses are in order. First, if firms establish internal channels for dissent, and treat such dissent seriously, then such external dissent will likely be relatively rare. Second, if respect for work-related employee speech is required by law, then no business will be at a relative competitive disadvantage. All will be subject to greater public scrutiny.

4

In this section I consider two further counterarguments to my thesis that employees have moral rights of free speech and conscience on work-related matters.

The first counterargument rests on the empirical claim that protecting such rights will result in lost productivity because their exercise will introduce disagreement and dissension into the workplace. If employees are permitted or encouraged to express their views on all of the moral matters relevant to the social production of goods and services, this will detract from the ability of management to give orders and have them promptly carried out. Also, the counterargument continues, however such speech and conscience are accommodated by employers, it will take time and energy away from that which might be used in the production of goods and services. Hence, unless we are prepared to embrace lower levels of productivity, and so fewer available goods and services, we should reject calls for the protection of employee speech and conscience.

Since all businesses would be required to respect such rights, the counterargument is most plausibly interpreted as focusing on the implications of such a policy for society as a whole. It is not a very interesting argument if it claims only that respecting such rights will result in a slightly lowered level of available goods and services. At least for nonutilitarian moral theorists, the mere fact (if it is a fact) that respecting some individuals' moral rights will result in a lower level of overall satisfaction in society is hardly sufficient grounds for declining to respect those rights.

However, Robert Ladenson interprets the counterargument in a more forceful fashion. He is concerned that "freedom of expression in the workplace must not extend so far as to undermine seriously the conditions of material prosperity upon which individuality also depends"[30] His contention appears to be that recognizing such rights could lower productivity to the point that the material conditions for the exercise of individuals' moral powers will be jeopardized. Since individuals presumably have even more basic rights to these material conditions, no scheme of work-related freedom of conscience and speech is defensible if it poses a threat to these more basic rights.[31]

Unfortunately, Ladenson offers little support for the claim that this threat is one we should take seriously. He rather cryptically remarks that "certain modes of discipline in a work setting ... are indispensable for the maintenance of efficient production or delivery of services."[32] This seems to equate conditions where free speech is protected with ones where discipline must be lacking. Yet, we might wonder why the two must go hand in hand. Ladenson does not develop his suggestion any further, and that is to be regretted. Even if we focus narrowly on the production of material goods and services, one question we would need answered is whether employees who find their moral powers more fully respected will, over a suitable period of time, produce more or fewer goods and services. Against the (allegedly) wasted time and energy the exercise of such powers will engender, we must weigh the possibility that employees whose moral powers are respected will have enhanced self-respect and self-esteem, will feel they have a greater stake in their work, and so as a result of both of these,

will be more motivated to work. Also, respect for employee conscience and speech might improve the quality of products. Employees could have valuable ideas about how to improve goods and services, how to market them, how to produce them in ways that more fully protect the environment, and so on.

Finally, if the affirmation of employee rights contributes to the development of responsible moral agency in the workplace, then employees, businesses, and society all stand to benefit. In short, if we are going to raise the issue of the costs to society of affirming employee rights, then these and other benefits to doing so must also be raised and carefully assessed.

The most formidable counterargument to the recognition of such employee rights focuses on the conflict between such rights and the rights of owners and shareholders to control the workplace. The latter rights are, in turn, grounded in rights to private property. Simply stated, the moral right to private property is held to entitle one to control the conduct of those inhabiting or using one's property. Hence, the counterargument holds that if the owners of a business do not wish to hear the opinions of employees on work-related matters, or if they wish to fire employees who refuse to follow orders for whatever reasons, then they ought to be able to do so without state (or other) interference.

It is important to clearly state where the conflict between employees' rights and owners' rights is alleged to lie. I have not argued that employees have a right to participation in work-related decisions as such a right is normally interpreted.[33] Such a right is one that goes well beyond the ones I have argued for in this paper. However, it might be argued that the measures I have urged would diminish employer control in subtle, yet important, ways. For one thing, these measures would deprive employers of some control over what is said in or about the workplace. The measures would also deprive employers of control over the treatment of employees who, in certain circumstances, refuse to follow orders. There is also the potential that employee speech will bring both internal and external pressure to bear on employers. Internal, because one employee's expressed concerns may spark others employees to raise questions that management feels called upon to respond to. External, because members of the general public may bring pressure to bear on management to explain their decisions and actions, or to alter them. It is these sorts of diminutions in control that the counterargument refers to.

Yet, as so far stated, the counterargument is question-begging. Even if institutionalized protection for employee speech and conscience does deprive owners and shareholders of some control over private economic organizations, the question is whether such exclusive control on their part is justified. Here we run up against questions about the nature, limits, and justification of moral rights. These are questions that deeply divide moral political theorists. Obviously, this is no place to begin defending a general theory of such rights—or what amounts to the same thing, a theory of social justice. Thus, I will respond to the counterargument in a limited way, utilizing the theoretical framework developed in this paper.

Simplifying matters, the choice we now face is one between two competing schemes of rights: (a) one which allows the owners of productive property to control the workplace in such a manner as to stifle employee freedom of conscience and speech; and (b) one which deprives the owners of productive property of such extensive control by protecting these employee rights. It seems clear that the latter option is more likely to establish social conditions that more fully support the moral powers of every individual. Such a scheme does not in any significant way threaten the moral powers of the owners of productive property. They can still have their say in the workplace (either directly or through management representatives) and outside of it about work-related matters. Indeed, their opinions are, absent a scheme of work participation, decisive. This greater efficacy to their speech and judgment is an advantage to them that is not eliminated by scheme (b). Still, scheme (b) would establish social conditions more supportive of the moral powers of many individuals, and, *ceteris paribus,* I think we ought to favor a more egalitarian scheme to a less egalitarian one. At the very least, it seems that the burden of argument ought to be on those who favor less egalitarian schemes.

Some will argue that even the scheme I favor does not go far enough. They will argue that employees whose speech and consciences are protected are only being given half a loaf, and one that is not likely to prove very filling in the long run. What is needed, they will argue, is a scheme of work participation that grants employees an explicit voice in the decisions of economic enterprises. Without a protected role in decision-making, employees will find themselves speaking out and being ignored by shareholders and management. Eventually, it is argued, employees will become frustrated and lose interest in the exercise of their rights of free speech and conscience.

While I am sympathetic to this argument, I think it is a mistake to hold that employees will gain no control over businesses under the more limited scheme that protects only their rights of speech and conscience. In theory, employers can, under such a scheme, choose to ignore what their employees say or conscientiously choose to do. However, employee speech and acts of conscience seem likely to create social pressure for an employer response. Since it is doubtful that employers will always be able to defend their decisions and practices in a manner which even they regard as satisfactory, we can expect them to occasionally alter their conduct. In short, employee speech and acts of conscience will likely be efficacious enough at times to produce economic institutions that more fully reflect the moral powers of all persons.

Notes

1. "Misery Market: Winos and Thunderbird Are a Subject Gallo Doesn't Like to Discuss," *The Wall Street Journal,* February 25, 1988.
2. The seminal work in this area is David Ewing's *Freedom Inside the Organization* (New York: E.P. Dutton, 1977). For more recent evidence of the, at best, ambivalent attitude of managers toward employee dissent within the workplace, see Robert Jackall, *Moral Mazes: The World of Corporate Mangers* (New York: Oxford University Press, 1988).
3 *Freedom Inside the Corporations,* p. 97.
4 See Thomas Donaldson, *Corporations and Morality* (Englewood Cliffs, NJ: Prentice-Hall, 1982), pp. 146–49; Patricia Werhane, *Persons, Rights, and Corporations* (Englewood Cliffs, New Jersey: Prentice-Hall, 1985), pp. 113–16; and Richard T. DeGeorge, *Business Ethics* (New York: Macmillan, 1990), pp. 338–39.

5. It seems likely that other theories of these rights will yield similar conclusions when applied to employees and their work-related speech and exercises of conscience.

6. *Toleration and the Constitution,* p. 168. Richards's analysis seems to presuppose, at the very least, that there are matters (for example, religious and moral beliefs) about which rational people can disagree. His analysis may presuppose more than this—that there are matters about which no rational resolution of disagreement is available. On the latter, see Thomas Nagel, "Moral Conflict and Political Legitimacy," *Philosophy and Public Affairs* Vol. 16 (1987): 215–40.

7. *Toleration and the Constitution,* p. 169.

8. *Toleration and the Constitution,* p. 167. In contrast, Frederick Schauer argues that experiences (for example, world travel) and action may develop our rationality as well, if not better, than speech and writing. Yet, it is difficult to conceive how either is likely to do so if unaccompanied by verbal or written narration, instruction, or criticism. See Schauer's *Free Speech: A Philosophical Inquiry* (Cambridge: Cambridge University Press, 1982), p. 57.

9. *Toleration and the Constitution,* p. 195.

10. *Toleration and the Constitution,* see p. 172.

11. *Toleration and the Constitution,* p. 173.

12. *Toleration and the Constitution,* see pp. 195ff.

13 See Donald L. Martin, "Is An Employee Bill of Rights Needed?" reprinted in Alan F. Westin and Stephan Salisbury, *Individual Rights in the Corporation* (New York: Pantheon Books, 1980), pp. 15–20.

14. See Christopher McMahon, "Managerial Authority," *Ethics* Vol. 100 (1989): 33–53.

15. See "Is An Employee Bill of Rights Needed?" p. 17.

16. Joel Feinberg, *Harm to Self* (New York: Oxford University Press, 1986), pp. 98–124.

17. David Zimmerman, "Coercive Wage Offers," *Philosophy and Public Affairs* Vol. 10 (1981): 121–45. See also Feinberg, *Harm to Self,* pp. 229–49.

18. *Toleration and the Constitution,* p. 85ff.

19. Arthur Kuflick, "The Inalienability of Autonomy," *Philosophy and Public Affairs* Vol. 13 (1984): 271–98.

20. *Business Ethics* (New York: Macmillan, 1990), p. 206.

21. *Business Ethics,* p. 207.

22. *Persons, Rights, and Corporations,* p. 156. Werhane's skepticism about the law leads her to favor the adoption by businesses of voluntary schemes of protection for employees' rights. It seems to me she slights the ways in which the law can act as a force for positive change in employer attitudes toward employees.

23. At the same time, I believe we should be skeptical of arguments against employee dissent based on the idea that such dissent disrupts employee morale. The tendency to disrupt morale may itself be a product of employer hostility to employee speech and conscience. In such a context, co-workers fear association with dissenters and are more likely to view dissent as an act of disloyalty. However, if employee speech and conscience were valued by employers, employee dissent would not be viewed as negatively by co-workers, and so would not be as disruptive to morale.

24. Through penalization of employees who refuse to carry out assigned tasks for idiosyncratic reasons should not be legally forbidden, employers might nevertheless attempt to accommodate employees' sincerely held beliefs. In many cases, other employees will be willing to carry out the tasks in question.

25. Of course, further questions arise when businesses engage in massive advertising campaigns aimed at creating favorable, and often misleading, public images. I will not discuss these issues here.

26. As Richard DeGeorge notes, there are cases where trade secrets perhaps ought to be made public. See his *Business Ethics,* pp. 243–49. There may also be cases where private information ought to be divulged.

27. There are difficult issues involved in determining what the appropriate penalty should be for any given transgression. I do not pursue these matters here.

28. *Toleration and the Constitution,* p. 244.

29. I am indebted to the account of the value of privacy developed by Joseph H. Kupfer in his "Privacy, Autonomy, and Self-Concept," *American Philosophical Quarterly* Vol. 24 (1987): 81–89.

30. Robert Ladenson, *A Philosophy of Free Expression* (Totowa, New Jersey: Rowman and Allanheld, 1983), p. 117.

31. It is unclear from Ladenson's text whether his argument is to be interpreted as a rights-based one or simply as a utilitarian one that claims that levels of overall utility will be greatly lowered by such a scheme of employee rights.

32. *A Philosophy of Free Expression,* p. 117.

33. See John J. McCall, "Participation in Employment," in Desjardins and McCall, *Contemporary Issues in Business Ethics,* pp. 250–58.

David R. Hiley /

Employee Rights and the Doctrine of At Will Employment

In a recent issue of *Management Review,* the president of the American Management Association described the erosion of the practice of "at will" employment and the employer's right to fire employees for whatever reason. He acknowledged that poor management practices were partly responsible for the increased legislation and litigation limiting the employer's right to fire, but he warned that the trend away from termination at will should concern all employers. The question he raised was how to balance the employer's need to terminate an employee against the need to treat employees fairly and responsibly. He concluded: "An organization must have the right to terminate incompetent personnel. Indeed, it has the obligation to its stockholders to do so. It must have the right to reduce its work force in hard times if that is what it needs to do to survive. But the organization behaves self-destructively when it tells its employees that it values the right to treat them capriciously."[1] The problem raised is how to balance an employer's right to terminate against an employee's right to be free from intimidation, retaliation, or caprice.

The erosion of the employer's right to terminate has become a common theme in business periodicals and management and supervision journals[2] as a result of a growing number of legal challenges to the common-law doctrine of employment at will that has allowed employers to terminate an employee without considerations of due process or just cause.[3] Employ-

ment at will is a uniquely American doctrine having its source in the common-law principle that where the employment relationship is not bound by a contract specifying the period of employment, the relationship is considered "at will" and can be terminated without cause by either party.[4] Currently, approximately 70 percent of workers in America are considered "at will" employees. Until relatively recently, courts have upheld the employer's right to terminate without cause or notice. In one frequently cited decision a court ruled that employers may dismiss their employees "for good cause, for no cause, or even for causes morally wrong, without being thereby guilty of legal wrong."[5]

Courts are increasingly finding in favor of employees, however. In a number of recent cases of wrongful discharge there have emerged three general grounds for exception to the "at will" doctrine:

1. when discharge violates explicit public policy or statute;
2. when discharge is a result of malice or bad faith; and
3. when discharge violates an implied contract between employer and employee.

With the first sort of exceptions, for example, courts have found that employers are not free to dismiss an employee for serving on a jury or for refusing to commit perjury. The second class of exceptions protects employees from retaliation from employers in such circumstances as sexual harassment or whistle-blowing, or in cases of discharge to avoid fulfilling an agreement on the part of the employer. The third category of cases is the latest legal development. Courts are finding that oral agreements, personnel policy manuals, and employee handbooks are implied contracts between employers and employees and that employers are not free to discharge employees in violation of these implied contracts.

Despite the fact that the employment-at-will doctrine has been the subject of considerable legal attention, it requires ethical analysis be-

From David R. Hiley, "Employee Rights and the Doctrine of At Will Employment," *Business and Professional Ethics Journal,* vol. 4 (1985). Reprinted by permission.

cause the law in this area is unstable as a result of recent significant challenges. More important, however, the law begins with the acceptance of the common-law tradition and the burden of proof is to justify exceptions to the employer's right to terminate at will; ethical analysis, however, must call the doctrine of employment at will, itself, into question and evaluate its justification in light of a commitment to more general ethical principles of fairness and due process. My initial thesis, then, is that the burden rests with those who defend the employer's unrestricted right to terminate. From a defense of this initial thesis, I will examine arguments that favor an employer's unrestricted right to terminate.

The burden-of-proof thesis rests on a series of claims supporting a *prima facie* right on the part of employees to be free from unfair or arbitrary dismissal and a defeasible right to job security in exchange for satisfactory job performance. It needs to be made clear initially, however, that my burden-of-proof argument requires only the minimal claim of a right to be free of unfair and arbitrary dismissal. These claims, themselves, require extended defense but for my present purpose it is necessary only that they provide a plausibility argument. The most general claim is that in a society that values and protects the rights we have as citizens—not the least of which are fair treatment and due process—it is unreasonable to think that we should not have these rights as workers.[6] Many recent arguments for employee rights are based on the idea that civil rights extend to the workplace. David Ewing, for example, has characterized American corporations as "the black hole of civil rights" and he argues against the idea that the rights we have as citizens should be left in the parking lot with our automobiles.[7] What makes this argument more compelling is the realization that American business is increasingly dominated by large corporate structures that exercise power over the lives of workers comparable to the power governments have over citizens. Lawrence Blades, in the most significant law article on the issue of employer right to terminate, begins his argument for the protection of worker freedom by stating that "large corporations now pose a threat to individual freedom comparable to that which would

be posed if governmental power were unchecked."[8] The claim that employees should have the right to fairness and due process, then, is part of the more general claim that employees have rights in the workplace.

In the context of our general commitment to fairness and due process, current practices in the United States regarding the right to be free from wrongful dismissal are all the more inconsistent. Thirty percent of the workforce is protected by collective bargaining agreements, civil service procedures, or tenure policies that prevent the employer from exercising an unrestricted right to terminate. It is implausible to think that the presence or absence of a contract alone entails the presence or absence of a right to fairness and due process.

Two other claims support my burden-of-proof thesis. First, an employee is not bound to his or her job simply through economic dependence. Some legal theorists are claiming that employees acquire a property right with respect to their jobs, thus as a property right, employment requires protection from wrongful or arbitrary violation.[9] The basis for this claim derives from a changing concept of property and from the realization that through seniority, pension plans, life-insurance benefits and the like, employees become "vested" in their employment. Charles Reich, in his influential article "The New Property," has argued that as the role of government has expanded, traditional forms of private wealth and private property are being transformed because we become dependent, as citizens and as businesses, on what he calls "government largess"—unemployment insurance, social security, government contracts, licensing regulations and so on. On Reich's analysis:

The significance of government largess is increased by certain underlying changes in forms of private wealth in the United States. . . . [T]oday more and more of our wealth takes the form of rights or status rather than tangible goods. An individual's profession or occupation is a prime example. To many others, a job with a particular employer is a principal form of wealth. A profession or a job is frequently far more valuable than a house or a bank account.[10]

If it is plausible to consider a profession or job as property, then workers acquire a right in their jobs that requires protection against wrongful dismissal or caprice.

Finally, perhaps the most important reason employees should be secure from wrongful and arbitrary termination is that such protection is a fundamental enabling right, constituting a condition for the protection of other employee rights. If employees are to be protected in the right of privacy in matters unrelated to their employment, or in their right of conscience or political liberty, then they must be protected from termination growing out of their possession or exercise of these and other important worker rights.

My thesis is that, because of these considerations, the burden of proof rests with those who maintain an employer's unrestricted right to terminate an employee at will. In turning to an examination of arguments that support the employer's rights, I must first point out that the claim that an employer has a right to terminate must be approached from a consideration of rights claims generally, as well as from consideration of the justification of this particular right. Obviously, rights claims must be grounded and the plausibility of the claim depends on the plausibility of the considerations upon which the right is grounded. Furthermore, the possession of a right entails claims on others—minimally the claim of noninterference—and it entails conditions of responsible exercise on the part of the one who possesses the right. My right to drive an automobile involves your obligation not to prevent me from exercising my right, and it involves an obligation on my part that I will exercise it within conditions described by the law and by considerations of safety. What is problematic about earlier legal precedents for the employer's right to terminate at will is that courts have supported the right as absolute and unconditioned. That is, the right has been assumed to be unrestricted and without conditions of responsible exercise. The effect of recent court decisions is that the right to terminate is increasingly treated as a defeasible right with both external and internal conditions for exception. Externally, public policy considerations can override the employer's right to terminate. Internally, employer irresponsibility through malice or breach of good faith are grounds for exception.

The employer's right to terminate at will has been grounded in three ways. First, of course, it is grounded historically in the common-law tradition of "at will" employment. That, however, does not constitute an adequate basis for meeting ethical challenge to the employer's right to terminate because the law itself is in the process of significant modification and, more obviously, because of the nonidentity of legality and morality.

Second, the right is grounded in considerations of mutuality between employee and employer drawn from contract theory. Since an "at will" employee has the right to resign at will, it is claimed that the employer has the corresponding right to terminate at will. It is argued that the employer's right to terminate is justified because both parties enter the relationship freely and both are equally free to terminate at will. In a frequently cited ruling, one court found that since "an employee is never presumed to engage his service permanently . . . if the contract of employment be not binding on the employee for the whole term of such employment, then it cannot be binding upon the employer; there would be lack of 'mutuality.' "[11]

This mutuality argument is problematic in two ways. First, applying the notion of "mutuality" from contract theory to the employment relationship assumes that the relationship is symmetrical in the relevant sense necessary to claim that whatever binds or fails to bind one party must bind or fail to bind the other. While there may be an abstract equality and freedom in the employer-employee relationship, there is a significant material inequality and lack of comparable freedom. Synoeyenbos and Roberts have pointed to the fact that there is an inequality of possible harm that slants in favor of the employer. "In times of high unemployment, or in fields of specialization or industries where there is a labor surplus, it will probably be more difficult for the discharged employee to find a new position that for the firm to hire a new employee, consequently, the harm to the employee, in terms of economic hardship and psychological disruption, is often greater than the harm to the firm."[12] In addition to the differential harm resulting from the general condition of the economy, an employee has an investment in his or her job in terms of economic dependency, benefit programs, pension plans and the like, and these, along with considerations of age, mobility, and family circumstance, imply a lack of mutuality. One might reasonably argue that a clerk's resignation without notice poses comparable harm to a mom and pop market, but the idea of mutuality of harm is simply implausible when comparing the harm to a fired head of household and Exxon Corporation. Work situations in the United States today are more like the latter than the former.

Besides consideration of differential harm, there is also an important asymmetry in relations of power and authority that affects the balance of freedom in the employment relationship. The growing defense of the idea that employees have rights in the workplace roughly parallel to civil rights is grounded, in part, by consideration of the way power is used and abused in organizations. This concern results from the realization mentioned above that large corporate organizations exercise power over workers similar to that of governments over citizens and from obvious abuses of employer power where termination is used as retaliation. Furthermore, differences in authority can exercise indirect coercive influences at the expense of employee rights. The use of polygraph tests as a condition of employment is a case in point. According to one line of argument, since a potential employee is always free to submit to the test or not, the use of a polygraph is not an abridgment of privacy. However, given that the potential employee and the employer do not meet as equals in the hiring setting because of differences in authority and control, and given that the potential employee's decision not to submit to the test is a decision not to be considered for the job, there is a fundamental lack of freedom. A similar situation is emerging in response to recent judgments in favor of employees for unfair dismissal. As one way of avoiding challenges to the right to terminate, some attorneys are advising employers to require employees to sign an "acknowledgment of waiver" agreeing that employment may be terminated without cause or notice. The assumption is that since the employee freely assents to the waiver, the employer will be protected from litigation. Apart from the fact that this response is rather like a restaurant posting a sign that it "reserves the right to refuse service to anyone" in response to desegregation laws, it is not obvious that a potential employee is any more free to refuse to sign such a waiver than he or she would be to refuse a polygraph test as a condition of employment.

The second problem that mutuality arguments raise for an employer's right to terminate is that mutuality considerations might reasonably be used as a defense *against* the claim that the employer can terminate without cause or notice. It has recently been argued that contract theory implies an obligation of good-faith dealings on the part of the contracting parties and that redress for wrongful discharge might be argued on the basis of a breach of good faith.[13] It is not my purpose to enter the legal issue of applying contract-theory considerations to wrongful dismissal, but rather to suggest that the mutuality argument provides dubious support for the claim that an employer has an unrestricted right to terminate.

The most promising basis for grounding the employer's right to terminate is the claim that it is an extension of private property rights. This argument is implied by the concern among businesspeople about the intrusion of government or the courts in the employment relationship. Although some of these concerns are clearly bad-faith defenses and special pleading, since government involvement is not opposed when it serves business interests—in price supports, protectionist policies concerning foreign trade, corporate bail-outs, for example—there is an important underlying argument that must be considered on its own terms. The most general form of the argument is that in a free economy of privately held businesses, employers have property rights entitling them—in the same way any owner of property is entitled—to do with, dispose of, or make decisions affecting the use of one's property free from interference. There are a pair of issues I do not want to engage in connection with this argument: I do not wish to consider whether free markets or private property are themselves morally justified; and I do not wish to debate the degree to which our economic system conforms to the model of free markets and private ownership. Rather, I am interested in examining the strongest possible case for the claim that the employer's right to terminate at will derives from the right of private ownership or private property on the methodological assumption that if it is not justified in the strongest case, then it will not be justified on the basis of whatever modified view of our current economic system one wants to maintain.

It is important to realize that this justification of the employer's right to terminate does not rest simply on the claim of private property rights. As is usually noticed, there is an important connection between rights and interests.[14] Support for the employer's right to terminate must rest not only on claimed property rights but on the claim that maintenance of the employer's unrestricted right fulfills important social interests. Thus this argument is coupled with the utilitarian justification that society's interests are best fulfilled by maintaining the employer's right to terminate at will. Less abstractly, this is the point of concern about the "erosion" of the employment-at-will doctrine in business and management periodicals. The assumption is that if employers are not free to fire, fear of litigation will bring about an increasing reluctance on the part of employers to terminate an employee even when there is just cause. The result, it is argued, is decreased efficiency, productivity, and profitability. Positively stated, the claim is that society has an interest in employers retaining the right to terminate since this right would contribute to a company's ability to maximize efficiency, productivity, and profitability— all of which contribute to social utility.

In examining this grounding of the employer's right to terminate, we must keep in mind that the property-rights argument cuts both ways. Given growing support for the idea that a worker can acquire a property right in his or her job, the issue is, at best, one of conflicting property-rights claims. Further, it is worth noticing that protecting the employer's property right cannot be defended on the basis of general claims about the efficiency of a system of private property. Frank I. Michelman has argued, for example, that the presumption that a system of private property is more efficient than any other system requires justification of the claim that any property system that is otherwise equivalent is less efficient. After considerable analysis, Michelman concludes that such a claim is unsupportable and that the justification of a system of private property must rest on noneconomic considerations.[15] More is required to defend the claim that the employer's unrestricted right to terminate serves the interests of efficiency than the argument that it is an extension of private property rights.

The burden rests on the following question: Is efficiency, productivity, and profitability diminished in proportion as an employer's right to terminate is modified? In approaching this question, we must distinguish a range of cases in order to sharpen the issue. First, no one could plausibly argue against an employer's right to terminate an employee for inadequate job performance or for gross misconduct related to job performance. Much of the argument in the "at will" controversy has turned on whether employers have the right to terminate at the other extreme of cases—for bad cause or for no cause at all. The most problematic cases for those who wish to limit the employer's right to terminate, however, fall between the extremes of termination for cause and termination from malice or caprice. Three sorts of cases seem particularly problematic: cases where job performance is adequate, but only minimally so; cases where job performance is adequate, but future growth and productivity is unlikely; and cases where performance and potential contribution are satisfactory, but other factors such as personal incompatibility disrupt efficiency and productivity. The question that must be considered is this: Will the limitation of the employer's right to terminate in the clearly irresponsible cases have the effect of restricting the employer's right to terminate in these more problematic cases? If the answer is yes, then there is plausibility to the claim that a restriction of the employer's right to terminate will constitute a social disutility since it will restrict that area of management judgment and foster mediocre employee performance.

This question can be approached from two directions. First, it could be argued that there are compelling counterexamples one way or the other. Second, the answer could turn on a consideration of whether an unrestricted right to terminate would be more beneficial than the policies and procedures required of an employer to demonstrate responsible judgment.

The United States is unique in its support of the doctrine of employment at will. One might look to other countries—West Germany or Japan, for example—where employees have security against termination without cause and consider whether the result has been reduced efficiency, productivity, or profitability. Norman Horton, in the article cited at the beginning of this paper, has appealed to the example of West Germany. He writes: "In West Germany, the law against unjust dismissal protects the employee rather than the employer. Although it doesn't prevent employers from firing for just cause, it has effectively created a corporate culture that avoids termination. A manager from a major German chemical company told me he envied the freedom American firms have to fire incompetents. 'You wouldn't believe some of the deadwood we support,' he said."[16] Managers in other countries may envy American employers' freedom to fire, but that is beside the point. The issue is solved neither anecdotally nor by appealing to management preference. Does the practice foster a social disutility? At best, counterexamples are inconclusive. On the one hand, recent literature on declining productivity in America has compared employer-employee relations in the United States unfavorably to those in West Germany and Japan and has placed at least part of the blame for the superior economic performance of Germany and Japan, when compared with that of the United States, on superior management. On the other hand, it is unclear to what extent the success of West German and Japanese business depends on the difference between free market economies and command economies. I am not in a position to enter either debate. It is enough, however, to see that the claim of social disutility will not be justified from obvious counterexamples. The most promising argument, then, must be that an employer's unrestricted right to terminate is more beneficial than the measures required of an employer to show cause and responsible judgment when terminating an employee.

Two different approaches have been recommended in the literature to assure the employer's right to fire and protection against wrongful-dismissal law suits. The defensive strategy is for employers to eliminate possible grounds for liability. Since, for example, courts are treating employee handbooks as binding contracts between employer and employee, some attorneys are recommending the elimination of anything in policy manuals or employee handbooks that could be construed as a commitment to job security that the employer does not intend. In addition, it is recommended that employers carefully document employee misconduct or inadequate job performance and provide the employee with notice of poor job performance. The affirmative strategy is to develop and implement clearly formulated personnel evaluation and review procedures, grievance procedures, and human resources development plans.[17] It seems plausible to expect that clarity of intention and responsibility in employee evaluation will, itself, contribute to efficiency and productivity—or at least it does not seem likely that it will diminish productivity. It also seems plausible to expect that within a framework of clearly articulated personnel policies and grievance procedures, managers would remain free to make personnel judgments for the good of the company—or at least the burden rests with employers to demonstrate why sound personnel policies and the need to show cause restricts their ability to deal effectively with their employees and produces a disutility that overrides an employee's right to fairness and due process.

I have argued that because employees have the right to be free from unfair and arbitrary dismissal, and because there is at least plausibility to the extended claim that they have a defeasible right to their jobs so long as satisfactory job performance is provided, employers do not have an unrestricted right to terminate an employee at will The arguments most frequently given for the employer's right to fire, do not justify the claimed right against a greater need to protect employees. Though certainly it is essential that employers have the right to make responsible personnel judgments, and though those judgments need not always turn simply on considerations of satisfactory job performance, the burden should rest with the employer to show either that termination is for just cause or that it is justified in terms of considerations of responsible business and personnel policy.

Notes

1. Norman R. Horton, "Dear New Hire: WE reserve the right to fire you . . .," *Management Review,* August 1984, p. 3.
2. See, for example, Jeffrey C. Pingpank and Thomas B. Mooney, "Wrongful Discharge: A New Danger for Employers," *Personnel Administrator,* March 1981, pp. 31–35; Anthony T. Oliver, Jr., "The Disappearing Right to Terminate Employees at Will," *Personnel Journal,* December 1982, pp. 910–17; Maria Leonard, "Challenges to the Termination-at-Will Doctrine," *Personnel Administrator,* February 1983, pp. 49–56; David W. Ewing, "Your Right to Fire," *Harvard Business Review,* March–April 1983, pp. 32–42; "Curtailing the Freedom to Fire," *Business Week,* March 19, 1984; and Charles G. Bakaly, Jr., and Joel M. Grossman, "How to Avoid Wrongful Discharge Suits," *Management Review,* August 1984, pp. 41–46.
3. For reviews of recent court cases see Lawrence E. Blades, "Employment At Will vs. Individual Freedom: On Limiting the Abusive Exercise of Employer Power," *Columbia Law Review* 67 (1967): pp. 1405–35; John D. Blackburn, "Restricting Employer Discharge Rights: A Changing Concept of Employment At Will," *American Business Law Journal* 17 (1980): pp. 467–92; and Brian Heshizer, "The Implied Contract Exception to At-Will Employment," *Labor Law Journal* 35, (1984): pp. 131–41.
4. The source of the common-law doctrine of employment at will is H. G. Wood, *A Treatise on Law of Master and Servant* (New York: John D. Parsons, 1887).
5. *Payne vs. Western & A. R.R.,* 81 Tennessee 507 (1884) pp. 519–20.
6. Patricia Werhane has made this the basis for her argument against the employer's unrestricted right to terminate in "Individual Rights in Business," in *Just Business: New Introductory Essays in Business Ethics,* ed. Tom Regan (New York: Random House, 1984), pp. 107f.
7. David Ewing, *Freedom Inside the Organization* (New York: Dutton Publishing Co., 1977).
8. Blades, "Employment At Will vs. Individual Freedom," p. 1409, cited in note 3.
9. See, for example, Mary Ann Glendon and Edward R. Lev, "Changes in the Bonding of the Employment Relationship: An Essay on the New Property," *Boston College Law Review* 20 (1979): pp. 457–84.
10. Charles Reich, "The New Property," *Yale Law Journal* 73 (1964). Citation is from reprint in *Property, Profits, and Economic Justice,* ed. Virginia Held (Belmont, CA: Wadsworth Publishing Co., 1980), p. 48.
11. *Pitcher vs. United Oil and Gas Syndicate Inc.,* 174 Louisiana 66 at 69, 139 So. 750 at 761 (1932).
12. Milton Snoeyenbos and John Wesley Roberts, "Ethics and the Termination of Employees," in *Business Ethics* (New York: Promoetheus Books, 1983), p. 249.
13. See Blackburn, "Restricting Employer Discharge Rights," pp. 482ff., for a review of this issue, cited in note 3.
14. See, for example, Virginia Held's recent book, *Rights and Goods* (New York: Free Press, 1984), chap. 10, where she connects property rights with interests of society.
15. Frank I. Michelman, "Ethics, Economics, and the Law of Property," *Ethics, Economics, & the Law,* Nomos XXIV, ed. J. Roland Pennock and John W. Chapman (New York: New York University Press, 1982), pp. 3–40.
16. Horton, "Dear New Hire," p. 3.
17. See, for example, Leonard, "Challenges to the Termination-at-Will Doctrine," and Charles G. Bakaly, Jr., and Joel M. Grossman, "How to Avoid Wrongful Discharge Suits," cited in note 2.

Frederick R. Post

Collaborative Collective Bargaining: Toward an Ethically Defensible Approach to Labor Negotiations

I. Introduction

The present legal and moral environment of current U.S. labor management relations can best be understood through the lens of history. Prior to the enactment of federal labor legislation in 1935, unions had no protection under the law. With a strident employer opposition to unionization coupled with an authoritarian management style, the predictable reaction was a militant labor movement. This produced a state of industrial warfare. As anyone familiar with labor history knows, the employers won almost all the battles.

Only under the umbrella of legal protection, consisting of the original Wagner Act[1] and its subsequent amendments,[2] collectively referred to as the National Labor Relations Act (The Labor Act), have unions and the collective bargaining process been legitimated. While free (meaning minimal governmental interference) collective bargaining is often applauded as the building block of our labor management relations system, it has been criticized recently from a moral and economic perspective.[3] Because the legal framework controlling the collective bargaining process was erected in response to a history of employer hostility towards and ex-

ploitation of employees to satisfy utilitarian ends, the legislature, in enacting the Labor Act, tried to balance the power between the two groups. However, the Labor Act does not encourage direct cooperation between an employer and employees; it merely prescribes a legal framework within which the employee representative bargains about the working conditions of represented employee groups.[4] Furthermore, both the administrative agency directed by congress to oversee the Labor Act, the National Labor Relations Board (The Labor Board), and reviewing federal courts consistently issue decisions that perpetuate an adversarial labor management environment.

While history provides both an explanation and an excuse for the present legal framework governing labor management relations, the present adversarial system may be less appropriate than the participatory management forms available for dealing with this critical internal business relationship. This is especially true for that aspect of the system which results in the labor contract. Since labor negotiations happen at least every three years, because the law only protects the incumbent relationship for that time period, any movement toward a more peaceful process would be advantageous for all concerned. Because the present system does not provide an optimal solution for this fundamental building block of labor management relations, it is time to consider an alternative approach.

This paper will explain the present adversarial collective bargaining process (ACB) and critique it on legal and ethical grounds. A new speculative methodology that I describe as the collaborative collective bargaining process (CCB) will then be explained and similarly critiqued. I will argue that replacing the present model with the CCB model will result in better long-term results for all parties concerned, those at the table and others whose lives are influenced by the outcome of bargaining.

Section II will examine the ACB model and describe strategies and tactics employed by the parties emblematic to ACB. Section III will

From Frederick R. Post, "Collaborative Collective Bargaining: Toward an Ethically Defensible Approach to Labor Negotiations," *Journal of Business Ethics,* Vol. 9, 1990. Reprinted by permission of Kluwer Academic Publishers.

contain a critique of ACB as a process on both legal and ethical grounds. In Section IV, I will propose a model for CCB that on both legal and ethical grounds can better accomplish both the tasks and needs of all parties influenced by both the process and the outcome of bargaining. In Section V, I will defend CCB on both legal and ethical grounds, respond to the anticipated arguments against it, and demonstrate that not only is it ethically defensible, but it may be the only viable alternative available for consensually harmonizing conflicting needs within the work places of today.

II. THE CURRENT ADVERSARIAL COLLECTIVE BARGAINING PROCESS (ACB)

ACB is comparable, in many respects, to the adversarial process used in litigation. There, two parties with a dispute as to the "true" facts and how the law would apply to whatever they are found to be, present their respective versions of the facts to a judge or a jury. This is accomplished by presenting witness testimony and exhibit evidence. Direct and cross examination of witnesses constitutes the method of identifying and clarifying perceptions of events. Technical, largely exclusionary, evidentiary rules, testing relevance, materiality and competency, are applied to the evidence to determine its admissability for review by the fact finder. This adversarial process is designed to uncover the "true" facts. Ultimately, the goal is to achieve justice.

A similar search for the "true" value of the employees' services and the quality of their working conditions is attempted during ACB but without the judge or jury as fact finder. The "safeguard" of the impartial fact finder used to search for the truth in litigation is foreclosed because there is no comparable safeguard in ACB. The efforts of the parties are directed solely toward concluding an agreement most favorable to their self interests based exclusively on their relative bargaining power. Not only is there no impartial decision maker like the judge or jury, but there are also no meaningful evidentiary rules determining the propriety of witness testimony or of offered documentation. So structured, ACB does not uncover any truths—

either the value of employee services or the quality of their working conditions. Finally, the expressed goal of ACB, as articulated in the Labor Act, is not justice or labor and management just but labor peace. So, the announced goal of the process is not the same as the goal in litigation. Furthermore, the Labor Act gives no indication of what labor peace is. With no direction as to what represents achieving this announced goal, how can the participants be expected to find it? I will elaborate on these flaws of ACB and show how CCB corrects them.

Since the much discussed 1968 article "Is Business Bluffing Ethical?" by Albert Carr,[5] which analogizes the game of poker with many types of business negotiations, including labor negotiations, several authors have agreed that Carr's poker game model is an accurate model for describing conventional collective bargaining.[6] I, however, find this analogy inadequate. ACB is more than the poker game analogy suggests. Though bluffing and deception do represent a portion of the behaviors, I will demonstrate that additional morally unsuitable behaviors are commonplace, thus making the picture represented by the poker game incomplete. If anything, it is too kind.

In their article, "Bluffing in Labor Negotiations: Legal and Ethical Issues," Carson et al.,[7] give a definition of lying as "... a deliberate false statement which is either intended to deceive others or foreseen to be likely to deceive others."[8] This definition of lying is encompassed within the broader concept of deception which is defined as "intentionally causing another person to have false beliefs"[9] although the authors point out that "only deception which involves making false statements can be considered lying."[10] With these contextually useful definitions of both deception and lying, which I agree are accurate descriptions of some of the actions of the parties, a definition of the process of ACB as seen by each party is necessary.

The goal of management within the framework of ACB is to negotiate terms and conditions of employment that will

a. restore or improve control over the employees,

b. reduce the labor costs of the employees, and

c. increase the productivity of the employees so that there will be an increase in profitability.

The employer seeks to achieve this goal through the skillful exercise of either actual or perceived power over the union. Management must demonstrate that it has the will and ability to wage a successful battle against the union during a strike to achieve an acceptable settlement. If the union recognizes the employer's will and ability to win such an economic battle, the employer will usually achieve its objectives without a strike.

Conversely, the goal of the union subjected to ACB is to obtain contract language by proposals made at the table that will

a. wrest away employer control over its members,
b. obtain wage and fringe benefit increases for its members and
c. protect its members from zealous management efforts to increase productivity by demanding rigid job classifications, increases in paid non-work time, and other methods.

I use the word "subjected" because the employer is normally the pro-active party and sets the tone for the negotiations. This will also be true for CCB, as I describe it in Section IV.

With the parties having such clearly contradictory goals, the structure of ACB is a combat model. It makes the battle lines clear, and it grants victory to the more convincing display of power, but it leaves casualties. Indeed, it cannot operate except upon the casualties of the opposing party, and those casualties are the basis for ever-renewed combat.

The legal framework within which the parties do battle is controlled by three deceptively simple sections of the Labor Act. Section 8(a)(5) and Section 8(b)(3) describe the respective duties of the employer and the union to meet and negotiate an agreement that will govern their relationship for the next three years. Failure to reach agreement can trigger the filing of unfair labor practice charges by either party against the other. The loose definition of collective bargaining is contained in Section 8(d) which specifies the type of conduct necessary:

[Collective bargaining entails] the performance of the mutual obligation of the employer and the representatives of the employees to meet at reasonable times and confer in good faith with respect to wages, hours, and other terms and conditions of employment, or the negotiation of an agreement . . . incorporating any agreement reached if requested by either party. . .

The Labor Board and reviewing federal courts have repeatedly held that the question of whether either party has met its statutory duty will be determined by the facts of each individual case. These three sections alone establish the parameters of the legality of ACB. There are no guiding regulations such as those employed by other federal regulatory agencies, for example OSHA, EPA, or SEC. Accordingly, whether or not conduct alleged to be illegal is found to be a violation of the law is a legal conclusion drawn by the Labor Board after analyzing the facts of the particular case. The decision will seldom be based upon one particular aspect of negotiations, but will be based upon "the totality of circumstances."[11]

After compliance with the strike notice provisions required by the Labor Act,[12] the process of ACB typically begins with the union submitting a written proposal to the employer containing requests for changes in the existing labor agreement. The employer follows with a similarly structured written proposal which reacts to some of the subjects raised by the union and requests other changes in the labor agreement. The negotiation process continues with several additional sessions during which the parties orally present proposals and counter-proposals covering the subject areas raised in their respective initial written proposals.

Both parties must participate in the process to comply with Section 8(d) of the Labor Act. Furthermore, each party must compromise some of its initial positions if it is to convince the Labor Board that it has engaged in good faith collective bargaining. When agreement is reached on subjects that have not been withdrawn, the parties must agree to execute a written contract incorporating any agreement reached if either party requests such a signed document. Written agreements are standard procedure.

Within this minimal statutory framework involving the interplay of only three sections of the Labor Act, the fabric of the law of collective bargaining has developed. Changes in how the Labor Board interprets the law are the byproduct of unfair labor practice charges filed alleging that conduct by a party violates the "intent" of the legislature (55 years earlier in 1935) as represented by the statutory language. With the Labor Board makeup determined politically, "intent" does shift back and forth—to the advantage or detriment of the parties. In spite of this further instability in the interpretation of the Labor Act, certain bargaining tactics do represent *per se* violations of the duty to bargain.[13] These acts are so obvious that avoiding them still leaves a great amount of latitude for manipulation and exploitation of the other party. Legally permissible deceptive behaviors include: padding proposals, proposing and then withdrawing unreasonable demands to pressure concessions, negotiating noneconomic proposals (language) extensively before ever addressing economic proposals to frustrate and delay, inundating the other party with lengthy confusing written proposals, extending bargaining sessions long into the evening, establishing negotiation locations which involve inconvenience, and reserving secret separate rooms for long caucuses to wear out the other party. These and other tactics are geared to make the negotiating process a thoroughly unpleasant and unrewarding experience for the recipient party.

Although such tactics are legal, there is some point at which the law can be violated if, based upon the totality of circumstances, the Labor Board determines that combinations of these types of conduct make out a violation. However, because of the minimal sanctions for a violation, there is little incentive for an employer to be concerned about where that point is. And, there is even less incentive for the union to be concerned because, practically speaking, there is no meaningful sanction for union violations. And, because both parties are very aware of this, few unfair labor practice charges are ever filed. As to the ineffectiveness of the law,

[u]nion officials have contended that the lack of significant remedies makes correction of good faith bargaining violations a farce. Since [The Labor Board] decisions can be appealed to the courts, it might take three or more years for a final determination.[14]

Considering the nature of the practices used in ACB, it would seem that bad faith bargaining charges would be frequently filed, but statistics show just the opposite. For example, in 1984, there were more than 190,000 separate labor contracts in the U.S.[15] Because of the customary three year duration, approximately one third or, 63,000, are re-negotiated each year. The Labor Board's own statistics in 1983 reveal that 42 percent (12,211 of 28,995) of the charges of employer violations involved employer refusals to bargain in good faith.[16] Therefore, out of approximately 63,000 negotiations, there were 12,211 charges of employer violations or about 19 percent of employers were alleged to have violated Section 8(a)(5) of the Labor Act. 5.6 percent (697) of 11,526 charges of union violations involved union refusals to bargain in good faith.[17] So, in these same number of negotiations, only 0.0009 percent of unions were alleged to have violated Section 8(b)(3) of the Labor Act. Only 19 percent of the time did unions file charges, and employers filed charges against unions less than 1 percent of the time. With little threat of charges being filed and the knowledge that there are no real sanctions anyway, the urge to do whatever is necessary to win is ever present. With the law so toothless, it has only nuisance value.[18]

III. LEGAL AND ETHICAL PROBLEMS WITH ACB

Many of the following criticisms of ACB have been presented before, specifically by Norman Bowie in his 1985 article "Should Collective Bargaining and Labor Relations Be Less Adversarial?"[19] However, I assert that there are additional criticisms that deserve attention and I will begin with them.

While the general nature of the adversarial system imposed by the Labor Act has been much discussed,[20] it is curious that no criticism has been made about the inability of the current system to accomplish what it has been asked to do. In an adversary setting, bargaining success is determined by combat. The party that best employs its power through skillful, and often deceptive, tactics wins. While the search for truth in a courtroom in the presence of a judge or jury may make sense, it is not logical to suggest that such combat has any way of accurately determining either the *value* of employees' services or the *quality* of their working conditions. In fact, it does not. These goals are not the outcome of simply who has (or who pays for) the best advocate. How can such a combat model determine these valued goals? It simply cannot.

Furthermore, as has been noted above, ACB is a largely unenforceable system. Remedies for employer misconduct at the bargaining table are minimal; remedies for union misconduct at the table are meaningless. Both parties know that bargaining violations will usually go unpunished because neither party ordinarily bothers to file charges. From the parties' perspective, filing charges only further complicates bargaining by introducing government investigators and creating additional disputed issues. The statistics suggest that only the party who is in a desperate condition and believe there has been egregious misconduct will make the effort. Therefore, each party is normally tempted to ignore the law in the effort to achieve its goals. As a result, both unethical and illegal behavior is rewarded.

Another seldom acknowledged yet typically experienced problem with ACB is an existing, often externally caused, bargaining power imbalance between the parties resulting in unfair combat *ab initio*. Often there are many variables beyond the control of one party which prevent it from entering bargaining on a "level playing field." Such variables often so imbalance power that one party begins with a decided advantage and easily exploits the other. Such types of imbalances often persist over time because of the particular relationship resulting in one party being gored continually.

Examples of employer problems placing it at a disadvantage include: a highly leveraged debt condition, a poor cash flow generating capability, inadequate inventory build-up capability, highly skilled irreplaceable employees, a high

percentage of employed employee spouses, substantial prior business commitments, short seasonal demand for products, other dependent facilities, or a highly competitive market for the product line.

Similar problems a union may face placing it at a disadvantage include: a small strike fund, a low percentage of employed employee spouses, a high unemployment rate in the geographical area, low skill levels among the employees, a winter month contract expiration date, or alternate employer production facilities.

If any number of these illustrative variables disadvantages one party, the negotiations start out imbalanced and the other party will easily exploit the situation under the ACB model. The predictable outcome is a negative ending to ACB. There is a winner and a loser or both parties believe they are losers. How can such a system have any moral value for the long-term relationship between the parties when precisely the wrong relationship is fostered and perpetuated?

In addition to my criticisms of ACB, there are other, equally significant criticisms outlined by Bowie,[21] which I will now review briefly to place them within the context of the overall destructive picture of ACB.

The subjects emphasized during the negotiations result in a distortion in favor of the extrinsic job conditions:[22] wages, fringes, seniority provisions, and grievance procedures. This occurs at the expense of possibly more important intrinsic job conditions[23] such as: job responsibility, recognition for work, advancement potential, personal growth, and job content. Often, the payback for emphasis upon extrinsic variables is that no attention is given to the intrinsic variables. This can result in a workplace of well paid but miserable employees who hate the job, and of subtle employer retribution through neglect of intrinsic conditions. In the short term, ACB is a zero sum game, and an embittered loser will seek to avenge those losses somehow.

Such a system frustrates the fundamental principle of commitment to quality that is deemed necessary for company success. The result is economic inefficiencies for the employer since the hostility that remains after the bargaining process is completed spills over into the workplace. Employees will seek recompense if they feel they lost. With such attitudes, how can employees be expected to make the effort to meet the quality standards necessary to compete with foreign competition? Too often they do not, and with predictable results. In fact, much of the recent literature on corporate management[24] has emphasized the necessity of working together. An internally divided employer cannot produce as a team.

Additionally, ACB frequently ignores the remaining stakeholders' interests due to its inherent myopia, and often even ignores stockholders' interests because the control of bargaining strategy is lodged in top management. This small group has much to gain by obtaining results directed to its specific short-run interests. Thus the management negotiating team is often compelled to advance positions that are irresponsible from a long-term perspective in order to satisfy short-term gains. For example, in the recent best seller *Iacocca: An Autobiography,* the author confesses:

Gradually, little by little, we gave in to virtually every union demand. We were making so much money that we didn't think twice. We were rarely willing to take a strike, and so we never stood on principle.

Our motivation was greed. The instinct was always to settle quickly, to go for the bottom line. In this regard, our critics were right—we were always thinking of the next quarter.

'What's another dollar an hour?' we reasoned. 'Let future generations worry about it. We won't be around then.'

But the future has arrived, and some of us are still around. Today we're all paying the price for our complacency.[25]

This shortsighted view by management almost destroyed the U.S. auto industry. Ironically, only when at the brink did these employers reconsider their approach to labor negotiations. However, these changes remain an anomaly now.

Ultimately, ACB undermines the importance to society of truth as a moral value. By promoting, and in effect, condoning deception, bluffing and lying as a function of the ACB process, it teaches the participants and other affected parties that truth and honesty as values are irrelevant in labor negotiations. While there is language in court decisions espousing the need for honesty, there are no sanctions for most forms of dishonesty in the bargaining process.[26]

ACB also assaults, because of the resentment, distrust and confusion it produces among employees, a basic human need for friendship among people. Employees simply do not know where their allegiances are. Do they work for the employer or the union? If they are pro-employer, that must make them anti-union; if they are pro-union, then they must be anti-employer. All of this creates an unsettling division of loyalty among employees and violates a basic human need for friendship and compatibility among both one's peer group and one's superiors in the work place.

Carson *et al.,*[27] argue that this state of affairs may be unavoidable "given the exigencies and harsh realities of economic bargaining in our society".[28] However, they continue, "competitive economic arrangements do not usually *cause* people to become dishonest or treacherous, etc."[29] Rather, they claim "that most of the 'undesirable moral effects' attributed to our economic institutions involve actualizing pre-existing disposition, rather than causing any fundamental changes in character."[30] I disagree. Even if some participants derived such tendencies from prior experiences, I contend that, in ACB labor negotiations, *the arrangements themselves* dictate that the parties act in morally unacceptable ways to survive. My proposed CCB model changes *the arrangements* and eliminates the necessity to become, as Carson *et al.,* state, "dishonest" or "treacherous" . . .

IV. The Proposed Collaborative Collective Bargaining Process (CCB)

The goal of parties who jointly elect to use CCB is to reach an agreement regarding the terms and conditions of employment for the employees represented by the union that *harmonizes* both the legitimate capitalist driven needs and wants of the employer as well as the needs and wants for economic justice of the employees.

The process is nonadversarial. There is no power manipulation between the parties involving efforts to win a battle and, through combat, defeat the other side. The CCB process contains five distinct stages. These are

a. the commitment stage,
b. the explanation stage,
c. the validation stage,
d. the prioritization stage, and
e. the negotiation stage.

Each stage builds upon every prior stage. While the process is now speculative, I submit that it represents a workable format because it is predicated upon an agreement made in advance to be candid and open; the use of the focusing influence of a mediator; and the value of a time format that, through structured intensity alone, greatly enhances the potential for reaching agreement.

The initial commitment process is critical because CCB cannot function without the voluntary consent between both parties to reject ACB and, instead, exercise candor, openness, and honesty in the negotiation process. Due to the political nature of every union, the leadership must firmly advocate CCB and sell the concept to the membership. Unless there is membership commitment, the union leadership will be chancing political suicide by advocating such an approach. For this reason, considerable effort must be expended by management to convince the union leadership that there are mutual benefits to be gained by the use of CCB.

A. The Commitment Stage

The commitment stage will begin by jointly convened meetings of management and union leadership one year before the expiration date of the labor agreement and again six months closer to the date. At these meetings, the new approach will be discussed in detail with emphasis on the benefits to both parties of collaborating on a new labor agreement. The many problems of ACB, reviewed in Section III of this paper, should be frankly discussed to emphasize the superiority of CCB because those problems are largely obviated through its use. The parties

should discuss performance targets for both management and the employees necessary for the proper growth of the company and ways in which gains beyond those targets may be shared. Documentation to support the basis for positions is available in our information intensive business world. A summarization of each of these meetings will be disseminated among the employees.

To ensure a legally binding commitment, a CCB agreement will be prepared and executed by the parties at their second meeting. This document will acknowledge that CCB will be the process used, prescribe a timetable for the five stages, contain a "collaboration compact," acknowledge the mediator selection mechanism to be used, indicate the scope of authority of the mediator, and designate sanctions for noncompliance. If the union will not (or can not) commit to the use of CCB, then the parties will resort to the conventional ACB as before.

The collaboration compact will consist of a jointly determined list of goals that the parties seek to accomplish during their labor negotiations. The preparation of this list is the initial phase of openness. These shared aspirations form the basis for the mediator's evaluation of the merit of positions expressed. Previously declared written goals will focus the mediator's efforts to push the parties toward an agreement.[31]

The mediator selection mechanism will be determined by the language already contained in the labor agreement that provides for arbitrator selection in the grievance procedure. This typically commences by providing for the parties to informally agree upon an arbitrator. Absent agreement, either the offices of the Federal Mediation and Conciliation Service (FMCS) or the American Arbitration Association (AAA) is contacted, with a request for a list of potential arbitrators from which the parties select an arbitrator. For use in the CCB process, either FMCS or AAA will also be capable of providing qualified persons from which the parties can select a mediator.

The mediator's authority will be designated in the CCB agreement. It will be limited to the authority to use mediating skills to aid the parties in achieving whatever common goals they have established in their collaboration compact. This will not include authority to decide between any two disputed positions, imposing one party's position upon the other party. The mediator will never assume the judicial function of an arbitrator. The CCB process is not a disguised form of the interest arbitration that is sometimes practiced in public sector labor negotiations.

B. The Explanation Stage

The next stage is the explanation stage which will consist of the first face-to-face bargaining meeting held one month before the contract expiration date. This will occur at what used to be the first negotiation meeting in ACB. The employer will present all non-economic and economic proposals with different package options within financially plausible ranges stated as possible objectives. The employer will explain noneconomic language proposals as well as anticipated supportable economic positions presented as ranges. The union will likewise explain its economic proposals as well as changes envisioned as necessary in noneconomic language.

The Validation Stage

Subsequent to this meeting, the validation stage will begin which will cover the time period between two to four weeks before the contract expiration date. The employer and union representatives will jointly prepare a questionnaire covering the ranges of all possible issues raised by each party. This questionnaire will be administered to the employees during company time. The content of the questionnaire will be determined by the specific proposals that were made by each party during the explanation stage. It will summarize all proposals presented in a forced-choice ranking format that will require the employees to evaluate proposals so that a collective consensus of prioritization will be evident. The exact content of the questionnaire will always be unique to the particular relationship. Generally, however, employer proposals can be expected to be geared toward expanding management rights to achieve increased flexibility and control over employee assignment choices. These goals are presumed to contribute to the ultimate objective of keeping wages and fringes as cost items in line in order to maintain profitability. Generally, union proposals will seek to structure mechanisms for either codetermination of or at least a voice in management decisions controlling its members as well as the typical proposals seeking improvements in wages and fringe benefits.

The greater the extent of harmony between the parties, the greater probability that the proposals of both parties will be directed toward decisions determined either jointly or made only after input from the union. The parties naturally come to the table with somewhat different agendas—the employer negotiating to maintain an acceptable level of profitability and the union negotiating to maintain an acceptable level of member acceptance. If both parties respect each other's goals and the role that the other party can have in better realizing those goals through harmonizing their aspirations, the CCB process can aid them in working together for the benefit of each of them.

Once the questionnaires have been filled out and turned in, the results will be tabulated by computer to obtain mean, median, and average scores for all responses where appropriate. These will then be posted for employee review to demonstrate an awareness of their need for involvement. Because employees have selected between different choice options available, the responses to employer and union proposals will provide important data for both parties. For example, responses to the employer proposals will enable the management negotiating team to better assess the level of dissatisfaction in the group toward certain language proposals or economic modification requests. Likewise, responses given to the union proposals will serve to better inform the union negotiating team as to the strength or weakness of its positions. And, by the posting process, the employee group will learn about its collective consensus on all of the issues placed on the table. Concurrently, each party will obtain any documentation requested during the prior explanation stage and obtain answers to questions raised during that stage.

D. The Prioritization Stage

The next meeting, held two weeks before the contract expiration date after the parties have obtained requested documentation and have enjoyed the benefit of separately assessing the results of the employee questionnaire, will mark the beginning of the prioritization stage. These proceedings will be conducted in the presence of the mediator they have selected. At this meeting, which is the second face-to-face meeting between the parties, they will again present their positions with the supporting documentation which has been obtained so that the mediator can not only understand what is being proposed but also understand the rationale for the proposals.

The mediator will then evaluate the merit of positions expressed based upon the respective presentations gauged with reference to the criteria appearing in the collaboration compact. The technique employed by the mediator will be the Socratic method of uncovering the bases for positions expressed, exposing their merit or lack thereof. For example: Why do you need that? Where else has that proposal been agreed to? Whose idea was that? What problem does that solve? How will implementation of that process increase productivity? How will the work group benefit by introducing that change? And similar inquiries seeking to expose the relative overall importance of each position to the party offering it. Through aggressive questioning by the mediator, and each party of the other, a frank and open discussion of the prioritized supportable needs and wants of each party will be possible. Further, supporting documentation will be scrutinized for its accuracy and relevance.

E. The Negotiation Stage

The final stage of CCB is the negotiation stage. This stage will begin between seven to ten days before the contract expiration date. Once the stage begins, strict time guidelines will govern each meeting in order to maximize work efforts and minimize any dilatory tactics or the customary posturing of traditional ACB. The meetings will be held during successive days. The negotiations will commence at 8:00 a.m. and

will include breakfast together to start the session in a pleasant setting. This meeting will last for two hours. At 10:00 a.m. there will be a two hour caucus during which each party will discuss separately the position alternatives proposed. The mediator will circulate between the parties' rooms and facilitate by asking questions and probing into the respective positions of each party. The parties will reconvene at 12:00 noon and meet again for two hours over lunch to discuss issues raised during the morning caucus. Precisely at 2:00 p.m., the parties will break for another two hour afternoon caucus. This process will continue with alternating two hour meetings and caucuses with the parties concluding their final meeting at 10:00 p.m. that evening, resulting in eight hours of face-to-face negotiation meetings and six hours of separate caucus meetings. The parties will resume the process the next morning and repeat the same schedule.

The mediator will continue the Socratic questioning about the basis for and necessity of each position proposed by a party. Further, to demonstrate the extent of progress, the mediator will prepare and maintain two lists, the "agreements agenda" and the "disagreements agenda." These two lists will serve as visual guidelines that structure the topics for discussion. The disagreements agenda represents unresolved proposals that remain to be negotiated to agreement. The agreements agenda contains all other proposals that have been already accepted as proposed, accepted as modified, or withdrawn. Posturing and procrastinating will be minimized when the agendas are kept in front of each party, especially during caucus meetings where, to prevent any private pontificating, the mediator can separately challenge each party's positions on all remaining unresolved proposals. And, by such challenges, the mediator can push the parties to compromise and consensus.

On the third day, the length of each type of meeting will be reduced by one hour, resulting in seven hours of face-to-face meetings and seven hours of separate caucus meetings. This should facilitate the progress of negotiations since the often necessary decisions about compromising or withdrawing positions are possible only during the privacy of the separate caucus.

This one hour alternating time period process will continue each successive day until the parties decide upon a new tentative labor agreement, subject to the ratification vote of the membership, or the expiration date is reached. Absent agreement at that time, the parties may either agree upon a new later expiration date and continue negotiating or exercise their respective economic weapons, such as a strike or a lockout, having failed to reach a satisfactory settlement.

The essence of CCB is to foster by commitment, structure, and format an environment which encourages open and frank discussion with the assistance of a skilled mediator to keep the parties' efforts properly directed much as a judge acts in a court of law. In this new environment, ranges of positions can be openly discussed and package options truly considered on their actual merits. Employee needs and wants, which have already been identified in the questionnaire, will be discussed between the parties and used as a form of prioritization. Employer positions, as supported by requested documentation, will be discussed to determine its priorities. As the negotiations progress, positions will be presented on a package basis. By structuring package proposals, the parties will be pressured to further prioritize options available and less important proposals will be exposed and compromised or withdrawn. The purpose of these intense continuing daily schedules is to lessen the incentive to engage in gamesmanship and tactical posturing, center energy on properly directed negotiations, and build the necessary team environment so the parties can collaborate together in good faith to complete the process before the expiration date. Mediator facilitation can enhance the parties' articulation of needs, wants, and frustrations with candor by drawing out reasons for positions advanced.

A model, illustrating the five-stage structure of the CCB process is given in *Figure 1*. As Figure 1 shows, the progressive movement through each stage narrows, specifies and prioritizes the respective positions. This will contribute to a harmonizing of the many initial conflicting needs and interests of the parties. The resulting labor contract will be truly indica-tive of both the employees' demonstrated wants and needs (as identified in the questionnaire and further presented and supported by the union) and the employer's supportable wants and needs (as presented by the employer and demonstrated through the validated documentation) so that both parties can leave bargaining with a feeling that each of them won because all positions proposed were debated, justified and considered in the process that led to the new labor agreement. The effect of full participation and consideration of one's views subjected to open debate cannot be overemphasized as a positive element of CCB.

V. CCB IS AN ETHICALLY DEFENSIBLE APPROACH TO LABOR NEGOTIATIONS

I will begin by addressing my choice of the word "collaborative" to describe the new model. This word was chosen as opposed to "cooperative" because it more accurately describes the nature of the CCB relationship, one that has evolved between former enemies to what now involves working together for a common shared goal. "Collaborate" is a broader term. It contains within it all of the operative elements of cooperate which, according to Webster's New Universal Unabridged Dictionary, Deluxe Second Edition, include: "to act or operate jointly with another or others, to the same end; to work or labor with mutual efforts to promote the same object . . . to practice economic cooperation," but goes further by accurately defining the *historical nature* of the specific relationship, namely, "cooperation with the enemy." For this reason, the descriptive label "collaborative" gives a more complete and contextual meaning to CCB.

What is it about CCB that is ethically justifiable? The process strips away the use of tactics such as bluffing, misrepresentation and lying. The parties cannot state their ranges on particular issues, address the justifications for their positions, and defend their positions in the presence of a skilled mediator and the other party, both of whom will ask probing questions, without openness and honesty. Also, being required to produce supporting documentation

Figure 1: Collaborative Collective Bargaining

Commitment Stage: 12 & 6 months before contract expiration date

Initial planning meeting convened
Follow-up planning meeting held
Collaboration compact goals determined
Mediator selection process completed
CCB Agreement drafted and executed
Summary of each meeting posted

Explanation Stage: 1 month before contract expiration date

First bargaining meeting held
Initial management proposal presented
Initial union proposal presented
Position basis questioning initiated
Support documentation inquiries raised
Timetable for remaining meetings determined

Validation Stage: 2 to 4 weeks before contract expiration date

Joint employee questionnaire prepared
Joint employee questionnaire administered
Questionnaire results calculated and posted
Requested support documentation assembled
Questionnaire results summaries analyzed
Position validation documentation obtained

Prioritization Stage: 2 weeks before contract expiration date

Second bargaining meeting held
Mediator CCB process facilitation initiated
Prioritized validated management proposal presented
Prioritized validated union proposal presented
Mediator position questioning commenced
Position validation documentation critiqued

Negotiation Stage: 1 week before contract expiration date

Continuous daily bargaining meetings commenced
CCB process daily timetable established
Mediator position questioning continued
Agreements and disagreements agendas drafted and updated
CCB process continued until settlement reached
Settlement agreement drafted and executed

NEW LABOR CONTRACT

for positions will require sober reflection about the basis for positions initially contemplated. The CCB process will preclude any effective use

of the most frequently criticized aspects of ACB. Due to the resulting free exchange of positions and ideas, the all too common hostility and distrust that permeates ACB will be eliminated or at least minimized. Because of employee awareness through the questionnaire and knowledge that such a process is being used on their behalf, there should be improved attitudes among employees since their input makes them a part of the CCB process. Consequently, their commitment to employer goals should improve. Better product quality can be anticipated as employees should no longer perceive themselves as separate and isolated from both the bargaining process and the employer.

Furthermore, because most bargaining table dishonesty is not punishable under the present legal framework, a voluntary policy of honesty through the whole CCB process sends a powerful message to the employees. This message should result in reciprocation on their part due to the example that has been set by the employer. Dissemination of the policy, as one important element of the overall corporate mission, will enhance the image of the employer as having moral values that represent the best in corporate citizenship.

Use of the CCB process also underscores the value of the teamwork so needed in our competitive world marketplace. Use of the word "collaborate" defines the working together process. As the current literature emphasizes, the same collaboration in all other aspects of corporate endeavors is necessary to compete effectively and CCB can set the tone for both management style and overall corporate policy.

In addition, CCB satisfies a basic human need for friendship in the workplace. Through the involvement of the employees, a desirable joint allegiance to employer and union *raison d'etre* [reason for being] is now understandable which can eliminate the current unsettling feelings of divided loyalties among employees.

Through the openness of CCB, the inclination to ignore stakeholders' interests is sharply reduced also. Justifications for positions taken will be debated in the presence of a mediator who will probe both parties as to the basis for their wants and needs. This will prevent the management group from prioritizing positions geared to their employment self-interest at the expense of the longer term interests of both stockholders, stakeholders, and the employees as one component of the stakeholder group.

Another value of the process is that intrinsic job variables, traditionally left unaddressed, may become a part of the negotiations. This will be to the distinct advantage of the affected employees. Elements of the job such as employee responsibility, opportunity for personal growth, recognition for good performance, and job content need more bargaining table discourse. This does not occur in ACB. The opportunity to consider these needs exists to a much greater degree under CCB.

As to the question of the value to be placed upon employees' services, there can be more meaningful comparisons made with wage rates of competitors, and a more thoughtful evaluation of cost of living concerns. The result will be that the union can more ably defend the need for wage and benefit increases. In the CCB process, the employer will have to make a better effort to understand whether there is merit to position advanced by the union. While it is difficult to determine the value of any group of employees' services, an open and frank discussion can certainly do more to promote understanding than having such matters determined by power and combat skills under ACB. Outcomes reached in that manner have little, if any, relation to the value of employees' services, as I have related earlier.

Finally, by the use of CCB, resort to the Labor Board for assistance against a wrongdoer's actions will normally be unnecessary. The parties will self-police their behaviors by compliance with the voluntarily agreed upon CCB process, monitored further by an impartial mediator selected by the parties to facilitate their negotiations.

VI. CONCLUSION

The legal system has fostered an adversarial collective bargaining process as an attempt to balance the power relationship between management and employees. This power relationship was out of balance due to the substantial changes in the economy brought about by the industrial revolution and the imbalance led to an exploitation of employees. ACB was an outgrowth of the adversarial search for the truth used in litigation. While the adversarial system did initially advance the economic well-being of employees, it also undermined their intrinsic worth by placing them continually at odds with their employer. It further sanctioned bluffing, deception, intimidation, coercion and other immoral conduct exercised as part of the power manipulation process needed to succeed.

The employer is also exploited because the problems caused by ACB impact directly on its competitiveness and profitability. ACB normally imposes losses on both sides. The workplace becomes a divided camp because of this internal combat. The outcome is economic inefficiency and a destruction of the intrinsic value of the employees.

An article[32] co-authored by several faculty in different disciplines of the Massachusetts Institute of Technology, from among a larger group who had formed the M.I.T. Commission on Industrial Productivity, has concluded that there are "five interconnected imperatives" that the U.S. must implement to achieve competitive industrial performance in the global marketplace of today. Two of these five imperatives reflect what I propose in the CCB process. One imperative is "to develop a new 'economic citizenship' in the marketplace."[33] The authors stress the need for increased employee involvement and responsibility and they emphasize that employees can no longer be treated as expendable parts of the production process but should be treated as long term assets to be nurtured and developed. Employees should become full participants in the destiny of the company.[34] Another imperative is to "strive to combine cooperation and individualism."[35] The authors note that the individualistic spirit that characterizes our culture is often counterproductive in the work places of today. It is largely absent in the most productive U.S. companies where, in its place," group solidarity, a feeling of community and a recognition of interdependence have led to important economic advantages.[36] These imperatives, the product of an extensive two year study involving 200 companies, 150 plant sites, and nearly 550 interviews in the U.S., Europe and Japan,[37] represent an indictment of the ACB process and graphically illustrate the need for several changes, including what is proposed in the CCB process.

The substitution of CCB can enable the parties to reorient their perspectives on labor negotiations. It should be clear by now that the value of employee services is not a predictable outcome of the combat model of ACB. By following the CCB model, the parties can avoid the negative and self-defeating elements of ACB and, in the process, work together to make the company an internally solidified entity, working toward mutually beneficial common goals, through the use of an ethically defensible approach to labor negotiations.

Notes

1. The National Labor Relations (Wagner) Act 49 Stat. 449 (1935), as amended, 29 U.S.C. Sections 141–97 (1958), as amended, 29 U.S.C. Sections 153–87 (Supp. I, 1959).
2. The Labor Management Relations (Taft-Hartley) Act, 61 Stat. 136 (1947), 29 U.S.C. Sections 141–97 (1958) and The Labor-Management Reporting and Disclosure (Landrum- Griffin) Act 73 Stat. 519 (1959), 29 U.S.C. Sections 153–87 (Supp. I, 1959).
3. Bowie, "Should Collective Bargaining and Labor Relations Be Less Adversarial?" *Journal of Business Ethics,* Vol. 4, 1985, p. 283; Koehn, "Commentary Upon Should Collective Bargaining and Labor Relations Be Less Adversarial," *Journal of Business Ethics,* Vol. 4, 1985, p. 293; Carson, Wokutch & Murrmann, "Bluffing in Labor Negotiations: Legal and Ethical Issues," *Journal of Business Ethics,* Vol. 1, 1982, p. 13.
4. Section 8(a)2 makes cooperation between most informal or formal employee groups and the employer an unfair labor practice under certain circumstances. If an employer is "cooperating" through certain types of assistance or preferential treatment, the Labor Board may find illegal domination since the definition of a "labor organization" in Section 2(5) is so general that most such groups would qualify.
5. Carr, "Is Business Bluffing Ethical?" *Harvard Business Review,* Jan.–Feb. 1968, at 143.
6. Carson *et al.,* supra, n.3.
7. Ibid.
8. Ibid. at 17.
9. Ibid. at 18.
10. Ibid.
11. Other than in instances where there has been a failure of one party to meet even the minimum requirements of good faith bargaining, or a specific *per se* violation, (see Note 13, *infra*) the Labor Board will investigate all conduct or the "totality of conduct" of a party which is the standard of conduct that determines whether a violation has occurred based upon a cumulation of actions. The original doctrine developed from the U.S. Supreme Court case of *NLRB v. Virginia Elec. & Power Co.,* 314 U S 469 (1941). Recent cases where the Labor Board has found violations under this standard include *Hyatt Regency New Orleans,* 281 NLRB No. 42 (1986) and *Walter A. Zlogar, Inc.,* 278 NLRB No. 149 (1986). To demonstrate the severity of bargaining misconduct required to violate this standard, a review of the recent case of *Roman Iron Works, Inc.,* 275 NLRB 449 (1985) is instructive. During bargaining management engaged in such hard bargaining tactics as reducing its wage offer from the initial proposal, denied a union request for employee addresses, demanded a subcontracting provision, and demanded significant economic concessions. In spite of these several tactics, because management also held several meetings with the union, made complete contract proposals, and offered its own concessions, the Labor Board found no violation of Section 8(a)5 of the Labor Act.
12. Section 8(d) of the Act was added as one of the Taft-Hartley Amendments, The Labor Management Relations (Taft-Hartley) Act, 61 Stat. 36 (1947), 29 U.S.C. Section 158(d) (1958).
13. Illustrative examples of *per se* violations of the Labor Act from the cases in which they occurred include: the refusal to bargain at all with the other party, which is considered tantamount to a refusal to even recognize the union, *NLRB v. Insurance Agents International Union,* 361 U.S. 477, (1960); to agree to bargain, but to insist that the bargaining be on subjects outside the scope of mandatory subjects, *NLRB v. Katz,* 369 U.S. 736 (1962); to unilaterally change some aspect of wages, hours, and the conditions of employment during the course of negotiations, without reaching a valid impasse and bypass the union, *Gas Machine Co.,* 221 NLRB No. 129, (1975); insistence on the presence of a court reporter to record all of the negotiating sessions, as a precondition to contract negotiations, *Barlett-Collins Co. v. NLRB,* 237 NLRB No. 106, 1978); insistence upon union bargaining committees' submission of the employer's last offer to the full union membership for a ratification vote as a condition precedent to employer reaching an agreement, *American Seating,* 176 NLRB 850, (1969); employer imposition of an absolute time limit on negotiations, for example, two hours per week, *A.J. Belo Corp. v. NLRB* 411 F.2d 959 (5th Cir. 1969) cert. den. 396 US 1007; insistence upon an illegal provision, *NLRB v. Reed and Prince Mfg. Co.,* F.2d 874 (1st Cir. 1941) cert.den. 313 US 595; refusal to incorporate matters previously agreed to by a party with no valid justification, *Amalgamated Clothing Workers v. NLRB* 324 F.2d 228 (2d Cir., 1963); intentional misrepresentations at the bargaining table which cause the other party to alter its position to its disadvantage, *Architectural Fiberglass,* 165 NLRB 238, (1967); and refusal to execute a written agreement between the parties prepared at the conclusion of negotiations, *Standard Oil Co. v. NLRB* 322 F.2d 40 (6th Cir. 1963).

14. W. Holley and K. Jennings, *The Labor Relations Process* 230 (3rd ed. 1988).

15. T. Kochan and T. Barocct, *Human Resource Management and Industrial Relations* 20 (1985).

16. National Labor Relations Board, *Forty-Eighth Annual Report,* Government Printing Office: Washington, D.C. (1986), p. 167.

17. Ibid.

18. "Nuisance value" in legal jargon represents the situation where potential liability is so remote for a defendant that the only real financial exposure is the cost of the defense. Therefore, if the plaintiff will accept an amount of money to settle the case that is less than the projected defense cost, the plaintiff should be paid that nuisance value to end the litigation. These types of settlement offers normally insult plaintiffs.

19. Bowie, *supra* n. 3, at 283.

20. See the following books, as illustrative of the literature describing the traditional adversarial model: B. Gray, *Collaborating,* (1989); C. Heckscher, *The New Unionism,* (1988); W. Ury, J. Brett and S. Goldberg, *Getting Disputes Resolved,* (1988); L. Susskind and J. Cruikshank, *Breaking The Impasse,* (1987); N. Chamberlain and J. Kuhn, *Collective Bargaining,* (3rd ed. 1986); C. Craypo, *The Economics of Collective Bargaining,* (1986); T. Kochan, H. Katz and R. McKersie, *The Transformation of American Industrial Relations,* (1986); J. Atleson, *Values and Assumption in American Labor Law,* (1983); H. Raiffa, *The Art and Science of Negotiation,* (1982); S. Bacharach and E. Lawler, *Bargaining,* (1981); R. Fisher and W. Ury, *Getting to Yes: Negotiating Agreement Without Giving in* (1981); R. Walton and R. McKersie, *A Behavioral Theory of Labor Negotiations,* (1965); T. Schelling, *The Strategy of Conflict,* (1960). Illustrative of the several articles appearing in journals discussing ACB and adversarial negotiations in general within the context of American law are: Hyman, "Trial Advocacy as an Impediment to Wise Negotiation," *Negotiation Journal,* Vol. 5, 1989, p. 237; Hyman, "Trial Advocacy and Methods of Negotiation: Can Good Trial Advocates be Wise Negotiators?" *UCLA Law Review,* Vol. 34, 1987, p. 863; Lax & Sebenius, "Three Ethical Issues in Negotiation," *Negotiation Journal,* Vol. 2, 1986, p. 363; Fisher, "Beyond Yes," *Negotiation Journal,* Vol. 1, 1985, p. 67; McCarthy, "The Role of Power and Principle in Getting to Yes," *Negotiation Journal,* Vol. 1, 1985, p. 59; Schuster, "Models of Cooperation and Change in Union Settings," *Industrial Relations,* Vol. 24, 1985, p. 382; Menkel-Meadow, "Toward Another View of Legal Negotiation: The Structure of Problem Solving," *UCLA Law Review,* Vol. 31, 1984, p. 754; Laventhal, "A General Theory of Negotiation: Process, Strategy and Behavior," *U. Kansas Law Review,* Vol. 69, 1982, p. 107; Scobel, "Business and Labor—From Adversaries to Allies," *Harvard Business Review,* Nov.–Dec., 1982, p. 129; White, "Machiavelli and the Bar: Ethical Limitations on Lying in Negotiations," *A.B.F. Res. J.,* 1980, p. 926.

21. Bowie, *supra* n. 3, at 283.

22. A. Szilagyi and M. Wallace, *Organizational Behavior and Performance,* 110 (2nd ed., 1980).

23. Ibid.

24. Illustrative of the numerous examples of contemporary management literature which emphasize participatory management, employee involvement, and empowerment in the workplace include: R. Waterman, Jr., *The Renewal Factor,* 71 (1987); T. Peters, *Thriving on Chaos,* 281 (1987); R. Kanter, *The Changemasters,* 180 (1983); W. Ouchi, *Theory Z,* 97 (1982); T. Peters and R. Waterman, Jr., *In Search of Excellence,* 235 (1982).

25. L. Iacocca, *Iacocca: An Autobiography,* 304 (1984).

26. A good example of this phenomenon is the case of *NLRB v. Truitt Manufacturing Co.,* 351 U.S. 149, 38 Lrrm 2024 (1956) where the Supreme Court stated that implicit in the meaning of "good faith bargaining" is honesty. The decision does not stand for that proposition, however, but for the principle of law that if an employer "pleads poverty" by basing its rejection of a union's economic proposals upon an inability to pay, the employer must allow the union's auditors access to the corporate financial records to substantiate the position. For this reason, an employer can say "NO" to union economic proposals, but better not claim inability to pay as the reason unless it is prepared to open its books.

27. Carson, *et al.,* supra, n.3.

28. Ibid at 20.

29. Ibid at 21.

30. Ibid.

31. An analysis of the process by which the parties structure common goals that can direct them toward consensus through the drafting of the collaboration compact is beyond the scope of this article. This process will be analyzed, referencing approaches based upon utilitarian, contractarian and deontological ethical theories, in another article entitled *Toward Consensual Labor Negotiations: Formulation of the Collaboration Compact* (forthcoming).

32. Berger, Dertouzos, Lester, Solow & Thurow, *Toward a New Industrial America,* 260 SCI. AM. 39 (1989).

33. Ibid.

34. Ibid.

35. Ibid.

36. Ibid.

37. Ibid at 40.

QUESTIONS

1. Do you agree with Lippke's claim that employees have no obligation to air moral concerns internally before expressing them publicly?

2. How would you define "idiosyncratic" speech and do you agree with Lippke that it ought to be protected?

3. Hiley mentions that if the doctrine of employment-at-will is eroded many employers may become reluctant to terminate an employee, even when there is just cause because of the fear of litigation. Is such a fear well-grounded? If it is, how would you suggest remedying the situation?
4. If we take seriously the claim that employers should not be able to terminate arbitrarily and without notice, must we also revise our views about whether an employee has the right to resign arbitrarily and without notice? Why or why not?
5. Is the duty to bargain in good faith consistent with the "bluffing" that takes place during negotiations? Explain. Do you agree with Post that present negotiating practices typically foster ill-will? How would you defend your view?
6. Do you think that collaborative collective bargaining could be made to work? Why or why not?

CASE 3:1 THE TERMINATED EMPLOYEE[1]

Ms. Laverty and Mr. Johnson lived together in a common-law relationship.

They were both friends of Mr. Cooper who ran a small metal plating business. In 1980 Cooper hired Leverty as his only salesperson. She had many key responsibilities; including costing, pricing and keeping customer accounts. By all reports, she was an effective employee and at least partially responsible for the prospering of Cooper's company.

A year or so after hiring Laverty, Cooper permitted Johnson the use of part of his premises to start a chemical-mixing business complementary to Cooper's metal plating. In 1984 Johnson moved his business to other premises.

In 1985 Cooper accidentally discovered that Johnson's business was no longer complementary, but had become a competitor. Although Cooper had no evidence that Johnson either through Laverty or by other means, had taken any business from him, Cooper dismissed Laverty without notice. Laverty sued Cooper for wrongful dismissal.

1. Based on *Laverty v. Cooper Plating Inc.*, 17 *Canadian Cases in Employment Law*, 44 (1987)

During the course of the proceedings it became clear that although there was no evidence that Laverty in any way directed existing or potential customers away from Cooper, she was aware that Johnson's new venture was in competition with Cooper.

QUESTIONS

1. Would you agree that Laverty's knowledge of Cooper's business, together with her responsibility as sales manager, were incompatible with her continuing relationship with Johnson and that her dismissal without notice was therefore justified?
2. Would it have been more fair for Cooper to have dismissed Laverty with notice?
3. Did Johnson act ethically?
4. Did Laverty have any obligation to inform Cooper of the new status of Johnson's business? If she had so informed him, should Cooper have then demanded her notice?

CASE 3:2 SUCCESSIVE EMPLOYERS AND THE DUTY TO BARGAIN[2]

In 1982 Sterlingwale Corporation, which had operated a textile dyeing and finishing plant in Fall River, Massachusetts for over thirty years, went out of business due to a combination of poor economic conditions and increased foreign competition. During the period of Sterlingwale's decline in the late 70s and early 80s, the Union representing employees met with company officials regarding layoffs and Sterlingwale's failure to pay premiums on

2. Based on *Fall River Dyeing & Finishing Corp. v. N.L.R.B.*, 107 *Supreme Court Reporter* 2225 (1987)

group-health insurance. The Union expressed its interests in keeping the company operating and in meeting with prospective buyers. In 1980 they also agreed to extend the expiration date of the Collective Agreement, due to expire April 1, 1981, for one year without any wage increase and to improve labor productivity.

Shortly after the plant's closing, Herbert Chase, former vice-president in charge of sales for Sterlingwale, and Arthur Friedman, president of one of Sterlingwale's major customers, formed the Fall River Dyeing and Finishing Corporation, and acquired the plant and its assets. Their plan was to use Sterlingwale's former assets and workforce to engage in the commission-dyeing business.

In September 1982 Fall River Dyeing and Finishing began operating the plant and hiring employees. Their initial goal was to hire one full shift of workers. They achieved this goal by mid-January 1983, at which time the large majority of their workers were former Sterlingwale employees. By mid-April 1983, they were hiring two shifts of workers and, for the first time, former Sterlingwale employees did not constitute the majority of their employees, though this was true only by the slimmest of margins. Working conditions for employees continued to be the same as under Sterlingwale and over half of the new company's business came from former Sterlingwale customers.

In October 1982 the Union requested that Fall River recognize it as the bargaining agent for employees and begin collective bargaining. Fall River refused, stating that the request had no legal basis. The Union subsequently filed an unfair labor practice charge with the National Labor Relations Board.

QUESTIONS

1. Do you agree with the Union's demand that Fall River should recognize it as the employee's bargaining agent? Why or why not.
2. Whether or not the original union should be recognized as the employees' bargaining agent depends on its continuity, and this in turn depends on whether the majority of employees were ex- Sterlingwale workers. Fall River insisted that the question of whether the majority of workers were ex-Sterlingwale workers should not be asked prior to its hiring a "full complement of workers," i.e. mid-April, at which time new employees outnumbered ex-Sterlingwale employees. The union insisted that the question should be asked as soon as the employer hired a "substantial and representative" complement of employees, i.e. mid-January, at which time ex-Sterlingwale employees outnumbered new employees. With whom do you agree and why?

FOR FURTHER READING

1. Richard D. Arvey and Gary L. Renz, "Fairness in the Selection of Employees," *Journal of Business Ethics,* Vol. 11, 1992, pp. 331–340.

2. Gertrude Ezorsky, ed., *Moral Rights in the Workplace* (Albany: State University of New York Press, 1987).

3. Mary Gibson, *Worker's Rights,* (Totowa, N.J.:Rowman & Allanheld, 1983).

4. Patricia Werhane, "Individual Rights in Business" in *Just Business,* Tom Regan ed. (New York: Random House, 1984).

Chapter Four

PRIVACY IN THE WORKPLACE

Introduction

Issues of privacy in the workplace have become increasingly important and controversial. New techniques of acquiring and processing information have focused attention on questions concerning what information may be gathered by an employer, the means by which it may be collected, and the uses that it may be put to. Increasingly sophisticated systems of data gathering and management have intensified and complicated concerns over their possible abuse.

Richard Lippke's "Work, Privacy, and Autonomy" sets the stage for our discussion of the more specific issues associated with drug-testing, and genetic and psychological screening. Lippke argues that the value of privacy derives from its relation to autonomy, i.e., the capacity to make genuine choices about one's goals and activities. Inasmuch as the inability to control information about oneself makes one more vulnerable to manipulation by others, lack of privacy tends to destroy autonomy.

It is often suggested that employers may justifiably gather information that is job relevant. As Lippke points out, however, the notion of "job relevance" raises more questions than it answers. Those who advocate it as a criterion do not want to include information concerning sexual orientation, political or religious beliefs, yet these may all conceivably affect how an employee interacts with other employees and hence job performance. Lippke suggests that the issue is not what information is relevant to the job, but how best to preserve the autonomy of the employee and yet meet the legitimate interests of the employer.

The problem, of course, is that an individual's autonomy is always qualified by the autonomy of other individuals. The legitimate interests of the employee are invariably conditioned by the legitimate interests of the employer and vice versa. Perhaps all that can be said in the abstract is that we should strive to maximize the autonomy not of one individual or group of individuals, but of all parties. How this is to be done with regard to specific technologies remains to be worked out.

Concerns raised by the technologies of drug testing and genetic screening are explored in our next two readings. In "Drug Testing in Employment," Joseph Desjardins and Ronald Duska examine the issue of whether drug testing violates employee privacy. In contrast to Lippke, they ground employee privacy in a contractualist view which holds that an employer is only entitled to information about an employee that is relevant to job performance or safety. They go on to argue that the knowledge of whether an employee is using drugs is not relevant to job performance and only rarely relevant to the issue of safety.

With respect to job performance, they argue that the issue is not whether an employee is taking drugs, but whether she is doing her job satisfactorily. If she is performing satisfactorily, there exists no reason to test her. If she is not, then one may terminate her employment regardless of the cause of nonperformance. In neither case is there any need to test for use of drugs.

With respect to safety, they are willing to agree that testing for drug use may sometimes be appropriate. They suggest that in situations where the potential for harm is clear and present, the employee has given reason to doubt his reliability, and the drugs being tested for really pose a hazard, then testing is appropriate if there exists no equally effective, less intrusive means of acquiring the information needed to ensure safety. They think, however, that such instances are very few in number.

David Resnik takes up the issue of genetic screening in his article "Genetic Privacy in Employment." His aim is to uncover the general criteria by which an employer is entitled to information she would not otherwise be entitled to. The development of such criteria permits their application to situations involving genetic information to determine the morality of genetic screening. Unlike some writers who reserve the term "invasion of privacy" for the wrongful gathering of information, Resnik is prepared to talk of legitimate "invasions" of privacy. Whether or not a particular "invasion" of privacy is justified or not will depend on whether the employer is entitled to the information that was acquired. This, in turn, will depend on whether the information is relevant to the employee's ability to perform the job.

He concludes that although many other questions must be answered before implementing any policy concerning the disclosure of genetic information to employers, it is possible to develop genetic privacy guidelines. These would place strong restrictions on what information employers could legitimately demand, but they would allow some instances in which employers could gain access to genetic information concerning employees.

Richard L. Lippke

Work, Privacy, and Autonomy

Employees today face what many believe are unjustified assaults on their privacy. At present, the most well-known and controversial such assault is the urine test. Estimates are that about 30% of the Fortune 500 companies in the United States require a urine test as part of the employment application process. Proponents of such testing warn of the dangers of rampant drug use and abuse in our society. They insist on the need to safeguard co-worker and consumer health and safety, and the need to maintain productivity. Opponents of testing conjure up images of Orwell's *1984*—of large and powerful institutions run amok, forcing innocent people to urinate while under the intense (and let us hope not prurient) supervision of official inspectors. Opponents lambast testing as an invasion of privacy and as a form of self-incrimination. Their most effective tactic has been to raise the specter of inaccurate tests; of persons unfairly scored with the scarlet letter of drug use.

Unfortunately, in the public debate over these issues there is little in the way of patient and careful analysis. In the recent philosophical literature, a good deal of attention has been focused on privacy and the right to privacy. Less attention has been paid to the privacy rights of employees and prospective employees. I will maintain that the philosophical defenses of employee privacy that have been offered are either incomplete or misguided. At times, they say too little about the value of privacy. Or, they offer suspect models of the employer/employee relationship. Or, they fail to convincingly show how

From Richard L. Lippke, "Work, Privacy, and Autonomy,"
Public Affairs Quarterly, Vol. 3, No. 2, April 1989.
Reprinted by permission.

we should deal with the conflict between privacy and other, competing values.

I will begin my analysis by arguing that privacy is valuable because of its relation to autonomy. For the purposes of this discussion, I will define autonomy as the capacity of persons to make rationally reflective choices about their ends and activities. All areas of persons' lives are assumed to be fit subjects for the exercise of their autonomy. Unless the relation between privacy and autonomy is kept clearly in view, we will not be able to establish the need for restrictions on the information employers may gather or on the means they may use. More importantly, I will argue that we must examine the privacy issue in the context of an understanding of how the contemporary organization of work in the United States affects the autonomy of workers. Simply put, workers in the U.S. face myriad assaults to their autonomy. I will show how failure to recognize this and to incorporate it into philosophical analyses of employee privacy inevitably weakens the case that can be made on behalf of employees. I will argue that when the reality of work is ignored, workers are more likely to be blamed for behavior that arguably stems (at least in part) from the system of private property rights in productive resources that deprives them of control over their working lives.

Though I will focus exclusively on the value of autonomy, I will not try to argue that it is the only value we should pay attention to in assessing the current organization of work in the U.S. I would contend that autonomy is an essential value, but I concede that other values are important as well. Others who have offered critiques of the current organization of work have tried to show that it undermines values like self-respect and welfare.[1]

At various points in my discussion, I will make empirical claims about the organization of work and its effects on workers. I will not try to support those claims in this paper, though I believe they can be supported. Much of what I say will only be true for most workers, not all. Also, I limit my claims to conditions in the U.S. Obviously, those claims might have to be modified or weakened if applied to other countries with different schemes of industrial organization.

Finally, those searching for simple "yes" or "no" answers on whether certain means of gathering information can legitimately be used by employers are likely to be frustrated with the conclusions I reach. I will not assume that the present organization of work is morally defensible, and so such answers are inappropriate. Also, I am more concerned with how we should approach and think about the whole issue of employee privacy than with making specific recommendations about which methods are or are not morally defensible.

There are difficulties in defining what privacy is. However, I do not think we need to be detained by them.[2] Generally, there is a consensus that it involves two things: (1) control over some information about ourselves; and (2) some control over who can experience or observe us.[3] In the abstract, it is hard to further specify how much control privacy involves and over what types of information it ranges. This is because whether any given piece of information about me is private in relation to someone else depends on the type of relationship I have to that individual. What is private in relation to my spouse is very different from what is private in relation to an employer or working associate.

Joseph Kupfer has recently offered a compelling analysis of the value of privacy.[4] Two of the ways in which privacy is valuable are especially relevant to the employer/employee relationship, so I will concentrate on them. First, Kupfer argues that privacy plays an essential role in individuals coming to have an "autonomous self-concept," that is, a concept of themselves as in control of their own lives:

An autonomous self-concept requires identifying with a particular body whose thoughts, purposes, and actions are subject to one's control . . . autonomy requires awareness of control over one's relation to others, including their access to us . . . privacy contributes to the formation and persistence of autonomous individuals by providing them with control over whether or not their physical and psychological existence becomes part of another's experience.[5]

Kupfer does not argue that privacy is intrinsically good. He argues that it is causally related to the formation and maintenance of an autonomous self-concept. An autonomous self-concept is, in turn, a necessary condition of the basic good of autonomy. In other words, unless individuals conceive of themselves as able to determine their own courses of action, their own life-plans, they cannot be autonomous. If individuals are to develop and maintain an autonomous self-concept, others must grant them control over information about themselves and control over who can experience them and when. Kupfer offers some empirical evidence to substantiate the claim that lack of privacy defeats the formation and maintenance of an autonomous self-concept.[6]

As Kupfer notes, the most autonomous person is one who evaluates his deepest convictions, or the most fundamental aspects of his life-plan. Privacy is essential to individuals having the concept that they can do this. It allows them to engage in this self-scrutiny without intrusion and distraction. When the most intimate aspects of their lives are up for scrutiny, individuals are vulnerable to ridicule or manipulation by others. It is vitally important for them to be able to remove themselves from observation and criticism by those they feel they cannot trust.

A second way in which privacy is valuable is that individuals subjected to invasions of their privacy seem less likely to conceive of themselves as *worthy* of autonomy:

Privacy is a trusting way others treat us, resulting in a conception of ourselves as worth being trusted. In contrast, monitoring behavior or collecting data on us, projects a disvaluing of the self in question.[7]

Close, intrusive supervision and constant correction (or the threat of it) are inimical to individuals developing and maintaining a sense of themselves as worthy of autonomy. In contrast, social practices that respect privacy give the individual a chance to make mistakes or do wrong, and thus convey the message that the individual is worthy of acting autonomously. The sense that they are worthy of acting autonomously may, as Kupfer notes, increase the confidence of individuals in themselves, and so they may exercise their autonomy to an even greater extent.

I might add that encouraging an individual to believe he is *worthy* of autonomy may be, in the end, the most effective way of protecting his autonomy. If he relies on others to protect his autonomy, he is more likely, it seems to me, to lose it.

With this brief characterization of some of the ways in which privacy is valuable in hand, I turn first to consider the issues raised by the *content* of information that businesses might acquire about employees or prospective employees. Both George Brenkert and Joseph Desjardins offer arguments designed to restrict the types of information employers may justifiably gather about employees to information that is "job relevant." Both also construe the employer/employee relationship in contractual terms, relying, apparently, on the fact that the courts are increasingly viewing the relationship in that fashion.

Desjardins argues that the contractual model is a marked improvement over the old principal/agent model, where the moral and legal rights seemed to be largely on the side of the employer and the moral and legal duties on the side of the employee. The contractual model presumes the existence of a legal framework to enforce the contract. More importantly, "contracts also must be noncoercive, voluntary agreements between rational and free agents."[8] And, they must be free from fraud and deception.

Desjardins explores the implications of this model for the issue of privacy in the employment context. He argues that the employer is entitled to make sure that the contract is free from fraud or deception. The employer can legitimately acquire information about the prospective employee's job qualifications, work experience, educational background, and "other information relevant to the hiring decision."[9] Information is "relevant" if it has to do with determining whether or not the employee is capable of fulfilling her part of the contract. In a similar vein, Brenkert argues that the "job relevance" requirement limits the information sought "to that which is directly connected with the job description."[10] Brenkert admits that aspects of a person's social and moral character (for example, honesty, ability and willingness to cooperate with others) are job relevant. What both Brenkert and Desjardins want to rule out as job relevant is information about such things as a prospective employee's political or religious beliefs and practices, her sexual preferences, marital status, credit or other financial data, and the like. One of Brenkert's complaints about the use of polygraph tests is that they often involve asking employees for information that is *not* job relevant.

I am sympathetic with the idea of such content restrictions, but I believe the arguments of Desjardins and Brenkert are seriously flawed. In the first place, we should be wary of the contractual model of the employer/employee relationship. Though it is an improvement over the traditional principal/agent model (especially for employees), and though the courts increasingly utilize it, I think that it is a very misleading model for understanding the interactions of most employers and employees in the U.S. today.

The danger in using this model is that it may lead us to ignore a crucial imbalance of power that exists in the marketplace. Individual employees rarely have bargaining power equal to that of their prospective employers. First, there are typically more potential employees available to firms than there are job openings available. Many jobs require little training or pre-existing expertise, and so workers can often be easily replaced. The threat that "there is always someone to take your place" is not an idle one for most workers. Unemployment in the economy generally and the problems workers face in moving to areas where there are jobs contribute to this buyers' market that is to the advantage of firms. Second, firms seem able to absorb underemployment more easily than workers can absorb unemployment. While firms need employees, they rarely need them as desperately as workers need jobs. As a result of these two factors, individual workers are rarely in a position to bargain on anything like equal terms with their prospective employers.[11]

This imbalance of power renders most workers practically unable to resist the demands for information that precede and accompany employment offers, and makes all the more urgent the content restrictions Desjardins and Brenkert advocate. After all, what is the point of urging such restrictions if the wage-labor agreement is one between relative equals? Why not just leave the sorts of information to be exchanged up to the negotiations between employer and employee?

Imagine the average worker actually going into "contract negotiations" with a company and asking for the information the *worker* needs to make sure the contract is free from fraud and deception: information about the company's health and safety or environmental record; information about its promotion practices, especially whether it has a record of promoting blacks and women (if one is a black or woman); information about whether the company has ever been convicted of any crimes; and information about company financial performance in the last ten years. According to the contractual model, just as the employer is entitled to ensure that the contract is free from fraud and deception, so should the worker be entitled to ensure that. Yet, is it realistic to believe that most workers who request such information during the employment interview will be given it, let alone hired? If not, then the contract is not a contract between equals in any meaningful sense.

Of course, Desjardins and Brenkert might insist that workers ought to be able to ask for this information without fears of any sort. They might claim to be offering a normative model, not a descriptive one. I do not think they are doing anything of the sort. In fact, they seem to be doing both at once. In any case, my point is that the contractual model is very misleading if used as a way to conceive of the reality of work in the U.S. It suggests a type of equality that does not exist, and if its descriptive and normative functions are run together, it distorts our perception of where the balance of power lies in the relationship between workers and employers.

Leaving aside the problems with the contractual model, it does not seem that Desjardins and Brenkert help us to understand the moral basis for the content restrictions they advocate. The appeal to the notion of "job relevance" raises more questions than it answers. Lots of information both would prevent employers from obtaining is, arguably, job relevant. For instance, if all of my employees are politically and religiously conservative, knowing where prospective employees stand on these matters may

very well be job relevant if my employees have to work closely together. After all, an atheist with socialist leanings may not get along at all with my employees and thereby disrupt productivity. Neither may a union supporter, a homosexual, or someone who is financially reckless or sexually promiscuous. I am not suggesting that we should cater to the prejudices of existing employees in making hiring decisions. What I am suggesting is that Brenkert's and Desjardins' arguments invoke a concept that is far from unproblematic.[12]

Even if the notion of "job relevance" was unproblematic, the argument would be incomplete. What we want is an argument that connects job relevance up with some moral value or values. In other words, why (morally speaking) limit employer access to only job relevant information? What is at stake in doing so?

If we turn back to the analysis of the value of privacy, the answer emerges. Suppose that employers are allowed to gather all of the sorts of information that the notion of "job relevance" is meant to exclude, and to use that information in making employment-related decisions. The result might be that business hiring and promotion decisions will wind up shaping peoples' lives in rather dramatic ways. Consider the likely chilling effects on employees. They may be reluctant to try out any new ideas or activities that may, at some future date, come back to haunt them. As we saw, privacy vitally contributes to our concept of ourselves as in control of our own lives. Part of this is that it protects our sense of self-determination by enabling us to engage in a "no holds barred" examination of all aspects of our lives. It allows us to experiment with different courses of our lives, if only in thought. These different courses may not be popular, especially to employers who are very conscious of the bottom line.

There is also the very real danger that all sorts of mistaken inferences about employee behavior will be made from access to such information. For instance, suppose that a polygraph test uncovers the fact that a person sometimes fantasizes about theft. It seems clear that a person who fantasizes about theft may be a long way from behaving as a thief. We do not understand the connections between the "inner workings" of peoples' minds and their behavior anywhere near well enough to allow employers to make such predictions in an accurate fashion.[13]

In short, the content restrictions Desjardins and Brenkert favor are morally justified as ways of limiting the perceived power that businesses have over the lives of their employees. We should discourage invasions of privacy that will likely result in individuals narrowing the exploration and examination of their lives, or that will decrease their sense that they control and are responsible for their lives. In a work environment without such restrictions, and where employers are already in a position to impose their wills on employees in other ways, it seems unlikely that employees will have as rich and lively a sense of their own autonomy. In turn, they will be less prone to exercise their auotonomy.

It seems clear that many of the most controversial *means* of acquiring information about employees may provide employers with information that is, on any reasonable interpretation of the notion, job relevant. Surveillance to prevent theft or to maintain productivity provides such information. Urine tests will provide such information, though they will also provide information about off-the-job drug or alcohol use that is, less obviously, job relevant. Searches of employee desks or lockers, and even polygraph tests (where the questions are suitably restricted) will provide such information. Physical exams and skills tests will do so, though few have seen these as controversial.

Numerous writers have argued against the use of at least some of these means. One popular objection to some of these means is that they are so inaccurate. Polygraph tests, in particular, seem gravely defective in this way, and to a lesser extent, so do urine tests. The concern about accuracy is a concern about fairness, about the possibility of unfairly accusing individuals of actions they are innocent of. I think that the inaccuracy issue is a very serious one, but I do not believe we should base our case against such tests on it alone, or even primarily. The reason for this is simple: suppose through various technological developments such tests are made *very* accurate. Are we then to conclude that there is nothing objectionable about them?

I think not. I will try to show that there are other objectionable features to such tests.

A second objection might be that such means of acquiring information are somehow too intrusive. It is important to ask what this means. Is it that such methods come too close to us, crossing some physical or psychological boundary that is morally significant? Administering the polygraph test does require that various devices be attached to our bodies, so maybe it is the actual physical contact that matters. It is hard to imagine anything more intrusive in this regard than a physical exam. Urine tests are not intrusive in this way, however, and neither are surveillance or forays through employee desks and lockers. Thus, physical contact does not seem to be a necessary condition of intrusiveness. It might be a sufficient condition, but we need to know precisely what is so objectionable about such contact. It does not seem objectionable in the same way that battery is, where the concern is with shielding individuals from physical harm.

Perhaps it is that such methods invade our "psychological space" in some objectionable fashion. Brenkert claims that employers are not entitled to "probe one's emotional responses, feelings, and thoughts."[14] Such an argument, if plausible, will rule out polygraph tests, but not most of the other ways of gathering information. And, is this argument really plausible? As we have seen, Brenkert admits that employers are entitled to information about the social and moral character of prospective employees, though he restricts this to information about their observable behavior in the past.[15] We need not be behaviorists to believe that finding out about a person's social and moral behavior in the past probably reveals quite a bit about his emotional responses, feelings, and thoughts. Will Brenkert prohibit employers from asking prospective employees about their career ambitions, or about what they "think" their strengths and weaknesses are? Moreover, why are employers not entitled to such information? Again, Brenkert does not tie his claim up in any way with moral values.[16]

More promising is Brenkert's argument that employers should avoid using any means that (like the polygraph) "operates by turning part of us over which we have little or no control against the rest of us."[17] Such means amount to a "subtle form of self-incrimination."[18]

In response to this, I begin by noting that Brenkert's line of reasoning will rule out not only polygraph and urine tests, but also physical exams, and more surprisingly, skills tests. After all, what does, for instance, a typing test do if not confirm or disconfirm a prospective employee's claims about her typing skills? Part of her may indeed turn against or incriminate the rest of her.[19] Also, though the disclosure of information about one's job qualifications, educational background, and the like, may not, strictly speaking, turn part of the worker against the rest of her, such information may contradict what she says about herself. If the "self against self" part of the argument is insisted upon, it is not clear how Brenkert will rule out surveillance or searches of employee desks and lockers. Furthermore, what is so bad about turning part of the self against the rest of the self?

What all of these methods of acquiring information seem to have in common is that they are ways of checking on the things employees say about themselves or the ways employees present themselves. In this regard, I do not see how a urine test or surveillance is all that much different than the required disclosure of information about work experience or educational background. Perhaps some methods are more intrusive, as a matter of degree, than others. Employees are increasingly finding that not even their own bodies are safe havens, let alone their desks and lockers. At every turn, they are hounded by employer efforts to catch them speaking or acting in ways contrary to what are deemed the employer's interests.

The proliferation of these methods of acquiring contradicting information seems likely to have two sorts of effects on workers. First, all such methods implicitly remind the worker where the balance of power lies in the working world. Again, most workers are not in a position to refuse to cooperate with the use of such methods and workers are highly vulnerable to any negative employer reactions to the information so gleaned.[20] The more a worker is checked on, tested, spied upon, and so on, the less likely she is to feel that she controls her own life in the working world. The aggregate and cumulative effects of many (by themselves seemingly innocent) attempts to check on workers might be an increased sense on the part of workers that the workplace is an oppressive environment. It is distressing that so many employees apparently submit to polygraph or urine tests without any reluctance. Can this be because they have already internalized the message that in the workplace their lives are not their own?

Second, random or across-the-board drug testing, or surveillance without "reasonable cause" implicitly tells employees that they are not trustworthy. It is important to keep in mind that in spite of statistics on the use of drugs by workers (estimates as high as one in six use drugs either on or off the job), the vast majority of workers are probably "clean" and honest. However, instead of there being a presumption that employees will act responsibly, the presumption behind the use of these methods of gathering information is that they cannot be trusted to act responsibly. Individuals who find themselves with a presumption of doubt against them may simply react with resentment. That is bad enough and a potential cost to employers. What is worse is the tendency such methods might have to undermine the employee's sense of trustworthiness, and therefore their sense that they are worthy of acting autonomously. Again, one valuable thing about privacy is that it affirms an individual's sense that she is worthy of autonomy. The more she lacks that sense, the more she is prone to tolerate invasions of her privacy, with the resulting debilitating effects on her autonomy.

In the abstract, concerns about the effects of such methods on employee autonomy might appear legitimate, but not of a sufficiently compelling nature to convince us that their use is wholly objectionable. If they are employed in a work environment that is otherwise supportive of employee autonomy, they might be only minor threats. Therefore, in order to strengthen the case against the use of such methods, it will help here to focus attention on how the organization of work in the U.S. *already* undermines the autonomy of most workers to an extraordinary extent.

As numerous critics of the organization of work in the U.S. have pointed out, the majority of workers are routinely subjected to a hierar-chical, authoritarian namagement structure that deprives them of any significant input into the economic decisions directly affecting their working lives. Most have very little input into decisions about the organization of work at even the shop-floor level, let alone at levels above it. As Adina Schwartz argues, most work-ers are subjected to a division of labor where they are confined to increasingly narrowly-defined tasks determined and supervised by others:

These routine jobs provide people with almost no opportunities for formulating aims, for deciding on means for achieving their ends, or for adjusting their goals and methods in light of experience.[21]

Work technology is decided by others, as are productivity quotas, criteria for evaluation, dis-cipline procedures, and plant closings or em-ployee lay-offs. Even the attitudes with which work is to be done are prescribed and pressures are put on workers to "be a loyal member of the team" or to "please the customer at all costs."

Also, as alluded to earlier, most workers are highly vulnerable to fluctuations in the demand for labor. If economic considerations so dictate, businesses lay off workers, cut their wages or benefits, or close down altogether. Labor unions are increasingly powerless to resist these deci-sions by management, especially in the face of threats by management to relocate if strikes are called. Unemployment compensation is both meager and short-term.[22]

Thus, each concession made to management's desire to gather information using the methods we have been discussing adds to an already impressive arsenal of weapons at its disposal for the assault on employee autonomy. The ques-tion is *not* whether we should endorse the use of methods that undermine employee autonomy in a setting where that autonomy is otherwise affirmed and nurtured. The question is whether we should endorse the use of methods that might further erode employee autonomy. For instant, random or across-the-board urine tests do not send a message to workers that they are untrustworthy in a context where their trust-worthiness is normally affirmed. Instead, it

sends a message that is likely repeated to work-ers in a thousand different ways throughout their working lives. A verdict wholly in favor of employees on all of the privacy issues we have been considering will, by itself, come nowhere near establishing working conditions supportive of employee autonomy.

Another way to put the preceding point about the organization of work in the U.S. is to say that property rights, with their supporting political-social institutions and practices, give some individuals a considerable amount of *power* over the lives of others. It is with this in mind that we should consider attempts to over-ride the privacy of employees by appeals to the property rights of the owners and stockholders.

Proponents of gathering information about employees may admit that privacy is a value and that it is threatened by the means employers want to use to gather information. But, they will argue, the property rights of the owners and stockholders are valuable as well. They will rightly demand to be shown that the privacy rights of workers ought to prevail over these property rights. Brenkert notes this problem, but says surprisingly little about how to deal with it.[23]

I think it is a mistake to even allow the issues here to be framed in terms of conflicting rights. In the first place, allowing this will make it far too easy for proponents of testing, surveillance, and the like, to make out what seems like a reasonable case for their side. Let me show how this is so. Suppose it is argued that the owners and stockholders are likely to feel that *their* autonomy is threatened if they cannot order management to gather information about work-ers. After all, the owners and stockholders may legitimately feel that their abilities to control the courses of their own lives are being undercut if they cannot take steps to protect their property. To strengthen their case, suppose they add that they are willing to adhere to the content restric-tions discussed earlier. What they want to know is why they should be prohibited from giving an occasional urine or polygraph test, or from engaging in surveillance from time to time. If the reply is that such means of gathering infor-mation undermine the autonomy of workers, the rejoinder will be that prohibiting such methods undermines the autonomy of the owners and stockholders. Framed in this way, the dispute looks like one about whose autonomy to affirm, and who the ultimate verdict should favor is anything but clear.

What this plausible-sounding argument ignores is how property rights in productive resources differ from privacy rights. The right to privacy is such that respecting it provides individuals with an increased sense of control (a necessary condition of autonomy) over their own lives. Respecting it does *not* provide individuals with increased control over the lives of others. Property rights as they exist in the U.S. are, as we have seen, not like this. They do give some power over the lives of others. And, importantly, a verdict in favor of the owners and stockholders will mean a further extension of that already considerable control.

Hence, the issue is not the rather abstract one of whether privacy rights are more or less important than property rights in relation to the autonomy of the bearers of those rights. Rather, since property rights as currently institutionalized give some power over the lives of others, the issue is whether to preserve or increase that power, *or* curtail it. Indeed, once the connection between property rights and power is revealed in this way, those rights become fit subjects for critical scrutiny. If we are concerned about the autonomy of workers, we can hardly ignore the existence of working conditions that systematically and pervasively undermine it.

A second reason for not allowing the issues to be framed simply in terms of conflicting rights is that this is likely to exonerate the existing organization of work from any blame for generating the employee behavior that is viewed as irresponsible. This irresponsible behavior is taken as a *given,* and various methods for collecting information about employees are proposed. The need to gather such information is implicitly attributed solely to defects in the character of employees. Those who seek to defend workers against invasions of their privacy are likely to be portrayed as condoning dishonesty, drug use, and the like. This portrayal is, of course, unfair, but it gains credence from the implicit assumption that such behaviors simply exist and must be countered. Thus,

the debate about conflicting rights begins, and employers are all too easily depicted as the innocent victims of their unscrupulous, irresponsible, and ungrateful employees.

Many critics of the organization of work in the U.S. will argue that it is the character of that work itself which is a very significant factor in producing such "problem" behaviors. The research that exists in this area strongly suggests that this is a possibility we should not ignore.[24] It is surprising that in the popular and philosophical discussions of these issues, the following sorts of questions are so rarely asked: Why is it that employees show up drunk or drugged for work? Why is it that they shirk work and responsibility? Why is it that they lie about their credentials or exaggerate them? Why is it that they engage in theft or sabotage? When the question asked is whether the employee privacy that is violated in order to counter such behaviors outweighs or is outweighed by the right to property, the preceding sorts of questions are suppressed. Behaviors which may be symptomatic of a morally sick organization of work are viewed as the underlying cause of the conflict. Then, in a twist of bitter irony, the property rights in which that organization of work is anchored are brought in to beat back the challenge posed by the employees' privacy rights.

Appeals to co-worker health and safety, or to the health and safety of consumers and members of the general public, are also used to justify invasions of worker privacy. No one wants their airline pilot to be high on cocaine or their nuclear power plant operator to be blitzed on Jim Beam. Moreover, protecting peoples' health and safety does *not* ipso facto give them power over the lives of others. Health and safety are obviously essential conditions for the preservation and exercise of autonomy, perhaps more essential than privacy. So, it would seem that health and safety considerations ought to prevail over privacy considerations.

In response to this, I begin by noting that we should not isolate the issue of whether or not we can invade the privacy of workers to protect health and safety from the larger issue of the role of the current organization of work in generating dangerous behavior. The issue is not simply whether health and safety outweighs privacy, but also whether fundamental changes in the organization of work would lessen or eliminate the behavior that makes overriding privacy seem so reasonable. It is hard to say whether and to what extent the means many would now use to gather information about employees would be used in a more democratically and humanely organized economy. Such an economy would eliminate or at least lessen the specter of unemployment, and so the felt need to lie about or exaggerate credentials in order to obtain work might be eliminated. Such an economy would give workers more real control over their working lives, and would eliminate the division between those who make decisions at work and those who simply implement the decisions of others. Such an economy would give workers more control over the products of their labor, and give them the power to discipline other workers. How such changes would affect employee morale, productivity, and the sense of responsibility for work performed are things we can only speculate about.

It seems likely that such changes will *not* eliminate all dangerous or destructive behavior on the part of workers. I do not wish to rule out, once and for all, the use of means of acquiring information that encroach on privacy. What I do want to suggest, in closing, is that in a more democratically and humanely organized economy, decisions about what measures to use and when to use them would not be made unilaterally by some people and then simply imposed on others. If we are going to respect the autonomy of persons, then we must give them input into decisions like this that vitally affect their lives.

Notes

1. See, for instance, David Schweickart, *Capitalism or Worker Control? An Ethical and Economic Appraisal* (New York: Praeger Publishers, 1980); Gerald Doppelt, "Conflicting Social Paradigms of Human Freedom and the Problem of Justification," *Inquiry*, vol. 27 (1984), pp. 51–86.
2. For a useful discussion of the difficulties in defining privacy, see H. J. McCloskey, "Privacy and the Right to Privacy," *Philosophy*, vol. 55 (1980), pp. 17–38.
3. For instance, see Joseph Kupfer, "Privacy, Autonomy, and Self-Concept, *American Philosophical Quarterly*, vol. 24 (1987), pp. 81–89. Also, Richard Wasserstrom, "Privacy," in *Today's Moral Problems*, Richard Wasser-

strom (ed.) (New York: Macmillan Publishing Co., 1979), pp. 392–408.
4. Kupfer, "Privacy, Autonomy, and Self-Concept," pp. 81–89. For a similar analysis, see Jeffrey H. Reiman, "Privacy, Intimacy, and Personhood," *Philosophy and Public Affairs*, vol. 6 (1976), pp. 26–44.
5. Kupfer, "Privacy, Autonomy, and Self-Concept," p. 82.
6. Ibid., pp. 81–82.
7. Ibid., p. 85.
8. Joseph R. Desjardins, "Privacy in Employment," in *Moral Rights in the Workplace*, Gertrude Ezorsky (ed.) (Albany, NY: State University of New York Press, 1987), pp. 127–139, p. 131.
9. Ibid., p. 132.
10. George G. Brenkert, "Privacy, Polygraphs, and Work," in *Contemporary Issues in Business Ethics*, Joseph R. Desjardins and John J. McCall (eds.) (Belmont, CA: Wadsworth, 1985), pp. 227–237, p. 231.
11. For those who might say that labor unions provide workers with such equality, I point out that, at present, less than 15% of U.S. workers are represented by labor unions.
12. Brenkert, "Privacy, Polygraphs, and Work," p. 231. Brenkert admits that the criterion of job relevance is "rather vague," yet proceeds to use it.
13. One of the more frightening prospects employees face is the availability of so-called "genetic marker" tests. These tests will allow employers to tell which individuals have genetic *tendencies* for such things as alcoholism, heart attacks, and cancer. Suppose businesses decide to gather and use such information in making employment-related decisions. Though there are things individuals can do to counteract their tendencies, they might find themselves labeled due to their genetic tendencies, and so denied jobs or promotions. This threatens their abilities to determine how their lives will go *in spite of* their genetic tendencies.
14. Brenkert, "Privacy, Polygraphs, and Work," p. 234.
15. Ibid., p. 231.
16. Desjardins suggests that employers should avoid using means of gathering information that bypass the employee's consent ("Privacy in Employment," p. 134). Of course, he sees the employee's divulging of information about his job qualifications, work experience, and so on, as unproblematically consented to. In any case, what we need to be shown is that employees have some rational ground for withholding their consent to the use of such means.
17. Brenkert, "Privacy, Polygraphs, and Work," p. 234.
18. Ibid., p. 234.
19. One way to distinguish skills tests and background checks from polygraphs and urine tests might be to say that the former are subject to much less interpretation than the latter. The results of, for instance, a typing test rather straightforwardly reveal whether or not a person can type. What the results of even very accurate polygraph tests reveal is notoriously more problematic. As with the concern about inaccuracy, this concern about interpretive latitude seems to be one about the possibility of being unfairly labeled in some derogatory fashion.

20. In light of this vulnerability, I think we can better understand the vocal opposition to polygraphs and drug tests based on their inaccuracy. Most workers who are victims of inaccurate tests cannot simply fall back on adequate unemployment compensation or secure comparable employment.

21. Adina Schwartz, "Meaningful Work," *Ethics,* vol. 92 (1982), pp. 634–646, p. 634. Cf. also Edward Sankowski, "Freedom, Work, and the Scope of Democracy," *Ethics,* vol. 91 (1981), pp. 228–242.

22. To the preceding points, we might add others such as the following: how inequalities in property ownership contribute to inequalities in political power and influence; how massive corporate advertising campaigns bombard individuals with one-sided and self-serving views about the nature of the good life and so interfere with their abilities to make rational choices about the courses of their lives; how inequalities in access to quality education confine many individuals to unemployment or underemployment; and so on.

23. Brenkert, "Privacy, Polygraphs, and Work," pp. 235–236. Some of his remarks suggest that he might allow health and safety concerns to override privacy.

24. See, for instance, *Work in America: Report of a Special Task Force to the Secretary of Health, Education, and Welfare* (Cambridge, MA: MIT Press, 1973); Harry Braverman, *Labor and Monopoly Capital: The Degradation of Work in the Twentieth Century* (New York: Monthly Review Press, 1974).

Joseph DesJardins and Ronald Duska

Drug Testing in Employment

According to one survey, nearly one-half of all Fortune 500 companies were planning to administer drug tests to employees and prospective employees by the end of 1987.[1] Counter to what seems to be the current trend in favor of drug testing, we will argue that it is rarely legitimate to override an employee's or applicant's right to privacy by using such tests or procedures.[2]

Opening Stipulations

We take privacy to be an "employee right" by which we mean a presumptive moral entitlement to receive certain goods or be protected from certain harms in the workplace.[3] Such a right creates a *prima facie* obligation on the part of the employer to provide the relevant goods or, as in this case, refrain from the relevant

From Joseph DesJardins and Ronald Duska, "Drug Testing in Employment," *Business and Professional Ethics Journal,* Vol. 6, No. 3, 1986. Reprinted by permission.

harmful treatment. These rights prevent employees from being placed in the fundamentally coercive position where they must choose between their job and other basic human goods.

Further, we view the employer-employee relationship as essentially contractual. The employer-employee relationship is an economic one and, unlike relationships such as those between a government and its citizens or a parent and a child, exists primarily as a means for satisfying the economic interests of the contracting parties. The obligations that each party incurs are only those that it voluntarily takes on. Given such a contractual relationship, certain areas of the employee's life remain their own private concern and no employer has a right to invade them. On these presumptions we maintain that certain information about an employee is rightfully private, i.e. the employee has a right to privacy.

The Right to Privacy

According to George Brenkert, a right to privacy involves a three-place relation between a person A, some information X, and another person B. The right to privacy is violated only when B deliberately comes to possess information X about A, and no relationship between A and B exists which could justify B's coming to know X about A.[4] Thus, for example, the relationship one has with a mortgage company would justify that company's coming to know about one's salary, but the relationship one has with a neighbor does not justify the neighbor's coming to know that information. Hence, an employee's right to privacy is violated whenever personal information is requested, collected and/or used by an employer in a way or for any purpose that is *irrelevant to* or *in violation of* the contractual relationship that exists between *employer and employee*.

Since drug-testing is a means for obtaining information, the information sought must be relevant to the contract in order for the drug testing not to violate privacy. Hence, we must first decide if knowledge of drug use obtained by drug testing is job-relevant. In cases where the knowledge of drug use is *not* relevant, there appears to be no justification for subjecting employees to drug tests. In cases where information of drug use is job-relevant, we need to consider if, when, and under what conditions using a means such as drug testing to obtain that knowledge is justified.

Is Knowledge of Drug Use Job Relevant Information?

There seem to be two arguments used to establish that knowledge of drug use is job relevant information. The first argument claims that drug use adversely affects job performance thereby leading to lower productivity, higher costs, and consequently lower profits. Drug testing is seen as a way of avoiding these adverse effects. According to some estimates twenty-five billion ($25,000,000,000) dollars are lost each year in the United States because of drug use.[5] This occurs because of loss in productivity, increase in costs due to theft, increased rates in health and liability insurance, and such. Since employers are contracting with an employee for the performance of specific tasks, employers seem to have a legitimate claim upon whatever personal information is relevant to an employee's ability to do the job.

The second argument claims that drug use has been and can be responsible for considerable harm to the employee him/herself, fellow employees, the employer, and/or third parties, including consumers. In this case drug testing is defended because it is seen as a way of preventing possible harm. Further, since employers can be held liable for harms done both to third parties, e.g. customers, and to the employee or his/her fellow employees, knowledge of employee drug use will allow employers to gain information that can protect themselves from risks such as liability. But how good are these arguments? We turn to examine the arguments more closely.

The First Argument: Job Performance and Knowledge of Drug Use

The first argument holds that drug use leads to lower productivity and consequently implies that a knowledge of drug use obtained through drug-testing will allow an employer to increase productivity. It is generally assumed that people using certain drugs have their performances affected by such use. Since enhancing productivity is something any employer desires, any use of drugs that reduces productivity affects the employer in an undesirable way, and that use is, then, job-relevant. If such production losses can be eliminated by knowledge of the drug use, then knowledge of that drug use is job-relevant information. On the surface this argument seems reasonable. Obviously some drug use in lowering the level of performance can decrease productivity. Since the employer is entitled to a certain level of performance and drug use adversely affects performance, knowledge of that use seems job-relevant.

But this formulation of the argument leaves an important question unanswered. To what level of performance are employers entitled? Optimal performance, or some lower level? If some lower level, what? Employers have a valid claim upon some *certain level* of performance, such that a failure to perform up to this level would give the employer a justification for disciplining, firing or at least finding fault with the employee. But that does not necessarily mean that the employer has a right to a maximum or optimal level of performance, a level above and beyond a certain level of acceptability. It might be nice if the employee gives an employer a maximum effort or optimal performance, but that is above and beyond the call of the employee's duty and the employer can hardly claim a right at all times to the highest level of performance of which an employee is capable.

That there are limits on required levels of performance and productivity becomes clear if we recognize that job performance is person related. It is person-related because one person's best efforts at a particular task might produce results well below the norm, while another person's minimal efforts might produce results abnormally high when compared to the norm. For example a professional baseball player's performance on a ball field will be much higher than the average person's since the average person is unskilled in baseball. We have all encountered people who work hard with little or no results, as well as people who work little with phenomenal results. Drug use in very talented people might diminish their performance or productivity, but that performance would still be better than the performance of the average person or someone totally lacking in the skills required. That being said, the important question now is whether the employer is entitled to an employee's maximum effort and best results, or merely to an effort sufficient to perform the task expected.

If the relevant consideration is whether the employee is producing as expected (according to the normal demands of the position and contract) not whether he/she is producing as much as possible, then knowledge of drug use is irrelevant or unnecessary. Let's see why.

If the person is producing what is expected, knowledge of drug use on the grounds of production is irrelevant since, *ex hypothesi* the production is satisfactory. If, on the other hand, the performance suffers, then, to the extent that it slips below the level justifiably expected, the employer has *prima facie* grounds for warning, disciplining or releasing the employee. But the justification for this is the person's unsatisfactory performance, not the person's use of drugs. Accordingly, drug use information is either unnecessary or irrelevant and consequently there

are not sufficient grounds to override the right of privacy. Thus, unless we can argue that an employer is entitled to optimal performance, the argument fails.

This counter-argument should make it clear that the information which is sub-relevant, and consequently which is not rightfully private, is information about an employee's level of performance and not information about the underlying causes of that level. The fallacy of the argument which promotes drug testing in the name of increased productivity is the assumption that each employee is obliged to perform at an optimal, or at least quite high, level. But this is required under few, if any, contracts. What is required contractually is meeting the normally expected levels of production or performing the tasks in the job-description adequately (not optimally). If one can do that under the influence of drugs, then on the grounds of job-performance at least, drug use is rightfully private. If one cannot perform the task adequately, then the employee is not fulfilling the contract, and knowledge of the cause of the failure to perform is irrelevant on the contractual model.

Of course, if the employer suspects drug use or abuse as the cause of the unsatisfactory performance, then she might choose to help the person with counseling or rehabilitation. However, this does not seem to be something morally required of the employer. Rather, in the case of unsatisfactory performance, the employer has a *prima facie* justification for dismissing or disciplining the employee.

Before turning to the second argument which attempts to justify drug testing, we should mention a factor about drug use that is usually ignored in talk of productivity. The entire productivity arugument is irrelevant for those cases in which employees use performance enhancing drugs. Amphetamines and steroids, for example, can actually enhance some performances. This points to the need for care when tying drug testing to job-performance. In the case of some drugs used by athletes, for example, drug testing is done because the drug-influenced performance is too good and therefore unfair, not because it leads to inadequate job-performance. In such a case, where the testing is done to ensure fair competition, the testing may be justified. But drug testing in sports is an entirely different matter than drug-testing in business.

To summarize our argument so far. Drug use may affect performances, but as long as the performance is at an acceptable level, the knowledge of drug use is irrelevant. If the performance is unacceptable, then that is sufficient cause for action to be taken. In this case an employee's failure to fulfill his/her end of a contract makes knowledge of the drug use unnecessary.

THE SECOND ARGUMENT: HARM AND THE KNOWLEDGE OF DRUG USE TO PREVENT HARM

Even though the performance argument is inadequate, there is an argument that seems somewhat stronger. This is an argument based on the potential for drug use to cause harm. Using a type of Millian argument, one could argue that drug testing might be justified if such testing led to knowledge that would enable an employer to prevent harm. Drug use certainly can lead to harming others. Consequently, if knowledge of such drug use can prevent harm, then, knowing whether or not one's employee uses drugs might be a legitimate concern of an employer in certain circumstances. This second argument claims that knowledge of the employee's drug use is job-relevant because employees who are under the influence of drugs can pose a threat to the health and safety of themselves and others, and an employer who knows of that drug use and the harm it can cause has a responsibility to prevent it. Employers have both a general duty to prevent harm and the specific responsibility for harms done by their employees. Such responsibilities are sufficient reason for an employer to claim that information about an employee's drug use is relevant if that knowledge can prevent harm by giving the employer grounds for dismissing the employee or not allowing him/her to perform potentially harmful tasks. Employers might even claim a right to reduce unreasonable risks, in this case the risks involving legal and economic liability for harms caused by employees under the influence of drugs, as further justification for knowing about employee drug use.

This second argument differs from the first in which only a lowered job performance was relevant information. In this case, even to allow the performance is problematic, for the performance itself, more than being inadequate, can hurt people. We cannot be as sanguine about the prevention of harm as we can about inadequate production. Where drug use can cause serious harms, knowledge of that use becomes relevant if the knowledge of such use can lead to the prevention of harm and drug testing becomes justified as a means for obtaining that knowledge.

As we noted, we will begin initially by accepting this argument on roughly Millian grounds where restrictions on liberty are allowed in order to prevent harm to others. (The fact that one is harming oneself, if that does not harm others is not sufficient grounds for interference in another's behavior according to Mill.) In such a case an employer's obligation to prevent harm may over-ride the obligation to respect an employee's privacy.

But let us examine this more closely. Upon examination, certain problems arise, so that even if there is a possibility of justifying drug testing to prevent harm, some caveats have to be observed and some limits set out.

JOBS WITH POTENTIAL TO CAUSE HARM

To say that employers can use drug-testing where that can prevent harm is not to say that every employer has the right to know about the drug use of every employee. Not every job poses a serious enough threat to justify an employer coming to know this information.

In deciding which jobs pose serious enough threats certain guidelines should be followed. First the potential for harm should be *clear* and *present*. Perhaps all jobs in some extended way pose potential threats to human well-being. We suppose an accountant's error could pose a threat of harm to someone somewhere. But some jobs like those of airline pilots, school bus drivers, public transit drivers and surgeons, are jobs in which unsatisfactory performance poses a clear and present danger to others. It would be much harder to make an argument that job performances by auditors, secretaries, executive vice-presidents for public relations, college teachers, professional athletes, and the like, could cause harm if those performances were carried on under the influence of drugs. They would cause harm only in exceptional cases.[6]

NOT EVERY PERSON IS TO BE TESTED

But, even if we can make a case that a particular job involves a clear and present danger for causing harm if performed under the influence of drugs, it is not appropriate to treat everyone holding such a job the same. Not every job-holder is equally threatening. There is less reason to investigate an airline pilot for drug use if that pilot has a twenty-year record of exceptional service than there is to investigate a pilot whose behavior has become erratic and unreliable recently, or than one who reports to work smelling of alcohol and slurring his words. Presuming that every airline pilot is equally threatening is to deny individuals the respect that they deserve as autonomous, rational agents. It is to ignore previous history and significant differences. It is also probably inefficient and leads to the lowering of morale. It is the likelihood of causing harm, and not the fact of being an airline pilot *per se,* that is relevant in deciding which employees in critical jobs to test.

So, even if knowledge of drug use is justifiable to prevent harm, we must be careful to limit this justification to a range of jobs and people where the potential for harm is clear and present. The jobs must be jobs that clearly can cause harm, and the specific employee should not be someone who is reliable with a history of such reliability. Finally, the drugs being tested should be those drugs, the use of which in those jobs is really potentially harmful.

LIMITATIONS ON DRUG TESTING POLICIES

Even when we identify those jobs and individuals where knowledge of drug use would be job relevant information, we still need to examine whether some procedural limitations should not be placed upon the employer's testing for drugs.

We have said that in cases where a real threat of harm exists and where evidence exists suggesting that a particular employee poses such a threat, an employer could be justified in knowing about drug use in order to prevent the potential harm. But we need to recognize that as long as the employer has the discretion for deciding when the potential for harm is clear and present, and for deciding which employees pose the threat of harm, the possibility of abuse is great. Thus, some policy limiting the employer's power is called for.

Just as criminal law places numerous restrictions protecting individual dignity and liberty on the state's pursuit of its goals, so we should expect that some restrictions be placed on an employer in order to protect innocent employees from harm (including loss of job and damage to one's personal and professional reputation). Thus, some system of checks upon an employer's discretion in these matters seems advisable. Workers covered by collective bargaining agreements or individual contracts might be protected by clauses on those agreements that specify which jobs pose a real threat of harm (e.g., pilots but not cabin attendants) and what constitutes a just cause for investigating drug use. Local, state, and federal legislatures might do the same for workers not covered by employment contracts. What needs to be set up is a just employment relationship—one in which an employee's expectations and responsibilities are specified in advance and in which an employer's discretionary authority to discipline or dismiss an employee is limited.

Beyond that, any policy should accord with the nature of the employment relationship. Since that relationship is a contractual one, it should meet the condition of a morally valid contract, which is informed consent. Thus, in general, we would argue that only methods that have received the informed consent of employees can be used in acquiring information about drug use.[7]

A drug-testing policy that requires all employees to submit to a drug test or to jeopardize their job would seem coercive and therefore unacceptable. Being placed in such a fundamentally coercive position of having to choose between one's job and one's privacy does not provide the conditions for truly free consent. Policies that are unilaterally established by employers would likewise be unacceptable. Working with employees to develop company policy seems the only way to insure that the policy will be fair to both parties. Prior notice of testing would also be required in order to give employees the option of freely refraining from drug use. It is morally preferable to prevent drug use than to punish users after the fact, since this approach treats employees as capable of making rational and informed decisions.

Further procedural limitations seem advisable as well. Employees should be notified of the results of the test, they should be entitled to appeal the results (perhaps through further tests by an independent laboratory) and the information obtained through tests ought to be kept confidential. In summary, limitations upon employer discretion for administering drug tests can be derived from the nature of the employment contract and from the recognition that drug testing is justified by the desire to prevent harm, not the desire to punish wrong doing.

EFFECTIVENESS OF DRUG-TESTING

Having declared that the employer might have a right to test for drug use in order to prevent harm, we still need to examine the second argument a little more closely. One must keep in mind that the justification of drug testing is the justification of a means to an end, the end of preventing harm, and that the means are a means which intrude into one's privacy. In this case, before one allows drug testing as a means, one should be clear that there are not more effective means available.

If the employer has a legitimate right, perhaps duty, to ascertain knowledge of drug use to prevent harm, it is important to examine exactly how effectively, and in what situations, the *knowledge* of the drug use will prevent the harm. So far we have just assumed that the *knowledge* will prevent the harm. But how?

Let us take an example to pinpoint the difficulty. Suppose a transit driver, shortly before work, took some cocaine which, in giving him a feeling of invulnerability, leads him to take undue risks in his driving. How exactly is drug-testing going to contribute to the knowledge which will prevent the potential accident?

It is important to keep in mind that; (1) if the knowledge doesn't help prevent the harm, the testing is not justified on prevention grounds; (2) if the testing doesn't provide the relevant knowledge it is not justified either; and finally, (3) even if it was justified, it would be undesirable if a more effective means for preventing harm were discovered.

Upon examination, the links between drug-testing, knowledge of drug use, and prevention of harm are not as clear as they are presumed to be. As we investigate, it begins to seem that the knowledge of the drug use even though relevant in some instances is not the most effective means to prevent harm.

Let us turn to this last consideration first. Is drug-testing the most effective means for preventing harm caused by drug use?

Consider. If someone exhibits obviously drugged or drunken behavior, then this behavior itself is grounds for preventing the person from continuing on the job. Administering urine or blood tests, sending the specimens out for testing and waiting for a response, will not prevent harm in this instance. Much drug testing because of the time lapse involved, is equally superfluous in those cases where an employee is in fact under the influence of drugs, but exhibits no or only subtley impaired behaviour.

Thus, even if one grants that drug testing somehow prevents harm an argument can be made that there might be much more effective methods of preventing potential harm such as administering dexterity tests of the type employed by police in possible drunk-driving cases, or requiring suspect pilots to pass flight simulator tests.[8] Eye-hand coordination, balance, reflexes, and reasoning ability can all be tested with less intrusive, more easily administered, reliable technologies which give instant results. Certainly if an employer has just cause for believing that a specific employee presently poses a real threat of causing harm, such methods are just more effective in all ways than are urinalysis and blood testing.

Even were it possible to refine drug tests so that accurate results were immediately available, that knowledge would only be job relevant if the drug use was clearly the cause of impaired job performance that could harm people. Hence, testing behavior still seems more direct and effective in preventing harm than testing for the presence of drugs *per se*.

In some cases, drug use might be connected with potential harms not by being causally connected to motor-function impairment, but by causing personality disorders (e.g. paranoia, delusions, etc.) that affect judgmental ability. Even though in such cases a *prima facie* justification for urinalysis or blood testing might exist, the same problems of effectiveness persist. How is the knowledge of the drug use attained by urinalysis and/or blood testing supposed to prevent the harm? Only if there is a causal link between the use and the potentially harmful behavior, would such knowledge be relevant. Even if we get the results of the test immediately, there is the necessity to have an established causal link between specific drug use and anticipated harmful personality disorders in specific people.

But it cannot be the task of an employer to determine that a specific drug is causally related to harm-causing personality disorders. Not every controlled substance is equally likely to cause personality changes in every person in every case. The establishment of the causal link between the use of certain drugs and harm-causing personality disorders is not the province of the employer, but the province of experts studying the effects of drugs. The burden of proof is on the employer to establish that the substance being investigated has been independently connected with the relevant psychological impairment and then, predict on that basis that the specific employee's psychological judgment has been or will soon be impaired in such a way as to cause harm.

But even when this link is established, it would seem that less intrusive means could be used to detect the potential problems, rather than relying upon the assumption of a causal link. Psychological tests of judgment, perception and memory, for example, would be a less intrusive and more direct means for acquiring the relevant information which is, after all, the likelihood of causing harm and not the presence

of drugs *per se*. In short, drug testing even in these cases doesn't seem to be very effective in preventing harm on the spot.

Still, this does not mean it is not effective at all. Where it is most effective in preventing harm is in its getting people to stop using drugs or in identifying serious drug addiction. Or to put it another way, urinalysis and blood tests for drug use are most effective in preventing potential harm when they serve as a deterrent to drug use *before* it occurs, since it is very difficult to prevent harm by diagnosing drug use *after* it has occured but before the potentially harmful behavior takes place.

Drug testing can be an effective deterrent when there is regular or random testing of all employees. This will prevent harm by inhibiting (because of the fear of detection) drug use by those who are occasional users and those who do not wish to be detected.

It will probably not inhibit or stop the use by the chronic addicted user, but it will allow an employer to discover the chronic user or addict, assuming that the tests are accurately administered and reliably evaluated. If the chronic user's addiction would probably lead to harmful behavior of others, the harm is prevented by taking that user off the job. Thus regular or random testing will prevent harms done by deterring the occasional user and by detecting the chronic user.

There are six possibilities for such testing:

1. regularly scheduled testing of all employees;
2. regularly scheduled testing of randomly selected employees;
3. randomly scheduled testing of all employees;
4. randomly scheduled testing of randomly selected employees;
5. regularly scheduled testing of employees selected for probable cause; or finally,
6. randomly scheduled testing of employees selected for probable cause.

Only the last two seem morally acceptable as well as effective.

Obviously, randomly scheduled testing will be more effective than regularly scheduled testing in detecting the occasional user, because the occasional users can control their use to pass the tests, unless of course tests were given so often (a practice economically unfeasible) that they needed to stop together. Regular scheduling probably will detect the habitual or addicted user. Randomly selecting people to test is probably cheaper, as is random scheduling, but it is not nearly as effective as testing all. Besides, the random might miss some of the addicted altogether, and will not deter the risk takers as much as the risk aversive persons. It is, ironically, the former who are probably potentially more harmful.

But these are merely considerations of efficiency. We have said that testing without probable cause is unacceptable. Any type of regular testing of all employees is unacceptable. We have argued that testing employees without first establishing probable cause is an unjustifiable violation of employee privacy. Given this, and given the expense of general and regular testing of all employees (especially if this is done by responsible laboratories), it is more likely that random testing will be employed as the means of deterrence. But surely testing of randomly selected innocent employees is as intrusive to those tested as is regular testing. The argument that there will be fewer tests is correct on quantitative grounds, but qualitatively the intrusion and unacceptability are the same. The claim that employers should be allowed to sacrifice the well-being of (some few) innocent employees to deter (some equally few) potentially harmful employees seems, on the face of it, unfair. Just as we do not allow the state randomly to tap the telephones of just any citizen in order to prevent crime, so we ought not allow employers to drug test all employees randomly to prevent harm. To do so is again to treat innocent employees solely as a means to the end of preventing potential harm.

This leaves only the use of regular or random drug-testing as a deterrent in those cases where probable cause exists for believing that a particular employee poses a threat of harm. It would seem that in this case, the drug testing is acceptable. In such cases only the question of effectiveness remains: Are the standard techniques of urinalysis and blood-testing more effective means for preventing harms than alternatives such as dexterity tests? It seems they are

effective in different ways. The dexterity tests show immediately if someone is incapable of performing a task, or will perform one in such a way as to cause harm to others. The urinalysis and blood-testing will prevent harm indirectly by getting the occasional user to curtail their use, and by detecting the habitual or addictive user, which will allow the employer to either give treatment to the addictive personality or remove them from the job. Thus we can conclude that drug testing is effective in a limited way, but aside from inhibiting occasional users because of fear of detection, and discovering habitual users, it seems problematic that it does much to prevent harm that couldn't be achieved by other means.

Consider one final issue in the case of the occasional user. They are the drug users who do weigh the risks and benefits and who are physically and psychologically free to decide. The question in their case is not simply "will the likelihood of getting caught by urinalysis or blood-testing deter this individual from using drugs?" Given the benefits of psychological tests and dexterity tests described above, the question is "will the rational user be more deterred by urinalysis or blood-testing than by random psychological or dexterity tests?" And, if this is so, is this increase in the effectiveness of a deterrent sufficient to offset the increased expense and time required by drug tests?[9] We see no reason to believe that behavioral or judgment tests are not, or cannot be made to be, as effective in determining what an employer needs to know (i.e., that a particular employee may presently be a potential cause of harm). If the behavioral, dexterity and judgment tests can be as effective in determining a potential for harm, we see no reason to believe that they cannot be as effective a deterrent as drug tests. Finally, even if a case can be made for an increase in deterrent effect of drug testing, we are skeptical that this increased effectiveness will outweigh the increased inefficiencies.

In summary, we have seen that deterrence is effective at times and under certain conditions allows the sacrificing of the privacy rights of innocent employees to the future and speculative good of preventing harms to others. However, there are many ways to deter drug use when that deterrence is legitimate and desirable to prevent harm. But random testing, which seems the only practicable means which has an impact in preventing harm is the one which most offends workers rights to privacy and which is most intrusive of the rights of the innocent. Even when effective, drug testing as a deterrent must be checked by the rights of employees.

ILLEGALITY CONTENTION

At this point critics might note that the behavior which testing would try to deter is, after all, illegal. Surely this excuses any responsible employer from being overly protective of an employee's rights. The fact that an employee is doing something illegal should give the employer a right to that information about his private life. Thus, it is not simply that drug use might pose a threat of harm to others, but that it is an *illegal* activity that threatens others. But again, we would argue that illegal activity itself is irrelevant to job performance. At best *conviction* records might be relevant, but, of course, since drug tests are administered by private employers we are not only exploring the question of conviction, we are also ignoring the fact that the employee has not even been arrested for the alleged illegal activity.

Further, even if the due process protections and the establishment of guilt is acknowledged, it still does not follow that employers have a claim to know about all illegal activity on the part of their employees.

Consider the following example: Suppose you were hiring an auditor whose job required certifying the integrity of your firm's tax and financial records. Certainly, the personal integrity of this employee is vital to the adequate job performance. Would we allow the employer to conduct, with or without the employee's consent, an audit of the employee's own personal tax return? Certainly if we discover that this person has cheated on his/her own tax return we will have evidence of illegal activity that is relevant to this person's ability to do the job. Given one's own legal liability for filing falsified statements, the employee's illegal activity also

poses a threat to others. But surely, allowing private individuals to audit an employee's tax returns is too intrusive a means for discovering information about that employee's integrity. The government certainly would never allow this violation of an employee's privacy. It ought not to allow drug testing on the same grounds. Why tax returns should be protected in ways that urine, for example, is not, raises interesting questions of fairness. Unfortunately, this question would take us beyond the scope of this paper.

VOLUNTARINESS

A final problem that we also leave undeveloped concerns the voluntariness of employee consent. For most employees, being given the choice between submitting to a drug test and risking one's job by refusing an employer's request is not much of a decision at all. We believe that such decisions are less than voluntary and thereby would hold that employers cannot escape our criticisms simply by including within the employment contract a drug-testing clause.[10] Furthermore, there is reason to believe that those most in need of job security will be those most likely to be subjected to drug testing. Highly skilled, professional employees with high job mobility and security will be in a stronger position to resist such intrusions than will less skilled, easily replaced workers. This is why we should not anticipate surgeons and airline pilots being tested, and should not be surprised when public transit and factory workers are. A serious question of fairness arises here as well.

Drug use and drug testing seem to be our most recent social "crises." Politicians, the media, and employers expend a great deal of time and effort addressing this crisis. Yet, unquestionably, more lives, health, and money are lost each year to alcohol abuse than to marijuana, cocaine and other controlled substances. We are well-advised to be careful in considering issues that arise due to such selective social concern. We will let other social commentators speculate on the reasons why drug use has received scrutiny while other white-collar crimes and alcohol abuse are ignored. Our only concern at this point is that such selective prosecution suggests an arbitrariness that should alert us to questions of fairness and justice.

In summary, then, we have seen that drug use is not always job-relevant, and if drug use is not job relevant, information about it is certainly not job-relevant. In the case of performance it may be a cause of some decreased performance, but it is the performance itself that is relevant to an employee's position, not what prohibits or enables him to do the job. In the case of potential harm being done by an employee under the influence of drugs, the drug use seems job relevant, and in this case drug testing to prevent harm might be legitimate. But how this is practicable is another question. It would seem that standard motor dexterity or mental dexterity tests, immediately prior to job performance, are more efficacious ways of preventing harm, unless one concludes that drug use invariably and necessarily leads to harm. One must trust the individuals in any system in order for that system to work. One cannot police everything. It might work to randomly test people, to find drug users, and to weed out the few to forestall possible future harm, but are the harms prevented sufficient to over-ride the rights of privacy of the people who are innocent and to overcome the possible abuses we have mentioned? It seems not.

Clearly, a better method is to develop safety checks immediately prior to the performance of a job. Have a surgeon or a pilot or a bus driver pass a few reasoning and motor-skill tests before work. The cause of the lack of a skill, which lack might lead to harm, is really a secondary issue.

Drug Testing for Prospective Employees

Let's turn finally to drug testing during a pre-employment interview. Assuming the job description and responsibilities have been made clear, we can say that an employer is entitled to expect from a prospective employee whatever performance is agreed to in the employment contract. Of course, this will always involve risks, since the employer must make a judgment

about future performances. To lower this risk, employers have a legitimate claim to some information about the employee. Previous work experience, training, education, and the like are obvious candidates since they indicate the person's ability to do the job. Except in rare circumstances drug use itself is irrelevant for determining an employee's ability to perform. (Besides, most people who are interviewing know enough to get their systems clean if the prospective employee is going to test them.)

We suggest that an employer can claim to have an interest in knowing (a) whether or not the prospective employee *can* do the job and (b) whether there is reason to believe that once hired the employee *will* do the job. The first can be determined in fairly straightforward ways: past work experience, training, education, etc. Presumably past drug use is thought more relevant to the second question. But there are straightforward and less intrusive means than drug-testing for resolving this issue. Asking the employee "Is there anything that might prevent you from doing this job?" comes first to mind. Hiring the employee on a probationary period is another way. But to inquire about drug use here is to claim a right to know too much. It is to claim a right to know not only information about what an employee *can* do, but also a right to inquire into whatever background information *might* be (but not necessarily *is*) causally related to what an employee *will* do. But the range of factors that could be relevant here, from medical history to psychological dispositions to family plans, is surely too open-ended for an employee to claim as a *right* to know.

It might be responded that what an employee is entitled to expect is not a certain level of output, but a certain level of effort. The claim here would be that while drug use is only contingently related to what an employee *can* do, it is directly related to an employee's *motivation* to do the job. Drug use then is *de facto* relevant to the personal information that an employee is *entitled* to know.

But this involves an assumption mentioned above. The discussion so far has assumed that drugs will adversely affect job performance. However, some drugs are performance *enhancing* whether they are concerned with actual *output* or *effort.* The widespread use of steroids, pain-killers, and dexadrine among professional athletes are perhaps only the most publicized instances of performance enhancing drugs. (A teacher's use of caffeine before an early-morning class is perhaps a more common example.) More to the point, knowledge of drug use tells little about motivation. There are too many other variables to be considered. Some users are motivated and some are not. Thus the motivational argument is faulty.

We can conclude, then, that whether the relevant consideration for prospective employees is output or effort, knowledge of drug use will be largely irrelevant for predicting. Employers ought to be positivistic in their approach. They should restrict their information gathering to measurable behavior and valid predictions, (What has the prospect done? What can the prospect do? What has the prospect promised to do?) and not speculate about the underlying *causes* of this behavior. With a probationary work period always an option, there are sufficient non-intrusive means for limiting risks available to employers without having to rely on investigations into drug use.

In summary, we believe that drug use is information that is rightfully private and that only in exceptional cases can an employer claim a right to know about such use. Typically, these are cases in which knowledge of drug use could be used to prevent harm. However, even in those cases we believe that there are less intrusive and more effective means available than drug testing for gaining the information that would be necessary to prevent the harm. Thus, we conclude that drug testing of employees is rarely justified, and mostly inefficacious.

Notes

Versions of this paper were read to the Department of Philosophy at Southern Connecticut State University and to the Society of Business Ethics. The authors would like to thank those people, as well as Robert Baum and Norman Bowie, the editors of *Business and Professional Ethics Journal* for their many helpful comments. Professor Duska wishes to thank the Pew Memorial Trust for a grant providing released time to work on this paper.

1. *The New Republic,* March 31, 1986.
2. This trend primarily involves screening employees for such drugs as marijuana, cocaine, amphetamines, barbituates, and opiates (e.g., heroin, methadone and morphine). While alcohol is also a drug that can be abused in the workplace, it seldom is among the drugs mentioned in conjunction with employee testing. We believe that testing which proves justified for controlled substances will, *a fortiori,* be justified for alcohol as well.
3. "A Defense of Employee Rights," Joseph Des Jardins and John McCall, *Journal of Business Ethics,* Vol. 4, (1985). We should emphasize that our concern is with the *moral* rights of privacy for employees and not with any specific or prospective *legal* rights. Readers interested in pursuing the legal aspects of employee drug testing should consult: "Workplace Privacy Issues and Employee Screening Policies" by Richard Lehe and David Middlebrooks in *Employee Relations Law Journal* (Vol. 11, no.3) pp. 407–21; and "Screening Workers for Drugs: A Legal and Ethical Framework" by Mark Rothstein, in *Employee Relations Law Journal* (vol. 11, no. 3) pp. 422–36.
4. "Privacy, Polygraphs, and Work," George Brenkert, *Business and Professional Ethics Journal,* vol. 1, #1 (Fall 1981). For a more general discussion of privacy in the workplace see "Privacy in Employment" by Joseph DesJardins, in *Moral Rights in the Workplace* edited by Gertrude Ezorsky, (SUNY Press, 1987). A good resource for philosophical work on privacy can be found in "Recent Work on the Concept of Privacy" by W. A. Parent, in *American Philosophical Quarterly* (Vol. 20, Oct. 1983) pp. 341–56.
5. *U.S. News and World Report* Aug. 1983; *Newsweek* May 1983.
6. Obviously we are speaking here of harms that go beyond the simple economic harm which results from unsatisfactory job performance. These economic harms were discussed in the first argument above. Further, we ignore such "harms" as providing bad role-models for adolescents, harms often used to justify drug tests for professional athletes. We think it unreasonable to hold an individual responsible for the image he/she provides to others.
7. The philosophical literature on informed consent is often concerned with "informed consent" in a medical context. For an interesting discussion of informed consent in the workplace, see Mary Gibson, *Worker's Rights* (Rowman and Allanheld, 1983) especially pp. 13–14 and 74–75.
8. For a reiteration of this point and a concise argument against drug testing see Lewis L. Maltby, "Why Drug Testing is a Bad Idea.", *Inc.* June, 1987, pp. 152–153. "But the fundamental flaw with drug testing is that it tests for the wrong thing. A realistic program to detect workers whose condition puts the company or other people at risk would test for the condition that actually creates the danger. The reason drunk or stoned airline pilots and truck drivers are dangerous is their reflexes, coordination, and timing are deficient. This impairment could come from many situations—drugs, alcohol, emotional problems—the list is almost endless. A serious program would recognize that the real problem is workers' impairment, and test for that. Pilots can be

tested in flight simulators. People in other jobs can be tested by a trained technician in about 20 minutes—at the job site." p. 152.

9. This argument is structurally similar to the argument against the effectiveness of capital punishment as a deterrent offered by Justice Brennen in the Supreme Court's decision in *Furman v Georgia.*

10. It might be argued that since we base our critique upon the contractual relationship between employers and employees, our entire position can be underminded by a clever employer who places within the contract a privacy waiver for drug tests. A full answer to this would require an account of the free and rational subject that the contract model presupposes. While acknowledging that we need such an account to prevent just any contract from being morally legitimate, we will have to leave this debate to another time. Interested readers might find "The Moral Contract between Employers and Employees" by Norman Bowie, in *The Work Ethic in Business,* edited by Hoffman and Wyly (Oelgeschlager and Gunn, 1981) pp. 195–202, helpful here.

David B. Resnik

Genetic Privacy in Employment

I. Introduction

Recent and projected advances in molecular genetics and in genetic screening technology will bring us a wealth of information regarding genetic diseases, abnormalities, and predispositions. This new knowledge will most certainly have positive effects on medicine and health care, but it could also have detrimental consequences for privacy. Employers, insurance companies, governments, and other agencies will try to gain access to genetic information in order to increase profits and efficiency and decrease liabilities and risks. In order to insure that these advances in genetics do not compromise privacy, it is important to formulate a policy regarding the use of genetic information before our brave new science and technology gets out of control. In this paper, I shall take some steps toward that goal by proposing some guidelines for the disclosure of genetic information in employment. I shall argue that the moral right to privacy allows employees to restrict their employers' access to genetic information in most situations, but that

From David B. Resnik, "Genetic Privacy in Employment." *Public Affairs Quarterly,* Vol. 7, No. 1, 1993. Reprinted by permission.

employers may invade an employee's genetic privacy[1] *only if* such an invasion meets criteria for a legitimate (or justified) invasion.

II. The Right to Privacy

It is not my aim in this paper to defend a definition of privacy or explore the moral basis of privacy. Instead, I shall adopt W. A. Parent's approach to privacy and apply it to the issues at hand. I recognize that some readers may disagree with Parent's views, but they do provide a clear and cogent framework for thinking about genetic privacy.[2] According to Parent, the right to privacy depends on a prior conception of privacy. Privacy, for Parent, "is the condition of not having undocumented personal knowledge about one possessed by others."[3] The key notions in this definition of privacy are "personal knowledge" and "documentation." Parent characterizes personal knowledge as information about an individual that most individuals choose to reveal only to family members and close friends, if they reveal it to anyone at all. What counts as personal knowledge may vary from culture to culture and from person to person. Not all personal knowledge is private, however, because some personal information belongs to the public record; it is information one can find in newspapers, court proceedings, and other public documents.[4]

Given this conception of privacy, Parent defines the moral right to privacy as a "right not to become the victim of wrongful invasions [of privacy]."[5] The moral right to privacy is not the right to not have privacy invaded, since there are legitimate invasions of privacy; it is a right not to have privacy *wrongly* invaded. If one assumes that moral rights imply moral obligations, it follows that we have an obligation to avoid wrongfully invading privacy. So what counts as a wrongful invasion of privacy? For the purposes of this paper, I shall define a wrongful invasion as one that is not legitimate (or justified). A legitimate invasion is an invasion of privacy which meets *all* of the following criteria (or necessary conditions); a wrongful one does not:[6]

a. *Justification.* Good reasons or purposes justify the invasion.
b. *Relevancy.* The information obtained by the invasion is relevant to the reasons or purposes of the invasion.
c. *Intrusiveness.* The invasion uses the least intrusive means of obtaining the information.[7]
d. *Specificity.* The invasion is discriminate and has procedural restraints and safeguards.[8]
e. *Secrecy.* The invasion has post-invasion safeguards to prevent the unwarranted disclosure of information.

III. PRIVACY IN EMPLOYMENT

Given that we have a right to privacy, how does employment affect this right? This question raises a number issues concerning employee rights and the employee-employer relationship. Again, I will not enter a lengthy discussion of these issues, but I will adopt an influential view in order to posit a conceptual framework for addressing the question of genetic privacy in employment. To this end, I shall utilize a contractarian model of the employee-employer relationship and employee rights.[9] In many respects my views will resemble George Brenkert's discussion of the use of polygraph tests in employment, since he also employs a contractarian model.[10]

According to the contractarian model, the employee-employer relationship is a business contract between consenting adults. In the contract, the employee agrees to provide the employer with goods and services in return for money, goods, or other forms of compensation. In addition, the employer may entrust the employee with tools, property, information, and various goods in order to enable her to do her job. This contract will be valid only if a) both parties are responsible and autonomous; and b) both parties respect the rights claims of other contractees. People do not loose their right to privacy when they gain or seek employment; on the contrary, people cannot become employees unless they have rights and these rights are respected.

Employers can legitimately gain access to personal information about their employees (or prospective employees), according to the contractarian approach, in order to insure the validity of the employee-employer contract. Employers need to have this information in order to determine whether their employees will be able to satisfactorily fulfill the duties and responsibilities outlined by the employee's job description in the contract. Employers can legitimately gain access to certain kinds of information about their employees, provided that they continue to respect their employees' privacy rights. In other words, employers can invade employee privacy only when this invasion would qualify as a legitimate invasion of privacy according to the criteria listed above. On the other hand, if an employee (or prospective employee) refuses to disclose certain kinds of information to her employer (or prospective employer), and this disclosure would qualify as a legitimate invasion, then her employer is justified in refusing to hire her (or in firing her).

Having established a conceptual framework for discussing privacy in employment, I am in a better position to answer the central question of this paper: what are the conditions for an employer's legitimate invasion of an employee's genetic privacy? Before answering this question, I need to discuss some facts about genetic information and how it is acquired, since these facts will help us determine what constitutes a legitimate invasion of genetic privacy.

IV. GENETIC INFORMATION

Nature vs. Nurture. Some traits, such as sex, are determined entirely by our genes, but most traits are determined by both genetic and environmental factors. Although one might claim that possession of a certain gene gives individuals a predisposition for developing a disease (or trait), whether this predisposition is realized depends on environmental factors.[11]

Causal vs. Statistical Connections. The causal pathway from genetic information, encoded in DNA, to an adult human being is incredibly complex, involving thousands of different genes and millions of different chemical reactions.[12] Most traits are not determined by one gene or one environmental factor, but by many different genes and environmental factors. Given this complex interplay of genes and the environment, we can rarely establish a strong causal connection between possessing a genetic characteristic and developing a phenotypic trait; more often than not we must settle for a statistical connection. We may be able to show that possessing a gene gives one a high probability or risk of developing a trait, but it is very difficult to show that a gene causes or determines a trait.

Timing. Although many genes produce their effects throughout a person's entire life, other genes produce their effects during specific times in a person's life span.[13] The important consequence of this fact is that a piece of genetic information might indicate that a person is likely to develop a disease at some time in their life, but this period may not coincide with their period of employment.

Treatment. We can use genetic information to cure or help people, rather than to stigmitize them or seal their fate. As we learn more about human genetics, we also learn how to treat (or prevent) genetic disease. In the future, we may be able to diagnose and treat a wide variety of genetically based illnesses, such as heart disease, diabetes, and cancer.[14]

Testing. In the past, the only way to acquire genetic information about a person would be to do a pedigree analysis of their family tree. However, pedigree analysis is unreliable and limited because it is an indirect method of detecting the presence of genes.[15] Due to advances in biotech-

nology, we now have a more reliable and powerful method for determining an individual's genetic constitution, genetic screening. Genetic screening is more reliable and powerful than predigree analysis because it allows scientists to directly examine an individual's genetic material through microscopy or biochemical analysis. In principle, one can give genetic screening tests during any stage of an individual's development, including the fetal stage. Genetic screening is still in its infancy, and it is not perfectly reliable or accurate, but in the foreseeable future it should be possible to use this technology to produce an entire genetic blueprint for any individual—the total gene screen.[16]

V. Legitimate Invasions of Genetic Privacy

Given this brief discussion of genetic information, I am in a position to apply my conceptual framework to the issue of genetic privacy in employment. My main thesis in this section is that invasions of genetic privacy are legitimate *only if* they meet all five of the criteria for invasion discussed in section II. If an invasion of genetic privacy fails to meet any one of these criteria, then it is a wrongful invasion. In order to defend my main thesis, I shall discuss each of criterion in the context of human genetics.

(1) Justification

The first criteria that an invasion needs to meet is that it must be done for good reasons or purposes. An employer's primary reason for invading genetic privacy is to validate the employee-employer contract. An employer may need to acquire information about an employee's genetic constitution in order to insure that she is able to satisfactorily fulfill her duties and obligations outlined in the job description. Since this reason already justifies the disclosure of many types of information to employers, such as education, work record, and so on, it could also be used to justify the disclosure of genetic information, provided that other conditions are met. This primary justification for invading genetic privacy can be strengthened by added concerns about worker health and safety, the welfare of others, and health care costs. However, concerns about worker health and safety or health care costs, cannot, by themselves, serve as good reasons for invading privacy; they must be combined with other reasons for to provide a sound justification for invading privacy. (I will provide more argument for this position in Section VI.)

(2) Relevancy

Assuming that the primary justification for invading genetic privacy is validation of the employee-employer contract, then the information sought must be relevant to this purpose. In other words, invasions of genetic privacy are legitimate provided that the information sought is job-relevant. Can genetic information ever be job-relevant? My preliminary answer to this question is "sometimes yes," although I hasten to add that the concept of "job-relevancy" is extremely context-dependent: it varies according to the job-description and the type of information sought.

Despite these misgivings, I do not think we must settle for a case-by-case approach to relevancy. My earlier discussion of genetic information should be useful in formulating some general guidelines for determining whether a piece of genetic information is job-relevant. Genetic information is job-relevant if and only the following conditions are met:

1. Possessing the genetic characteristic in question gives one a statistically significant task of not satisfactorily performing duties outlined by the job-description.
2. The characteristic is likely to produce its phenotypic effects during the employee's period of employment.
3. The characteristic's effects cannot be satisfactorily altered, modified, or treated through medicine or therapy.

The conditions are based, in large part, on the nature of genetic information. Condition (1) requires that there be a sound scientific basis for seeking the genetic information. As discussed in section IV, it is rarely the case that one can establish a strong causal connection between possessing a genetic characteristic and manifesting a certain trait. But given the current state of molecular genetics, we can frequently establish at least a statistical connection (or risk) between possessing a genetic characteristic and developing a trait.

The next question that naturally arises is, "what is a statistically significant (or relevant) connection (or risk)?" Since one cannot answer this query without more information about the job and the genetic characteristic in question, I will not answer it here. But I will make a few remarks about statistical significance and genetic risk factors. In evaluating genetic risk factors, we should treat them no differently than other risk factors, such as lifestyle, attitude, and health. We are justified in focusing on genetic risk factors only when they carry a higher risk than other factors which might also be job-relevant. If we do not treat all risk factors equally, we will be unjustly discriminating against people on the basis of genetic characteristics.

Condition (2) is important because genetic characteristics that do not manifest themselves during an employee's period of employment should not be considered job-relevant. For example, scientists have speculated that Alzheimer's disease may have a genetic basis. But since this disease usually does not manifest itself until most employees have retired, employers are not justified in screening for an Alzheimer's gene (if there is such a gene).

Condition (3) is important because if the effects a genetic characteristic can be treated (i.e. prevented, ameliorated, or satisfactorily overcome), then the characteristic should not be job-relevant. Often people who have genetic diseases can lead healthy, normal lives with proper care and treatment. People who may have treatable genetic diseases may wish to voluntarily participate in genetic screening to protect their own health, but employers are not justified in invading genetic privacy in order to find out about treatable diseases.

(3) Intrusiveness

This condition for a legitimate invasion can be easily satisfied, since employers can use genetic screening, a technique which is the least intrusive (available) means of gaining genetic information.

(4) Specificity

Although this condition is not as easily satisfied as condition (3), it can be met provided that appropriate safeguards are in place. In performing a genetic screening test on an individual, the screener will have access to a wealth of genetic information. Employers can make their genetic screening discriminate by instructing testers to ignore the excess information and focus on the information in question.

(5) Secrecy

This condition, like condition (4), can also be met, provided that appropriate safeguards are in place. While no one can prevent all information leaks, employers can minimize leaks by enacting policies to protect the secrecy of genetic information. Information from genetic tests should be distributed on a need to know basis, and those who do not need the information should not have access to it. The people who should have access to the genetic information include people who make personnel decisions, and especially the person who has been tested. If you submit to a genetic test, then you have the right know the results of the test, since these results may provide you with important health information.

VI. DISCUSSION OF HYPOTHETICAL CASES

The following hypothetical cases serve to illustrate my views on genetic privacy and allow me to address some pertinent objections.

Case 1: The Narcolepsy Gene. Suppose it is discovered that a small percentage of the population possess a gene, gene *X*, that makes them highly susceptible to narcolepsy. People with gene *X* have a significant risk of falling asleep during normal waking hours, and there is no effective treatment for this disorder. A major airline company, Safe Air, has had some trouble with pilots falling asleep, and narcolepsy has become an important safety concern. The company decides to require its pilots (and prospective pilots) to submit to a genetic screening test for gene *X*. The test will focus only on gene *X*, and

the company will provide safeguards to protect the secrecy of the results.

In this case, Safe Air's invasion of privacy is legitimate since the invasion meets all the criteria for legitimacy. The airline has a strong justification for genetic screening: it wants to validate the employee contract and insure the safety of its employees and customers. The information sought is relevant to the purpose of the invasion: people with gene *X* run a high risk of succumbing to narcolepsy, and narcoleptics cannot satisfactorily pilot airplanes.

Case 2: The Cancer Gene. In the second case, suppose that a chemical company, Acme Industries, exposes its workers to a small amount of a carcinogenic substance, carconine, during the production of plastics. Most people run a very small risk (0.1% chance) of contracting lung cancer when exposed to a small amount of carconine, but a small percentage of the population possesses a gene, gene *Y*, which gives them a significant risk (33% chance) of developing lung cancer after being exposed to carconine. Also suppose that Acme Industries has taken all reasonable steps to avoid exposing its employees to carconine; in order to further reduce carconine exposure it would have to stop producing plastic, its most profitable operation. Acme Industries decides to institute a genetic screening program for gene *Y* in order to protect its employees and reduce health care costs. The program focuses only on gene *Y*, and steps are taken to maintain secrecy.

Although this case is not as clear-cut as the first one, it still meets the criteria for a legitimate invasion of privacy. Relevancy, intrusiveness, specificity, and secrecy would not seem to be at issue in the case, but the justification would appear to be controversial. The problem with the justification is that the invasion is not done for the purpose of validating the employee-employer contract, assuming that lung cancer does not affect one's job performance until it reahes its final stages.[17] The two stated reasons for invading genetic privacy are to protect employees and to reduce health care costs. Although neither of these reasons, by itself, could justify an invasion of privacy, taken together, they form a good justification for invading privacy in this case.

Some might object that Acme Industries should improve the safety of the workplace instead of screening its employees, but we have already supposed that it has done its best to minimize exposure to carconine. In this example, the only way Acme Industries can reduce carconine exposure is to completely shut down one of its important operations, which could be considered an unreasonable cost. (Given the enormous cost of genetic screening, it is likely that most companies will try to improve the work environment before resorting to genetic screening.)

Some might object that Acme Industries is adopting a paternalistic policy: employees, being autonomous decision-makers, should be able to decide whether they want to expose themselves to dangers or harms. However, one might argue that autonomy can be restricted in this case because employees who do not submit to a genetic screening tests are not fully informed, and hence, not fully autonomous.[18] A person who is not fully autonomous with respect to a certain kind of decision loses the right to make that decision for themselves. Furthermore, one might argue that autonomy can be restricted in this case because the employee who refuses a test is not the only person who could be harmed: the company (as whole) and other employees could be harmed. If an employee gets lung cancer, she could create enormous health care costs for the company, and she might even bring a lawsuit against the company. These costs will result in diminished profit for the company and fewer benefits for other employers.

Case 3: The Heart Attack Gene. Suppose we discover that individuals with gene Z run a high risk of having a heart attack by the time they are 40 years old, but their risk is not significantly greater than the risk run by individuals without gene Z who lead an unhealthy lifestyle (smoke, drink, eat meat, etc . . .) Nevertheless, a toy manufacturer, Fun Industries, decides to screen potential employees for gene Z for the purpose of avoiding health care costs and maxmizing its investment in training costs. It will make sure that its screening program is discriminate and protects secrecy.

Can Fun Industries legitimately request individuals to take a test for gene Z? My answer is a definite "no." Fun Industries' main reason for invading privacy in this case is to minimize health care and training costs. Information about gene Z could not be considered necessary to validate the employment contract or protect employees. Employees with gene Z should be able to do their work as well as people without gene Z, and they will impose no significant risks or hardships on others.

One might object that health can be part of a person's job description and that the purpose of invasion is to validate the employment contract. However, allowing health to be a part of a person's job description would create a slippery slope that would eventually lead to discrimination and bias against the unhealthy.[19] Allowing genetic screening in this case opens the door to a broad range of cases in which employers seek to discriminate against individuals deemed "health risks." Allowing genetic screening in cases 1 and 2, on the other hand, would not result in such disastrous consequences. In cases 1 and 2 the screening is done for highly specific reasons directly related to job performance or genuine safety concerns, while in case 3 the screening is done for more general reasons relating to cost minimization and profit. Screening in cases 1 and 2 is not based on reasons which could also justify screening in a wide range of cases, while screening in cases 3 is based on reasons which could justify screening in a wide range of cases. Hence, allowing screening in cases 1 and 2 would probably not lead us down a "slippery slope" toward unjust discrimination and stigmatization.[20]

VI. CONCLUSION: GENETIC PRIVACY GUIDELINES

Given this analysis of privacy, genetic information, and hypothetical cases, I draw the following general conclusions (or guidelines) for genetic privacy in employment. Employers may legitimately gain access to genetic information *only if* all of the following conditions are met:

1. The information is sought to (a) validate the employment contract, or (b) to protect employees and minimize costs (or both a and b).

2. There is a sound statistical connection between possessing the genetic characteristic in question and manifesting a disorder/trait relevant to the purpose of the invasion.

3. The disorder/trait in question manifests itself during the employee's period of employment.

4. The disorder/trait in question is not currently treatable.

5. A scientifically valid and non-intrusive kind of test is used, e.g., genetic screening.

6. The employers adopt safeguards to insure that the tests are discriminate and to protect secrecy.

Many other questions need to be answered before we can establish a sound policy regarding the disclosure of genetic information in employment, such as "When is information statistically relevant?," "What counts as taking reasonable measures to improve the work place?," "How can ____? protect secrecy?," and so on. I will not explore these questions in much depth here, but I think these guidelines serve as a good first step toward a sound policy on genetic privacy in employment.[21]

Notes

1. By "genetic privacy" I mean privacy relating to genetic information.
2. This paper will focus on moral, not legal aspects of privacy. The points I make in this paper should not be affected by metaethical disputes concerning the foundation of moral rights. Although I am using the term "rights" in this paper, I do not appeal to a theory of natural rights. It should make no difference to my discussion if its turns out that rights are derived from other moral concepts, such as duties or obligations.
3. W. A. Parent, "Privacy, Morality, and the Law," *Philosophy and Public Affairs*, vol. 12 (1983), p. 269.
4. This point brings up some interesting questions about documentation. For instance, should we consider in-

formation that appears in *The National Enquirer* to be properly documented?
5. Parent, *op. cit.*, p. 273.
6. I have derived these criteria from Parent's position; these are not his exact words.
7. I will not attempt to define "intrusive" but I shall assume that we can judge whether some technique is more or less intrusive than another technique.
8. I will also not attempt to define the word "discriminate" but I will assume that we can tell the difference between discriminate and indiscriminate methods. Indiscriminate methods yield much more information than is desired or needed, while discriminate methods can pinpoint specific types of information.
9. See Norman E. Bowie, "The Moral Contract Between Employer and Employee," in Tom Beauchamp and Norman Bowie (eds.), *Ethical Theory and Business* (Englewood Cliffs, NJ: Prentice-Hall, 1983), pp. 150–161.
10. George Brenkert, "Privacy, Polygraphs, and Work," *Business and Professional Ethics Journal*, vol. 1 (1981), pp. 19–35.
11. David Suzuki and Peter Knudson, *Genethics* (Cambridge, MA: Harvard University Press, 1989), pp. 25–45.
12. Ibid., pp. 48–70.
13. Ibid., pp. 70–94.
14. Ibid., pp. 167–68.
15. Ibid., pp. 164–165.
16. Ibid., pp. 165–176.
17. If lung cancer does significantly affect job performance, then Acme Industries' justification would be stronger.
18. Gerald Dworkin, *The Theory and Practice of Autonomy* (New York: Cambridge University Press, 1988), pp. 17–20.
19. One of the ironies of this case (and others like it) is that the employment discrimination would result from a particular way of allocating health care resources, i.e. via employer-provided health insurance. This type of discrimination probably would not occur in countries that have socialized medicine.
20. For more on slippery slope arguments, see Leon Kass, *Toward a More Natural Science: Biology and Human Affairs* (New York: The Free Press, 1985).
21. I would like to thank Ed Sherline and an anomymous referee for *Public Affairs Quarterly* for helpful comments. Research for this paper was supported, in part, by a grant from the University of Wyoming.

QUESTIONS

1. Lippke considers the argument that the autonomy of owners and stockholders is at risk if they cannot protect their property by instructing management to gather information about employees. His reply is that autonomy is furthered by invoking the notion of a right to privacy, since respecting the right to privacy does not provide individuals with increased control over the lives of others. Invoking the notion of property rights, however, allows individuals increased control over the lives of others and thus, does not further autonomy. Is he correct in asserting that the ability to keep information secret, e.g. whether or not an employee uses drugs, has no

potential to curtail the autonomy of others? Why or why not?

2. In response to the argument that health and safety are even more essential than privacy for the preservation and exercise of autonomy, and hence that drug testing can be justified on the basis of health and safety considerations, Lippke responds that we cannot address this question in isolation from the larger issue of the role of the current organization of work in generating dangerous behavior. He suggests that a more humane workplace might lessen or eliminate the need to override privacy concerns in the interests of health and safety. Given that such a reorganization of work has not yet occurred, to what degree is it legitimate to override privacy concerns to protect health and safety in the workplace as it now exists?

3. DesJardins and Duska argue that one of the necessary conditions to justify drug testing of employees is that the potential for clear and present harm exists. How would you define the "potential for clear and present harm"? Could an worker under the influence of drugs on an auto assembly line conceivably present a potential for clear and present harm?

4. Drug testing might be viewed not primarily as a means of detecting impaired job performance, but rather as a way to verify its occurrence. If drug testing can be made accurate, might it be legitimately used as a means to verify what might otherwise be regarded as the subjective and perhaps unreliable impression of a manager or supervisor? Explain.

5. Resnik claims that genetic information is job-relevant if and only if the following conditions are met:

a. Possessing the genetic characteristic in question gives one a statistically significant risk of not satisfactorily performing duties outlined by the job-description.

b. The characteristic is likely to produce its phenotypic effects during the employee's period of employment.

c. The characteristic's effects cannot be satisfactorily altered, modified, or treated through medicine or therapy.

Suppose that conditions (a) and (b) pertain, but that the characteristic's effect is treatable through medicine or therapy. Suppose further, that although the characteristic can be satisfactorily treated, the treatment is so expensive that the potential employee cannot afford it. How ought the company conduct itself in deciding whether or not to hire the potential employee?

6. Resnik argues in Case 2 that an individual who refused to submit to a test to reveal whether she possessed a genetic disposition for lung cancer could be viewed as infringing on the autonomy of fellow employees, inasmuch as she could create enormous health costs they would have to help bear. In Case 3 he argues that health is not relevant to a person's job description, since it would create a slippery slope that would lead to discrimination and bias against the unhealthy. Are these two statements consistent? How would you defend your view.

CASE STUDY 4:1 DRUG TESTING AND THE REFUSE COLLECTOR[1]

In the spring of 1990 Mr. Halischuk had been employed as a refuse helper by the city of Winnipeg for approximately five and a half years. As part of a crew consisting of a driver and one or two helpers, his job was to pick up refuse and load it into a rear collector, which has a compactor in the back of the hopper. In performing this job, it is important that the helper exhibit good judgment, since the potential for harm is great if individuals are not clear of the compactor during operation.

On the morning of May 1, 1990, Halischuk was driven by another employee in the city refuse truck to Halischuk's home where they picked up three bottles of beer. While in the truck, they consumed the beer and smoked two marijuana cigarettes.

Upon this incident coming to light, Halischuk confirmed a lengthy history of marijuana use and that he had previously used marijuana during working hours and before starting work.

Halischuk was suspending pending a discipline hearing on June 4, 1990. During the intervening five weeks, he attended a three-week out-patient rehabilitation program for drug use. He also apologized to his district supervisor and made clear his intention to stay clear of drugs.

G. K. Stewart, director of operations at the city, was impressed with Halischuk's sincerity and cooperation, but was concerned by the issue of workplace safety. Unlike alcohol, drug usage is difficult to detect and is often not apparent until there is a serious addiction. Without revealing Halischuk's identity, Stewart consulted with Dr. William Davis, a Ph.D in psychology and manager of employee occupations safety and health unit.

Davis was of the view that the facts indicated a drug dependence, if not an addiction. He recommended random testing, in order to eliminate the possibility of the user planning around the testing. He suggested that mandatory testing was a "win-win" situation for both parties, since it gave the employee an opportunity to retain his job, yet addressed the employer's legitimate concerns over safety.

Stewart decided that he would require Halischuk to submit to random drug testing for a period of one year and that Halischuk's continuing employment would be contingent upon not testing positive for drug use. The test involved would only indicate the presence of drugs, it would not indicate whether Halischuk was impaired at the time of testing. Periodic usage on weekend or outside work hours could cause a positive result at the time of testing.

The union protested this decision maintaining that the intrusion into Halischuk's privacy was not justified. It argued that not only was the process of taking urine samples a violation of privacy, but that the nature of the test illegitimately regulated Halischuk's private life for the period he was subject to testing.

CASE STUDY QUESTIONS

1. Should Halischuk's voluntary participation in a rehabilitation program have any bearing on Stewart's decision? Why or why not?
2. Should Halischuk's admission of other delinquent incidents have any bearing on Stewart's decision? How would you defend your view?
3. Was it right for the union to protest Stewart's decision? How would you argue in support of your view?

CASE STUDY 4:2 PUBLIC SAFETY AND THE RIGHT TO PRIVACY[2]

James Hennessey worked for Coastal Eagle Point Oil Company in Westville, New Jersey as an at-will employee in its oil refinery. His job was what is known as a "lead pumper." It consisted of supervising the "gaugers" who blend gasoline with various additives and manage the flow of petroleum products through the refinery. The gaugers take their directions from the lead pumper who translates orders and instructions into gauge levels the gaugers then set. The job of lead pumper carries a high degree of responsibility, since there is little direct supervision of the lead pumper, and misjudgment on his or her part can result in spills with the potential for major explosions and environmental damage.

When Coastal Eagle acquired the refinery in 1985, it conducted physical examinations, including drug tests, on all employees. At this time, Hennessey tested negative for drug use. Coastal Eagle also issued a written policy in which it prohibited the on-premise use of alcohol, drugs, and controlled substances. It also required that employees advise their supervisors if they had occasion to use medication that could impair judgment or job performance. Further, it notified employees that at any time they might be required to give a urine or blood sample to determine compliance with the policy. Part of Coastal Eagle's policy at this time was that it would help employees who voluntarily disclosed drug problems.

After discovering evidence of on-site marijuana use in January 1986, Coastal Eagle decided to conduct random urine testing in the spring. It chose urine testing on the basis that it would be less intrusive than blood testing. It also took steps to ensure that the testing was truly random, that the samples would not be counterfeited, that the samples would not be tested for physiological characteristics other than those indicating drug use, and that positive results be confirmed by a separate test. It did not, however, notify employees that the tests would be conducted or describe the methodology that would be used. Neither did it directly notify non-management employees that it was rescinding its informal policy of allowing those who tested positive to avoid termination through entering a rehabilitation program. Apparently its expectation was that non-management employees would learn of this change in informal policy through the chain of command.

Hennessey was randomly chosen for testing and his urine tested positive for marijuana and diazepam, the active ingredient in Valium. He neither challenged the accuracy of the results nor suggested he had medical reasons justifying the use of diazepam. Coastal Eagle dismissed him.

Hennessey brought suit against Coastal Eagle. He alleged that the company had violated his constitutional right of privacy under New Jersey law.

He also argued that urine tests detect only drug use, not degree of impairment, and some other means of testing, either by observation or performance, would be both more effective and less intrusive.

CASE STUDY QUESTIONS

1. Hennessey's immediate supervisor evaluated Hennessey's work as "above average," stating that his job "always got done well." Given this,

should Hennessey have been dismissed or simply reprimanded?
2. Do you think that the claim that drug tests detect only the use of drugs and not actual impairment is relevant to the questions of whether drug tests should be allowed?

Notes

1. Selected from *City of Winnipeg and Canadian Union of Public Employees, Local 500* as found in *Labour Arbitration Cases*, Vol. 23, 4th series, 1991, pp. 441–44.
2. Based on *Hennessey v. Coastal Eagle Point Oil Co.* 609 Atlantic Reporter, 2nd Series 11 (N.J. 1992).

FOR FURTHER READING

1. George G. Brenkert, "Privacy, Polygraphs and Work," *Business and Professional Ethics Journal* Vol. 1, No. 1, 1981, pp. 19–35.

2. Gertrude Ezorsky, ed., *Moral Rights in the Workplace* (Albany: State University of New York Press, 1987).

3. Julie Inness, "Information, Access, or Intimate Decisions About One's Actions? The Content of Privacy," *Public Affairs Quarterly* Vol. 5, No. 3, July 1991 pp. 227–242.

4. Jeffery L. Johnson, "A Theory of the Nature and Value of Privacy," *Public Affairs Quarterly*, Vol. 6, No. 3, July 1992, pp. 271–288.

5. Alan Westin, *Privacy and Freedom* (New York: Atheneum Publishers, 1976).

Chapter Five

SEXUAL HARASSMENT

Introduction

A good definition should be neither too narrow, excluding what should be included, nor too broad, including what should be excluded. With respect to defining sexual harassment, this proves to be no easy matter. Initially, at least, when we first think of sexual harassment, we probably think of what seem to be clear-cut examples, e.g. a male supervisor threatening a female subordinate with dismissal if she does not grant him sexual favors. But even in cases of what seem to be obvious instances of sexual harassment, it is not always easy to articulate the precise grounds for our opinion. Also, we are in danger of constructing a definition that is too narrow if we concentrate only on dramatic and straightforward examples. What is needed is a definition which not only clearly captures obvious instances of sexual harassment, but also provides guidance in more ambigious cases.

With regard to the workplace, the courts have treated sexual harassment as a form of discrimination and distinguished two types. The first, *quid pro quo,* occurs when sexual favors are made the condition of employment opportunities. The second occurs when a sexually hostile environment affects an employee's ability to function effectively. The *quid pro quo* form of sexual harassment is easiest to define, though even here the courts have insisted that it must be shown that the victim suffered a tangible economic loss. It is a far more difficult task to define what constitutes a sexually hostile environment and establish its effect upon an employee.

What is clear is that the legal issues surrounding sexual harassment cannot be resolved independently of the moral issues surrounding it. What constitutes an implicit threat? Can sexual harassment be judged to have occurred only if the victim has suffered a tangible loss? Can one person unintentionally harass another? Questions such as these must be addressed if the law is to be just and fair both in theory and application.

The readings for this chapter reveal the diversity of views that exists as regards defining sexual harassment. Edmund Wall, in his article "The Definition of Sexual Harassment," defends the view that sexual harassment is to be defined primarily in terms of intention. He attempts to refute the view that sexual harassment can be defined in terms of behavior. His argument is that physically identical actions may be distinguished on the basis of motive. A "sensual touch" might be physically indistinguishable from a "friendly touch," yet one might constitute sexual harassment and the other not. Wall would admit that, especially in more extreme instances, behavior can often be an indicator of motive, but he would insist that motive is the essential element in judging the morality of an action.

For Wall, sexual harassment amounts to violating a person's privacy rights. What is immoral in sexual harassment is not what is proposed, but the inappropriateness of the approach. The sexual harasser engages in intimate communication in a manner and context which does not respect the dignity and autonomy of the victim.

Anita Superson takes quite a different approach in her article "A Feminist Definition of Sexual Harassment." She defines sexual harassment as "any behavior (verbal or physical) caused by a person, A, in the dominant class directed at another, B, in the subjugated class, that expresses and perpetuates the attitude that B or members of B's sex is/are inferior because of their sex, thereby causing harm to either B and/or members of B's sex." Underlying this definition is the conviction that instances of sexual harassment must be viewed not primarily in terms of harm to the immedi-

ate victim, but rather as attacks upon all women.

A consequence of this definition, and in sharp contrast to Wall's view, is that the question of motive is not central. According to Superson, a man may sexually harass a woman without ever intending to. Also irrelevant is the question of whether the victim finds the behavior in question offensive. A woman may be so unaware of her oppression that she does not find harassing behavior offensive. A further implication of this definition, and one to which Superson is careful to draw attention, is that assuming men are dominant in society, it is impossible for women to sexually harass men.

In our final reading on this topic, "Sexual Harassment: Offers and Coercion," Nancy Tuana discusses the difficult issue of what constitutes a coercive offer. Standard accounts of coercion suggest that only actions which involve threats of harm can be viewed as coercive. How then, can promises of rewards for sexual favors be taken as coercive? If, as Tuana insists, sexual harassment is to be defined in terms of the coercion of sexual activity, this seems to rule out attempts to procure sexual favors by offers of rewards as constituting sexual harassment.

Her answer is that standard accounts of coercion are deficient, inasmuch as they do not take into account the important issue of the context in which offers of rewards for sexual favors take place. They ignore, for example, the fact that a common response to a refusal of a sexual advance is to feel hurt and upset and that this frequently leads to a desire to retaliate. They thus fail to consider the very real possibility that the rejection of a sexual proposal may cause a threat to come into existence, even though no such threat existed initially. Tuana's proposal is that offers of rewards for sexual favors which involve no initial threat or intention to harm can nevertheless be coercive if it is reasonable to believe that their denial will cause retaliation.

Edmund Wall

The Definition of Sexual Harassment

As important as current managerial, legal and philosophical definitions of sexual harassment are, many of them omit the interpersonal features which define the concept. Indeed, the mental states of the perpetrator and the victim are the essential defining elements. In this essay arguments are presented against mere behavior descriptions of sexual harassment, definitions formulated in terms of the alleged discriminatory and coercive effects of a sexual advance, and the federal legal definition which omits reference to relevant mental states. It is argued that sexual harassment is essentially a form of invasive communication that violates a victim's privacy rights. A set of jointly necessary and sufficient conditions of sexual harassment are defended which purport to capture the more subtle instances of sexual harassment while circumventing those sexual advances that are not sexually harassive. [If *X* is a *necessary condition* of *Y* then the absence of *X* guarantees the absence of *Y*. Note, however, that the presence of *X* does not guarantee the presence of *Y*. For example, in humans a necessary condition of being a mother is being female, but being female does not guarantee that one is a mother. If *X* is a *sufficient condition* of *Y* then the presence of *X* guarantees the presence of *Y*. Note, however, that the absence of *X* does not guarantee the absence of *Y*. For example, in humans a sufficient condition of being male is being a father, but not being a father does not guarantee that one is not male.]

There are many types of behavior that may be classified as instances of sexual harassment, and some people, such as Kenneth Cooper, have

From Edmund Wall, "The Definition of Sexual Harassment," *Public Affairs Quarterly*, Vol. 5, No. 4, 1991. Reprinted by permission.

proposed that managers explain the concept to their employees primarily through descriptions of various behavior patterns. Cooper addresses the sexual harassment of female employees by male managers in an essay which describes what he terms "six levels of sexual harassment." He seems to order these levels according to what he assumes to be two complementary considerations: a third party's ability to identify the perpetrator's behavior as sexually harassive and the severity of the infraction. The categories are presented in ascending order with the first category ostensibly representing the least flagrant type of behavior, the sixth category representing the most flagrant type of behavior. He writes that "obvious and blatant harassment may be decreasing, but borderline harassment behavior has never let up."[1] He takes the first four categories to be accounts of "borderline" cases.

He refers to the first type of behavior as "aesthetic appreciation." This refers to comments which "express a non-aggressive appreciation of physical or sexual features." For example, an alleged perpetrator says to a co-worker: "Gee... sigh... you're looking better every day!"[2] Cooper refers to such examples as the most "innocent" type of sexual harassment, but believes that these examples, nevertheless, constitute sexual harassment. In such cases the harassment is concealed.

Does managerial behavior which falls under "aesthetic appreciation" necessarily constitute sexual harassment? Cooper argues that "regardless of how harmless these appreciative comments may seem, they are put-downs which lower the group stature of the target." The offender, he tells us, is in a "superior position" from which to judge the employee's physical attributes.[3]

Comments of "aesthetic appreciation" made by male managers to female employees may not be appropriate, but all such comments are not, as Cooper suggests, necessarily instances of sexual harassment. Cooper argues that managerial comments of "aesthetic appreciation" made to employees are sexually harassive because they are "put-downs which lower the group stature of the target." There is a problem here. Such comments are not necessarily a reflection of any group differential.[4] Of course, the manager is in a "superior position" in relation to his employee, but only with respect to her coporate duties—not with respect to her physical attributes. The manager may try to use his corporate authority in order to force his employee to listen to his assessment of her physical attributes. Furthermore, the employee may feel as though she must submit to the manager's remarks, even if he does not openly attempt to coerce her. However, his sexually harassive behavior need not inherently be an exercise of corporate authority. It could simply be misguided human behavior which utilizes his corporate authority.

The second type of behavior which, according to Cooper, constitutes sexual harassment is "active mental groping." Under this heading Cooper places "direct verbal harassment," which evidently includes sexual jokes about the employee, and also the type of staring that may leave an employee feeling as though managers are "undressing them with their eyes."[5] This is followed by "social touching." Cooper maintains that, along with the first two categories of behavior, this type of behavior is "borderline," since the offender remains "within normal social touching conventions." In other words this behavior misleadingly appears "totally innocent" to a "third party."[6]

As far as "social touching" is concerned, he distinguishes an innocent "friendly touch" from a "sensual touch." He does not provide an example of a "friendly touch," but an example of a "sensual touch" would be "a caressing hand laid gently on the [employee]," or the movement of the manager's hand up and down his employee's back.[7] Unfortunately, Cooper offers no defense of his distinction between two types of touching. Neither does he clearly relate this distinction to his account of sexual harassment, although he seems to assume that a manager's "friendly touch" does not constitute sexual harassment, whereas his "sensual touch" would. He merely warns managers against any "social touching."

The reason why the distinction between an innocent "friendly touch" and a "sensual touch"

makes sense is also the reason why behavior descriptions are not central to the definition of sexual harassment. The basis for the distinction lies in the manager's mental state. A sincerely "friendly touch" would depend, among other things, upon the manager's motive for touching his employee. Sexual harassment refers to a defect in interpersonal relations. Depending upon the manager's and employee's mental states, it is possible that some examples of managerial behavior which satisfy Cooper's first, most "innocent" category (i.e., "aesthetic appreciation"), would actually be more objectionable than his second and third categories (i.e., "active mental groping" and "social touching," respectively). Indeed, depending upon the manager's and employee's mental states, cases which fall under any of Cooper's first three categories of sexual harassment could be characterized as "innocent."

Consider the case in which a manager finds that one of his employees strikingly resembles his mother. He has managed this employee for three years without incident, and one day in the corporate dining room they begin to discuss their parents. He may tell her of the resemblance between her and his mother. He may stare at her for a long while (this would constitute "active mental groping" on Cooper's view). He may tell her that her cheek bones are as pretty as those of his mother (an example of "aesthetic appreciation" according to Cooper). Finally, he may put his hand on her shoulder (i.e., an example of friendly "social touching" on Cooper's view) and say "Oh well, I must be getting back to my desk." Given this scenario, it is obvious that at least some employees would take no offense at the manager's behavior. Such a case need not involve sexual harassment, even though mere behavior descriptions would lead up to the opposite conclusion.

Cooper refers to his fourth and final "borderline" category as "foreplay harassment." Unlike "social touching," the touching here is not "innocent in nature and location," although its inappropriateness is still concealed.[8] Examples of "foreplay harassment" include a manager noticing that a button on an employee's blouse is undone. Instead of telling her about it, he buttons it. Another example would be brushing up against her "as if by accident."[9]

Cooper suggests that the "scope, frequency, and feel" of the touching "shows an obvious intent on the part of the offender to push the limits of decency . . ."[10] In this description of sexual harassment Cooper alludes to the importance of the manager's motive, but does not make its importance explicit. He does not express it as one of the essential descriptions of sexual harassment. Accidental physical contact between a manager and his employee is not, of course, sexual harassment. When the manager deliberately makes contact with his employee from a certain motive or due to his negligence, then he becomes an offender. Whether or not he makes physical contact, he may still be an offender. Indeed, as Cooper recognizes an employee could be sexually harassed without *any* physical contact between her and her manager.

Cooper overlooks the possibility that what appears to be "foreplay harassment" of an employee may not be. Even when a manager is sexually "petting" an employee in his office, as inappropriate as this behavior could be, he is not necessarily sexually harassing her. Consider the case in which a manager and an employee form an uncoerced agreement to engage in such inappropriate office behavior.[11] This is not sexual harassment. The general problem with behavior descriptions of sexual harassment can be seen when we attempt to construct examples of sexual harassment. The application of any of Cooper's four "borderline" categories to our examples may yield false determinations, depending upon the mental states involved.

Cooper's fifth and sixth categories are not "borderline," but involve flagrant sexual advances. They are "sexual abuse" and "ultimate threat," respectively. The latter which refers to a manager's coercive threats for sexual favors will be discussed later.[12] The former obviously involves sexual harassment.

Probably any behavior which constitutes sexual harassment (i.e., which satisfies certain descriptions of the manager's and employee's mental states) would probably constitute sexual abuse—whether physical or verbal. When an individual is maliciously or negligently responsible for unjustified harm to someone, it would seem that he has abused that person. Abuse can be subtle. It may include various ways of inflicting psychological harm. In fact, there is a more subtle form of sexual harassment accomplished through stares, gestures, innuendo, etc. For example, a manager may sexually harass his employee by staring at her and "undressing her with his eyes." *In light of this and the other limitations of behavior descriptions we need a set of jointly necessary and sufficient conditions of sexual harassment capable of capturing all subtle instances of sexual harassment while filtering out (even overt) sexual behavior which is not harassive.*

Wherein X is the sexual harasser and Y the victim, the following are offered as jointly necessary and sufficient conditions of sexual harassment:

1. X does not attempt to obtain Y's consent to communicate to Y, X's or someone else's purported sexual interest in Y.
2. X communicates to Y, X's or someone else's purported sexual interest in Y, X's motive for communicating this is some perceived benefit that he expects to obtain through the communication.
3. Y does not consent to discuss with X, X's or someone else's purported sexual interest in Y.
4. Y feels emotionally distressed because X did not attempt to obtain Y's consent to this discussion and/or because Y objects to the content of X's sexual comments.

The first condition refers to X's failure to attempt to obtain Y's consent to discuss someone's sexual interest in Y. X's involvement in the sexual harassment is not defined by the sexual proposition that X may make to Y. If the first condition was formulated in terms of the content of X's sexual proposition, then the proposed definition would circumvent some of the more subtle cases of sexual harassment. After all, Y may actually agree to a sexual proposition made to her by X and still be sexually harassed by X's attempting to discuss it with her. In some cases Y might not feel that it is the proper time or place to discuss such matters. In any event *sexual harassment primarily involves wrongful communication.* Whether or not X attempts to obtain Y's consent to a certain type of communication is crucial. What is inherently repulsive about sexual harassment is not the possible vulgarity of *X*'s sexual comment or proposal, but his failure to show respect for *Y*'s rights. It is the obligation that stems from privacy rights that is ignored. *Y*'s personal behavior and aspirations are protected by *Y*'s privacy rights. The intrusion by *X* into this moral sphere is what is so objectionable about sexual harassment. If *X* does not attempt to obtain *Y*'s approval to discuss such private matters, then he has not shown *Y* adequate respect.

X's lack of respect for *Y*'s rights is not a sufficient condition of sexual harassment. *X*'s conduct must constitute a rights violation. Essentially, the second condition refers to the fact that *X* has acted without concern for *Y*'s right to consent to the communication of sexual matters involving her. Here *X* "communicates" to *Y* that *X* or someone else is sexually interested in *Y*. This term includes not only verbal remarks made by *X*, but any purposeful conveyance such as gestures, noises, stares, etc. that violate its recipient's privacy rights. Such behavior can be every bit as intrusive as verbal remarks.

We need to acknowledge that *X* can refer to some third party's purported sexual interest in *Y* and still sexually harass *Y*. When he tells her, without her consent, that some third party believes she is physically desirable, this may be a form of sexual harassment. *Y* may not approve of *X* telling her this—even if *Y* and the third party happen to share a mutual sexual interest in each other. This is because *X*'s impropriety lies in his invasive approach to *Y*. It does not hinge upon the content of what he says to *Y*. *X* may, for example, have absolutely no sexual interest in *Y*, but believes that such remarks would upset *Y*, thereby affording him perverse enjoyment. Likewise his report that some third party is sexually interested in *Y* may be inaccurate but this does not absolve him from his duty to respect *Y*'s privacy.

X's specific motive for communicating what he does to *Y* may vary, but it always includes some benefit *X* may obtain from this illegitimate communication. *X* might or might not plan to have sexual relations with *Y*. Indeed, as we have seen, he might not have a sexual interest in *Y* at all and still obtain what he perceives to be beneficial to himself, perhaps the satisfaction of

disturbing *Y*.[13] Perhaps, as some contemporary psychologists suggest, *X*'s ultimate motive is to mollify his feelings of inferiority by controlling *Y*'s feelings, actions, environment, etc. Yet another possibility is that *X* wants to conform to what he believes to be parental and/or peer standards for males. The proposed first and second conditions can account for these various motives. The point is that, whatever the perceived benefit, it is the utility of the approach as perceived by *X*, and not necessarily the content of his message, that is important to the harasser. Furthermore, the "benefit" that moves him to action might not be obtainable or might not be a genuine benefit, but, nevertheless, in his attempt to obtain it, he violates his victim's rights.

The third condition refers to *Y*'s not consenting to discuss with *X*, *X*'s or someone else's purported sexual interest in *Y*. Someone might argue that the first condition is now unnecessary, that *X*'s failure to obtain *Y*'s consent to the type of discussion outlines in the third condition will suffice; the provision concerning *X*'s failure to *attempt* to obtain *Y*'s consent is, therefore, unnecessary. This objection would be misguided, however. The first condition insures that some sexual comments will not be unjustly labelled as "harassive." Consider the possibility that the second and third conditions are satisfied. For example, *X* makes a sexual remark about *Y* to *Y* without her consent. Now suppose that the first condition is not satisfied, that is, suppose that *X* *did attempt* to obtain *Y*'s consent to make such remarks. Furthermore, suppose that somewhere the communication between *X* and *Y* breaks down and *X* honestly believes he has obtained *Y*'s consent to this discussion when, in fact, he has not. In this case, *X*'s intentions being what they are, he does not sexually harass *Y*. *X* has shown respect for *Y*'s privacy. *Y* may certainly *feel* harassed in this case, but there is no offender here. However, after *X* sees *Y*'s displeasure at his remarks, it is now his duty to refrain from such remarks, unless, of course, *Y* later consents to such a discussion.

The case of the ignorant but well-intentioned *X* demonstrates the importance of distinguishing between accidents (and merely unfortunate circumstances) and sexual harassment. The remedy for avoiding the former is the encouragement of clear communication between people. Emphasis on clear communication would also facilitate the identification of some offenders, for some offenders would not refrain from making sexual remarks after their targets clearly expressed their objections to those remarks. The above case also reveals that the alleged victim needs to clearly express her wishes to others. For example, when she wishes not to discuss an individual's sexual interest in her, it would be foolish for her to make flirting glances at this individual. Such gestures may mislead him to conclude that she consents to this communication.

The first three conditions are not jointly sufficient descriptions of sexual harassment. What is missing is a description of Y's mental state. In sexual harassment cases the maligned communication must distress Y for a certain reason. Let us say that X has expressed sexual interest in Y without any attempt to obtain her consent. She, in fact, does not consent to it. However, perhaps she has decided against the discussion because she finds X too refined and anticipates that his sexual advances will not interest her. Perhaps she welcomes crass discussions about sexual matters. In this case she might not be sexually harassed by X's remarks. As the fourth condition indicates, Y must be distressed because X did not attempt to insure that it was permissible to make sexual comments to Y which involve her, or because the content of X's sexual comments are objectionable to Y. Yet another possibility is that both the invasiveness of X's approach and the content of what X says causes Y emotional distress. In this case, however, it would appear that Y would neither object to the content of X's sexual remarks nor to the fact that X's sexual remarks nor to the fact that X did not attempt to obtain Y's consent to make these remarks to her. Due to Y's views concerning sexual privacy this case is similar to one in which X does not attempt to obtain Y's consent to discuss with Y how well she plays tennis, or some other mundane discussion about Y.

You may recall that we postponed a discussion of the relation of sexual harassment to coercion and discrimination against women. Let us now explore this relation.

The fact that male employers and managers represent the bulk of the reported offenders has caused some legal theorists and philosophers to conclude that sexual harassment necessarily involves discrimination against women as a class. This approach is unacceptable. The proposed description of sexual harassment in terms of interpersonal relations is incompatible with this account, and, it seems that sexual harassment is not necessarily tied to discrimination or to coercion.

In an essay entitled "Is Sexual Harassment Coercive" Larry May and John C. Hughes argue that sexual harassment against women workers is "inherently coercive"—whether the harassment takes the form of a threat or an offer. They also maintain that the harm of sexual harassment against women "contributes to a pervasive pattern of discrimination and exploitation based upon sex."[14] They begin by defining sexual harassment as "the intimidation of persons in subordinate positions by those holding power and authority over them in order to exact sexual favors that would ordinarily not have been granted."[15]

May and Hughes recognize that male employees may be sexually harassed, but choose to limit their discussion to the typical case in which a male employer or manager sexually harasses a female employee. They choose this paradigm because it represents the "dominant pattern" in society and because they believe that, as a class, women have been conditioned by society to acquiesce "to male initiative."[16] According to May and Hughes women represent an injured class. The fact that men dominate positions of authority and status in our society renders women vulnerable to sexual harassment. Furthermore, the sexual harassment of female employees by male employers and managers sparks a general increase in the frequency of the crime, since such behavior reinforces male stereotypes of women as sexual objects.[17]

Even if May's and Hughes' social assumptions are accepted, that would not entail that their definition of sexual harassment is adequate. Their definition includes a power differential between the offender and the victim. Unhappily, this circumvents the sexual harassment between employees of equal rank, capabilities and recognition. Suppose that X and Y are co-workers for some company. X makes frequent comments concerning Y's sexual appeal and repeatedly propositions Y despite Y's refusals. Authority and rank are superfluous here. Y may be sexually harassed regardless of X's or Y's corporate status. As argued above in the critique of Cooper's article, the harassment at issue is not an extension of X's corporate authority, nor is the harassment essentially explained by the exercise of his authority. Rather, it is essentially explained by X's lack of respect for Y's right to refuse to discuss sexual matters pertaining to Y. If Y chooses not to enter X's discussion or is upset by X's refusal to recognize Y's privacy rights, then sexual harassment has occurred. X's and Y's mental states are essential, not some power differential between them.

Although the law vaguely recognizes the significance of Y's mental state in its sexual harassment definitions, the same is not true of X's mental state. For example, the California Department of Fair Employment and Housing (DFEH) completely omits the alleged perpetrator's mental state in their brief definition. Acknowledging that sexual harassment can occur between co-workers, they define it as "unwanted sexual advances, or visual, verbal or physical conduct of a sexual nature."[18] The difficulty with the DFEH's omission can be seen in the following counter-example. Y may be a paranoid individual who believes that any social advance by a member of the opposite sex somehow harms her. Perhaps X asks Y for a date and Y feels sexually harassed. Let us say that X is not yet planning to discuss with Y anyone's sexual interest in Y and that X terminates the discussion as soon as he notices Y's displeasure. On their definition the DFEH would be forced to consider this sexual harassment when clearly it is not. Although it involves an "unwanted sexual advance," X's mental state points to the innocence of his proposal.

Many of the examples that the DFEH use to illustrate their definition are also ambiguous. Unwanted "touching" is one example. In this case the commission might be referring to unwanted "sensual touching," but they offer no way of distinguishing a sensual from a merely friendly touch. Suppose that Y works in the sales office of some company and X works in the maintenance department. Y may object to X's touching her, but only because she does not want to stain her clothing. She knows that her friend, X, is not sexually interested in her and, if his hands were clean, she would have no objections to his occasional "friendly touch." This is not a case of sexual harassment, although it may, if it persists, show a lack of consideration on X's part. By ignoring the importance of mental states, the DFEH not only fails to identify the perpetrator's lack of respect for Y in genuine sexual harassment cases, but also fails to acknowledge the importance of Y's concerns. In this example Y did not feel sexually harassed, although she may have been upset because of her friend's inconsideration. In this subtle way California law does not do justice to the concerns of this alleged victim.

May's and Hughes' inaccurate definition of sexual harassment skews their inquiry. Their main objective is to illustrate the coercive nature of sexual harassment; more specifically, the coercive nature of sexual threats and offers made to women employees by male corporate authorities. They focus on the type of sexual advances that are tied to hiring, promotions or raises.[19] They briefly refer to a third type of sexual advance, one which is "merely annoying" and one which is "without demonstrable sanction or reward."[20] However, after introducing this third category the authors circumvent it. This oversight is a serious one. The essence of sexual harassment lies not in the content of the offender's proposal, but in the innappropriateness of his approach to the victim. It lies in the way he violates the victim's privacy. This is the "annoying" aspect of his approach which needs elucidating. May and Hughes could not pursue this third type of sexual advance because they had defined sexual harassment in terms of someone in authority acquiring some sexual favor from his employee. They set themselves the task of proving that sexual harassment is necessarily coercive. Their definition thereby hinged on the alleged coercive effects of the harasser's proposal, rather than on his mental state.

We still need to examine May's and Hughes' position that all sexual threats and offers made by male employers or managers to female employees are sexually harassive as well as coercive. They describe a conditional sexual threat from the employer's position: "If you don't provide a sexual benefit, I will punish you by withholding a promotion or raise that would otherwise be due, or ultimately fire you."[21] According to their "baseline" approach "sexual threats are coercive because they worsen the objective situation the employee finds herself in." Before the threat the retention of her job only depended upon "standards of efficiency," whereas, after the threat, the performance of sexual favors becomes a condition of employment.[22] Presumably, these same "baseline" considerations also render the threat sexually harassive.

May and Hughes acknowledge that their "baseline account" of coercive threats is essentially Nozickian. Elsewhere, I have defended an interpersonal description of coercive threats against "baseline accounts."[23] According to my description X issues Y a coercive threat (in his attempt to get Y to do action "A") when X intentionally attempts to create the belief in Y that X will be responsible for harm coming to Y should Y fail to do A. X's coercive threat is described primarily in terms of his intentions. His motive for attempting to create this belief in Y is his desire to bring about a state of affairs in which Y's recognition of this possible harm to himself influences Y to do A. May and Hughes are correct that every conditional sexual threat issued by a male superior to a female subordinate is a coercive threat. (Indeed, a conditional sexual threat issued against anyone is a coercive threat.) The male employer would be trying to create the belief in the female employee that he will be responsible for harm coming to her (i.e. her termination, demotion, etc.) should she fail to comply with his sexual request. He would do this because he wants the prospect of this harm to motivate her to comply. Nevertheless, it is not true that every conditional sexual threat *as May and Hughes describe these threats* would be coercive. If, for example, the employer and the employee are playfully engaging in "banter" when he tells her that without her compliance he will fire her, then she is not being threatened. He does not intend to create the belief in her

that harm will come to her. In this scenario she would not be sexually harassed either because the employer has a good faith belief that she consents to this "banter." Therefore, May and Hughes need a more rigorous description of coercive threats which includes the intentions of the person making the threat.

May and Hughes argue that if the employee wants to provide sexual favors to her employer regardless of the employer's demand, she is still coerced. They maintain that her objective baseline situation is still made worse, for now it would be very difficult for her to cease a sexual relationship with her employer should she choose to do so.[24] May and Hughes do not tell us who or what would specifically be making the coercive proposal if the *employee* propositioned the employer. After all, on their view, her offer would worsen her objective situation for the same reason his threat would. Perhaps they would refer to this as a coercive situation, or would find the employer's consent to the sexual relationship to include some sort of a coercive stance, but, nevertheless, their external analysis overlooks the mental state of the individual who is supposedly victimized. Depending upon her values and personal outlook she may, without reservation, accept her employer's demand as a "career opportunity." By excluding the employee's mental state in their "baseline analysis" they overlook the fact that her situation may improve after the demand and that, to her, the prospect of a permanent sexual relationship with her employer is no problem. According to this "baseline account" she would not be coerced or harassed. Unlike May's and Hughes' account, the proposed interpersonal account of sexual harassment maintains that an employee who receives a sexual threat from her employer is not necessarily sexually harassed. Let us say that he told her she must have sex with him or else be demoted. Still, she may welcome his demand as a "career opportunity." If she is not offended by his demand, then she is not sexually harassed by the threat.

As we have seen May and Hughes maintain that the sexual harassment of a female employee by a male corporate authority is coercive because it worsens the employee's employment situation. They say that sexual harassment by an employer erects an unfair employment condition against women as a class. May and Hughes therefore believe that the discriminatory nature of sexual harassment against female employees is tied to these "coercive" dimensions. They argue that, in general, men do not have to endure the maligned "job requirement" generally foistered upon women and that when men make sexual threats to their female subordinates they "establish a precedent for employment decisions based upon the stereotype that values women for their sexuality . . ."[25] Because the sexual harassment of female employees by male employers worsens the employment situation of women by stereotyping them, we supposedly have a necessary relation between ("coercive") sexual harassment and discrimination.

May and Hughes are not alone in their belief that sexual harassment and discrimination are necessarily related. When they describe their arguments for the coercive-discriminatory effects of a male employer's sexual threat on a female employee, they refer to such a threat as an "instance of discrimination in the workplace."[26] Here they follow federal law by claiming that sexual threats in the workplace fall under the rubric of Title VII of the Civil Rights Act of 1964. They are relying on the fact that in 1980 the Equal Employment Opportunity Commission (EEOC) set a precedent by finding that sexual harassment is a form of sex discrimination.[27]

The prevailing belief that the sexual harassment of women is a form of sex discrimination is ill-founded. Even if we follow May and Hughes and limit our discussion to the sexual harassment of female employees by male employers, something that the EEOC cannot do, a male employer's sexual threat is not necessarily an "instance" of sex discrimination. For a given sexual harassment case, gender may not be a consideration at all. Picture the bisexual employer who is not in control of his sexual desires. He might indiscriminately threaten or proposition his employees without giving consideration to the gender of his victims. The additional "job requirement" referred to by May and Hughes would, in this case, apply to all employees male and female. Indeed, since, as argued above, sexual harassment is primarily a

matter of communication which infringes on basic privacy rights, there is no presumption of gender. Now, the EEOC does make reference to a candidate losing a job because another candidate who is less qualified has acquiesced to an employer's sexual threat, but this is not necessarily a case of sex discrimination as May and Hughes contend. Gender need not be the motive behind the employer's sexual threat. If the qualified candidate has been discriminated against, this may occur for a variety of reasons. Although the proposed interpersonal account is compatible with the assumptions that sexual harassment against women generally *contributes* to discrimination against women and that prejudice against women *may* be the motive of most male employers when they sexually harass female employees, we should avoid *defining* sexual harassment in terms of these assumptions.

Of course, the possibility that federal authority was misdirected when the EEOC set policy for sexual harassment in the workplace, does not entail that the EEOC's definition is incorrect. They maintain that: unwelcome sexual advances, requests for sexual favors, and other verbal or physical conduct of a sexual nature constitute sexual harassment when

1. submission to such conduct is made either explicitly or implicitly a term or condition of an individual's employment
2. submission to or rejection of such conduct by an individual is used as the basis for employment decisions affecting such an individual, or
3. such conduct has the purpose or effect of unreasonably interfering with an individual's work performance or creating an intimidating, hostile, or offensive working environment.

The EEOC's conditions of sexual harassment not only appear to capture sexual threats and offers, but, also, "annoyances" and other more subtle violations. The EEOC's definition thereby avoids May's and Hughes' mistake. Their third condition also allows for sexual harassment between employees, something also lacking in May's and Hughes' account. Unfortunately, the

EEOC's first two conditions seem to suggest that all sexual threats and offers made by employer's to employees are sexually harassive. As argued above, not all sexual threats made by employers to employees must be sexually harassive, their inappropriateness notwithstanding. The EEOC's definition of sexual harassment is too inclusive because it fails to capture precisely the victim's mental state and the way that she reacts to the threat. In omitting a description of her mental state the EEOC's definition encourages the FDEH's oversight in allowing a paranoid "victim" to claim sexual harassment against a well-intentioned employer. Moreover, the EEOC makes no provision for the intentions of the employer.

Some states such as California maintain that sexually explicit materials which disturb employees are sexually harassive. This stance seems to be in line with the EEOC's definition. According to the EEOC the employer or employee who, for example, displays a sexually explicit poster may exhibit "physical conduct of a sexual nature" which creates an "offensive working environment." This is a difficult example, but it seems that an employee's mere disapproval of such materials does not entail that she is sexually harassed. Even if the disgruntled employee disapproves of the poster's explicit sexual representations, this does not mean that the person displaying the poster is intending to communicate anything to her and about her. Of course, in many cases he may be making a subtle statement to her about her sexual appeal. For example he may be using the poster in order to communicate his or someone else's sexual interest in her. According to the interpersonal account these cases would involve sexual harassment. If he is merely displaying the poster for his own benefit, however, then his behavior is rude, but not sexually harassive. There is a difference between the disrespect involved in rudeness, which indicates poor taste or a breach of etiquette, and the disrespect involved in sexual harassment. In the latter case the privacy of some specific individual has not been respected.

If May's and Hughes' position that all conditional sexual threats by male employers to female employees are sexually harassive and discriminatory in nature has successfully been overturned, their contention that the same considerations also apply to sexual offers collapses. They describe a sexual offer from the male employer's position: "If you provide a sexual benefit, I will reward you with a promotion or a raise that would otherwise not be due."[28] Since the benefit would ostensibly improve the employee's baseline situation, she is made an offer by her employer. Without the offer, she would not get the promotion or raise. Interestingly, May and Hughes argue that such offers actually worsen the employee's baseline situation and are, therefore, coercive offers. They do not explain how the employee's situation is simultaneously improved and worsened, but perhaps they have the following in mind: the employer's proposal is an offer because it may improve the employee's strategic status, whereas his offer is coercive because of certain social considerations. May and Hughes tell us that the employer's sexual offer changes the work environment so that the employee "is viewed by others, and may come to view herself, less in terms of her work productivity and more in terms of her sexual allure." Moreover, they say that, since women are more "economically vulnerable and socially passive than men," they are inclined to "offset [their] diminished status and to protect against later retaliation" by acquiescing to employer demands. Thus, according to May and Hughes, they are necessarily coerced by a male employer's sexual offer.[29]

May and Hughes argue that there is usually an implicit threat concealed in an employer's sexual offer and that this makes the offer coercive. Of course, here it may be the threat that is coercive and not the offer. What we are interested in is their argument that the employer's sexual offer itself is coercive because it reduces the female employee's self-esteem, and also raises the spectre of some future threat (should the employee fail to comply or otherwise fall victim to the employer's "bruised" ego). Even if May and Hughes are correct and these are the general social effects of these sexual offers, this does not entail that a sexual offer made by a male employer to a female employee is coercive in nature. It would be unreasonable to suggest that every female employee would experience these hardships following a male employer's sexual offer. As mentioned in the discussion of sexual threats, the employee's values and personality contribute to the effects of an employer's presumably coercive proposal. Moreover, May's and Hughes' claim about the coercive effects of these sexual offers hinges upon their "baseline account" of coercion (which has been criticized above).

There is a more plausible alternative to a "baseline account" of coercive offers. An interpersonal account is possible. X makes Y a coercive offer when X intends to create the belief in Y that he will not prevent harm from coming to Y unless Y complies with his request. A genuine offer, on the other hand, would be limited to a mutual exchange of perceived benefits, or it may be a gift. This offer could become coercive if X attempts to cause Y to believe that her rejection of his request will result in some harm to her. Essentially, the coercive element is that X makes his proposed assistance in preventing this harm conditional upon Y's agreement to his request. He tries to use her belief that harm will occur as a way of controlling her. Not all offers by male employers to female employees are like this. Thus, on this interpersonal account, a male employer's offer is not coercive by nature.

We still need to address May's and Hughes' account of the implications of an employer's sexual offer to an employee. We are told that a non-compliant employee may worry that a disgruntled employer may threaten or harm her at some future date. This is certainly possible. However, such proposals are not coercive unless they involve the relevant intentions. The proposed account does acknowledge that an employer's non-coercive sexual offer might be sexually harassive. As argued above this depends upon the legitimacy of his approach to the employee and upon the employee's wishes. Moreover, the fact that, according to the proposed view, some of these sexual offers are not coercive or sexually harassive does not alter the fact that an employer who is both considerate and prudent would avoid any behavior that could be construed as sexually harassive.[30]

Notes

1. Kenneth C. Cooper, "The Six Levels of Sexual Harassment," *Contemporary Moral Controversies in Business*, ed. A. Pablo Iannone (New York: Oxford University Press, 1989), p. 190.
2. Ibid.
3. Ibid.
4. See especially pp. 381ff. for a detailed discussion of sexual harassment and discrimination.
5. Cooper, *op. cit.*, p. 191.
6. Ibid.
7. Ibid.
8. Ibid.
9. Cooper, *op. cit.*, pp. 191–92.
10. Cooper, *op. cit.*, p. 192.
11. See pp. 377ff. for a discussion of coercion and sexual harassment.
12. Cooper, *op. cit.*, p. 192; see pp. 379–81.
13. Some sociologists would disagree with me. They believe that the offender must have set himself a "sexual goal" in order for sexual harassment to occur. See K. Wilson and L. Kraus, "Sexual Harassment in the University." This paper was presented at the annual meetings of the American Sociological Association (Toronto, 1981).
14. Larry May and John C. Hughes, "Is Sexual Harassment Coercive?," *Moral Rights in the Workplace*, ed. Gertrude Ezorsky (Albany, NY: State University of New York, 1987), pp. 115–22.
15. May and Hughes, *op. cit.*, p. 115.
16. Ibid.
17. May and Hughes, *op. cit.*, p. 118.
18. Pamphlet entitled "Sexual Harassment" (1990), distributed by the California Department of Fair Employment and Housing.
19. May and Hughes, *op. cit.*, pp. 116–17.
20. May and Hughes, *op. cit.*, p. 117.
21. May and Hughes, *op. cit.*, pp. 116–17.
22. May and Hughes, *op. cit.*, pp. 117–18.
23. "Intention and Coercion," *Journal of Applied Philosophy*, vol. 5 (1988), pp. 75–85.
24. May and Hughes, *op. cit.*, p. 118.
25. May and Hughes, *op. cit.*, pp. 118–19.
26. May and Hughes, *op. cit.*, p. 118.
27. Equal Employment Opportunity Commission, *Federal Register*, vol. 45, no. 219 (10 November, 1980), Rules and Regulations, 74676–7.
28. May and Hughes, *op. cit.*, p. 117.
29. May and Hughes, *op. cit.*, p. 120.
30. I am grateful to Burleigh Wilkins for helpful comments on this paper.

Anita M. Superson

A Feminist Definition
of Sexual Harassment

I. INTRODUCTION

By far the most pervasive form of discrimination against women is sexual harassment (SH). Women in every walk of life are subject to it, and I would venture to say, on a daily basis.[1] Even though the law is changing to the benefit of victims of SH, the fact that SH is still so pervasive shows that there is too much tolerance of it, and that victims do not have sufficient legal recourse to be protected.

The main source for this problem is that the way SH is defined by various Titles and other sources does not adequately reflect the social nature of SH, or the harm it causes all women. As a result, SH comes to be defined in subjective ways. One upshot is that when subjective definitions infuse the case law on SH, the more subtle but equally harmful forms of SH do not get counted as SH and thus not afforded legal protection.

My primary aim in this paper is to offer an objective definition of SH that accounts for the group harm all forms of SH have in common. Though my aim is to offer a moral definition of SH, I offer it in hopes that it will effect changes in the law. It is only by defining SH in a way that covers all of its forms and gets at the heart of the problem that legal protection can be given to all victims in all circumstances.

I take this paper to be programmatic. Obviously problems may exist in applying the definition to cases that arise for litigation. In a larger project a lot more could be said to meet those objections. My goal in this paper is merely

From Anita M. Superson, "A Feminist Definition of Sexual Harassment," *Journal of Social Philosophy,* Vol. 24, No. 1, 1993. Reprinted by permission of the *Journal of Social Philosophy.*

to defend my definition against the definitions currently appealed to by the courts in order to show how it is more promising for victims of SH.

I define SH in the following way:

Any behavior (verbal or physical) caused by a person, A, in the dominant class directed at another, B, in the subjugated class, that expresses and perpetuates the attitude that B or members of B's sex is/are inferior because of their sex, thereby causing harm to either B and/or members of B's sex.

II. CURRENT LAW ON SEXUAL HARASSMENT

Currently, victims of SH have legal recourse under Title VII of the Civil Rights Act of 1964, Title IX of the 1972 Education Amendments, and tort law.

The Civil Rights Act of 1964 states:

a) It shall be an unlawful employment practice for an employer—
   (1) to fail or refuse to hire or to discharge any individual, or otherwise to discriminate against any individual with respect to his compensation, terms, conditions, or privileges of employment because of such individual's race, color, religion, sex, or national origin. . . .[2]

Over time the courts came to view SH as a form of sex discrimination. The main advocate for this was Catharine MacKinnon, whose book, *Sexual Harassment of Working Women,*[3] greatly influenced court decisions on the issue. Before it was federally legislated, some courts appealed to the Equal Employment Opportunity Commission (EEOC) *Guidelines on Discrimination Because of Sex* to establish that SH was a form of sex discrimination. The *Guidelines* (amended in 1980 to include SH) state that

Harassment on the basis of sex is a violation of Sec. 703 of Title VII. Unwelcome sexual advances, requests for sexual favors, and other verbal or physical conduct of a sexual nature constitute sexual harassment when (1) submission to such conduct is made either explicitly or implicitly a term or condition of an individual's employment, (2) submission to or rejection of such conduct by an individual is used as the basis for employment decisions affecting such individual, or (3) such conduct has the purpose or effect of unreasonably interfering with an individual's work performance or creating an intimidating, hostile, or offensive working environment.[4]

In a landmark case,[5] *Meritor Savings Bank, FSB v. Vinson* (1986),[6] the Supreme Court, relying on the EEOC *Guidelines,* established that SH was a form of sex discrimination prohibited under Title VII. The case involved Mechelle Vinson, a teller-trainee, who was propositioned by Sidney Taylor, vice president and branch manager of the bank. After initially refusing, she agreed out of fear of losing her job. She allegedly had sexual relations with Taylor 40 or 50 times over a period of four years, and he even forcibly raped her several times, exposed himself to her in a restroom, and fondled her in public.[7]

Sexual harassment extends beyond the workplace. To protect students who are not employees of their learning institution, Congress enacted Title IX of the Education Amendments of 1972, which states:

No person in the United States shall, on the basis of sex, be excluded from participation in, be denied the benefits of, or be subjected to discrimination under any educational program or activity receiving federal financial assistance.[8]

Cases of litigation under Title IX have been influenced by *Meritor* so that SH in educational institutions is construed as a form of sex discrimination.[9]

The principles that came about under Title VII apply equally to Title IX. Under either Title, a person can file two different kinds of harassment charges: *quid pro quo,* or hostile environment. *Quid pro quo* means "something for something."[10] *Quid pro quo* harassment occurs when "an employer or his agent explicitly ties the terms, conditions, and privileges of the victim's employment to factors which are arbitrary and unrelated to job performance."[11] Plaintiffs must show they "suffered a tangible economic detriment as a result of the harassment."[12] In con-

trast, hostile environment harassment occurs when the behavior of supervisors or co-workers has the effect of "unreasonably interfering with an individual's work performance or creates an intimidating, hostile, or offensive environment."[13] Hostile environment harassment established that Title VII (and presumably Title IX) were not limited to economic discrimination, but applied to emotional harm, as well. The EEOC *Guidelines* initiated the principle of hostile environment harassment which was used by the courts in many cases, including *Meritor.*

For each kind of SH (*quid pro quo* or hostile environment), courts can use one of two approaches: disparate treatment, or disparate impact. *Black's Law Dictionary* defines disparate *treatment* as "[d]ifferential treatment of employees or applicants on the basis of their race, color, religion, sex, national origin, handicap, or veteran's status."[14] The key is to establish that the person was harassed because of her sex, and not because of other features (e.g., hair color). Disparate *impact,* in contrast, "involves facially neutral practices that are not intended to be discriminatory, but are discriminatory in effect. . . ."[15] Disparate impact came about because the facts did not always show that an employer blatantly discriminated on the basis of sex,[16] but the employer's practices still worked to the disadvantage of certain groups. Allegedly, "[f]or both *quid pro quo* and hostile environment sexual harassment, courts use disparate treatment theory."[17]

For women who are harassed other than in an employment or an educational setting, tort law [A *tort* is a private or civil, as opposed to public, wrong. We thus speak of civil as opposed to criminal offenses in the law.] can offer legal remedy. Also, torts can accompany a claim invoking Title VII (and presumably, Title IX).[18] Criminal suits apply only if the victim of harassment "is a victim of rape, indecent assault, common assault, assault causing bodily harm, threats, intimidation, or solicitation,"[19] and in these cases the suit will usually be for one of these charges, not harassment. To be taken seriously, the action requires police charges, a difficulty in SH cases.

Civil torts are a more promising way to go for victims of SH, though with limitations. The battery tort prohibits battery which is defined as "an intentional and unpermitted contact, other than that permitted by social usage."[20] The intent refers to intent to contact, not intent to cause the harm that may result from the contact. The assault tort prohibits assault, which is defined as "an intentional act, short of contact, which produces *apprehension* of battery."[21] The defendant must have intended to arouse psychic apprehension in his victim.[22] Victims can also appeal to the tort of intentional infliction of emotional distress. According to Section 46 of the *Restatement of Torts,*

Liability has been found only where the conduct has been so outrageous in character, and so extreme in degree, as to go beyond all possible bounds of decency, and to be regarded as atrocious, and utterly intolerable in a civilized community. Generally, the case is one in which the recitation of the facts to an average member of the community would arouse his resentment against the actor, and lead him to exclaim, "Outrageous."[23]

"[M]ere insults, indignities, threats, annoyances, petty oppression, or other trivialities" will not result in tort action because a person must be "hardened to a certain amount of rough language."[24] The *Restatement of Torts* invokes the reasonable man standard, claiming that the emotional distress must be "so severe that no reasonable man could be expected to endure it."[25] Moreover, the conduct must be done intentionally or recklessly.

Despite major advances made in the last few decades in the law on SH, I believe the law is still inadequate. The main problem in my view is that the law, reflecting the view held by the general public, fails to see SH for what it is: an attack on the group of *all* women, not just the immediate victim. Because of this, there is a failure to recognize the group harm that all instances of SH, not just the more blatant ones, cause all women. As a result, the law construes SH as a subjective issue, that is, one that is determined by what the victim feels and (sometimes) what the perpetrator intends. As a result, the burden of proof is wrongly shifted to the victim and off of the perpetrator with the result that many victims are not legally protected.

For instance, victims filing complaints under Title VII (and presumably Title IX) are not protected unless they have a fairly serious case. They have to show under hostile environment harassment that the behavior unreasonably interfered with their work performance, and that there was a pattern of behavior on the defendant's behalf. Regarding the latter point, the EEOC *Guidelines* say that:

In determining whether alleged conduct constitutes sexual harassment, the Commission will look at the record as a whole and at the totality of the circumstances, such as the nature of the sexual advances and the context in which the alleged incidents occurred.[26]

It seems unlikely that the victim of isolated incidents of SH could have her complaint taken seriously under this assessment. Under *quid pro quo* harassment, the victim must show she suffered a tangible economic detriment. Disparate treatment cases might be difficult to show because not *all* members of the victim's class (e.g., the group of all females) are likely to be harassed by the defendant. This makes it unlikely that the victim will be able to show she was harassed because of her sex, and not because of some personal feature she has that others lack. Victims who are harassed outside of the workplace and educational institutions have to rely on tort law to make their case, but under it, defendants have a way out by claiming innocence of intention. Under the tort of intentional infliction of emotional distress, victims must have an extreme case in order to get protection.

Victims not protected include the worker who is harassed by a number of different people, the worker who suffers harassment but in small doses, the person who is subjected to a slew of catcalls on her two mile walk to work, the female professor who is subjected to leering from one of her male students, and the woman who does not complain out of fear. The number of cases is huge, and many of them are quite common.

To protect all victims in all circumstances, the law ought to treat SH as it is beginning to treat racial discrimination. In her very interesting paper, Mari Matsuda has traced the history of the law regarding racist speech.[27] Article 4 of the International Convention on the Elimination of All Forms of Racial Discrimination which was unanimously adopted by the General Assembly December 21, 1965, prohibits not only acts of violence, but also the "mere dissemination of racist ideas, without requiring proof of incitement."[28] Apparently many states have signed and ratified the signing of the Convention, though the United States has not yet done so because of worries about freedom of speech protected by the First Amendment.[29] Aside from the Convention, the United Nations Charter, the Universal Declaration of Human Rights, the European Convention for the Protection of Human Rights and Fundamental Freedoms, the American Declaration of the Rights and Duties of Man, as well as the domestic law of several nations, have all recognized the right to equality and freedom from racism. In these and other codes, racist ideas are banned if they are discriminatory, related to violence, or express inferiority, hatred, or persecution.[30] On my view, some forms of SH are related to violence, and they *all* express inferiority whether or not they express hatred. At the root of the standard on racism that is gaining worldwide recognition is the view that racist speech "interferes with the rights of subordinated-group members to participate equally in society, maintaining their basic sense of security and worth as human beings."[31] Sexual harassment has the same effect, so it, too, should be prohibited. But I think SH can be afforded the best legal protection under antidiscrimination law instead of tort law, as this misses the social nature of SH. The world-wide standard against racist speech recognizes the group harm of racism by realizing that racist speech expresses inferiority; a similar standard against SH should be adopted.

III. The Social Nature of Sexual Harassment

Sexual harassment, a form of sexism, is about domination, in particular, the domination of the group of men over the group of women.[32] Domination involves control or power which can be seen in the economic, political, and social spheres of society. Sexual harassment is not simply an assertion of power, for power can be used in beneficial ways. The power men have over women has been wielded in ways that oppress women. The power expressed in SH is oppression, power used wrongly.

Sexual harassment is integrally related to sex roles. It reveals the belief that a person is to be relegated to certain roles on the basis of her sex, including not only women's being sex objects, but also their being caretakers, motherers, nurturers, sympathizers, etc. In general, the sex roles women are relegated to are associated with the body (v. mind) and emotions (v. reason).

When A sexually harasses B, the comment or behavior is really directed at the group of all women, not just a particular woman, a point often missed by the courts. After all, many derogatory behaviors are issued at women the harasser does not even know (e.g., scanning a stranger's body). Even when the harasser knows his victim, the behavior is directed at the particular woman because she happens to be "available" at the time, though its message is for all women. For instance, a catcall says not (merely) that the perpetrator likes a woman's body but that he thinks women are at least primarily sex objects and he—because of the power he holds by being in the dominant group—gets to rate them according to how much pleasure they give him. The professor who refers to his female students as "chicks" makes a statement that women are intellectually inferior to men as they can be likened to non-rational animals, perhaps even soft, cuddly ones that are to serve as the objects of (men's) pleasure. Physicians' using Playboy centerfolds in medical schools to "spice up their lectures" sends the message that women lack the competence to make it in a "man's world" and should perform the "softer tasks" associated with bearing and raising children.[33]

These and other examples make it clear that SH is not about dislike for a certain person; instead, it expresses a person's beliefs about women as a group on the basis of their sex, namely, that they are primarily emotional and bodily beings. Some theorists—Catharine MacKinnon, John Hughes and Larry May—have recognized the social nature of SH. Hughes and May claim that women are a disadvantaged group because

1. they are a social group having a distinct identity and existence apart from their individual identities,
2. they occupy a subordinate position in American society, and
3. their political power is severely circumscribed.[34]

They continue:

Once it is established that women qualify for special disadvantaged group status, all practices tending to stigmatize women as a group, or which contribute to the maintenance of their subordinate social status, would become legally suspect.[35]

This last point, I believe, should be central to the definition of SH.

Because SH has as its target the group of all women, this *group* suffers harm as a result of the behavior. Indeed, when any one woman is in any way sexually harassed, all women are harmed. The group harm SH causes is different from the harm suffered by particular women as individuals: it is often more vague in nature as it is not easily causally tied to any particular incident of harassment. The group harm has to do primarily with the fact that the behavior reflects and reinforces sexist attitudes that women are inferior to men and that they do and ought to occupy certain sex roles. For example, comments and behavior that relegate women to the role of sex objects reinforce the belief that women *are* sex objects and that they *ought to* occupy this sex role. Similarly, when a female professor's cogent comments at department colloquia are met with frowns and rolled eyes from her colleagues, this behavior reflects and reinforces the view that women are not fit to occupy positions men arrogate to themselves.

The harm women suffer as a group from any single instance of SH is significant. It takes many forms. A Kantian analysis would show what is wrong with being solely a sex object. Though there is nothing wrong with being a caretaker or nurturer, etc., *per se*, it is sexist—

and so wrong—to assign such roles to women. In addition, it is wrong to assign a person to a role she may not want to occupy. Basically women are not allowed to decide for themselves which roles they are to occupy, but this gets decided for them, no matter what they do. Even if some women occupy important positions in society that men traditionally occupy, they are still viewed as being sex objects, caretakers, etc., since all women are thought to be more "bodily" and emotional than men. This is a denial of women's autonomy, and degrading to them. It also contributes to women's oppression. The belief that women must occupy certain sex roles is both a cause and an effect of their oppression. It is a cause because women are believed to be more suited for certain roles given their association with body and emotions. It is an effect because once they occupy these roles and are victims of oppression, the belief that they *must* occupy these sex roles is reinforced.

Women are harmed by SH in yet another way. The belief that they are sex objects, caretakers, etc., gets reflected in social and political practices in ways that are unfair to women. It has undoubtedly meant many lost opportunities that are readily available to men. Women are not likely to be hired for jobs that require them to act in ways other than the ways the sex roles dictate, and if they are, what is expected of them is different from what is expected of men. Mothers are not paid for their work, and caretakers are not paid well in comparison to jobs traditionally held by men. Lack of economic reward is paralleled by lack of respect and appreciation for those occupying such roles. Certain rights granted men are likely not to be granted women (e.g., the right to bodily self-determination, and marriage rights).

Another harm SH causes all women is that the particular form sex stereotyping takes promotes two myths: (1) that male behavior is normally and naturally predatory, and (2) that females naturally (because they are taken to be primarily bodily and emotional) and even willingly acquiesce despite the appearance of protest.[36] Because the behavior perpetuated by these myths is taken to be normal, it is not seen as sexist, and in turn is not counted as SH.

The first myth is that men have stronger sexual desires than women, and harassment is just a natural venting of these desires which men are unable to control. The truth is, first, that women are socialized *not* to vent their sexual desires in the way men do, but this does not mean these desires are weaker or less prevalent. Masters and Johnson have "decisively established that women's sexual requirements are no less potent or urgent than those of men."[37] But second, SH has nothing to do with men's sexual desires, nor is it about seduction; instead, it is about oppression of women. Indeed, harassment generally does not lead to sexual satisfaction, but it often gives the harasser a sense of power.

The second myth is that women either welcome, ask for, or deserve the harassing treatment. Case law reveals this mistaken belief. In *Lipsett v. Rive-Mora*[38] (1987), the plaintiff was discharged from a medical residency program because she "did not react favorably to her professor's requests to go out for drinks, his compliments about her hair and legs, or to questions about her personal and romantic life."[39] The court exonerated the defendant because the plaintiff initially reacted favorably by smiling when shown lewd drawings of herself and when called sexual nicknames as she thought she had to appease the physician. The court said that "given the plaintiff's admittedly favorable responses to these flattering comments, there was no way anyone could consider them as 'unwelcome.' "[40] The court in *Swentek v. US Air*[41] (1987) reacted similarly when a flight attendant who was harassed with obscene remarks and gestures was denied legal recourse because previously she used vulgar language and openly discussed her sexual encounters. The court concluded that "she was the kind of person who could not be offended by such comments and therefore welcomed them generally."[42]

The idea that women welcome "advances" from men is seen in men's view of the way women dress. If a woman dresses "provocatively" by men's standards, she is said to welcome or even deserve the treatment she gets. One explanation harassing professors give for their behavior is that they are bombarded daily with the temptation of physically desirable young women who dress in what they take to be revealing ways.[43] When the case becomes public, numerous questions arise about the attractiveness of the victim, as if she were to blame for being attractive and the consequences thereof. Catcallers often try to justify their behavior by claiming that the victim should expect such behavior, given her tight-fitting dress or shorts, low-cut top, high heels, etc. This way of thinking infests discussions of rape in attempts to establish that women want to be raped, and it is mistaken in that context, too. The myth that women welcome or encourage harassment is designed "to keep women in their place" as men see it. The truth of the matter is that the perpetrator alone is at fault.

Both myths harm all women as they sanction SH by shifting the burden on the victim and all members of her sex: women must either go out of their way to avoid "natural" male behavior, or establish conclusively that they did not in any way want the behavior. Instead of the behavior being seen as sexist, it is seen as women's problem to rectify.

Last, but certainly not least, women suffer group harm from SH because they come to be stereotyped as victims.[44] Many men see SH as something they can do to women, and in many cases, get away with. Women come to see themselves as victims, and come to believe that the roles they *can* occupy are only the sex roles men have designated for them. Obviously these harms are quite serious for women, so the elimination of all forms of SH is warranted.

I have spoken so far as if it is only men who can sexually harass women, and I am now in a position to defend this controversial view. When a woman engages in the very same behavior harassing men engage in, the underlying message implicit in male-to-female harassment is missing. For example, when a woman scans a man's body, she might be considering him to be a sex object, but all the views about domination and being relegated to certain sex roles are absent. She cannot remind the man that he is inferior because of his sex, since given the way things are in society, he is not. In general, women cannot harm or degrade or dominate men *as a group*, for it is impossible to send the message that one dominates (and so cause group harm) if one does not dominate. Of course, if the sexist roles predominant in our society were reversed, women *could* sexually harass men. The way things are, any bothersome behavior a woman engages in, even though it may be of a sexual nature, does not constitute SH because it lacks the social impact present in male-to-female harassment. Tort law would be sufficient to protect against this behavior, since it is unproblematic in these cases that tort law fails to recognize group harm.

IV. SUBJECTIVE V. OBJECTIVE DEFINITIONS OF SEXUAL HARASSMENT

Most definitions of 'sexual harassment' make reference to the behavior's being "unwelcome" or "annoying" to the victim. *Black's Law Dictionary* defines 'harassment' as a term used "to describe words, gestures and actions which tend to annoy, alarm and abuse (verbally) another person."[45] The *American Heritage Dictionary* defines 'harass' as "to disturb or irritate persistently," and states further that "[h]arass implies systematic persecution by besetting with annoyances, threats, or demands."[46] The EEOC *Guidelines* state that behavior constituting SH is identified as "unwelcome sexual advances, requests for sexual favors, and other verbal or physical conduct of a sexual nature."[47] In their philosophical account of SH, Hughes and May define 'harassment' as "a class of annoying or unwelcome acts undertaken by one person (or group of persons) against another person (or group of persons)."[48] And Rosemarie Tong takes the feminists' definition of noncoercive SH to be that which "denotes sexual misconduct that merely annoys or offends the person to whom it is directed."[49]

The criterion of "unwelcomeness" or "annoyance" is reflected in the way the courts have handled cases of SH, as in *Lipsett, Swentek,* and *Meritor,* though in the latter case the court said that the voluntariness of the victim's submission to the defendant's sexual conduct did not mean that she welcomed the conduct.[50] The criterion of unwelcomeness or annoyance present in these subjective accounts of harassment puts the burden on the victim to establish that she was sexually harassed. There is no doubt that many women *are* bothered by this behavior, often with serious side-effects including anything from anger, fear, and guilt,[51] to lowered self-esteem and decreased feelings of competence and confidence,[52] to anxiety disorders, alcohol and drug abuse, coronary disturbances, and gastro-intestinal disorders.[53]

Though it is true that many women are bothered by the behavior at issue, I think it is seriously mistaken to say that whether the victim is bothered determines whether the behavior constitutes SH. This is so for several reasons.

First, we would have to establish that the victim was bothered by it, either by the victim's complaints, or by examining the victim's response to the behavior. The fact of the matter is that many women are quite hesitant to report being harassed, for a number of reasons. Primary among them is that they fear negative consequences from reporting the conduct. As is often the case, harassment comes from a person in a position of institutional power, whether he be a supervisor, a company president, a member of a dissertation committee, the chair of the department, and so on. Unfortunately for many women, as a review of the case law reveals, their fears are warranted.[54] Women have been fired, their jobs have been made miserable forcing them to quit, professors have handed out unfair low grades, and so on. Worries about such consequences means that complaints are not filed, or are filed years after the incident, as in the Anita Hill v. Thomas Clarence case. But this should not be taken to imply that the victim was not harassed.

Moreover, women are hesitant to report harassment because they do not want anything to happen to the perpetrator, but just want the behavior to stop.[55] Women do not complain because they do not want to deal with the perpetrator's reaction when faced with the charge. He might claim that he was "only trying to be friendly." Women are fully aware that perpetrators can often clear themselves quite easily, especially in tort law cases where the perpetrator's intentions are directly relevant to whether he is guilty. And most incidents of SH occur without any witnesses—many perpetrators plan it this way. It then becomes the harasser's word against the victim's. To complicate matters, many women are insecure and doubt themselves. Women's insecurity is capitalized upon by harassers whose behavior is in the least bit ambiguous. Clever harassers who fear they might get caught or be reported often attempt to get on the good side of their victim in order to confuse her about the behavior, as well as to have a defense ready in case a charge is made. Harassers might offer special teaching assignments to their graduate students, special help with exams and publications, promotions, generous raises, and the like. Of course, this is all irrelevant to whether he harasses, but the point is that it makes the victim less likely to complain. On top of all this, women's credibility is very often questioned (unfairly) when they bring forth a charge. They are taken to be "hypersensitive." There is an attitude among judges and others that women must "develop a thick skin."[56] Thus, the blame is shifted off the perpetrator and onto the victim. Given this, if a woman thinks she will get no positive response—or, indeed, will get a negative one—from complaining, she is unlikely to do so.

Further, some women do not recognize harassment for what it is, and so will not complain. Sometimes this is because they are not aware of their own oppression, or actually seem to endorse sexist stereotypes. I recall a young woman who received many catcalls on the streets of Daytona Beach, Florida during spring break, and who was quite proud that her body could draw such attention. Given that women are socialized into believing their bodies are the most important feature of themselves, it is no surprise that a fair number of them are complacent about harassing behavior directed at them. Sandra Bartky provides an interesting analysis of why every woman is not a feminist, and I think it holds even for women who understand the issue.[57] Since for many women having a body felt to be "feminine" is crucial to their identity and to their sense of self "as a sexually desiring and desirable subject," feminism "may well be apprehended by a woman as something that threatens her with desexualization, if not outright annihilation."[58] The many women who resist becoming feminists are not likely to per-

ceive harassing behavior as bothersome. It would be incorrect to conclude that the behavior is not harassment on the grounds that such victims are not bothered. What we have is a no-win situation for victims: if the behavior bothers a woman she often has good reason not to complain; and if it does not bother her, she will not complain. Either way, the perpetrator wins. So we cannot judge whether women are bothered by the behavior on the basis of whether they *say* they are bothered.

Moreover, women's *behavior* is not an accurate indicator of whether they are bothered. More often than not, women try to ignore the perpetrator's behavior in an attempt not to give the impression they are encouraging it. They often cover up their true feelings so that the perpetrator does not have the satisfaction that his harassing worked. Since women are taught to smile and put up with this behavior, they might actually appear to enjoy it to some extent. Often they have no choice but to continue interacting with the perpetrator, making it very difficult to assert themselves. Women often make up excuses for not "giving in" instead of telling the perpetrator to stop. The fact that their behavior does not indicate they are bothered should not be used to show they were not bothered. In reality, women are fearful of defending themselves in the face of men's power and physical strength. Given the fact that the courts have decided that a lot of this behavior should just be tolerated, it is no wonder that women try to make the best of their situation.

It would be wrong to take a woman's behavior to be a sign that she is bothered also because doing so implies the behavior is permissible if she does not seem to care. This allows the *perpetrator* to be the judge of whether a woman is harassed, which is unjustifiable given the confusion among men about whether their behavior is bothersome or flattering. Sexual harassment should be treated no differently than crimes where harm to the victim is assessed in some objective way, independent of the perpetrator's beliefs. To give men this power in the case of harassment is to perpetuate sexism from all angles.

An *objective* view of SH avoids the problems inherent in a subjective view. According to the objective view defended here, what is decisive in determining whether behavior constitutes SH is not whether the victim is bothered, but whether the behavior is an instance of a practice that expresses and perpetuates the attitude that the victim and members of her sex are inferior because of their sex. Thus the Daytona Beach case counts as a case of SH because the behavior is an instance of a practice that reflects men's domination of women in that it relegates women to the role of sex objects.[59]

The courts have to some extent tried to incorporate an objective notion of SH by invoking the "reasonable person" standard. The EEOC *Guidelines,* as shown earlier, define SH partly as behavior that "has the purpose or effect of *unreasonably* interfering with an individual's work performance. . . ."[60] The *Restatement of Torts,* referring to the tort of intentional infliction of emotional distress, states that the emotional distress must be "so severe that no *reasonable* man could be expected to endure it."[61]

In various cases the courts have invoked a reasonable man (or person) standard, but *not* to show that women who are not bothered still suffer harassment. Instead, they used the standard to show that even though a particular woman *was* bothered, she would have to tolerate such behavior because it was behavior a reasonable person would not have been affected by. In *Rabidue v. Osceola Refining Co.*[62] (1986), a woman complained that a coworker made obscene comments about women in general and her in particular. The court ruled that "a reasonable person would not have been significantly affected by the same or similar circumstances,"[63] and that "women must expect a certain amount of demeaning conduct in certain work environments."[64]

But the reasonable man standard will not work, since men and women perceive situations involving SH quite differently. The reasonable person standard fares no better as it becomes the reasonable man standard when it is applied by male judges seeing things through male eyes. Studies have shown that sexual overtures that men find flattering are found by women to be insulting. And even when men recognize behavior as harassment, they think women will be flattered by it.[65] The differences in perception

only strengthens my point about the group harm that SH causes all women: unlike women, men can take sexual overtures directed at them to be complimentary because the overtures do not signify the stereotyping that underlies SH of women. A reasonable man standard would not succeed as a basis upon which to determine SH, as its objectivity is outweighed by the disparity found in the way the sexes assess what is "reasonable."

Related to this last topic is the issue of the harasser's intentions. In subjective definitions this is the counterpart to the victim's being bothered. Tort law makes reference to the injuror's intentions: in battery tort, the harasser's intent to contact, in assault tort, the harasser's intent to arouse psychic apprehension in the victim, and in the tort of intentional emotional distress, the harasser's intent or recklessness, must be established in order for the victim to win her case.

But like the victim's feelings, the harasser's intentions are irrelevant to whether his behavior is harassment. As I just pointed out, many men do not take their behavior to be bothersome, and sometimes even mistakenly believe that women enjoy crude compliments about their bodies, ogling, pinching, etc. From perusing cases brought before the courts, I have come to believe that many men have psychological feelings of power over women, feelings of being in control of their world, and the like, when they harass. These feelings might be subconscious, but this should not be admitted as a defense of the harasser. Also, as I have said, many men believe women encourage SH either by their dress or language, or simply by the fact that they tolerate the abuse without protest (usually out of fear of repercussion). In light of these facts, it would be wrongheaded to allow the harasser's intentions to count in assessing harassment, though they might become relevant in determining punishment. I am arguing for an objective definition of SH: it is the attitudes embedded and reflected *in the practice* the behavior is an instance of, not the attitudes or intentions *of the perpetrator,* that makes the behavior SH.

Yet the idea that the behavior must be directed at a certain person in order for it to count as harassment, seems to suggest that intentions *do* count in assessing harassment. This feature is evident both in my definition, as well as in that found in *Black's Law Dictionary,* which takes harassment to be conduct directed against a specific person causing substantial emotional distress. If conduct is directed at a particular individual, it seems that the person expressing himself must be intentionally singling out that individual, wanting to cause her harm.

I think this is mistaken. Since the harasser can subconsciously enjoy the feeling of power harassing gives him, or might even consider his behavior to be flattering, his behavior can be directed at a specific person (or group of persons) without implying any ill intention on his part. By 'directed at a particular individual,' I mean that the behavior is in some way observed by a particular person (or persons). This includes, for example, sexist comments a student hears her professor say, pornographic pictures a worker sees, etc. I interpret it loosely enough to include a person's overhearing sexist comments even though the speaker has no idea the person is within earshot (sometimes referred to as "nondirected behavior"). But I interpret it to exclude the bare knowledge that sexist behavior is going on (e.g., female employees knowing that there are pornographic pictures hidden in their boss's office). If it did not exclude such behavior it would have to include knowledge of *any* sexist behavior, even if no person who can be harmed by it ever observes it (e.g., pornographic magazines strewn on a desert island). Though such behavior is sexist, it fails to constitute SH.

V. Implications of the Objective Definition

One implication of my objective definition is that it reflects the correct way power comes into play in SH. Traditionally, SH has been taken to exist only between persons of unequal power, usually in the workplace or an educational institution. It is believed that SH in universities occurs only when a professor harasses a student, but not *vice versa.* It is said that students can cause "sexual hassle," because they cannot "destroy [the pro-

fessor's] self-esteem or endanger his intellectual self-confidence," and professors "seldom suffer the complex psychological effects of sexual harassment victims."[66] MacKinnon, in her earlier book, defines SH as "the unwanted imposition of sexual requirements in the context of a relationship of unequal power."[67]

Though it is true that a lot of harassment occurs between unequals, it is false that harassment occurs *only* between unequals: equals and subordinates can harass. Indeed, power is irrelevant to tort law, and the courts now recognize harassment among coworkers under Title VII.

The one sense in which it is true that the harasser must have power over his victim is that men have power—social, political, and economic—over women as a group. This cannot be understood by singling out individual men and showing that they have power over women or any particular woman for that matter. It is power that all men have, in virtue of being men. Defining SH in the objective way I do allows us to see that *this* is the sense in which power exists in SH, in *all* of its forms. The benefit of not restricting SH to cases of unequal institutional power is that *all* victims are afforded protection.

A second implication of my definition is that it gives the courts a way of distinguishing SH from sexual attraction. It can be difficult to make this distinction, since "traditional courtship activities" are often quite sexist and frequently involve behavior that is harassment. The key is to examine the practice the behavior is an instance of. If the behavior reflects the attitude that the victim is inferior because of her sex, then it is SH. Sexual harassment is not about a man's attempting to date a woman who is not interested, as the courts have tended to believe; it is about domination, which might be reflected, of course, in the way a man goes about trying to get a date. My definition allows us to separate cases of SH from genuine sexual attraction by forcing the courts to focus on the social nature of SH.

Moreover, defining SH in the objective way I do shifts the burden and the blame off the victim. On the subjective view, the burden is on the victim to prove that she is bothered significantly enough to win a tort case, or under Title VII, to show that the behavior unreasonably interfered with her work. In tort law, where the perpetrator's intentions are allowed to figure in, the blame could easily shift to the victim by showing that she in some way welcomed or even encouraged the behavior thereby relinquishing the perpetrator from responsibility. By focusing on the practice the behavior is an instance of, my definition has nothing to do with proving that the victim responds a certain way to the behavior, nor does it in any way blame the victim for the behavior.

Finally, defining SH in a subjective way means that the victim herself must come forward and complain, as it is her response that must be assessed. But given that most judges, law enforcement officers, and even superiors are men, it is difficult for women to do so. They are embarrassed, afraid to confront someone of the same sex as the harasser who is likely not to see the problem. They do not feel their voices will be heard. Working with my definition will I hope assuage this. Recognizing SH as a group harm will allow women to come to each other's aid as co-complainers, thereby alleviating the problem of reticence. Even if the person the behavior is directed at does not feel bothered, other women can complain, as they suffer the group harm associated with SH.

VI. Conclusion

The definition of SH I have defended in this paper has as its main benefit that it acknowledges the group harm SH causes all women, thereby getting to the heart of what is wrong with SH. By doing so, it protects all victims in all cases from even the most subtle kinds of SH, since all cases of SH have in common group harm.

Of course, as with any definition, problems exist. Though space does not allow that I deal with them, a few are worth mentioning. One is that many behaviors will count as SH, leading perhaps to an unmanageable number of claims. Another is that it will still be a matter of interpretation whether a given behavior meets the criteria for SH. Perhaps the most crucial objection is that since so many kinds of behavior count as SH, the right to free speech will be curtailed in unacceptable ways.[68]

I believe there are at least partial solutions to these problems. My proposal is only programmatic, and a thorough defense of it would include working through these and other problems. Such a defense will have to wait.

Notes

I would like to thank John Exdell and Lois Pineau for helpful discussions and many insightful comments on an earlier draft of this paper.

1. Rosemarie Tong, "Sexual Harassment," in *Women and Values,* Marilyn Pearsall, ed., (Belmont, CA: Wadsworth Publishing Company, 1986), pp. 148–166. Tong cites a *Redbook* study that reported 88 percent of 9,000 readers sampled experienced some sort of sexual harassment (p. 149).
2. Civil Rights Act of 1964, 42 U.S.C. Sec. 2000e-2(a) (1982).
3. Catharine A. MacKinnon, *Sexual Harassment of Working Women: A Case of Sex Discrimination* (New Haven: Yale University Press, 1979).
4. EEOC *Guidelines on Discrimination Because of Sex,* 29 C.F.R. Sec. 1604.11(a) (1980).
5. The case was a landmark case because it established (1) federal legislation that SH is a form of sex discrimination, (2) that just because the victim "voluntarily" submitted to advances from her employer, it did not mean she welcomed the conduct, (3) that victims could appeal on grounds of emotional harm, not merely economic harm. For an excellent discussion of the history of the case as it went through the courts, see Joel T. Andreesen, "Employment Discrimination— The Expansion in Scope of Title VII to Include Sexual Harassment as a Form of Sex Discrimination: *Meritor Savings Bank, FSB v. Vinson, The Journal of Corporation Law,* Vol. 12, No. 3 (Spring, 1987), pp. 619–638.
6. *Meritor Savings Bank, FSB v. Vinson,* 477 U.S. 57 (1986).
7. Joyce L. Richard, "Sexual Harassment and Employer Liability," *Southern University Law Review,* Vol. 12 (1986), pp. 251–279. See pp. 272–275 for an excellent discussion of the case.
8. Title IX of the Education Amendments of 1972, 20 U.S.C. Sec. 1681 (1982).
9. For a very good discussion of the case law regarding Title IX, see Walter B. Connolly, Jr., and Alison B. Marshall, "Sexual Harassment of University or College Students by Faculty Members," *The Journal of College and University Law,* Vol. 15 (Spring, 1989), pp. 381–403.
10. *Black's Law Dictionary,* 6th Ed. (St. Paul, MN: West Publishing Co., 1990), p. 1248.
11. Michael D. Vhay, "The Harms of Asking: Towards a Comprehensive Treatment of Sexual Harassment," *The University of Chicago Law Review,* Vol. 55 (Winter, 1988), p. 334.
   In the case of students, *quid pro quo* harassment can take the form of a professor threatening the student with a lower grade if she does not comply with his demands.

12. Ellen Frankel Paul, "Sexual Harassment as Sex Discrimination: A Defective Paradigm," *Yale Law & Policy Review,* Vol. 8, No. 2 (1990), p. 341.

13. EEOC *Guidelines, Op. cit.,* at Sec. 1604.11(a).

14. *Black's Law Dictionary, Op.cit.,* p. 470. It cites *Rich v. Martin Marietta Corp.,* D.C.Colo., 467 F.Supp. 587, 608.

15. *Topical Law Reports.* (New York: Commerce Clearing House, Inc., 1988), p. 3030.

16. John C. Hughes and Larry May, "Sexual Harassment," *Social Theory and Practice,* Vol. 6, No. 3 (Fall, 1980), p. 260.

17. Frankel Paul, *Op.cit.,* p. 337.

18. See Frankel Paul, Ibid., pp. 359–360, for a list of cases invoking torts along with Title VII claims.

19. Rosemarie Tong, *Women, Sex, and the Law.* (Savage, MD: Rowman & Littlefield Publishers, Inc., 1984), p. 71.

20. Frank J. Till, *Sexual Harassment: A Report on the Sexual Harassment of Students.* (Washington, D.C.: National Advisory Council on Women's Educational Programs, 1980), pt. II, p. 13.

21. Ibid., p. 14.

22. Tong, *Women, Sex, and the Law, Op.cit.,* p. 73.

23. *Restatement (Second) of Torts* Sec. 46 (1965) comment a.

24. Ibid.

25. Ibid., comment j.

26. EEOC *Guidelines,* 29 C.F.R., Sec. 1604.11(b) (1985).

27. Mari J. Matsuda, "Public Response to Racist Speech: Considering the Victim's Story," *Michigan Law Review,* Vol. 87, No. 8 (August, 1989), pp. 2320–2381.

28. Ibid., pp. 2345, 2344.

29. Ibid., p. 2345.

30. Ibid., p. 2346.

31. Ibid., p. 2348.

32. This suggests that only men can sexually harass women. I will defend this view later in the paper.

33. Frances Conley, a 50-year-old distinguished neurophysician at Stanford University, recently came forward with this story. Conley resigned after years of putting up with sexual harassment from her colleagues. Not only did they use Playboy spreads during their lectures, but they routinely called her "hon," invited her to bed, and fondled her legs under the operating table. *Chicago Tribune,* Sunday, June 9, 1991, Section 1, p. 22.

34. Hughes and May, *Op.cit.,* pp. 264–265.

35. Ibid., p. 265.

36. These same myths surround the issue of rape. This is discussed fruitfully by Lois Pineau in "Date Rape: A Feminist Analysis," *Law and Philosophy,* Vol. 8 (1989), pp. 217–243.

37. MacKinnon, *Op.Cit.,* p. 152, is where she cites the study.

38. *Lipsett v. Rive-Mora,* 669 F.Supp. 1188 (D. Puerto Rico 1987).

39. Dawn D. Bennett-Alexander, "Hostile Environment Sexual Harassment: A Clearer View," *Labor Law Journal,* Vol. 42, No. 3 (March, 1991), p. 135.

40. Lipsett, Ibid., Sec. 15.

41. *Swentek v. US Air,* 830 F.2d 552 (4th Cir. 1987).

42. *Swentek v. US Air,* Ibid., 44 EPd at 552.

43. Billie Wright Dziech and Linda Weiner, "*The Lecherous Professor: Sexual Harassment on Campus.* (Boston: Beacon Press, 1984), p. 63.

44. This harm is similar to the harm Ann Cudd finds with rape. Since women are the victims of rape, "they come to be seen as in need of protection, as weak and passive, and available to all men." See Ann E. Cudd, "Enforced Pregnancy, Rape, and the Image of Woman," *Philosophical Studies,* Vol. 60 (1990), pp. 47–59.

45. *Black's Law Dictionary, Op.cit.,* p. 717.

46. *American Heritage Dictionary of the English Language.* (New York: American Heritage Publishing Co., Inc., 1973), p. 600.

47. EEOC *Guidelines, Op.cit.,* Sec. 1604.11(a).

48. Hughes and May, *Op.cit.,* p. 250.

49. Tong, *Women, Sex, and the Law, Op.cit.* p. 67.

50. *Meritor, Op.cit.,* at 1113–16.

51. MacKinnon, *Op.cit.,* p. 83.

52. Stephanie Riger, "Gender Dilemmas in Sexual Harassment Policies and Procedures," *American Psychologist,* Vol. 46 (1991), pp. 497–505.

53. Martha Sperry, "Hostile Environment Sexual Harassment and the Imposition of Liability Without Notice: A Progressive Approach to Traditional Gender Roles and Power Based Relationships," *New England Law Review,* Vol. 24 (1980), p. 942, fns. 174 & 175.

54. See Catharine MacKinnon, *Feminism Unmodified: Discourses on Life and Law.* (Cambridge: Harvard University Press, 1987), Chapter Nine, for a nice discussion of the challenges women face in deciding whether to report harassment. See also Ellen Frankel Paul, *Op.cit.,* for an excellent summary of the case law on sexual harassment.

55. MacKinnon, *Sexual Harassment of Working Women, Op.cit.,* p. 83.

56. See Frankel Paul, *Op.cit.,* pp. 333–365. Frankel Paul wants to get away from the "helpless victim syndrome," making women responsible for reporting harassment, and placing the burden on them to develop a tough skin so as to avoid being seen as helpless victims (pp. 362–363). On the contrary, what Frankel Paul fails to understand is that placing these additional burdens on women *detracts* from the truth that they *are* victims, and implies that they deserve the treatment if they do not develop a "tough attitude."

57. Sandra Bartky, "Foucault, Femininity, and the Modernization of Patriarchal Power," in Sandra Bartky, *Femininity and Domination: Studies in the Phenomenology of Oppression.* (New York: Routledge, Chapman, and Hall, Inc., 1990), pp. 63–82. See especially pp. 77–78.

58. Ibid., p. 77.

59. This case exemplifies my point that the behavior need not be persistent in order to constitute harassment, despite the view of many courts. One catcall, for example, will constitute SH if catcalling is shown to be a practice reflecting domination.

60. EEOC *Guidelines, Op.cit.,* Sec. 1604.11(a), my emphasis.

61. *Restatement (Second) of Torts,* Sec. 146, (1965), comment j, my emphasis.

62. *Rabidue v. Osceola Refining Co.,* 805 F.2d (1986), Sixth Circuit Court.

63. Ibid., at 622.
64. Ibid., at 620–622.
65. Stephanie Riger, "Gender Dilemmas in Sexual Harassment Policies and Procedures," *American Psychologist,* Vol. 46, No. 5 (May 1991), p. 499 is where she cites the relevant studies.
66. Wright Dziech and Weiner, *Op.cit.,* p. 24.
67. MacKinnon, *Sexual Harassment of Working Women, Op.cit.,* p. 1. It is actually not clear that MacKinnon endorses this definition throughout this book, as what she says seems to suggest that harassment can occur at least between equals. In her most recent book, she recognizes that harassment "also happens among co-workers, from third parties, even by subordinates in the workplace, men who are women's hierarchical inferiors or peers." Catharine A. MacKinnnon, *Feminism Unmodified: Discourses on Life and Law.* (Cambridge: Harvard University Press, 1987), p. 107.

68. For an excellent analysis on sexist speech and the limits of free speech as guaranteed by the Constitution, see Marcy Strauss, "Sexist Speech in the Workplace," *Harvard Civil Rights and Civil Liberties Law Review,* Vol. 25 (1990), pp. 1–51. She cites the relevant case law concerning sexist speech that is not protected by First Amendment rights. She defends the view that the Constitution can prohibit speech demanding or requesting sexual relationships, sexually explicit speech directed at the woman, and degrading speech directed at the woman, but not sexually explicit or degrading speech that the woman employee knows exists in the workplace, even though it is not directed at her. (p. 43) She employs an interesting and useful distinction between speech that discriminates, and speech that merely advocates discrimination, recognizing that the state has an interest in regulating the former, given the harm it can cause.

Nancy Tuana

Sexual Harassment: Offers and Coercion

In the last ten years, sexual harassment within the workplace and academe has been the subject of numerous studies.[1] The large majority of such studies which categorize types of activities which are to be classified as sexual harassment include the attempt on the part of the instructor or employer to procure sex or sex related behavior by promise of rewards as a type of sexual harassment. For example, the study of sexual harassment of postsecondary students compiled by the National Advisory Council on Women's Educational Programs contains the category of "solicitation of sexual activity or other sex-linked behavior by promise of rewards" within its list of five types of activity which are to be classified as sexual harass-

ment.[2] The University of Washington's official policy concerning sexual harassment states that sexual harassment may include "requests for sexual favors."[3] The government of the District of Columbia's policy on sexual harassment issued in 1979 included the action of "demanding sexual favors accompanied by implied or overt promise of preferential treatment with regard to an individual's employment status" as one of the categories of sexual harassment.[4] Catharine MacKinnon, in her study of sexual harassment of working women, views the act of an employer offering a job opportunity in exchange for sexual favors as constituting sexual harassment.[5]

Sexual harassment has as its central meaning the coercion of sexual activity. Charges of sexual harassment are most generally raised when an employee or student feels that his or her employer, supervisor, or instructor has used his or her institutional authority over them to coerce sexual favors from them. However, current analyses of coercion reject the possibility of offers being coercive. Such analyses thus call into question the status of attempts to procure sexual favors by offers of rewards. Are we to classify such actions as cases of sexual harassment?

From Nancy Tuana, "Sexual Harassment: Offers and Coercion," *Journal of Social Philosophy,* Vol. 19, No. 2 (Summer 1988). Reprinted by permission of the *Journal of Social Philosophy.*

THE CASE AGAINST COERCIVE OFFERS

The main attack upon the possibility of coercive offers was developed by Michael Bayles[6] who argued that only actions which involve threats can be viewed as coercive. By claiming that offers do not involve threats, he was able to conclude that offers cannot be coercive. His attempt to illustrate this position is directly applicable to the issue of sexual harassment. In his rejection of Virginia Held's[7] position that inducements can be coercive, Bayles offers the following example to illustrate his position:

Assume there is a mediocre woman graduate student who would not receive an assistantship. Suppose the department chairman offers her one if she goes to bed with him, and she does so. In what sense has the graduate student acted against her will? She apparently preferred having an assistantship and sleeping with the chairman to not sleeping with him and not having an assistantship. So it would appear that she did what she wanted in the situation. Held may mean that the woman acted against her will in that she would rather have had the assistantship and not slept with the chairman; that is, there was a consequence of her choice which she found undesirable. But the fact that a choice has an undesirable consequence does not make it against one's will. One may prefer to have clean teeth without having to brush them; nonetheless, one is not acting against one's will when one brushes them.[8]

From this analysis, Bayles would have us conclude that offers to students by instructors (or by extrapolation, to employees by employers) do not involve sexual harassment if sexual harassment is viewed as involving coercion. In fact, Bayles would have us believe that in such situations, students and employees experience no impairment of their freedom of choice.

Such an analysis of offers or rewards in return for sexual favors does not fit well with the experiences of students and employees who have been in such situations. A classification of the results of a 1978 study of sexual harassment at the University of California at Berkeley, in which students who felt that they had been harassed were asked to describe that harassment, includes sexual bribery as one of the self-reported types of sexual harassment.[9] A number of students, in reporting the events they perceived to constitute harassment, described grade offers in exchange for affairs. A survey conducted at the University of California at Santa Barbara in 1981 which consisted of student reactions to a series of vignettes, revealed that the inclusion, within such a vignette, of the instructor indicating that sexual cooperation would improve the student's grade dramatically, increased the sexual harassment rating of that vignette.[10] In fact, the survey revealed that the addition of sexual bribery to a vignette increased the sexual harassment rating of a vignette more than did the addition of a warning by the instructor that the student's success in the class could be affected if he or she did not consent to sexual activity with the instructor.

Thus we see a clear tension between philosophical analyses which reject the possibility of coercive offers and the experiences of students and employees. In order to reconcile the tension between these two positions, it would be helpful to look at the standard analysis of coercion.

THE STANDARD ANALYSIS OF COERCION

According to the accepted analysis of coercion, there are six criteria which must be satisfied to classify an action as coercive. The analysis of a person, X, having coerced another person, Y, to do an action, A, would be the following:

1. X intends that Y do A
2. X further intends to harm Y if Y does not do A
3. X threatens Y with harm if Y does not do A
4. Y does A
5. Y would have done otherwise had Y so chosen
6. Y would have chosen otherwise had Y not been threatened by X.[11]

Given this analysis of coercion, it becomes clear why one might reject the possibility of offers being coercive. If we examine the illustration given above, we can see that Bayles is claiming that the offer merely makes the action of sex with the chair more desirable or less undesirable to the student than it had been prior to the offer, or makes available a choice not previously available to the student. Such an offer then, according to this analysis, presents no harm to the recipient. It would seem to follow from this that, if in order for there to be coercion, there must be a person (or group of people) who threatens to harm the coerced individual and intends to so harm her or him, then it would appear that offers could not be coercive. In order for an action to be threatening, that act must make a victim's choice situation less desirable or more undesirable, and this is done either by adding some undesirable consequence to, or removing a desirable consequence from, one of the victim's alternative choices, which will result in harm to him or her if he or she refuses to act as is desired. Bayles claims that the offer made by the chair made the student's choice situation more desirable by providing her the option of an assistantship which would not otherwise have been available. If sexual harassment is defined as involving coercion, one could use the analysis above to deny that solicitation of sexual favors by promise of rewards falls under the category of sexual harassment.

It is my contention that the attempt to procure sexual contact through the promise of rewards can be and often is coercive when the person who makes the offer is in a position of authority over the person to whom he or she makes the offer. I believe that the above illustration could be classified as coercive even though there is no threat to harm the student and the chair has no intention of harming the student should she refuse. I will therefore show that the standard analysis of coercion is not complete, for it omits a very important and common type of coercion.

OFFERS AND COERCION

Let us look again at the above illustration of solicitation of sexual favors. Bayles spends no time considering the context in which the offer was made nor does he consider the beliefs or reactions of the student to whom the offer was made. I will show that this is a significant omission which, when rectified, will demonstrate the possibility of coercive offers.

In this case the person who has made the offer is the chairperson of the department. The chairperson of this department has a variety of powers, including the ability to offer or refuse assistantships. Given typical department politics it would be fair to assume that the chairperson also has the power to make other very important decisions which could affect the career of this graduate student, such as assigning the members of her dissertation committee, deciding on the jobs for which she will receive a departmental recommendation, and the like. In other words, the chair has the power to make it very difficult for this student to receive her degree and to succeed in her career. We have to add to this the fact that this graduate student is "mediocre." What this means is that if the chairperson wishes to, he would have a less difficult time getting this student dropped out of the program than he would if she had been a star student. Given her record, there are probably no instructors who are willing to support her case should she complain, for it would be difficult to make a case for her given her less than excellent record. Also, as all of us know who have been a part of academia, the decisions of retention or expulsion in borderline cases are difficult and anything but objective. It would be very easy for the chairperson of a department to recommend against retention when the student's record is reviewed, using her mediocre performance as the sole reason for this recommendation, and probably not raise anyone's suspicions in so doing. Had the student an excellent record it would be more difficult for the chairperson to recommend against retention without casting suspicion upon his motives. But given her mediocre record, should she protest such an action or claim that it was the result of her refusal to grant sexual favors, most people would tend to discredit her complaint as "sour grapes." Now let us assume that the student believes all of this.

In addition to the above beliefs about the power of the chairperson of one's department, given that the chairperson has offered this student a position better than she deserves in return for sexual favors, she now knows that the chairperson of her department feels neither morally nor legally obliged to promote fairly.

The very fact that the chairperson was willing to give her a position for which she did not qualify is good reason to believe that he might be the type of person who would be willing to abuse a student who displeases him. So the student now knows that the chairperson is the type of person who is willing to misuse his power to obtain what he wants, and thus has good reason to believe that this misuse of power might extend to penalizing a student who gets in the way of his wants.

An additional aspect of this situation which must be taken into consideration is the nature of the action being requested by the chair and the social attitudes surrounding such an action. We live in a culture in which people are often very sensitive about another person's response to their request for sexual contact. People generally have very fragile egos concerning rejections of sexual advances. A very common response to a refusal of a sexual proposition is to feel hurt and upset. Furthermore, many people who experience such hurt then develop the desire to retaliate. The graduate student will be well aware of this and will probably start thinking about all the instances she has heard of in which instructors retaliated against students who refused their sexual advances by misusing their authority to hurt the student.

So the graduate student accepts the chairperson's offer. Notice that Bayles' explanation is that she did so because "she apparently preferred having an assistantship and sleeping with the chairman to not sleeping with him and not having an assistantship.[12] If that was all there was to the situation (the student was quite willing to have sex with the chairperson in order to acquire the assistantship), then I would be willing to say that there was no coercion and that the situation involved no sexual harassment, though I would want to fault the chairperson for immoral and unprofessional conduct. But it is not acceptable to assume that this explanation will fit all cases. I would like to suggest another plausible scenario, which happens quite frequently, which does involve coercion and should be classified as sexual harassment.

Given the context of the situation as I have spelled it out in the above paragraphs, the student finds herself in a situation where she is very vulnerable to being harmed by the chairperson, well knowing that there is a very good chance that if she rejects his proposition, he will be upset enough to want to hurt her in turn. The student has no desire to have any sexual contact with the chairperson, and she does not think that getting the assistantship is a good reason for having the sexual contact. However, being aware of the power of the chairperson and the vulnerability of her position in the department, she fears that a refusal of the offer will upset and anger the chairperson, making him want to retaliate. Furthermore, she believes that such retaliation could result in her being failed out of the program, thus ending her hopes for an academic career. Because of her fear of such harm, the student accepts the offer.

If we were to analyze this case based on the above model, where X is the chair, Y the student, and A the act of sexual involvement, the result would be the following:

1. X intends that Y do A
2. Y does A
3. Y would have done otherwise had Y so chosen
4. Y would have done otherwise had he or she not feared that Y would harm him or her if he or she did not do A.

It is important to notice that this analysis is significantly different from the standard analysis of coercion. There is no initial intention to harm on the chairperson's part, nor does the student think that the chair has the intention to harm her when the chair makes the offer. Also there is no threat made by the chairperson, nor does the student think that the chairperson has threatened her. One cannot thus object that the case that I am describing is a case of a mixed offer and threat where the student is offered an inducement for submitting to the sexual involvement, and threatened with a harm if she refuses. I have no doubt that such situations do occur, but such an analysis does not fit the above situation in that it is not the case, nor does the student believe that it is the case, that the chair has the *intention* to threaten the student with harm, or to harm the student should she refuse *when the offer is made.*

Despite the absence of a threat or any intention to harm on the part of the chair, what makes this action coercive and thus a case of sexual harassment is that the student's choice situation is made less desirable or more undesirable because of her fear of harm if she refuses to act as is desired. What is significantly different about this case, and what the standard analysis of coercion misses completely is that a person can reasonably believe that her refusal of an offer, like the one above, would result in a situation in which she would be harmed. As I am describing it, the above situation is one in which the student believes that there is a very high probability that her rejection of the offer will *cause* the chairman to have the desire to harm her. So the situation is one in which the threat of harm which the student fears is not made prior to or at the time of the offer, but will *come into existence* as a result of her refusal. One thing which is overlooked on the standard analysis of coercion is a person's reaction to having his or her offer rejected. Some offers are so loaded that a refusal may cause a desire to retaliate. In the words of a lawyer who was a junior member of a law firm, regarding the sexual proposition of one of the senior members of that firm:

... I also recognized I was in a compromising and extremely dangerous position. I definitely didn't want to have an affair with Mr. Scott ... however, Mr. Scott's ego was on the line. Terribly frightened of offending him and possibly ruining my chances for success in the firm, I knew I was treading on thin ice ... Mr. Scott had a reputation for extreme ruthlessness when crossed.[13]

What my depiction of the "offer" scenario illustrates is that in certain situations, a student's situation after an offer can be worse than it was before the offer. Accounts which consider offers non-coercive deny that even unwelcome offers are coercive, "... for one would not have done or chosen otherwise had they not been made. Nor are they turned into threats, for they do not make any of the alternative choices less desirable or more undesirable."[14] I have, on the contrary, shown that this need not be the case. In the present situation, if the student consents to a sexual involvement in order to avoid the harm in which she thinks a refusal will result, *then the offer does modify her choice.* The offer also makes alternative choices less desirable, for the student reasonably believes that the choice of rejecting the offer will result in harm which she would not have experienced had the offer never been made. Hence, I conclude that the above described situation is an offer situation involving coercion, and is the type of situation that we would want to classify as sexual harassment.

What I have shown is that the standard analysis of coercion is inadequate in that it omits sufficient reference to the context, the situation in which the action is performed. Once this omission is remedied, it can be shown that offers can be coercive whenever the background context is such that it is reasonable for the victim to believe that her refusal to accept the offer will result in harm

RESPONSIBILITY FOR COERCIVE OFFERS

A question might be raised at this point concerning responsibility for coercive offers. Consider the previous example. Since the chairperson intended no harm and was unaware that the student would perceive her refusal to consent to a sexual relation as ultimately resulting in his desiring to harm her, is the chairperson to be held responsible for the coercion? The answer to this question can only be obtained by considering the context of the offer.

In this case, the person in question is the chairperson of a department and a faculty member in a university. So we must look at the obligations of holding such a position. Each faculty member in taking his or her job signs a contract which binds him or her to a set of obligations. One group of these requirements concerns professional ethics. Many universities have adopted the American Association of University Professors' statement of professional ethics to make these requirements explicit. Concerning the relationship of instructors to their students, the statement says the following:

As teachers, professors encourage the free pursuit of learning in their students ... they demonstrate respect for students as individuals, and adhere to their proper role as intellectual guide and counselor. They make every reasonable effort to foster honest academic conduct and to assure that the evaluation of students reflects their true merit ... they avoid any exploitation of students for their private advantage and acknowledge significant assistance from them. They protect students' academic freedom.[15]

As an instructor and the chairperson of a department, one is obliged to work to create a situation in which students in classes and graduate students in the department work in an atmosphere which promotes intellectual development. It thus follows from this that the chairperson has the obligation to do nothing which could reasonably be seen by students as an inhibition to their intellectual development. The chair's intention alone is not sufficient.

Given this, I would argue that the example, as I have developed it, is one involving negligence on the part of the chairperson. Despite the fact that he did not intend his action to be coercive, or to be seen as coercive by the student, he should have known that his actions could reasonably be so construed given the circumstances. Thus the chairperson failed to take account of the coercive nature of the situation. Given his professional obligations, he should have known better. Because of this, I contend that we should hold the chairperson responsible for the coercion even though it was not his intention. Any claims of ignorance of the nature of the situation would not be justifiable given professional responsibilities to protect students' academic freedom, and would thus be classified as negligence. This would thus be a case in which the chairperson would be responsible for the coercion of the graduate student.[16]

From my development of this example, we can derive the following conclusions. In order to determine whether a person or group of people are to be held responsible for setting up a coercive situation, the context must be carefully examined. Relevant features of the context would include the following. First, the obligations that the person or group of people, Y, has to the person or persons, X, who are coerced. If the relationship is one of teacher/student, then the instructor's professional obligations, as dis-

cussed above, must be considered. If the relationship is that of employer/employee, then the employer's legal obligations to their employees, such as equal pay for equal work, must be considered. Second, the dominant cultural attitudes surrounding the action of Y which led to the coercive situation must be examined. In the above case, the fact that most people in our culture view rejections of requests for sexual contact as an insult was relevant, for such a fact explains why the student might reasonably believe that her refusal to accept the offer would lead to the chairperson desiring to hurt her. Third, in addition to considering the dominant cultural attitudes which apply to the relevant acts, we must determine Y's knowledge of these attitudes. If, for example, Y is from another country which has a different set of attitudes about the acts in question, and was not familiar with the attitudes of X's culture, then we may not want to hold Y responsible for the coercive situation which was the result of his offer. Fourth, we would also need to take into consideration Y's knowledge of X's personal attitudes. Any information Y might have about X's socio-economic position as this might affect his or her personal attitudes about the act in question, or any knowledge of X's personal attitudes which Y might have obtained through conversations with X or with people who had contact with X would also be relevant. To illustrate this, modify the above example by imagining that the chairperson had discussed this graduate student with other faculty in the program and had been told that she had happily accepted such offers in the past and had herself approached faculty with the offer of sexual favors in return for grades higher than she deserved. Given this modification we would be much less likely to hold the chairperson responsible should a coercive situation result from his offer, for he had good reason to believe that she would not be uninterested in the offer.

The general conclusion I would derive from this discussion is that the attempt to determine responsibility for coercive situations will require a careful examination of the context. Determining responsibility will be a complicated matter involving consideration of the beliefs and attitudes of those involved in that situation.

CONCLUSIONS

It is now obvious that the tension between, on the one hand, sexual harassment guidelines and the reports of self-identified victims of sexual harassment and, on the other hand, the rejection of offers as coercive, has been resolved by pointing out the inadequacies of the standard analysis of coercion. From this investigation we can derive two conclusions. First, that the standard analysis of coercion is inadequate because it omits any reference to the context of the situation and must be reformulated. My discussion then provides the beginning of a more adequate analysis of coercion. Second, that offers can be, but are not always, coercive. My analysis then supports the common view that sexual bribery is, in certain situations, a form of sexual harassment.

An additional consequence of my analysis goes far beyond the issue of sexual harassment. By recognizing that the refusal to do something can cause someone to have the intention to harm, a variety of types of actions can be seen as coercive which would not have been classified as coercive on the standard analysis. In other words, my analysis here is not just limited to offers. Promises, requests, advice, and a variety of different types of speech acts can be coercive. To illustrate this I shall describe a situation in which a request is coercive though there is no threat of harm nor intention to harm when the request is made.

Two people, Troy and Pat, are both close friends and business partners. They have known each other for over ten years during which time Troy has come to see Pat as his closest friend, as well as trusting her with the major financial decisions of the business. One day Pat confides to Troy that she is having an affair. Troy does not approve of Pat's affair for Troy knows that Pat has explicitly agreed to a monogamous relationship with her spouse. In addition Pat is intending to keep the affair secret from her spouse, thus violating their commitment of honesty. Though disapproving of the affair for these reasons, Troy decides not to say anything to Pat.

The next day Troy arrives at work to find a message from Pat saying that she has decided to spend the weekend in San Antonio with her new lover. In addition to informing Troy of the decision, Pat has asked Troy to "cover" for her should her spouse contact Troy. Now Troy has no desire to deceive Pat's spouse in this way and feels that doing so would constitute an implicit acceptance of the affair. Given this, Troy's initial response is to refuse to cover for Pat. However, Troy begins to think about what Pat's response would be to his refusal to cover the weekend. Troy and Pat have talked a lot about trust and support, and Pat has made it very clear that anyone she considers to be a friend must be willing to back her up even if they do not always agree with her decisions. The refusal to offer such support is viewed by Pat as an indication that the other person is not a true friend. Given such discussions Troy realizes that a refusal to "cover" for Pat will be interpreted by her as a lack of commitment to the friendship. Troy realizes that the consequences of refusing Pat's request will be a loss of their friendship. This recognition startles Troy for he remembers that Pat, though extremely supportive of her friends, believes it important to get even with anyone who she believes has tried to hurt her. What this means is that Troy's act of refusing to cover for Pat will be interpreted by Pat as an act of sabotage on the part of Troy. Such an interpretation would thus make Pat want to get even with Troy—to hurt him in turn. Troy realizes that Pat has enough control over Troy's investments that she could use her power to seriously hurt Troy financially.

So Troy finds himself in a dilemma. He does not want to "cover" for Pat and thinks that doing so would be immoral. On the other hand, should he refuse Pat's request, he believes that he will not only lose Pat's friendship, but also will risk a serious financial loss. Let's say that Troy decides to "cover" for Pat because he does not want to lose Pat's friendship nor suffer a financial setback. He has done an action which he would not have otherwise done, and has done so for fear of the consequences of refusing the request. Troy does not think that Pat is threatening him, or is in anyway intending to threaten him. Rather, Troy thinks that the action of refusing the request will cause Pat to desire to harm him. Despite the absence of any threat or intention to harm on Pat's part, this is a case where Troy has been coerced to cover for Pat. Troy did other then he would have otherwise chosen for fear of harm which would come to him if he refused the request.

The basic model then is that acts which involve no threat or intention to harm can be coercive if there is good reason to believe that to refuse to act as is desired will cause the other person or persons to desire to harm the person refusing. We thus see that a variety of speech acts, including offers, can be coercive. The basic lesson of this model is that any attempt to determine whether an act is coercive must take into consideration the context in which the act occurs.

Notes

1. Such studies include: Backhouse, Constance, and Cohen, Lea. *Sexual Harassment On the Job,* New Jersey: Prentice Hall, 1981. Benson, Donna Jean, and Thomson, Gregg E. "Sex, Gender, and Power: Sexual Harassment on a University Campus," Unpublished research paper, University of California at Berkeley, 1979. Farley, Lin. *Sexual Shakedown: Sexual Harassment of Women at Work,* New York: McGraw Hill, 1971. MacKinnon, Catharine. *Sexual Harassment of Working Women,* New Haven: Yale University Press, 1979. Meyer, M. C., Oestreich, J., Collins, F., and Berchtold, I. *Sexual Harassment,* New York: Petrocelli, 1981. Neugarten, D. A. and Shafritz, J. M. *Sexuality in Organizations: Romantic and Coercive Behaviors at Work,* Illinois: Moore Publishing Co., 1980. Project on the Status and Education of Women. *Sexual Harassment: A Hidden Issue,* Washington, D.C.: Association of American Colleges, 1978. Till, Frank. *Sexual Harassment: A Report on the Sexual Harassment of Students,* Washington, D.C.: National Advisory Council on Women's Educational Programs, 1980. Women Students' Coalition. *The Quality of Women's Education at Harvard University: A Survey of Sex Discrimination in the Graduate and Professional Schools,* Harvard University, 1980. Since this essay was written, additional studies have been published including: Russell, Diana. *Sexual Exploitation: Rape, Child Sexual Abuse and Workplace Harassment,* Beverly Hills, CA: Sage, 1984. Wright, Dziech and Linda Weiner. *The Lecherous Professor: Sexual Harassment on Campus,* Boston: Beacon Press, 1984. Brandenburg, Judith Berman. "Sexual Harassment in the University: Guidelines for Establishing a Grievance Procedure," *Signs* 8 (1982): 320–336. Lott, Bernice, Mary Ellen Reilly, and Dale R. Howard. "Sexual Assault and Harassment: A Campus Community Case Study," *Signs* 8 (1982): 296–319. Crocker, Phyllis. "An Analysis of Universal Definations of Sexual Harassment," *Signs* 8 (1983): 696–707.
2. Fill, Frank. *Sexual Harassment: A Report on the Sexual Harassment of Students,* Washington, D.C.: National Advisory Council on Women's Educational Programs, 1980, p. 8.
3. University of Washington, "Policy Prohibiting Sexual Harassment," 1980.
4. Government of the District of Columbia, "Government of the District of Columbia Policy on Sexual Harassment," Mayor's Order 79–89, May 24, 1979.
5. MacKinnon, Catherine. *Sexual Harassment of Working Women,* New Haven: Yale University Press, 1979, p. 32.
6. Bayles, Michael. "Coercive Offers and Public Benefits," *The Personalist,* Vol. LV, No. 2, Spring 1974, pp. 139–44.
7. Held, Virginia. "Coercion and Coercive Offers," in *Coercion: Nomos XIV,* Ed. J. Roland Pennock and John Chapman, Chicago: Aldine-Atherton, 1972, pp. 49–62.
8. Bayles, Michael. "Coercive Offers and Public Benefits," *The Personalist,* Vol. LV, No. 2, Spring 1974, pp. 142–43.
9. Reported in Benson, D. and Thomson, G. "Sexual Harassment on a University Campus: The Confluence of Authority Relations, Sexual Interest, and Gender Stratification," *Social Problems,* Vol. 29, No. 3, Fall 1982, p. 242.
10. Reported in Reilly, T., Carpenter, S., Dull, V., and Bartlett, K. "The Factorial Survey: An Approach to Defining Sexual Harassment on Campus," *Journal of Social Issues,* Vol. 38, No. 4, 1982, pp. 99–110.
11. Bayles, Michael. "A Concept of Coercion," in *Coercion: Nomos XIV,* Ed. J. Roland Pennock and John Chapman, Chicago: Aldine-Atherton, 1972, p. 24. Most current discussions that involve the notion of coercion have employed Bayles' analysis or a variant of it. See for example: Golash, D. "Exploitation and Coercion," *Journal of Value Inquiry,* Vol. 15: 319–328, 1981. Philips, M. "Are Coerced Agreements Involuntary?," *Law and Philosophy,* Vol. 3:133–145, 1984. Ryan, C. "The Normative Concept of Coercion," *Mind,* Vol. 89: 481–498, 1980.
12. Bayles, Michael. "Coercive Offers and Public Benefits," *The Personalist,* Vol. LV, No. 2, Spring 1974, p. 142.
13. Backhouse, Constance and Cohen, Leah. *Sexual Harassment On the Job,* New Jersey: Prentice Hall, 1981, p. 19.
14. Bayles, Michael. "Coercive Offers and Public Benefits," *The Personalist,* Vol. LV, No. 2, Spring 1974, p. 142.
15. American Association of University Professors Bulletin, 55 (1969), pp. 86–87.
16. The coercive aspect of solicitation of sexual activity by promise of rewards may not constitute the only harm done to the students by this type of action. Additional harm is done to the students whether or not they accept the offer. Such an offer may damage the students' self-image and cause them to question their intellectual abilities. The students may come to believe that other instructors were not judging them according to their merit, but rather because of that instructor's sexual interest in them. Furthermore, such an action may make the students fearful and distrustful of faculty members in general. They may avoid one-on-one learning situations, visits during office hours, etc. with their

instructors in order to avoid being again confronted with such a situation. In addition, if other students or faculty members become aware of the offer, they may lose their respect for that student, believing that the student procured some of their grades through offers of sexual contact. Similar harm may result from such an offer in the workplace. In the words of one such victim: "personally, I was devastated. I began to wonder why I had got the job in the first place. Here I thought I was hired for my ability, and now it turned out that my major attraction may have been my body . . . my health began to suffer." (Backhouse, Constance and Cohen, Leah. *Sexual Harassment On the Job*, New Jersey: Prentice Hall, 1981, p. 20.)

QUESTIONS

1. Consider Wall's example of a woman employee who receives a sexual threat from her employer that she will be demoted if she does not have sex with him. The woman, far from being offended, welcomes the opportunity, convinced that it provides her with opportunities for career advancement. Wall maintains that such a woman has not been sexually harassed. Do you agree? Why or why not? How would Superson respond to Wall's claim?

2. Wall argues that if there exists no intent to harass, there can be no sexual harassment, even though the "victim" may feel sexually harassed. Explain why you agree or disagree.

3. Superson argues that in society as it presently exists women cannot sexually harass men. She suggests that "any bothersome behavior a woman engages in, even though it may be of a sexual nature, does not constitute sexual harassment because it lacks the social impact present in male-to-female harassment." Suppose a female superior threatens a male employee with dismissal if he refuses to have sex with her. Do you agree with Superson that such behavior does not deserve to be called sexual harassment? How would you defend your answer?

4. Superson claims that a person overhearing sexist comments even though the speaker has no idea the person is within earshot constitutes sexual harassment. How would you define sexist comments and do you agree that this constitutes sexual harassment?

5. Explain why you agree or disagree with Tuana's claim that "sexual harassment has as its central meaning the coercion of sexual activity." How do you think Wall and Superson would respond to this claim?

6. On what grounds does Tuana claim that a person should sometimes not be held responsible for the coercive situation resulting from his or her offer?

CASE STUDY 5:1 SEXUAL HARASSMENT AND AN EMPLOYER'S RESPONSIBILITY[1]

In the fall of 1986, Elizabeth Paroline applied for a job as a word processor at Unisys. She was interviewed by Charles Peterson, who had overall responsibility for the office, and by Edgar Moore. Unknown to Paroline, Peterson has already received complaints that Moore, as well as other men in the office, had made sexually suggestive remarks and engaged in unwelcome touching of female employees. In response to these complaints, Peterson had convened a staff meeting in which he warned male workers not to engage in behavior that could be construed as sexual harassment. He had also met privately with Moore to caution him concerning his inappropriate behaviour.

During Paroline's interview, Moore asked her what she would do if subjected to sexual harassment. Although Peterson thought the question inappropriate, he never criticized or reprimanded Moore for asking it. Moore recommended Paroline for the job and she was subsequently hired.

Shortly after her hiring, Moore started to make sexually suggestive remarks to Paroline that she found offensive. In December of 1986, Moore approached Paroline as she was working and started rubbing his hands on her back. He continued, even though she indicated she wished him to stop.

On January 22, 1987, a severe snowstorm forced the early closing of the office in which Paroline worked. Since she had no ride home, Paroline accepted Moore's offer of a ride. During the ride home, Moore made remarks she interpreted as sexually suggestive, kissed her, and repeatedly tried to hold her hand. When they reached her apartment, he insisted on coming in despite her objections. After several minutes in the apartment, he grabbed Paroline and began kissing her and rubbing his hand up and down her back, despite her demands that he stop. Initially, he refused to remove his hands from her body, but she eventually persuaded him to leave.

The next day, Paroline reported the incident to Peterson. According to Paroline, Peterson indicated there had been previous reports of sexual harassment in the office and promised to eliminate such behavior. Subsequently, Unisys launched a formal investigation of Moore's conduct. As a result, it warned Moore that any recurrence of sexual harassment, or any retaliation against female employees, would be grounds for immediate termination. Unisys further insisted that Moore seek counselling and limit contact with female employees to official company business. It also terminated his access to the company's Sensitive Compartmented Intelligence Facility (SCIF).

On January 29, 1987, Unisys notified Paroline of its disciplining of Moore. Paroline, having learned of Moore's alleged sexual harassment of other female workers and the failure of previous warnings to deter Moore, considered the actions of Unisys inadequate. She also expressed concern that banning Moore from the SCIF area would increase her contact with him because she had not yet obtained a security clearance to enter the SCIF and would thus be forced to remain in the same part of the office where Moore would be working. There is no evidence that Moore made any inappropriate remarks or sexual overtures toward Paroline after she complained to Peterson.

Knowing she was upset, company officials offered Paroline two weeks off. Although Unisys officials asked her not to quit, she submitted her resignation on February 15, 1987 and later filed suit against Moore and Unisys.

CASE STUDY QUESTIONS

1. Unisys argued that it should not be held liable for Moore's actions because it took prompt and adequate remedial steps once Paroline complained to try to deter Moore from further harassment. Explain why you agree or disagree.
2. Evidence exists that after Peterson's staff meeting in which he warned male employees not to engage in behavior which could be construed as sexual harassment, a number of men, including Peterson himself, began joking about the women's complaints of sexual harassment. In court it was argued that the male employees' response cast doubt on the effectiveness and sincerity of the warnings. Do you agree? Why or why not?
3. To succeed in a hostile environment claim, a plaintiff must show that he or she was not unreasonably sensitive to the working environment, and that the harassment interfered with his or her ability to perform the work, or significantly affected his or her psychological well-being. If Moore's behavior had not escalated and if Moore had not been in a position of authority over Paroline, could she have reasonably claimed that she was sexually harassed? Why or why not?

CASE STUDY 5:2 SEXUAL HARASSMENT AND CONFLICTING REPORTS [2]

Brenda Purdy began working for Marwick Manufacturing Company early in March 1984 as an assembler of wallpaper sample books. In a complaint to the Ontario Human Rights Commission, she alleged that on April 23, 1984, she was sexually harassed by two co-workers, Paul Arthur and Don Bianco. Purdy alleges that Arthur grabbed her "rear end" when he walked by the work station at which she and co-workers were assembling sample books and commented that if she would go to bed with him he would suggest to his brother-in-law, the foreman, that she be moved to a better job. Purdy states that she rejected Arthur's advance. She reports that Arthur and Bianco a little later called her back to a remote area of the plant where they worked to show her something. Upon her arrival, she claims that they showed her a book of naked women. She reports that she told them she found it uninteresting and returned to her station. She further reports that Bianco a little later walked by her table and also grabbed her rear end.

She alleges that a shortly after this incident Arthur again asked her to come to the remote area where he and Bianco worked. She claims that when she arrived Bianco pulled down his pants in front of her, upon which she turned around and returned to her work area. According to Purdy, Arthur and Bianco passed her table a few minutes later, at which point Bianco commented that he had won the bet. Purdy understood him to mean that he had bet Arthur he would pull down his pants in front of her.

Purdy complained to the foreman who advised that she talk to the company president. She did so, and after talking with him, was moved to a separate company in the same building with which the president was also associated. She quit after two days, complaining that the work was boring.

Arthur and Bianco denied that any of the events took place as Purdy described them. They admit that Purdy did come to the remote area where they worked, but insisted that it was she who brought and displayed a pornographic magazine. They denied grabbing her posterior and Bianco denied dropping his pants.

A subsequent investigation revealed that female employees reported finding Purdy in the washroom, visibly upset, on the afternoon in question. When questioned as to the cause of her distress, she reported that Bianco had exposed himself to her. It also revealed that Purdy was correct in her assertion that Bianco was wearing yellow underwear that day. Less in keeping with Purdy's account, however, is that the investigation also revealed that young girls who worked on the premises complained that Purdy had shown them pornographic materials.

Also disturbing was the fact that Purdy made no attempt to have fellow workers at her work station corroborate her story of Arthur and Bianco grabbing her posterior.

Case Study Questions

1. How would you attempt to determine whether Arthur and Bianco were guilty of sexual harassment? Does the difficulty of determining who is telling the truth have any bearing on what punishment should be contemplated?

2. If the reports of Purdy showing pornographic material to young girls are true, is she guilty of sexual harassment?

Notes

1. From *Paroline v. Unisys Corp.* 879 Federal Reporter 2d series 100 (4th Cir. 1989).

2. Based on *Purdy v. Marwick Manufacturing Co.* as reported in Canadian Human Rights Reporter, Vol. 9, Decision 757, Paragraphs 37425–37461 July 1988, pp. D/4840–D4845.

For Further Reading

1. Jan Crosthwaite and Christine Swanton, "On the Nature of Sexual Harassment," *Women and Philosophy: Australasian Journal of Philosophy,* supp. to Vol 64, 1986, pp. 91–106.

2. Natalie Dandekar, "Contrasting Consequences: Bringing Charges of Sexual Harassment Compared with Other Cases of Whistleblowing," *Journal of Business Ethics,* Vol. 9, No. 2, February 90, pp. 151–158.

3. Susan M. Dodds and Lucy Frost, Robert Pargetter and Elizabeth W. Prior, "Sexual Harassment," *Social Theory and Practice,* Vol. 14, Summer 1988, pp. 111–130.

4. Loann S. Lublin, "Thomas Battle Spotlights Harassment," *Wall Street Journal,* October 9, 1991, B1 & B5. Also his article "Harassment: Views in the Workplace," *Wall Street Journal,* October 10, 1991, B1.

5. Catherine MacKinnon, *Sexual Harassment of Working Women* (New Haven, Conn.: Yale University Press, 1979).

Chapter Six

Safety in the Workplace

Introduction

The issue of safety in the workplace is obviously an important one. Employees in many professions routinely work with hazardous materials and dangerous machinery. Even when this is not the case, there remain legitimate concerns with regard to the environment employees work in. The health of a clerical worker may be just as much at risk due to a poorly ventilated office building or an improperly shielded video-terminal, as that of a construction worker operating heavy machinery.

The selections in this chapter deal with questions of the rights of employees with regard to the materials they work with and the conditions under which they work. In "The Employer-Employee Relationship and the Right to Know," Anita Superson argues that although it has not been commonly recognized, employers have the duty to inform employees and prospective employees of all safety and health hazards associated with their workplace. She further argues that the reason employees' right to such information has not been generally recognized, lies in the fact that the employer-employee relationship is nonfiduciary, i.e. there exists little or no trust on behalf of each party in the actions of the other. There is, therefore, a strong tendency for employer and employee to treat each other merely as means to an end. Superson recommends reconceiving the employer-employee relationship so that it becomes fiduciary in nature, and she thinks this is consistent with retaining a free market system.

Robert Sass, in his article "The Workers' Right to Know, Participate and Refuse Hazardous Work: A Manifesto Right" broadens the discussion. He feels that not only do employees have the right to be informed of hazards in the workplace, they have the right to participate in designing and controlling the work environment and process. He argues that the present legal concept of risk should be broadened to apply to work environment matters such as organization, pace of work, scheduling, and job cycle. In his view, workers' lack of control over their work environment is a major cause of accidents. Although he does not explicitly address the issue, his view seems to require considerable modification of any theory of a free market of labor.

Quite a different point of view is expressed by Tibor Machan in "Human Rights, Workers' Rights, and the 'Right' to Occupational Safety."

In contrast to Sass, who contends that the employer-employee relationship involves special duties owed by employers to employees, Machan argues that there do not exist special workers' rights. He holds that workers possess the same basic rights as other human beings and defends a free labor market. He denies that a free labor market need lead to the exploitation of workers. In his view, taking seriously the basic rights that all human beings possess is sufficient to address the evils which motivate many to invoke the notion of workers' rights. He argues that the moral force of most attacks on the free labor market theory are a result of the fact that many presumed examples of the free labor market really constitute violations of that theory.

Anita M. Superson

The Employer-Employee Relationship and the Right to Know

I

Dangers lurk in the workplace. It has been reported that more than 2,200,000 workers are disabled, and more than 14,000 are killed annually as a result of accidents on the job.[1] The causes include safety hazards such as fires, explosions, electrocution, dangerous machinery, as well as health hazards such as loud noise, harmful dusts, asbestos particles, toxic gases, carcinogens, and radiation.[2] The fact that these and other dangers exist is problem enough; but even more problematic is that an employee's

awareness of such dangers, prior to being exposed to them, is often minimal, at best. If an employee is to have any say in what happens to his person, what needs to be established—at least more firmly than it is currently—is an employee's[3] right to know about the presence of health and safety hazards in the workplace.

In what follows, I shall first examine the current status of an employee's right to know. I shall argue that it is the very nature of the employer-employee relationship that gives rise to an employee's limited awareness of on-the-job hazards. Next, I shall offer what I think are the philosophical justifications for an employee's right to know. Finally, in light of these justifications, I shall argue that establishing an employee's right to know will, in fact, benefit both the employee and the employer, and be one step toward achieving a fiduciary relationship.

Throughout this essay, I compare the employer-employee relationship to that of the physician and patient. Although there are some disparities between the two, the comparison is helpful in that it points out that the moral basis for establishing a right to know for a patient is the same as for an employee, yet the two are not accorded the same recognition by the law. To

From Anita M. Superson, "Employer-Employee Relationship and the Right to Know," *Business and Professional Ethics Journal,* Vol. 3, No. 4 (Fall, 1983). Reprinted by permission.

show that the right to know for patients is not recognized as being the same for employees, yet that it is based on the same philosophical foundation for the same reasons, only strengthens the argument for establishing a right to know in the workplace.

II

In the medical setting a person's right to know about risks involved in different kinds of treatment has been recognized under the guise of informed consent. Recently, there have been many attempts in the law and in various health codes to ensure that patients have given informed consent to medical treatments or experimentation. In *Canterbury* v. *Spence,* 1972, Circuit Court Judge Spotswood W. Robinson III rules that since "every human being of adult years and sound mind has a right to determine what shall be done with his own body," a physician has a "duty of reasonable disclosure of the choices with respect to proposed therapy and the dangers inherently and potentially involved."[4] Similarly, the American Hospital Association's *Patient's Bill of Rights* (1973) states that "The patient has the right to receive from his physician information necessary to give informed consent prior to the start of any procedure and/or treatment."[5] Again, the Nuremberg Code, which focuses on guidelines used in human experimentation carried out in Nazi Germany, specifies that the human subject "should have sufficient knowledge and comprehension of the elements of the subject matter involved as to enable him to make an understanding and enlightened decision."[6] These and other such examples show that through informed consent, a patient's or research subject's right to know about the risks and hazards involved in medical procedures is firmly entrenched. We shall see later that this right is protected by the law. Though the amount of information given to patients may vary among physicians, consent forms must be signed by the patient or by his next of kin. This is true for all patients undergoing most invasive forms of treatment (e.g., surgery).

But the headway that has been made in the medical setting is, unfortunately, unparalleled in the workplace. It was not until 1980 that the Occupational Safety and Health Administration (OSHA) of the United States Department of Labor established the legal right of an employee to "access to employer maintained exposure and medical records relevant to employees exposed to toxic substances and harmful physical agents."[7] In 1983, OSHA issued a final rule requiring

chemical manufacturers and importers to assess the hazards of chemicals which they produce and import, and all employers having workplaces in the manufacturing division. . . to provide information to their employees concerning hazardous chemicals by means of hazard communication programs including labels, material safety data sheets, training, and access to written records. In addition, distributors of hazardous chemicals are required to ensure that containers they distribute are properly labeled, and that a material safety data sheet is provided to their customers. . . .[8]

On the same note, the National Institute for Occupational Safety and Health (NIOSH) reported that workers had the right to know whether or not they were exposed to hazardous chemical and physical agents regulated by the Federal Government.[9] Finally, the National Labor Relations Act (NLRA) recognizes a labor union's right to information that is relevant to a collective bargaining issue, including safety rules and practices.[10] Although these regulations are a step in the direction of securing a worker's right to know, they are insufficient.

First, though the OSHA rulings recently have been expanded from simply permitting access to an employer's exposure and medical records to requiring assessment of the hazards of chemicals and providing information about such chemicals to an employee by means of labels and material safety data sheets, they fail to extend protection through information to many workers. The 1983 regulation applies only to employees in the manufacturing division, yet does not apply to employees in other divisions such as mining, construction, trade, etc. The reasoning underlying OSHA's restriction to manufacturing is that it has determined that the employees in this division "are at the greatest risk of experiencing health effects from exposure to hazardous chemicals.[11] The agency thus hoped to regulate that sector in which it could be most effective for the greatest number of employees. So, although warning labels and safety data sheets, as well as the assessment of hazards which they necessitate, certainly are positive steps toward securing a worker's right to know, they apply to about only fifty percent of all workers.[12]

Second, the OSHA rulings apply only to employees which the agency defines as "a current employee, a former employee, or an employee being assigned or transferred to work where there will be exposure to toxic substances or harmful physical agents."[13] The rulings exclude provision of information regarding hazards to the *prospective* employee. This is problematic because the prospective employee is often faced with a similar choice, that is, the choice of whether or not to take on a job which entails working in hazardous conditions. Yet providing this information to prospective employees may raise problems in itself. Employers may find this too time-consuming a task to perform for *each* person contending for a position; or, they may feel an obligation to provide this information only to employees since it is this group of persons which has pledged some degree of loyalty to the company. These problems, though, should be worked around for the sake of the prospective employee who will avoid the trouble of committing himself to a job if he knows in advance that the hazardous working conditions outweigh the benefits of taking on the job.

Third, the OSHA rulings do not apply to all safety and health hazards. The 1980 ruling regulates "toxic substances and harmful physical agents," and the 1983 ruling regulates "hazardous chemicals." Clearly, these rulings do not account for a whole spectrum of on-the-job hazards, some of which were mentioned at the outset of this essay. A worker's right to know of these hazards has yet to be firmly established.

This is not to imply that an employer has no responsibility to keep his workplace safe. In fact, in 1970, the Occupational Safety and Health Act (OSHAct) was passed, establishing safety and health standards for all workers other than those employed by federal, state, and local governments. The Act requires an employer to ensure that his workplace is "free from recognized hazards that are causing or likely to cause death or serious physical harm."[14] But this act, too, is insufficient. It has been reported[15] that the Act protects against only "recognized hazards," defined as those which "can be detected by the common human senses, unaided by testing devices, and which are generally known in the industry to be hazards." Indeed, this leaves many hazards unaccounted for. It is those hazards not prohibited by law about which the employee may not be informed.

The NIOSH report is inadequate in similar ways. The Institute recognizes a worker's right to know only whether or not they were *exposed* to hazardous chemical and physical agents regulated by the Federal Government. Its inadequacies are that it does not recognize a right to know of hazards prior to exposure to them, and that like the OSHA rulings, it applies only to chemical and physical agents, rather than all on-the-job hazards.

Finally, the National Labor Relations Act accords some protection to employees who belong to labor unions but is also limited. It established that labor unions had a right to "information that is in the hands of the employer and is relevant to bargainable issues."[16] An employee's right to know about hazardous working conditions is usually recognized as being "relevant to bargainable issues." But what sometimes occurs is a conflict between the employee's right to know and the company's right to keep trade secrets. A trade secret has been defined under the Restatement of Torts as "any formula, device, or information, used in a business which gives its holder a competitive advantage over those without the secret."[17] Now if a labor union requests information about job hazards, but this information will expose an employer's trade secrets, thereby jeopardizing his competitive advantage, the employer need not necessarily release this information. And in different cases, the law has favored both sides.

In *Borden Chemical,* an administrative law judge of the National Labor Relations Board determined that Borden had refused to bargain in good faith when it failed to release information to the labor union. It was then ordered to supply the information to the union. The reason behind the ruling was that Borden failed to show that disclosure of the information would damage its competitive position.[18] Essentially, Borden failed to show how its trade secrets would reach its competitors.[19] In *Colgate-Palmolive,* however, an administrative law judge ruled that the employer was obliged to reveal a list of chemicals in the workplace *except* those constituting trade secrets.[20] Colgate-Palmolive apparently showed how it would be disadvantaged were its trade secrets to be revealed. We can surmise from these two cases and from the OSHA and NIOSH rulings that an employee's right to know is not accorded full protection by the law, and, in fact, may be denied by the law.

III

Why is the right to know in the workplace not firmly grounded? It is the argument of this section that protection of such a right is limited because of the very nature of the employer-employee relationship.

This relationship can be best defined as a nonfiduciary one, meaning that there is little or no trust on behalf of each party in the actions of the other party. This lack of trust stems from the expectations each party has for forming a personal relationship. In most cases, the expectations dictate a non-personal interaction. The employee often feels the same; he views himself as a person for hire, whose function is to perform a certain job for the company or institution in exchange for wages and perhaps a few fringe benefits. If the employee does not like his job for whatever reason, he is free to leave. The employer is also free (for the most part) to fire any employee who is not performing his job in what the employer judges to be a favorable way. As a result, many employees remain with a certain company for only a short period of time, thus making it difficult to come to know their employer personally, if this be at all possible.

Both the employer and employee normally do not enter into their relation thinking that they can trust each other to look out for the other's best interests. Probably the only form of trust existent between the two parties is that the employer will pay the employee a wage that at least matches the work he puts out, and that the employee will perform the job he is asked to do in a way that is normally expected. These are the roles both the employer and employee expect each other to take on. It would be difficult to establish a fiduciary relationship under such expectations. What adds to the difficulty is that often the employer and employee do not even know each other at any kind of personal level. I ask rhetorically: How can a fiduciary relationship be established if no relationship has been established?

Another feature of the employer-employee relationship which adds to its nonfiduciary nature is the reasons both the employee and the employer have for entering into their relationship. The employee enters a relationship with his employer primarily for monetary reasons; he seeks employment in order to earn wages with which he can secure the goods he needs to live. The employer, on the other hand, enters a relationship primarily for the sake of profit-making. His position in respect to that of the employee is one of power. It derives its power from the fact that the employer offers the employee a benefit—wages—if he accepts and performs a job. The employer stands to benefit directly from his employee. He needs a certain job to be done; the company's profits depend upon whether the task is accomplished. And the financial success of the company is directly related to the employer.

Both the expectations of the employee and employer, as well as the reasons for each entering into the relationship, make it likely that an employer would use his employee merely as a means to his own end, to borrow a notion from Kant. That is, the employer, seeking to augment his profits (the end), may use the employee merely as a means to achieve that end. One way in which he could do this is to fail to inform an employee about hazardous work conditions. Failure to inform an employee about these hazards is to deny him information that may affect his decision to stay on the job. And by remaining on the job, the employee works in part for the employer's benefit, that is, to increase the company's profits. In this way, the employee is used as a means to the employer's end.

More specifically, if the expectations of both the employer and employee of each other are as I have described, it is easy for the former to use the latter as a means to an end because being so far removed on a personal level form the employee, he does not feel a sense of obligation towards the employee's welfare. All he has invested in the relationship is that the job gets done. And since the employee does not view the relationship as a fiduciary one, he has no basis for trusting the employer to ensure that the workplace is free from hazards, or at least to inform him of the hazards that do exist. Indeed it would be nice for the employer to do either; yet the employee probably does not expect it, and certainly cannot trust his employer to do so.

And, if the reasons the employer and employee have for entering their relationship are as I have described, this is another reason why an employer may use his employee merely as a means to his own end. If the employer is aware of the power he holds over his employee, that is, that he to a large extent controls the employee's means of livelihood, he may feel no obligation to inform the employee about on-the-job hazards. In fact, somewhat ironically, the employer may even go so far as to view the employee as using *him*, the *employer*, as a means to an end. This belief is based upon the fact that the employee may take on a job solely for the purpose of obtaining money, perhaps with minimum effort put forth, and that the employee is free to leave when he so desires. If the employer has this attitude toward his employee, it becomes easier for him not to inform the employee of hazards in the workplace.

The nature of the employer-employee relationship differs from that of the physician-patient in these two respects. Specifically, the expectations of the physician and patient are of a much more trusting nature. Oftentimes, the physician and patient have established a personal relationship; they, for example, know somewhat about each other's life-styles, values, etc. Patients generally expect and trust their physician to act in their best interests. They expect that physicians will inform them of the hazards and risks involved in various medical treatments, and that together they will arrive at a decision about what is the best course of action to take. And if the physician fails to inform his patient about these hazards and risks, the patient usually assumes that the information was withheld for his, the patient's own benefit.

Furthermore, the reasons for the patient and physician entering a relationship are different from that of the employer and employee. Patients seek the advice of a physician because, simply put, they want to be treated for an illness. They expect that the physician will do this, and will give the patient information on forms of treatment. This is what the patient pays for, and thus expects to receive. The physician, in turn, should feel that he has an obligation to provide this information to the patient, unless he can justify withholding it.

The physician's reasons for entering the relationship are different from the employer's. Rather than being solely, or at least primarily, profit-motivated, physicians often view their role as one of benefitting the sick. Certainly there are many physicians who enter the profession for monetary reasons: I do not wish to deny this. Yet, as any physician would admit, there are easier ways to make money. Still, the physician, like the employer, is in a power position. But the source of the physician's power is different. He does not stand to benefit from performing a certain therapy on any *particular* patient (unless, of course, the patient is indeed unique), for it is likely that another patient will choose to undergo that treatment. And, more importantly, physicians will always have patients seeking their services because persons will always get sick. Unless a physician is so inadequate, he can rest assured that he will be in business for a long time. This gives him less reason to deny patients information they need concerning the hazards of treatment. Thus, a physician's power position is not as threatened by loss of profit as is an employer's. He therefore has less reason than an employer to use a person merely as a means to his own end.

Moreover, an employer's reasons for withholding information are often different from those of the physician. While the physician may feel he is acting in the patient's best interests (whether or not he is certainly is open to debate) when he withholds information concerning the risks of treatment, this is not often the case with the employer. The employer withholds information about on-the-job hazards not because he wishes to protect the employee, or to act in the employee's best interests, but because he want to protect his *own* interests. He wants the company to profit, and this may be possible only if certain hazardous assignments are made. The employer may feel that he is justified in withholding information about risks from the employee. After all, the employee does not have to stay on *this* job; he is free to leave. The employer's reasons for withholding information are thus, unlike those of most physicians, self-interested.

It is these features of the employer-employee relationship, namely, the expectations of both parties, their reasons for entering into the relationship, and the employer's reasons for withholding information, which all contribute to the nonfiduciary nature of this relationship. These features may, of course, all be a result of the capitalist system. If this be so, some persons may argue that the very nature of the employer-employee relationship can be changed only by changing the socio-economic system. I believe this is false, and in Section V I will argue that establishing an employee's right to know will, in fact, make headway in changing the relationship into one that is fiduciary in nature.

IV

We have seen that the nature of the employer-employee relationship is such that it is difficult to establish an employee's right to know. Employers, on the one hand, find little or no reason to give their employees information about hazards in the workplace. In turn, employees find little or no reason to expect to receive this information. The differences in the nature of the relationship are, in all probability, responsible for the dissimilarities in the establishment of the right to know. But should this difference exist? Is there a difference in the choices faced by a person as patient versus a person as employee that will justify the difference in the recognition of the right to know?

I suggest that there is not. Although many disparities exist between the relationships, an important similarity grounds the right to know. It is this: in both cases, the person wants to know the dangers involved for the *same* reasons. He wants to know the risks that may be incurred to his body so that he can decide whether or not to expose himself to those risks. The information is needed for him to make a reasonable choice.

In both situations, the moral basis of the right to know lies in the principle of autonomy. Much talk has been generated about this principle since Mill and Kant recognized its importance. Although the literature offers a variety of definitions, this principle is usually defined in such a way as to include the notion of making one's own decisions affecting one's own life without coercion from others. In order for one to make a responsible decision, he must be informed about the choices with which he is faced. Just as a patient must be informed about the risks involved in a certain treatment in order for him to decide if he wants that treatment, an employee, too, must be informed about the hazards involved in working under certain conditions if he is to make a responsible, autonomous choice about whether or not to subject his person to such risks. In either case, if such information is not disclosed, the person's autonomy has been placed in jeopardy.

The choice faced by both the patient and the employee is one of whether or not to subject one's person to risk of harm. It may be objected that the harms which may be incurred in the workplace are less serious than those which may be incurred in the medical setting. But this is simply not true. The harms incurred in the workplace may be just as serious, and may not be as immediate as those incurred in the medical setting. For example, side-effects from an operation or from taking certain drugs are often known by the patient and/or his physician soon after they are incurred. Harms resulting from on-the-job hazards, however, often take considerable time to manifest themselves, and often require long-term exposure to take effect. For example, chronic berylliosis, constituted by coughing, dyspnea, and anorexia, may appear years after exposure to beryllium.[21] And cancer may take years to manifest itself after exposure to coal tar, paraffin, asbestos, vinyl chloride, and benzene. Other toxic materials do not produce side-effects in the exposed person, but instead in his or her children. These are either mutagenic in nature, in which case they change the genetic makeup of the offspring, or teratogenic, in which case they are capable of causing birth defects in the offspring.[22] This is not to imply that all harms incurred in the medical setting are immediate, and those incurred on the job are made manifest years after exposure; instead, the point is that many do follow this pattern.

Because the harms incurred in the workplace often are made manifest years later, it is more difficult for an employer to face liability charges. In the medical realm, patients can be awarded damages either in battery or in negligence. Traditionally, patients can sue physicians for damages in battery if they are touched, treated, or researched upon without consent.[23] In a British Columbia case, it was reported[24] that a patient who suffered loss of smell and partial loss of taste after surgery was awarded damages in battery because she was unaware of these risks at the time of her consent. In America, failure to disclose risks to patients "is considered a breach of the physician's general duty to care to give reasonable information and advice to his patient."[25] To be awarded damages in battery, the patient need only establish that "what was done differed substantially from that to which he assented."[26]

Patients can sue also for damages in negligence. In Canada, it is reported that the physician should inform the patient of the nature and seriousness of treatment lest he be held negligent. The duty in negligence "is based on the nature of the physician-patient relationship as a trust," thus imposing a basic requirement of honesty upon the physician."[27] In order for a physician to be found negligent, the patient must show that there was a breach of the duty of disclosure and that he, the patient, would not have consented had the required disclosure been given, and that he suffered a loss as a result.[28]

Although a patient can sue for damages in either battery or negligence, an employee has no such privilege. Establishment of workmen's

compensation has prevented the right to sue in tort.[29] Prior to the establishment of workmen's compensation, employees could settle under tort law and receive payments for both loss of income as well as for "pain and suffering." Workmen's compensation statutes, however, include payment for loss of income, but only limited payment for "pain and suffering."[30] One source reports that *no* payment for pain and suffering is included.[31] Thus, employers do not have to pay for the full consequences of their negligence. Employees themselves must shoulder most of the burden of costs for employer negligence. This seems especially unjust when we are reminded of the fact that an employee's right to know is not firmly established.

One basis, then, for establishing a right to know in the workplace is that it ensures that an employee is given information necessary for him to be able to make a choice which may significantly affect his life. Informing an employee of workplace hazards puts him in the position of deciding whether or not he wants to be exposed to hazards, and thereby is one step in the direction of promoting his autonomy. Establishment of a right to know is especially important for the workers since he does not have much recourse against his employer if damages ensue.

Another basis for establishing this right lies in the notion of fairness of contract. When a person is hired for a job, there is an implicit contract made between the employer and employee, the terms of which spell out that person X will do job A and will be paid by person Y. This contract requires, like any fair contract, that both parties know what they are contracting to. It is insufficient that an employee know he is consenting to do a certain job in a certain way at a certain pace, and so on. If hazards which may produce harm to his person are involved, he should be made aware of them before he enters the contract. If he is not made aware of the hazards, and enters the contract with the employer, he is not giving fully informed consent to the relevant terms of the contract. The contract is thus unfair.

A third basis for establishing an employee's right to know is partly economic, partly moral. It lies in Milton Friedman's notion of business' social responsibility, namely "to use its resources and engage in activities designed to increase its profits so long as it stays within the rules of the game, which is to say, engages in open and free competition, without deception or fraud."[32] The moral justification for the right to know, using Friedman's terms of business' social responsibility, lies in his normative judgment that business should not engage in deceptive practices. Though Friedman does not spell out what this entails, surely withholding information from the prospective employee-information which is likely to influence his decision—is a deceptive practice, prohibited even on Friedman's libertarian analysis of business in the free market system.

An economic justification for the right to know also can be found in Friedman and other free market advocates. It is this: in order to ensure that the free market really *is* free, persons should be able to enter the occupation of their choosing (at least insofar as they meet the qualifications). This choice must be informed. If information about job hazards is withheld, the choice will not be fully informed. And if the choice is not fully informed, it is not truly free. Thus, ignoring the right to know, besides violating moral principles such as autonomy and fairness of contract, violates one of the fundamental economic bases of the free market system.

V

If an employee's right to know becomes firmly established, certain implications are likely to follow. On the negative side, the employer will be faced with the difficult task of determining how much and what kind of information ought to be given to the employee. The employer will have to devote time and effort to find out just what hazards exist, and to convey the results of his findings to the employee. And if the risks involved in taking on a certain job are very high, or very serious, the employer may have difficulty in hiring someone for the job. Also, the company's trade secrets undoubtedly will sometimes be revealed.

While I do not wish to diminish the inconvenience these implications bring to the employer,

none is too important to override the employee's right to know. Indeed, there certainly are ways to lessen the inconvenience while still bringing about the desired effects.

More importantly though, it is reasonable to assume that both parties are likely to benefit by establishing an employee's right to know.

It benefits the employee in several ways. First, since the employer will have to ascertain what are hazards in the workplace, he may eliminate at least some of them for the sake of attracting employees. Thus, the environment may be safer for the employee. Second, if the employee is presented with the relevant information about on-the-job hazards, it places into the hands of the *employee* the informed decision of whether or not to accept a position. The employee can then make his *own* choice of whether or not to expose himself to those hazards. Moreover, informing the employee of hazards in the workplace ensures him that the contract made with his employer is fair and not based upon deception. In these ways, it establishes trust in the employer.

The employer, too, benefits. Once he has given such information to his employee, if the employee willingly accepts the job knowing that to which he has consented, and is in some way harmed, the employer would decrease his liability in many cases. After all, it was the employee's decision to expose himself to the hazards. He knew what to expect, and is responsible for his decision. The employer, in many cases, will avoid paying compensation.

Most important is that the right to know may go so far as to establish a fiduciary relationship between employer and employee, much the same as that existent between many patients and their physicians. Part of what is involved in such a relationship is that both parties trust each other to look after each other's best interests. The employer can accomplish this by improving his work environment, by informing his employee of existent hazards, and the like.

The employee, also, can look out for his employer's best interests by unifying his goals with the goals of his employer. If the employee is made aware of risks involved in taking on a certain job, and yet he consents to taking on that job (assuming, of course, that he understands the risks and is not coerced into the job perhaps by another person or because he is unable to find an alternative), he has invested a part of himself into that relationship. He admits his willingness to work for an employer to achieve his employer's goals. The goals of the employer are then shared with the employee. And since the employee knows he is not being deceived about the conditions under which he works, he may have more incentive to do his job well. This, too, is likely to benefit the employer.

It is interesting to note, in conclusion, that the very nature of the employer-employee relationship which makes it difficult to secure an employee's right to know can, in fact, be changed into one of a fiduciary nature through the establishment of a right to know. We have seen that though the philosophical basis for securing a right to know in the workplace is the same as in the medical setting and that the harms which may possibly be incurred are similar, this right is more firmly grounded in the medical setting than in the workplace. What needs to be firmly established for the benefit of both the employer and employee in order to make headway in achieving a fiduciary relationship is an employee's right to know.

Notes

I am greatly indebted to George Brenkert for his initial suggestion to write this paper, for his very helpful comments on earlier versions, as well as for his encouragement to send it out.

1. Manuel G. Velasquez, *Business Ethics: Concepts and Cases* (Englewood Cliffs, NJ: Prentice-Hall, Inc., 1982), p. 311.
2. See Nicholas A. Ashford, *Crisis in the Workplace: Occupational Disease and Injury* (Cambridge, MA: The MIT Press, 1976), pp. 68–83, for a thorough and interesting description of these hazards.
3. Although I shall use the term 'employee' throughout this essay, my arguments shall apply also to the prospective employee since he is faced with a similar choice, that is, whether nor not to accept a job in a hazardous work environment.
4. *Canterbury v. Spence,* US Court of Appeals, District of Columbia Circuit, May 19, 1972, 464 Federal Reporter, 2nd Series, 772.
5. "A Patient's Bill of Rights," American Hospital Association, reprinted in Mappes & Zembaty (eds.), *Biomedical Ethics* (New York: McGraw-Hill, Inc., 1981), pp. 87–89.
6. "Declaration of Helsinki," World Medical Association, reprinted in Mappes & Zembaty, ibid., pp. 145–147.
7. *Federal Register,* Vol. 45 no. 102, Friday, May 23, 1980, Rules and Regulations, Dept. of Labor, Occupational Safety and Health Administration, 23CFR Part 1910, 35212.
8. *Federal Register,* Vol. 48 no. 228, Friday, November 25, 1983, Rules and Regulations, Dept. of Labor, Occupational Safety and Health Administration, 29CFR Part 1910, 53280.
9. Ruth R. Faden and Tom L. Beauchamp, "The Right to Risk Information and the Right to Refuse Health Hazards in the Workplace," in *Ethical Theory of Business* (2nd Ed.), Tom L. Beauchamp and Norman E. Bowie (eds.), (Englewood Cliffs, NJ: Prentice-Hall, Inc., 1983), pp. 196–206.
10. Time D. Wermager, "Union's Right to Information vs. Confidentiality of Employer Trade Secrets: Accommodating the Interests Through Procedural Burdens and Restricted Disclosure," 66 *Iowa Law Review,* 1333–51, July, 1981.
11. *Federal Register,* Vol. 48 no. 228, Friday, November 25, 1983, Rules and Regulations, Dept. of Labor, Occupational Safety and Health Administration, 29CFR Part 1910, 53284.
12. Ibid., Table 1, p. 53285.
13. Ibid., Vol. 45, p. 35215.
14. The Occupational Safety and Health Act of 1970 (Public Law 91-596), Section 5(a)(1), reprinted in Ashford, pp. 545–75.
15. Robert Stewart Smith, *The Occupational Safety and Health Act: Its Goals and Its Achievements* (Washington, D.C.: American Enterprise Institute for Public Policy Research, 1976), p. 9.
16. Wermager, *op. cit.,* p. 1333.
17. David Carey Fraser, "Trade Secrets and the NLRA: Employee's Right to Health and Safety Information," 14 *University of San Francisco Law Review,* 495–524, Spring, 1980.
18. Wermager, *op. cit.,* pp. 1335–36.
19. Wermager, *op. cit.,* pp. 1343.
20. Wermager, *op. cit.,* pp. 1345.
21. Ashford, *op. cit.,* pp. 76.
22. Ashford, *op. cit.,* pp. 78.
23. Karen Lebacqz and Robert J. Levine, "Informed Consent in Human Research: Ethical and Legal Aspects," in *Encyclopedia of Bioethics,* Vol. 2, Warren T. Reich, ed.-in-chief, (New York: The Free Press, 1978), pp. 754–762.
24. Gilbert Sharpe, LLM, "Recent Canadian Court Decisions on Consent," *Bioethics Quarterly,* Vol. 2 No. 1 (Spring, 1980), 56–63.
25. Sharpe, ibid., p. 58.
26. Sharpe, ibid., p. 61.
27. Janice R. Dillon, "Informed Consent and the Disclosure of Risks of Treatment: The Supreme Court of Canada Decides," *Bioethics Quarterly,* Vol. 3 No. 3&4, (Fall/Winter, 1981), 156–162.
28. Dillon, ibid., p. 160.
29. Ashford, *op. cit.,* p. 350.
30. Ashford, *op. cit.,* p. 392.

31. "Occupational Health Risks and the Worker's Right to Know," 90 *Yale Law Journal*, 1792–1810, July, 1981.

32. Milton Friedman, *Capitalism and Freedom* (Chicago: The University of Chicago Press, 1962), p. 133.

Robert Sass

The Workers' Right to Know, Participate and Refuse Hazardous Work: A Manifesto Right

I. INTRODUCTION

Worker rights in workplace health and safety is crucial in bringing about necessary reforms in working conditions, especially their right to know about the chemicals they work with, and to participate on a daily basis regarding work environment matters—both quantitative (noise, dust, etc.) and qualitative (work organization and job design questions), and their right to refuse a job believed (not known) to be dangerous to their well-being.

It can also be argued that existing worker rights (to know, participate and refuse) should be extended and deepened to legally permit workers in industry to deal with work organization (as a social concept) and job design (individual relation to machine) matters, including pace of work, monotony, scheduling, sexual harassment, job cycle, etc., as well as those work environment matters which are important to workers (i.e. daily punishments and humiliations). The extension of the present-day legal concept of "risk" to ensure worker involvement

From Robert Sass, "The Workers' Right to Know, Participate and Refuse Hazardous Work: A Manifesto Right," *Journal of Business Ethics* Vol. 5 (1986) 129–136. © 1986 by D. Reidel Publishing Company. Reprinted by permission of Kluwer Academic Publishers.

and increased control of their working conditions can also be argued as a moral right derived from a "fundamental need" (health and safety) in the same way arguments were made on behalf of universal medical care. The extension of present-day limited or partial worker rights in occupational health and safety statutes and regulations ought to be "stretched" to deal with greater worker control over work environment matters and the work process.

While this development can be argued as a practical consideration, we must, nonetheless classify this cluster of proposed right as *manifesto rights* for the obvious reason that they are not generally accepted at the present time.

Presently, management and corporate *interests* go beyond what is necessary to maximize efficiency in production with equity. What is, therefore, desirable is the extension of certain civil rights into industry. And by increasing worker rights, we also increase productivity and efficiency, and, more importantly ensure greater justice in industry. This paper will specifically focus on the need to increase worker rights in regard to work environment matters. That is the right of the worker to participate in work environment issues, and to have greater control over the work process. After all, if you neglect and debase workers in order to increase efficiency, you will in the end decrease productivity and make our society poorer. Present day worker "punishments" and humiliations cannot be justified by appeals to increased productivity and economic "law." An individual worker is more than a "hand", commodity or factor of production only, but something greater, more precious and sacred than material wealth.

A. Productivity Versus Equity

While it is morally necessary to increase production and equitable distribution of wealth in a world where there is enormous impoverishment and wide-spread starvation, there is no reason why this wealth should be based upon the commodification of labour. Especially, when this form of production and organization of industry results in the de-skilling and dehumanizing of a large part of the workforce.

Current employment relations evolved during the transition from feudalism to capitalism (from simple to composite production. In jurisprudential terms, from a status to a contract society. This development by the law is based upon a "relationship of services"[1] (in contrast to commitment or obligation). According to H. Glasbeek:

This accords with the notion that an entrepreneur in a competitive society should be free to invest and to dispose of his capital as he sees fit and to be subjected to as little external noneconomic restraint as is consonant with social needs. The upshot of legal acquiescence with this approach is the imposition of onerous duties on the employee as compared with those which burden the employer.
. . . even under collective bargaining regimes all the initial decisions remain an employer's to make. Thus, how much to invest, where to do so, what products shall be made, what amount, what quality, what processes are to be used, what *substances* are to be employed, and so on, are all decisions left to the employer.[2] [Emphasis mine].

In essence, employer freedom of disposition with respect to capital ownership is the supreme legitimizing principle of private ownership. This includes the right not to use, to destroy, to alienate capital ("flight of capital") and the right to buy, to organize, and to control the labour of others, as well as to make decisions concerning the goals of production and the use of surplus value.

While collective agreements and regulation may limit these rights, private ownership remains essentially undisturbed. In Canada today, it is generally accepted by arbitrators that the rights to "manage and operate the enterprise, assign work, determine work methods, procedures and equipment, schedule production, and direct the workplace" are reserved to management.[3] It is "not unusual for unions to withdraw entirely from management decisions at this level."[4]

In a recent study entitled 'The Limits of Trade Union Power in Organizational Decision Making,' the authors conclude that

Despite the popular image of powerful unions, such tangential evidence that does exist suggests that the actual power of trades unions over organizational level decisions is relatively low, irrespective of desired or actual participation in the decision making process.[5]

The prevailing residual or reserved rights theory is different from the "status quo" approach which supports the view that the *status quo* should prevail if workers or their bargaining agent oppose or disagree with a management decision until the matter is mutually resolved[6], even though the contract is silent.

Management's rights under the common law explicitly vested the employer with sole control over the business and management of its affairs, infusing the employment contract with the traditional law of "master-servant." This, in effect, divests the employer of any sense of duty, obligation and responsibility toward those he employs. The employment contract in law emphasizes the *limited* nature of the parties to each other while reserving full authority of direction and control to the employer. The result is, of course, the *limited* rights of workers.

In effect, the employment contract is in large part a legal device for guaranteeing to management the unilateral power to make rules and exercise discretion. Thus, ownership carries with it the right of "freedom of contract."[7]

This "market theory" of labour incorrectly assumes an approximate *equality* of individuals to function in the market environment, which "is an inappropriate assumption on which to base the actual right to participate."[8] The contract law of employment is partially based upon a fundamental and "empirically absurd" understanding of equality.[9]

Secondly, a major underlying assumption supporting the buying and selling of labour and management's "excessive" prerogatives under common law is our socially accepted conception of work as instrumental rather than self-fulfilling, enabling the worker to sustain status and self-respect. The acceptance of hierarchy and privilege in the organization of production reinforces the "cycle of inequality" in society.[10]

Within a prevailing class structure, the privileged view ordinary blue-collar, manual workers as 'fit' for dirty work. Harry Glasbeek states that

in as much as the argument is that the contract of employment doctrines display an assumption that a *superior-inferior relationship* is to be accepted, and that collective bargaining regimes do not share this assumption, it is also of dubious merit. This characterization of the common law is justified on the basis that employers could (and can) treat their employees as servants, as commodities, as a matter of law.[11] [Emphasis mine]

Finally, the acceptance of inequality, the instrumentality of work, and a prejudice towards ordinary workers as having "strong backs and weak minds" reinforces the present dehumanizing organization of industry and judicial and legal constructs pertaining to the employment relationship. The further acceptance of this situation is positively argued by the social value of the freedom of contract doctrine which construes the relationship between employee and employer as a *voluntary* agreement. The "lack of parity cannot be adduced as a reason for questioning this doctrine in behalf of worker rights, unless one is prepared to question it in all instances where parity is lacking."[12]

Critics of increased worker rights also argue that the establishment of such rights:

. . . will generate gross inefficiency since it will ensnarl simple employee proceedings with procedural red tape. With special rights, no employee can simply be fired or demoted; he must be given a formal hearing; and to ensure that due process is realized, complicated organizational mechanisms must be established, mechanisms that will require time and effort that might otherwise contribute to productive activities.[13]

Clearly, as Donaldson correctly observes,

such critics envision a straightjacketed corporation management, working in an environment in which penalizing and firing workers is all but impossible. The result, presumably, will be lower working standards, lazier employees, and *widespread inefficiency*.[14] [Emphasis mine]

and so equity must be sacrificed by a supposedly greater good: efficiency.

B. Participation and Productivity

To this argument one can reply that worker rights and participation might enhance efficiency. After an extensive review of the literature on this issue, Bruce Stokes states that "ample experience exists to quell most fears that employee involvement in day-to-day company decisions leads to declining economic efficiency."[15] Further, Stokes reported that:

A 1975 National Science Foundation survey of 57 field studies of worker participation experiences in the United States found that four out of five reported productivity increases. A 1977 study by Dr. Raymond Katzell of New York University of 103 U.S. worker productivity experiments confirmed these findings. Karl Frieden, in a 1978 study for the National Center for Economic Alternatives, concluded that, "the scientific rigor of many of the studies on workers' participation is less than ideal. However, a clear pattern emerges . . . supporting the proposition that increases in workers' participation results in improvements in productivity.[16]

Even The Trilateral Commission's Task Force on Industrial Relations, an important management research body, admitted that "nothing in the literature suggests that participation significantly harms productivity."[17]

There is a vast body of literature which confirms the positive correlation between worker involvement and productivity. Nonetheless, strong resistance exists against the widening of existing "partial" worker rights in industry.

During my ten year tenure as Associate Deputy Minister of Labour in the Province of Saskatchewan, I sat on a number of Boards of Directors which included union and/or worker representation. The contribution of workers and their representatives was of enormously high quality, and in regard to the bi-partite Work Environment Board of the Potash Corporation of Saskatchewan, of which I was chairperson, the worker and union contribution was, in my opinion, of greater practical and intellectual merit than that of the senior management. This might be because the terms of reference of the Work Environment Board centered upon working conditions with which management was less familiar. This applies to the worker members of the mandatory joint occupational health and safety committees in Saskatchewan.[18]

Consequently, I believe that worker rights should be extended by statute in all areas of production, but full rights be accorded in matters relating to workplace health and safety. This paper will argue the necessity to "stretch" the present legal concept of risk covering dust, chemicals, lighting and other quantifiable and measureable aspects of the workplace to all work environment matters including: how the work is organized, the design of the job, pace of work, monotony, scheduling, sexual harrassment, job cycle and similar work environment matters which matter to workers.

II. WORKER PARTICIPATION AND OCCUPATIONAL SAFETY

A. Introduction

Lack of worker "rights" to control work processes is a major contributor to both increased adverse stress and a worsening of accident rates. Whereas, meaningful participation and greater control has a positive effect on worker health and safety. While worker participation is viewed as a "political" goal, it is also a means to come to grips with bad working conditions.

B. Management Prerogatives and the Impovershment of Job Content

Trade unionism represents a collective act of protecting and improving living standards by people who sell their labour power against people who buy it. This protective function is performed in various ways, but primarily through a method of determining conditions of employment by negotiations or collective bargaining between representatives of the employer and union representatives of the employees. The results of the bargaining are set forth in a written agreement covering "wages, hours and working conditions."

Historically, "working conditions" have come to mean overtime provisions, holiday pay, vaca-

tions, and other issues which generally deal with the *extrinsic* nature of work, or time away from work as opposed to the *intrinsic nature* of work, or time-inwork. The latter refers to the intensity of work which includes: the length of the work cycle, task variety, skills demanded, the rhythm of work, machine pacing, monotonous and repetitive work which activates only a limited part of the workers' capabilities. When these conditions are part of an authoritarian work setting and a severe structure of command, workers experience a feeling of powerlessness and alienation. They have a limited degree of self-control over their methods of work, and are even restricted in their possibilities for leaving their work station without a stand-in. The "partial" rights of labour limit workers in their involvement in decision-making at the shop-floor level. These job characteristics deny workers control over planning and work methods and are the substantive issues that define the *intrinsic nature* of work which is part of managements' rights and prerogatives. Unfortunately, neither collective agreements nor existing government statutes have pierced this impenetrable fortress. The result adversely effects both worker health and safety.

C. Worker Participation and Safety

In 1971 a British researcher, J. B. Cronin published an article, 'Cause and Effect Investigations into Aspects of Industrial Accidents in the United Kingdom.'[19] Studying the accident rates of 41 factories, which were essentially alike in most respects, he found that "the 'worst' factory had an accident ratio ten times that of the 'best'." Of the 41 factories, six were selected—three pairs which were very similar in plant and size and very different in accident ratio—for more careful study. Cronin found that ". . . there was clearly no relationship in the factories concerned between the standard of compliance with the Factories Act and the accident ratio."[20] What was the operant factor then? The results of the study "appeared to indicate some sort of direct relationship between good safety record and successful joint consultation."[21] Cronin further concluded, "Such indications as there are show the accident rate to be a function of industrial relations. What is more, of a special aspect of industrial relations: communications and participation."[22]

In the mid-1970's, as Executive Director of the Occupational Health and Safety Branch in the Saskatchewan Department of Labour I wrote a letter to Mr. Cronin seeking futher empirical information in support of his thesis. On March 15, 1976, I received a response stating:

I gave up research in this field many years ago now because I found it totally impossible to get cooperation from employers once they realized the lines on which I was working. So far as they were concerned "investigation into the causes of accidents" meant bigger and better statistics and closer and closer examination of working conditions. Once they realized that I was concerned with attitudes and management methods they would have nothing of it. Revans has had much the same experience. It is much the same with publication. The editorial board of the ILR had to have a special meeting before they could pluck up courage to print that little article!

Some times ago Otto Kahn-Freund, of whom you must have heard, was anxious that Penguin Books should publish a short book on the whole of my work. But even with all the weight of Otto's reputation behind it, and that—as they say out here—is quite something, they would not touch it. And I don't think it was the writing. Similarly with Sweet ad Maxwell who actually went back on the contract.

The last meaningful thing that I was able to do was with a large local firm in Southampton which, the exception that proves the rule, was interested in what I was trying to do. I was able to do quite a complicated attitude survey of a ten per cent weighted random sample of their employees and found a quite astonishing correlation between the employees who had suffered more than one reportable accident and what might be described as "anti-social" attitudes. Indeed, the link-up was almost enbarrassingly complete from a statistical point of view—made even me wonder if the computer had cooked the results![23]

In 1971 the British researchers Philip Powell, Mary Hale, Jean Martin, and Martin Simon published a study entitled, '2,000 Accidents: A Shop Floor Study of Their Causes Based on 42 Months' Continuous Observation.'[24] This exhaustive study exposed many of the myths accepted by "safety professionals" today. I will quote just one of their conclusions:

... A general social pressure to do something about risks might embarrass industrial management because it can see itself as the executive of the action required. If the management of a factory sets up a training programme which teaches people that certain of the systems in the factory involve risk of injury, it lays itself open to allegations that it is not doing enough to re-design the systems and eliminate the risks. This might be a root of the apathy we observed. In some cases, it may need strong governmental and public pressure to overcome it.[25]

Another British study, *Safety or Profit*[26] was published by researchers Theo Nichols and Pete Armstrong in 1973. They found that there exists a fundamental conflict in conventional factories between safety and profit, and that, despite lip-service to safety rules, there is tremendous pressure on workers to place production ahead of safety:

... each of the accidents we have reviewed occurred in context of a process failure and whilst the men concerned were trying to maintain or restore production. In every case the dangerous situation was created in order to make it quicker and easier to do this. In every case the company's safety rules were broken. The process failures involved were not isolated events. Nor were the dangerous means used to deal with them. The men acted as they did in order to cope with the pressure from foremen and management to keep up production. This pressure was continual, process failures were fairly frequent and so the short-cutting methods used to deal with them were repeatedly employed. In each case it was only a matter of time before somebody's number came up.[27]

They further concluded:

... All this suggests that what is needed is some way of counteracting the *pressure for production* on the shop floor. It was just because management were not prepared to relax this pressure that men did not believe their propaganda; for in the long run such propaganda can only be effective to the extent that management *does* put safety before production.[28]

These and other studies indicate that the working conditions for every job are determined totally by the organization of work and the degree of control (or lack of control) that workers have over the means of work and the process of work. The prevailing ideology describes working conditions as a miscellaneous collection of the "physical" and "social" features of a particular job. The reality of the situation is just the opposite: the social organization of work produces both each job and its environment. What is important is the *control* over the work process.

Further it is work organization and the social relations—more particularly the power relations—within the workplace that determine the work environment with which the individual worker is faced, within which he must work—and all too often, which he must endure and suffer.

Once the power relations are seen for what they are, and once it is admitted that the preponderance of power, by far, lies with management, then it follows that "accident proneness"[29] is far more likely to lie, not with an individual worker whose power is very limited, but with a supervisor or manager, whose power is much greater.

For example, I was informed of an experiment conducted in two maintenance departments in the Vancouver Transit Company. They were five miles apart. In one department they had a high percentage of accidents while in another there was a low percentage. They switched the supervisors, and found out that the accident rates switched also. The accident rate followed the respective supervisors. Perhaps the supervisor whom the high accident rate followed should be called an "accident prone" supervisor! In all technical questions there is a social dimension.

D. The Conventional Wisdom of Accident Causation

The present widely-held management view of accident causation implies a tacit assumption that workers are primarily responsible for accidents through their "carelessness," "accident proneness," or "bad attitudes"—and that they can therefore stop accidents form happening merely by resolving to "be careful," to "obey their superiors," or to "have a positive attitude towards safety." Such an assumption is either naive or perverse. It is naive to believe that

workers willingly suffer accidents and injuries, that they seek out dangerous situations just to spite management. There is no valid reason to believe that workers are any more childish, silly, or self-destructive than are accountants, bureaucrats, doctors, lawyers, scientists, managers, safety professionals—or any other group in society. On the other hand, it is perverse to avoid spending money on needed safety improvements in the plant by dogmatically adopting a victim-blaming ideology.

I want to emphasize the fact that unsafe act theories of accident causation are ideology not science. I have been at pains over a number of years to refute these ideologies. I realize, of course, that any number of articles by me will not succeed in eradicating a myth which has become so ingrained in management ideology over the better part of century. However, I would like to quote in full the abstract of an article by me published in the *International Journal of Health Services:*

The "accident proneness" thesis has been with us since the early 1900s. The early statistical studies that reputedly provided the scientific basis for this notion are examined and found to be lacking due to methodological errors and fragemented view of industrial life. Accident proneness, as originally envisioned, has no empirical foundations. It has, however, become part of the tactical armamentarium [i.e. weaponry] used in "blaming the victim" for industrial accidents. It focuses on the personal characteristics of workers in relation to accident causation, while de-emphasizing the role of dangerous work environments. In this respect, it has acted as a barrier in the development of preventive occupational health and safety principles and practices. The notion has endured not only because it is tactically advantageous, but also because many members of the professions that deal with workplace accidents have accepted it without reservation and lent it credence. For the purpose of industrial accident prevention, however, it would be more appropriate to discard this notion in favor of a more integrated and broader understanding of the nature of the interaction between workers and their socio-technical work environment.[30]

In rejecting the prevailing management ideology on safety I do not want to leave the impression that I am "tearing down" and not "building up," that I can see what is wrong but cannot offer something better. On the contrary, I believe there is a need to emphasize, in regard to accident prevention, worker rights—the right to know, the right to participate, and the right to refuse as a sound theoretical foundation.

Notes

1. Glasbeek, Harry J., "The Contract of Employment at Common Law," in Anderson and Gunderson, *Union-Management Relations in Canada* (Addison-Wesley, 1982), p. 73.
2. Ibid., p. 73-74.
3. Swan, Kenneth P., "Union Impact on Management of the Organization: A Legal Perspective," in Anderson and Gunderson, *op. cit.,* p. 280.
4. Ibid., p. 280.
5. Wilson, David C., Butler, Cray, Hickson and Mallory, "The Limits of Trade Union Power in Organizational Decision Making," *British Journal of Industrial Relations* XX, No. 3 (November 1982), p. 323.
6. A leading proponent of this approach was Bora Laskin, former Chief Justice in Canada. See: Re Peterboro Lock Mfg. Co. Ltd. (1953), 4 L.A.C. 1499, at p. 1502 (Laskin). Also see Freedman, S., *Report of Industrial Inquiry Commission on Canadian National Railway "Run-Throughs,"* (Ottawa: Queen's Printer), 1965.
7. See Alan Fox, *Beyond Contract: Work, Power and Trust Relations,* (Faber, London) 1974), especially pp. 181–190.
8. Beatty, David M., "Labour Is Not a Commodity" in Reiter and Swan *Studies in Contract Law,* 1980, p. 316.
9. Ibid., pp. 340–1. See also R. H. Tawney, *Equality* (London: Unwin Brooks), 1964.
10. Fox, Alan, "The Meaning of Work," in *The Politics of Work and Occupations,* edited by Geoff Island and Graheme Salaman (University of Toronto Press), 1980, pp. 172–173.
11. Glasbeek, H., *op. cit.,* p. 74.
12. Thomas Donaldson, "Employee Rights," Ch. 7, in *Corporations and Morality* (Prentice-Hall, Inc., Englewood Cliffs, New Jersey), 1982, p. 138.
13. Ibid., p. 138.
14. Ibid., p. 138.
15. Stokes, Bruce, "Worker Participation—Productivity and the Quality of Work Life," *Worldwatch Paper 25* (December, 1978), p. 33.
16. Ibid., p. 33.
17. Ibid., p. 33.
18. In 1972, the Government in Saskatchewan passed an *Occupational Health and Safety Act* which required a joint labour-management committee to be set up in places of employment with ten or more employees (Section 20). As former Executive Director of the Occupational Health and Safety Branch within the Department of Labour from 1973 to 1982, I met with many of these committees and reviewed the Occupational Health and Safety Committee *Minutes* meetings throughout my tenure in government.
19. J. B. Cronin, "Cause and Effect? Investigations into Aspects of Industrial Accidents in the United Kingdom," *International Labor Review 103,* 2 (Feb. 1971), pp. 99–115.
20. Ibid., p. 106.
21. Ibid., p. 108.
22. Ibid., p. 115.
23. Letter from John B. Cronin to Robert Sass dated March 14, 1976.
24. Philip Powell, Mary Hale, Jean Martin and Martin Simon, *2,00 Accidents: A Shop Floor of their Cases Based on 42 Months' Continuous Observation.* (London: National institute of Industrial Psychology, 1971).
25. Ibid., p. 37.
26. Theo Nichols and Pete Armstrong, *Safety or Profit: Industrial Accidents and the Conventional Wisdom.* (England: Falling Wall Press, 1973).
27. Ibid., p. 20.
28. Ibid., p. 25.
29. Carelessness and Accident proneness are false accident causation theories which blame the victim, the worker, for accidents and deflect attention from unsafe conditions.
30. Robert Sass and Glen Crook, "Accident Proneness: Science or Non-Science?" *International Journal of Health Services* Vol. 11, No. 2 (Nov. 1981), p. 175.

Tibor R. Machan

Human Rights, Workers' Rights, and the "Right" to Occupational Safety

INTRODUCTION

I take the position of the nonbeliever.[1] I do not believe in special workers' rights. I do believe that workers possess rights as human beings, as do publishers, philosophers, disc jockeys, students, and priests. Once fully interpreted, these rights may impose special standards at the workplace, as they may in hospitals, on athletics fields, or in the marketplace.

HUMAN RIGHTS

Our general rights, those we are morally justified to secure by organized force (e.g., government), are those initially identified by John Locke: life, liberty, and property. [*John Locke* (1632–1704), an English philosopher, was the first systematic theorist of *liberalism,* the view that the state's purpose is to preserve the natural rights of its citizens to life, liberty and property.] That is, we need ask no one's permission to live, to take actions, and to acquire, hold, or use peacefully the productive or creative results of our actions. We may, morally, resist (without undue force) efforts to violate or infringe upon our rights. Our rights are

1. absolute,
2. unalienable, and
3. universal:

a. in social relations no excuse legitimatizes their violation;
b. no one can lose these rights, though their exercise may be restricted (e.g., to jail) by what one chooses to do; and
c. everyone has these rights, whether acknowledged or respected by others or governments or under different descriptions (within less developed conceptual schemes).[2]

I defend this general rights theory elsewhere.[3] Essentially, since adults are rational beings with the moral responsibility to excel as such, a good or suitable community requires these rights as standards. Since this commits one to a virtuously self-governed life, others should respect this as equal members of the community. Willful invasion of these rights—the destruction of (negative) liberty—must be prohibited in human community life.

So-called positive freedom—that is, the enablement to do well in life—presupposes the prior importance of negative freedom. As, what we might call, self-starters, human beings will generally be best off if they are left uninterfered with to take the initiative in their lives.

WORKERS' RIGHTS

What about special workers' rights? There are none. As individuals who intend to hire out their skills for what they will fetch in the marketplace, however, workers have the right to offer these in return for what others, (e.g., employers) will offer in acceptable compensation. This implies free trade in the labor market.

Any interference with such trade workers (alone or in voluntary cooperation) might want to engage in, with consent by fellow traders, would violate both the workers' and their traders' human rights. Freedom of association would thereby be abridged. (This includes freedom to organize into trade associations, unions, cartels, and so forth.)

From Tibor R. Machan, "Human Rights, Workers' Rights, and the "Right" to Occupational Safety," in *Moral Rights in the Workplace,* ed. Gertrude Ezorsky (Albany: State University of New York Press, 1987). Reprinted by permission.

Workers' rights advocates view this differently. They hold that the employee-employer relationship involves special duties owed by employers to employees, creating (corollary) rights that governments, given their purpose, should protect, Aside from negative rights, workers are owed respect of their positive rights to be treated with care and consideration.

This, however, is a bad idea. Not to be treated with care and consideration can be open to moral criticism. And lack of safety and health provisions may mean the neglect of crucial values to employees. In many circumstances employers should, morally, provide them.

This is categorically different from the idea of enforcible positive rights. (Later I will touch on unfulfilled reasonable expectations of safety and health provisions on the job!) Adults aren't due such service from free agents whose conduct should be guided by their own judgments and not some alien authority. This kind of moral servitude (abolished after slavery and serfdom) of some by others has been discredited.

Respect for human rights is necessary in a moral society—one needn't thank a person for not murdering, assaulting, or robbing one—whereas being provided with benefits, however crucial to one's well being, is more an act of generosity than a right.

Of course moral responsibilities toward others, even strangers, can arise. When those with plenty know of those with little, help would ordinarily be morally commendable. This can also extend to the employment relationship. Interestingly, however, government "regulation may impede risk-reducing change, freezing us into a hazardous present when a safer future beckons."[4]

My view credits all but the severely incapacitated with the fortitude to be productive and wise when ordering their affairs, workers included. The form of liberation that is then vital to workers is precisely the bourgeois kind: being set free from subjugation to others, including governments. Antibourgeois "liberation" is insultingly paternalistic.[5]

ALLEGING SPECIAL WORKERS' RIGHTS

Is this all gross distortion? Professor Braybrooke tells us, "Most people in our society . . . must look for employment and most (taking them one by one) have no alternative to accepting the working conditions offered by a small set of employers—perhaps one employer in the vicinity."[6] Workers need jobs and cannot afford to quibble. Employers can wait for the most accommodating job prospects.

This in part gives rise to special workers' rights doctrines, to be implemented by government occupational safety, heath and labor-relations regulators, which then "makes it easier for competing firms to heed an important moral obligation and to be, if they wish, humane."[7]

Suppose a disadvantaged worker, seeking a job in a coal mine, asks about safety provision in the mine. Her doing so presupposes that (1) she has other alternatives, and (2) it's morally and legally optional to care about safety at the mine, not due to workers by right. Prior to government's energetic prolabor interventions, safety, health, and related provisions for workers had been lacking. Only legally mandated workers' rights freed workers from their oppressive lot. Thus, workers must by law be provided with safety, health care, job security, retirement, and other vital benefits.

Workers' rights advocates deny that employers have the basic (natural or human) private property rights to give them full authority to set terms of employment. They are seen as nonexclusive stewards of the workplace property, property obtained by way of historical accident, morally indifferent historical necessity, default, or theft. There is no genuine free labor market. There are no jobs to offer since they are not anyone's to give. The picture we should have of the situation is that society should be regarded as a kind of large team or family; the rights of its respective parts (individuals) flow not from their free and independent moral nature, but from the relationship of the needs and usefulness of individuals as regards the purposes of the collective.

By this account, everyone lacks the full authority to enter into exclusive or unilaterally determined and mutual agreements on his or her terms. Such terms—of production, employment, promotion, termination, and so on—would be established, in line with moral propriety, only by the agency (society, God, the party, the democratic assembly) that possesses the full moral authority to set them.

Let us see why the view just stated is ultimately unconvincing. To begin with, the language of rights does not belong within the above framework. That language acknowledges the reality of morally free and independent human beings and includes among them workers, as well as all other adults. Individual human rights assume that within the limits of nature, human beings are all efficacious to varying degrees, frequently depending upon their own choices. Once this individualist viewpoint is rejected, the very foundation for rights language disappears (notwithstanding some contrary contentions).[8]

Some admit that employers are full owners of their property, yet hold that workers, because they are disadvantaged, are owed special duties of care and considerateness, duties which in turn create rights the government should protect. But even if this were right, it is not possible from this position to establish enforcible *public* policy. From the mere existence of *moral* duties employers may have to employees, no enforcible public policy can follow; moral responsibilities require freely chosen fulfillment, not enforced compliance.

Many workers' rights advocates claim that a free labor market will lead to such atrocities as child labor, hazardous and health-impairing working conditions, and so forth. Of course, even if this were true, there is reason to think that OSHA-type regulatory remedies are illusionary. As Peter Huber argues, "regulation of health and safety is not only a major obstacle to technological transformation and innovation but also often aggravates the hazards it is supposed to avoid."[9]

However, it is not certain that a free labor market would lead to child labor and rampant neglect of safety and health at the workplace. Children are, after all, dependents and therefore have rights owed them by their parents. To subject children to hazardous, exploitative work, to deprive them of normal education and health care, could be construed as a violation of their individual rights as young, dependent human beings. Similarly, knowingly or negligently subjecting workers to hazards at the workplace

(of which they were not made aware and could not anticipate from reasonable familiarity with the job) constitutes a form of actionable fraud. It comes under the prohibition of the violation of the right to liberty, at times even the right to life. Such conduct is actionable in a court of law and workers, individually or organized into unions, would be morally justified, indeed advised, to challenge it.

A consistent and strict interpretation of the moral (not economic) individualist framework of rights yields results that some advocates of workers' rights are aiming for. The moral force of most attacks on the free labor market framework tends to arise from the fact that some so-called free labor market instances are probably violations of the detailed implications of that approach itself. Why would one be morally concerned with working conditions that are fully agreed to by workers? Such a concern reflects either the belief that there hadn't been any free agreement in the first place, and thus workers are being defrauded, or it reflects a paternalism that, when construed as paternalism proper instead of compassion, no longer carries moral force.

Whatever its motives, paternalism is also insulting and demeaning in its effect. Once it is clear that workers can generate their own (individual and/or collective) response to employers' bargaining power—via labor organizations, insurance, craft associations, and so on—the favorable air of the paternalistic stance diminishes considerably. Instead, workers are seen to be regarded as helpless, inefficacious, inept persons.

THE "RIGHT" TO OCCUPATIONAL SAFETY

Consider an employer who owns and operates a coal mine. (We could have chosen any firm, privately or "publicly" owned, managed by hired executives with the full consent of the owners, including interested stockholders who have entrusted, by their purchase of stocks, others with the goal of obtaining economic benefits for them.) The firm posts a call for jobs. The mine is in competition with some of the major coal mines in the country and the world. But it is much less prosperous than its competitors. The employer is at present not equipped to run a highly-polished, well-outfitted (e.g., very safe) operation. That may lie in the future, provided the cost of production will not be so high as to make this impossible.

Some of the risks will be higher for workers in this mine than in others. Some of the mine-shafts will have badly illuminated stairways, some of the noise will be higher than the levels deemed acceptable by experts, and some of the ventillation equipment will be primitive. The wages, too, will be relatively low in hopes of making the mine eventually more prosperous.

When prospective employees appear and are made aware of the type of job being offered, and its hazards they are at liberty to

a. accept or reject
b. organize into a group and insist on various terms not in the offing,
c. bargain alone or together with others and set terms that include improvements, or
d. pool workers' resources, borrow, and purchase the firm.

To deny that workers could achieve such things is not yet to deny that they are (negatively) free to do so. But to hold that this would be extraordinary for workers (and thus irrelevant in this sort of case) is to

1. assume a historical situation not in force and certainly not necessary,
2. deny workers the capacity for finding a solution to their problems, or
3. deny that workers are capable of initiative.

Now suppose that employers are compelled by law to spend the firm's funds to meet safety requirements deemed desirable by the government regulators. This increased cost of production reduces available funds for additional wages for present and future employees, not to mention available funds for future prospect sites. This is what has happened: The employee-employer relationship has been unjustly in-truded upon, to the detriment not only of the mine owners, but also of those who might be employed and of future consumers of energy. The myth of workers' rights is mostly to blame.

CONCLUSION

I have argued that the doctrine of special workers' rights is unsupported and workers, accordingly, possess those rights that all other humans possess, the right to life, liberty, and property. Workers are not a special species of persons to be treated in a paternalistic fashion and, given just treatment in the community, they can achieve their goals as efficiently as any other group of human beings.[10]

Notes

1. I wish to thank the Earhart, Jon M. Olin, and Reason Foundations for making it possible, in part, for me to work on this project. I also wish to thank Bill Puka and Gertrude Ezorsky for their very valuable criticism of an earlier draft of this essay, despite their very likely disapproval of my views.
2. This observation rests, in part, on epistemological insights available, for example, in Hanna F. Pitkin, *Wittgenstin and Justice* (Berkeley, Calif.: University of California Press, 1972).
3. Tibor R. Machan, "A Reconsideration of Natural Rights Theory," *American Philosophical Quarterly 19* (January 1980): 61–72.
4. Peter Huber, "Exorcists vs. Gatekeepers in Risk Regulations," *Regulation* (November/December 1983), 23.
5. But see Steven Kelman, "Regulation and Paternalism," *Rights and Regulation,* ed. T. R. Machan and M. B. Johnson (Cambridge, Mass.: Ballinger Publ. Co., 1983), 217–248.
6. David Braybrooke, *Ethics in the World of Business* (Totawa, N.J.: Rowman & Allanheld, 1983), 223.
7. Ibid., 224.
8. For an attempt to forge a collectivist theory of rights, see Tom Campbell, *The Left and Rights* (London and Boston: Routledge & Kegan Paul, 1983).
9. Huber, "Exorcists vs. Gatekeepers," 23.
10. Ibid. Huber observes that "Every insurance company knows that life is growing safer, but the public is firmly convinced that living is becoming every more hazardous" (p. 23). In general, capitalism's benefits to workers have simply not been acknowledged, especially by moral and political philosophers! It is hardly possible to avoid the simple fact that the workers of the world believe differently, judging by what system they prefer to emigrate to whenever possible.

1. Explain why you find Superson's analogy between a doctor and a patient and an employer and an employee either persuasive or unpersuassive?

2. How should an employee's right to know if he or she is working with hazardous materials be balanced with an employer's right to protect trade secrets?

3. What does Sass mean by the term "manifesto right"?

4. Do you agree with Sass's claim that employees have the right to participate in designing their jobs? Why or why not?

5. Machan claims that "from the mere existence of *moral* duties employers may have to employees, no enforcible public policy can follow." Do you agree or disagree? How does Machan support his claim?

6. Why does Machan think that workers' rights imply paternalism? Do you agree? Why or why not?

CASE 6:1 SAFETY AND SIGNIFICANT RISK[1]

In 1979 producers of benzene filed petition for review of a new health standard put forth by the Occupational Safety and Health Administration (OSHA) limiting occupational exposure to benzene. Under the Occupational Safety and Health Act of 1970, the Secretary of Labor, through the agency of OSHA, is to ensure safe and healthy working conditions. Where toxic materials are concerned, the Act directs setting "the standard which most adequately assures, to the extent feasible, on the basis of the best available evidence, that no employee will suffer material impairment of health or functional capacity." With regard to carcinogens, OSHA has held that no safe exposure level can be determined and that the exposure level should thus be set at the lowest technologically feasible level that will not impair the viability of the industry in question. In the present instance, having determined a causal connection between benzene and leukemia, OSHA reduced the permissible exposure limit to airborne concentrations of benzene from ten parts per million to one part per million and prohibited skin contact with benzene solutions.

Producers of benzene protested the imposition of this new standard on the grounds that OSHA had not shown that the one part per million exposure level was "reasonably necessary or appropriate to provide safe and healthful employment." They further argued that a safe workplace is not the equivalent of a risk-free workplace, and that OSHA had exceeded its authority in seeking a risk-free workplace regardless of cost to the industry.

CASE STUDY QUESTIONS

1. OSHA's decision to lower the exposure standard was based not on an empirical study indicating that leukemia is caused by exposure to ten parts per million of benzene, but on a series of assumptions that some cases of leukemia might result from exposure to ten parts per million of benzene and that the number of cases would be reduced by lowering the exposure level to one part per million. Would OSHA's decision be justified if the evidence plausibly suggested a link between benzene exposure at the level of ten parts per million and leukemia, even though firmly documented proof was lacking?

2. Do you agree that a safe working environment is compatible with an environment in which there are risks? How would you define a safe working environment?

3. The Occupational Safety and Health Act was not designed to require employers to provide risk-free workplaces whenever it is technologically feasible to do so, so long as the cost is not great enough to destroy the entire industry, but to eliminate, when feasible, significant risks of harm. Do you think its mandate should be strengthened?

CASE 6:2 RISK AND THE NORMAL CONDITIONS OF EMPLOYMENT[2]

In 1987 John Walton was a corrections officer employed at Kingston Penitentiary. At that time, correctional officers rotated through different assignments, one of these being hospital duty. On May 19, 1987 Walton, along with a colleague, was assigned to work in the hospital. Part of his duties was to escort inmates who were kept in isolation cells with no modern plumbing facilities to the washroom each morning, where they emptied the contents of the portable toilets kept in their rooms. These wastes often contained semen because of the incidence of masturbation among inmates. Three of the inmates were suspected of having AIDS or Hepatitis B.

Out of concern that they might contact one of these diseases through these three inmates throwing their waste upon them, Walton and his colleague refused to open their cells. Walton and his colleague also felt that the protective equipment of light-weight surgical gloves covering only hands and wrists and light-weight paper gowns covering only the torso, issued to guards to prevent infection, was not sufficient protection from contacting these diseases through being bitten or spat upon by infected inmates. They requested that they be issued equipment that better protected them and that they be vaccinated against Hepatitis B. They also requested that the practice of storing protective equipment in areas accessible to prisoners be discontinued.

CASE STUDY QUESTIONS

1. Our knowledge of AIDS has increased and we now know that it can be contracted in more ways than was formerly thought. Was Walton's request a reasonable one, given the knowledge available at the time?
2. Should an employee have the right to refuse work that is extremely unpleasant, as opposed to unsafe? At the time, should Walton's work have been characterized as unsafe or simply as extremely unpleasant?

Notes

1. Based on *Industrial Union v. American Petroleum* as found in 100 Supreme Court Reporter, 844 (1980).
2. Based on *Walton v. Treasury Board (Correctional Services Canada)* as found in *Canadian Cases of Employment Law*, vol 16, pp. 190–200.

FOR FURTHER READING

1. Carl F. Cranor, "Some Moral Issues in Risk Assessment," *Ethics*, Vol. 101, Oct. 1990, pp. 123–143.

2. Gertrude Ezorsky, editor, *Moral Rights in the Workplace* (Albany: State University of New York Press, 1987).

3. Theodore S. Glickman and Michael Gough, editors, *Readings in Risk* (Washington, D.C.: Resources for the Future, 1990).

Chapter Seven

WHISTLEBLOWING AND EMPLOYEE LOYALTY

Introduction

Whistleblowing can be defined in various ways, but it is basically an attempt by an employee, or a former employee to bring a wrongful practice to the attention of those who have power to remedy the situation. In most instances, whistleblowers act not out of a desire for personal gain or a vendetta against a disliked employer, but out of a concern for public welfare and the integrity of the company they work for. On this basis, one might expect that whistleblowers are both admired and respected by the public and their employers. Unfortunately, this is not the case. Most whistleblowers are ostracized by fellow workers, and are subject to lowered evaluations by supervisors, demotions, punitive transfers, loss of jobs, and blacklisting in their profession. For example, Roger Boisjoly, a senior engineer at Morton Thiokol, who strongly recommended that the space shuttle *Challenger* not be launched and testified to that effect before the Rogers Commission, found that he was unable to continue working at Morton Thiokol because of alienation from his coworkers and that other companies were unwilling to hire a known whistleblower.

In his article "Avoiding the Tragedy of Whistleblowing," Michael Davis argues that whistleblowing typically exacts a high price not only from whistleblowers, who suffer the most severe consequences, but also from employers and fellow employees. In Davis' view, whistleblowing seems to be analogous to major surgery. Although it may in certain circumstances be necessary, it takes a high toll on those undergoing it and if there exists a way of preventing the condition that necessitates it, this should be vigorously pursued. At best, whistleblowing is the lesser of two evils.

Davis observes that a good deal of the persecution whistleblowers undergo lies in the irrational human tendency to blame the messenger for bad news. He is probably correct in this observation, but it seems clear persecution of whistleblowers has deeper roots. Whistleblowing is often described by employers and fellow employees as a betrayal of trust; a lack of loyalty where loyalty is owed. It is this feeling of betrayal which best explains the depth of feeling typically aroused by whistleblowing.

In "Whistleblowing and Employee Loyalty," Robert Larmer discusses the the view commonly held by employers and fellow workers that the whistleblower is disloyal and thus morally deficient. Larmer argues that whistleblowing is consistent with loyalty to one's employer and fellow employees. The view that whistleblowing involves a betrayal of loyalty is based on the assumption that to be loyal to someone is to act in a way that accords with what that person believes to be in her best interests. This implies that if a whistleblower's employer or fellow employees do not believe whistleblowing to be in their best interests, the whistleblower has acted disloyally. In Larmer's view, this common assumption is mistaken. To act loyally towards someone is not necessarily to act in a manner which that person believes to be in his interest, but rather to act in a manner which is genuinely in his interest, whether he believes so or not. Larmer goes on to argue that to the degree that an action is genuinely immoral, it is impossible that it is in the agent's best interests. It follows that an employer or fellow worker who is acting immorally in not ultimately acting in the best interests of either the company or herself, and that the whistleblower does not act disloyally in blowing the whistle.

Natalie Dandekar further explores the tendency to view whistleblowing as a betrayal of trust. In her article "Can Whistleblowing be FULLY Legitimated," she notes that whistleblowers often find themselves in the embarrassing position of questioning superiors who would ordinarily be regarded as persons of good will and ethical moral judgment. A problem whistleblowers often face is that ethical issues are not always recognized as such, even by persons of good will and acknowledged moral competency in other matters. She suggests that at the level of practical response, adjusting the disparity of resources between the corporation and the whistleblower in instances of litigation, focusing on educational sensitizing sessions, and acknowledging the fact that wrongdoing may not be the result of evil intent, will help mitigate the persecution whistleblowers receive.

Michael Davis

Avoiding the Tragedy of Whistleblowing

[T]he strength of the pack is the Wolf, and the strength of the Wolf is the pack.
—Rudyard Kipling, "The Law of the Jungle"

Most discussions of whistleblowing seek to justify whistleblowing or to distinguish justified from unjustified whistleblowing; or they report who blows the whistle, how, and why; or they advise on how to blow the whistle or how to respond to an employee about to blow the whistle or what to do once she has; or they make recommendations for new laws to protect whistleblowers. In one way or another, they treat whistleblowing as inevitable. I shall not do that. Instead, I shall try to help individuals and organizations *avoid* whistleblowing.

That purpose may suggest that I oppose whistleblowing. I do not. I think whistleblowing is, on balance, at least a necessary evil (and sometimes even a good thing). I certainly think whistleblowers should have legal protection.[1] They should not be fired for their good deed or punished for it in any other way. But I doubt that much can be done to protect them. I shall use much of this paper to explain why.

That explanation will bring out the destructive side of whistleblowing, making it easier for most of us to see ourselves in the role of those who mistreat whistleblowers. Insofar as it does that, it will give the organization's case for mistreatment. The explanation will, however, also show the importance of avoiding whistleblowing. We should try to get the benefits of whistleblowing without making people and or-

From Michael Davis, "Avoiding the Tragedy of Whistleblowing," *Business & Professional Ethics Journal,* Vol. 8, No. 4, 1988. Reprinted with permission.

ganizations pay the enormous price whistleblowing typically exacts.[2]

This paper is addressed *both* to those who have a substantial say in how some organization runs *and* to those who could some day have to blow the whistle on their own organization. These groups overlap more than most discussions of whistleblowing suggest.[3] That, however, is not why I have chosen to address both here. My reason runs deeper. I believe that, even if those two groups did not overlap, they would still share an interest in making whistleblowing unnecessary; that both groups can do much to make whistleblowing unnecessary; and that each will be better able to do its part if it understands better what the other group can do.

THE INFORMAL ORGANIZATION WITHIN THE FORMAL

Let us begin with the obvious. No matter how large or small, every formal organization includes one or more informal groups. An academic department, for example, is a network of poker buddies, movie buffs, cooks, and so on. Departmental conversation is not limited to what must be said to carry on departmental business. Ordinary life, ordinary attitudes, permeate the formal structure. Much of what makes the formal organization succeed or fail goes on within and between these informal groups. Who likes you is at least as important in most organizations as what you are. Success is not simply a matter of technical skill or accomplishment. You must also have enough friends properly placed—and not too many enemies. Perhaps only at hiring time do academics talk much about personality but every academic knows of a department that fell apart because certain members did not get along and others that survived financial troubles, campus disorders, and tempting offers to individual members in part at least because the faculty got along so well together.

Though my example is an academic department, nonacademics will, I think, confirm that much the same is true of corporate offices and even of government bureaus. Most of what makes such organizations work, or fail to work, can't be learned from the table of organization, formal job descriptions, or even personnel evaluations. Thinking realistically about whistleblowing means thinking about the informal aspects of formal organization as well as the formal. I shall focus on those informal aspects here.

II. BLAMING THE MESSENGER

"Whistleblower" is a capacious term. Whistleblowers can, it seems, be anonymous or open, internal or external, well-intentioned or not so well-intentioned, accurate or inaccurate, justified or unjustified. Perhaps strictly speaking, some of these are not whistleblowers at all.[5] But I have no reason to speak strictly here. For my purposes, "whistleblower" may refer to any member of a formal organization who takes information *out of channels* to try to stop the organization from doing something he believes morally wrong (or to force it to do something he believes morally required).[6]

Most organizations will fire a whistleblower if it can, whether she was right or not; will ruin her job prospects if it can; and, if it can do neither, will still do what it can to make her life miserable. Otherwise humane organizations can treat a whistleblower savagely.[7] Why?

The most common answer is that those who mistreat whistleblowers do so because they expect to benefit from having fewer whistleblowers. The self-interest of individuals or their organization explains the mistreatment.

Though no doubt part of the truth, this explanation is, I think, only a small part. We are in general far from perfect judges of self-interest. Our judgment does not improve simply because we assume an organizational role. We can still be quite irrational. Recall how Shakespeare's Cleopatra responds to her messenger's report that Antony has married Octavia:

. . . Hence,
Horrible villian! or I'll spurn thine eyes
Like balls before me; I'll unhair thy head:
Thou shalt be whipp'd with wire and stew'd in
brine. . .

. . . let ill tidings tell
Themselves when they be felt.[8]

Though Cleopatra had ordered him to spy on Antony, the messenger will hear more harsh words, receive hard blows, and have a knife angrily put to this throat before he is allowed to leave with a small reward.

Today's formal organizations can treat the bringer of bad news much as Shakespeare's love-sick Cleopatra did. So, for example, in a recent book on corporate life, Robert Jackall grimly recounts what happened to several executives with bad news to tell their respective organizations. Though each discovered wrongdoing it was his duty to discover, reported it through channels, and saw the wrongdoer punished, though none of them was responsible for the wrong reported, and though the organization was better off for the report, the lucky among Jackall's executives had their part in the affair forgotten. Some paid with their careers.[9]

We generally think of information as power—and it is. But thinking of information that way is no small achievement when the information wrecks our plans. Even experienced managers can find themselves telling subordinates, "I don't want to hear any more bad news."

The rationality of formal organization is an ideal never more than partially achieved. We must keep that in mind if we are to understand what happens to so many whistleblowers. An organization that would "whip with wire and stew in brine" the simple bringer of bad news is not likely to respond well to the whistleblower—even if, as often happens, the whistleblower serves the organization's long-term interests. The whistleblower is, after all, not only a bearer of bad news; he *is* bad news.

III. WHISTLEBLOWING AS BAD NEWS ALL AROUND

Discussion of whistleblowing tend to emphasize the undeniable good the accurate whistleblower does. The incidental harm tends to be overshadowed, perhaps because so much of it seems deserved. The harm done by inaccurate whistleblowing has received much less attention. Why?[10]

Whatever the reasons for ignoring the bad news about whistleblowing, the fact remains that much of it is ignored and, for our purposes, the bad news is crucial. So, let us recall how much bad news there is.

Whistleblowing is always proof of organizational trouble. Employees do not go out of channels unless the channels at least seem inadequate.

Whistleblowing is also proof of management failure. Usually several managers directly above the whistleblower will have heard his complaint, tried to deal with it in some way, and failed to satisfy him. However managers view the whistleblower's complaint, they are bound to view their own failure to "keep control" as a blot on their record.

Whistleblowing is also bad news for those on whom the whistle is blown. What they were peacefully doing in obscurity is suddenly in the spotlight. They will have to participate in "damage control" meetings, investigations, and the like that would not otherwise demand their scarce time. They will have to write unusual reports, worry about the effect of publicity on their own career, and face the pointed questions of spouse, children, and friends. And they may have to go on doing such things for months—or even years.

Insofar as whistleblowing has such effects, no one within the organization will be able to hear the whistleblower's name without thinking unpleasant thoughts. No manager will be able to make a decision about the whistleblower without having bad associations color her judgment. The whistleblower not only makes conscious enemies within his organization, he can also create enormous biases against himself, biases very hard to cancel by any formal procedure.

And that is not all the bad news. What must the whistleblower have become to blow the whistle? At the very least, he must have lost faith in the formal organization. If he had kept faith, he would have accepted whatever decision came through formal channels—at least once he had exhausted all formal means of appeal.

For anyone who has been a loyal employee for many years, losing faith in the organization is likely to be quite painful—rather like the disintegration of a marriage. My impression is that few whistleblowers take their job thinking that they might some day have to blow the whistle. They seem to start out as loyal employees—perhaps more loyal than most. One day something happens to shake their loyalty. Further shocks follow until loyalty collapses, leaving behind a great emptiness. While managers tend to think of whistleblowers as traitors to the organization, most whistleblowers seem to feel that, on the contrary, it is the organization that has betrayed them.[11]

This bad news implies more. Before the whistleblower was forced to blow the whistle, she trusted the formal organization. She took its good sense for granted. That is no longer possible. Faith has become suspicion. Since what we call "organizational authority" is precisely the ability of the organization to have its commands taken more or less on faith, the "powers that be" now have as much reason to distrust the whistleblower as she has to distrust them.[12] She no longer recognizes their authority. She is much more likely to blow the whistle than before. She is now an enemy within.

Something equally bad has happened to relations between the whistleblower and her coworkers. Whistleblowing tends to bring out the worst in people. Some friends will have become implaccable enemies. Others will hide, fearing "guilt by association." Most, perhaps, simply lose interest, looking on the whistleblower as they would someone dying of cancer. These desertions can leave deep scars. And even when they do not, they leave the whistleblower an outsider, a loner in an organization in which isolation for any reason makes one vulnerable.

All this bad news suggests some hard questions: How can a whistleblower work as before with people whose loyalty he no longer shares? How can coworkers treat him as they did before when he is no longer quite one of them? How can he hope for promotion, or even retention, in an organization in which he can put no trust, in which he has no friends, and for which he is likely to make further trouble? These, I think, are plainly not questions a law can answer.

IV. Helping the Whistleblower and the Organization

How do they know that they are a ✓

What then can be done for the whistleblower? One option is to find her another job. That is not easy. Potential employers generally shun known whistleblowers. That alone makes finding a new job hard. Then too, the whistleblower may not be as good an interviewee as before. Many whistlblowers seem to signal the bad news even when they do their best to conceal it. They may, for example, sound emotionally exhausted, ask questions that suggest distrust, or just seem prickly. They are like people going through a bad divorce.

Since few potential employers want someone else's troubles, we must draw this paradoxical conclusion: the whistleblower's best hope for continuing her career may be her old employer. That the old employer may be her best hope is the chief reason to support laws protecting whistleblowers. Though a law can offer the whistleblower little direct protection, it can prod the organization to think about making peace with the whistleblower.

This, however, is still a slim hope. The organization can make peace with the whistleblower *only if* it can reestablish his loyalty to the organization and his trust in those with whom he must work. That is not easy.

Clearly, the formal organization itself must change enough for the whistleblower to have good reason to believe that he will not have to go out of channels again. The changes will probably have to be substantial, something most organizations automatically resist. But formal changes alone will not be enough to reestablish the whistleblower's informal relations with superiors, subordinates, and coworkers. What is needed in addition is something like marriage counseling, some sort of group therapy to expose and resolve all the feelings of betrayal, distrust, and rejection whistleblowing inevitably generates. The whistleblower will not be safe until he is reintegrated into the formal organization.

Some government agencies have required employees involved in a whistleblowing case to participate in such group therapy. The results so far have not been good. Managers, especially, seem to view such therapy as just one more hoop to jump through on the way to the inevitable.[13] To work, the therapy probably needs to be voluntarily undertaken by all participants, something not easily legislated.

That is why even this best hope for the whistleblower, reconciliation with the organization, is so slim. We need to find better ways to protect whistleblowers. In the long run at least, peace between the whistleblower and the organization is as good for the organization as for the whistleblower. The whistleblower is not really an enemy. An organization that has whistleblowers needs them. The whistleblower is like the knock at the door that wakes one in a house on fire—unwelcome, but better than sleeping till the fire reaches the bed. An organization that punishes its whistleblowers blinds itself to troubles better faced.

To say that is not to deny the disadvantages of whistleblowing described earlier but to explain why we should try to make whistleblowing unnecessary rather than try to prevent whistleblowing in other ways. It is to the chief means of making whistleblowing unnecessary that I now turn.

V. How Organizations Can Avoid Whistleblowing

If whistleblowing means that an organization has trouble using bad news, one way for an organization to avoid whistleblowing is to improve the organization's ability to use bad news. We may distinguish three approaches.

One approach, what we might call the "procedural," builds invitations to report bad news into the ordinary ways of doing business. These procedures can be quite simple, for example, a space on a form for "disadvantages" or "risks." Such a blank almost forces the person filling out the form to say something negative. Those above him are also more likely to treat bad news reported in this way as part of "doing the job" than they would the same bad news reported without that specific invitation.[14]

The first approach also includes more complicated procedures, for example, "review meetings" the purpose of which is to identify problems. The review meeting works like a blank space. Where the emphasis is on revealing bad news, more bad news is likely to come out. Revealing bad news is more likely to seem part of the job.

Of course, how things will seem is in part a matter of the mental set the people involved bring to the procedure. That set will be determined in large part by what has happened in the organization before. Organizational atmosphere can turn any procedure into a mere formality. If, for example, people who fill in the disadvantage blank or speak up at a review meeting are commonly treated like Cleopatra's messenger, the procedures will bring in little bad news. Part of making procedures work is making sure those involved think about them in the right way. This is especially important when the procedures are new and patterns of response have not yet developed.[15]

In a way, then, my first approach, the procedural, presupposes others. Those participating in various procedures need to understand how important bad news can be. They also need regular reminders, because everyday experience tends to teach them how much bad news hurts. Education can provide one reminder; a structure of formal incentives can provide another.

I intend "education" to be understood broadly (so broadly in fact that the line between education and formal incentives all but disappears). Training sessions in which superiors or special trainers stress the importance of hearing the worst is only part of what I have in mind. Everyday experience is also part of education. Subordinates are more likely to take the formal training to heart if they are regularly thanked for giving superiors bad news, if they see that bringing bad news is treated much as bringing good news is, and so on.

Superiors are, of course, more likely to treat well subordinates who bring bad news if the organization makes it rational to do so. But treating such subordinates well will generally be rational only if the organization routinely uses bad news in ways that encourage reporting it—or, at least, do not discourage reporting it. An organization's ability to do this routinely depends on its structure.

For example: Suppose that an organization holds a manager responsible only for what gets reported "on her watch." Suppose too that her subordinate informs her that her predecessor improved the division's profits by skipping routine maintenance and now much of the machinery is in poor condition. The manager will *not* want to report this to her superiors. She would be bringing news that will threaten everyone who must pass it on. She will therefore not want to hear the bad news herself. She will have good reason to tell her subordinate, "Let sleeping dogs lie." Perhaps the dogs will not howl until her successor takes over.

Now, suppose instead that the organization has routine ways of assigning responsibility to a manager for what she does while in a position even if the bad consequences only become apparent later. In such an organization, a manager has good reason to want subordinates to report the bad news about her predecessor's work as soon as they learn of it. She need not fear such "sleeping dogs." They will not wake to howl for her blood. And, if she lets them lie, she may later have to explain how *she* could have missed them.

Most organizations tend to treat the person in charge as responsible for whatever bad news he must report. Few have any routine for assigning responsibility to anyone else (perhaps because such a routine would be quite expensive).[16] Hence, in that respect at least, most organizations have structures tending to discourage bad news. Leaving managers in charge for long terms, say, ten or twenty years, would probably compensate for this tendency. Few problems lie dormant that long. Today, however, managers seldom stay in one position for even five years. If they do not rise quickly within an organization, they are likely to move to another. This mobility means that most organizations must rely on other means of giving managers reason to welcome bad news.

The most common approach these days is to create alternative channels for bad news so that no one in an organization is in position to block its flow upward. The most traditional of these alternative channels is the regular outside audit. Another is an "open door" policy allowing subordinates to go directly to a senior official, by passing several layers of management. Another is changing the traditional chain of command into something much more like a lattice, so that subordinates have less to fear from any particular superior and have routine access to more than one. Such arrangements give a manager reason to be thankful that he has heard the bad news from a subordinate rather than from a superior and reason to try to respond in a way likely to satisfy the subordinate. The subordinate has saved the manager from being "blindsided." Such arrangements tend to make whistleblowing unnecessary.

That, I think, is enough for now about how organizations can make whistleblowing unnecessary. We are ready to consider how individuals can avoid becoming whistleblowers.

VI. How to Avoid Having to Blow the Whistle

The simplest way to avoid having to blow the whistle may seem to be joining an organization in which whistleblowing will never be necessary. Unfortunately, things are not that simple. Organizations are human contrivances; none is perfect.

Still, organizations do differ quite a bit. By choosing the right organization, one can reduce substantially the chance one will have to blow the whistle (much as one can reduce substantially the chance of divorce by not "marrying in haste"). The question is how the organization handles bad news. The answer will be found in the organization's procedures, educational programs, and structure, not the ones "on paper" but the ones actually in effect. The difference can be crucial. For example, if the organization has an open door policy, is the door ever used? Since organizations always work imperfectly, an open door that is never used is probably a channel no one dare use, not an unnecessary channel. Using such a channel will probably be treated as whistleblowing.

Any organization described as "one happy family" should be examined with special care. Organizations, like families, generally have arguments, tensions, and the like. That is how they grow. The organization that recalls only good times is not the one that had no bad times but the one that has no use for bad news. It is exactly the kind of organization in which whistleblowing is most likely to be necessary. Personally, I would prefer an organization in which old battles are recalled blow by blow and the general happiness must be inferred from the fact that all participants survived to work together again.[17]

Having chosen the right organization, can one do anything more to reduce the chance he will some day have to blow the whistle? Certainly, But he will have to think in strikingly political terms.

He will, first of all, want to develop his own informal channels to augment formal channels. So, for example, a new employee W officially reports to A. But if B carries more weight with their common superior, W might want to get to know B. Perhaps they share an interest in chess. Once W is friends with B, W is in position to pass information around A should A try to suppress it. A can hardly object to W playing chess with B. Yet, once A knows W and B are chess buddies, A will be less likely to suppress information W wants passed up. A knows W has a channel around him.

Second, one should form alliances with colleagues and subordinates, people who share one's responsibilities. One should not have to stand along against a superior. Whenever possible, the superior should have to respond to a common recommendation. Managers are likely to treat a group concern much more seriously than a single individual's. One should try to work through groups as much as possible.

But, third, not any group will do. The group should be sensitive to the moral concerns likely to force one to blow the whistle. The organizations most in need of whistleblowers are also most likely to be so organized that employees become morally less sensitive the longer they work for the organization.[18] So, one will probably need to cultivate the moral sensitivity of potential allies. There are many ways to do this. The simplest is to bring in items from the newspaper raising problems similar to those the organization could face and pass them around at lunch, asking how "we" could handle them. If potential allies share the same profession, one might try getting the local professional society to host discussions dealing with the ethical problems that come up in work they do.[19]

Last, but not least, one needs to cultivate one's own ability to present bad news in a way most likely to get a favorable response. Part of doing that is, of course, presenting the information clearly, with enough technical detail and supporting evidence. But there is more to it than that. Some people have, I think, become whistleblowers for lack of a pungent phrase.[20] A master of words is less likely to have to blow the whistle than someone who, though understanding a peril, has trouble communicating it.

And that is not all. Presenting bad news in a way likely to get a favorable response also includes what used to be called "rhetoric." A little sugar helps the medicine go down. Is there a good side to the bad news? If so, why not present that first? If there is no good side, how about presenting the bad news in a way likely to bring out the personal stake the decision-maker has in responding favorably? Such tactics are usually not mentioned in a discussion of whistleblowing. Yet, it seems to me, many people end up as whistleblowers because they did not pay enough attention to the feelings of their audience.

Those who have substantial say in how an organization runs might, then, want to consider some educational programs our earlier discussion of education may not have suggested. In particular, they might want to consider training employees in such political skills as how to present bad news effectively and how to maneuver it through channels. They also might want to review their hiring practices. For example, will the personnel office reject an applicant who asks whether the company has an open door policy, treat such a question with indifference, or consider it as a plus? Any organization that does not treat such questions as a plus will not select *for* people with the skills needed to make whistleblowing unnecessary.

VII. Concluding Remarks

The world can be a hard place. One can do everything in her power and still end having to choose between blowing the whistle on her organization and sitting by while innocent people suffer harm she can prevent. The whistleblower is a tragic character. Her decency pushes her to bring great suffering on herself and those about whom she cares most. Her only alternative, sitting by, would save those she cares about most from harm—but at an incalculable cost (failing to do what she has a duty to do). Her organization will probably be better off in the long run—if it survives. But, in the short run, it too will suffer.

When events leave only this choice, most of us—at least when we are not directly involved—would hope the person upon whom that choice is forced will find the strength to blow the whistle. Heroism is the best we can hope for then. But, looking up from this chain of unhappy events, we can see how much better off everyone would have been had heroism been unnecessary. That is why I have focused on making whistleblowing unnecessary.

Notes

Versions of this paper were presented at the Neil Staebler Conference, Insitute of Public Policy Studies, University of Michigan, Ann Arbor, February 17, 1988; at Aquinas College, Grand Rapids, Michigan, September 21, 1989; and at the Mechanical Engineering Bi-Weekly Seminar Series, Western Michigan University, Kalamazoo, Michigan, October 3, 1989. I [Michael Davis] should like to thank those present, as well as my colleague, Vivian Weil, for helping me to see the many sides of whistleblowing. I should also like to thank the editor of this journal for his helpful comments and some useful references.

1. For a good summary of what is (or could be) offered, see Martin H. Malin, "Protecting the Whistleblower from Retaliatory Discharge," *Journal of Law Reform* 16 (Winter 1983): 277–318. For some suggestion of how ineffective that protection is, see Thomas M. Devine and Donald G. Aplin, "Whistleblower Portection—The Gap Between the Law and Reality," *Howard Law Journal* 31 (1988): 223–239; or Rosemary Chalk, "Making the World Safe for Whisleblowers," *Technology Review* 91 (January 1988): 48–57.

2. The literature describing the suffering of whistleblowers is, of course, large. For a good scholarly summary, see Myron Peretz Glazer and Penina Migdal Glazer, *The Whistleblowers: Exposing Corruption in Government and Industry* (Basic Books: New York, 1989). There is, in contrast, very little about how the organization suffers (or benefits). Why?

3. The holder of a "professional position" is much more likely to become a whistleblower than an ordinary employee is. See, for example, Marcia P. Miceli and

Janet P. Near, "Individual and Situational Correlates of Whistle-Blowing," *Personnel Psychology* 41 (Summer 1988): 267–281.

4. Compare Chester A. Barnes, *The Function of the Executive* (Harvard University Press: Cambridge, Mass., 1938).

5. For a good discussion of the problems of defining "whistleblowing," see Frederick Elliston et al., *Whistleblowing Research: Methodological and Moral Issues* (Praeger: New York, 1985), esp. pp. 3–22 and 145–161.

6. Even this definition should be read liberally. In most organizations, there are "ordinary" channels the use of which gives no offense and "extraordinary" channels the use of which will give offense. Sometimes one can only determine that a channel is extraordinary by using it. Those using an extraordinary channel will be treated as whistleblowers (and, indeed, will often be so labeled even when they are not whistleblowers according to this—or any other standard—definition). Similarly, the dispute between a whistleblower and her organization may in part be over whether her objection is a moral rather than a technical one (everyone agreeing that *if* the objection is moral, she would be justified). But, since they think the objection is not a moral one, they consider her a "disgruntled employee," not a whistleblower. I do not intend what I say here to turn on how we resolve such difficult cases. For a good summary of the recent literature of definition, see Marian V. Heacock and Gail W. McGee, "Whistleblowing: An Ethical Issue in Organizational and Human Behavior," *Business & Professional Ethics Journal* 6 (Winter 1987): 35–46.

7. I have in mind especially the response to whistleblowers within academic institutions such as my alma mater: see, for example, Bruce W. Hollis, "I Turned in My Mentor," *The Scientist* 1 (December 14, 1987): 1–13.

8. William Shakespeare, *Anthony and Cleopatra* Act II: Sc. 5.

9. Robert Jackall, *Moral Mazes* (Oxford University Press: New York, 1988), esp. 105–112 & 119–133.

10. One reason may be that inaccurate whistlblowing is less likely to make news. Newspapers, police departments, and senior managers are constantly receiving "tips" that don't pan out. These are not news. Another reason inaccurate whistleblowing has received little attention may be that reliably determining that a particular whistleblower is inaccurate can be quite difficult. The whistleblower's evidence may establish only a presumptive case against an organization. The organization may not be able to reply in full without revealing proprietary information or violating the privacy of other employees, leaving outsiders no way to know that the whistleblower is mistaken. Even the organization in question may not be able to make such a determination without great expense—and may therefore never bother. Much whistleblowing seems enveloped in the organizational equivalent or what Clausewitz called "the fog of battle." If we knew more

about cases of inaccurate, mistaken, or otherwise flawed whistleblowing, perhaps our assessment of the overall good effect of whistleblowing would change. Perhaps whistleblowing, like tyrannicide, is so likely to hit the wrong target that it cannot in practice be justified. This is a subject about which we need to know more.

11. See, for example, Dick Polman, "Telling the truth, paying the price," *Philadelphia Inquirer Magazine,* June 18, 1989, pp. 16ff.

12. For an interesting analysis of this traditional view of organizational authority (and related issues), see Christopher McMahan, Managerial Authority," *Ethics* 100 (October 1989): 33–53.

13. I owe this observation to Thomas Devine. I have found no research to confirm it.

14. For a procedure I doubt will do much good, see Theodore T. Herbert and Ralph W. Estes, "Improving Executive Decisions by Formalizing Dissent: The Corporate Devil's Advocate," *Academy of Management Review* 2 (October 1977): 662–667. Dissent is likely to be more effective if the dissenter is not viewed as "just going through the motions" and likely to be more common if not the job of just one person.

15. Compare James Water, "Catch 20.5: Corporate Morality as an Orgainzational Phenomenon," *Orgainzational Dynamics* 6 (Spring 1978): 3–19.

16. *Moral Mazes, for example, pp. 105–112.*

17. These are, of course, matters of what is now often called "culture." For a good discussion, see Charles O'Reilly, "Corporations, Culture, and Commitment: Motivation and Social Control in Organizations." *California Management Review* (Summer 1989): 9–25.

18. This claim is defended in: Michael Davis, "Explaining Wrongdoing," *Journal of Social Philosophy* 20 (Spring/Fall 1989): 74–90. See also M. Cash Matthews, "Ethical Dilemmas and the Disputing Process: Organizations and Societies," *Business & Professional Ethics Journal* 8 (Spring 1989): 1–11.

19. Michael Davis, *One Social Responsibility of Engineering Societies: Teaching Managers About Engineering Ethics,* Monograph #88-WA/DE-14 (The American Society of Mechanichal Engineers: New York, 1988).

20. Perhaps the best example of such a person would be Roger Boisjoly (if his required testimony before Congress was whistleblowing at all). The warnings Boisjoly gave on the might before the *Challenger* exploded were (though technically accurate) in the bloodless language in which engineers generally communicate. He never said anything like "This decision could kill seven human beings." How might things have gone had Boisjoly (or anyone else present) said something of that sort when NASA pressured Thiokol to approve a launch? A hard question, to be sure, but one that at least suggests the potential power of language at the moment of decision. For details, see *The Presidential Commission on the Space Shuttle Challenger Disaster* (Washington, DC: June 6, 1986).

Robert A. Larmer

Whistleblowing and Employee Loyalty

Whistleblowing by an employee is the act of complaining, either within the corporation or publicly, about a corporation's unethical practices. Such an act raises important questions concerning the loyalties and duties of employees. Traditionally, the employee has been viewed as an agent who acts on behalf of a principal, i.e., the employer, and as possessing duties of loyalty and confidentiality. Whistleblowing, at least at first blush, seems a violation of these duties and it is scarcely surprising that in many instances employers and fellow employees argue that it is an act of disloyalty and hence morally wrong.[1]

It is this issue of the relation between whistleblowing and employee loyalty that I want to address. What I will call the standard view is that employees possess *prima facie* duties of loyalty and confidentiality to their employers and that whistleblowing cannot be justified except on the basis of a higher duty to the public good. Against this standard view, Ronald Duska has recently argued that employees do not have even a *prima facie* duty of loyalty to their employers and that whistleblowing needs, therefore, no moral justification.[2] I am going to criticize both views. My suggestion is that both misunderstand the relation between loyalty and whistleblowing. In their place I will propose a third more adequate view.

Duska's view is more radical in that it suggests that there can be no issue of whistleblowing and employee loyalty, since the employee has no duty to be loyal to his employer. His reason for suggesting that the employee owes the employer, at least the corporate employer, no loyalty is that companies are not the kinds of things which are proper objects of loyalty. His argument in support of this rests upon two key claims. The first is that loyalty, properly understood, implies a reciprocal relationship and is only appropriate in the context of a mutual surrendering of self-interest. He writes,

It is important to recognize that in any relationship which demands loyalty the relationship works both ways and involves mutual enrichment. Loyalty is incompatible with self-interest, because it is something that necessarily requires we go beyond self-interest. My loyalty to my friend, for example, requires I put aside my interests some of the time. . . . Loyalty depends on ties that demand self-sacrifice with no expectation of reward, e.g., the ties of loyalty that bind a family together.[3]

The second is that the relation between a company and an employee does not involve any surrender of self-interest on the part of the company, since its primary goal is to maximize profit. Indeed, although it is convenient, it is misleading to talk of a company having interests. As Duska comments,

A company is not a person. A company is an instrument, and an instrument with a specific purpose, the making of profit. To treat an instrument as an end in itself, like a person, may not be as bad as treating an end as an instrument, but it does give the instrument a moral status it does not deserve . . .[4]

Since, then, the relation between a company and an employee does not fulfill the minimal requirement of being a relation between two individuals, much less two reciprocally self-sacrificing individuals, Duska feels it is a mistake to suggest the employee has any duties of loyalty to the company.

This view does not seem adequate, however. First, it is not true that loyalty must be quite so reciprocal as Duska demands. Ideally, of course, one expects that if one is loyal to another person that person will reciprocate in kind. There are, however, many cases where loyalty is

From Robert A. Larmer, "Whistleblowing and Employee Loyalty," *Journal of Business Ethics*, Vol. 11, 1992.
Reprinted by permission of Kluwer Academic Publishers.

not entirely reciprocated, but where we do not feel that it is misplaced. A parent, for example, may remain loyal to an erring teenager, even though the teenager demonstrates no loyalty to the parent. Indeed, part of being a proper parent is to demonstrate loyalty to your children whether or not that loyalty is reciprocated. This is not to suggest any kind of analogy between parents and employees, but rather that it is not nonsense to suppose that loyalty may be appropriate even though it is not reciprocated. Inasmuch as he ignores this possibility, Duska's account of loyalty is flawed.

Second, even if Duska is correct in holding that loyalty is only appropriate between moral agents and that a company is not genuinely a moral agent, the question may still be raised whether an employee owes loyalty to fellow employees or the shareholders of the company. Granted that reference to a company as an individual involves reification and should not be taken too literally, it may nevertheless constitute a legitimate shorthand way of describing relations between genuine moral agents.

Third, it seems wrong to suggest that simply because the primary motive of the employer is economic, considerations of loyalty are irrelevant. An employee's primary motive in working for an employer is generally economic, but no one on that account would argue that it is impossible for her to demonstrate loyalty to the employer, even if it turns out to be misplaced. All that is required is that her primary economic motive be in some degree qualified by considerations of the employer's welfare. Similarly, the fact that an employer's primary motive is economic does not imply that it is not qualified by considerations of the employee's welfare. Given the possibility of mutual qualification of admittedly primary economic motives, it is fallacious to argue that employee loyalty is never appropriate.

In contrast to Duska, the standard view is that loyalty to one's employer is appropriate. According to it, one has an obligation to be loyal to one's employer, and consequently, a *prima facie* duty to protect the employer's interests. Whistleblowing constitutes, therefore, a violation of duty to one's employer and needs strong justification if it is to be appropriate.

Sissela Bok summarizes this view very well when she writes

the whistleblower hopes to stop the game; but since he is neither referee nor coach, and since he blows the whistle on his own team, his act is seen as a violation of loyalty. In holding his position, he has assumed certain obligations to his colleagues and clients. He may even have subscribed to a loyalty oath or a promise of confidentiality. Loyally to colleagues and to clients comes to be pitted against loyalty to the public interest, to those who may be injured unless the revelation is made.[5]

The strength of this view is that it recognizes that loyalty is due one's employer. Its weakness is that it tends to conceive of whistleblowing as involving a tragic moral choice, since blowing the whistle is seen not so much as a positive action, but rather the lesser of two evils. Bok again puts the essence of this view very clearly when she writes that "a would-be whistleblower must weigh his responsibility to serve the public interest *against* the responsibility he owes to his colleagues and the institution in which he works" and "that [when] their duty [to whistleblow] . . . *so overrrides loyalties to colleagues and institutions,* they [whistleblowers] often have reason to fear the results of carrying out such a duty."[6] The employee, according to this definition of whistleblowing, must choose between two acts of betrayal, either of her employer or the public interest, each in itself reprehensible.

Behind this view lies the assumption that to be loyal to someone is to act in a way that accords with what that person believes to be in her best interests. To be loyal to an employer, therefore, is to act in a way which the employer deems to be in his or her best interests. Since employers very rarely approve of whistleblowing and generally feel that it is not in their best interests, it follows that whistleblowing is an act of betrayal on the part of the employee, albeit a betrayal made in the interests of the public good.

Plausible though it initially seems, I think this view of whistleblowing is mistaken and that it embodies a mistaken conception of what constitutes employee loyalty. It ignores the fact that the great majority of corporate whistleblowers ... [consider] themselves to be very loyal employees who ... [try] to use "direct voice" (internal whistleblowing), ... [are] rebuffed and punished for this, and then ... [use] "indirect voice" (external whistleblowing). They ... [believe] initially that they ... [are] behaving in a loyal manner, helping their employers by calling top management's attention to practices that could eventually get the firm in trouble.[7]

By ignoring the possibility that blowing the whistle may demonstrate greater loyalty than not blowing the whistle, it fails to do justice to the many instances where loyalty to someone constrains us to act in defiance of what that person believes to be in her best interests. I am not, for example, being disloyal to a friend if I refuse to loan her money for an investment I am sure will bring her financial ruin; even if she bitterly reproaches me for denying her what is so obviously a golden opportunity to make a fortune.

A more adequate definition of being loyal to someone is that loyalty involves acting in accordance with what one has good reason to believe to be in that person's best interests. A key question, of course, is what constitutes a good reason to think that something is in a person's best interests. Very often, but by no means invariably, we accept that a person thinking that something is in her best interests is a sufficiently good reason to think that it actually is. Other times, especially when we feel that she is being rash, foolish, or misinformed we are prepared, precisely by virtue of being loyal, to act contrary to the person's wishes. It is beyond the scope of this paper to investigate such cases in detial, but three general points can be made.

First, to the degree that an action is genuinely immoral, it is impossible that it is in the agent's best interests. We would not, for example, say that someone who sells child pornography was acting in his own best interests, even if he vigorously protested that there was nothing wrong with such activity. Loyalty does not imply that we have a duty to refrain from reporting the immoral actions of those to whom we are loyal. An employer who is acting immorally is not acting disloyally in blowing the whistle.[8] Indeed, the argument can be made that the employee who blows the whistle may be demonstrating greater loyalty than the employee who simply ignores the immoral conduct, inasmuch as she is attempting to prevent her employer from engaging in self-destructive behaviour.

Second, loyalty requires that, whenever possible, in trying to resolve a problem we deal directly with the person to whom we are loyal. If, for example, I am loyal to a friend I do not immediately involve a third party when I try to dissuade my friend from involvement in immoral actions. Rather, I approach my friend directly, listen to his perspective on the events in question, and provide an opportunity for him to address the problem in a morally satisfactory way. This implies that, whenever possible, a loyal employee blows the whistle internally. This provides the employer with the opportunity to either demonstrate to the employee that, contrary to first appearances, no genuine wrongdoing had occurred, or, if there is a genuine moral problem, the opportunity to resolve it.

This principle of dealing directly with the person to whom loyalty is due needs to be qualified, however. Loyalty to a person requires that one acts in that person's best interests. Generally, this cannot be done without directly involving the person to whom one is loyal in the decision-making process, but there may arise cases where acting in a person's best interests requires that one act independently and perhaps even against the wishes of the person to whom one is loyal. Such cases will be especially apt to arise when the person to whom one is loyal is either immoral or ignoring the moral consequences of his actions. Thus, for example, loyalty to a friend who deals in hard narcotics would not imply that I speak first to my friend about my decision to inform the police of his activities, if the only effect of my doing so would be to make him more careful in his criminal dealings. Similarly, a loyal employee is under no obligation to speak first to an employer about the employer's immoral actions, if the only response of the employer will be to take care to cover up wrongdoing.

Neither is a loyal employee under obligation to speak first to an employer if it is clear that by doing so she placed herself in jeopardy from an employer who will retaliate if given the opportunity. Loyalty amounts to acting in another's best interests and that may mean qualifying what seems to be in one's own interests, but it cannot imply that one take no steps to protect oneself from the immorality of those to whom one is loyal. The reason it cannot is that, as has already been argued, acting immorally can never really be in a person's best interests. It follows, therefore, that one is not acting in a person's best interest if one allows oneself to be treated immorally by that person. Thus, for example, a father might be loyal to a child even though the child is guilty of stealing from him, but this would not mean that the father should let the child continue to steal. Similarly, an employee may be loyal to an employer even though she takes steps to protect herself against unfair retaliation by the employer, e.g., by blowing the whistle externally.

Third, loyalty requires that one is concerned with more than considerations of justice. I have been arguing that loyalty cannot require one to ignore immoral or unjust behavior on the part of those to whom one is loyal, since loyalty amounts to acting in a person's best interests and it can never be in a person's best interests to be allowed to act immorally. Loyalty, however, goes beyond considerations of justice in that, while it is possible to be disinterested and just, it is not possible to be disinterested and loyal. Loyalty implies a desire that the person to whom one is loyal take no moral stumbles, but that if moral stumbles have occurred that the person be restored and not simply punished. A loyal friend is not only someone who sticks by you in times of trouble, but someone who tries to help you avoid trouble. This suggests that a loyal employee will have a desire to point out problems and potential problems long before the drastic measures associated with whistleblowing become necessary, but that if whistleblowing does become necessary there remains a desire to help the employer.

In conclusion, although much more could be said on the subject of loyalty, our brief discussion has enabled us to clarify considerably the relation between whistleblowing and employee loyalty. It permits us to steer a course between the Scylla of Duska's view that, since the primary link between employer and employee is economic, the ideal of employee loyalty is an oxymoron, and the Charybdis of the standard view that, since it forces an employee to weight conflicting duties, whistleblowing inevitably involves some degree of moral tragedy. The solution lies in realizing that to whistleblow for reasons of morality is to act in one's employer's best interests and involves, therefore, no disloyalty.[In Greek mythology *Scylla* and *Charybdis* were two sea monsters living in caves on opposite sides of the narrow straits of Messina separating Italy and Sicily. Reference to the myth is often made by those attempting to steer a middle course between equally unpleasant extremes.]

Notes

1. The definition I [Robert A. Larmer] have proposed applies most directly to the relation between privately owned companies aiming to realize a profit and their employees. Obviously, issues of whistleblowing arise in other contexts, e.g., governmental organizations or charitable agencies, and deserve careful thought. I do not propose, in this paper, to discuss whistleblowing in these other contexts, but I think my development of the concept of whistleblowing as positive demonstration of loyalty can easily be applied and will prove useful.

2. Duska, R: 1985, "Whistleblowing and Employee Loyalty," in J. R. Desjardins and J. J. McCall, eds., *Contemporary Issues in Business Ethics* (Wadsworth, Belmont, California), pp. 295–300.

3. Duska, p. 297.

4. Duska, p. 298.

5. Bok, S: 1983, "Whistleblowing and Professional Responsibility," in T. L. Beauchamp and N. E. Bowie, eds., *Ethical Theory and Business,* 2nd ed. (Prentice-Hall Inc., Englewood Cliffs, New Jersey), pp. 261–269, p. 263.

6. Bok, pp. 261–2, emphasis added.

7. Near, J. P. and P. Miceli: 1985, "Organizational Dissidence: The Case of Whistle-Blowing," *Journal of Business Ehtics* 4, pp. 1–16, p. 10.

8. As Near and Miceli note "The whistle-blower may provide valuable information helpful in improving organizational effectiveness ... the prevalence of illegal activity in organizations is associated with declining organizational performance" (p. 1).

   The general point is that the structure of the world is such that it is not in a company's long-term interests to act immorally. Sooner or later a company which flouts morality and legality will suffer.

Natalie Dandekar

Can Whistleblowing Be FULLY Legitimated? A Theoretical Discussion

Whistleblowing as a phenomenon seems puzzling. The whistleblower presumably acts to bring a wrongful practice to public attention so that those with power are enabled to correct the situation. Bok observes, "Given the indispensable services performed by so many whistleblowers, strong public support is often merited."[1] Yet Myron and Penina Glazer[2] report that in over two thirds of the sixty-four cases they documented whistleblowers suffered severe negative consequences.[3] When a social practice issues in consequences which marginalize or endanger the agent, when the agent may become a pariah for "committing the truth" it is impossible to claim that practice is regarded as fully legitimate. I am interested in exploring the paradox. Why, in the case of whistleblowing, does committing truth result in punitive sanctions? How might we, as a society, increase the probability that this virtue is rewarded rather than punished? Why have we been so slow to do just that?

To answer these questions, I consider all four topics Duska[4] considers central to a theoretical discussion of whistleblowing,

1. definition,[5]
2. whether and when whistleblowing is permissible; or
3. obligatory; and

From Natalie Dandekar, "Can Whistleblowing be FULLY Legitimated? A Theoretical Discussion," *Business & Professional Ethics Journal*, Vol. 10, No. 1, 1991. Reprinted with permission.

4. appropriate mechanisms for institutionalizing whistleblowing.

In Section 1, I discuss two important recent definitions of whistleblowing, concluding that whistleblowing is a specific type of action; going public with privileged information about a legitimate organization in order to prevent nontrivial public harm. In Section 2, I explore the moral ambiguity inherent in whistleblowing and the complications this affords to Goldberg's persuasive case for seeing a case of potential whistleblowing as either inappropriate or obligatory.[6] In Section 3, citing studies which show that whistleblowers often suffer outrageous costs, I explore legitimation factors which might safeguard the morally responsible whistleblower.

I. Whistleblowing Defined

Two recent books about whistleblowing differ in their definition of the term. For the Glazers, whistleblowing is defined by Norman Bowie's six ideal requirements:

B1. the act stems from appropriate moral motives of preventing unnecessary harm to others;
B2. the whistleblower uses all available internal procedures for rectifying the problematic behavior before public disclosure (except when special circumstances preclude this);
B3. the whistleblower has evidence that would persuade a reasonable person;
B4. the whistleblower perceives serious danger that can result from the violation;
B5. the whistleblower acts in accordance with his or her responsibilities for avoiding/ exposing moral violations; and
B6. the whistleblower's action has some reasonable chance of success.[7]

In contrast, Deborah Johnson, writing as a consultant for an NSF project on whistleblowing research[8] concluded that a full defined case of whistleblowing occurs when

J1. an individual performs an action or series of actions intended to make information public;

J2. the information is made a matter of public record;

J3. the information is about possible or actual nontrivial wrongdoing in an organization; and

J4. the individual who performs the action is a member or former member of the organization.[9]

As Heacock and McGee point out, managers define whistleblowing to include going outside the normal chain of command even if not actually gong public with damaging information. Thus, whistleblowing can include internal reporting of wrongdoing in or by the organization.[10] Like Davis,[11] I am willing to see going outside the normal chain of command as a form of going public.[12]

The definitions offered by Johnson and Bowie differ with respect to whether a whistleblower's motivation should be included (B1), whether whistleblowing will succeed (B6), and whether the whistleblower is a member or former member of the organization (J4). Johnson's focus on action, exclusive of any reference to the whistleblower's motivation seems preferable since, as Johnson observes,

reasons for acting, the degree of certainty that the whistleblower has about the wrongdoing and whether or not the whistleblower has tried to remedy the wrongdoing by internal mechanisms . . . will bear on our understanding of when whistleblowing is permissible and when it is morally obligatory, but these factors should not be confused with definitional features.[13]

An additional reason for adopting Johnson's perspective arises when one considers a case of mixed motives. The *Wall Street Journal*[14] describes a former GE employee who spoke about time card fraud in a GE sponsored assertiveness training session. For six years afterward, Mr. Gravitt

confronted executives with evidence . . . (until he) was fired (or laid off) . . . (He also) testified before the House subcommittee about mischarging as a way of life at GE.

Now he hopes to win a bountiful settlement, so "people will know they can do something to correct what isn't right."

Mr. Gravitt meets Johnson's definitional criteria though not those of Bowie. Since, it seems wrong to dismiss his case simply because he might realize monetary gain, it seems appropriate to dismiss motivation as a definitional issue. The action—going public with possible or actual nontrivial wrongdoing—seems the more appropriate focus for definition.

There are however two points on which I think Johnson's definition could be improved. First, Johnson's stipulation that "whistleblowing always takes place in the context of an organization"[15] should be amended to include the point that the wrongdoers be persons of presumed respectability and the organization a legitimate one. This seems a little noted aspect of whistleblowing, but as with Gravitt's case where the reporter notes GE "prides itself on a favorable public image," presumptive organizational respectability consistently characterizes whistleblowers' self-reports. When they suspect wrongful practices, they feel surprise. Knowing the organization values its good reputation, the whistleblower sees the wrongful practice as a sign of deterioration but remediable.[16] Amazed that higher management avoids imposing remedies to restore reputable practice, the whistleblower is moved to protest.

Second, where Johnson stipulates the actor is a member or former member of the organization, I think the criterion should be broadened. The whistleblower must have privileged access and be trusted to maintain the confidentiality of this information. But not every privileged insider must be a member or former member of the organization. A rough survey of the ways whistleblowers have obtained incriminating information shows privileged access can result from six distinct relationships.[17]

Most often the whistleblower is a member/ former member trusted with privileged information. Yet within the category of trusted employee, distinctions can be usefully drawn isolating four subcategories.

First, the whistleblower may have earned access to incriminating information through quite legal acts of loyalty. For example, when he brought charges against Senator Thomas Dodd, James Boyd was Dodd's chief aide and had worked devotedly on Senator Dodd's behalf for eleven years.

A second pattern involves a worker who colludes with the criminal practice. Thus, Dr. Arthur Console, medical director of Squibb, pressured by profit oriented superiors, pushed others to certify drugs they had not fully tested. After changing careers, he conscientiously reported the ongoing practice at Squibb.[18]

Third, a worker afraid to face reprisals may share data with a less obviously assailable colleague. A staff psychologist at the Veterans Administration Hospital in Leavenworth, Kansas learned that a staff physician was conducting a drug-testing project using patients who could suffer harm from the drug's side effects. Believing the opinion of a trained physician would carry more weight with hospital administrators, he asked Dr. Mary McAnaw, then chief of surgery at the hospital to accompany him when he discussed his concerns. In this way she learned of the hospital administration's complicity and eventually blew the whistle.[19]

Fourth, company arrogance may lead to information about wrongful practices being available to all employees, though the company hides these practices from the public. Karen Silkwood seems to have worked for such an arrogantly abusive corporation.

However my rough survey also reveals two patterns by which a whistleblower may learn of an incriminating practice without being a member of an organization. Fifth, someone who is not a member of the organization, may be given access to their records. Thus, Dr. Carl Johnson, a public health physician established the probability of wrongful practices at the Rocky Flats nuclear weapons plants.[20] The company never gave him direct access to specifically incriminating information[21] but accepted that he had a right to acquire health-related data about their employees. In another such instance, Thomas Applegate, a private detective "hired by Cincinnati Gas and Electric to investigate timecard fraud among workers at the construction site of the Zimmer nuclear power plant in Ohio . . . inadvertently uncovered much more serious construction problems."[22] After utility officials ignored his warning, he alerted the NRC. When no official body would pay attention, he sought help from GAP, a public interest watchdog group,[23] which forced additional investigations uncovering such gross violations the plant was cancelled.[24]

Sixth, the whistleblower may be a relative of the victim of wrongful practices, even if neither are members of the supposedly respectable organization. For example, in cases of nursing home abuse, drugged/senile patients are in no position to bring charges of wrongdoing. But some relatives have done so on their behalf. Mental patients too require someone else act e.g. to prevent fiscally wasteful practices, since testimony of the mentally deranged is unlikely to be believed trustworthy. Thus, a concerned relative may become a whistleblower on a wrongful organizational practice even when generally grateful for the care provided by the organization to the needy relative.

Gaining access to information, the whistleblower must be an insider in some sense, but it seems too restrictive to require the whistleblower be a member/former member of the organization accused of wrongdoing. Of the six distinct patterns of acquiring privileged information, two—the clue follower, who is not made directly privy to information about a wrongful practice but is given an opportunity to obtain clues, and the caring relative who, like the clue follower, discerns the outlines of a wrongful practice by observation—find themselves in possession of information because both have been trusted with privileged access though they are not members of the organization. Yet even these, when they go public, in some sense betray the trust which led to confidentiality.

II. The Moral Ambiguity of Whistleblowing

The whistleblower's act is intrinsically liable to moral ambiguity because whistleblowing (a) involves betrayal of confidentially and (b) the organization is presumptively legitimate. Because the organization accused is legitimate and so presumably staffed by persons of at least ordinary moral probity, whistleblowing shares the moral ambiguity of insubordinate accusations which reject the judgement of a majority of normally competent moral individuals who find a dubious practice at least minimally acceptable.

In a case of price-fixing those charged include some "described as having high moral character ..."[25] A sympathetic analysis of their motivation showed these morally respectable perpetrators generally practiced some form of self-deception, excusing their wrongdoing as only trivially wrong, or offset by some non-trivial good. Knowing pricefixing to be illegal, some claimed that it helps stabilize the market, or serves the corporate good, ends which outweigh illegality. Others claimed the law was wrong, and pricefixing should not be illegal.[26]

When respectable persons go along, their behavior suggests that the apparently wrongful practice is not thoroughly vicious. This undercuts the impetus to whistleblowing, and may also explain some of the anger that those who go along feel toward the whistleblower who won't.

The premise that private vices produce public goods, as in Adam Smith's theoretical conclusion that individual greed works through an Invisible Hand to produce the common welfare, may also promote hanging back in this respect. When respectable persons, obviously competent to engage in moral reasoning, have chosen to go along, an onlooker may wonder if this wrong nonetheless serves the common welfare in the long run, with whistleblowing morally compromised by that possibility.

Core elements of whistleblowing foster a condition of moral ambiguity. The whistleblower perceives the wrongful practice as a source of non-trivial public harm and the effort to bring the practice to public attention as serving the public interest. But from the perspective of ordinary citizens, the organization accused is respectable, so there is some doubt about the degree to which the wrongful practice will harm the public. Moreover, the person bringing the charge is betraying a trust on behalf of protecting the public interest. Paradoxically the one who betrays a trust claims to be more trustworthy than those who remain loyal to an apparently respectable corporation.

Apart from these sources of moral ambiguity, whistleblowing is liable to two other kinds of moral defect. The first stems from the motivation and character of the whistleblower:

(T)he disappointed, the incompetent, the malicious and the paranoid all too often leap to accusations in public . . . (while) ideological persecution throughout the world traditionally relies on insiders willing to inform on their colleagues or even on their family members.[27]

HUAC operated in an environment characterized by two factors: the communist party was illegal and ordinary citizens feared that communism might lead to society-wide harm. Thus those who chose to inform on communists acted in accordance with the definition of whistleblowing suggested above: bringing unlawful practices presumed harmful to the general public to the attention of those in a position to protect the public against the continuance of the practice. Even under Bowie's idealistic description of whistleblowing, the issue persists. For during that period of public hysteria, some testimony was motivated by a concern for preventing the spread of communism. However, the illegality reported and the harm feared seem less dangerous to the public than the practice of reporting and the climate thus engendered. Witchhunts illustrate the necessity to limit the powers of a wrongly aroused public opinion.

As Johnson noticed, once whistleblowing is defined, it remains worthwhile to discover under what circumstances it is permissible and when it is morally obligatory.[28] It may also be worth exploring the conditions under which whistleblowing is simply not the morally correct response to a situation. DeGeorge[29] suggests whistleblowing is *permissible* when

  a. a practice or product does or will cause serious harm to individuals or society at large;
  b. the charge of wrongdoing has been brought to the attention of immediate superiors; and
  c. no appropriate action has been taken to remedy the wrongdoing.

If, in addition

    d. there is documentation of the potentially harmful practice or defect; and

    e. there is good reason to believe public disclosure will avoid the present or prevent similar future wrongdoing,

then according to DeGeorge whistleblowing becomes increasingly *obligatory*. But, since it is common knowledge that whistleblowers frequently suffer extreme retaliation, De George concludes that whistleblowing is to be understood as morally permissible, rather than obligatory.[30] Against this, Goldberg convincingly argues that if employees are to have a right, then they must be protected from reprisals in exercising the right. If conditions (a) trough (e) are met and (d) and (e) are unavailable so too is the right.[31] It follows that some whistleblowing is obligatory. So, it is more than ever important to distinguish situations in which it does not pander to the wrongful arousal of public opinion or witchhunting. DeGeorge's conditions, unfortunately compatible with anti-communist witchhunts, need supplementation. Legitimate whistleblowing must be limited to cases where the wrongfulness ascribed is not the product of emotional distortion, rationalization, or prejudice.[32]

Whistleblowing is a morally ambiguous activity on a complex concatenation of grounds: it necessarily involves a betrayal of trust on behalf of a public interest which itself is on some occasions morally ambiguous; it indicts otherwise morally competent individuals and organizations concerned with being perceived as legitimate; sometimes it arouses public opinion, a frequently contaminated process. Understandably, whistleblowers are not always perceived as moral heros.

Nonetheless when an outsider—an investigative reporter, or a political opponent, or a lawyer on behalf of a defendant—proves a corporation or government bureaucracy is wasting public funds, or endangering the lives of those who rely upon their integrity, the exposer reaps social rewards. Reporters enhance a valued reputation for sleuthing. Political opponents generally realize gains from masking a case against corruption. Lawyers earn money and respect for success in prosecuting wrongdoing.

However, privileged insiders do best to serve as valuable but anonymous informants for outsiders. For if identified, they suffer outrageous costs. Once the charge becomes a threat to some superior, whistleblowers risk retaliation. Westin[33] suggests every whistleblower suffers loss of reputation. Supervisors redescribe them as disgruntled troublemakers, people who make an issue out of nothing, self-serving publicity seekers or troubled persons who distort and misinterpret situations due to their own psychological imbalance and irrationality.[34]

Yet character assassination barely begins to describe the consequences of submitting well-founded important alerts, serving to prevent harm in obvious ways. Some who work in private industry are fired, even black-listed so they cannot continue in their profession. Of sixty four, the Glazers found forty one lost their jobs; twenty eight suffered long periods of idleness, and eighteen of these changed careers entirely. A " . . . career switch usually meant . . . a reduction in their standard of living . . . or a painful realization that closure was still beyond their farthest reach."[35] Others suffered transfer with prejudice, or demotion. Staff were transferred away. Letters of recommendation subtly or overtly mentioned the trouble caused by this employee's actions. When possible, the letter attacked professional competence and impugned professional judgement.

Even when evidence entirely supports the rightness of whistleblowing and the public benefit accruing therefrom, whistleblowers may find themselves unemployable in their chosen fields. Dr. Carl Johnson, after alerting the public to negligent practices at Rocky Flats nuclear weapons plants, had been "horribly mistreated and discredited" for many years, only finding rehabilitation after death.[36]

As mentioned earlier, other employees often feel that with respect to loyalty, they are morally superior. They are loyal. The whistleblower is disloyal. For this, other employees may shun, vilify, or physically attack whistleblowers.[37] Death threats may be aimed at the whistleblower and her family.[38]

Analysis shows whistleblowing is morally ambiguous. It is a betrayal of trust, and an accusation against a respectable person, corporate or natural. But when legitimate; it is also morally obligatory. So, the original puzzle remains: too often praiseworthy whistleblowing, deserving societal reward, results in severe social penalties for the whistleblower. As one writer put it, "It's a hell of a commentary on our contemporary society when you must . . . become an insolvent pariah . . . to live up to your own ethical standards by 'committing the truth' and exercising your First Amendment rights."[39]

Where whistleblowing is a legitimate, responsible, morally obligatory action, this must be remedied. But how?

III. SAFEGUARDING LEGITIMATE WHISTLEBLOWING

In the early 1970s one who brought a charge of sexual harassment suffered character assassination and reprisals from more "loyal" employees, just as other whistleblowers of that period did. But, by the middle of the 1980s one who brings a charge of sexual harassment is less likely to be perceived as a disloyal employee.[40] Her supervisor may even confront a harasser on her behalf.[41] Courts often support the legitimate complainant with continued job security and awards.

The difference in outcome can be related to several specific and to some extent imitable factors. First, the power imbalance between the one bringing the charge, and the respectable institution, is mitigated:

   a. because of consciousness raising techniques, those bringing charges of sexual harassment have a well-defined constituency willing to offer support;
   b. sexual harassment offers a specific legal ground; and
   c. organizations like the Women's Rights Litigation Clinic at Rutgers University Law School offer litigants well trained legal help, at a more affordable cost than is otherwise generally available.

Thus, the disparity of resources between the corporation and the claimant is made less overwhelming. Second, susceptible bureaucracies

have established internal procedures for sensitizing employee to the issues that give rise to these complaints.[42] Two factors may be noted:

   a. education about sexual harassment is mandated as part of the legal settlement for a proven sexual harassment case; and
   b. sexual harassment is a "new" form of wrong.

By contrast, with respect to the power imbalance, only one organization correlates efforts on behalf of most whistleblowers

"organized . . . by a group of young attorneys to defend and investigate problems of national security resisters, such as Daniel Ellsberg. By the mid-1970s, their mission had expanded to . . . issues concerning waste and mismanagement . . . in large organizations (and) . . . gave whistleblowers an institutional home."[43]

Perhaps, in imitation of sexual harassment litigation, the Government Accountability Project (GAP) would do well to train lawyers in a variety of locations, and for a variety of specific purposes. The approach taken by CAP's Kohn in focussing on environmental whistleblowers suggests specificity is possible.[44]

A second potentially imitable factor pertaining to the protecting whistleblowers relates to the law itself. While an employee who discovers criminal behavior is enjoined to blow the whistle or become personally liable to criminal penalties, only five states prohibit private employers from retaliating.[45] All but nine states have a public policy exception that limits an employer's right to fire at will[46] nevertheless, state by state exceptions limit the effectiveness of this tort. For example, Maryland law does not require any investigation into underlying charges of wrongdoing. California law protects whistleblowers who testify before special legislative committees[47] but those who give depositions may not be covered.[48]

Public sector employees under the Civil Service Reform Act of 1978 fall under language which seems to protect them for disclosures within a wide latitude. In addition to crimes, "an employee may now complain of mismanagement, gross waste of funds, abuse of authority or substantial and specific danger to public health and safety."[49] But those charged with protecting confidentiality of public sector employees apparently put whistleblowers at risk of reprisal, and "courts have struck an uneasy balance between the employee's First Amendment right to freedom of speech and the efficient operation of government agencies. Thus public employee's First Amendment rights . . . vary from court to court."[50] Unions and professional societies generally fail to defend members who live up to professional codes of ethics by blowing the whistle.[51] Arbitrators, too, tend to see whistleblowing as an act of disloyalty which disrupts business and injures the employer's reputation.[52]

Unpredictability of legal protection may reflect the vagueness of the law enjoining that "possible acts of dishonest, improper actions or behavior, . . . should be reported."[53] MacKinnon found that when company policies were unspecific, cases alleging sexual harassment tended to be dismissed as personal rather than job related difficulties. This suggests that a vague law might promote dismissive court responses. Thus, more specificity both of lawyers and laws might eventuate in a more protective environment for legitimate whistleblowing.

Another category of imitative practice might focus on educational sensitizing sessions, to establish some practices as no longer subject to social toleration. Educational procedures which create sensitivity about sexual harassment have been among the most productive means of fostering community tolerance. It therefore seems appropriate to suggest that the institution of procedures sensitizing and empowering employees to prevent other kinds of wrongful practices should be included among punishments meted out for corporate wrongdoing. It is important that others within the company be persuaded that loyalty to the company does not entail support of wrongful behavior.[54]

Another possibly imitable factor may be called "moral newness." As Calhoun[55] points out feminist moral critique begins in an abnormal moral context where moral ignorance is the norm and only a limited group are morally aware. Under these circumstances one need neither be morally defective nor morally corrupt

to be at risk of wrongdoing. As public consensus emerges on the wrongness of the newly sensitive area, wrongdoers become the subject of reproach, yet there is an excusatory element, an acknowledgement that at the level of social practice, the wrongdoer is part of an oppressive system. The complications of accomodating to a new consciousness allows for educational lapses. Normally ethical individuals might be ignorant; they occupy an abnormal moral context in process of being normalized. To realize a new level of moral behavior in the workplace, when presumably this level reflects new sensitivities makes it easier for individuals to accept responsibility for change.

In 1974 when Catherine MacKinnon undertook to establish that sexual harassment fit the legal contours of discrimination she created a kind of moral newness as the draft copy of her book circulated. Courts came to agree with her analysis, so that by 1979, her published book cites favorable precedents establishing sexual harassment as a legal claim.[56] The very term, sexual harassment, is a neologism which "facilitate(s) . . . seeing moral issues where we had not previously and drawing connections between these and already acknowledged moral issues."[57]

Newness seems paradoxically to smooth the path for those bringing the charge. Where the accusation focusses upon a newly normalized moral context, the wrongdoer is accused more of ignorance than of vice, willful complicity, or self-deception. The wrongdoing is real, yet the wrongdoer is not ipso facto morally flawed. Rather, moral newness raises "the possibility of morally unflawed individuals committing serious wrongdoing."[58]

In pursuit of moral newness, perhaps the foolish sounding term whistleblowing should be replaced with a neologism of more apparent dignity. The Glazers suggest "ethical resistance." Other routes to moral newness, such as institution ombuds or compliance officers, offer hope.[59] But they also pose risks since moral newness is endangered by familiarity/friendship within an organization. Bok warns that "many a patient representative in hospitals (experiences) . . . growing loyalty to co-workers and to the institution."[60] So the method for remedying defects within the corporate structure turns into a management tool, leaving the dissenter "little choice between submission and open revolt." Another risk involves what James Thomson calls domestication[61] co-opting the dissenter as the insider who might eventually persuade. Then the doubter's conscience is assuaged. But his position is made predictable. Hirschman concludes this predictability means a fatal loss of power with the dissenter left hoping even the tiniest influence is worth exerting.

Sensitivity to the need for remedy against deterioration can be blunted by the familiar and domesticated. As sexual harassment becomes a normal moral concept and newness thins, potential wrongdoers may practice techniques of self-deception. A colleague mentioned hearing an instance of sexual harassment that began with the offender saying "you will probably call this sexual harassment, but . . . " This demonstrates how fragile it is and yet how important it is to retain the lens of moral newness.

Re-inventing newness might serve as a means in restoring quality in legitimate organizations. One step to legitimating whistleblowing may be recognition that legitimate organizations suffer remediable deteriorations in quality. Perhaps eventually we could realize the ideal in which loyalty to an organization means loyalty to ethical standards characteristic of the organization at its finest. But until then whistleblowing deserves far greater legitimation than it evokes.

CONCLUSION

To answer the questions asked at the beginning of this paper, not all whistleblowing should be fully legitimated. The moral ambiguities of whistleblowing preclude any assumption that all whistleblowing is intrinsically virtuous. However, some whistleblowing is morally justified and of indispensable service to society. Such whistleblowers should find legitimacy in new forms of social practice. At least they should be saved from suffering punitive sanctions. I argue two sorts of changes might promote such legitimation. The first requires redressing the power imbalance by means of specificity in laws and

educational methods. The second, closely allied with the first, requires recognition that organizations suffer quality deterioration. Moral newness can serve to disintegrate misplaced familiarity and help repair quality deterioration within an organization by means of rhetorical neologisms, educational and legal consensus building techniques.

Notes

I [Natalie Dandekar] should like to thank the anonymous readers and the editor for their helpful suggestions through several revisions.

 1. Sissela Bok, "Whistleblowing and Professional Responsibility," *New York University Education Quarterly*, Vol. 11, #4 Summer 1980, p. 2.
 2. Myron Peretz Glazer and Penina Migdal Glazer, *The Whistleblowers, Exposing Corruption in Government and Industry* (New York: Basic Books, 1989).
 3. Glazer and Glazer, p. 206.
 4. Ronald Duska, "Whistleblowing and Employee Loyalty," in J. R. Desjardins and J. J. McCall, *Contemporary Issues in Business Ethics* (Belmont, CA: Wadsworth, 1985), pp. 295–300.
 5. A good summary of the recent literature of definition is provided by Marian V. Heacock and Gail W. McGee, "Whistleblowing: An Ethical Issue in Organizational and Human Behavior," *Business & Professional Ethics Journal*, Vol. 6, No. 4, pp. 35–45.
 6. David Theo Goldberg, "Tuning in To Whistleblowing," *Business & Professional Ethics Journal*, Vol. 7, No. 2, pp. 85–94.
 7. Norman Bowie, *Business Ethics* (Englewood Cliffs, N. J.: Prentice-Hall, 1982), p. 143, cited in Glazer and Glazer, p. 4.
 8. Frederick Elliston, John Keenan, Paula Lockhart and Jane van Schaick, *Whistleblowing Research: Methodological and Moral Issues* (New York: Praeger, 1984), work conducted under a grant from NSF jointly sponsored by the National Endowment for the Humanities.
 9. Elliston, *et. al.*, p. 15. (In the text, the authors attribute the definition to Dr. Johnson who worked as a consultant on the project. p. 23)
10. However, with reference to the legitimation of the practice, Heacock and McGee suggest that the external whistleblower may suffer most. "External whistleblowing, in the absence of specific mechanisms to facilitate it, may be construed as a violation of the privilege of employment with a firm." (p. 37.) Alternatively, Lee suggests that with respect to job loss in the private sector, the whistleblower is more fortunate than many in that all but nine states allow plaintiffs to use the law of personal injury in case of unjust discharge by private sector employers if and only if the employer discharges an employee without just cause and the employee can articulate a claim involving the public good. For discussion of these and related points, see Barbara A. Lee, *Something Akin to a Property Right: Protections for*

Employee Job Security" in *Business & Professional Ethics Journal,* Vol. 8, No. 3, pp. 63–82.

11. Davis appropriately notices that "taking the information out of channels to try to stop the organization from doing something he believes is morally wrong" is sufficient to cause organizational members to regard the informer as a whistleblower, cf. Michael Davis, "Avoiding the Tragedy of Whistleblowing," *Business & Professional Ethics Journal,* Vol. 8, No. 3, pp. 3–20.

12. I think that Davis' observation can be accomodated to the claim that the whistleblower goes public by noticing the onionlike structure of the public-private distinction: what is private belongs on the inside of each enveloping segment, all the surrounding outer layers are perceived as public from that perspective.

13. Elliston, *et al.,* p. 17.

14. Gregory Stricharchuk, "Bounty Hunter, Ex-Foreman May Win Millions for His Tale about Cheating at GE," *Wall Street Journal,* June 23, 1988, pp. 1 and 12.

15. Elliston, *et al.,* p. 13.

16. cf. Albert O. Hirschman's discussion of remediable flaws in deteriorating institutions growing out of an effort to connect economic and political theorizing. Albert O. Hirshman, *Exit, Voice and Loyalty, Responses to Decline in Firms, Organizations and States,* (Cambridge, MA: Harvard University Press, 1970).

17. Ralph Nader, Peter J. Petkas and Kate Blackwell, eds. *Whistle Blowing* (New York: Bantam, 1972); Charles Peters and Taylor Branch, *Blowing the Whistle* (New York: Praeger, 1972); Alan Westin, ed., *Whistle Blowing! Loyalty and Dissent in the Corporation* (New York: McGraw-Hill, 1981); Greg Mitchell, *Truth . . . and Consequences* (New York: Dembner Books, 1981).

18. Glazer and Glazer, pp. 97ff.

19. Glazer and Glazer, pp. 84–85. This point may hold against one of Davis' suggestions about the way in which a conscientious employee may avoid the tragedy of whistleblowing by using some alternative informant to pass information cf. Davis, p. 14.

20. Pamela Reynolds, "Respected in Death, For Nuclear Safety He Took a Stand" *Boston Globe,* Jan. 11, 1989, p. 1.

21. Reynolds, p. 47.

22. Glazer and Glazer, pp. 30–31.

23. This is described more fully on pp. 11 ff. below.

24. Glazer and Glazer, p. 31.

25. Mike W. Martin, *Self-Deception and Morality,* (Lawrence, Kansas: University Press of Kansas, 1986) p. 7.

26. Martin, p. 17.

27. Bok, p. 3.

28. In Elliston, *et al.,* p. 17.

29. Richard De George, *Business Ethics,* (New York: Macmillan, 1982).

30. Richard DeGeorge, "Ethical Responsibilities of Engineers in Large Organizations," *Business & Professional Ethics Journal,* Vol. 1, No. 1, pp. 1–14, and *Business Ethics* (New York: Macmillan, 1982), p. 161.

31. Goldberg, Ibid.

32. Ronald Dworkin, "Should Homosexuality and Pornography be Crimes?" *The Yale Law Journal,* Vol. 75, p. 986, reprinted in A. K. Bierman and James A. Gould,

eds., *Philosophy for a New Generation,* (New York: Macmillan, 1981), pp. 279–292.

33. Alan F. Westin, Ibid.

34. Westin, pp. 22 ff, 34–5, 50 and 102; Elliston, *et al.,* pp. 99ff.

35. Glazer and Glazer, p. 210.

36. Reynolds, p. 47.

37. cf. Hirschman, Westin and Salisbury. Also, Albert Robbins, "Dissent in the Corporate World: When Does an Employee have the Right to Speak out?" *Civil Liberties Review* 5, (Sept/Oct 1978), pp. 6–10, 15–17; Phillip I. Blumberg, "Corporate Responsibility and the Employee's Duty of Loyalty and Obedience: A Preliminary Inquiry," *Oklahoma Law Rev.* 24, (Aug. 1971), pp. 297–318.

38. Glazer and Glazer, p. 160.

39. Cited in Glazer and Glazer, p. 207.

40. Natalie Dandekar, "Contrasting Consequences: Bringing Charges of Sexual Harassment Compared with Other Cases of Whistleblowing," *Journal of Business Ethics,* Vol. 9, No. 2 (1990), pp. 151–158.

41. Danielle Coviello, "Interviews with students who have reported sexual harassment from employers," unpublished paper, Bentley College, Women and Society course, Ph. 291 Sec. 002, May 1989.

42. Dandekar, p. 156.

43. Glazer and Glazer, p. 61.

44. Steven Kohn, *Protecting Environmental and Nuclear Whistleblowers: A Litigation Manual,* Nuclear Information and Resource Service, GAP, 1985.

45. David Lindorff, "How to Blow the Whistle—Safely, *Working Mother,* June, 1987, p. 25; John Conway, "Protecting the Private Sector At Will Employee Who 'Blows the Whistle': A Cause of Action Based Upon Determinants of Public Policy," *Wisconsin Law Review* 77 (1977), pp. 777–812; Alfred Feliu, "Discharge of Professional Employees: Protecting Against Dismissal for Acts Within a Professional Code of Ethics" *Columbia Human Rights Law Review* 11, (1980), pp. 149–187.

46. Stephen M. Kohn and Michael D. Kohn, "An Overview of Federal and State Whistleblower Protections," *Antioch Law Journal,* (Summer, 1986), pp. 102–11.

47. Elliston, *et al.,* p. 106.

48. Rosemary Chalk, "Making the World Safe for Whistleblowers" *Technology Review,* Jan. 1988, pp. 48–58.

49. Elliston, *et al.,* p. 109.

50. Elliston, p. 112.

51. Glazer and Glazer, pp. 97ff.

52. Martin H. Marlin, "Current Status of Legal Protection for Whistleblowers," paper delivered at the Second Annual Conference on Ethics in Engineering, Illinois Institute of Technology, 1982, cited in Gene James, "In Defense of Whistle Blowing" in W. Michael Hoffman and Jennifer Mills Moore, eds., *Business Ethics, Readings and Cases in Corporate morality,* (New York: McGraw Hill, 1984), pp. 249–252.

53. Bank of America policy as cited for *Miller v. Bank of America,* cited in Mackinnon, p. 62.

54. Michael Davis, whose interest coincides with mine in trying to support organizational change which would obviate the tragedies of whistleblowing suggests in

addition that employees should receive training in how to present bad news effectively. I think there is merit in this suggestion, and I would like to see him explore the means by which this might actually be accomplished. (Davis, p. 15.) Perhaps Hirschman's conception of remediable defects in an organization also deserves more attention than those who discuss whistleblowing have yet given it. (Hirshman, pp. 33, 45–53, 59 and 77–106).

55. Cheshire Calhoun, "Responsibility and Reproach," *Ethics*, 99 (January 1989), p. 396.
56. Catherine A. MacKinnon, *Sexual Harassment of Working Women*, (New Haven: Yale University Press, 1979), p. xi.
57. Calhoun, p. 397.
58. Calhoun, p. 389.
59. cf. also, Monte Throdahl, "Anyone Can Whistle," describing the internal institutionalization of whistleblowing activities at Monsanto through the Environmental Policy Staff, in A. Pablo Iannone, ed. *Contemporary Moral Controversies in Business*, (Oxford University Press, New York, 1989), pp. 219–220.
60. Bok, p. 8.
61. James C. Thomson, Jr. "How Could Vietnam Happen? An Autopsy," *Atlantic Monthly*, (April, 1968), pp. 45–57 cited in Hirschman, p. 115.

Questions

1. Davis suggests certain procedural and structural strategies to reduce the necessity of whistleblowing on the basis that an ounce of prevention is worth a pound of cure. Given that it is unlikely that the necessity for whistleblowing can ever be entirely removed, what recommendations would you make to help reduce the problems associated with whistleblowing?

2. Is Davis correct in his claim that whistleblowing must exact inevitable high costs both from employee and employer? Why or why not?

3. What is Larmer's argument for suggesting that "blowing the whistle may demonstrate greater loyalty than not blowing the whistle"?

4. Do you agree with Larmer's claim that to the degree an action is genuinely immoral, it is impossible that it is in the agent's best interests? Defend your answer.

5. Do you agree with Dandekar's claim that the whistleblower betrays a trust on behalf of protecting the public interest? Explain and defend your view.

6. What does Dandekar mean by the term "moral newness"?

Case 7:1 The Challenger Disaster

Morton Thiokol, an aerospace corporation, manufactured the solid fuel booster rocket used to propel the space shuttle *Challenger*. This booster rocket was constructed in segments which progressively burn away during a launch and which need to be sealed from one another to prevent unburned fuel from exploding and destroying the shuttle. Research showed that the seals had a significantly higher failure risk at low temperatures and Thiokol's contract with NASA specified that the boosters should not be operated at temperatures under 40 degrees F.

The *Challenger's* launch, which had already been delayed several times, was scheduled for January 28, 1986. NASA, under funding pressure, and needing a successful mission to help justify its program, was anxious to avoid the bad publicity associated with another aborted launch. Unfortunately, January 28 turned out to be a cold cloudy day. NASA, wishing to launch to proceed, contacted Thiokol and pressured them to approve the launch, despite the cold weather. Thiokol executives were anxious to accommodate an important customer. They overruled the warning of their engineers working on the project and approved a launch at 30 degrees F. The launch took place, even though the temperature was below 30 degrees F, with disastrous results.

Roger Boisjoly, the chief engineer, testified to a presidential commission that he had made his opposition to the launch known to both Thiokol executives and NASA officials. He was subsequently "reassigned to other responsibilities" and isolated from NASA. He experienced alienation from his coworkers and despite his experience and former high position at Thiokol, was unable to find a job with other engineering companies. He later took medical leave for post-traumatic stress disorder and subsequently left the company.

1. Does NASA or Thiokol bear the greater degree of blame for allowing the launch to go forward? Explain your answer.

2. Suppose you were Roger Boisjoly and you knew the consequences of whisleblowing. Would you whistleblow? Why or why not? What were Boisjoly's other options?

Case 7:2 Company Suspicion and Changed Working Conditions[1]

Charles G. Oxford worked for the National Laboratories Division of Lehn and Fink Industrial Products Division Inc., a division of Sterling Drug Inc., from 1963 to October 31, 1983 under a contract for an indefinite term. In the late seventies and early eighties Sterling was prosecuted for submitting false information to the General Services Administration during contract negotiations. As a result of these pricing violations, Sterling eventually had to pay $1,075,000 to the federal government. Ray Mitchell, president of the Lehn and Fink Division, expressed in October 1981 his belief that Oxford was responsible for reporting Sterling's pricing violations.

In October 1981 Oxford was advised that his position as manager of contract sales would be eliminated effective January 1, 1982, as a result of company restructuring. Oxford accepted a new position as a district sales manager, the lowest position in the National Laboratories Division hierarchy. Coincident with his accepting this new position, Oxford received an "EEO" letter from his supervisor, this being the nickname for a letter used to set an employee up for termination. This letter detailed Oxford's new responsibilities, one of which included conducting floor care demonstrations five nights a week after business hours.

Oxford's supervisor, who repeatedly criticized Oxford's performance of these new duties, later testified that he had been asked to write the EEO letter by Bill Milliron, a Lehn and Fink executive, and that his repeated criticism of Oxford following the company procedure outlined by Milliron to document an employee's termination. The supervisor also testified that he had only written two other EEO letters in his career, one to a district manager and one to a regional manager, and that both men had resigned under pressure.

Oxford, who consistently denied reporting Sterling to the General Services Administration, maintained that his supervisor also reprimanded him for performing acts he had not done and that he failed to receive stock he had won in a company sales contest. He left his territory in August 1983 without approval from Sterling and did not return to work. Sterling officially discharged him on Oct 31, 1983. In 1984 he brought a suit against Sterling, alleging that it had engaged in a systematic campaign to force his resignation.

Case Study Questions

1. Do you have a duty as a citizen to inform the government if it is being cheated of large sums of money by your employer? Does the government have a duty to protect citizens who do this from retaliation by their employers?
2. Supposing Oxford had asked you if he should blow the whistle on Sterling, and if so, how. What advice would you have given him?
3. If you were a fellow employee of Oxford and he had asked you to support him in his whistleblowing how would you have replied?

Notes
1. Based on Sterling Drug Inc. v. Charles G. Oxford as described in 743 *South Western Reporter*, 2nd series, pp. 380–389.

1. Sissela Bok "Whistleblowing and Professional Responsibility," *New York Education Quarterly,* Vol. 4, 1980, pp. 2–7.

2. Richard T. De George "Ethical Responsibilities of Engineers in Large Organizations: The Pinto Case," *Business & Professional Ethics Journal,* Vol. 1, No. 1, 1981, pp. 1.–14.

3. Ronald Duska "Whistleblowing and Employee Loyalty," in *Contemporary Issues in Business Ethics,* 2nd ed., edited by Joseph R. Des Jardins and John J. McCall (Belmont, CA: Wadsworth, 1990) pp. 142–146.

4. Myron Glazer "Ten Whistleblowers and How They Fared," *Hastings Center Report,* Vol. 13, No. 6, 1983, pp. 33–41.

INSIDER TRADING

Introduction

Insider trading can be defined as the buying or
selling of stocks on the basis of privileged information available only to a select few. It is
widely regarded as unethical and is illegal in
the United States and Canada, as well as a
large number of European and Asian countries. Nevertheless, some economic and ethical
theorists have insisted that insider trading is
morally acceptable and ought not to be illegal.[1] They argue that insider trading can in
many instances be viewed as good for the
economy, the corporation whose shares are
traded, the insiders who trade the shares,
and that it does not necessarily involve defrauding investors. They also note that many
countries that either do not have laws or do
not enforce laws against insider trading, nevertheless function as effective business cultures.
The challenge they pose to defenders of the
traditional view is to make clear exactly
why insider trading should be regarded as
unethical.

Jennifer Moore, in "What is Really Unethical
About Insider Trading?" takes the position that
insider trading is unethical, but finds many of
the traditional objections unconvincing. She
rejects as unpersuasive criticisms based on
considerations of fairness, property rights to
information, and harm to ordinary investors.
She argues that insider trading is to be rejected
on the basis that it threatens the fiduciary
relationship that lies at the heart of business
organization.

In "The Ethics of Insider Trading" Patricia
Werhane contends that insider trading is both
immoral and economically inefficient. She argues that it violates standards of fairness and

undermines competition, which is the very basis of any free market. She defends the view that a free market should not be conceived as permitting the operation of unrestrained self-interest, but rather self-interest qualified by reason, moral sentiment, and human sympathy. Adam Smith's famous Invisible Hand[2] is not, therefore, to be conceived as acting independently of the requirements of morality.

Richard Lippke in "Justice and Insider Trading" argues that the morality of insider trading must be evaluated in the context of discussing the broad principles of justice that should be adopted by society and the degree to which existing institutions apply these principles. He claims that once this is done, the arguments held to justify insider trading are revealed as deficient, inasmuch as they beg the question of whether the existing structures of wealth and power are morally defensible. He goes on to propose an egalitarian theory of justice and to argue that insider trading cannot be defended within such a theory.

Notes

1. See, for example, Henry Manne, *Insider Trading and the Stock Market* (New York: The Free Press, 1966) and William Shaw, "Shareholder Authorized Insider Trading: A Legal and Moral Analysis," *Journal of Business Ethics*, Vol. 9, 1990, pp. 913–928.
2. Adam Smith (1723–1790), the founder of modern economics, argued that, although those in business primarily seek their own benefit, a free market produces "as if by an invisible hand," the overall good of society.

Jennifer Moore

What is Really Unethical About Insider Trading?

" Insider trading," as the term is usually used, means the buying or selling of securities on the basis of material, non-public information. It is popularly believed to be unethical, and many, though not all, forms of it are illegal. Insider trading makes for exciting headlines, and stories of the unscrupulousness and unbridled greed of the traders abound. As it is reported in the media—complete with details of clandestine meetings, numbered Swiss bank accounts and thousands of dollars of profits carried away in plastic bags—insider trading has all the trappings of a very shady business indeed.[1] For many, insider trading has become the primary

From Jennifer Moore, "What is Really Unethical About Insider Trading?" *Journal of Business Ethics* Vol. 9: 171–182, 1990. Reprinted by permission of Kluwer Academic Publishers.

symbol of a widespread ethical rot on Wall Street and in the business community as a whole.[2]

For a practice that has come to epitomize unethical business behavior, insider trading has received surprisingly little ethical analysis. The best ethical assessments of insider trading have come from legal scholars who argue against the practice. But their arguments rest on notions such as fairness or ownership of information that require much more examination than they are usually given.[3] Proponents of insider trading are quick to dismiss these arguments as superficial, but offer very little ethical insight of their own. Arguing almost solely on grounds of economic efficiency, they generally gloss over the ethical arguments or dismiss them entirely.[4] Ironically, their refusal to address the ethical arguments on their merits merely strengthens the impression that insider trading is unethical. Readers are left with the sense that while it might reduce efficiency, the prohibition against insider trading rests on firm *ethical* grounds. But can we assume this? Not, I think, without a good deal more examination.

This paper is divided into two parts. In the first part, I examine critically the principal ethical arguments against insider trading. The arguments fall into three main classes: arguments based on fairness, arguments based on property rights in information, and arguments based on harm to ordinary investors or the market as a whole. Each of these arguments, I contend, has some serious deficiencies. No one of them by itself provides a sufficient reason for outlawing insider trading. This does not mean, however, that there are no reasons for prohibiting the practice. Once we have cleared away the inadequate arguments, other, more cogent reasons for outlawing insider trading come to light. In the second part of the paper, I set out what I take to be the real reasons for laws against insider trading.

The term insider trading" needs some preliminary clarification. Both the *SEC* [SEC is an acronym for the Securities and Exchange Commission] and the courts have strongly resisted pressure to define the notion clearly. In 1961, the SEC stated that corporate insiders—such as officers or directors—in possession of material, non-public information were required to disclose that information or to refrain from trading.[5] But this "disclose or refrain" rule has since been extended to persons other than corporate insiders. People who get information from insiders ("tippees") and those who become "temporary insiders" in the course of some work they perform for the company, can acquire the duty of insiders in some cases.[6] Financial printers and newspaper columnists, not "insiders" in the technical sense, have also been found guilty of insider trading.[7] Increasingly, the term "insider" has come to refer to the kind of information a person possesses rather than to the status of the person who trades on that information. My use of the term will reflect this ambiguity. In this paper, an "insider trader" is someone who trades in material, non-public information—not necessarily a corporate insider.

I. ETHICAL ARGUMENTS AGAINST INSIDER TRADING

Fairness

Probably the most common reason given for thinking that insider trading is unethical is that it is "unfair." For proponents of the fairness argument, the key feature of insider trading is the disparity of information between the two parties to the transaction. Trading should take place on a "level playing field," they argue, and disparities in information tilt the field toward one player and away from the other. There are two versions of the fairness argument: the first argues that insider trading is unfair because the two parties do not have *equal* information; the second argues that insider trading is unfair because the two parties do not have equal *access* to information. Let us look at the two versions one at a time.

According to the equal information argument, insider trading is unfair because one party to the transaction lacks information the other party has, and is thus at a disadvantage. Although this is a very strict notion of fairness, it has its proponents,[8] and hints of this view appear in some of the judicial opinions.[9] One proponent of the equal information argument is Saul Levmore, who claims that "fairness is achieved when insiders and outsiders are in equal positions. That is, a system is fair if we would not expect one group to envy the position of the other." As thus defined, Levmore claims, fairness "reflects the 'golden rule' of impersonal behavior—treating others as we would ourselves."[10] If Levmore is correct, then not just insider trading, but *all* transactions in which there is a disparity of information are unfair, and thus unethical. But this claim seems overly broad. An example will help to illustrate some of the problems with it.

Suppose I am touring Vermont and come across an antique blanket chest in the barn of a farmer, a chest I know will bring $2500 back in the city. I offer to buy it for $75, and the farmer agrees. If he had known how much I could get for it back home, he probably would have asked a higher price—but I failed to disclose this information. I have profited from an informational advantage. Have I been unethical? My suspicion is that most people would say I have not. While knowing how much I could sell the chest for in the city is in the interest of the farmer, I am not morally obligated to reveal it. I am not morally obligated to tell those who deal with me *everything* that it would be in their interest to know.

U.S. common law supports this intuition. Legally, people are obligated not to lie or misrepresent a product they are selling or buying. But they are not required to reveal everything it is in the other party's interest to know.[11] One might argue that this is simply an area in which the law falls short of ethical standards. But there is substantial ethical support for the law on these matters as well. There does seem to be a real difference between lying or misrepresentation on the one hand, and simple failure to disclose information on the other, even though the line between the two is sometimes hard to draw.[12] Lying and misrepresentation are forms of deception, and deception is a subtle form of coercion. When I successfully deceive someone, I cause him to do something that does not represent his true will—something he did not intend to do and would not have done if he had known the truth. Simply not revealing information (usually) does not involve this kind of coercion.

In general, it is only when I owe a *duty* to the other party that I am legally required to reveal all information that is in his interest. In such a situation, the other party believes that I am looking out for his interests, and I deceive him if I do not do so. Failure to disclose is deceptive in this instance because of the relationship of trust and dependence between the parties. But this suggests that trading on inside information is wrong, *not* because it violates a general notion of fairness, but because a breach of fiduciary duty is involved. Cases of insider trading in which no fiduciary duty of this kind is breached would not be unethical.

Significantly, the Supreme Court has taken precisely this position: insider trading is wrong because, and when, it involves the violation of a fiduciary duty to the other parties to the transaction.[13] The Court has consistently refused to recognize the general duty to *all* investors that is argued for by proponents of the fairness argument. This is particularly clear in *Chiarella v. US,* a decision overturning the conviction of a financial printer for trading on inside information:

At common law, misrepresentation made for the purpose of inducing reliance upon the false statement is fraudulent. But one who fails to disclose

material information prior to the consummation of a transaction commits fraud *only when he is under a duty to do so.* And the duty to disclose arises when one party has information "that the other party is entitled to know because of a fiduciary or other similar relation of trust and confidence between them." . . . The element required to make silence fraudulent—a duty to disclose—is absent in this case. . . .

We cannot affirm petitioner's conviction without recognizing a general duty between all participants in market transactions to forgo actions based on material, nonpublic information. Formulation of such a broad duty, which departs radically from the established doctrine that duty arises from a specific relationship between two parties . . . Should not be undertaken absent some explicit evidence of congressional intent. . . .[14]

The court reiterated that "there is no *general* duty to disclose before trading on material nonpublic information" in *Dirks v. SEC.*[15] It is worth noting that if this reasoning is correct, the legal and ethical status of insider trading depends on the understanding between the fiduciary and the party he represents. Insider trading would not be a violation of fiduciary duty, and thus would not be unethical, unless

1. it were clearly contrary to the interests of the other party or
2. the other party had demanded or been led to expect disclosure.

We shall return to this point below.

There is a second ethical reason for not requiring all people with informational advantages to disclose them to others: there may be relevant differences between the parties to the transaction that make the disparity of information "fair." Perhaps I invested considerable time, effort and money in learning about antiques. If this is true, I might deserve to reap the benefits of these efforts. We frequently think it is fair for people to benefit from informational advantages of their own making; this is an important justification for patent law and the protection of trade secrets. "Fairness" is often defined as "treating equals equally." But equals in what respect? Unless we know that the two parties to a transaction *are* equal in the relevant way, it is difficult to say that an informational advantage held by one of them is "unfair."

My point here is different from the frequently heard claim that people should be allowed to profit from informational advantages because this results in a more efficient use of information. This latter claim, while important, does not really address the fairness issue. What I am arguing is that the notion of fairness offered by proponents of the equal information argument is itself incomplete. We cannot make the notion of fairness work for us unless we supply guidelines explaining who are to count as "equals" in different contexts. If we try, we are likely to end up with results that seem intuitively *unfair*.

For these reasons, the "equal information" version of the fairness argument seems to me to fail. However, it could be argued that insider trading is unfair because the insider has information that is not *accessible* to the ordinary investor. For proponents of this second type of fairness argument, it is not the insider's information advantage that counts, but the fact that this advantage is "unerodable," one that cannot be overcome by the hard work and ingenuity of the ordinary investor. No matter how hard the latter works, he is unable to acquire non-public information, because this information is protected by law.[16]

This type of fairness argument seems more promising, since it allows people to profit from informational advantages of their own making, but not from advantages that are built into the system. Proponents of this "equal access" argument would probably find my deal with the Vermont farmer unobjectionable, because information about antiques is not in principle unavailable to the farmer. The problem with the argument is that the notion of "equal access" is not very clear. What does it mean for two people to have equal access to information?

Suppose my pipes are leaking and I call a plumber to fix them. He charges me for the job, and benefits by the informational advantage he has over me. Most of us would not find this transaction unethical. True, I don't have "equal access" to the information needed to fix my pipes in any real sense, but I could have had this information had I chosen to become a plumber. The disparity of information in this case is simply something that is built into the fact that

people choose to specialize in different areas. But just as I could have chosen to become a plumber, I could have chosen to become a corporate insider with access to legally protected information. Access to information seems to be a relative, not an absolute, matter. As Judge Frank Easterbook puts it:

> People do not have or lack "access" in some absolute sense. There are, instead, different costs of obtaining information. An outsider's costs are high; he might have to purchase the information from the firm. Managers have lower costs (the amount of salary foregone); brokers have relatively low costs (the value of the time they spent investigating). . . . The different costs of access are simply a function of the division of labor. A manager (or a physician) always knows more than a shareholder (or patient) in some respects, but unless there is something unethical about the division of labor, the difference is not unfair.[17]

One might argue that I have easier access to a plumber's information than I do to an insider trader's, since there are lots of plumbers from whom I can buy the information I seek.[18] The fact that insiders have a strong incentive to keep their information to themselves is a serious objection to insider trading. But if insider trading were made legal, insiders could profit not only from trading on their information, but also on selling it to willing buyers. Proponents of the practice argue that a brisk market in information would soon develop—indeed, it might be argued that such a market already exists, though in illegal and clandestine form.[19]

The objections offered above do not show conclusively that *no* fairness argument against insider trading can be constructed. But they do suggest that a good deal more spadework is necessary to construct one. Proponents of the fairness argument need to show how the informational advantages of insider traders over ordinary investors are different in kind from the informational advantages of plumbers over the rest of us—or, alternatively, why the informational advantages of plumbers are unfair. I have not yet seen such an argument, and I suspect that designing one may require a significant overhaul of our traditional ideas about fairness. As it stands, the effectiveness of the fairness argument seems restricted to situations in which the insider trader owes a duty to the person with whom he is trading—and as we will see below, even here it is not conclusive because much depends on how that duty is defined.

The most interesting thing about the fairness argument is not that it provides a compelling reason to outlaw insider trading, but that it leads to issues we cannot settle on the basis of an abstract concept of fairness alone. The claim that parties to a transaction should have equal information, or equal access to information, inevitably raises questions about how informational advantages are (or should be) acquired, and when people are entitled to use them for profit. Again, this understanding of the limits of the fairness argument is reflected in common law. If insider trading is wrong primarily because it is unfair, then it should be wrong no matter *who* engages in it. It should make no difference whether I am a corporate insider, a financial printer, or a little old lady who heard a takeover rumor on the Hudson River Line. But it does make a difference to the courts. I think this is because the crucial questions concerning insider trading are not about fairness, but about how inside information is acquired and what entitles people to make use of it. These are questions central to our second class of arguments against insider trading, those based on the notion of property rights in information.

Property Rights in Information

As economists and legal scholars have recognized, information is a valuable thing, and it is possible to view it as a type of property. We already treat certain types of information as property: trade secrets, inventions, and so on— and protect them by law. Proponents of the property rights argument claim that material, non-public information is also a kind of property, and that insider trading is wrong because it involves a violation of property rights.

If inside information is a kind of property, whose property is it? How does information come to belong to one person rather than another? This is a very complex question, because information differs in many ways from other, more tangible sorts of property. But one

influential argument is that information belongs to the people who discover, originate or "create" it. As Bill Shaw put it in a recent article, "the originator of the information (the individual or the corporation that spent hard-earned bucks producing it) owns and controls this asset just as it does other proprietary goods."[20] Thus if a firm agrees to a deal, invents a new product, or discovers new natural resources, it has a property right in that information and is entitled to exclusive use of it for its own profit.

It is important to note that it is the firm itself (and/or its shareholders), and not the individual employees of the firm, who have property rights in the information. To be sure, it is always certain individuals in the firm who put together the deal, invent the product, or discover the resources. But they are able to do this only because they are backed by the power and authority of the firm. The employees of the firm—managers, officers, directors—are not entitled to the information any more than they are entitled to corporate trade secrets or patents on products that they develop for the firm.[21] It is the firm that makes it possible to create the information and that makes the information valuable once it has been created. As Victor Brudney puts it,

The insiders have acquired the information at the expense of the enterprise, and for the purpose of conducting the business for the collective good of all the stockholders, entirely apart from personal benefits from trading in its securities. There is no reason for them to be entitled to trade for their own benefit on the basis of such information. . . .[22]

If this analysis is correct, then it suggests that insider trading is wrong because it is a form of theft. It is not exactly like theft, because the person who uses inside information does not deprive the company of the use of the information. But he does deprive the company of the *sole* use of the information, which is itself an asset. The insider trader "misappropriates," as the law puts it, information that belongs to the company and uses it in a way in which it was not intended—for personal profit. It is not surprising that this "misappropriation theory" has begun to take hold in the courts, and has become one of the predominant rationales in prosecuting insider trading cases. In *U.S. v. New-*

man, a case involving investment bankers and securities traders, for example, the court stated:

In *US v. Chiarella*, Chief Justice Burger . . . said that the defendant "misappropriated"—stole to put it bluntly—valuable nonpublic information entrusted to him in the utmost confidence." That characterization aptly describes the conduct of the connivers in the instant case. . . . By sullying the reputations of [their] employers as safe repositories of client confidences, appellee and his cohorts defrauded those employers as surely as if they took their money.[23]

The misappropriation theory also played a major role in the prosecution of R. Foster Winans, a *Wall Street Journal* reporter who traded on and leaked to others the contents of his "Heard in the Street" column.[24]

This theory is quite persuasive, as far as it goes. But it is not enough to show that insider trading is always unethical or that it should be illegal. If insider information is really the property of the firm that produces it, then using that property is wrong *only when the firm prohibits it*. If the firm does not prohibit insider trading, it seems perfectly acceptable.[25] Most companies do in fact forbid insider trading. But it is not clear whether they do so because they don't want their employees using corporate property for profit or simply because it is illegal. Proponents of insider trading point out that most corporations did not prohibit insider trading until recently, when it became a prime concern of enforcement agencies.[26]

If insider trading is primarily a problem of property rights in information, it might be argued, then it is immoral, and should be illegal, only when the company withholds permission to trade on inside information. Under the property rights theory, insider trading becomes a matter of *contract* between the company, its shareholders and its employees. If the employment contract forbids an employee from using the company's information, then it is unethical (and illegal) to do so.

A crucial factor here would be the shareholders' agreement to allow insider information. Shareholders may not wish to allow trading on inside information because they may wish the employees of the company to be devoted simply to advancing shareholder interests. We will return to this point below. But if shareholders did allow it, it would seem to be permissible. Still others argue that shareholders would not need to "agree" in any way other than to be told this information when they were buying the stock. If they did not want to hold stock in a company whose employees were permitted to trade in inside information, they would buy that stock. Hence they could be said to have "agreed."

Manne and other proponents of insider trading have suggested a number of reasons why "shareholders would voluntarily enter into contractual arrangements with insiders giving them property rights in valuable information."[27] Their principal argument is that permitting insider trading would serve as an incentive to create more information—put together more deals, invent more new products, or make more discoveries. Such an incentive, they argue, would create more profit for shareholders in the long run. Assigning employees the right to trade on inside information could take the place of more traditional (and expensive) elements in the employee's compensation package. Rather than giving out end of the year bonuses, for example, firms could allow employees to put together their own bonuses by cashing in on inside information, thus saving the company money. In addition, proponents argue, insider trading would improve the efficiency of the market. We will return to these claims below.

If inside information really is a form of corporate property, firms may assign employees the right to trade on it if they choose to do so. The only reason for not permitting firms to allow employees to trade on their information would be that doing so causes harm to other investors or to society at large. Although our society values property rights very highly, they are not absolute. We do not hesitate to restrict property rights if their exercise causes significant harm to others. The permissibility of insider trading, then, ultimately seems to depend on whether the practice is harmful.

Harm

There are two principal harm-based arguments against insider trading. The first claims that the practice is harmful to ordinary investors who engage in trades with insiders; the second claims that insider trading erodes investors' confidence in the market, causing them to pull out of the market and harming the market as a whole. I will address the two arguments in turn.

Although proponents of insider trading often refer to it as a "victimless crime," implying that no one is harmed by it, it is not difficult to think of examples of transactions with insiders in which ordinary investors are made worse off. Suppose I have placed an order with my broker to sell my shares in Megalith Co., currently trading at $50 a share, at $60 or above. An insider knows that Behemoth Inc. Is going to announce a tender offer for Megalith shares in two days, and has begun to buy large amounts of stock in anticipation of the gains. Because of his market activity, Megalith stock rises to $65 a share and my order is triggered. If he had refrained from trading, the price would have risen steeply two days later, and I would have been able to sell my shares for $80. Because the insider traded, I failed to realize the gains that I otherwise would have made.

But there are other examples of transactions in which ordinary investors *benefit* from insider trading. Suppose I tell my broker to sell my shares in Acme Corp., currently trading at $45, if the price drops to $40 or lower. An insider knows of an enormous class action suit to be brought against Acme in two days. He sells his shares, lowering the price to $38 and triggering my sale. When the suit is made public two days later, the share price plunges to $25. If the insider had abstained from trading, I would have lost far more than I did. Here, the insider has protected me from loss.

Not all investors buy or sell through such "trigger" orders. Many of them make their decisions by watching the movement of the stock. The rise in share price might have indicated to an owner of Megalith that a merger was imminent, and she might have held on to her shares for this reason. Similarly, the downward movement of Acme stock caused by the insider might have suggested to an owner that it was time to sell. Proponents of insider trading argue that large trades by insiders move the price of shares closer to their "real" value, that is, the value that reflects *all* the relevant information about the stock. This makes the market more efficient and provides a valuable service to all investors.[28]

The truth about an ordinary investor's gains and losses from trading with insiders seems to be not that insider trading is never harmful, but that it is not systematically or consistently harmful. Insider trading is not a "victimless crime," as its proponents claim, but it is often difficult to tell exactly who the victims are and to what extent they have been victimized. The stipulation of the law to "disclose *or* abstain" from trading makes determining victims even more complex. While some investors are harmed by the insider's trade, to others the insider's actions make no difference at all; what harms them is simply *not having complete information* about the stock in question. Forbidding insider trading will not prevent these harms. Investors who neither buy nor sell, or who buy or sell for reasons independent of share price, fall into this category.

Permitting insider trading would undoubtedly make the securities market *riskier* for ordinary investors. Even proponents of the practice seem to agree with this claim. But if insider trading were permitted openly, they argue, investors would compensate for the extra riskiness by demanding a discount in share price:

> In modern finance theory, shareholders are seen as investors seeking a return proportionate with that degree of systematic or market-related risk which they have chosen to incur. . . . [The individual investor] is "protected" by the price established by the market mechanism, not by his personal bargaining power or position. . . . To return to the gambling analogy, if I know you are using percentage dice, I won't play without an appropriate adjustment of the odds; the game is, after all, voluntary.[29]

If insider trading were permitted, in short, we could expect a general drop in share prices, but no net harm to investors would result. Moreover, improved efficiency would result in a bigger pie for everyone. These are empirical claims, and I am not equipped to determine if they are true. If they are, however, they would defuse one of the most important objections to insider trading, and provide a powerful argument for leaving the control of inside information up to individual corporations.

The second harm-based argument claims that permitting insider trading would cause ordinary investors to lose confidence in the market and cease to invest there, thus harming the market as a whole. As former SEC Chairman John Shad puts it, "if people get the impression that they're playing against a marked deck, they're simply not going to be willing to invest."[30] Since capital markets play a crucial role in allocating resources in our economy, this objection is a very serious one.

The weakness of the argument is that it turns almost exclusively on the *feelings* or *perceptions* of ordinary investors, and does not address the question of whether these perceptions are justified. If permitting insider trading really does harm ordinary investors, then this "loss of confidence" argument becomes a compelling reason for outlawing insider trading. But if, as many claim, the practice does not harm ordinary investors, then the sensible course of action is to educate the investors, not to outlaw insider trading. It is irrational to cater to the feelings of ordinary investors if those feelings are not justified. We ought not to outlaw perfectly permissible actions just because some people feel (unjustifiably) disadvantaged by them. More research is needed to determine the actual impact of insider trading on the ordinary investor.[31]

II. Is There Anything Wrong With Insider Trading?

My contention has been that the principal ethical arguments against insider trading do not, by themselves, suffice to show that the practice is unethical and should be illegal. The strongest arguments are those that turn on the notion of a fiduciary duty to act in the interest of shareholders, or on the idea of inside information as company "property." But in both arguments, the impermissibility of insider trading depends on a contractual understanding among the company, its shareholders and its employees. In both cases, a modification of this understanding could change the moral status of insider trading.

Does this mean that there is nothing wrong with insider trading? No. If insider trading is

unethical, it is so *in the context* of the relationship among the firm, its shareholders and its employees. It is possible to change this context in a way that makes the practice permissible. But *should* the context be changed? I will argue that it should not. Because it threatens the fiduciary relationship that is central to business management, I believe, permitting insider trading is in the interest neither of the firm, its shareholders, nor society at large.

Fiduciary relationships are relationships of trust and dependence in which one party acts in the interest of another. They appear in many contexts, but are absolutely essential to conducting business in a complex society. Fiduciary relationships allow parties with different resources, skills and information to cooperate in productive activity. Shareholders who wish to invest in a business, for example, but who cannot or do not wish to run it themselves, hire others to manage it for them. Managers, directors, and to some extent, other employees, become fiduciaries for the firms they manage and for the shareholders of those firms.

The fiduciary relationship is one of moral and legal obligation. Fiduciaries, that is, are bound to act in the interests of those who depend on them even if these interests do not coincide with their own. Typically, however, fiduciary relationships are constructed as far as possible so that the interests of the fiduciaries and the parties for whom they act *do* coincide. Where the interests of the two parties compete or conflict, the fiduciary relationship is threatened. In corporations, the attempt to discourage divergences of interest is exemplified in rules against bribery, usurping corporate opportunities, and so forth. In the past few years, an entire discipline, "agency theory," has developed to deal with such questions. Agency theorists seek ways to align the interests of agents or fiduciaries with the interests of those on behalf of whom they act.

Significantly, proponents of insider trading do not dispute the importance of the fiduciary relationship. Rather, they argue that permitting insider trading would *increase* the likelihood that employees will act in the interest of shareholders and their firms.[32] We have already touched on the main argument for this claim.

Manne and others contend that assigning employees the right to trade on inside information would provide a powerful incentive for creative and entrepreneurial activity. It would encourage new inventions, creative deals, and efficient new management practices, thus increasing the profits, strength, and overall competitiveness of the firm. Manne goes so far as to argue that permission to trade on insider information is the only appropriate way to compensate entrepreneurial activity, and warns: "[I]f no way to reward the entrepreneur within a corporation exists, he will tend to disappear from the corporate scene."[33] The entrepreneur makes an invaluable contribution to the firm and its shareholders, and his disappearance would no doubt cause serious harm.

If permitting insider trading is to work in the way proponents suggest, however, there must be a direct and consistent link between the profits reaped by insider traders and the performance that benefits the firm. It is not at all clear that this is the case—indeed, there is evidence that the opposite is true. There appear to be many ways to profit from inside information that do not benefit the firm at all. I mention four possibilities below. Two of these (2 and 3) are simply ways in which insider traders can profit without benefitting the firm, suggesting that permitting insider trading is a poor incentive for performance and fails firmly to link the interests of managers, directors and employees to those of the corporation as a whole. The others (1 and 4) are actually harmful to the corporation, setting up conflicts of interest and actively undermining the fiduciary relationship.[34]

(1) Proponents of insider trading tend to speak as if all information were positive. "Information," in the proponents' lexicon, always concerns a creative new deal, a new, efficient way of conducting business, or a new product. If this were true, allowing trades on inside information might provide an incentive to work ever harder for the good of the company. But information can also concern *bad* news—a large lawsuit, an unsafe or poor quality product, or lower-than-expected performance. Such negative information can be just as valuable to the insider trader as positive information. If the freedom to trade on positive information encourages acts that are

beneficial to the firm, then by the same reasoning the freedom to trade on negative information would encourage harmful acts. At the very least, permitting employees to profit from harms to the company decreases the incentive to avoid such harms. Permission to trade on negative inside information gives rise to inevitable conflicts of interest. Proponents of insider trading have not satisfactorily answered this objection.[35]

(2) Proponents of insider trading also assume that the easiest way to profit on inside information is to "create" it. But it is not at all clear that this is true. Putting together a deal, inventing a new product, and other productive activities that add value to the firm usually require a significant investment of time and energy. For the well-placed employee, it would be far easier to start a rumor that the company has a new product or is about to announce a deal than to sit down and produce either one—and it would be just as profitable for the employee. If permitting insider trading provides an incentive for the productive "creation" of information, it seems to provide an even greater incentive for the non-productive "invention" of information, or stock manipulation. The invention of information is in the interest of neither the firm nor of society at large.

(3) Even if negative or false information did not pose problems, the incentive argument for insider trading overlooks the difficulties posed by "free riders"—those who do not actually contribute to the creation of the information, but who are nevertheless aware of it and can profit by trading on it. It is a commonplace of economic theory that if persons can benefit from a good without paying for it, they will generally do so. If there is no way to exclude those who do not "pay" from enjoying a benefit, no one will have an incentive to pay for it, there will be no incentive to produce it, and the good will not be supplied. In the case of insider trading, an employee's contribution to the creation of positive information constitutes the "payment." Unless those who do not contribute can be excluded from trading on it, there will be no incentive to produce the desired information; it will not get created at all.

(4) Finally, allowing trading on inside information would tend to deflect employees' atten-

tion from the day-to-day business of running the company and focus it on major changes, positive or negative, that lead to large insider trading profits. This might not be true if one could profit by inside information about the day-to-day efficiency of the operation, a continuous tradition of product quality, or a consistently lean operating budget. But these things do not generate the kind of information on which insider traders can reap large profits. Insider profits come from dramatic changes, from "news"—not from steady, long-term performance. If the firm and its shareholders have a genuine interest in such performance, then permitting insider trading creates a conflict of interest for insiders. The ability to trade on inside information is also likely to influence the types of information officers announce to the public, and the timing of such announcements, making it less likely that the information and its timing is optimal for the firm. And the problems of false or negative information remain.[36]

If the arguments given above are correct, permitting insider trading does not increase the likelihood that insiders will act in the interest of the firm and its shareholders. In some cases, it actually causes conflicts of interest, undermining the fiduciary relationship essential to managing the corporation. This claim, in turn, gives corporations good reason to prohibit the practice. But insider trading remains primarily a private matter among corporations, shareholders, and employees. It is appropriate to ask why, given this fact about insider trading, the practice should be *illegal*. If it is primarily corporate and shareholder interests that are threatened by insider trading, why not let corporations themselves bear the burden of enforcement? Why involve the SEC? There are two possible reasons for continuing to support laws against insider trading. The first is that even if they wish to prohibit insider trading, individual corporations do not have the resources to do so effectively. The second is that society itself has a stake in the fiduciary relationship.

Proponents of insider trading frequently point out that until 1961, when the SEC began to prosecute insider traders, few firms took steps to prevent the practice.[37] They argue that this fact indicates that insider trading is not truly harmful to corporations; if it were, corporations would have prohibited it long ago. But there is another plausible reason for corporations' failure to outlaw insider trading: they did not have the resources to do so, and did not wish to waste resources in the attempt to achieve an impossible task.[38] There is strong evidence that the second explanation is the correct one. Preventing insider trading requires continuous and extensive monitoring of transactions and the ability to compel disclosure, and privately imposed penalties do not seem sufficient to discourage insider trading.[39] The SEC is not hampered by these limitations. Moreover, suggests Frank Easterbrook, if even a few companies allow insider trading, this could make it difficult for other companies to prohibit it. Firms that did not permit insider trading would find themselves at a competitive disadvantage, at the mercy of "free riders" who announce to the public that they prohibit insider trading but incur none of the enforcement costs.[40] Outlawing the practice might be worth doing simply because it enables corporations to do what is in all of their interests anyway—prohibit trading on inside information.

Finally, the claim that the fiduciary relationship is purely a "private" matter is misleading. The erosion of fiduciary duty caused by permitting insider trading has social costs as well as costs to the corporation and its shareholders. We have already noted a few of these. Frequent incidents of stock manipulation would cause a serious crisis in the market, reducing both its stability and efficiency. An increase in the circulation of false information would cause a general decline in the reliability of information and a corresponding decrease in investor trust. This would make the market less, not more efficient (as proponents of the practice claim). Deflecting interests away from the task of day-to-day management and toward the manipulation of information could also have serious negative social consequences. American business has already sustained much criticism for its failure to keep its mind on producing goods and services, and for its pursuit of "paper profits."

The notion of the fiduciary duty owed by managers and other employees to the firm and its shareholders has a long and venerable history in our society. Nearly all of our important activities require some sort of cooperation, trust, or reliance on others, and the ability of one person to act in the interest of another—as a fiduciary—is central to this cooperation. The role of managers as fiduciaries for firms and shareholders is grounded in the property rights of shareholders. They are the owners of the firm, and bear the residual risks, and hence have a right to have it managed in their interest. The fiduciary relationship also contributes to efficiency, since it encourages those who are willing to take risks to place their resources in the hands of those who have the expertise to maximize their usefulness. While this "shareholder theory" of the firm has often been challenged in recent years, this has been primarily by people who argue that the fiduciary concept should be widened to include other "stakeholders" in the firm.[41] I have heard no one argue that the notion of managers' fiduciary duties should be eliminated entirely, and that managers should begin working primarily for themselves.

III. CONCLUSION

I have argued that the real reason for prohibiting insider trading is that it erodes the fiduciary relationship that lies at the heart of our business organizations. The more frequently heard moral arguments based on fairness, property rights in information, and harm to ordinary investors, are not compelling. Of these, the fairness arguments seem to me the least persuasive. The claim that a trader must reveal everything that it is in the interest of another party to know, seems to hold up only when the other is someone to whom he owes a fiduciary duty. But this is not really a "fairness" argument at all. Similarly, the "misappropriation" theory is only persuasive if we can offer reasons for corporations not to assign the right to trade on inside information to their employees. I have found these in the fact that permitting insider trading threatens the fiduciary relationship. I do believe that lifting the ban against insider trading would cause harms to shareholders, corporations, and society at large. But again, these harms stem primarily from the cracks in the fiduciary relationship caused by permitting insider trading, rather than from actual trades with insiders. Violation of fiduciary duty, in short, is at the center of insider trading offenses, and it is with good reason that the Supreme Court has kept the fiduciary relationship at the forefront of its deliberations on insider trading.

Notes

1. See, for example, Douglas Frantz, *Levine & Co.* (Avon Books, NY, 1987).
2. This is certainly true of former SEC chair John Shad, one of the leaders of the crusade against insider trading, who recently donated millions of dollars to Harvard University to establish a program in business ethics. Also see Felix Rohatyn of the investment banking house Lazard Frères: ". . . [A] cancer has been spreading in our industry. . . . Too much money is coming together with too many young people who have little or no institutional memory, or sense of tradition, and who are under enormous economic pressure to perform in the glare of Hollywood-like publicity. The combination makes for speculative excesses at best, illegality at worst. Insider trading is only one result." *The New York Review of Books*, March 12, 1987.
3. An important exception is Lawson, "The Ethics of Insider Trading," 11 *Harvard Journal of Law and Public Policy* 727 (1988).
4. Henry Manne, for example, whose book *Insider Trading and the Stock Market* stimulated the modern controversy over insider trading, has nothing but contempt for ethical arguments. See "Insider Trading and the Law Professors," 23 *Vanderbilt Law Review* 549 (1969): "Morals, someone once said, are a private luxury. Carried into the area of serious debate on public policy, moral arguments are frequently either a sham or a refuge for the intellectually bankrupt." Or see Jonathan R. Macey, "Ethics, Economics and Insider Trading: Ayn Rand Meets the Theory of the Firm," 11 *Harvard Journal of Law and Pubic Policy* 787 (1988): "[I]n my view the attempt to critique insider trading using ethical philosophy—divorced from economic analysis—is something of a non-starter, because ethical theory does not have much to add to the work that has already been done by economists."
5. *In re Cady, Roberts*, 40 SEC 907 (1961).
6. On tippees, see *Dirks v. SEC*, 463 US 646 (1983) at 659; on "temporary insiders," see *Dirks v. SEC*, 103 S. Ct. 3255 (1983), at 3261 n. 14, and *SEC v. Musella* 578 F. Supp. 425.
7. See *Materia v. SEC*, 725 F. 2d 197, involving a financial printer and the Winans case, involving the author of the *Wall Street Journal's* "Heard on the Street" column, *Carpenter v. US*, 56 LW 4007; *U.S. v. Winans*, 612 F. Supp. 827. It should be noted that the Supreme Court has not wholeheartedly endorsed these further extensions of the rule against insider trading.

8. See Kaplan, "*Wolf v. Weinstein:* Another Chapter on Insider Trading," 1963 *Supreme Court Review* 273. For numerous other references, see Brudney, "Insiders, Outsiders and Informational Advantages Under the Federal Securities Laws," 93 *Harvard Law Review* 339, n. 63.

9. See *Mitchell v. Texas Gulf Sulphur Co.,* 446 F. 2d. 90 (1968) at 101; *SEC v. Great American Industries,* 407 F. 2d. 453 (1968) at 462; *Birdman v. Electro-Catheter Corp.,* 352 F. Supp. 1271 (1973) at 1274.

10. Saul Levmore, "Securities and Secrets: Insider Trading and the Law of Contracts," 68 *Virginia Law Review* 117.

11. See Anthony Kronman, "Mistake, Disclosure, Information, and the Law of Contracts," 7 *Journal of Legal Studies* 1 (1978). The Restatement (Second) of Torts § 551(2)e (Tent. Draft No. 11, 1965) gives an example which is very similar example to the one above, involving a violin expert who buys a Stradivarius (worth $50,000) in a second-hand instrument shop for only $100.

12. It seems clear that sometimes failure to disclose can *be* a form of misrepresentation. Such could be the case, for example, when the seller makes a true statement about a product but fails to reveal a later change in circumstances which makes the earlier statement false. Or if a buyer indicates that he has a false impression of the product, and the seller fails to correct the impression. A plausible argument against insider trading would be that failure to reveal the information to the other party to the transaction allows a false impression of this kind to continue, and thus constitutes a form of deception. It is not clear to me, however, that insider trading is a situation of this kind.

13. An important question is whether trades involving the violation of *another kind* of fiduciary duty, constitute a violation of 10b–5. I address this second type of violation below.

14. *Chiarella v. US,* 445 U.S. 222, at 227–8; 232–233. Italics mine.

15. 445 US at 233. Italics mine.

16. The equal access argument is perhaps best stated by Victor Brudney in his influential article, "Insiders, Outsiders and Informational Advantages Under the Federal Securities Laws," 93 *Harvard Law Review* 322.

17. Easterbrook, *Insider Trading, Secret Agents, Evidentiary Privileges, and the Production of Information,* 1981 Supreme Court Review 350.

18. Robert Frederick brought this point to my attention.

19. Manne, *Insider Trading and the Stock Market* (Free Press, New York, 1966), p. 75.

20. Bill Shaw, "Should Insider Trading Be Outside The Law," *Business and Society Review,* Vol. 66, p. 34. See also Macey, "From Fairness to Contract: The New Direction of the Rules Against Insider Trading," 13 *Hofstra Law Review,* Vol. 9 (1984).

21. Easterbrook points out the striking similarity between insider trading cases and cases involving trade secrets, and cites *Perrin v. US,* 444 US 37 (1979), in which the court held that it was a federal crime to sell confidential corporate information.

22. Brudney, "Insiders, Outsiders, and Informational Advantages," 344.

23. *U.S. v. Newman,* 664 F. 2d 17.

24. *U.S. v. Winans,* 612 F. Supp. 827. The Supreme Court upheld Winans' conviction, but was evenly split on the misappropriation theory. As a consequence, the Supreme Court has still not truly endorsed the theory, although several lower court decisions have been based on it. *Carpenter v. US,* 56 LW 4007.

25. Unless there is some other reason for forbidding it, such as that it harms others. See p. 176 first column below.

26. Easterbrook, "Insider Trading As An Agency Problem," *Principals and Agents: The Structure of Business* (Harvard University Press, Cambridge, MA, 1985).

27. Carlton and Fischel, "The Regulation of Insider Trading," 35 *Stanford Law Review* 857. See also Manne, *Insider Trading and the Stock Market.*

28. Manne, *Insider Trading and the Stock Market;* Carlton and Fischel, "The Regulation of Insider Trading."

29. Kenneth Scott, "Insider Trading: Rule 10b–5, Disclosure and Corporate Privacy," 9 *Journal of Legal Studies* 808.

30. "Disputes Arise Over Value of Laws on Insider Trading," *The Wall Street Journal,* November 17, 1986, p. 28.

31. One area that needs more attention is the impact of insider trading on the markets (and ordinary investors) of countries that permit the practice. Proponents of insider trading are fond of pointing out that insider trading has been legal in many overseas markets for years, without the dire effects predicted by opponents of the practice. Proponents reply that these markets are not as fair or efficient as U.S. markets, or that they do not play as important a role in the allocation of capital.

32. See Frank Easterbrook, "Insider Trading as an Agency Problem." I speak here as if the interests of the firm and its shareholders are identical, even though this is sometimes not the case.

33. Manne, *Insider Trading and the Stock Market,* p. 129.

34. For a more detailed discussion of the ineffectiveness of permitting insider trading as an incentive, see Roy Schotland, "Unsafe at any Price: A Reply to Manne, *Insider Trading and the Stock Market,*" 53 *Virginia Law Review* 1425.

35. Manne is aware of the "bad news" objection, but he glosses over it by claiming that bad news is not as likely as good news to be provide large gains for insider traders. *Insider Trading and the Stock Market,* p. 102.

36. There are ways to avoid many of these objections. For example, Manne has suggested "isolating" non-contributors so that they cannot trade on the information produced by others. Companies could also forbid trading on "negative" information. The problem is that these piecemeal restrictions seem very costly—more costly than simply prohibiting insider trading as we do now. In addition, each restriction brings us farther and farther away from what proponents of the practice actually want: unrestricted insider trading.

37. Frank Easterbrook, "Insider Trading as an Agency Problem."
38. Ibid.
39. Penalties did not begin to become sufficient to discourage insider trading until the passage of the Insider Trading Sanctions Act in 1984. Some argue that they are still not sufficient, and that that is a good reason for abandoning the effort entirely.
40. Easterbrook, "Insider Trading as an Agency Problem."
41. See Freeman and Gilbert, *Corporate Strategy and the Search for Ethics* (Prentice-Hall, Englewood Cliffs, NJ, 1988).

Patricia H. Werhane

The Ethics of Insider Trading

Insider trading is the reverse of speculation. It is reward without risk, wealth generated—and injury done to others—by an unfair advantage in information ... [T]he core principle is clear: no one should profit from exploitation of important information not available to the public.[1]

Insider trading in the stock market is characterized as the buying or selling of shares of stock on the basis of information known only to the trader or to a few persons. In discussions of insider trading it is commonly assumed that the privileged information, if known to others, would affect their actions in the market as well, although in theory this need not be the case. The present guidelines of the Securities and Exchange Commission prohibit most forms of insider trading. Yet a number of economists and philosophers of late defend this kind of activity both as a viable and useful practice in a free market and as a practice that is not immoral. In response to these defenses I want to question the value of insider trading both from a moral and an economic point of view. I shall argue that insider trading both in its present illegal form

From Patricia H. Werhane, "The Ethics of Insider Trading," *Journal of Business Ethics*, Vol. 8: 841–845, 1989. Reprinted by permission of Kluwer Academic Publishers.

and as a legalized market mechanism violates the privacy of concerned parties, destroys competition, and undermines the efficient and proper functioning of a free market, thereby bringing into question its own raison d'etre. [i.e., reason for being.] It does so and therefore is economically inefficient for the very reason that it is immoral.

That insider trading as an illegal activity interferes with the free market is pretty obvious. It is like a game where there are a number of players each of whom represents a constituency. In this sort of game there are two sets of rules—one ostensive set and another, implicit set, functioning for some of the players. In this analogy some of the implicit rules are outlawed, yet the big players manage to keep them operative and actually often in control of the game. But not all the players know all the rules being played or at least they are ignorant of the most important ones, ones that determine the big wins and big losses. So not all the players realize what rules actually manipulate the outcome. Moreover, partly because some of the most important functioning rules are illegal, some players who do know the implicit rules and could participate do not. Thus not everyone in a position to do so plays the trading game the same way. The game, then, like the manipulated market that is the outcome, is unfair—unfair to some of the players and those they represent—unfair not only because some of the players are not privy to the most important rules, but also because these "special" rules are illegal so that they are adopted only by a few of even the privileged players.

But suppose that insider trading was decriminalized or not prohibited by SEC regulations.

Then, one might argue, insider trading would not be unfair because anyone could engage in it with impunity. Although one would be trading on privileged knowledge, others, too, could trade on *their* privileged information. The market would function more efficiently since the best-informed and those most able to gain information would be allowed to exercise their fiscal capabilities. The market itself would regulate the alleged excesses of insider trading. I use the term "alleged" excesses because according to this line of reasoning, if the market is functioning properly, whatever gains or losses are created as a result of open competition are a natural outcome of that competition. They are not excesses at all, and eventually the market will adjust the so-called unfair gains of speculators.

There are several other defenses of insider trading. First, insider information, e.g. information about a merger, acquisition, new stock issue, layoffs, etc., information known only to a few, *should* be and remain private. That information is the property of those engaged in the activity in question, and they should have the right to regulate its dissemination. Second and conversely, even under ideal circumstances it is impossible either to disseminate information to all interested parties equally and fairly, or alternately, to preserve absolute secrecy. For example, in issuing a new stock or deciding on a stock split, a number of parties in the transaction from brokers to printers learn about that information in advance just because of their participation in making this activity a reality. And there are always shareholders and other interested parties who claim they did not receive information of such an activity or did not receive it at the same time as other shareholders even when the information was disseminated to everyone at the same time. Thus it is, at best, difficult to stop insider trading or to judge whether a certain kind of knowledge is "inside" or privileged. This is not a good reason to defend insider trading as economically or morally desirable, but it illustrates the difficulties of defining and controlling the phenomenon.

Third, those who become privy to inside information, even if they take advantage of that information before it becomes public, are trading on probabilities, not on certainties, since they are trading before the activity actually takes place. They are taking a gamble, and if they are wrong the market itself will "punish" them. It is even argued that brokers who do not use inside information for their clients' advantage are cheating their clients.

Finally, and more importantly, economists like Henry Manne argue that insider trading is beneficial to outsiders. Whether it is more beneficial than its absence is a question Manne admits he cannot answer. But Manne defends insider trading because, he argues, it reduces the factor of chance in trading both for insiders and outsiders. When shares are traded on information or probabilities rather than on rumor or whim, the market reflects more accurately the actual economic status of that company or set of companies. Because of insider trading, stock prices more closely represent the worth of their company than shares not affected by insider trading. Insider trading, then, actually improves the fairness of the market, according to this argument, by reflecting in stock prices the fiscal realities of affected corporations thereby benefitting all traders of the stocks.[2]

These arguments for insider trading are persuasive. Because outsiders are allegedly not harmed from privileged information not available to them and may indeed benefit from insider trading, and because the market punishes rash speculators, insider trading cannot be criticized as exploitation. In fact, it makes the market more efficient. Strong as these arguments are, however, there is something amiss with these claims. The error, I think, rests at least in part with the faulty view of how free markets work, a view which stems from a misinterpretation that derives from a misreading of Adam Smith and specifically a misreading of Smith's notions of self-interest and the Invisible Hand.

The misinterpretation is this. It is sometimes assumed that the unregulated free market, driven by competition and self-interest, will function autonomously. The idea is that the free market works something like the law of gravity—autonomously and anonymously in what I would call a no-blooded fashion. The interrelationships created by free market activities based on self-interested competition are similar to the gravitational relationships between the planets and the sun: impersonal, automatic interactions determined by a number of factors including the distance and competitive self-interest of each of the market components. The free market functions, then, despite the selfish peculiarities of the players just as the planets circle the sun despite their best intentions to do otherwise. Given that picture of the free market, so-called insider trading, driven by self-interest but restrained by competitive forces, that is, the Invisible Hand, is merely one gravitational mechanism—a complication but not an oddity or an aberration in the market.

This is a crude and exaggerated picture of the market, but I think it accounts for talk about the market *as if* it functioned in this independent yet forceful way, and it accounts for defenses of unrestrained self-interested actions in the market place. It allows one to defend insider trading because of the positive market fall-out from this activity, and because the market allegedly will control the excesses of self-interested economic activities.

The difficulty with this analysis is not so much with the view of insider trading as a legitimate activity but rather with the picture of economic actors in a free market. Adam Smith himself, despite his 17th century Newtonian background, did not have such a mechanical view of a laissez-faire [i.e., to let do. In the present context it refers to the principle of non-interference by government in commercial enterprise.] economy. Again and again in the *Wealth of Nations* Smith extols the virtues of unrestrained competition as being to the advantage of the producer and the consumer.[3] A system of perfect liberty he argues, creates a situation where "[t]he whole of the advantages and disadvantages of the different employments of labour and stock . . . Be either perfectly equal or continually tending to equality."[4] Yet for Smith the greatest cause of inequalities of advantage is any restrictive policy or activity that deliberately gives privileges to certain kinds of businesses, trades, or professions.[5] The point is that Smith sees perfect liberty as the necessary condition for competition, but perfect competition occurs only when both parties in the exchange are on more or less on equal grounds, whether it be competition for labor, jobs, consumers, or capital. This is not to imply that Smith favors equality of outcomes. Clearly he does not. But the market is most efficient and most fair when there is competition between equally matched parties.

Moreover, Smith's thesis was that the Invisible Hand works because, and only when, people operate with restrained self-interest, self-interest restrained by reason, moral sentiments, and sympathy, in Smith's case the reason, moral sentiments and sympathies of British gentlemen. To operate otherwise, that is, with unrestrained self-interest, where that self-interest causes harm to others would "violate the laws of justice"[6] or be a "violation of fair play,"[7] according to Smith. This interferes with free competition just as government regulation would because the character of competition, and thus the direction of the Invisible Hand, depends on the manner in which actors exploit or control their own self-interests. The Invisible Hand, then, that "masterminds" the free market is not like an autonomous gravitational force. It depends on the good will, decency, self-restraint, and fair play of those parties engaging in market activities.[8] When self-interests get out of hand, Smith contends, they must be regulated by laws of justice.[9]

Similarly, the current market, albeit not Smith's ideal of laissez-faire, is affected by how people operate in the market place. It does not operate autonomously. Unrestrained activities of insider traders affect competition differently than Smithian exchanges which are more or less equal exchanges between self-interested but restrained parties. The term "insider trading" implies that some traders know more than others, that information affects their decision-making and would similarly affect the trading behavior of others should they become privy to that information. Because of this, the resulting market is different than one unaffected by insider trading. This, in itself, is not a good reason to question insider trading. Henry Manne, for example, recognizes the role of insider trading in influencing the market and finds that, on balance, this is beneficial.

Insider trading, however, is not merely a complication in the free market mechanism.

Insider trading, whether it is legal or illegal, affects negatively the ideal of laissez-faire of *any* market, because it thwarts the very basis of the market: competition, just as "insider" rules affect the fairness of the trader even if that activity is not illegal and even if one could, in theory, obtain inside information oneself. This is because the same information, or equal information, is not available to everyone. So competition, which depends on the availability of equal advantage by all parties is precluded. Insider trading allows the insider to indulge in greed (even though she may not) and that, by eschewing stock prices, works against the very kind of market in which insider trading might be allowed to function.

If it is true, as Manne argues, that insider trading produces a more efficient stock market because stock prices as a result of insider trading better reflect the underlying economic conditions of those companies involved in the trade, he would also have to argue that competition does not always produce the best results in the marketplace. Conversely, if competition creates the most efficient market, insider trading cannot, because competition is "regulated" by insiders. While it is not clear whether outsiders benefit more from insider trading than without that activity, equal access to information would allow (although not determine) every trader to compete from an equal advantage. Thus pure competition, a supposed goal of the free market and an aim of most persons who defend insider trading, is more nearly obtained without insider trading.

Insider trading has other ethical problems. Insider trading does not protect the privacy of information it is supposed to protect. To illustrate, let us consider a case of a friendly merger between Company X and Company Y. Suppose this merger is in the planning stages and is not to be made public even to the shareholders for a number of months. There may be good or bad reasons for this secrecy, e.g., labor problems, price of shares of acquired company, management changes, unfriendly raiders, competition in certain markets, etc. By law, management and others privy to knowledge about the possible merger cannot trade shares of either company during the negotiating period. On the other hand, if that information is "leaked" to a trader (or if she finds out by some other means), then information that might affect the merger is now in the hands of persons not part of the negotiation. The alleged privacy of information, privacy supposedly protected by insider traders, is now in the hands of not disinterested parties. While they may keep this information a secret, they had no right to it in the first place. Moreover, their possession of the information has three possible negative effects.

First, they or their clients in fact may be interested parties to the merger, e.g., labor union leaders, stockholders in competing companies, etc., the very persons for whom the information makes a difference and therefore are the objects of Company X and Y's secrecy. Second, insider trading on privileged information gives unfair advantages to these traders. Even if outsiders benefit from insider trading, they are less likely to benefit as much nor as soon as insider traders for the very reason of their lack of proximity to the activity. Insider traders can use information to their advantage in the market, an advantage neither the management of X or Y nor other traders can enjoy. Even if the use of such information in the market makes the market more efficient, this is unfair competition since those without this information will not gain as much as those who have such knowledge. Even if insider trading does contribute to market stabilization based on information, nevertheless, one has also to justify the fact that insider traders profit more on their knowledge than outsiders, when their information becomes an actuality simply by being "first" in the trading of the stock. Do insider traders deserve this added profit because their trading creates a more propitious market share knowledge for outsiders? That is a difficult position to defend, because allowing insider trading also allows for the very Boeskyian greed that is damaging in any market.

Third, while trading X and Y on inside information may bring their share prices to the value most closely reflecting their real price-earnings ratio, this is not always the case. Such trading may reflect undue optimism or pessimism about the possible outcome of the merger, an event that has not yet occurred. So the prices of X and

Y may be overvalued or undervalued on the basis of a probability, or, because insider traders seldom have all the facts, on guesswork. In these cases insider trading deliberately creates more risk in the market since the stock prices or X or Y are manipulated for not altogether solid reasons. So market efficiency, the end which allegedly justifies insider trading is not guaranteed.

What Henry Manne's defenses of insider trading do show is what Adam Smith well knew, that the market is neither independent nor self-regulatory. What traders do in the market and how they behave affects the direction and kind of restraint the market will exert on other traders. The character of the market is a product of those who operate within it, as Manne has demonstrated in his defense of insider trading. Restrained self-interest creates an approximation of a self-regulatory market, because it is that that allows self-interested individuals and companies to function as competitively as pos-

sible. In the long run the market will operate more efficiently too, because it precludes aberrations such as those exhibited by Ivan Boesky's and David Levine's behavior, behavior that created market conditions favorable to no one except themselves and their clients.

Notes

1. George Will, "Keep Your Eye on Guiliani," *Newsweek*, March 2, 1987, p. 84.
2. See Henry Manne, *Insider Trading and the Stock Market* (The Free Press, New York, 1966), especially Chapters X and XI.
3. Adam Smith, *The Wealth of Nations*, ed. R. A. Campbell and A. S. Skinner (Oxford University Press, Oxford, 1976), I.x.c, II.v.8–12.
4. *Wealth of Nations*, I.x.a.1.
5. *Wealth of Nations*, I.x.c.
6. *Wealth of Nations*, IV.ix.51.
7. Adam Smith, *The Theory of Moral Sentiments*, ed.D. D. Raphael and A. L. Macfie (Oxford University Press, Oxford, 1976), II.ii.2.1.
8. See Andrew Skinner, *A System of Social Science* (Clarendon Press, Oxford, 1979), especially pp. 237ff.
9. See, for example, *The Wealth of Nations*, II.ii.94, IV, v.16.

Richard L. Lippke

Justice and Insider Trading

Long illegal in the United States, insider trading in securities markets is increasingly being legally proscribed in European and Asian countries. France led the way in prohibiting insider trading, outlawing it in 1970, but the United Kingdom, Italy, Sweden, Norway, Spain, Greece, and others have since followed suit.[1] Pressure

From Richard L. Lippke, "Justice and Insider Trading," *Journal of Applied Philosophy*, Vol. 10, No. 2, 1993. Reprinted by permission of Society for Applied Philosophy, 1993, Blackwell Publishers, 108 Cowley Road, Oxford, OX4 IJF, UK and 3 Cambridge Center, Cambridge, MA 02142, USA.

from the European Community has recently forced Germany to enact laws against such trading, and even Japan and Hong Kong have taken steps to limit its occurrence in their formerly wide-open securities markets.[2]

Meanwhile, the morality of insider trading remains a hotly contested topic in a variety of scholarly journals. Many scholars enthusiastically defend it, and some, while not wholeheartedly defending it, seek to debunk the many arguments against it. The focus of this paper will be on the fairness arguments against insider trading. The underlying idea behind these arguments is that to permit insider trading would be to set up stock market trading rules that are unfair to non-insiders, individuals who do not possess or have access to the sorts of material, non-public information that insiders do. These arguments have been widely discussed. I will lay bare the largely unstated assumptions about fairness behind these discussions and then attempt to show that these assumptions yield, at best, a truncated conception of justice. At worst, these assumptions legitimise, without argument, the political and economic *status quo* in countries with large inequalities. I argue that a defensible treatment of the fairness of insider trading requires both a complete conception of justice and its thoughtful application to existing political and economic institutions.

The discussion is in three main sections. In the first, I summarise the fairness debate about insider trading as that debate has been presented in the recent scholarly literature. In the second section, I reveal the assumptions about fairness implicit in that debate and argue that these assumptions cannot be defended independently of a larger conception of justice. In the third section, I briefly summarise and then use an egalitarian conception of justice to analyse insider trading. By doing so, I hope to illustrate how a more systematic approach to the analysis of insider trading, one that invokes a complete theory of justice, transforms the debate about the fairness of insider trading. I should add that the conception I employ is one that most commentators would find unappealing. However, one of the points I wish to make is that their discussions do little more than beg the question against such a conception.

Before proceeding further, let me clarify two matters. First, the insiders with which I will most concern myself throughout the paper are corporate managers. They are the individuals most likely to have inside information, and as such, their actions are the principal focus of most discussions of the fairness of insider trading. I won't say much about the other individuals who might come to possess inside information, referred to in the literature as tippees and misappropriators.[3] Second, I will use the term "non-insiders" to refer to those individuals who do not possess any inside information relevant to a particular stock purchase or sale. Non-insiders might be insiders with regard to some stock transactions. And, of course, non-insiders might be and often are corporate employees.

I

As long as insider trading is legally proscribed, there is a fairly simple argument that shows how

its existence is unfair to non-insiders.[4] Insiders who trade on material, non-public information, rather than disclosing the information or abstaining from trading as the rules typically prescribe, will be doing little more than cheating. They will be acting in a manner that violates the social expectations fostered by the rules. It is not convincing to argue, as some do, that since non-insiders " know" insider trading takes place, they realise that the official (legal) rules are not the actual rules; therefore their participation in the investing game must condone insider actions. First, it is likely that not all non-insiders know that insider trading takes place or how frequently it occurs. Second, the fact that insider trading is legally prohibited and socially disapproved surely muddies the waters for those who maintain that non-insiders "know" it occurs. At best, non-insiders may be confused about how insiders actually behave. At worst, they may assume that most insiders will abstain from trading or disclose material information.

The more interesting question is whether, morally speaking, insider trading should be legally proscribed. In particular, is there something unfair about such trading such that it ought to be a legitimate target of state action? Now the debate begins in earnest.

The most plausible case to be made that there is something unfair about insider trading emphasis the notion of "equal access to information.[5] It seems a mistake to hold that all parties to a market transaction must have equal information. To require this would be, in effect, to deprive persons of informational advantages they may have acquired through diligent effort. What seems bothersome about insider trading is that non-insiders lack *access* to the information on which insiders are trading. The informational advantage that insiders have is not "erodable" by the diligence or effort of non-insiders. No matter how carefully or exhaustively non-insiders study the available public information about firms in which they invest, they cannot really compete against those insiders who have access to material non-public information.[6]

A typical scenario described by opponents of insider trading is as follows: insiders known of an impending takeover bid for another firm by their firm. In anticipation of the rise in stock prices that usually results from such bids, they purchase shares of the target firm's stock. Often, such insider trading activity will send the target firm's stock price up slightly. Non-insiders who hold stock in the target firm, believing there is no plausible reason for the rise in the share price, may decide to cash in by selling their stock. Though the non-insiders were able to sell their stock at a higher price than they would have received had the insiders not been active, opponents of insider trading argue that the non-insiders lose out on the further gains that typically result once a takeover bid is publicly announced. Non-insiders, because they lacked access to the information about the takeover bid prior to the public announcement, lose out on the opportunity to receive the additional gain.[7] Instead, the gain goes to insiders and this, opponents argue, is unfair to the non-insider.

Some commentators argue that insider trading is not likely to result in such losses (or unrealised gains) for non-insiders.[8] Yet none of these arguments seems to address the equal access objection head on. It seems likely that there will be some occasions where non-insiders do sell in response to a price rise caused by insider trading activity. The fact that this may not necessarily happen or happen often seems beside the point. If insider trading is legally permitted, non-insiders can reasonably complain that the rules are set up in ways that are unjustifiably advantageous to insiders and so likely to the disadvantage of non-insiders. The possibility that the informational advantages insiders have and might use work out to the advantage of non-insiders does not explain why insiders should be allowed to have and use those advantages.[9]

Frank Easterbrook and Jennifer Moore contend that non-insiders really cannot justifiably complain—that they do (or did) not have equal access to this information.[10] Non-insiders could have made career choices to become corporate executives, choices that would have given them access to inside information. Such information is, on this view, one of the perquisites of being a corporate insider. Moore draws an analogy. Plumbers have access to certain kinds of information that non-plumbers do not have (or to

which they have more difficult access). Yet, no one complains when plumbers use their informational advantages to their own benefit by charging non-plumbers for their services. Similarly, non-insiders should not complain when insiders use informational advantages to their benefit. Easterbrook maintains that the different costs of access to information are simply a function of the division of labour: "A manager (or a physician) always knows more than a shareholder (or patient) in some respects, but unless there is something unethical about the division of labour, the difference is not unfair."[11]

This is a dubious argument for a number of reasons. Critics of insider trading who rely on the equal access argument clearly have in mind a different point of equal access than the one proffered by Moore and Easterbrook. The critics have in mind equal access via the typical ways in which corporations make information about themselves matters of public record—press releases, trade journals, reports to shareholders, etc. They might argue that there is a great deal of difference between saying that non-insiders should have researched their investment decisions more carefully and saying that non-insiders should have made different career choices.

Still, Easterbrook and Moore may simply be challenging the critics' conception of equal access and offering a substitute. However, there are problems with this substitute. What the non-insiders need is not simply the sort of knowledge that comes with the career choice of becoming a corporate manager. After all, some non-insiders (with respect to particular trades) might indeed be corporate managers and so they presumably have that kind of knowledge. Non-insiders need the specific information insiders have enabling them to deal on the stock market with an advantage over others. The claim that non-insiders cannot reasonably complain about the fairness of particular transactions because they too "could" have chosen to become corporate managers is not to the point. It is not insiders' career skills that non-insiders need but the insiders' information about particular business events.[12]

Also, the informational advantages insiders have over non-insiders have no clear analogue in the case of plumbers and non-plumbers. What non-plumbers pay plumbers for is plumbers' knowledge about plumbing. What shareholders pay managers for is managers' knowledge about managing. But plumbers do not seem to have an additional way of gaining an advantage over non-plumbers as do insiders in relation to non-insiders if insider trading is permitted. Insiders are already being compensated for their labour by the shareholders. Insider trading would give them something extra. If that something extra is "taken" without the shareholders' knowledge and consent, then it seems that the shareholders would have two different grounds for complaint. They could complain about their lack of equal access to information, or they could complain that the managers who take advantage of them via insider trades are failing to live up to their fiduciary responsibilities, which are to promote shareholder interests.

Still, both grounds for complaint can be undermined *if* insider trading is authorised by the shareholders. In effect, the shareholders would give their consent to an arrangement whereby corporate managers would be allowed, under certain conditions, to take advantage of their superior access to information.[13] Remember, we are no longer assuming that insider trading is illegal. Instead, we are trying to determine what set of rules regarding insider trading would be fair to all interested parties. Advocates of insider trading contend that it should be up to the shareholders to decide whether insider trading is to be permitted. After all, the information that is being traded on is their property. They should be allowed to determine how this information will best be put to use.

This leads to the question of why the shareholders would ever agree to permit managers to take advantage of the information to which they are privy, especially when the resultant trades might lead to losses (or failures to gain) by shareholders. Also, why would potential investors in a company purchase shares if they knew that the company permitted insider trading? Wouldn't investors be inclined to steer clear of such firms?

The boldest response to these questions is provided by Henry Manne and his followers.[14] Manne argues that if firms allowed insider trad-ing as part of the management compensation package, this would enable them to attract managers who are likely to be more creative, productive, risk-takers. Allowing managers to trade on inside information would provide them the incentive to undertake riskier ventures, try out innovative production techniques, develop new products or services—in general, to engage in those activities that would create more value, in the long run, for the shareholders. Insider trading would allow these managers to reap the benefits of the new information they create and firms would save money by having to pay managers less base compensation. Of course, shareholders would not know precisely when insiders of their own firm were trading based on material non-public information, so shareholders might occasionally lose out in trades where insiders are involved. However, this is something the shareholders might consent to in the hopes of finding managers who will increase the long-term value of their shares.[15]

Consistent with Manne's argument, others have suggested that as long as a firm's rules about insider trading are a matter of public record, individuals who invest in such firms will have voluntarily assumed the risk of trading in situations where insiders may be operating. Indeed, some argue that investors will react to this prospect by altering their own behavior. They may try to compensate for the possibility of future losses to insiders by paying less for stocks initially.[16] Or, when they see a stock's price rising, anticipating that insiders may know something, they may demand a higher price to induce them to sell. Moreover, most investors seek to reduce their risks by diversifying their stock portfolios. As Kenneth Scott points out, such investors will be less interested in the details of the buying and selling of particular stocks than in the overall performance of their portfolios.[17]

This general line of argument is both limited in its scope and has been subjected to withering criticism by various commentators. Its scope is limited because it seems to justify insider trading only by those employees who have a role in creating the information. It would not justify such trading by tippees or misappropriators. Also, some have suggested that since insiders can profitably trade on negative information, the shareholders would have to be careful to limit any incentives for managers to create such information.[18] Criticisms of the argument have focused on whether there are not other, more effective ways shareholders might use to provide incentives to managers to create value; on whether there are ways to ensure that managers do not derive "too much" compensation from insider trading; and on whether managers themselves are likely to find the prospect of cashing in on inside information attractive enough to agree to compensation packages that permit such trading.[19]

As Easterbrook and Shaw both note, it is no easy task to weigh all of the pros and cons that have been unearthed by the various commentators.[20] In large part, this is due to the debate turning on the answers to a variety of empirical questions about the effects of firms permitting insider trading versus the effects of their not doing so—questions about which we have little evidence to go on. In any case, there seems a great deal to be said at this point for allowing shareholders to experiment with permitting insider trading if that is what they so desire. After all, it is their property, and the costs and benefits to third parties seem pretty speculative at this point. Investors who wish to steer clear of firms that permit forms of insider trading will presumably be able to do so, at least as long as corporate policies on the subject are made clear. In short, the debate about whether insider trading is fair seems to have been transformed into one about what it is reasonable for shareholders and their hired managers to negotiate amongst themselves.

II

In the preceding section, I explicated the logic of the fairness debate about insider trading as that debate has been recently carried on by scholars in various fields. In this section, I will highlight the assumptions about fairness that seem implicit in that debate and show how they are, if not problematic, at least controversial.

The place to begin is by noting that none of the commentators referred to in the previous section raises any questions about the fairness of the distribution of wealth, income, opportunities, and power that is the broader social context for decisions about what the rules regarding insider trading will be. Their discussions are simply divorced from the larger and more difficult questions that have been raised by moral and political theorists about the nature of social justice. They are also divorced from the implications the various theories offered have for an analysis of existing political and economic institutions. The existing distribution of property and other goods is taken as given and so, implicitly at least, legitimised.

One point at which this assumption of the legitimacy of the *status quo* is most clearly revealed is in Moore and Easterbrook's contention that non-insiders do have access to inside information at the point when they make their career choices. As we saw, this is a poor argument as a response to the equal access objection to insider trading. It is also an argument that seems rife with assumptions about the justice of the political and economic system in which people in countries like the United States live. I say "seems rife" because it is not altogether clear what Moore or Easterbrook are assuming. Are they assuming, for instance, that no questions of fairness can be raised about the existing division of labour which distributes income, wealth, opportunities, and prestige in certain ways? Or, are they assuming that all peoples' career paths are, in a meaningful sense, matters of choice, such that coal miners could just as easily have "chosen" to be lawyers or investment bankers? Are they assuming that everyone in society has equal access to insider information, at least at the point at which they "choose" their careers?

Again, it is not apparent which, if any, of these assumptions Moore or Easterbrook are making, though their willingness to defend insider trading by invoking the division of labour and the career choices with which it presents individuals certainly suggests that they do not see anything problematic about either notion. If so, their assumptions are obviously at odds with the views of welfare liberals and radical egalitarians about the justice of institutions that tolerate significant disparities in peoples' income, wealth, and life-prospects. Moore and Easterbrook's underlying assumptions about justice or fairness seem quite controversial given the current state of discussion of these matters by moral and political theorists.

However, since their argument is of scant value in the debate about insider trading, perhaps we should turn our attention to the argument that seems to command more respect. That argument holds that as long as insider trading is consented to by the shareholders, there is nothing unfair about the unequal access to information had by insiders. It might seem that such a notion is not in the least controversial, that regardless of one's theory of justice, one will endorse the idea that these sorts of transactions between people are paradigms of fairness. What could be more fair than an informed exchange between parties none of whom is in any way forced to participate in the exchange or accept terms they find unreasonable? Doesn't this show that we can separate the debate about insider trading from the larger, more contentious debates about social justice?

Not really. I suspect that the notion of "voluntary informed consent" will play some important role in almost any plausible theory of justice. However, part of what distinguishes theories of justice is that they say very different things about the conditions that must be satisfied in a voluntary exchange is to be regarded as fully fair. Judgments about the fairness of particular transactions between or among persons are, I would argue, always defeasible in light of judgments about the extent to which the relevant conditions are satisfied. For moderate egalitarians like John Rawls, the focus will be on the extent to which the basic structure of the society in question satisfies his two principles of justice, especially the Difference Principle.[21] To the extent that the two principles are not satisfied, judgments about the fairness of particular transactions between or among persons are problematic. Moderate egalitarians like Rawls will emphasise that exchanges between parties vastly unequal in bargaining power (owing to wealth or social status) are likely to be fair in only a qualified sense even if they involve no overt deception or force.

In contrast, for libertarians, the conditions that must be satisfied if a voluntary informed exchange between persons is to be deemed just are less structural and more historical in character.[22] To the extent that a particular distribution of property holdings came about in ways that violate libertarian principles of property acquisition and transfer, reference to the fairness of voluntary informed exchanges among individuals whose holdings depend on that distribution is problematic. For instance, suppose that recently released slaves, individuals who have been forcibly deprived of the fruits of their labour, reach wage-labour agreements with their comparatively wealthy former owners, the terms of which greatly favour the former owners. Even libertarians might acknowledge that because of the historical conditions leading up to them, these wage-labour agreements are not paradigms of fairness.

Now, if it is true that judgments about the fairness of voluntary informed exchanges amongst persons cannot meaningfully be separated from theory-dependent judgments about the extent to which certain other conditions are satisfied, what implications does this have for the debate about the fairness of insider trading? It is not that those who have written about insider trading all seem to favour one larger theory of justice over another, or that they do so without really arguing for their preferred theory. It is rather that none of them appears to be operating with any such theory at all—or if they are, it is one that rather simply implies that the social and economic *status quo* in countries like the United States is unproblematically just. I know of no plausible theory that implies this. My hunch is that the commentators wish to avoid delving into the difficulties that discussions of these larger theories of justice inevitably raise. Yet, by avoiding these difficulties, they deprive themselves of the sort of theoretical framework which can alone make an analysis and evaluation of insider trading maximally well-grounded and coherent.[23]

In the next section, I will show how an analysis of insider trading grounded in a larger theory of justice might look. I hope this will further develop and illuminate the points I have made in this section.

III

Egalitarian theories of justice are a diverse lot, ranging from the moderate types like that of Rawls to the more radical types like that of Kai Nielsen.[24] All, however, share certain features, the most important of which for our purposes I will briefly summarise.

First, egalitarian theories generally hold that inequalities in things like income, wealth, power, opportunities, the social conditions for self-respect, etc., ought to be limited. Egalitarians are concerned that people's life-prospects should not differ too significantly along these dimensions affected by humanly alterable institutions and practices. Inequalities can be constrained by the designing of political and economic institutions that maintain certain structural features in society. For instance, while egalitarians may believe competitive markets can play important roles in a just society, they are reluctant to let markets wholly determine the distribution of goods like income and opportunities. Hence, they will favour state involvement in ensuring for all persons not only traditional civil liberties but also goods like subsistence, education and medical care. Or, to take another example, egalitarians are likely to be concerned about the ways in which social and economic power can be exercised to the detriment of some peoples' interests. Thus, they are likely to favour rather strict limits on the extent to which wealth can be transferred between generations and on the extent to which or economic power is able to influence democratic political decisions. Also, some egalitarians favour extending democratic decision-making structures into the economic sphere. This would entail the institutionalisation of schemes of worker participation, if not control.

Obviously, the preceding depiction of egalitarianism rather brutally oversimplifies it and leaves a great deal of the conception unexplained and undefended. However, I think it will serve to introduce an egalitarian analysis of insider trading.

First, egalitarians would attempt to gauge the extent to which the basic institutional structures of societies accord with their favoured principles of justice. Obviously, different egalitarians will employ slightly different principles, and even among egalitarians who are in rough agreement about principles of justice, there will be room for disagreement about what these principles imply about the justice of actual societies. In any case, I think it is fair to say that most egalitarians would be greatly dismayed by the distribution of income, wealth, opportunities, and power in many advanced capitalist societies.[25]

Consider the United States, for instance. The existence of significant segments of the population that cannot satisfy their basic needs for subsistence and health care; of large disparities in access to quality education and meaningful work; the ability of those with wealth and economic power to exercise inordinate political and cultural power; and the evidence that the gap between rich and poor is growing, with many in the middle class slipping into poverty, would, for egalitarians, be among the most disturbing features of U.S. society.[26]

Second, egalitarians might note that both corporate insiders and shareholders are likely to be among the most advantaged members of advanced capitalist societies. Corporate executives, those most likely to be in a position to have access to inside information, are handsomely paid and enjoy other perquisites such as prestigious work, power over others, and access to political influence. Those who invest in stocks, corporate executives among them, are also likely to be quite well off. Recent studies of wealth in the US, for instance, suggest that approximately 80% of families own no stocks.[27] These studies also suggest that about 95% of all stocks are owned by families with incomes of more than $96,000 per year—that is, by about 3% of all families. Thus, those who are in the top income-bracket are also those able to invest in stocks and accumulate even more wealth.

Egalitarians will note the many attendant effects of this concentration of stock ownership, and with it, legal control of corporations. Though actual control over the day-to-day operations of corporations is typically ceded to hired managers, these managers will generally seek to advance the shareholders' interests. Historically, managements' attempts to do this have resulted in "costs" being passed onto other members of society. For instance, corporations have often sought to evade or weaken environmental regulations, with the result that the costs of pollution, hazardous wastes, and the depletion of scarce resources fall on those with less economic power and influence (including members of future generations). Or, to take another example, corporations have often resisted attempts to provide employees with clearer and safer working environments because doing so would increase costs of production. The result, however, is that employees then bear greater costs owing to the resulting injuries and illnesses.

Supporters of the current scheme of property rights might respond by saying that corporations are answerable to a much broader constituency than the shareholders. First, they must conform to laws and regulations that are, directly or indirectly, democratically enacted. These laws and regulations constrain corporate decision-making in ways that make it more conducive to the interests of all in society. Second, corporations are answerable to the public in other ways. They must produce goods and services that the public is willing to buy—that is, they must be responsive to consumer "votes." Also, corporations are vulnerable to consumer boycotts if their actions are perceived by many as socially irresponsible. The fact that such boycotts are rare suggests that corporations are generally perceived as acting in the interests of all members of society. Finally, supporters of the *status quo* will argue that the stock market performs an invaluable service to society, generating capital funds for businesses that provide jobs and goods and services for many people.

Let me indicate, briefly, what I believe would be the egalitarian response to this line of argument. First, they would repeat their concerns about the extent to which wealth and economic power influence democratic decision-making in advanced capitalist societies. This influence significantly dilutes the actual democratic control that ordinary citizens have over large corporations, arguably to the detriment of those citizens. Second, they will argue that it is naive to think that corporations simply respond to consumer "votes." Instead, they actively seek to shape consumer attitudes, preferences, and val-

ues through massive persuasive advertising. It is at least an open question whether the resulting consumer "votes" reflect consumers' autonomous beliefs and preferences (those they would have if the conditions for critical reflection on them were not undermined by massive persuasive advertising) or whether they reflect the economic interests of large corporations. Also, corporations are very active in their efforts to shape public perceptions about their character and conduct as economic enterprises. It is no easy matter for the average consumer to get accurate information about the actual conduct of large corporations, even assuming that the average consumer had the time or inclination to engage in the monitoring of corporate conduct. Last, while the current scheme of stock ownership does generate investment funds for economic enterprises, the point of the egalitarian critique of that scheme is to raise the question whether there might be a more desirable alternative scheme. In particular, might there be a scheme that does not rest on and so reflect the influence of considerable inequality, one that would generate investment funds in ways that better advance the interests of *all* members of society?

In the light of the preceding discussion, it might be suggested that egalitarians would view the debate over insider trading as one of little significance—that the "negotiations" between management and shareholders that proponents of insider trading favour are little more than ways for unjustly advantaged members of society to determine how best to divide, or perhaps increase, the spoils of their advantages.

However, it seems to me that egalitarians could offer more than this to the insider trading debate. They could point out that most who have written about insider trading simply presuppose that those most directly affected by the rules about insider trading are managers and shareholders. Occasionally, in discussions of insider trading, reference is made to its broader effects on the efficiency of the market. But typically, the focus of most analyses is on the motivations, interests, expectations, and behaviour of managers and shareholders. Yet this leaves out of the reckoning how other' interests are potentially affected by whatever agreements are reached by managers and shareholders. In particular, employees of corporations, especially those not in the top managerial classes, may be affected by those agreements.

For instance, suppose that the shareholders are convinced by Manne's arguments that insider trading will offer valuable incentives to managers to be less risk-averse and so they agree to allow managers to take advantage of the information they "create" through their activities by engaging in insider trading. There are risks here, to be sure, for the shareholders, for their less risk-averse managers may undertake ventures that ultimately cost the shareholders money. Still, the shareholders, at least, take this chance with their eyes open. But what of the other employees of the corporation who lose their jobs or have their wages and benefits cut when the inevitable belt-tightening occurs as a result of failed ventures? Or, to take another possible scenario, what of the employees who lose their jobs or have them downgraded when top management decides to "create value" by taking over another company only then to cut the target's labour costs by eliminating mid-level management positions? These examples make clear that what top managers and shareholders negotiate with regard to insider trading can affect other members of the organisation, not to mention members of the surrounding communities. Less risk-averse managers may be a boon to the shareholders, but not necessarily to other employees or members of society.

Perhaps the interests of other employees are ignored in the debate over insider trading because analysts simply assume that another, independent set of negotiations takes place between corporations and their non-executive employees. Corporations that permit insider trading by their top-level managers could make this clear to other prospective employees, and the latter could be understood to give their consent to the risks involved by agreeing to work for the corporation. Or perhaps most analysts are simply assuming that whatever the negative effects on employees due to the incentives created by insider trading, they are, in principle, no different from the ones that might occur because of other ways of compensating top-level managers. All compensation schemes

for top-level managers may contain incentives that lead to decisions that adversely affect certain other employees. What is the difference, it might be asked, between top-level decisions to close plants based on the usual profit-considerations and decisions to lay off employees due to risky ventures (spurred by the lure of insider trading profits) gone sour?

Neither assumption is likely to be seen as defensible from an egalitarian perspective. Egalitarians will regard the claim that employees "consent" to whatever rules corporations have about insider trading (and so to the decisions that may adversely affect them resulting from those rules) as insensitive to the lack of bargaining power most employees find themselves with in relation to large corporations. The inability of prospective employees to do anything but simply accept what the shareholders and managers have negotiated will be seen as especially severe where the alternatives to gainful employment are few and unattractive. Most workers are not as mobile as shareholders who can easily take their investments elsewhere if they do not like the rules regarding insider trading that corporations adopt. Also, if many corporations decide to permit insider trading, the options open to many workers will be greatly limited.

Moreover, it seems that most analysts are simply assuming that employees are to have no say in whether the businesses for which they work permit insider trading. The claim that the possible negative effects of corporate policies permitting insider trading are no different from other policies designed to keep businesses operating efficiently, and at a profit, rests on this assumption. The traditional powers and prerogatives that go with the ownership of property in many advanced capitalist societies are thereby simply reaffirmed. Yet many egalitarians regard the current distribution of power in the workplace as deeply suspect morally because it fails to affirm the autonomy of workers and results in business decisions that fail to advance impartially the interests of all affected. To assume the legitimacy of this distribution without argument is simply question-begging.[28]

It may seem that discussion in the preceding section strays quite a way from the simpler question about the fairness of insider trading with which we began this paper. However, the point I have attempted to make throughout this paper, illustrated in the preceding section, is precisely that the simpler question is too simple. It presupposes that we can intelligently discuss what the rules for insider trading should be independent of a discussion of the broader principles of justice that should be adopted and the extent to which existing institutions realise those principles. If my argument is correct, it points the discussion away from the simple question about the fairness of insider trading to the more complex and contested questions discussed by theorists of social justice. Current analyses of the fairness of insider trading simply beg all of these questions, and to that extent are philosophically facile.

Notes

I am grateful to Sharon O'Hare for many helpful comments on an earlier draft of this paper.

1. Pierre Lemieux, "Exporting the Insider Trading Scandal," *The Wall Street Journal*, October 13, 1992.
2. For developments in Germany, see "Behind the Times," *The Economist*, July 13, 1991, p. 86; for developments in Japan, see "Over to the Men in Uniform," *The Economist*, May 19, 1990, pp. 91–2; for developments in Hong Kong, see Michael Taylor, "Lifting the Veil," *Far Eastern Economic Review*, November 28, 1991, pp. 63–4.
3. Tippees are individuals who are typically not corporate employees but who are given inside information by corporate employees. Misappropriators are individuals who are typically not corporate managers but who come across inside information (e.g. financial printers temporarily employed by corporations).
4. For a useful summary of the legal status of insider trading in the United States, see Bill Shaw, "Shareholder Authorized Inside Trading: A Legal and Moral Analysis," *Journal of Business Ethics*, Vol. 9 (1990): 913–928.
5. Victor Brudney was one of the first to articulate the equal access argument. See his "Insiders, Outsiders, and Informational Advantages Under the Federal Securities Laws," *Harvard Law Review*, Vol. 93 (1979): 322–376.
6. Also, Patricia Werhane argues that if we value competition on the assumption that it will lead to the most socially beneficial results, then we should favour those rules which promote more vigorous competition. If we allow insiders to trade on their informational edge, competition will be systematically diminished because non-insiders will predictably lose out to insiders. See her "The Ethics of Insider Trading," *Journal of Business Ethics*, Vol. 8 (1989): 841–845.
7. Cf. Richard DeGeorge, "Ethics and the Financial Community," in Oliver Williams, Frank Reilly, and John Houck, *Ethics and the Investment Industry* (Savage, MD: Rowman and Littlefield, 1989), p. 203.

8. For instance, Jennifer Moore argues that insider trading can sometimes actually benefit non-insiders by enabling them to avoid losses, and so is not systematically harmful to non-insiders. See her "What is Really Unethical About Insider Trading?" *Journal of Business Ethics*, Vol. 9 (1990): 171–182. For arguments that insider trading is not likely to harm non-insiders, see Deryl W. Martin and Jeffrey H. Peterson, "Insider Trading Revisited," *Journal of Business Ethics*, Vol. 10 (1991): 57–61.
9. Bill Shaw points out that the current rules with regard to insider trading already give insiders an edge in relation to non-insiders. If nothing else, insiders with material, non-public information know when not to trade, and the disclose-or-abstain rule permits this. See his "Shareholder Authorized Inside Trading: A Legal and Moral Analysis," p. 916. Still, allowing insiders to trade on such information might tilt things even more in their favour, so the equal access argument could be modified to say that insiders should not be given any more advantages than they already have.
10. Frank H. Easterbrook, "Insider Trading, Secret Agents, Evidentiary Privileges, and the Production of Information," *Supreme Court Review* (1981): 309–365, especially pp. 323–330. Moore, "What Is Unethical About Insider Trading?" pp. 172–4.
11. Easterbrook, "Insider Trading, Secret Agents, Evidentiary Privileges, and the Production of Information," p. 330.
12. Indeed, the reason why tippees, free riders, and misappropriators can make use of inside information to their advantage is precisely that its usefulness has little to do with having made the career choice to become a corporate manager. Such information is thoroughly "detachable" from the division of labour.
13. For the most explicit presentation of the shareholder authorisation argument, see Shaw, "Shareholder Authorized Inside Trading: A Legal and Moral Analysis," pp. 920–1.
14. Henry G. Manne, *Insider Trading and the Stock Market* (New York: The Free Press, 1966); see also Dennis W. Carlton and Daniel R. Fischel, "The Regulation of Insider Trading," *Stanford Law Review*, Vol. 35 (May 1983): 857–895.
15. In response to Werhane's argument that insider trading undermines competition (*supra* note 6), Manne might argue that permitting it may reduce competitiveness in one area but heighten it in others. The market for corporate managers will heat up as firms that permit insider trading compete for those individuals who will take more risks and be more innovative. Also, within firms, allowing managers to profit from insider trading may spur them to try to outdo one another so that they can trade on any information "created."
16. See Kenneth E. Scott, "Insider Trading: Rule 10b–5, Disclosure, and Corporate Privacy," *The Journal of Legal Studies*, Vol. 9 (1980): 801–818.
17. Ibid., p. 809.

18. Negative information might include such things as news of an impending major lawsuit against the corporation, news of poor earnings, or news of a product failure.

19. There is also considerable speculation about the effects of insider trading on the efficiency of the stock market. However, the concerns with efficiency is different from the concern with fairness.

20. Easterbrook, "Insider Trading, Secret Agents, Evidentiary Privileges, and the Production of Information," p. 338; see also his "Insider Trading as an Agency Problem," in John W. Pratt and Richard J. Zeckhauser, *Principals and Agents: The Structure of Business* (Boston: Harvard Business School Press, 1985): 81–100; Shaw, "Shareholder Authorized Inside Trading: A Legal and Moral Analysis," pp. 921–2.

21. John Rawls, *A Theory of Justice* (Cambridge, MA: Harvard University Press, 1971). See also his essay "The Basic Structure As Subject," in Alvin I. Goldman and Jaegwon Kim, *Values and Morals* (Boston: D. Reidel, 1978): 47–71.

22. Cf. Robert Nozick, *Anarchy, State, and Utopia* (New York: Basic Books, 1974).

23. For more on the tendency of those who write about business ethics to avoid the problems raised by competing theories of justice, see my "A Critique of Business Ethics," *Business Ethics Quarterly," Vol. 1 (October 1991): 367–384.

24. Rawls, *A Theory of Justice;* Kai Nielsen, *Equality and Liberty: A Defense of Radical Egalitarianism* (Totowa, NJ: Rowman and Allanheld, 1984).

25. Of course, advanced capitalist societies differ from one another in some of their structural features. Any egalitarian analysis will have to take these differences into account in assessing the impact of various insider trading rules.

26. On the last point, in particular, see Denny Braun, *The Rich Get Richer* (Chicago: Nelson-Hall Publishers, 1991), pp. 137–197.

27. See the three wealth studies analysed by Richard T. Curtin, F. Thomas Juster, and James N. Morgan, "Survey Estimates of Wealth: An Assessment of Quality," in Robert E. Lipsey and Helen Stone Tice, *The Measurement of Saving, Investment, and Wealth* (Chicago: The University of Chicago Press, 1989): 473–548.

28. Of course, this extension of democratic decision-making into the economic sphere that many egalitarians favour may seem unattractive if divorced from the other, collateral changes urged by egalitarians. These changes will include better education for many workers, along with the enforcement of due process and the protection of free speech in the workplace.

QUESTIONS

1. Moore suggests that so long as one does not engage in deception, there is nothing unethical in buying an item for $75 knowing that one can with little expense or effort resell it for $2500. Do you agree? How do you think Lippke would respond to this claim?

2. One frequent criticism of insider trading is that it is unfair because the advantage the insider possesses is "unerodable," i.e. it could not be overcome by the hard work and ingenuity of an ordinary investor. Moore dismisses this argument on the grounds that just as one could have chosen to become a plumber and hence possess information not possessed by non-plumbers, so one could have chosen to become a corporate insider and thus possess information not possessed by the ordinary investor. In neither case, she argues, is the possession and use of specialized information unfair. How persuasive do you find her analogy? How do you think Werhane would respond to this analogy? What is Lippke's response to this analogy?

3. Is Werhane correct in her claim that since insider trading undermines competition, it undermines an efficient market? Why or why not?

4. Werhane claims that competition is a precondition of an efficient market. She also claims that competition declines as inequality between individuals increases and that the market is most efficient when there is competition between equally matched parties. What are the implications of this as regards market regulation?

5. Critically assess Lippke's claim that insider trading can only be evaluated in the context of a comprehensive theory of justice.

CASE 8:1 THE VENGEFUL TIPPEE[3]

In the mid-1980s Carl F. Berner sought damages against Bateman Eichler, Hill Richards, Incorporated. Berner alleged that he had suffered substantial trading losses because a security broker employed by Bateman Eichler, Hill Richards, in collusion with the officer of a corporation, fraudulently induced Berner to purchase stock in the corporation by revealing false and materially incomplete information about the company and claiming it was accurate inside information.

1. Are tippees, i.e. those receiving inside information, less blameworthy than tippers, i.e. those divulging inside information? Why or why not?
2. Should tippees be allowed to bring suit against defrauding tippers? Explain your answer.

CASE 8:2 FRIENDSHIP AND INSIDER TRADING[4]

In the late 1980s, Plastic Engine Technology Corporation (PETCO) was a small firm listed on the Toronto Stock Exchange, attempting to exploit promising technology in the area of producing small plastic engines. PETCO had received orders for hundreds of thousands of these engines, but needed venture capital to meet costs associated with filling so large a demand. Gerald McKendry, president and CEO of PETCO, approached Woods, a director of PETCO, and president of Head Start Capital Corporation, a company in the business of venture capital for start-up companies.

In October 1988 Woods approached James Richardson, a long-time business associate, for a bridge loan of $500,000 to help PETCO to try and deal with its chronic cash shortage. Richardson loaned PETCO the money; his loan being secured by a fixed charge on PETCO's assets. PETCO, in the midst of negotiations for equity financing with Samuel Manutech Inc., the Middlefield Capital fund, and a group of individual investors, arranged for the sale and leaseback of substantially all its equipment. With the money obtained from the sale of its equipment, PETCO repaid Richardson's loan in late November 1988.

On December 21, 1988 Manutech, Middlefield, and the group of individual investors signed a letter of intent with PETCO to provide equity financing of $11.25 million. Around the same time, Woods arranged for a second bridge loan from Richardson; to be repaid by PETCO by mid-January 1989. As before, the loan was to be secured by a charge on the assets of PETCO. Woods did not reveal, however, that PETCO was now leasing the equipment it had formerly owned and that Richardson's loan was therefore at much greater risk.

On January 19, 1989, one day prior to the proposed equity financing taking effect, Middlefield advised PETCO it could not proceed. Manutech and the group of individual investors were able to interest Davidson Tisdale Mines Ltd., but the new financial package they put together was conditional on PETCO receiving a federal government grant of approximately $2 million. Initially, it looked probable that the federal government would provide assistance and the deal closed in escrow on February 7, 1989 with PETCO issuing a press release to that effect. By February 17, 1989, however, it became clear that the federal government would not provide aid and the new financing package collapsed.

Desperate for funds, PETCO asked Woods to propose to Richardson that Richardson convert his bridge loan into equity. On February 22, 1989, Richardson agreed, but on Wood's recommendation, instructed Woods to arrange to short-sell some PETCO shares in order to hedge his risk. (A short sale takes place when someone sells shares prior to owning them by selling shares borrowed from a broker. If the shares decrease in value, allowing the seller to pay a lower price to the broker from whom they were borrowed than what he or she sold them for, the seller will realize a profit.)

On February 24, 1989 PETCO issued a press release stating that although no formal agreement had been reached, they had tentative commitments for approximately $8.5 million in equity financing. Unfortunately for investors, this was simply false. Woods, aware of the misleading nature of the press release, and with full knowledge of PETCO's precarious situation, arranged further short-selling of PETCO shares on Richardson's behalf to minimize Richardson's loss on his loan in the event of PETCO failing. This was done without consulting Richardson.

CASE STUDY QUESTIONS

1. Woods argued that he was not guilty of insider trading, since he received no personal financial benefit from his activities. How would you respond to his argument?

2. Perhaps part of Woods' reason for short-selling stock on Richardson's behalf is that Richardson had originally been misled that his second loan to PETCO was as fully secured as the first. Would this in any way excuse Woods' actions? Why or why not?

3. Was Richardson guilty of any wrongdoing?

Notes

3. Based on *Berner v. Bateman Eichler, Hill Richards Inc.* as found in 105 Supreme Court Reporter 2622 (1985).

4. Based on *Regina v. Plastic Engine Technology Corporation* as found in Canadian Criminal Cases, Vol. 88, 3rd series, pp. 287–333.

FOR FURTHER READING

1. William B. Irvine, "Insider Trading: An Ethical Appraisal," *Business and Professional Ethics Journal,* Vol. 6, No. 4, 1986, pp. 3–33.

2. Gary Lawson, "The Ethics of Insider Trading," *Harvard Journal of Law and Public Policy,* Vol. 11, No. 3, 1988, pp. 727–783.

3. Henry Manne, *Insider Trading and the Stock Market* (New York: The Free Press, 1966).

4. William Shaw, "Shareholder Authorized Inside Trading: A Legal and Moral Analysis," *Journal of Business Ethics,* Vol. 9, 1990, pp. 913–928.

5. Patricia Werhane, "The Indefensibility of Insider Trading," *Journal of Business Ethics,* Vol. 10, 1991, pp. 729–731.

Chapter Nine

INTELLECTUAL PROPERTY

Introduction

Most of us at one time or another have copied
a favorite cassette or compact disk so that we
may have a copy not only in our home, but
also in our car. Many of us have photocopied
magazine or journal articles to give to a friend
or colleague. We are familiar with the fact that
it is cheaper to buy a clone computer than the
famous brands they so closely imitate, and we
probably know people who use pirated software on their computers. These activities raise
questions concerning copyrights, patents,
trademarks, and trade secrets that are becoming increasingly important and complex as our
ability to copy, distribute, and process information grows at an exponential rate.

Traditionally, such questions have been addressed in the context of appealing to intellectual property and the rights of property owners to control how their property is used. This
raises at least two very complex issues. The
first is how we are to conceive ownership of
property. The notion of physical property often
proves difficult—do I, for example, own the
water in the aquifer below my farm—but the
concept of intellectual property seems even
more puzzling. How can I be said to own a
certain arrangement of machine parts, i.e. its
design, and how does someone arranging machine parts in an identical or very similar way
violate my property right, since it in no way
prohibits my continuing to use that design.
Often it is suggested that we must distinguish
between an idea and its expression, and that
an idea cannot be intellectual property, i.e.
copyrightable, but its expression can be. Unfortunately, this distinction frequently breaks
down; in many instances style and content,

application and general principle, interpenetrate one another and cannot be easily distinguished.

Second, even if we can make clear the notion of intellectual property, the issue of how such property rights are qualified by public utility or the rights of others arises. Pharmaceutical companies, for example, spend large sums to research and develop new drugs. On this basis, they argue that their patents should extend over large periods of time in order for them to recoup their development costs and finance further research. This argument should not be too quickly dismissed, but in many instances long patent periods result in huge profits and keep drug prices much higher than they would otherwise be. Granting the existence of intellectual property rights in such instances, does not resolve the question of whether such long patent periods can be justified.

Whether traditional justifications of intellectual property rights are firmly grounded is the subject of Edwin C. Hettinger's article "Justifying Intellectual Property." He argues that because intellectual property is nonexclusive in nature, i.e. unlike physical property, its possession and use does not hinder its possession and use by others, we should not attempt to develop a theory of intellectual property analogous to theories of exclusive and private ownership of physical property. He further argues that it is far from clear that the concept of intellectual property is consistent with the value society places on freedom of thought and expression. He thinks that the most persuasive argument in support of intellectual property is one based on social utility, but suggests that even this argument is weak, since it is not obvious that the current system provides the best means of ensuring the availability and dissemination of knowledge.

Lynn Sharp Paine replies to Hettinger in her article "Trade Secrets and the Justification of Intellectual Property: A Comment on Hettinger." In Paine's view, Hettinger's failure to find a justification for intellectual property rights lies in the fact that he tries to treat intellectual property as analogous to physical property and thus focuses his attention on the traditional arguments for private property. She argues that intellectual property rights are best justified not on the grounds of a dubious analogy with tangible property, but rather by virtue of the essential role they play in defining personality and social relationships. Their foundation lies in the right of a person to keep her ideas to herself, disclose them to a select few, or disseminate them widely. In contrast to Hettinger's focus on social utility, Paine focuses on the autonomy of the individual and its implications as regards control over his or her ideas. She also suggests that Hettinger ignores the possibility that different intellectual property institutions may be justified in different ways. What justifies one intellectual property institution, e.g. copyright, need not be construed as the only possible means of justifying another institution, e.g. trade secrets.

Mark Alfino in "Intellectual Property and Copyright Ethics" takes the position that any adequate theory of intellectual property will have to take into account both the historical circumstances which gave rise to the concept and the present circumstances in which it is applied. He argues that current fair use guidelines, which attempt to operate on the basis of distinguishing between individual and systematic use, are increasingly *ad hoc* in view of the fact that emerging technologies make this distinction difficult to maintain. For example, through new technologies libraries are increasingly making use of interlibrary loans and cooperative acquisitions to reduce costs, yet maximize resources available to users.

Alfino sees the problem in terms of tension between individual and social values. On the one hand, there is a legitimate concern to respect private property, on the other, a legitimate desire to further the availability of knowledge. His approach is to try to develop a *via media* by which information producers recognize an obligation to employ technologies which facilitate wide distribution of their work and by which consumers recognize an obligation to consider the effect of these technologies upon information producers.

For further discussion on this topic as it arises in an international context, students should consult Paul Steidlmeier's article "The

Edwin C. Hettinger

Justifying Intellectual Property

Property institutions fundamentally shape a society. These legal relationships between individuals, different sorts of objects, and the state are not easy to justify. This is especially true of intellectual property. It is difficult enough to determine the appropriate kinds of ownership of corporeal objects (consider water or mineral rights); it is even more difficult to determine what types of ownership we should allow for noncorporeal, intellectual objects, such as writings, inventions, and secret business information. The complexity of copyright, patent, and trade secret law reflects this problem.

According to one writer "patents are the heart and core of property rights, and once they are destroyed, the destruction of all other property rights will follow automatically, as a brief postscript."[1] Though extreme, this remark rightly stresses the importance of patents to private competitive enterprise. Intellectual property is an increasingly significant and widespread form of ownership. Many have noted the arrival of the "post-industrial society"[2] in which the manufacture and manipulation of physical goods is giving way to the production and use of information. The result is an ever-increasing strain on our laws and customs protecting intellectual property.[3] Now, more than ever, there is a need to carefully scrutinize these institutions.

As a result of both vastly improved information-handling technologies and the larger role information is playing in our society, owners of intellectual property are more frequently faced with what they call "piracy" or information theft (that is, unauthorized access to their intellectual property). Most readers of this article have undoubtedly done something considered piracy by owners of intellectual property. Making a cassette tape of a friend's record, videotaping television broadcasts for a movie library, copying computer programs or using them on more than one machine, photocopying more than one chapter of a book, or two or more articles by the same author—all are examples of alleged infringing activities. Copyright, patent, and trade secret violation suits abound in industry, and in academia, the use of another person's ideas often goes unacknowledged. These phenomena indicate widespread public disagreement over the nature and legitimacy of our intellectual property institutions. This article examines the justifiability of those institutions.

COPYRIGHTS, PATENTS, AND TRADE SECRETS

It is commonly said that one cannot patent or copyright ideas. One copyrights "original works of authorship," including writings, music, drawings, dances, computer programs, and movies; one may not copyright ideas, concepts, principles, facts, or knowledge. Expressions of ideas are copyrightable; ideas themselves are not.[4] While useful, this notion of separating the content of an idea from its style of presentation is not unproblematic.[5] Difficulty in distinguishing the two is most apparent in the more artistic forms of authorship (such as fiction or poetry), where style and content interpenetrate. In these mediums, more so than in others, *how* something is said is very much part of *what* is said (and vice versa).

A related distinction holds for patents. Laws of nature, mathematical formulas, and methods of doing business, for example, cannot be patented. What one patents are inventions—that is, processes, machines, manufacturers, or compositions of matter. These must be novel (not previously patented); they must constitute nonobvious improvements over past inventions; and they must be useful (inventions that do not work cannot be patented). Specifying what sorts of "technological recipes for production"[6] constitute patentable subject matter involves distinguishing specific applications and utilizations from the underlying unpatentable general principles.[7] One cannot patent the scientific principle that water boils at 212 degrees, but one can patent a machine (for example, a steam engine) which uses this principle in a specific way and for a specific purpose.[8]

Trade secrets include a variety of confidential and valuable business information, such as sales, marketing, pricing, and advertising data, lists of customers and suppliers, and such things as plant layout and manufacturing techniques. Trade secrets must not be generally known in the industry, their nondisclosure must give some advantage over competitors, and attempts to prevent leakage of the information must be made (such as pledges of secrecy in employment contracts or other company security policies). The formula for Coca-Cola and bids on government contracts are examples of trade secrets.

Trade secret subject matter includes that of copyrights and patents: anything which can be copyrighted or patented can be held as a trade secret, though the converse is not true. Typically a business must choose between patenting an invention and holding it as a trade secret. Some advantages of trade secrets are

1. they do not require disclosure (in fact they require secrecy), whereas a condition for granting patents (and copyrights) is public disclosure of the invention (or writing);
2. they are protected for as long as they are kept secret, while most patents lapse after seventeen years; and

3. they involve less cost than acquiring and defending a patent.

Advantages of patents include protection against reverse engineering (competitors figuring out the invention by examining the product which embodies it) and against independent invention. Patents give their owners the *exclusive* right to make, use, and sell the invention no matter how anyone else comes up with it, while trade secrets prevent only improper acquisition (breaches of security).

Copyrights give their owners the right to reproduce, to prepare derivative works from, to distribute copies of, and to publicly perform or display the "original work of authorship." Their duration is the author's life plus fifty years. These rights are not universally applicable, however. The most notable exception is the "fair use" clause of the copyright statute, which gives researches, educators, and libraries special privileges to use copyrighted material.[9]

INTELLECTUAL OBJECTS AS NONEXCLUSIVE

Let us call the subject matter of copyrights, patents, and trade secrets "intellectual objects."[10] These objects are nonexclusive: they can be at many places at once and are not consumed by their use. The marginal cost of providing an intellectual object to an additional user is zero, and though there are communications costs, modern technologies can easily make an intellectual object unlimitedly available at a very low cost.

The possession or use of an intellectual object by one person does not preclude others from possessing or using it as well.[11] If someone borrows your lawn mower, you cannot use it, nor can anyone else. But if someone borrows your recipe for guacamole, that in no way precludes you, or anyone else, from using it. This feature is shared by all sorts of intellectual objects, including novels, computer programs, songs, machine designs, dances, recipes for Coca-Cola, lists of customers and suppliers, management techniques, and formulas for genetically engineered bacteria which digest crude oil. Of course, sharing intellectual objects does prevent the original possessor from selling the intellectual object to others, and so this sort of use is prevented. But sharing in no way hinders *personal* use.

This characteristic of intellectual objects grounds a strong *prima facie* case against the wisdom of private and exclusive intellectual property rights. Why should one person have the exclusive right to possess and use something which all people could possess and use concurrently? The burden of justification is very much on those who would restrict the maximal use of intellectual objects. A person's right to exclude others from possessing and using a physical object can be justified when such exclusion is necessary for this person's own possession and unhindered use. No such justification is available for exclusive possession and use of intellectual property.

One reason for the widespread piracy of intellectual property is that many people think it is unjustified to exclude others from intellectual objects.[12] Also, the unauthorized taking of an intellectual object does not feel like theft. Stealing a physical object involves depriving someone of the object taken, whereas taking an intellectual object deprives the owner of neither possession nor personal use of that object—though the owner is deprived of potential profit. This nonexclusive feature of intellectual objects should be kept firmly in mind when assessing the justifiability of intellectual property.

OWNING IDEAS AND RESTRICTIONS ON
THE FREE FLOW OF INFORMATION

The fundamental value our society places on freedom of thought and expression creates another difficulty for the justification of intellectual property. Private property enhances one person's freedom at the expense of everyone else's. Private intellectual property restricts methods of acquiring ideas (as do trade secrets), it restricts the use of ideas (as do patents), and it restricts the expression of ideas (as do copyrights)—restrictions undesirable for a number of reasons. John Stuart Mill argued that free thought and speech are important for the acquisition of true beliefs and for individual

growth and development.[13] Restrictions on the free flow and use of ideas not only stifle individual growth, but impede the advancement of technological innovation and human knowledge generally.[14] Insofar as copyrights, patents, and trade secrets have these negative effects, they are hard to justify.

Since a condition for granting patents and copyrights is public disclosure of the writing or invention, these forms of intellectual ownership do not involve the exclusive right to possess the knowledge or ideas they protect. Our society gives its inventors and writers a legal right to exclude others from certain uses of their intellectual works in return for public disclosure of these works. Disclosure is necessary if people are to learn from and build on the ideas of others. When they bring about disclosure of ideas which would have otherwise remained secret, patents and copyrights enhance rather than restrict the free flow of ideas (though they still restrict the idea's widespread use and dissemination). Trade secrets do not have this virtue. Regrettably, the common law tradition which offers protection for trade secrets encourages secrecy. This makes trade secrets undesirable in a way in which copyrights or patents are not.[15]

LABOR, NATURAL INTELLECTUAL PROPERTY
RIGHTS, AND MARKET VALUE

Perhaps the most powerful intuition supporting property rights is that people are entitled to the fruits of their labor. What a person produces with her own intelligence, effort, and perseverance ought to belong to her and to no one else. "Why is it mine? Well, it's mine because I made it, that's why. It wouldn't have existed but for me."

John Locke's version of this labor justification for property derives property rights in the product of labor from prior property rights in one's body.[16] A person owns her body and hence she owns what it does, namely, its labor. A person's labor and its product are inseparable, and so ownership of one can be secured only by owning the other. Hence, if a person is to own her body and thus its labor, she must also own what she joins her labor with—namely, the product of her labor.

This formulation is not without problems. For example, Robert Nozick wonders why a person should gain what she mixes her labor with instead of losing her labor. (He imagines pouring a can of tomato juice into the ocean and asks whether he thereby ought to gain the ocean or lose his tomato juice.)[17] More importantly, assuming that labor's fruits are valuable, and that laboring gives the laborer a property right in this value, this would entitle the laborer only to the value she added, and not to the *total* value of the resulting product. Though exceedingly difficult to measure, these two components of value (that attributable to the object labored on and that attributable to the labor) need to be distinguished.

Locke thinks that until labored on, objects have little human value, at one point suggesting that labor creates 99 percent of their value.[18] This is not plausible when labor is mixed with land and other natural resources. One does not create 99 percent of the value of an apple by picking it off a tree, though some human effort is necessary for an object to have value for us.

What portion of the value of writings, inventions, and business information is attributable to the intellectual laborer? Clearly authorship, discovery, or development is necessary if intellectual products are to have value for us; we could not use or appreciate them without this labor. But it does not follow from this that all of their value is attributable to that labor. Consider, for example, the wheel, the entire human value of which is not appropriately attributable to its original inventor.[19]

The value added by the laborer and any value the object has on its own are by no means the only components of the value of an intellectual object. Invention, writing, and thought in general do not operate in a vacuum; intellectual activity is not creation *ex nihilo*. Given this vital dependence of a person's thoughts on the ideas of those who came before her, intellectual products are fundamentally social products. Thus even if one assumes that the value of these products is entirely the result of human labor, this value is not entirely attributable to *any particular laborer* (or small group of laborers).

Separating out the individual contribution of the inventor, writer, or manager from this historical/social component is no easy task. Simply identifying the value a laborer's labor adds to the world with the market value of the resulting product ignores the vast contributions of others. A person who relies on human intellectual history and makes a small modification to produce something of great value should no more receive what the market will bear than should the last person needed to lift a car receive full credit for lifting it. If laboring gives the laborer the right to receive the market value of the resulting product, this market value should be shared by all those whose ideas contributed to the origin of the product. The fact that most of these contributors are no longer present to receive their fair share is not a reason to give the entire market value to the last contributor.[20]

Thus an appeal to the market value of a laborer's product cannot help us here. Markets work only after property rights have been established and enforced, and our question is what sorts of property rights an inventor, writer, or manager should have, given that the result of her labor is a joint product of human intellectual history.

Even is one could separate out the laborer's own contribution and determine its market value, it is still not clear that the laborer's right to the fruits of her labor naturally entitles her to receive this. Market value is a socially created phenomenon, depending on the activity (or nonactivity) of other producers, the monetary demand of purchasers, and the kinds of property rights, contracts, and markets the state has established and enforced. The market value of the same fruits of labor will differ greatly with variations in these social factors.

Consider the market value of a new drug formula. This depends on the length and the extent of the patent monopoly the state grants and enforces, on the level of affluence of those who need the drug, and on the availability and price of substitutes. The laborer did not produce these. The intuitive appeal behind the labor argument—"I made it, hence it's mine"—loses its force when it is used to try to justify owning something others are responsible for (namely, the market value). The claim that a laborer, in virtue of her labor, has a "natural right" to this socially created phenomenon is problematic at best.

Thus, there are two different reasons why the market value of the product of labor is not what a laborer's labor naturally entitles her to. First, market value is not something that is produced by those who produce a product, and the labor argument entitles laborers only to the products of their labor. Second, even if we ignore this point and equate the fruits of labor with the market value of those fruits, intellectual products result from the labor of many people besides the latest contributor, and they have claims on the market value as well.

So even if the labor theory shows that the laborer has a natural right to the fruits of labor, this does not establish a natural right to receive the full market value of the resulting product. The notion that a laborer is naturally entitled as a matter of right to receive the market value of her product is a myth. To what extent individual laborers should be allowed to receive the market value of their products is a question of social policy; it is not solved by simply insisting on a moral right to the fruits of one's labor.[21]

Having a moral right to the fruits of one's labor might also mean having a right to possess and personally use what one develops. This version of the labor theory has some force. On this interpretation, creating something through labor gives the laborer a *prima facie* right to possess and personally use it for her own benefit. The value of protecting individual freedom guarantees this right as long as the creative labor, and the possession and use of its product, does not harm others.

But the freedom to exchange a product in a market and receive its full market value is again something quite different. To show that people have a right to this, one must argue about how best to balance the conflicts in freedoms which arise when people interact. One must determine what sorts of property rights and markets are morally legitimate. One must also decide when society should enforce the results of market interaction and when it should alter those result (for example, with tax policy). There is a gap—requiring extensive argumentative filler—between the claim that one has a natural right to possess and personally use the fruits of one's labor and the claim that one ought to receive for one's product whatever the market will bear.

Such a gap exists as well between the natural right to possess and personally use one's intellectual creations and the rights protected by copyrights, patents, and trade secrets. The natural right of an author to personally use her writings is distinct from the right, protected by copyright, to make her work public, sell it in a market, and then prevent others from making copies. An inventor's natural right to use the invention for her own benefits is not the same as the right, protected by patent, to sell this invention in a market and exclude others (including independent inventors) from using it. An entrepreneur's natural right to use valuable business information or techniques that she develops is not the same as the right, protected by trade secret, to prevent her employees from using these techniques in another job.

In short, a laborer has a *prima facie* natural right to possess and personally use the fruits of her labor. But a right to profit by selling a product in the market is something quite different. This liberty is largely a socially created phenomenon. The "right" to receive what the market will bear is a socially created privilege, and not a natural right at all. The natural right to possess and personally use what one has produced is relevant to the justifiability of such a privilege, but by itself it is hardly sufficient to justify that privilege.

DESERVING PROPERTY RIGHTS BECAUSE OF LABOR

The above argument that people are naturally entitled to the fruits of their labor is distinct from the argument that a person has a claim to labor's fruits based on desert. If a person has a natural right to something—say her athletic ability—and someone takes it from her, the return of it is something she is *owed* and can rightfully demand. Whether or not she deserves this athletic ability is a separate issue. Similarly, insofar as people have natural property rights in the fruits of their labor, these rights are something they are *owed,* and not something they necessarily deserve.[22]

The desert argument suggests that the laborer deserves to benefit from her labor, at least if it is an attempt to do something worthwhile. This proposal is convincing, but does not show that what the laborer deserves is property rights in the object labored on. The mistake is to conflate the created object which makes a person deserving of a reward with what that reward should be. Property rights in the created object are not the only possible reward. Alternatives include fees, awards, acknowledgment, gratitude, praise, security, power status, and public financial support.

Many considerations affect whether property rights in the created object are what the laborer deserves. This may depend, for example, on what is created by labor. If property rights in the very things created were always an appropriate reward for labor, then as Lawrence Becker notes, parents would deserve property rights in their children.[23] Many intellectual objects (scientific laws, religious and ethical insights, and so on) are also the sort of thing that should not be owned by anyone.

Furthermore, as Becker also correctly points out, we need to consider the purpose for which the laborer labored. Property rights in the object produced are not a fitting reward if the laborer does not want them. Many intellectual laborers produce beautiful things and discover truths as ends in themselves.[24] The appropriate reward in such cases is recognition, gratitude, and perhaps public financial support, not full-fledged property rights, for these laborers do not want to exclude others from their creations.

Property rights in the thing produced are also not a fitting reward if the value of these rights is disproportional to the effort expended by the laborer. "Effort" includes

1. how hard someone tries to achieve a result,
2. the amount of risk voluntarily incurred in seeking this result, and
3. the degree to which moral consideration played a role in choosing the result intended.

The harder one tries, the more one is willing to sacrifice, and the worthier the goal, the greater are one's deserts.

Becker's claim that the amount deserved is proportional to the value one's labor produces is mistaken.[25] The value of labor's results is often significantly affected by factors outside a person's control, and no one deserves to be rewarded for being lucky. Voluntary past action is the only valid basis for determining desert.[26] Here only a person's effort (in the sense defined) is relevant. Her knowledge, skills, and achievements insofar as they are based on natural talent and luck, rather than effort expended, are not. A person who is born with extraordinary natural talents, or who is extremely lucky, *deserves* nothing on the basis of these characteristics. If such a person puts forward no greater effort than another, she deserves no greater reward. Thus, two laborers who expend equal amounts of effort deserve the same reward, even when the value of the resulting products is vastly different.[27] Giving more to workers whose products have greater social value might be justified if it is needed as an incentive. But this has nothing to do with giving the laborer what she deserves.

John Rawls considers even the ability to expend effort to be determined by factors outside a person's control and hence a morally impermissible criterion for distribution.[28] How hard one tries, how willing one is to sacrifice and incur risk, and how much one cares about morality are to *some extent* affected by natural endowments and social circumstances. But if the ability to expend effort is taken to be entirely determined by factors outside a person's control, the result is a determinism which makes meaningful moral evaluation impossible. If people are responsible for anything, they are responsible for how hard they try, what sacrifices they make, and how moral they are. Because the effort a person expends is much more under her control than her innate intelligence, skills, and talents, effort is a far superior basis for determining desert. To the extent that a person's expenditure of effort is under her control, effort is the proper criterion for desert.[29]

Giving an inventor exclusive rights to make and sell her invention (for seventeen years) may provide either a greater or a lesser reward than she deserves. Some inventions of extraordinary market value result from flashes of genius, while others with little market value (and yet great social value) require significant effort.

The proportionality requirement may also be frequently violated by granting copyright. Consider a five-hundred-dollar computer program. Granted, its initial development costs (read "efforts") were high. But once it has been developed, the cost of each additional program is the cost of the disk it is on—approximately a dollar. After the program has been on the market several years and the price remains at three or four hundred dollars, one begins to suspect that the company is receiving far more than it deserves. Perhaps this is another reason so much illegal copying of software goes on: the proportionality requirement is not being met, and people sense the unfairness of the price. Frequently, trade secrets (which are held indefinitely) also provide their owners with benefits disproportional to the effort expended in developing them.

The Lockean Provisos

We have examined two versions of the labor argument for intellectual property, one based on desert, the other based on a natural entitlement to the fruits of one's labor. Locke himself put limits on the conditions under which labor can justify a property right in the thing produced. One is that after the appropriation there must be "enough and as good left in common for others."[30] This proviso is often reformulated as a "no loss to others" precondition for property acquisition.[31] As long as one does not worsen another's position by appropriating an object, no objection can be raised to owning that with which one mixes one's labor.

Under current law, patents clearly run afoul of this proviso by giving the original inventor an exclusive right to make, use, and sell the invention. Subsequent inventors who independently come up with an already patented invention cannot even personally use their invention, much less patent or sell it. They clearly suffer a great and unfair loss because of the original patent grant. Independent inventors should not be prohibited from using or selling their inventions. Proving independent discovery of a pub-

licly available patented invention would be difficult, however. Nozick's suggestion that the length of patents be restricted to the time it would take for independent invention may be the most reasonable administrative solution.[32] In the modern world of highly competitive research and development, this time is often much shorter than the seventeen years for which most patents are currently granted.

Copyrights and trade secrets are not subject to the same objection (though they may constitute a loss to others in different ways). If someone independently comes up with a copyrighted expression or a competitor's business technique, she is not prohibited from using it. Copyrights and trade secrets prevent only mimicking of other people's expressions and ideas.

Locke's second condition on the legitimate acquisition of property rights prohibits spoilage. Not only must one leave enough and as good for others, but one must not take more than one can use.[33] So in addition to leaving enough apples in the orchard for others, one must not take home a truckload and let them spoil. Though Locke does not specifically mention prohibiting waste, it is the concern to avoid waste which underlies his proviso prohibiting spoilage. Taking more than one can use is wrong because it is wasteful. Thus Locke's concern here is with appropriations of property which are wasteful.

Since writings, inventions, and business techniques are nonexclusive, this requirement prohibiting waste can never be completely met by intellectual property. When owners of intellectual property charge fees for the use of their expressions or inventions, or conceal their business techniques from others, certain beneficial uses of these intellectual products are prevented. This is clearly wasteful, since everyone could use and benefit from intellectual objects concurrently. How wasteful private ownership of intellectual property is depends on how beneficial those products would be to those who are excluded from their use as a result.

Sovereignty, Security, and Privacy

Private property can be justified as a means to sovereignty. Dominion over certain objects is important for individual autonomy. Ronald Dworkin's liberal is right in saying that "some sovereignty over a range of personal possessions is essential to dignity."[34] Not having to share one's personal possessions or borrow them from others is essential to the kind of autonomy our society values. Using or consuming certain objects is also necessary for survival. Allowing ownership of these things places control of the means of survival in the hands of individuals, and this promotes independence and security (at least for those who own enough of them). Private ownership of life's necessities lessens dependence between individuals, and takes power from the group and gives it to the individual. Private property also promotes privacy. It constitutes a sphere of privacy within which the individual is sovereign and less accountable for her actions. Owning one's own home is an example of all of these: it provides privacy, security, and a limited range of autonomy.

But copyrights and patents are neither necessary nor important for achieving these goals. The right to exclude others from using one's invention or copying one's work of authorship is not essential to one's sovereignty. Preventing a person from personally using her own invention or writing, on the other hand, would seriously threaten her sovereignty. An author's or inventor's sense of worth and dignity requires public acknowledgment by those who use the writing or discovery, but here again, giving the author or inventor the exclusive right to copy or use her intellectual product is not necessary to protect this.

Though patents and copyrights are not directly necessary for survival (as are food and shelter), one could argue that they are indirectly necessary for an individual's security and survival when selling her inventions or writings is a person's sole means of income. In our society, however, most patents and copyrights are owned by institutions (businesses, universities, or governments). Except in unusual cases where individuals have extraordinary bargaining power, prospective employees are required to give the rights to their inventions and works of authorship to their employers as a condition of employment. Independent authors or inventors who earn their living by selling their writ-

ings or inventions to others are increasingly rare.[35] Thus arguing that intellectual property promotes individual security makes sense only in a minority of cases. Additionally, there are other ways to ensure the independent intellectual laborer's security and survival besides copyrights and patents (such as public funding of intellectual workers and public domain property status for the results).

Controlling who uses one's invention or writing is not important to one's privacy. As long as there is no requirement to divulge privately created intellectual products (and as long as laws exist to protect people from others taking information they choose not to divulge—as with trade secret laws), the creator's privacy will not be infringed. Trying to justify copyrights and patents on grounds of privacy is highly implausible given that these property rights give the author or inventor control over certain uses of writings and inventions only after they have been publicly disclosed.

Trade secrets are not defensible on grounds of privacy either. A corporation is not an individual and hence does not have the personal features privacy is intended to protect.[36] Concern for sovereignty counts against trade secrets, for they often directly limit individual autonomy by preventing employees from changing jobs. Through employment contracts, by means of gentlemen's agreements among firms to respect trade secrets by refusing to hire competitors' employees, or simply because of the threat of lawsuits, trade secrets often prevent employees from using their skills and knowledge with other companies in the industry.

Some trade secrets, however, are important to a company's security and survival. If competitors could legally obtain the secret formula for Coke, for example, the Coca-Cola Company would be severely threatened. Similar points hold for copyrights and patents. Without some copyright protection, companies in the publishing, record, and movie industries would be severely threatened by competitors who copy and sell their works at lower prices (which need not reflect development costs). Without patent protection, companies with high research and development costs could be underpriced and driven out of business by competitors who simply mimicked the already developed products. This unfair competition could significantly weaken incentives to invest in innovative techniques and to develop new products.

The next section considers this argument that intellectual property is a necessary incentive for innovation and a requirement for healthy and fair competition. Notice, however, that the concern here is with the security and survival of private companies, not of individuals. Thus one needs to determine whether, and to what extent, the security and survival of privately held companies is a goal worth promoting. That issue turns on the difficult question of what type of economy is most desirable. Given a commitment to capitalism, however, this argument does have some force.

THE UTILITARIAN JUSTIFICATION

The strongest and most widely appealed to justification for intellectual property is a utilitarian argument based on providing incentives. The constitutional justification for patents and copyrights—"to promote the progress of science and the useful arts"[37]—is itself utilitarian. Given the shortcomings of the other arguments for intellectual property, the justifiability of copyrights, patents, and trade secrets depends, in the final analysis, on this utilitarian defense.

According to this argument, promoting the creation of valuable intellectual works requires that intellectual laborers be granted property rights in those works. Without the copyright, patent, and trade secret property protections, adequate incentives for the creation of a socially optimal output of intellectual products would not exist. If competitors could simply copy books, movies, and records, and take one another's inventions and business techniques, there would be no incentive to spend the vast amounts of time, energy, and money necessary to develop these products and techniques. It would be in each firm's self-interest to let others develop products, and then mimic the result. No one would engage in original development, and consequently no new writings, inventions, or business techniques would be developed. To avoid this disastrous result, the argument

claims, we must continue to grant intellectual property rights.

Notice that this argument focuses on the users of intellectual products, rather than on the producers. Granting property rights to producers is here seen as necessary to ensure that enough intellectual products (and the countless other goods based on these products) are available to users. The grant of property rights to the producers is a mere means to this end.

This approach is paradoxical. It establishes a right to restrict the current availability and use of intellectual products for the purpose of increasing the production and thus future availability and use of new intellectual products. As economist Joan Robinson says of patents: "A patent is a device to prevent the diffusion of new methods before the original investor has recovered profit adequate to induce the requisite investment. The justification of the patent system is that by slowing down the diffusion of technical progress it ensures that there will be more progress to diffuse. . . . Since it is rooted in a contradiction, there can be no such thing as an ideally beneficial patent system, and it is bound to produce negative results in particular instances, impeding progress unnecessarily even if its general effect is favorable on balance."[38] Although this strategy may work, it is to a certain extent self-defeating. If the justification for intellectual property is utilitarian in this sense, then the search for alternative incentives for the production of intellectual products takes on a good deal of importance. It would be better to employ equally powerful ways to stimulate the production and thus use of intellectual products which did not also restrict their use and availability.

Government support of intellectual work and public ownership of the result may be one such alternative. Governments already fund a great deal of basic research and development, and the results of this research often become public property. Unlike private property rights in the results of intellectual labor, government funding of this labor and public ownership of the result stimulate new inventions and writings without restricting their dissemination and use. Increased government funding of intellectual labor should thus be seriously considered.

This proposal need not involve government control over which research projects are to be pursued. Government funding of intellectual labor can be divorced from government control over what is funded. University research is an example. Most of this is supported by public funds, but government control over its content is minor and indirect. Agencies at different governmental levels could distribute funding for intellectual labor with only the most general guidance over content, leaving businesses, universities, and private individuals to decide which projects to pursue.

If the goal of private intellectual property institutions is to maximize the dissemination and use of information, to the extent that they do not achieve this result, these institutions should be modified. The question is not whether copyrights, patents, and trade secrets provide incentives for the production of original works of authorship, inventions, and innovative business techniques. Of course they do. Rather, we should ask the following questions: Do copyrights, patents, and trade secrets increase the availability and use of intellectual products more than they restrict this availability and use? If they do, we must then ask whether they increase the availability and use of intellectual products more than any alternative mechanism would. For example, could better overall results be achieved by shortening the length of copyright and patent grants, or by putting a time limit on trade secrets (and on the restrictions on future employment employers are allowed to demand of employees)? Would eliminating most types of trade secrets entirely and letting patents carry a heavier load produce improved results? Additionally, we must determine whether and to what extent public funding and ownership of intellectual products might be a more efficient means to these results.[39]

We should not expect an across-the-board answer to these questions. For example, the production of movies is more dependent on copyright than is academic writing. Also, patent protection for individual inventors and small beginning firms makes more sense than patent protection for large corporations (which own the majority of patents). It has been argued that patents are not important incentives for the research and innovative activity of large corporations in competitive markets.[40] The short-term advantage a company gets from developing a new product and being the first to put it on the market may be incentive enough.

That patents are conducive to a strong competitive economy is also open to question. Our patent system, originally designed to reward the individual inventor and thereby stimulate invention, may today be used as a device to monopolize industries. It has been suggested that in some cases "the patent position of the big firms makes it almost impossible for new firms to enter the industry"[41] and that patents are frequently bought up in order to suppress competition.[42]

Trade secrets as well as can stifle competition, rather than encourage it. If a company can rely on a secret advantage over a competitor, it has no need to develop new technologies to stay ahead. Greater disclosure of certain trade secrets—such as costs and profits of particular product lines—would actually increase competition, rather than decrease it, since with this knowledge firms would then concentrate on one another's most profitable products.[43] Furthermore, as one critic notes, trade secret laws often prevent a former employee "from doing work in just that field for which his training and experience have best prepared him. Indeed, the mobility of engineers and scientists is often severely limited by the reluctance of new firms to hire them for fear of exposing themselves to a lawsuit."[44] Since the movement of skilled workers between companies is a vital mechanism in the growth and spread of technology, in this important respect trade secrets actually slow the dissemination and use of innovative techniques.

These remarks suggest that the justifiability of our intellectual property institutions is not settled by the facile assertion that our system of patents, copyrights, and trade secrets provides necessary incentives for innovation and ensures maximally healthy competitive enterprise. This argument is not as easy to construct as one might at first think; substantial empirical evidence is needed. The above considerations suggest that the evidence might not support this position.

CONCLUSION

Justifying intellectual property is a formidable task. The inadequacies of the traditional justifications for property become more severe when applied to intellectual property. Both the nonexclusive nature of intellectual objects and the presumption against allowing restrictions on the free flow of ideas create special burdens in justifying such property.

We have seen significant shortcomings in the justifications for intellectual property. Natural rights to the fruits of one's labor are not by themselves sufficient to justify copyrights, patents, and trade secrets, though they are relevant to the social decision to create and sustain intellectual property institutions. Although intellectual laborers often deserve rewards for their labor, copyrights, patents, and trade secrets may give the laborer much more or much less than is deserved. Where property rights are not what is desired, they may be wholly inappropriate. The Lockean labor arguments for intellectual property also run afoul of one of Locke's provisos—the prohibition against spoilage or waste. Considerations of sovereignty, security, and privacy are inconclusive justifications for intellectual property as well.

This analysis suggests that the issue turns on considerations of social utility. We must determine whether our current copyright, patent, and trade secret statutes provide the best possible mechanisms for ensuring the availability and widespread dissemination of intellectual works and their resulting products. Public financial support for intellectual laborers and public ownership of intellectual products is an alternative which demands serious consideration. More modest alternatives needing consideration include modifications in the length of intellectual property grants or in the strength and scope of the restrictive rights granted. What the most efficient mechanism for achieving these goals is remains an unresolved empirical question.

This discussion also suggests that copyrights are easier to justify than patents or trade secrets. Patents restrict the actual usage of an idea (in making a physical object), while copyrights restrict only copying an expression of an idea.

One can freely use the ideas in a copyrighted book in one's own writing, provided one acknowledges their origin. One cannot freely use the ideas a patented invention represents when developing one's own product. Furthermore, since inventions and business techniques are instruments of production in a way in which expressions of ideas are not, socialist objections to private ownership of the means of production apply to patents and trade secrets far more readily than they do to copyrights. Trade secrets are suspect also because they do not involve the socially beneficial public disclosure which is part of the patent and copyright process. They are additionally problematic to the extent that they involve unacceptable restrictions on employee mobility and technology transfer.

Focusing on the problems of justifying intellectual property is important not because these institutions lack any sort of justification, but because they are not so obviously or easily justified as many people think. We must begin to think more openly and imaginatively about the alternative choices available to us for stimulating and rewarding intellectual labor.

Notes

The original research for this article was completed while I worked for the National Telecommunications and Information Administration of the United States Department of Commerce. I am grateful to Roger Salaman and the Department of Commerce for stimulating and encouraging my work on intellectual property. I wish to thank Beverly Diamond, Margaret Holmgren, Joseph Kupfer, Martin Perlmutter, Hugh Wilder, and the Editors of *Philosophy & Public Affairs* for valuable assistance.

1. Ayn Rand, *Capitalism: The Unknown Ideal* (New York: New American Library, 1966), p. 128.
2. See, for example, John Naisbitt's *Megatrends* (New York: Warner Books, 1982), chap. 1.
3. See R. Salaman and E. Hettinger, *Policy Implications of Information Technology*. NTIA Report 84–144, U.S. Department of Commerce, 1984, pp. 28–29.
4. For an elaboration of this distinction see Michael Brittin, "Constitutional Fair Use," in *Copyright Law Symposium*, no. 28 (New York: Columbia University Press, 1982), pp. 142ff.
5. For an illuminating discussion of the relationships between style and subject, see Nelson Goodman's *Ways of Worldmaking* (Indianapolis: Hackett, 1978), chap. II, esp. sec. 2.
6. This is Fritz Machlup's phrase. See his *Production and Distribution of Knowledge in the United States* (Princeton: Princeton University Press, 1962), p. 163.

7. For one discussion of this distinction, see Deborah Johnson, *Computer Ethics* (Englewood Cliffs, N.J.: Prentice-Hall, 1985), pp. 100–101.

8. What can be patented is highly controversial. Consider the recent furor over patenting genetically manipulated animals or patenting computer programs.

9. What constitutes fair use is notoriously bewildering. I doubt that many teachers who sign copyright waivers at local copy shops know whether the packets they make available for their students constitute fair use of copyrighted material.

10. "Intellectual objects," "information," and "ideas" are terms I use to characterize the "objects" of this kind of ownership. Institutions which protect such "objects" include copyright, patent, trade secret, and trademark laws, as well as socially enforced customs (such as sanctions against plagiarism) demanding acknowledgment of the use of another's ideas. What is owned here are objects only in a very abstract sense.

11. There are intellectual objects of which this is not true, namely, information whose usefulness depends precisely on its being known only to a limited group of people. Stock tips and insider trading information are examples.

12. Ease of access is another reason for the widespread piracy of intellectual property. Modern information technologies (such as audio and video recorders, satellite dishes, photocopiers, and computers) make unauthorized taking of intellectual objects far easier than ever before. But it is cynical to submit that this is the major (or the only) reason piracy of information is widespread. It suggests that if people could steal physical objects as easily as they can take intellectual ones, they would do so to the same extent. That seems incorrect.

13. For an useful interpretation of Mill's argument, see Robert Ladenson, "Free Expression in the Corporate Workplace," in *Ethical Theory and Business*, 2d ed., ed. T. Beauchamp and N. Bowie (Englewood Cliffs, N.J.: Prentice-Hall, 1983), pp. 162–69.

14. This is one reason the recent dramatic increase in relationships between universities and businesses is so disturbing: it hampers the disclosure of research results.

15. John Snapper makes this point in "Ownership of Computer Programs," available from the Center for the Study of Ethics in the Professions at the Illinois Institute of Technology. See also Sissela Bok, "Trade and Corporate Secrecy," in *Ethical Theory and Business*, p. 176.

16. John Locke, *Second Treatise of Government*, chap. 5. There are several strands to the Lockean argument. See Lawrence Becker, *Property Rights* (London: Routledge and Kegan Paul, 1977), chap. 4, for a detailed analysis of these various versions.

17. Robert Nozick, *Anarchy, State, and Utopia* (New York: Basic Books, 1974), p. 175.

18. Locke, *Second Treatise*, chap. 5, sec. 40.

19. Whether ideas are discovered or created affects the plausibility of the labor argument for intellectual property. "I discovered it, hence it's mine" is much less persuasive than "I made it, hence it's mine." This issue also affects the cogency of the notion that intellectual objects have a value of their own not attributable to intellectual labor. The notion of mixing one's labor with something and thereby adding value to it makes much more sense if the object preexists.

20. I thank the Editors of *Philosophy & Affairs* for this way of making the point.

21. A libertarian might respond that although a natural right to the fruits of labor will not by itself justify a right to receive the market value of the resulting product, that right plus the rights of free association and trade would justify it. But marketplace interaction presupposes a set of social relations, and parties to these relations must jointly agree on their nature. Additionally, market interaction is possible only when property rights have been specified and enforced, and there is no "natural way" to do this (that is, no way independent of complex social judgments concerning the rewards the laborer deserves and the social utilities that will result from granting property rights). The sorts of freedoms one may have in a marketplace are thus socially agreed-upon privileges rather than natural rights.

22. For a discussion of this point, see Joel Feinberg, *Social Philosophy* (Englewood Cliffs, N.J.: Prentice-Hall, 1973), p. 116.

23. Becker, *Property Rights*, p. 46.

24. This is becoming less and less true as the results of intellectual labor are increasingly treated as commodities. University research in biological and computer technologies is an example of this trend.

25. Becker, *Property Rights*, p. 52. In practice, it would be easier to reward laborers as Becker suggests, since the value of the results of labor is easier to determine than the degree of effort expended.

26. This point is made nicely by James Rachels in "What People Deserve," in *Justice and Economic Distribution*, ed. J. Arthur and W. Shaw (Englewood Cliffs, N.J.: Prentice-Hall, 1978), pp. 150–63.

27. Completely ineffectual efforts deserve a reward provided that there were good reasons beforehand for thinking the efforts would pay off. Those whose well-intentioned efforts are silly or stupid should be rewarded the first time only and then counseled to seek advice about the value of their efforts.

28. See John Rawls, *A Theory of Justice* (Cambridge: Harvard University Press, 1971), p. 104; "The assertion that a man deserves the superior character that enables him to make the effort to cultivate his abilities is equally problematic; for his character depends in large part upon fortunate family and social circumstances for which he can claim no credit." See also p. 312; "the effort a person is willing to make is influenced by his natural abilities and skills, and the alternatives open to him. The better endowed are more likely, other things equal, to strive conscientiously."

29. See Rachels, "What People Deserve," pp. 157–58, for a similar resistance to Rawl's determinism.

30. Locke, *Second Treatise*, chap. 5, sec. 27.

31. See Nozick, *Anarchy,* pp. 175–82, and Becker, *Property Rights,* pp. 42–43.
32. Nozick, *Anarchy,* p. 182.
33. Locke, *Second Treatise,* chap. 5, sec. 31.
34. Ronald Dworkin, "Liberalism," in *Public and Private Morality,* ed. Stuart Hampshire (Cambridge: Cambridge University Press, 1978), p. 139.
35. "In the United States about 60 per cent of all patents are assigned to corporations" (Machlup, *Production,* p. 168). This was the case twenty-five years ago, and I assume the percentage is even higher today.
36. Very little (if any) of the sensitive information about individuals that corporations have is information held as a trade secret. For a critical discussion of the attempt to defend corporate secrecy on the basis of privacy see Russell B. Stevenson, Jr., *Corporations and Information* (Baltimore: Johns Hopkins University Press, 1980), chap. 5.
37. U.S. Constitution, sec. 8, para. 8.
38. Quoted in Dorothy Nelkin, *Science as Intellectual Property* (New York: Macmillan, 1984), p. 15.
39. Even supposing our current copyright, patent, and trade secret laws did maximize the availability and use of intellectual products, a thorough utilitarian evaluation would have to weigh all the consequences of these legal rights. For example, the decrease in employee freedom resulting from trade secrets would have to be considered, as would the inequalities in income, wealth, opportunity, and power which result from these socially established and enforced property rights.
40. Machlup, *Production,* pp. 168–69.
41. Ibid., p. 170.
42. See David Noble, *America by Design* (New York: Knopf, 1982), chap. 6.
43. This is Stevenson's point in *Corporations,* p. 11.
44. Ibid., p. 23. More generally, see ibid., chap. 2, for a careful and skeptical treatment of the claim that trade secrets function as incentives.

Lynn Sharp Paine

Trade Secrets and the Justification of Intellectual Property: A Comment on Hettinger

In a recent article Edwin Hettinger considers various rationales for recognizing intellectual property.[1] According to Hettinger, traditional justifications for property are especially problematic when applied to intellectual property because of its nonexclusive nature.[2] Since possessing and using intellectual objects does not preclude their use and possession by others, there is, he says a "strong prima facie case

against the wisdom of private and exclusive intellectual property rights." There is, moreover, a presumption against allowing restrictions on the free flow of ideas.

After rejecting several rationales for intellectual property, Hettinger finds its justification in an instrumental, or "utilitarian,"[3] argument based on incentives.[4] Respecting rights in ideas makes sense, he says, if we recognize that the purpose of our intellectual property institutions is to promote the dissemination and use of information. To the extent that existing institutions do not achieve this result, they should be modified.[5] Skeptical about the effectiveness of current legal arrangements, Hettinger concludes that we must think more imaginatively about structuring our intellectual property institutions—in particular, patent, copyright, and trade secret laws—so that they increase the availability and use of intellectual products. He ventures several possibilities for consideration: eliminating certain forms of trade secret protections, shortening the copyright and patent protection periods, and public funding and ownership of intellectual objects.

Hettinger's approach to justifying our intellectual property institutions rests on several problematic assumptions. It assumes that all of our intellectual property institutions rise or fall

From Paine, Lynn Sharp, "Trade Secrets and the Justification of Intellectual Property: A Comment on Hettinger," *Philosophy and Public Affairs,* vol. 20, No. 3. Copyright © 1991 by Princeton University Press. Reprinted by permission of Princeton University Press.

together—that the rationale for trade secret protection must be the same as that for patent and copyright protection.[6] This assumption, I will try to show, is unwarranted. While it may be true that these institutions all promote social utility or well-being, the web of rights and duties understood under the general heading of "intellectual property rights" reflects a variety of more specific rationales and objectives.[7]

Second, Hettinger assumes that the rights commonly referred to as "intellectual property rights" are best understood on the model of rights in tangible and real property. He accepts the idea, implicit in the terminology, that intellectual property is like tangible property, only less corporeal. This assumption leads him to focus his search for the justification of intellectual property on the traditional arguments for private property. I will try to show the merits of an alternative approach to thinking about rights in ideas—one that does not depend on the analogy with tangible property and that recognizes the role of ideas in defining personality and social relationships.

The combined effect of these assumptions is that trade secret law comes in for particular serious criticism. It restricts methods of acquiring ideas; it encourages secrecy; it places unacceptable restrictions on employee mobility and technology transfer; it can stifle competition; it is more vulnerable to socialist objections. In light of these deficiencies, Hettinger recommends that we consider the possibility of "eliminating most types of trade secrets entirely and letting patents carry a heavier load". He believes that trade secrets are undesirable in ways that copyrights and patents are not.

Without disagreeing with Hettinger's recommendation that we reevaluate and think more imaginatively about our intellectual property institutions, I believe we should have a clearer understanding of the various rationales for these institutions than is reflected in Hettinger's article. If we unbundle the notion of intellectual property into its constituent rights,[8] we find that different justifications are appropriate for different clusters of rights.[9] In particular, we find that the rights recognized by trade secret law are better understood as rooted in respect for individual liberty, confidential relationships, common morality, and fair competition than in the promotion of inno-vation and the dissemination of ideas. While trade secret law may serve some of the same ends as patent and copyright law, it has other foundations which are quite distinctive.[10]

In this article, I am primarily concerned with the foundations of trade secret principles. However, my general approach differs from Hettinger's in two fundamental ways. First, it focuses on persons and their relationships rather than property concepts. Second, it reverses the burden of justification, placing it on those who would argue for treating ideas as public goods rather than those who seek to justify private rights in ideas. Within this alternative framework, the central questions are how ideas may be legitimately acquired from others, how disclosure obligations arise, and how ideas become part of the common pool of knowledge. Before turning to Hettinger's criticisms of trade secret principles, it will be useful to think more broadly about the rights of individuals over their undisclosed ideas. This inquiry will illustrate my approach to thinking about rights in ideas and point toward some of the issues at stake in the trade secret area.

THE RIGHT TO CONTROL DISCLOSURE

If a person has any right with respect to her ideas, surely it is the right to control their initial disclosure.[11] A person may decide to keep her ideas to herself, to disclose them to a select few, or to publish them widely. Whether those ideas are best described as views and opinions, plans and intentions, facts and knowledge, or fantasies and inventions is immaterial. While it might in some cases be socially useful for a person to be generous with her ideas, and to share then with others without restraint, there is no general obligation to do so. The world at large has no right to the individual's ideas.[12]

Certainly, specific undertakings, relationships, and even the acquisition of specific information can give rise to disclosure obligations. Typically, these obligations relate to specific types of information pertinent to the relationship or the subject matter of the undertaking. A seller of goods must disclose to potential buyers latent defects and health and safety risks associated with the use of the goods. A person who undertakes to act as an agent for another is obliged to disclose to the principal information she acquires that relates to the subject matter of the agency. Disclosure obligations like these, however, are limited in scope and arise against a general background right to remain silent.

The right to control the initial disclosure of one's ideas is grounded in respect for the individual. Just as a person's sense of herself is intimately connected with the stream of ideas that constitutes consciousness, her public persona is determined in part by the ideas she expresses and the ways she expresses them. To require public disclosure of one's ideas and thoughts—whether about "personal" or other matters—would distort one's personality and, no doubt, alter the nature of one's thoughts.[13] It would seriously interfere with the liberty to live according to one's chosen life plans. This sort of thought control would be an invasion of privacy and personality of the most intrusive sort. If anything is private, one's undisclosed thoughts surely are.[14]

Respect for autonomy, respect for personality, and respect for privacy lie behind the right to control disclosure of one's ideas, but the right is also part of what we mean by freedom of thought and expression. Frequently equated with a right to speak, freedom of expression also implies a *prima facie* right not to express one's ideas or to share them only with those we love or trust or with whom we wish to share.[15] These observations explain the peculiarity of setting up the free flow of ideas and unrestricted access as an ideal. Rights in ideas are desirable insofar as they strengthen our sense of individuality and undergird our social relationships. This suggests a framework quite different from Hettinger's, one that begins with a strong presumption against requiring disclosure and is in favor of protecting people against unconsented-to acquisitions of their ideas.[16] This is the moral backdrop against which trade secrecy law is best understood.

CONSEQUENCES OF DISCLOSURE

Within this framework, a critical question is how people lose rights in their ideas. Are these rights forfeited when people express their ideas or communicate them to others? Surely this depends on the circumstances of disclosure. Writing down ideas in a daily journal to oneself or recording them on a cassette should not entail such a forfeiture. Considerations of individual autonomy, privacy, and personality require that such expressions not be deemed available for use by others who may gain access to them.[17]

Likewise, communicating an idea in confidence to another should not render it part of the common pool of knowledge. Respect for the individual's desire to limit the dissemination of the idea is at stake, but so is respect for the relationship of trust and confidence among the persons involved. If A confides in B under circumstances in which B gives A reason to believe she will respect the confidence, A should be able to trust that B will not reveal or misuse the confidence and that third parties who may intentionally or accidentally discover the confidence will respect it.[18]

The alternative possibility is that by revealing her ideas to B, A is deemed to forfeit any right to control their use or communication. This principle is objectionable for a couple of reasons. First, it would most certainly increase reluctance to share ideas since our disclosure decisions are strongly influenced by the audience we anticipate. If we could not select our audience, that is, if the choice were only between keeping ideas to ourselves and sharing them with the world at large, many ideas would remain unexpressed, to the detriment of individual health as well as the general good.

Second, the principle would pose an impediment to the formation and sustenance of various types of cooperative relationships—relationships of love and friendship, as well as relationships forged for specific purposes such as education, medical care, or business. It might be thought that only ideas of an intimate or personal nature are important in this regard. But it is not only "personal" relationships, but cooperative relationships of all types, that are at stake. Shared knowledge and information of varying types are central to work relationships and communities—academic departments and disciplines, firms, teams—as well as other organizations. The possession of common ideas and information, to the exclusion of those outside the relationship or group, contributes to the group's self-definition and to the individual's sense of belonging. By permitting and protecting the sharing of confidences, trade secret principles, among other institutions, permit "special communities of knowledge" which nurture the social bonds and cooperative efforts through which we express our individuality and pursue common purposes.[19]

Of course, by disclosing her idea to B, A runs the risk that B or anyone else who learns about the idea may use it or share it further. But if B has agreed to respect the confidence, either explicitly or by participating in a relationship in which confidence is normally expected, she has a *prima facie* obligation not to disclose the information to which she is privy.[20] Institutions that give A a remedy against third parties who appropriate ideas shared in confidence reduce the risk that A's ideas will become public resources if she shares them with B. Such institutions thereby support confidential relationships and the cooperative undertakings that depend on them.

Yet another situation in which disclosure should not be regarded as a license for general use is the case of disclosures made as a result of deceit or insincere promises. Suppose A is an entrepreneur who has created an unusual software program with substantial sales potential. Another party, B, pretending to be a potential customer, questions A at great length about the code and other details of her program. A's disclosures are not intended to be, and should not be deemed, a contribution to the general pool of knowledge, nor should B be permitted to use A's ideas.[21] Respect for A's right to disclose her ideas requires that involuntary disclosures—such as those based on deceit, coercion, and theft of documents containing expressions of those ideas—not be regarded as forfeitures to the common pool of knowledge and information. In recognition of A's right to control disclosure of her ideas and to discourage appropriation of her ideas against her wishes, we might expect our institutions to provide A with a remedy against these sorts of appropriation. Trade secret law provides such a remedy.

Competitive fairness is also at stake if B is in competition with A. Besides having violated standards of common morality in using deceit to gain access to A's ideas, B is in a position to exploit those ideas in the marketplace without having contributed to the cost of their development. B can sell her version of the software more cheaply since she enjoys a substantial cost advantage compared to A, who may have invested a great deal of time and money in developing the software. Fairness in a competitive economy requires some limitations on the rights of firms to use ideas developed by others. In a system based on effort, it is both unfair and ultimately self-defeating to permit firms to have a free ride on the efforts of their competitors.[22]

Problematic Issues

Respect for personal control over the disclosure of ideas, respect for confidential relationships, common morality, and fair competition all point toward recognizing certain rights in ideas. Difficult questions will arise within this system of rights. If A is not an individual but an organization or group, should A have the same rights and remedies against B or third parties who use or communicate information shared with B in confidence? For example, suppose A is a corporation that hires an employee, B, to develop a marketing plan. If other employees of A reveal in confidence to B information they have created or assembled, should A be able to restrain B from using this information to benefit herself (at A's expense)? Does it matter if A is a two-person corporation or a corporation with 100,000 employees? What if A is a social club or a private school?

Hettinger seems to assume that corporate A's should not have such rights—on the grounds that they might restrict B's employment possibilities. It is certainly true that giving A a right against B if she reveals information communicated to her in confidence could rule out certain jobs for B. However, the alternative rule—that corporate A's should have no rights in ideas they reveal in confidence to others—has problems as well.

One problem involves trust. If our institutions do not give corporate A's certain rights in ideas they reveal in confidence to employees, A's will seek other means of ensuring that competitively valuable ideas are protected. They may contract individually with employees for those rights, and if our legal institutions do not uphold those contracts, employers will seek to hire individuals in whom they have personal trust. Hiring would probably become more dependent on family and personal relationships and there would be fewer opportunities for the less well connected. Institutional rules giving corporate A's rights against employees who reveal or use information given to them in confidence are a substitute for personal bonds of trust. While such rules are not cost-free and may have some morally undesirable consequences, they help sustain cooperative efforts and contribute to more open hiring practices.

Contrary to Hettinger's suggestion, giving corporate A's rights in the ideas they reveal in confidence to others does not always benefit the strong at the expense of the weak, or the large corporation at the expense of the individual, although this is surely sometimes the case.[23] Imagine three entrepreneurs who wish to expand their highly successful cookie business. A venture capitalist interested in financing the expansion naturally wishes to know the details of the operation—including the prized cookie recipe—before putting up capital. After examining the recipe, however, he decides that it would be more profitable for him to sell the recipe to CookieCo, a multinational food company, and to invest his capital elsewhere. Without money and rights to prevent others from using the recipe, the corporate entrepreneurs are very likely out of business. CookieCo, which can manufacture and sell the cookies much more cheaply, will undoubtedly find that most of the entrepreneurs' customers are quite happy to buy the same cookies for less at their local supermarket.

Non-Property Foundations of Trade Secret Law

To a large extent, the rights and remedies mentioned in the preceding discussion are those recognized by trade secret law. As this discussion showed, the concept of property is not necessary to justify these rights. Trade secret law protects against certain methods of appropriating the confidential and commercially valuable ideas of others. It affords a remedy to those whose commercially valuable secrets are acquired by misrepresentation, theft, bribery, breach or inducement of a breach of confidence, espionage, or other improper means.[24] Although the roots of trade secret principles have been variously located, respect for voluntary disclosure decisions and respect for confidential relationships provide the best account of the pattern of permitted and prohibited appropriations and use of ideas.[25] As Justice Oliver Wendell Holmes noted in a 1917 trade secret case, "The property may be denied but the confidence cannot be."[26] Trade secret law can also be seen as enforcing ordinary standards of morality in commercial relationships, thus ensuring some consistency with general social morality.[27]

It may well be true, as Hettinger and others have claimed, that the availability of trade secret protection provides an incentive for intellectual labor and the development of ideas. The knowledge that they have legal rights against those who "misappropriate" their ideas may encourage people to invest large amounts of time and money in exploring and developing ideas. However, the claim that trade secret protection promotes invention is quite different from the claim that it is grounded in or justified by this tendency. Even if common law trade secret rights did not promote intellectual labor or increase the dissemination and use of information, there would still be reasons to recognize those rights. Respect for people's voluntary disclosure decisions, respect for confidential relationships, standards of common morality, and fair competition would still point in that direction.

Moreover, promoting the development of ideas cannot be the whole story behind trade secret principles, since protection is often accorded to information such as customer data or cost and pricing information kept in the ordinary course of doing business. While businesses may need incentives to engage in costly research and development, they would certainly keep track of their customers and costs in any event.

The rationale for giving protection to such information must be other than promoting the invention, dissemination, and use of ideas. By the same token, trade secret principles do not prohibit the use of ideas acquired by studying products available in the marketplace. If the central policy behind trade secret protection were the promotion of invention, one might expect that trade secret law, like patent law, which was explicitly fashioned to encourage invention, would protect innovators from imitators.

The fact that Congress has enacted patent laws giving inventors a limited monopoly in exchange for disclosure of their ideas without at the same time eliminating state trade secret law may be a further indication that trade secret and patent protection rest on different grounds.[28] By offering a limited monopoly in exchange for disclosure, the patent laws implicitly recognize the more fundamental right not to disclose one's ideas at all or to disclose them in confidence to others.[29]

REASSESSING HETTINGER'S CRITICISM OF TRADE SECRET LAW

If we see trade secret law as grounded in respect for voluntary disclosure, confidential relationships, common morality, and fair competition, the force of Hettinger's criticisms diminishes somewhat. The problems he cites appear not merely in their negative light as detracting from an ideal "free flow of ideas," but in their positive role as promoting other important values.

Restrictions on Acquiring Ideas

Hettinger is critical, for example, of the fact that trade secret law restricts methods of acquiring ideas. But the prohibited means of acquisition—misrepresentation, theft, bribery, breach of confidence, and espionage—all reflect general social morality. Lifting these restrictions would undoubtedly contribute to the erosion of important values outside the commercial context.

How much trade secrecy laws inhibit the development and spread of ideas is also open to debate. Hettinger and others have claimed that trade secrecy is a serious impediment to innovation and dissemination because the period of permitted secrecy is unlimited. Yet, given the fact that trade secret law offers no protection for ideas acquired by examining or reverse-engineering products in the marketplace, it would appear rather difficult to maintain technical secrets embodied in those products while still exploiting their market potential. A standard example used to illustrate the problem of perpetual secrecy, the Coke formula, seems insufficient to establish that this is a serious problem. Despite the complexity of modern technology, successful reverse-engineering is common. Moreover, similar technical advances are frequently made by researchers working independently. Trade secret law poses no impediment in either case. Independent discoverers are free to exploit their ideas even if they are similar to those of others.

As for nontechnical information such as marketing plans and business strategies, the period of secrecy is necessarily rather short since implementation entails disclosure. Competitor intelligence specialists claim that most of the information needed to understand what competitors are doing is publicly available.[30] All of these considerations suggest that trade secret principles are not such a serious impediment to the dissemination of information.

Competitive Effects

Hettinger complains that trade secret principles stifle competition. Assessing this claim is very difficult. On one hand, it may seem that prices would be lower if firms were permitted to obtain cost or other market advantages by using prohibited means to acquire protected ideas from others. Competitor access to the Coke formula would most likely put downward pressure on the price of "the real thing." Yet, it is also reasonable to assume that the law keeps prices down by reducing the costs of self-protection. By giving some assurance that commercially valuable secrets will be protected, the law shields firms from having to bear the full costs of protection. It is very hard to predict what would happen to prices if trade secret protection were eliminated. Self-protection would be more costly and would tend to drive prices up, while increased competition would work in the opposite direction. There would surely be important differences in morale and productivity. Moreover, as noted, any price reductions for consumers would come at a cost to the basic moral standards of society if intelligence-gathering by bribery, misrepresentation, and espionage were permitted.

Restrictions on Employee Mobility

Among Hettinger's criticisms of trade secret law, the most serious relate to restrictions on employee mobility. In practice, employers often attempt to protect information by overrestricting the postemployment opportunities of employees. Three important factors contribute to this tendency: vagueness about which information is confidential; disagreement about the proper allocation of rights to ideas generated by employees using their employers' resources; and conceptual difficulties in distinguishing general knowledge and employer-specific knowledge acquired on the job. Courts, however, are already doing what Hettinger recommends, namely, limiting the restrictions that employers can place on future employment in the name of protecting ideas.[31] Although the balance between employer and employee interests is a delicate one not always equitably struck, the solution of eliminating trade secret protection altogether is overbroad and undesirable, considering the other objectives at stake.

Hypothetical Alternatives

Hettinger's discussion of our intellectual property institutions reflects an assumption that greater openness and sharing would occur if we eliminated trade secret protection. He argues that trade secret principles encourage secrecy. He speaks of the "free flow of ideas" as the ideal that would obtain in the absence of our intellectual property institutions. This supposition strikes me as highly unlikely. People keep secrets and establish confidential relationships for a variety of reasons that are quite independent of any legal protection these secrets might have. The psychology and sociology of secrets have been explored by others. Although much economic theory is premised on complete information, secrecy and private information are at the heart of day-to-day competition in the marketplace.

In the absence of something like trade secret principles, I would expect not a free flow of ideas but greater efforts to protect information through contracts, management systems designed to limit information access, security equipment, and electronic counterintelligence devices. I would also expect stepped-up efforts to acquire intelligence from others through espionage, bribery, misrepresentation, and other unsavory means. By providing some assurance that information can be shared in confidence and by protecting against unethical methods of extracting information and undermining confidentiality, trade secret principles promote cooperation and security, two important conditions for intellectual endeavor. In this way, trade secret principles may ultimately promote intellectual effort by limiting information flow.

THE BURDEN OF JUSTIFICATION

We may begin thinking about information rights, as Hettinger does, by treating all ideas as part of a common pool and then deciding whether and how to allocate to individuals rights to items in the pool. Within this framework, ideas are conceived on the model of tangible property.[32] Just as, in the absence of social institutions, we enter the world with no particular relationship to its tangible assets or natural resources, we have no particular claim on the world's ideas. In this scheme, as Hettinger asserts, the "burden of justification is very much on those who would restrict the maximal use of intellectual objects."

Alternatively, we may begin, as I do, by thinking of ideas in relation to their originators, who may or may not share their ideas with specific others or contribute them to the common pool. This approach treats ideas as central to personality and the social world individuals construct for themselves. Ideas are not, in the first instance, freely available natural resources. They originate with people, and it is the connections among people, their ideas, and their relationships with others that provides a baseline for discussing rights in ideas. Within this conception, the burden of justification is on those who would argue for disclosure obligations and general access to ideas.

The structure of specific rights that emerges from these different frameworks depends not only on where the burden of justification is located, but also on how easily it can be discharged.[33] It is unclear how compelling a case is required to overcome the burden Hettinger sets up and, consequently, difficult to gauge the depth of my disagreement with him.[34] Since Hettinger does not consider the rationales for trade secret principles discussed here, it is not clear whether he would dismiss them altogether, find them insufficiently weighty to override the presumption he sets up, or agree that they satisfy the burden of justification.

One might suspect, however, from the absence of discussion of the personal and social dimension of rights in ideas that Hettinger does not think them terribly important, and that his decision to put the burden of justification on those who argue for rights in ideas reflects a fairly strong commitment to openness. On the assumption that our alternative starting points reflect seriously held substantive views (they are not just procedural devices to get the argument started) and that both frameworks require strong reasons to overcome the initial presumption, the resulting rights and obligations are likely to be quite different in areas where neither confidentiality nor openness is critical to immediate human needs. Indeed, trade secrecy law is an area where these different starting points would be likely to surface.

The key question to ask about these competing frameworks is which is backed by stronger reasons. My opposition to Hettinger's allocation of the burden of justification rests on my rejection of his conception of ideas as natural resources and on different views of how the world would look in the absence of our intellectual property institutions. In contrast, my starting point acknowledges the importance of ideas to our sense of ourselves and the communities (including work communities) of which we are a part. It is also more compatible with the way we commonly talk about ideas. Our talk about disclosure obligations presupposes a general background right not to reveal ideas. If it were

otherwise, we would speak of concealment rights. To use the logically interesting feature of nonexclusiveness as a starting point for moral reasoning about rights in ideas seems wholly arbitrary.

CONCLUSION

Knives, forks, and spoons are all designed to help us eat. In a sense, however, the essential function of these tools is to help us cut, since without utensils, we could still consume most foods with our hands. One might be tempted to say that since cutting is the essential function of eating utensils, forks and spoons should be designed to facilitate cutting. One might even say that insofar as forks and spoons do not facilitate cutting, they should be redesigned. Such a modification, however, would rob us of valuable specialized eating instruments.

Hettinger's train of thought strikes me as very similar. He purports to examine the justification of our various intellectual property institutions. However, he settles on a justification that really only fits patent and, arguably, copyright institutions. He then suggests that other intellectual property rights be assessed against the justification he proposes and redesigned insofar as they are found wanting. In particular, he suggests that trade secret principles be modified to look more like patent principles. Hettinger fails to appreciate the various rationales behind the rights and duties understood under the heading "intellectual property," especially those recognized by trade secret law.

I agree with Hettinger that our intellectual property institutions need a fresh look from a utilitarian perspective.[35] The seventeen-year monopoly granted through patents is anachronistic given the pace of technological development today. We need to think about the appropriate balance between employer and employee rights in ideas developed jointly. Solutions to the problem of the unauthorized copying of software may be found in alternative pricing structures rather than in fundamental modifications of our institutions. Public interest considerations could be advanced for opening access to privately held information in a variety of areas. As we consider these specific questions, however, I would urge that we keep firmly in mind the variety of objectives that intellectual property institutions have traditionally served.[36] If, following Hettinger's advice, we single-mindedly reshape these institutions to maximize the short-term dissemination and use of ideas, we run the risk of subverting the other ends these institutions serve.

Notes

1. Edwin C. Hettinger, "Justifying Intellectual Property," *Philosophy & Public Affairs* 18, no. 1 (Winter 1989): 31–52.

2. Thomas Jefferson agrees. See Jefferson's letter to Isaac McPherson, 13 August 1813, in *The Founder's Constitution*, ed. Philip B. Kurland and Ralph Lerner (Chicago: University of Chicago Press, 1987), 3:42.

3. Hettinger uses the term *utilitarian* is a very narrow sense to refer to a justification in terms of maximizing the use and dissemination of information. Some utilitarians might see intellectual property institutions as promoting objectives other than information dissemination. My discussion of the roots of trade secret principles is perfectly consistent with a utilitarian justification of those principles. Indeed, a utilitarian could argue (as many economists do) that giving people certain rights in ideas they generate through their own labor advances social well-being by promoting innovation. See, e.g., Robert U. Ayres, "Technological Protection and Piracy: Some Implications for Policy," *Technological Forecasting and Social Change* 30 (1986):5–18.

4. In Hettinger's paper and in mine, the term *justification, goal, purpose, rationale,* and *objective* are used loosely and somewhat interchangeably. But, of course, identifying the purpose or goal of our intellectual property institutions does not automatically justify them. Some further legitimating idea or ultimate good, such as the general welfare or individual liberty, must be invoked. A difficulty with Hettinger's argument is that he identifies an objective for our intellectual property institutions—promoting the use and dissemination of ideas—and concludes that he has justified them. However, unless maximizing the use and dissemination of ideas is an intrinsic good, we would expect a further step in the argument linking this objective to an ultimate good. Hettinger may think this step can be made or is self-evident from his terminology. However, it is not clear whether he calls his justification "utilitarian" because of its consequentialist form or because he means to appeal to social well-being or some particular good he associates with utilitarianism.

5. Hettinger seems to think that he has provided a clear-cut objective against which to measure the effectiveness of our intellectual property institutions. Yet, a set of institutions that maximized the "dissemination and use of information" would not necessarily be most effective at "promoting the creation of valuable intellectual works" or promoting " 'the progress of science and the useful arts' ". A society might be quite successful at disseminating information, but rather mediocre at creating valuable intellectual works.

There is an inevitable tension between the objectives of innovation and dissemination. The same tension is present in other areas of law concerned with rights in information—insider trading, for example. For discussion of this tension, see Frank H. Easterbrook, "Insider Trading, Secret Agents, Evidentiary Privileges, and the Production of Information," *1981 Supreme Court Review*, p. 309. While we struggle to piece together a system of information rights that gives due consideration to both objectives, we must be wary of the notion that there is a single optimal allocation of rights.

Indeed, the very idea of a "socially optimal output of intellectual products" is embarrassingly imprecise. What is a socially optimal output of poems, novels, computer programs, movies, cassette recordings, production processes, formulations of matter, stock tips, business strategies, etc.? How we allocate rights in ideas may affect the quality and kinds of intellectual products that are produced as well as their quantity and dissemination. Hettinger seems concerned primarily with quantity. The use of general terms like *intellectual product* and *socially optimal output* obscures the complexity of the empirical assessment that Hettinger proposes.

6. Hettinger mentions trademark as another of our intellectual property institutions, along with our social sanction on plagiarism, but his central discussion focuses on copyright, patent, and trade secret concepts. Neither trademark principles nor the prohibition on plagiarism fits comfortably with his justification in terms of increasing the dissemination and use of ideas. Both are more closely related to giving recognition to the source or originator of ideas and products.

7. It may be helpful to think of two levels of justification: (1) an intermediate level consisting of objectives, purposes, reasons, and explanations for an institution or practice; and (2) an ultimate level linking those objectives and purposes to our most basic legitimating ideas such as the general good or individual liberty. Philosophers generally tend to be concerned with the ultimate level of justification while policymakers and judges more frequently operate at the intermediate level. Hettinger has, I think, mistaken an intermediate-level justification of patents and copyrights (promoting the dissemination and use of ideas) for an ultimate justification of intellectual property institutions.

8. Hettinger, of course, recognizes that various rights are involved. He speaks of rights to possess, to personally use, to prevent others from using, to publish, and to receive the market value of one's ideas. And he notes that one might have a natural right to possess and personally use one's ideas even if one might not have a natural right to prevent others from copying them. But he does not consider the possibility that the different rights involved in our concept of intellectual property

may rest on quite varied foundations, some firmer than others.

9. It is generally accepted that the concept of property is best understood as a "bundle of rights." Just as the bundle of rights involved in home ownership differs substantially from the bundle of rights associated with stock ownership, the bundle of rights involved in patent protection differs from the bundle of rights involved in trade secret protection.

10. Today we commonly speak of copyright protection as providing incentives for intellectual effort, while at the same time ensuring widespread dissemination of ideas. As Hettinger notes, the effectiveness of copyright protection in achieving these aims may depend partly on the period of the copyright grant. Historically, at least before the first English copyright act, the famous 1710 Act of Anne, it appears that the dissemination of ideas was not so central. The common law gave the author an exclusive first right of printing or publishing her manuscript on the grounds that she was entitled to the product of her labor. The common law's position on the author's right to prohibit subsequent publication was less clear. See generally *Wheaton v. Peters*, 8 Pet. 591 (1834), reprinted in *The Founders' Constitution* 3:44–60.

11. Hettinger recognizes a right not to divulge privately created intellectual products, but he does not fit this right into his discussion. If the right is taken seriously, however, it will, I believe, undermine Hettinger's own conclusions.

12. We would hope that the right to control disclosure would be exercised in a morally responsible way and that, for example, people with socially useful ideas would share them and that some types of harmful ideas would be withheld. But the potential social benefits of certain disclosures cannot justify a general requirement that ideas be disclosed.

13. Here, I am using the term *personal* to refer to ideas about intimate matters, such as sexual behavior.

14. The right to control disclosure of one's thoughts might be thought to be no more than a reflection of technical limitations. Enforcing a general disclosure requirement presupposes some way of identifying the undisclosed thoughts of others. Currently, we do not have the technology to do this. But even if we did—or especially if we did—respect for the individual would preclude any form of monitoring people's thoughts.

15. On the relation between privacy and intimate relationships, see Charles Fried, "Privacy," *Yale Law Journal* 77 (1968): 475–93. Below, I will argue that confidentiality is central to other types of cooperative relationships as well.

16. Whether the presumption is overcome will depend on the importance of the objectives served by disclosure, and the degree of violence done to the individual or the relationship at stake.

17. Technically, of course, others have access to ideas that have been expressed whereas they do not have access to undisclosed thoughts. But ease of access is not the criterion for propriety of access.

18. This is the fundamental principle behind the prohibition on insider trading.

19. The phrase "special communities of knowledge" comes from Kim Lane Scheppele, *Legal Secrets* (Chicago: University of Chicago Press, 1988), p. 14.

20. In practice, this prima facie obligation may sometimes be overridden when it conflicts with other obligations, e.g., the obligation to prevent harm to a third party.

21. An actual case similar to this was litigated in Pennsylvania. See *Continental Data Systems, Inc. v. Exxon Corporation*, 638 F. Supp. 432 (D.C.E.D. Pa. 1986).

22. For the view that fair and honest business competition is the central policy underlying trade secret protection, see Ramon A. Klitzke, "Trade Secrets: Importing Quasi-Property Rights," *Business Lawyer* 41 (1986): 557–70.

23. It appears that Hettinger is using the term *private company* in contrast to individuals rather than to public companies—those whose shares are sold to the public on national stock exchanges. If one wishes to protect individuals, however, it might be more important to distinguish small, privately held companies from large, publicly held ones than to distinguish individuals from companies. Many individuals, however, are dependent on large, publicly held companies as their livelihood.

24. *Uniform Trade Secrets Act with 1985 Amendments*, sec. 1, in *Uniform Laws Annotated*, vol. 14 (1980 with 1988 Pocket Part). The Uniform Trade Secrets Act seeks to codify and standardize the common law principles of trade secret law as they have developed in different jurisdictions.

25. See Klitzke, "Trade Secrets." Different theories of justification are discussed in Ridsdale Ellis, *Trade Secrets* (New York: Baker, Voorhis, 1953). Kim Lane Scheppele is another commentator favoring the view that breach of confidence is what trade secret cases are all about. See *Legal Secrets*, p. 241. In their famous article on privacy, Warren and Brandeis find the roots of trade secret principles in the right to privacy. Samuel D. Warren and Louis D. Brandeis, *Harvard Law Review* 4 (1890):212.

26. E. I. DuPont de Nemours Powder Co. v. Masland, 244 U.S. 100 (1917).

27. One commentator has said, "The desire to reinforce 'good faith and honest, fair dealing' in business is the mother of the law of trade secrets." Russell B. Stevenson, Jr., *Corporations and Information* (Baltimore: Johns Hopkins University Press, 1980), p. 19.

28. Support for this interpretation is found in Justice Thurgood Marshall's concurring opinion in *Kewanee Oil Co. v. Bicron Corp.*, 416 U.S. 470, 494 (1974). The court held that the federal patent laws do not preempt state trade secret laws.

29. Congress may have realized that trying to bring about more openness by eliminating tarde secret protection, even with the added attraction of a limited monopoly for inventions that quality for patent protection, would be inconsistent with fundamental moral notions such as respect for confidential relationships, and would probably not have worked anyway.

30. See, e.g., the statement of a manger of a competitor surveillance group quoted in Jerry L. Wall, "What the Competition Is Doing: Your Need to Know," *Harvard Business Review* 52 (November-December 1974): 34. See generally Leonard M. Fuld, *Competitor Intelligence: How to Get It—How to Use IT* (New York: John Wiley and Sons, 1985).

31. See, e.g., John Burgess, "Unlocking Corporate Shackles," *Washington Business,* 11 December 1989, p. 1.

32. Hettinger speaks of ideas as objects, and of rights in ideas as comparable to water or mineral rights. Indeed, according to Hettinger, the difficulty in justifying intellectual property rights arises because ideas are not in all respects like tangible property, which he thinks is more easily justified.

33. The Editors of *Philosophy & Public Affairs* encouraged me to address this point.

34. His argument from maximizing the production and dissemination of ideas suggests that the presumption in favor of free ideas is not terribly strong: it can be overridden by identifying some reasonable objective likely to be served by assigning exclusive rights.

35. That is, we should look at the effects of these institutions on social well-being in general and select the institutions that are best on the whole.

36. A utilitarian assessment will also include consideration of the various interests that would be affected by alternative allocations of intellectual property rights. For example, denying authors copyright in their works may increase the power and profit of publishers and further impair the ability of lesser-known writers to find publication outlets. One scholar has concluded that America's failure to recognize the copyrights of aliens before 1891 stunted the development of native literature. For fifty years before the passage of the Platt-Simmonds Act, publishing interests vigorously and successfully opposed recognition of international copyright. This is understandable since the works of well-known British authors were available to publishers free of charge. Publishers were not terribly concerned with the artistic integrity of these works. They sometimes substituted alterative endings, mixed the works of different authors, and edited as economically necessary. There were few reasons to take the risks involved in publishing the works of unknown and untested American writers who might insist on artistic integrity. See generally Aubert J. Clark, *The Movement for International Copyright in Nineteenth Century America* (Westport, Conn.: Greenwood Press. 1973).

Mark Alfino

Intellectual Property and Copyright Ethics

Philosophers have given relatively little attention to the ethical issues surrounding the nature of intellectual property in spite of the fact that for the past ten years the public policy debate over "fair use" of copyrighted materials in higher education has been heating up. This neglect is especially striking since copyright ethics are at stake in so many aspects of academic life: the photocopying of materials for classroom use and scholarly work, access to electronic texts, and the cost and availability of single-source information technology such as

Dialogue, library card catalogues, the *Oxford English Dictionary,* and a variety of other print and electronic resources. Of course, the ethics of copyright are not only an issue for those of us in the business of education: recent allegations of copyright infringement by Texaco, which regularly photocopied articles from scientific and technical journals for its employees, suggests that questions about copyright ethics may arise regularly for every corporation and business. While the recent lawsuits against Kinko's Copies[1] and Texaco may settle some public policy questions in the short run, the legal discourse on fair use depends upon competing ethical institutions which are not likely to be resolved soon.

The ethical quandaries surrounding fair use will not be resolved by appealing to well known principles of property rights. One reason for this is that copying a book involves an act of labor which, one might allege, creates property in the copy. Unlike the act of labor involved in theft, copying does not, in any obvious way, involve

From Mark Alfino, "Intellectual Property and Copyright Ethics," *Business & Professional Ethics Journal,* vol. 10, No. 2 (Summer 1991). Reprinted with permission.

the removal of someone else's property or the violation of their privacy. In the course of our discussion, I will show that there are strong counter arguments to this argument. But here, at the outset, a labor theory of property offers no decisive answer. Second, the electronic transmission of data throws the whole notion of what a "copy" is into confusion: Is text from a database on a terminal a copy? Is an electronic copy of a data file analogous to a paper copy of a printed work? Third, the development of computer software threatens to blur the distinction between a copyright and a patent. Traditionally, patents protect processes or products of processes which show genuine technical innovation. In return for registering (and making public) the process, society grants a limited monopoly to the inventor. Copyrights involve similar protections (though of a longer duration) for the novel expression of ideas. Computer software is a hybrid, combining both novel expressions of old ideas (e.g. displaying a print spreadsheet on a video terminal) and new processes for doing things (e.g. the transformation of a calendar into an algorithm for displaying and printing calendars. There is no escaping the fact that computer software and hardware is transforming the distinction between processes of production (candidates for patents) and expressions of ideas (candidates for copyright).

Finally, new developments in scholarship such as the growth of film studies and the development of video technology as an instructional medium, raise difficult problems for handling copyrights to videotapes and video broadcasts. Typically the more "commercial" a product is the more the courts have been willing to protect copyright holders. When a commercial object seen as a movie or documentary becomes an object of study, a confusion arises as to whether fair use should be determined by looking at the motives for its production or the demands of education and scholarship. The 1978 copyright law is far more generous in exempting from protection classroom texts rather than video and broadcasts.

It took several centuries for public discourse to evolve a coherent way of balancing the property claims of print publishers with the society's legitimate claim to have access to cultural works and knowledge. In little more than three decades, the discourse on copyright has been challenged in ways in which the first writers of copyright laws and the most prominent philosophers of property rights could not have imagined. It is hard to imagine John Locke responding to *droit morale* [i.e., moral right] issues such as the artist's right to prevent colorization of films, the reinstallation of contemporary sculptures, or the effect of remodeling a building on the architect's reputation. All of these cases involve copyright issues.

My central contention in this paper is that settling intellectual property questions requires us to attend to the development of the technology of intellectual production and to an ongoing social discourse about the production and value of knowledge and culture. I think these two social processes, technology and discourse about the status of knowledge, are always at work in the emergence of ethical problems and copyright[2] and I think they are also the place to look for solutions. If I am right then policy arguments which proceed primarily by a retrieval of abstract thought on the metaphysical principles of property are inadequate. I will demonstrate my thesis first by showing that our basic understanding of copyright is itself a product of clashes between technological development and social discourse about the value of knowledge and culture. Then I will discuss efforts which focus either exclusively or primarily on a retrieval of property rights talk. I find Edwin Hettinger's work particularly important in this regard, because I think he has a keen sense of the inadequacy of traditional arguments about property rights. Finally, I will show how new copyright policy can be forged by attending to the actual social process (both technological and conversational) which create our difficulties in the first place.

I. Historical and Critical Studies of Copyright and Authorship

In order to show how policy questions arise and are settled, I would like to recount a significant episode in the history of the development of modern copyright law. My specific claim in relating this history is that social values about technology, knowledge, and culture are the real determinants of our thinking about copyright. Of course, a mere history does not tell us that these *should* be the determinants of our thinking. I will not be prepared to make that claim until I show the inadequacy of some other approaches, which I will do in Section II. Still, I think the story I am about to tell goes some way toward *showing* the reasonableness of my general claim.

The best general history of the development of copyright in England remains Lyman Patterson's *Copyright in Historical Perspective,* which traces the development of copyright from the origin of the printing press to the refinement of the modern copyright statues as a result of the 18th century "Battle of the Books." Copyright began as a royal prerogative granted to the main publishing guild, the Stationers Company. The granting of a license to control copy was originally motivated by the crown's desire to control the spread of potentially threatening religious or political ideas.[3] Until the first modern copyright statute, the 1709 Statute of Anne, the Stationers Company enjoyed an unlimited monopoly over copy, including at times, the right to search buildings and seize copy.[4]

Modern copyright laws, which recognize, as a matter of moral principle, a limit to the monopoly which control of copy entails, begin with the Statute of Anne in 1709, subtitled "An Act for the Encouragement of Learning, by Vesting the Copies of Printed Books in the Authors or Purchasers of such Copies, during the Times herein mentioned." The act first gave legal expression to the idea that the social value of disseminating information and culture was great enough to justify limiting the property interests of publishers. The act also prepared the way for an author's copyright.

The Stationers argued for and received extensions to the statutory limits of copyright in the act. They continued to charge exorbitant prices for classics of English literature and editions of the Bible, to which they owned the copyright. The "Battle of the Books" took place during the first three quarters of the 18th century[5] as independent publishers, in sympathy with the "Society for the Encouragement of Learning,"

challenged copyright holders by producing unauthorized editions of popular English literature. In the celebrated case of *Donaldson v. Beckett* (1774), a lasting precedent against perpetual copyright was established.

Mark Rose[6] rightly takes the Donaldson case as a turning point in our thinking about copyright. He shows, quite successfully, that behind the Donaldson case lay a variety of changes including a new attitude toward authorship, the development of a market for intellectual labor, and the application of the justification of private property to intellectual labor.

In the Donaldson case, owners of the copyright to James Thompson's *The Seasons* sued Alexander Donaldson for producing unauthorized copies of the popular work. The defense argued that the statutory period of monopoly granted by the Statute of Anne had run out and that the copy was therefore not protected. The plaintiff argued that copyright is a common-law property right and that statutes merely supplement, but do not absolutely limit, the enjoyment of the right. After a three week hearing before the House of Lords, which featured packed galleries and daily attention from the press, the defense won and the statutory basis of copyright was never again challenged in either England or the United States.

The legal principle at stake in the Donaldson case has significant ethical implications. If copyright is a form of limited monopoly granted through statute, based on policy considerations, and not an absolute common law right, the ethical burden of proof shifts to copyright holders to show that their property interests are more important than the public good of having access to information. The ethical issue takes a metaphysical turn when we ask, as we shall in section II, just what it is that constitutes the intellectual property protected by copyright. Again, if the "substance" of intellectual property is constituted by statutory fiat, then the limitations of the right are not analogous to limitations of natural rights.

Two kinds of arguments for perpetual copyright were offered during the 18th century. First, the Stationers alleged, especially with regard to literature, that authors are entitled to a perpetual property right because their work is an original invention. Second, many claimed that intellectual property is analogous to real estate and that the right of ownership derives from a right of "occupation." William Blackstone argued in his *Commentaries* (1765–1769) that in publishing a book one is not offering something for public use, as when land is given for use as a highway. Rather, "In such a case, it is more like making a way through a man's own private grounds, which he may stop at pleasure; he may give out a number of keys, by publishing a number of copies; but no man who receives a key, has thereby a right to forge others, and sell them to other people."[7] Thus, Blackstone asserted an analogy between intellectual property and real property over which one has a right of occupation. If Blackstone is right then public access to copyrighted works is not a public right but a kind of visitation right. Copyright infringement is thus not so much theft as trespassing.

The argument from invention, on the other hand, identifies the production of the text with the person of the author. The text is uniquely tied to its origin in the personality of the author. As an extension of the person of the author, the expression embodied in the printed text is quintessentially [essentially] personal property. The argument from occupation satisfies a similar intuition in a different way. It harkens back to a notion of original appropriation. Prior to its expression by the author, the work was like unowned property. Expression is a way of "staking out" or "homesteading" a territory. The peculiar strength to this argument is that it doesn't have to explain how appropriation remains legitimate once all land is originally occupied. As long as there are infinitely many ways to express something, the author's occupation of his intellectual estate cannot be considered an unjust monopoly.

If these seem like metaphysically extravagant arguments we should look briefly at how great a burden of proof is assumed in any argument for copyright as a natural property right. While there is no question that the physical text is a piece of physical property, the proponent of copyright as a common law right must claim that a right exists in the ownership of the ideal expression which lies "behind" the text. The

argument will not succeed without an appeal to some metaphysical entity which is related to the personality of the author in some way that is relevant to the author's most fundamental interests. In the following passage, William Enfield, a contemporary of Blackstone's, identifies that interest as the profitability of the work. Intellectual property is justified because it is as real a means of making a livelihood as cultivating land:

In this various world different men are born to different fortunes: one inherits a portion of land; he cultivates it with care, it produces him corn and fruits and wool: another possesses a fruitful mind, teeming with ideas of every kind; he bestows his labor in cultivating *that*; the produce is reason, sentiment, philosophy. It seems but equitable, that a fair exchange should be made of these goods; and that one man should live by the labor of his brain, as well as another by the sweat of his brow.[8]

Ultimately, the argument from invention and the argument from original appropriation dovetail, since behind both lie the intuition that through intellectual labor one makes an original acquisition of a profitable object. The difficult part of the justification is to show that one is morally entitled to the profit which can be made from regarding the ownership of the expression of ideas as an exclusive entitlement. The claim of a just property interest in the potential distribution of the object depends upon *first* regarding that object as an abstract metaphysical entity, but neither argument really justifies the existence of such an entity. The form of the argument is: If we regard intellectual property as an ideal object, then it is analogous to productive land. Alternatively, we could hold to the view that the production of a book is like the production of any other object which requires some ingenuity and labor to produce. Then the form of the argument would be: If we regard intellectual property as the objects produced by the joint labor of authors and printers, then it is analogous to the sale of a commodity. In the case of a book, the commodity happens to be reproducible, whether by copying the book longhand or by printing or photocopying. We can compare the book's reproducibility to the reproducibility of any other object. Of course, these alternatives don't tell us which way we should frame the argument, but they show that we could think quite coherently of intellectual property without the metaphysical abstraction which Blackstone's argument entails. We either need a way of choosing between the two ways of framing the argument or we need to recognize that the general argument itself is based on a consideration of social and personal interests extrinsic to the nature of intellectual activity itself.[9]

Before moving to a philosophical consideration of copyright ethics, we should identify some of the specific virtues of critical historical research on this topic. It is a commonplace of much work in ethics that the historical justifications for our ethical intuitions do not settle ethical issues in any ultimate way. The arguments put forward by Blackstone and others during the "Battle of the Books" have a kind of historical interest, but do they reveal the direction which philosophical argumentation should take?

While it is surely naive to suppose that history simply reveals fundamental ethical principles (at least without the interpretive activity of the historical philosopher), it is also unreasonable to suppose that ethical norms which *have histories* are always justifiable apart from the actual social practices to which their histories refer. At a minimum the history of a norm reveals the changing needs to which the norm responds. We may decide that it was historically accidental that certain values were not recognized as fundamental long before they were in fact recognized, but in other cases we cannot help but feel that the value itself is largely motivated by historical circumstance, even if it is logically related to other, more "primary" values which seem less contingent.

In the case of copyright, this tension between *a priori* justification and historical contingency is particularly acute. In the context of the history of the West, it is significant that the ethical values which underlie copyright law emerge alongside the development of economic markets for intellectual labor, the decline of the patronage system, a change in the correlation between literacy and membership in an upper class or clerical class, and the development of a new explanation of intellectual production which emphasized "invention" and "original genius."

The connection between the rise of the modern understanding of copyright and the decline of older more traditional ways of thinking about the credit one deserves for intellectual achievement and the social reward system for the same is well documented.[10] Doubtless, we are a long way from Martin Luther's warning to printers not to be covetous of the proceeds from distributing intellectual works. Luther argued, "I have freely received, freely do I give and expect nothing in return."[11] However, an awareness of the variety of ways of thinking about the values and obligations associated with intellectual production cannot help but persuade the reader that there may be no unique, ahistorical formula for understanding copyright ethics. Rather, a coherent and justified ethical understanding of copyright will have to take into account the actual historical practices governing intellectual production and the value of intellectual activity. This includes an analysis of the technological, political, and economic conditions under which copyrights are claimed. While I certainly do not think that current practices are "self-justifying," I do believe that the justifiability of our ethical intuitions about copyright are so closely connected to current institutional practices that no adequate analysis of the former can ignore the latter. That is why my own position in section III is constructed in relation to concrete problems posed by the institutional practices of publishers, libraries, and educators.

In the next section, I consider two efforts by philosophers to give abstract justifications for positions in copyright ethics. In my criticisms of these efforts I will give further support to the claim made above, that no coherent understanding of copyright can be achieved which does not consider the actual historical conditions under which intellectual labor takes place.

II. PHILOSOPHICAL APPROACHES TO COPYRIGHT ETHICS

Selmer Bringsjord[12] argues on purely logical grounds that since we have strong intuitions that some forms of copying are permissible and since we cannot make a logical distinction between various forms of copying, therefore all forms of copying are morally permissible.[13]

When scholars think about whether it is morally permissible to photocopy a text, they cannot help but be struck by how much of their everyday activity involves copying in the general sense of the word. Even without considering copying technology (which really includes everything from the pencil to the text scanner), mental activity itself seems to be a form of copying. Surely no one believes that when I jot down a few notes to aid my memory, I am violating any ethical norm. Even if I make several longhand copies of a lengthy passage[14] and distribute them to my friends, it is hard to identify, at first glance, a moral harm. The introduction of copy technology, it might be alleged, doesn't introduce any new logical features. After all, at one level of use, the copying machine merely replaces the laborious work of copying text longhand. At another level, it merely obviates the need to lug large bound journals back to one's study. Apart from the speed and efficiency of the copying, there seems to be little difference between:

a. reciting from memory a long poem for several friends on different occasions;
b. sending them longhand copies; and
c. sending them photocopies.

If we consider enough cases, we may come to the same conclusion which Bringsjord does that it is morally permissible to copy anything that is in public circulation as long as you don't plan to sell the copy. Because his argument, like the one above, depends upon a gradation of similar cases, I will call such arguments *gradation arguments*. While gradation arguments show us some interesting features of the activity of copying, I think they are fundamentally inadequate as a means of deciding any ethical issues concerning copyright.

The actual argument schema for Bringsjord's argument is a little different than the example above. The basic idea is to argue from a case in which we have no qualms about copying through a series of cases which are not different in any obvious logical or moral sense to a case,

finally, which most people (including the framers of the copyright law) would consider unethical. Since there are no logical differences among the particular cases, the conclusion is that the judgement that the last case is unethical is unjustified. The presupposition of this approach is that there can be no differences in our moral appraisal of two cases of copying unless there is a logical difference between the two cases. To illustrate the argument schema, Bringsjord considers twelve cases of "renting a video" beginning with a person who watches the video and "replays" the events in memory, moving through cases in which the viewer has more and more vivid recollections and more and more fantastic abilities to reproduce the movie for friends, ending finally with a case in which the viewer has devised a machine for replaying the movie. It is perhaps relevant that in the fantasy of the thought experiment, we are requested to imagine that the machine has made its recording directly from the brain of the well-situated viewer. This makes the ultimate copy much like the spontaneous reproduction from memory with which the gradation of cases began.

Bringsjord's argument is quite clever and really does capture our feeling that different cases of copying really don't have different morally relevant logical features. One striking example of this concerns the distinction between fair use in scholarly research and fair use in classroom distribution of copyrighted materials. Current guidelines governing the former are much more liberal than those governing the latter. If someone were to challenge my distribution of a packet of readings, I could place the readings on reserve and require each student to copy them individually. But is there really a moral principle at issue here? We could imagine a gradation of cases between purely spontaneous individual copying, which is protected, and systematic copying, which is not, and not find a single step in the succession of cases in which a morally relevant logical difference occurred. As long as we focus on the copying activity itself, the bottom line is that a copy is a copy is a copy.

But this is just where the limitation of Bringsjord's argument becomes apparent. He assumes uncritically that the issue of the moral permissibility of copying is to be decided by looking at the logical structure of the copying activity itself. This approach ignores the fact that the same activity performed in different situations may have different moral implications. If the goal of copyright law (and with it copyright ethics) is to promote invention, discovery and intellectual achievement within the context of a free market, then some copying (e.g. systematic copying, even if not for sale) might be judged immoral even though it is no more or less an instance of copying which under other circumstances is judged moral. For example, suppose that one day I am copying from Plato's *Sophist* and, being scrupulous, I determine that there are no living relatives of the copyright owners (in this case the translator). The next day I copy the complete text of a new best selling novel by an up and coming young author. The two cases are logically equivalent, yet there are morally relevant contextual differences.

Bringsjord also makes a rather weak defense against an objection to the logical apparatus behind the argument. One might object, drawing on a paradox from Plato, that by the addition of incremental features, none of which by itself is morally objectionable, one can conclude, fallaciously, that the whole sum of these increments introduces no morally objectionable feature. To use Bringsjord's example, if I claim that a one inch tall man is short and that after adding one billionth of an inch to him he is still short, I might deduce from these premises that a 500 foot tall man is short. The "paradox" is that the argument "is formally valid and has apparently obviously true premises, yet the conclusion is absurd."[15] The author excuses his own argument from this fallacy because he feels the conclusion (that copying is morally permissible) is not absurd. Of course, one's choice of words in an argument is almost always crucial. The fallacy occurs not only when the conclusions are "absurd" but also when they are simply not necessarily true. While the author's conclusion is not absurd, it may or may not be true. Therefore, I think it does commit the fallacy.

But the more serious flaw in the argument was the first one. We cannot assume that moral questions about copying can be resolved without considering the substantive moral issues which underlie our intuitions. In the case of

copyright ethics these issues include respect for the author's achievement, respect for property interests, and a recognition of the social claim to fruits of intellectual activity and the social right of free access to information.

Since many of these values are incorporated into natural rights and utilitarian arguments for property, we might have better luck with Edwin Hettinger's consideration of such arguments.[16] Hettinger gives a critical assessment of two traditional justifications of copyright:

1. Copyrights are justified as personal property rights; and
2. Copyrights provide incentives to produce knowledge and cultural works and are justified on utilitarian grounds.

The first claim needs to be discussed because one of our principle texts for the justification of property rights, Locke's *Two Treatises,* is remarkably silent about intellectual property. One possible reason for this is that Locke lived and wrote in an age in which authorship was not proprietary. Intellectual labor was motivated by the independent production of a leisure class or a production sponsored by that class. Locke himself disclaimed authorship and property interests in the very text justifying private property. He is reported to have found the entire book selling industry objectionable on aesthetic, if not moral, grounds.[17] Because proprietary authorship, and with it the very notion of intellectual property, is a more recent notion than private property, a question naturally arises over the possibility of justifying intellectual property with traditional arguments for private property.

Hettinger argues that natural rights arguments justifying intellectual property are weaker than one might suppose, for the following reasons: 1. Intellectual objects are "nonexclusive;" they are not consumed by their use. Since sharing them in no way hinders one's personal use of the object, the burden of proof falls on those who would justify their exclusivity. As Hettinger puts it, "Why should one person have the exclusive right to possess and use something which all people could possess and use concurrently?"[18] 2. There is a fundamental and longstanding ethical tradition recognizing the social value of free (or at least affordable) access to information. 3. Property rights guarantee people an interest in the value added to an object by their acts of labor. But in intellectual objects it is impossible to determine in what portion of the object the author deserves a property interest. "A person who relies on human intellectual history and makes a small modification to produce something of great value should no more receive what the market will bear than should the last person needed to lift a car receive full credit for lifting it."[19] 4. In a market economy driven in part by information, one might argue that copyrights are a means by which individuals provide for their survival and security. But since most copyrights are owned by institutions, Hettinger finds this argument unpersuasive. In addition to these arguments, he argues that copyrighted works may violate Locke's proviso against waste and spoilage (if the copyright holder charges an excessive fee, for instance), but since that argument depends upon argument 1 above, we do not need to address it specifically.

In arguing against the claim that recognizing an *absolute* (perpetual and unrestricted) copyright is necessary to guarantee an individual's human dignity, Hettinger is quite persuasive. But some of the arguments above are not very persuasive. While I agree that the non-exclusivity of intellectual objects is an important logical feature of them, it does not follow from their nonexclusivity that the widespread availability of a copyrighted work would not limit the uses its author *might* make of the work if he *were* entitled to exploit the profitability of the work. Of course, that is not an argument that the author is so entitled, but Hettinger's argument is only valid if one has already excluded "earning money" as one of the legitimate uses of the object.[20] The question of whether limiting the profitability of the object is justified is still open. Therefore, we would do well not to base our arguments on a conception of non-exclusivity which begs the answer to that question.

The second argument is right on the mark and correctly identifies the ethical tension between individual and social values which lies at the heart of copyright ethics. It also supports Hettinger's basic intuition, with which I also agree, that justifying intellectual property by

appeal to the natural rights tradition is not as simple a matter as some would have us believe.

However, I do not think the third argument is very strong. On the traditional view, we are entitled to whatever we get through original appropriation and as a result of adding value to an appropriated object through our labor. The non-exclusivity of intellectual objects guarantees, ideally,[21] that every individual can make can appropriation of his or her intellectual tradition. Thus, we are not giving undeserved credit to individuals who make an innovation in some intellectual endeavor precisely because we do not normally need to take credit away from someone else to do so. Only an absolutist agenda for intellectual property, which no one but an Objectivist[22] would argue for, would result in a wholly proprietary intellectual tradition in which even lending rights were not recognized.

The fourth argument, that the security interests people have in copyright might not be sufficient to justify intellectual property rights, is especially weak. The fact that institutions own many copyrights and patents does not show that individuals do not derive a livelihood from intellectual property. Also, I think a good case can be made that individual proprietary authors *do* depend for their livelihood upon the ability to control the distribution of their work for a limited period of time. The very emergence of proprietary authorship is tied to the growth of economically independent writing careers.[23] I certainly agree that security interest do not justify *unlimited* copyright, but again, who is really trying to justify that position?

In discussing utilitarian justifications for copyright, which are by far the most persuasive, Hettinger claims that he finds it paradoxical that a right which restricts access to intellectual property could actually promote intellectual production. I agree that there is nothing necessary about this relationship. Historically, great intellectual production occurred in the absence of any notion of copyright whatever. However, in the context of a market economy, it is not at all paradoxical that incentives, which may require copyright protection, might promote activity. If people are indeed motivated by the prospect of gain, and if gain is only possible through a control of copying, then a restriction of some uses of intellectual property might really promote production.

Hettinger concludes by arguing for greater government funding of intellectual activity and by urging that public ownership of intellectual property might replace private ownership. I think this proposal makes a certain amount of sense in some areas: for instance, if a company gained exclusive rights to a database which, because it was constantly changing, could in effect become perpetually copyrighted, we might make a strong argument that the monopolistic effect of such a system justified its regulation. This is in fact what occurred in the case of the copyright clearinghouses for the recording industry. Also, I think the government might be too uncritical (or just not business wise) in disclaiming rights to the results of the research which it currently finances.

A government program for funding intellectual and artistic production shares some features with the older patronage system under which authors worked for centuries. Government patronage might be abusive or liberating, depending upon the circumstances. If the funds are given to professionals with a tradition of academic freedom, like the university professors or independent artists, perhaps the results would be good. Of course, governments have interests that may be expressed in funding decisions no matter who the recipient is and governments may have to observe restrictions in funding decisions that private patrons do no (consider the recent controversies over government funding of the arts). But the general claim that private copyright should be weakened by re-introducing a patronage system for intellectual production is quite reactionary. After all, the traditional system for intellectual production was based on such a patronage system (variously controlled by guilds, aristocracies, church and state). Whatever the dangers of proprietary authorship, it emerged in the seventeenth and eighteenth centuries partly because intellectuals wanted to be free from the constraints of a patronage system.[24]

While I have been somewhat critical of Hettinger's arguments, I should add that they become quite persuasive if one takes them as arguments against a perpetual and unrestricted copyright. Also, he correctly locates one of the major philosophical tensions in the copyright ethics debate—the tension between a social ethic which values the availability of knowledge and the ethical foundations of private property. Still, his approach is too divorced from social practices to provide an adequate analysis of the direction which copying practices should take in the future. The interesting question for a philosopher of public policy is whether philosophy can go any further in providing an analysis of this tension which is also sensitive to the role of technology and the social values embodied in marketplace incentives. I think that it can, but not by going back to the general tenets of a theory of private property written at the dawn of the capitalist era and prior to the emergence of contemporary information technology. If the history of proprietary authorship holds any lessons, one is that our ethical intuitions need to be worked out in relation to the concrete social circumstances which pose the ethical problem in the first place. In the 18th century and again in the 20th century the changing economics of the book industry were a guide to courts and legislators trying to weight the harmfulness to information producers of liberalizing copyrights against the harm to society of restricting them. In the late seventies, U.S. copyright reform had to contend with the additional complications of new technologies (e.g. inexpensive copying, video and computer technology) and new uses of older media (e.g. educational uses of visual media and musical recordings). In order to get past the general thesis that neither society nor rights holders have an absolute claim on each other, we shall have to look at concrete social practices affecting the copyright debate today. That is what the next section of this paper proposes to do.

III. PROPERTY RIGHTS, PUBLIC ACCESS, AND THE TASK OF A FUTURE-ORIENTED COPYRIGHT ETHIC

Like most ethical controversies, copyright ethics emerges in its contemporary form because of the breakdown of a traditional social structure or matrix of social practices within which ethical questions have either been resolved or lack a motivation. Faced with such a breakdown, we try alternately to retrieve insights from the ethical traditions which precede us and to develop new ways of formulating our justified intuitions for the future. Philosophical work on copyright ethics has so far done the former without sufficient attention to the latter. In copyright ethics, a future-oriented ethical analysis requires some familiarity with the technology and legal thinking within which many of our practices and ethical intuitions are embodied. Future-oriented copyright policy requires further the articulation of *obligations to move toward those technologies which allow us to meet competing demands.*

Current legal and public policy controversies over intellectual property have their origin in the development of xerography and electronic information technology during the sixties and seventies. Prior to that, the most serious area of dispute concerned the fair handling of copyrights to music. Radio broadcasting and sound recording technology made possible social practices similar to the broadcasting of information through telecommunications networks and the duplication of printed works through photocopying.

We might expect, therefore, that the music industry offers a model for handling problems in other areas. Two clearinghouses for collecting copyright royalties, ASCAP and BMI, emerged in the 50's and 60's and soon became recognized as the means for radio stations, bar owners and any public performer of copyrighted music to satisfy their legal (and ethical) obligations to copyright holders. As a result of monopolistic practices in the setting and collecting of royalty fees, both associations were forced by courts to adopt flat-fee pricing schemes and fair rules for imposing and collecting those fees. The flat fee format has had a generally positive impact on the availability of music to a listening public.

No such structure currently exists for the print publishing industry, although the fledgling Copyright Clearance Center is hoping to establish itself in this capacity. However, before discussing this and other approaches to resolving copyright issues in information technology, we should look more closely at the ways in which recent technology is breaking down the traditional approaches to print and information copyrights.

The social value of free access to information is embodied in public lending practices developed during the free public library movement and in "fair use" guidelines which emerged through court cases since the turn of the century[25] and which are currently embodied in section 107 of the current U.S. copyright law (U.S. 17) passed in 1978. They allow specific exemptions for the use of copyrighted material for personal and educational purposes provided such uses pass three tests:

1. Brevity;
2. Spontaneity; and
3. Cumulative Effect.

The point of the tests is to distinguish the occasional and narrowly focused *individual* use of materials from uses which are *systematic* in the sense that they create a significant impact on the market for the copyrighted works. A similar test underlies the provisions of the same copyright law governing fair use in interlibrary loan agreements which libraries use to share resources. Interlibrary loan schemes are more prone to copyright infringement as they become systematic means of avoiding the purchase of books and journals and less infringing as they merely provide a means for individual users to request materials which the local library cannot afford to maintain. Curiously, the fair use guidelines do not apply directly to videotapes, broadcast transmissions, and software, even though the increase in educational use of these media would seem to demand some articulation of the doctrine for them.[26]

The philosophical justification for focusing on the distinction between individual and systematic use is obvious. The more systematic the use, the less one can reasonably claim that the purpose of the use is to gain personal access to information. At one extreme, the individual who systematically copies tapes and books and distributes them for sale is doing more than securing his or her own right to gain access to information. At the other extreme, the individual who photocopies even a fairly lengthy text for personal study has no intent to infringe on the original market for that text. The fair use test of "cumulative effect" suggests that as long as the cumulative effect of *that individual's* activity is not materially detrimental, then the use is fair. Current discussions of fair use are therefore directly connected to the historical tension between property interests and the social utility of information. A direct line can be traced from the original limitations on perpetual copyright during the "Battle of the Books" to the current exemption allowing individuals to photocopy from books for personal use.

From a philosophical (as well as public policy) point of view, fair use guidelines are interesting because they try to preserve a distinction which is clearly vanishing in the face of current and emerging technology. The distinction between individual and systematic use is increasingly *ad hoc* in the following cases.

1. Interlibrary loan schemes are essentially systematic. Libraries are increasingly using "cooperative acquisitions" programs[27] to reduce spending and increase the range of texts available to users. In a related development, the great number and diversity of scientific and technical journals has led many hospital libraries to use low cost document supply houses, which provide information on a per document basis. These highly efficient behaviors cannot help but affect the market for print materials. It seems regressive to allow property considerations to slow down an inevitable and desirable shift to a system of production which depends less on the sale of hard copies of texts than on the sale of access to texts through networks. On the other hand, by merely shifting to a fee-for-use system, the notion of free access is imperiled. New means of satisfying producers' interests may need to be developed but that cannot occur by continuing to tie fair use to an outdated paradigm in which individual users retrieve individual texts without involving a complex system of distribution.

2. While fair use offers extensive protections to individual scholars, it does not address the reasonable needs of communities of scholarship (including classroom instruction, seminars and professional scholarly societies), which can only function by systematically distributing texts. By orienting fair use to individual scholarly activity, we perpetuate the myth that scholars are not working more and more in community through conferences and telecommunications. Again, what seems like an inevitable and desirable social trend may be retarded by confused and increasingly outdated distinctions between individual and systematic use.

Current legal challenges to "professor's publishing"[28] schemes are based on the notion that such activity systematically undermines the property interests of producers of anthologies and texts for the college market. Clearly, publishers have a right not to have the market for their products systematically eroded by the activities of infringing (if well intentioned) scholars. On the other hand, by limiting an instructor's ability to assemble the best available texts in an affordable and convenient form we compromise our commitment to the social value of free access to learning.

The optimal ethical balance will not be struck merely by setting arbitrary limits to the use of photocopied anthologies, as currently copyright guidelines do.[29] It is important to realize that the ethical conflict itself is exacerbated by the practice of some publishers who hold to a marketing strategy which packages educational materials in costly anthologies. To their credit, some publishers are promoting "custom publishing" services through which they offer to assemble anthologies to suit the customer's needs. The publisher may then collect the royalties lost to the local copy center.

The existence of professor's publishing schemes is evidence of an unmet need in the market and the "custom publishing" program may be a good effort to satisfy that need while preserving author's royalties. If we focus on the places in the market at which copyright conflict emerges, I think we will see that the problem lies in the conflict between the technologies of information production and information use or consumption. The solution to these conflicts does not involve a rereading of Locke; rather, it involves a transition to new technologies and marketing practices and a recasting of our traditional intuitions in the terms of the new technologies. Only by looking forward to a future arrangement of technologies and practices in which producers receive a nominal fee for use of copyrighted materials can we overcome the current stalemate in fair use thinking. Thus, an arrangement similar to the copyright clearance houses for the recording industry may be the best future solution to the current controversy.

The Copyright Clearance Center, which operates a growing clearinghouse for print works (primarily from journals), is one part of the solution. However, its approach is fatally flawed because it collects whatever fees producers set for their works. While at first glance this practice appears entirely consistent with the ethics of the marketplace, it provides no room in the new equation for fair use or public access. If the free market pricing structure of the CCC is upheld in court, the notion of fair use on a practical level will be left further and further behind as information technology advances. As libraries and educational institutions increasingly rely on systematic practices (e.g. electronic media, library networking, faxing, and photocopying) which take us away from the traditional domain of fair use, the practical value of free or affordable access to information will be eroded.

The challenge in copyright ethics is, on the one hand, not to hold on to traditional practices when change is immanent and desirable, and, on the other hand, to reconstruct the traditional values in the new technological configuration. The move to an absolutely proprietary information system would represent a failure to meet the second challenge, and the retrenchment of the publishing industry and traditional fair use advocates would represent a failure to meet the first challenge. A flat-fee clearinghouse for photoduplicating of print materials appears to be a good solution because it would add a nominal charge to users (which would be more than offset by likely decreases in the cost of duplication) while allowing producers to recover costs at a high margin of profit (because they would not actually have to produce the copies). A computerized billing service could be established in major copy centers (such as Kinko's Copies stores, corporate copying facilities, and university copy centers) while leaving alone incidental copiers such as individual library patrons.

I think a similar arrangement could be made for videotapes and software, though these media do have special characteristics which affect our concern for producers' interests. Where production overhead for major software packages and major movie and documentary works is high, more concern might be shown for the market for these products. Economic modelling of producers' rates of return for various types of electronic media might govern decisions to include such media in a flat-fee clearinghouse.

In general then, I recommend that information producers see themselves as socially obligated to move toward technologies which facilitate the wide distribution of their works. At the same time, consumers should allow that the new information technologies they use obligate them to consider the effect of their use on information producers.

IV. CONCLUSION

In addition to providing a general introduction to the subject of copyright ethics, I hope I have shown that thinking about copyright cannot be divorced from the history of social practices which originally constituted it. We cannot begin to understand the competing claims of private property owners and society, unless we look at the tension between these competing interests in historical detail. On the other hand, such a history is in no way prescriptive or prospective. Philosophical approaches to copyright are needed and I considered two: Bringsjord's and Hettinger's. However, we will not succeed by merely attending to the logical features of copying (as Bringsjord does). Our ethical intuitions do not posses such precision or generality. Failing that, we might hope that the philosophical tradition justifying property will guide us in thinking about intellectual property. But Hettinger successfully shows that the tradition cannot do this. I suggest the reason for this is, in part, that abstract justifications are too divorced from actual social practices to arbitrate between competing ethical values. In the case of copyright ethics we need to look at current and emerging technology and try to understand how our best intuitions about rewarding personal achievement and allowing public access can be satisfied.

Notes

The author would like to acknowledge the assistance of Mead Data Central's LEXIS research service.

1. The Kinko's suit (*Basic Books, Inc. v. Kinko's Graphics Corporation*) was recently decided by U.S. District court in New York. The court ruled for the plaintiff, rejecting Kinko's argument that because its clients are educators, its service is protected under the fair use guidelines. As this article goes to press the judge's ruling is not available, but news reports indicate that the decision against Kinko's was based in part upon the fact that Kinko's "Professor's Publishing" service is commercial. This leaves open the question of whether nonprofit university run copy centers could operate within the fair use exemption.

2. To give a simple example, the dilemma over film colorization doesn't occur until the technology for colorizing film develops. Also, the question about how to treat videos in educational contexts doesn't emerge until educators place a value on them as instructional media.

3. The first three major copyright acts, the *Star Chamber Decrees of 1586 and 1637*, the *Ordinances of 1643 and 1647*, and the *Licensing Act of 1662* were all primarily censorship acts. Lyman Patterson, *Copyright in Historical Perspective* (Nashville, TN: Vanderbilt UP, 1968) 82.

4. The right to copy remained with the individual guild member who registered it. It was his property in perpetuity. The copyright could be transferred to widows of Guild members, but if the widow remarried outside the Guild, she lost the copyright and it reverted to the company. Patterson 111.

5. The Statute of Anne (1709) and its extension in 1734 set the stage for the Donaldson case (1774), described below. In addition to traditional stationers and renegades like Donaldson, groups like the Society for the Encouragement of Learning (1734) played a part in the "battle."

6. Mark Rose, "The Author as Proprietor: *Donaldson v. Beckett* and the Genealogy of Modern Authorship," Representations 23 (1988) 51–85.

7. William Blackstone, *Commentaries on the Laws of England* 4 vols. (Oxford, 1765–1769) 2:406.

8. William Enfield, *Observation on Literary Property* (London, 1774) 21–22.

9. To set this argument in context one should read Kenneth Vandevelde's "The New Property of the Nineteenth Century: The Development of the Modern Concept of Property," *Buffalo Law Review* 29.2 (1980): 325–367, in which he argues that the conceptual difficulties of extending natural property rights to non-physical objects requires an appeal to the public policy benefits of recognizing such property. Thus, in the interest of logical coherence, the argument for natural property rights shifts in character to an argument about social utility.

10. Martha Woodmansee, "The Genius and the Copyright: Economic and Legal Conditions of the Emergence of the Author," *Eighteenth Century Studies* 17 (1984) 425–448.

11. Woodmansee 434 (19n), from Martin Luther's "Warning to Printers."

12. Selmer Bringsjord, "In Defense of Copying," *Public Affairs Quarterly* 3 (1989) 1–9.

13. I realize that this simple reconstruction is perhaps not as sympathetic as it could be; however, I think this is an accurate representation of the structure of Bringsjord's argument.

14. For the sake of this argument, suppose I copy more than 250 words from a long poem, thus exceeding the copyright guidelines for photocopying associated with the current U.S. copyright law.

15. Bringsjord 6.

16. Edwin Hettinger, "Justifying Intellectual Property," *Philosophy and Public Affairs* 18 (1989) 31–52.

17. Peter Laslett, Introduction, *Two Treatises of Government*, John Locke (Cambridge: Cambridge UP, 1988) 7.

18. Hettinger, p. 35.

19. Hettinger, p. 38.

20. This is why it is not adequate, for example, for educators to base claims to fair use solely on the notion that their use is "not for profit". Such arguments ignore the fact that widespread photocopying *does* diminish potential returns to rights holders.

21. I recognize that if basic opportunities for education and advancement are not available then this counterargument will not succeed.

22. See for example the Objectivist position as it is articulated in "What is the Objectivist position in regard to patents and copyrights?" *The Objectivist Newsletter*, May, 1964, 19–20.

23. Samuel Taylor Coleridge, William Wordsworth, and Charles Dickens were among the first great English language authors to attempt to earn their living from the relatively new "author's copyright" which the 1834 revision of the Statute of Anne gave expression to. Dickens was especially vocal in his defense of the value of an independent profession of authorship. This trend is also noted in Rose's and Woodmansee's articles.

24. Of course, this is not to deny that any particular market may be structured in a way that imposes oppressive constraints also.

25. Leo Raskind traces the development of the U.S. fair use doctrine from the mid-19th century. However, detailed legal opinion does not emerge until cases involving the use of copyrighted material on radio, television, and film. For an excellent review of the case history, see Leo Raskind, "A Functional Interpretation of Fair Use," *The Journal of the Copyright Society of the USA* (1984) 601–639.

26. A recent bill before the Senate (S. 198, 101st Congress) addressing software copyrights contained a fair use exemption allowing libraries to lend software to patrons. The exemption was justified by the need to combat illiteracy and promote education, especially in rural and impoverished communities (see S. Rept. 101–265). Cited in *ALA Washington Newsletter*, April 30, 1990, 7–8.

27. Under cooperative acquisitions schemes libraries agree to supplement rather than duplicate each others holdings.

28. "Professor's publishing" is a term coined, as far as I know, by Kinko's Copies to describe its service of duplicating packets of readings for college course instruction.

29. Current guidelines allow professors not more than 9 copyrighted works per classroom anthology and prohibit the repeated use of the same anthologies semester after semester. Since no individual article or essay may exceed 2500 words, many packets in use today do in fact violate the guidelines. These guidelines are not part of the actual legislation of *1978 Copyright Act* (PL 94–553, U.S. 17), but were published as a House report (H. Repts. 94–1476 and 94–1733). Excerpts of the reports are available in the American Library Association's *Librarian's Guide to the New Copyright Law* (Chicago, 1978) or from Copyright Information Services, *The Official Fair-Use Guidelines: complete texts of four official documents arranged for use by educators,* 3rd edition (Friday Harbor, Washington) 1987.

QUESTIONS

1. What is Hettinger's argument for claiming that trade secrets are undesirable in a way in which copyrights or patents are not?
2. Do you agree with Hettinger's claim that the goal of private intellectual property institutions is to maximize the dissemination and use of information? Explain your answer.
3. Paine claims that "even if common law trade secret rights did not promote intellectual labor or increase the dissemination and use of information, there would still be reasons to recognize those rights." What reasons does she mention?
4. How does Paine's framework for addressing the issue of intellectual property rights differ from Hettinger's?
5. What does Alfino mean when he claims that with regard to intellectual property, "policy arguments which proceed primarily by a retrieval of abstract thought on the metaphysical principle of property are inadequate"? Do you agree?
6. Do you agree with Alfino's claim that the fair use guidelines cannot be maintained in the face of current and emerging technology? Why or why not?

CASE 9:1 THE CONTESTED STATUE[1]

In the fall of 1985, the Community for Creative Non-Violence (CCNV) approached sculptor James Earl Reid to produce a statue to dramatize the plight of the homeless. During the time Reid worked on the statue, CCNV officials visited him several times to monitor progress and to coordinate CCNV's construction of the sculpture's base. In the process of the statue's construction, CCNV members made a number of suggestions and directions concerning the statue's appearance, which Reid, for the most part adopted. Upon completion and delivery of the statue, Reid and CCNV, neither of whom had ever discussed copyright of the sculpture, filed competing copyright registration certificates.

CCNV argued that the sculpture was a "work made for hire" and that they possessed copyright. This would entitle them to reproduce and sell copies of the statue without Reid receiving any royalties. Reid argued that the statue was not created by an employee within the scope of employment, but rather as the work of an independent contractor, and so he possessed copyright. The right to reproduce and sell copies of the statue was his alone.

CASE STUDY QUESTIONS

1. Is Reid morally entitled to copyright on the statue?
2. Does CCNV have a valid claim to joint copyright?
3. Should the distinction between an employee and independent contractor make a difference as to who is entitled to copyright?

In 1981 Omnitech Graphics Systems Ltd. sold computer-aided drafting equipment to Cadco Graphics Ltd. This hardware required specific software owned by Omnitech to be of any use. Omnitech agreed to provide the necessary software, in the form of floppy disks, on the conditions that Cadco recognize that the software remained the exclusive property of Omnitech, that it was non-transferable, and that Cadco would ensure its employees did not copy or permit its unauthorized use or disclosure.

In 1985 Perry Engineering acquired the assets of Cadco. Perry transferred the information on the floppy disks Cadco had acquired from Omnitech to the hard drive of the drafting equipment. This was done without Omnitech's consent.

Perry subsequently sold the hardware into which they had integrated Omnitech's software to Farrage Ltd. Part of the conditions of the sale was that Perry would transfer to Farrage the title to possess and use Omnitech's software. Upon learning that Perry had integrated the software into the drafting equipment without Omnitech's consent, Farrage refused to pay the balance owing. Perry sued Farrage for breach of contract.

CASE STUDY QUESTIONS

1. Perry argued that since the hardware in question cannot be used without the software, Omnitech's prohibition on transfer should not be allowed, inasmuch as it constitutes an illegitimate restraint of trade. Do you agree or disagree and why?
2. Do you agree that Perry's contract with Farrage should be enforceable in the circumstances described? Why or why not?
3. Does Omnitech have any moral obligation to allow Farrage access to the necessary software? Explain your reasoning.

Notes

1. Based on *Reid v. Community for Creative Non-Violence* as found in 109 Supreme Court Reporter 2166 (1989).
2. Based on *Perry Engineering Ltd. v. Farrage et al.; Cadco Graphics Ltd. et al* (third parties) as described in Canadian Intellectual Property Reports, Vol. 26, 1990, pp. 89–95.

FOR FURTHER READING

1. S. M. Besen and L. J. Raskind, "An Introduction to the Law and Economics of Intellectual Property," *Journal of Economic Perspectives*, Vol. 5, No. 1, 1991, pp. 3–27.

2. Selmer Bringsjord, "In Defense of Copying," *Public Affairs Quarterly*, Vol. 3, 1989, pp. 1–9.

3. Russell B. Stevenson, Jr., *Corporations and Information* (Baltimore: Johns Hopkins University Press, 1980).

Chapter Ten

Bribery

Introduction

We focus in this chapter on two difficult issues. The first is that of how bribery should be defined. As in the case of sexual harassment, we are liable to think we have a clear idea of what constitutes bribery, only to find on closer analysis that arriving at an adequate definition is more complicated than we first realized. For example, if a salesperson sends a Christmas present to a valued customer is she offering a bribe? Is a company offering a bribe if it holds a promotional seminar at a popular Caribbean resort and pays the travel costs of the sales representatives in the hope of persuading them to order its product? Is a person guilty of taking a bribe if he accepts such a Christmas present or expense-paid seminar?

Second, the acceptability of bribery varies widely from culture to culture. Despite the fact that virtually all cultures officially condemn bribery, there are many societies in which bribery is an informally accepted commercial tradition. On pain of lapsing into an untenable relativism we cannot suggest that a company should simply follow the practices of whatever culture it finds itself in, but it is no easy matter to give practical advice to companies trying to operate in cultures where bribery is an established part of doing business.

Our first two selections by Michael Philips and Kendall D'Andrade focus on the issue of how bribery should be defined. Philips' aim, in his article "Bribery," is to develop a definition and by using that definition to distinguish bribery from related practices with which it is often confused. He attempts to make clear the essential differences between payment or services as an act of bribery and payment or services as a result of extortion, an appreciative gift, or a symbol of a special relationship.

Like Philips, Kendall D'Andrade attempts to develop a definition of bribery in his article "Bribery." D'Andrade and Philips agree on many points, but whereas Philips defines taking a bribe as accepting payment or the promise of payment to act in a manner such that one fails to fulfil what was expected of one as a participant in a certain practice, D'Andrade defines it as an alienation of agency. In D'Andrade's view, bribery is essentially the subversion of a contract. One contracts with an employer to be a loyal agent, i.e. to pursue the interests of the employer, but then undermines the legitimate expectations of one's employer by secretly pursuing the contrary interests of a second employer.

Our third reading focuses on the practical issue of how businesses should react to an environment in which bribery is prevalent. Jeffrey Fadiman, in his article "A Traveler's Guide to Gifts and Bribes," makes clear the importance of understanding the society in which one wishes to do business. He notes for example, that it is a mistake to view the requests for bribes and payoffs characteristic of many non-Western business environments as always motivated by personal greed of corrupt officials. Many times requests for bribes are at least partly motivated by a desire to fulfil communal obligations. Similarly, the meaning of a gift in these cultures, and the obligations it either creates or discharges, is quite different than in Canada or the United States. Failure to understand the different context in which apparently similar practices take place makes it impossible to assess their morality.

Michael Philips

Bribery

Although disclosures of bribery have elicited considerable public indignation over the last decade, popular discussions of the morality of bribery have tended largely to be unilluminating. One reason for this is that little care has been taken to distinguish bribes from an assortment of related practices with which they are easily confused. Before we can be in a position to determine what to do about the problem of bribery, we need to be clearer about what count and ought to count as bribes. Unfortunately, there is as yet very little philosophical literature on this topic.[1] In this essay I shall remedy this defect by presenting an account of the concept

From Michael Philips, "Bribery," *Ethics,* Vol. 94, 1984. Copyright © 1984 by The University of Chicago. Reprinted by permission.

of bribery and by employing that account to clarify matters in three areas in which there is public controversy and confusion.

At least some confusion in discussions of bribery arises from a failure adequately to appreciate the distinction between bribery and extortion. This is true, for example, of accounts of the notorious case of Lockheed in Japan. I shall attempt to show that the morality of this and similar transactions is better assessed if we are clear on that distinction.

A second problem area arises out of the fact of cultural variability. As is generally recognized, the conduct of business, government, and the professions differs from culture to culture. In some places transactions that many Americans would consider bribes are not only expected behavior but accepted practice as well. That is, they are condoned by the system of rules governing the conduct of the relevant parties. Are they bribes? Are only some of them bribes? If so, which?

A third problem arises out of the general difficulty of distinguishing between bribes, on the one hand, and gifts and rewards, on the other. Suppose that a manufacturer of dresses keeps a buyer for a catalog company happy by supplying him with any tickets to expensive shows and athletic events that he requests. Are these bribes? Or suppose that a special interest group rewards public administrators who rule in its favor with vacations, automobiles, and jewelry. May we correctly speak of bribery here?

I

To answer such questions we need to say more precisely what bribes are. A bribe is a payment (or promise of payment) for a service. Typically, this payment is made to an official in exchange for her violating some official duty or responsibility. And typically she does this by failing deliberately to make a decision on its merits. This does not necessarily mean that a bribed official will make an improper decision; a judge who is paid to show favoritism may do so and yet, coincidentally, make the correct legal decision (i.e., the bribe offerer may in fact have the law on her side). The violation of duty consists in deciding a case for the wrong sorts of reasons.

Although the most typical and important cases of bribery concern political officials and civil servants, one need not be a political official or a civil servant to be bribed. Indeed, one need not be an official of any sort. Thus, a mortician may be bribed to bury a bodyless casket, and a baseball player may be bribed to strike out each time he bats. Still, baseball players and morticians are members of organizations and have duties and responsibilities by virtue of the positions they occupy in these organizations. It is tempting, then, to define a bribe as a payment made to a member of an organization in exchange for the violation of some positional duty or responsibility. This temptation is strengthened by our recognition that we cannot be bribed to violate a duty we have simply by virtue of being a moral agent. (Hired killers, e.g., are not bribed to violate their duty not to kill.) And it is further strengthened when we recognize that we may be paid to violate duties we have by virtue of a nonorganizationally based status without being bribed. (I am not

bribed if—as a nonhandicapped person—I accept payment to park in a space reserved for the handicapped; nor am I bribed if—as a pet owner—I accept payment illegally to allow my dog to run free on the city streets.)

Still, it is too strong to say that occupying a position in an organization is a necessary condition of being bribed. We may also speak of bribing a boxer to throw a fight or of bribing a runner to lose a race. These cases, however, are importantly like the cases already described. Roughly both the boxer and the runner are paid to do something they ought not to do given what they are. What they are, in these cases, are participants in certain practices. What they are paid to do is to act in a manner dictated by some person or organization rather than to act according to the understandings constitutive of their practices. Civil servants, business executives, morticians, and baseball players, of course, are also participants in practices. And their responsibilities, as such, are defined by the rules and understandings governing the organizations to which they belong. At this point, then, we are in a position to state a provisional definition of bribery. Thus, P accepts a bribe from R if and only if P agrees for payment to act in a manner dictated by R rather than doing what is required of him as a participant in his practice.[2]

One advantage of this account is that it enables us to deal with certain difficult cases. Suppose that a high-ranking officer at the Pentagon is paid by a Soviet agent to pass on defense secrets. The first few times he does this we would not hesitate to say that he is bribed. But suppose that he is paid a salary to do this and that the arrangement lasts for a number of years. At this point talk of bribery appears less appropriate. But why should something that has the character of a bribe if done once or twice (or, perhaps, on a piecework basis) cease to have that character if done more often (or, perhaps, on a salaried basis)? In my account the explanation is that the frequency or basis of payment may incline us differently to identify the practice in question. Thus, if an American officer works for the Soviet Union long enough, we begin to think of him as a Soviet spy. In any case, to the extent to which we regard his practice as spying we are inclined to think of the payments in question as payments of a salary as opposed to so many bribes. A similar analysis holds in the case of industrial spies, undercover agents recruited from within organizations, and so forth.[3] We do not think of them as bribed because we do not think of them as full-fledged practitioners of the practices in which they appear to engage.

This practice conception is further supported by the fact that a person may satisfy my account of bribery on a long-term and regularized basis and still be said to be a recipient of bribes. This is so where his continued and regularized acceptance of payments does not warrant any change in our understanding of the practices in which he participates. Thus, we do not think of a judge who routinely accepts payments for favors from organized crime as participating in some practice other than judging, even if he sits almost exclusively on such cases. This may be arbitrary: perhaps we ought rather think of him as an agent of a criminal organization (a paid saboteur of the legal system) and treat him accordingly. My point, however, is that because we do not think of him in this way—because we continue to think of him as a judge—we regard each fresh occurrence as an instance of bribery.

The present account, however, is not entirely adequate as it stands. Consider the following counterexamples:

a. an artist is offered $5,000 by an eccentric to ruin a half-completed canvas by employing an unsuitable color and
b. a parent is paid $500 for the use of his eight-year-old son in a pornographic film.

It might be argued in relation to *a* that it is consistent with the practice of being an artist that one accept payment to produce whatever a client is willing to pay for. However, the conception of a practice that underlies this response seems to me questionable. What seems to me counterintuitive about speaking of bribery in *a* is that the act in question is private. By this I mean, roughly, that it affects no one who is not a party to the transaction. If I pay an artist to ruin a painting that has been commissioned by a museum, the oddity of speaking of bribery

disappears. In general, where there is no violation of an organizational duty, we might say that a payment is a bribe only if it affects the interests of persons or organizations who are not parties to the transaction. To forestall counterexamples based on remote or indirect consequences, we must add that the parties affected must be parties whose interests are normally affected by the conduct of the practice in question and that they must be affected in the manner in which they are normally affected.

It is tempting to go further than this and claim that a bribe occurs only when the act agreed to by the bribed party violates the moral rights of some third party or organization. But this seems to me mistaken. We may speak of bribing officers of terribly corrupt institutions (e.g., concentration camps), but it is not at all clear that these officeholders necessarily violate the rights of any person or organization by violating their institutional duties (e.g., by allowing prisoners to escape). Or consider a society in which slaves are used as boxers and masters wager on the bouts. It seems clear that one can bribe a slave to lose a fight here, but it is not at all clear that a slave violates anyone's rights by accepting payment for so doing. (To say this would be to imply that a slave boxer has a *prima facie* duty to try to win his fight, and this seems to me untenable.)

What, then, of the second counterexample? Why are we reluctant to speak of bribery in the case of parents? One way to deal with this case is to attribute this reluctance to an anachronistic linguistic habit developed and sustained by centuries of thinking according to which children are the property of parents. According to this outmoded way of thinking, either there is no such thing as the practice of parenting or that practice far more resembles an account that Thrasymachus might offer of it than an account most of us would now accept. [Thrasymachus (459–413 B.C.) was an early Greek philosopher who held that "justice is nothing other than the advantage of the stronger," i.e., might makes right.] It sounds odd to speak of bribing parents, then, because our linguistic habits have not caught up with our new vision of parenting. But this is something we should change: we ought to allow that parents may be bribed.

But I am uncomfortable with this reply. Most of us now agree that children have rights which ought to be protected by law and/or community pressure and that parents have duties not to violate these rights. To this extent, we are coming to understand families as organizations. Thus, if we allow that parents are bribed, we will almost certainly hold that they are bribed in the way that members of organizations are typically bribed, namely, they are paid to violate their positional duties. But there is something disturbing about this. For despite our conviction that children have rights, many of us are uncomfortable thinking of the family as just another organization and thinking of a parent as just another functionary. Our reluctance to maintain that parents may be bribed, then, may express a healthy resistance to thinking of a parent on the model of an official. Just how we ought to think of the family, I cannot say; the challenge is to arrive at a conception that acknowledges that children have legally enforceable rights without reducing the family to just another institution.

If we exempt the family from consideration and we build in the condition required by the second counterexample, we are now in a position to present a tentative definition of bribery. Thus, P is bribed by R if and only if

1. P accepts payment from R to act on R's behalf,[4]
2. P's act on R's behalf consists in violating some rule or understanding constitutive of a practice in which P is engaged, and
3. either P's violation is a violation of some official duty P has by virtue of his participation in that practice or P's violation significantly affects the interests of persons or organizations whose interests are typically connected to that practice.

At least two additional important features of bribery deserve mention. The first is a consequence of the fact that bribes are payments. For, like other kinds of payments (e.g., rent), bribes presuppose agreements of a certain kind.[5] That is, it must be understood by both parties that the payment in question is exchanged, or is to be exchanged, for the relevant conduct. In the most typical and important cases, the bribed party is an official and the conduct in question is the violation of some official duty. In these cases we may say simply that an official P is bribed by R when she accepts payment or the promise of payment for agreeing to violate a positional duty to act on R's behalf. This agreement requirement is of great importance. As I shall argue in Section IV, without it we cannot properly distinguish between bribes and gifts or rewards.

Such agreements need not be explicit. If I am stopped by a policeman for speeding and hand him a fifty-dollar bill along with my driver's license, and he accepts the fifty-dollar bill, it is arguable that we have entered into such an agreement despite what we might say about contributions to the Police Benevolence Association. As I shall argue, some of the difficulties we have in determining what transactions to count as bribes may stem from unclarity concerning the conditions under which we are entitled to say an agreement has been made.

It is a consequence of this account that someone may be bribed despite the fact that she subsequently decides not to perform the service she has agreed to perform. Indeed, we must say this even if she has never been paid but has been only promised payment, or even if she has been paid but returns this payment after she decides not to abide by her part of the agreement. I see nothing strange about this. After all, if one accepts a bribe it seems natural to say that one has been bribed. Still, I have no strong objection to distinguishing between accepting a bribe and being bribed, where a necessary condition of the latter is that one carries out one's part of the bribery agreement. As far as I can see, no important moral question turns on this choice of language.

A final interesting feature of bribery emerges when we reflect on the claim that offering and accepting bribes is *prima facie* wrong. I will begin with the case of officials. The claim that it is prima facie wrong for someone in an official position to accept a bribe is plausible only if persons in official capacities have *prima facie* obligations to discharge their official duties. The most plausible argument for this claim is grounded in a social contract model of organizations. By accepting a position in an organization, it might be argued, one tacitly agrees to abide by the rules of that organization. To be bribed is to violate that agreement—it is to break a promise—and is, therefore, *prima facie* wrong.[6] While I concede that this argument has merit in a context of just and voluntary institutions, it seems questionable in a context of morally corrupt institutions (e.g., Nazi Germany or contemporary El Salvador). And even were it technically valid for those contexts, its conclusion would nonetheless be a misleading half-truth.

It is beyond the scope of this paper to discuss, in detail, the problems with the tacit consent argument in a context of corrupt institutions. In brief, my position is that actions which create *prima facie* moral obligations in just or ideal contexts do not necessarily create comparable obligations in unjust or corrupt contexts. Thus, for example, it does not seem to me that, if I join the Mafia with the intention of subverting its operations and bringing its members to justice, I have thereby undertaken a *prima facie* obligation to abide by the code of that organization. Of course, one could say this and add that the obligation in question is typically overridden by other moral considerations. But this seems to me an ad hoc move to defend a position. We use the expression "*prima facie* duty" to point to a moral presumption for or against a certain type of action. And surely it is strange to insist that there is a moral presumption, in the present case, in favor of carrying out the commands of one's Don.

But even if we grant that there is a *prima facie* duty here, we must be careful to qualify this assertion. For it is also clear that participants in unjust institutions have a *prima facie* right to interfere with the normal functioning of those institutions (at least where these functionings can be reasonably expected to produce unjust outcomes). Indeed, where the injustice is great enough they have a *prima facie* duty to interfere. And in some cases, the strength of this *prima facie* obligation will exceed the strength of any promise-keeping obligation generated by tacit consent. Thus we may say, other things equal, that the commandant of a concentration camp ought to act in a manner that frustrates the genocidal purpose of that institution. And,

assuming that that institution is "rationally" designed to serve its purpose, there will be a strong moral presumption in favor of the violation of his positional duty.

What, then, of the morality of accepting bribes in such cases? If an official has no *prima facie* duty to satisfy her positional duties—or if the presumption in favor of satisfying them is outweighed by the presumption against so doing—then, other things being equal, it is difficult to see why it is *prima facie* wrong to accept payment for violating them. After all, there may be serious risks involved. This at least is so where the case against carrying out the purposes of one's organization is strong enough to permit one to violate one's positional duty but is not so strong that one has a *prima facie* obligation to do this. For it does seem *prima facie* wrong to make compliance with a *prima facie* duty contingent on payment (it ought rather to be contingent on an assessment of what one ought to do, all things considered). And it certainly seems wrong to demand payment for doing what is one's duty, all things considered.

Still, this may be too quick. Consider a concentration camp guard who lacks the courage to help inmates escape but who would be courageous enough to undertake the risks involved were he assured of sufficient funds to transport his family to another country and comfortably to begin a new life. If he is in fact reasonably certain that he would be brave enough to do what is required of him were he paid, it seems not improper of him to demand payment. In general, if the wrong of demanding payment for doing one's duty is outweighed by the importance of doing it and if demanding payment for doing it is causally necessary for doing it, then, all things considered, it is not wrong to demand payment.

If it is not wrong for an official to accept a bribe, one does not induce him to do something wrong by offering him one. Thus, we cannot say in all contexts that it is *prima facie* wrong to offer someone a bribe *because* this is an attempt to induce him to do something wrong or to corrupt him.[7] On the other hand, there may be cases in which it is *prima facie* wrong to offer a bribe despite the fact that it is perfectly acceptable for the bribed party to accept one. Recall the case of the boxer slave. Despite the fact that the slave has no obligation to try to win, a wagering master may have a *prima facie* obligation not to pay him to lose. For by so doing the master may gain an unfair advantage over his fellow wagerers. It might be objected that the master's obligation in this case is misleadingly described as an obligation not to bribe. He is obligated, rather, not to fix fights; or, more generally, not to take unfair advantage of his fellow wagerers. This objection raises issues we need not consider here. It is enough to point out that the purpose of offering a bribe is very often to seek some unfair or undeserved benefit or advantage and that this is one reason we are rightly suspicious of the morality of bribe offers.

We are now in a position to state a fifth interesting feature of bribery. Even if it is not *prima facie* wrong to offer and to accept bribes in all contexts, it is *prima facie* wrong to do so in morally uncorrupted contexts. Accordingly, a bribe offerer or a bribe taker must defend the morality of his act either by showing that there are countervailing moral considerations in its favor or alternatively by showing that the moral context is so corrupt that the factors that generate *prima facie* duties in uncorrupted contexts do not apply here. This strategy of moral justifications, of course, is not unique to bribery. It may hold in relation to a wide range of what are ordinarily taken to be *prima facie* duties. In the case of bribery, however, arguments to the effect that the moral context is corrupted will have a certain characteristic form. Thus, in the most important case—the case of officials—they will be arguments that challenge the legitimacy of an institution.

II

I now turn to the first of three problem areas I shall address in this paper, namely, the problem of distinguishing between bribery and extortion. Compare the following cases:

a. Executive P hopes to sell an airplane to the national airline of country C. The deal requires the approval of minister R. P knows that R can make a better deal elsewhere and that R knows this as well. P's researchers have discovered that R has a reputation for honesty but that R is in serious financial difficulties. Accordingly P offers R a large sum of money to buy from him. R accepts and abides by the agreement.

b. The same as *a* except that P knows that he is offering the best deal R can get, and R knows this too. Nonetheless, P is informed by reliable sources that R will not deal with P unless P offers to pay him a considerable sum of money. P complies, and R completes the deal.

According to my analysis *a* is bribery; *b* is not. The difference between *a* and *b* is clear enough. In *a* P pays R to violate R's duty (in this case, to make the best deal that R can). In *b* P does no such thing. Instead, he pays R to do what is required of R by his institutional commitments in any case. Moreover, he does so in response to R's threat to violate those commitments in a manner that jeopardizes P's interests. Accordingly, *b* resembles extortion more than it does bribery. For, roughly speaking, R extorts P if R threatens P with a penalty in case P fails to give R something to which R has no rightful claim.

If this is true it may be that American corporate executives accused of bribing foreign officials are sometimes more like victims of extortion than offerers of bribes. For in at least some cases they are required to make payments to assure that an official does what he is supposed to do in any case. This is especially true in the case of inspectors of various kinds and in relation to government officials who must approve transactions between American and local companies. An inspector who refuses to approve a shipment that is up to standards unless he is paid off is like a bandit who demands tribute on all goods passing through his territory.

It does not follow that it is morally correct for American companies to pay off such corrupt officials. There are cases in which it is morally wrong to surrender to the demands of bandits and other extortionists. But it is clear that the moral questions that arise here are different sorts of questions than those that arise in relation to bribery. The moral relations between the relevant parties differ. The bribery agreement is not by its nature an agreement between victims and victimizers. The extortion agreement is. Moral justifications and excuses for complying with the demands of an extortionist are easier to come by than moral justifications and excuses for offering bribes.

Of course, the distinction in question is often easier to draw in theory than in practice. An inspector who demands a payoff to authorize a shipment is likely to fortify his demand by insisting that the product does not meet standards. In some cases it may be difficult to know whether or not he is lying (e.g., whether the shipment has been contaminated in transit). And given the high cost of delays, a company may decide that it is too expensive to take the time to find out. In this case, a company may decide to pay off without knowing whether it is agreeing to pay a bribe or surrendering to extortion. Since the morality of its decisions may well turn on what it is in fact doing in such cases, a company that does not take the time to find out acts in a morally irresponsible manner (unless, of course, it is in a position to defend both courses of action).

What sorts of justifications can a company present for offering bribes? It is beyond the scope of this paper to provide a detailed discussion of this question. However, I have already mentioned a number of considerations that count as moral reasons against bribery in a variety of contexts. To begin with, in reasonably just contexts, officials ordinarily are obligated to discharge the duties of their offices. In these cases bribe offers are normally attempts to induce officials to violate duties. Moreover, if accepted, a bribe offer may make it more likely that that official will violate future duties. Accordingly, it may contribute to the corruption of an official. In addition, the intent of a bribe offer is often to secure an unfair advantage or an undeserved privilege. Where this is the case, it too counts as a reason against bribery. To determine whether a bribe offer is wrong in any particular case, then, we must decide:

1. whether these reasons obtain in that case;
2. if they obtain, how much weight we ought to attach to them; and

3. how much weight we ought to attach to countervailing considerations. (Suppose, e.g., that it is necessary to bribe an official in order to meet an important contractual obligation.)

It is worth remarking in this regard that, where officials routinely take bribes, the presumption against corrupting officials normally will not apply. Similarly, to the extent that bribery is an accepted weapon in the arsenal of all competitors, bribe offers cannot be construed as attempts to achieve an unfair advantage over one's competitors.

III

It is sometimes suggested that an environment may be so corrupt that no payments count as bribes. These are circumstances in which the level of official compliance to duty is very low, and payoffs are so widespread that they are virtually institutionalized. Suppose, for example, that the laws of country N impose very high duties on a variety of products but that it is common practice in N for importers and exporters to pay customs officials to overlook certain goods and/or to underestimate their number or value. Suppose, moreover, that the existence of this practice is common knowledge but that no effort is made to stop it by law enforcement officials at any level;[8] indeed, that any attempts to stop it would be met by widespread social disapproval. One might even imagine that customs officials receive no salary in N but earn their entire livelihood in this way. One might further imagine that customs officials are expected to return a certain amount of money to the government every month and are fired from their jobs for failure to do so. Finally, one might suppose that the cumulative advantages and disadvantages of this way of doing things is such that the economy of N is about as strong as it would be under a more rule-bound alternative. Are these officials bribed?

In my analysis, the answer to this question depends on how we understand the duties of the customs officer. If the official job description for the customs officer in N (and the written laws of N) is like those of most countries, the customs officer violates his official duties according to these codes by allowing goods to leave the country without collecting the full duty. The question, however, is how seriously we are to take these written codes. Where social and political practice routinely violates them, nothing is done about it, and few members of the legal and nonlegal community believe that anything ought to be done about it, it is arguable that these codes are dead letters. If we find this to be true of the codes governing the duties of the customs officials in country N, we have good reason for saying that the real obligations of these officials do not require that they impose the duties described in those written codes (but only that they return a certain sum of the money they collect to the central government each month). Anything collected in excess of that amount they are entitled to keep as salary (recall that they are officially unpaid). In reality we might say that duties on exports in country N are not fixed but negotiable.

Of course if we decide that the written law of N is the law of N, we must describe the situation otherwise. In that case, the official obligations of the customs officials are as they are described, and the system in N must be characterized as one of rampant bribery condoned both by government and by popular opinion. In seems to me that the philosophy of law on which this account rests is implausible. However, there is no need to argue this to defend my analysis of this case. My position is simply that whether or not we describe what goes on here as bribery depends on what we take the real legal responsibilities of the customs official to be. To the extent that we are inclined to identify his duties with the written law we will be inclined to speak of bribery here. To the extent that we are unwilling so to identify his duties we will not.[9]

IV

Let us now consider the problem of distinguishing bribes from rewards and gifts. The problem arises because gifts are often used in business and government to facilitate transactions. And to the degree to which a business person, pro-fessional person, or government official is influenced in her decision by gifts, it is tempting to conclude that she is violating her duties. In such cases we are tempted to speak of these gifts as bribes.

If I am correct, however, this temptation should be resisted. A bribe, after all, presupposes an agreement. A gift may be made with the intention of inducing an official to show favoritism to the giver, but unless acceptance of what is transferred can be construed as an agreement to show favoritism, what is transferred is not a bribe.

In some cases, of course, the acceptance of what is offered can be so construed. Again, if I offer fifty dollars to a policeman who has stopped me for speeding, he has a right to construe my act as one of offering a bribe, and I have a right to construe his acceptance in the corresponding manner. If I regularly treat the neighborhood policeman to a free lunch at my diner and he regularly neglects to ticket my illegally parked car, we have reason to say the same. Agreements need not be explicit. My point is just that to the degree that it is inappropriate to speak of agreements, it is also inappropriate to speak of bribes.

It follows from this that, if I present an official with an expensive item to induce him to show favoritism on my behalf, in violation of his duty, I have not necessarily bribed him. It does not follow from this, however, that I have done nothing wrong. So long as you are morally obligated to perform your official duty, normally it will be wrong of me to induce you to do otherwise by presenting you with some expensive item. Moreover, if you have any reason to believe that accepting what I offer will induce you not to do your duty, you have done something wrong by accepting my gift. To prevent such wrongs we have laws prohibiting persons whose interests are closely tied to the decisions of public officials from offering gifts to these officials. And we have laws forbidding officials to accept such gifts.

It might be objected that this account is too lenient. Specifically, it might be argued that wherever P presents Q with something of value to induce Q to violate Q's official duties P has offered a bribe.

But this is surely a mistake. It suggests, among other things, that an official is bribed so long as she accepts what is offered with this intent. Yet an official may accept such a gift innocently, believing that it is what it purports to be, namely, a token of friendship or goodwill. And she may do so with justifiable confidence that doing so will not in any way affect the discharge of her duty.

It may be replied that officials are bribed by such inducements only when they are in fact induced to do what is desired of them. But again, it may be the case that an official accepts what is offered innocently, believing it to be a gift, and that she believes falsely that it will not affect her conduct. In this case she has exercised bad judgment, but she has not been bribed. Indeed, it seems to me that it is improper to say that she accepts a bribe even when she recognizes the intent of the inducement and believes that accepting it is likely to influence her. There is a distinction between accepting a drink with the understanding that one is agreeing to be seduced and accepting a drink with the knowledge that so doing will make one's seduction more likely. To be bribed is to be bought, not merely to be influenced to do something.

From a moral point of view, whenever failure to perform one's official duties is wrong it may be as bad to accept a gift that one knows will influence one in the conduct of one's duty as it is to accept a bribe. And clearly we are entitled morally to criticize those who offer and accept such inducements. Moreover, we are right to attempt to prevent this sort of thing by legally restricting the conditions under which persons may offer gifts to officials and the conditions under which officials may accept such gifts. Nonetheless, such gifts ought not to be confused with bribes. If P accepts a gift from R and does not show the desired favoritism, R may complain of P's ingratitude but not of P's dishonesty (unless, of course, P led him on in some way). If P accepts a bribe from R and does not show the desired favoritism, P has been dishonest (perhaps twice).

This point is not without practical importance. People who work in the same organization or in the same profession often form friendships despite the fact that some of them are in a position to make decisions that affect the interests of others. Here, as everywhere, friendships are developed and maintained in part by exchanges of favors, gifts, meals, and so forth. Were we to take seriously the inducement theory of bribery, however, this dimension of collegial and organizational existence would be threatened. In that case, if P's position is such that he must make decisions affecting R, any gifts, favors, *et cetera* from R to P should be regarded with at least some suspicion. To guard against the accusation that he has been bribed by R, P must be in a position to offer reasons for believing that R's intent in inviting him to dinner was not to induce him to show favoritism. And for R to be certain that he is not offering P a bribe in this case, R must be certain that his intentions are pure. All of this would require such vigilance in relation to one's own motives and the motives of others that friendships in collegial and organizational settings would be more difficult to sustain than they are at present.

Since decision makers are required to show impartiality they must in any case be careful not to accept gifts and favors that will influence them to show favoritism. Moreover, if they are required by their position to assess the moral character of those affected by their decisions, they may be required to assess the intent with which such gifts or favors are offered. Most officials, however, are not required to assess character in this way. In order to avoid doing wrong by accepting gifts and favors they need only be justly confident of their own continued impartiality. Thus, they are ordinarily entitled to ignore questions of intent unless there is some special reason to do otherwise. If the intent to influence were sufficient for a bribe, however, they would not be at liberty to bestow the benefit of the doubt in this way.

Again, there are cases in which impartiality is so important that decision makers should be prohibited both from accepting gifts or favors from any persons likely to be directly affected by their decisions and from forming friendships with such persons. And they should disqualify themselves when they are asked to make a decision that affects either a friend or someone from whom they have accepted gifts or favors in the reasonably recent past. Judges are a case in point. In other cases, however, institutions and professions should be willing to risk some loss in impartiality in order to enjoy the benefits of friendship and mutual aid. For these are essential to the functioning of some organizations and to the well-being of the people within them. Consider, for example, universities. The practical disadvantage of the inducement account is that it may require us to be unnecessarily suspicious of certain exchanges constitutive of mutual aid and friendship (at least if we take it seriously).

V

An interesting related problem arises in cultures in which a more formal exchange of gifts may be partly constitutive of a special relationship between persons, namely, something like friendship. In such cultures, so long as certain other conditions are satisfied, to make such exchanges is to enter into a system of reciprocal rights and duties. Among these duties may be the duty to show favoritism toward "friends," even when one acts in an official capacity. Moreover, the giver may be expected to show gratitude for each occasion of favoritism by further gift giving. On the face of it, this certainly looks like bribery. Is that description warranted?

To begin with, we need to distinguish between cases in which the special relationships in question are genuine and cases in which they are not. In the latter case certain ritual or ceremonial forms may be used to dress up what each party regards as a business transaction of the standard Western variety in a manner that provides an excuse for bribery. I shall say more about this presently. But let me begin with the first case.

Where the relationships in question are genuine and the laws of the relevant society are such that the official duties of the relevant official do not prohibit favoritism, this practice of gift giving cannot be called bribery. For in this case there is no question of the violation of duty. All that can be said here is that such societies condone different ways of doing business than we do. Specifically, they do not mark off a

sphere of business and/or bureaucratic activity in which persons are supposed to meet as "abstract individuals," that is, in which they are required to ignore their social and familial ties. Their obligations, rather, are importantly determined by such ties even in the conduct of business and governmental affairs. Favoritism is shown, then, not in order to carry out one's part of a bargain but, rather, to discharge an obligation of kinship or loyalty. Failure to show favoritism would entitle one's kinsman or friend to complain not that one reneged on an agreement but, rather, that one had wronged him as an ally or a kinsman.

This is not to say that one cannot bribe an official in such a society. One does this here, as elsewhere, by entering into an agreement with him such that he violates his official duties for payment. The point is just that favoritism shown to friends and kinsmen is not necessarily a violation of duty in such societies. Indeed, one might be bribed not to show favoritism.

The official duties of an official, of course, may not be clear. Thus, the written law may prohibit favoritism to kin and ally, though this is widely practiced and condoned and infrequently prosecuted. This may occur when a society is in a transitional state from feudalism or tribalism to a Western-style industrial society, but it may also occur in an industrial society with different traditions than our own. To the extent that it is unclear what the official duties of officials are in such cases it will also be difficult to say what count as bribes. Indeed, even if we decide that an official does violate his duty by showing favoritism to kin and allies who reciprocate with gifts, we may not be justified in speaking of bribery here. For the official may not be acting as he does in order to fulfill his part of an agreement. Rather, he may be acting to fulfill some obligation of kinship or loyalty. Again, his failure so to act may not entitle his kinsmen or allies to complain that he had welched on a deal; rather, it would entitle them to complain that he wronged them as kinsmen or allies.

Of course, all this is so only when the relationships in question are genuine. In some cases, however, the rhetoric and ceremonial forms of a traditional culture may be used to camouflage what are in fact business relations of the standard Western variety. To the extent that this is so, the favoritism in question may in fact be bribery in ethnic dress. The relationships in question are not genuine when they are not entered into in good faith. It is clear, moreover, that when American executives present expensive gifts to foreign businessmen or foreign government officials they do so for business reasons. That is, they have no intention of entering into a system of reciprocal rights and duties that may obligate them in the future to act contrary to their long-term interest. Rather, they perform the required ceremonies knowing that they will continue to base their decisions on business reasons. Their intention is to buy favoritism. And the foreign officials and companies with whom they do business are typically aware of this. This being the case, invitations of the form "First we become friends, then we do business" cannot plausibly be construed as invitations to participate in some traditional way of life. Typically, both parties recognize that what is requested here is a bribe made in an appropriate ceremonial way.

VI

On the basis of this analysis it seems clear that American officials are not always guilty of bribery when they pay off foreign officials. In some cases they are victims of extortion; in other cases, the context may be such that the action purchased from the relevant official does not count as a violation of his duty. The fact that American executives engaged in international commerce are innocent of some of the charges that have been made against them, however, does not imply that those who have made them are mistaken in their assessment of the character of these executives. One's character, after all, is a matter of what one is disposed to do. If these executives are willing to engage in bribery whenever this is necessary to promote their perceived long-term business interests, whatever the morality of the situation, it follows (at very least) that they are amoral.

Notes

1. At the time this paper was written there were no references to bribes or bribery in the *Philosopher's Index*. Since

that time one paper has been indexed—Arnold Berleant's "Multinationals, Local Practice, and the Problems of Ethical Consistency" (*Journal of Business Ethics* 1 [August 1982]: 185–93)—but, as the title of this short paper suggests, Berleant is not primarily concerned with providing an analysis of the concept of bribery. However, three presentations on the topic of bribery were made at the 1983 "Conference for Business Ethics" (organized by the Society for Business Ethics at DePaul University, July 25–26) and have subsequently been accepted for publication. These are: Kendall D'Andrade's "Bribery" (forthcoming in a special issue of the *Journal of Business Ethics*, devoted to the DePaul conference, 1984); John Danley's "Toward a Theory of Bribery" (forthcoming in the *Journal of Business and Professional Ethics*, 1984); and Tom Carson's "Bribery, Extortion and the Foreign Corrupt Practices Act" (forthcoming in *Philosophy and Public Affairs*, Summer 1984). Where my position on substantive questions differs significantly from D'Andrade's, Carson's, or Danley's, I shall discuss this in the notes.

2. Danley defines "bribing" as "offering or giving something of value with a corrupt intent to induce or influence an action of someone in a public or official capacity." Carson defines a bribe as a payment to someone "in exchange for special consideration that is incompatible with the duties of his position." Both go on to discuss bribery as if it were restricted to officials of organizations. Since these are the most typical and important cases of bribery, their focus is understandable. But it does have at least one unfortunate consequence. For it leads both Danley and Carson to think that the question of whether it is *prima facie* wrong to offer or accept bribes reduces to the question of whether officials have obligations to satisfy their positional duties. Danley argues that they do not if the institutions they serve are illegitimate. Carson argues that they do on the ground that they have made a tacit agreement with their institution to discharge those duties (accepting a bribe, for Carson, is an instance of promise breaking). Whatever the merits of their arguments concerning the responsibilities of officials, both approach the question of the *prima facie* morality of bribery too narrowly. For different issues seem to arise when we consider bribery outside the realm of officialdom. Clearly it is more difficult for Carson to make his tacit consent argument in relation to the bribed athlete. For it is not clear that a runner who enters a race tacitly agrees to win it (if so, he would be breaking a promise by running to prepare for future races or by entering to set the pace for someone else). Nor is it clear that a boxer who accepts payment not to knock out his opponent in the early rounds violates a tacit agreement to attempt a knockout at his earliest convenience. Danley must expand his account to accommodate such cases as well. For it is not clear what it means to say that a practice such as running or boxing is legitimate.

3. Such cases present a problem for the accounts of both Danley and Carson. At the very least they must expand their accounts of positional duties such that we can distinguish between a bribe, on the one hand, and a

salary paid to a spy recruited from within an organization, on the other.

4. Thus D'Andrade defines bribery as "alienation of agency." In his account bribery occurs when someone is seduced into abandoning his role as an agent of one person or organization and, for a price, becomes the agent of another. This highlights an important feature of bribery that is ignored by Carson and Danley and that was neglected in my own earlier thinking on this subject, namely, that a bribe taker acts on behalf of someone. But D'Andrade's claim that agency is alienated when one accepts a bribe implies that the bribe taker necessarily is committed to act on behalf of some person or organization before he is in a position to accept a bribe. And it is difficult to see what helpful truth this might express in relation to the scientist, runner, or boxer of my examples. Surely it is not helpful to say that a bribe taker begins as his own agent in these cases and, for pay, alienates that agency to another. This applies to anyone who takes a job. Nor is it helpful to say—as D'Andrade did say at one point—that he may begin as an agent of some abstraction (e.g., truth). Surely the point behind this obscure claim is better made by speaking of what is expected of someone as a participant in a practice. It is also worth noting that D'Andrade's alienation of agency account offers no basis for distinguishing between bribed officials, on the one hand, and undercover agents and spies, on the other. For these too alienate agency.

5. Carson fails to recognize the significance of this feature of bribery. This view of bribery, moreover, is inconsistent with Danley's account. Danley understands a bribe as an attempt to induce or influence someone. In this matter he appears to have most dictionaries on his side (including the OED). However, as I argue in more detail in Sec. IV he is mistaken.

6. This is Carson's argument.

7. Nor can we say that it is *prima facie* wrong because it is an attempt to get someone to do something that is prima facie wrong. This argument is flawed in two ways. To begin with, as we have seen, the premise expresses what is at best a dangerous half-truth. Were we to reason from the whole truth we must conclude that there are some contexts in which the presumption in favor of violating one's official duties is stronger than the presumption against it. In the second place, moreover, the inference is invalid: it is not necessarily *prima facie* wrong to induce someone to do something that is *prima facie* wrong. Rather, it is *prima facie* wrong to induce someone to do something that is wrong, all things considered. Thus, if it is *prima facie* wrong for P to do A, but P ought to do A, all things considered, there is no presumption against my inducing P to do A; I do not need to justify this by appealing to countervailing moral considerations. I require such justification only when it is wrong for P to do so. Cases of this sort are interesting but typically neglected by philosophers. (The following are examples: a. P is a soldier in a war in which each side has equal claim to justice; R is a guard on the opposite side. Though it might be wrong for R to accept a bribe from P, it is not wrong for P to offer R a bribe. b. P's father is certain to be convicted of a crime he did not commit because the evidence is overwhelmingly against him. It is permissible for P to offer a bribe to R, an assistant district attorney, to "lose" some evidence; but it is wrong for R to accept the bribe.) In any case, the upshot of this is that even if there were a general moral presumption against accepting bribes it would not follow that there is a comparable presumption against offering bribes.

8. In D'Andrade's account bribes are necessarily secret, so these could not count as bribes.

9. A corresponding point holds in relation to bribery outside the realm of officialdom. Consider the case of professional wrestling. Most of us believe that the outcome of professional wrestling matches is determined in advance. Are the losers bribed? (To simplify matters let us assume that they are paid a bit of extra money for losing.) The answer here depends on how we understand their practice. If we take them to be participating in a wrestling competition, we must say that they are bribed. In that case, by failing to compete they violate an understanding constitutive of their practice. It is reasonably clear, however, that professional wrestlers are not engaged in an athletic competition. Rather, they are engaged in a dramatic performance. This being the case the losers are not bribed. They are merely doing what professional wrestlers are ordinarily paid to do, namely, to play out their part in an informal script.

Kendall D'Andrade

Bribery

I

Bribery is wrong. It is immoral almost by definition in the same way that murder is. But what exactly is wrong with bribery? Let's look at some examples,[1] really stereotypes, of bribes, then search for a common factor.

1. Bribing a cop, say, to let you out of a speeding ticket.
2. Bribing an inspector or auditor, say a building inspector who you want to overlook some hazardous code violation.
3. Bribing a politician, whether elected or appointed, say to gain a favorable zoning change.
4. Bribing a purchasing agent to buy from you at a price which is inflated at least enough to cover the costs of bribing him.
5. Bribing a voter, usually to vote for your candidate for governmental office.

Working from such standard instances we obtain, not surprisingly, the standard model of bribery: a transaction between two people with one offering money (or other goods) to a second in order to induce that person to commit an improper act. In most cases the person bribed would not have acted as he did without the inducement of the bribe; in the remaining cases the bribe helps to reinforce a tendency already present, with the briber hoping to purchase a virtual guarantee that the person bribed will perform the desired act. It's easy to isolate the immoral aspect of bribery in this picture: solicitation to commit an immoral act. Borrowing some terminology from law, we may view the

From Kendall D'Andrade, "Bribery," *Journal of Business Ethics,* Vol. 4, 1985. Reprinted by permission of Kluwer Academic Publishers.

person offering a bribe as an accessory to the improper act committed by the person accepting that bribe. As an accessory before the fact[2] the briber is at least as culpable as his hired agent.

Still following the legal model, the degree of impropriety of the act solicited in tendering a bribe will generally determine the degree of impropriety of the act of bribery soliciting commission of that act. Secretly discharging massive amounts of toxic wastes, thereby causing numerous birth defects, is clearly much worse than arranging to have some corporate properties grossly underassessed. Our intuition here is that buying a person's silence about the nature and extent of the polluting is far worse than bribing someone to keep quiet about the company's big tax savings because bribery "inherits" its wrongness from the wrongness of the act one bribes another to commit. This is why being an accessory through bribery to deforming people is worse than being an accessory to tax fraud.[3]

To persuade another to become your accessory you influence him through the offer of some good. This kind of offer is therefore improper, but that hardly shows that all such offers are. Payment of money (or other goods) to obtain another good or service cannot by itself be immoral since that would render all commerce improper. One might seek to escape this conclusion by claiming that commerce was essentially an exchange of goods while bribery was less of a mutual trade than an attempt by one person to change or even control the behavior of another. Even this characterization is too broad; all work for pay can be viewed as the result of inducing one person, the employee, to act differently than he would have had the employer not offered him cash. And for examples where no direct trade is involved we have only to look to our own profession and the grants we receive which enable us to do work we could not otherwise afford to do. Offers of money clearly changed our behavior, and perhaps are intentions as well, yet nothing immoral occurred. These considerations seem to suggest that we look for bribery only when the act "paid for" is wrong and the payment is an important cause of that wrong act.[4]

Have we reached an adequate definition of bribery? One direction seems obvious; if the conditions are fulfilled then the act looks wrong. Put another way, we will certainly not be able to find straightforward examples of payments to induce a person to do an immoral act where the act of offering the payment was itself morally acceptable.[5] But we can find cases which go the other way: where our intuitions are that the act is permissible but the offer of a bribe to perform that act is impermissible. I offer you a bribe to vote for a particular candidate. You have the right to vote, so you certainly have the right to vote for that candidate. You have the legal right to cast your ballot for whatever reasons seem best to you without regard to anyone's judgment about those reasons, whether they are good, relevant, trivial, even wrong-headed. Hence the act of voting for my candidate is permissible, yet few would condone my act of bribing you to vote for that candidate. If it is objected that this case trades on a difference between legally and morally permissible we can change the example slightly. Now you have determined that one candidate is the best using the best possible criteria. All the relevant evidence is currently available, you have reviewed all appropriate material exhaustively, and your decision is firm because the weight of evidence is clear. To eliminate time for changing your mind, this is election day and you are about to vote. I, knowing nothing about you beyond the apparent fact that you are a potential voter, offer you a bribe to vote for my candidate, who also happens to be your choice. I press money on you and disappear. Your act of voting for your choice still seems beyond reproach while mine is morally unsavory.[6]

The preceding suggests that the simple accessory model will not capture all our intuitions concerning what is immoral about bribery. One obvious next step would be to search for more complicated models with extra conditions to include just those examples we felt belonged to the condemned class. But I will not take that path. Instead I offer a different model of bribery: a three-party relation where the offense against that third-party is the source of the extra immo-

rality bribery adds to whatever immorality may result from being an accessory to another's immoral act.

II

The most visible parties to a bribe are the person offering the bribe and the person accepting it. In this simple picture, the only one we have examined so far (which I labeled the accessory model), the accessory offering the bribe acts as a special kind of employer. In most of the stock examples he is someone who "hires" another to commit an illegal and/or immoral act, though he is not likely to formalize such a relationship or observe other niceties of contemporary management practice. As an employer of this type I might hire you to help me rob a bank by recruiting you to hold a gun on the people present while I am busy gathering money from the safe. Since it is highly unlikely that you would have volunteered to restrain people for the sheer fun of it, my offer has certainly affected your behavior, another way of saying that my payment of money to you changed your mind (and thus your actions as well). Your act is clearly wrong, therefore my enticing you to commit your act is also wrong. Here we have all the elements usually thought needed for a bribe even though our pretheoretic intuitions would not lead us to call my employing you as an assistant bank robber bribing you. So let's change the example slightly. I am still intent on robbing the same bank and I still want your help, but now I simply want you to "forget" to lock a few doors. You comply and I enter unobserved and clean out the cash. Here my payment to you qualifies as a bribe. Not everyone has the necessary keys to get him into that bank's vault. In fact you must be a trusted employee (or owner) who for simplicity we may assume works directly for the bank. But according to the accessory model you are also my employee, giving you two employers. The bank expects you to defend its interests (in this case by defending it from robbers), I expect precisely the opposite. Clearly you cannot satisfy both of us, and in this scenario the bank is disappointed because, contrary to their expectations, you secretly acted as *my* agent while appearing to continue acting as the bank's agent. I call your behavior alienation of agency and locate the special immorality of bribery there.[7]

What, precisely, *is* wrong in this last example? Employment by itself is hardly immoral.[8] Apparently the only immoral component was my invitation to commit an illegal (and immoral) act, precisely what the accessory model says. But as I suggested above,[9] that is an illusion fostered by our choice of examples. Consider the bribery of a purchasing agent understood as the purchase of his services in aiding a manufacturer to secure a desired contract with the agent's firm. *Under that description* the purchasing agent does nothing immoral since he is merely acting as another salesman for the manufacturer. Of course we don't really believe in his innocence, despite what the analogy suggests. What is missing from that story is an account of the conflict of interest between his loyalty to the firm which is his regular employer and his special loyalty to the manufacturer purchased just for this occasion. Our intuition that he is not acting properly towards his regular employer might be expressed by the employer as, "He let me down."

To better display this impropriety I want to make several simplifying assumptions. For the moment let us ignore any possible conflicts between the employee's loyalty to his employer and any other obligations he might have; with regard to the act he is bribed to do, his only relevant obligation derives from his employee status and the resulting obligation to act in the employer's interest as the employer perceives that interest. We may also eliminate ignorance; the employer understands the situation sufficiently to perceive what is in fact in his interest and the employee is fully informed about that interest and how to act to best realize the employer's aims. Finally, there are no mitigating factors; the contract of employment is a fair one, fully understood by the employee prior to the first moment of employment; he was not coerced into accepting those terms; all relevant activity occurs during normal business hours as a normal part of the employee's work; the situation is a standard one for this type of employee.[10]

In the unemployed state[11] a person is free to act in his own interests or to volunteer his time and effort to aid another in pursuit of that person's interests. But he always retains the freedom to help when he chooses, and so to withdraw that help when he chooses, even to pretend to help while not actually doing anything helpful at all. Here trickery and inconstancy are not immoral since we are assuming that no commitments exist or are implied—my somewhat extended use of the term unemployed.[12] But when he accepts employment he enters into a contractual relationship (whether formal or implied) which does limit his original, primitive freedom. In the language of contracts, he has exchanged his freedom to act just as he chooses (in particular, without considering anyone else's interests) for some other goods. Generally these are economic goods which he receives as compensation for services performed for his employer. While working in accordance with his contract the employee acts as the agent of the employer in the sense that he does what the employer wishes to have done but for some reason does not perform himself.[13] In this sense he is his employer's agent. Insofar as he acts as an agent he should act to further the employer's interest without regard to his own, or to any third party's; and he should be perceived as an agent rather than a principal. As long as the employment relationship continues, the employee continues to be obligated to his employer. Any deviation from the role of faithful agent creates an essential change in the (employment) contract, and since our simplifying assumptions imply that no moral reasons exist permitting subversion of the contract, the employee has only two acceptable choices: continue faithfully in the agent's role or publicly suspend the contract. Whatever the mechanism for achieving the appropriate publicity, it cannot include remaining on the job, performing the same sorts of tasks and receiving the customary rewards for that performance, or generally representing himself as a continuing agent of the former employer. Yet these are just what the bribed person normally does, and what he must do if he is to successfully carry out the task he was bribed to do.[14] Moreover, the typical bribetaker hopes to retain his present position along with all the rewards given to one who had never ceased acting simply as an employee (specifically, as the employer's agent).

If we think of bribing as a form of employing then the person bribed has two separate employers. In that situation he can only act as a faithful agent of both if he is able to strictly separate the times he acts as agent for each employer, or if the interests of the two employers never even potentially conflict whenever he might have to act as the agent of both simultaneously. In the first case no bribery occurs, the employee has simply taken a second job.[15] In the second we might wonder why the second employer found it worth his while to employ a person to continue doing what he had already obligated himself to do.[16] But typically bribes are offered to obtain the *reverse* of what a person would otherwise do as an employee. Think of the most common examples, the person bribed acts against the interests of his original employer by substituting the second (bribing) employer's desires for his presumed concern for the first employer's business.[17] Some bribes do not seem intended to change behavior, only to reinforce already settled plans. Yet this class of bribes is also offered in the hope of influencing behavior, at least potential behavior. Before accepting the bribe the employee might have planned to act in harmony with the bribe-payer's wishes but he retained the freedom to reconsider those plans in the light of new information or changing interests of his employer. Accepting the bribe is accepting a limitation on that freedom, and so limiting his fidelity to his original employer. If he stays bribed he has agreed to fix in advance decisions which his original employer might wish him to reconsider, and perhaps revise, later on. In this he has become the agent of the one who bribed him rather than remaining his employer's agent. And this he has no right to do, having already 'sold' his agency to his first employer, i.e., contractually giving over his freedom to sell that same agency in the same situation again.

On this analysis accepting a bribe is like selling your car to two different dealers without bothering to retrieve your title by repurchase (or other legitimate means) from the first dealer. If we think of selling agency instead of selling cars then what the briber does when he supplants the original employer is to alienate the agency of the employee by improperly seducing him to covertly switch principals. By hypothesis, the employee had lost this right; and his only obligation was to act as agent of his original employer, and this includes not accepting any other commissions which might dilute his faithfulness or efficiency.[18]

III

In introducing a third party[19] into the analysis my theory helps explain why secrecy is such an essential element in successful bribery. Of course the accessory model also assumes secrecy, but there it is invoked simply for the protection of the two parties from legal and/or social pressures, not as an integral part of the act of bribery itself. The problem (for the one being bribed) is how to continue to be treated as a trusted employee when you are no longer one. Recall the bank robbery scenario. The nightwatchman who leaves doors unlocked so that burglars may enter and loot the place simply could not retain his opportunity to aid in the robbery if he was known to have been "bought." He would lose his keys, and the chance to be alone in the bank unwatched by anyone more trustworthy. Probably he would lose his job, and maybe his freedom for a few years as well, both consequences that loom large in his desire for secrecy. But beyond questions of motivation of the various wrongdoers, which the accessory model handles perfectly well, there is a need to account for the continuing trust of the bribed employee by the employer who, in hindsight, finds himself 'sold out'. Assuming that the first employer is rational, only ignorance of the employee's covert switch in loyalty will explain the continuing trust of the (in fact) untrustworthy person, and ignorance on the employer's part practically demands secrecy by the bribe-taker and the bribe-giver about their "special arrangement."

Even when a person is not in any sense bribed, merely hired, his credibility depends in great measure on our "forgetting" about his special status, and the conflict of interest resulting from his conflicting commitments. Very few believe the used car salesman's claims about his clunkers. Similarly, most other paid agents are not taken at face value because we believe their commitment to telling the truth is compromised by their acceptance of the position of advocate for their company, product, and/or client. Such a person is ordinarily not free to form, and then publicize, his own opinion; rather he has agreed in advance to defend as if it were his own the position of his employer. As long as he is open about that fact there need be nothing immoral about his job. But when he pretends to objectivity and a degree of independence which he has in fact sold then he is guilty of alienation of agency in acting as if he were our[20] employee while "covertly" acting as his employer's agent. The expert witness paid for his testimony can all too easily be caught in this bind.

Up to this point almost every person bribed was the employee of a private corporation. But when a public official is bribed the description gets a bit more complicated because we often want to overturn the effects of past actions as well as guard against future abuses. When someone leaves the bank open we also hope to protect ourselves from being robbed (again), but there is no attempt to 'reverse' the robbery. All we can hope for is restitution (possibly accompanied by some form of punishment, if only loss of his job as a guard in that bank). But public officials can do more than help others raid the treasury, they can create relations by their actions (and decisions), and these consequences remain even when the official is long gone.[21] This is one of the major classes of performatives noticed by John Austin.[22] Many employees of private businesses have a similar, quasi-official status: the purchasing agent who awards a contract, the museum director who hangs my work while denying you space, the critic who praises (or pans) a restaurant, and the judges who award first place in a pie-eating contest all make decisions which are not overturned simply by showing that the "official" accepted a bribe which influenced his decision.

The bank guard is rendered harmless (to the bank) by discharging him or, failing that, by setting some other guard over him (either by assigning another person to that duty or effecting a change of duty for the first guard, thus removing his power to leave the bank open, and vulnerable, at night). Similarly the paid advocate loses much of his effectiveness when we learn that he may be more interested in his fee than in revealing the truth. But while "everybody may know" that a legislator has sold his vote, still that vote is routinely counted *even if* it is, effectively, a tie-breaker and hence the decisive vote. Secrecy, understood as general public ignorance of the act, is certainly not preserved, though the act is not completely open either in the sense that very few people have sufficient evidence, say to convict the legislator or the person offering the bribe of the crime of bribing a public official. The two criminals have exercised what I will call discretion in that they have done nothing to provide sufficient grounds for nullifying the act the official was bribed to do, or for motivating someone to (successfully) overturn that act.[23]

Consider a judge who has been bought. The accessory model helps us to identify two parties to this transaction: the judge who becomes the covert employee and the one who offers the bribe and thus becomes the covert, real, employer. But who is the first employer that the judge has betrayed? Since the judge receives a salary from the government it is tempting to think of him as an employee of that government, either that government as a whole or the particular unit which pays him directly. But this won't do. If the judge sells his loyalty to the government then he can never properly sit on a case where the government is a party, a result which would either require all judges to disqualify themselves in such circumstances or leave them with an irreconcilable conflict between loyalty to the government and their duty to act fairly and impartially.[24] But if the judge ought to put fairness, impartiality and justice above all other commitments then those ideals function as his real (first) employer.[25] When the judge accepts a bribe to act as the bribe-offerer wishes him to act he is subverting his commitment to justice, etc. while pretending that he is (still) acting fairly and impartially. Thus he is guilty of alienation of agency in that he no longer acts as the "agent" of justice while continuing to act as a judge, using his judicial power (to decide authoritatively), the exercise of which assumes his impartiality and commitment to fairness (which he has, unfortunately, sold for that case). But he must be discrete in that he must avoid any action which will result in his decision being reversed.[26]

IV

When is it impossible for *A* to bribe *B*? The obvious replay is "When *B* is a moral hero, for then he will automatically resist temptation." But when is there no temptation to be resisted? One easy answer, given my theory, is when there aren't three parties to the transaction; since the bribe-offerer and the bribe-taker will have to be present in any situation that looks even remotely like a bribe, the only party who can be absent is the first employer to whom the putative bribe-taker owes allegiance. Without a first employer the "bribe-taker" is his own agent, so he is really a free agent, free to consider whether the proffered "bribe" sweetens the deal enough to make it advantageous. In the most obvious class of cases no one would suggest the presence of a first employer behind the "agent"; for instance, while shopping for a new lens (for myself) the salesman may offer me an extra $30 but that cannot be a bribe. In accepting a bribe the bribe-taker thinks it more profitable (in the wider meaning of being more desirable for him) to desert his original employer for the fee offered in the bribe. But that makes no sense if I act for myself; for I would then have to judge the bribe sufficiently advantageous to me that it was worth acting against my own interest in making the purchase. That notion is incoherent.

Where I clearly act only for myself there is no suggestion of bribery; but that obvious ontological fact only distracts us from the serious moral problem of deciding *when I may legitimately* act as an independent agent[27] (rather than the faithful agent of another). At issue here is the kind of payments prohibited under the Foreign Corrupt Practices Act,[28] as well as grease payments made in this country.[29] Much of the debate seems to assume that all such payments are bribes, perhaps relying on the official position of most recipients, but claiming necessity on the part of the payer as sufficient excuse for such conduct.

I would suggest that both sides of this issue are assuming the wrong paradigm; many of these acts are not bribes at all[30] but tips.[31] A tip is very much like a bribe in that it is payment for service but unlike it in that the recipient of a tip is not an unfaithful employee, despite his simultaneous employee status. Many employers permit employees to solicit tips from customers, with the understanding that the employee's primary loyalty must be to the employer; any conflicts of interest is expected to be resolved in the company's favor.[32] For example, the waiter who provides superior service serves both the restaurant and the diner, properly *earning* both his salary and his tip; but if he sells one of the restaurant's secret recipes he is accepting a bribe, even when it is left on the table with the tip. In principle, there is no reason why a government employee could not have a similar dual role: as both a faithful bureaucrat and an independent entrepreneur; and in these cases he must keep his two jobs separate[33] *and* he must have at least the tacit permission of his first employer to operate as an independent businessman in his role as tip solicitor. The second condition must be fulfilled in cultures which virtually require "bribery" at every level of government. Whether the officials actually separate their independent and official roles is a question for each individual official.

It should be clear that this last paragraph is not a defense of bribery, whether in foreign or domestic contexts, but an argument showing why these practices may not be bribes at all. If the employee can be a faithful employee while selling his services to his (and his employer's) customers then his is not, *and cannot be*, bribed to provide the customers the services he provides as an independent contractor, even if they are the same services he provides as part of his faithful service to his (first) employer. So if your "bribe" isn't an invitation to alienation of agency in the culture where it is offered, you act of offering it isn't immoral. This "defense," though sufficient to excuse some foreign corporate "bribers," is still not strong enough for most opponents of the FCPA; they claim that American corporations would really prefer not to offer bribes[34] but are forced into making payments by the structure of the society where they are doing business. In other words, they are innocent victims of an extortion which they are powerless to resist. That opens a whole new truly large can of worms, for extortion is not simply bribery from the other side of the dollar.[35] In some ideal world we would certainly prefer that no one ever offered a bribe, no matter how worthy the objective and how necessary the bribe was to achieving that end; similarly we would prefer that no one ever yield to an extortion threat. But in *this* world we can occasionally justify both bribes and the payment of extortion, though on quite different grounds, since paying extortion is metaphysically more complex then paying a bribe. Both our sympathy (which is more with the victim of extortion than the man claiming he "needed" to bribe another)[36] and the practical application of the law favor the (to my mind reasonable) view that paying extortion is excusable in some circumstances where offering a bribe would be condemned. Basically, we just do not expect moral heroism to the extent of losing one's business (or home or even job) just to fight official extortion, though we would not condone offering an unsolicited bribe to evade a similar trivial infraction. Supporting these intuitions requires a surprising amount of machinery.

In "Extortion" I find a possibility of six different parties to the crime.[37] The extortion victim decides whether he should resist by deciding whether he is faithful to his first employer in so resisting the extortioner's demands. Correct identification of the appropriate first employer is crucial here, which is another way of saying that you need to know where your obligations lie. Metaphysical analysis will only provide tools; you must make the decisions; you as an individual must decide between the rivals for the title "First Employer." (This existentialist commonplace seems to be the primary motivation behind Danley's paper.)[38]

All bribes are instances of alienation of agency. But one can wrongly commit alienation of agency without being bribed; conflict of interest should be avoided when following the wrong interest is tantamount to accepting a bribe. Further, assume that I have an obligation to my future self. Then choosing the lesser, but more accessible, good while sacrificing my real interests is both foolish (irrational) and another example of alienation of agency (where the bribe[39] is the nearer, smaller, good). Here we are back to the classical problem of *akrasia* (weakness of the will); which in the context of this paper[40] can be rendered as the question: "Why would anyone ever accept a bribe?"

Notes

1. These divide neatly into two classes: (1) and (2) are instances of what I call Cover-ups; (3), (4), and (5) are attempts to buy Favors. We can state this distinction in terms of the whistle-blowing each class might require. Any offer of a bribe creates the possibility of blowing the whistle on the person making the offer simply for offering a bribe, and if that offer is accepted, on the recipient just for accepting a bribe. But bribes which attempt to cover up some wrong also invite whistle-blowing to call attention to the very wrong the briber was trying to conceal by offering the bribe. Neither class distinguishes official from unofficial acts. Favors can be solicited from officials of the government (#3) and from private citizens (#5). The same violation may be known to a municipal official (#2) any my neighbor, and I may attempt to secure the silence of each by bribery. In fact I may offer the neighbor a bribe to keep quiet about my unorthodox, but morally permissible, life-style; in this last case no one can be impeded in performing his official duty since by hypothesis no official has any reason for any *official* interest in my life-style.

2. Even when a bribe is given to insure the continuance of a pattern of actions already in progress the effect of the bribe can only be to influence future performance. These shade into generalized bribes. When a lawyer regularly pays off members of the appeals board he is not seeking a specific ruling on any *particular* case. No specific action is solicited from the bribe-taker; only "good will" and generally favorable treatment. The attorney may even realize that he will continue to lose a few cases. This class of bribes has no specific actions as its end, unlike the five examples of bribes noted earlier, but this does not mitigate its wrongness.

Only in very exceptional circumstances is the briber an accessory during or after the fact, namely when he offers a bribe as an inducement to perform an act which he believes has not yet been performed when the act has in fact already occurred and cannot be effectively negated. Such cases are degenerate in that the bribe *cannot* have influenced the person bribed in any relevant manner, yet the offer of the bribe is still improper. These cases can be very illuminating; see pp. 240–241 and my story of such an attempt to bribe a voter.

3. Readers who classify moral actions into only two, or three, essentially homogeneous categories (namely

morally required, morally forbidden, and, perhaps, morally neutral) need only accept an interpretation of inheritance which says that an act of bribery is wrong *because* the act the bribe is meant to induce is morally forbidden.

4. This is probably Nozick's position in his "Coercion," first published in 1969 and reprinted with minor changes in Peter Laslett, W. G. Runciman and Quentin Skinner (ed.), *Philosophy, Politics and Society, Fourth Series,* Basil Blackwell, 1972; see pp. 112–117 and especially 127–128 where he insists on the noncoercive aspect of all offers.

5. But even here there are puzzles, especially when the induced act promotes a morally permissible (or even obligatory) goal.

6. *Why* is my act wrong? To summarize an argument I've developed at much greater length elsewhere, from a Rousseauian position, I should cast my vote to express the general will, not simply my percentage of input into the will of all. Society thus becomes what I will call (in the next section) your first employer, my bribe could only be an attempt to turn you into my agent when you should be society's. The oddity of this example is that I obtain the intended result, your vote for my candidate, without the expected means; having you vote your interest (in this case your interest in my money) rather than your best judgment.

But to those inclined towards a more libertarian theory of voting, I suggest embedding voting in general, public, elections within the context of voting in other, more limited contexts: voting in a legislature, or a jury, or for a prestigious award. In all these contexts we have a clear obligation to support the *best* candidate without regard to our personal preferences or profit.

7. This three-party analysis may soon become the standard interpretation of bribery. Similar ontological positions were espoused by all four panalists at the first DePaul conference on Business Ethics (see Note 40). Scott Turow's paper is published in this issue, pp. 249–251. Tom Carson's paper has recently appeared as "Bribery, Extortion, and the Foreign Corrupt Practices Act" in *Philosophy and Public Affairs* (Winter, 1985) 14.1, pp. 66–90. John Danley's "Toward a Theory of Bribery" was published by the *Business and Professional Ethics Journal* in Volume 2, Number 3, pp. 19–39, followed by commentaries from Turow and myself in Volume 3, Number 1, pp. 80–86. Note 38 hints at the direction of those remarks. Michael Philips heard at least early versions of each of these papers while at the conference and has since published his analysis in *Ethics*. 94.4, pp. 621–636, under the title "Bribery." At present there are no *published* criticisms of the basic ontology known to me, though a few doubts have been mentioned in conversations. The major division among those who accept this approach is over the issue of whether bribery is a prima facie wrong.

8. Cf. p. 240 above. Changing employers is not immoral, having two different employers is not immoral. It is even arguable that one may accept employment from a second source while concealing the second job from your first employer. The legitimacy of such behavior

would follow from an employee's right to privacy in his private (off the job) life and the consequent limitation on the employer's right to even know about such activity, much less control it.

9. P. 239.

10. If any of these conditions are not fulfilled that fact may provide some excuse for accepting the bribe, even justify reducing an otherwise appropriate punishment. But on my view such circumstances will rarely render the acts of bribing and being bribed morally acceptable.

11. An economic version of the state of nature. My account obviously borrows heavily from social contract theorists, particularly Hobbes's account (*Leviathan,* Chapter 16) of how actions can be performed by one person yet owned by another. Later on we will have to extend the notions of employee and employer developed thus far to include all agents and all those principals for whom they act. Still, many of my examples occur in a business context so I will continue to refer to agents of all kinds as employees and the entity to which they are obligated as the employer.

12. Thinkers who see obligations everywhere will have to impose further limits on my primitive free spirit until his behavior falls within their understanding of morally acceptable limits.

13. Or in the case of a corporate employer, acts which the corporation *cannot* perform directly. Cf. Larry May: "Vicarious Agency," *Philosophical Studies* (January, 1983), pp. 69–82.

14. We can construct a little Kantian-style argument justifying the requirements of publicity in terminating or suspending a contractual relationship. What if there were no such requirement? Then an agent would be free to pretend to continue in his capacity as an agent while secretly "changing sides," leaving both his principal and those he might encounter as a putative agent of that principal with absolutely no means of distinguishing genuine agents from phonies. Since it is often profitable to pretend to be an agent when one is not, the phonies might easily outnumber the true agents—in concrete terms, imagine not being able to determine whether the "salesman" took your money on behalf of the store or simply to pocket it himself. Authorizing a person to act as ones agent and acceptance of that authorization at face value would cease. Without the requirement of public termination the very notion of agency becomes incoherent.

Since the employee who fails to inform his old employer that he is at least temporarily giving up his job is in fact deceiving that employer we can see the previous argument as simply a translation of Kant's famous argument that lying is immoral because it would be impossible, or at least impractical, to deceive others were it known that there were no constraints on ones speech (cf. the *Foundation of the Metaphysics of Morals,* p. 403).

15. See Section IV for an all too brief discussion of when an act is, or can be, a bribe.

16. Research grants are the closest legitimate instance of this kind of offer that I can imagine, but even here the

dispenser of the grant expects the recipient to do more than he would have done without it, although he generally only hopes to increase the quantity and/or improve the quality of the same type of research already in progress (or planning).

17. For example, in my story of the bank employee who enabled me to enter the bank after hours and rob it, p. 241 above.

18. The courts have recognized this as a type of fraud: "The normal relationship of employer and employee implies that the employee will be loyal and honest in all his actions with or on behalf of his employer. . . . When one tampers with that relationship for the purpose of causing the employee to breach his duty he in effect is defrauding the employer of a lawful right. The actual deception that is practiced is in the continued representation of the employee to the employer that he is honest and loyal to the employer's interests. . . ." United States v. Procter & Gamble Co. et al., cited in W. Michael Reisman, *Folded Lies: Bribery, Crusades, and Reforms*. The Free Press, 1979, p. 176. Reisman's book is a mine of information about bribery, particularly on the extent of bribery in "normal" contexts. He makes a number of observations which can be taken as evidence for my view, though it is not certain that he would endorse my basic position that there must be three parties to a bribe. In fact, he most often characterizes bribery as an economic transaction between only two parties, the briber and the recipient of the bribe; see especially his first two chapters.

19. The original employer, the one to which the employee owes the faithfulness which he sells to the bribe-offer.

20. Or he might pretend he was only serving the truth. Any university, or university employee, who does contractual research for a business or governmental agency needs to watch for this trap as well. How credible is drug advertising which cites "a major medical study" or "research at a major hospital"?

21. Whether through resignation, defeat in an election, failure to be reappointed, transfer, or other removal.

22. In *How to Do Things With Words*, Oxford University Press, 1962.

23. Subsequent reappraisals of an artist's importance, the retroactive return of Robert E. Lee's U.S. citizenship, printing a retraction, and awarding damages for slander are all overturnings of a previous act (though not always on a showing of bribery, or even alienation of agency).

24. The same line of argument would prove that no ombudsman could ever simultaneously be appropriately loyal to his employer and an advocate for another employee opposing their common employer.

25. My method of determining the putative employer is an obvious adaptation of Hobbes's method of determining who is sovereign in a given community (*Leviathan*, Chapter 18). But in allowing commitment to ideals as well as individuals and groups many more cases can be analyzed as instances of alienation of agency.

26. The most obvious, least analogical, instance of overturning an act.

27. Legitimacy makes all the difference; every bribe-taker is in fact acting as an independent agent when he accepts the bribe and helps the bribe-giver accomplish his objectives, but in so acting he is doing wrong.

28. Hereafter, the more conventional FCPA.

29. Whether to dock bosses for safe speedy unloading of one's cargo or to the multitude of inspectors many businesses face regularly.

30. Hence neither justified bribes nor inexcusable bribes.

31. I develop this position in much greater detail in an expanded version of this paper and in a forthcoming article: "Extortion."

32. Drawing on the initial simplifying assumption that the employee has no other relevant moral duties which conflict with his promise of loyal service to his employer.

33. An impossible demand when conflict of interest can spring out of the most unlikely places, no matter how one tries to avoid it. Rather than a requirement, I propose it as an ideal.

34. A factual claim that needs some considerable substantiation, but which ultimately appeals to the motives of the many corporate executives who will have to answer that charge within their own private consciences.

35. Tom Carson and I agree on this, and on the conclusion that it can license paying extortion when bribery would not be morally acceptable. But we will surely part company over the precise analysis of extortion, though I cannot yet figure out just what his view is. (A full citation for his paper is in Note 7.)

36. Examples abound, from Lockheed in Japan to lawyers practicing before the Chicago Board of Tax Appeals; as Scott Turow says, the jury just couldn't feel sorry for the plight of attorneys who *needed* to earn around half a million annually.

37. The extorter, his victim, and the first and second employers of each (though two pairs are usually identified, reducing the actual number to four).

38. Cited in note 7. His three-person analysis is similar to my own, but his principal claim—that bribery is in itself morally neutral—is one I cannot accept. Alienation of agency is a breach of a previous good-faith agreement. Both of us can easily find instances where one is morally obligated to abandon previous commitments: whistleblowing is the obvious, classic example. Danley seems to believe that the obligation to go public obliterates the whistleblower's earlier obligations to his employer. From the social contract perspective, which I realize Danley doesn't share, this is needless overkill. Contracts, and promises in general, don't create absolute obligations, but they do create some obligations. When we can't keep our previous promises, or when we must entice others into not keeping theirs, we should also have the moral courage to admit that we have dirtied our hands, and we should see that it would be better if we could have achieved the same desirable outcome at less moral cost, even if we cannot find a path to this moral paradise.

39. In that one is guilty of alienation of agency; I have often used the term bribery in this extended sense as if

it were a synonym for the clumsier but more precise alienation of agency.

40. The most recent version of this paper was part of a symposium on bribery, itself part of a program of the Society for Business Ethics held at DePaul University, July 25–26, 1983; the earliest was a talk at Moorhead State University in July 1981. In between there was a presentation to the Business Ethics Study Group at Loyola (led by Kathy Hockenberry) and several very useful discussions with Gerald Dworkin. I am grateful to all for their comments, criticisms, etc.

Jeffrey A. Fadiman

A Traveler's Guide to Gifts and Bribes

"What do I say if he asks for a bribe?" I asked myself while enduring the all-night flight to Asia. Uncertain, I shared my concern with the man sitting beside me, a CEO en route to Singapore. Intrigued, he passed it on to his partners next to him. No one seemed sure.

Among American executives doing business overseas, this uncertainty is widespread. Consider, for example, each of the following situations:

You are invited to the home of your foreign colleague. You learn he lives in a palatial villa. What gift might both please your host and ease business relations? What if he considers it to be a bribe? What if he *expects* it to be a bribe? Why do you feel uneasy?

Your company's product lies on the dock of a foreign port. To avoid spoilage, you must swiftly transport it inland. What "gift," if any, would both please authorities and facilitate your business? What if they ask for "gifts" of $50? $50,000? $500,000? When does a gift become a bribe? When do you stop feeling comfortable?

From Jeffrey A. Fadiman, "A Traveler's Guide to Gifts and Bribes," *Harvard Business Review*, May-June 1986. Reprinted by permission of *Harvard Business Review*.

Negotiations are complete. The agreement is signed. One week later, a minister asks your company for $1 million—"for a hospital"—simultaneously suggesting that "other valuable considerations" might come your way as the result of future favors on both sides. What response, if any, would please him, satisfy you, and help execute the signed agreement?

You have been asked to testify before the Securities and Exchange Commission regarding alleged violations of the Foreign Corrupt Practices Act. How would you explain the way you handled the examples above? Would your explanations both satisfy those in authority and ensure the continued overseas operation of your company?

Much of the discomfort Americans feel when faced with problems of this nature is due to U.S. law. Since 1977, congressional passage of the Foreign Corrupt Practices Act has transformed hypothetical problems into practical dilemmas and has created considerable anxiety among Americans who deal with foreign governments and companies. The problem is particularly difficult for those conducting business in the developing nations, where the rules that govern payoffs may differ sharply from our own. In such instances, U.S. executives may face not only legal but also ethical and cultural dilemmas: How do businesspeople comply with customs that conflict with both their sense of ethics and this nation's law?

One way to approach the problem is to devise appropriate corporate responses to payoff requests. The suggestions that follow apply to those developing Asian, African, and Middle Eastern nations, still in transition toward industrial societies, that have retained aspects of their communal traditions. These approaches do not assume that those who adhere to these ideals exist in selfless bliss, requesting private payments only for communal ends, with little thought of self-enrichment. Nor do these suggestions apply to situations of overt extortion, where U.S. companies are forced to provide funds. Instead they explore a middle way in which non-Western colleagues may have several motives when requesting a payoff, thereby providing U.S. managers with several options.

DECISIONS AND DILEMMAS

My own first experience with Third World bribery may illustrate the inner conflict Americans can feel when asked to break the rules. It occurred in East Africa and began with this request: "Oh, and Bwana, I would like 1,000 shillings as Zawadi, my gift. And, as we are now friends, for Chai, my tea, an eight-band radio, to bring to my home when you visit."

Both *Chai* and *Zawadi* can be Swahili terms for "bribe." He delivered these requests in respectful tones. They came almost as an afterthought, at the conclusion of negotiations in which we had settled the details of a projected business venture. I had looked forward to buying my counterpart a final drink to complete the deal symbolically in the American fashion. Instead, after we had settled every contractual aspect, he expected money.

The amount he suggested, although insignificant by modern standards, seemed large at the time. Nonetheless, it was the radio that got to me. Somehow it added insult to injury. Outwardly, I kept smiling. Inside, my stomach boiled. My own world view equates bribery with sin. I expect monetary issues to be settled before contracts are signed. Instead, although the negotiations were complete, he expected me to pay out once more. Once? How often? Where would it stop? My reaction took only moments to formulate. "I'm American," I declared. "I don't pay bribes." Then I walked away. That walk was not the longest in my life. It was, however, one of the least commercially productive.

As it turned out, I had misunderstood him—in more ways than one. By misinterpreting both his language and his culture, I lost an opportunity for a business deal and a personal relationship that would have paid enormous dividends without violating either the law or my own sense of ethics.

Go back through the episode—but view it this time with an East African perspective. First, my colleague's language should have given me an important clue as to how he saw our transaction. Although his limited command of English caused him to frame his request as a command—a phrasing I instinctively found offensive—his tone was courteous. Moreover, if I had listened more carefully, I would have noted that he had addressed me as a superior: he used the honorific *Bwana,* meaning "sir," rather than *Rafiki* (or friend), used between equals. From his perspective, the language was appropriate; it reflected the differences in our personal wealth and in the power of the institutions we each represented.

Having assigned me the role of the superior figure in the economic transaction, he then suggested how I should use my position in accord with his culture's traditions—logically assuming that I would benefit by his prompting. In this case, he suggested that money and a radio would be appropriate gifts. What he did not tell me was that his culture's traditions required him to use the money to provide a feast—in my honor—to which he would invite everyone in his social and commercial circle whom he felt I should meet. The radio would simply create a festive atmosphere at the party. This was to mark the beginning of an ongoing relationship with reciprocal benefits.

He told me none of this. Since I was willing to do business in local fashion, I was supposed to know. In fact, I had not merely been invited to a dwelling but through a gateway into the maze of gifts and formal visiting that linked him to his kin. He hoped that I would respond in local fashion. Instead, I responded according to my cultural norms and walked out both on the chance to do business and on the opportunity to make friends.

The Legal Side

Perhaps from a strictly legal perspective my American reaction was warranted. In the late 1970s, as part of the national reaction to Watergate, the SEC sued several large U.S. companies for alleged instances of bribery overseas. One company reportedly authorized $59 million in contributions to political parties in Italy, including the Communist party. A second allegedly paid $4 million to a political party in South Korea. A third reportedly provided $450,000 in "gifts" to Saudi generals. A fourth may have diverted $377,000 to fly planeloads of voters to the Cook Islands to rig elections there.

The sheer size of the payments and the ways they had been used staggered the public. A U.S. senate committee reported "corrupt" foreign payments involving hundreds of millions of dollars by more than 400 U.S. corporations, including 117 of the *Fortune* "500." The SEC described the problem as a national crisis.

In response, Congress passed the Foreign Corrupt Practices Act in 1977. The law prohibits U.S. corporations from providing or even offering payments to foreign political parties, candidates, or officials with discretionary authority under circumstances that might induce recipients to misuse their positions to assist the company to obtain, maintain, or retain business.

The FCPA does not forbid payments to lesser figures, however. On the contrary, it explicitly allows facilitating payments ("grease") to persuade foreign officials to perform their normal duties, at both the clerical and ministerial levels. The law establishes no monetary guidelines but requires companies to keep reasonably detailed records that accurately and fairly reflect the transactions.

The act also prohibits indirect forms of payment. Companies cannot make payments of this nature while "knowing or having reason to know" that any portion of the funds will be transferred to a forbidden recipient to be used for corrupt purposes as previously defined. Corporations face fines of up to $1 million. Individuals can be fined $10,000—which the corporation is forbidden to indemnify—and sentenced to a maximum of five years in prison. In short, private payments by Americans abroad can mean violation of U.S. law, a consideration that deeply influences U.S. corporate thinking.

The Ethical Side

For most U.S. executives, however, the problem goes beyond the law. Most Americans share an aversion to payoffs. In parts of Asia, Africa, and the Middle East, however, certain types of bribery form an accepted element of their commercial traditions. Of course, nepotism, shakedown, and similar practices do occur in U.S. business; these practices, however, are both forbidden by law and universally disapproved.

Americans abroad reflect these sentiments. Most see themselves as personally honest and professionally ethical. More important, they see themselves as preferring to conduct business according to the law, both American and foreign. They also know that virtually all foreign governments—including those notorious for corruption—have rigorously enforced statutes against most forms of private payoff. In general, there is popular support for these anticorruption measures. In Malaysia, bribery is publicly frowned on and punishable by long imprisonment. In the Soviet Union, Soviet officials who solicit bribes can be executed.

Reflecting this awareness, most U.S. businesspeople prefer to play by local rules, competing in the open market according to the quality, price, and services provided by their product. Few, if any, want to make illegal payments of any kind to anybody. Most prefer to obey both local laws and their own ethical convictions while remaining able to do business.

The Cultural Side

Yet, as my African experience suggests, indigenous traditions often override the law. In some developing nations, payoffs have become a norm. The problem is compounded when local payoff practices are rooted in a "communal heritage," ideals inherited from a preindustrial past where a community leader's wealth—however acquired—was shared throughout the community. Those who hoarded were scorned as antisocial. Those who shared won status and authority. Contact with Western commerce has blurred the ideal, but even the most individualistic businesspeople remember their communal obligations.

Contemporary business practices in those regions often reflect these earlier ideals. Certain forms of private payoff have endured for centuries. The Nigerian practice of *dash* (private payments for private services), for example, goes back to fifteenth century contacts with the Portuguese, in which Africans solicited "gifts" (trade goods) in exchange for labor. Such solicitation can pose a cultural dilemma to Americans who may be unfamiliar with the communal nuances of non-Western commercial conduct. To cope, they may denigrate these traditions, perceiving colleagues who solicit payments as unethical and their culture as corrupt.

Or they may respond to communal business methods by ignoring them, choosing instead to deal with foreign counterparts purely in Western fashion. This approach will usually work—up to a point. Non-Western business-people who deal with U.S. executives, for example, are often graduates of Western universities. Their language skills, commercial training, and professional demeanor, so similar to ours, make it comfortable to conduct business. But when these same colleagues shift to non-Western behavior, discussing gifts or bribes, Americans are often shocked.

Obviously, such reactions ignore the fact that foreign businesspeople have more than one cultural dimension. Managers from developing countries may hold conflicting values: one instilled by exposure to the West, the other imposed by local tradition. Non-Western business-people may see no conflict in negotiating contracts along Western lines, then reverting to indigenous traditions when discussing private payments. For Americans, however, this transition may be hard to make.

My experience suggests that most non-Westerners are neither excessively corrupt nor completely communal. Rather, they are simultaneously drawn to both indigenous and Western ideals. Many have internalized the Western norms of personal enrichment along with those of modern commerce, while simultaneously adhering to indigenous traditions by fulfilling communal obligations. Requests for payoffs may spring from both these ideals. Corporate

responses must therefore be designed to satisfy them both.

Background for Payoffs

Throughout non-Western cultures, three traditions form the background for discussing payoffs: the inner circle, future favors, and the gift exchange. Though centuries old, each has evolved into a modern business concept. Americans who work in the Third World need to learn about them so they can work within them.

The Inner Circle

Most individuals in developing nations classify others into some form of "ins" and "outs." Members of more communal societies, influenced by the need to strive for group prosperity, divide humanity into those with whom they have relationships and those with whom they have none. Many Africans, for instance, view people as either "brothers" or "strangers." Relationships with brothers may be real—kin, however distant—or fictional, extending to comrades or "mates." Comrades, however, may both speak and act like kin, address one another as family, and assume obligations of protection and assistance that Americans reserve for nuclear families.

Together, kin and comrades form an inner circle, a fictional "family," devoted to mutual protection and prosperity. Like the "old boy networks" that operate in the United States, no single rule defines membership in the inner circle. East Africans may include "age mates," individuals of similar age; West Africans, "homeboys," all men of similar region; Chinese, members of a dialect group; Indians, members of a caste. In most instances, the "ins" include extended families and their friends.

Beyond this magic circle live the "outs": strangers, aliens, individuals with no relationship to those within. Communal societies in Southern Africa, for example, describe these people in all their millions as "predators," implying savage creatures with whom the "ins" lack any common ground. The motives of outsiders inspire fear, not because there is danger but simply because they are unknown. Although conditioned to display courtesy, insiders prefer to restrict both social and commercial dealings to those with whom they have dependable relationships. The ancient principle can still be found in modern commerce; non-Western businesspeople often prefer to restrict commercial relationships to those they know and trust.

Not every U.S. manager is aware of this division. Those who investigate often assume that their nationality, ethnic background, and alien culture automatically classify them as "outs." Non-Western colleagues, however, may regard specific Westerners as useful contacts, particularly if they seem willing to do business in local fashion. They may, therefore, consider bringing certain individuals into their inner circles in such a manner as to benefit both sides.

Overseas executives, if asked to work within such circles, should find their business prospects much enhanced. These understandings often lead to implicit quid pro quos. For example, one side might agree to hire workers from only one clan; in return the other side would guarantee devoted labor. As social and commercial trust grows, the Westerners may be regarded less and less as aliens or predators and more and more as comrades or kin. Obviously, this is a desirable transition, and executives assigned to work within this type of culture may wish to consider whether these inner circles exist, and if so, whether working within them will enhance business prospects.

The Future Favor

A second non-Western concept that relates to payoffs is a system of future favors. Relationships within the inner circles of non-Western nations function through such favors. In Japan, the corresponding system is known as "inner duty" or *giri*. On Mt. Kenya, it is "inner relationship," *uthoni*. Filipinos describe it as "inner debt," *utani na loob*. All systems of this type assume that any individual under obligation to another has entered a relationship in which the first favor must be repaid in the future, when convenient to all sides.

Neither side defines the manner of repayment. Rather, both understand that some form of gift or service will repay the earlier debt with interest. This repayment places the originator under obligation. The process then begins again, creating a life-long cycle. The relationship that springs from meeting lifelong obligations builds the trust that forms a basis for conducting business.

My own introduction to the future favors system may illustrate the process. While conducting business on Mt. Kenya in the 1970s, I visited a notable local dignitary. On completing our agenda, he stopped my rush to leave by presenting me a live and angry hen. Surprised, I stammered shaky "thank-yous," then walked down the mountain with my kicking, struggling bird. Having discharged by obligation—at least in Western terms—by thanking him, I cooked the hen, completed my business, eventually left Kenya, and forgot the incident.

Years later, I returned on different business. It was a revelation. People up and down the mountain called out to one another that I had come back to "return the dignitary's hen." To them, the relationship that had sprung up between us had remained unchanged throughout the years. Having received a favor, I had now come back to renew the relationship by returning it.

I had, of course, no such intention. Having forgotten the hen incident, I was also unaware of its importance to others. Embarrassed, I slipped into a market and bought a larger hen, then climbed to this homestead to present it. Again I erred, deciding to apologize in Western fashion for delaying my return. "How can a hen be late?" he replied. "Due to the bird, we have *uthoni* [obligations, thus a relationship]. That is what sweetens life. What else was the hen for but to bring you here again?"

These sentiments can also operate within non-Western commercial circles, where business favors can replace hens, but *uthoni* are what sweetens corporate life. Western interest lies in doing business, non-Western, in forming bonds so that business can begin. Westerners seek to discharge obligations; non-Westerners, to create them. Our focus is on producing short-term profit; theirs, on generating future favors. The success of an overseas venture may depend on an executive's awareness of these differences.

The Gift Exchange

One final non-Western concept that can relate to payoffs is a continuous exchange of gifts. In some developing nations, gifts form the catalysts that trigger future favors. U.S. executives often wish to present gifts appropriate to cultures where they are assigned, to the point where at least one corporation has commissioned a special study of the subject. They may be less aware, however, of the long-range implications of gift giving within these cultures. Two of these may be particularly relevant to CEOs concerned with payoffs.

In many non-Western commercial circles, the tradition of gift giving has evolved into a modern business tool intended to create obligation as well as affection. Recipients may be gratified by what they receive, but they also incur an obligation that they must some day repay. Gift giving in these cultures may therefore operate in two dimensions: one meant to provide short-term pleasure; the other, long-range bonds.

This strategy is common in Moslem areas of Africa and Asia. Within these cultures, I have watched export merchants change Western clientele from browsers to buyers by inviting them to tea. Seated, the customers sip at leisure, while merchandise is brought before them piece by piece. The seller thus achieves three goals. His clients have been honored, immobilized, and placed under obligation.

In consequence, the customers often feel the need to repay in kind. Lacking suitable material gifts, they frequently respond as the merchant intends: with decisions to buy—not because they need the merchandise but to return the seller's gift of hospitality. The buyers, considering their obligation discharged, leave the premises believing relations have ended. The sellers, however, hope they have just begun. Their intent is to create relationships that will cause clients to return. A second visit would mean presentation of another gift, perhaps of greater value. That, in turn, might mean a second purchase, leading to further visits, continued gifts, and a gradual deepening of personal and commercial relations intended to enrich both sides.

The point of the process, obviously, is not the exchanges themselves but the relationships they engender. The gifts are simply catalysts. Under ideal circumstances the process should be unending, with visits, gifts, gestures, and services flowing back and forth among participants throughout their lives. The universally understood purpose is to create reciprocal good feelings and commercial prosperity among all concerned.

Gift giving has also evolved as a commercial "signal." In America, gifts exchanged by business colleagues may signal gratitude, camaraderie, or perhaps the discharge of minor obligations. Among non-Westerners, gifts may signal the desire to begin both social and commercial relationships with members of an inner circle. That signal may also apply to gifts exchanged with Westerners. If frequently repeated, such exchanges may be signals of intent. For Americans, the signal may suggest a willingness to work within a circle of local business colleagues, to assume appropriate obligations, and to conduct business in local ways. For non-Western colleagues, gifts may imply a wish to invite selected individuals into their commercial interactions.

Approaches to Payoffs

While U.S. corporations may benefit from adapting to local business concepts, many indigenous business traditions, especially in developing regions, are alien to the American experience and therefore difficult to implement by U.S. field personnel—as every executive who has tried to sit crosslegged for several hours with Third World counterparts will attest.

Conversely, many non-Western administrators are particularly well informed about U.S. business practices, thus permitting U.S. field representatives to function on familiar ground. Nonetheless, those willing to adapt indigenous commercial concepts to U.S. corporate needs may find that their companies can benefit in several ways. Through working with a circle of non-Western business colleagues, and participating fully in the traditional exchange of gifts and favors, U.S. executives may find that their companies increase the chance of preferential treatment; use local methods and local contacts to gain market share; develop trust to reinforce contractual obligations; and minimize current risk, while maximizing future opportunities by developing local expertise.

Corporations that adapt to local business concepts may also develop methods to cope with local forms of payoff. Current approaches vary from culture to culture, yet patterns do appear. Three frequently recur in dealings between Americans and non-Westerners: gifts, bribes, and other considerations.

Gifts: The Direct Request

This form of payoff may occur when key foreign businesspeople approach their U.S. colleagues to solicit "gifts." Solicitations of this type have no place in U.S. business circles where they could be construed as exploitation. Obviously, the same may hold true overseas, particularly in areas where shakedown, bribery, and extortion may be prevalent. There is, however, an alternative to consider. To non-Western colleagues, such requests may simply be a normal business strategy, designed to build long-term relationships.

To U.S. businesspeople, every venture is based on the bottom line. To non-Western colleagues, a venture is based on the human relationships that form around it. Yet, when dealing with us they often grow uncertain as to how to form these relationships. How can social ties be created with Americans who speak only of business, even when at leisure? How can traditions of gift giving be initiated with people unaware of the traditions? Without the exchange of gifts, how can obligations be created? Without obligation, how can there be trust?

Faced with such questions, non-Western business colleagues may understandably decide to initiate gift-giving relationships on their own. If powerful, prominent, or wealthy, they may simply begin by taking on the role of giver. If less powerful or affluent, some may begin by suggesting they become recipients. There need be no dishonor in such action, since petitioners know they will repay with future favors whatever inner debt they incur.

The hosts may also realize that, as strangers, Americans may be unaware of local forms of gift giving as well as their relationship to business norms. Or they may be cognizant of such relationships but may have no idea of how to enter into them. In such instances, simple courtesy may cause the hosts to indicate—perhaps obliquely—how proper entry into the local system should be made. Such was the unfortunate case with my East African colleague's request for the eight-band radio.

Cultural barriers can be difficult to cross. Most Americans give generously, but rarely on request. When solicited, we feel exploited. Solicitations may seem more relevant, however, if examined from the perspective of the non-Western peoples with whom we are concerned.

Often, in societies marked by enormous gaps between the rich and the poor, acts of generosity display high status. To withhold gifts is to deny the affluence one has achieved. Non-Western counterparts often use lavish hospitality both to reflect and to display their wealth and status within local society. When Americans within these regions both represent great wealth through association with their corporations and seek high status as a tool to conduct business, it may prove more profitable for the corporation to give than to receive.

In short, when asked for "gifts" by foreign personnel, managers may consider two options. The first option is to regard each query as extortion and every petitioner as a potential thief. The second is to consider the request within its local context. In nations where gifts generate a sense of obligation, it may prove best to give them, thereby creating inner debts among key foreign colleagues in the belief that they will repay them over time. If such requests indeed reflect a local way of doing business, they may be gateways into the workings of its commercial world. One U.S. option, therefore, is to consider the effect of providing "gifts"—even on direct request—in terms of the relationships required to implement the corporation's long-range plans.

Bribes: The Indirect Request

A second approach to payoffs, recurrent in non-Western business circles, is the indirect request. Most Third World people prefer the carrot to the stick. To avoid unpleasant confrontation, they designate third parties to suggest that "gifts" of specified amounts be made to those in local power circles. In explanation they cite the probability of future favors in return. No line exists, of course, dividing gifts from bribes. It seems that direct solicitation involves smaller amounts, while larger ones require go-betweens. On occasion, however, the sums requested can be staggering: in 1976, for example, U.S. executives in Qatar were asked for a $1.5 million "gift" for that nation's minister of oil.

U.S. responses to such queries must preserve both corporate funds and executive relationships with those in power. While smaller gifts may signal a desire to work with the local business circles, a company that supplies larger sums could violate both local antipayoff statutes and the FCPA. Conversely, outright rejection of such requests may cause both the go-betweens and those they represent to lose prestige and thus possibly prompt retaliation.

In such instances, the FCPA may actually provide beleaguered corporate executives with a highly convenient excuse. Since direct compliance with requests for private funds exposes every U.S. company to threats of negative publicity, blackmail, legal action, financial loss, and damage to corporate image, it may prove easy for Americans to say no—while at the same time offering nonmonetary benefits to satisfy both sides.

U.S. competitors may, in fact, be in a better situation than those companies from Europe and Japan that play by different rules. Since the principle of payoffs is either accepted or encouraged by many of their governments, the companies must find it difficult to refuse payment of whatever sums are asked.

Nor should the "right to bribe" be automatically considered an advantage. Ignoring every other factor, this argument assumes contracts are awarded solely on the basis of the largest private payoff. At the most obvious level, it ignores the possibility that products also compete on the basis of quality, price, promotion, and service—factors often crucial to American success abroad. U.S. field representatives are often first to recognize that payoffs may be only one of many factors in awarding contracts. In

analyzing U.S. competition in the Middle East, for instance, one executive of an American aircraft company noted: "The French have savoir faire [sophistication] in giving bribes discreetly and well, but they're still not . . . backing up their sales with technical expertise." The overseas executive should consider to what degree the right to bribe may be offset by turning the attention of the payoff seekers to other valuable considerations.

Other Considerations: The Suggested Service

A third approach, often used by members of a non-Western elite, is to request that U.S. companies contribute cash to public service projects, often administered by the petitioners themselves. Most proposals of this type require money. Yet if American executives focus too sharply on the financial aspects, they may neglect the chance to work other nonmonetary considerations into their response. In many developing nations, nonmonetary considerations may weigh heavily on foreign colleagues.

Many elite non-Westerners, for example, are intensely nationalistic. They love their country keenly, deplore its relative poverty, and yearn to help it rise. They may, therefore, phrase their requests for payoffs in terms of a suggested service to the nation. In Kenya, for example, ministerial requests to U.S. companies during the 1970s suggested a contribution toward the construction of a hospital. In Indonesia, in the mid-1970s, a top executive of Pertamina, that nation's government-sponsored oil company, requested contributions to an Indonesian restaurant in New York City as a service to the homeland. In his solicitation letter, the executive wrote that the restaurant was in fact intended to "enhance the Indonesian image in the U.S.A., . . . promote tourism, . . . and attract the interest of the U.S. businessmen to investments in Indonesia."

Westerners may regard such claims with cynicism. Non-Westerners may not. They recognize that, even if the notables involved become wealthy, some portion of the wealth, which only they can attract from abroad, will still be shared by other members of their homeland.

That belief is worth consideration, for many elite non-Westerners share a second concern: the desire to meet communal obligations by sharing wealth with members of their inner circle. Modern business leaders in communal cultures rarely simply hoard their wealth. To do so would invite social condemnation. Rather, they provide gifts, funds, and favors to those in their communal settings, receiving deference, authority, and prestige in return.

This does not mean that funds transferred by Western corporations to a single foreign colleague will be parceled out among a circle of cronies. Rather, money passes through one pair of hands over time, flowing slowly in the form of gifts and favors to friends and kin. The funds may even flow beyond this inner circle to their children, most often to ensure their continued education. Such generosity, of course, places both adult recipients and children under a long-term obligation, thereby providing donors both with current status and with assurance of obtaining future favors.

In short, non-Western colleagues who seek payoffs may have concerns beyond their personal enrichment. If motivated by both national and communal idealism, they may feel that these requests are not only for themselves but also a means to aid much larger groups and ultimately their nation.

A DONATION STRATEGY

Requests for payoffs give executives little choice. Rejection generates resentment, while agreement may lead to prosecution. Perhaps appeals to both communal and national idealism can open up a third alternative. Consider, for example, the possibility of deflecting such requests by transforming private payoffs into public services. One approach would be to respond to requests for private payment with well-publicized, carefully tailored "donations"—an approach that offers both idealistic and practical appeal.

This type of donation could take several forms. The most obvious, a monetary contribution, could be roughly identical to the amount requested in private funds. Donating it publicly, however, would pay off important foreign colleagues in nonmonetary ways.

At the national level, for instance, the most appropriate and satisfying corporate response to ministerial requests for "contributions" toward the construction of a hospital, such as occurred in Kenya, might be actually to provide one, down to the final door and stethoscope, while simultaneously insisting that monetary payments of any kind are proscribed by U.S. law.

The same principle can apply at local levels. Top executives of smaller companies, faced with requests for funds by influential foreign counterparts, might respond by donating to medical, educational, or agricultural projects at the provincial, district, or even village level, focusing consistently on the geographic areas from which those associates come. The donation strategy can even operate at interpersonal levels. How, for example, would my African colleague have reacted had I responded to his request by offering to "donate" whatever would be needed for a special feast—including a radio?

U.S. executives could also weave "other considerations" into the donation, encouraging foreign colleagues to continue business interaction. Many U.S. companies now simply donate funds. Those in Bali, Indonesia, contribute large sums to local temples. Those in Senegal donate to irrigation projects. Companies in South Africa support 150 Bantu schools for black Africans.

Yet donations alone seem insufficient. To serve as an alternative to payoffs, the concept should have practical appeal. Consider, for example, the story of a Western company in Zaire. During the 1970s, Zaire's economy decayed so badly that even ranking civil servants went unpaid. As a result, key Zairian district officials approached officers of the Western company, requesting private funds for future favors. Instead, the company responded with expressions of deference and "donations" of surplus supplies, including goods that could be sold on the black market. The resulting cash flow enabled the officials to continue in their posts. This in turn allowed them to render reciprocal services, both to their district and to the company. By tailoring their contribution to local conditions, the company avoided draining its funds, while providing benefits to both sides.

There are many ways to tailor donations. At the most obvious level, funds can support social projects in the home areas of important local colleagues. Funds or even whole facilities can be given in their names. Production centers can be staffed by members of their ethnic group. Educational, medical, and other social services can be made available to key segments of a target population based on the advice of influential foreign counterparts. Given the opportunity, many non-Westerners would direct the contributions toward members of their inner circles profiting from local forms of recognition and prestige. These practices, often used in one form or another in the United States, can provide non-Western counterparts with local recognition and authority and supply a legal, ethical, and culturally acceptable alternative to a payoff.

Donating Services

U.S. companies may also deflect payoff proposals by donating services, gratifying important foreign colleagues in nonmonetary fashion, and thus facilitating the flow of future business. In 1983, for example, a British military unit, part of the Royal Electrical and Mechanical Engineers, planned an African overland vehicle expedition across the Sahara to Tanzania. On arrival, they were "expected" to make a sizable cash donation to that nation to be used in support of its wildlife.

Usually this meant meeting a minister, handing over a check, and taking a picture of the transfer. Instead, the British assembled thousands of dollars worth of tools and vehicle parts, all needed in Tanzanian wildlife areas for trucks on antipoaching patrols. Tanzania's weakened economy no longer permitted the import of enough good tools or parts, which left the wildlife authorities with few working vehicles. As a result, wild-game management had nearly halted. By transporting the vital parts across half of Africa, then working alongside local mechanics until every vehicle was on the road, the British reaped far more goodwill than private payments or even cash donations would have gained. More important, they paved the way for future transactions by providing services meant to benefit both sides.

Donating Jobs

A third alternative to private payoffs may be to donate jobs, particularly on projects meant to build goodwill among a host nation's elite. In the 1970s, for example, Coca-Cola was the object of a Middle Eastern boycott by members of the Arab League. Conceivably, Coca-Cola could have sought to win favor with important individuals through gifts or bribes. Instead, the company hired hundreds of Egyptians to plant thousands of acres of orange trees. Eventually the company carpeted a considerable stretch of desert and thereby created both employment and goodwill.

More recently, Mexico refused to let IBM become the first wholly owned foreign company to make personal computers within its borders. Like Coca-Cola in Egypt, IBM employed a strategy of national development: it offered a revised proposal, creating both direct and indirect employment for Mexican nationals, in numbers high enough to satisfy that nation's elite. Such projects do more than generate goodwill. Those able to involve key foreign colleagues in ways that lend prestige on local terms may find they serve as viable alternatives to bribery.

Good Ethics, Good Business

Three strategies do not exhaust the list. U.S. executives in foreign countries should be able to devise their own variants based on local conditions. Each approach should further social progress while offering local status instead of U.S. funds. Americans may find their non-Western colleagues more inclined to do business with corporations that lend prestige than with those whose representatives evade, refuse, or simply walk away. It should not harm a company to gain a reputation for providing social services instead of bribes. A corporation that relies too much on payoffs will be no more respected within non-Western business circles than developing nations that rely too much on payoffs are now respected in U.S. business circles.

Similarly, since the legal dilemma would be resolved, home offices might respond more favorably to overseas requests for funds. Whereas funding for private payments remains illegal, proposals to "donate" the same amounts toward host-nation development could be perceived as public relations and cause-related marketing. Home offices should not fear legal action. While the FCPA prohibits payments to foreign political parties, candidates, or officials with discretionary authority, nowhere does it prohibit the use of funds to aid developing societies, and it requires only that companies keep detailed records that accurately and fairly reflect the transactions.

Businesspeople can also resolve the ethical dilemma. Turning private payoffs into public services should meet both U.S. and corporate moral standards. While one measure of corporate responsibility is to generate the highest possible returns for investors, this can usually be best achieved within a climate of goodwill. In contemporary Third World cultures, this climate can more often be created by public services than by private payoffs. To sell cola, Coke did not bribe ministers, it planted trees. Certainly, host governments will look most favorably on companies that seek to serve as well as to profit, especially through "gifts" that show concern for local ways.

Finally, the cultural dilemmas can also be resolved. Non-Western business practices may be difficult to comprehend, especially when they involve violations of U.S. legal, commercial, or social norms. Nonetheless, U.S. business options are limited only by our business attitudes. If these can be expanded through selective research into those local concepts that relate to payoffs, responses may emerge to satisfy both congressional and indigenous demands. What may initially appear as begging, bribery, or blackmail may be revealed as local tradition, cross-cultural courtesy, or attempts to make friends. More important, when examined from a non-American perspective, mention of "gifts," "bribes," and "other valuable considerations" may signal a wish to do business.

QUESTIONS

1. To Philips does it make any sense to talk of parents bribing their children? Do you think it is possible for parents to bribe their children?
2. Philips' rejects the claim that "wherever P presents Q with something of value to induce Q to violate Q's official duties P has offered a bribe." What is Philips argument in support of this? Is it a good argument?
3. What is a tip? On what basis does D'Andrade distinguish between bribes and tips?
4. In D'Andrade's view is it possible for an employer to be bribed? Explain.
5. Consider the following passage from Fadiman's article:

Most individuals in developing nations classify others into some form of "ins" and "outs". . . . Like the "old boy networks" that operate in the United States . . . beyond this magic circle live the "outs": strangers, aliens, individuals with no relationship to those within. . . .

Overseas executives, if asked to work within such circles, should find their business prospects much enhanced. These understandings often lead to implicit quid pro quos. For example, one side might agree to hire workers from only one clan; in return the other side would guarantee devoted labor. As social and commercial trust grows, the Westerners may be regarded less and less as aliens or predators and more and more as comrades or kin. Obviously, this is a desirable transition, and executives assigned to work within this type of culture may wish to consider whether these inner circles exist, and if so, whether working within them will enhance business prospects.

Does this comment do justice to the ethical concerns implicit in such a situation?

6. What are some of the alternatives that Fadiman suggests as alternatives to payoffs and bribes? Do you find these alternatives morally acceptable?

In the mid 1980s William Lamb and Carmon Willis, both tobacco growers in Kentucky, brought suit against Phillip Morris, Inc. and B.A.T. Industries, alleging that these companies had violated federal antitrust laws and the Foreign Corrupt Practices Act. The basis of their suit was that Phillip Morris and B.A.T., who buy tobacco not only from Kentucky growers but from foreign producers, had through subsidiaries, entered into a contract with La Fundacion Del Nino (the Children's Foundation) of Caracas, Venezuela. The contract was signed by the Foundation's president, the wife of the then President of Venezuela. Under the contract's terms the subsidiaries were to make periodic donations to the Children's Foundation totalling approximately $12.5 million dollars. In addition to tax deductions for the donations, the subsidiaries received guarantees of price controls on Venezuelan tobacco, the elimination of controls on retail cigarette prices in Venezuela, and assurances that existing tax rates to tobacco companies would not increase. Lamb and Willis claimed that similar contracts had been arranged by Phillip Morris and B.A.T. in Argentina, Brazil, Costa Rica, Mexico, and Nicaragua. They asserted that such contracts amount to unlawful inducements designed to restrain trade and result in manipulation of tobacco prices to the detriment of domestic growers.

CASE STUDY QUESTIONS

1. Is there anything immoral in companies signing contracts such as those signed by the subsidiaries of Phillip Morris, Inc. and B.A.T. Industries?
2. Would you classify such contracts as bribes? Why or why not?

CASE 10:2 AN INFLUENTIAL FRIEND[2]

In October 1986 Metropolitan Inc. was awarded a $38 million contract whereby it became the exclusive supplier of diesel fuel for the Chicago Transit Authority's vehicles. It won the contract by agreeing to give the CTA substantial discounts if fuel invoices were paid for within specified time periods and by agreeing to meet the CTA's Minority Business Requirement by employing a minority-run subcontracting firm.

Metropolitan entered into the contract believing that the CTA would not find it possible to pay its fuel bills promptly enough to entitle it to the agreed upon discounts. Unfortunately for Metropolitan, this did not prove to be the case, and the company began losing money on its sales to the CTA. In an effort to remedy this, Metropolitan began to send the invoices late in order to prevent the CTA from taking advantage of the discount. When this did not work, Metropolitan attempted to artificially inflate the invoices so that CTA would still pay full price even after the discount had been applied.

The CTA, becoming suspicious, launched an investigation. This alarmed Metropolitan's head, Brian Flisk, who then contacted Howard Medley, a member of the CTA's Board of Directors. During the subsequent conversation concerning the CTA investigation, Medley indicated to Flisk that he (Medley) would stand to gain a $300,000 commission if he were to sell a warehouse for some friends. Flisk indicated he was prepared to enter into negotiations for the warehouse, since Medley was helping him with the CTA investigation. At the time this took place a CTA ethics regulation explicitly prohibited board members from doing business with CTA vendors.

The CTA's investigation resulted in a report documenting Metropolitan's billing irregularities and raised questions whether the subcontracting firm was a legitimate minority enterprise or a fraudulent pass-through corporation. Despite the fact that other board members spoke in favor of terminating Metropolitan's contract, and despite the fact that Metropolitan never satisfactorily answered the report's allegations, Medley strongly defended Metropolitan and no action was taken by the Board.

A short while later, a second investigation was undertaken by the CTA. The subsequent report indicated numerous problems with the quality of the diesel fuel being sold by Metropolitan. At Flisk's request, Medley again intervened and was again successful in preventing the termination of Metropolitan's contract.

CASE STUDY QUESTIONS

1. Suppose Flisk thought the warehouse deal was a good deal entirely on its own merits, but was also aware that buying the warehouse would influence Medley's decisions in his favor. Would there be anything wrong in Flisk's pursuing the deal? Would pursuing the deal constitute offering a bribe?

2. Suppose Medley actively pursued Flisk and suggested that Flisk's problems could be solved through an appropriate "donation." Would Flisk be morally wrong to provide such "a donation"? Explain.

Notes

1. Based on *Lamb v. Phillip Morris, Inc.* as found in 915 *Federal Reporter,* 2nd series, 1024, (6th Cir. 1990).
2. Based on *U.S. v. Medley* as found in 913 *Federal Reporter,* 2nd series, 1248 (7th Cir. 1990).

FOR FURTHER READING

1. Arnold Berleant, "Multinationals, Local Practice, and the Problem of Ethical Consistency," *Journal of Business Ethics*, Vol. 1, No. 3, August 1982, pp. 185–193.

2. Tom Carson, "Bribery, Extortion, and the Foreign Corrupt Practices Act," *Philosophy and Public Affairs,* Vol. 14, No. 1, Winter 1985, pp. 66–90.

3. John Danley, "Toward a Theory of Bribery," *Business and Professional Ethics Journal,* Vol. 2, No. 3, pp. 19–39. (Note that *Business and Professional Ethics Journal*, Vol. 3, No. 1, pp. 80–86, contained commentaries on Danley's article by Scott Turow and Kendall D'Andrade).

Part III

Business and the Consumer

Chapter Eleven

ADVERTISING

Introduction

Chapter Eleven marks a shift in focus from the relationship between employer and employee to the relationship between business and consumer. We begin our examination of the ethical issues involved with this relationship by considering some of the ethical concerns associated with advertising.

Advertising is usually defended on the grounds that the exchange of information is a necessary condition of an efficient free market. It is argued that if advertising were not available consumers would find it difficult to become aware of significant new products or to compare the merits of competing products, and manufacturers would find it hard to capture enough consumers to lower production costs. This argument fails to address the issue that advertising is not primarily an attempt to present information, but is rather an attempt to persuade or influence consumers. There are many instances in which little or no relevant information is presented to the consumer. Questions concerning the moral legitimacy of advertising must focus, therefore, not simply on the necessity of exchanging information in the marketplace, but on the techniques of persuasion advertisers typically employ.

By way of introduction to the topic, Paul F. Camenisch's article, "Marketing Ethics: Some Dimensions of the Challenge" treats the question of the marketer's responsibility to the customer in the broad context of business' role in society. His goal is not so much to offer specific instruction on how those marketing a product ought to conduct themselves, but rather to make clear the foundation which needs to underlie consideration and discussion of their duties. In Camenisch's view, marketing is a societal enterprise, depending on society's permission and support to occur, and is, therefore, to some extent, subject to the moral expectations of society. It follows that marketing practices cannot be evaluated solely on the basis of their effectiveness in promoting sales, but must also take into account the goals of the society in which they take place. Given the value society places on individual autonomy, marketing practices which undermine the consumer's capacity to make free and informed decisions should be avoided.

Our next two selections by Tibor Machan and John Waide focus on general questions raised by advertising's emphasis on persuasion. Machan, in his article "Advertising: The Whole or Only Some of the Truth?," criticizes the assumption that advertising's primary purposes should be to convey information and provide help to consumers. He defends the doctrine of *caveat emptor*, i.e., let the buyer beware, suggesting that so long as an advertiser does not deceive the customer she has acted ethically. She has no duty to provide further information that will help the customer make a reasoned decision, e.g., that the product is obsolete or the price has been grossly inflated.

In support of his view, Machan espouses a form of egoism which he terms classical. Appealing to Aristotle, he suggests that each individual should seek to promote his or her interests as a human being and an individual. He argues that we need not fear that such an egoism implies the permissibility of lying or cheating as sales practices, since such activities cannot be seen as fulfilling human nature and thus promoting one's interests as a human being.

In "The Making of Self and World in Advertising" John Waide criticizes the practice of marketing products by associating them with deep non-market desires, e.g., friendship, acceptance, and esteem of others, that they cannot possibly fulfil. He finds such associative advertising morally problematic on two counts. First, because the desire to sell the product is largely independent of a sincere concern to improve the life of the consumer, associative advertising undermines in its practitioners the concern and sympathy that are essential to moral virtue. Second, insofar as it is effective, it leads consumers to substitute market goods for the development of virtues. Associating friendship with the type of beer one drinks or the brand of mouthwash one uses, devalues the development of virtues such as empathy and loyalty, that are the true basis of friendship. In Waide's view, the central issue is not whether the consumer in some sense retains autonomy, but whether in order to sell a product, it is morally desirable to encourage individuals to live lives in which the development of character and virtue is hindered or undermined. Although Waide makes no explicit reference to Aristotle, his emphasis on the development of character and virtue is certainly in the Aristotelian tradition. A question worth pondering is whether Waide's position is consistent with the *caveat emptor* approach taken by Machan, who also claims to find his inspiration in Aristotle, and if not, which writer more accurately reflects Aristotle's ethical thinking.

Classified advertising tends to be informational rather than persuasive in nature. We might on this account, think it presents fewer moral problems than other forms of advertising. Tomlinson's "Choosing Social Responsibility Over Law: The *Soldier of Fortune* Classified Advertising Cases" demonstrates that we should not be too quick to draw this conclusion. Through analysis of two notorious cases in which professional hit men were hired through classified advertisements in *Soldier of Fortune* magazine, he explores the social responsibility of those who subsidize their publications through classified advertising. His conclusion is that publishers have concerned themselves too much with questions of legality and not enough with questions of moral responsibility.

Paul F. Camenisch

Marketing Ethics: Some Dimensions of the Challenge

The tension between the imperatives of economic survival in the competitive marketplace and ethics is a very real one for many individuals and corporations. Any such tensions can be magnified and complicated in marketing since the marketing firm must not only survive in its own market, but must, as one factor in that survival, deal with the question of what it must do, or what its clients *think* it must do to ensure the clients' survival in their marketplaces. Practitioners must vividly portray these complex and difficult situations for academic ethicists from time to time, lest the ethical analysis and recommendations offered by the latter lose all touch with the harsh realities business people actually face.

At the same time, the integrity of the ethicists' own profession requires that they keep pressing practitioners not to relax the tension they feel by abandoning ethics and capitulating to the demands of the marketplace. Confronting practitioners with hard questions about such matters is not, or certainly need not be, the attack of hostile outsiders determined to expose the soft underbelly of business to a critical public. It can also be the challenge of the loyalist who believes that businesspersons are often sufficiently sensitive to such issues and that business can be sufficiently creative to find ways to be simultaneously successful and ethical.

One way to press such a concern about ethics in business, and specifically in marketing is by

From Paul F. Camenisch, "Marketing Ethics: Some Dimensions of the Challenge," *Journal of Business Ethics*, Vol. 10, No. 4, 1991. Reprinted by permission of Kluwer Academic Publishers.

holding up the issue of the social responsibility of business, which I understand to refer to the doing of societal good unrelated or minimally related to the business activity in view. It is in some ways a kind of "add-on" ethic for business. Following Milton Friedman many business persons dismiss such social responsibility as an inappropriate add-on for business people and organizations operating in the competitive marketplace. They often maintain not that business does no social good, but that business that does its business well is already performing a number of positive services to society and its members through the creation of jobs, the paying of taxes, and the generating of beneficial and/or desired products and services. Additional social responsibility is simply seen as excessive and inappropriate. While I think the issue of corporate social responsibility cannot be dismissed this easily, I will here focus on another dimension of the business-society relationship by raising the question of the ethics of business activity itself, the question of the ethics which is in some sense internal to that activity. In our current case, that means the ethic that is internal to marketing. Here we deal not with some add-on to business but with an element integral to business activity.

One can begin thinking about an ethic internal to a given kind of activity by asking what the goal or purpose of that activity is. By this I mean not the goals or purposes of the various parties engaged in that activity; those are almost unlimited in their variety. I mean rather the purpose or goal of the activity itself, specifically its *societal* purpose, the reason that society permits, encourages, even facilitates such activity.

The goals of marketing have been variously stated and I will not here conclusively answer the question of which is its definitive goal. The goal perhaps most often assumed and supported by common sense observation of the business enterprise is that marketing's goal is to increase the company's profits by increasing the sales of its product. Some students of business and marketing, either because they fear that a focus on profit will give too much of a toehold to the critic, or because they know a company's profits depend on many factors other than marketing, prefer to see the goal of marketing as creating a market, or creating a customer. But to this amateur observer such ideas do not really change the thrust of the first answer. They only buffer it by putting another layer between the activity and its ultimate goal. Why does a company want to create a market except to increase its sales? And why create a customer except to buy its products or services?

However put, such answers may be more or less adequate when marketing is viewed from the side of the marketer. But marketing is a societal enterprise. It occurs in society, with society's permission and support, and purportedly, in part for society's benefit. Presumably it is therefore to some extent subject to the moral regulations and expectations society and potential customers attach to it.

But what is marketing's purpose when seen from other perspectives, specifically those of the larger society and of the customer? These two perspectives are not identical. But given that all of us are customers in much of our lives, this perspective represents the larger society better than does the perspective of businesspersons who represent only a portion of the population.

To speak of the goal of marketing from this perspective we must go beyond the simple idea of moving the product or increasing sales, since these as such serve the larger society only indirectly at best. One might attempt to bring together the goals of marketing as seen by business and as seen by the customer or the larger society by suggesting that the goal of responsible marketing is to inform the customer about the product so that sales will increase. This goal of informing the potential customer can be brought one step closer to specifically moral considerations by drawing on philosopher Richard DeGeorge and others who have suggested that transactions are more likely to be morally defensible if both parties enter it freely and fully informed. Assuming that marketing and marketers want to be part of morally defensible transactions, one might then say that viewed societally, the goal of marketing should be to increase the likelihood and frequency of free and informed transactions in the marketplace. Or, to put it negatively, marketing ought not to decrease the likelihood of such free and informed market transactions.

The information requirement is easy enough to state, even if determining what constitutes being fully informed is not. Unfortunately we are also familiar with the various ways it can be compromised. Blatant untruths would seem to be relatively rare in current advertising. But partial truths, the misleading embellishing of the facts (the fixed focus camera becomes "focus free," the unsized bathrobe becomes "one-size-fits-all"), propositions intentionally implied to be true but not actually stated, still abound. Here we meet a variety of unresolved and perhaps unresolvable matters: How much hard information do customers want and deserve? How much of the relevant information are marketers obligated to provide and how much should potential customers be left to seek out on their own? In planning advertising so as not to mislead the public, are marketers to envision the average citizen, however that elusive will 'o the wisp is defined, or the especially vulnerable or gullible citizen—the child, the aged, the simple-minded? How much of the policing of advertising should be taken on by the government and how much left up to the industry.

But in spite of these and related questions, the most complex part of the problem of morally defensible transactions probably has to do with the question of freedom. Clear, honest information relevant to the goods or services being marketed is almost certain to enhance the potential customer's freedom in the transaction, or at least it will not diminish that freedom. But except for the highly technical information aimed at limited markets such as stereophiles, and price advertising of grocery specials and automobile deals, very little of marketing has to do with hard information about the product. Any student of marketing knows that much of contemporary marketing consists of techniques which can be used to "hook" the potential customer on the product in a way that potentially diminishes clear, rational decision-making about the product or service being offered. These of course include enhancing the symbolic value of products by associating them with celebrities, including them in sexually provocative advertising campaigns, linking them with deeply held values and commitments, or presenting them as solutions to widely shared insecurities and fears. This is not to say that all puffery is inappropriate. But it is to say that the lines between legitimate puffery, distortion, deception and the psychological "hooking" of the potential customer are not easy to draw, and that the more the interaction is cluttered by irrelevant "information," the more likely the seller is trying to prevent a fully informed and free decision by the customer.

Of course some will dismiss this goal of marketing as the recommendation of a well-meaning but idealistic academician. But before doing that, one should consult that almost perennial final appeal of the defender of the marketplace, Adam Smith. The market he was willing to defend is one in which there is no fraud or coercion and in which all participants are adequately informed about the transaction. Of course we will not always agree on what constitutes adequate information. But here we are more interested in the principle of adequate information for the participant than we are in the details of definition or the mechanics of enforcement.

But perhaps most decisive for the argument being made here is the point made by many marketers that the marketplace is not turned into a moral reality only by moral considerations brought to it from the outside—the moral convictions of the various participants, or the societal guidelines established for its conduct. Rather, the marketplace is itself already a moral as well as an economic mechanism even prior to any externally imposed moral requirements. There are moral constraints built into the very dynamics through which marketing works. For example, contemporary marketing practitioners often argue that dishonest marketing will be unsuccessful marketing, that the market will weed out those who violate the common morality. I am not entirely convinced that that is true, at least in the short run. Products that conspicuously and almost immediately fail to perform have been rejected by the public in spite of aggressive and clever marketing campaigns. But

that is a very limited category of test cases. Increasingly we deal more in very complex products and services whose performance, especially long-run performance, and potential negative impacts are not easily assessed by the layperson. Just what sort of performance level, length of service, and maintenance and repair costs are reasonable for such products as modern automobiles, or the electronic products which now flood our lives? What are the truly significant potential harms of the countless chemical products from pharmaceuticals to fertilizers we now scatter freely through our lives and our environment? These are much more complex judgements than whether the miracle knife advertised on television can slice both tin cans and ripe tomatoes in that order with equal aplomb, or whether the new copier really does produce X copies per minute with greater clarity than the old machine. The variety and complexity of products most of us now purchase in the consumer society mean that virtually no unassisted layperson can make truly informed rational decisions about such purchases. The question then is whether marketing will be an ally or an obstacle in our making such decisions. Where it is the latter it is clearly morally indefensible on the criteria suggested here. But even if marketing is merely neutral in terms of its impact on the freedom and informed character of the transaction, it is not clear how one would justify the increase it generates in the ultimate cost of the product.

There is another set of concerns which are an element in the issues raised above, but which also have a life of their own in the discussion of advertising ethics. These concerns arise in relation to advertising that critics see as appealing to our baser, darker, less admirable side—our penchant towards violence, exploitative sex, and the desire to control and manipulate other persons. The usual defense of such advertising is that marketers here are simply offering us what we want, whether in the product or service offered, or in the marketing which sells it. Such a defense is backed by the claim that they have discovered what we want both by experience and by marketing research through surveys and focus groups. But given the more than 100 billion dollars poured annually into advertising and the shaping of the consumer's view of the world, it should hardly surprise us that advertisers find in the minds and psyches of many consumers what they have been helping put there for decades. It is no trick to pull a rabbit from a hat as long as one chooses the hat into which one has previously put the rabbit. Nor are advertisers cleared of responsibility for such advertising even if this baser side is rooted in something other than prior marketing efforts, which it no doubt is. The question still remains whether marketing and its clients should not only exploit that side of us for the sake of sales, but legitimate it and give it respectable, public standing by making it seem to be not only a natural and universal, but even the dominant dimension of the human self.

Of course if these questions are to be answered and the answers then enforced by agencies outside the marketing enterprise, we encounter the very complex and troubling issues of censorship in a free society. It is much to be preferred for everyone's sake that marketers and their clients raise these questions in a serious manner that can, where indicated, lead to self-regulation. This is most likely to happen if they look at these issues not just from the perspective of business, but as responsible citizens of a society in which they, their children, families and friends must also join with the rest of us in building and sustaining liveable, humane communities.

This raises the issue, met by many occupational and professional groups, of how we relate our work or our professional roles to our other roles in the society—our roles as responsible citizens, as members of communities responsible for the raising and moral formation of children, as members of religious communities and other voluntary associations. Do these other dimensions of our selves figure into our reflec-

tions on appropriate marketplace activity? If so, then economic survival, whether individual or corporate, cannot be the only, or even the last and decisive consideration. Or do we recommend a compartmentalization, a walling off of these various roles from each other that denies the marketer a consistency, an integrity among the various things she is and does? Little need be said here about the individual and societal pathologies that result from such an approach. The only viable alternative seems to be a proper vision of the world which subordinates marketing to business, and business to the goals and purposes of the larger society, so that the tensions among these and the other spheres of one's life are reduced to a minimum and one can fulfill one's various roles with a sense of personal integrity.

My focus has been on the possible moral problems posed by contemporary marketing. That is not because there is no positive case to be made for marketing. It rather reflects my assigned task and the fact that the interesting ethical discussions occur there rather than around the positive side of advertising, such as its alerting us to the availability of new products, the helpful information it does sometimes convey, and the possible reduction in price resulting from the larger volume of sales generated.

It would be an impossible and a pointless task to attempt a cost/benefit analysis on the basis of the above considerations to decide if advertising as a whole is morally defensible. It should be neither impossible nor pointless to do such a calculus about some specific forms of advertising for those who are prepared to acknowledge that marketing must be seen in the context of the larger society, of the sorts of human communities we are trying to build and of the sorts of persons we are trying to become.

Tibor R. Machan

Advertising: The Whole or Only Some of the Truth?

When commercial advertising is criticized, often some assumption surfaces that should be explored more fully. I have in mind in particular the hidden premises that advertising is first and foremost a means for conveying information. Another assumption which lingers in the background of criticisms of advertising is that ethics requires that those who sell goods and services should first of all help customers.

My aim here is to defend the approach to advertising that does not require of merchants that they tell all. So long as merchants are honest, do not mislead or deceive, they are acting in a morally satisfactory manner. It is not good for them—and there is nothing in morality that requires it of them—to take up the task of informing consumers of the conditions most favorable to them in the market place, to aid them in their efforts to find the best deal.

The following passage will help introduce us to the topic. It illustrates the kind of views that many philosophers who work in the field of business ethics seem to find convincing.

Merchants and producers have many ways of concealing truth from the customers—not by lying to them, but simply by not telling them facts that are relevant to the question of whether they ought to purchase a particular product or whether they are receiving full value for their money.[1]

The author goes on to state that "it is certainly unethical for (salesmen and businessmen) to fail to tell their customers that they are

From Tibor R. Machan, "Advertising: The Whole or Only Some of the Truth," *Public Affairs Quarterly,* Vol. 1, No. 4, 1987. Reprinted with permission.

not getting full value for their money."[2] He cites David Ogilvy, a successful advertiser, admitting that "he is 'continuously guilty of *suppressio veri,* the suppression of the truth.'"[3] In other words, what advertisers do ethically or morally wrong is to fail to tell all, the whole truth, when they communicate to others about their wares, services, goods, products, or what not.

Yet there is something unrealistic, even farfetched, about this line of criticism. To begin with, even apart from advertising, people often enough advance a biased perspective on themselves, their skills, looks, and so on. When we go out on a first date, we tend to deck ourselves out in a way that certainly highlights what we consider our assets and diminishes our liabilities. When we send out our resumes in our job search efforts, we hardly tell all. When we just dress for the normal day, we tend to choose garb that enhances our looks and covers up what is not so attractive about our whole selves.

Burton Leiser, the critic we have been using to illustrate the prevailing view of advertising, is not wholly unaware of these points, since he continues with his quotation from Ogilvy, who says, "Surely it is asking too much to expect the advertiser to describe the shortcomings of his produce. One must be forgiven for 'putting one's best foot forward'." To this Leiser exclaims, "So the consumer is *not* to be told all the relevant information; he is *not* to be given all the facts that would be of assistance in making a reasonable decision about a given purchase ... "[4] Nevertheless, Leiser does not tell us what is ethically wrong in such instances of *suppressio veri.* In fact, the claim that in all advertising one must present the whole truth, not just be truthful about one's subject matter, presupposes the very problematic ethical view that one ought to devote oneself *primarily* to bettering the lot of other people. What commerce rests on ethically, implicitly or explicitly, is the very different doctrine of *caveat emptor* (let him [the purchaser] beware), which assumes that prudence is a virtue and should be practiced by all, including one's customers. I will argue here that the merchant's ethical stance is more reasonable than that of the critics.

I. The Vice of *Suppressio Veri*

Leiser and many others critical of business and sales practices assume that in commercial transactions persons owe others the whole truth and nothing but the truth. This is why they believe that merchants act unethically in failing to tell their customers something that customers might ask about if they would only think of everything relevant to their purchasing activities. Leiser gives a good example:

Probably the most common deception of this sort is price deception, the technique some high-pressure salesmen use to sell their goods by grossly inflating their prices to two, three, and even four times their real worth. Again, there may be no "untruth" in what they say; but they conceal the important fact that the same product, or one nearly identical to it, can be purchased for far less at a department or appliance store . . . [5]

Before I discuss the ethical points in these remarks, a word, first, about the alleged simplicity of learning whether some item for sale by a merchant is in fact available for purchase "for far less" elsewhere. The idea is, we may take it, that the customer will indeed obtain what he or she wants by purchasing this item from some other seller. This ignores the fact that it may be quite important for customers to purchase some items in certain places, in certain kinds of environments, even from certain types of persons (e.g., ones with good manners). Sheer accessibility can be crucial, as well as atmosphere, the merchant's demeanor, and so on. If it is legitimate for customers to seek satisfaction from the market, it is also legitimate to seek various combinations of satisfaction, not simply product or price satisfaction.

Let us, however, assume that a customer could have obtained all that she wanted by going elsewhere to purchase the item at a price "far less" than what it costs at a given merchant's store. Is there a responsibility on the merchant's part (if she knows this) to make the information available to the customer? Or even more de-mandingly, is it ethically required that the merchant become informed about these matters and convey the information to potential customers?

The answer depends on a broader ethical point. What are the standards by which human beings should conduct themselves, including in their relationship to others? If something on the order of the altruist's answer is correct, then, in general, *suppressio veri* is wrongful. Telling the whole truth would help other people in living a good human life. Altruism here means not the ideal of equal respect for everyone as a human being, advocated by Thomas Nagel.[6] Rather it is the earlier sense of having one's primary duty to advance the interest of others.[7] A merchant need not be disrespectful toward his customers by not informing them of something that perhaps they ought to have learnt in the first place. By volunteering information that quite conceivably a customer should, as a matter of his personal moral responsibility (as a prudent individual), have obtained, a merchant might be meddling in matters not properly his own, which could be demeaning.

But an altruism in terms of which one is responsible to seek and obtain the well-being of his fellow human beings would render *suppressio veri* morally wrong. Such an altruism is certainly widely advocated, if not by philosophers then at least by political reformers. For example, Karl Marx states, in one of his earliest writings, that "The main principle . . . which must guide us in the selection of a vocation is the welfare of humanity . . ." and that "man's nature makes it possible for him to reach his fulfillment only by working for the perfection and welfare of his society."[8] Here he states precisely the morality of altruism initially espoused by August Comte, who coined the term itself and developed the secular "religion" by which to promote the doctrine.[9]

Now only by the ethics of altruism does it follow unambiguously that a merchant who does not tell all "is certainly unethical." Neither the more common varieties of utilitarianism, nor Kant's theory, as it is often understood, implies this. If we are to live solely to do good for others, then when we have reason to believe that telling the whole truth will promote others' well-being (without thwarting the well-being of yet some other person), we morally ought to tell the whole truth to this person. So when a merchant has reason to believe that telling his customer about lower prices elsewhere (for goods which he sells at higher price) will benefit his customer, he ought morally to do so.

But for it to be established that this is what a merchant ought morally to do for any customer, and that not doing so "is certainly unethical," the sort of altruism Marx and Comte defended would have to be true. No other ethical viewpoint seems to give solid support to the above claim abut what "is certainly unethical."

Still, might one perhaps be able to show the whole truth thesis correct by other means than depending on a strong altruistic moral framework? Not very plausibly.

Intuitionism, as generally understood, would not override the well entrenched belief that when one embarks on earning a living and deals with perfect strangers, one should *not* promote one's weaknesses, one should *not* volunteer information detrimental to one's prospects. I doubt anyone would seriously advise job seeking philosophers to list on their C.V.s rejected articles and denied promotions—that would be counterintuitive.

It is also doubtful that most versions of utilitarianism would support a very strong general principle of self-sacrifice from which it can be shown that it "is certainly unethical" not to tell the whole truth. There could be many good utilitarian reasons to support at least a substantial degree of *caveat emptor* in the marketplace. For example, if the classical and neo-classical defenses—and the Marxian explanation of the temporary necessity—of the unregulated market of profit seeking individuals have any merit, it is for utilitarian reasons that the competitive, self-interested conduct of market agents should be encouraged. This would preclude giving away information free of charge, as a matter of what is right from a utilitarian perspective of maximizing the good of society, which in this case would be wealth.

Even a Kantian deontological ethics, as generally understood, advises against taking over what is very plausibly another person's moral responsibility, namely, seeking out the knowledge to act prudently and wisely. The Kantian idea of moral autonomy may not require seeking one's personal happiness in life, as the Aristotelian concept of the good moral life does, but it does require leaving matters of morality to the discretion of the agent. Meddling with the agent's moral welfare would conceivably be impermissibly intrusive. By reference to the categorical imperative it is difficult to imagine why one should invite commercial failure in one's market transactions, a failure that is surely possible if one is occupied not with promoting one's success but with the success of one's potential customers.

It seems then, that the altruist ethics, which makes it everyone's duty to further the interests of other people, is indeed the most plausible candidate for making it "certainly unethical" to suppress the truth in commercial transactions. Yet, of course, troubles abound with altruism proper.

When properly universalized, as all *bona fide* moralities must be, the doctrine in effect obligates everyone to refuse any help extended. Such a robust form of altruism creates a veritable daisy-chain of self-sacrifice. None is left to be the beneficiary of human action. Perhaps, therefore, what should be considered is a less extreme form of altruism, one which obligates everyone to be helpful whenever he or she has good reason to think that others would suffer without help.

Specifically, the altruism that might be the underpinning of the criticism of advertising ethics illustrated above should be thought of more along Rawlsian lines. According to this view we owe help to others only if they are found in special need, following the lead of Rawls's basic principle that "All social values—liberty and opportunity, income and wealth, and the bases of self-respect—are to be distributed equally unless an unequal distribution of any, or all, of these values is to everyone's advantage."[10]

But this form of moderate egalitarianism no longer supports the prevailing idea of proper business ethics.[11] In complying with this principle the merchant should, in the main—except when informed of special disadvantages of potential customers—put a price on his product that will sell the most of his wares at the margin. That is exactly what economists, who assume that merchants are profit maximizers, would claim merchants will do. And this is the kind of conduct that the merchant has reason to believe will ensure the equal distribution of values, as far as she can determine what that would be. The reason is that from the perspective of each merchant *qua* merchant it is reasonable in the course of commerce to consider potential customers as agents with equal status to merchants who are interested in advancing their economic interests. From this, with no additional information about some possible special disadvantage of the customer, merchants must see themselves as having equal standing to customers and as having legitimate motives for furthering their own interests.[12]

Thus, the Rawlsian egalitarian moral viewpoint will not help to support the doctrine that merchants owe a service to customers. Only the robust form of altruism we find in Marx and some others is a good candidate for the morality that, for example, Leiser assumes must guide our merchant. Ethical views other than altruism might support the view that the merchant ought to be extra helpful to special persons—family, friends, associates, even neighbors—but not to everyone. Even a narrow form of subjective "ethical" egoism can lead merchants to regard it as their responsibility to be helpful toward *some* other people. For instance, a merchant might consider most of his customers close enough friends that the morality of friendship, which need not be altruistic and may be egoist, would guide him to be helpful even to the point of risking the loss of business. Or, alternatively, were it the case that having the reputation of being helpful leads to increased patronage from members of one's community, then in just such a community such a subjective egoist would properly engage in helping behavior, including now and then informing his customers of more advantageous purchases in other establishments.

II. The Morality of Caveat Emptor

In contrast to the assumption of altruism as a guide to business conduct, I wish to suggest a form of egoism as the appropriate morality in terms of which to understand commerce. I have in mind a form of egoism best called "classical" because, as I have argued elsewhere,[13] it identifies standards of (egoistic) conduct by reference to the teleological conception of the human self spelled out in the works of classical philosophers, especially Aristotle, but modified in line with an individualism that arises from the ontology of human nature.[14] The idea, briefly put, is that each individual should seek to promote his interests as a human being *and* as the individual he is. . . . Classical egoism regards the individual person as the ultimate, though not sole, proper beneficiary of that individual's own moral conduct. The standards of such conduct are grounded on the nature of the individual *as a human being,* as well as that particular person, thus in a moral universe which is coherent there need be no fundamental conflict between the egoistic conduct of one person and the egoistic conduct of another.

Accordingly, in the case of our merchant, he should abide by the basic moral principle of right reason, and the more particular implication of this, namely the virtue of honesty, as he answers the questions his customer puts to him. He might, for example, even refuse to answer some question instead of either giving help or lying. It is a person's moral responsibility to promote his rational self-interest. And taking up the task of merchandising goods and services can qualify, for various individuals with their particular talents and opportunities in life, as promoting one's rational self-interest. So a merchant could be acting with perfect moral propriety in not offering help to a customer with the task of information gathering (especially when it is clear that competing merchants are doing their very best to publicize such information as would be valuable to customers). The responsibility of merchants is to sell conscientiously their wares, not to engage in charitable work by carrying out tasks that other persons ought to carry out for themselves.

It might be objected that if someone asks an informed merchant, "Is this same product available for a lower price somewhere else?" no other alternative but letting the customer know the answer exists—it could be rather strained to refuse to answer. But there are many ways to deflect answering that do not mark someone as a deceiver. Smiling at the customer, the merchant might quietly put a question in response to the question: "Well, do you actually want me to help you to take your business elsewhere?" Should it be clear to a merchant that the customer isn't going to be satisfied with the wares available in his or her establishment, it would make perfectly good sense to offer help—as indeed countless merchants do frequently enough. Thus, when one looks for shoes, one frequently finds that one merchant will guide a customer to another where some particular style or size is likely to be available. Both good merchandising and ordinary courtesy would support such a practice, although it is doubtful that any feasible ethical system would make it obligatory!

In terms of the classical egoism that would seem to give support to these approaches to ethical issues in business, it does not follow that one would be acting properly by lying to avoid putting oneself at a competitive disadvantage. One's integrity, sanity, reputation, generosity and one's respect for others are more important to oneself than competitive advantage. Yet neither is prudence merely a convenience, and seeking a competitive advantage in the appropriate ways would indeed be prudent.[15]

Of course showing that this morality is sound would take us on a very long journey, although some work has already been done to that end.[16] As I have noted already, in numerous noncommercial situations human beings accept the form of conduct which characterizes ordinary but decent commercial transactions as perfectly proper. In introducing ourselves to people we have never met, for example, we do not advance information that would be damaging to the prospects of good relations. We do not say, "I am John Doe. When I am angry, I throw a fit, and when in a bad mood I am an insufferable boor." When we send an invitation to our forthcoming party, we do not say, "While this party may turn out to be pleasant, in the past we have had some very boring affairs that also set out to be fun." Innumerable non-commercial endeavors, including professional ones, are characterized by "putting but our best foot forward," leaving to others the task of making sure

whether they wish to relate to us. The fields of romance, ordinary conversation, political advocacy, and so forth all give ample evidence of the widespread practice of putting our best foot forward and letting others fend for themselves. We do not lie, mislead or deceive others by not mentioning to them, unsolicited, our bad habits, our foibles. As suggested before, we are not lying or misleading others when in sending along our resumes or C.V.s we do not list projects that have been rejected.

The exceptions to this are those cases in which we have special obligations arising out of special moral relationships such as friendship, parenthood, collegiality, and so on. In these—as well as in contractual relationships where the obligations arise out of explicitly stated intent instead of implied commitments and promises—one can have obligated oneself to be of assistance even in competition or contest. Friends playing tennis could well expect one another to lend a hand when skills are quite uneven. Parents should not allow their children to fend for themselves, with limited information, as the children embark upon various tasks. And in emergency cases it is also reasonable to expect strangers to set aside personal goals that ordinarily would be morally legitimate.

Commercial relationships usually take place between strangers. The only purpose in seeking out other persons is for the sake of a good deal. Even here, sometimes further bonds emerge, but those are essentially beside the point of commerce. So the moral aspects of personal intimacy would not be the proper ethics for commercial relationships, anymore than they would be for sport or artistic competitions.

Some, of course, envision the good human community as a kind of large and happy family, the "brotherhood of man," as Marx did (not only early in his life but, insofar as his normative model of the ultimately good human society was concerned, for all of his career). For them the fact that some human beings interact with others solely for "narrow," "selfish" economic purposes will be a lamentable feature of society—to be overcome when humanity reaches maturity, perhaps, or to be tolerated only if out of such selfishness some public good can be achieved.[17]

But this alleged ideal of social life cannot be made to apply to human beings as they in fact are found among us. That vision, even in Marx, is appropriate only for a "new man," not the actual living persons we are (in our time). For us this picture of universal intimacy must be rejected in favor of one in which the multifaceted and multidimensional possibility of pursuing personal happiness—albeit in the tradition of Aristotle, not Bentham or contemporary microeconomists—is legally protected (not guaranteed, for that is impossible). For them commercial interaction or trade does not place the fantastic burden on the parties involved that would be required of them if they needed to "be forgiven for putting one's best foot forward."

I have tried to offer some grounds for conceiving of trade in such a way that the unreasonable burden of having to tell others the whole truth, blemishes and all, need not be regarded as morally required. None of the above endorses cheating, deception, false advertising, and the like. It does recommend that we look at the practice of commercial advertising—as well as other practices involving the presentation of oneself or one's skills and wares in a favorable light—as morally legitimate, justified, even virtuous (insofar as it would be prudent).

III. PRODUCT LIABILITY: SOME CAUTION

One line of objection that has been suggested to the above approach is that failing to tell all about the features of a commercial transaction on the part of those embarking on it is like not telling someone about a defect in a product. When a merchant sells an automobile tire, if he is aware that this tire is defective, the mere fact that his customer does not explicitly inquire about defects does not appear to be, on its face, sufficient justification for suppression of the truth of the fact. But is this not just what my analysis above would permit, on egoistic grounds? And would that not be sufficient ground, as James Rachels argues[18] in another context against egoism, for rejecting the argument?

Without embarking on a full discussion of the topic of product liability, let me point out

some possible ways of approaching the issues that are consistent with the moral perspective I have taken on truth telling. First, as in law, so in morality there is the "reasonable man" standard which can be appealed to in considering personal responsibility. After all, a merchant is selling an automobile tire and it is implicit in that act that he is selling something that will, to the best of available knowledge, function in that capacity when utilized in normal circumstances.

One problem with this response is that it comes close to begging the question. Just what the reasonable expectation is in such cases of commercial transaction is precisely at issue. If it is true that *caveat emptor* is justified, then why not go the full distance and make the buyer beware of all possible hitches associated with the transaction?

The answer to that question introduces the second approach to handling the product liability issue. . . . I am thinking here of the need for a distinction between what is essential about some item and what is incidental or merely closely associated with it. And when we are concerned about truth telling—and I have not tried to reject the requirement of honesty, only that of telling everything that one knows *and* that may be of help to the buyer—it is more than likely that in the very identification of what one is trading, one commits oneself to having to give any information that is pertinent to the nature of the item or service at hand. Concerning automobile tires, their function as reliable equipment for transport on ordinary roads is a good candidate for an essential feature. So not telling of a defect in tires pertaining to this feature would amount to telling a falsehood, that is, saying one is trading x when in fact one is trading not-x (inasmuch as the absence of an essential feature of x would render whatever is identified as x a fake, something that would in the context of commercial transactions open the party perpetrating the misidentification to charges of fraud).

This is not to claim what is essential about items must remain static over time. The context has a good deal to do with the determination of essential attributes of items and services, and convention and practice are not entirely inapplicable to that determination. Here is where a certain version of the theory of rational expectations would be useful and may indeed already function in some instances of tort law. As J. Roger Lee puts it,

I have rights. They do not come out of agreements with others, being prior to and presupposed by such agreements. But standard relations with others, which I will call "rational expectations frameworks," fix the criteria of their application to situations in everyday life. And rational expectation frameworks are a guide to those criteria.

... For example, if I go into a bar and order a scotch on the rocks, then it is reasonable to expect that I'll get what I order and that neither it nor the place where I sit will be boobytrapped. There are countless examples of this.[19]

It is possible to show that from a robust or classical ethical egoist standpoint, *the truth about an item or service being traded should be told.* But this does not show that the whole truth should be told, including various matters associated with the buying and selling of the item or service in question—such as, its price elsewhere, its ultimate suitability to the needs of the buyer, its full value and so on. This perspective, in turn, does not imply that defective products or incompetent service are equally suitable objects of trade in honest transactions.[20,21]

Notes

1. Burton Leiser, "Deceptive Practices in Advertising," in Tom L. Beauchamp and Norman Bowie (eds.), *Ethical Theory and Business* (Englewood Cliffs: Prentice-Hall, 1979), p. 479. Leiser's rendition of this view is perhaps the most extreme. Others have put the matter more guardedly, focusing more on the kind of suppression that conceals generally harmful aspects of products than on failure to inform the public of its comparative disadvantage vis a vis similar or even identical substitutes. Yet the general statements of the ethical point, in contrast to the examples cited, are very close to Leiser's own. See, e.g., Vincent Barry, *Moral Issues in Business* (Belmont: Wadsworth Publishing Company, 1983), Chapter 8. Barry chides advertisers for concealing "a fact ... when its availability would probably make the desire, purchase, or use of the product less likely than in its absence" (p. 278).
2. Leiser, op. cit.
3. Ibid., p. 484.
4. Ibid., p. 479.
5. Ibid., p. 481.
6. Thomas Nagel, *The Possibility of Altruism* (Oxford: Clarendon Press, 1970).
7. This is the sense of the term as it occurs in the writings of August Comte who reportedly coined it. Thus the *Oxford English Dictionary* reports that the term was "introduced into English by the translators and expounders of Comte," e.g., Lewes, *Comte's Philosophy,* Sc. 1. xxi. 224: "Dispositions influenced by the purely egotistic impulses we call popularly 'bad,' and apply the term 'good' to those in which altruism predominates" (1853), *The Compact Edition,* 65.
8. Loyd D. Easton and Kurt H. Guddat (eds.), *Writings of the Young Marx on Philosophy and Society* (Garden City: Anchor Books, 1967), p. 39. See, for a recent statement, W. G. Maclagan, "Self and Others: A Defense of Altruism," *The Philosophical Quarterly,* vol. 4 (1954), pp. 109–27. As Maclagan states it, "I call my view 'altruism' *assuming* a duty to relieve the distress and promote the happiness of our fellows." He adds that such a view requires "that a man may and should discount altogether his own pleasure or happiness as such when he is deciding what course of action to pursue" (p. 110).
9. Wilhelm Windelband, *A History of Philosophy,* Vol. II (New York: Harper Torchbooks, 1968), pp. 650ff.
10. John Rawls, *A Theory of Justice* (Cambridge, Mass.: Harvard University Press, 1971), p. 62.
11. Because of the intimate association of ethics and altruism (self-sacrifice), some defenders of the value of commerce or business have settled for a total disassociation of business and morality. See, e.g., Albert Carr, "Is Business Buffing Ethical?" in Thomas Donaldson and Patricia H. Werhane (eds.), *Ethical Issues in Business* (Englewood Cliffs: Prentice-Hall, 1979), pp. 46–52.
12. I [Tibor R. Machan] believe that this point about the compatibility of Rawlsian egalitarianism and the market economy has been argued in James Buchanan, "A Hobbesian Interpretation of the Rawlsian Difference Principle," *Kyklos,* vol. 29 (1976), pp. 5–25.
13. Tibor R. Machan, "Recent Work in Ethical Egoism," *American Philosophical Quarterly,* vol. 16 (1979), pp. 1–15. See also T. R. Machan, "Ethics and the Regulation of Professional Ethics," *Philosophia,* vol. 8 (1983), pp. 337–348.
14. *Nicomachean Ethics,* 119a 12. This point is stressed in W. F. R. Hardie, "The Final Good in Aristotle's *Ethics,*" *Philosophy,* vol. 40 (1965), pp. 277–95.
15. For more elaborate development of these points, see Tibor R. Machan, *Human Rights and Human Liberties* (Chicago: Nelson-Hall, 1975), Chapter 3.
16. See., e.g., Eric Mack, "How to Derive Ethical Egoism," *The Personalist,* vol. 52 (1971), pp. 735–43.
17. The entire tradition of classical economics embodies this point, made most forcefully by Mandeville's *The Fable of the Bees* and Adam Smith's *The Wealth of Nations.*
18. James Rachels, "Two Arguments Against Ethical Egoism," *Philosophia,* vol. 4 (1974), pp. 297–314.
19. J. Roger Lee, "Choice and Harms," in T. R. Machan and M. Bruce Johnson (eds.), *Rights and Regulations Economic, Political, and Economic Issues* (Cambridge, MA: Ballinger, 1983), pp. 168–69.

20. For more on product liability, see Richard A. Epstein, *A Theory of Strict Liability* (San Francisco; Cato Institute, 1980). See, also, Tibor R. Machan, "The Petty Tyranny of Government Regulations," in M. B. Johnson and T. R. Machan (eds.), *Rights and Regulations op. cit.*
21. This paper was presented to the American Association for the Philosophic Study of Society, San Francisco, California, March 27, 1987. I [Tibor R. Machan] wish to express my appreciation for the opportunity to give this paper to a very receptive and helpful audience at that meeting. I want also to thank the anonymous reviewer for the *Public Affairs Quarterly* for very helpful suggestions.

John Waide

The Making of Self and World in Advertising

In this paper I will criticize a common practice I call associative advertising. The fault in associative advertising is not that it is deceptive or that it violates the autonomy of its audience—on this point I find Arrington's arguments persuasive.[1] Instead, I will argue against associative advertising by examining the virtues and vices at stake. In so doing, I will offer an alternative to Arrington's exclusive concern with autonomy and behavior control.

Associative advertising is a technique that involves all of the following:

1. The advertiser wants people[2] to buy (or buy more of) a product. This objective is largely independent of any sincere desire to improve or enrich the lives of the people in the target market.

2. In order to increase sales, the advertiser identifies some (usually) deep-seated non-market good for which the people in the target market feel a strong desire. By "non-market good" I mean something which cannot, strictly speaking, be bought or sold in a marketplace. Typical non-market goods are friendship, acceptance and esteem of others. In a more extended sense we may regard excitement (usually sexual) and power as non-market goods since advertising in the U.S.A. usually uses versions of these that cannot be bought and sold. For example, "sex appeal" as the theme of an advertising campaign is not the market-good of prostitution, but the non-market good of sexual attractiveness and acceptability.

3. In most cases, the marketed product bears only the most tenuous (if any) relation to the non-market good with which it is associated in the advertising campaign. For example, soft drinks cannot give one friends, sex, or excitement.

4. Through advertising, the marketed product is associated with the non-market desire it cannot possibly satisfy. If possible, the desire for the non-market good is intensified by calling into question one's acceptability. For example, mouthwash, toothpaste, deodorant, and feminine hygiene ads are concocted to make us worry that we stink.

5. Most of us have enough insight to see both

   a. that no particular toothpaste can make us sexy and
   b. that wanting to be considered sexy is at least part of our motive for buying that toothpaste.

Since we can (though, admittedly, we often do not bother to) see clearly what the appeal of the ad is, we are usually not lacking in relevant information or deceived in any usual sense.

From John Waide, "The Making of Self and World in Advertising," *Journal of Business Ethics,* Vol. 6, 1987. Reprinted by permission of Kluwer Academic Publishers.

6. In some cases, the product actually gives at least partial satisfaction to the non-market desire—but only because of advertising.[3] For example, mouthwash has little prolonged effect on stinking breath, but it helps to reduce the intense anxieties reinforced by mouthwash commercials on television because we at least feel that we are doing the proper thing. In the most effective cases of associative advertising, people begin to talk like ad copy. We begin to sneer at those who own the wrong things. We all become enforcers for the advertisers. In general, if the advertising images are effective enough and reach enough people, even preposterous marketing claims can become at least partially self-fulfilling.

Most of us are easily able to recognize associative advertising as morally problematic when the consequences are clear, extreme, and our own desires and purchasing habits are not at stake. For example, the marketing methods Nestlé used in Africa involved associative advertising. Briefly, Nestlé identified a large market for its infant formula—without concern for the well-being of the prospective consumers. In order to induce poor women to buy formula rather than breastfeed, Nestlé selected non-market goods on which to base its campaigns—love for one's child and a desire to be acceptable by being modern. These appeals were effective (much as they are in advertising for children's clothing, toys, and computers in the U.S.A.). Through billboards and radio advertising, Nestlé identified parental love with formula feeding and suggested that formula is the modern way to feed a baby. Reports indicate that in some cases mothers of dead babies placed cans of formula on their graves to show that the parents cared enough to do the very best they could for their children, even though we know the formula may have been a contributing cause of death.[4]

One might be tempted to believe that associative advertising is an objectionable technique only when used on the very poorest, most powerless and ignorant people and that it is the poverty, powerlessness, and ignorance which are at fault. An extreme example like the Nestlé case, one might protest, surely doesn't tell us much about more ordinary associative advertising in the industrialized western nations. The issues will become clearer if we look at the conceptions of virtue and vice at stake.

Dewey says "the thing actually at stake in any serious deliberation is not a difference of quantity [as utilitarianism would have us believe], but what kind of person one is to become, what sort of self is in the making, what kind of a world is making."[5] Similarly, I would like to ask who we become as we use or are used by associative advertising. This will not be a decisive argument. I have not found clear, compelling, objective principles—only considerations I find persuasive and which I expect many others to find similarly persuasive. I will briefly examine how associative advertising affects a. the people who plan and execute marketing strategies and b. the people who are exposed to the campaign.

a. Many advertisers[6] come to think clearly and skillfully about how to sell a marketable item by associating it with a non-market good which people in the target market desire. An important ingredient in this process is lack of concern for the well-being of the people who will be influenced by the campaign. Lloyd Slater, a consultant who discussed the infant formula controversy with people in both the research and development and marketing divisions of Nestlé, says that the R&D people had made sure that the formula was nutritionally sound but were troubled or even disgusted by what the marketing department was doing. In contrast, Slater reports that the marketing people simply did not care and that "those guys aren't even human" in their reactions.[7] This evidence is only anecdotal and it concerns an admittedly extreme case. Still, I believe that the effects of associative advertising[8] would most likely be the same but less pronounced in more ordinary cases. Furthermore, it is quite common for advertisers in the U.S.A. to concentrate their attention on selling something that is harmful to many people, e.g., candy that rots our teeth, and cigarettes. In general, influencing people without concern for their well-being is likely to reduce one's sensitivity to the moral motive of concern for the well-being of others. Compassion, concern, and sympathy for others, it seems to me, are clearly central to moral virtue.[9] Associative advertising must surely undermine this sensitivity in much of the advertising industry. It is, therefore, *prima facie* morally objectionable.

b. Targets of associative advertising (which include people in the advertising industry) are also made worse by exposure to effective advertising of this kind. The harm done is of two kinds:

1. We often find that we are buying more but enjoying it less. It isn't only that products fail to live up to specific claims about service-life or effectiveness. More often, the motives ("reasons" would perhaps not be the right word here) for our purchases consistently lead to disappointment. We buy all the right stuff and yet have no more friends, lovers, excitement or respect than before. Instead, we have full closets and empty pocket books. Associative advertising, though not the sole cause, contributes to these results.

2. Associative advertising may be less effective as an advertising technique to sell particular products than it is as an ideology[10] in our culture. Within the advertising which washes over us daily we can see a number of common themes, but the most important may be "You are what you own".[11] The quibbles over which beer, soft drink, or auto to buy are less important than the over-all message. Each product contributes its few minutes each day, but we are bombarded for hours with the message that friends, lovers, acceptance, excitement, and power are to be gained by purchases in the market, not by developing personal relationships, virtues, and skills. Our energy is channeled into careers so that we will have enough money to *be* someone by buying the right stuff in a market. The not very surprising result is that we neglect non-market methods of satisfying our non-market desires. Those non-market methods call for wisdom, compassion, skill, and a variety of virtues which cannot be bought. It seems, therefore, that insofar as associative advertising encourages us to neglect the non-market cultivation of our virtues and to substitute market goods instead, we become worse and, quite likely, less happy persons.

To sum up the argument so far, associative advertising tends to desensitize its practitioners to the compassion, concern, and sympathy for others that are central to moral virtue and it encourages its audience to neglect the cultivation of non-market virtues. There are at least five important objections that might be offered against my thesis that associative advertising is morally objectionable.

First, one could argue that since each of us is (or can easily be if we want to be) aware of what is going on in associative advertising, we must want to participate and find it unobjectionable. Accordingly, the argument goes, associative advertising is not a violation of individual autonomy. In order to reply to this objection I must separate issues.

a. Autonomy is not the main, and certainly not the only, issue here. It may be that I can, through diligent self-examination neutralize much of the power of associative advertising. Since I can resist, one might argue that I am responsible for the results—*caveat emptor* with a new twist.[12] If one's methodology in ethics is concerned about people and not merely their autonomy, then the fact that most people are theoretically capable of resistance will be less important than the fact that most are presently unable to resist.

b. What is more, the ideology of acquisitiveness which is cultivated by associative advertising probably undermines the intellectual and emotional virtues of reflectiveness and self-awareness which would better enable us to neutralize the harmful effects of associative advertising. I do not know of specific evidence to cite in support of this claim, but it seems to me to be confirmed in the ordinary experience of those who, despite associative advertising, manage to reflect on what they are exposed to.

c. Finally, sneer group pressure often makes other people into enforcers so that there are penalties for not going along with the popular currents induced by advertising. We are often compelled even by our associates to be enthusiastic participants in the consumer culture. Arrington omits consideration of sneer group pressure as a form of compulsion which can be (though it is not always) induced by associative advertising.

So far my answer to the first objection is incomplete. I still owe some account of why more people do not complain about associative advertising. This will become clearer as I consider a second objection.

Second, one could insist that even if the non-market desires are not satisfied completely, they must be satisfied for the most part or we would stop falling for associative advertising. This objection seems to me to make three main errors:

a. Although we have a kind of immediate access to our own motives and are generally able to see what motives an advertising campaign uses, most of us lack even the simple framework provided by my analysis of associative advertising. Even one who sees that a particular ad campaign is aimed at a particular non-market desire may not see how all the ads put together constitute a cultural bombardment with an ideology of acquisitiveness—you are what you own. Without some framework such as this, one has nothing to blame. It is not easy to gain self-reflective insight, much less cultural insight.
b. Our attempts to gain insight are opposed by associative advertising which always has an answer for our dissatisfactions—buy more or newer or different things. If I find myself feeling let down after a purchase, many voices will tell me that the solution is to buy other things too (or that I have just bought the wrong thing). With all of this advertising proposing one kind of answer for our dissatisfactions, it is scarcely surprising that we do not usually become aware of alternatives.
c. Finally, constant exposure to associative advertising changes[13] us so that we come to feel acceptable as persons when and only when we own the acceptable, fashionable things.

By this point, our characters and conceptions of virtue already largely reflect the result of advertising and we are unlikely to complain or rebel.

Third, and perhaps most pungent of the objections, one might claim that by associating mundane marketable items with deeply rooted non-market desires, our everyday lives are invested with new and greater meaning. Charles Revson of Revlon once said that "In the factory we make cosmetics; in the store we sell hope."[14] Theodore Levitt, in his passionate defense of associative advertising, contends that [15]

Everyone in the world is trying in his [or her] special personal fashion to solve a primal problem of life— the problem of rising above his [or her] own negligibility, of escaping from nature's confining, hostile, and unpredictable reality, of finding significance, security, and comfort in the things he [or she] must do to survive.

Levitt adds: "Without distortion, embellishment, and elaboration, life would be drab, dull, anguished, and at its existential worst."[16] This objection is based on two assumptions so shocking that his conclusion almost seems sensible.

a. Without associative advertising would our lives lack significance? Would we be miserable in our drab, dull, anguished lives? Of course not. People have always had ideals, fantasies, heroes, and dreams. We have always told stories that captured our aspirations and fears. The very suggestion that we require advertising to bring a magical aura to our shabby, humdrum lives is not only insulting but false.
b. Associative advertising is crafted not in order to enrich our daily lives but in order to enrich the clients and does not have the interests of its audience at heart. Still, this issue of intent, though troubling, is only part of the problem. Neither is the main problem that associative advertising images somehow distort reality. Any work of art also is, in an important sense, a dissembling or distortion. The central question instead is whether the

specific appeals and images, techniques and products, enhance people's lives.[17]

A theory of what enhances a life must be at least implicit in any discussion of the morality of associative advertising. Levitt appears to assume that in a satisfying life one has many satisfied desires—*which* desires is not important.[18] To propose and defend an alternative to his view is beyond the scope of this paper. My claim is more modest—that it is not enough to ask whether desires are satisfied. We should also ask what kinds of lives are sustained, made possible, or fostered by having the newly synthesized desires. What kind of self and world are in the making, Dewey would have us ask. This self and world are always in the making. I am not arguing that there is some natural, good self which advertising changes and contaminates. It may be that not only advertising, but also art, religion, and education in general, always synthesize new desires.[19] In each case, we should look at the lives. How to judge the value of these lives and the various conceptions of virtue they will embody is another question. It will be enough for now to see that it is an important question.

Now it may be possible to see why I began by saying that I would suggest an alternative to the usual focus on autonomy and behavior control.[20] Arrington's defense of advertising (including, as near as I can tell, what I call associative advertising) seems to assume that we have no standard to which we can appeal to judge whether a desire enhances a life and, consequently, that our only legitimate concerns are whether an advertisement violates the autonomy of its audience by deceiving them or controlling their behavior. I want to suggest that there is another legitimate concern—whether the advertising will tend to influence us to become worse persons.[21]

Fourth, even one who is sympathetic with much of the above might object that associative advertising is necessary to an industrial society such as ours. Economists since Galbraith[22] have argued about whether, without modern advertising of the sort I have described, there would be enough demand to sustain our present levels of production. I have no answer to this ques-

tion. It seems unlikely that associative advertising will end suddenly, so I am confident that we will have the time and the imagination to adapt our economy to do without it.

Fifth, and last, one might ask what I am proposing. Here I am afraid I must draw up short of my mark. I have no practical political proposal. It seems obvious to me that no broad legislative prohibition would improve matters. Still, it may be possible to make small improvements like some that we have already seen. In the international arena, Nestlé was censured and boycotted, the World Health Organization drafted infant formula marketing guidelines, and finally Nestlé agreed to change its practices. In the U.S.A., legislation prohibits cigarette advertising on television.[23] These are tiny steps, but an important journey may begin with them.

Even my personal solution is rather modest. *First,* if one accepts my thesis that associative advertising is harmful to its audience, then one ought to avoid doing it to others, especially if doing so would require that one dull one's compassion, concern, and sympathy for others. Such initiatives are not entirely without precedent. Soon after the surgeon general's report on cigarettes and cancer in 1964, David Ogilvy and William Bernbach announced that their agencies would no longer accept cigarette accounts and *New Yorker* magazine banned cigarette ads.[24] *Second,* if I am even partly right about the effect of associative advertising on our desires, then one ought to expose oneself as little as possible. The most practical and effective way to do this is probably to banish commercial television and radio from one's life. This measure, though rewarding,[25] is only moderately effective. Beyond these, I do not yet have any answers.

In conclusion, I have argued against the advertising practice I call associative advertising. My main criticism is two-fold:

a. Advertisers must surely desensitize themselves to the compassion, concern, and sympathy for others that are central emotions in a virtuous person, and

b. associative advertising influences its audience to neglect the non-market cultivation of our virtues and to substitute market goods instead, with the result that we become worse and, quite likely, less happy persons.

Notes

An earlier draft of this paper was presented to the Tennessee Philosophical Association, 10 November 1984. I [John Waide] am indebted to that group for many helpful comments.

1. Robert L. Arrington, "Advertising and Behavior Control," *Journal of Business Ethics* 1, pp. 3–12.
2. I prefer not to use the term "consumers" since it identifies us with our role in a market, already conceding part of what I want to deny.
3. Arrington, p. 8.
4. James B. McGinnis, *Bread and Justice* (New York: Paulist Press, 1979) p. 224. McGinnis cites as his source INFACT Newsletter, September 1977, p. 3. Formula is often harmful because poor families do not have the sanitary facilities to prepare the formula using clean water and utensils, do not have the money to be able to keep up formula feeding without diluting the formula to the point of starving the child, and formula does not contain the antibodies which a nursing mother can pass to her child to help immunize the child against common local bacteria. Good accounts of this problem are widely available.
5. John Dewey, *Human Nature and Conduct* (New York: Random House, 1930), p. 202.
6. This can be a diverse group including (depending upon the product) marketing specialists, sales representatives, or people in advertising agencies. Not everyone in one of these positions, however, is necessarily guilty of engaging in associative advertising.
7. This story was told by Lloyd E. Slater at a National Science Foundation Chatauqua entitled "Meeting World Food Needs" in 1980–81. It should not be taken as a condemnation of marketing professionals in other firms.
8. One could argue that the deficiency in compassion, concern, and sympathy on the part of advertisers might be a result of self-selection rather than of associative advertising. Perhaps people in whom these moral sentiments are strong do not commonly go into positions using associative advertising. I doubt, however, that such self-selection can account for all the disregard of the audience's best interests.
9. See Lawrence A. Blum, *Friendship, Altruism and Morality* (Boston: Routledge and Kegan Paul, 1980) for a defense of moral emotions against Kantian claims that emotions are unsuitable as a basis for moral judgement and that only a purely rational good will offers an adequate foundation for morality.
10. I use "ideology" here in a descriptive rather than a pejorative sense. To be more specific, associative advertising commonly advocates only a part of a more comprehensive ideology. See Raymond Geuss, *The Idea of a Critical Theory* (Cambridge University Press, 1981), pp. 5–6.
11. For an interesting discussion, see John Lachs, "To Have and To Be," *Personalist* 45 (Winter, 1964), pp. 5–14;

reprinted in John Lachs and Charles Scott, *The Human Search* (New York: Oxford University Press, 1981), pp. 247–255.
12. This is, in fact, the thrust of Arrington's arguments in "Advertising and Behavior Control."
13. I do not mean to suggest that only associative advertising can have such ill effects. Neither am I assuming the existence of some natural, pristine self which is perverted by advertising.
14. Quoted without source in Theodore Levit, "The Morality (?) of Advertising," *Harvard Business Review,* July-August 1970; reprinted in Vincent Barry, *Moral Issues in Business,* (Belmont, CA: Wadsworth Publishing Company, 1979), p. 256.
15. Levitt (in Barry), p. 252.
16. Levitt (in Barry), p. 256.
17. "Satisfying a desire would be valuable then if it sustained or made possible a valuable kind of life. To say this is to reject the argument that in creating the wants he [or she] can satisfy, the advertiser (or the manipulator of mass emotion in politics or religion) is necessarily acting in the best interests of his [or her] public." Stanley Benn, "Freedom and Persuasion," *Australasian Journal of Philosophy* 45 (1969); reprinted in Beauchamp and Bowie, *Ethical Theory and Business,* second edition (Englewood Cliffs, NJ: Prentice-Hall, 1983), p. 374.
18. Levitt's view is not new. "Continual success in obtaining those things which a man from time to time desires—that is to say, continual prospering—is what men call felicity." Hobbes, *Leviathan* (Indianapolis: Bobbs-Merrill, 1958), p. 61.
19. This, in fact, is the principal criticism von Hayek offered of Galbraith's argument against the "dependence effect." F. A. von Hayek, "The *Non Sequitur* of the 'Dependence Effect,' " *Southern Economic Journal,* April 1961; reprinted in Tom L. Beauchamp and Norman E. Bowie, *Ethical Theory and Business,* second edition (Englewood Cliffs, New Jersey: Prentice-Hall, 1983), pp. 363–366.
20. Taylor R. Durham, "Information, Persuasion, and Control in Moral Appraisal of Advertising," *The Journal of Business Ethics* 3, 179. Durham also argues that an exclusive concern with issues of deception and control leads us into errors.
21. One might object that this requires a normative theory of human nature, but it seems to me that we can go fairly far by reflecting on our experience. If my approach is to be vindicated, however, I must eventually provide an account of how, in general, we are to make judgments about what is and is not good (or life-enhancing) for a human being. Clearly, there is a large theoretical gulf between me and Arrington, but I hope that my analysis of associative advertising shows that my approach is plausible enough to deserve further investigation.
22. The central text for this problem is *The Affluent Society* (Houghton Mifflin, 1958). The crucial passages are reprinted in many anthologies, e.g., John Kenneth Galbraith, "The Dependence Effect," in W. Michael

Hoffman and Jennifer Mills Moore, *Business Ethics: Readings and Cases in Corporate Morality* (New York: McGraw-Hill, 1984), pp. 328–333.

23. "In March 1970 Congress removed cigarette ads from TV and radio as of the following January. (The cigarette companies transferred their billings to print and outdoor advertising. Cigarette sales reached new records.)"

Stephen Fox, *The Mirror Makers: A History of American Advertising and its Creators,* (New York: William Morrow and Co., 1984), p. 305.

24. Stephen Fox, pp. 303–4.

25. See, for example, Jerry Mander, *Four arguments for the Elimination of Television* (New York: Morrow Quill Paperbacks, 1977).

Don E. Tomlinson

Choosing Social Responsibility Over Law: The *Soldier of Fortune* Classified Advertising Cases

. . . [T]he media . . . tend to be preoccupied with their rights more than with their responsibilities.[1]

INTRODUCTION

Only classified ads . . . do we presume to contain solid, unembellished fact.[2]

Classified advertising is "a tremendous revenue producer"[3] for American daily and weekly newspapers. "[It] is regarded almost as fondly [as display advertising] . . . ."[4] Revenue from classified advertising is extremely important to newspapers, and any perceived threat to its unfettered continuation is viewed with great seriousness.[5] Likewise, magazines view any perceived threat to the viability of classified advertising as quite serious.[6] While magazines gross less from classified advertising than do newspa-

By Don E. Tomlinson, Texas A&M University (reprinted from *Business & Professional Ethics Journal*). Revised © 1995 by Don E. Tomlinson.

pers, classified advertising is nonetheless a very important part of the magazine business.

In general, classified advertising has been viewed as different from display advertising in that it has been almost completely informational in nature. Display advertising certainly can be and often is informational but is distinguished from classified advertising by its frequent "verbal and graphic hyperbole."[7] The non-puffery nature of classified advertising has earned the respect and loyalty of buyers and sellers alike.[8]

The classifications in classified advertising are broad in their number and narrow in their individual scope. In many general circulation newspapers, there may be more than a hundred classifications.[9] Classified advertisements in special interest magazines involve fewer categories because of the magazines' limited types of readers, among other reasons. In either case, almost all the classifications seem innocuous (e.g., "Garage Sales" and "Musical Instruments") and the advertising itself seems innocuous, as well (e.g., "Furniture, baby furniture, clothing . . ." and "Yamaha Alto Saxophone. With case. Like new . . .").[10] But there is one classified advertising category that is giving rise to ethical and legal concerns. It is called the "personals" classification.[11]

In many publications, the "personals" classification has been around for a long time, its content mainly having been items such as "I will be responsible for no debts other than my own" and "Honey, please come home" and "Love Pumpkin to Garden Guru: The frost is on the vine."[12] Sometimes, a circulation ploy involving classified advertising in general and the "personals" classification in particular is used to try to help a daily newspaper compete better with its cross-town rival.[13] The theory is that while an extra page or two of newsprint is not cheap, allowing people to put free "personals" on those pages and calling them "happy ads" would much more than make up for any added cost by significantly increasing circulation.

There have been problems with some of these "happy ads," including problems relating to physical violence and crime. In the *Fort Worth Star-Telegram*, for example, there was an allegation that a rape occurred as the result of a "happy ad."[14] As shall be seen, legal liability may not attach to the publication in such a situation, but what of the newspaper's moral responsibility[15] to its readers and others? Some publications try to screen the "personals." *Newsday*, for instance, one of the largest circulation newspapers in the United States, has a "personals" section, but it also has a policy of rejecting any "personals" it deems "flaky" or "kinky."[16]

As publications, magazines in particular, become more specialized, they also can become more bizarre—until they reach the real fringes of society. On the fringes of the publishing world, moral responsibility, more particularly described here as social responsibility,[17] is a concept for which there may be little respect. *Hustler* magazine, for example, published an article in 1981 about the ecstasy of and how to engage in "autoerotic asphyxiation."[18] Not long after the article was published, a 14-year-old Texas boy was found hanging in the closet of his bedroom, nude, with the magazine open to the article and laying on the floor beneath him. When the boy's mother sued, *Hustler* argued it should have no liability in the case because, among other reasons, it had led the article with a "disclaimer" warning readers not to try the masturbation stunt because it had proved fatal for some who had tried it and because the magazine felt it owed no further duty to its readers.[19] A three-judge panel of the U.S. Court of Appeals for the Fifth Circuit agreed with *Hustler.*[20]

Soldier of Fortune magazine openly states that its intended readers are "professional adventurers." The magazine began publication in 1975. From its inception, it contained a classified advertising section, including a "personals" classification. Over the ten-year period it published classified "personals" (1975–85), it published some 2,000 such advertisements. A number of them, fairly comparatively small though it may be, have unquestionably led to murders, attempted murders, arson, and crimes of other types.[21]

The *Eimann* and *Norwood* cases[22] provide two excellent examples of the consequences of some of the "personals" advertising in *Soldier of Fortune* and of one point at which law and ethics can diverge.

In 1985, a Bryan, Texas woman was murdered in cold blood by a "hit man" hired by her husband through the pages of *Soldier of Fortune* to murder her. The husband was convicted of capital murder and executed by lethal injection in 1993 at a state prison facility in Huntsville, Texas. The "hit man" pleaded guilty and is serving a life sentence.[23] In the trial of the husband, the "hit man" testified that he was contacted by the husband on the basis of the advertisement, which read:

EX-MARINES - 67-69 'Nam vets - ex-DI - weapons specialist - jungle warfare, pilot, M.E., high risk assignments U.S. or overseas. [Phone number].[24]

In 1987, the slain woman's mother, Marjorie Eimann, filed a wrongful death lawsuit against *Soldier of Fortune* in a Houston federal court.[25]

In the other *Soldier of Fortune* case noted here, the victim, Douglas Norwood, was not murdered but not because his assailants did not try to kill him. In 1985, he was ambushed, assaulted, the victim of a car-bomb blast and shot—each time by would-be killers hired through classified advertisements published in *Soldier of Fortune*. Six persons, including the one who hired the other five through the advertisements, were indicted and eventually received federal prison sentences ranging from five to 25 years. The two advertisements from which the would-be killers were hired read:

GUN FOR HIRE: 37-year-old—professional mercenary desires jobs. Vietnam Veteran. Discreet and very private. Bodyguard, courier, and other special skills. All jobs considered. [Phone number].

and

GUN FOR HIRE: Nam sniper instructor. SWAT. Pistol, rifle, security specialist, bodyguard, courier plus. All jobs considered. Privacy guaranteed. Mike [Phone number].[26]

Norwood sued *Soldier of Fortune* in 1986. The parties settled out of court in 1987 by way of a private agreement.[27]

ADVERTISING TORT LAW IN CASES INVOLVING PHYSICAL INJURY

Nearly all human acts . . . carry some recognizable possibility of harm to another.[28]

In general, the print media are not legally responsible for physical injury to their readers or to others based on advertising.[29] There have been comparatively few reported cases on the subject.[30] In the usual case, the injured plaintiff would have a better suit against the *advertiser* than against the *advertising medium.*[31] Generally, to sustain a cause of action against the publication requires a showing that the publication was something more than merely the medium through which the advertising message was disseminated.[32]

In 1988, a jury awarded the plaintiffs in *Eimann* $1.9 million in actual damages and $7.5 million in punitive damages against the magazine.[33] In 1989, a three-judge panel of the United States Court of Appeals for the Fifth Circuit reversed the case (and the U.S. Supreme Court later declined to review the decision).[34] The Fifth Circuit ruled that notwithstanding its assumption that *Soldier of Fortune* owed "a duty of reasonable care to the public,"[35] the minimally necessary standard of conduct required to satisfy the obligation of reasonableness in this case was met by *Soldier of Fortune* and that, consequently, no liability could attach.[36]

The court did not say what *Soldier of Fortune* did to satisfy the minimum standard of conduct necessary to live up to the duty of acting reasonably toward the general public in terms of the classified advertisement it published. Rather, the court couched its language in negative terms, stating what the standard of conduct in the case did not involve having to do in order to live up to the duty of acting reasonably toward the public. It stated that the standard of conduct necessary to live up to the duty did not involve an obligation to investigate or to recognize and refuse to publish ambiguous advertisements that could be interpreted as offers to engage in illegal activity.[37] The standard of conduct necessary to live up to the duty did not reach that high in *Eimann,* the court said, because the particular advertisement was "facially innocuous."[38] Nor would the court recognize the "context" argument that *Soldier of Fortune* was on actual or constructive notice in the situation because of its knowledge of its own publication of a number of previous similar advertisements having led to various serious crimes.[39] "Context" could not help define the appropriate minimum standard of conduct the court said, because of "the pervasiveness of advertising in our society."[40]

The plaintiffs had generated a considerable body of evidence in relation to why *Soldier of Fortune* should have known the advertiser's intentions, but the court said requiring publications to discern such intentions is too high a burden as weighed against the risk that some injury might result from the publication of a particular advertisement, especially, the court said, given the social utility of advertising.[41]

But while the "context" argument proved not to carry any legal weight in *Eimann,* the facts that give rise to the argument certainly bear on the ethics of the situation. For ten years prior to Mrs. Black's murder, the "personal" classified advertising pages of *Soldier of Fortune* contained advertising of the sort used to contact the advertiser who committed the murder.[42] The plaintiffs had presented evidence showing that at the time of the publication of the advertisement in question nine previous such advertisements in the magazine had resulted in crimes from extortion to jailbreaks, two of which situations also had resulted in staff members of the magazine assisting police investigations of the crimes, including acknowledgements that the crimes had been arranged through the *Soldier of Fortune* advertisements.[43] Cited as sources were the Associated Press, United Press International,

The Rocky Mountain News, The Denver Post, Time, and *Newsweek.*[44]

Although not mentioned in *Eimann,* it was argued in *Norwood* that the federal appellate court decisions handed down earlier in the 1980s had upheld criminal convictions of persons who advertised their criminal availability through *Soldier of Fortune,* one of which cases was tried in Denver, 30 miles from *Soldier of Fortune's* corporate headquarters in Boulder.[45]

In terms of the impact of *Eimann* on journalism, the practices of mainstream American publishers of print advertising, principally general and special circulation newspapers and magazines, will go unchanged—as it would have had the Fifth Circuit upheld the lower court decision in a properly narrowly worded opinion, which it easily could and should have done. But "sleaze factor" in American journalism now has a new federal appeals court precedent that says publishers can publish any kind of advertisement they want with virtual immunity from civil liability.[46] Any publisher of classified advertising could publish dozens of advertisements on the same pages of the publication issue after issue which, taken together, a school child could see were in contemplation of criminal activity, but a plaintiff desiring to prove actual harm resulted from one of those advertisements would be effectively estopped from introducing contextual and historical evidence, i.e., the advertisement which allegedly caused the harm would have to be discussed in a vacuum. Given the likelihood of the advertisement being found to be "facially ambiguous" while in that vacuum, the duty might as well not be owed because the standard of conduct necessary to breach the duty would have to involve the advertisement, at a minimum, singularly and directly stating the advertiser's intention to engage in criminal activity.

THE LAW/SOCIAL RESPONSIBILITY DICHOTOMY

The defenses of unrestrained press freedom found in contemporary journalism seldom explicitly consider the range of moral rights and responsibilities that confront the press, and these defenses often *amount to a demand for privileged treatment that moral analysis will not support. Journalists need not be moral philosophers, of course, but they should be aware that competing values may have moral weight equal to or greater than press freedom.*[47]

It has been argued that based on the fear of the massive loss of advertising revenue, the American press has not covered the "cigarettes cause cancer" controversy with nearly as much rigor as it reserves for other subjects.[48] When journalism is accused of this double standard, it routinely ducks behind the First Amendment.[49] In 1985, when the American Newspaper Publishers Association and the Magazine Publishers Association trotted out the First Amendment in response to criticism over journalism's alleged lack of rigor in covering the story, the ombudsman for *The Washington Post* called the organizations to task for not distinguishing between what is legally correct and what is socially responsible:

In this era of voluntarism, when the business community is constantly urging Congress and regulatory agencies to stand aside and "let us take care of this problem ourselves," couldn't the newspapers of the country agree—voluntarily and collectively—to refuse cigarette advertising? Couldn't they do what is right rather than only what is not prohibited by law?[50]

Interestingly, the ANPA and the MPA were two of the journalism organizations which participated in the filing of a friends of the court brief in *Eimann* supporting *Soldier of Fortune's* First Amendment position.

Law aside, however, the media must assume the responsibility for operating on principles of social responsibility because no one else can do it for them:

The First Amendment bars any outside authority from imposing responsibility on the media, so the authority must come from within. However, none of the various "codes" adopted by media institutions indicates any willingness to impose responsibility. So "within the profession" really means "within the individuals practicing the profession."[51]

Those who look to law for moral reasoning must surely be disappointed much of the time for ". . . the law permits many immoralities . . . a great variety of deceptions."[52]

Law does not take up where morality leaves off nor vice versa. Much of the reasoning process that discovers the law is applicable to moral reasoning but much of it is not. Ethics is broader, for while ethics in the broadest sense is not subject to legal scrutiny, " . . . law . . . is always subject to moral scrutiny and moral criticism."[53] The public, many times, views legal disputes as essentially moral questions, but, many times, they are not. For example, the law-abiding person is not necessarily morally virtuous, and if an act is legally acceptable, that fact alone does not make it morally acceptable."[54]

Some mass communicators would have society believe, and perhaps believe themselves, that when a mass communicator has complied with "the law," the mass communicator has complied with "the ethics" of the situation as well. While the First Amendment and tort law sometimes permit journalists to be irresponsible, no lack of moral obligation should be implied therefrom; indeed, that journalism is largely free from the otherwise long reach of the law would seem to indicate a greater obligation of more responsibility—not a smaller one.[55]

Choosing Social Responsibility Over Law

Certainly one measure of a society's strength is the degree of justice and civility with which it settles disputes between its citizens . . . . [But] court decisions often create, or leave open, ethical issues for the journalist, quite apart from the legal limits they may attempt to define.[56]

Assume, then, that no plaintiff will even win a case like this. Just because tort law and the First Amendment may protect against *legal* liability, does anything about that make this kind of behavior *ethically* correct? Should not social responsibility play a role here? More specifically, notwithstanding its legal definition, is not "duty" the real ethics issue here?

There are different kinds of duties. In corporations, there is a duty to the entity itself, and in sole proprietorships, there is a duty to oneself, but these duties alone cannot be determinative of one's actions in every case for there also is a duty to society. Social responsibility must be dealt with if one is to act ethically. And in situations involving the real potential of real harm "our loyalty to society warrants preeminence."[57] Perhaps there was a time when the problem of harm caused to others through advertising simply did not come up—through ignorance or through the prevalence of a sort of "let the buyer beware" attitude, but given the sophistication of society today, " . . . a sincere sense of social responsibility and a genuine concern for the citizenry [should] become characteristic marks of all contemporary media."[58]

Legal and ethical thought processes can be the same, as in the case of the consideration of whether a duty is owed and to what lengths an actor should go not to breach an existing duty. In this specific situation, " . . . the weight of the harm and the degree of risk should be balanced directly against the public benefit of the [communication]."[59]

It is true that advertising is more valued than reporting by many people.[60] Certainly, most advertising constitutes a public benefit. But the harm in *Eimann* and *Norwood* was death and attempted death and the degree of risk very high given the reasonable conclusion that *Soldier of Fortune* knew that previous advertisements had resulted in criminal activity.

Some publications feel a real sense of duty; others, such as grocery store rags like the *National Enquirer*, seem not to—and their reputations precede them in many quarters. But Sandra Black's and Doug Norwood's opinions of *Soldier of Fortune* were of no consequence; after all, they were not even readers, they were completely innocent third-party victims.

Publications are known by the company they keep. The editorial matter in a publication normally sets the tone for the publication, but the advertising it publishes can play a major role in that regard, as well.[61] Some publications, in fact, use advertising as a serious means of fostering an image. Clearly, *Soldier of Fortune* wanted a "macho" image.

But rather than discussing the publication as though it actually possessed human life and was the only actor, what of the individuals involved? In the final ethics analysis, after all, it is individuals, not organizations, which are accountable.[62]

Media executives are aware that circulation depends in large measure on consumers who are just as interested in the advertisements in the publication, including classified, as they are in the publication's editorial content.[63] Media executives, in other words, live in a world where duty to human beings very easily can get confused with or overshadowed by duty to one's company. There once was a time when most publishers had a real reverence for the concept of journalism, but as media mergers cause the media to be more centralized and media managers to be responsible to lenders and shareholders for huge amounts of indebtedness, the bottom line naturally looms larger and larger in the minds of media managers who want to continue to be employed.[64] This is acutely true in advertising departments where there never has been quite the same reverence for journalism and what it classically means as there has been on the editorial side.[65]

One of the ramifications, of course, of not accepting an advertisement on ethical grounds is a loss of revenue, but that is the price one must pay.[66] Sometimes choices are easy, but most of the time they are not; in this case the choice is between money and social responsibility.[67] It would be nice if one's sense of duty to the publication and one's sense of duty to society could always peacefully co-exist; alas, however, they cannot, meaning here the impossibility of accepting every classified advertisement that is offered and being selective at the same time.[68]

Not every individual working in media, though, is a publisher or an executive. Most employees, in fact, are not personally accountable for profit. Some work on the editorial side; some on the advertising side. Does employment on the advertising side as opposed to the editorial side mean such employees need not feel any sense of social responsibility? What logic would there be in freeing the employees on the advertising side of a publication from social responsibility? The compromises people make usually are thought by them to be small ones, but the consequences of such actions are cumulative, resulting in " . . . a working environment where short-run advantage triumphs over long-term integrity, personal gain over fairness."[69]

Mass communication is a business, of course, like any other business, or is it? Supreme Court Justice Potter Stewart once noted that the press is the only business specifically singled out for protection by the Constitution.[70] But the responsibility that goes along with the constitutional protection should override, in appropriate situations, concerns related to profit.[71] While duty is the principal moral idea being discussed here, it is not the only moral idea that should be given consideration in the moral resolution of the issue of whether to publish.

Another perspective from which to view such advertisements is harms versus goods, i.e., did (could) any good result from the publication of this advertisement in particular or the previous similar advertisements in general? Does the potential good outweigh the potential harm and to what extent? The fact is that some good did result from the publication of the Hearn advertisement (and likely from some of the previous similar advertisements). One of Hearn's "professed goals" was the " . . . recruiting [of] candidates for bodyguard jobs. Hearn performed precisely that function for at least one client who contacted him through the ad."[72] But it seems abundantly clear from the circumstances that the gravity of the harms which could (and did) result would far outweigh (outweighed) any good that could (did) come from the publication of the advertisement. Bodyguards, it should be said, can be hired through non-harmful means.

The conflict in this case between freedom of expression and the idea of "greatest good" also should be considered. As a moral or a legal principle, freedom of expression is not and never has been absolute.[73] It has many exceptions. Many of the exceptions are based on situations where the principle of freedom of expression collides with another principle—for example, doing what results in the greatest good.

At least morally, freedom of expression should not be used as a license to aid and abet the taking of human life. There is no good greater than the preservation of human life. And while there are many examples of society sacrificing life-preserving ideas in favor of other ideas (e.g., raising the speed limit on interstate highways from 55 m.p.h. to 65 m.p.h.), the freedom to express a classified advertisement should not be one of them.

Conclusions

How many deaths will it take 'til we know that too many people have died?[74]

Can duty be compromised; in other words, are there degrees of duty? Tort-law scholarship indicates no shades of gray in the concept of duty,[75] and ethics scholarship also recognizes that a duty either exists or it does not.[76]

The real question here is to what lengths, ethically, should mass communicators go in upholding the duty of lack of harm to the public once a decision has been made that a duty exists? One answer is that where publication of an advertisement reasonably and foreseeably could result in serious physical injury or death, the very highest standard of conduct is owed. Assuming ambiguity in the advertisements discussed here, which given the nature of the magazine itself seems charitable, should *Soldier of Fortune* reasonably and foreseeably have known that the first such advertisement that did lead to crime would lead to crime?

In the law, dogs generally get to bite one human "free," in that their owners would have had no reason to believe the dogs were predisposed to bite humans. The second bite, however, is far less excusable, given history.[77] In these situations, the owner of the dog is "strictly liable,"[78] meaning that keeping a vicious dog generates liability without regard to considerations of fault, like negligence, and can more easily result in awards of punitive damages.[79]

Ambiguity aside, then, what causes *Soldier of Fortune* to have not lived up to the *ethics* standard of conduct was its obvious knowledge that in the neighborhood of nine felonies involving physical violence had been committed as a result of similar advertising in the magazine. Upon acquiring knowledge of the *second*

such incident, Soldier of Fortune should have shut down the personals classification, or at least stopped taking advertisements relating to personal services of the type discussed here.

Investigation of the advertisements, pre-publication, an idea at which the court in *Eimann* bristled, would not be necessary. Had *Soldier of Fortune* felt any real sense of duty to the Sandra Blacks and Doug Norwoods of the world, the decision not to have run the advertisements which resulted in her death and his attempted death would have been made on the basis of the very real experience with the previous advertisements and not on an investigation to determine whether the advertiser meant by the advertisement to be soliciting to engage in criminal behavior.

Standards of acceptability in the classified advertising industry are anything but new, dating at least to the late 1940s.[80] It may have been a simpler time, but it was a less violent one, as well. In a 1952 book, the national classified advertising trade organization called for all newspapers to formalize procedures for dealing with unacceptable classified advertisements:

Eternal vigilance is the price to be paid for a "clean" Classified Advertising section.[81]

Newspapers can consistently oppose and support censorship at one and the same time. They can oppose it in their editorial and news columns on the grounds that it withholds information vital to public welfare. They can support it in the Want Ad columns because it forces the advertiser to use facts and honest statements, so necessary for reader protection. The goal in each case is identical—the publication of complete statements and facts.[82]

The book, published under the auspices of the Association of Newspaper Classified Advertising Managers, Inc. (ANCAM), went on to propose a censorship manual to newspapers. One of the sections was called "Injurious Advertisements":

Advertisements containing statements that injure the health ... of ... readers, either directly or indirectly, ... are not acceptable.[83]

It was followed by another section called "Illegal Advertising":

Any advertisement fostering the evasion or violation of any law or making a direct or indirect offer of any article or service that violates a city, State or Federal statute is not acceptable.[84]

ANCAM still publishes suggested standards. One of its latest versions is a 28-page handbook published in 1982 called "Standards of Acceptance for Classified Advertising." The language is a bit more modern, but the spirit is the same, i.e., *be ethical.* Given that context, it is worth noting that ANCAM, too, participated in the filing of the friends of the court brief in *Eimann* supporting *Soldier of Fortune's* legal position.

Perhaps the time has come for all publications publishing classified advertising, clearly including those operating on the fringes of society, to consider once more the promise of a more socially responsible time. There is a current need for some real soul-searching with regard to how much movement there has been, inadvertent or otherwise, away from classified advertising standards of acceptability grounded on the ethic of social responsibility, especially regarding the "personals" classification.

A return to a simpler, less legalistic and clearer sense of social responsibility might well be in order. Duty calls, and given all the circumstances of the *Soldier of Fortune* "personals" classification, the magazine should have abolished the classification long before it did (which was a few months after Mrs. Black's murder). Abolishing the classification would not have been beyond the call of duty; indeed, it would have been nothing more than the exercise of the duty every human being owes every other human being.

At some point in the career of most every professional mass communicator, the question arises as to whether the person is a mass communicator first and a human being second or *vice versa.* The answer, of course, is that being a human being always should come first. Unfortunately it took several deaths and considerable other mayhem for *Soldier of Fortune,* specifically its owners and executive employees, to learn the lesson. When *Soldier of Fortune* was justifying its actions on the freedoms embodied in the First Amendment (and, as it turns out, tort law, as well), its sense of social responsibility was sorely lacking. At least on a philosophical level, *Soldier of Fortune's* assertion that it owed no duty to Sandra Black—that the First Amendment and tort law acted as a shield against such a duty—was bereft of reason.

Law cannot shield anyone from the most basic duty all human beings owe all other human beings: respect for life. Law and ethics are not one and the same. Further, using law as a justification for conduct which is socially irresponsible is socially irresponsible in itself.

Notes

1. Klaidman, Stephen, and Beauchamp, Tom L., *The Virtuous Journal,* New York: Oxford University Press, 1987, p. 150.
2. Levitt, Tom, "The Morality (?) of Advertising," *Harvard Business Review,* July/August, 1970, pp. 84–92 at 84.
3. Tremblay, Catherine, "Classified Advertising," in Newsom, D. Earl, ed., *The Newspaper,* Englewood Cliffs, N.J.: Prentice-Hall, 1981, pp. 133–142 at 142.
4. Meyer, Philip, *Ethical Journalism,* New York: Longman, Inc., 1982, p. 146.
5. "Responsibility for ad content," *Editor & Publisher,* March 12, 19 p. 6.
6. Metcalf, Slade, "Ad Liability: How Real Is the Threat?" *Folio: The Magazine for Magazine Management,* January, 1989, p. 195.
7. Christians, Clifford G., Rotzoll, Kim B., and Fackler, Mark, *Media Ethics: Cases and Moral Reasoning,* 2nd ed., New York: Longman, Inc., 19 p. 199.
8. Ibid.
9. Tremblay, *supra* note 3, p. 133.
10. *The Houston Post,* August 20, 1989, p. L-11.
11. The first "personals" section debuted in a New York newspaper in the mid-19th century (Tremblay, *supra* note 3, p. 133). It was called "infamous" even then (Fleming, Thomas, "How It Was in Advertising: 1776–1976," in *How It Was in Advertising: 1776–1976,* Chicago: Crain Books, 1976, pp. 5–14 at 9).
12. See, for example, *The Houston Post,* August 20, 1989, p. B-17.
13. Morton, John, "Dueling Dailies: A Short History," *Washington Journalism Review,* November, 1988, p. 48.
14. Polilli, Steve, "Date Through Personal Ad Results in Rape, Police Say," *Fort Worth Star-Telegram,* January 31, 1988, p. 1–22.
15. Klaidman, *supra* note 1, pp. 14–16.
16. Fink, Conrad C., *Media Ethics: In the Newsroom and Beyond,* New York: McGraw-Hill, 1988, p. 131.
17. Christians, *supra* note 7, p. 18.
18. Milner, Richard, "Orgasm of Death," *Hustler,* August, 1981, pp. 33–34.
19. See *Herceg v. Hustler Magazine, Inc.,* 814 F.2d 1017 (5th Cir. 1987); *cert. denied* 108 S.Ct. 1219 (1988).
20. Ibid.
21. Tomlinson, Don E., "The *Soldier of Fortune* Classified Advertising Cases: First Amendment and Common Law

Tort Considerations," *Southwestern Mass Communication Journal*, 4–1 (1988): 42–54 at 51.

22. In the first *Soldier of Fortune* case to reach the appellate level, *Eimann v. Soldier of Fortune Magazine, Inc.*, 880 Fed.2d 830 (5th Cir. 1989); *cert. denied* 110 S.Ct. 729 (1990), quite a number of print journalism organizations joined forces to submit an *amici curiae* brief to the court. They include: The American Newspaper Publishers Association, the American Society of Newspaper Editors, the Association of Area Business Publications, the Association of Newspaper Classified Advertising Managers, the *Dallas Times Herald*, the Hearst Corporation, the Louisiana Press Association, Magazine Publishers of America, The Mississippi Press Association, National Newspaper Association, Scripps-Howard, Inc., the Texas Daily Newspaper Association, and Time, Inc. The other *Soldier of Fortune* case discussed in this article is *Norwood v. Soldier of Fortune Magazine, Inc.*, 651 F.Supp. 1397 (W.D. Ark. 1987). (Since the original publication of this article, one of the several other cases filed against *Soldier of Fortune* based on similar facts has resulted in a multi-million-dollar judgment *affirmed* by a federal appellate court because the ad, it said, was *not* facially ambiguous.)

23. Tomlinson, *supra* note 21, p. 42.

24. Ibid.

25. Ibid. p. 43.

26. Ibid. p. 42–43.

27. Ibid. p. 43.

28. *Prosser and Keeton on Torts*, Sec. 31 at 170 (5th ed., 1984).

29. See Shapiro, Neil L., and Olson, Karl, "Advertiser Liability: *Soldier of Fortune* Cases Take Deadly Aim at Publishers," 11 *Hastings Comm/Ent Law Journal* 383 (1989); Caswell, Kimberly, "Soldiers of Misfortune: Holding Media Defendants Liable for the Effects of Their Commercial Speech," 41 *Federal Communications Law Journal* 217 (1989); Allegro, Donald B., and La-Due, John D., "*Eimann v. Soldier of Fortune* and 'Negligent Advertising' Actions: Commercial Speech in an Era of Reduced First Amendment Protection," 64 *Notre Dame Law Review* 157 (1989); Lee, Debbie, " 'Gun for Hire' Advertisement that Backfired and Hit the Publisher in the Pocketbook," 8 *Loyola Entertainment Law Journal* 439 (1988); Smith, Gerald R., "Media Liability for Physical Injury Resulting from the Negligent Use of Words," 72 *Minnesota Law Review* 1193 (1988); Diamond, John L., and Primm, James L., "Rediscovering Traditional Tort Typologies to Determine Media Liability for Physical Injuries: From the *Mickey Mouse Club* to *Hustler* Magazine," 10 *Hastings Comm/Ent Law Journal* 969 (1988); Lane, Daniel M., Jr., "Publisher Liability for Material that Invites Reliance," 66 *Texas Law Review* 1155 (1988); Drechsel, Robert E., "Media Tort Liability for Physical Harm," *Journalism Quarterly*, 64–1 (Spring 1987): 99–105, 177; Stevens, George E., "Newspaper Tort Liability for Harmful Advertising," *Newspaper Research Journal*, 8–1 (Fall 1986): 37–41; Hoffman, Jonathan M., "From Random House to Mickey Mouse: Liability for Negligent Publishing and Broadcasting," 21 *Tort and Insurance Law Journal* 65 (1985); Weingarten, Steven, "Tort Liability for Nonlibelous Negligent Statements: First Amendment Considerations," 93 *Yale Law Journal* 744 (1984); and Spak, Michael, "Predictable Harm: Should the Media Be Liable?" 42 *Ohio State University Law Journal* 671 (1981).

30. See, e.g., *Pittman v. Dow Jones & Co.*, 662 F.Supp. 921 (E.D. La. 1986), *aff'd.*, 834 F.2d 1171 (5th Cir. 1987); *Walters v. Seventeen Magazine, Inc.*, 241 Cal. Rptr. 101 (Ct.App. 1987); *News and Sun-Sentinel Co. v. Board of County Comm'rs*, 693 F.Supp. 1066 (S.D. Fla. 1987); *Loveday v. FCC*, 707 F.2d 1443 (D.C. Cir. 1983); *Pressler v. Dow Jones & Co.*, 450 N.Y.S.2d 884 (App.Div. 1982); *Yuhas v. Mudge*, 322 A.2d 824 (N.J.Sup.Ct.App.Div. 1974); *Goldstein v. Garlick*, 318 N.Y.S.2d 370 (Sup.Ct. 1971); and *MacKown v. Illinois Publishing and Printing Co.*, 6 N.E.2d 526 (Ill.App.Ct. 1937). But see *South Carolina State Ports Authority v. Booz-Allen & Hamilton, Inc.*, 676 F.Supp. 346 (D. D.C. 1987).

31. Stevens, *supra* note 29, p. 37.

32. See *Hanberry v. Hearst Corporation*, 276 Cal.App.2d 680, 81 Cal. Rptr. 519 (1969).

33. Tomlinson, *supra* note 21, p. 43.

34. *Eimann, supra* note 22.

35. Ibid. p. 835.

36. Ibid. p. 837.

37. Ibid. p. 835.

38. Ibid. p. 836.

39. Ibid.

40. Ibid. p. 838.

41. Ibid.

42. Ibid. p. 832.

43. Ibid.

44. Ibid.

45. *Norwood, supra* note 22, Plaintiff's Response to Motion for Summary Judgment and Memorandum in Support, pp. 2 and 14.

46. While it is true that the media have gained some of their greatest First Amendment victories in cases involving such magazines as *Penthouse* and *Hustler*, it nonetheless seems a rather dubious distinction (see, e.g., Denniston, Lyle, "Larry Flynt, Freedom Fighter," *Washington Journalism Review*, May, 1988, p. 16).

47. Klaidman, *supra* note 1, p. 10.

48. Warner, Kenneth E., "Cigarette Advertising and Media Coverage of Smoking and Health," *New England Journal of Medicine*, February 7, 1985, pp. 384–388.

49. "The use of words like *obligation*, *duty*, and *requirement* sends most journalists running for cover under the First Amendment. The operative assumption seems to be that if obligations are accepted, regulations will follow (Klaidman, *supra* note 1, p. 129)."

50. Zagoria, Sam, "Smoking and the Media's Responsibility," *The Washington Post*, December 18, 1985, p. A26.

51. Mathews, Cleve, and Rivers, William L., *Ethics for the Media*, Englewood Cliffs, N.J.: Prentice-Hall, 1988, p. 5.

52. Callahan, Joan C., ed., *Ethical Issues in Professional Life*, New York: Oxford University Press, 1988, p. 11.

53. Ibid.

54. Klaidman, *supra* note 1, p. 12.
55. Ibid. p. 11.
56. Lambeth, Edmund B., *Committed Journalism: An Ethic for the Profession,* Bloomington: Indiana University Press, 1986, p. 132.
57. Christians, *supra* note 7, p. 18.
58. Ibid.
59. Klaidman, *supra* note 1, p. 136.
60. " . . . [T]he particular consumer's interest in the free flow of commercial information. . . may be as keen, if not keener by far, than his interest in the day's most urgent political debate. . . (*Virginia State Board of Pharmacy v. Virginia Citizens Consumer Council, Inc.* 425 U.S. 748 at 763 [1976])."
61. Smith, R. P., "Advertising Acceptability Policies Protect Newspaper's Credibility," *INAME News,* June, 1984, p. 11.
62. Christians, *supra* note 7, p. 20.
63. Fink, *supra* note 16, p. 125.
64. Ibid. p. 139.
65. Ibid. p. 125.
66. Ibid. p. 128.
67. Ibid. p. 122.
68. Smith, *supra* note 61.
69. Christians, *supra* note 7, p. 201.
70. Franklin, Marc A., ed., *Mass Media Law,* 2d ed., Mineola, NY: Foundation Press, 1982, p. 39, quoting Justice Stewart from his address at the Yale Law School Sesquicentennial Convocation, November 2, 1974.
71. Klaidman, *supra* note 1, pp. 217–218.
72. *Eimann, supra* note 22, at 838.
73. See, for example, *Near v. Minnesota,* 283 U.S. 697, 51 S.Ct. 625, 75 L.Ed. 1357 (1931).
74. Dylan, Bob, "Blowin' in the Wind," copyright 1962, Warner Bros. Music Publishing Co., Inc.
75. White, G. Edward, *Tort Law in America,* New York: Oxford University Press, 1985, p. 38 and generally.
76. Klaidman, *supra* note 1, p. 99.
77. The doctrine may have had its origin in the Old Testament: "But if the ox were wont to push with his horn in time past, and it hath been testified to his owner, and he hath not kept him in, but that he hath killed a man or woman; the ox shall be stoned, and his owner shall be put to death (Exodus 21: 28–29)."
78. See, e.g., *Holt v. Leslie,* 116 Ark. 433, 173 S.W. 191 (1915).
79. See, generally, 4 *Am.Jur.* 2d Animals 93 and 3A *C.J.S.* Animals 232 (c).
80. *Principles and Practices of Classified Advertising* was first published in 1947 as *Encyclopedia of Classified Advertising.*
81. Reh, Bert, "Censorship," in McDonald, Morton J. A. ed., *Principles and Practices of Classified Advertising,* Culver City, CA: Murray & Gee, Inc., 1952, pp. 167–209 at 171.
82. Ibid. p. 167.
83. Ibid. p. 179–180.
84. Ibid.

QUESTIONS

1. Do you agree with Camenisch's claim that "the marketplace is itself already a moral as well as an economic mechanism even prior to any externally imposed moral requirements"? What argument does he give in support of this claim?

2. Camenisch seems to suggest that marketing techniques are only defensible insofar as they do not diminish customer freedom. Is this consistent with his claim that "puffery" is sometimes permissible? How would you define "puffery" and to what degree do you think it is permissible?

3. Compare Machan's approach to advertising with the position taken by Waide. Which do you find more defensible and why?

4. Consider the practice of advertising prices customarily charged as dramatic markdowns, e.g., 50 or 75 percent, from "suggested retail prices" that are artificially inflated. Would Machan feel such a practice is ethical? Do you feel such a practice is ethical?

5. What does Waide mean by the term "associative advertising"?

6. Do you agree with Waide's claim that consumer autonomy is not the central issue in evaluating the morality of associative advertising? Why or why not?

7. Could *Soldier of Fortune* magazine reasonably be expected to realize that the advertisements in question were liable to lead to crime? If so, did they have a duty not to print them? What if the crime in question was not murder, but some lesser offense?

8. Do you agree with the claim that competing values have moral weight equal to or greater than freedom of the press? How would you defend your answer?

CASE 11:1 SELLING SUGARED CEREALS[1]

On June 30, 1977 five organizations (The Committee on Children's Television, Inc., the California Society of Dentistry for Children, The American G.I. Forum of California, the Mexican-American

Political Association, and the League of United Latin American Citizens) brought a class action on behalf of California residents against General Foods, concerning General Foods marketing of sugared cereals. These cereals (Alpha Bits, Honeycomb, Fruity Pebbles, Sugar Crisp, and Cocoa Pebbles) contain from 38 to 50 percent sugar by weight.

One of the allegations of the plaintiffs was that these cereals are marketed on the basis of deceptive advertising. They charged that advertisements for these cereals are typically both implicitly and explicitly misleading. At the implicit level the advertisements suggest that children who eat sugared cereals "are bigger, stronger, more energetic, happier, more invulnerable and braver than they would have been if they did not eat candy breakfasts." At the explicit level they suggest that the cereals are healthful, nutritious grain products forming the most important element of a well-balanced breakfast. The plaintiffs also charged that the advertisements concealed the facts that there is no honey in Honeycomb, no fruit in Fruity Pebbles, and that sugared cereals contribute to tooth decay, as well as

more serious medical consequences. They also noted the failure of the advertisements to note that these cereals cost more per serving than breakfast foods of greater nutritional value.

CASE STUDY QUESTIONS

1. Does General Foods have any responsibility to reveal the fact that sugar cereals cost more per serving than breakfast foods of greater nutritional value? Explain.
2. Does the fact that there is no honey in a product called "Honeycomb" and no fruit in a product called "Fruity Pebbles" constitute deception? Why or why not? Does the fact that such products are marketed to children have any relevance to how this question should be answered? Why or why not?
3. How would you distinguish between "puffery" and "deception"? How would you describe the advertisements in question?

CASE 11:2 THE BETTE MIDLER SOUND ALIKE[2]

In 1985, the Ford Motor Company and its advertising agency, Young and Rubicam Inc., promoted the Ford Lincoln Mercury by means of nineteen television commercials. These commercials, known in the agency as "The Yuppie Campaign" attempted to make a favorable impression on Yuppies, by bringing back college memories associated with popular songs of the seventies. The agency attempted to contract with the original artists responsible for popularizing the songs, but were successful in only nine cases. In the other ten cases, the songs were sung by "sound alikes."

One of the songs used was "Do You Want To Dance," a song associated with Bette Midler and her 1973 album *The Divine Miss M*. The agency approached Midler, but she was not interested in doing the commercial. The agency then approached Ula Hedwig who had been a backup singer for Midler for ten years. Hedwig recorded the commercial, imitating Midler to the best of her ability.

Hedwig's imitation was so good that Midler was told by a number of people that it sounded exactly like her. Hedwig was told by friends that they thought it was Midler singing the commercial, and Ken Fritz a personal manager in the entertainment

business and not associated with Midler, testified in an affidavit that he thought Midler had done the singing.

The agency was careful to use neither Midler's name or picture in the commercial, and to obtain a license from the copyright holder to use the song. Nevertheless, Midler sued on the grounds that she had a right to protect her voice from imitation.

CASE STUDY QUESTIONS

1. Given that Midler was offered first opportunity to sing, that the song was one she had previously sung, and that the product and commercial were attractive, would you agree that Midler was exploited?
2. In the course of the trial it was argued that

[not] every imitation of a voice to advertise merchandise is actionable. ... only ... when a distinctive voice of a professional singer is widely known and deliberately imitated in order to sell a product, [have] the sellers ... committed a tort ...

In view of the fact that there is little point to imitating a voice that is not widely known and associated with a famous individual, does this argument undermine the grounds on which it held Midler to be exploited?

Notes

1. Based on The Children's Committee on Television Inc. v. General Founds as found in 673 *Pacific Reporter* 2nd 660 (Cal. 1983).
2. Based on Midler v. Ford Motor Co. as found in 849 *Federal Reporter,* 2nd series, 460.

FOR FURTHER READING

1.   Robert Arrington, "Advertising and Behavior Control," *Journal of Business Ethics,* Vol. 1, (1982) pp. 3–12.

2.   Tom Beauchamp, "Manipulative Advertising," *Business and Professional Ethics Journal,* Vol. 3, Spring/Summer (1984) pp. 1–22.

3.   Roger Crisp, "Persuasive Advertising, Autonomy, and the Creation of Desire," *Journal of Business Ethics,* Vol. 6, (1987) pp. 413–418.

4.   Virginia Held, "Advertising and Program Content," *Business and Professional Ethics Journal,* Vol. 3, (1983) pp. 61–76.

5.   Robert Lippke, "Advertising and the Social Conditions of Autonomy," *Business and Professional Ethics Journal,* Vol. 8, No. 4, 1988, pp. 35–58.

Chapter Twelve

CORPORATE RESPONSIBILITY

Introduction

Individual employees act as agents for their employers. As we have seen in our discussion on whistleblowing in Chapter 7, this does not imply that the employee has the obligation to act immorally on behalf of his or her employer. Equally clear is the fact that the employer who asks an employee to perform an immoral action should be punished at least as harshly, and probably more harshly, than the employee who simply carries out the employer's request. In many cases, however, employees are employed by corporations. Are corporations moral agents that can be held guilty of wrongdoing? If so, how does one go about punishing a corporation? They can scarcely be imprisoned, and monetary fines are liable to be ultimately passed on to the consumer. It is to this important issue of corporate responsibility that we turn our attention in Chapter Twelve.

In his article "The Moral Status of the Corporation," R. E. Ewin addresses the very difficult conceptual problem of whether, and to what degree, corporations can be conceived as moral agents. It is usually held that only persons can have duties, possess rights, or be capable of acting virtuously. This raises the question of whether a corporation can in any sense be conceived as a person, or should talk of a company as a moral agent be understood as a shorthand way of referring to the moral agents which make up the company? Ewin takes the position that corporations can legitimately be conceived as moral agents, but as severely truncated ones, incapable of virtue or vice. Thus, although they can possess rights and duties, they remain merely instruments incapable of developing or exhibiting moral character. How well or how poorly they are used is a reflection of the character of the full-blooded moral agents whose instrument they are.

Robert J. Rafalko, in his article "Corporate Punishment: A Proposal," examines the moral status of corporations and how they can be punished. With regard to the question of the moral status of corporations, his thesis is that they are in some important respects sufficiently like persons so that we should treat them as if they do have rights. He emphasizes, however, that the rights we accord them are not grounded in the fact that corporations are persons, but that it is expedient to human interests to treat them as possessing such rights. Any "rights" a corporation possesses derive not from the fact that it is a moral agent, but from the interests of those moral agents it was created to serve.

With regard to the issue of punishment, he proposes that we consider a form of what he calls "corporate corporal punishment." He suggests that, in cases where the usual judicial sanctions fail and where the wrongdoing is serious, that a complete reorganization of the decision-making process at or above the level of vice-president take place. He further recommends the dissolution of shareholders' stock for all shareholders who possess 1% or more of the outstanding stock of the corporation; the confiscated stock to be turned over to the company employees in equal shares. His proposal for corporate punishment is not developed in great detail and there are major theoretical and practical obstacles that would have to be overcome if it were to be implemented. It does, however, raise the question of the responsibilities of corporate executives. This question is further explored in our third and fourth articles.

In "The Moral Responsibility of Corporate Executives for Disasters," John D. Bishop explores the conditions under which senior executives can be held accountable for disasters. As is customary, he absolves executives of any blame resulting from disasters caused by "acts of God" or actions not performed on behalf of the corporation. Where he parts company with the standard view is his willingness to hold senior executives responsible in any instance in which the information necessary to prevent the disaster was possessed by company personnel. Usually it is thought that a senior executive is absolved of any responsibility for a disaster, if, despite the executive's best efforts to obtain information that could have prevented the disaster, subordinates fail to convey that information. Bishop, relying on a concept he terms "professional responsibility," insists that executives have not only a moral responsibility to try to avoid disasters, but a professional responsibility to be successful in their endeavors.

Robert Larmer, in "Corporate Executives, Disasters and Moral Responsibility," criticizes Bishop on the basis that Bishop's position runs counter to our intuition that individuals should not be held responsible for events they have no way of anticipating or preventing. Larmer suggests that Bishop cannot escape this difficulty by invoking the notion of professional responsibility, since this notion cannot ground his claim that we are justified in such instances in holding executives responsible based on moral considerations. Larmer goes on to argue that the notion of professional responsibility is itself open to ethical evaluation, and that its presumed authority ultimately derives from moral responsibility.

R. E. Ewin

The Moral Status of the Corporation

Peter French's persuasive arguments to show that corporations[1] have rights and duties, and to that extent have a moral personality,[2] establish at best a Kantian sort of moral personality for them. His claim that ". . . corporations can be full-fledged moral persons and have whatever privileges, rights and duties as are, in the normal course of affairs, accorded to moral persons"[3] is misleading: the moral personality of corporations is severely limited. Corporations, as artificial persons, can have all sorts of rights and duties,[4] but they lack the emotional life without which there can be no possession of virtues and vices. The moral personality of a corporation can be no more than a Kantian moral personality, restricted to issues of rights and duties; it cannot be the richer moral life of generosity and courage, meanness and cowardice, that is lived by "natural" people. The moral personality of a corporation is exhausted by its legal personality,[5] and that fact, taken together with the representative function of a corporation's management, places important limitations on what constitutes ethical behavior on the part of management. Those limitations are interesting because a common misunderstanding of them can lead ethical managers to behave in quite unethical ways and can lead members of the public to have quite improper expectations of corporations and management.

I. ACTING ON A CORPORATION'S BEHALF: LIMITATIONS

A corporation cannot act without some particular person acting on its behalf. That does not

From R. E. Ewin, "The Moral Status of the Corporation," *Journal of Business Ethics,* Vol. 10, 1991. Reprinted by permission of Kluwer Academic Publishers.

exclude it from being a moral person: there is a large range of things that the insane, the comatose, or babes in arms cannot do without some other person acting on their behalf, and people in those classes retain rights. It does, on the other hand, limit the sorts of actions that are open to corporations. In this section, I intend to examine those limitations and to show that they tend to restrict the moral concerns of corporations and their managers to matters of rights and duties.

On the face of it, corporations can act only through representatives and can do only those things that representatives can do. What representatives can do is work in terms of rights and duties.[6] Representatives can commit one to various things. In a democracy, our political representatives commit us to certain laws; by their actions on our behalf (even if not at our behest), they change what it is that we have a right or a duty to do. Somebody authorized by the corporation to buy bolts for the manufacture of tractors, by her actions, commits the corporation to paying the bill for the supply of bolts, that is, creates a duty for the corporation by her exercise of one of the corporation's rights that she has been authorized to exercise. If she decides also to buy flowers for her mother, then the corporation can properly require that she pay that bill from her private funds.

A representative exercises the rights of whomever he or she is representing. The control exercised by the represented might be quite direct: the buyer might be sent out to buy a certain number of bolts at a certain price from a certain supplier and authorized to do nothing else, so that unavailability of bolts at that price from that supplier means a wasted trip or phone call. The representative in such a case is nothing more than a delegate.

Some representatives become representatives without any authorization from the people they represent. As an example, it was not uncommon in colonial times for the colonial government to appoint somebody to represent the natives. The representative was appointed by the colonial governor, let us say, and in the standard case was certainly not appointed by the natives. Any authorization came from the government, not from the people represented. How, then, can this sort of representation be distinguished from simple theft of rights? There is a limitation on what the representative can do with the rights of those he or she represents;[7] insofar as the rights and duties of the represented allow, the representative must act so as to further their interests. If I simply take over your rights and make them mine (perhaps I buy them from you, or you forfeit them as a penalty for something), then I can quite properly use them to further my own interests, since they have ceased to be your rights and have become mine. If, instead of taking over your rights and making them mine, I represent you with respect to those rights, then I must use them to further your interests rather than my own. We see the same sort of relationship between a guardian and an infant ward when the guardian must act as the infant's representative with respect to an inheritance the infant has received:[8] that the guardian is the guardian and thus the infant's representative is not a matter of authorization from the two-year-old, but, because of that, what the guardian can do in exercising the infant's rights is severely limited.

For the same reason, one would expect the same principle to hold when the authorization is a wide one so that the representative, though authorized, is much more than a mere delegate. There might be the further point here that the authorization could reasonably be taken to imply that sort of limitation. If the buyer is sent off to buy bolts, then *of course* she is expected not to pay a higher price for the same bolts that she could have bought for less, because she is supposed to be acting as a representative of the corporation and acting in its interests.[9]

The executive officers of a corporation are (at least, usually) elected by the shareholders or appointed by people who were elected by the shareholders. They do not attain their position in the same sort of way as does the colonial representative of native interests. But that is a matter of how they attain their positions as representatives, not of what it is to be a representative. The point about representation without consent is that it brings out what the job of

a representative is. The point about voting or any other method of appointing representatives is that it goes on to the important question of who is to be the judge of the interests of the people represented. The function of the representative of a corporation is still that of furthering the interests of the members of the corporation as much as possible within the limitations imposed by their rights and duties.[10]

The guardian who has to look after the infant ward's inheritance may properly invest the money in something safe. If, as things turn out, the long-odds investments do pay off better, that is simply unfortunate; the infant will have to struggle through with less money than she might have had otherwise and, if the investments were reasonable, will not be able to sue the guardian for the difference. The ward, in the end, will have to live with the consequences of the guardian's proper action. If, on the other hand, the guardian uses the money to set up a fraud, even if he does so solely to further the ward's interests and with no though of personal gain, then the *guardian* has to live with the consequences of that. Not everything done to further the interests of the represented is done in the capacity of representative, even if representatives should act so as to further the interests of those they represent; a representative can act as such only when acting within the limits imposed by the rights of the represented. It can be *my* act only if I could have authorised it, and I cannot hand over rights that I do not possess.

The ward, when she comes of age and takes over her inheritance, will have the rights to do all sorts of things with the money and may act in or against her own interests as she sees fit. The guardian, as we have seen, is more limited in what he can do. He is not precluded only from perpetrating fraud on his ward's behalf; he is not allowed to do various sorts of good on her behalf, either. When she takes over the inheritance, the ward can give it all to charity; the guardian cannot, when the ward is still two years old, give all her money to charity. But the law might allow a conservative imputation of authorization from a ward still to young to authorize anything: it might allow that the guardian, from the income on the inheritance, make contributions to charity which the ward, if capable, might be expected to authorize if she is a decent person.

The basis of that imputed authorization would be that the ward could be expected to make it if she were capable of deciding such matters. Adult shareholders are quite capable of deciding such matters for themselves, so the same justification for doing good on behalf of those represented rather than pursuing their interests will not apply in the case of those representing the shareholders. For a corporation to be charitable, *prima facie,* is simply for some people (the executives of the corporation) to be "generous" with money belonging to other people (the shareholders), and that is a very dubious form of generosity. If those people who are being forced into "generosity" want to be generous with their own money, then they are quite capable of doing it for themselves and exercising their own judgment about which charitable enterprises are most worthy of support. There is no obvious ground here for a relaxation of the principle that the representative should act so as to further the interests of the represented as far as possible within the limits imposed by the rights and duties of the represented.[11]

Because corporations are legal persons, they have at least some moral personality: they can have rights and duties. Corporations, therefore, can act justly or unjustly. Beyond that, when it comes to such matters as acting generously or charitably, it looks as though there might be a problem. Corporations can act only through representatives, and representatives must act, so far as the rights and duties of the corporation allow, so as to further the interests of the corporation as far as possible. So it looks as though corporations might be logically locked into selfishness, which would leave them with a very limited and unsatisfactory moral personality. Of course, it might be very imprudent for them to *look* as though they were entirely selfish and might, with such a poor corporate image, have deleterious efforts on their trading performance, but that is not sufficient to defeat the point and solve the problem. All that shows is that an efficient firm would be *subtle* about its selfishness, considering what promoted its interests in the long run, and would employ a good advertising agency.

II. The Corporation's Inability to Exhibit Any Virtue or Vice

What matters with rights and duties is simply that the job be done and the requirements met, so I can employ somebody else to do the job for me in such cases. My debts are paid when they are paid, even if I pay them with very bad grace and only under the threat of legal penalty; I have then met the requirements of justice and done what justice requires, even if I have not shown myself to be a possessor of the virtue of justice. Duties can be carried out and rights recognized quite cold bloodedly. I can do my duty from any of many motivations: because I shall not be paid if I do not; because I want a reputation as a reliable person; because I think I owe it to others to do my duty; and so on. I can do my duty simply from habit and without thinking about it at all. In each of those cases, my duty has been done no matter what the motivation or lack of motivation. There is no problem at all about corporations doing their duties, and the same sort of point applies to corporations insisting on their rights. Corporations can behave justly or unjustly. What I shall proceed to show now is that, despite the possibility of their acting justly or unjustly, they cannot really exhibit any virtue or vice, including the virtue of justice. They lack the virtues and vices that make up the moral character of a natural person.

Corporations clearly have interests: it is those interests that the representatives who act for the corporation are supposed to serve. Since corporations have interests and can act, even if they act only through representatives, it at least looks as though they could be prudent or imprudent. Prudence is a virtue, so this might provide a move to a wider moral personality than seems to have been allowed for corporations so far.

It is not only the buying of bolts that corporations can do only through representatives or the activities of particular people. Decisions, too, must be made by particular people (or groups of people voting according to certain rules) if the corporation is to make any decisions at all, so what is considered in making those decisions will be considered by particular people and not by the corporation in some other form. There is, then, an important sense in which the corporation, as such, cannot think for itself; it can think only through the people who act for it. Hence, a corporation, as such, cannot give proper (or improper) consideration to its own interests. If the representatives of the corporation put the corporation's interests first, that might be selfless devotion rather than prudence on their part; if they do it because that will further their own personal interests in the long run, then that might be prudence on their part but is not prudence on the part of the corporation.[12]

This is a long way short of anything that would allow us to attribute the virtue of prudence to the corporation: the corporation, unlike its representatives, does not *care* about its interests, and possession of a virtue is a matter of what one cares about. Prudence is a matter of having a proper concern for one's interests; it requires a *concern,* though a proper concern that puts one's interests in the context of many other things and gives them only their proper importance. Corporations, as such, and as distinct from the people who act for them, have no feelings of that sort.

Virtues generally are a matter of caring about certain sorts of things,[13] so there is a general problem about whether a corporation can have any virtues (or any vices) if they cannot really care about things.[14] There might be no problem about whether corporations can *behave* justly or unjustly, but there is a real problem about whether they can *possess the virtue* of justice. If I pay what I recognize to be my debts, but do so with bad grace and only because I want to avoid time in jail, then I do what justice requires but I do not exhibit the virtue of justice. The just person does what justice requires *because justice requires it*[15] and because he or she cares about justice.

If I owe you $20 but am the irresponsible sort of person who regards his debts as being of no importance and consistently forgets them, and if I am also a good-hearted soul, then, when I see you sad because you lack the $20 you need to carry out some project that you have, I might give you the money to help you out. In fact, I shall then have repaid my debt and done what justice required, but if I exhibited a virtue at all

it was a virtue something more like generosity than like justice because of what it was that moved me. I was moved by my concern for your well-being, not by any concern for justice. Had I owed the money to somebody else instead, to somebody who needed it but was not present so that their plight could touch my heart, then, being the sort of person I am in this story, I should have given you the money then, too, despite the injustice involved. I should have exhibited a sense of justice and the virtue of justice had I given you the money because I owed it to you, and only if I gave it to you for that reason.

The point is more obvious with something such as kindness. Kindness is quite clearly a matter of motivation, of performing the act because the other person is suffering or needs help and because one cares about that fact, not simply of performing a helpful act cold-bloodedly because it will help to win one a good reputation or another Boy Scout badge. A kind person, though the point needs a lot of qualifications to make it an accurate one,[16] is somebody who cares about the well-being of others and is therefore inclined to choose the well-being of others as an end for its own sake.

Corporations can give large donations to War on Want or Oxfam; there is no question that they can do what a kind person with their resources would do. Those resources are limited to the fairly impersonal: corporations can do helpful things such as providing a clean water supply or more beds for the hospital, but they cannot give a kind word or the personal touch that makes clear that somebody cares, and it is the kind word and personal touch that is really central to kindness. Nevertheless, there are actions that a kind person would perform which a corporation can also perform. Still, since the corporation cannot care, it cannot be exhibiting the virtue of kindness in performing those helpful acts. We regard the issue of motivation as crucial when we are concerned with the kindness of a natural person, and we should do the same when considering a corporation. Motivation is at the core of kindness.

Corporations, unlike the people who run them, have no emotional life. Corporations operate at the level of reason and requirement, but they do not get angry at being mistreated, they are not sickened by tales of the squalor in which some people have to live, and, generally, they simply do not have the emotional life required of a being that is to care about things as things must be cared about if one is to possess a virtue. Still, one might ask, does that matter so long as the corporation is run by people who do have that sort of emotional life and so long as the corporation is capable of performing helpful and other relevant sorts of actions?

III. The Corporation and Charitable Intentions

It might even be the case that a corporation was formed for charitable purposes—the Anti-Poverty Corporation, formed to raise money to lift some people from the squalor in which they are forced to live. That speaks well of the people who form and run such a corporation, no doubt, but it does not mean that the corporation itself possesses the virtue of charity. It does mean that the people running the corporation will have a fine chance to exercise their charitable instincts.

The more ordinary sort of corporation, one formed, say, to make a profit from the production of tractors, is not in the same position and does not give the same opportunity for those running it to exercise their charitable instincts. If the corporation is successful then the money will be there, and the board of directors might decide to give a lot of it to various worthy causes. Nevertheless, that is quite different from a case in which the Anti-Poverty Corporation does the same thing. The Anti-Poverty Corporation was formed for that purpose, advertises itself in those terms, and gives people a chance, by acting cooperatively, to raise money for anti-poverty projects that they could not raise if they were acting alone. The Big Red Tractor Corporation was formed to make profits by producing tractors and to give its shareholders a chance to make money for themselves that they could not have made by acting alone. They might then, of course, choose to donate that money to the Anti-Poverty Corporation, but that is a matter for them to decide.

Those who act for the Big Red Tractor Corporation have the job of furthering its interests insofar as they can do so while carrying out its duties and acting within the limitations of its rights. The interests of the corporation are determined by its point:[17] the point of the Big Red Tractor Corporation is to make the greatest possible return to its shareholders, so the people who act for the corporation have the job of making the greatest possible return to the shareholders and whatever will help them to do so will be in the interest of the corporation. The profit made by the corporation is, at first blush, the shareholders' money. The managers of the corporation are acting for the shareholders, as their representatives.

If those who act for the corporation have the duty of furthering its interests, and if that means that they have the duty of producing the greatest possible return to the shareholders, then they are in breach of their duty, and are therein acting unjustly, if they fail to make the best return to the shareholders that they can. That means that they can exercise their charitable instincts with the corporation's money only at the expense of acting unjustly.

Nor is it the case that they have a choice between generosity and justice, because the injustice infects the generosity. I can be generous only with what is *mine*; giving away what is somebody else's is merely irresponsible and does not show any willingness on my part to make myself worse off for the good of another.[18] If the profits belong to the shareholders, then those who act for the corporation, in exercising their charitable instincts, would be merely confused about charity and would be giving away what was somebody else's. The decision about whether to give it away should lie with the people who own it.[19]

The Anti-Poverty Corporation is not in a significantly different position from the Big Red Tractor Corporation as far as this point goes. If the executive officers, instead of putting the income of the corporation to charitable use, decide instead to raise their own salaries, then they have not merely been mean: they have failed to do their duty. The points about corporations apply to the Anti-Poverty Corporation, too; its officers deal in terms of doing their duties or failing to do so. It is simply that the duties of officers of the Anti-Poverty Corporation are different from those of the officers of the Big Red Tractor Corporation.

There is, of course, a quite separate point: if the Big Red Tractor Corporation gives large donations to good causes, that might give it a better image, give other people a more favorable attitude to it, and improve business so that profits were larger because of the money that was given away.[20] That motivation has nothing to do with the motivation required for a case of generosity or charity; if it exhibited a virtue at all, it would be the virtue of prudence. What it is more likely to show is conscientiousness and careful planning on the part of those who act for the corporation.

The same sort of point applies if one considers other facts about the behavior of the corporation such as whether it adopts only environmentally friendly policies or whether it looks after its employees well. Such considerations might pay off in terms of corporate image, or they might show that the shareholders are jolly nice people who would rather give up some of their profits[21] than have the corporation pollute the air and the waterways;[22] it might lead to improved loyalty of employees, who are thus better motivated to do their duty when they could get away with doing less and might even be willing to do more,[23] thus improving corporate performance; but it will not show that the corporation as such cares about anything and will not show any virtue in the corporation. Such things might be good business practice, but they are not exhibitions of any moral virtue residing in the corporation itself.

People who run corporations can have virtues and vices just like anybody else, and they can show their virtues and vices in the work that they do in the corporation: they can be honest or corrupt; they can show fortitude or cowardice; they can show any of a range of virtues and vices. Corporations might behave much better when they are run by virtuous people, by people who consider such issues as the consequences of the corporation's activities and whether the shareholders have a right to inflict those consequences on others. But corporations themselves can possess no virtues; as far as that sort of consideration

goes, they are merely instruments for others to use. Shareholders can use them to raise money to give to the poor, which they can do whether the corporation be the Anti-Poverty Coverty Corporation or the Bid Red Tractor Corporation, or they can use them to raise money to spend on riotous living. The morality is in the people who use the instrument, not in the instrument. And the managers are limited in the virtues that they can exhibit when acting on behalf of the corporation by the fact that they act as representatives of the shareholders: they do not act in their personal capacities, but in professional capacities, representing other people whose actions they are performing.

And that morality can, clearly, go wrong if the people using the instrument mistake their moral categories and take it that all the moral categories that apply to natural people also apply to corporations. It does not take ill-will to misuse the shareholders' money: good will might well be the explanation of why a corporate officer gives some of the corporation's money to charity, or provides excessive services to employees, or does a number of things that do not constitute acting in the interests of the shareholders as much as that can be done within the limits of their rights and duties. That corporations can come to be improperly accused of selfishness and other such vices is not the only problem arising from this sort of mistake about the moral categories that can appropriately be applied to corporations; it can also lead to corporate officers' failing to do their duties.

IV. Conclusion

If the morality is in the people who use the instrument and not in the corporation itself, then the corporation is rescued from the suggestion that it is logically tied into selfishness. The reason is plain: selfishness is not merely a matter of acting in one's own interests, as a corporation should do, but having an undue care for one's own interests at the expense of those of others. If corporations do not care, then they do not have an undue care for their own interests.

From all of this, it follows as well that descriptions of corporations as greedy are mistaken: that is not greed, it is the officers of the corporation doing their duty. If one objects to that, then one objects to the existence of corporations; presumably, shareholders do not so object. If greater profits are to be made by trading with South Africa, then that is what the officers of the corporation should do provided that it is not illegal for them to do so. On the other hand, in the normal run of things people have no duty to deal with any particular corporation. If people want to boycott that corporation so that trade with South Africa becomes unprofitable, then they are fully entitled to do so. Policies of ethical investing (as it has been called) attempt to exert that sort of pressure.

Because they are artificial people and not "natural" people, corporations lack the emotional makeup necessary to the possession of virtues and vices. Their moral personality is exhausted by their legal personality. Corporations can have rights and duties; they can exercise the rights through their agents, and they can in the same way fulfill their duties. If necessary, they can be forced to fulfil their duties. The moral personality of a corporation would be at best a Kantian sort of moral personality, one restricted to issues of requirement, rights, and duties. It could not be the richer moral life of virtues and vices that is lived by the shareholders, the executives, the shopfloor workers, the unemployed, and "natural" people in general.

Notes

1. My [R. E. Ewin] concern in this paper is with ordinary listed corporations. An interesting project would be to consider different sorts of corporations with different sorts of points (an ordinary listed corporation, a private family company, Oxfam, a state-owned corporation, perhaps even the state) and what effects their different points have for the ethical requirements to be imposed on people acting for those corporations. That project must wait for another time.
2. French (1979 and 1984).
3. French (1979, p. 207).
4. On the relationship between legal and moral rights, see Ewin (1987) *passim.*
5. In arguing for this claim, I shall be both agreeing and disagreeing with the conclusion for which Peter A. French argues (on quite different grounds) in French (1979). His claim is that ". . . corporations can be full-fledged moral persons and have whatever privileges, rights and duties as are, in the normal course of

affairs, accorded to moral persons" (p. 207). My claim is that corporations can have rights and duties, but that being a fully-fledged moral person involves substantially more.
6. On the subject of representation, see A. Phillips Griffith (1960). My discussion of representation draws heavily on this paper.
7. See Griffith.
8. A similar analogy is used in introducing the explanation of the duties of directors and other officers in Ford (1986).
9. Other things being equal, of course. It might be better to pay a higher price this time to retain good relations with that supplier because only that supplier can provide the bolts in times of shortage, or for some reason of that sort.
10. This is an important limitation of which I shall not make much here. It deserves another paper.
11. The sort of points that have been made will apply also when the issue that comes up is one of the relationship between the corporation's interest and the national interest. Except insofar as there is a specific duty to act in the national interest, a duty which would limit the actions that were open to the corporation, the job of the corporation will be to look after the shareholders' interests and leave them to concern themselves with whatever they think is the national interest to whatever extent they, personally, see fit. If the money is to be made in the domestic market, then corporations will be under no special obligation to try to produce export goods because the government has allowed a huge build-up of foreign debt.
12. Whether a corporation can exhibit virtues and vices by having (say) its executive officers do so when they act for it is an issue that I shall take up in Section III. Certainly one would often take reference to a corporation's virtues or vices as shorthand for reference to the virtues and vices of its officers when they act for it.
13. On virtues generally, see Ewin (1981).
14. We do read claims that certain corporations care. These might best be read as claims that the people who run those corporations care, or they might be more accurately read as expressing a desire that we should think well (no matter how confusedly) of the corporation so that we shall be more likely to buy its product or less likely to oppose its other activities.
15. Or, of course, some other version of that (because it was owed, because it was my duty, etc.) filling out the details of which would require reference to justice.
16. A great many qualifications are needed: somebody who goes around helping willy-nilly, with no concern about what is his or her business and what is not, is an interfering busy-body rather than a kind person. If help is needed and I care about that fact, it is still possible that I am not the right or best person to give the help; if your appendix has to be removed, it might be better if I wait for the surgeon. Helping might sometimes do no more in the long run than make people dependent; one needs good judgment about all sorts of things. And so on.

17. Which leaves the interesting possibility that it might be in the interests of the Anti-Poverty Corporation to put itself out of business by removing everybody from squalor.

18. The exception, of course, is when my giving what is somebody else's means my knowingly letting myself in for a lot of trouble. The generosity then lies in my taking that risk to make somebody better off.

19. An interesting side-issue here is the extent to which these points apply to governments and their officers. Hobbes's sovereign was an artificial man, so my arguments seem to apply against what he says of the sovereign and charity (p. 387): "And whereas many men, by accident unevitable, become unable to maintain themselves by their labour; they ought not to be left to the Charity of private persons; but to be provided for, (as far-forth as the necessities of Nature require), by the Lawes of the Common-wealth. For as it is uncharitable-nesse in any man to neglect the impotent; so it is in the Soveraign of a Common-wealth, to expose them to the hazard of such uncertain Charity."

20. Or things might not work out that way. Cf. Michael Milken's remarks about owner-managership, quoted in Bruck (1988, p. 273). See Love (1986) for an account of a corporation that is confident that its involvement in community and charitable activities has paid off.

21. Assuming unanimity amongst the shareholders, otherwise the problem about some giving away what belongs to others will arise again.

22. There might be more to it than that. If the corporation executives are acting on behalf of the shareholders, acting as their representatives, then they must further the interests of those shareholders *insofar as they can do so while fulfilling the duties of the shareholders and acting within the limitations of their rights*. That leaves argument to be had about whether the shareholders have the right to pollute the air and the waterways; if they have not, then the executives may not do so on their behalf.

23. But compare the judgment of Justice Plowman in *Parke v. Daily News Ltd.* ([1962] 1 Ch. 927) as reported in *Company Directors' Duties: Report on the Social and Fiduciary Duties and Obligations of Company Directors* by the Australian Senate Standing committee on Legal and Constitutional Affairs (Canberra: Australian Government Publishing Service, 1989), p 11. The *Report's* account of the case is: "In that case, directors of a company about to be wound up decided to pay compensation and other benefits to employees about to lose their jobs. The court held that according to law the directors were unable to do so. Their primary duty was to the shareholders."

Robert J. Rafalko

Corporate Punishment: A Proposal

A disturbing anomaly exists in the way U.S. law treats American corporations. Ever since Chief Justice John Marshall described the corporation as "an artificial being, invisible, intangible, and existing only in the contemplation of the law."[1] the boundaries for the rights and responsibilities of corporations have been hotly and, for the most part, inconclusively disputed. Never have we encountered a more misused metaphor than Marshall's, but few others have been quoted more often. Perhaps, just because of the metaphor's lack of illumination, it can mean all things to all people and, subsequently, each of us can quote it to his own purpose. In any case, that's undoubtedly why answers to questions about corporate rights and liabilities are so muddled in business, legal and philosophical discussions. The following essay is an exercise in logic and creative thinking. I shall argue that no good reasons exist for the supposition that corporations have rights independent of the rights and interests of the persons they serve and that the error of treating corporations as though they do have autonomous rights derives from a sloppy argument from analogy. I shall further argue that the analogy of corporations to citizens, though pushed too far by some courts and lawmakers, remains a useful analogy if its logical relations can be cleaned up and clarified. Finally, I shall conclude this essay by employing the refurbished analogy in such a way that it yields a proposal for more effective criminal punishment for corporate wrongdoing.

From Robert J. Rafalko, "Corporate Punishment: A Proposal," *Journal of Business Ethics*, Vol. 8, 1989.
Reprinted by permission of Kluwer Academic Publishers.

Part of my intent in writing this paper is satirical. I believe that much of the analysis on this subject has been due to pressing some faulty analogies too far. When we allow metaphors and analogies to get out of control, the result can be humor as well as confusion. We've taken the confused thesis too seriously too long. I hope the reader will find that my proposal has a humorous as well as an insightful side to it.

I. SETTING UP THE PROBLEM

The problem is one of moral and legal liability where corporations have transgressed acceptable bounds of conduct. The problem of corporate legal liability is one of justification, and the familiar hardware of legal justification is precedent and the calculation of competing interests and rights. Precedent is, in the last analysis, a special sort of appeal to authority, and authority in this instance rests on no more than prior pronouncements made on like cases. These pronouncements presumably rest on further moral types of justification. Therefore, the problem of legal liability reduces in the last instance to a problem of moral liability.

The difficulty, however, arises when we ask questions about the nature of the corporation. Can an abstract, collective entity be the sort of thing that assumes moral identity? If we answer "Yes," and we are able to make good our answer, then most moral and legal theoreticians instinctively view the problem of the justification of corporate moral liability claims as a clash of competing interests—most often, as a clash between the rights of the corporation and the interests of workers, consumers, and the community-at-large. If we answer "No," then, for many, the problem ends rights there. The corporation is a creature bound by its charter. Regulations and restrictions may be (or may not be) appropriate, but no further talk about liability or punishment is conceptually appropriate.[2]

My contention is that the adherents of the arguments on both sides of this position are mistaken. First, the stubbornly persistent manner of viewing claims about liability and punishment as a weighting of competing rights and interests will get us nowhere; but, second, the analogy of corporations to moral persons is useful if not exact, and without appeal to such an analogy we are destined to succumb to a blind moral debility whose catastrophic effects to the environment, the community, and the worker no free market jingoism can palliate.

Regarding corporations as analogous to moral persons has one overriding drawback. Corporations are designed to limit liability, whereas no moral person is so exempted. The history of the evolution of the corporation is quite clear on this matter. Many people commonly think of the corporation as existing solely or exclusively for the purpose of making a profit, but this view is clearly mistaken. Corporate charters were originally granted to universities, monasteries, the guilds and boroughs in order to separate jurisdictions and divide responsibilities.[3] As early as the 15th century, English courts had come to recognize the corporate principle of limited liability: "*Si quid universitati debetur, singulis non debetur, nec quod debet universitas, singuli debent.*"[4] [i.e., If anything is owed to a corporation it is not owed to the individual, and the individuals do not owe what the corporation owes.] Later, companies such as the Hudson Bay Company and the East India Company were incorporated with the intention of encouraging investment by means of the principle of limited liability. The sharing of responsibility among shareholders served three purposes: first, a creditor usually stood to gain more by suing the shareholders as a unit than he would be suing any one individual; secondly, the shareholder became liable only to the extent of his original investment—his other assets could not be touched; and thirdly, these limits on liability served to make investment more attractive, thus establishing the modern close link between profit and shared liability.

Moreover, even modern corporations do not exist solely—and many, not at all—for the purpose of reaping profits. Some corporations, for example, the University of North Carolina, are chartered as nonprofit, their corporate status serving to define responsibilities and to place limits on the liability of their members.

The corporation, I submit, is best defined as a liability-limiting mechanism. Given this definition, no wonder the courts have so much difficulty meting out just punishment to corporations when they engage in misconduct! Rarely can the courts legally pierce the corporate veil to prosecute individuals thought responsible for corporate wrongdoing. Even when they can, the courts tend to display a reluctance to do so—we may suspect that that reluctance is the result of confusion regarding the range of liability pertaining to corporations and the well-entrenched personification of the corporation as moral agent.

When the courts attempt to place responsibility on the corporation itself, the appropriate punishment is deemed to be monetary. However, when a corporation engages in repeated instances of gross misconduct, the courts are reluctant to levy truly heavy fines—as in the case of Hooker Chemical Company, despite a history of repeated violations of the law over a period of four decades. Good reason exists for the court's caution. A truly ponderous fine, the sort of fine necessary to act as a deterrent . . . [might leave a] community . . . stranded without its major industry, or consumers might be deprived of a much-needed or much-wanted product.

At the heart of the problem is the inability of legislators, jurists, businessmen, and philosophers to find innovative solutions to these and like problems.

One of the misconceptions that we may judge to be in part responsible for this sort of inflexible thinking is the supposition that if indeed corporations are like moral agents, then corporations have moral rights which must be weighted against the interests of the community. In the next section, I question this assumption and argue that we more properly ought to regard the existence of the corporation as a socially conferred privilege, which does not entail any supposition of a corporation's moral right to exist, or moral rights of any other kind.

II. Do Corporations have Rights?

Our question concerns the normative justifications for the supposition that corporations have rights analogous to First Amendment guarantees offered to all citizens of the United States. If corporations do have such rights, then we may be tempted to infer that they also possess a right to exist analogous to a human's right to life. Were that so, it would have a significant impact on any considerations we might devise regarding the proper punishment to be accorded incorrigibly law-breaking corporations. However, let us see if that is really so.

If we were to phrase our question as, "Do corporations have *human* rights?"—the answer would be, "No," for obvious reasons: corporations do not eat, drink, breath, sleep or procreate; they are not human beings. Some philosophers even cogently dispute the contention that human beings have such rights as "Human Rights," but that is not at issue here. What is at issue is whether there is good and compelling reason to offer the guarantees of the Bill of Rights to American corporations.

Some philosophers, such as Thomas Donaldson, believe the issue is already settled: corporations *do* enjoy such guarantees. Donaldson's strategy is an admirable one: he hopes that by making such concessions to the ownership of such rights, then, by the force of analogy, corporations can be brought into tow, morally speaking. Rights entail moral responsibilities, so, by making such a concession, Donaldson constructs a social contract basis for moral censures against irresponsible and incorrigible corporations. However, as is clear from the passage quoted below from his book, *Corporations and Morality*, Donaldson concedes far too much:

With the passage of the Fourteenth Amendment to the Constitution, U.S. corporations acquired full status as abstract persons, complete with rights to life, liberty, and state citizenship. (Most U.S. corporations are citizens of the state of Delaware). Although modern U.S. corporations do not possess certain features of personhood—i.e. they neither eat, require medical attention, nor vote—they are treated as persons in a multitude of ways: they must pay taxes, are liable for damages, can enter into legal agreements, and have the right to freedom of speech. Modern corporations are created by persons, but they are created in the image of their creators.[5]

This is a beguiling passage, but we see at once what's wrong with it: it is not an argument; it is an assertion, coupled with a few factual references. Moreover, Donaldson has some of his facts wrong. If the Fourteenth Amendment "grants" such rights as free speech to the corporation, it does so only in a way that is derivative from the rights of the persons whom the corporation serves.

Corporations are not persons, and cannot thereby be entitled to the rights of persons. However, we grant some of the protections of the Fourteenth Amendment to corporations because we find such actions suitable on occasion—especially the due-process and equal protection provisions, and especially where they pertain to the deprivation of *property*. But where we find such *ad hoc* applications suitable, we can also find other applications unsuitable. For example, we do not find First Amendment guarantees for freedom of assembly suitable whenever corporations engage in collusion over price fixing. And God forbid that we should ever grant U.S. corporations the inalienable right to bear arms!

Sometimes people (mostly corporation lawyers, but sometimes philosophers as well) argue that corporations are deserving of due process and equal protection of all First Amendment rights because so esteemed a personage as Justice Marshall said that they are "invisible persons," but we are already wise to this rhetorical device; it is a run-away metaphor, and a fallacious appeal to authority as well. Sometimes it is useful to think of the corporation as though it were an "invisible person," but an actual person, decidedly, it is not. If we wish to grant such rights to the corporation, we must always in the first instance ask the simple question, "Why? Is such a declaration expedient? In the national interest? In the interests of the individuals served by the corporation?" The answers will vary with the circumstances: sometimes treating corporations as though they have certain rights is expedient in some of these ways; sometimes not.

Donaldson is also incorrect when he supposes that the courts have recognized that American-based corporations have the First Amendment rights of free speech. Nothing I have been able to uncover in Supreme Court decisions corroborate that belief. In the landmark case of *First National Bank of Boston v. Bellotti,* for example,—the case that I surmise Donaldson had in mind when he made his assertion—the Court did not rule that corporations (meaning *all* corporations, or even *all U.S. based* corporations) have the right of freedom of speech. Nor did the Court—interestingly enough—rule that First National Bank of Boston had the right to free speech. The majority opinion, written by Justice Powell, is especially enlightening in this regard. Justice Powell writes:

The proper question therefore is not whether corporations have First Amendment rights and, if so, whether they are coextensive with those of natural persons. Instead the question must be whether "the statute in question" abridges expression that the First Amendment was meant to protect. We hold that it does. . . .[6]

Justice Powell clearly did not mean to commit the Court to the ascription of Human Rights to abstract entities—a wise precaution to my mind. In a fashion that would please William of Occam, Justice Powell avoided ontological commitment to abstract entities. Justice Powell ruled just that, *in this instance,* abridging free speech to First National Bank of Boston would be less expedient than prohibiting such expression. Yet, we also infer from the decision that in other cases, prudence might dictate the need to abridge corporate free expression—for example, Justice Powell mentions the restrictions on trading on the basis of inside information.

I take Judge Powell's decision to be based on an appeal to the principle of the greatest liberty compatible with a like liberty for all. That may be relevantly applicable in the case of *First National Bank of Boston V. Bellotti,* but improper where price-fixing or inside trading is concerned. Each case must be taken on its respective merits with regard to the principle of greatest liberty.

The lesson to be learned from this case is that we *can* make good sense of the corporation as a legal entity, a *persona ficta* with *iures fictus* (rights of a certain but derivative sort). Yet, any conclusion which supposes that a corporation has an autonomous right to exist apart from the interest it serves is unwarranted. Therefore, the corporation is enough like a moral person to make moral and legal demands of it—that would seem to follow from any grant of *rights* to it, for the correlative of rights is responsibilities; but no basis exists for the supposition that the corporation is somehow entitled to the same degree of protection or of compassion or of mercy that the courts accord to real persons when they break the law. Surely, the faulty conclusion which portrays corporations as bearers of autonomous rights could only follow as a result of a misplaced reliance on the strength of the analogy involved when corporations are compared to persons, and a greater understanding of the worth of argument by analogy is necessary to clarify the degree to which we should credence the personification of the modern corporation. This is a subject which I shall develop in the next section.

III. THE ARGUMENT FROM ANALOGY

We now know that arguments from analogy have special strengths and special drawbacks. Monroe Beardsley sums up the difficulties with analogical argument, saying that it is indeed "a distinctive form of argument" but "not a cogent (one)."[7] Because arguments from analogy have the virtue of plausibility, and wide acceptance in popular use, we must know how to deal with them, but in fact analogical arguments do not render the conclusion any probability whatever.

Consider just how the argument from analogy fails on the test of cogency: Compare two entities *A* and *B* by searching for whatever properties they share. If entities *A* and *B* share properties *X, Y,* and *Z,* we are in no way justified in leaping to the conclusion that if *A* has further property *a,* then so also will *B.* The only way we could be sure that *B* had *a* is if we knew in advance of the argument the truth of the further premise that *B* and *A* are identical. Then, by virtue of Leibnitz' Law of the Identity of Indiscernibles; we would then and only then be justified in inferring that *B* also has *a* [*Leibniz* (1646-1716) was a German philosopher, scientist, mathematician and historian. He proposed a view called the identity of indiscernibles. According to Leibniz, it is not possible for two objects to be identical in all respects and yet to be numerically different.].

However, critical inquiry is not the only basis for argument. We have the familiar distinction between critical thought and creative thought. Beardsley suggests that analogies can helps us put objects in a new light, and they can prompt new and creative hypotheses.[8] Such is the real value of analogical arguments.

We would do well to draw a distinction here between the use of the argument from analogy as "deductively binding," and the argument from analogy as "critically explorative." When an analogical argument is used in a deductively binding way, it is faulty. . . . Such an argument speculates on the independent existence of certain relations or entities—but this is speculation only; such relations or entities are not *observed,* nor is any evidence offered beyond the analogical exercise itself which confers any degree of likelihood or certainty on the conclusion of the argument.

We may detect, however, a more legitimate basis for this argument form: we may say that an analogical argument is "critically explorative" just in case it is used in a manner which opens up new avenues of thought, or if it employed in a way that expands our options in finding solutions to problems, or in clarifying relations between otherwise unlike objects. The difference between "critically explorative" and "deductively binding" uses of the argument from analogy is very much the difference between mapmaking and consulting a ready-made map (except that, in the former case, we also may be creating some of the landscape even as we're charting it).

Recall, once more, Justice Marshall's personification of the corporation as "an artificial being." The problem is twofold: First, Marshall's juridical descendants used the analogy in precisely the form of which Monroe Beardsley disapproves—what we've called here, "the deductively binding form. The analogy is taken much too literally and we run the danger of looking for (or, worse: assuming the existence of) attributes of personhood in the corporation where none exist. The danger is compounded by the second feature of the Marshall definition of the corporation: the fact that the analogy is case in a *metaphorical* form. Metaphors, we must emphasize, have especially regrettable propensities in such critical contexts since they may be said to be "analogies in disguise."

What separates the metaphor from the more clearly analogical simile is the implicit suggestion in the metaphor that the analogy to be made entails a correspondingly tight fit between shared properties of distinct entities. A stronger presumption exists, then, that if A has property a, then so also will B. Such figures of speech are fraught with perils from a logical point of view, especially when argumentative appeals are made to the metaphors coined by illustrious personages on the part of individuals in a legal system that is by its nature exceedingly literal-minded. Beardsley wisely cautions us that metaphors have two hidden dangers: first, metaphors are hard to control. They often run away from us, and cause us to seem to be saying more than we intended. Second, we can get locked into favorite metaphors, causing us to see matters only through the point of view which the metaphor prompts. Such metaphors may obscure other possible interrelationships, so that coming to think in new and more productive ways becomes more and more difficult.[9] The greatest contribution that analogies have to make to our thinking—their potential for creativity—can be defeated by a metaphor that has too familiar a use. I fear that both of these drawbacks are present in the legal, moral and business reliance on the Marshall metaphor, and I attribute our inability to find new and creative solutions to the problem of corporate misconduct tied to the worn-out and over-used metaphor of corporations as "abstract beings."

We may rush to Justice Marshall's defense, and rightly so, for he clearly shows us the dissimilarities between persons and corporations within the very context of these oft-quoted remarks: persons are not invisible, neither are they intangible nor existing only in the contemplation of law. But this metaphor has, in the first place, entranced subsequent users into disregarding the dis-analogies. Even so cautious a thinker as Thomas Donaldson sometimes inadvertently slips into the habit of describing corporations as "invisible persons."[10] The problem is that Justice Marshall's metaphor has controlled our thinking too rigidly: it has attained the status of a legal presupposition. As a result,

solutions to problems of corporate wrongdoing continue to elude us.

Philosophy may well be defined as the discipline which seeks to uncover, and challenge, basic presuppositions about life, conduct, knowledge and reality—presuppositions which may be widely shared, largely unrecognized, and stand as roadblocks to appropriate or innovative solutions. It is my contention that such unrecognized presuppositions have hold of us here.

The method by which philosophers most often uncover these presuppositions is through the device known as a "thought-experiment." Thought-experiments share both a critical and a creative function. Once a presupposition of import is uncovered, then constructive critical analysis can begin, but in the first instance thought-experiments are creative enterprises. They may pose the question, "What if matters were otherwise?" By so asking, a philosopher can look at a problem from a new vantage point. . . . Thereupon, critical analysis can proceed. However, I repeat, in the first instance the exercise is always a creative one, and that usually proceeds along an analogical base.

My proposal is to do some creative thinking of our own. If some corporations act irresponsibly and threaten the life and well-being of law-abiding citizens in the community, then surely some device more effective than the levying of fines can be found as a way of deterring such misconduct in the future. To find the answer, treating recalcitrant corporations as on a par to hardened criminals might well be an illuminating analogy. Notice that by so proposing such an analogy, I do not endorse an exact correspondence. That would be to miss the point of the thought-experiment. The analogy proposed has a creative, not a critical, intention.

IV. CIVIL VS. CRIMINAL PROSECUTION

Consider the familiar case history of Hooker Chemical Company. In a period that stretches from 1942 to 1979, Hooker Chemical and Plastics Corporation demonstrated a remarkable disregard for the health and well-being of residents living adjacent to disposal sites and chemical discharges. Most notable of these transgressions was the incident at Love Canal, but a long series of such abuses is on record. In 1972, at Hyde Park, N.Y., the manager of an adjacent plant complained to Hooker of "an extremely dangerous condition affecting our plant and employees. . . ." The manager traced the source to a Hooker disposal site. In 1976, the New York Department of Environmental Conservation was forced to ban consumption of several species of fish from Lake Ontario because of discharges of the chemical Mirex from the Hooker Niagara Falls Plant. In 1976–1977, Hooker was named as a defendant for supplying raw materials for the manufacture of Kepone dust, which had induced illness in employees of Life Science Company, Virginia. In 1977, Hooker paid a fine of $176,000 for discharging HCCPD into a lake in Michigan. Michigan officials also sued Hooker in 1979 for pollution around its plant in Montague. In 1979, the town of Niagara Falls filed suit against Hooker based on a NY State Health Department survey of residents near Hyde Park.[11] Again, in 1979, Hooker was convicted of polluting the air with fluoride at White Springs, Florida.[12]

Despite these cases, Hooker Chemical and Plastics Company has shown no evidence of a "change of heart" in its policies regarding chemical discharges and disposal sites. In fact, as far as we are able to determine, to date no fine or suit has been able to deter Hooker from its *modus operandi*. The fines have been negligible in both amount and in effect.

Union Carbide's Bhopal incident serves as another case in point, where 2000 people lost their lives. Less than one year later, an accident occurred at the Union Carbide site in West Virginia, and just prior to the Bhopal incident, Union Carbide was fined $3.9 million for delaying reporting of new carcinogenicity information on the chemical, diethyl sulfate, to the Environmental Protection Agency. In these cases, fines have proved (and may continue to be) costly to Union Carbide. Nevertheless, a pattern of abuses has developed in the company's safety procedures.[13]

There are some promising developments in prosecutorial aggressiveness directed against individuals in the corporation who may be made out to be more responsible than others when the decision-making process results in grievous transgressions of the law. For instance, in the case of the General Dynamics Corporation overcharges to the U.S. Military, attempts have been made to pierce the "corporate veil" and prosecute the individuals who are allegedly responsible for the decision which led the company into wrongdoing. Such charges have been leveled at three senior executives of General Dynamics regarding the overcharges. Even more aggressive is the set of charges leveled against Lester Crown, owner of 23% of General Dynamics' 65 million shares of stock, with respect to an Illinois bribery case which may result in the suspension of his security clearance.[14] Such attempts are not entirely without precedent, but they do represent a challenge to the very boundary lines of corporate liability sharing. Nevertheless, good reasons exist for those boundaries, and, by virtue of those good reasons, nothing may come of those attempts by the courts. Moreover, such legal actions are the exception to the rule and, as Neil Gilxon argues, that is a major reason such corporations remain recalcitrant. He writes:

The idea of personal responsibility is evidently passe. Responsibility is diffused into the corporation, and finally fades away into misdemeanors whose perpetrators must perform community service, as if they had been guilty of writing graffiti on subway walls.[15]

Glixon goes on to point out that Union Carbide's Chairman, Warren M. Anderson, begged off from any blame, either for himself or for his company, for the accident at Bhopal, India. Glixon comments: "The problem is that in today's corporate structures the causal chain is always extended. One can easily understand how a Warren Anderson may find it difficult to identify himself as a culprit in so extended a chain. . . ."[16] However, Glixon here overlooks Anderson's earlier pronouncements of personal moral responsibility for the accident, when he claimed he would devote the rest of his life to helping the people who suffered during the tragedy. He reversed himself a year later, in an interview for *Business Week,* where he stated that when he made his remarks about moral responsibility, he had "overreacted." What brought on this hardening of the heart? The issue is insightfully discussed in the "Notes and Comment" heading of the New Yorker magazine:

His company, pursued by lawyers seeking billions of dollars in compensation for the dead and injured (and sizable fees), is facing a critical court decision about whether the case will be tried in India or in America, where damage awards are expected to be higher. . . .

What Mr. Anderson meant . . . , perhaps, is that at first he reacted as a private man but in the intervening months he has remembered—or been reminded—that he is the head of a corporation. Murray Kempton pointed out in a recent edition of Newsday that has Mr. Anderson was talking about the "moral responsibilities" of his company its stock was collapsing; now the company, defiant . . . has seen its shares rise to a price more than a third above their level on the day before Bhopal.[17]

Such are the problems with attempts to pierce the corporate veil for the purpose of attaching responsibility to private individuals. We may find convincing the claim that as a CEO of Union Carbide, Warren Anderson never acts as an autonomous decision maker, no matter the great authority he undoubtedly wields. True, the lesson of the Nuremberg Trials is that guilt is individual; the notion of collective guilt has no place in American law. Yet, this is precisely the problem with attempts at the prosecution of individuals in many cases of corporate wrongdoing, for placing the blame is an exceedingly difficult undertaking, made more complicated by the corporation's very structure. For some corporations at least, no provision is made to accommodate issues of the public good. In such circumstances, an executive may find that resisting the tide of impending corporate decisions can take exceptional moral willpower. Moreover, we may have no way of knowing whether a given executive dissented from the board's joint decision. The matter of diffused responsibility is intimately connected with the corporation's internal structure of shared liability, but if everybody shares liability, then surely nobody does.

The judgments of the courts in these matters amply demonstrate their debility in handling prosecution of corporate wrongdoing. Once again, the courts are reluctant to utilize the full weight of the law against such corporations because too many innocent parties stand to suffer, whereas CEO's are largely protected from prosecution due to the corporation's traditional composition which diffuses personal responsibility. The result is that many corporations continue their abuses much in the manner as a repeat criminal or psychopathic individual would.

The problem is that such corporations may be criminally liable, but we exact mainly civil penalties. We've already considered why civil penalties are self-defeating—for one thing, the punishment exacted tends to ricochet, depriving workers of jobs, communities of their major industry, and consumers of needed products and optimal prices derived from the possible absence of competition should such fines effectively close a company down.

Yet, the history of the prosecution of corporate wrongdoing is the fullest exemplification of "thinking in a rut." If one fine doesn't work, and a company's transgression is repeated, then the court's policy is to levy another fine—usually not much greater than the one that preceded it. Companies write off these fines as external dis-economies, and learn that they are less costly than the technology needed to correct the abuses. As a result, the abuses continue. Commenting on the apparent lack of moral responsibility exercised by corporations, The New Yorker editorialized, "Corporations need to function the way they function—it is the only way they make sense. Yet there is no point in denying that they feel less responsibility to the people of, say, Bhopal than to the people who hold their stocks and bonds. This is neither good nor bad; it is merely a fact."[18]

We would do well to be skeptical of such laments of moral impotence. Corporations are, after all, made in the image and likeness of man; they are what we make them to be. They exist or perish at the sufferance of broader social interests. Corporations, like governments, are human institutions; that is sufficient cause to judge them on the basis of morality.

As a result of incidents like those at Bhopal, we loudly cry out for greater governmental regulation. The prosecutorial attempts against

Lester Crown of General Dynamics also offer us some hope for changes in the conduct of corporate officers and powerbrokers. Whether such attempts will succeed—or whether even they should succeed—remain to be seen, but I will propose yet another way.

Let us return to the metaphor struck a few paragraphs above, comparing corporations to repeat criminals or psychopathic individuals. We find a useful ambiguity here. Corporations are not persons, but they sometimes behave *like* persons. In some respects, the recalcitrant corporation acts much like a repeat criminal in bearing some measure of responsibility for its conduct; in other respects, the corporation behaves like a psychopathic individual, breaking the law much as a person does who is out of control.

This ambiguity has confused the issue in the minds of many theorists, some of whom argue too tightly the "repeat criminal" analogy, while others argue too closely to the "psychopath" analogy. But the confusion is really very easy to resolve. The analogies have been pushed too far. Recalcitrant corporations can be viewed either way, depending on which point of view better serves the public interest. The courts cannot find human beings both criminally insane and morally responsible for their actions, but corporations are not human beings and sometimes good reasons will be found for treating them as "out of control," and sometimes as morally responsible.

In what ways are corporations like repeat criminal offenders? For one thing, certain intentional constructs can be discerned in corporate behavior. These intentions are collectively emergent from the corporation's charter, its executive leadership and statement of goals. These serve as the corporation's "rationale" for (sometimes) engaging in illegal conduct. To the extent that this rationale can be amended or changed, corporations can be said to be morally responsible for their actions.

In what ways are corporations like psychopathic individuals? This is a little more complicated. Psychopathic behavior in individuals is characterized as "spasmodic anti-social behavior," according to Brendan A. Maher in *Principles of Psychopathology: An Experimental Approach*. Many bases of comparison can be found between the psychopathic personality and the incorrigible corporation. Recall our discussion about the ineffectuality of fines levied against corporations (especially in the case of Hooker Chemical and Plastics Corporation), and contrast this with the following comment from Maher: "... in spite of frequent punishments for impulsive antisocial activity, the psychopath appears not to learn anything from his own experience."[19]

Maher describes several traits as characteristic of the psychopathic individual:

... we should notice that the positive attributes, such as antisocial behavior, emotional shallowness, and vanity, are accompanied by certain negative attributes. Notable among these are the absence of overt anxiety and the absence of guilt. Also, the psychopath's behavioral insensitivity to punishment requires explanation in any satisfactory account of the determinates of this pathological pattern.[20]

Recalling our cautions about metaphors, we must not be too strongly taken up by the analogies drawn here. For example, no relevant comparison comes to mind about the psychopath's trait of vanity and the makeup of the modern corporation. Yet, when Warren Anderson backs off from claims of moral responsibility by Union Carbide for the Bhopal accident, one is tempted to draw a comparison between this and the psychopath's absence of guilt. The environmental record of Hooker Chemical aptly exemplifies the psychopath's insensitivity to punishment. The analogy suggested here is straightforward enough: the incorrigible corporation is to the law-abiding corporation in the way that the criminal psychopath is to the moral person. If we sometimes find comparing the average corporation to a moral person a useful, if sometimes misleading, analogy, then the comparison between the recalcitrant corporation and the psychopathic individual may also serve us here. The question, "What is the *nature* of the corporation," is misdirected when discussing moral corporate conduct.... We should be asking instead, "How should we *treat* corporations?" The answer here is obvious enough. We treat them as constructs set up to serve the public good. Now we can carry the insight one step further. When the corporation obstructs rather than advances the public good, when the corporation acts more like a criminal psychopath than as a model citizen, the offender ought to be confined in the interests of public safety. Unfortunately, a corporation is not sufficiently like a human being to allow for conventional methods of confinement; we are left to the devices of fines and regulations—the very devices we had assumed at the outset to have been ineffective when used against the recalcitrant corporation. Stronger measures are apparently called for.

In so suggesting, however, we return to the familiar problem of the effects any disruption of the corporation may have on its workers, its neighboring community, or the consumer deprived of its goods or services. However, now that we're clear about the role of the analogy in clarifying our thinking and in offering creative options, we see there is really no need to cling to our analogy too tightly. What we may propose for corporations which engage in repeated, calculated moral and legal wrongdoing is a sentence of "corporate corporal punishment." Therefore, we can propose something analogous to a "beheading."

The decision-making apparatus of most large corporations is a complicated and involved construction, including not only the President and the Chairman of the Board, but also the Board of Directors itself, the legions of Vice-Presidents and other important Corporate Executive Offiers, and stockholders who carry large holdings in the corporation. At least on paper, this is correct (actual practice may vary). Yet, we may well agree that each of them ought to have a voice in the conduct of the corporation. When they do not exercise that prerogative, and the corporation engages in wrongdoing, then they are remiss in their duties to the corporation and to the public at large. This proposal will insure that they do not commit such sins of omission in the future.

The proposal sketched here remains, above all, a proposal. I offer it in the spirit of further discussion. As such, I do not offer detailed guidelines for how such a corporate "beheading" should take place (though I will make some general suggestions). I do not consider in any depth the sorts of legal obstacles that stand in the way. I do however assert that sufficient justification exists for implementing a proposal of this general sort.

How might this punishment be meted out? We may suggest a complete reorganization of the decision-making organization, including the Company President, the Chairman of the Board, the Board of Directors itself, and every executive officer at or above the level of Vice-President. We can further recommend the dissolution of shareholders' stock for all shareholders who possess 1% or more of the outstanding stock of the corporation. The figure as it is presented here is arbitrary, but the idea is to minimize the effects of this decision on the smallest shareholders, who presumably have little or no voice in the corporation's conduct (unlike the case of Lester Crown, who holds a sizable portion of General Dynamics stock). The confiscated stocks will then be turned over to the company's employees in equal shares, provided (say) that the employee has been working for this company for six months or more.

Clearly, this proposal calls for drastic action. We can conceive of the idea as a last resort measure, to be taken when all other reasonable recourse has been exhausted. The point is, however, that the usual sorts of judicial sanctions, while they work well enough against most corporations, completely fail to modify the behavior of those corporations we compared to repeat criminal offenders or psychopathic individuals. The sanctions proposed here are directed at an aberrant minority of corporations. However, when appropriate, these penalties should not be invoked lightly. Therefore, several conditions must be prevalent for this recommendation to take effect. First, the transgressions a corporation commits must be sufficiently grievous, involving loss of life or extreme environmental damage. There must be some correlation to criminal justice's concept of a capital offense. Second, the implementation of this proposal should not apply to first-time offenders. Our main goal is behavior modification, and the conventional sanctions (fines and regulations) may be sufficient to accomplish that job with regard to most corporate legal transgressions. However, we may think of "corporate corporal punishment" as another instrument the court can draw out of its judicial toolbox when the corporation has repeatedly shown disdain for the law, and little likelihood exists for its rehabilitation.

One advantage to this proposal is that it provides relief to the innocent. Closing down a company altogether is an unsavory proposition, but the "beheading" called for here has a surgical benefit: removing the head, while leaving the body unharmed. Workers have the opportunity, at least, to continue their employment without relocating. As a further benefit, communities that rely on the corporation's plants as their main industry will continue to hold on to their main industry. And consumers will continue to have access to the corporation's products and services, and to the pricing effects of its competitive impact such as it might be.

A further advantage to this proposal is that it can be seen as a way to advance what many regard as an economic ideal: corporate democracy. Corporate democracy or (as it is sometimes called) "economic democracy" is the organization of economic authority according to a Rousseauean interpretation of the social contract when applied to a business [Rousseau (1712-1778) was a French political philosopher who urged that individual sovereignty is given up to the state in order to achieve freedom, equality, and justice within society. This social contract between the individual and the state is valid only insofar as the state genuinely pursues these aims.].[21] It is a hypothetical contract between the company, workers and consumers. The Rousseauean interpretation demands an identification between the "rulers" and the "ruled"—in this instance, an identification of management with the workers.

Usually, in the West, economic democracy comes into play where no conflicts of private property rights stand in the way. For example, a company may shut down a plant which serves as the major industry in a community, giving the employees the dismal choice of relocation or unemployment. Economic democracy stands as a broadening of options, nullifying the apparent dilemma, and offering a chance for a community and its workers to buy the company from its parent and keep it in operation.

In much the same way, worker controlled factories offer a broadening of options where a corporation's transgressions of the law are grievous and repetitive. Furthermore, a precedent may be in the making for this sort of activity in the proposal made by New Orleans councilmen to "municipalize" their power company. I offer this discussion as an extension of, and a justification of, the New Orleans example. The New Orleans case also represents a possible response to the anticipated charge that the proposal is "socialistic" in its outlook. Like the councilmen of New Orleans, many of whom are elected, conservative Republicans, I share their answer that the proposal is not ideologically-tied; it is merely a practical response to an aggravated problem.[22]

One might object, however, that I have strayed from the terms of the original analogy. We compared the recalcitrant corporation to a psychopathic individual. But the courts do not execute psychopaths, they restrain them. Objectors may point out that I am engaging in a species of fallacious special pleading by appealing for unusual and inappropriate modes of punishment, or of begging the question because I sometimes compare such corporations to repeat criminals and sometimes as criminal psychopaths. However, I do not think these are serious objections.

My answer is that the objections fail to take cognizance of the role of the analogy. We do not need a point-by-point correspondence between the offending corporation and the psychopath or repeat offender. We need to know only that there is enough of a likeness between the two to warrant more drastic action to be taken than is conventionally applied: the offending corporation, like the criminal psychopath, represents a great danger to society; we have compassionate ways of restraining psychopaths, but no effective way of restraining the incorrigible corporation. The object in employing the analogy to criminal psychopaths is one of exploring creative options, not metaphysical analysis about the nature of the corporation. For the same reason, the objection of special pleading is also ill-conceived. The purpose of a thought-experiment is not critical discovery (and it is in this context that charges of special pleading carry the most weight), but creative exploration of options. I do grant, however, that my position has metaphysical import. I am bringing a nominalist outlook to bear on the problem, employing Occam's razor in the effort to avoid the proliferation of unnecessary entities. Corporations really *aren't* persons; they are only somewhat *like* persons when corrective action is called for.

This difference in outlook makes all the difference in the world. For example, with regard to human beings, I have strong, personal moral reservations about the use of capital punishment. I question the truth of its adherent's strongest claim in the defense of its use—viz., its supposed deterrent powers.[23] Moreover, I object to capital punishment on the grounds of moral compassion, and because of the "de-civilizing" effects I believe wide-spread executions have on the moral fabric of society at large. This might well surprise the reader, since I openly advocate something similar for the corporation when it grievously breaks the law. However, the object of my proposal is not deterrence so much as it is protection from the menace of "psychopathic" corporations. My proposal may sound overly harsh, but the corporation, I repeat, is *not* a person; it is a human artifact.

There is a sense in which I want to pattern my sentiments after a remark made by John Kenneth Galbraith to the effect that, where financial dealings are concerned, "nothing is being lost but someone else's money."[24] In this context, however, the remark proves to be a bit cavalier. The financial insanity of incorrigible corporations can cause terrible tragedies, as in the cases of Bhopal and Love Canal. Moreover, given the implementation of the proposal, not only is money being lost, but in many cases the careers of executives. The consolation I offer is small, but perhaps adequate: this measure is directed at no individual in the corporation; it is directed against the chartered corporation itself—a corporation which sometimes enjoys rights and other protections, and must accordingly conduct itself in a socially responsible manner. The liability of individual executives in the corporation may be limited, but we discern enough responsibility on their parts to be liable to at least this extent.

No stigma need attach to any executive who is displaced under the terms of this proposal, but its implementation is only the other side of the coin from when an executive comes to benefit (whether through her efforts or not) from those conditions under which a corporation becomes prosperous. I expect, moreover, that most executives who are disenfranchised by the implementation of this proposal will find niches in other companies. In any case, the (usually temporary) setback in their careers is justly proportionate to the advantages they enjoyed by corporate veils of liability and equal to their responsibility for their sin of omission, their failure to speak for the record in protest.

Notes

1. *Dartmouth College v. Woodward,* 4 Wheat 518.636 (1819).
2. See, for example, Milton Friedman's discussion of "The Social Responsibility of Business," in *The New York Times Magazine,* September 13, 1970 reprinted in Hoffman and Moore, *Business Ethics: Readings and Cases in Corporate Morality* (McGraw-Hill, New York: 1984, pp. 126–131).
3. In what may be the definitive history of the origins of business enterprise in England, Ephraim Lipson devotes a lengthy discussion to the struggle between the towns and the Church to gain separate legal jurisdiction. Lipson writes:
   There appear to be no indications that English towns ever formed confederacies for their mutual support after the manner of continental towns, but there are signs of sporadic co-operation. We also get occasional glimpses of the process by which their efforts to achieve emancipation forced the townsmen to recognize the need for corporate action. The men of Bury St. Edmunds assessed themselves for a sum of money to maintain their contest with the abbey, and we may infer that in other towns a growing sense of corporate consciousness was fostered by the pressure of like circumstances. Ephraim Lipson, *The Economic History of England,* "The Middle Ages," Vol. 1 (Barnes and Noble, New York) 12th Ed., 1962, p. 208.
4. "Corporation, Business," *The Encyclopedia Britannica,* Vol. 5, pp. 182–189.
5. Thomas Donaldson, *Corporations and Morality* (Prentice-Hall, Englewood Cliffs, NJ) 1982, p. 3.
6. *First National Bank of Boston v. Bellotti,* 435 U.S. 765, April 26, 1978; reprinted in Hoffman and Moore, *op. cit.,* pp. 215–221.
7. Monroe Beardsley, *Thinking Straight* (Prentice-Hall, Englewood Cliffs, NJ) 4th Ed., 1975, p. 113.
8. Ibid., p. 112.
9. Ibid., p. 165.
10. Donaldson, *op. cit.,* p. 18. See also Justice Rehnquist's dissent in *First National Bank of Boston v. Bellotti,*

where he also makes use of the metaphor of "invisible persons" in a "deductively binding" use of the metaphor. (Reprinted in Hoffman and Moore, *op. cit.*, pp. 220–221).

11. Gary Whitney, "Case Study—Hooker Chemical and Plastics," reprinted in Thomas Donaldson, *Cases Studies in Business Ethics* (Prentice-Hall, Englewood Cliffs, NJ) 1984, pp. 66–70. See also "Hooker Chemical and Love Canal" in Tom L. Beauchamp, *Case Studies in Business, Society, and Ethics*, (Prentice-Hall, Englewood Cliffs, NJ) 1983, pp. 107–115.

12. Donaldson, *op. cit., Corporations and Morality*, p. 11.

13. A timely example of the need for more stringent powers of enforcement against corporate wrongdoing may be seen in the aftermath of the Exxon Valdez accident of March, 1989. Regarding Exxon's irresponsibility in the matter, *The Los Angeles Times* editorialized: "The Exxon Valdez spill has demonstrated that Americans cannot rely on the good will of corporations to clean up their own messes adequately, although there are companies that value their public image so highly that they will do the right thing. The Alaskan tragedy makes the case for strong federal regulations and controls closely monitored and strongly enforced. There must be stiff penalties for failure to comply." "The Risks of Underregulation," *The Los Angeles Times*, May 6, 1989.

14. *Business Week,* No. 2925, December 16, 1985, p. 28; See also: "Lester Crown Blames the System; General Dynamics' Biggest Shareholder Steps Forward to Defend His Troubled Company and Its Departing Chief," *The New York Times,* June 16, 1985, Sec. 3.

15. Neil Glixon, "Uncollared Crime; The Riddle of Guiltlessness," *Commonweal*, November 29, 1985, p. 662.

16. Ibid.

17. "The Talk of the Town," *The New Yorker,* January 13, 1986, p. 18.

18. Ibid., p. 18.

19. Brendan A. Maher, *Principles of Psychopathology: An Experimental Approach,* (McGraw-Hill, New York) 1966, p. 213.

20. Ibid., p. 213.

21. For a survey article on this subject, see Drew Christie, "Recent Calls for Economic Democracy," in *Ethics,* Vol. 95, October, 1984, pp. 112–128.

22. "New Orleans Begins Plan Toward Utility Takeover," *The Wall Street Journal,* Western edition, January 30, 1985, p. 16.

23. For a representative discussion of the arguments for and against capital punishment, see Hugo A. Bedau, Ed., *The Death Penalty in America,* (Oxford University Press, Oxford) 3rd, Ed., 1982.

24. John Kenneth Galbraith, *The Great Crash 1929* (Houghton-Mifflin, Boston) 1979, p. xiv

John D. Bishop

The Moral Responsibility of Corporate Executives for Disasters

I. INTRODUCTION

When large corporations are criticized for causing disasters, the senior executives of those corporations usually protest their personal in-

From John D. Bishop, "The Moral Responsibility of Corporate Executives for Disaster," *Journal of Business Ethics*, Vol. 10, 1991. Reprinted by permission of Kluwer Academic Publishers.

nocence, and deny that they should bear any moral responsibility for the tragedy. They often protest that they were not given information which could have warned them of impending problems even though they made honest efforts to obtain such information. Subsequent investigations have sometimes revealed that others in the corporation (often engineers) knew of safety problems, but that this information failed to reach decision making executives. Examples of this phenomenon include the cargo door problem on the DC-10, and the explosion of the Challenger—both tragedies involving loss of life.

This denial of moral responsibility intuitively conflicts with the high remuneration that CEOs and other executives receive in return for being responsible for corporations. In particular, it conflicts with the bonus remuneration which they receive if the corporation performs well. If they benefit when the corporation flourishes, should they not accept responsibility when things go horribly wrong?

The denial also conflicts with the current trend in our society of holding senior executives more socially responsible (Brooks, 1989). To note a single example, a U.S. District Judge recently insisted that the CEO of Pennwalt Corp. should personally attend his court to enter a guilty plea on a toxic spill charge. Note that the judge was not making a legal point, (corporate lawyers could have just as easily entered the plea), but a point about social responsibility (Globe and Mail, 1989).

This paper will analyse to what extent we can or should hold executives morally responsible for disasters. In particular, it will examine the case in which knowledge indicating impending problems is available to someone in the corporation, but has failed to reach decision making executives.

To help clarify the issues that the rest of the paper will deal with, the next section will eliminate some cases in which executives clearly are not responsible. Section III will elaborate on the reasons executives give for denying responsibility; in particular this paper concentrates on the case in which executives claim that they did not have and could not be expected to have had information vital to preventing the disaster. The reasons why apparently powerful executives cannot get information from their own corporation needs to be examined carefully (Section IV) before moving on in the final two sections to analysing to what extent we are justified in holding executives morally responsible.

It perhaps should be made clear at the outset that moral responsibility, or the lack of it, does not have direct implications for legal liability. The legal aspects of this problem are complicated, especially when the tragedy is in one country, and the corporate head office is in another. Legal issues are not dealt with in this paper.

II. LIMITS ON EXECUTIVE RESPONSIBLITY

It is commonplace in discussing morality that people should not be held responsible for events over which they have no influence or control. In this section, several types of events over which executives have no influence are eliminated from discussion. Executives cannot be held responsible for acts of God, nor, in their role as executives, for actions which are not performed on behalf of the corporation. Events not excluded in this section are not necessarily the moral responsibility of executives, but they are the actions which will be the basis of discussion in the rest of this article.

It can be accepted that executives are not responsible for obvious "acts of God". This does not mean that they should not be held accountable for the results of a natural event, for they may well be in a position to determine the outcome even when the event itself is inevitable. For example, suppose an earthquake causes a factory to collapse, killing several workers. Obviously, we cannot hold the executives of the company which owns the factory responsible for the earthquake itself; earthquakes are natural events which are beyond human control. However, we might hold the executives responsible for the factory being built in an earthquake zone, or we might hold them responsible for the use of money saving construction methods which caused the building to collapse. In these cases, we would consider the executives at least partly responsible for the workers' deaths. The fact that a person has no influence or control over an event does not necessarily exempt him or her from responsibility for the consequences of that event. What we hold him or her responsible for are the actions which determined those consequences.

Corporate executives, in their role as executives, should also not be held responsible for events which are not the result of the corporation's activities. The concepts of the "executive's role" and of the "corporation's activities" both need explaining.

Executives, because they are people, have more responsibilities, as citizens, neighbours, parents. Such responsibilities, while not being denied, will not be discussed in this paper. The purpose of this present discussion is limited to the moral responsibility of executives in their role as executives. However, this should not be taken to mean that the moral principles that apply to persons acting in the role of executives are any different from those that apply in the rest of their lives. Although it is sometimes argued that the morality of professional activities differs from the morality of everyday life (Carr 1968), that is a position which cannot be applied to executives without the most careful examination (Callahan, 1988-A; Gillespie, 1983; Nagel, 1978). I will not go into this debate here; since this paper does not discuss the actual moral duties of executives as executives, we need not discuss how they differ from their other duties.

The notion of "corporate activities" also needs expanding. It has been argued that corporations are moral entities in their own right, and that corporations can commit actions (French, 1977). This is a position which I reject for the sorts of reasons outlined in Danley (1980). However, in this paper I will avoid further discussion of this issue because it is not relevant to the current topic. Even if corporations are moral agents and as such are held responsible for corporate activities, this does not exempt the people in the corporation from also being held responsible for their role in those activities. Moral responsibility is not a fixed quantity; its assignment to one moral entity does not necessarily reduce the responsibility of other moral agents. Thus corporate executives can be held morally accountable to the same events for which the corporation is also accountable, though not necessarily to the same degree or for the same reasons. Because of this, I do not have to decide on corporate moral responsibility to discuss the issue of the responsibility executives [have] for their role in corporate actions.

"Corporate activities" can also refer to the actions of the corporation's employees which are done in their capacity as employees. Presumably, executives are in a position to influence such actions on the part of employees, and it is their responsibility for such actions that the rest of this paper will be concerned with. Executives may, for social reasons, be in a position to influence employee behaviour off the job, but the use of such influence does not concern us here. We will confine our examination to events which result from the actions of employees while on the job. To hold the executives responsible for such events (if we decide to do so) is to

hold them responsible for the actions of others, but it is assumed that executives have some influence or control over the actions of employees. The question we need to discuss is to what extent the executive has such influence and control, and whether it extends only to actions the executive directly instigates, or to all actions and omissions of employees as employees.

Even though we will confine the discussion to executive responsibility for actions employees commit in their capacity as employees, for convenience sake such employee actions will sometimes be referred to as the actions of the corporation. This should not be taken to imply that corporations can actually commit actions; the phrase is used as shorthand. Similarly, by employee actions, we mean only those committed as employees.

III. WHY EXECUTIVES MAY NOT BE MORALLY RESPONSIBLE

When things go horribly wrong, executives sometimes deny responsibility on the grounds that they did not know, and could not be expected to know, the information they needed to prevent the disaster. They maintain this even when some of the corporation's employees knew, or ought to have known, the relevant information.

Consider the case of DC-10 Ship 29, which crashed near Paris on March 3, 1974 when its cargo doors flew off. All 346 people aboard were killed. Subsequent investigations revealed that McDonnell-Douglas, the manufacturer of the aircraft, was aware of the cargo door problem, and that Ship 29 had been returned to the corporation for FAA ordered corrections to the door locking mechanism (French, 1984; Eddy *et al.*, 1976). These corrections were never made, though stamped inspection sheets indicated they had been. John Brizendine, President of the Douglas division of McDonnell-Douglas, denied all knowledge of this failure to fix the doors (French, 1982), though it is clear that at least some people in the company must have known. Since there is no reason to question Brizendine's honesty, we will assume that the information that could have prevented the disaster failed to reach him. (We will also assume that he would have acted on the information if he had received it).

As a second example, consider the explosion of the Challenger space shuttle, again with loss of life. Engineers at Morton Thiokol, which manufactured the solid rocket booster, had repeatedly expressed concerns, in written memos and verbally, about possible failure of O-ring seals on cold weather launches (Grossman, 1988). These concerns failed to reach decision making management at NASA, who maintain that they would have stopped the launch had they been aware of the engineers' opinion (Callahan, 1988-B). Again, vital information that could have prevented disaster failed to reach executives responsible for the final decision.

I do not want to raise the issue of the honesty of the executives when they claim they did not know. It has transpired in some cases that executives knew more than they were willing to admit—such was the case in the Dalkon shield tragedy (Mintz, 1985), or the knowledge of tobacco executives about early cancer studies (White, 1988). However, it is clear that executives often do not know, and are not told even if others in the corporation have the information. The immorality of lying, and of being able to stop a disaster and not doing so, are beyond doubt; the responsibility (if any) of executives when they actually are not told is more problematic, and is the central topic of this paper. It will be assumed that in the cases cited (the DC-10 cargo door problem and the Challenger disaster), executives were in fact in the dark about impending problems.

IV. Negative Information Blockage

Can executives be taken seriously when they claim that they cannot be expected to know about impending tragedy? After all, they have the authority to demand that information be given to them. And it is their job to know what is going on in their corporation. If someone in the company has or can get the information (which is the most interesting case), then why cannot the executives simply send a memo to all employees saying such information is to be sent

directly to their attention? This question needs to be examined carefully if we are to determine whether executives are responsible when disaster strikes, or whether we should accept the claim that they did not know and could not have known the information needed to prevent the tragedy.

The problem with getting information to executives is a well-known phenomenon in corporate and other hierarchical organizations which I will call "negative information blockage." In brief, information regarding the riskiness of a corporation's plans is stifled at source or by intervening management, even when senior executives have demanded that such information be sent on to them. This phenomenon needs to be analysed further.

The notion of negative information requires the distinction between a corporation's objectives and its constraints. The objectives (or goals—I will use the two words interchangeably) of a corporation are what its senior executives are perceived as wanting to achieve. These objectives are, of course, the executive's, but it is convenient to refer to them as the corporation's. These goals may or may not be what the executives think they want to achieve, or what they say they want to achieve; corporate mission statements may not be honest or may not be believed. The actual goals of the executives (or the corporation) can only be identified by examining what sorts of behaviour the executives reward, as will be discussed below.

The constraints on a corporation are those facts which affect the pursuit of its goals, and which cannot be changed, at least in the short run. Some constraints are physical, and cannot be violated by anyone in the corporation even if they wanted to. For example, the cabins on jet aircraft need to be pressurized—that need is a fact which no manufacturer can do anything about. Other constraints are moral, legal, or mandated by safety. These constraints can be ignored by a corporation or its employees, and it is these sorts of constraints which interest us.

Objectives and constraints are very different concepts, though sometimes constraints are recognized in statements of a company's objectives. For example, the objective of an aircraft manufacturing corporation might be stated as: "To produce aircraft which can be safely operated." Here safety, which is a constraint, looks like it is part of the objective, but this appearance does not stand up to analysis. The objective is to produce operable aircraft; safety is actually a constraint on that goal because airplanes cannot be operated if they fall out of the sky. Safety is not a separate or secondary goal, but a condition of achieving the actual goal of making operable aircraft.

Within a corporation, goals and constraints are treated very differently. Rewards are given for employee behaviour which appears to help the company achieve its goals. Observing legal, moral, and safety constraints is seldom rewarded; it tends to be assumed that employees will observe such constraints without reward. Instead, employees in companies which enforce constraints are usually punished when violation of the constraint is discovered; they are not usually rewarded just for observing constraints. Complete failure of a corporation to enforce legal, moral or safety constraints raises obvious moral problems; this discussion will be centered on the more interesting case in which constraints are enforced by the corporation (i.e., by the executives), but ignored by some of the employees. Why they are ignored, even under the threat of punishment, has to do with the different ways in which executives encourage employees to pursue goals, and discourage them from violating constraints.

In general, employee behaviour which enhances corporate goals is rewarded, observing constraints is not. Hindering objectives is almost always punished. Constraints are constraints on the pursuit of the company's goals, and hence observing them can threaten an employee's rewards. In fact, observing constraints and asking one's management to do so as well may impede the company's goals to the point where the behaviour itself is punished. Surely this encourages violation of constraints.

There are other pressures on employees to put rewards for pursuing goals before the observance of constraints. Violation of constraints is only punished if one is caught; hence there is an element of gamble involved. The time factor also plays a major role; rewards are usually immediate, while discovery of violated constraints may be months or years away, by which time the employee has had his promotion and is safely elsewhere.

To complicate matters further, corporations are hierarchical. If an employee does resist temptation and observes constraints at the risk of losing rewards, his manager, or his manager's manager, may not. If getting a company to observe a constraint requires escalating concerns to the senior executive level (and this is the case we are concerned with in this article), then a single failure to resist temptation may block the concern from reaching the executives. This is the phenomenon of negative information blockage.

Since negative information blockage is inherent in the nature of goals, constraints, rewards and punishments, then to what extent can executives be held resonsible for getting information past the blockage? The next section will consider two possible views on this topic.

V. EXECUTIVE RESPONSIBILITY AND NEGATIVE INFORMATION BLOCKAGE

The first of the two views is that executives are responsible for doing whatever they can to prevent negative information blockage. They have a moral duty to structure the corporation to ensure that risks of disaster are discovered and made known to themselves (and then, of course, to act on the information). They have a moral responsibility to do as much as they can to prevent tragedy.

What exactly executives can do I will not discuss in detail; a few examples will suffice. They can offer rewards for information brought to them; they can keep an "open door" policy so junior employees can go around the blockages; they can set a personal example of concern for moral, legal, and safety constraints. These ideas are generally discussed in business ethics literature under the topic of whistleblowing, since whistleblowing is often the result of frustration with negative information blockage. (See, for example, Callahan, 1988-C). Without going into further detail on what executives can do, we can summarize the first view of corporate executive responsibility by suggesting they should do whatever is reasonably possible to prevent knowledge of potential disasters from being blocked before it reaches them.

The second view is that executives, especially CEOs, are responsible for preventing tragedy, excepting only those cases, such as acts of God, which were discussed above in Section II. This view is radically different from the first; just how different can be seen if we consider how executives would be judged in the event of a tragedy. On the first view, the impartial spectator making moral judgements would inquire what steps the executives had taken prior to the tragedy to make sure information on the impending disaster had been conveyed to them. And, of course, they would ask whether the executives had acted on anything they knew. On the second view, the impartial spectator would hold the executive morally responsible for the failure to acquire sufficient information to prevent the tragedy, regardless of whether or not steps had been taken to circumvent negative information blockage. This view is essentially holding that since the tragedy happened, the steps taken were obviously not sufficient, and hence the executives are morally culpable.

It should be noted that on the second view, we are holding executives morally responsible even though they did not know the disaster might happen, and even though they may have taken some steps to acquire the knowledge. We are holding them morally responsible for the result, not the effort. The first view holds them responsible only for the effort.

There are many cases in life where people are held responsible for results rather than effort: it is one of the painful lessons we learn as children. For example, on examinations, students, especially in such subjects on medicine and engineering, are quite rightly marked on results, not the amount of effort they put into studying. And executives themselves do not hesitate to hold employees responsible for getting results.

Demanding results on the job, not just effort, is acceptable because it is necessary. When an engineer designs a bridge, it is important to society that it does not collapse. It is important to society that doctors are competent, not just that they are doing their best. We are often justified in holding people responsible for doing their job well.

If people fail in their jobs, they may or may not be held legally liable depending on the circumstances, but in any case their careers suffer, and they may lose their jobs. The fact that they are held responsible is reflected in the impact on their professional standing when they succeed or fail. To distinguish this type of responsibility from legal and moral responsibility, I will refer to it as professional responsibility.

The case of professional responsibility that best parallels the situation of executives is that of cabinet ministers in a parliamentary system. When things go wrong in an area of ministerial responsibility, the minister is held accountable and is expected to resign. They are not supposed to argue that they tried, that they have not been negligent, or that they are not legally liable. Thus Lord Carrington resigned when Argentina invaded the Falklands; he did not stay on protesting that it was not his fault (though it probably was not). The questions we must now deal with are: should we apply professional responsibility to executives? And secondly, how does professional responsibility relate to moral responsibility?

VI. PROFESSIONAL RESPONSIBILITY

The concept of professional responsibility applies when the outcome of a professional activity is of great concern to a person or people other than the person doing the activity. It especially applies if the outcome is of concern over and above any contract the professional has with some other person, or if the outcome is of great concern to bystanders. Let me illustrate these points with an example.

When I buy a pair of shoes and find them faulty, I take them back to the shoe store and generally will be satisfied if I am given back my money. The responsibility is limited to reversing the contract. When I go to a doctor for an operation, I am not interested in hearing that he or she will refund me the cost of the operation if it goes wrong, especially if I die. We can say in this case that the doctor has a professional responsibility which goes beyond the "contract." It goes beyond because the consequences of failure go beyond the contract. Similarly, if an engineer designs a bridge that collapses, then refunding the money he or she received for the design hardly helps those who were on the bridge when it collapsed. It helps so little that that course of action is seldom pursued. The engineer, in this case, has a professional responsibility.

Liability laws generally reflect the fact that responsibility can extend far beyond reversing the original contract, but this discussion is not an attempt to define legal liability. The point is that professional responsibility arises when the consequences of failure have effects on other people (customers or bystanders) which exceed the confines of the initial contract.

Clearly, this applies to executives. If they fail to create a corporate culture which overcomes negative information blockage and disaster results, it often involves the death of their customers (or of their customers' customers, as in the case of the DC-10s). It is clear that we are justified in holding executives professionally responsible when tragedy happens. In other words, we hold them professionally responsible for failing to obtain the information needed to prevent the disaster, whether or not they tried to.

But is holding executives professionally responsible different from holding them morally responsible? In the cases we have been examining, there is a close connection between the two.

Executives and everyone else have a moral responsibility to ensure that their activities do not result in the deaths of others if that result can be prevented. Executives, therefore, have a moral responsibility to do their best to obtain the information needed to prevent disasters. They have a professional responsibility, as we have seen, not just to do their best, but to actually succeed in preventing avoidable disasters. The latter grows out of the former in the sense that executives have a professional responsibility to succeed in fulfilling their moral responsibilities. (Of course, they also have professional responsibilities with other origins as well). Thus, although normally a person only has a moral responsibility for trying to avoid immoral results, in this case (and in others) a person has a professional responsibility to succeed in fulfilling the underlying moral responsibility.

This conclusion has a major implication for judging executives; namely, when tragedy happens, we are justified in holding them responsible based on moral values. If they object that they did not have the information necessary to prevent the disaster and that they had made an honest effort to obtain that information, then we can accept that as individuals they have fulfilled their moral obligations. (We are assuming honesty). But as professional executives, they have failed to fulfil their professional obligation to carry out moral requirements. We are still justified in holding them responsible based on moral considerations.

References

1. Brooks, L. J.: 1989, "Corporate Ethical Performance: Trends, Forecasts, and Outlooks," *Journal of Business Ethics* 8, No. 1, pp. 31–8.
2. Callahan, J. C.: 1988-A, *Ethical Issues in Professional Life* (Oxford University Press, Oxford), pp. 49–50.
3. Callahan, J. C.: 1988-B, *Ethical Issues in Professional Life* (Oxford University Press, Oxford), p. 342.
4. Callahan, J. C.: 1988-C, *Ethical Issues in Professional Life* (Oxford University Press, Oxford), pp. 337–39.
5. Carr, A. Z.: 1968, "Is Business Bluffing Ethical?," *Ethical Issues in Professional Life*, C. Callahan, ed. (Oxford University Press, Oxford), pp. 69–72.
6. Danley, J. R.: 1980, "Corporate Moral Agency: the case for Anthropological Bigotry," *Ethical Issues in Professional Life*, J. C. Callahan, ed. (Oxford University Press, Oxford), pp. 269–74.
7. French, Peter A.: 1977, "Corporate Moral Agency," *Ethical Issues in Professional Life*, J. C. Callahan, ed. (Oxford University Press, Oxford), pp. 265–69.
8. Gillespie, Norman Chase: 1983, "The Business of Ethics," *Ethical Issues in Professional Life*, J. C. Callahan, ed. (Oxford University Press, Oxford), pp. 72–6.
9. Globe and Mail: 1989, "Polluting firm's chairman hauled into court by U.S. judge," Associated Press, Globe and Mail, August 10 1989, p. B10.
10. Grosman, Brian A.: 1988, *Corporate Loyalty: A Trust Betrayed* (Penguin Books, Markham Ont.), pp. 177–79.
11. Mintz, Morton: 1985, *At Any Cost: Corporate Greed, Women, and the Dalkon Shield* (Random House, Inc., New York).
12. Nagel, Thomas: 1978, "Ruthlessness in Public Life," *Ethical Issues in Professional Life*, J. C. Callahan, ed. (Oxford University Press, Oxford), pp. 76–83.
13. White, Larry C.: 1988, *Merchants of Death: The American Tobacco Industry* (Beech Tree/Morrow, New York).

Robert Larmer

Corporate Executives, Disasters, and Moral Responsibility

In a recent paper, John Bishop has explored the question of whether corporate executives can be held morally responsible for disasters.[1] His thesis is that they cannot be held responsible for acts of God, i.e. events which are beyond human control and could not reasonably be foreseen, and actions which are not performed on behalf of the corporation. They can be held responsible, however, both in instances in which they possessed the information needed to prevent the disaster, and in instances in which, although it was not personally available, the necessary information was possessed by company personnel.

Bishop's claim that corporate executives should not be held accountable for "acts of God," nor for actions which are not performed on behalf of the corporation seems uncontroversial, as does his claim that they should be held accountable in cases where they possessed the information needed to prevent the disaster but failed on act on it. What is controversial is his claim that corporate executives can be held accountable in instances where, although they did not personally possess the information needed to avert disaster, such information was in company hands. It is to this latter claim that he devotes the bulk of his attention and upon which he focuses his argument.

Prima facie, the view that corporate executives can be held accountable for disasters, even in the absence of the information needed to prevent them, seems to run counter to Kant's commonly accepted dictum that *ought* implies *can.* It seems to make no sense to hold individuals responsible for preventing events they could not anticipate or forestall.

It might be replied that we often hold individuals responsible for fulfilling tasks they are incapable of performing. Intoxicated drivers, for example, are held morally culpable for failing to drive safely, even though it is clear they are incapable of doing so. Such cases however, do not refute the claim that ought implies can, since the only reason we hold the drunk driver morally culpable is that although it is not within his power to drive safely once intoxicated, it was within his power not to become intoxicated in the first place. The possibility is suggested that at least in some instances, we may legitimately hold corporate executives responsible for disasters they lacked the information to prevent, if the corporate executive was in a position to acquire the relevant information and could reasonably be expected to have done so.

I think this latter argument has merit and that it refutes the facile claim that a corporate executive's ignorance of the information needed to prevent a disaster is never morally culpable. It will not, however, serve Bishop's purposes. He wants to hold that so long as the necessary information was possessed by anyone within the company, the corporate executives of that company can be held accountable for the disaster. He further argues that it is not always reasonable to think that corporate executives are, or could be, in a position to obtain such information. He notes in this regard that the phenomenon of "negative information blockage," the stifling at the source or by intervening management of information regarding the riskiness of a corporation's plans, is characteristic of even well-run companies. He thinks that this phenomenon is inherent in any system of business and occurs even when senior executives have demanded that such information be brought to their attention.[2]

How then, does it make any sense to hold that even in the absence of the information needed to prevent a disaster, a corporate executive is always and inevitably to be held accountable so long as the requisite information was possessed by someone within the company? It is one thing to claim that a corporate executive's ignorance is no excuse in instances where she could reasonably be expected to have such information; it is quite another to suggest that she be held accountable even in instances where she could not reasonably be expected to have obtained it.

Bishop's answer is that we must distinguish between moral and professional responsibility. He notes that there are many instances where we hold individuals accountable not simply for doing their best, but for the success or failure of their efforts. Thus a cabinet minister may feel compelled to resign when a policy fails, even though he may be innocent of any negligence or moral laxness.[3]

He maintains that the concept of professional responsibility is relevant "when the outcome of a professional activity is of great concern to a person or people other than the person doing the activity [and] it especially applies if the outcome is of concern over and above any contract the professional has with some other person, or if the outcome is of great concern to bystanders."[4] He cites the example of an engineer designing a bridge, suggesting that the engineer's responsibilities go far beyond refunding her fee if the bridge collapses.[5]

Under these criteria, he argues we are justified in holding corporate executives professionally responsible for failing to obtain the information necessary to prevent disasters. The question of whether or not they tried to obtain the necessary information is pertinent to the issue of whether they are morally culpable, but irrelevant to questions of professional responsibility. He concludes that, since corporate executives not only have a moral obligation to seek to avoid disasters but a professional obligation to be successful in avoiding disasters, we are justified in holding them responsible on moral considerations.[6]

The concept of professional responsibility is interesting and deserves further explanation. It will not, however, bear the weight of Bishop's argument. There are at least three reasons this is so.

First, if as Bishop insists, professional responsibility must be distinguished from both legal and moral responsibility,[7] it is difficult to see how invoking the notion of professional responsibility can support the conclusion that in cases where corporate executives are not morally cul-

pable for lacking the information necessary to prevent a disaster, we are nevertheless "justified in holding them responsible based on moral considerations."[8] How, if the corporate executive is not morally culpable, do moral considerations enter the picture?

His answer is that, although professional responsibility must be distinguished from moral responsibility, part of a corporate executive's professional responsibility is to fulfill certain moral requirements. He comments that

Executives . . . have a moral responsibility to ensure that their activities do not result in the deaths of others if that result can be prevented. . . . They have a professional . . . responsibility . . . not just to do their best, but to actually succeed in preventing avoidable disasters. The latter grows out of the former in the sense that executives have a professional responsibility to succeed in fulfilling their moral responsibilities.[9]

It may be agreed that one of a corporate executive's professional responsibilities is to fulfill certain moral obligations and that one of these is to do his best to avoid disasters. Let us suppose, however, that despite a corporate executive's best efforts, he is not successful in obtaining from company personnel information that could have prevented a disaster. On what grounds can we judge him as failing to fulfill his professional obligation? Certainly not on the grounds that he has failed to fulfill the moral requirements built into his professional responsibility, since all that morality requires is that he have done his best to avoid the tragedy.

Bishop insists that "although normally a person only has a moral responsibility for trying to avoid immoral results, . . . [in the case of a corporate executive] a person has a professional responsibility in fulfilling the underlying moral responsibility."[10] But what is required to fulfill this underlying moral responsibility? Bishop claims that it includes actually preventing avoidable disasters. The problem is that what is avoidable by one person in a certain set of circumstances may be unavoidable by another, or even the same, person in a different set of circumstances. A disaster which is avoidable if certain information is passed on to a corporate executive may be unavoidable if that information never reaches her. Whether or not that information ever reaches her is, in many instances, beyond her ability to control. Her moral responsibility is to make every reasonable effort to be in possession of the information needed to prevent disasters; it is not actually to possess information she cannot obtain. Any judgement that she has failed to meet her professional obligation in such instances is grounded not in the fact that she has failed to meet the requirements of morality, but in the insistence that executives be successful in what they undertake. It is a mistake, therefore, to claim that moral considerations can justify the claim that so long as the information needed to avert a disaster was possessed by someone within the company, we can always hold its corporate executives responsible.

I have argued that any decision to hold corporate executives responsible for obtaining information they could not reasonably have been expected to gather must be based not on moral considerations, but on purely non-moral aspects of professional responsibility. This brings us to a second problem in Bishop's argument. The issue is not whether as a matter of fact we hold corporate executives legally or professionally responsible in certain situations, but whether we are morally justified in doing so. Put a little differently, our interest is in whether present notions of legal and professional responsibility need to be altered to fit the requirements of morality. Bishop's claim that corporate executives should be held professionally responsible for disasters, even in cases where they could not reasonably be expected to acquire the information needed to prevent the disaster, is a normative claim not about how in fact professional responsibility is presently understood, but how it *should* be understood. The understanding of professional responsibility it advocates should only be accepted if we find it acceptable to hold individuals morally responsible for events which they could not anticipate and over which they had no control.

The problem, as Bishop notes early in his paper, is that we do not hold people responsible for events over which they have no influence or control. If there are instances in which individuals are held professionally responsible for events they could not reasonably be expected to have taken precautions against, this is an indication that we should reform our understanding of professional responsibility, not that we should abandon our basic moral intuitions.[11]

A third problem with Bishop's position is that, in the final analysis, the notion of professional responsibility is dependent upon the notion of moral responsibility. Initially, this does not seem the case: assignment of moral responsibility for a disaster can only occur if the individual was lax in taking efforts to avoid it; assignment of professional responsibility makes no such requirement. Things are not so simple, however. No one would want to hold corporate executives professionally responsible for disasters resulting from "acts of God," yet if professional responsibility does not require moral culpability why should such events be excluded? It seems clear that if no one could reasonably have been expected to have acquired the information necessary to have prevented a disaster we could never be justified in holding a corporate executive professionally responsible for its occurrence.

I suspect that what drives the notion of professional responsibility is that in complex situations it is very difficult to accurately judge degrees of moral culpability. Questions of whether all reasonable steps were taken to prevent a disaster and whose responsibility it was to take those various steps are notoriously hard to answer. Given the human tendency to pass the buck, it is useful to have a practical rule that in cases where it may possibly be doubted that he took all reasonable steps to prevent the disaster, a corporate executive be judged as failing in his professional duties, even though it is far from clear that he is actually morally culpable. Should it become clear, however, that he did take all reasonable steps to prevent the disaster and that he is in no way morally culpable, it also becomes clear that he cannot be held professionally responsible. It cannot be denied, therefore, that professional responsibility derives from moral responsibility and that any assignment of professional responsibility for a disaster implies that there is at least the possibility of ascribing moral culpability for its occurrence. Contrary to Bishop, questions of professional responsibility cannot be treated independently of questions of moral responsibility.

I have been attacking Bishop's view that corporate executives can be held accountable for disasters so long as the information necessary to prevent the disaster was possessed by company personnel on the basis that it does not do justice to the fact that in many instances it is unreasonable to expect a corporate executive to obtain such information. My own view is that although it is often difficult to say whether a corporate executive could have done better in seeking to obtain the information necessary to prevent a disaster, we cannot sever the notion of professional responsibility from the notion of what can reasonably be expected. It is no easy matter to say what can reasonably be expected in the way of acquiring such information, but unless we attempt to do so the notion of professional responsibility becomes morally monstrous.

Two practical comments are in order. First, if we should be cautious to blame corporate executives for disasters, we should also be cautious to attribute a company's success to them. The idea that a company's success should automatically be attributed to its corporate executives and that this justifies extremely high salaries and bonuses strikes me as no more defensible than the suggestion that they should automatically be blamed if disasters occur. It seems far more likely that both the attribution of blame and credit should be spread more evenly through the corporation.

Second, there is a moral obligation on the part of corporate executives to know their capabilities and limitations. Even if one is doing one's best, one may be acting immorally if one insists on acting in an area where one knows oneself to be less qualified or competent than the job requires. A corporate executive is morally required to assess both the impact of her decisions and her competency in making decisions. A humble heart and a desire to act only in areas one knows oneself effective scarcely guarantee the avoidance of disasters, but they are a good beginning.

Notes

1. John D. Bishop, "The Moral Responsibility of Corporate Executives for Disasters," *Journal of Business Ethics*, Vol. 10, 1991, pp. 377-83.
2. Ibid., pp. 380-81.
3. Ibid., pp. 381-82.
4. Ibid., p. 382.
5. Ibid., p. 382.
6. Ibid., p. 382.
7. Ibid., p. 381.
8. Ibid., p. 382.
9. Ibid., p. 382.
10. Ibid., p. 382.
11. Bishops slips very quickly from the observation that professional responsibility is often understood in a fashion that holds individuals accountable for events over which they had no control to the position that such a concept of professional responsibility is morally acceptable. The question of whether he has fallen victim to the naturalistic fallacy arises.

QUESTIONS

1. Ewin thinks that it is possible for corporations to possess rights and duties, but not virtues. Why?
2. What is Ewin's argument for rejecting the claim that corporations are logically tied into selfishness?
3. In your view, does Rafalko suggest that corporations have rights or only that we should, in certain circumstances, treat them as if they did? How would you defend your answer?
4. What are some of the difficulties you would foresee in attempting to implement Rafalko's proposal concerning "corporate corporal punishment"? Could such punishment be made fair?
5. On what basis does Bishop distinguish professional and moral responsibility?
6. Given that Bishop distinguishes professional and moral responsibility, does it make any sense to hold executives morally culpable in instances where they fail in their professional obligation to prevent disasters? Explain.
7. What does it mean to claim that "ought implies can"? Why does Larmer think that Bishop's claim runs counter to this principle?
8. Larmer suggests that questions of professional responsibility cannot be treated independently of questions of moral responsibility. What is his argument in support of this claim?

Case 13:1 How Safe a Gun?[1]

On June 19, 1983, the barrel of Robert Loitz's shotgun exploded during a trapshooting competition, injuring his left hand and thumb. Loitz subsequently brought suit against Remington, the manufacturer of his shotgun.

At issue was the safety of the Model 1100 12-gauge shotgun he had been using. This model, a semiautomatic gas-operated shotgun designed for hunting and target shooting, first marketed in 1963, had subsequent sales of over three million. The particular gun used by Loitz was purchased secondhand in 1972 and had presented no problems prior to the explosion. Loitz, as is common with experienced competitors, was using shells he had reloaded.

Loitz alleged that the explosion was a result of Remington using unsuitable steel for the shotgun barrel. An expert witness, Dr. David Levinson, a professor of metallurgy at the University of Illinois, testified that in his view, the gun barrel exploded in response to a normal-pressure shell as a result of metal fatigue. Levinson suggested that the high sulphur content of the steel used by Remington permits the formation of fatigue cracks that under repeated use may eventually cause the barrel to fail under normal pressure loads.

Remington alleged that the explosion was the result of an overloaded shell. Their expert witness, Dr. Richard Hertzberg, a professor of metallurgy at Lehigh University, testified that the explosion was probably the result of an overloaded shell. He based his view on his own tests of the strength of the steel used by Remington and on a comparison of Loitz's gun with guns that had been deliberately exploded by discharging overloaded shells. Hertzberg was not aware until trial that a Remington barrel had failed during proof-testing and was unable to explain why this could occur.

Testing of Loitz's unused reloaded shells revealed none that was overloaded. Evidence was also brought that by the time of Loitz's accident, Remington had received reports of 94 other barrel explosions of Model 1100 barrels resulting in injury. In five of these cases, the persons involved claimed to be using factory-made ammunition. Remington maintained that in all cases, the result of the explosion was an overloaded shell. In addition, evidence was brought that by 1979, Remington had received reports of over 100 barrel explosions not resulting in injury.

Case Study Questions

1. Did Loitz deserve to receive damages? Why or why not?
2. To what degree, if any, do you regard Remington as morally culpable in regard to Loitz's accident? How would you justify your answer?

Case 13:2 The Untrustworthy Encyclopedia[2]

Wilhelm Winter and Cynthia Zheng enjoyed eating mushrooms. Wishing to harvest some of the edible wild varieties, they bought *The Encyclopedia of Mushrooms*, a reference guide on the habitat, collection, and cooking of mushrooms. This book is the work of two British authors and was originally published by a British firm. An American publishing firm, G.P. Putnam's Sons, later purchased copies of the book from the British firm and distributed it in the United States. Putnam played no part in the writing or editing of the book.

Relying on the *Encyclopedia*'s descriptions to determine which varieties were safe to harvest, Winter and Zheng went mushroom hunting. Unfortunately, after cooking and eating the mushrooms they collected, they both became critically ill. They subsequently required liver transplants.

Alleging that the *Encyclopedia* contained erroneous and misleading information with regard to identifying some of the most deadly species of mushrooms, they brought suit against Putnam on the grounds of product liability, breach of warranty, negligence, negligent misrepresentation, and false representation.

With regard to product liability, they argued that although product liability is customarily held to extend only to tangible items, the *Encyclopedia* was analogous to aeronautical charts, which several jurisdictions have treated as "products" for the purposes of product liability. Their argument was that like aeronautical charts, the *Encyclopedia* represents natural features of the world and is intended to be used while engaged in hazardous activity.

With regard to breach of warranty, negligence, negligent misrepresentation, and false representation, they argued that Putnam either had a duty to investigate the accuracy of the books it publishes or a duty to investigate the accuracy of the books it publishes or a duty to warn the consumer that either the information in the book cannot be relied on, or that it has not investigated the text and cannot, therefore, guarantee its accuracy.

CASE STUDY QUESTIONS

1. The court has noted that computer software that fails to yield the result for which it was designed might be considered a "product" for the purposes of product liability. Might it be plausibly argued that the *Encyclopedia* is analogous to such software inasmuch as it, like the software, is designed, with proper use, to yield certain results?

2. Does a publisher have any moral, as opposed to legal, duty to try and ensure the accuracy of the works it publishes?

3. Should a publisher have a legal duty to ensure the accuracy of the books it publishes? What would be the implications of creating such a legal duty?

Notes

1. Based on Loitz v. Remington Arms Co., Inc. as found in 563 *North Eastern Reporter*, 2nd. series, 397 (Ill. 1990).
2. Based on Winter v. G.P. Putnam's Sons as found in 938 *Federal Reporter*, 2nd series, pp. 1033 (9th Cir. 1991).

FOR FURTHER READING

1. Angelo J. Corlett, "Corporate Responsibility and Punishment," *Public Affairs Quarterly*, Vol. 2, No. 1, January 1988, pp. 1–16.

2. Peter French, "The Corporation As A Moral Person," *American Philosophical Quarterly*, Vol. 3, 1979, pp. 207–215.

3. John Ladd, "Corporate Mythology and Individual Responsibility," *The International Journal of Applied Philosophy*, Vol. 2, Spring 1984, pp. 1–21.

4. David T. Risser, "Punishing Corporations: A Proposal," *Business & Professional Ethnics Journal*, Vol. 8, No. 3, 1988, pp. 83–91.

5. Jere Surber, "Individual and Corporate Responsibility," *Business & Professional Ethics Journal*, Vol. 2, No. 4, 1982, pp. 67–88.

Chapter Thirteen

RESPONSIBILITIES OF PROFESSIONALS

Introduction

Professionals such as doctors, engineers, law-yers, and academics enjoy a great deal of power and prestige in society. Because of their specialized knowledge and their ability to af-fect basic issues of human life, professionals are commonly perceived as subject to more rigorous standards of conduct than non-professionals. Although it is no easy matter to say how a profession should be defined, or precisely what distinguishes a profession from other occupations, we are accustomed to speak of "professional ethics," meaning some special set of rules or guidelines designed by which moral conduct is measured within a particular profession.

Without a doubt, the notion of a profes-sional ethic has played an important role in the development and self-understanding of the professions. It has, however, both a bright and dark side. At its best, a special set of rules or guidelines remind men and women of good will of their special responsibilities, and pro-vides a repository of accumulated wisdom of what constitutes ethical practice within their professions. At its worst, such rules or guide-lines may become a poor substitute for proper ethical motivation, or represent the attempt of an elite group to escape public accountability.

The selections in this chapter focus on the issue of what it means to be a professional and act ethically. Bruce Jennings' general discussion in "The Regulation of Virtue; Cross Currents in Professional Ethics" sets the stage for our consideration of specific issues in the medical and engineering professions.

Jennings examines three interrelated issues. The first concerns the dual emphasis that pro-fessional ethics must place on discerning both what is right and motivating right behavior. Although there are instances in professional life where it may be difficult to discern what is morally correct, there are many instances where the problem is not to understand what is right but rather to motivate individuals to do the right thing. The second issue Jennings addresses concerns the distinction between moral dilemmas inherent in the human condition and moral dilemmas created by institutional structures. The first type of moral dilemma is unavoidable, the second can often be avoided by altering institutional structure. An important part of professional ethics is to be open to the possibility of avoiding moral dilemmas by modifying the institutions within which professionals function. Jennings' third issue concerns whether an emphasis on rules and regulations, which is typical of professional codes of conduct, undermines the emphasis on character and virtue that lies at the heart of professional ethics. A question arising out of this third concern is whether professionals should regulate themselves or be subject to external regulation.

Judith P. Swazey, in her article "Are Physicians a 'Delinquent Community?: Issues in Professional Competence, Conduct and Self-Regulation," examines some of the concerns associated with the insistence of physicians that they be granted a large degree of autonomy and self-regulation. She notes that the treatment whistleblowers typically receive when they report cases of wrongdoing to fellow physicians renders suspect the view that self-regulation effectively guards morality. She suggests that the notion of self-regulation is typically concerned more with etiquette than ethics, and has come to characterize an autonomy that rejects moral accountability.

Stephen E. Lammers, in his "Commentary," suggests that a part of the problem pointed out by Swazey lies in the fact that connections between the profession and the larger society which it is supposed to serve tend to be cut rather than reinforced in the training of professionals. He argues that we must pose the question of "how do we build and sustain individuals who will be the appropriate sorts of people to have when persons will be forced to act to defend professional standards?" and that we cannot divorce questions of character from considerations of entrance into a profession.

In his article "Technical Decisions: Time to Rethink the Engineer's Responsibilities," Michael Davis argues that the common view that engineers typically work in a highly compartmentalized environment with little power to affect decisions made by management is false. He suggests that engineers generally exert a lot more influence than they commonly perceive and play a large role in non-compartmentalized decision-making procedures. He maintains that in developing a professional ethic for engineers, we should pay more attention to the role of the engineer as advocate and the ethical issues implicit in reaching moral decisions by consensus.

Bruce Jennings

The Regulation of Virtue: Cross-Currents in Professional Ethics

Professional ethics is based on an optimistic wager best made by a subdued heart. The wager is that something of important ethical substance can be learned about the conduct of the professions in modern society from an interdisciplinary dialogue and, beyond that, ultimately from an even more inclusive public dialogue. The discourse of professional ethics is most successful when it achieves a public dimension—when it addresses matters of genuine public concern in a way accessible to the public at large. It is less successful when it is limited to professionals talking to other professionals about the ethics of their colleagues, and least successful of all when limited to philosophers talking to other philosophers about the ethics of everybody else.

Now if the success of professional ethics rests upon its ability to cross boundaries, as it were, to be interdisciplinary and public, then it may be useful to step back and ask what must be the case in order for those boundaries to be crossed. What assumptions do we have to make in order for professional ethics to achieve "uptake" (as the ordinary language philosophers used to say)? What functions does discourse in professional ethics perform and what keeps it meaningful or communicative? What keeps it from misfiring? For misfire it can, and often does— when it is hived off into an academic ghetto called "applied ethics"; when it becomes an ideological *apologia* for professional domination and power, or when it is trivialized by an

From Bruce Jennings, "The Regulation of Virtue: Cross-Currents in Professional Ethics," *Journal of Business Ethics*, Vol. 10, No. 8, 1991. Reprinted by permission of Kluwer Academic Publishers.

excessive concern with legal and financial issues so that most of the human moral drama inherent in professional practice—the drama of trust, dependency, vulnerability, fallibility, uncertainty, tragic choices—is overlooked.

I contend that professional ethics can and should be a medium through which we come to explore and to appreciate that moral drama richly. It can and should provide a forum for a critical and historical assessment of the social roles and influences of the professions in relation to the technologies and specialized knowledge the professions produce and reproduce. It can offer ethical critique and guidance by evaluating professional conduct in light of well reasoned and justified principles and rules. Finally, professional ethics can be a kind of ongoing conversation and renegotiation of the social contract between the professions and society.

One objection arises immediately. To say that this is a possible vision for what the discourse of professional ethics should aspire to be is to say that something like a public philosophy is still possible in what we euphemistically call our "pluralistic" society. Yet how can a rich public philosophy prosper in our divided, fragmented, Babelesque world, where increasingly small units of cultural cohesion can only communicate with one another in a *lingue franca* [i.e., any language serving as a medium of communication between different people.] of interests and imperialistic rights-claims, and where, in order to avoid outright hostility, the most one can aspire to is an equilibrium of mutual avoidance, indifference, and the kind of toleration that signifies a desire not to be bothered oneself? The present dispensation does not seem propitious for the emergence of a professional ethics nurtured by a public philosophy.[1]

The question of how professional ethics is possible is closely related to the question of what professional ethics is for. How are we to think about what can reasonably be expected from professional ethics? What framework of concepts and categories can we use to articulate its goals and purposes? In what follows I shall try to get a purchase on these questions by reflecting on three interrelated issues that tacitly inform and color much work in professional ethics. The first of these issues has to do with the difference (if there is one) between understanding and motivation. The second issue concerns how we interpret what I will call the situation of moral agency in the professions, and in particular whether the dilemmas moral agents face are somehow inherent in moral agency itself or are artifacts of specific institutional structures. The third issue involves the ambiguity captured in my title: it is the paradox that professional ethics regulation—i.e., general, rule-governed attempts to deter ethical misconduct and to encourage right conduct—must rely on a kind of motivation that is undermined by the very existence of the regulations that motivation is necessary to sustain. Professional ethics has not yet come to grips with this paradox because it has not really come to grips with the implications of the notion of moral virtue. And the reasons for this, in turn, lead us back to the problem of professional ethics as civic discourse.

SEEING THE RIGHT AND WANTING TO DO RIGHT

Consider first the distinction between seeing the right versus motivating right conduct. What I have in mind is this. There are times in the moral life of professionals (and everybody else too) when it is absolutely clear what is right and what is wrong, and the problem is not knowing but acting; the problem is to get people to do what is right and to avoid doing what is wrong. At issue here is not really an ethical quandary or dilemma; the problem is more one of how to create the commitment to the right thing within the psyches and self-identities of moral agents.[2] And outwardly, how do we structure our institutions in such a way that on the whole people acting without a policeman looking over their shoulder will do the right thing rather than the wrong thing? For no conceivable institution, not even the worst Gulag, can possibly police everyone all the time.

Seeing the right, on the other hand, is a problem that arises in those situations in life where reasonable people of good will look at the same circumstances and facts, just don't know what is right and what is wrong. Reasonable people of good will can disagree about what the right thing to do is.

Both of these situations arise in professional practice. Professional ethics has to address the challenge of teaching professionals how to see the right, and it also has to figure out how to motivate right conduct. Many times professional ethics tends to err on the side of worrying excessively about motivating right conduct. This is scandal ethics; it is still probably the most publicly visible face of the discourse of professional ethics today. But one can go only so far with public ethical discourse in this mode. Talking about taking bribes is really not an interesting ethical question because there is no interesting argument in favor of taking bribes. There must be more to professional ethics than that.

At the same time, it is possible to be too idealistic and to forget about real world exigencies and demands. As students of professional ethics it is not open for us to say: "The only things I'm concerned about as an ethicist are the really interesting moral dilemmas of life. Don't bother me with the details about regulation and how to get people motivated. That's somebody else's problem; leave that to the educators or the psychologists or the lawyers or the bureaucrats. As an ethicist, as a philosopher, I am interested only in those moral dilemmas where we really have to agonize, balancing right versus right and figuring out how to choose the lesser of evils. My *metier* [i.e., trade or profession.] is illumination and enlightenment, not moral police work; my task is to win through to some clarity and resolution in precisely those situations that initially present themselves to us as deep quandaries."

A great deal of time teaching, writing, and talking about professional ethics is quite properly spent in grappling with hard cases of precisely this kind. But so much time is spent in trying to sort out what the values are, what the rights and wrongs are, that no time is given over to figuring out how to change the world, how to actually affect professional behavior or how to make things better for clients, patients, or fellow citizens.

So we can err on both sides: a scandal ethics that is philosophically banal, or an exquisite, almost sublime brand of ethics that is essentially irrelevant to the actually existing world of professional practice. In my estimation, professional ethics has not yet decided which side it wants to err on, nor has it discovered how to cover moral understanding and moral motivation equally well.

THE SITUATION OF MORAL AGENCY

A second important issue for professional ethics has to do with how we interpret the situation of the moral agent. What is the source of the moral dilemmas the agent faces, what is impinging on her range of moral choice, and what is the appropriate response to these dilemmas? Here it is useful to distinguish between what we might call "natural dilemmas" and "institutional dilemmas."

There are situations in the moral life where dilemmas flow just from the nature of things and from enduring features of what can only be called human nature. In any conceivable situation, in any conceivable institutional arrangement, human beings being what they are, they are bound to face certain kinds of moral choices and moral dilemmas. I simply cannot care for my ailing, elderly father and my six year old son in the same way, to the same degree, at the same time. In a completely just welfare state, neither my father in his nursing home nor my son in his day care center would be deprived of care and comfort. But it would be care and comfort from strangers, not from me, which is not the same, and the dilemma would remain.

On the other hand, we also face certain kinds of moral dilemmas that are just as clearly artifacts of a particular institutional arrangement. We face hard choices and tradeoffs figuring out how best to distribute burdens among people equitably because we are faced with artificial scarcity imposed by the nature of our institutions or the nature of regulations and laws. A physician working in an intensive care unit, for example, is in a situation where someone else has made a determination that there are going to be ten beds in that unit, not eleven or twelve,

and not fifteen. If you have eleven or twelve patients in need of those beds, you face a rationing or a triage ethical dilemma. But it is not inherent in the nature of things; it is an artifact of the health care system at a given time.

The distinction between natural dilemmas and institutional dilemmas has an important bearing on how we interpret what a moral agent is up against and what the appropriate response on her part would be. Professional practice is clearly embedded in a particular institutional and historical context. It is mostly contingent in the sense that the available resources, and even the very way the professionals view their reality and the choices they face, are best comprehended in relation to cultural and institutional patterns that are subject to deliberate, purposive change. For a professional as a moral agent to bow to the givens of the situation by appeal to these contingent conditions of his practice strikes us as an unduly accommodationist stance at best, or a kind of willful moral blindness at worst; and in any case as an exceedingly weak ethical justification for his conduct. Moral agents must not be too quick to interpret the situation of their moral agency as one in which it is necessary to embrace a tragic choice, or to settle for the lesser of two evils. Sometimes the proper response is to reject the limits and the choice, to reconstrue the situation of agency such that the givens are challenged and overthrown, not accepted. There are times when a solution to professional misconduct or ethical problems in professional life requires institutional change; at other times it requires some effort to change the people or attitudes that produce the (false) dilemma or tragic choice. Construing the situation of moral agency in this way does not put an end to moral problems and difficulties, to be sure. Very difficult matters of judgment and prudence remain, as do basic moral principles that should govern the means employed to bring about the morally requisite social change. But embracing these difficulties is surely preferable to the failure of moral nerve one commits when one accepts the intolerable as a given and tries to make the most of it.

The opposite error is somewhat harder to specify, but is just as morally problematic in its own way. It is characterized by a kind of moral hubris, [i.e., pride] an unwillingness or an inability to see the limits and the tragic side to human life. Such a temperament is all too quick to sacrifice the interests of others in a vain quest for some kind of perfection in the human character or institutions that is not to be had. When professionals, in particular, are entrusted with the lives, resources, and interests of others, this kind of moral cowboy mentality is particularly reprehensible. We do not admire the crusading attorney who jeopardizes his client's freedom or assets in order to obtain a ruling that would be an important precedent, unless the client freely and knowledgeably consents to that legal strategy. Nor do we condone a physician who places a patient at greater risk than a standard therapy would in order to advance medical science, unless the benefit to the patient is proportionately great and the patient has given informed consent. In other words, there is something in the kind of moral agents that professionals are called to be, and something in the moral situation of professional practice that weighs heavily in favor of moral humility and even conservatism.

BEYOND REGULATORY ETHICS

The paradox of the regulation of virtue lies at the heart of professional ethics. The paradox is that effective ethics regulation (that which deters improper conduct and encourages good conduct) may have to presuppose an underlying cultural ethos that cannot subsist in the face of regulation.[3] The notion of the regulation of virtue also suggests a kind of ambivalence that runs through much work in professional ethics these days, because both regulation and virtue are desirable things to promote, and professional ethics is unwilling or unable to do without either one.

It is not easy to have it both ways, however. Regulation talk and virtue talk inhabit two different universes of discourse, two different language games, two different ways of seeing the world and the moral life. Regulation talk has mostly behind it a model of rational self-interest on the part of actors. Regulation involves creating a structure of incentives or disincentives that will impact on the interests of individuals

and will channel their behavior in one direction or another in accordance with some rational calculus that we presume agents do undertake. That is the essence of the notion, at least the modern notion, of regulation. The idea is that if you appeal to rational self-interest you can structure incentives in a way that will get people to orient their behavior in good ways rather than bad ways, in ways that serve the common welfare rather than in ways that are destructive and simply self-serving. Private vices, public virtues, as Mandeville put it.[4]

Now within this universe of discourse of regulation talk, there is a lowbrow version and a highbrow version. The lowbrow version of regulation talk is what you usually hear from economists; it is the straightforward kind of rational choice theory which many would say has very little to do with ethics at all. (This seems to me to be wrong because the entire tradition of utilitarianism is built along the same kind of theoretical and psychological lines.) But in any event, it is lowbrow in the sense that it does not require any highfalutin moral principles or motivation. As a planner or a regulator, you've got good old-fashioned self-interest and you use it; it's your tool, it's your raw material, it is the key to social control, the structuring of social order, and the achievement of good ends.

Highbrow regulation talk, by contrast, involves much of what we see today in the field of ethics and moral philosophy, particularly in its non-utilitarian variants—rights theory, neo-Kantianism, and deontological theory. John Rawls is probably the leading contemporary example of the perspective I have in mind. Highbrow regulation is regulation of and by moral principles. The goal is to use internalized moral commitments, what Rawls calls the sense of justice, much as the lowbrow regulators would use legal and economic incentives. The idea here is that human behavior is shaped by dint of the moral commitments moral agents make. If you internalize a commitment to justice, you will act as a just individual. And the principle is thereby made regulatory through this expanded conception of human motivation and psychology, expanded to include more than self-interest. A commitment to moral ideals and principles becomes a part of one's self-interest as an agent, a part of one's identity as a professional. This highbrow version of regulatory ethics is still within the universe of discourse of regulation talk, and I would still counterpoise it to virtue talk. Highbrow regulatory ethics, no less than the lowbrow version, is essentially concerned with the rewarding and punishing, the judging and guiding aspects of the rules and principles it develops.

Virtue talk stands in contrast to regulatory ethics mainly because it is as concerned with the agent's being as with his doing. Virtue talk involves notions of character, habit, disposition, inclination. It implies a way of being in the world, a general orientation toward the good on the part of the self in the living of a whole life. Alasdair MacIntyre relates virtues to goods that are internal to practices, and by practices he means activities such as we find professionals often engaged in.[5] Practices are structured, traditionbound kinds of activities that have a point to them, that have their own internal sets of rules, that can be done well or badly, according to criteria that people generally (or at least the members of the professional community generally) understand. The things that you get out of this kind of discipline—this living of your life according to these criteria and these notions of excellence and worth—are the goods that are internal to practices. You are not—or should not be—practicing medicine, say, or practicing law, just to get something external out of it, just to make money. You are doing it because it's a worthy way of life—because there's an intrinsic excellence in the doing of it.

Thus understood, virtue talk is less common in our moral vocabulary today than regulation talk. It is certainly less common in the idiom and discourse of professional ethics, but it is not absent altogether. In fact in the field of professional ethics right now there are interesting arguments and tensions between those who feel generally more comfortable working within the idiom of regulation talk, either highbrow or lowbrow, and those who feel more comfortable within the idiom of virtue talk. Among ethical theorists there are significant and interesting philosophical debates taking place about whether a principle-based ethical theory or virtue ethics is more adequate and desirable as a philosophical framework.[6] Equally important, as one moves into the arena of applied ethics and professional practice, one finds some interesting splits there as well.

Generally, although there are many exceptions to this, the academic philosophers and ethicists tend to favor regulatory ethics while many practitioners, especially those of an older generation, favor virtue talk. They want their professional ethics to be channeled through the filter and the lens of concepts and categories such as virtue, character, excellence, and calling. That produces some very interesting arguments and tension within bioethics, for example, between philosophers and lawyers who want to talk about regulation and physicians who want to talk about the virtuous physician. It produces disagreements about the best approach to take to solve certain kinds of problems, such as the use of life-sustaining technology. Do we need more regulations, more hospital policies and protocols, more laws to clarify things? Or is the problem that we need more courage, more conviction, and more virtue among our physicians so that they would not be so hesitant to do the right thing. (Assuming that we know in those cases what the right thing to do is.)

So the arguments go back and forth. There's a certain kind of politics behind this line of argument. And the politics, of course, has to do with professional autonomy versus external control. Those are the stakes. In my reading of it, those who argue for an approach to professional ethics that relies on virtue talk are those who favor more internal autonomy by the profession; if not by the individual professional then at least self-regulation by the profession itself. Whereas those who look to a regulatory ethic usually tend to come up with notions of external regulation, legal accountability, administrative review, and the like. It is a very live question in our society today whether the professions are generally sufficiently accountable to the public, or whether they are overly regulated.

TOWARD A CIVIC CONCEPTION OF PROFESSIONAL ETHICS

However this question should be settled, one thing is clear. What we now see as the academic discourse of professional ethics has been—and remains—dominated by regulatory talk and regulatory ethics at the expense of virtue talk and virtue ethics, or some third alternative yet to be devised. Why is this so?

The answer seems to me to lie in the general orientation and stance of professional ethics. One of the reasons professional ethics has trouble appreciating virtue talk is that professional ethics has been characterized by a kind of judicial outlook.[7] By and large, professional ethics is the exercise of judicial reason. What I mean by that is as follows.

The task of judicial reason is the application of general moral principles to specific dilemmas and decisions arising in professional practice. Three ideas are central to this conception. First, in professional ethics, the primary unit of analysis is the activity of the individual professional practitioner rather than the collective practices of many practitioners or the traditions, norms and institutions of the profession as a whole. Professional ethics is concerned with individual moral agency, not communal moral practice. Second, the focus of professional ethics is not on professional activity in a broad sense, activity as a shape of a life, a pattern of conduct revealing character, a vocation, a practice of virtue and excellence. Instead the focus is on activity understood as decision making and choice. The moral agent envisioned by professional ethics generally is a weigher of options and a balancer of conflicting values and interests.

Finally, this conception of applying principles to choice situations is fundamentally juridical in method and spirit. The professional ethicist is supposed to stand in judgment on professional decision making, and the grounds of this evaluation is supposed to come from outside the field of knowledge of the profession itself. The principles applied by professional ethicists are both universal moral principles and principles of universal morality. As such their justification can come only from some exogenous or external standpoint of enlightened reason. Indeed, professional ethics, at least during recent years, has been built on the assumption that endogenous sources of law and authority, internal sources of law and authority within the professions, are incapable of regulating the profes-

sions, or of providing the basis for the necessary evaluations and judgments we want to make of the professions. Thus the professional ethicist provides a moral view from afar. Even if professional ethics were to focus on a community of moral practice rather than individual acts of moral choice, according to the judicial conception of professional ethics, the ethicists as ethicist would be in, but not of that community.

The focus on individual decision making and choice, the notion that the unit of analysis is not a whole pattern of conduct but rather particular decisions and particular choices and the separation between the ethicist who judges and the professional practitioners who are being judged—these three things make it very difficult for the discourse of professional ethics to come to grips with notions of character and virtue. Still, an interesting question which the proponents of virtue ethics have not adequately answered would be what alternative model of professional ethics, and what alternative stance of the ethicist would be necessary in order to take virtue talk seriously? I think that at the very least what we would want to see is a less distanced and a less adversarial relationship between the ethicist and the principles and knowledge that the ethicist brings to bear, on the one side, and the profession and professionals, on the other.

I do not mean that ethicists should be uncritically immersed in the traditions, norms, and codes of the professions they are studying. One of the great liberating aspects of professional ethics in recent years is that it has gotten us beyond the generally banal and self-serving moral talk that is internal to so many professions. But we must be careful not to throw the baby out with the bath. In those segments of the professions that have been interested in ethics over the years, and in the record they left in professional journals and other internal professional sources going back into the nineteenth century in some cases, is revealed a kind of internal moral life and tradition. This is true in each one of our professions, I daresay; some richer and older than others, of course. But none of these occupations that we reasonably call a profession today is totally lacking in such an internal moral tradition.

Granting this, one may ask if this is of any philosophic value or interest?[8] And if the internal moral life and heritage of the professions are not in very good shape today, to what extent should we as ethicists be attempting to build upon it, to revitalize it, to reshape it? Or to what extent should we be saying: "Well, professions are not different from any other occupation because they have a kind of special tradition or a moral calling of their own. Let's just treat professionals like any other seller of services; let's just treat the professions as any other business enterprise or collective group that is trying to get its own way in society and pursue its own interest, and let's regulate it accordingly." The alternative as far as professional ethics is concerned then would also have to take stock of where it is the ethicist stands when she passes moral judgment. Where are we coming from when we talk about ethics? Are we coming from our own personal history? Are we coming somehow from practices and experiences that we ourselves have had in our society? Is ethics a kind of universal and timeless knowledge that some can gain and then apply to those who lack it?

These are fundamental questions that professional ethics at some point has to ask of itself. I think professional ethics by and large has taken those questions for granted. We have assumed that the principles that we argue with, and use come from someplace that is valid, that we do not have to scrutinize their theoretical basis or foundations, but we can just apply them without further ado. William May once made the following delightful characterization of a professional ethicist: "A professional ethicist is somebody who carries water from wells he had not dug, to fight fires he cannot find."[9] The professional ethicist is caught between the ethical theorist who comes up with the moral principles in the first place (digs the well), and professional practitioners who know from their practical experience what the problems are (where the fires are to be found). Professional ethicists have neither credential to bring to the enterprise. So wherein does our own legitimacy reside? Why should anyone take us seriously? What's the payoff of doing professional ethics? What moral and even political authority ought it have in our culture?

An alternative to what I call the judicial model of professional ethics might be something that we can call professional ethics as civic discourse.[10] We have now returned to our starting point. Professional ethics should be a part of a broader dialogue in our society that takes place between professional elites and citizens. This dialogue should be about the role of the professions in this society, the nature, extent, and limits of professional power, and the social effects of those technologies the professions create and control and through them shape our entire way of life. That's what civic discourse is all about. It is about the kind of society we want to have and to build. How do we want to distribute power and authority? To what ends do we want to use technology and professional expertise?

This is a kind of conversation that professional ethics must be one voice in. Of course, ethicists are not the only participants in such a conversation. The professions have to have a voice in it. Citizens at large at the grassroots level have to have a voice in it. Other academic disciplines need to have a voice in it as well. Professional ethics would be greatly strengthened if we were able somehow to broaden and enrich the context within which we do our work in order to create something like a contribution to a broader civic discourse about those sorts of questions. We cannot regulate virtue in the professions unless we first nurture it, both there and in the wider civil society.

Notes

1. Sullivan, W.: 1982, *Reconstructing Public Philosophy* (University of California Press, Berkeley).
2. Pincoffs, E. L.: 1986, *Quandaries and Virtues* (University Press of Kansas, Lawrence).
3. Stone, C. D.: 1975, *Where the Law Ends: The Social Control of Corporate Behavior* (Harper and Row, New York).
4. Hirschman, A. O.: 1977, *The Passions and the Interests* (Princeton University Press, Princeton).
5. MacIntyre, A.: 1981, *After Virtue* (University of Notre Dame Press, Notre Dame), pp. 178ff.
6. Cf. Clarke, S. G. and Simpson, E., eds.: 1989, *Anti-Theory in Ethics and Moral Conservatism* (State University of New York Press, Albany).
7. Cf. Rorty, A. O.: 1988, "Three Myths of Moral Theory," in *Mind in Action* (Beacon Press, Boston), pp. 271–98.
8. Camenisch, P. F.: 1983, *Grounding Professional Ethics in a Pluralistic Society* (Haven Publication, New York).

9. May, W. F.: 1980, "Professional Ethics: Setting, Terrain, and Teacher," in Daniel Callahan and Sissela Bok, eds.: 1980, *Teaching Ethics in Higher Education* (Plenum Press, New York), p. 239.

10. I discuss this at greater length in "Bioethics and Democracy," *The Centennial Review* XXXIV (Spring 1990), pp. 207–225.

Judith P. Swazey

Are Physicians a "Delinquent Community"?: Issues in Professional Competence, Conduct, and Self-Regulation

INTRODUCTION

Rather than prepare a formal scholarly paper for my presentation, I thought it might be more interesting and instructive to discuss the moral responsibility of physicians as professionals through the lens of some of my own experiences in medical education, medical research, and the practice of medicine. These experiences are not examples of the many positive encounters I have had over the years, but they have stimulated my interest in, and taught me a great deal about, how doctors sometimes define and handle problems of physicianly conduct and competence, and some of the problems that the medical profession—like other professions—has in governing itself.

The idea of examining such topics through a partly autobiographical account was suggested to me by Dr. Mark Frankel, head of the AAAS'

From Judith P. Swazey, "Are Physicians a 'Delinquent Community'?: Issues in Professional Competence, Conduct, and Self-Regulation," *Journal of Business Ethics*, Vol. 10, No. 8, 1991. Reprinted by permission of Kluwer Academic Publishers.

Office of Scientific Freedom and Responsibility, when he asked me to give a talk for a 1987 AAAS workshop on the "state of the art" in science, engineering, and ethics.[1] He felt that it would be useful to the workshop participants if I served as a "living case study" of how one becomes involved in studying, teaching, and writing about ethics and values in science and medicine. I accepted the invitation, even though it made me feel as though I was teetering on the brink of retirement, and found that the exercise of thinking about my own "personal encounters and professional journeys" provided a useful perspective on issues that have concerned me for many years.

Before providing some vignettes, let me place them in a framework, that also will help us consider why sociologist Eliot Freidson has used the term "delinquent community" to refer to the norms and actions of a group of physicians that he studied.[2] The two key concepts I want to touch on are "profession" and "social controls." There is a large sociological literature on the subject of professions, including a great deal of controversy as to how a profession should be defined, and why, and whether professions are really distinct from other occupations.[3] Skirting that ongoing debate among sociologists, let me assume that there are certain characteristics distinguishing people we call professionals. These characteristics are seen most strikingly in the so-called learned or higher professions, which philosopher John Ladd has also termed the "moral professions"[4]— law, medicine, divinity, and university faculty. Ladd points out that "three distinctive features separate these higher professions from other occupations that are often called professions . . . . First, members of the higher professions provide personal services to individuals with whom they have a special professional relationship, namely clients, patients, parishioners, or students. Second, these professions have traditionally almost completely controlled the services they offer, the standards of evaluation of these services, and the qualifications for membership in the profession. This autonomy and self-government has given them a virtual monopoly over areas in which they claim competence. Third, . . . the members of these professions often assume the role of *moral entrepreneurs:* they take it to be part of their job as professionals . . . to be moral arbiters of what, in respect to professional services provided, is morally good for their clients and perhaps even of what is morally good for society."[5]

In considering the moral responsibility of professionals, another important perspective is provided by theologian James Gustafson, who has written eloquently about the value dimensions of being a professional, particularly those involving commitment or "calling." In its deepest and most ideal sense, Gustafson reminds us, medicine and other professions are vocations, not just jobs. As vocations, they are embedded in a wide context of significance and meaning, and it is this context that he terms the "calling" dimension of a profession.[6]

The concept of "social controls" also is a subject that has been written about extensively in the sociological literature, and, to a lesser extent, in writings on medical ethics. As used by sociologists, the term "social controls" has two distinct meanings.[7] First, it refers to the capacity of an individual or group to regulate itself; this is termed self-regulation or internal controls, which can involve informal or formal methods. The second category of social controls is called external social controls: these are the informal and formal means that can be used by outside agencies to influence, regulate, or discipline particular individuals or groups of individuals.[8]

Medicine and physicians have been at the epicenter of writings, studies, and policy actions dealing with social controls and the professions, particularly with respect to how well or poorly doctors exercise their prerogative of self-regulation.[9] There are at least three reasons why medicine, among all professions and occupations, has received so much attention. First,

medicine is viewed as the archetype of a "powerful profession," with physicians, sometimes described as "dominant professionals," standing at the peak of and exercising authority over a large hierarchy of other people working in health care. Due to their real and symbolic authority, doctors, more than other professionals, acquired the right to largely govern themselves and each other, and to behave as a self-regulating "company of equals."[10] Second, we are particularly concerned about standards of technical, cognitive, and moral competence and conduct for physicians, and what happens when those standards are not met, because health and illness, life and death are literally and symbolically central aspects of our lives, and we are all, at some point, going to be a patient. Third, medicine typifies the dilemmas and difficulties of adequately controlling a profession both from within and without.

PERSONAL AND PROFESSIONAL "CLOSE ENCOUNTERS"

The four topics in social controls and the medical profession I want to discuss involve, at their core, the moral responsibility of professionals, towards themselves and their colleagues, their students, the clients they serve, and ultimately, the society that has invested such trust and authority in them. The four are research misconduct; behavioral impairment or deviance—in this case linked with medical education; incompetence; and what physician and ethicist Edward Pellegrino calls practices at "the moral margins."[11]

Research Misconduct

Until my junior year in college, when I took an intensive year-long course in the history of science, my images of science and scientists had been formed, as is often the case, by the brief descriptions students are exposed to in textbooks. These descriptions portray the nature of scientific research and discovery in stereotyped and often inaccurate ways.[12] Similarly, the values or norms of scientists and of the scientific community, and the ways scientists enact those norms in their professional work, are presented in abstract, idealized ways: the way science *should* operate, and the way we like to think it always does. In addition to integrity or "honor in science,"[13] the ethos of modern science that we learn in textbooks has been characterized in a now-classic paper by sociologist Robert K. Merton as involving four central values: universalism, communalism, disinterestedness, and organized skepticism.[14]

The fact that science and scientists do not always function according to such ideal images was forcefully brought home to me during college by my first real-world, in-the-laboratory encounter with research misconduct. The incident involved the disappearance of a series of photomicrographs we had prepared in connection with experiments on the functions of a particular endocrine organ. After several fruitless searches, we decided that, somehow, the slides had been discarded, repeated the experiment, and went on with our work. Months later, reading a newly published paper by a rising young researcher who was doing similar studies of the same gland, and with whom our professor occasionally discussed their respective projects, we were shocked to find the missing photomicrographs in the pages of Dr. X's article. It was a hard but instructive way for student-researchers, and their teacher to learn that scientists do not always live by the moral code of "honor in science." The incident, as best I remember it, was dealt with in a fairly typical fashion, by the use of informal internal social controls: we figured out the most likely way the slides had gotten from our lab to Dr. X's, and our professor quietly let him, and his "accomplice," know that we knew, and would be on guard henceforth.

Since I am focusing on physicians, I should note that my "greening" in professional ethics also began from an idealized set of beliefs and attitudes about medicine and physicians, formed by the kinds of fine doctors I grew up knowing through my physician-father, and the fact that I was a medical novel junkie, who inhaled the "dear and glorious physician" novels that were best-sellers in those days. Medicine, I believed, was the noblest of callings, and physicians were all extraordinarily intelligent, committed people, dedicated to fighting illness and disease, and going so with what my colleague Renée Fox has called "caring competence."[15] [I

still hold these beliefs about many aspects of medicine, and about many but by no means all doctors, but my views have certainly become more tempered over the years.]

It was many years after college when I had my second close encounter with research misconduct, as a medical school professor teaching social science and ethics in the late 1970s. That encounter dragged on for several years, and proved to be a wrenching experience in participant observation that I hope never to repeat. To the extent I could step back from it, and certainly in retrospect, it was an informative case, which taught many people in medical centers and federal agencies some important early lessons about the good and bad ways to deal with research misconduct and those who are involved in its as alleged perpetrators or as whistleblowers. The 1980s made the subject of research misconduct a familiar one, but this case, now so relatively long ago, was one of the first major research fraud cases that exploded beyond the confines of the institution.

To quickly summarize a very involved plot line, the misconduct involved a physician, recruited to the medical center from NIH as a likely "superstar," who, with the aid of others, fabricated data about experimental drug treatments for cancer patients. Other types of misconduct in this case included doing research that had not been approved, as required by federal regulations, by the institution's human subjects committee. The first whistleblowing occurred when several junior physicians and nurses involved in the research decided they could no longer accept what was being done, or participate in it, and told their story to a more senior physician, who was a medical oncologist and also taught in our department. She was profoundly upset at what she heard, and deeply worried about the sanctions that these whistleblowers might incur, and came to discuss the situation with our department chairman and myself, since I was both a friend and the person who "did medical ethics" at the institution. She and I, and a third colleague who is a health-lawyer, became the "senior whistleblowers" in the affair, first within the institution, and then, having hit the stone walls that most whistleblowers encounter, to outside sources.

Becoming a whistleblower, I assure you, is not a decision that people take lightly; for me, and others I know, it involves many days and nights of wrestling with your conscience, assessing your moral responsibilities, wondering whether you are, just perhaps, being a "tattletale" or too morally arrogant, and worrying about what the professional repercussions of your actions may be.[16]

In any event, the three of us, somewhat naively and optimistically, sallied forth. We were, we heard, viewed as an unholy trio within the institution, and our actions were explained away by who we were: the doctor who, many people whispered, clearly was envious of Dr. S's statute and was after his job; the lawyer who, everyone "knew" was always out to get doctors; and the "ethicist" who . . . . Here, people, had trouble explaining my motives, and only a couple of colleagues suggested it might have something to do with my professional and personal sense of medical ethics. Alternative explanations for my involvement, though, were quickly thought of; they ranged from the suggestion that I was after material for another book, to the definitive announcement that I was seeking to "punish the institution" because I had been having an affair with a senior administrator that he had terminated.

Our objective in becoming whistleblowers was to have the institution investigate and resolve the allegations against Dr. S in a timely and fair manner, with due process for all involved. An inquiry was started, though the process and procedures left something to be desired, even in those days when institutions were much less familiar with the thought that misconduct could occur within their walls, and with how such allegations should be handled. When the inquiry was going on, the dean did take the admirable step of notifying, in-person, the funding agency in Washington of what seemed to have transpired, but they clearly signalled they did not want to know any more about it, and preferred that it all be handled quietly and decorously in-house. Then, to the relief of the medical and administrative leaders of the hospital and medical school, Dr. S. decided to resign, and with his departure, the case was considered "closed." This was, and still is, a too common way for hospitals and academic institutions to handle misconduct and other forms of deviance. But some of us felt it was not an acceptable resolution for what, by that time, had become an exceedingly complicated and unpleasant affair. At times it was like living out a Robin Cook melodrama: I was getting copies of falsified patient records and research findings delivered to my office in plain brown rappers, a couple of offices were broken in to and attempts made to alter other doctors' records, threats of physical violence were being made against some nurses, and, for a time and to the bewilderment and alarm of the patients, armed guards patrolled the oncology unit and escorted the threatened nurses to the bathroom and cafeteria.

After weeks of being "buffed and turfed" from one authority figure or group to another, and often being denied access to them, we perceptively concluded that the case was not, after all, going to be dealt with willingly by the medical school, hospital, or parent university. Everyone, for reasons we could understand though not agree with, hoped it would just be forgotten and certainly not become known outside the institution, even though the oncology grapevine had been abuzz for weeks about the "scandal." The human subjects committee decided that, if some of the research had been done without their review and approval, it was beyond their jurisdiction or concern. The medical school decided it was really the university hospital's case, since Dr. S. had had his primary appointment at the hospital. The hospital trustees and administrator declined further discussion or action, because Dr. S. had left. The university president declared it was a hospital matter, in which the university need not be involved. And the vice-president for medical affairs, in a memorable meeting with the three of us, declared that a term like "fudge it," which Dr. S. had written in response to a nurse's written query about how they should handle data on a patient resuming treatment with an experimental drug, whose earlier records had been falsified, was a "very ambiguous phrase," which could have several meanings. That matter disposed of, we then were told about the "much worse things that go on in surgery."

Our next strategy was to report Dr. S. to the state board of registration in medicine. But the board was overwhelmed with too many cases to investigate, some of them seen as much more serious than a "little data falsification," and had too few staff for a timely response to most complaints it received. And by the time someone began looking into our complaint, Dr. S. was working at a medical center in another state, so the board decided the whole case was not outside of their jurisdiction.

As weeks went by with no response from the board of registration, our frustration and exhaustion levels increased; we wanted somebody to listen to us, review the documents we had acquired, and do something. It was not that Dr. S. had committed the most heinous act we had ever heard of in medicine, but we felt, very deeply, that he had done things that were fundamentally wrong, and that our institution had not responded as it should or could have. And so, we, and chiefly I, committed what whistleblowers know is the ultimate act of disloyalty to an organization:[17] I took the story "outside," to channels where rumors had already been circulating for many weeks. Soon, the case was receiving prominent media coverage, including a well-documented series by a team of investigative reporters; became the subject of lengthy investigations by the Food and Drug Administration and National Institutes of Health, which led, several years later, to Dr. S's being debarred from receiving federal research grants for several years; and the immediate participants were enmeshed in drawn out suits and counter-suits involving charges of libel, defamation of character, etc.

I could discuss this case in much more detail, but let me end this vignette by noting some of the lessons I began to learn about social controls and the medical profession.

1. It is a complex, fascinating, and practically important field of study, which, partly as a coping mechanism in the wake of this case, I began to pursue. Having moved from the medical school to a small nonprofit organization, I directed a two-year study on the subject, funded by the National Science Foundation. As part of that project, we organized the first major workshop on fraud and whistleblowing in biomedical research, cosponsored by the AAAS and the President's Commission for the Study of Ethical Problems in Medicine and Biomedical and Behavioral Research.[18]

2. This case, and other cases that have been documented in the 1980s and analyzed by scholars like Patricia Woolf, show the difficulties that physicians, other university faculty, and their institutions have in facing the fact that misconduct does occur, and in devising and using appropriate policies and procedures to deal with such deviations from proper professional conduct. That is, professionals and their institutions have problems using the self-regulatory social controls available to them. The ways that research misconduct have been defined and dealt with since the late 1970s has improved. But in the words of Dr. Paul Friedman, a member of the Institute of Medicine's Committee on the Responsible Conduct of Research,[19] the academic community has exhibited an "indecisive response" to "well publicized cases of research fraud or serious misconduct,"[20] and there are many less dramatic and unpublicized incidents that point to the complexities and difficulties of adequate self-regulation.

Physicians, and the academic research community more generally, still tend to treat each instance of misconduct as an isolated, idiosyncratic event, and often try to explain it away by "medicalizing" the reasons for its occurrence. That is, they decide that the individual who engaged in misconduct did so because he or she had some sort of psychiatric aberration, was under great stress, etc. In effect, this not only makes the case a unique event, but places the perpetrator in the sick role and thus absolves him of personal blame or moral responsibility for his act. As one looks at misconduct cases, however, there are patterns involved in their occurrence that make it hard to view each incident as unique. And, given the fallout from failures of self-regulation in these cases, institutions are beginning to realize that it is not, in fact, in their "best interests" to try to define such incidents as isolated events that can simply be swept under the rug.

3. One of the strong impressions I got from my involvement in this early misconduct case

was that many physicians did not view various types of "data massaging," or even outright fabrication, as terribly serious violations of professional standards, as long as it caused no direct harm to patients. This was a value judgment I heard many times in off-the-record conversations, usually prefaced with a "don't quote me, but . . ." Hopefully, with the consciousness-raising that has gone on in the 1980s, those same physicians I talked with a decade ago would now treat "cooking, fudging, or trimming" data as morally serious events, because they violate basic ethical principles of professional integrity. I am concerned, however, that there is still too much consequentialist moral reasoning abroad in the medical community with respect to research misconduct. An indicator is that one of the most publicized cases of the 1980s, which for the first time led to the criminal prosecution and conviction of a researcher for falsifying data in a federally funded research project, was eventually treated as a particularly "serious" event because of the possibility that it could have resulted in harm to patients—in this case, children. The case, long suppressed by the researcher's institution and his funder, the National Institutes of Mental Health, involved a massive and multi-year falsification of data on the use of drugs to treat mentally retarded children, by one of the country's most influential researchers in that field, Dr. Stephen Breuning. When the charges of misconduct against Dr. Breuning were finally and slowly investigated, and eventually verified, the major wrongdoing was defined as his having deceptively influenced both the actual treatment of severely retarded patients, and social policies concerning such treatment.[21] A second consequentialist judgment about the seriousness of Dr. Breuning's misconduct, and the legal grounds for his criminal indictment, was that he had used his falsified data to obtain a large grant from the NIMH. This is not to argue that such consequences are not very serious, but to raise the question of whether Dr. Breuning's transgressions would have been judged so severely had he falsified data with no apparent medical or financial consequences.

4. Another lesson I learned from my own involvement in a misconduct case was one that

scores of whistleblowers, in academia, government agencies, and private industry, have learned only too well. Within the organization, whistleblowers are often viewed as more deviant than those on whom they blow the whistle, the responses to their action often are more angry and enduring, and the sanctions against them more severe, especially if they take their concerns and allegations to outside sources. Dr. Robert Sprague, who blew the whistle on Stephen Breuning, bears deep personal and professional scars for acting on his moral convictions; one of his sanctions, for example, was to have his research support from NIMH abruptly deferred, after 17 years of funding and a unanimous recommendation for continuing funding from the study section that reviewed his proposal.[22] Focusing on moral responsibility and social controls, the major point I want to make about whisleblowers concerns self-regulation. It explains, in part, why whistleblowers are defined as deviant, and points to the need to change that definition and the actions that follow from it, if physicians and other professionals are to do a better job, morally and operationally, of self-regulation.

The act of whistleblowing calls into question the capacity of scientists and physicians to regulate themselves effectively . . . . [It] threatens both the individual self-esteem of members of the research community and the continued prestige and existence of that community as a self-regulating company of equals, especially when the whistleblower makes his charges public.

The negative reactions to and sanctions against the whistleblower also . . . serve as an *ad hominen* defense by the [group] against charges that imply a failure of individual and group norms. That is, by focusing attention on the whistleblower as the deviant group member and attacking his motivations and actions, attention may be diverted, at least for a time, from the substance of the disclosure to the discloser himself.[23]

Behavioral Deviance and Gatekeeping

A third case, in which I participated less directly, raises questions of moral responsibility and the exercise of professional social controls in two categories, which in this instance were interrelated. First, what should constitute acceptable standards of professional behavior, and how should departures from those standards be dealt with? Second, by virtue of their autonomy and expertise, physicians control access to their professional community. They are the gatekeepers who decide which applicants merit admission to professional training, set the standards of cognitive, technical, and moral competency that trainees are expected to meet, and decide if they have met those requirements and thus should be granted a professional degree, certification, or licensure.

The case, I think, speaks for itself: The teenage son of a friend and colleague was admitted to the inpatient psychiatric unit of a university hospital with an acute psychotic break. His prognosis was guarded, at best, and several weeks after his admission, his parents were notified that he had run away from the hospital. He was found, and told his parents that one of the reasons he had left the hospital was because he had been homosexually assaulted by a medical student who was doing a clinical rotation on the unit. Granting that their son was a seriously disturbed young man, the parents still felt his story had a ring of truth to it, and pressed the medical school to investigate the charges.

Because the parents were well-educated and persistent, the school did, however reluctantly, look into the allegations. They proved to be substantially correct, and it turned out that several of the student's teachers and clinical preceptors had flagged him as having behavioral problems as a medical trainee related to his homosexuality. Ultimately, the powers-that-be at the medical school decided that the student's conduct did not warrant dismissal, or even disciplinary action. He would be warned against any similar acts and offered counseling, but allowed to complete medical school and become a physician. The dean of students and other officials, however, assured the aghast parents that they would track the student through his internship and residency training, and try to guide him into a specialty such as pathology where he would not have direct contact with patients. In the words of Charles Bosk, they felt

that their moral responsibility as gatekeepers was to "forgive and remember."[24]

Medical Competence

From 1983–1988, Renée Fox and I conducted a detailed first-hand study of the social, ethical, and policy issues involved in attempts to use the Jarvik 7 artificial heart as both a permanent and temporary replacement for the human heart. One of our major conclusions was that the use of the artificial heart, considered as an experiment in which a very risky device was implanted into human subjects primarily for research purposes, should not have been initiated, or, once started, allowed to continue.[25] In our judgment, the artificial heart experiment, from beginning to end, demonstrated inadequacies in the exercise of social controls by every gatekeeper involved, including individuals in key decisionmaking roles, institutional bodies such as the human subjects committees that were charged with reviewing and approving the experiment, the FDA as the responsible federal regulatory agency, and the larger community of cardiac surgeons.

The major reason for reaching this conclusion about the artificial heart experiment and the lack of an adequate exercise of professional responsibility has to do with medical competence. This case involved the competence to do medical research with patients, but the issues are equally relevant to how the profession often deals with colleagues whom they know are not competent in regular medical practice.

To make a very long and complicated story extremely brief, the "fatal flaw" in the experiment with the Jarvik 7 heart was that physicians responsible for designing the experiment, conducting it, and evaluating the results, were not adequately trained to do clinical research. Thus, they were not competent for the task they wanted to do and were authorized to do. We heard this judgement repeatedly in private interviews and conversations with many people in a position to evaluate the experiment, such as members of the teams that were involved in the artificial heart implant for Barney Clark at the University of Utah, and in the implants for "bionic Bill Scroeder" and two other patients at the Human Hospital Audubon in Louisville, Kentucky. These individuals, for example, described that data gathering and analysis that went on as "garbage in, garbage out," and asked us, the sociologists, to tell them what clinical research is and whether they were doing it. Members of the human subjects committee at Urah characterized the research approach of Drs. DeVries and Jarvik as "put the device in and see if it works," and members of the committee spent a year rewriting the artificial heart protocol to make it a scientifically acceptable research plan that they could approve. The justifiability of the experiment also was questioned, in private, by some of the country's most eminent figures in cardiovascular surgery, research, and the use of mechanical cardiac replacement or assistance devices. One prominent surgeon, for example, said to us that were the Jarvik heart team working for him, the first thing he would do is teach them to do good clinical research.

There are many reasons why the various gatekeepers who could have blocked the initiation of the artificial heart experiment, or shortened its duration, chose not to exercise the social controls at their disposal. Among them were a strong desire to "win the race" to implant a permanent replacement for the human heart, and put their institution "on the map" of pioneering medical work; the belief of FDA regulators that they would "look bad" in the eyes of the public if they blocked a dramatic venture like the Jarvik heart; and the reluctance of knowledgeable, senior physicians not directly involved in the Jarvik heart's use to openly criticize fellow-physicians. Sociologically, each reason is understandable, and forms part of a recurring pattern of what I believe is the failure of the medical professionals to regularly exercise one of their cardinal moral responsibilities: to try to prevent harm or wrong-doing by ensuring, to the best of their ability, that they and their colleagues are competent physicians. As professionals, physicians are the gatekeeper or guardians for competency and conduct. When we ended our long study of the artificial heart, one of the questions that troubled us most is, "Who shall guard the guardians?"

The "Moral Margins" of Professional Practice

A final example deals with what physicians and other professionals define as the content and boundaries of their "calling." It relates to professional conduct in the broadest sense, because it asks the individual professional, and his or her collective professional community, to decide what falls within the scope of their duties or responsibilities to those they serve.

One of my encounters with this question happened in 1988, when I was asked to meet with the staff and members of a state Board of Registration in Medicine to discuss some ethical issues they were finding deeply troubling. The issues were not, as I first supposed, the usual fare for Boards of Registration, such as how to deal with impairment, incompetence, or Medicaid fraud. Rather, the staff and members of the Board wanted to explore the question of whether physicians have a duty to treat patients with AIDS, or whether they have a right to refuse giving such care, if, for whatever reason, this is a class of patients they do not want to treat. Second order questions, which joined ethics and law, were whether, if physicians have such a duty, it can be stipulated through regulations, and what sanctions, if any, a state board could impose on doctors who violated their duty.

From the perspective of this syposium these questions focus our attention on a cardinal aspect of professional self-regulation: the responsibilities of a profession as a "moral enterprise."[26]

The refusal of some physicians to treat HIV-infected patients, whether from fear of contagion or a personal distaste for the lifestyles of many AIDS sufferers, is what Pellegrino aptly calls a practice at the "moral margin."[27] By that phrase, he refers not to the flagrant violations of professional ethics, but to a whole series of professional actions that are legally permissible, generally tolerated within a profession, and, overall, socially acceptable. Other examples within medicine that Pellegrino cites include denying service to the indigent or underinsured, turning away complicated cases because of fears of malpractice, and various forms of medical entrepreneurship, like marketing ventures to increase the demand for worthless or dubious devices and procedures. What concerns Pellegrino so deeply about these practices at the moral margins is that he believes they demonstrate a growing conviction among the learned professions that they must give greater weight to their own self-interest, rather than the traditional ethics governing their professions. The warning he sounds, which I hope will be heeded, is that "the professions today are afflicted with a species of moral malaise that may prove fatal to their moral identities and fatal to our whole society."[28]

Physicians as a "Delinquent Community"

Finally, let me turn to the question posed in the title of my presentation: with respect to the ways they exercise self-regulation to govern the competence and conduct of their members, are physicians what Freidson termed a "delinquent community"? My answer is, "yes," which needs some explanation. Freidson uses this characterization in his 1975 book, *Doctoring Together: A Study of Professional Social Controls*. It describes and analyses the workings and behaviors of a large group practice of physicians whom Friedson studied in depth in the early 1960s. I first read it when I was immersed in the oncology research fraud case, and it helped me make sense of the events and patterns in which I was caught up. Rereading this book in 1990, I am impressed by how current it seems, despite all the changes that have taken place in medicine in the intervening years. For, as Freidson wrote, it is a book about "the underlife of social policy" about the "day-to-day work of doctoring" that is "controlled, if controlled at all, by professionals"[29]

The physicians Freidson studied work as a group of colleagues, or what he calls a "collegium," who governed themselves by a set of largely informal norms or "rules." These norms provided them with the basis for deciding "why some forms of behavior and work performance and not others [were] considered to require control of some kind." What Freidson documented, in a nutshell, and what other first-hand studies also have described, is that "at the core of

the professional control system of the medical group was a set of rules [i.e., norms] for defining the limits of acceptable performance by reference to conceptions of self, one's colleagues, and the nature of medical work and work performance. These norms blurred and weakened the notion of collegial accountability upon which the effective operation of a control system must rely . . . . The professional was treated as an individual free to follow his own judgement without restraint, so long as his behavior was short of blatant and gross deficiencies in performance and inconvenience to his colleagues."

The way that the norms of the collegium were designed and operated, to give each physician maximum autonomy in his work performance and behavior, is the reason that Freidson placed them in a taxonomy called the "delinquent community." Here, he drew on sociological studies of French school children and personnel in French bureaucracies, which researchers characterized as "delinquent communities" because their members showed a "jealous equalitarianism," a "conspiracy of silence against superior authority," and a "defensive solidarity [that] involves the collective obligation to protect each colleague's independence."

Looking at the history and traditions of the medical profession, Freidson argued that "at best, its delinquent community may be explained by reference to a sense of vulnerability to the possible imposition of [rigid external] controls, an *anticipatory* response." However, as he noted and as we saw with the regulation of medical practice and legistlative and regulatory responses to research misconduct during the 1970s and 1980s, that "the irony is that rather than defending the profession against the imposition of a rigid authoritarian framework, the anticipatory responses of the medical community have created part of the pressure for the institution of such a framework."

As Freidson commented at the end of *Doctoring Together,* and as I have illustrated through briefly describing some of my encounters with problems in medical conduct and competence and how they were dealt with, "a new blueprint" is needed for the content of and ways that physicians engage in self-governance. Our society has granted physicians the prerogative and privilege of working as a "self-regulating company of equals." But all too often, that self-regulation is concerned more with etiquette than with ethics, and demonstrates the "deliberately uncritical and permissive individualism" characterizing a "delinquent community." The medical professions, and I believe all professions, need to constantly remind themselves about the "calling" that is involved in their work, and about the moral responsibilities they should exercise in the name of the vocation they have chosen. Part of that moral responsibility is to assume an individual and collective responsibility for true self-governance. This may be an idealistic statement, but it is part of the vocation of medicine that physicians, for centuries, have inscribed in their special prayers, oaths, creeds, and codes.

Notes

1. Frankel, M., ed.: 1988, *Science, Engineering, and Ethics. State-of-the-Art and Future Directions* (American Association for the Advancement of Science, Publication 88–28, Washington, DC).
2. Freidson, E.: 1975, *Doctoring Together. A Study of Professional Social Control* (Elsevier, NY).
3. For a concise discussion of the debate over "professions," and an examination of the literature on the professions of medicine and nursing, see Fox, R. C.: 1989, *The Sociology of Medicine. A Participant Observer's View* (Prentice Hall, Englewood Cliffs, NJ).
4. Ladd, J.: 1985, "Philosophy and the Moral Professions," in J. P. Swazey and S. R. Scher, eds., *Social Controls and the Medical Profession* (Oelgeschlager, Gunn, & Hain, ch. 1, Boston, MA).
5. Ibid. pp. 11–12.
6. Gustafson, J. M.: 1982, "Professions as 'Callings,' " *Social Service Review* 56 (Dec.), pp. 501–515.
7. Janowitz, M.: 1975, "Sociological Theory and Social Control," *American Journal of Sociology* 81 (1), pp. 82–108.
8. See chs. 6–15 in J. P. Swazey and S. R. Scher, eds., *Social Controls and the Medical Profession* (op. cit.), which examines a variety of topics concerning the nature and effectiveness of informal and formal/internal and external controls in relation to competence and impairment.
9. See, for example, Bosk, C.: 1979, *Forgive and Remember, Managing Medical Failure* (University of Chicago Press, Chicago); Freidson, E., *Doctoring Together* (op. cit.); J. P. Swazey and S. R. Scher, eds., *Social Controls and the Medical Profession* (op. cit), especially ch. 2.
10. Barber, B.: 1952, *Science and the Social Order* (Free Press, Glencoe, IL), pp. 139–156.
11. Pellegrino, E. D.: 1989, "Character, Virtue, and Self-Interest in the Ethics of the Professions," *Journal of Contemporary Health Policy and Law* 5 (Spring), pp. 53–73.
12. Kuhn, T. S.: 1970, *The Structure of Scientific Revolutions,* 2d edn. (University of Chicago Press, Chicago); Swazey J. P. and Reeds, K.: 1978, *Today's Medicine, Tomorrow's Science. Essays on Paths of Discovery in the Biomedical Sciences* (DHEW Publication No, (NIH) 78–244, Washington, DC).
13. Sigma Xi: 1986 *Honor in Science* (Sigma Xi, New Haven, CT); see alo the National Academy of Science's recent publication, *On Being a Scientist* (National Academy Press, 1989, Washington, DC).
14. Merton, R. K.: 1942, "The Normative Structure of Science." Reprinted in Merton, R. K.: 1973, *The Sociology of Science, theoretical and Empirical Investigations* (University of Chicago Press, Chicago).
15. Fox, R. C.: 1990, "Training in Caring Competence in North American Medicine: Reforming the Reforms," *Humane Medicine* 6 (Winter): pp. 15–21.
16. There is an extensive literature on the roles and results of whistleblowing in various organizational settings. See, for example, Bowman, J. S., Elliston, F. and Lockhart, P.: 1984, *Professional Dissent, An Annotated Bibliography and Guide* (Garland Publisher, Inc., NY); Chalk, R.: 1988, "Making the World Safe for Whistleblowers," *Technology Review* (Jan.), pp. 48–57; Swazey, J. P. and Scher, S. R., eds.: 1982, *Whistleblowing in Biomedical Research* (President's Commission for the Study of Ethical Issues in Medicine and Biomedical Research, Washington, DC).
17. Westin, A.: 1981, *Whistle-Blowing! Loyalty and Dissent in the Corporation* (McGraw Hill, NY).
18. Swazey J. P. and Scher, SD. R., eds., op. cit. *Social Controls and the Medical Profession;* Swazey J. P. and Scher, S. R., eds., op. cit. *Whistleblowing in Biomedical Research.*
19. Institute of Medicine: 1989, *The Responsible Conduct of Research in the Health Sciences* (National Academy Press, Washington, DC).
20. Freidman, P. J.: 1989, "A Last Call for Self-Regulation of Biomedical Research," *Academic Medicine* 64, pp. 502–504.
21. On the Breuning case, see: Holden, C.: 1987, *NIMH Finds a Case of 'Serious' Misconduct,*" *Science* 235 (27 March), pp. 1566–1567; "Researcher Indicted on Charges of Falsifying Data," *NY Times,* April 17, 1988, "Scientist Given a 60-Day Term for False Data," *NY Times,* Nov. 12, 1988.
22. For accounts of Dr. Robert Sprague's experiences as the whistleblower in the Breuning case, see: "Researcher sounds fraud alarm and loses NIMH grant," *Science & Government Report* 16 (April 1, 1987): 1–3; R. L. Sprague: "I trusted the research system [special section on whistleblowing]," *The Scientist* 1 (Dec. 14, 1987: 11ff). In recognition of the moral responsibility he exercised in the Breuning case, at great personal and professional costs, the AAAS gave its annual award for outstanding work in Scientific Freedom and Responsibility to Dr. Sprague in 1988.
23. Swazey, J. P., and Scher, S. R.: 1982, "The Whistleblower as a Deviant Professional: Professional Norms and Responses to Fraud in Clinical Research," in *Whistleblowing in Biomedical Research,* op. cit., p. 188.

24. Bosk, op. cit.
25. Swazey, J. P., Fox, R. C., and Watkins, J. C.: 1986, "Assessing the Artificial Heart: the Clinical Moratorium Revisited," *International Journal of Technology Assessment in Health Care* 2(3), pp. 387–410; Swazey, J. P.: 1988, "The Social Context of Medicine. Lessons from the Artificial Heart Experiment," *Second Opinion* 8 (July), pp. 44–65.

26. Zuger, A. and Miles, S. H.: 1987, "Physicians, AIDS, and Occupational Risk: Historic Traditions and Ethical Obligations," *Journal of American Medical Association* 258 (9 Oct.), pp. 1924–1928.
27. Pellegrino, op. cit.
28. Ibid, p. 55.
29. The quotations in this section are drawn from Freidson, op. cit.

Stephen E. Lammers

Are Physicians a "Delinquent Community?" Issues in Professional Competence, Conduct, and Self-Regulation: Commentary

Introduction

I would like to thank Dr. Swazey for her paper. It seems to me that it is a valuable contribution, valuable because it is a candid and thoughtful reflection on the profession of medicine by someone who is informed by a conception of a profession as something more than a career. It is valuable too because it does not privilege, or in this case, deprivilege, any profession, in its discussion of the failures she recounts. Let me say further that the paper rings true, rings true in the sense that I can think of like examples both from my experience of following around physicians as well as my experience of spending

From Stephen E. Lammers, "Are Physicians a 'Delinquent Community?' Issues in Professional Competence, Conduct, and Self-Regulation: Commentary," *Journal of Business Ethics,* Vol. 10, No. 2, 1991. Reprinted by permission of Kluwer Academic Publishers.

some thirty years in higher education. I would like to be clear about one difference in experience between Dr. Swazey and myself. Her stories concern academic medicine, although there are clear clinical components. My focus will be community clinical medicine, on the one hand, and the academy, on the other. Rather than asking questions about some central premise or argument of the paper, I propose instead to reflect on a number of themes contained within the paper and try to develop a point about which the paper was silent. In that way, I hope that we might have some discussion. Let me try to develop three points around some of the difficulties which Dr. Swazey identified. The three issues which are of interest to me are the following. First, the excessive individualism of modern professions such that the modern professional thinks of him or herself as a self-sufficient monad [i.e. self-sufficient unit] in terms of their professional practice. Second, there is the corresponding lack of any kind of societal vision within professions and no sense that there is any promise, covenant, or contract between society at large and the profession. Third, I would like to take a moment and reflect upon whistleblowing in our society and why it is such an endangered practice. In the midst of this discussion, I will be making a suggestion about one of the reasons why professions are in such difficulty today. Let me begin.

The Self-Sufficiency of Professionals

The first matter that needs comment is the perception, on the part of the professional, that he or she is self-sufficient. At one level, that of etiquette, physicians in the clinical setting know that they are dependent upon one another. Thus the elaborate rituals of thanking referring physicians for consultations that appear over and over in charts. However, at the level of peer review or peer inspection, matters are different. Physicians resist mightily any attempt to have anyone look over their shoulders in any way that might appear to be judgmental. They know that medicine is practiced in many ways in a very public arena in the modern hospital. They tolerate this and try to control it as much as they can.

It is the medicine in the office, where there is no organizational pressure for change or maintenance of standards, which offers the possibility of real abuse in the clinical setting. This should be of real concern, since as a result of changes in practice in response to cost containment measures, more and more procedures have been shifted from the hospital to clinics or outpatient facilities, and many procedures that used to be the reason for overnight stays are now routinely done in physician's offices. In this sense, there is less formal or informal professional or organizational control of performance. Performance is often not seen, except by partners, if there are any. When it is seen, as Professor Swazey suggests, initially there is an impetus to overlook poor performance.

Physicians are not alone as professionals in resisting peer review, nor are they alone in using consequential reasoning in thinking about professional peer control. I have heard colleagues talking about a colleague who was known to be doing inadequate teaching. These colleagues not only overlooked the fact that there was poor teaching; they excused it by saying that he was not doing a great deal of harm to students. These same colleagues would be outraged if physicians spoke of not doing a great deal of harm to patients, yet we ourselves tolerate the same kind of moral reasoning in ourselves that is used by the physicians whom we would be ready to criticize.

In fact, it seems to me that the real controls that are effective in medicine today are those that work in the external organizational or institutional context, and not those controls, informal or formal, which are supposed to work

within the profession. I am also convinced that ultimately these organizational controls will not be effective, since too much medicine is practiced outside of the organizational environment, where only peers will know, if anyone does. If there are going to be controls, they will have to be developed within the professions, and it seems to me that is a task yet to be accomplished once again, or perhaps, for the first time.

PROFESSIONS AND A SOCIAL CONTRACT

Professionals today often think that it is something beyond their ken to serve the community outside of their professional institution; indeed, given the ethos which I see in institutions of higher education and in hospitals, it is beyond their ken to serve even their own communities.

Let me relate just one example which will make this clear. Recently, the American Medical Association and the American Bar Association published an editorial in their main professional journals, asking that each professional donate 50 hours, that is, one hour a week, of their time, to serving those persons who could not otherwise afford their services. When I spoke about this with a young physician friend, he pointed out to me that he already met this criterion because he took Medicaid patients, whose reimbursement did not meet his costs. When I pointed out to him that I thought that the editorial required a bit more than this, he was outraged, pointing out, correctly it turns out, that his group was the only one serving these patients in the area. What gets lost in all of this is some sense that the professional owes a great deal to the society which educated him or her and allows the professional the quasi monopoly that professionals enjoy. The practice of not taking Medicaid patients is another example of what Pellegrino refers to as practices at the moral margin. No wonder the proposal that lawyers and physicians spend 50 hours a year in the community did not meet with overwhelming approval within these professional communities.

Just to make it clear that I am not blaming those professions alone, I would like to point out that the professionals in higher education have to ask themselves some questions on this matter. Whereas it used to be the expectation that teachers would lend their expertise to the larger community, this is no longer the case. What has become clear is that we no longer think that what we do as educators has any relevance to the larger community and we no longer think that what we do in the larger community is worth considering when we are thinking about ourselves as professionals. In this fashion, we cut, rather than reinforce, the connections between the profession and the larger society within which it finds itself and which it is supposed to be serving.

WHISTLEBLOWING AS A PRACTICE IN OUR SOCIETY TODAY

I do not want to lose the personal touch which Dr. Swazey has offered us, since it seems to me the story is a great gift which we should receive with appreciation. There are two features of the story that intrigue me. As with most first person stories of whistleblowers, the story is told calmly; we find none of the passion and the intrigue that undoubtedly marked this event. For reasons of my own, I think of this as positive. Most often, it is the second hand account of the whistleblower which is lurid and full of danger. The persons actually doing the good work see matters much differently.

There is a second feature of this story to which I would also like to attend. It is the sense, which Dr. Swazey rightly identifies as held by most whistleblowers, the sense that the larger world treats them as more of a problem than the offenders. This is often a surprise for the whistleblower. It is not clear that it was a surprise for Dr. Swazey.

I had to ask myself why I was not surprised, indeed, why I am not surprised when I read essentially the same story again and again. Why was it that I expected this kind of behavior? What did that tell me, not necessarily about the world, but about myself? Was it cynicism or was it something else? In trying to answer that question, I find myself reflecting on what we need to sustain professions, and worrying that we do not have it. What do I mean?

It seems that the important difference here is that persons who have been shaped by a theological account of the world as fallen and hopefully redeemed might see this problem differently. The difficulties that whistleblowers face would come as no surprise at all. Disappointment yes, but not a surprise. To put this in a slightly different way, persons trained to see the world in this fashion would not be surprised that the world was not necessarily going to approve of anyone when those persons did the correct thing. It may, or it may not, but one should not act in the expectation that the world would welcome what you did. That did not mean that one should not do the right thing, one of the points of telling saints stories in my own community was to remind persons that the rewards of this world were ephemeral and passing.

Why do I tell this? It brings in particularity, and worse, religious particularity into the discussion. Nothing appears more distasteful to modern sensibilities.

It seems to me that an important question which must be addressed by persons who wish to sustain professions as understood by Dr. Swazey will be, "How do we build and sustain individuals who will be the appropriate sorts of people to have when persons will be forced to act to defend professional standards?" What I am suggesting is that we once had communities which did those sorts of things. Absent those communities, and I insist on the word communities here, since there were many different communities that did this, it seems to me that there always will be difficulties with the professions. For being a professional means learning the capacity to tell the truth to another, a truth which is potentially destructive, while at the same time accepting that person. That has always struck me as extraordinarily difficult.

It has been suggested that since we no longer have communities which teach this skill, we must go different ways. One alternative is to try and instill those virtues necessary for the professional within professional training; another is to demand those virtues as a prerequisite for entrance into the profession. For reasons which seem to me obvious, neither of those strategies is likely to meet with success today.

In my own view, it is this divorce of character from considerations of entrance into professions which is a sign of our problem. What it means is that we can no longer count on the presence of persons among us who are committed to the welfare of their parents, clients, students because that commitment is good in and of itself. That commitment always has to be seen in the light of something else, some reward that will come from the practice of the profession.

At this juncture, I am not optimistic about how all of this will turn out. For one thing, I do not think that the current emphasis upon medical ethics will help very much. Recently medical ethics has focused upon moral reasoning and not very often upon the development of those virtues necessary to practice medicine in a societal context which will be constantly tempting the professional to act for him or herself and not for their patient. Further, the professional is ill-prepared for professional practice in which one has to expose the errors of oneself and one's fellow professionals. It seems to me that only when medicine begins to ask itself what kind of institutions it needs to sustain and support those persons who will take seriously their professional responsibilities, that we will be at the point where we can be optimistic once again about professional practice within clinical or academic medicine.

Professionals will fail to meet the standards of their professions; that it seems to me, is the human condition. However, if the message is that you will suffer ostracism and opprobrium for reminding your professional colleagues of their professional obligations, and that is all you know, then I am not sanguine that many persons will defend professional standards. When that happens, we are in a sorry mess indeed. For we will still need the help of physicians, attorneys, and teachers, that is, we will be vulnerable and need healing, education, and assistance with the law. Only now, we shall not be able to count on their using their professional authority to make sure that other professionals, and themselves, live up to their responsibilities to all of us.

This leads me to my central point. It is my belief that among the contributing factors to all of this has been the lack of attention to matters of virtue and character in the training of professionals, even earlier than the medical school and the residency, but in the undergraduate environment as well. Let me relate a story. Some years ago I had the duty of serving on the pre-medical advisory committee, the committee that at that time was responsible for the single letter that was sent by Lafayette about medical school applicants. We had before us an applicant who made it clear that he sought entrance into the medical profession so that he could make a lot of money and live a very comfortable life. He was not apologetic about this but thought of it as a perfectly sensible business decision.

The committee was not pleased that this person wanted to go to medical school, but felt that it could not comment on what it took to be his obvious personal deficiencies. It did not think that commenting on the character of the applicant was relevant, unless that person had committed some violation of academic dishonesty. All other forms of morally reprehensible behavior were outside of our purview, including seeking admission to medical school for monetary reasons.

In my own view, it is this divorce of character from considerations of entrance into professions which is a sign of our problem. What it means is that we can no longer count on the presence of persons among us who are committed to the welfare of their patients, clients, students because that commitment is good in and of itself. That commitment always has to be seen in light of something else, some reward that will come from the practice of the profession. I am not for a moment suggesting that professionals should do what they do for no pay; what is at stake here is a consideration of what are to be thought of as the central rewards of the profession. Pellegrino has made the point on any number of occasions that without attention to matters of character, the profession of medicine is bound to come into disrepute, if not disarray.

It is worth observing that Dr. Swazey has presented us with a high conception of the professions and of professional responsibility. Opposed to those who would substitute the word "career" for profession, Dr. Swazey argues instead that professionals should line up to the best that can be demanded of them, rather than the worst of what might be expected. In other words, she demands that they live up to what they have tried to have the American public believe that they were about. In doing this, they make the rest of us better. The question is, how to sustain persons who make these kinds of commitments?

Michael Davis

Technical Decision: Time to Rethink the Engineer's Responsibilities?

The study of professional ethics belongs to a wider field, what we might call "philosophy of professions." Like other philosophy-ofs (philosophy of law, philosophy of science, philosophy of art, and so on), the philosophy of professions attempts to understand its subject as a rational undertaking. Because professions are not abstract entities but contingent activities, each with a distinct history, social context, and internal dynamic, the philosophy of professions necessarily presupposes knowledge philosophers as such lack. To do the philosophy of any particular profession, philosophers need empirical knowledge of the sort historians, sociologists, and other social scientists typically provide. In its absence, philosophers will, at best, see nothing philosophically interesting in professions or, at worst, waste much time on problems that do not exist.

I shall illustrate that point here. First, I shall describe the common view of the way engineers work, "the received view." Second, I shall describe an alternative view of the way engineers work, one derived from recent empirical research. Last, I shall consider how this alterna-

From Michael Davis, "Technical Decisions: Time to Rethink the Engineer's Responsibilities," *Business & Professional Ethics Journal*, Vol. 11, Nos. 3 & 4, 1992. Reprinted with permission.

tive view should change the questions we ask in engineering ethics in particular and philosophy of engineering in general.

I should add that I am not singling out the social sciences for blame. The underdeveloped state of philosophy of engineering is probably as much the cause as the effect of the underdeveloped state of our empirical knowledge of engineering. Social scientists have been working with very primitive conceptions of engineering. Philosophers and social scientists need to cooperate more closely than they have if the study of engineering is to advance. I hope this paper, itself the product of such cooperation, will encourage more.

I. THE RECEIVED VIEW OF THE ENGINEER'S ROLE

Most engineers work in large organizations. On the received view, such organizations leave engineers little room for moral choice. Engineers are a "captive profession" in a highly compartmentalized environment. Managers choose what to do, divide work into small jobs, and assign each job to one engineer or small group. Communication between engineers is kept to a minimum to assure management control. An engineer may need permission from his boss even to discuss a project with an engineer in another department or working group. Engineers identify options, test them, and report the results to managers. Managers combine these reports with business information they alone have. Managers decide. Engineers merely advise.

That is the received view. Here is an example of it in practice. At a conference on engineering ethics about ten years ago, John Ladd, a philosopher at Brown University, advised his audience:

"Compare in this regard a company physician who has a degree of 'autonomy' in what he does, with a company engineer, who has almost none."[1]

On the received view, the major ethical question engineers face is when to blow the whistle. And here the situation is, according to Ladd, "[comparable] to that of people living under a totalitarian regime, where responsible action involving remonstrance leads to extermination."[2] On the received view, engineering ethics is a domain with a few martyred heroes and a great silent majority of the morally compromised.

Recently, Rosalind Williams, not only an historian of technology at MIT but the daughter, granddaughter, and niece of engineers, suggested that the situation of engineers is becoming worse. On the one hand, she noted, "Now business schools, not engineering staffs, are the favored source of managerial expertise."[3] On the other hand, "as consolidations and mergers tend to strengthen managerial authority, engineers have less and less weight in decision-making."[4] "The organizational structure of engineering today does not," she concluded, "encourage practitioners to ask questions beyond narrowly technical ones—much less to raise objections."[5]

One problem with any received view is that it generally passes without objection and therefore without defense. Ladd, for example, gave no evidence for his claims. Williams did little more. Her only evidence was one parenthetical sentence: "The now-classic example is the way engineer Roger Boisjoly was overruled by Morton-Thiokol management when he advised against launching the Challenger space shuttle in cold weather."[6]

Williams' evidence is revealing. In fact, the Challenger disaster is not a case in which mere managers overruled engineers. Those doing the overruling, three of Thiokol's vice-presidents, all had degrees in engineering.[7] Mason had a bachelor's in aeronautical engineering; Lund, a bachelor's in mechanical engineering. Though Kilminster's bachelors was in math, not engineering, he had a masters in mechanical engineering. The Challenger is a case of engineers with management responsibility ignoring the advice of other engineers, their technical staff, not of MBAs run amok.[8]

Equally revealing is the relationship between the three engineer-managers. Mason, Senior Vice President of the Wasatch Operations, was the highest-ranking Thiokol officer among those present the night before the Challenger exploded. Kilminster, Vice President for Space Booster Programs, was in charge of operations. Kilminster reported to Mason (through another vice president). Lund, Boisjoly's boss twice removed, was Vice President for Engineering. Lund reported directly to Mason.[9] Lund advised Mason (and, through him, Kilminster). Technically, Kilminster's signature was all that mattered (unless Mason intervened). Kilminster and Mason were line managers; Lund, staff. Yet, even after Mason had decided to launch, Kilminster would not sign the launch order until Lund approved. Lund, the staff engineer, not the line managers, Mason and Kilminster, seems to have had the last word on whether to launch.

The Challenger case thus provides evidence against Williams' claim, not an illustration of it. Engineers, though admittedly engineers managing other engineers, had a decisive role in the Challenger disaster.[10]

If the Challenger launch is in fact an example of typical engineering decision-making, although an example of that process flawed in an important way, then engineers have much greater autonomy than the received view suggests. Engineering advice may not be so different from management decision; and engineering ethics may be much more like medical or legal ethics. The traditional emphasis on whistle-blowing in engineering ethics may be badly misplaced.[11]

II. Empirical Work on Engineering Practice

What evidence is there that the decision-making leading to the Challenger disaster is not typical of engineering decision-making generally? The answer is: none. The received view seems to be the creature of an empirical vacuum. Though engineers are far more numerous than physicians, engineering decision-making has received far less study than medical decision-making. Indeed, it has received almost no study. We know more about decision-making among chimpanzees in the wild than about technical decisions-making among engineers in an ordinary company, American, European, or Japanese.[12]

But that has begun to change. Thanks to a grant from the Hitachi Foundation, a few colleagues and I recently interviewed 60 employees of 10 companies as part of a study of technical communication between engineers and their managers. About a third of our interviewees were managers; about a third, "bench engineers;" and the remainder, "group leaders" and others who combined some managing with a good deal of their own engineering. The companies in our sample ranged from two with a few engineers to several companies employing thousands. While most of the companies were American, one was a German transplant and another a Japanese transplant. Our sample included only one woman engineer, but a significant number of foreign-born engineers, including at least one trained in England, Holland, Germany, Poland, Japan, or Canada. All major fields of engineering were represented: mechanical, chemical, electrical, metallurgical, and civil. All interviews were conducted on site during the working day with full cooperation of the company. Interviewees were promised anonymity and seemed to speak frankly. No company refused to let us interview, but we only asked companies where we had contacts. Most interviews were conducted in the Chicago metropolitan area. Since our sample is relatively small, geographically limited, and perhaps biased by the way we selected companies, our findings must be considered tentative.

One finding concerns the common view that MBA's are replacing engineers in management. Though we interviewed many engineers with MBA's, we never interviewed a manager without an engineering degree (or its equivalent) until we explicitly sought them out. The company at which we did that, though we went there because it was reputed to have a good many non-engineers in technical management, had trouble finding them for us. Several managers the company initially identified as non-engineers reported a bachelors in engineering that an advanced degree in something else

seemed to have made invisible to the personnel department.[13]

Though our sample is too small to disprove the supposed shift from engineer-managers to MBA's without engineering degrees, it is enough to make an important point about method. Any study of the shift that relies on what companies report must be viewed with suspicion. Companies may not be very good at keeping track of engineers in their employ.

This finding is, however, only a byproduct of our interviews. We undertook the interviews to learn how engineers and managers work together to make technical decisions. What did we find?

III. How Engineers and Managers Work Together

Asked how technical decisions get made at their company, some of our interviewees initially described what sounded like the received view of how engineers and managers work together. For example, one manager told us, "Managers nearly always make the decisions;" another, "Managers have the most weight." One engineer put it this way: "[The engineer] gives the best advice he can but it's their money." Another told us that, in case of disagreement, "The boss typically wins."

Such comments were, however, largely contradicted by what even these interviewees went on to tell us about decision-making in their respective companies. For example, the same manager who told us managers nearly always make the decisions also told us: "If an engineer has a good case, a manager seldom, if ever, would overrule—that is, if the engineer really feels it won't work. However, a manager might step in regarding costs, customer preference, or some life cycle strategy—that is, something that is not absolutely engineering in nature." In the same way, the engineer who told us the boss typically wins added, "I haven't experienced this."

What in fact emerged from our interviews was a process one manager called "negotiation," a process much more reminiscent of an academic department than of a totalitarian state. Engineers' "recommendations" were often indistinguishable from decisions. Managers generally "overruled" engineers' recommendations only when non-engineering reasons (such as cost or schedule) seemed to outweigh engineering considerations. And even when they "overruled" an engineering recommendation for non-engineering reasons, managers did not literally overrule it. Instead, they presented the additional reasons to the engineer and sought the engineer's concurrence, either by winning him over with the new information or by seeking some compromise. Consensus seemed to be the mark of a good decision; outright overrule, something to be avoided at almost any cost.

This process of seeking consensus, a better term than "negotiation," seemed to rest on three assumptions:

1. that disagreement about any engineering or related management question is ultimately factual;
2. that where reasonable technically-trained people with the same information cannot reach consensus on a factual question, there is not enough information for a good decision; and
3. that, except in an emergency, putting off a decision until there is enough information (or a better understanding of the information available) is better than making a bad decision.

Our interviews suggest that these assumptions are widely shared by engineers and their managers.[14]

The power of the these assumptions can be seen in comments like the following. Asked whether he and his engineers always see eye to eye on technical decisions, one manager, having answered "no," went on to explain: "There are different ways to approach a problem. Young engineers are often inexperienced and need to learn from their mistakes. There are no real differences, though, on matters of safety and quality—these are pretty much black and white." Asked how much weight an engineer's recommendation should have, he responded "100%" and added, "I've always reached agreement with my engineers." Another manager informed us that if a manager and engineer disagree over a major technical decision, "engineers and managers go to a boss together . . . . The boss then decides. But we haven't had major problems here."

Engineers sketched a similar picture. Asked how engineering decisions were made in his company, one engineer responded, "I'm handed a design and asked, 'How do we produce this?' Eventually I make a recommendation. My boss, a supervising engineer, says yes or no. If he says no, he gives reasons. If I'm not convinced, there's no stand-off; we just go out and test." Note that the "boss" seems to have no more weight in the decision than the engineer. The ultimate arbiter is another "test." Another engineer, the one who said he gave the best advice he could, "but it's their money," nonetheless reported that he and management "always see eye to eye in the end." He had in fact never been overruled.

IV. Some Differences Among Companies

This process of reaching consensus seems to presuppose that engineers and managers have the same information. Having the same information in turn seems to presuppose a good deal of openness about technical and related business matters. How much openness is there? Before answering that question, we need to distinguish between two "types" of company. Some companies at which we interviewed seemed more *engineering-oriented;* others, more *customer-oriented.* We're not happy with either of these terms, but they are the best we've come up with so far.

Both engineers and managers in an engineering-oriented company might, for example, take pride in refusing customer requests that mean sacrificing the company's ideal of quality. In customer-oriented companies, on the other hand, both engineers and managers would be more likely to stress the lengths to which they go to satisfy customers. Such companies have no ideal of quality independent of what will satisfy a particular customer (and applicable law).

The role of engineers in customer-oriented companies differs somewhat from that in engineering-oriented companies. Customer-oriented companies seem

1. to assign greater importance to the engineer's role as advocate;
2. to place more emphasis on non-engineering considerations in decision-making;
3. to be more explicitly concerned with safety (even though the technology was no riskier); and
4. to have more difficultly maintaining open communication.

Let's consider these differences in order. They will bring us back to the *Challenger*.

At most of the customer-oriented companies where we interviewed, relations between individual engineers and managers seemed as good as the engineering-oriented companies. Yet, unlike their counterparts engineering-oriented companies, managers at customer-oriented companies repeatedly stressed the need for engineer to "hammer" on their recommendations. One manager at a small company thought: "An engineer should be willing to go to the mat if he feels strongly that quality is violated." A manager at a large company agreed: "Engineers should never be content to see their professional judgment superseded. If there's a good reason for the manager's decision, the engineer should agree. If the engineer doesn't agree, something must be wrong. Everyone should keep talking."[15]

The managers clearly thought of their engineers as advocates of a point of view which, though different from their own, had to be weighed against it—or rather, integrated with it. There was no mystery about how the two points of view differed. According to one manager, "[satisfying] the customer's needs [involves] three factors. . . : quality (which is a technical matter); timing (which is a concern of sales); and specs/cost." The engineers speak for the "techinical." A manager at another company contrasted his role with the engineers' in this way: "It has to be decided where the line is on a specification. For example, how 'perfect' does something have to be. I occasionally have to explain, 'Hey guys, it doesn't have to be absolutely perfect.' . . . [T]he customer's needs are the most basic consideration." Another manager

at this company gave the same picture but using a phrase now infamous: "The most important factors in company decisions are business issues: what does the customer want? What are his expectations? Often, it's time versus quality. And then you have to decide which hat to wear—engineer's or manager's."

Engineers in most customer-oriented companies seem to accept—or at least be resigned to—the conflict between technical and business considerations. As one engineer put it, "Cost issues are constraints I can understand."[16]

In engineering-oriented companies, "safety" and "quality" were mentioned in the same breath—when "safety" was mentioned at all. That, however, was not true in customer-oriented companies. In such companies, safety had the same absolute priority as in engineering-oriented companies, but it was mentioned much more often, So, for example, the same engineer who said quality was sacrificed to get products "out the door," stressed that he "never felt safety was being sacrificed." Many engineers also told us that they should have the "last word" on safety (even though they did not claim the last word on anything else). Managers agreed: "It's okay to overrule an engineer's recommendation on a business issue. But on safety, exposure to dangerous materials, etc., the engineer should have the last word."

Given the importance assigned consensus in all the companies at which we interviewed, open communication in customer-oriented companies should be as important as in engineering-oriented companies. Many managers seemed to believe so. Indeed, generally, they were more emphatic about being open with engineers than the managers at the engineering-oriented companies. Thus, one manager, asked about withholding information, observed, "I never withhold technical information. That's dumb." Another (at another company), answered, "Never. That's dangerous." A third: "There's no need. . . . We've got strict rules on use of information."

Yet, in each company where some managers answered this way, others reported withholding information relevant to technical decisions. For example, one manager admitted: "I have withheld proprietary information, for example, relating to preparations for a joint venture that might mean using a different technology." Others, while denying that they had withheld information, reported superiors withholding information from them: "I should add," said one, "that engineers are often in the dark and are subject to last minute surprises. Our department last year was working on existing products, things that were familiar. We were not told about any new possibilities or any new product challenges. We were provided only with vague clues. I don't know why."

Managers in customer-oriented companies also seemed more concerned about engineers withholding information from them than were their counterparts at engineering-oriented companies. Thus, one manager reported; "Engineers tend to give me a rosier picture than is factual just to continue getting my support. I try to counteract that by MBWA [Management By Wandering Around]. This is a lot more effective than formal performance reviews." Another manager at the same company stressed the dark side of such withholding: "Yes, but it only happens when they don't know enough to know what to tell. For example, now and then, a guy gets into trouble and thinks he can fix it himself. The result is I find out when it's too late to help—and I get burned too. That's happened a couple of times in my career." A manager at another company put it more succinctly: "Do they withhold information from me? When they screw up, yes."

Yet, other managers at these same companies denied that their engineers ever withheld technical information from them. One manager was more cautious: "This is the toughest question on the list. I've occasionally had the feeling there was more there than I could see in the engineer's report."

Engineers gave an equally mixed report on communications at customer-oriented companies. For example, on engineer told us of a "recent survey" that indicated that "people believe upper management holds back information from the company," adding, "My current manager does not withhold information from me." An engineer at another company admitted to the "feeling" his superior was withholding technical information. Yet, most engineers reported that they did not think their managers withheld technical information from them.

Interestingly, unlike engineers in engineering-oriented companies, engineers in some customer-oriented companies did report withholding information from managers. One observed, "I have, but I'm not sure it was necessary. I have withheld a theory or brainstorm until it was tested to verify it positively. I have delayed bad news in order to retest first." A group leader at another company admitted, "I sometimes don't tell my manager about a decision if I am already quite comfortable with it."

So, it seems, technical communication in customer-oriented companies tends to be somewhat less open than in engineering-oriented companies. Given how much customer-oriented companies differ from one another and from engineering-oriented companies, the cause of that apparent tendency is probably complex. Still, two factors seem relevant.

First, the relatively greater importance of business information in decisions of customer-oriented companies is likely to change the effect of withholding business information. Even if the same amount of business information were withheld in a customer-oriented company as in an engineering-oriented company, its withholding would be more likely to threaten consensus in a customer-oriented company (where it would be a more prominent part of the big picture). Hence, its withholding would be more likely to be noticed.

Second, the greater emphasis on the engineer as advocate in customer-oriented companies may tempt engineers to engage in lawyerly tactics. Hence, the greater tendency of engineers in customer-oriented companies to withhold information.

Whatever the cause, a customer-oriented company that wants to decide by consensus will, it seems, have to take more care to keep information flowing than an otherwise similar engineering-oriented one.

V. CONCLUSION: BEYOND THE RECEIVED VIEW

On the received view, engineering work is highly compartmentalized, making engineers mere tools of those for whom they must work.

Engineers generally cannot be responsible for what they do because they generally lack the control necessary for responsibility. Some companies may approximate the received view. One engineer we interviewed recalled work at a previous employer (more than ten years before): "There I would often be assigned a job by a P.E. [a licensed Professional Engineer] I never saw and send him a written report. Occasionally, the report came back with written comments. Usually, I had no idea what happened to it."

Though there may be some truth in the received view, we found little evidence of it at the companies where we interviewed. Instead of the rigid, hierarchical, and compartmentalized decision process of the received view, we found a highly fluid process depending heavily on meetings and less formal exchange of information across even departmental boundaries. Managers seemed to have little control over what information would reach their engineers. Indeed, they seemed anxious to get their engineers to hook up with others on their own. Their only complaints were about remaining compartmentalization, especially the parochialism of their own engineers.

While we heard many complaints about remaining compartmentalization from engineers too, we also heard a few complaints arising from attempts to reduce compartmentalization. One example will be enough. Asked what he would change if he had full control of his company, one engineer at an engineering-oriented company answered, "I wouldn't show up at a field meeting with so many engineers we outnumber the customer." Such outnumbering was, it seemed, a common consequence of sending one engineer from each department likely to be involved in a particular a project.[17]

If we now look again at the meeting the night before the *Challenger* exploded, we will see two more ways in which events do not fit the received view. First, there is no question of compartmentalization. Boisjoly knew everything his superiors did. Second, his attempt to make them understand his objections to launching is not as extraordinary as the received view would have us suppose. If Thiokol Boisjoly was doing what an engineer is supposed to do if he disagrees "hammering" away, "going to the

mat." What is unusual is the managers' reaction. Instead of letting the engineers have the last word on safety, or seeking consensus with them on quality or related business issues, the managers closed the engineers out of the process, seeking consensus only among themselves. The *Challenger* disaster is not an example of the small role engineers have in ordinary technical decisions. Instead, it is an object lesson in the dangers of reducing the large role engineers ordinarily have in such decisions.[18]

This new reading of the critical events of the night before the *Challenger* exploded suggests the need to change the focus of work in engineering ethics. We need to pay more attention to the engineer's role as advocate. We need, for example, to answer such questions as these: What information, if any, may an engineer ethically withhold from a manager? When should an engineer join a consensus? When refuse? Beyond these questions lie deeper ones, for example, whether engineers should make decisions by consensus. These deeper questions should link work in the philosophy of engineering with work in the philosophy of other professions.[19]

That I, a philosopher, gave up almost two hundred hours to interview engineers and managers is evidence of how keenly I felt the absence of empirical knowledge of the practice of engineering. What I learned in consequence shows the importance of such work for engineering ethics, for philosophy of engineering, and (by generalization) for philosophy of professions. I hope this paper will encourage others to do something similar.

Notes

Versions of this paper were read at the National Conference on Ethics and the Professions, University of Florida, Gainesville, 1 February 1992, and at a seminar sponsored by the Department of Mechanical Engineering, Texas A & M University, 12 March 1992. I [Michael Davis] should like to thank those present at one or the other of these readings for their comments.

1. John Ladd, "Collective and Individual Moral Responsibility in Engineering: Some Questions," in *Beyond Whistleblowing: Defining Engineers' Responsibilities,* ed. by Vivian Weil, Center for the study of Ethics in the Professions, Illinois Institute of Technology: Chicago, 1982), 95.
2. Ibid.

3. Rosalind Williams, "Engineer's image problem," *Issues in Science and Technology* 6 (Spring 1990), p. 86.

4. Ibid.

5. Williams, 86. For much the same point recently made by a professor of engineering graphics, see Richard Devon, "New Paradigms for Engineering Ethics," published by the IEEE (1990) as document #89CH2931-4/90/0000/0081.

6. Williams, 86.

7. Information obtained from Bob Barker (801 863-3601), Human Relations Department, Thiokol (Wasatch, Utah).

8. The engineer-manager who overruled ordinary engineers seems to be a common character in engineering disasters. For a bit more on this point, see my "One Social Responsibility of Engineering Societies: Teaching Managers About Engineering Ethics," monograph 88-WA/DE-14 (American Society of Mechanical Engineers: New York, 1988), pp. 2–3. Other professions may face similar problems. For an example involving a physician (but without a disaster), see *Pierce v. Ortho Pharmaceuticals Corp.*, 84 N.J. 58, 417 A. 2d. 505 (1980).

9. *Report of the Presidential Commission on the Space Shuttle Challenger Accident* (Washington, D.C.: U.S. Government Printing Office, 1986), vol. I, p. 230 (organization chart).

10. There is another way in which this case seems to be evidence against the received view rather than evidence for it: When the *Challenger* exploded, the managers had to explain why they overruled the recommendation of their engineers. No one argued that engineers should be restricted to narrowly technical advice.

11. For some idea how the emphasis might be shifted, see my "Avoiding the Tragedy of Whistleblowing," *Business & Professional Ethics Journal* 8 (4):3–19.

12. The best work in this area is probably still Tom Burns and G. M. Stalker, *The Management of Innovation* (London: Tavistock Publications, 1966). But like others who have written on managing production, development, or research, Burns and Stalker tend to lump engineers with scientists in research and with managers or mechanics in the shop. They do not even raise the question whether engineers have a special role, much less investigate what that role might be.

13. Interestingly, these "secret engineers" invariably described themselves as engineers early in our initial telephone contact. They considered themselves to be "engineers with management responsibilities," not "managers." "Manager" was either a job description (rather than a profession) or the default designation of managers without another profession. This self-identification deserves more study.

14. These assumptions were thought to apply to some matters philosophers do not think of as factual, for example, safety and quality. Whether such matters are literally factual is a philosophical question we may ignore now. What "factual" means here is simply that experience has taught those disagreeing about such matters to expect to settle their disagreements by further testing, other new information, or reconsidering information already available. For our purposes, what is important is that engineers and their managers do expect to agree on such matters. These "factual matters" were routinely contrasted with others, especially personnel matters, about which the same could not be said. Engineers and managers did not expect to agree on who should get a raise, a better office, or a promotion.

15. Compare Richard T. De George, "Ethical Responsibilities of Engineers in Large Organizations: The Pinto Case," *Business & Professional Ethics Journal* 1 (Fall 1981): 1–14, esp. 5: "Engineers in large firms have an ethical responsibility to do their jobs as best they can, to report their observations about safety and improvement of safety to management. But they do not have the obligation to insist that their perceptions or their standards be accepted. They are not paid to do that, they are not expected to do that, and they have no moral or ethical obligation to do that." While all this may have been true at Ford in the 1970's, De George (uncharacteristically) offers no evidence even for that. He seems simply to have assumed the received view.

16. There was, however, one company in which the engineers showed no such resignation. This was a traditionally customer-oriented company that had begun a quality enhancement program because senior management had concluded that the company could not survive in the long run unless its products met standards of quality beyond what the market was then demanding. Here one engineer told us: "Technical questions get short-changed to make schedule. 'We can do it better,' I say, but my manager says, 'No time!'" Another engineer at the same company reported in evident disgust, "They'll sacrifice quality to get it out the door," adding, "Why not do it right the first time rather than taking a lot of time later to patch up a system?" Apparently, the managers found adapting to the new quality standards harder than the engineers did. In effect, the company was becoming more engineering-oriented.

17. The most common complaint of this sort was simply "too many meetings."

18. I am, I should add, not trying to offer a full explanation of what went wrong that night. For some suggestions about what might have contributed to the managers' conduct, see Saul W. Gellerman's generic list, "Why 'good' managers make bad ethical choices," *Harvard Business Review* (July–August 1986): 85–90; or, better yet, my discussion of the *Challenger* in "Explaining Wrongdoing," *Journal of Social Philosophy* 20 (Spring/Fall 1989): 74–90.

19. For an example of recent work on decision by consensus in another profession from which philosophy of engineering might benefit, see the entire August 1991 issue of *The Journal of Medicine and Philosophy*.

1. What does Jennings mean when he claims that contemporary professional ethics has not come to grips with the notions of character and virtue? Do you agree? Why or why not? Does an emphasis on rules and regulation inevitably undermine an emphasis on character and virtue? Explain your answer.

2. Which do you take to be the bigger problem in professional ethics: discerning what is right or motivating people to do what is right? Defend your view.

3. What does Swazey mean when she suggests that whistleblowers are often viewed as more deviant than those on whom they blow the whistle? How does she explain for this tendency?

4. On what basis does Swazey term physicians a "delinquent community"?

5. Why does Lammers suggest that organizational controls are not effective in controlling medical practices?

6. What is Lammers positive suggestion for improving the moral climate in the professions?

7. What is Davis' criticism of the "received view" of the way engineers work?

8. What does Davis mean when he suggests that "to do the philosophy of any particular profession, philosophers need empirical knowledge of the sort historians, sociologists, and other social scientists typically provide"?

CASE 13:1 MEDICAL RESEARCH AND THE INTERESTS OF THE PATIENT [1]

On October 5, 1976 shortly after being diagnosed with a rare disease known as hairy-cell leukemia, John Moore travelled from Seattle to the UCLA Medical Center to confirm the diagnosis. At the time, Dr. David W. Gold, the physician who attended Moore at the UCLA Medical Center, confirmed the accuracy of the original diagnosis. On October 8, 1976 Golde informed Moore that Moore had reason to fear for his life and recommended the removal of Moore's spleen to slow down the progress of the disease. On Golde's advice, Moore gave written consent authorizing a splenectomy. The operation was performed on October 20, 1976. During the period between November 1976 and September 1983, Moore travelled from his home in Seattle to the UCLA Medical Center several times. On each of these visits, Golde took samples of blood, blood serum, skin, bone marrow aspirate, and sperm. Moore made these trips on the understanding that they were essential for his health and that the procedures involved should only be performed under Golde's supervision.

What Golde did not reveal to Moore was the large commercial value of Moore's blood and bodily substances, and Golde's plans to benefit financially from his exclusive access to Moore's cells. Golde, along with Shirley G. Quan, a researcher employed by the University of California, planned using recombinant DNA technology, to use Moore's cells to help them produce lymphokines, i.e., proteins that regulate the immune system. Golde and Quan made arrangements prior to the removal of Moore's spleen to obtain portions of it following Moore's splenectomy so that it would provide them with material for research. Neither Golde nor Quan informed Moore of these plans or requested his permission to perform research. Moore alleges that in reply to his subsequent inquiries as to whether his cells might be of financial value, Golde repeatedly informed him they had no commercial value and actively discouraged him from further investigation.

Sometime prior to August 1979, Golde and Quan were successful in establishing what is called a cell line from Moore's T'lymphocytes. On January 30, 1981 the University of California applied for a patent of the cell line, listing Golde, Quan, and the University. With the University's assistance, Golde negotiated agreements for commercial development of the cell line. Through an agreement with Genetics Institute Inc., Golde became a paid consultant and acquired 75,000 shares of common stock. Genetics Institute also agreed to pay Golde and the University at least $330,000 over three years. On June 4, 1982 Sandoz Pharmaceuticals Corporation was added to the agreement and the compensation payable to Golde and the University was increased by $110,000.

Upon becoming aware of these developments, Moore sued on thirteen grounds. Among these were lack of informed consent, a breach of fiduciary duty, fraud, and deceit and unjust enrichment.

1. Golde held that Moore had no cause for complaint, inasmuch as the research activities in no way affected the qualify of his medical treatment.Supposing Moore's medical treatment was in no way compromised, are Golde's actions justified?

2. What moral responsibilities, if any, did Quan, the University, and the companies have with respect to Moore?
3. Is Moore morally entitled to a share of the profits from products developed from his cells?

CASE 13:2 A LAWYER WHISTLEBLOWS[2]

Robert W. Herbster was employed as chief legal officer and vice-president in charge of the legal department for North American Company for Life and Health Insurance under an oral contract terminable at will. In 1984 Herbster brought a suit for retaliatory discharge against North American. According to Herbster, he had been discharged for failing to remove or destroy documents in North American's files that had been requested in law suits pending in the Federal court in Alabama against North American. These documents tended to support allegations of fraud in the sale of annuities by North American. Herbster also claimed that if he had not refused to remove or destroy these documents he would have defrauded the Federal court of Alabama and violated his Code of Professional Responsibility.

North American claimed that there was no cause of action for retaliatory discharge by an attorney terminated by his client, that Herbster was discharged because of the inferior quality of his work,

and that they had never directed Herbster to destroy or remove any discovery information.

CASE STUDY QUESTIONS

1. Can you think of safeguards which would protect the special attorney-client relationship, yet would also protect lawyers from retaliation by employers who ask them to perform unethical actions?
2. How would you have acted in Herbster's circumstances?

Notes

1. Based on Moore v. Regents of the Univ. of Cal. as found in 793 *Pacific Reporter,* 2nd series, 479 (Cal. 1990).
2. Based on Herbster v. North American as found in 501 North *Eastern Reporter,* 2nd series, 343 (Ill. App. 2 Dist. 1986).

FOR FURTHER READING

1. J. C. Callahan, editor *Ethical Issues in Professional Life* (New York: Oxford University Press, 1988)

2. Michael Davis, "Conflict of Interest," *Business and Professional Ethics Journal* Summer, 1982, 17–27.

3. A. Flores and D. G. Johnson "Collective Responsibility and Professional Roles," *Ethics,* Vol. 93, April, 1983, pp. 537–545.

4. Karl J. Mackie, "Business Regulation, Business Ethics and the Professional Employee," *Journal of Business Ethics,* Vol. 8, 1989, pp. 607–616.

Part IV

BUSINESS AND SOCIETY

Chapter Fourteen

Affirmative Action and Comparable Worth

Introduction

The topics of affirmative action, (sometimes called reverse discrimination) and comparable worth, (also known as pay equity) generate heated debate. Many proponents argue that programs of affirmative action and comparable worth are the only way to bring about a more just society. But critics just as vigorously contend that such programs undermine any attempt to make society more just.

What makes it possible for men and women of good will to disagree so vehemently on these issues? The explanation lies, I think, in the fact that both affirmative action and pay equity programs pose a host of complicated factual and moral questions. It is no easy matter, for example, to determine to what degree the occupational and wage differences between men and women are a result of sex discrimination, just as it is no easy matter to resolve the moral question of how far we may depart from what seem just procedures of hiring or promotion (procedural justice) in the interests of what seems to be a just result (substantive justice) of placing minority members in positions from which they have been historically excluded. It is important in approaching these difficult topics to discern whether our disagreements are a result of weighing moral values differently, holding different factual beliefs, or a combination of both.

The title of the first selection "What is Wrong with Reverse Discrimination" by Edwin C. Hettinger, is misleading, inasmuch as it seems to suggest that Hettinger does not think programs of affirmative action can by morally justified. Hettinger argues that common objections to affirmative action fail, and that although affirmative action involves judging people on the basis of involuntary characteristics and forcing young white males to shoulder a disproportionate share of the costs associated with achieving an egalitarian society, these minor evils are easily outweighed by the good accomplished by such programs.

Louis P. Pojam in his article, "The Moral Status of Affirmative Action," examines the history of affirmative action and the arguments both for and against affirmative action programs of preferential treatment. He concludes that despite being well-intentioned, such programs are morally unjustified and pragmatically ineffective.

Programs of comparable worth are based on the claim that women's jobs are consistently undervalued. Proponents of such programs point to the undeniable fact that on the average women make far less money than men. They suggest that the explanation for this fact is systematic discrimination against women, resulting in women being paid less than men in comparable jobs, and that justice requires intervention to ensure equal remuneration.

Opponents of such programs point out that we cannot simply assume that the fact that women on the average earn less than men is the result of discrimination. It has been argued for example, that as early as 1971, single women in their thirties who had worked continuously since leaving school earned slightly more than single men of the same age, and that female academics who never married earned more than male academics who never married.[1] In this view, most of the income differences between men and women turn out to be differences between married women who interrupt their working career and all other categories.

Wil Waluchow in his article, "Pay Equity: Equal Value to Whom," argues that although other factors may partially explain the gap between the average wages of men and women, a significant portion can only be explained on the hypothesis of unjust discrimination. In Waluchow's view, the question is not whether programs of comparable worth are justified, but rather the criteria by which we judge different jobs to be of equal value. His concern is that the phrase "work of equal value" will focus attention on the functional worth of the worker's work, rather than upon the merit of the worker considered as a person working under difficult conditions.

June O'Neill in her article, "An Argument Against Comparable Worth," argues that proponents of comparable worth typically overestimate the effects of discrimination. She suggests that both occupational differences and the wage gap are the result of differences in the roles of men and women in the family. She also argues that when we can identify discriminatory barriers these are better dealt with by policies other than comparable worth.

Notes

1. See, for example, Walter Block "Economic Intervention, Discrimination and Unforeseen Consequences" in *Discrimination, Affirmative Action, and Equal Opportunity* (Vancouver: The Fraser Institute, 1982) p. 51, p. 112.

Edwin C. Hettinger

What is Wrong with Reverse Discrimination?

Many people think it obvious that reverse discrimination is unjust. Calling affirmative action reverse discrimination itself suggests this. This discussion evaluates numerous reasons given for this alleged injustice. Most of these accounts of what is wrong with reverse discrimination are found to be deficient. The explanations for why reverse discrimination is morally troubling show only that it is unjust in a relatively weak sense. This result has an important consequence for the wider issue of the moral justifiability of affirmative action. If social policies which involve minor injustice are permissible (and perhaps required) when they are required in order to overcome much greater injustice, then the mild injustice of reverse disimination is easily overridden by its contribution to the important social goal of dismantling our sexual and racial caste system.[1]

By "reverse discrimination" or "affirmative action" I shall mean hiring or admitting a slightly less well qualified woman or black, rather than a slightly more qualified white male,[2] for the purpose of helping to eradicate sexual and/or racial inequality, or for the purpose of compensating women and blacks for the burdens and injustices they have suffered due to past and ongoing sexism and racism.[3] There are weaker forms of affirmative action, such as giving preference to minority candidates only when qualifications are equal, or providing special educational opportunities for youths in disadvantaged groups. This paper seeks to defend the more controversial sort of reverse dis-

crimination defined above. I begin by considering several spurious objections to reverse discrimination. In the second part, I identify the ways in which this policy is morally troubling and then assess the significance of these negative features.

SPURIOUS OBJECTIONS

1. Reverse Discrimination as Equivalent to Racism and Sexism

In a discussion on national television, George Will, the conservative news analyst and political philosopher, articulated the most common objection to reverse discrimination. It is unjust, he said, because it is discrimination on the basis of race or sex. Reverse discrimination against white males is the same evil as traditional discrimination against women and blacks. The only difference is that in this case it is the white male who is being discriminated against. Thus if traditional racism and sexism are wrong and unjust, so is reverse discrimination, and for the very same reasons.

But reverse discrimination is not at all like traditional sexism and racism. The motives and intentions behind it are completely different, as are its consequences. Consider some of the motives underlying traditional racial discrimination.[4] Blacks were not hired or allowed into schools because it was felt that contact with them was degrading, and sullied whites. These policies were based on contempt and loathing for blacks, on a feeling that blacks were suitable only for subservient positions and that they should never have positions of authority over whites. Slightly better qualified white males are not being turned down under affirmative action for any of these reasons. No defenders or practitioners of affirmative action (and no significant segment of the general public) think that contact with white males is degrading or sullying, that white males are contemptible and loathsome, or that white males—by their nature—should be subservient to blacks or women.

From Edwin C. Hettinger, "What is Wrong with Reverse Discrimination?" *Business and Professional Ethics Journal,* Vol. 6, No. 3, 1986. Reprinted with permission.

The consequences of these two policies differ radically as well. Affirmative action does not stigmatize white males; it does not perpetuate unfortunate stereotypes about white males; it is not part of a pattern of discrimination that makes being a white male incredibly burdensome.[5] Nor does it add to a particular group's "already overabundant supply" of power, authority, wealth, and opportunity, as does traditional racial and sexual discrimination.[6] On the contrary, it results in a more egalitarian distribution of these social and economic benefits. If the motives and consequences of reverse discrimination and of traditional racism and sexism are completely different, in what sense could they be morally equivalent acts? If acts are to be individuated (for moral purposes) by including the motives, intentions, and consequences in their description, then clearly these two acts are not identical.

It might be argued that although the motives and consequences are different, the act itself is the same: reverse discrimination is discrimination on the basis of race and sex, and this is wrong in itself independently of its motives or consequences. But discriminating (i.e., making distinctions in how one treats people) on the basis of race or sex is not always wrong, nor is it necessarily unjust. It is not wrong, for example, to discriminate against one's own sex when choosing a spouse. Nor is racial or sexual discrimination in hiring necessarily wrong. This is shown by Peter Singer's example in which a director of a play about ghetto conditions in New York City refuses to consider any white applicants for the actors because she wants the play to be authentic.[7] If I am looking for a representative of the black community, or doing a study about blacks and disease, it is perfectly legitimate to discriminate against all whites. Their whiteness makes them unsuitable for my (legitimate) purposes. Similarly, if I am hiring a wet-nurse, or a person to patrol the women's change rooms in my department store, discriminating against males is perfectly legitimate.

These examples show that racial and sexual discrimination are not wrong in themselves. This is not to say that they are never wrong; most often they clearly are. Whether or not they are wrong, however, depends on the

purposes, consequences, and context of such discrimination.

2. Race and Sex as Morally Arbitrary and Irrelevant Characteristics

A typical reason given for the alleged injustice of all racial and sexual discrimination (including affirmative action) is that it is morally arbitrary to consider race or sex when hiring, since these characteristics are not relevant to the decision. But the above examples show that not all uses of race or sex as a criterion in hiring decisions are morally arbitrary or irrelevant. Similarly, when an affirmative action officer takes into account race and sex, use of these characteristics is not morally irrelevant or arbitrary. Since affirmative action aims to help end racial and sexual inequality by providing black and female role models for minorities (and non-minorities), the race and sex of the job candidates are clearly relevant to the decision. There is nothing arbitrary about the affirmative action officer focusing on race and sex. Hence, if reverse discrimination is wrong, it is not wrong for the reason that it uses morally irrelevant and arbitrary characteristics to distinguish between applicants.

3. Reverse Discrimination as Unjustified Stereotyping

It might be argued that reverse discrimination involves judging people by alleged average characteristics of a class to which they belong, instead of judging them on the basis of their individual characteristics, and that such judging on the basis of stereotypes is unjust. But the defense of affirmative action suggested in this paper does not rely on stereotyping. When an employer hires a slightly less well qualified woman or black over a slightly more qualified white male for the purpose of helping to overcome sexual and racial inequality, she judges the applicants on the basis of their individual characteristics. She uses this person's sex or skin color as a mechanism to help achieve the goals of affirmative action. Individual characteristics of the white male (his skin color and sex) prevent him from serving one of the legitimate goals of employment policies, and he is turned down on this basis.

Notice that the objection does have some force against those who defend reverse discrimination on the grounds of compensatory justice. An affirmative action policy whose purpose is to compensate women and blacks for past and current injustices judges that women and blacks on the average are owed greater compensation than are white males. Although this is true, opponents of affirmative action argue that some white males have been more severely and unfairly disadvantaged than some women and blacks.[8] A poor white male from Appalachia may have suffered greater undeserved disadvantages than the upper-middle class women or black with whom he competes. Although there is a high correlation between being female (or being black) and being especially owed compensation for unfair disadvantages suffered, the correlation is not universal.

Thus defending affirmative action on the grounds of compensatory justice may lead to unjust treatment of white males in individual cases. Despite the fact that certain white males are owed greater compensation than are some women or blacks, it is the latter that receive compensation. This is the result of judging candidates for jobs on the basis of the average characteristics of their class, rather than on the basis of their individual characteristics. Thus compensatory justice defenses of reverse discrimination may involve potentially problematic stereotyping.[9] But this is not the defense of affirmative action considered here.

4. Failing to Hire the Most Qualified Person is Unjust

One of the major reasons people think reverse discrimination is unjust is because they think that reverse discrimination is unjust the most qualified person should get the job. But why should the most qualified person be hired?

a. Efficiency One obvious answer to this question is that one should hire the most qualified person because doing so promotes efficiency. If job qualifications are positively

correlated with job performance, then the more qualified person will tend to do a better job. Although it is not always true that there is such a correlation, in general there is, and hence this point is well taken. There are short term efficiency costs of reverse discrimination as defined here.[10]

Note that a weaker version of affirmative action has no such efficiency costs. If one hires a black or woman over a white male only in cases where qualifications are roughly equal, job performance will not be affected. Furthermore, efficiency costs will be a function of the qualifications gap between the black or woman hired, and the white male rejected: the larger the gap, the greater the efficiency costs.[11] The existence of efficiency costs is also a function of the type of work performed. Many of the jobs in our society are ones which any normal person can do (e.g., assembly line worker, janitor, truck driver, etc.). Affirmative action hiring for these positions is unlikely to have significant efficiency costs (assuming whoever is hired is willing to work hard). In general, professional positions are the ones in which people's performance levels will vary significantly, and hence these are the jobs in which reverse discrimination could have significant efficiency costs.

While concern for efficiency gives us a reason for hiring the most qualified person, it in no way explains the alleged injustice suffered by the white male who is passed over due to reverse discrimination. If the affirmative action employer is treating the white male unjustly, it is not because the hiring policy is inefficient. Failing to maximize efficiency does not generally involve acting unjustly. For instance, a person who carries one bag of groceries at a time, rather than two, is acting inefficiently, though not unjustly.

It is arguable that the manager of a business who fails to hire the most qualified person (and thereby sacrifices some efficiency) treats the owners of the company unjustly, for their profits may suffer, and this violates one conception of the manager's fiduciary responsibility to the shareholders. Perhaps the administrator of a hospital who hires a slightly less well qualified black doctor (for the purposes of affirmative action) treats the future patients at that hospital unjustly, for doing so may reduce the level of health care they receive (and it is arguable that they have a legitimate expectation to receive the best health care possible for the money they spend). But neither of these examples of inefficiency leading to injustice concern the white male "victim" of affirmative action, and it is precisely this person who the opponents of reverse discrimination claim is being unfairly treated.

To many people, that a policy is inefficient is a sufficient reason for condemning it. This is especially true in the competitive and profit oriented world of business. However, profit maximization is not the only legitimate goal of business hiring policies (or other business decisions). Businesses have responsibilities to help heal society's ills, especially those (like racism and sexism) which they in large part helped to create and perpetuate. Unless one takes the implausible position that business' only legitimate goal is profit maximization, the efficiency costs of affirmative action are not an automatic reason for rejecting it. And as we have noted, affirmative action's efficiency costs are of no help in substantiating and explaining its alleged injustice to white males.

b. The Most Qualified Person has a Right to the Job One could argue that the most qualified person for the job has a right to be hired in virtue of superior qualifications. On this view, reverse discrimination violates the better qualified white male's right to be hired for the job. But the most qualified applicant holds no such right. If you are the best painter in town, and a person hires her brother to paint her house, instead of you, your rights have not been violated. People do not have rights to be hired for particular jobs (though I think a plausible case can be made for the claim that there is a fundamental human right to employment). If anyone has a right in this matter, it is the employer. This is not to say, of course, that the employer cannot do wrong in her hiring decision; she obviously can. If she hires a white because she loathes blacks, she does wrong. The point is that her wrong does not consist in violating the right some candidate has to her job (though this would violate other rights of the candidate).

c. The Most Qualified Person Deserves the Job It could be argued that the most qualified person should get the job because she deserves it in virtue of her superior qualifications. But the assumption that the person most qualified for a job is the one who most deserves it is problematic. Very often people do not deserve their qualifications, and hence they do not deserve anything on the basis of those qualifications.[12] A person's qualifications are a function of at least the following factors:

   a. innate abilities,
   b. home environment,
   c. socio-economic class of parents,
   d. quality of the schools attended,
   e. luck, and
   f. effort or perseverance.

A person is only responsible for the last factor on this list, and hence one only deserves one's qualifications to the extent that they are a function of effort.[13]

It is undoubtedly often the case that a person who is less well qualified for a job is more deserving of the job (because she worked harder to achieve those lower qualifications) than is someone with superior qualifications. This is frequently true of women and blacks in the job market: they worked harder to overcome disadvantages most (or all) white males never faced. Hence, affirmative action policies which permit the hiring of slightly less well qualified candidates may often be more in line with considerations of desert than are the standard meritocratic procedures.

The point is not that affirmative action is defensible because it helps insure that more deserving candidates get jobs. Nor is it that desert should be the only or even the most important consideration in hiring decisions. The claim is simply that hiring the most qualified person for a job need not (and quite often does not) involve hiring the most deserving candidate. Hence the intuition that morality requires one to hire the most qualified people cannot be justified on the grounds that these people deserve to be hired.[14]

d. The Most Qualified Person is Entitled to the Job One might think that although the most qualified person neither deserves the job nor has a right to the job, still this person is entitled to the job. By "entitlement" in this context, I mean a natural and legitimate expectation based on a type of social promise. Society has implicitly encouraged the belief that the most qualified candidate will get the job. Society has set up a competition and the prize is a job which is awarded to those applying with the best qualifications. Society thus reneges on an implicit promise it has made to its members when it allows reverse discrimination to occur. It is dashing legitimate expectations it has encouraged. It is violating the very rules of a game it created.

Furthermore, the argument goes, by allowing reverse discrimination, society is breaking an explicit promise (contained in the Civil Rights Act of 1964) that it will not allow race or sex to be used against one of its citizens. Title VII of that Act prohibits discrimination in employment on the basis of race or sex (as well as color, religion, or national origin).

In response to this argument, it should first be noted that the above interpretation of the Civil Rights Act is misleading. In fact, the Supreme Court has interpreted the Act as allowing race and sex to be considered in hiring or admission decisions.[15] More importantly, since affirmative action has been an explicit national policy for the last twenty years (and has been supported in numerous court cases), it is implausible to argue that society has promised its members that it will not allow race or sex to outweigh superior qualifications in hiring decisions. In addition, the objection takes a naive and utopian view of actual hiring decisions. It presents a picture of our society as a pure meritocracy in which hiring decisions are based solely on qualifications. The only exception it sees to these meritocratic procedures is the unfortunate policy of affirmative action. But this picture is dramatically distorted. Elected government officials, political appointees, business managers, and many others clearly do not have their positions solely or even mostly because of their qualifications.[16] Given the widespread acceptance in our society of procedures which are far from meritocratic, claiming that the most qualified person has a socially endorsed entitlement to the job is not believable.

5. Undermining Equal Opportunity for White Males

It has been claimed that the right of white males to an equal chance of employment is violated by affirmative action.[17] Reverse discrimination, it is said, undermines equality of opportunity for white males.

If equality of opportunity requires a social environment in which everyone at birth has the roughly the same chance of succeeding through the use of his or her natural talents, then it could well be argued that given the social, cultural, and educational disadvantages placed on women and blacks, preferential treatment of these groups brings us closer to equality of opportunity. White males are full members of the community in a way in which women and blacks are not, and this advantage is diminished by affirmative action. Affirmative action takes away the greater than equal opportunity white males generally have, and thus it brings us closer to a situation in which all members of society have an equal chance of succeeding through the use of their talents.

It should be noted that the goal of affirmative action is to bring about a society in which there is equality of opportunity for women and blacks without preferential treatment of these groups. It is not the purpose of the sort of affirmative action defended here to disadvantage white males in order to take away the advantage a sexist and racist society gives to them. But noticing that this occurs is sufficient to dispel the illusion that affirmative action undermines the equality of opportunity for white males.[18]

LEGITIMATE OBJECTIONS

The following two considerations explain what is morally troubling about reverse discrimination.

a. Judging on the Basis of Involuntary Characteristics

In cases of reverse discrimination, white males are passed over on the basis of membership in a group they were born into. When an affirmative action employer hires a slightly less well qualified black (or woman), rather than a more highly qualified white male, skin color (or sex) is being used as one criterion for determining who gets a very important benefit. Making distinctions in how one treats people on the basis of characteristics they cannot help having (such as skin color or sex) is morally problematic because it reduces individual autonomy. Discriminating between people on the basis of features they can do something about is preferable, since it gives them some control over how others act towards them. They can develop the characteristics others use to give them favorable treatment and avoid those characteristics others use as grounds for unfavorable treatment.[19]

For example, if employers refuse to hire you because you are a member of the American Nazi party, and if you do not like the fact that you are having a hard time finding a job, you can choose to leave the party. However, if a white male is having trouble finding employment because slightly less well qualified women and blacks are being given jobs to meet affirmative action requirements, there is nothing he can do about this disadvantage, and his autonomy is curtailed.[20]

Discriminating between people on the basis of their involuntary characteristics is morally undesirable, and thus reverse discrimination is also morally undesirable. Of course, that something is morally undesirable does not show that it is unjust, nor that it is morally unjustifiable.

How morally troubling is it to judge people on the basis of involuntary characteristics? Notice that our society frequently uses these sorts of features to distinguish between people. Height and good looks are characteristics one cannot do much about, and yet basketball players and models are ordinarily chosen and rejected on the basis of precisely these features. To a large extent our intelligence is also a feature beyond our control, and yet intelligence is clearly one of the major characteristics our society uses to determine what happens to people.

Of course there are good reasons why we distinguish between people on the basis of these sorts of involuntary characteristics. Given the goals of basketball teams, model agencies, and employers in general, hiring the taller, better

looking, or more intelligent person (respectively) makes good sense. It promotes efficiency, since all these people are likely to do a better job. Hiring policies based on these involuntary characteristics serve the legitimate purposes of these businesses (e.g. profit and serving the public), and hence they may be morally justified despite their tendency to reduce the control people have over their own lives.

This argument applies to reverse discrimination as well. The purpose of affirmative action is to help eradicate racial and sexual injustice. If affirmative action policies help bring about this goal, then they can be morally justified despite their tendency to reduce the control white males have over their lives.

In one respect this sort of consequentialist argument is more forceful in the case of affirmative action. Rather than merely promoting the goal of efficiency (which is the justification for businesses hiring naturally brighter, taller, or more attractive individuals), affirmative action promotes the non-utilitarian goal of an egalitarian society. In general, promoting a consideration of justice (such as equality) is more important than is promoting efficiency or utility.[21] Thus in terms of the importance of the objective, this consequentialist argument is stronger in the case of affirmative action. If one can justify reducing individual autonomy on the grounds that it promotes efficiency, one can certainly do so on the grounds that it reduces the injustice of racial and sexual inequality.

2. Burdening White Males Without Compensation

Perhaps the strongest moral intuition concerning the wrongness of reverse discrimination is that it is unfair to job seeking white males. It is unfair because they have been given an undeserved disadvantage in the competition for employment; they have been handicapped because of something that is not their fault. Why should white males be made to pay for the sins of others?

It would be a mistake to argue for reverse discrimination on the grounds that white males deserve to be burdened and that therefore we should hire women and blacks even when white males are better qualified.[22] Young white males who are now entering the job market are not more responsible for the evils of racial and sexual inequality than are other members of society. Thus, reverse discrimination is not properly viewed as punishment administered to white males.

The justification for affirmative action supported here claims that bringing about sexual and racial equality necessitates sacrifice on the part of white males who seek employment. An important step in bringing about the desired egalitarian society involves speeding up the process by which women and blacks get into positions of power and authority. This requires that white males find it harder to achieve these same positions. But this is not punishment for deeds done.

Thomas Nagel's helpful analogy is state condemnation of property under the right of eminent domain for the purpose of building a highway.[23] Forcing some in the community to move in order that the community as a whole may benefit is unfair. Why should these individuals suffer rather than others? The answer is: Because they happen to live in a place where it is important to build a road. A similar response should be given to the white male who objects to reverse discrimination with the same "Why me?" question. The answer is: Because job-seeking white males happen to be in the way of an important road leading to the desired egalitarian society. Job-seeking white males are being made to bear the brunt of the burden of affirmative action because of accidental considerations, just as are homeowners whose property is condemned in order to build a highway.

This analogy is extremely illuminating and helpful in explaining the nature of reverse discrimination. There is, however, an important dissimilarity that Nagel does not mention. In cases of property condemnation, compensation is paid to the owner. Affirmative action policies, however, do not compensate white males for shouldering this burden of moving toward the desired egalitarian society. So affirmative action is unfair to job-seeking white males because they are forced to bear an unduly large share of the burden of achieving racial and sexual equality without being compensated for this sacrifice.

Since we have singled out job-seeking white males from the larger pool of white males who should also help achieve this goal, it seems that some compensation from the latter to the former is appropriate.[24]

This is a serious objection to affirmative action policies only if the uncompensated burden is substantial. Usually it is not. Most white male "victims" of affirmative action easily find employment. It is highly unlikely that the same white male will repeatedly fail to get hired because of affirmative action.[25] The burdens of affirmative action should be spread as evenly as possible among all the job seeking white males. Furthermore, the burden job-seeking white males face—of finding it somewhat more difficult to get employment—is inconsequential when compared to the burdens ongoing discrimination places on women and blacks.[26] Forcing job seeking white males to bear an extra burden is acceptable because this is a necessary step toward achieving a much greater reduction in the unfair burdens our society places on women and blacks. If affirmative action is a necessary mechanism for a timely dismantlement of our racial and sexual caste system, the extra burdens it places on job seeking white males are justified.

Still the question remains: Why isn't compensation paid? When members of society who do not deserve extra burdens are singled out to sacrifice for an important community goal, society owes them compensation. This objection loses some of its force when one realizes that society continually places undeserved burdens on its members without compensating them. For instance, the burden of seeking efficiency is placed on the shoulders of the least naturally talented and intelligent. That one is born less intelligent (or otherwise less talented) does not mean that one deserves to have reduced employment opportunities, and yet our society's meritocratic hiring procedures make it much harder for less naturally talented members to find meaningful employment. These people are not compensated for their sacrifices either.

Of course, pointing out that there are other examples of an allegedly problematic social policy does not justify that policy. Nonetheless, if this analogy is sound, failing to compensate job-seeking white males for the sacrifices placed on them by reverse discrimination is not without precedent. Furthermore, it is no more morally troublesome than is failing to compensate less talented members of society for their undeserved sacrifice of employment opportunities for the sake of efficiency.

Conclusion

This article has shown the difficulties in pinpointing what is morally troubling about reverse discrimination. The most commonly heard objections to reverse discrimination fail to make their case. Reverse discrimination is not morally equivalent to traditional racism and sexism since its goals and consequences are entirely different, and the act of treating people differently on the basis of race or sex is not necessarily morally wrong. The race and sex of the candidates are not morally irrelevant in all hiring decisions, and affirmative action hiring is an example where discriminating on the basis of race or sex is not morally arbitrary. Furthermore, affirmative action can be defended on grounds that do not involve stereotyping. Though affirmative action hiring of less well qualified applicants can lead to short run inefficiency, failing to hire the most qualified applicant does not violate this person's rights, entitlements, or deserts. Additionally, affirmative action hiring does not generally undermine equal opportunity for white males.

Reverse discrimination is morally troublesome in that it judges people on the basis of involuntary characteristics and thus reduces the control they have over their lives. It also places a larger than fair share of the burden of achieving an egalitarian society on the shoulders of job seeking white males without compensating them for this sacrifice. But these problems are relatively minor when compared to the grave injustice of racial and sexual inequality, and they are easily outweighed if affirmative action helps alleviate this far greater injustice.[27]

Notes

I thank Cheshire Calhoun, Beverly Diamond, John Dickerson, Jasper Hunt, Glenn Lesses, Richard Nunan, and Martin Perlmutter for helpful comments.

1. Thomas Nagel uses the phrase "racial caste system" in his illuminating testimony before the Subcommittee on the Constitution of the Senate Judiciary Committee, on June 18, 1981. This testimony is reprinted as "A Defense of Affirmative Action" in *Ethical Theory and Business,* 2nd edition, ed. Tom Beauchamp and Norman Bowie (Englewood Cliffs, NJ: Prentice-Hall, 1983), pp. 483-487.

2. What should count as qualifications is controversial. By "qualifications" I refer to such things as grades, test scores, prior experience, and letters of recommendation. I will not include black skin or female sex in my use of "qualification," though there are strong arguments for counting these as legitimate qualifications (in the sense of characteristics which would help the candidate achieve the legitimate goals of the hiring or admitting institution). For these arguments see Ronald Dworkin, "Why Bakke Has No Case," *The New York Review of Books,* November 10th, 1977.

3. This paper assumes the controversial premise that we live in a racist and sexist society. Statistics provide immediate and powerful support for this claim. The fact that blacks comprise 12% of the U.S. population, while comprising a minuscule percentage of those in positions of power and authority is sufficient evidence that our society continues to be significantly racist in results, if not in intent. Unless one assumes that blacks are innately less able to attain, or less desirous of attaining, these positions to a degree that would account for this huge under-representation, one must conclude that our social organizations significantly disadvantage blacks. This is (in part) the injustice that I call racism. The argument for the charge of sexism is analogous (and perhaps even more persuasive given that women comprise over 50% of the population). For more supporting evidence, see Tom Beauchamp's article "The Justification of Reverse Discrimination in Hiring" in *Ethical Theory and Business,* pp. 495-506.

4. Although the examples in this paper focus more on racism than on sexism, it is not clear that the former is a worse problem than is the latter. In many ways, sexism is a more subtle and pervasive form of discrimination. It is also less likely to be acknowledged.

5. This is Paul Woodruff's helpful definition of unjust discrimination. See Paul Woodruff, "What's Wrong With Discrimination," *Analysis,* vol. 36, no. 3, 1976, pp. 158-160.

6. This point is made by Richard Wasserstrom in his excellent article "A Defense of Programs of Preferential Treatment," *National Forum* (The Phi Kappa Phi Journal), vol. viii, no. 1 (Winter 1978), pp. 15-18. The article is reprinted in *Social Ethics,* 2nd edition, ed. Thomas Mappes and Jane Zembaty (New York: McGraw-Hill, 1982), pp. 187-191. The quoted phrase is Wasserstrom's.

7. Peter Singer, "Is Racial Discrimination Arbitrary?" *Philosophia,* vol. 8 (November 1978), pp. 185-203.

8. See, for example, Robert Simon, "Preferential Hiring: A Reply to Judith Jarvis Thomson," *Philosophy and Public Affairs,* vol. 3, no. 3 (Spring 1974).

9. If it is true (and it is certainly plausible) that every black or woman, no matter how fortunate, has suffered from racism and sexism in a way in which no white male has suffered from racism and sexism, then compensation for this injustice would be owed to all and only blacks and women. Given this, arguing for affirmative action on the grounds of compensatory justice would not involve judging individuals by average features of classes of which they are members. Still it might be argued that for certain blacks and women such injustices are not nearly as severe as the different type of injustice suffered by some white males. Thus one would have to provide a reason for why we should compensate (with affirmative action) any black or woman before any white male. Perhaps administrative convenience is such a reason. Being black or female (rather than white and male) correlates nicely with the property of being more greatly and unfairly disadvantaged, and thus race and sex are useful rough guidelines for determining who most needs compensation. This does, however, involve stereotyping.

10. In the long run, however, reverse discrimination may actually promote overall societal efficiency by breaking down the barriers to a vast reservoir of untapped potential in women and blacks.

11. See Thomas Nagel, "A Defense of Affirmative Action," p. 484.

12. This is Wasserstrom's point. See "A Defense of Programs of Preferential Treatment," in Social Ethics, p. 190.

13. By "effort" I intend to include (1) how hard a person tries to achieve certain goals, (2) the amount of risk voluntarily incurred in seeking these goals, and (3) the degree to which moral considerations play a role in choosing these goals. The harder one tries, the more one is willing to sacrifice, and the worthier the goal, the greater are one's deserts. For support of the claim that voluntary past action is the only valid basis for desert, see James Rachels, "What People Deserve," in Justice and Economic Distribution, ed. John Arthur and William Shaw (Englewood Cliffs, NJ: Prentice-Hall, 1978), pp. 150-163.

14. It would be useful to know if there is a correlation between the candidate who is most deserving (because she worked the hardest) and the one with the best qualifications. In other words, are better qualified candidates in general those who worked harder to achieve their qualifications? Perhaps people who have the greatest natural abilities and the most fortunate social circumstances will be the ones who work the hardest to develop their talents. This raises the possibility, suggested by John Rawls, that the ability to put forward effort is itself a function of factors outside a person's control. See his A Theory of Justice (Cambridge, MA: Harvard University Press, 1971), pp. 103-104. But if anything is under a person's control, and hence is something a person is responsible for, it is how hard she tries. Thus if there is an appropriate criterion for desert, it will include how much effort a person exerts.

15. See Justice William Brennan's majority opinion in United Steel Workers and Kaiser Aluminum v. Weber, United States Supreme Court, 443 U.S. 193 (1979). See also Justice Lewis Powell's majority opinion in the University of California v. Bakke, United States Supreme Court, 483 U.S. 265 (1978).

16. This is Wasserstrom's point. See "A Defense of Programs of Preferential Treatment," p. 189.

17. This is Judith Thomson's way of characterizing the alleged injustice. See "Preferential Hiring," Philosophy and Public Affairs, vol. 2, no. 4 (Summer 1973).

18. If it is true that some white males are more severely disadvantaged in our society than are some women and blacks, affirmative action would increase the inequality of opportunity for these white males. But since these individuals are a small minority of white males, the overall result of affirmative action would be to move us closer toward equality of opportunity.

19. James Rachels makes this point in "What People Deserve," p. 159. Joel Feinberg has also discussed related points. See his Social Philosophy (Englewood Cliffs, NJ: Prentice-Hall, 1973), p. 108.

20. He could work harder to get better qualifications and hope that the qualifications gap between him and the best woman or black would become so great that the efficiency cost of pursuing affirmative action would be prohibitive. Still he can do nothing to get rid of the disadvantage (in affirmative action contexts) of being a white male.

21. For a discussion of how considerations of justice typically outweigh considerations of utility, see Manuel Velasquez, Business Ethics (Englewood Cliffs, NJ: Prentice-Hall, 1982), Chapter Two.

22. On the average, however, white males have unfairly benefited from the holding back of blacks and women, and hence it is not altogether inappropriate that this unfair benefit be removed.

23. Nagel, "A Defense of Affirmative Action," p. 484.

24. It would be inappropriate to extract compensation from women or blacks since they are the ones who suffer the injustice affirmative action attempts to alleviate.

25. This is a potential worry, however, and so it is important to insure that the same white male does not repeatedly sacrifice for the goals of affirmative action.

26. Cheshire Calhoun reminded me of this point.

27. Of course one must argue that reverse discrimination is effective in bringing about an egalitarian society. There are complicated consequentialist arguments both for and against this claim, and I have not discussed them here. Some of the questions to be addressed are: (1) How damaging is reverse discrimination to the self-esteem of blacks and women? (2) Does reverse discrimination promote racial and sexual strife more than it helps to alleviate them? (3) Does it perpetuate unfortunate stereotypes about blacks and women? (4) How long are we justified in waiting to pull blacks and women into the mainstream of our social life? (5) What sorts of alternative mechanisms are possible and politically practical for achieving affirmative action goals (for instance, massive early educational funding for children from impoverished backgrounds)?

Louis P. Pojman

The Moral Status of Affirmative Action

Hardly a week goes by but that the subject of Affirmative Action does not come up. Whether in the guise of reverse discrimination, preferential hiring, non-traditional casting, quotas, goals and time tables, minority scholarships, or race-norming, the issue confronts us as a terribly perplexing problem. . . .

There is something salutary as well as terribly tragic inherent in this problem. The salutary aspect is the fact that our society has shown itself committed to eliminating unjust discrimination. Even in the heart of Dixie there is a recognition of the injustice of racial discrimination. Both sides of the affirmative action debate have good will and appeal to moral principles. Both sides are attempting to bring about a better society, one which is color blind, but they differ profoundly on the morally proper means to accomplish that goal.

And this is just the tragedy of the situation: good people on both sides of the issue are ready to tear each other to pieces over a problem that has no easy or obvious solution. And so the voices become shrill and the rhetoric hyperbolic. . . .

In this paper I will confine myself primarily to Affirmative Action policies with regard to race, but much of what I say can be applied to the areas of gender and ethnic minorities.

I. Definitions

First let me define my terms:

Discrimination is simply judging one thing to differ from another on the basis of some crite-

From Louis P. Pojman, "The Moral Status of Affirmative Action," *Public Affairs Quarterly,* Vol. 6, No. 2, 1992. Reprinted with permission.

rion. "Discrimination" is essentially a good quality, having reference to our ability to make distinctions. As rational and moral agents we need to make proper distinctions. To be rational is to discriminate between good and bad arguments, and to think morally is to discriminate between reasons based on valid principles and those based on invalid ones. What needs to be distinguished is the difference between rational and moral discrimination, on the one hand, and irrational and immoral discrimination, on the other hand.

Prejudice is a discrimination based on irrelevant grounds. It may simply be an attitude which never surfaces in action, or it may cause prejudicial actions. A prejudicial discrimination in action is immoral if it denies someone a fair deal. So discrimination on the basis of race or sex where these are not relevant for job performance is unfair. Likewise, one may act prejudicially in applying a relevant criterion on insufficient grounds, as in the case where I apply the criterion of being a hard worker but then assume, on insufficient evidence, that the black man who applies for the job is not a hard worker.

There is a difference between *prejudice* and *bias*. Bias signifies a tendency towards one thing rather than another where the evidence is incomplete or based on non-moral factors. For example, you may have a bias towards blondes and I towards red-heads. But prejudice is an attitude (or action) where unfairness is present—where one *should* know or do better, as in the case where I give people jobs simply because they are red-heads. Bias implies ignorance or incomplete knowledge, whereas prejudice is deeper, involving a moral failure—usually a failure to pay attention to the evidence. But note that calling people racist or sexist without good evidence is also an act of prejudice. I call this form of prejudice "defamism," for it unfairly defames the victim. . . .

Equal Opportunity is offering everyone a fair chance at the best positions that society has at its disposal. Only native aptitude and effort should be decisive in the outcome, not factors of race, sex or special favors.

Affirmative Action is the effort to rectify the injustice of the past by special policies. Put this way, it is Janus-faced or ambiguous, having both a backward-looking and a forward-looking feature [In Roman mythology, *Janus* was a god with two faces.]. The backward-looking feature is its attempt to correct and compensate for past injustice. This aspect of Affirmative Action is strictly deontological. The forward-looking feature is its implicit ideal of a society free from prejudice; this is both deontological and utilitarian.

When we look at a social problem from a backward-looking perspective we need to determine who has committed or benefited from a wrongful or prejudicial act and to determine who deserves compensation for that act.

When we look at a social problem from a forward-looking perspective we need to determine what a just society (one free from prejudice) would look like and how to obtain that kind of society. The forward-looking aspect of Affirmative Action is paradoxically race-conscious, since it uses race to bring about a society which is not race-conscious, which is color-blind (in the morally relevant sense of this term).

It is also useful to distinguish two versions of Affirmative Action. *Weak Affirmative Action* involves such measures as the elimination of segregation (namely the idea of "separate but equal"), widespread advertisement to groups not previously represented in certain privileged positions, special scholarships for the disadvantaged classes (e.g., all the poor), using underrepresentation or a history of past discrimination as a tie breaker when candidates are relatively equal, and the like.

Strong Affirmative Action involves more positive steps to eliminate past injustice, such as reverse discrimination, hiring candidates on the basis of race and gender in order to reach equal or near equal results, proportionate representation in each area of society.

II. A Brief History of Affirmative Action

1. After a long legacy of egregious racial discrimination the forces of civil justice came to a head during the decade of 1954-1964. In the 1954 U.S. Supreme Court decision, *Brown v. Board of Education,* racial segregation was declared inherently and unjustly discriminatory, a violation of the constitutional right to equal protection, and in 1964 Congress passed the Civil Rights Act which banned all forms of racial discrimination.

During this time the goal of the Civil Rights movement was equal opportunity. The thinking was that if only we could remove the hindrances to progress, invidious segregation, discriminatory laws, and irrational prejudice against blacks, we could free our country from the evils of past injustice and usher in a just society in which the grandchildren of the slave could play together and compete with the grandchildren of the slave owner. We were after a color-blind society in which every child had an equal chance to attain the highest positions based not on his skin color but on the quality of his credentials. In the early '60s when the idea of reverse discrimination was mentioned in civil rights groups, it was usually rejected as a new racism. The Executive Director of the NAACP, Roy Wilkins, stated this position unequivocally during congressional consideration of the 1964 civil rights law. "Our association has never been in favor of a quota system. We believe the quota system is unfair whether it is used for [blacks] or against [blacks] ... [We] feel people ought to be hired because of their ability, irrespective of their color. .. We want equality, equality of opportunity and employment on the basis of ability."[1]

So the Civil Rights Act of 1964 was passed outlawing discrimination on the basis of race or sex.

Title VII, Section 703(a) Civil Rights Act of 1964: It shall be an unlawful practice for an employer—(1) to fail or refuse to hire or to discharge any individual or otherwise to discriminate against any individual with respect to his compensation, terms, conditions, or privileges of employment, because of such individual's race, color, sex, or national origin; or
(2) to limit, segregate, or classify his employees or applicants for employment in any way which would deprive or tend to deprive any individual of employment opportunities or otherwise adversely affect his status as an employee because of such individual's

race, color, religion, sex, or national origin. [42 U.S.C.2000e-2(a).]

. . . Nothing contained in this title shall be interpreted to require any employer . . . to grant preferential treatment to any individual or to any group . . . on account of an imbalance which may exist with respect to the total numbers or percentage of persons of any race . . . employed by any employer . . . in comparison with the total or percentage of persons of such race . . . in any community, State, section, or other areas, or in the available work force in any community, State, section, or other area. [42 U.S.C.2000e-2(j)]

The Civil Rights Act of 1964 espouses a meritocratic philosophy, calling for equal opportunity and prohibits reverse discrimination as just another form of prejudice. The Voting Rights Act (1965) was passed and Jim Crow laws throughout the South were overturned. Schools were integrated and public accommodations opened to all. Branch Rickey's promotion of Jackie Robinson from the minor leagues in 1947 to play for the Brooklyn Dodgers was seen as the paradigm case of this kind of equal opportunity—the successful recruiting of a deserving person.

2. But it was soon noticed that the elimination of discriminatory laws was not producing the fully integrated society that leaders of the civil rights movement had envisioned. Eager to improve the situation, in 1965 President Johnson went beyond equal opportunity to Affirmative Action. He issued the famous Executive Order 11246 in which the Department of Labor was enjoined to issue government contracts with construction companies on the basis of race. That is, it would engage in reverse discrimination in order to make up for the evils of the past. He explained the act in terms of the shackled runner analogy.

Imagine a hundred yard dash in which one of the two runners has his legs shackled together. He has progressed 10 yds., while the unshackled runner has gone 50 yds. How do they rectify the situation? Do they merely remove the shackles and allow the race to proceed? Then they could say that "equal opportunity" now prevailed. But one of the runners would still be forty yards ahead of the other. Would it not be the better part of justice to allow the previously shackled runner to make-up the forty yard gap; or to start the race all over again? That would be affirma-

tive action towards equality. (President Lyndon Johnson 1965 inaugurating the Affirmative Action Policy of Executive Order 11246).

In 1967 President Johnson issued Executive order 11375 extending Affirmative Action (henceforth "AA") to women. Note here that AA originates in the executive branch of government. Until the Kennedy-Hawkins Civil Rights Act of 1990, AA policy was never put to a vote or passed by Congress. Gradually, the benefits of AA were extended to Hispanics, native Americans, Asians, and handicapped people.[2]

The phrase "An Equal Opportunity/Affirmative Action Employer" ("AA/EO") began to appear as official public policy. But few noticed an ambiguity in the notion of "AA" which could lead to a contradiction in juxtaposing it with "EO," for there are two types of AA. At first AA was interpreted as, what I have called, "Weak Affirmative Action," in line with equal opportunity, signifying wider advertisement of positions, announcements that applications from blacks would be welcomed, active recruitment and hiring blacks (and women) over *equally* qualified men. While few liberals objected to these measures, some expressed fears of an impending slippery slope towards reverse discrimination.

However, except in professional sports—including those sponsored by universities—Weak Affirmative Action was not working, so in the late 60's and early 70's a stronger version of Affirmative Action was embarked upon—one aimed at equal results, quotas (or "goals"—a euphemism for "quotas"). In *Swann v. Charlotte-Mecklenburg* (1971), regarding the busing of children out of their neighborhood in order to promote integration, the Court, led by Justice Brennan, held that Affirmative Action was implied in *Brown* and was consistent with the Civil Right Act of 1964. The NAACP now began to support reverse discrimination.

Thus began the search for minimally qualified blacks in college recruitment, hiring, and the like. Competence and excellence began to recede into second place as the quest for racial, ethnic, and gender diversity became the dominant goals. The slogan "We have to become race conscious in order to eliminate race consciousness" became the paradoxical justification for reverse discrimination.

3. In 1968 the Department of Labor ordered employers to engage in utilization studies as part of its policy of eliminating discrimination in the work place. The office of Federal Contract Compliance of the U.S. Department of Labor (Executive Order 11246) stated that employers with a history of *underutilization* of minorities and women were required to institute programs that went beyond passive nondiscrimination through deliberate efforts to identify people of "affected classes" for the purpose of advancing their employment. Many employers found it wise to adopt policies of preferential hiring in order to preempt expensive government suits.

Employers were to engage in "utilization analysis" of their present work force in order to develop "specific and result-oriented procedures" to which the employer commits "*every good-faith effort*" in order to provide "relief for members of an '*affected class*,' who by virtue of *past discrimination* continue to suffer the present effects of that discrimination." This self-analysis is supposed to discover areas in which such affected classes are underused, considering their availability and skills. "*Goals and time-tables* are to be developed to guide efforts to correct deficiencies in the employment of affected classes people in each level and segment of the work force." Affirmative Action also calls for "rigorous examination" of standards and criteria for job performance, not so as to "dilute necessary standards" but in order to ensure that "arbitrary and discriminatory employment practices are eliminated" and to eliminate unnecessary criteria which "have had the effect of eliminating women and minorities" either from selection or promotion.[3]

4. In 1969 two important events occurred. (a) The Philadelphia Plan—The Department of Labor called for "goals and time tables" for recruiting minority workers. In Philadelphia area construction industries, where these companies were all white, family run, businesses, the contractor's union took the case to court on the grounds that Title VII of the Civil Rights Act prohibits quotas. The Third Circuit Court of Appeals upheld the Labor Department, and the Supreme Court refused to hear it. This case became the basis of the EEOC's aggressive pursuit of "goals and time tables" in other business situations.

(b) In the Spring of 1969 James Forman disrupted the service of Riverside Church in New York City and issued the Black Manifesto to the American Churches, demanding that they pay blacks $500,000,000 in reparations. The argument of the Black Manifesto was that for three and a half centuries blacks in America have been "exploited and degraded, brutalized, killed and persecuted" by whites; that this was part of the persistent institutional patterns of first, legal slavery and then, legal discrimination and forced segregation; and that through slavery and discrimination whites had procured enormous wealth from black labor with little return to blacks. These facts were said to constitute grounds for reparations on a massive scale. The American churches were but the first institutions to be asked for reparations.[4]

5. The Department of Labor issued guidelines in 1970 calling for hiring representatives of *underutilized* groups. "*Nondiscrimination* requires the elimination of all existing discriminatory conditions, whether purposeful or inadvertent . . . *Affirmative action* requires . . . the employer to make additional efforts to recruit, employ and promote qualified members of groups formerly excluded" (HEW Executive Order 22346, 1972). In December of 1971 Guidelines were issued to eliminate underutilization of minorities, aiming at realignment of job force at every level of society.

6. In *Griggs v. Duke Power Company* (1971) the Supreme Court interpreted Title VII of the Civil Rights Act as forbidding use of aptitude tests and high school diplomas in hiring personnel. These tests were deemed presumptively discriminatory, employers having the burden of proving such tests relevant to performance. The notion of *sufficiency* replaced that of excellence or best qualified, as it was realized (though not explicitly stated) that the social goal of racial diversity required compromising the standards of competence.

7. In 1977, the EEOC called for and *expected* proportional representation of minorities in every area of work (including universities).

8. In 1978 the Supreme Court addressed the Bakke case. Alan Bakke had been denied admis-

sion to the University of California at Davis Medical School even though his test scores were higher than the 16 blacks who were admitted under the Affirmative Action quota program. He sued the University of California and the U.S. Supreme Court ruled (*University of California v. Bakke,* July 28, 1978) in a 5 to 4 vote that reverse discrimination and quotas are illegal except (as Justice Powell put it) when engaged in for purposes of promoting diversity (interpreted as a means to extend free speech under the First Amendment) and restoring a situation where an institution has had a history of prejudicial discrimination. The decision was greeted with applause from anti-AA quarters and dismay from pro-AA quarters. Ken Tollett lamented, "The affirmance of Bakke would mean the reversal of affirmative action; it would be an officially sanctioned signal to turn against blacks in this country. . . . Opposition to special minority admissions programs and affirmative action is anti-black."[5]

But Tollett was wrong. The Bakke case only shifted the rhetoric from "quota" language to "goals and time tables" and "diversity" language. In the '80s affirmative action was alive and well, with preferential hiring, minority scholarships, and "race norming" prevailing in all walks of life. No other white who has been excluded from admission to college because of his race has even won his case. In fact only a year later, Justice Brennan was to write in *U.S. Steel v. Weber* that prohibition of racial discrimination against "any individual" in Title VII of the Civil Rights Act did not apply to discrimination against whites.[6]

9. Perhaps the last step in the drive towards equal results took place in the institutionalization of grading applicants by group related standards, race norming. Race norming is widely practiced but most of the public is unaware of it, so let me explain it.

Imagine that four men come into a state employment office in order to apply for a job. One is black, one Hispanic, one Asian and one white. They take the standard test (a version of the General Aptitude Test Battery or VG-GATB). All get a composite score of 300. None of them will ever see that score. Instead the numbers will be fed into a computer and the applicants'

percentile ranking emerges. The scores are group-weighted. Blacks are measured against blacks, whites against whites, Hispanics against Hispanics. Since blacks characteristically do less well than other groups, the effect is to favor blacks. For example, a score of 300 as an accountant will give the black a percentile score of 87, an Hispanic a percentile score of 74 and a white or oriental a score of 47. The black will get the job as the accountant. See [table]:

PERCENTILE CONVERSION TABLES

Jobs are grouped into five broad families: Family I includes, for example, machinists, cabinet makers, and tool makers; Family II includes helpers in many types of agriculture, manufacturing, and so on; Family III includes professional jobs such as accountant, chemical engineer, nurse, editor; Family IV includes bus drivers, bookkeepers, carpet layers; Family V includes exterminators, butchers, file clerks. A raw score of 300 would convert to the following percentile rankings:

	I	II	III	IV	V
Black	79	59	87	83	73
Hispanic	62	41	74	67	55
Other	39	42	47	45	42

Sources: Virginia Employment Commission: U.S. Department of Labor. Employment and Training Administration, Validity Generalization Manual (Section A: Job Family Scoring).

This is known as race norming. Until an anonymous governmental employee recently blew the whistle, this practice was kept a secret in several state employment services. Prof. Linda Gottfredson of the University of Delaware, one of the social scientists to expose this practice, has since had her funding cut off. In a recent letter published in the New York Times she writes:

One of America's best-kept open secrets is that the Employment Service of the Department of Labor has unabashedly promulgated quotas. In 1981 the service recommended that state employment agencies adopt a race-conscious battery to avoid adverse impact when referring job applicants to employers. . . . The score adjustments are not trivial. An unadjusted score that places a job applicant at the 15th percentile among whites would, after race-norming, typically place a black near the white 50th percentile.

Likewise, unadjusted scores at the white 50th percentile would, after race-norming, typically place a black near the 85th percentile for white job applicants.... [I]ts use by 40 states in the last decade belies the claim that *Griggs* did not lead to quotas.[7]

10. In the *Ward Cove, Richmond,* and *Martin* decisions of the mid-80's the Supreme Court limited preferential hiring practices, placing a greater burden of proof on the plaintiff, now required to prove that employers have discriminated. The Kennedy-Hawkins Civil Rights Act of 1990, which was passed by Congress last year, sought to reverse these decisions by requiring employers to justify statistical imbalances not only in the employment of racial minorities but also that of ethnic and religious minorities. Wherever underrepresentation of an "identified" group exists, the employer bears the burden of proving he is innocent of prejudicial behavior. In other words, the bill would make it easier for minorities to sue employers. President Bush vetoed the bill, deeming it a subterfuge for quotas. A revised bill is now in Congressional committee.

Affirmative Action in the guise of underutilized or "affected groups" now extends to American Indians, Hispanics—Spaniards (including Spanish nobles) but not Portuguese, Asians, the handicapped, and in some places Irish and Italians. Estimates are that 75% of Americans may obtain AA status as minorities: everyone except the white non-handicapped male. It is a strange policy that affords special treatment to the children of Spanish nobles and illegal immigrants but not the children of the survivors of Russian pogroms or Nazi concentration camps....

III. ARGUMENTS FOR AFFIRMATIVE ACTION

Let us now survey the main arguments typically cited in the debate over Affirmative Action. I will briefly discuss seven arguments on each side of the issue.

1. Need for Role Models

This argument is straightforward. We all have need of role models, and it helps to know that others like us can be successful. We learn and are encouraged to strive for excellence by emulating our heroes and role models.

However, it is doubtful whether role models of one's own racial or sexual type are necessary for success. One of my heroes was Gandhi, an Indian Hindu, another was my grade school science teacher, one Miss DeVoe, and another was Martin Luther King. More important than having role models of one's own type is having genuinely good people, of whatever race or gender, to emulate. Furthermore, even if it is of some help to people with low self-esteem to gain encouragement from seeing others of their particular kind in leadership roles, it is doubtful whether this need is a sufficient condition to justify preferential hiring or reverse discrimination. What good is a role model who is inferior to other professors or business personnel? Excellence will rise to the top in a system of fair opportunity. Natural development of role models will come more slowly and more surely. Proponents of preferential policies simply lack the patience to let history take its own course.

2. The Need of Breaking the Stereotypes

Society may simply need to know that there are talented blacks and women, so that it does not automatically assign them lesser respect or status. We need to have unjustified stereotype beliefs replaced with more accurate ones about the talents of blacks and women. So we need to engage in preferential hiring of qualified minorities even when they are not the most qualified.

Again, the response is that hiring the less qualified is neither fair to those better qualified who are passed over nor an effective way of removing inaccurate stereotypes. If competence is accepted as the criterion for hiring, then it is unjust to override it for purposes of social engineering. Furthermore, if blacks or women are known to hold high positions simply because of reverse discrimination, then they will still lack the respect due to those of their rank. In New York City there is a saying among doctors, "Never go to a black physician under 40," referring to the fact that AA has affected the medical system during the past fifteen years.

The police use "Quota Cops" and "Welfare Sergeants" to refer to those hired without passing the standardized tests. (In 1985 180 black and Hispanic policemen, who had failed a promotion test, were promoted anyway to the rank of sergeant.) The destruction of false stereotypes will come naturally as qualified blacks rise naturally in fair competition (or if it does not— then the stereotypes may be justified.) Reverse discrimination sends the message home that the stereotypes are deserved—otherwise, why do these minorities need so much extra help?

3. Equal Results Argument

Some philosophers and social scientists hold that human nature is roughly identical, so that on a fair playing field the same proportion from every race and gender and ethnic group would attain to the highest positions in every area of endeavor. It would follow that any inequality of results itself is evidence for inequality of opportunity. John Arthur, in discussing an intelligence test, Test 21, puts the case this way.

History is important when considering governmental rules like Test 21 because low scores by blacks can be traced in large measure to the legacy of slavery and racism: segregation, poor schooling, exclusion from trade unions, malnutrition, and poverty have all played their roles. Unless one assumes that blacks are naturally less able to pass the test, the conclusion must be that the results are themselves socially and legally constructed, not a mere given for which law and society can claim no responsibility.

The conclusion seems to be that genuine equality eventually requires equal results. Obviously blacks have been treated unequally throughout US history, and just as obviously the economic and psychological effects of that inequality linger to this day, showing up in lower income and poorer performance in school and on tests than whites achieve. Since we have no reason to believe that differences in performance can be explained by factors other than history, equal results are a good benchmark by which to measure progress made toward genuine equality.[8]

The result of a just society should be equal numbers in proportion to each group in the work force.

However, Arthur fails even to consider studies that suggest that there are innate differences between races, sexes, and groups. If there are genetic differences in intelligence and temperament within families, why should we not expect such differences between racial groups and the two genders? Why should the evidence for this be completely discounted?

Perhaps some race or one gender is more intelligent in one way than another. At present we have only limited knowledge about genetic differences, but what we do have suggests some difference besides the obvious physiological traits.[9] The proper use of this evidence is not to promote discriminatory policies but to be *open* to the possibility that innate differences may have led to an over-representation of certain groups in certain areas of endeavor. It seems that on average blacks have genetic endowments favoring them in the development of skills necessary for excellence in basketball.

Furthermore, on Arthur's logic, we should take aggressive AA against Asians and Jews since they are over-represented in science, technology, and medicine. So that each group receives its fair share, we should ensure that 12% of the philosophers in the United States are Black, reduce the percentage of Jews from an estimated 15% to 2%--firing about 1,300 Jewish philosophers. The fact that Asians are producing 50% of Ph.D's in science and math and blacks less than 1% clearly shows, on this reasoning, that we are providing special secret advantages to Asians.

But why does society have to enter into this results game in the first place? Why do we have to decide whether all difference is environmental or genetic? Perhaps we should simply admit that we lack sufficient evidence to pronounce on these issues with any certainty--but if so, should we not be more modest in insisting on equal results? Here is a thought experiment. Take two families of different racial groups, Green and Blue. The Greens decide to have only two children, to spend all their resources on them, to give them the best education. The two Green kids respond well and end up with achievement test scores in the 99th percentile. The Blues fail to practice family planning. They have 15 children. They can only afford 2 children, but lack of ability or whatever prevents them from keeping their family down. Now they need help for their large family. Why does society have to step in and help them? Society did not force them to have 15 children. Suppose that the achievement test scores of the 15 children fall below the 25th percentile. They cannot compete with the Greens. But now enters AA. It says that it is society's fault that the Blue children are not as able as the Greens and that the Greens must pay extra taxes to enable the Blues to compete. No restraints are put on the Blues regarding family size. This seems unfair to the Greens. Should the Green children be made to bear responsibility for the consequences of the Blues' voluntary behavior?

My point is simply that Arthur needs to cast his net wider and recognize that demographics and childbearing and -rearing practices are crucial factors in achievement. People have to take some responsibility for their actions. The equal results argument (or axiom) misses a greater part of the future.

4. The Compensation Argument

The argument goes like this: blacks have been wronged and severely harmed by whites. Therefore white society should compensate blacks for the injury caused them. Reverse discrimination in terms of preferential hiring, contracts, and scholarships is a fitting way to compensate for the racist wrongs.

This argument actually involves a distorted notion of compensation. Normally, we think of compensation as owed by a specific person A to another person B whom A has wronged in a specific way C. For example, if I have stolen your car and used it for a period of time to make business profits that would have gone to you, it is not enough that I return your car. I must pay you an amount reflecting your loss and my ability to pay. If I have only made $5,000 and only have $10,000 in assets, it would not be possible for you to collect $20,000 in damages—even though that is the amount of loss you have incurred.

Sometimes compensation is extended to groups of people who have been unjustly harmed by the greater society. For example, the United States government has compensated the Japanese-Americans who were interred during the Second World War, and the West German government has paid reparations to the survivors of Nazi concentration camps. But here a specific people have been identified who were wronged in an identifiable way by the government of the nation in question.

On the face of it the demand by blacks for compensation does not fit the usual pattern. Perhaps Southern states with Jim Crow laws could be accused of unjustly harming blacks, but it is hard to see that the United States government was involved in doing so. Furthermore, it is not clear that all blacks were harmed in the same way or whether some were *unjustly* harmed or harmed more than poor whites and others (e.g. short people). Finally, even if identifiable blacks were harmed by identifiable social practices, it is not clear that most forms of Affirmative Action are appropriate to restore the situation. The usual practice of a financial payment seems more appropriate than giving a high level job to someone unqualified or only minimally qualified, who, speculatively, might have been better qualified had he not been subject to racial discrimination. If John is the star tailback of our college team with a promising professional future, and I accidentally (but culpably) drive my pick-up truck over his legs, and so cripple him, John may be due compensation, but he is not due the tailback spot on the football team.

Still, there may be something intuitively compelling about compensating members of an oppressed group who are minimally qualified. Suppose that the Hatfields and the McCoys are enemy clans and some youths from the Hatfields go over and steal diamonds and gold from the McCoys, distributing it within the Hatfield economy. Even though we do not know which Hatfield youths did the stealing, we would want to restore the wealth, as far as possible, to the McCoys. One way might be to tax the Hatfields, but another might be to give preferential treatment in terms of scholarships and training programs and hiring to the McCoys.[10]

This is perhaps the strongest argument for Affirmative Action, and it may well justify some weak versions of AA, but it is doubtful whether it is sufficient to justify strong versions with quotas and goals and time tables in skilled positions. There are at least two reasons for this. First, we have no way of knowing how many people of group G would have been at competence level L had the world been different. Secondly, the normal criterion of competence is a strong *prima facie* consideration when the most important positions are at stake. There are two reasons for this:

1. society has given people expectations that if they attain certain levels of excellence they will be awarded appropriately and
2. filling the most important positions with the best qualified is the best way to insure efficiency in job-related areas and in society in general.

These reasons are not absolutes. They can be overridden. But there is a strong presumption in their favor so that a burden of proof rests with those who would override them.

At this point we get into the problem of whether innocent non-blacks should have to pay a penalty in terms of preferential hiring of blacks. We turn to that argument.

5. Compensation from Those who Innocently Benefited from Past Injustice

White males as innocent beneficiaries of unjust discrimination of blacks and women have no grounds for complaint when society seeks to rectify the tilted field. White males may be innocent of oppressing blacks and minorities (and women), but they have unjustly benefited from that oppression or discrimination. So it is perfectly proper that less qualified women and blacks be hired before them.

The operative principle is: He who knowingly and willingly benefits from a wrong must help pay for the wrong. Judith Jarvis Thomson puts it this way. "Many [white males] have been direct beneficiaries of policies which have down-graded blacks and women . . . and even those who did not directly benefit . . . had, at any rate, the advantage in the competition which comes of the confidence in one's full membership [in the community], and of one's right being recognized as a matter of course."[11]

That is, white males obtain advantages in self respect and self-confidence deriving from a racist system which denies these to blacks and women.

Objection. As I noted in the previous section, compensation is normally individual and specific. If A harms B regarding x, B has a right to compensation from A in regards to x. If A steals B's car and wrecks it, A has an obligation to compensate B for the stolen car, but A's son has no obligation to compensate B. Furthermore, if A dies or disappears, B has no moral right to claim that society compensate him for the stolen car—though if he has insurance, he can make such a claim to the insurance company. Sometimes a wrong cannot be compensated, and we just have to make the best of an imperfect world.

Suppose my parents, divining that I would grow up to have an unsurpassable desire to be a basketball player, bought an expensive growth hormone for me. Unfortunately, a neighbor stole it and gave it to little Lew Alcindor, who gained the extra 18 inches—my 18 inches—and shot up to an enviable 7 feet 2 inches. Alias Kareem Abdul Jabbar, he excelled in basketball, as I would have done had I had my proper dose.

Do I have a right to the millions of dollars that Jabbar made as a professional basketball player—the unjustly innocent beneficiary of my growth hormone? I have a right to something from the neighbor who stole the hormone, and it might be kind of Jabbar to give me free tickets to the Laker basketball games, and perhaps I should be remembered in his will. As far as I can see, however, he does not *owe* me anything, either legally or morally.

Suppose further that Lew Alcindor and I are in high school together and we are both qualified to play basketball, only he is far better than I. Do I deserve to start in his position because I would have been as good as he is had someone not cheated me as a child? Again, I think not. But if being the lucky beneficiary of wrong-doing does not entail that Alcindor (or the coach) owes me anything in regards to basketball, why should it be a reason to engage in preferential hiring in academic positions or highly coveted jobs? If minimal qualifications are not adequate to override excellence in basketball, even when the minimality is a consequence of wrongdoing, why should they be adequate in other areas?

6. The Diversity Argument

It is important that we learn to live in a pluralistic world, learning to get along with those of other races and cultures, so we should have fully integrated schools and employment situations. Diversity is an important symbol and educative device. Thus preferential treatment is warranted to perform this role in society.

But, again, while we can admit the value of diversity, it hardly seems adequate to override considerations of merit and efficiency. Diversity for diversity's sake is moral promiscuity, since it obfuscates rational distinctions, and unless those hired are highly qualified the diversity factor threatens to become a fetish. At least at the higher levels of business and the professions, competence far outweighs considerations of diversity. I do not care whether the group of surgeons operating on me reflect racial or gender balance, but I do care that they are highly qualified. And likewise with airplane pilots, military leaders, business executives, and, may I say it, teachers and professors. Moreover, there are other ways of learning about other cultures besides engaging in reverse discrimination.

7. Anti-Meritocratic (Desert) Argument to Justify Reverse Discrimination: "No One Deserves His Talents"

According to this argument, the competent do not deserve their intelligence, their superior character, their industriousness, or their discipline; therefore they have no right to the best positions in society; therefore society is not unjust in giving these positions to less (but still minimally) qualified blacks and women. In one form this argument holds that since no one deserves anything, society may use any criteria it pleases to distribute goods. The criterion most often designated is social utility. Versions of this argument are found in the writings of John Arthur, John Rawls, Bernard Boxill, Michael Kinsley, Ronald Dworkin, and Richard Wasser-

strom. Rawls writes, "No one deserves his place in the distribution of native endowments, any more than one deserves one's initial starting place in society. The assertion that a man deserves the superior character that enables him to make the effort to cultivate his abilities is equally problematic; for his character depends in large part upon fortunate family and social circumstances for which he can claim no credit. The notion of desert seems not to apply to these cases."[12] Michael Kinsley is even more adamant:

Opponents of affirmative action are hung up on a distinction that seems more profoundly irrelevant: treating individuals versus treating groups. What is the moral difference between dispensing favors to people on their "merits" as individuals and passing out society's benefits on the basis of group identification?

Group identifications like race and sex are, of course, immutable. They have nothing to do with a person's moral worth. But the same is true of most of what comes under the label "merit." The tools you need for getting ahead in a meritocratic society—not all of them but most: talent, education, instilled cultural values such as ambition—are distributed just as arbitrarily as skin color. They are fate. The notion that people somehow "deserve" the advantages of these characteristics in a way they don't "deserve" the advantage of their race is powerful, but illogical.[13]

It will help to put the argument in outline form.

1. Society may award jobs and positions as it sees fit as long as individuals have no claim to these positions.
2. To have a claim to something means that one has earned it or deserves it.
3. But no one has earned or deserves his intelligence, talent, education or cultural values which produce superior qualifications.
4. If a person does not deserve what produces something, he does not deserve its products.
5. Therefore better qualified people do not deserve their qualifications.
6. Therefore, society may override their qualifications in awarding jobs and positions as it sees fit (for social utility or to compensate for previous wrongs).

So it is permissible if a minimally qualified black or woman is admitted to law or medical school ahead of a white male with excellent credentials or if a less qualified person from an "underutilized" group gets a professorship ahead of a far better qualified white male. Sufficiency and underutilization together outweigh excellence.

Objection Premise 4 is false. To see this, reflect that just because I do not deserve the money that I have been given as a gift (for instance) does not mean that I am not entitled to what I get with that money. If you and I both get a gift of $100 and I bury mine in the sand for 5 years while you invest yours wisely and double its value at the end of five years, I cannot complain that you should split the increase 50/50 since neither of us deserved the original gift. If we accept the notion of responsibility at all, we must hold that persons deserve the fruits of their labor and conscious choices. Of course, we might want to distinguish moral from legal desert and argue that, morally speaking, effort is more important than outcome, whereas, legally speaking, outcome may be more important. Nevertheless, there are good reasons in terms of efficiency, motivation, and rough justice for holding a strong *prima facie* principle of giving scarce high positions to those most competent.

The attack on moral desert is perhaps the most radical move that egalitarians like Rawls and company have made against meritocracy, but the ramifications of their attack are far reaching. The following are some of its implications. Since I do not deserve my two good eyes or two good kidneys, the social engineers may take one of each from me to give to those needing an eye or a kidney—even if they have damaged their organs by their own voluntary actions. Since no one deserves anything, we do not deserve pay for our labors or praise for a job well done or first prize in the race we win. The notion of moral responsibility vanishes in a system of levelling.

But there is no good reason to accept the argument against desert. We do act freely and, as such, we are responsible for our actions. We deserve the fruits of our labor, reward for our noble feats and punishment for our misbehavior.

We have considered seven arguments for Affirmative Action and have found no compelling case for Strong AA and only one plausible argument (a version of the compensation argument) for Weak AA. We must now turn to the arguments against Affirmative Action to see whether they fare any better.[14]

IV. ARGUMENTS AGAINST AFFIRMATIVE ACTION

1. Affirmative Action Requires Discrimination Against a Different Group

Weak Affirmative Action weakly discriminates against new minorities, mostly innocent young white males, and Strong Affirmative Action strongly discriminates against these new minorities. As I argued in III.5, this discrimination is unwarranted, since, even if some compensation to blacks were indicated, it would be unfair to make innocent white males bear the whole brunt of the payments. In fact, it is poor white youth who become the new pariahs on the job market. The children of the wealthy have no trouble getting into the best private grammar schools and, on the basis of superior early education, into the best universities, graduate schools, managerial and professional positions. Affirmative Action simply shifts injustice, setting blacks and women against young white males, especially ethnic and poor white males. It does little to rectify the goal of providing equal opportunity to all. If the goal is a society where everyone has a fair chance, then it would be better to concentrate on support for families and early education and decide the matter of university admissions and job hiring on the basis of traditional standards of competence.

2. Affirmative Action Perpetuates the Victimization Syndrome

Shelby Steele admits that Affirmative Action may seem "the meagerest recompense for centuries of unrelieved oppression" and that it helps promote diversity. At the same time, though, notes Steele, Affirmative Action reinforces the spirit of victimization by telling blacks that they can gain more by emphasizing their suffering, degradation and helplessness than by discipline and work. This message holds the danger of blacks becoming permanently handicapped by a need for special treatment. It also sends to society at large the message that blacks cannot make it on their own.

Leon Wieseltier sums up the problem this way.

The memory of oppression is a pillar and a strut of the identity of every people oppressed. It is no ordinary marker of difference. It is unusually stiffening. It instructs the individual and the group about what to expect of the world, imparts an isolating sense of aptness. . . . Don't be fooled, it teaches, there is only repetition. For that reason, the collective memory of an oppressed people is not only a treasure but a trap.

In the memory of oppression, oppression outlives itself. The scar does the work of the wound. That is the real tragedy: that injustice retains the power to distort long after it has ceased to be real. It is a posthumous victory for the oppressors, when pain becomes a tradition. And yet the atrocities of the past must never be forgotten. This is the unfairly difficult dilemma of the newly emancipated and the newly enfranchised: an honorable life is not possible if they remember too little and a normal life is not possible if they remember too much.[15]

With the eye of recollection, which does not "remember too much," Steele recommends a policy which offers "educational and economic development of disadvantaged people regardless of race and the eradication from our society—through close monitoring and severe sanctions—of racial and gender discrimination.[16]

3. Affirmative Action Encourages Mediocrity and Incompetence

Last Spring Jesse Jackson joined protesters at Harvard Law School in demanding that the Law School faculty hire black women. Jackson dismissed Dean of the Law School, Robert C. Clark's standard of choosing the best qualified person for the job as "Cultural anemia." "We cannot just define who is qualified in the most narrow vertical academic terms," he said. "Most people in the world are yellow, brown, black, poor, non-Christian and don't speak English, and they can't wait for some White males with

archaic rules to appraise them."[17] It might be noted that if Jackson is correct about the depth of cultural decadence at Harvard, blacks might be well advised to form and support their own more vital law schools and leave places like Harvard to their archaism.

At several universities, the administration has forced departments to hire members of minorities even when far superior candidates were available. Shortly after obtaining my Ph.D. in the late '70s I was mistakenly identified as a black philosopher (I had a civil rights record and was once a black studies major) and was flown to a major university, only to be rejected for a more qualified candidate when it discovered that I was white.

Stories of the bad effects of Affirmative Action abound. The philosopher Sidney Hook writes that "At one Ivy League university, representatives of the Regional HEW demanded an explanation of why there were no women or minority students in the Graduate Department of Religious Studies. They were told that a reading of knowledge of Hebrew and Greek was presupposed. Whereupon the representatives of HEW advised orally:" Then end those old fashioned programs that require irrelevant languages. And start up programs on relevant things which minority group students can study without learning languages.[18]

Government programs of enforced preferential treatment tend to appeal to the lowest possible common denominator. Witness the 1974 HEW Revised Order No. 14 on Affirmative Action expectations for preferential hiring: "Neither minorities nor female employees should be required to possess higher qualifications than those of the lowest qualified incumbents."

Furthermore, no tests may be given to candidates unless it is *proved* to be relevant to the job.

No standard or criteria which have, by intent or effect, worked to exclude women or minorities as a class can be utilized, unless the institution can demonstrate the necessity of such standard to the performance of the job in question.

Whenever a validity study is called for . . . the user should include . . . an investigation of suitable alternative selection procedures and suitable alternative methods of using the selection procedure which have as little adverse impact as possible. . . . Whenever the user is shown an alternative selection procedure with evidence of less adverse impact and substantial evidence of validity for the same job in similar circumstances, the user should investigate it to determine the appropriateness of using or validating it in accord with these guidelines.[19]

At the same time Americans are wondering why standards in our country are falling and the Japanese are getting ahead. Affirmative Action with its twin idols, Sufficiency and Diversity, is the enemy of excellence. I will develop this thought below (IV.6).

4. Affirmative Action Policies Unjustly Shift the Burden of Proof

Affirmative Action legislation tends to place the burden of proof on the employer who does not have an "adequate" representation of "underutilized" groups in his work force. He is guilty until proven innocent. I have already recounted how in the mid-eighties the Supreme Court shifted the burden of proof back onto the plaintiff, while Congress is now attempting to shift the burden back to the employer. Those in favor of deeming disproportional representation "guilty until proven innocent" argue that it is easy for employers to discriminate against minorities by various subterfuges, and I agree that steps should be taken to monitor against prejudicial treatment. But being prejudiced against employers is not the way to attain a just solution to discrimination. The principle: innocent until proven guilty, applies to employers as well as criminals. Indeed, it is clearly special pleading to reject this basic principle of Anglo-American law in this case of discrimination while adhering to it everywhere else.

5. An Argument from Merit

Traditionally, we have believed that the highest positions in society should be awarded to those who are best qualified. . . . Rewarding excellence both seems just to the individuals in the competition and makes for efficiency. Note that one of the most successful acts of integration, the recruitment of Jackie Robinson in the late '40s, was done in just this way, according to

merit. If Robinson had been brought into the major league as a mediocre player or had batted .200 he would have been scorned and sent back to the minors where he belonged.

Merit is not an absolute value. There are times when it may be overridden for social goals, but there is a strong *prima facie* reason for awarding positions on its basis, and it should enjoy a weighty presumption in our social practices.

In a celebrated article Ronald Dworkin says that "Bakke had no case" because society did not owe Bakke anything. That may be, but then why does it owe anyone anything? Dworkin puts the matter in Utility terms, but if that is the case, society may owe Bakke a place at the University of California/Davis, for it seems a reasonable rule-utilitarian principle that achievement should be rewarded in society. We generally want the best to have the best positions, the best qualified candidate to win the political office, the most brilliant and competent scientist to be chosen for the most challenging research project, the best qualified pilots to become commercial pilots, only the best soldiers to become generals. Only when little is at stake do we weaken the standards and content ourselves with sufficiency (rather than excellence)—there are plenty of jobs where "sufficiency" rather than excellence is required. Perhaps we now feel that medicine or law or university professorships are so routine that they can be performed by minimally qualified people—in which case AA has a place.

But note, no one is calling for quotas or proportional representation of *underutilized* groups in the National Basketball Association where blacks make up 80% of the players. But if merit and merit alone reigns in sports, should it not be valued at least as much in education and industry?

6. The Slippery Slope

Even if Strong AA or Reverse Discrimination could meet the other objections, it would face a tough question: once you embark on this project, how do you limit it? Who should be excluded from reverse discrimination? Asians and Jews are over-represented, so if we give blacks positive quotas, should we place negative quotas to these other groups? Since white males, "WMs," are a minority which is suffering from reverse discrimination, will we need a New Affirmative Action policy in the 21st century to compensate for the discrimination against WMs in the late 20th century?

Furthermore, Affirmative Action has stigmatized the *young* white male. Assuming that we accept reverse discrimination, the fair way to make sacrifices would be to retire *older* white males who are more likely to have benefited from a favored status. Probably the least guilty of any harm to minority groups is the young white male—usually a liberal who has been required to bear the brunt of ages of past injustice. Justice Brennan's announcement that the Civil Rights Act did not apply to discrimination against white shows how the clearest language can be bent to serve the ideology of the moment.[20]

7. The Mounting Evidence Against the Success of Affirmative Action

Thomas Sowell of the Hoover Institute has shown in his book *Preferential Policies: An International Perspective* that preferential hiring almost never solves social problems. It generally builds in mediocrity or incompetence and causes deep resentment. It is a short term solution which lacks serious grounding in social realities.

For instance, Sowell cites some disturbing statistics on education. Although twice as many blacks as Asians students took the nationwide Scholastic Aptitude Test in 1983, approximately fifteen times as many Asian students scored above 700 (out of a possible 800) on the mathematics half of the SAT. The percentage of Asians who scored above 700 in math was also more than six times higher than the percentage of American Indians and more than ten times higher than that of Mexican Americans—as well as more than double the percentage of whites. As Sowell points out, in all countries studied, "intergroup performance disparities are huge" (108).

There are dozens of American colleges and universities where the median combined verbal SAT score and mathematics SAT score total 1200 or above. As of 1983 there were less than 600 black students in the entire US with combined SAT scores of 1200.

This meant that, despite widespread attempts to get a black student "representation" comparable to the black percentage of the population (about 11%), there were not enough black students in the entire country for the Ivy League alone to have such a "representation" without going beyond this pool-- even if the entire pool went to the eight Ivy League colleges.[21]

Often it is claimed that a cultural bias is the cause of the poor performance of blacks on SAT (or IQ tests), but Sowell shows that these test scores are actually a better predictor of college performances for blacks than for Asians and whites. He also shows the harmfulness of the effect on blacks of preferential acceptance. At the University of California, Berkeley, where the freshman class closely reflects the actual ethnic distribution of California high school students, more than 70% of blacks fail to graduate. All 312 black students entering Berkeley in 1987 were admitted under "Affirmative Action" criteria rather than by meeting standard academic criteria. So were 480 out of 507 Hispanic students. In 1986 the median SAT score for blacks at Berkeley was 952, for Mexican Americans 1014, for American Indians 1082 and for Asian Americans 1254. (The average SAT for all students was 1181.)

The result of this mismatching is that blacks who might do well if they went to a second tier or third tier school where their test scores would indicate they belong, actually are harmed by preferential treatment. They cannot compete in the institutions where high abilities are necessary.

Sowell also points out that Affirmative Action policies have mainly assisted the middle class black, those who have suffered least from discrimination. "Black couples in which both husband and wife are college-educated overtook white couples of the same description back in the early 1970s and continued to at least hold their own in the 1980s" (115).

Sowell's conclusion is that similar patterns of results obtained from India to the USA wherever preferential policies exist. "In education, preferential admissions policies have led to high attrition rates and substandard performances for those preferred students . . . who survived to graduate." In all countries the preferred tended to concentrate in less difficult subjects which lead to less remunerative careers. "In the employment market, both blacks and untouchables at the higher levels have advanced substantially while those at the lower levels show no such advancement and even some signs of retrogression. These patterns are also broadly consistent with patterns found in countries in which majorities have created preferences for themselves. . ." (116).

The tendency has been to focus at the high level end of education and employment rather than on the lower level of family structure and early education. But if we really want to help the worst off improve, we need to concentrate on the family and early education. It is foolish to expect equal results when we begin with grossly unequal starting points—and discriminating against young white males is no more just than discriminating against women, blacks or anyone else.

CONCLUSION

Let me sum up. The goal of the Civil Rights movement and of moral people everywhere has been equal opportunity. The question is: how best to get there. Civil Rights legislation removed the legal barriers to equal opportunity, but did not tackle the deeper causes that produced differential results. Weak Affirmative Action aims at encouraging minorities in striving for the highest positions without unduly jeopardizing the rights of majorities, but the problem of Weak Affirmative Action is that it easily slides into Strong Affirmative Action where quotas, "goals," and equal results are forced into groups, thus promoting mediocrity, inefficiency, and resentment. Furthermore, Affirmative Action aims at the higher levels of society—universities and skilled jobs—yet if we want to improve our society, the best way to do it is to concentrate on families, children, early education, and the like. Affirmative Action is, on the one hand, too much, too soon and the other hand, too little, too late.

Martin Luther said that humanity is like a man mounting a horse who always tends to fall off on the other side of the horse. This seems to be the case with Affirmative Action. Attempting to redress the discriminatory iniquities of our history, our well-intentioned social engineers engage in new forms of discriminatory iniquity and thereby think that they have successfully mounted the horse or racial harmony. They have only fallen off on the other side of the issue.[22]

Notes

1. Quoted in William Bradford Reynolds, "Affirmative Action is Unjust" in D. Bender and B. Leone (eds.), *Social Justice* (St. Paul, MN, 1984), p. 23.

2. Some of the material in this section is based on Nicholas Capaldi's *Out of Order: Affirmative Action and the Crisis of Doctrinaire Liberalism* (Buffalo, NY, 1985), chapters 1 and 2. Capaldi, using the shackled runner analogy, divides the history into three stages: a *platitude stage* "in which it is reaffirmed that the face is to be fair, and a fair race is one in which no one has either special disadvantages or special advantages (equal opportunity)"; a *remedial stage* in which victims of past discrimination are to be given special help in overcoming their disadvantages; and a *realignment stage* "in which all runners will be reassigned to those positions on the course that they would have had if the race had been fair from the beginning" (p. 18f).

3. Wanda Warren Berry, "Affirmative Action is Just" in D. Bender, *op. cit.,* p. 18.

4. Robert Fullinwider, *The Reverse Discrimination Controversy* (Totowa, NJ, 1970), p. 25.

5. Quoted in Fullinwider, *op, cit.,* p. 4f.

6. See Lino A. Graglia, " 'Affirmative Action,' " the Constitution, and the 1964 Civil Rights Act," *Measure*, no. 92 (1991).

7. Linda Gottfredson, "Letters to the Editor," *New York Times*, Aug. 1, 1990 issue. Gender-norming is also a feature of the proponents of Affirmative Action. Michael Levin begins his book *Feminism and Freedom* (New Brunswick, 1987) with federal Court case *Beckman v. NYFD* in which 88 women who failed the New York City Fire Department's entrance exam in 1977 filed a class-action sex discrimination suit. The court found that the physical strength component of the test was not job-related, and thus a violation of Title VII of the Civil Rights Act, and ordered the city to hire 49 of the women. It further ordered the fire department to devise a special, less-demanding physical strength exam for women. Following EEOC guidelines if the passing rate for women is less than 80% of that of the passing rate of men, the test is presumed invalid.

8. John Arthur, *The Unfinished Constitution* (Belmont, CA, 1990), p. 238.

9. See Philip E. Vernon's excellent summary of the literature in *Intelligence: Heredity and Environment* (New York, 1979) and Yves Christen "Sex Differences in the Human Brain" in Nicholas Davidson (ed.) *Gender Sanity* (Lanham, 1989) and T. Bouchard, *et al.,* "Sources of

Human Psychological Differences: The Minnesota Studies of Twins Reared Apart," *Science*, vol. 250 (1990).

10. See Michael Levin, "Is Racial Discrimination Special?" *Policy Review*, Fall issue (1982).
11. Judith Jarvis Thomson, "Preferential Hiring" in Marshall Cohen, Thomas Nagel and Thomas Scanlon (eds.), *Equality and Preferential Treatment* (Princeton, 1977).
12. John Rawls, *A Theory of Justice* (Cambridge, 1971), p. 104; See Richard Wasserstrom "A Defense of Programs of Preferential Treatment," *National Forum* (Phi Kappa Phi Journal), vol. 58 (1978). See also Bernard Boxill, "The Morality of Preferential Hiring," *Philosophy and Public Affairs*, vol. 7 (1978).
13. Michael Kinsley, "Equal Lack of Opportunity," *Harper's*, June issue (1983).
14. There is one other argument which I have omitted. It is one from precedence and has been stated by Judith Jarvis Thomson in the article cited earlier:
"Suppose two candidates for a civil service job have equally good test scores, but there is only one job available. We could decide between them by cointossing. But in fact we do allow for declaring for *A* straightaway, where *A* is a veteran, and *B* is not. It may be that *B* is a non-veteran through no fault of his own. . . Yet the fact is that *B* is not a veteran and *A* is. On the assumption that the veteran has served his country, the country owes him something. And it is plain that giving him preference is not an unjust way in which part of that debt of gratitude can be paid" (p. 379f).
The two forms of preferential hiring are analogous. Veteran's preference is justified as a way of paying a debt of gratitude; preferential hiring is a way of paying a debt of compensation. In both cases innocent parties
bear the burden of the community's debt, but it is justified.

My response to this argument is that veterans should not be hired in place of better qualified candidates, but that benefits like the GI scholarships are part of the contract with veterans who serve their country in the armed services. The notion of compensation only applies to individuals who have been injured by identifiable entities. So the analogy between veterans and minority groups seems weak.

15. Quoted in Jim Sleeper, *The Closest of Strangers* (New York, 1990), p. 209.
16. Shelby Steele, "A Negative vote on Affirmative Action," *New York Times*, May 13, 1990 issue.
17. *New York Times*, May 10, 1990 issue.
18. Nicholas Capaldi, *op. cit.*, p. 85.
19. Ibid.
20. The extreme form of this New Speak is incarnate in the Politically Correct Movement ("PC" ideology) where a new orthodoxy has emerged, condemning white, European culture and seeing African culture as the new savior of us all. Perhaps the clearest example of this is Paula Rothenberg's book *Racism and Sexism* (New York, 1987) which asserts that there is no such thing as black racism; only whites are capable of racism (p. 6). Ms. Rothenberg's book has been scheduled as required reading for all freshmen at the University of Texas. See Joseph Salemi, "Lone Star Academic Politics," no. 87 (1990).
21. Thomas Sowell, *op. cit.*, p. 108.
22. I am indebted to Jim Landesman, Michael Levin, and Abigail Rosenthal for comments on a previous draft of this paper. I am also indebted to Nicholas Capaldi's *Out of Order* for first making me aware of the extent of the problem of Affirmative Action.

Wil Waluchow

Pay Equity: Equal Value to Whom?

A fundamental principle of justice upon which many of our moral and legal practices are founded is that equals should be treated equally:

From Wil Waluchow, "Pay Equity: Equal Value to Whom?" *Journal of Business Ethics*, Vo. 7, 1988. Reprinted by permission at Kluwer Academic Publishers.

that in the absence of relevant differences between them, people should be treated the same. This principle, associated with the Greek philosopher Aristotle, accounts for many of our beliefs about fairness and underlies the common law doctrines of legal precedent. It is also a principle which lies at the heart of the pay equity controversy. Work of equal value performed by men and women in the workplace (traditionally conceived) does not always appear to be rewarded with equal or even comparable pay. There is a wage gap (some estimate it as high as 36%) which seems undeniably due, in part, to the persistent, wholly unwarranted undervaluation of work performed by women. An irrelevant difference, sex, has been and is functioning as though it were relevant. The result is injustice; equals are not being treated equally.

The major difficulties in overcoming these injustices through social or legal means seem to fall largely into four categories. First, there has been much controversy over the nature or cause of the wage gap and therefore over how best and whether to tackle it. We cannot, the critics rightly point out, simply infer from the fact that there is a gap between the wages of men and women that sexual discrimination is the cause or even a significant part of the cause of its existence.[1] Some argue that only a very small percentage of the gap is attributable to this factor. Alternative explanations range from the premise that women, as the marriage partners largely responsible, traditionally, for maintaining homes and rearing children have in comparison with men been able to invest less "human capital" in the market-place, thus accounting for their lower wages;[2] to the premise that the relatively sudden influx of women onto the job market in post-war years resulted in a fierce competition for the relatively few, lower paying jobs more established participants—i.e, the men—were inclined to avoid.[3] But however much of the wage gap we can attribute to such additional factors, it is clear that there is a considerable remainder which can be explained only by the fact of discrimination.[4]

A second set of objections is based on the high, and in the view of some unfair, costs to business and government (and ultimately the taxpayer) of increased wages for women in the private and public sectors respectively. To this there is a simple reply. If business, government, and the male work force are, and have been for some time, profiting from the suppressed wages of women, then we have a clear case of unjust enrichment; and it is anything but unfair to demand the return of unjustly appropriated goods.

A third set of objections follows from the second. Increased wages for women will result, it has been argued, in a decreased demand for labour, especially in those sectors of the job market in which women happen to be concentrated. Thus we encounter a dilemma: our well-intentioned efforts will bring about more harm than good for those very people we are trying to help. To this there are at least three replies. First, the objection seems analogous to ones often formulated by people who were opposed to the abolition of slavery. To be sure, many Blacks did suffer in the short run; but there is no denying the long term gains. Secondly, when personal welfare competes with justice even the victim will often choose the latter. Witness the reluctance of many strikers to relinquish their cause even in the face of grave financial burdens. A third reply is that it is far from clear that the harmful consequences will be all that severe. The experience of Australia, which took major steps towards pay equity in the 1970s offers some grounds for hope. As Paul Weiler notes: "Although we cannot hold out comparable worth as an unqualified boon for women . . . the fact is that when one sums up both . . . wage and employment effects, there was a sharp net improvement in the condition of Australian women on the whole."[5] So there is hope that the choice isn't quite as bleak as all that.

A fourth set of objections to movements toward pay equity involves a questions which Aristotle's principle leaves entirely unanswered. We are instructed to treat equals equally. But precisely how do we determine who is equal and who is therefore entitled to equal or comparable pay? What criteria should we use in determining relevant and irrelevant differences? The conceptual and practical difficulties encountered in answering these questions have led many to condemn pay equity out of hand. According to Clarence Pendleton, chairman of the United States Civil Rights Commission, equal or comparable worth is the "looniest idea since Looney Tunes came on the screen."[6] Were we unable to unearth conceptually sound and workable criteria, Pendleton would have a strong case. Unless we have appropriate criteria and are confident that they can be applied in a consistent, principled manner, we run the risk of perpetuating, even increasing, the injustice we set out to eradicate. If we have the wrong criteria, then equals may be treated even more unequally.

On what basis, then, should we determine whose work is equal in value to whose? I'm afraid I have no easy solution—mainly worries and difficulties, in particular worries about a phrase which has figured in several landmark American legal cases and which one sometimes encounters in Canadian media reports: "work of equal value *to the employer.*"[7] My concern is that continued use of this phrase may lead to the continued undervaluation of certain forms of work. It may result in the very same injustices we are trying to eliminate. In what follows I shall try to make clear the sources of my concern.

In beginning, we must first distinguish two very different principles as they apply to women and pay equity. The first, the "Equal Work Principle" (EWP) states that women should receive equal pay for equal—i.e. identical—work. The second, the "Equal [or Comparable] Value Principle" (EVP) says that women should receive equal pay, not only for identical work, but for different work of equal value. The EWP applies, of course, in cases where men and women perform precisely the same tasks, more or less equally well. Some men might perform the relevant tasks better than some women; but the reverse applies as well. Here we encounter no significant difficulties. We have a clear-cut criterion: The work performed is equal; so the value of the work must be equal; and so it follows from the EWP that women who do this work are, all else being equal, entitled to the same pay as men. How valuable the work in question really is and how much each should therefore receive are difficult questions, of course. But they are also ones which are beyond the scope of the EWP. It is purely comparative and specifies one limited circumstance in which men and women should receive equal pay. It says nothing about the absolute value of those equal forms of work or about how much they merit in the way of financial reward.

It's a well-documented fact that the EWP is a relatively powerless tool in addressing the wage gap. For a number of reasons, women and men as a whole have tended to land in different jobs and different industries, though we can hope that pay equity will go some way towards eliminating this feature of our society in future. In such cases, we lack the clear-cut criterion provided by the EWP and must instead invoke the EVP with all its attendant difficulties. How do we compare very different jobs? Is it really like comparing apples and oranges, as the critics are so fond of saying? If not, how can we determine whether and how the differences between two different types of work are relevant for purposes of value and pay? One thing seems clear. We cannot, as we could with the EWP, answer these questions without asking *how much* a particular task is worth as compared with another. We cannot help asking whether, in terms of the relevant criteria, the value of a particular level or brand of secretarial work is greater than, equal to, or less than, the value of warehouse work or the work of electricians and carpenters. And so we inevitably encounter serious conceptual difficulties. These difficulties result largely from the fact that many different conceptions and associated criteria seem to be suggested by the amorphous phrase "equal value." At least that's what I'd now like to argue.

Consider for a moment the range of possible answers to the following question:

How does one determine the worth or value of someone's work so as to compare it with the work of others?

Here is a partial list of possible answers suggesting different criteria not all of which yield the same evaluations in all cases.

a. By whatever the *existing market*—i.e. an employer—will pay for it;
b. By whatever a *fair market* would pay for it;
c. By what she *deserves* for doing it;
d. By how much her work *contributes to the success of the firm;*
e. By how much her work *contributes to the community or society;*
f. By whatever is *the going rate in "the industry"* for people who do the same work;
g. By whatever value her work is assigned by her employer's *declared or explicit wage policy;*
h. By whatever value her work is assigned by her employer's *implicit wage policy.*

Answers A and B are favorites of those enamoured of neo-classical economic theory. Answer

C appeals to desert, D and E to one's contribution to an enterprise broadly construed. Answers F–H, like the EWP, are purely comparative. They require the consistent enforcement of existing standards or policies.

Much needs to be said about these eight competing, and possibly overlapping, criteria. Each has its merits; though each has its obvious problems as well. A is neat and tidy, but of no use in dealing with pay inequities. The existing market is unfair to women and largely responsible for the present wage gap. B allows us to purge the market of at least some of its undesirable forces, but it is anything but neat and tidy. The criterion suggested involves counterfactual speculation about what a fair market—i.e. one which, among other things, did not pander to prejudice against women—*would* pay for one's work *if* a whole set of non-existent conditions obtained. Such counterfactual speculation should be avoided if at all possible. Answer C seems *prima facie* appealing and acceptable, but it begs all sorts of questions, desert being an eminently contestable notion. D and E are very popular and often used to justify, for instance, very high wages for corporate executives and doctors. F and H pose problems of their own. To the extent that they appeal to existing standards which themselves may be based on prejudice, they will of course be of no help. F also ignores such things as regional differences, the different histories of collective bargaining within particular firms, and possibly even the different levels of productivity among different companies within the same industry.[8] G is often invoked by defenders of pay equity. Firms, at least sizeable ones, often have sophisticated internal procedures for ranking labour and management positions. These involve criteria which, if consistently applied without latent prejudice against women and so-called women's work, could sometimes eliminate inequities. But there are at least two problems with this solution. First, as noted earlier, to the extent that the internal standards are themselves biased, the result of their unbiased enforcement will still be unjust. A second problem is that many firms, in particular many smaller ones, simply lack explicit standards and procedures. This is one reason in favour of criterion H, a version of which has

been developed by Treiman, Hartman and Roos.[9] On this model, one sets out to discover the implicit values underlying an employer's wage structure for its various non-female (i.e. predominantly male or mixed) positions, on the assumption that the values the employer actually places on various job factors will not be skewed by sexual prejudice in such instances. Once found, these values can then be used to compare what the employer actually pays for these same factors when they are found in the predominantly female jobs. One could, in this way, discover how an employer objectively valued, say, educational credentials versus the assumption of risk of injury. The unbiased values might be revealed by what he pays for such jobs as electrician as opposed to predominantly male administrative or professional jobs like engineer.[10] Whatever values we discovered we would then have a basis for comparing how much the employer pays for these same factors when they figure in the predominantly female positions such as secretary or plant nurse. If we found a difference, we would have a clear case for equalization.

This seems to be a promising proposal which deserves serious consideration, especially given the general reluctance of governments to allow anything more than comparisons of how men and women fare on existing pay structures within one and the same firm of "establishment." But its limitations are obvious and must be acknowledged. First, it applies only to large firms with a wide variety of different jobs upon the basis of which the appropriate comparisons can be made. Second, it fails to provide a solution for companies where the employees are almost exclusively women. Here something more than this entirely internal, comparative test is required. And third, the values discovered in the non-female jobs might still be skewed by other non-sexual forms of bias.

One could go on discussing the eight criteria in some detail. But instead I should now like to turn to my main worry, which can now be expressed in terms of the desert and contribution criteria (C–E). Once we distinguish these different criteria, it is clear that the phrase "work of equal value" is radically ambiguous. The contribution criteria suggest that a work's value is instrumental in nature; it depends on, or exists in relation to, its *functional role* in bringing about desired states of affairs. These states of affairs can include such things as satisfactory production levels, profits, or as in the case of public nurses and doctors, a healthy population. On such a model, it is principally one's *work* which is of value, a value which can properly be expressed as its value to the employer or to society. The more a person's work contributes to securing the relevant desired states of affairs, the more valuable it is. We might call this *functional value,* and (somewhat tentatively) add that, all else being equal, work of higher skill and responsibility (two of the four factors normally mentioned in discussions of pay equity; effort and working conditions being the others) will be functionally more valuable. The contribution criteria, then, provide the best explanation of their relevance.

The desert criterion, however, operates very differently. Here, we might say, the value lies not so much in *the work* and its functional role in achieving desired states of affairs. Rather the value—more precisely, the *merit*—lies in *the worker herself.* The work of an employee who toils under conditions of physical or mental danger or miscomfort, or who puts in a much greater effort in preparing for a job or in carrying it out, it not *necessarily* of greater value to her employer. Her work may actually be of little functional value as compared with, say, the relatively cushy work of the corporate executive. The latter may score high in terms of responsibility and skill, i.e. in terms of the contribution criteria, but not necessarily the desert criterion. As for the former, her *work* might score very low on the contribution criterion, but *she herself* will rate very high on the desert criterion. And the reason is clear. All else being equal, one who makes a greater effort or endures undesirable conditions to achieve desirable ends, merits greater reward, regardless of the functional value of her work, of how much it *contributes* to securing those ends. This again, is because desert, unlike functional value, attaches principally to the worker not her work.

In so far as the desert and contribution criteria apply to different things—the worker vs. her work—they involve very different conceptions of value and often yield crucially different results. These important differences are masked by the phrase "work of equal value." We should always ask: "Equal with respect to what or to whom?" How we rank different jobs will depend crucially on how we answer this question.

I am now in a position to formulate my worry about the phrase "equal value to the employer." These words strongly suggest *functional value* (and the contribution criterion) at the expense of *worker's* value (and the desert criterion). It follows that use of this phrase in formulating, describing or even conceiving pay equity policy can easily lead to the undervaluation of important factors such as effort and working conditions. The result can only be injustice: workers will still be treated unequally. One final point: to the extent that many women are at present clustered in so-called "ghetto jobs", a number of which could well score very low on the contribution criteria but comparatively high on the desert criterion, this result should be of particular concern to proponents of pay equity for women. We have here a case where our choice of words might make a considerable difference both in conception and ultimately practice.[11]

Notes

1. C.f. R. Abella, *Equality in Employment: A Royal Commission Report,* Government of Canada, 1984.
2. See G. Becker, "Human Capital, Effort, and the Sexual Division of Labor, *J. Lab. Econ.* Vol. 2. No. 33 (1985).
3. This argument is outlined in "Comparable Worth: Theory, Policy and Equity Issue," Christian Dick, M. A. Thesis, McMaster University, 1986, p. 48-58.
4. See Paul Weiler, "The Wages of Sex: The Uses and Limits of Comparable Worth," *Harvard Law Review* Vol. 99: 1728 (1986) at 1790–91. See also, Corcoran & Duncan, "Work History, Labor Force Attachment, and Earnings Differences Between the Races and Sexes," *J. Human Resources* Vol. 3, (1979); England, "The Failure of Human Capital Theory to Explain Occupational Sex Segregation," *J. Hum. Resources* Vol. 17; 358 (1982); Roos. "Sex Stratification in the Workplace: Male Female Differences in Economic Returns to Occupation," *Soc. Sci. Research* Vol. 10 (1981); Treiman, Hartman, and Roos, "Assessing Pay Discrimination Using National Data," in *Comparable Worth and Wage Discrimination: Technical Possibilities and Political Realities,* ed. H. Remick (1984); and *Women, Work, and Wages: Equal Pay for Jobs of Equal Value,* ed. Treiman & Hartmann (Washington, D.C.: National Academy Press, 1981).
5. Weiler, p. 1777. Weiler's conclusions are based on Gregory & Duncan, "Segmented Labor Market Theo-

ries and the Australian Experience of Equal Pay for Women," *J. Post-Keynesian Econ.* Vol. 3, 403 (1981); and Gregory, McMahon, and Whittingham, "Women in the Australian Labor Force: Trends, Causes, and Consequences," *J. Lab. Econ.* Vol. 3, S293 (1985).

6. *New York Times*, Sept. 5, 1985, A25. Cited in Weiler, p. 1729.

7. See, for example, *AFSCME v. Washington*, 770 F.2d 1401 (9th Cir. 1985) where the court claimed that "the value of a particular job *to an employer* is but one factor influencing the rate of compensation for that job" (emphasis added). See also, *Christensen v. Iowa*, 563 F.2d 353 (8th Cir. 1977), where a similar claim was made. Comparable worth, the court said, would "ignore economic realities. The value of a job *to an employer* represents but one factor affecting wages . . ." (emphasis added). In the first of a series of articles on Ontario's proposed new pay equity legislation, (Bills 105 and 154), the *Hamilton Spectator* explained that "Pay equity, also known as equal pay for work of equal value, means paying women the same as men for doing different jobs that are judged to be of the same value *to*

the employer." (Nov. 25, 1986, A1, emphasis added). Interestingly enough, the phrase "equal value to the employer" is nowhere to be found in either bill. Nor is it employed in comparable legislation in Manitoba or in the *Canadian Human Rights Act*. But its use in explaining or interpreting these provisions (in conjunction with American precedent) could lead to a belief that this is what is meant by "equal value."

8. This may pose a problem for the EWP too, if the equal work in question is not restricted to one and the same "establishment," to use the phrase adopted in the *Canadian Human Rights Act*.

9. See Treiman, Hartman, and Roos; and Treiman and Hartman, *supra* Note 4. The model is outlined and defended by Weiler in *supra* Note 2.

10. The example is borrowed from Weiler, *Supra* Note 2.

11. An earlier version of this paper was read at a conference entitled "Women and Economic Equity: The Canadian Context," which was held on January 23—5 at Mount St. Vincent University, Halifax. I wish to acknowledge the assistance of several of the participants, in particular Deborah Poff and Alex Michalos.

June O'Neill

An Argument Against Comparable Worth

The traditional goal of feminists has been equal opportunity for women—the opportunity for women to gain access to the schools, training, and jobs they choose to enter, on the same basis as men. This goal, however, basically accepts the rules of the game as they operate in a market economy. In fact the thrust has been to improve the way the market functions by removing discriminatory barriers that restrict the free supply of workers to jobs. By contrast, the more recent policy of "comparable worth" would dispense with the rules of the game. In place of the

goal of equality of opportunity it would substitute a demand for equality of results, and it would do this essentially through regulation and legislation. It proposes, therefore, a radical departure from the economic system we now have, and so should be scrutinized with the greatest care.

The topics I will cover in this paper and the main points I will make are as follows:

1. The concept of comparable worth rests on a misunderstanding of the role of wages and prices in the economy.

2. The premises on which a comparable worth policy is based reflect a misconception about the reasons why women and men are in different occupations and have different earnings. Both the occupational differences and the pay gap to a large extent are the result of differences in the roles of women and men in the family and the effects these roles differences have on the accumulation of skills and other job choices that affect pay. Discrimination by employers may account for some of the occupational differences, but

From June O'Neill, "An Argument Against Comparable Worth," *Comparable Worth: An Issue for the 80's*, vol. 1 (Washington, D.C.: U.S. Commission on Civil Rights, 1984). Reprinted by permission.

it does not, as comparable worth advocates claim, lower wages directly in women's occupations.

3. Comparable worth, if implemented, would lead to capricious wage differentials, resulting in unintended shortages and surpluses of workers in different occupations with accompanying unemployment. Moreover, it would encourage women to remain in traditional occupations.

4. Policies are available that can be better targeted than comparable worth on any existing discriminatory or other barriers. These policies include the equal employment and pay legislation now on the books.

THE CONCEPT OF COMPARABLE WORTH

By comparable worth I mean the view that employers should base compensation on the inherent value of a job rather than on strictly market considerations. It is not a new idea—since the time of St. Thomas Aquinas, the concept of the "just price," or payment for value, has had considerable appeal. Practical considerations, however, have won out over metaphysics. In a free market, wages and prices are not taken as judgments of the inherent value of the worker or the good itself, but reflect a balancing of what people are willing to pay for the services of these goods with how much it costs to supply them. Market prices are the efficient signals that balance supply and demand. Thus, in product markets we do not require that a pound of soybeans be more expensive than a pound of Belgian chocolates because it is more nutritious, or that the price of water be higher than that of diamonds because it is so much more important to our survival. If asked what the proper scale of prices should be for these products, most people—at least those who have taken Economics I—would give the sensible answer that there is no proper scale—it all depends on the tastes and needs of millions of consumers an the various conditions that determine the costs of production and the supplies of these products.

What is true of the product market is equally true of the labor market. There is simply no independent scientific way to determine what pay should be in a particular occupation without recourse to the market. Job skills have "costs of production" such as formal schooling and on-the-job training. Different jobs also have different amenities that may be more or less costly for the employer to provide—for example, part-time work, safe work, flexible hours, or a pleasant ambience. And individuals vary in their talents and tastes for acquiring skills and performing different tasks. The skills required change over time as the demand for products changes and as different techniques of production are introduced. And these changes may vary by geographic region. In a market system, these changing conditions are reflected in changing wage rates, which in turn provide workers with the incentive to acquire new skills or to migrate to different regions.

The wage pattern that is the net outcome of these forces need not conform to anyone's independent judgment based on preconceived notions of comparability or of relative desirability. The clergy, for example, earn about 30 percent less than brickmasons.[1] Yet the clergy are largely college graduates; the brickmasons are not. Both occupations are more than 95 percent male—so one cannot point to sex discrimination. Possibly the reason for the wage disparity lies in unusual union power of construction workers and is an example of market imperfections. But other explanations are possible too. The real compensation to the clergy, for example, may include housing and spiritual satisfaction as fringe benefits. On the other hand, the high risk of unemployment and exposure to hazards of brickmasons may be reflected in additional monetary payments. If enough people require premiums to become brickmasons and are willing to settle for nonmonetary rewards to work as clergy, and if the buyers of homes are willing to pay the higher costs of brickmasons, while churchgoers are satisfied with the number and quality of clergy who apply, the market solution may well be satisfactory.[2]

One can also think of examples of jobs that initially may seem quite comparable but that would not command the same wage, even in nondiscriminatory and competitive markets. The following example is based on a case that has been used before, but it illustrates the point so well it bears repeating.[3] Consider two jobs—one a Spanish-English translator and the other a French-English translator. Most job evaluators would probably conclude that these jobs are highly comparable and should be paid the same. After all, the skills required, the mental demands, the working conditions, and responsibility would seem to be nearly identical. But "nearly" is not equal, and the difference in language may in fact give rise to a legitimate pay differential. The demand for the two languages may differ—for example, if trade with Spanish-speaking countries is greater. But the supply of Spanish-English translators may also be greater. And this would vary by geographic area. It would be difficult to predict which job will require the higher wage and by how much in order to balance supply and demand.

What the market does is to process the scarcity of talents, the talents of heterogeneous individuals and the demands of business and consumers in arriving at a wage. The net outcome would only coincidentally be the same as a comparable worth determination. There are simply too many factors interacting in highly complex ways for a study to find the market clearing wage.

Why Abandon the Market?

The argument for abandoning market determination of wages and substituting "comparable worth," where wage decisions would be based on an independent assessment of the "value" of occupations, is based on the following premises:

1. the pay gap between women and men is due to discrimination and has failed to narrow over time;
2. this discrimination takes the form of occupational segregation, where women are relegated to low-paying jobs; and
3. pay in these female-dominated occupations is low simply because women hold them.

The Pay Gap

In 1983 the pay gap, viewed as the ratio of women's to men's hourly pay, was about 72 percent overall (Table 1).[4] Among younger groups the ratio is higher (and the pay gap smaller)—a ratio of 89 percent of 20–24-year-olds and 80 percent for the age 25–34 years old. Among groups age 35 and over the ratio is about 65 percent.

What accounts for the pay gap? Clearly, not all differentials reflect discrimination. Several minorities (Japanese and Jewish Americans, for example) have higher than average wages, and I do not believe anyone would ascribe these differentials to favoritism towards these groups and discrimination against others.

A growing body of research has attempted to account for the pay gap, and the researchers have come to different conclusions. These studies, however, use different data sources, refer to different populations and control for many, but not always the same set of variables. Even the gross wage gap—the hourly earnings differential before adjusting for diverse characteristics—varies from study to study, ranging from 45 to 7 percent of depending on the type of population considered. Studies based on national samples covering the full age range tend to show a gross wage gap of 35 to 40 percent. Studies based on more homogeneous groups, such as holders of advanced degrees or those in specific professions, have found considerably smaller gross wage gaps.

After adjusting for various characteristics, the wage gap narrows. Generally, the most important variables contributing to the adjustment are those that measure the total number of years of work experience, the years of tenure on current job, and the pattern or continuity of previous work experience.

Traditional home responsibilities of married women have been an obstacle to their full commitment to a career. Although women are now combining work and marriage to a much greater extent than in the past, older women in the labor force today have typically spent many years out of the labor force raising their families. Data from the National Longitudinal Survey (NLS) indicate that in 1977 employed white women in their forties had worked only 61 percent of the years after leaving school, and employed black women had worked 68 percent of the years.[5] By contrast, men are usually in the labor force or the military on a continuing basis after leaving school.

In a recent study I examined the contribution of lifetime work experience and other variables using the NLS data for men and women aged 25 to 34. White women's hourly wage rate was found to be 66 percent of white men's—a wage gap of 34 percent. This wage gap narrowed to 12 percent after accounting for the effects of male-female differences in work experience, job tenure, and schooling, as well as differences in plant size and certain job characteristics, such as the years of training required to learn a skill, whether the occupation was hazardous, and whether the occupation has a high concentration of women.

The gross wage gap between black men and black women was 18 percent. The gross wage gap was smaller for blacks than for whites because job-related characteristics of black women and black men are closer than those of white women and white men. Black women have somewhat fewer years of work experience in their teens and early twenties than white women, which may be related to earlier child-bearing. They are more likely to work continuously and full time later on, however, and thus accumulate more total work experience and longer tenure on their current jobs than white women. The adjustment for differences in the measured characteristics cited above narrowed the wage gap of black men and women to 9 percent.

Are the remaining unaccounted-for differences a measure of discrimination in the labor market?

If all the productivity differences between women and men are not accurately identified and measured, labor market discrimination would be overestimated by the unexplained residual. Many variables were omitted from this analysis and from other studies because relevant data are not available. These include details on the quality and vocational orientation of education; on the extent of other work-related investments, such as job search; and on less tangible factors, such as motivation and effort. Differences in these factors could arise from the priority placed on earning an income versus fulfilling home responsibilities. If women, by tradition, assume the primary responsibility for homemaking and raising children, they may be reluctant to take jobs that demand an intense work commitment.

On the other hand, the unexplained residual may underestimate discrimination if some of the included variables, such as years of training to learn a job, or the sex typicality of occupations, partially reflect labor market discrimination. Some employers may deny women entry into lengthy training programs or be reluctant to hire them in traditionally male jobs. It is difficult with available data to distinguish this situation from one where women choose not to engage in training because of uncertainty about their long-run career plans or choose female occupations because they are more compatible with competing responsibilities at home.

Occupational Segregation

Although occupational segregation clearly exists, it is in large part the result of many of the same factors that determine earnings: years of schooling, on-the-job training, and other human capital investments, as well as tastes for particular job characteristics. In a recently completed study, I found that women's early expectations about their future life's work—that is, whether they planned to be a homemaker or planned to work outside the home—are strongly related to the occupations they ultimately pursue.[6] Many women who initially planned to be homemakers, in fact, become labor force participants, but they were much more likely to purse stereotyped female occupations than women who had formed their plans to work at younger ages. Early orientation influences early training and schooling decisions, and as a result women may be locked into or out of certain careers. Some women, however, by choice, maintain an ongoing dual career—combining work in the home with an outside job—and this leads to an accommodation in terms of the number of hours that women work and other conditions that influence occupational choice.

Women and men were also found to differ sharply in the environmental characteristics of their occupations. Women were less likely to be

TABLE 1 *Female-Male Ratios of Median Usual Weekly Earnings of Full-Time Wage and Salary Workers, by Age, 1971–1983*

1. *Unadjusted Ratios*

| Age | May 1971 | May 1973 | May 1974 | May 1975 | May 1976 | May 1977 | May 1978 | 2nd Quarter 1979 | Annual Average | | |
									1979	1982	1983
16–19	.89	.82	.82	.86	.86	.88	.86	.85	.87	.88	.94
20–24	.78	.77	.76	.76	.80	.78	.75	.75	.76	.83	.84
25–34	.65	.64	.65	.66	.67	.65	.66	.67	.66	.72	.73
35–44	.59	.54	.55	.57	.55	.56	.53	.58	.58	.60	.60
45–54	.57	.57	.57	.59	.57	.56	.54	.57	.56	.59	.58
55–64	.62	.63	.60	.63	.61	.59	.60	.60	.58	.60	.62
Total, 16 years and over	.62	.62	.61	.62	.61	.61	.61	.62	.62	.65	.66

II. *Adjusted for Male-Female Differences in Full-time Hours*[1]

| Age | May 1971 | May 1973 | May 1974 | May 1975 | May 1976 | May 1977 | May 1978 | 2nd Quarter 1979 | Annual Average | | |
									1979	1982	1983
16–19	.94	.86	.87	.90	.90	.92	.91	.96	.92	.91	.96
20–24	.85	.83	.82	.82	.86	.84	.80	.81	.82	.88	.89
25–34	.73	.72	.72	.73	.74	.72	.73	.74	.73	.79	.80
35–44	.66	.61	.61	.63	.61	.62	.59	.64	.64	.66	.66
45–54	.62	.62	.62	.63	.62	.61	.59	.63	.61	.64	.63
55–64	.67	.69	.65	.67	.67	.65	.65	.66	.64	.65	.67
Total, 16 years and over	.68	.68	.67	.68	.68	.67	.67	.68	.68	.71	.72

[1]Female-male earnings ratios were adjusted for differences in hours worked by multiplying by age-specific male-female ratios of average hours worked per week (for nonagricultural workers on full-time schedules).

Source: [Data from] Earnings by age and sex are from unpublished tabulations from the Current Population Survey provided by the Bureau of Labor Statistics, U.S. Department of Labor. Hours data are from U.S. Bureau of Labor Statistics, Employment and Earnings series, January issues, annual averages.

in jobs with a high incidence of outdoor work, noisy or hazardous work, or jobs requiring heavy lifting. These differences may reflect employer prejudice or the hostile attitudes of male coworkers, but they may also reflect cultural and physical differences.

In sum, a substantial amount of the differences in wages and in occupations by sex has been statistically linked to investments in work skills acquired in school or on the job. Varied interpretations of these results are possible, however. Thus, the precise amount that can be labeled as the result of choices made by women and their families rather than the result of discrimination by employers is not known.

The Trend in the Pay Gap

A major source of frustration to feminists and a puzzle to researchers has been the failure of the gap to narrow over the post-World War II period, despite large increases in women's labor force participation. In fact, the gap in 1982 is somewhat larger than it was in 1955.

The wage gap would not, however, narrow significantly over time unless the productivity or skill of women in the labor force increased relative to men's, or discrimination in the workplace diminished. Because the gross wage gap widened somewhat after 1955, either discrimination increased or women's skills decreased relative to men's. Findings from a recent study suggest that changes in skill, as measured by the changes in the education and work experience of men and women in the labor force, strongly contributed to an increase in the wage gap.[7]

In 1952 women in the labor force had completed 1.6 more years of schooling than men. This difference narrowed sharply so that by 1979 it had disappeared. One reason for this is that the educational level of men advanced more rapidly than that of women during the 1950s. Aided by the GI bill educational benefits, more men attended college. Another reason is that the labor force participation of less educated women increased more rapidly than the participation of highly educated women. Thus, the female labor force became increasingly less selective over time in terms of schooling attainment.

The rise in the number of women in the labor force may also have had an effect on the lifetime work experience of the average working women. A large number of less experienced women entering the labor force may have diluted the experience level of the working women. Although the total number of years of work experience of women is not available for periods of time before the late 1960s, data on job tenure—years with current employer—show that in 1951 men's job tenure exceeded women's job tenure by 1.7 years. This difference widened to 2.7 years in 1962 and then slowly declined, reaching 1.9 years in 1978 and 1.5 years in 1981.

The decline in working women's educational level relative to men's alone would have caused the pay gap to widen by 7 percentage points. The initial widening in the job tenure differential contributed another 2 percentage points to the gap. Together the change in education and job tenure would have increased the wage gap by more than it actually increased. Possibly then, discrimination declined during this period even though the wage gap widened. Since the mid-1960s, educational and work experience differences have moved in different directions. Male educational attainment rose slightly more than that of working women, which alone would have widened the pay gap slightly. Difference in work experience declined overall. Recently (between 1979 and 1983), a narrowing has occurred in the wage gap, from 68 percent to 72 percent overall.

Evidence from the NLS and other sources suggests that the pay gap is likely to narrow perceptibly in the next decade. Not only are young women working more continuously, but they are also getting higher pay for each year of work experience than they were in the late 1960s. This could reflect a reduction in sex discrimination by employers or a greater willingness of women to invest in market skills, or both. Women's career expectations also seem to be rising. In response to an NLS question asked in 1973, 57 percent of women between 25 and 29 indicated their intention to hold jobs rather than be homemakers when they reach age 35. Among women reaching ages 25 to 29 in 1978, 77 percent expressed their intention to work.

Young women have also greatly increased their educational level relative to men. Female college enrollment increased significantly during the 1970s, while male enrollment fell between 1975 and 1980. Moreover, women have made impressive gains in professional degrees during the 1970s. Work roles and work expectations of women and men may well be merging. As these younger women become a larger component of the female labor force, it is anticipated that the overall wage gap will be reduced.

Are Women's Occupations Underpaid?

A major contention of comparable worth supporters is that pay in women's occupations is lower because employers systematically downgrade them. The argument differs from the idea that pay in women's occupations is depressed because of an oversupply to these occupations. An oversupply could arise either because large numbers of women entering the labor force choose these occupations (which is compatible with no discrimination) or because women are barred from some causing an oversupply in others (a discriminatory situation). Although comparable worth advocates have taken the view that overcrowding is caused by restrictive measures, they have lately come to believe that this explanation is not the whole cause of "low payment" in women's jobs.[8] The argument is made that employers can pay less to women's jobs regardless of supply considerations, simply reflecting prejudice against such jobs because they are held by women.

The ability of firms to wield such power is highly questionable. If a firm underpaid workers in women's occupations, in the sense that their wages were held below their real contributions to the firm's receipts, other firms would have a strong incentive to hire workers in these occupations away, bidding up the wages in these occupations. Thus, competition would appear to be a force curtailing employer power. This process could only be thwarted by collusion, an unrealistic prospect considering the hundreds of thousands of firms.

Killingsworth (1984) has suggested that the market for nurses may be an example of collusion by a centralized hospital industry that has conspired to hold wages down. Without more careful analysis of the hospital industry, it is difficult to verify whether this is a valid hypothesis. Basic facts about wages and supply in nursing, however, suggest that collusion either does not exist or is ineffective. Despite a perennial "shortage" of nurses that seems to have existed as far back as one can go, the number of nurses has increased dramatically, both absolutely and as a percentage of the population. In 1960 there were 282 registered nurses per 100,000 population. In 1980 there were 506 nurses per 100,000. This rate of increase is even more rapid than the increase in doctors over the past decade, and the supply of doctors has been rapidly increasing. Why did the increase occur? Were women forced into nursing because they were barred from other occupations? That does not seem to be the case in recent times. What has happened is that nursing, along with other medical professions, has experienced a large increase in demand since the middle 1960s when medicare and medicaid were introduced, and private health insurance increased. As a result, the pay of nurses increased more rapidly than in other fields. Between 1960 and 1978 the salary of registered nurses increased by 250 percent, while the pay of all men rose by 206 percent and the pay of all women rose by 193 percent. During the 1970s the rate of pay increase for nurses slowed, which is not surprising considering the increase in supply. And entry of women into nursing school has recently

slowed, suggesting a self-correcting mechanism is at work.

Another way to attempt to evaluate the contention that lower pay in female-dominated occupations reflects discrimination is through statistical analysis of the determinants of earnings in occupations. In a recent study, I asked the question—after accounting for measurable differences in skill, do these predominantly female occupations still pay less? In an analysis of data on more than 300 occupations, I found that after adjusting for schooling, training, part-time work, and environmental conditions (but not actual years of work experience or job tenure, which were not available), the female proportion in an occupation was associated with lower pay in that occupation for both women and for men. But the effect was not large. For each 10 percentage point increase in the percent female in an occupation, the wage in the occupation went down by 1.5 percent. Again, however, one is left with a question mark. Are there other characteristics of occupations that women, on the average, may value more highly than men because of home responsibilities or differences in tastes and for which women, more so than men, are willing to accept a lower wage in exchange? Characteristics that come to mind might be a long summer vacation, such as teaching provides, or a steady 9 to 5 job close to home that certain office or shop jobs may provide. The true effect of sex on occupational differences or wage rates is, therefore, another unresolved issue. There are many good reasons why women would be in lower paying occupations than men, even in the absence of sex discrimination on the part of employers. That does not rule out the existence of discrimination, but it weakens the case for seeking an alternative to the market determination of occupational wage rates.

COMPARABLE WORTH IN PRACTICE—THE WASHINGTON STATE EXAMPLE

What would happen if wages were set in accordance with comparable worth standards and independently of market forces? Any large-scale implementation of comparable worth would necessarily be based on job evaluations that assign points for various factors believed to be common to disparate jobs. For example, in the State of Washington, where a comparable worth study was commissioned, a job evaluation firm assisted a committee of 13 politically chosen individuals in rating the jobs used as benchmarks in setting pay in State employment. The committee's task was to assign points on the basis of knowledge and skills, mental demands, accountability, and working conditions. In the 1976 evaluation a registered nurse at level IV was assigned 573 points, the highest number of points of any job—280 points for knowledge and skills, 122 for mental demands, 160 for accountability, and 11 for working conditions. A computer systems analyst at the IV level received a total of only 426 points—212 points for knowledge and skills, 92 points for mental demands, 122 points for accountability, and no points for working conditions. In the market, however, computer systems analysts are among the highest paid workers. National data for 1981 show that they earn 56 percent more than registered nurses. The Washington job evaluation similarly differs radically from the market in its assessment of the value of occupations throughout the job schedule. A clerical supervisor is rated equal to a chemist in knowledge and skills and mental demands, but higher than the chemist in accountability, thereby receiving more total points. Yet the market rewards chemists 41 percent higher pay. The evaluation assigns an electrician the same points for knowledge and skills and mental demands as a level I secretary and 5 points less for accountability. Auto mechanics are assigned lower points than the lowest level homemaker or practical nurse for accountability as well as for working conditions. Truckdrivers are ranked at the bottom, assigned lower points on knowledge and skills, mental demands, and accountability than the lowest ranked telephone operator or retail clerk. The market, however, pays truckdrivers 30 percent more than telephone operators, and the differential is wider for retail clerks.

Should the market pay according to the comparable worth scale? Or is the comparable worth scale faulty? In Washington State, AF-SCME, the American Federation of State, Coun-

try, and Municipal Employees, brought suit against the State on the grounds that failure to pay women according to the comparable worth scale constituted discrimination. Judge Jack E. Tanner agreed and ruled in favor of the union. The decision was based largely on the fact that the State had conducted the study. Whether or not the study was a reasonable standard for nondiscriminatory wage patterns was never an issue. The State, in fact, was disallowed from presenting a witness who would have critically evaluated the study.

What would happen if comparable worth were to be adopted as a pay-setting mechanism? Take the example of registered nurses and computer systems analysts. Nurses are 95 percent female. If a private firm employing both occupations were required to adopt the rankings from the Washington State comparable worth study, it would likely have to make a significant pay adjustment. It could either lower the salary of systems analysts below that of nurses or raise the pay of nurses above systems analysts. If it lowered the pay of systems analysts, it would likely find it impossible to retain or recruit them. The more popular remedy would be to raise the pay of nurses. If the firm did so, it would also be compelled to raise its prices. Most likely, demand for the firm's product would fall, and the firm would of necessity be required to cut back production. It would seek ways of lowering costs—for example, by reducing the number of registered nurses it employed, trying to substitute less skilled practical nurses and orderlies where possible. Some women would benefit—those who keep their jobs at the higher pay. But other women would lose—those nurses who become unemployed, as well as other workers who are affected by the cutback.

Of course, if the employer is a State government, the scenario may be somewhat different. The public sector does not face the rigors of competition to the same extent as a private firm. I suspect this is one reason why public sector employees seem to be in the forefront of the comparable worth movement. The public sector could not force workers to work for them if the remedy was to lower the wage in high-paying male jobs. But that is not usually what employee groups request. It can, however, pay the bill for the higher pay required to upgrade wages in female-dominated occupations by raising taxes. But in the long run, the State may have financing problems, since taxpayers may not be willing to foot the bill, and the result would be similar to that in the private firm—unemployment of government workers, particularly women in predominantly female occupations, as government services are curtailed.

Concluding Remarks

Advocates of comparable worth see it as a way of raising women's economic status and, quite expectedly, tend to minimize costs. A typical comment is as follows (Center for Philosophy and Public Policy):

Certainly, the costs incurred would vary widely depending on the scope of the approach chosen. But the economic costs of remedying overt discrimination should not prove staggering. Employers and business interests have a long history of protesting that fair treatment of workers will result in massive economic disruption. Similar claims were made preceding the abolishment of child labor and the establishment of the minimum wage, and none of the dire predictions came to pass.

Evidently the author is unaware of the numerous economic studies showing the disemployment effects of the minimum wage. However, what this statement fails to see is that comparable worth is in a bigger league than the child labor law or the minimum wage laws that have actually been implemented. It is far more radical. Instituting comparable worth by means of studies such as the one conducted in Washington State could be more like instituting a $15 an hour minimum wage or passing sweeping legislation like Prohibition. Moreover, the costs in terms of economic distortion would be much more profound than the dollars required to pay the bills. Curiously, this is recognized by one comparable worth proponent,[9] who then suggests "that we give very serious consideration to the idea that firms that do raise pay for 'disadvantaged occupations' get special tax incentives for capital equipment that will raise the productivity of these workers. We can't expect firms to

swallow these losses; that's crazy." Barrett is willing to go to these lengths because she thinks it might be a way to raise the incomes of poor women heading families on welfare. Long-term welfare recipients, however, are not the women holding the jobs covered by comparable worth schemes. The work participation of women in this situation is very low. Moreover, the lesson of studies of minimum wage effects has been that those who are most vulnerable to disemployment as a result of wage hikes that exceed national market rates are the disadvantaged—those with little education, poor training, and little work experience. Comparable worth would hurt, not help, these women. Subsidies to try to prevent these effects from occurring would be impractical to implement and prohibitively costly.

With all the difficulties that would ensue from implementing comparable worth, it is striking that it would not achieve many of the original goals of the women's movement such as the representation of women as electricians, physicists, managers, or plumbers. In fact, it would likely retard the substantial progress that has been made in the past decade. Younger women have dramatically shifted their school training and occupational choices. They have been undertaking additional training and schooling because the higher pay they can obtain from the investment makes it worthwhile. Raising the pay of clerical jobs, teaching, and nursing above the market rates would make it less rewarding to prepare for other occupations and simply lead to an oversupply to women's fields, making it still harder to find a stable solution to the problem of occupational segregation.

Another byproduct of comparable worth is that it diverts attention away from the real problems of discrimination that may arise. Such problems need not be confined to women in traditional jobs. Pay differences between men and women performing the same job in the same firm at the same level of seniority may no longer be an important source of discrimination. The form discrimination more likely takes is through behavior that denies women entry into on-the-job training or promotions on the same basis as men. The obvious solution is the direct one—namely, allowing or encouraging women whose rights are being denied to bring suit. Existing laws were intended to cover this very type of problem.

The pay-setting procedure in all levels of government employment is another area where remedies other than comparable worth would be more direct and effective. Governments usually do not have the flexibility to meet market demands. The need to adhere to rigid rules under considerable political pressure may result in paying wages that are too high in some occupations and too low in others. (By "too high" I mean that an ample supply of workers could be obtained at a lower wage). This could occur if the private plants covered in a pay survey for a particular occupation are themselves paying above market—for example, as the result of a powerful union. Such a situation could lead to unnecessary pay differentials between certain occupations that are male dominated (which are more likely to be represented by such strong unions) and other male, mixed, and female occupations whose private sector wages are more competitive. Comparable worth is not the solution, however, since it does not address the problem. Paysetting procedures can be improved by changing the nature of the pay surveys and by introducing market criteria—for example, by considering the length of the queue to enter different government jobs and the length of time vacancies stay open. Such changes may help women and also improve the efficiency of government.

Dramatic changes have occurred in women's college enrollment, in labor force participation, and in entrance into formerly male occupations, particularly in the professions. These changes are taking place because of fundamental changes in women's role in the economy and in the family—changes that themselves reflect a response to rising wage rates as well as changing social attitudes. Pay set according to comparable worth would distort wage signals, inducing inappropriate supply response and unemployment. If women have been discouraged by society or barred by employers from entering certain occupations, the appropriate response is to remove the barriers, not try to repeal supply and demand. Comparable worth is no shortcut to equality.

Notes

1. These statistics are based on the median hourly earnings of workers in these occupations in 1981. Rytina, 1982.
2. If brickmasons' wages ware artificially high because of union power, the market would be unstable. More workers would desire to be brickmasons than would be hired at the artificially high wage. Would comparable worth policy help the situation? Not likely. A comparable worth solution would likely require higher pay for clergy than for brickmasons because of the heavy weight placed on readily measured items like education. A wage for clergy that is too high would also be unstable. Only the removal of the union power or restrictions on unions would satisfactorily resolve the issue.
3. This example was originated by Sharon Smith and described in Killingsworth (1984), who notes it is cited in Gold (1983).
4. The commonly cited pay gap—where women are said to earn 59 cents out of every dollar earned by men—is based on a comparison of the annual earnings of women and men who work year round and are primarily full time. In 1982 this ratio was 62 percent. This figure is lower than the figure of 72 percent cited above because the annual earnings measure is not adjusted for differences in hours worked during the year, and men are more likely than women to work overtime or on second jobs.
5. O'Neill, 1984.
6. O'Neill, 1983.
7. O'Neill, 1984.
8. Hartmann, 1984.
9. Barrett, 1983.

QUESTIONS

1. Hettinger argues for strong affirmative action (reverse discrimination) on the basis that although it is to some degree undesirable, it is nevertheless justified inasmuch as it is required to achieve the important goal of dismantling our sexual and social caste system. What moral theory appears to underlie this claim?

2. Do you agree with Hettinger's claim that failing to compensate job-seeking white males for the sacrifices placed on them by reverse discrimination is no more morally troublesome than failing to compensate less talented members of society for their undeserved sacrifice of employment

opportunities for the sake of efficiency? Why or why not?

3. What is "race norming"? Is it morally justified? Why or why not?

4. How does Pojman respond to the argument made by Hettinger and others that since qualifications for a job are largely undeserved, the most qualified candidate for the job does not necessarily deserve the position?

5. What does Waluchow feel is the difference between pay equity based on the criterion of desert and pay equity based on the criterion of function?

6. Waluchow suggests that we should concentrate not on measuring the value of a person's work,

but on the merit of the person working. Do you agree? Would it be more or less difficult to establish the merit of the person working, i.e., what s/he deserves, than the functional value of the work performed?

7. What is O'Neill's argument for suggesting that programs of comparable worth may lead to higher unemployment of women?

8. Why does O'Neill think that programs of comparable worth tend to discourage rather than encourage women to pursue employment in non-traditional fields?

CASE 14:1 GROUP COMPOSITION, DISCRIMINATION AND HIRING PRACTICES[1]

Jobs at Ward's Cove Packing Company's Alaskan salmon cannery fall into two general categories: lower paying unskilled "cannery" jobs, which are predominantly filled by nonwhites, and higher paying skilled "noncannery" jobs, predominantly filled by white workers. The cannery is in operation only during the salmon runs in the summer; the rest of the time it is inoperative and unstaffed. A few weeks before the annual salmon runs, workers filling "noncannery" jobs arrive to prepare the plant for canning operations. When the salmon runs begin, the workers who operate the cannery lines arrive and remain as long as there are fish to can. Upon completion of the runs, these "cannery" positions are terminated, the workers leave, and the plant is shut down and winterized by the noncannery workers. Due to the fact that the location is remote and the work intense, both groups of workers are housed at the cannery and have their meals provided by the company. The two groups live in separate dormitories and eat in separate mess halls.

In 1974 a group of nonwhite cannery workers brought action against Ward's Cove alleging that among other things, separate hiring channels, a

lack of objective hiring criteria, and the practice of not promoting from within, had produced a racially stratified workforce in which they were denied skilled "noncannery" jobs on the basis of race.

Case Study Questions

1. Approximately 17% of Ward Cove's new hires for medical jobs at the cannery were nonwhite, and approximately 15% of the new hires for office worker positions were nonwhite. Supposing it to be the case that less than 15 to 17% of applicants for these jobs were nonwhite. Would this indicate that Ward's Cove is non-discriminatory in its employment practices? Would the question of whether the minorities represented in the "noncannery" jobs are the same as the minorities represented in the "cannery" jobs have any relevance to your decision? Explain your answer.

2. Is Ward's Cove policy of housing "noncannery" and "cannery" workers in separate dormitories and mess halls defensible? Why or why not?

CASE 14:2 AFFIRMATIVE ACTION AND SENIORITY[2]

In the early 1980s certain job classifications at Brass Craft Canada Ltd. were exclusively occupied by men and others by women, even though most of the jobs could be performed equally well by either sex. This pattern of employment had given rise to separate seniority lists for male and female employees. As a result, it would sometimes happen following a lay-off that a female employee with less seniority than a male might be called back to work earlier. The reverse would also sometimes happen. The union was well aware of this practice and had never raised any objection.

The situation changed after a recession caused a layoff more extensive than any formerly experienced.

At the end of the layoff, the company hired four additional female employees into a traditionally female classification. At this point, all the employees on the female seniority list had been recalled, but three employees on the male seniority list had not. The four female employees had previously been employed as replacement workers during an earlier strike. When the strike ended, Brass Craft had terminated their employment in compliance with the Collective Agreement, but because the Agreement did not forbid rehiring such persons, felt it was permitted to rehire them.

Initially, the union complained on the grounds that it violated the "spirit" of the return to work agreement to expect union members to work alongside "scabs" who had filled their jobs during a strike. They later grieved on the basis that segregated seniority lists had unfairly discriminated against the three male employees who had not been recalled.

Brass Craft responded by retaining its four new female employees and requested the three male employees who remained on layoff to signify in writing their willingness to take jobs traditionally classified as female. They then assigned them jobs as they became available, whether those jobs were in male or female classifications. After discussion, Brass Craft also agreed to integrate their seniority lists. They did not feel, however, that compensation was owed to these workers for the interval of time between the four new hires and the opening of positions those laid off eventually filled.

Case Study Questions

1. Are there instances in which segregated seniority lists are more fair than nonsegregated lists?
2. Given that the union had made no objection to segregated lists in the past, should Brass Craft have been obligated to pay compensation to the three laid off male employees?
3. Would Brass Craft have been justified in terminating the four new female employees in order to meet the demands of the union as regards the three laid off male employees?

Notes

1. Based on *Ward Cove Packing Co., Inc. v. Atonio* as found in 109 Supreme Court Reporter, 2115, (1989).
2. Based on *Brass Craft Canada, Ltd. and the International Association of Machinists and Aerospace Workers,* Local 2446 (1983), as found in 11 *Labour Arbitration Cases* 3rd series, 236.

For Further Reading

1. Tanis Day "Pay Equity: Some Issues In The Debate." (Background Paper for the Canadian Advisory Council on the Status of Women) March 1987, pp. 1-17.

2. Sidney Hook, "Rationalizations for Reverse Discrimination," *New Perspectives,* Vol. 17, Winter 1985, pp. 9-11.

3. William Shaw "Affirmative Action: An Ethical Evaluation," *Journal of Business Ethics,* Vol. 7, 1988, pp. 763-770.

4. Laurie Shrage "Some Implication of Comparable Worth," *Social Theory and Practice,* Vol. 13, No. 1, Spring 1987, pp. 77-102.

5. Thomas Sowell, *Preferential Policies: An International Perspective* (New York: 1990).

6. Richard Wasserstrom, "A Defense of Programs of Preferential Treatment," *National Forum: The Phi Kappa Phi Journal,* Vol. 58, No. 1, Winter 1978, pp. 15-18.

Chapter Fifteen

BUSINESS AND THE FAMILY

Introduction

Chapter Fifteen explores the relationship between business and the family. Although there is a wide interest on the part of psychologists and sociologists concerning the interrelationships of family and work, those in the field of business ethics have paid comparatively little attention to this topic. Indeed, a number of reviewers who evaluated the text, expressed doubts as to whether such a topic should be included in a business ethics text. Nevertheless, business and the family is a topic that deserves more attention from business ethicists than it has received. Work and family interpenetrate one another and cannot fail to raise important issues concerning not only prioritizing employment and family responsibilities, but how work and family institutions are to be structured.

The first selection, "Toward a Policy and Program Agenda for Working Parents" is taken from Chapter Seven of Sheila B. Kamerman's *Parenting in an Unresponsive Society.* She surveys the experience of two hundred women, [the Maplewood women] half of whom were white, half of whom were black, who either continued to work after the birth of a child or who re-entered the labor market some years after a child's birth. Two-thirds of the women were married, the other third were single mothers and the sole wage-earners in their families.

The greatest problem faced by these women was child-care, with single mothers facing the most difficult challenge. The survey also found that although the type of job influences work-family strain, the relevant distinctions lie not in the areas of pay or professional versus nonprofessional status, but in terms of flexibility and time. Kamerman goes on to suggest ways in which society and employers can help ease the conflict so many women experience between work and family responsibilities.

In "Men and the Politics of Gender," a selection from chapter ten of her book *No Man's Land,* Kathleen Gerson argues that there has been a decline of cultural consensus on the meaning of manhood. As a result, there is a great diversity of parenting models from which men must choose. She suggests that we should accept this diversity and not make the mistake of insisting there is only one correct model of male parenting. She also argues that if men are to have a genuine opportunity to be equally involved in parenting this implies a reorganization of the workplace, since the current structure of the workplace makes it difficult for a parent, regardless of gender, to combine employment and parenting.

Although some theorists have argued that the family as it exists in modern industrial society is inevitably oppressive to women, Domènec Melé in his article "Organization of Work in the Company and Family Rights of the Employees," repudiates neither capitalism nor the contemporary family. He argues that the organization of work within a capitalist system must recognize a number of family rights. In his view, employees have legitimate family duties that employers must recognize and not make harder to fulfill.

In our final selection, "Work and Family: Should Parents Feel Guilty," Lynn Sharp Paine explores the issue of parental guilt as regards entrusting children to caregivers in order to pursue careers. Paine argues that many discussions of this issue are superficial, inasmuch as they simply assume that these absence-related guilt feelings are irrational and inappropriate. This ignores the possibility that these feelings of guilt might very well be appropriate. She goes on to argue that the guilt feelings of many parents are a rational response to falling short of what they have good reason to regard as their parental responsibilities. She suggests that parents who feel guilty should not be treated as neurotic or mistaken. Rather, they should be encouraged, along with employers, to seek patterns of employment compatible with fulfilling what they understand to be their parental duties.

Sheila B. Kamerman

Toward a Policy and Program Agenda for Working Parents

WHAT WE LEARNED FROM THE STUDY

The most significant social phenomenon in the industrial societies of the mid-twentieth century is the large-scale entry of women into the labor force, in particular the accelerated labor force participation rate of young married women with preschool children. This development is generating a social revolution in family life-styles in the United States. Almost half of husband-wife families have two wage-earners; 60 percent of the women of childbearing age are in the work force; and by the end of the 1980s this group is likely to increase to 70 percent. Seventy percent of the working women hold jobs because of economic necessity, and with continued inflation this percentage is likely to increase. Furthermore, a significant additional percentage work for compelling family economic reasons, if not out of absolute necessity.

Two hundred women, half of them white, half of them black, and all with at least one preschool-age child, were interviewed in order to obtain insights and new information on how these women are coping with this life-style, which is increasingly emerging as the modal life-style for American families—as for most other families living in advanced Western industrial countries. The women interviewed were either continuing work after the birth of a child or reentering the labor market some years after a child's birth. Two-thirds of the women were married and living with their husbands; the remaining third were single mothers and the sole wage-earners in their families. Approximately half of the women can be described as professionals, middle-level managers or executives; the other half as office workers, blue-collar workers, or paraprofessionals. A significant number of single mothers in transition from public assistance to earned income only were also involved in the study. The women were interviewed twice, once at the point of the major life-style transition (childbirth; returning to the labor force as a parent) and then a second time six months later to review the adjustment and adaptation process.

Despite the rhetoric in the United States that emphasizes concern for children and families, the reality which surfaces in this study of women trying to cope with both family and work lives suggests very little sensitive response. It seems clear that our world is not set up to make it easy to manage home, children, and work simultaneously.

Child care is by far the most important problem these women have to contend with. Neither the problem of child care nor the solutions are very different among professional or nonprofessional women, middle- or low-income mothers, regardless of race or family structure. The most significant factor in determining the type of child care used—and preferred—by working mothers is the age of their child. School—preschool, nursery school, prekindergarten, kindergarten—is the single most important child-care mode for children aged three to five, just as it is for children of this age nationally. Regardless of its prevalence and popularity, however, it is rarely the sole care mode, primarily because preschool is often a short day or at most a normal school day, and this does not cover the full working day for mothers. For this

reason, as well as certain others mentioned below, child care for the children of working mothers can best be described as a "package involving elements such as kindergarten, day care, family day care, a spouse, a relative's home, or a teenage babysitter. More than half of the preschool children experience two or more forms of child care during a routine week. Children aged three, four, or five are particularly likely to experience multiple forms of child care. Moreover, over 25 percent of the families coordinate a complicated multimode child-care package, since the presence of two or more children substantially increases the likelihood of requiring multiple child-care arrangements. Inevitably, the tensions attendant on keeping the system functioning are ever present for these women.

The greatest diversity is found in types of child care used for infants and toddlers (children under the age of three). White professional two-parent families are likely to use in-home, paid child care. Working-class two-parent families are likely to share child care between parents who work different shifts, use some form of relative care either in their own homes or in the home of the relative, or use family day care. One-parent families are most likely to use a day care center, either because they prefer such care or because they are more likely to be eligible for subsidized care, which is more available in centers.

There is extensive use of relatives in providing child care for at least some portion of the time care is needed, and husbands play an important role in two-parent families.

Child-care needs and problems continue to weigh heavily on working mothers. Nor does there seem to be any easing of the situation in sight. There is a shortage of subsidized group programs—both preschool programs for three- to five-year-olds and infant and toddler child-care programs. Many preschools are part-day, and almost all kindergartens are, which creates additional problems for mothers who may have had a three- or four-year-old in a full-day nursery school and now, at five, this child is suddenly experiencing a shorter day. Many suburban schools refuse to permit children who live within a mile of the school to have lunch at school, and other schools still do not provide a school lunch or permit any child to remain at school at lunchtime! Few schools provide programs for children during the short or long school vacations.

There is little in the way of infant and toddler child-care programs for those who are interested in using such programs. Moreover, little reliable information is available to parents regarding family day care mothers, or, equally important, competent women who can take over in an emergency if a regular caregiver is ill or if a child is ill and cannot attend his/her usual program or school that day.

A significant amount of child care is informal and free, or at least nonmonetized. Much of the informal monetized care is quasi-market and, therefore, still low-cost. A relatively small amount of child care is paid for at full market value.

Although modified traditional gender roles continue to dominate in the allocation of most household tasks, a majority of the women interviewed described some movement toward greater equity in fulfilling household responsibilities. In particular, they stressed more sharing than was true in their parental households or in their own families before they worked or before the birth of their child. Furthermore, regardless of who has responsibility for these chores, and how much is done by the woman, these women stressed equity between spouses as a central value in marriage, even though the reality may still be very different. No one likes to relinquish power, but it would seem that men are realizing that when a woman contributes substantially to the family's income, she is entitled to some help along the way. A major finding of the study is that when there is a sense of equity in the sharing of tasks women describe their marriage and households as much happier than otherwise.

Although "family" continues to be primary in the lives of these women, "work" plays an increasingly important role in their lives, too. Most of the women interviewed expect to work all their adult lives, just as most adult men do. Although clearly the overwhelming majority state that they are working for economic reasons, most also say that they would continue to work even if there were no longer any financial need. Professional women stress the importance of careers or work as a central source of personal gratifications. Single mothers emphasize the role of work as the basis of social relationships and supplementary life experiences. Only among the two-parent working-class families do a majority of the women say they would stop working if the family no longer needed their earnings. And even within this group half of those indicated that, if part-time work were available, they would take such employment in order to continue obtaining the personal satisfaction that work can provide while alleviating the pressure on family life coming from full-time employment.

Thus, child-care problems are a source of constant stress and are only partially solved by existing resources. Intrafamily household and home problems are just beginning to respond to some increased role equity within the family. Purchased services are far outside the reach of most families, but husband's help and the help of other relatives attenuate some of the strain. In contrast, there has been almost no adaptation on the part of the work place. As a consequence, work pressures continue to impinge severely on parenting and family-related needs and conditions.

Neither statutory provisions nor employment-related fringe benefits provide much in the way of parent-related benefits. Very few of these women—or women in the country generally—possess any real entitlements to maternity benefits and leaves, and none have any right to a sickness benefit related to caring for an ill child at home. Although some women use their own sickness and vacation benefits to cover maternity or other child-related needs, this is implemented on an informal basis at best and sometimes is done *sub rosa*. As a consequence, those women who continued work after childbirth took off an average of six weeks after childbirth, half of the minimum statutory entitlement of almost all other industrialized countries and one-quarter of what is becoming the standard benefit in Northern Europe. Although some women returned quickly to work because of career pressures, the majority of those who took off a very short time after birth did so because of intense economic needs.

In addition to the obvious lack of child-parenting and family-related benefits at work, employers continue to be unsympathetic and often downright hostile to mothers at the workplace. The women report that in applying for jobs they encounter employers of an older generation (with at-home wives) who quiz them on their plans for taking care of their children. These questions are illegal, but they are still asked. Employers create an inevitable double bind for working mothers. They provide no benefits to facilitate women's coping with parenting responsibilities. Yet if women make such a request, this is used to underscore the "secondary" nature of women's employment and their lack of serious commitment to a job and the labor market generally.

We mentioned earlier that although the supply of child-care services at reasonable cost continues to be inadequate, the choice of child-care mode is more a factor of the child's age than anything else and that only for younger children do class, race, and family structure influence choice around such issues as the use of paid in-home care, relative care, or out-of-home care, respectively. Clearly, family structure influences the patterns of how household responsibilities are fulfilled, since by definition there is rarely any person to share tasks within a one-parent family. Even if there is no assurance of sharing in a two-parent family, a far greater possibility for sharing does exist. In contrast, neither race, class, nor family structure influence the extent of work-related problems and pressures. Furthermore, although the type of job does affect the extent and intensity of work-family strain, it is more a question of specific jobs rather than a distinction between professional and less skilled occupations. Thus, low-skilled work such as family day care or teacher aide may lead to less strain between home and work. The same is true for teaching generally and for work done at home (e.g., a practicing psychotherapist whose office is at home, a freelance writer.) On the other hand, for many professionals, work is a seven-day-a-week occupation, including many evenings as well. Thus, some combination of specific jobs, occupations which permit autonomy and flexibility, and individual personality may be the determining factors in attenuating work-family stress, given the current unresponsiveness of the work situation for most employees.

In analyzing the pattern of needs, problems, and solutions of working mothers across race, class, and family structure, we were struck most by the significance of family structure and less by race and class, except as exacerbating factors. For example: The major problems faced by the black families when compared to the white families are lower income and less job satisfaction. Although clearly of major importance, neither of these is unique to black working mothers. Indeed, the black two-parent families had incomes well above national and state median income levels, because two earners make a difference in all families. The significant differences in family income are more a factor of male wage differentials, higher unemployment rates, or high rates of female-headed families. On the other hand, the black working-class families and one-parent families are far more likely to have extensive informal supports available to them. These families see more of their relatives and make greater use of them in providing child care as well as a variety of other forms of help and reassurance.

The major difference between the professional and working-class families is primarily one of income and attitude toward work. Clearly, the financial rewards of work are greater for the professional families. In part, this leads to a greater use in purchased services, in contrast to working-class families whose major source of help is nonmonetized—through relatives, friends, or neighbors. However, this does not mean that either type of service is by definition better service. Furthermore, although their attitude toward work may be expressed in different ways, work plays a significant role in the values and sense of personal worth of all these women regardless of class.

The most significant differences in the problems of the working mothers in our study are primarily related to family structure and, to a much lesser extent, to marital satisfaction in our two-parent families. For all the women in our study, managing child care, household tasks and responsibilities, and job-related pressures presents a constant strain—a combination of time and energy pressures that often seems almost insurmountable. Most of the families described—and the women we interviewed—seem to be coping with a stressful life-style with incredible ingenuity and creativity. Their solutions are tenuous and complicated and often acceptable only because they are clearly transitory. Many women maintain an attitude like that of the mother who said, "Problems? Problems? Who has time for problems?" At best the situation is difficult, and the women are astonishing in their capacity to cope with relative equanimity.

But for some the situation is particularly bad. For the married woman whose husband continues to assume a traditional male role in the home, expecting his wife to fulfill all household responsibilities despite a full-time job outside the home, the situation is very tough. We looked at some women's time budgets and wondered: How could they manage an eight-hour work day, one hour or more of travel time to and from work, and six hours every weekday of child and household responsibilities in addition to full-time child care on weekends? If their husbands were ambivalent about their working—let alone opposed to it—this created major problems. Indeed, two wives in family situations such as this separated from their husbands during the course of our study. However, these extreme family situations were in the minority for two-parent families.

In contrast, almost all our single mothers lived under constant time and energy pressures, and most had to contend with economic strain too. Obviously, the major difference between our one- and two-parent families is economic. Family income is significantly reduced when there is only one wage-earner in a family, and the reduction is even more marked when the sole wage-earner is a woman. However, the problems of occupational segregation, job training, and wage equity, although of great importance, would be significant whether these women were mothers or not. The problem of inadequate family income when children are present is, however, of great significance, and will be discussed again later in this chapter.

For the most part, two-parent families can be assured of two sources of income. In addition, these families have four hands and two persons

available for tasks instead of two hands and one person. Thus they share tasks, expand time availability, permit the division of responsibilities and the alleviation of emotional stress and strain. They even have the potential of two sources of informal supports in the form of a double set of relatives.

In contrast, single mothers have less of almost everything, except, perhaps, problems. They are, of course, saved the possible additional load of a husband's problems at the same time as they are deprived of all such possible help. In addition to the probability of less income, single working mothers have at their disposal less time, less energy, fewer skills, and less support both in and out of the home.

If a marriage is bad, these women find their single status relieves them of the additional strain of fighting, conflict, tension—and often of husbands who gave no help anyway. But coping with child care, childrearing, home responsibilities, and work pressures when you are alone is very difficult. And most of these women have no options. They must work. Hearing them describe how they managed their homes, their jobs, and their children (often in isolation and loneliness) was painful and poignant. Their daily lives often seemed incredibly difficult, and they received little support anywhere.

In essence, for all of these women and their families, it seems quite clear: Being a member of the labor force and a full-time parent means trying to manage against overwhelming odds in an unresponsive society.

IMPLICATIONS FOR A POLICY AND
PROGRAM AGENDA

Nothing we would say here is original or unique. Our focus is clearly on the needs of wage-earning adults who also happen to be parents, on working mothers when they are the sole parent, and on working mothers and fathers when both parents in a two-parent family are employed. As stated earlier, we are not here addressing broader social policy issues, which require attention regardless of whether the adults are parents or not. Thus, the income, employment, and training needs of blacks in general or women regardless of race require attention with or without the presence of children.

However, the income needs of families with young children—and of adults rearing children—clearly are of particular significance as we identify the problems of working parents.

Women who are sole parents are likely to suffer major financial hardships with consequences for their children.[1] Thirty-six percent of all female-headed families in the United States had incomes below the poverty level in 1977. Although female-headed families constitute 15 percent of the total number of families in the United States, they represent over half of the families living in poverty. Moreover, more than half of the 10 million children living in families with incomes below the poverty level were in one-parent families. In 1977, 861,000 families of the 8.2 million families headed by women had only one source of income—public assistance—and almost all of them were living below the poverty level. Of the 675,000 families headed by women that had earnings and also received public assistance, over 61 percent were below the poverty level. Among families with children, the median income of $6,358 for families headed by women was only one-third of the median income of husband-wife families.

Regardless of what else is done to improve the wage-earning capacities of women, it is time to address the low-income status of female-headed families even when the women are in the labor force and work full time. For these families, as well as for the other 5 million children in families with an employed father and income below the poverty level, surely it is time to provide a child or family allowance—a cash benefit provided to families based on the presence and number of minor children in the family. The United States is the only one of sixty-five industrialized countries that does not provide such a benefit—which would assure a direct cash income supplement to all families with children. Although the benefit provided in other countries varies in size, even a small amount can help in a family with very low income. This benefit can be provided as a direct cash transfer or indirectly, as a refundable tax credit.

The recently expanded earned income tax credit in the United States represents a variation on this approach for low-income working parents. But we would urge the need now to develop some form of income transfer for all families with children, not just families with working mothers, even if the policy were to make such a benefit taxable.

In contrast, one way to provide an income support benefit specific to working mothers would be to offer a paid maternity or parental leave for employed women (or perhaps a benefit to be shared between employed husbands and wives). Such a policy, assuring wage replacement and full job protection for a specified period of time following childbirth, would be of enormous importance in protecting income for families dependent on two wages or on the sole wage of a mother. In addition, women would be assured that their jobs would be held for them, and that they would not risk unemployment if they remained home for some weeks after childbirth. Recently passed legislation in the United States provides such benefits only to women covered under private disability insurance. Approximately 40 percent of the working women in the United States have such coverage as a result. (A much smaller percentage were covered among the women interviewed.)

At present, in Europe, three months is the minimum paid leave provided under law for all employed women. The average leave in the Northern and Eastern European countries is six months, and Sweden provides nine months. Moreover, Sweden and Norway provide for fathers under their legislation through a kind of "parent insurance."

Similarly, neither as a part of federal nor state legislation nor even as part of labor union negotiations has there been an interest expressed in assuring parents a specified number of days of paid sick leave to cover caring for an ill child at home. This too is an employment benefit that is emerging increasingly in several European countries and would be of help to working parents here.

Child care continues to be the central problem for all employed mothers. Our own analyses of national census data suggest that close to 60 percent of the three- to five-year-olds attend some form of out-of-home group programs.[2] Another recent report on child-care arrangements in the United States reports similar figures.[3] Our Maplewood families report the same trend and, perhaps even more important, stress the preference of parents for preschool programs. Parents are clearly using this type of care for three- to five-year-olds. The problem is that most of it is market care and thus inaccessible to a significant portion of the working-class and middle-class families who cannot afford to pay the full market costs of a high-quality preschool program. Of equal importance, however, is the finding that these children are particularly likely to be cared for in multiple arrangements during the week—because many of the preschool programs are part-day, not even as long as the normal school day. At the very least, it should be possible to expand the availability of publicly subsidized preschool programs to make them available to any child of this age whose parents wish him or her to participate.

Furthermore, for these children in preschool and for children aged six to eight in primary schools whose two parents or single parents work, the problem of supplementary school care is crucial also. Parents may need to leave for work before the child leaves for school and return home after school closes, or cope with child care on days that school is closed and the work place is open. We have no data in the United States which indicate how primary school children are cared for now when their parents' work day does not coincide with the normal school day. We need to learn how parents are coping now, and we need to begin to identify different models for supplementary school programs. There are simple things that could be done to make life easier for working families. For example, all schools could provide lunch; schools could open one hour earlier and stay open one or two hours longer, with informal recreational activities available for children who wish to participate. Schools could lower their age of entry and develop a preschool program. The supplementary programs could be administered and operated separately from the regular school program. These are just a few of the possibilities that could be instituted to respond to the changing life-styles of American families.

Finally, with regard to child care, we need to expand the options for infant and toddler care.[4] We are only now beginning to learn about such care; and we are only now beginning to recognize the growing demand for this care. If paid maternity leave were available for some portion of the first year after a child was born, our major concern would be for children from about six months or one year of age to two and a half or so. Parental preferences are not yet clear for child care of children of this age, but it seems highly likely that a variety of types of care will be used and should be available. This suggests the need to expand group care but also to improve the quality of family day care for parents who prefer more informal care. Of particular importance, however, would be some expansion in child-care information and referral services, since many parents say they have great difficulty learning about reliable family day care providers.

Apart from child care, little mention is made of other formal resources as significant family supports. In contrast, great stress is placed on the need for more flexibility and responsiveness at the work place. Flexitime, part-time employment, and shared jobs were mentioned by many as offering possible relief from work/family pressures. Any efforts in this direction should be encouraged.

Our study has highlighted the problems of the single mother. Inadequate income, although central, is only one facet of the problem. It seems clear, also, that work—a job—is essential for these women, not only for obvious economic reasons but for nonpecuniary reasons as well. Work offers a potential source of gratification and often the only source of social contact and relationships in what is frequently a lonely and isolated life. Adequate child-care arrangements become even more important when work is central to both economic and noneconomic needs. In addition, however, single mothers suffer from a lack of time and a lack of physical and emotional support. There is only one person to do all the routine family and household tasks. Friends, neighbors and relatives help, but at best this help is limited, and unless relationships already exist and are very strong these single mothers have little time to cultivate new relationships. Community agencies interested in responding to the needs of single mothers would do well to experiment with a range of different types of programs, including innovative approaches to providing brief supplementary child care, occasional home-help or other concrete services, information and advice services, and the development of self-help networks.

The recommendations made thus far stem directly from the findings of our study. The women interviewed were clear about the problems and tensions they experienced as part of their daily lives and what would really make a difference—and would really be of help. We would summarize now the questions our study did not answer or those that emerged in the course of the study itself and we would hope to see explored in further work. One major regret at the end of the study is that we did not have a budget that would have permitted systematic interviewing of fathers (husbands, cohabitants). A few were interviewed informally, because they were present at the time of the scheduled interview, or because they expressed a special interest. Any subsequent attempt at exploring the family and work lives of working families should include both parents in order to obtain a more complete picture of what daily life is like and the extent to which father's and mother's views of daily routines, problems, and needs do—or do not—coincide.[5]

The descriptions many of the Maplewood women gave their average or "typical" days—the complicated arrangements, the multiplicity of responsibilities, the constant juggling of time and tasks—underscored how little we know about what Urie Bronfenbrenner has referred to as the natural ecology of children. As important as data on sickness or health, behavior or misbehavior may be for quantitative measures of growth, learning, and understanding what is happening to children in our society, we also need to learn more about the actual daily lives of children, as they experience their life. We would urge more ethnographic studies of parenting and childbearing within the home environment in order to provide data about families in real life situations.[6] Similarly, we would urge more use of time studies with

working families.[7] Our own efforts in this study convinced us of the difficulties in obtaining valid and reliable time-use data. Time is used in multiple ways simultaneously, and there are consequent problems in allocating time segments to discrete tasks. "The laundry is put into the machine and while the wash is done I get dinner ready. The four-year-old likes to help so she puts the plates and silver on the table. The baby is in the high chair and we sing songs and play together. Sometimes I give the baby supper then." How are we to allocate this half-hour? Yet despite the difficulty we need to know more about how working parents use their time. In particular, we should be trying to monitor any increase in the amount of time men invest in household and family tasks and whether some of the overload is being removed from women. We might hypothesize increasing problems in those families in which women continue to maintain full responsibility for home and family even though they are also full-time workers. We might also hypothesize some positive consequences of an increased involvement in "fathering" or "parenting" roles by men.

In conclusion, we would remind our readers that in their interviews and in their reports on their daily lives, these Maplewood women emphasized once more the centrality and significance of families. Much rhetoric is directed at the value of the family in our society, but little real attention is paid it. For these women, their families—their husbands and children first, and then other family members—are the most important part of their lives. Their jobs, whatever they may be, are a significant part too, but in no way supersede their family relationships. They are trying in every way possible to cope with complicated and demanding routines in order to satisfy what they view as essential responsibilities and obligations in both domains. If their family responsibilities constrain what they can do in the world of work, their families also offer them support which permits them to cope with both worlds. In contrast, however, the world of work continues to impinge on family and home life. As women move increasingly into the work place, both women and men will become more aware of the difficulties in coping with these two domains, unless some modification and adaptation occur.[8] Family life-styles are changing and adapting. Male and female relationships are changing and adapting. If men and women are to become productive adults at home and work—if they are to be parents as well as workers and wage-earners—society too must respond more actively to these changes. In short, there is a policy agenda. Given what is happening to families in our society today, it is time now to respond.

Notes

1. See Beverly L. Johnson, "Women Who Head Families, 1970–1977: Their Numbers Rose, Income Lagged," *Monthly Labor Review*, February 1978. See also Heather L. Ross and Isabell V. Sawhill, *Time of Transition: The Growth of Families Headed by Women* (Washington, D.C.: The Urban Institute, 1975); Clarie Vickery, "Economics and the Single Mother Family," *Public Welfare*, Vol. 36, No. 1 (Winter 1978), and "The Changing Household: Implications for Devising an Income Support Program," *Public Policy*, Vol. XXVI, No. 1 (Winter 1978).

2. Sheila B. Kamerman and Alfred J. Kahn, "Day Care: A Wider View," *The Public Interest* (Winter 1979).

3. Mary Jo Bane *et al.*, "Child Care Arrangements of Working Parents," *Monthly Labor Review*, Vol. 102, No. 10 (October 1979).

4. For an overview of child-care policy for the very young children of employed parents in five European countries, see Sheila B. Kamerman, "Work and Family Life in Industrialized Countries," *SIGNS: The Journal of Women in Culture and Society* (Summer, 1979). For an extensive discussion of these policies and related programs, see Sheila B. Kamerman and Alfred J. Kahn, *Child Care, Family Benefits and Working Parents* (New York: Columbia University Press, 1980).

5. The Working Family Project and the Families and Community Project, at the Wellesley College Center for Research on Women, Laura Lein, Principal Investigator, is one illustration of a study employing such an approach.

6. The current research of Urie Bronfenbrenner involves such an approach.

7. Joseph H. Pleck, Associate Director, Center for the Family, University of Massachusetts, is involved in such an effort now, as is Elliott A. Medrich, Director, Children's Time Study, University of California, Berkeley.

8. For some discussion of this issue, see Kamerman, "Work and Family Life in Industrialized Societies," and Kamerman and Kahn, *Child Care, Family Benefits and Working Parents*.

Kathleen Gerson

Men and the Politics of Gender

We are in a period of sustained and deeply rooted diversity in men's lives—one in which breadwinners, involved fathers, and single and childless men are contending for economic and social support. This transformation extends well beyond the confines of the so-called underclass or other minorities pursuing "alternative life-styles." The fundamental social and economic changes propelling this revolution have affected most men, and especially those under the age of forty. Even if they have not personally experienced declining economic fortunes or been involved with work-committed women, men have felt the ripple effects of changes that have spread outward in unforeseeable ways.

Men are facing new dilemmas as well as new choices. Those who withdraw from work or share economic obligations with a woman face being labeled inadequate providers. Those who decide not to have children are seen as irresponsible or selfish. Those who become primary breadwinners confront the charge that they are male chauvinists. Diversity has thus generated ambivalence and disagreement about the appropriate obligations and legitimate rights of men. It is time for the national debate to address the cultural, political, and social policy implications of changes in men's lives.

. . .

MEN'S PARENTING AND SOCIAL POLICY

The decline of male breadwinning poses significant dangers, but it also offers an unprecedented opportunity to bring greater equality to family and work life while expanding men's and women's range of choice and enhancing the well-being of children. Accomplishing these ends, however, requires more than the efforts of ordinary men. Just as individuals develop strategies to respond to unavoidable change, so must societies. While changes in the organization of the economy, marriage, and child rearing make the decline of breadwinning inevitable, social policies can help shape the forms that emerge to take its place. We have seen how opportunities and barriers at work and in the home can either thwart or encourage men's family involvement. Since men's choices are shaped by social circumstances, the challenge is to build social institutions that support the best aspects of change (such as the expansion of equality, choice, and family involvement) and discourage the worst (such as the abandonment of children and the overburdening of women). In the best American tradition, we need to build policies that respect diversity, encourage responsibility, and create equal opportunity.

Diversity in men's choices is here to stay. A new cultural consensus on the meaning of manhood appears no more imminent than the emergence of a new dominant pattern of behavior. In light of these new realities, we need to avoid replacing one dogma with another. Tolerance for diversity is central to American political culture. On the other hand, a cultural politics of division and blame draws attention away from the social challenge to adapt to inevitable change. It is time to abandon the search for one, and only one, correct pattern for all men. It is time not only to accept diversity but to respect it.

In rejecting rigid definitions of manhood, we need to include new responsibilities along with an expanded range of choice. Among men who retain a breadwinning identity, there is a difference between those who are actually supporting nonemployed wives and those who refuse to admit that their wives are breadwinners, too. Among men who have moved away from parenthood, there is a difference between those who have decided that the responsible choice is to remain childless and those who have abdicated responsibility for their children. Among involved fathers, there is a difference between those who have accepted equal responsibility for domestic work and those who remain helpers. Clearly, some choices are more responsible than others.

We can uphold the ideal of diversity and choice without sacrificing responsible standards of behavior. In a world where marital and parenting commitments have become fragile, this does not mean that everyone should get married or have children. It does, however, mean that choosing marriage or parenthood implies assuming serious responsibilities and making necessary sacrifices. If a man chooses to marry, he is agreeing to uphold the principles of justice and fairness. If he chooses to become a father, he is making a lifelong commitment to caring for his children.

Upholding standards of justice and sharing in personal commitments is neither a punishment nor an unmitigated loss to men. We have seen that men have much to gain from more equal relationships with women and more caring connections to children. Economic and social changes may require men to relinquish some long-standing privileges, but they also offer men a chance to claim new rights and surrender old burdens. No longer held solely responsible for the economic health of their families, men can look forward to sharing the obligations of breadwinning and enjoying the pleasures of care. Moreover, if men become more involved in the care of their children, they gain the moral authority to fight for parental rights inside and outside of marriage. Not only do involved fathers have a greater claim to parental rights in the event of divorce, but they are also less likely to abandon their children.[1] If marriage becomes more just and equal, then so can divorce. On the other hand, if men want parental rights, they must earn them the way women do—by being responsible, caring, sharing parents who meet their children's needs in myriad ways every day.

Institutions can foster or discourage responsible choices. If we want men to behave responsibly, then we must build social policies that support and encourage such an outcome. Effective social supports could transform men's family involvement from a latent, incipient possibility to expected, unremarkable behavior. Given the growing proportion of women struggling to balance work and family obligations and the growing proportion of children living without the economic or emotional contributions of men, men's commitment to care and equality has become greatly needed as well as morally desirable. Such a profound transformation in men's lives will require equally fundamental changes in the organization of the workplace and the economic opportunities available to women.

Women's movement into the labor force has made it clear that the home and the workplace are interacting rather than separate spheres. Yet conflicts between work and family have typically been viewed as a woman's problem. The current organization of the workplace makes it difficult for any parent, regardless of gender, to combine employment and parenting. Work also poses obstacles to men's family involvement, and to ignore these obstacles is to leave the problem unfairly resting on women's shoulders.

In addition, the historical bargain between employers and families has broken down. When employers paid their male workers enough to support a homemaking wife, they could argue that children's needs were not their concern. Since employers are now less likely to pay men a family wage that subsidizes female caretakers, the time has come to admit that most families depend on either two earners or one parent. These revolutionary changes in gender and family life require a new bargain between employers and workers based on the principle that parenthood is a right, not just a privilege, for all.

What does this mean in practical terms? At the least, it means no longer penalizing employed fathers or mothers for providing the care and attention that children require. Even more, it means offering workers greater flexibility in how they choose to balance work and family contributions over the course of the week, the year, and the career. Caretaking demands ebb and flow in unpredictable ways that cannot be addressed via rigid work schedules and career tracks. We need to create a more flexible boundary between family and work. Yet only about 3,500 companies address family policy issues at all, and most do so in a piecemeal fashion. Only about 50 companies have developed fully integrated work/family benefits, including appointing someone with designated responsibility to develop and oversee a package of policies.[2]

Bringing the workplace into a new partnership with family life will require more than the goodwill of employers, most of whom are unlikely to institute change unless compelled to do so. And it will require more than *de jure* policies that formally allow family involvement but informally penalize those who choose it. If involved parenting remains a formal option that few feel entitled to take without great sacrifice to their careers, the most ambitious among us—women as well as men—will resist involved parenthood and reject the programs that exist on paper but punish those who utilize them.[3] Instead, we need "family support" policies that allow involvement for all parents. If men and women unite to fight for the parental rights of all workers, then the conflicts between work and family may begin to dissolve.

Creating genuine family support policies to replace the patchwork of company-initiated programs that now exist will require political and legislative action. The federal family leave law that requires larger firms to offer their workers three months of unpaid leave in the event of a child's birth or a family medical emergency is certainly an important start, but it needs to become the floor on which we build more fundamental programs rather than the ceiling above which family policies cannot rise. Sweden, for example, guarantees all workers six weeks of paid vacation each year, three months paid leave when children are sick, the right to work part-time without losing one's job until one's children are seven years old, and eighteen months of parental leave to fathers as well as mothers. A quarter of Swedish fathers take paternity leave.[4] To move beyond family leave to secure the broader range of parental rights that many Europeans now take for granted may ultimately depend on a "parents' movement" comparable to the movements for workers' rights that once secured limits on the length of the work week, safer working conditions, and minimum wage guarantees. This means bringing men into the fight that women have pioneered in pursuit of a more family-supportive workplace.

A reorganized workplace is necessary, but not sufficient, to bring men into family life. Men's family involvement also depends on equal economic opportunities for women. Women's economic resources give them the leverage to insist that men parent more. They also make it possible for men to work less. A father's involvement depends on economic opportunities for his female partner. Thus, policies that promote economic opportunity for women also promote men's parental involvement.

Of course, economic opportunity and family obligation are related. Women cannot enjoy equal employment opportunities until men shoulder equal family obligations, and men are not likely to become equal parents until women enjoy equal economic opportunities. Indeed, when parenthood becomes as costly to men's work careers as it is to women's, then men, too, will have a stake in reducing the economic and social penalties for taking care of children.[5]

Equal opportunity and a reorganized workplace will be difficult to achieve, and the struggle to achieve them will surely remain politically controversial.[6] But the costs of *not* creating family-friendly workplaces, equal economic opportunities for women, and equal family opportunities for men will be much worse. Even if these were not worthy goals in themselves, our economic and social health depends on achieving them. The costs of a system that has put parenthood, along with women and children, last have already proved to be far too high.[7]

Why should men support institutional changes that respect diversity and promote responsibility and equality? Because policies that offer men an equal opportunity to parent and offer women an equal opportunity to support their families will reduce the dilemmas and expand the range of choices for all. Even more important, the long-run fates of men, women, and especially children will depend on how our political and social institutions respond to the spreading dilemmas of family life that have been created in no small measure by changes in the lives of men.

Revolutionary change has produced confusion and disagreement among men and dilemmas for which there are few clear resolutions. Some men are opposing challenges to their power and privilege, labeling them threats to the social order and moral fabric. Others are welcoming the chance to escape the narrow and stringent demands of twentieth-century masculinity. Inevitably, conflicts are emerging between those who see change as a threat and those who see it as an opportunity, and between those for whom opportunity means more freedom and those for whom it means more sharing. As new conflicts develop among men, new alliances may also develop between men and women who share a similar vision of the future they would like to create.[8] Indeed, men and women face a historic opportunity to forge new alliances based on their common ground as parents and workers.

Will future generations of men—the children of those who have created and coped with the current transformation—emulate, rebel against, or ignore the choices made by this one? Will they steadfastly declare themselves to be the only breadwinners and breadwinners only, even as they watch their female friends and partners build strong work commitments? Will they eschew family obligations in ever-rising numbers, deciding not to father children or to care for those they have? Or will they join with women to create a more equal and flexible balance between family and work, caretaking and breadwinning? These are all ways for men to claim the no man's land created by social change. Which vision becomes predominant in reality depends on which alternatives men are offered. Either we create the conditions for equality and caring or we live with the consequences of failing to do so.

Notes

1. Numerous studies have noted that when divorced fathers are estranged from their children or from making decisions about their children's lives, they are likely to withhold or withdraw economic support as well. By allowing and encouraging fathers' participation, we increase the chances that children will also receive economic support. [See the following:
Hanson, Shirley, M. H. 1986. "Father/Child Relationships: Beyond Kramer v. Kramer." In Men's Changing Roles in the Family, pp. 135–50. Edited by Robert A.

Lewis and Marvin B. Sunnar. New York: Haworth Press. McLurahan, Sara, Judith Seltzer, Tom Hannon and Elizabeth Thomson. 1992, "Child Support Enforcement and Child Well-Being: Greater Security or Greater Conflict?" Paper presented at the Annual Meeting of the American Sociological Association (August), Pittsburgh.

Wallerstein, Judith S, and Sarah Blakerlee. 1989 Second Chances: Men, Women, and Children a Decade After Divorce. New York: Tickner and Fields.

Weitzman, Lenore J. 1985. The Divorce Revolution: The Unexpected Social and Economic Consequences for Women and Children in America. New York: Free Press.]

2. These estimates are based on a study by the Families and Work Institute reported in Smith et al., 1990. Smith et al., 1990, and Schor, 1992, argue that social policies need to redress the time imbalance caused by "greedy" work institutions.

To imagine a more flexible integration of family and work, we need only look to the world before the advent of industrialism, when work and family were more closely integrated and parenthood was not rigidly divorced from other productive activities. (See Stacey, 1990 and 1991, on the "postmodern family" and Hochschild with Machung, 1989, on modern women as "urbanized peasants.")

3. Schwartz, 1989, proposed that employers offer women a "mommy track." By relegating mothers, and mothers only, to a second tier in the managerial structure of organizations, this proposal provides a remarkably regressive response to new family dilemmas. It allows employers to avoid addressing the twin dilemmas of gender inequality and work/family conflicts; it reinforces an unequal division of labor between women and men; it forces women, but not men, to make wrenching decisions between employment and parenting; and it maintains the historic obstacles to male parental involvement. In other words, the idea of a mommy track perpetuates the idea that work and parenthood are in conflict and that caring for children is an indication of low work commitment. As Capek (1990: 1) notes: "The issues for a viable, competitive workforce—ultimately the same issues for a viable, competitive American economy—are not 'mommy tracks' but managing diversity; not 'letting in a few women without rocking the boat,' but radically rethinking the future American workplace in an increasingly multiracial, multicultural global economy." Other critiques of the mommy-track approach include Smith et al., 1990, and Rodgers and Rodgers, 1989.

4. Hobson (1991: 846–48). Studies that document the comparative lack of family and child-care policies in the United States include Hofferth, 1990; Hofferth and Phillips, 1987; Kamerman and Kahn, 1987; Moen, 1989; and Pleck, 1989 and 1993.

5. Okin, 1989, argues that our notions of justice should encompass themes of both care and abstract rights. For women, care has all too often meant relinquishing rights and becoming dependent on men within marriage. Since marriage can no longer offer women economic security, the philosophy of individual rights must encompass women and the obligation to care for others must include men.

6. Some feminists have expressed discomfort with those aspects of change that require women to forfeit some privileges in order to obtain other rights. For example, Smart and Seven-Huijsen, 1989, and Chesler, 1988, argue that women should retain priority in child custody decisions, even though redefining men's and women's parental rights is a logical consequence of the movement toward gender equality (Kingson, 1988). Other feminists have argued that equality requires recognizing diversity among men and women rather than perpetuating a principle based on gender difference. See Vogel, 1990.

7. The heavy social costs of *not* implementing family support policies have been well documented by Edelman, 1987; Folbre, 1987; Hewlett, 1991; and Sidel, 1986 and 1990. Less obvious is the mounting evidence that companies also incur higher costs by denying family support, such as parental leave, than by offering it. See Spalter-Roth and Hartmann, 1990, and Roel, 1991.

8. The development of political divisions among men may also involve the emergence of coalitions between men and women who share similar world views. Numerous studies have found that a "marriage gap" in voting behavior is larger than the more highly publicized gender gap. Breadwinners and homemakers tend to vote in similar ways, while single men and women also show similar voting patterns. See Brackman and Erie, 1986; Fleming, 1988; Gerson, 1987a; Goertzel, 1983; Greenberg, 1985; Kingston and Finkel, 1987; Klein, 1985; Luker, 1984; Mansbridge, 1985 and 1986; Mason and Lu, 1988; and Weisburg, 1987.

Domènec Melé

Organization of Work in the Company and Family Rights of the Employees

Businessmen are well aware of the marked relationship between family affairs of employees and their behavior in the company. The organization of work and activities in the company considerably affect family life. Some work set-ups can lead to family problems, and family problems, in turn, affect employee performance in the company. This intrinsic relationship between the family and organization of work makes it a subject of great concern to both employees and managers.

In countries such as Spain, where the family is a deep-rooted institution, the family-company relationship arouses considerable concern. According to a survey recently conducted by IESE among two hundred Spanish managers, the study of the family-work relationship came out as one of the four or five most important subjects that must be taught in the business ethics courses.[1]

Until now, very little attention has been given to the study of the relationship between the organization of work in the company and the family rights and duties of the employee. However, a number of interesting works are available, albeit focussed only on some particular problems and referring specifically to American society.[2]

Some people consider that the family, by being a part of the employee's personal life, has no bearing on the company. Thus, any interfer-

ence by the company in the employee's family life, is seen as an intrusion into the personal life of the employee. As such, it must be avoided. But in doing so, companies fail to take into account the importance of the family as the basic unit of society and its corresponding rights.

Others consider that it is sufficient to have flexible agreements between the company and its employees concerning family issues. In this situation, the rights of the family are taken into account only if the negotiating parties are conscious of them. Many times the family duties of the employees are viewed only as interests which are in conflict with the company's interests. They fail to realize, however, that the family is a source of real rights.

It must be pointed out that in the "Universal Declaration of Human Rights" and in the "International Agreement of Civil and Political Rights," it is categorically stated that "the family is the natural and fundamental unit of society and is entitled to the protection of society and the State".[3] Other international texts on human rights are couched in similar terms,[4] showing the existence of a wide international consensus on the intrinsic value of the family. In addition, a detailed Charter of the Rights of Family[5] was published by Roman Catholic Church in 1983 and a European Charter of Family Rights is being prepared at the moment.[6]

Nevertheless, some family rights can easily be infringed upon as a result of the organizational work within the company. These rights can be enumerated as follows:

a. The right to find the necessary social support to consolidate the unity and stability of the family so that it may carry out its specific task.
b. The right to socio-economic conditions that enable it to carry out its duties with respect to the procreation and upbringing of children.
c. The right to working hours and periods necessary to devote to the other spouse, the children and to just being together.

From Domènec Melé, "Organization of Work in the Company and Family Rights of the Employees," *Journal of Business Ethics*, Vol. 8, 1989. Reprinted by permission of Kluwer Academic Publishers.

d. The right to a quality of work life that does not affect the workers' genetic heritage nor their physical or mental health nor the necessary attention to their respective families.

e. The right to a sufficient compensation to start and maintain a family.

The following discussion deals with some aspects of work organization connected with the above-mentioned family rights illustrated in several scenarios taken from cases that have been published or that the author has direct knowledge of.

BUSINESS AND WORKING ENVIRONMENT MUST FAVOR MARITAL UNITY AND STABILITY

Company policy on work organization may attack the family's unity and stability in a variety of situations such as those illustrated in the following scenarios:

a. Bribery or Extortion Using Extra-Marital Sexual Relations

The use of sexual favour is a well known way of bribery or extortion.

Scenario 1: A company invites several managers from client companies to a convention at which its latest products will be presented. The reception includes all kinds of entertainment, including callgirls, which are supposed to smooth the way for sales to the potential buyers.

b. Sexual Harassment

Sexual harassment within the company is, of course, another form against the unity and stability of marriage. It usually happens with extortion from someone superior.

Scenario 2: A male supervisor sexually harasses a female subordinate. The subordinate is aware of the unfavorable consequences that would result from rejecting the supervisor's advances: loss of promotion, misleading information on her performance to their superiors, effect on salary increases, and perhaps, dismissal in a future restructuring.

c. Situations that Favor Sexual Attraction in the Company

Moreover, some company practices—work arrangement, business trips, etc.—can also lead to immoderate sexual attraction among employees, although, these company practices are not conceived to lead to such consequences.

Scenario 3: A fast-moving finance company specialising in high-risk loans wishes to recruit a recent Harvard MBA graduate. On his first visit to the company, the young MBA realised that most of the women in the office were young and very attractive. In fact, he had never seen so many pretty women in one place before. Later he learned that the company's vice-president (only him?) usually had some employee accompany him on his business trips, suggesting that they sleep together to "save the firm the price of a second room."

The executives earned a lot of money but if they wanted to get to the top they had to work Saturdays and Sundays. With all this, it is not surprising that the company's divorce rate was somewhat high.[7]

In all these situations, in addition to damaging the family, the business organization itself will suffer adverse consequences: distorted communications, hostile self-interest that go against the company's interest, impairment of the work unit's reputation, greater slowness in decision-taking, etc.

d. Dual Careers and Prolonged Separation of Spouses

In cases where both husband and wife work, a good working opportunity which requires relocation to another city, may come to either of the two. The overall success, however, can only be guaranteed if the other spouse can be permitted to relocate to the same city. Otherwise, the family may suffer temporary separation or the professional life of one may suffer to give in to the other.

A better alternative can be found if firms could take into account the family issues in dual careers.

Scenario 4: A large group of companies has recruited Antonio to turn around one of its ailing companies near Barcelona. Antonio is then asked to do the same in another company in the south of Spain. It is planned that he will spend three to five years in the new company. Antonio may have a very good career before him in this group of companies but he must be prepared to accept all the changes the company requires.

Antonio is married with three children aged less than 14. His wife Montse is an architect and works for the regional government. Her career prospects are also good. Montse also takes an active part in political life and knows a lot of people in the Barcelona area. Their children are happily enrolled in a school in Barcelona. Montse and Antonio also think that such a dramatic cultural change would not be good for the children. Antonio's bosses have pressured him a lot on this change and have made him understand that if he does not accept their demands, he can expect little future in the company. Antonio faces a dilemma and fears that he would not be able to find such a good job in another company.

It is hard to say just how much a company can pressure its employees in defense of its legitimate interests but it is clear that if it does not act with a certain consideration for family circumstances, it will be favoring the breakup of the family. Also, the prolonged separation of spouses gives rise to a lot of problems, especially when this separation is accompanied by frequent dealings with people of the other sex for work or social reasons, which may also undermine the unity and stability of the family.

On this point, the comment made by R. Quinn[8] is interesting in that he states that in 74% of the love affairs that occur at work, the man holds a higher position than the woman and, in almost half of the cases, the woman involved is his secretary.

In all these scenarios, of course, the person involved is free to refuse the proposition of infidelity but the company's policy, the work environment or the behaviour of its managers may significantly influence the preservation of the unity and stability of the marriage.

The company can make it easier to fulfill the duties of marital unity and stability by acting in the following areas:

1. Forbidding its employees to use all forms of bribery including the exploitation of the sexual instincts of potential customers.

2. Penalizing those who take advantage of their power by extorting people in exchange for sexual gratification.
3. Taking steps to prevent sexual harassment between employees, especially those occurring from the abuse of power. It should be borne in mind that, according to the Merit System Protection Board, sexual harassment has little to do with mutual physical attraction, provocative behaviour or even sex.[9] It is above all an expression of dominance and nonreciprocal behaviour directed by the strongest at the weakest.
4. Acting with care in the design of work organization and avoiding, as much as possible, forms of business activity that may easily result in thoughtless sexual provocation among its employees.
5. Creating an appropriate atmosphere within the company in order to avoid sexual harassment and to encourage managers to exercise care in their relations with the people with whom they work the most.
6. Taking into account the effects of dual careers on the families, avoiding the considerable pressure on the employees resulting in discrimination.
7. Avoiding as much as possible prolonged separations of spouses.

COMPATIBILITY OF WORK WITH THE OBLIGATIONS OF PARENTHOOD

Attention given to the family, and especially to the bringing up of children, can be unacceptably low as a result of the ineffective work organization in the company. The organization itself can hinder, and in some cases, even prevent the parents from freely choosing the type of education their children should receive. Here are a few situations:

a. Moving Employees or Managers to Another City or Country

This may affect the professional or social interests of the concerned spouse or of the rest of the family, as well as affecting the children's education (change of school, educational system or culture).

Scenario 5. A leading leather tanning factory in Valencia (Spain) opened a factory in Indonesia. The factory had to be managed by someone trusted by the company, who knew the tanning process and the leather-tanning trade well. The company management was convinced that this person had to be one of its employees. However, moving the employee with his family not only meant having to live in a different country and culture but also the impossibility of finding a school that would educate his children in accordance with his wishes. In fact, in spite of the promotion and the good pay, there was no-one willing to accept the position and relocate.

The company saw two alternatives: pressure the person concerned in various ways until he was persuaded to move or find alternative solutions that respect the family rights. The final solution was to appoint two managers who would work alternately on three month periods in Indonesia and Valencia.

b. Business Trips that Excessively Shorten the Amount of Time Available to the Family

Scenario 6. A Barcelona company is in the turnkey business of building and selling ceramic and earthenware plants. It has projects all over the world. Part of its staff of 1,500 employees work on the assembly and start-up of the new plants and, where necessary, on repairing those already existing.

These travelling workers spend from six months to two years away from their city (normally abroad). Their allowances are not excessive and they are not given more vacation time than their non-travelling colleagues. If necessary, the return from one country is tied up with the departure for an assignment in another country, as a result the worker is hardly able to spend any time with his family. Of course, his employment contract includes the obligation to travel as often as necessary.

On occasions, especially when the stay is going to be long, the workers take their families with them. The educational problems that arise are heightened by the cultural and religious differences in the customer-countries, some of which have communist governments.

The trips abroad are organized without any consideration for the worker's personal situation.

Obviously, moving away is not equally distressing for all employees. Consider the case of a bachelor, or of a man whose children are already grown up or of a man whose children are of school age.

It does not seem reasonable to exclude an employee's family situation unless no consideration is made of the personal aspect of work.

A totally liberal approach would argue that business trips and work abroad are within the contractual provisions and previously freely agreed upon. However, such circumstances harm family rights. And because family rights are natural rights, they must obviously come before any other kinds of commitment, including working commitments.

On the other hand, contracts that contain elements of coercion may lead one to question their fairness. This would be the case of a contract that did not respect the worker's family rights if the freedom of choice was reduced, as occurs, for example, in situations of excess supply of labor.

c. Rigidity in Working Hours and the Possibility of Working at Home

It is becoming increasingly common for both wife and husband to work outside the home. In the USA, more than two-fifths of the work force (47 million employees) are composed of spouses in working households.[10] In Europe, the proportion of this kind of people could vary widely according to the country but is important enough to pay attention to.[11]

Rigid working hours adversely affect mothers who wish or need to work out of home, especially when the children are still young. This is perhaps one of the most pressing problems for many young families. The problems that usually arise when both parents work are well known: the care of small children, the mismatch between work and school vacations and working hours, the care of children when they fall ill and above all, the deficiencies in upbringing that usually arise because of lack of time and the parents being too tired to give enough attention to their children.

There seems to be no doubt that the best solution to these problems is to spend more time working at home, especially when the children are very young. However, this is not always possible for a number of reasons.

Some companies have proposed various solutions ranging from locating kindergartens and schools next to companies to flexible working hours. They are solutions that each have their pros and cons and respond rather to a compromise of interest than to a social recognition of the rights and duties of parents, foremost among which is the care and upbringing of their children.

On the other hand, working outside of home with a reasonable degree of flexibility may also provide very suitable solutions.[12]

Nancy R. Pearcy, a writer resident in Canada and a former feminist, advocates work in the house and not just housework. This would be compatible with the mother's important task of bringing up her children. She thinks that women who work at home can have the best of both worlds: earn a living while being able to freely organize their working hours, in accordance with the number and age of their children.[13] The idea is interesting and even feasible in some situations; however, when there is no appropriate labor legislation, there may be companies that take advantage of conscientious and hardworking mothers to exploit them using the well-known practices of the underground economy:

Scenario 7. An imitation jewelry firm contracts out assembly work to homeworkers. Without any employment contract, social security, abnormally low piece rates and tax avoidance, this firm is able to make large profits while the workers—mothers with small children in almost all cases—are able to look after their offspring while working at home but with a ridiculously low pay.

It does not seem fair that labor legislation prevents flexible working schedule or homeworking. Perhaps this justifies some forms of black economy but, in any case, business ethics demands that abuses be avoided and that alternatives be devised to solve this problem which, for many families, has serious effects.

d. Excessive Working Hours and Lack of Vacation Periods which Hinder Family Life and Especially the Care of Children

Inflexible and prolonged working hours and rigidity at work in general (prohibition of part-time working, vacation periods dictated by the company, etc.) all too often affect family duties, especially those of mothers who work out of home. This situation largely depends on the company management. Even though working hours can be influenced by labor legislation, companies usually still have ample room for maneuver.

Scenario 8. Arturo Garcia, the managing director of a Spanish firm employing 90 people, usually has his lunch outside of the office and, after a long rest, returns to his office at about 5:30. He then starts to work at a feverish pace. He wants his immediate subordinates to extend their working day until very late to help him. One of his secretaries, who is an excellent worker, has stated her desire not to extend her working hours beyond the normal time because she must go to fetch her children from school. This attitude has upset Mr. Garcia who is not prepared to promote that person nor increase her salary beyond that stated in the collective agreement because, according to him, "she can't be counted on."

Arturo Garcia places his convenience and habits before the legitimate rights of his employees. Mr. Garcia could probably organize his work without interfering with the family rights of his employees.

e. Overwork to the Detriment of Family Life

In some occasions, temporary increases in the workload make it necessary to do a lot of overtime work. And this at times becomes a habit and the person is forced to do overtime work on a regular basis. Without guidance, he may lose sight of the fact that work is not an end in itself.

Scenario 9. Juan is a top executive in a Spanish automobile company. He is married and has three children aged 6, 8 and 11. He leaves home at 6:30 a.m. and gets back exhausted at about 10 p.m. when the children are already in bed. He also goes to the office on many weekends or takes work home. His job requires frequent travel. In order to make the best use of time, he often starts his trips on a Sunday.

Juan earns a lot of money which he uses to try to satisfy all his wife's and children's desires. His wife, Maria, often complains that she has everything except a husband. The few times she is with her husband to talk about their children, she tries to explain to him that he cannot delegate to her his part of the children's upbringing. Juan justifies himself by saying that the amount of work he has to do is due to the pace set by the company's president and that he has to work as hard as the president does to maintain his position, earn enough money and maintain the, admittedly high, standard of living of his family.

In the situation of overwork shown in the previous situation, the initial responsibility lies with the employee. Juan should reconsider his scale of values, his duties as father and husband, his behavior towards his family and the organization of his own work. However, the company may also be partly responsible. Could Juan alone change the situation without giving up his job? Perhaps, but the management style imposed by the president no doubt has a significant influence.

Working Conditions in Relation to Family Duties

Hygiene and safety conditions at work primarily affect the worker. However, working conditions may have effects that go beyond the individual worker, involving his family life.

The following two situations, while not intended to be exhaustive, illustrate two types of inadequate working conditions and their relation to family rights.

a. Physical, Chemical or Psychological Conditions that Affect the Employee's Health

This obviously affects to a greater or lesser extent the real possibilities of carrying out family activities.

Scenario 10. In Spain, as in other countries, in the mid-'60s there was no protection against the deafening noise in the cement factory mills. The people who worked there ended up completely deaf. In exchange, the company paid them a bonus for dangerous work. It is not difficult to imagine the problems of oral communication that occur in the family.

Today, this situation has been overcome in most industrialized countries by thick insulating walls and remote control. It is a point that is usually well protected by legislation in industri-

alized countries. The problem lies in the enforcement of this legislation and, above all, in the working conditions in certain developing nations.

b. Lack of Protection of Fertility and Genetic Heritage or Inadequate Working Conditions for Pregnant Mothers

The protection of the transmission of life derives from the right of the new being already conceived to life or the genetic heritage which may be altered as a result of the action of certain substances present at the place of work. It also derives from the inalienable right of parents to responsibly transmit life, which should not be harmed by working conditions.

Scenario 11. AT&T detected a high rate of miscarriages among the female workers in the chip manufacturing lines. Consequently, in 1986, AT&T decided to transfer those pregnant workers who were working on the semiconductor production lines.[14]

Respect of Independence and Family Privacy

The company, as also the rest of society, should not interfere in family privacy nor in its future prospects. Nor should it pressure or discriminate due to:

a. the status of the spouse and the number of children
b. the type of education or school chosen by the parents
c. the family's moral or religious values

Scenario 12. In 1978, the American Cyanamid Company in Willow Island (West Virginia) had a dye production plant which used lead chromate, a fetotoxic substance. Eight women worked in this section. As a result of legislation, the company drew up a series of safety regulations which included removing women from this section unless they could certify they were sterile. In fact, of the eight women employed in the lead dye section, five had themselves surgically sterilized. This drastic decision was probably influenced by the poor economic conditions in the area, the small size of the Willow Island facilities and the non-existence of jobs available for the women in the immediate short term. In subsequent lawsuits, the company argued that it had tried to dissuade the five women from sterilizing themselves and that it had offered them suitable alternatives in the form of jobs of similar rank and pay. If this is true, the offer was either not convincing or the regulations made did not take into account sufficiently the logical consequences in those female workers who destroyed all possibility of having children in order to keep their jobs.[15]

In cases such as this, the organization of work may violate family privacy and one of the most important family rights: the right of responsible procreation. This type of situation shows the inadequacy of a system of ethics that does not take into account the foreseeable consequences.

SUFFICIENT COMPENSATION FOR A DECENT FAMILY LIFE

Paying unjustly low wages is another way of violating family independence. It is well-known that remuneration for work done is the principle means of living for most employees.

If real pay is insufficient to bring up a family, then a basic right is trampled under foot which, to a large extent, conditions all the rest.

Scenario 13. A Spanish company employs 60 workers. Its financial situation is good. Most of the workers hold positions that require little skill or experience. However, wages are scaled above all according to years of service (for historical reasons and union pressure) and to date, very few benefits have been given to workers and their families. Unfortunately, economic protection of the family in Spain is one of the lowest in Europe (an annual allowance of 2000 pesetas per child and tax deduction of 16000 pesetas per child, in 1987).

Some of the workers in this company with large families are in serious financial difficulties. Others see in the current pay system an effective coercion tool against procreation. Obviously, these problems affect the working atmosphere.

Management is considering restructuring wage rates taking into account not only production but also the worker's family situation.

In several international human rights documents, the need has been stated to provide economic protection for the family.[16] John Paul II, following a long tradition of social teaching by the Roman Catholic Church, insists in the encyclical *Laborem exercens* on the need for a sufficient level of remuneration to enable the employee to lead a decent family life.[17]

The State, mainly through welfare benefits and tax deductions, can provide a certain economic protection for the family. However, the company cannot remain aloof from the economic rights of its employees' families, especially when State aid is insufficient. This consideration gives rise to two statements:

a. The wages paid should not be less than those required by an average family to live a decent life within the context of the time and place concerned.
b. The benefits granted by the company to its workers should cover all members of their families. These benefits should be greater the lesser the protection given by society in general to families. It is not always easy to give these family-weighted benefits. It requires a lot of solidarity not only from the company with respect to its employees, but also among the individual employees, taking into consideration the over all financial capability of the firm to grant the benefits.

Efforts should also be made to prevent a particular company from being excessively affected by the size of its workers' families.

Also, those workers with large families may be discriminated against. It therefore seems advisable to create special funds for families from certain groups of companies or economic sectors. Thus, it would be possible to better respect the economic rights of the family without resorting to the State or overburdening individual companies.

CONCLUSION

The narrow attitude towards work which separates the worker from his family life should be dispelled. The worker is not just "labor" but a person who has family duties of crucial importance for himself and for society.

Family duties fall primarily upon the members of the family itself but, by being natural rights of all those who have chosen marriage and family, they should be respected and even promoted by the firm to ensure social justice in employer-employee relations.

It is one of the company's ethical obligations to organize work, taking into account the family duties of its employees and their subsequent compliance.

The idea that the loose agreement between employee and employer is insufficient, and unjust without the explicit consideration of the rights of the family. When the negotiating parties do not have the same power or there exists the need to work, family rights and other rights may be disregarded in the name of freedom of negotiation.

Family rights must be enforced with care and not just as a mere legalism in the organization or work in the firm. By doing so, the efforts to respect family rights will lead to corresponding improvements in labor relations.

Finally, when employees feel hindered to comply with their family duties because of excessive work, they become unmotivated and less efficient. Hence, the organization is worse off.

Notes

1. It will be published.
2. Such as those by Cfr. R. M. Kanter: 1977, "Work and Family in the United States" (Russell Suge, New York). R. Bailyn: 1978, "Accommodations of Work to Family" in *Working Couples* ed. by R. Rapoport and R. N. Rapoport (Harper and Row, New York).
J. P. Fernández; 1986, *Child Care and Corporation Productivity: Resolving Family/Work Conflicts.* (Lexington Books, Lexington).
A. C. Michalos: 1986, "Job Satisfaction, Marital Satisfaction and the Quality of Life: A Review and a Preview in," *Research and the Quality of Life,* ed. by F. M. Andres (University of Michigan Press, Ann Arbor Michigan), pp. 57–83.
3. U.N.O.: *Universal Declaration of Human Rights,* art. 16,3 (Paris, 12.10.1948); *International Agreement of Economic, Social and Cultural Rights,* Art. 10,1 and Art. 23,1, adopted by the General Assembly of the UN in its resolution 2200 A (XXI) on 11.16.1966. Came into effect on 12.30.1976.
4. *American Declaration of Human Rights* (1948), Art. 6; *European Social Charter* (1961), Art. 16; *American Convention of Human Rights* (1969), Art. 17,1. Recommendation 2018 (XX) adopted by the General Assembly of the UN on 12.1.1965; *Declaration on social progress and development* proclaimed by the General Assembly of the UN in its resolution 2542 (XXIV) on 12.11.1969.
5. Holy See: 1983, *Charter of the Rights of the Family* (London, Catholic Truth Society). In 1981, the Pope John Paul II pointed out some basic family rights and committed the Holy See to prepare a Charter on the Rights of the Family (Exh. Apost. *Familiaris consortio,* n. 46. London, Catholic Truth Society). This Charter has been the first monographic international document on the rights of the family.
6. This European Charter of Family Rights was proposed by Mr. Oreja, the Secretary General of the Council of Europe in his address to the 20th Conference of European Ministries responsible for the family. (Allocution du Secrétaire Général pour la 20c Conférence des Ministers Européen chargés des Affaires familiaires. Brussels, May 19, 1987).
7. C. P. Dredge and V. Sathe, *Mike Miller (A),* Case Study of Harvard Business School, ICCM 9.482.061.
8. R. E. Quinn: March 1977, "Coping with Cupid: The Formation, Impact and Management of Organizational Romance," in *Administrative Science Quarterly.*
9. Merit System Protection Board: 1981, "Sexual Harassment in the Federal Workplace," (U.S. Government Printing Office).
10. Conference Board: 1985, "Corporations and Families: Changing Practices and Perspectives," Report No. 868. (Conference Board, New York).
11. On the employment of women by age group in different European countries: *vid.* 1986, "Year Book of Labour Statistics," 46th Issue, pp. 35–42. (International Labour Office, Geneva).
12. K. Ropp: 1987, "Case Studies" in *Personnel Administrator,* Vol. 32, No. 8, pp. 72–79.
13. Cfr. N. R. Pearcey: 1987, "Why I Am Not a Feminist (Any More)," *The Human Life Review* New York, March, pp. 80–88.
14. Cfr. *La Actualidad Electrónica,* Barcelona, January, 1987, p. 20.
15. Cfr. J. B. Matthews, K. E. Goodpaster and L. L. Nash: 1985, *Policies and Personas. A Casebook in Business Ethics.* (McGraw-Hill, New York) pp. 72ff.
16. Cfr. U.N.O. *Universal Declaration of Human Rights,* art. 23.3; *European Social Charter,* art. 4.1; U.N.O. *International Agreement on Human Rights,* art. 11.1, etc.
17. John Paul II, Enc. *Laborem exercens,* No. 19 (Boston: St. Paul Press, 1981).

Lynn Sharp Paine

Work and Family: Should Parents Feel Guilty?

Many working parents feel guilty about the time they spend away from their children.[1] Until recently, judging from media coverage, career-minded women seemed to be the primary sufferers. It is increasingly clear, however, that fathers, too, feel conflict and guilt about their children's care.[2] A recent Stanford University study found that among couples whose members both hold graduate business degrees, husbands have *more* anxiety about the children than their wives.[3] Advertisers have discovered that parental guilt is a theme with sales potential, and entrepreneurs have discovered that it is a source of economic opportunity.[4]

Employers are concerned about the effects of parental guilt on productivity. "Executive Guilt: Who's Taking Care of the Children?" appeared recently as a cover story for *Fortune* magazine.[5] The article, which describes corporate responses to employees' child care problems, quotes Dr. Lee Salk, professor of psychology and pediatrics at New York Hospital-Cornell Medical Center. Says Salk, "Guilt is what parents are coming to talk to me about.[6]

What, exactly, do these parents feel guilty about? According to these articles and studies, many parents believe they are not giving their children enough personal time and attention. Many who aspire to traditional careers in the professions and business, or to high levels of achievement in other fields, entrust their young children to caretakers for most of the child's waking hours. As a result, some parents carry

with them a nagging sense of guilt.[7] Even when their children appear to be developing normally and have the best child care money can buy, some parents feel they are not fulfilling their parental responsibilities.

Are such feelings appropriate? Is it reasonable for parents to feel guilty about their absences when their children are well cared for by others?[8] The thrust of the popular literature on parental guilt is that absence-related guilt feelings are generally irrational and inappropriate.[9] This view, I will argue, rests on failure to acknowledge the moral foundations of guilt feelings and on a very narrow conception of parents' obligations. On a different conception of parental obligations and values, a conception I will elaborate, absence-related guilt can be seen to be a morally fitting response to the situation of working parents.

My ultimate aim is practical. I want to know how parental guilt feelings are best dealt with. But to answer this practical question we must understand the basis of these feelings. If parental guilt is a neurosis with no rational basis, as suggested by some commentators, counseling or psychiatric treatment may be called for. But if, as I argue, guilt is a morally fitting response to the situation of working parents, efforts to address the situation, not simply the feelings, will be in order.

I. MORALITY AND GUILT FEELINGS

Concerned about employment opportunities for women, many popular writers have urged mothers to dismiss their feelings of guilt. Perhaps they fear that acknowledging the possible legitimacy of guilt will cause mothers to flee the workplace and justify employers in refusing to hire them.[10] One approach to undermining the seriousness of guilt feelings is to redescribe them as non-moral feelings—as unhappiness, regret, or anxiety, for example.[11] Another is to explain them as vestiges, like the human appendix, which no longer serve any identifiable function but survive as a reminder of the past.[12]

From Lynn Sharp Paine, "Work and Family: Should Parents Feel Guilty?" *Public Affairs Quarterly*, Vol. 5, No. 1, 1991. Reprinted by permission.

Both approaches are ultimately unsatisfying because they neglect essential attributes of guilt feelings, attributes such as the self-criticism and sense of moral failure that are part of feeling guilty. The truth that these accounts fail to acknowledge is that guilt feelings are moral feelings. They cannot be understood apart from the unsatisfied moral imperative or unrealized moral ideal underlying them.

For example, one commentator redescribes guilt as excessive anxiety. The author of a *Glamour* magazine piece asserts that "guilt is nothing but good, healthy, loving concern taken a step too far."[13] This account, however, neglects the element of self-criticism implicit in guilt feelings.[14] When I am anxious about my children, I am concerned about *them*. I imagine what they may do or what may happen to them, and I may take steps to assure myself that they are all right. It is entirely possible for me to feel anxious about my children even if I am confident that I have made the right decision to, for example, permit them to bicycle to school. Anxiety may exist quite independently of guilt. When I feel guilty, I may also be anxious, but more importantly and, in addition, I believe I have fallen short morally. Perhaps I have failed to teach the children bicycle safety, or I have neglected to warn them about a dangerous crossing. When I feel guilty my concern focuses on *me* as well as on them. Any explanation of guilt that leaves out the element of moral self-criticism is conceptually inadequate. Excessive anxiety can, of course, be destructive in its own right. But it is quite a different thing from guilt.[15]

Disregard for the moral basis of guilt feelings is also seen in other attempts to explain maternal guilt. One psychologist, for example, attributes mothers' guilt to "a mismatch between the current realities of family life and ideas about motherhood and children that suited the late-nineteenth and early-twentieth centuries."[16] The author argues that today's mothers suffer guilt because they are not living up to the nineteenth-century ideal of exclusive attachment between mother and child.[17]

This account of maternal guilt is unsatisfactory for many reasons. Besides leaving fathers' guilt untouched, its historical accuracy is questionable. Among the Victorian middle and upper classes, children were often looked after by relatives, nannies, wet nurses, and various domestics, while their mothers attended to the myriad aspects of household management and family and social life.[18] But setting aside historical accuracy, the account fails to explain why the ideal of exclusive attachment should persist while other nineteenth-century ideals have been abandoned with changing circumstances. Moreover, if parents were only clinging wistfully to outmoded conceptions of parenthood, why would they describe themselves as feeling guilty rather than nostalgic or regretful?

The answer is found by noticing the moral imperative implicit in the governing ideal of parenthood. Parents feel guilty because they see themselves as failing to be the kind of parent they believe they *ought* to be, not simply the kind of parent they would *like* to be. Unlike nineteenth-century ideals of entertaining or landscaping which are also impractical in today's world, the purportedly nineteenth-century ideal of motherhood has a moral dimension which is ignored by the vestige theory of maternal guilt. Once we notice this dimension, we cannot simply discard the ideal as impractical and inconvenient. We must look more deeply at its foundations and its relationship to human well-being.

"Guilt" is a popular and perhaps overused word. No doubt, some parents mistakenly describe as "guilt," feelings that are more accurately described as "regret," or "sadness," arising from missing their children. Some parents may falsely report feeling guilty when, in fact, they are relieved to spend most of their time in a professional environment in the company of adults. Some reports of guilt may reflect simple hypocrisy driven by the desire to present oneself as a dutiful parent. Still, the existence of spurious claims does not eliminate the problem. Parents who feel guilty about not seeing enough of their children are expressing feelings of moral inadequacy. If these feelings are genuine, they cannot be resolved by redescriptions and explanations of the sort commonly found in the popular literature. Fashioning a suitable and effective response to parents' guilt feelings requires that we take them seriously and acknowledge their moral foundations.

II. Resolving Feelings of Guilt

Guilt is not altogether a bad thing. A testament to our commitment to important values, guilt feelings have a positive role in moral life. They can lead to conduct that affirms important moral standards, restores human relationships, and improves the well-being of others. Guilt feelings aroused by the contemplation of forbidden conduct can sometimes deter it. But unresolved guilt can have a destructive effect on personality and on the ability to function effectively. Gnawing guilt can interfere with concentration and with the self-esteem and hope necessary to forge ahead with one's projects and daily activities. In extreme cases, it can lead to personality disorders involving obsessive behavior and even to madness.[19] It is thus understandable that many people are concerned about parental guilt and would like to reduce its frequency.

The first step toward a fitting and effective resolution of parental guilt is to assess its moral appropriateness. The goal is not simply to eliminate guilt feelings—an objective which could probably be achieved in many cases through a program of belief or behavior modification—but to do so while acknowledging guilt's positive role in upholding morality. This more complex aim demands that morally appropriate guilt be resolved in a way that affirms the moral standards at stake. Affirmation may take many forms: an apology, a change in behavior, reparation or compensation for harm done, confession, acceptance of punishment.[20] Even a symbolic affirmation may be fitting. The important point is that the suitability of a resolution depends on the nature of the moral deficiency in question.

Fashioning an effective resolution thus depends centrally on correct identification of the moral standards and factual beliefs behind the feelings. Failure to appreciate the full range of parents' moral concerns, is, I suggest, another problem with much of the mass-media advice and many employer-sponsored child-care programs intended to help parents.[21] The prevailing assumption seems to be that parental guilt is driven by a moral principle of avoiding harm to children, where harm is thought of narrowly in terms of children's present interests in physical, intellectual, social, or emotional health, and is measured by the degree of departure from some standard of normalcy.

The assumption that parents' central concern is their children's interests in "normal" or "average" development along these discrete dimensions is implicit in much popular advice. One writer, for instance, instructs that, "Reality guilt is when you have neglected or abused your children. Neurotic guilt is the conflict you feel between what you want to do and what you feel you have to do."[22] Other commentators reassure parents by pointing to studies showing "that children in quality daycare don't suffer any cognitive loss or feel any less attached to their parents."[23] The same assumption influences the direction of child-care research, which tends to focus on finding out whether daycare is harmful to children's physical, cognitive, or socio-emotional development.[24] Studies typically test hypotheses about the intellectual achievement and ability, or the emotional and social development of daycare children as compared to non-daycare children.

Assumptions about the moral norms behind guilt feelings affect our assessment of their appropriateness and shape our approach to resolving them. If we assume that parental guilt is based on concerns about children's physical, intellectual, and socio-emotional development, its appropriateness becomes an empirical question to be resolved, at the general level, by social scientists. On the evidence to date, a case can be made that the guilt feelings we are exploring here—absence-related guilt felt by parents whose children enjoy high-quality substitute care—are simply inappropriate. Research on the effects of daycare is inconclusive in many respects, and much debate centers on its effects, especially the effects of infant daycare.[25] But, as yet, it does not appear that children cared for by parent substitutes suffer identifiable cognitive, physical, social, or emotional deficiencies.[26] Children looked after in quality daycare centers perform as well, and sometimes better, than non-daycare children on the chosen dimensions.[27]

Within this moral framework, the central, perhaps the only, issue is the quality of substitute care. Guilt felt by parents whose care arrangements lead to sub-normal child development is seen as appropriate and suitably resolved by improving the quality and availability of substitute care. On the other hand, guilt feelings of parents whose children are developing normally along the defined dimensions are regarded as inappropriate and best dealt with through reasoning, counseling, or therapy. Such parents are advised to recognize how others—their parents, doctors, and children—"make them" feel guilty.[28] They are exhorted to examine the scientific studies showing that daycare is not harmful and can actually enhance their children's social skills. Their guilt feelings come to be seen as psychological aberrations rather than morally appropriate feelings calling for an affirmation of their moral ideals.[29]

Some parents may find this line of reasoning comforting. For a variety of reasons, others will find it interesting but unsatisfying. The evidence—the long-term evidence—is not really "in." We know little about the effects of child-rearing practices on adult development. Perhaps, the social, emotional, or cognitive harms will show up later. Many parents feel that parental obligation goes beyond protecting children from harm—that is, protecting them from falling below a minimal standard defined by statistical averages—and requires the positive promotion of each child's cognitive, physical, and social capabilities. Even those with a more minimal conception of parental obligation may continue to be concerned about the possibly harmful effects, not of daycare in general, but of the particular arrangements they have devised for their children.

Still other parents will find this line of reasoning largely irrelevant because it rests on a faulty assumption about the moral standard at issue. For these parents, guilt persists in the face of excellent substitute care not because of concerns about their children's cognitive, physical, or socio-emotional health, but because they have a moral ideal of parenthood that calls for greater personal involvement with their children. Departures from this ideal are problematic not because of the effects typically measured in studies of substitute care, but because of the moral harm involved—moral harm to both children and their parents. On this alternative con-

ception of the underlying moral imperative, I suggest, parental guilt feelings are a very appropriate response to a situation in which parents have little time to spend with their children. As I will explain, the persuasiveness of this suggestion depends on the strength of the case for the ideal.

III. MORALLY APPROPRIATE GUILT

Guilt feelings can fail to be appropriate in one of two ways.[30] They may be inappropriate because based on a moral standard for which there is no reasonable justification. Or they may be inappropriate because based on mistaken factual beliefs about, among other things, the consequences of conduct, the availability of morally preferable alternatives, or the degree of fault. As we have seen, one line of reasoning about parental guilt treats it as inappropriate because based on false beliefs about the effects of substitute care.

Assessing the appropriateness of guilt feelings thus requires inquiry into both the relevant facts and the underlying moral standards. This assessment may sometimes be a straightforward, though not necessarily simple, matter of ascertaining the truth of critical beliefs and matching conduct against moral requirements, as the legal model of criminal guilt might suggest. But in other cases, perplexing problems attend our judgments about the moral standards to which we hold ourselves. There is, for instance, the problem of conflicting obligations. Sometimes I have no choice but to violate some general moral obligation, even though, after careful consideration, I decide that I ought, all things considered, to take one course of action rather than another. Are my feelings of guilt appropriate if I have done the best I can?

A similar problem arises when I am forced by others to do something which is morally wrong. I may not be culpable, strictly speaking, but I have nevertheless done something which ought not be done. Should I feel guilty? The best response is that guilt is understandable even though perhaps inappropriate under the specific circumstances. My character as such that I have an aversion to doing things that generally I ought not do, and feel guilty when I do those things even for a good reason. A little extra guilt may be the price of a good character. Of course, if I have arranged things in a way that makes it likely that conflicts will arise, my feelings of culpability are more appropriate.[31]

Problematic cases aside for the moment, feeling guilty is sometimes clearly appropriate: if, for example, I knowingly lie about my qualifications to gain an advantage in a job competition. My subsequent feelings of guilt are perfectly appropriate because, very simply, I did what I ought not to have done under the circumstances—namely, lie. The conclusion that guilt is appropriate is unproblematic in this case. The link between the breach of a morality and the feelings of guilt is straightforward. The general prohibition against lying is widely accepted and easily justifiable by almost any standard of moral justification. Even the most minimal morality contains a prohibition on lying. The case involves no factual questions and there appear to be no factors mitigating blameworthiness. My lie was not an act of desperation intended to secure the only available opportunity for a livelihood for my dependents. It was simply a means of capturing for myself an advantage over similarly situated competitors.

More difficult are questions about the appropriateness of guilt in cases involving standards that are not so widely accepted because they are thought to be supererogatory or simply different. For example, some people believe they are obligated to contribute a tenth of their income to charity and may feel guilty when their contributions fall below this standard. Others would regard such a standard as far too onerous. Some people are more inclined than others to impose moral requirements on themselves. It is very likely that these people will more frequently see themselves as falling short and thus carry a heavier burden of guilt than those who demand less of themselves.[32]

This example resembles the case of parental guilt: both involve moral standards that are far from universally accepted. Unlike the principle of honesty or fidelity to promises, for example, the standards seem somewhat optional. How are we to assess the appropriateness of guilt in this sort of case? Herbert Morris has suggested that we ask

1. whether there is common acceptance of the reported feeling without a corresponding widespread inclination to seek some explanation other than that offered by the person; and
2. whether there is widespread respect for the moral ideal underlying the feeling.[33]

Morris's recommendation is not very helpful in the case of parental guilt. This case is problematic just because there is no consensus on the ideal underlying the feelings. Knowing that there is no general agreement on the ideal will not help us determine whether guilt is appropriate. More importantly, Morris's approach is unsatisfying for the same reasons that all relativistic theories are unsatisfying: there is no way to distinguish what is accepted from what ought to be accepted. We must, instead, examine the basis for the underlying moral ideal and decide whether it makes sense to hold oneself to such a standard.

IV. PARENTAL LOVE AND PARENTAL PRESENCE

Feelings of guilt associated with parental absence can be explained by a moral ideal of parenthood calling for attentive love and personal engagement with one's children. This ideal has a variety of closely related sources. As I will elaborate, it flows from parents' responsibilities for their children's moral education and their obligations as fiduciaries for their children's interests. It also has roots in the needs and interests of adults and the community. But it rests fundamentally on a judgment that deep personal commitments, relationships of love involving personal engagement with other human beings, have intrinsic moral value. A life with such relationships, and the joys and hardships they entail, is morally better than a life without them.

Relationships of love offer the most thoroughgoing experience of sympathetic identification with another that we are likely to encounter. These relationships are enriching, enlarging, a source of unique joy. They are onerous, trying, and a source of unique pain. But they are our link with other human beings as ends in themselves and in this respect have intrinsic moral worth. The giving of oneself and the appreciation of the other at the core of these relationships are the sources of their moral value. Although parental love lacks the mutuality of love between friends or spouses, it is based, like other love relationships, on concern for the other for his own sake. The very absence of mutuality is perhaps a reason to see in parental love greater moral value than in relationships between equals.

Insofar as the ideal of parenthood outlined here depends upon the intrinsic moral value of personal relationships of love, there can be no substitute for some degree of personal interaction between parent and child. Parents cannot delegate to others the responsibility for providing love and attention as they delegate the responsibility for providing transportation, medical care, or music education. For the parent, the moral value of personal involvement lies not just in bringing about a certain result for the child but also from the giving of himself and actively caring for the child. Only through direct involvement can the parent enjoy this moral good.[34]

Personal involvement also has instrumental moral value for parents. By testing and enhancing their capacity to care deeply and continuously for others, parenthood can propel adults into a new phase of their own moral development. Parents who take seriously their role as moral example and teacher are bound to experience moral growth through the reassessment of moral beliefs and commitments that goes with personal involvement in child care. Moreover, personal involvement enhances parents' performance as fiduciaries for their children. Without a substantial core of shared experience, it is doubtful that parents could know their children well enough to make intelligent decisions in their behalf.

These are compelling reasons to think that personally caring for one's children can be a source of great moral value for a parent. There are also reasons to think that the moral good for children is promoted by personal involvement with their parents. These reasons can be seen by looking more closely at some tasks of parenthood.

One of the central tasks of parenthood is to prepare children for life by nurturing the capacities and interests that will permit them to flourish when no longer dependent on their parents. A great deal has been made of the centrality of autonomous decision-making.[35] In this connection, the ability to relate to others and moral behavior are equally important. The capacity to participate in intimate relationships of love later in life[36] and the capacity to engage in moral thought and action appear to be closely linked, both causally and conceptually, with each other[37] and with the experience of being loved by one's parents.[38]

For children, the moral importance of parental love rests not only on its causal role in contributing to dispositions to be honest and responsible and to trust others, but also on its role as exemplar. A child's conception of what it is to love another has its earliest roots in the experience of being the recipient of parental love and an observer of the love between her parents. Besides being the child's first sustained love relationship, the parent-child relationship provides a uniquely intimate commitment. The importance of parental love as an example—positive or negative—of what love requires may only surface in adulthood.

A parent's engagement with this child is not only an expression of love for the child, it is also an indication of how much the parent values intimate relationships. Parents' choices reflect their conception of the good and provide children with an example of how diverse goals and values—love, self, work, achievement, money, morality—can and should be integrated into a coherent life.[39] In many cases, parents are the only adults to whom children can look for such an example, for they are the only adults children know well enough. Others—teachers, doctors, family members, friends—are seen only in their particular roles or seen too infrequently to provide useful examples of how life might be lived. It is not surprising that absence-related guilt seems to afflict career-oriented professionals whose work, while perhaps socially valuable, is also a source of self-gratification and for whom the giving up of work-related opportunities may require self-sacrifice. At the margin—after fulfilling legitimate material requirements—the decision to take on more work rather than to attend to one's children may reflect the choice of a lesser moral good over a greater one, and the choice of self-interest over the interests of others. For the parent who subscribes to the ideal of parenthood I have described, all-consuming work may be a source not only of absence-related guilt but of guilt related to the discrepancy between professed moral values and conduct.

A certain amount of parental presence is necessarily required for parental love to fulfill the functions outlined here. If parental love is to serve as an example of a relationship of love, it must be accessible to the child and the child must perceive it to be such a relationship. Parents' personal involvement is also important if parental love is to fulfill its causal role in strengthening moral dispositions and preparing children for participation in later love relationships. This is, quite simply, because what matters from the child's perspective is not only that she is loved, but that she also believe herself to be loved.[40]

Unfortunately, a child can feel unloved and quite alone at the same time his parents see themselves as deeply loving. The discrepancy may arise because of the child's level of cognitive and emotional development. He may not be able to appreciate the depth of a parent's abstract love or impersonal expressions of concern: the trouble a parent may take, for instance, in finding a daycare provider. Children's limited knowledge of the world, their shorter time horizons, and their emerging conceptions of self—all affect their perceptions of their parents' love and concern. There is a risk that impersonally expressed concern for a child's well-being will be inadequate to support the child's belief that she is loved.

The importance of parental presence is not due exclusively to children's limited cognitive capacities, however. Most of us, children and adults alike, feel loved and valued by those who seek out our companionship, take our perspectives and problems seriously, give us a high priority in their scheme of things, and support us even in difficult times. Aristotle's idea that loving entails caring for another for that person's sake captures an important motivational element in genuine love: it must proceed from concern for the beloved and not from the lover's concern for herself. Our belief that we are loved depends on our perception of the lover's motives and on the presence of certain expressions of love. I will not believe you love me if your attentions appear to be a means to your own advantage. Nor will I believe you love me if you show insufficient interest in me as a person.

An example may be helpful. Suppose, while assuring me of his love, my husband regularly arranges to have his personal agent or substitute join me for dinner or evenings out, counsel me on problems, and perhaps occasionally even spend the night. At some point, no matter how carefully and efficiently he manages the coming and going of his substitutes, no matter how much I like them, and no matter how much he protests that he really loves me, I will begin to doubt him. I will begin to think his excuses of responsibilities at work are bogus or that he loves his work first and foremost. Or I may think his attentions to me spring from some source other than love of me.

These same difficulties are present when parents delegate to others too much of the responsibility for providing their children with loving care and attention. The child's understanding of his parents' reasons for delegating his care are very important. The child who realizes that the family's very livelihood depends on his parents' being away from home is quite likely to feel differently from the child who sees his parents' absence as selfish expressions of their desire for self-fulfillment. It is impossible to assess the effects of parental absence without including the motives and perceived motives of parents. The precise amount of personal attention required to sustain a child's trust in the parent's love is probably quite variable since it depends in part on the child's ability to comprehend and interpret the parents' conduct and motives as well as on the child's conceptual maturity. As the child's capacity for abstract thought matures, the amount of personal attention required could be expected to diminish. Nevertheless, as with adult love, there would appear to be some minimum amount of personal attention necessary for a parent to love his child in a way that the child recognizes as love.

As noted, delegating too much of the responsibility to give children love and attention may jeopardize their trust in their parents' love. But one might wonder why parents' love should matter so much if children believe they are loved by the nannies, daycare providers, and other caregivers hired by parents. The difficulty with all these parent surrogates is the very limited nature of their love and commitment.[41] The employment relationship is a tenuous foundation for bonds of love. This is especially true given the low pay, high turn-over, and low morale characteristic in today's child-care and domestic labor markets. The more serious problem, however, stems from fundamentals of the employment relationship.

Except in extraordinary cases, the child's welfare occupies quite a different position in a parent's and an employee's scheme of priorities. Usually, no matter how much an employee loves her charges, her attachment is contingent on receipt of adequate compensation. Assisting the child—as teacher, nanny, babysitter—is a job and must be seen in that context. Employment mobility and the needs of the employee's own family limit the commitment most are willing to make. If fulfilling parental responsibilities requires a stable, constant and relatively permanent attachment, all non-family parent substitutes suffer a comparative disadvantage.[42] The parents' affection for the child and the relative permanence of the parent/child attachment give parents a stake in the child's welfare much greater than the stake any employee could be expected to have. This differential, coupled with the other factors noted, may translate into less rigorous protection and promotion of the child's interests.[43] While the caretaker may well be affectionate, she probably will not and should not be expected to demonstrate the level of personal commitment normally associated with a love relationship.

If the child does become attached to the parent substitute, the substitute's departure for a better job may be that much more problematic. The consequences for the child's self-esteem must be considered but also his developing conception of love hangs in the balance. What sort of love can be so easily withdrawn? The serious question is how much of the responsibility for giving children love and attention can be delegated to others without unacceptably distorting the love. It is perfectly possible to hire someone to give a child affection and attention within the confines of an employment relationship. The risk is that this form of limited love will provide an inadequate foundation for a conception of fully committed love, and that the parents' more permanent, but less involved, expressions of will be inadequate, too. There may be no one the child perceives as fully committed and from whom he learns what it means to love.

Instrumental justifications for spending time with one's children must not obscure this basic value judgment: that relationships of love are intrinsically valuable as elements of a morally good and satisfying life. Acceptance of this judgment is perhaps the central, though not the only, reason many parents both want and feel they ought to spend more time with their children than their jobs and professional commitments permit.

V. Conceptions of the Family

Guilt associated with parental absence rests centrally on parents' obligation to give their children love. But it is also linked to a conception of the family as the primary source of the individual's sense of self-worth and sense of morality. Within such a conception, parents have a special responsibility to show children they are valued for themselves and not just for the role they fulfill or for their achievements.[44] In contrast, for example, to business firms in which individuals are valued primarily for their contribution to the firm's goals, the family is a place where ideally they are also valued for themselves and for their personal qualities. Parents communicate this sense of individual worth through the love and friendship they extend to their children and through their attitudes toward themselves and their roles in the family. To the extent that parents willingly delegate parental responsibilities to others, they reflect a view of themselves as replaceable functionaries rather than uniquely important members of the family unit.

No less important is the family's special responsibility for moral education. The fundamental moral capacities for trust and for caring, as well as the dispositions to respect certain basic principles of honesty and fidelity to one's word must be nurtured from the beginnings of life. Given the existing structure of social institutions, there is no practical alternative to the family for this basic grounding in morality. The family is the only organization in which membership is sufficiently permanent to provide the constancy and consistency conducive to the development of these basic moral capacities and dispositions. Ideally, of course, morality will be reinforced by other social institutions. But it is doubtful that other institutions can make up for the family's failures in moral education.

In summary, the connections among parental love, parental involvement, and morality are multifaceted. Insofar as morality rests on willingness to care for others for their own sake, it rests on an attitude of love which receives its earliest nurturing through parental example. To the extent that morality involves dispositions to act in certain ways and not others, it is nurtured through the example, instruction, and consistent discipline provided by parents over the long term. Insofar as morality raises questions about how to live and what is valuable, parents can be children's greatest resource.

Parental involvement is essential if the family is to fulfill its role as the primary source of the individual's self-worth and sense of morality. Within this conception, the parent is both a source of love and a moral teacher, and as such, cannot be replaced. While these particular parental responsibilities are not delegable in the ways that many others are, they are not in principle inconsistent with parents' roles as breadwinners, household managers, overseers of childrens' education and health, or with parents' roles outside the family. But they depend on a personal commitment of time that may in practice conflict with the demands of other roles and responsibilities.

A managerial conception of parenthood which appears to be taking hold among some parents permits an easier reconciliation of these competing demands.[45] Unlike the ideal outlined here, the managerial ideal is, in principle, consistent with the delegation of all parental responsibilities.[46] The parental role becomes that of a manager who delegates, coordinates, and monitors performance. Inconsistent with commitment to the intrinsic value of love, the managerial conception also reflects an instrumental view of the individual. Good management dictates that every member of an organization be regarded as replaceable and that substitution of one individual for another not affect its functioning.

Managing children's activities is a very essential task of parenthood, but it is not the only one. If parents come to see themselves primarily as managers of their children's upbringing, not involved personally but only as higher-order supervisors, there is a danger that the distinctive competencies and roles of the family will be lost—that the family will come to be just another organization and the parent, just another functionary.[47] Adopting the managerial conception of parenthood may lead to a reduction in the guilt experienced by parents who spend little time with their children, but it may also lead to morally diminished quality of life for children, parents, and society.[48] To the extent parental love provides the foundation for the moral community in which we live as adults, widespread adoption of the managerial conception of parenthood is a threat to that community.[49]

If this argument is correct, employment practices incompatible with family life must be reassessed. We must recognize that the economic benefits yielded by these practices are won at considerable moral and social expense. Insofar as the operation of the economy depends on the moral fabric of the community, we must consider whether these practices may not be ultimately self-defeating, even from an economic point of view.

VI. PRACTICAL IMPLICATIONS: RESOLVING PARENTAL GUILT

I have outlined a case for the moral ideal of parenthood which I believe lies behind the guilt feelings reported by middle-class professionals. Many parents who are experiencing guilt may not have articulated for themselves these ideals and responsibilities, so pervasive is the view that guilt feelings are irrational and inappropriate. I have tried to show not only that these ideals are not irrational, but that there are strong arguments in their favor. There appear to be very good reasons to regard some parental responsibilities as non-delegable and to support parents who believe that they ought to spend more time with their children. Guilt-plagued parents should not be treated as neurotic or mistaken and sent for counseling to overcome their guilt. Instead, they should be encouraged to reorganize their lives to give expression to deeply held and important familial values and to speak up for patterns of employment that are compatible with fulfilling parental responsibilities as they see them.[50]

From a social point of view, serious reconsideration must be given to the organization of work and to the usual child-care benefits offered by government and private employers. Birth leave, tax breaks through "cafeteria" benefit plans, full-time child-care services, employer-sponsored referral services, sick leave for children's illnesses—the usual benefits discussed—will do nothing to assuage the guilt aroused by regular day-to-day parental absences. That will be dealt with only by rather radical changes in patterns of work and career development. Opportunities for part-time work, self-directed work, job-sharing, and career breaks represent path-breaking steps in the right direction, but these practices must become more widely available and fully institutionalized as normal and acceptable if they are to make a significant contribution to the problem of parental guilt.

The nation's child-care policy must include support for daycare for the many families that need it. However, a policy that focuses only on daycare will not resolve the guilt problem discussed here. This problem will require public policy initiatives that encourage employers to accommodate variable work commitments as well as insurance and benefit plans that do not rigidly exclude part-time workers. It will require employers to take the lead in creating and permitting their employees to create new career patterns. Ultimately, however, such initiatives will succeed only if there is widespread recognition of the moral importance of the parent-child relationship and the value of parents' involvement with their children.

Given the various factors involved in each family situation, it is impossible to say, in general, just how much time it takes to satisfy the parental ideal I have described.[51] However, there is no reason to think that being a good parent takes just the amount of time left over after work is finished or even after normal working hours as conventionally defined in today's business world. Ideological blinders and women's desires to enter the professional and managerial work force on a par with men have made the issue of time for children a taboo topic. Now that women's competence is no longer in question and now that men are taking on more parental responsibilities, we can perhaps give this matter the attention it deserves.[52]

Notes

1. In testimony before the Senate Subcommittee on Children, Family, Drugs, and Alcoholism, Dana E. Friedman of the Conference Board reported that "Millions of men and women are going to work, each day carrying in their lunch pails and briefcases, the right amount of private guilt, the proper level of subdued expectation, and the perfect amount of stress which serves as the fulcrum for what is called 'balancing work and family life.'" Hearing on S. 1985, The Act for Better Child Care Services, March 15, 1988.
2. E.g., Cathy Trost, "Men, Too, Wrestle with Career-Family Stress," *Wall Street Journal* (November 1, 1988), p. B1, col. 3; David Wessell, "Working Fathers Feel New Pressures Arising From Child-Rearing Duties," *Wall Street Journal* (September 7, 1984), p. 29, col. 4
3. Fern Schumer Chapman, "Executive Guilt: Who's Taking Care of the Children?" *Fortune* (February 16, 1987), p. 30.
4. The idea behind upscale daycare, according to one investor, is "to rid white-collar executives of the guilt of leaving their children." Lawrence Ingrassia, "Day-Care Business Lures Entrepreneurs," *Wall Street Journal* (June 3, 1988), p. 21, col. 3.
5. Chapman, "Executive Guilt."
6. Ibid.
7. Take the New York executive described in the Fortune magazine article mentioned earlier. For a time, when his one-year-old daughter was spending eleven hours a day in a child care center, he was profoundly unhappy. His feelings of guilt overwhelmed his ability to concentrate on his work, and he considered quitting to stay home with his child. When his parents moved next door and took over as babysitters, he found that he could focus on his work again, but even in those circumstances, his guilt feelings did not completely disappear.

8. One may, of course, be guilty without feeling guilty and feel guilty without being guilty. However, in the standard case involving violations of generally accepted and justifiable ethical standards one hopes that objective attributions of guilt and subjective feelings of guilt coincide. The words "guilt" and "parental guilt" are used throughout this paper to mean "guilt feelings."

9. See, e.g., Sandra Scarr, *Mother Care/Other Care* (New York: Basic Books, Inc., 1984); Gloria Norris and Joann Miller, "Motherhood and Guilt," *Working Woman* (April 1984), p. 159.

10. Hostility to the idea that absence-related guilt feelings may be morally appropriate is understandable. Historically, the idea that children need the personal attention of their parents has served as a rationale for keeping women in the home and out of the workplace, since mothers have traditionally been assigned the role of custodial parent. And research on maternal deprivation has been misused to show that full-time maternal care is essential to children's well-being. See generally Ann Dally, *Inventing Motherhood: The Consequences of an Ideal* (New York: Schocken Books, 1982), p. 162. See also Michael Rutter, *Maternal Deprivation Reassessed* (Hammondsworth, England: Penguin Books, Ltd., 1972).

11. For a discussion of the difference between regret and moral feelings, see R. M. Hare, *Moral Thinking* (New York: Oxford University Press, 1981), pp. 28–30.

12. See, e.g., the following comment by a pediatric psychologist: "For so many years there was this ethic that if you don't care for your own child, you're doing something wrong. Although that has dissipated considerably, many mothers still carry remnants of that in their heads." Diane Granat, "Are You My Mommy?" *Washingtonian* (October 1988), p. 182.

13. Louise Lague, "The Good News About Working Moms and Guilt," *Glamour* (May 1984), p. 234.

14. Gabrielle Taylor emphasizes the element of self-assessment in her account of guilt in *Pride, Shame and Guilt* (Oxford: Clarendon Press, 1986), pp. 85–107.

15. Herbert Morris, too, makes the point that guilt cannot be reduced to anxiety. See The Decline of Guilt," *Ethics*, vol. 99, no. 1 (October 1988), pp. 66–67.

16. Sandra Scarr, *Mother Care/Other Care*, p. 54.

17. Ibid., p. 105.

18. Scarr, by her own account, seems to confuse Victorian with Freudian ideas about motherhood. See ibid, pp. 81–105. Jerome Kagan gives a contrasting account of nineteenth-century attitudes toward the mother-child relationship. He attributes the emphasis on the child's attachment to the mother to Freud and, more recently, to John Bowlby. See Jerome Kagan, *The Nature of the Child* (New York: Basic Books, Inc., 1984), pp. 50–63. See also Ann Dally, *Inventing Motherhood: The Consequences of an Ideal*, pp. 104–42, for an historical account different from Scarr's.

19. For an enlightening discussion of the effects of guilt, see Taylor, *Pride, Shame and Guilt*, pp. 93–7.

20. Guilt need not be linked with liability to punishment or the possibility of reparation, as argued by Anthony O'Hear in "Guilt and Shame as Moral Concepts," *Proceedings of the Aristotelian Society,* vol. 77 (1976–77), pp. 73–86. Guilt feelings that arise from forgetting a promise to a friend, for instance, do not typically involve liability to punishment or even necessarily, the possibility of reparation.

21. I have in mind corporations that have responded to parental concerns by providing financial or other assistance in securing child care rather than restructuring work so that parents can be more involved with their children's upbringing. According to Chapman, "Executive Guilt," p. 33, some 3000 companies offer subsidized day care centers, financial assistance for child care or child care referral services.

22. Lague, "The Good News About Working Moms and Guilt," p. 234.

23. Bettye M. Caldwell, quoted in Chapman, "Executive Guilt," p. 36.

24. See, for example, Bengt-Erik Andersson, "Effects of Public Day-Care: A Longitudinal Study," *Child Development,* vol. 60 (1989), pp. 857–66. For reviews of research on daycare, see, for example, Alison Clarke-Stewart, *Daycare* (Cambridge, MA: Harvard University Press, 1982), pp. 63–77; Thomas J. Gamble and Edward Zigler, "Effects of Infant Day Care: Another Look at the Evidence," *American Journal of Orthopsychiatry,* vol. 56 (January 1986), pp. 26–42.

25. See K. Alison Clarke-Stewart, "Infant Day Care Maligned or Malignant?" *American Psychologist,* vol. 44 (February 1989), pp. 266–273; Gamble and Zigler, "Effects of Infant Day Care."

26. See T. Berry Brazelton, "Issues for Working Parents," *American Journal of Orthopsychiatry,* vol. 56, n. 1 (January 1986), at p. 23. ("Most studies to date have not found negative consequences, but these studies tend to be biased in one of several ways.") See also, Clarke-Stewart, *Daycare,* pp. 63–77. Of course, much depends on the operative conception of harm and how it is measured, and some researchers claim that certain types of group arrangements do have undesirable effects such as increasing children's aggressiveness and assertivencess. Certainly, particular care arrangements can have detrimental effects on the cognitive and emotional development of the children involved. Even the most ardent critics of maternal guilt reluctantly acknowledge that "If your child is truly suffering under your present child care arrangements, perhaps you should consider lowering your life-style and paying for better care." Norris and Miller, "Motherhood and Guilt," pp. 159–60.

27. See, e.g., Bengt-Erik Anderson, "Effects of Public Day-Care;" Clarke-Stewart, *Daycare,* pp. 63–77; and research reported in Ruth J. Moss, "Good Grades for Day-Care," *Psychology Today* (February 1987), p. 21.

28. Norris and Miller, "Motherhood and Guilt," pp. 159–60.

29. The observation of Dr. Salk, quoted above, indicates the extent to which parents are seeking psychological help with their feelings of guilt. See Chapman, "Executive Guilt," p. 30.

30. Herbert Morris discusses the ways guilt can fail to be appropriate. His concern is to argue that guilt can be

appropriate despite the absence of moral culpability. See Herbert Morris, "Nonmoral Guilt," in *Responsibility, Character, and the Emotions,* ed. by Ferdinand Schoeman (New York: Cambridge University Press, 1987), pp. 222–25.

31. Ruth Barcan Marcus argues that we ought to conduct our lives and arrange our institutions so as to minimize situations of moral conflict. See Ruth Barcan Marcus, "Moral Dilemmas and Consistency," *Journal of Philosophy,* vol. 77, no. 3 (1980), p. 121.

32. See Herbert Fingarette, "Feeling Guilty," *American Philosophical Quarterly,* vol. 16, no. 2 (April 1979), p. 159.

33. Morris, "Nonmoral Guilt," p. 224.

34. I was advised by a partner in the law firm where I worked before the birth of my second child not to take a long maternity leave. Otherwise, he said, "I would begin to love the baby."

35. Several writers treat the capacity for autonomous choice as the central capacity parents should be concerned with. See, for example, Jeffrey Blustein, *Parents and Children: The Ethics of the Family* (New York: Oxford University Press, 1982), pp. 120–36. Blustein devotes only a brief paragraph to the capacity to develop deep personal relationships.

36. E. H. Erikson, *Childhood and Society* (New York: W. W. Norton, 1963).

37. I am grateful to Joseph Fletcher for bringing to my attention the following quotation from R. M. Hare: "To think that love and morality have different languages, so that the one can be at variance with the other, is a mistake often made by those to whom love means sex, and morality means a book of rules the reasons for which everyone has forgotten. But in truth morality is love. For the essence of morality is to treat the interests of others as of equal weight with one's own." "Community and Communication," in *Applications of Moral Philosophy* (London: Macmillan, 1972), p. 115. See also Annette Baier, "Trust and Antitrust," *Ethics,* vol. 96 (1986), pp. 231–60.

38. Psychologists have said that family affection is an important factor in the development of children's sense of honesty, responsibility, and moral courage. See, e.g., the following works cited in Michael Schulman and Eva Mekler, *Bringing up a Moral Child* (Reading, Mass: Addison-Wesley Publishing Company, Inc., 1985), p. 132; Brown, A. W., Morrison J., and Couch, G. B., "Influence of Affectional Family Relationships on Character Development," *Journal of Abnormal and Social Psychology* (1947), pp. 422–28; McCord, W., McCord, J., and Howard, A., "Familial Correlates of Aggression in Non-Delinquent Male Children," *Journal of Abnormal and Social Psychology* (1961), pp. 62, 79–93.

39. Of course, one cannot simply "read off" values from choices. The constraints under which certain choices are made may make them quite unreflective of the agent's actual values. This seems to be the case for many parents who entrust their children to the care of others in order to work.

40. For discussion of the importance of the partiality parents show their children, see Elizabeth Newson, "Unreasonable Care: The Establishment of Selfhood," in *Human Values,* ed. by Godfrey Vesey (Atlantic Highlands, NJ: Humanities Press, Inc., 1976), pp. 1–26. She argues that parent partiality is important for the development of self-esteem.

41. The problem of limited commitment would seem more acute in some situations than others. Child care provided by extended family members whose involvement with the child is likely to be relatively permanent would not pose the problem I discuss here.

42. See Newson, "Unreasonable Care," for discussion of distinctive characteristics of the parent-child relationship important for the child's well-being. She focuses on its long-term nature and the shared history behind continuing interactions.

43. Rousseau argued against delegating parental responsibilities for education on the grounds that no hired teacher would be sufficiently dedicated to the child's interests. *Emile,* trans. by Allan Bloom (New York: Basic Books, 1979), pp. 49–50.

44. See generally Newson, "Unreasonable Care."

45. Women in management compare running their families with running their companies. One mother quoted in the *Washingtonian* article cited earlier notes that supervising the care of her children "requires as much management as running my own company." Diane Granat, "Are You My Mommy?" p. 168. The similarities between parents and executives is discussed by Kenneth Keniston and the Carnegie Council on Children in *All Our Children* (New York: Harcourt Brace Jovanovich, 1977), pp. 17–18.

46. Cynthia Fuchs Epstein concludes from her study of women lawyers that "The women who seemed to thrive the most on the challenge of managing multiple roles were those who experienced the least guilt about delegating duties at work and at home ... These women did not tend to brood about the amount of time they spent with their children, but rather defined circumscribed times with children as adequate... " Cynthia Fuchs Epstein, "Multiple Demands and Multiple Roles: The Conditions of Successful Management," in *Spouse, Parent, Worker,* ed. by Faye J. Cosby (New Haven: Yale University Press, 1987), pp. 23–43 at 30.

47. I would agree with philosopher Michael Phillips who notes in passing in his article, "Bribery," ". . . many of us are uncomfortable thinking of the family as just another organization and thinking of a parent as just another functionary." *Ethics* (July 1984), p. 625.

48. Epstein cites the correspondence between reduction of guilt and willingness to delegate in "Multiple Demands, Multiple Roles."

49. Annette Baier is quoted as observing that "Rawls' theory like so many other theories of obligation, in the end must take out a loan . . . on the natural virtue of parental love . . . if the just society is to last beyond the first generation." See Owen Flanagan and Kathryn Jackson, "Justice, Care, and Gender: The Kohlberg-Gilligan Debate Revisited," *Ethics,* vol. 97 (1987), pp. 622–37; see p. 630.

50. Herbert Morris notes that the desire to minimize social disruption is a powerful force behind the tendency to devalue guilt in contemporary society. Parents should realize that resistance to changing the workplace to accommodate the needs of parents and children may account for ready acceptance of the idea that parental guilt is irrational in today's world. See generally Morris, "The Decline of Guilt," p. 73.

51. Graduate students at the University of Virginia's Darden School of Business Administration were asked how much time parents should spend with pre-school children each week. The most popular response was 31–50 hours, the answer selected by 47% of the male respondents and 69% of the female respondents. A third of the men and 16% of the women indicated that children should have more than 50 hours a week with a parent. Memorandum, "Results of Survey on Family and Career Issues," Center for the Study of Applied Ethics (now The Olsson Center), The Darden School, Charlottesville, Virginia (May 4, 1984).

52. Earlier versions of this paper were presented at the 1986 annual meeting of the Society for Applied Philosophy and the March 15, 1988, Scholars Luncheon at Georgetown University's Kennedy Institute of Ethics. I want to thank members of both groups for their criticisms and helpful suggestions. In particular, I am grateful to Henry Richardson for urging me to reconsider the relationships between the intrinsic and instrumental value of parental love. I also appreciate the valuable comments I received from Judith Areen, Normal Bowie, Sidney Callahan, Joseph Fletcher, Kenneth Goodpaster, R. M. Hare, Joel Kupperman, Dennis Thompson, and this journal's anonymous referee.

QUESTIONS

1. Kamerman suggests that the problem of child-care and its solutions are not very different among professional or nonprofessional women, middle- or low-income mothers, regardless of race or family structure. Do you agree? Is Kamerman's suggestion consistent with her claim that one-parent families are most likely to use a day care center?

2. Some two-parent families make financial sacrifices in order to have one parent stay in the home and care for the children. Should such families be forced to help pay the costs of subsidized day care for other two-parent families? Why or why not?

3. Gerson suggests that we recognize the legitimacy of a number of different styles of male parenting. Do you agree that all these different styles are equally legitimate? Explain.

4. Gerson argues that we need effective social supports which can transform men's family involvement from a latent, incipient possibility to expected, unremarkable behavior. Would such policies discriminate against families which have chosen to structure themselves on the "male as breadwinner" model? Do you agree with the claim that if the male is the sole or primary breadwinner he cannot be deeply involved in his family? Why or why not?

5. What does Melé mean when he asserts that the family is a source of real rights? Can a family possess rights or can rights only be possessed by particular individuals?

6. What does Melé think are the rights of the family as regards employment? Do you agree that these are genuine rights? Why or why not?

7. Paine suggests that personal involvement in child-rearing has instrumental moral value for parents. What does she mean and what is her argument in support of this claim?

8. What is Paine's criticism of the prevailing assumption that parental guilt is driven by a moral principle of avoiding harm to children?

CASE 15:1 MEN AND CHILDREARING LEAVE[1]

Gerald Schafer was employed as a teacher by the Board of Public Education of the School District of Pittsburgh, Pennsylvania from August 1978 until December 14, 1981. In the early fall of 1981, Schafer requested an unpaid leave of absence for the 81–82 school year so he might pursue childrearing. Although female employees were routinely granted such leaves, Schafer was advised that males were never granted childrearing leaves and was told to apply for ninety-day unpaid emergency leave. Schafer applied for the emergency leave and also for a childrearing leave to take effect at the end of his emergency leave. He was granted an emergency leave, but towards its end, informed that no childrearing leave would be forthcoming. On November 30, 1981, Schafer submitted a letter of resignation in which he stated that in light of inability to obtain appropriate child care or childrearing leave, he was forced to resign in order to care for his son.

Near the end of December 1981, Schafer did locate daycare for his son, but did not at that time request reinstatement. He alleges that he did not believe he had the option to return to his former job. On June 23, 1982 he wrote the Board requesting the Board reconsider its denial of his leave so he could return to work in September 1982. The Board responded that he was no longer an employee.

Schafer then filed a charge of discrimination against the Board. The Board subsequently introduced a policy of granting male employees childrearing leave on the same basis as it is granted to female employees, but refused to grant Schafer reinstatement and back pay.

CASE STUDY QUESTIONS

1. Should childrearing leaves be legislated or a matter of negotiation between employers and employees? Justify your answer.
2. Are men equally entitled to childrearing leaves as women? Why or why not?

CASE 15:2 FAMILY RESPONSIBILITIES AND CAREER ADVANCEMENT

Large law firms have high overhead costs and as a consequence, often expect employees to produce high billable hours. Employees are encouraged to put in long hours and to make commitment to work their first priority. This frequently results in employees, especially those beginning their careers, experiencing tension between work and family responsibilities. Typically, part-time work is not encouraged since there is a perception that the overhead applicable to a part-time lawyer is only slightly less than a full-time position, but the billable hours produced by a part-timer are far less than those produced by a full-time employee. Those employees who choose part-time work do not tend to be promoted quickly or advance so far as those who work full time.

A recent report *Touchstones for Change,*[2] prepared by The Canadian Bar Association Task Force on Gender Equality, challenges a number of common assumptions. It argues that given the high cost of recruiting and retraining, it makes good sense to facilitate more job flexibility, explore work sharing, and provide greater opportunity for part-time employees to be promoted. It also argues that models of compensation other than billable hours be considered, such as client satisfaction, quality of work, or area of specialization. One of its more controversial suggestions is that lawyers with child-rearing responsibilities should receive reductions of 20% or more in hours of work with no reduction in salary. Specifically, it recommended "that law firms provide parental leave benefits and that an employee's entitlement to or eligibility for consideration for available raises, compensation benefits, seniority, admission to partnership, and other advancement not be affected while they are on paid parental leave."[3] A further recommendation was that law firms recognize the need for alternate work arrangements for all lawyers with parental responsibilities and that they provide emergency back-up child care for their employees.

CASE STUDY QUESTIONS

1. The Task Force felt that its recommendations would be beyond the ability of small firms or the legal profession to support economically and suggested that the government provide support either through tax exemption or direct subsidy. Does society, through government, have an obligation to provide such support? Is such government support practical if we extend the Report's suggestions to other occupations? In light of government deficits, is such support desirable?
2. The Task Force noted that men are assuming an increasingly greater role in family responsibilities and recognized that male lawyers are also concerned about balancing their professional and family responsibilities. It argued, however, that women typically bear the lion's share of family responsibilities and therefore, the emphasis in the short term should be on altering workplace policies to accommodate women with family responsibilities. Do you agree? Why or why not?
3. Do you feel that it is fair to suggest that a single man or woman who has devoted his or her time and energy to his or her career should enjoy no advantage in career advancement over someone who has chosen to work part time? Explain your answer.

Notes

1. Based on *Schafer v. Board of Public Education of the School District of Pittsburgh, PA.*, 903 Federal Reporter, 2nd series 243 (3rd Cir. 1990).

2. *Touchstones for Change: Equality, Diversity and Accountability*, Report of the Canadian Bar Association Task Force on Gender Equality in the Legal Profession (August 1993, The Canadian Bar Association, Ottawa, Ontario).

3. *Touchstones for Change,* p. 100.

FOR FURTHER READING

1. Rosanna Hertz, *More Equal Than Others: Women and Men in Dual-Career Marriages* (Berkeley: University of California Press, 1986).

2. J. H. Greenhaus and N. J. Beutell, "Sources of Conflict Between Work and Family Roles," *Academy of Management Review,* Vol. 10, 1967, pp. 76–88.

3. Kathleen B. Jones, "Socialist-Feminist Theories of the Family," *Praxis International,* Vol. 8, Oct. 1988, pp. 284–300.

4. Peter Moss and Nickie Fonda, (editors) *Work and the Family* (Great Britain: Maurice Temple Smith Ltd., 1980).

Chapter Sixteen

Business and the Community

Introduction

In chapter Sixteen the issue of the social responsibility of business is explored. Although
the term "social responsibility of business," is
widely used, its meaning is not entirely clear.
In a very general sense, almost any of the ethical constraints upon the pursuit of profit can
be viewed as a social responsibility of business. Thus, for instance, fair and honest advertising seems a social responsibility of business.
Construed in this way, the term should not be
taken to refer to a specific issue, but rather to
any obligations arising out of its interactions
with society. When the term is understood in
this general sense, discussion of the social responsibility of business focuses on the extent
of the ethical constraints on business' pursuit
of profit. Some theorists claim that business
will fulfil its obligations if it avoids causing
harm, or makes reparation for any harm it
causes. Other theorists think business has additional obligations; suggesting that these further constraints on the pursuit of profit are
grounded in an implicit social contract between business and society.

In a narrower sense, some take the term not
to refer to ethical constraints upon the pursuit
of profit, but rather to business' presumed obligation to pursue certain social goods independently of seeking profit. Understood in this
way, the term "social responsibility of business" generally refers to questions of whether
business should act philanthropically and to
what degree.

We need, therefore, to distinguish two types
of questions in discussing the issue of the social responsibility of business. The first concerns the type and extent of the ethical con-

straints that govern business' pursuit of profit; the second, whether business has moral responsibilities beyond pursuing profit in an ethical manner. Our first two articles deal with the concept of social responsibility defined in what I have called the general sense, i.e., questions of what are the ethical constraints upon business' pursuit of profit. Our third article discusses the issue of corporate philanthropy.

In our first selection, Milton Friedman argues that the only social responsibility of business is to achieve profits through open and free competition without deception or fraud. He emphatically rejects any notion of social responsibility defined in what I have called the narrow sense, i.e., pursuing social goods independently of seeking profit. In Friedman's view, executives of a company who pursue objectives other than profit, act immorally. The money they spend amounts to a tax on the shareholders and the policies they implement have not been authorized by the democratic process. In effect, they impose taxes and social policy for which they have no mandate.

Robert L. Lippke, in his article "Setting the Terms of the Business Responsibility Debate," contrasts Friedman's view with a conflicting view which holds that there exists a social contract between business and society, requiring business to do more than maximize profits while avoiding deception or fraud. Lippke finds neither view satisfactory. He proposes what he considers a viable compromise. On the one hand, he sides with Friedman in insisting that business should not implement social policy, but rather pursue profits in a principled way. On the other hand, he sides with the social contract approach in insisting that business' unique position in society generates special duties. His basic claim is that we cannot conceive of agents abstractly in discussing their moral responsibilities. In Lippke's view, Friedman is correct to insist that the sole goal of business is to pursue profit through free and open competition. Where Friedman goes wrong, according to Lippke, is conceiving employer and employee as rough equals in terms of their abilities to affect one another. This may sometimes be the case, but it is often not. In such instances, the more powerful party should take into account that there is more to preserving another's autonomy, i.e., the ability to take part in free and open competition, than simply avoiding violence or deception.

George Brenkert, in his article "Private Corporations and Public Welfare," argues that the suggestion that business has moral responsibilities beyond pursuing profit in an ethical manner fails to take account of important considerations in the setting of public policy. The basic problem he points to is that those receiving corporate aid typically lack any constitutional voice in the organization helping them. This tends to undermine the democratic setting of public policy, since the policies which are being pursued are not set by individuals who may be voted in or out of office, but rather by private corporations with an agenda that may not reflect the public will.

Milton Friedman

The Social Responsibility of Business is to Increase Its Profits

When I hear businessmen speak eloquently about the "social responsibilities of business in a free-enterprise system," I am reminded of the wonderful line about the Frenchman who discovered at the age of 70 that he had been speaking prose all his life. The businessmen believe that they are defending free enterprise when they declaim that business is not concerned "merely" with profit but also with promoting desirable "social" ends; that business has a "social conscience" and takes seriously its responsibilities for providing employment, eliminating discrimination, avoiding pollution and whatever else may be the catchwords of the contemporary crop of reformers. In fact they are—or would be if they or anyone else took them seriously— preaching pure and unadulterated socialism. Businessmen who talk this way are unwitting puppets of the intellectual forces that have been undermining the basis of a free society these past decades.

The discussions of the "social responsibilities of business" are notable for their analytical looseness and lack of rigor. What does it mean to say that "business" has responsibilities? Only people can have responsibilities. A corporation is an artificial person and in this sense may have artificial responsibilities, but "business" as a whole cannot be said to have responsibilities, even in this vague sense. The first step toward clarity in examining the doctrine of the social responsibility of business is to ask precisely what it implies for whom.

Presumably, the individuals who are to be responsible are businessmen, which means individual proprietors or corporate executives. Most of the discussion of social responsibility is directed at corporations, so in what follows I shall mostly neglect the individual proprietor and speak of corporate executives.

In a free-enterprise, private-property system, a corporate executive is an employee of the owners of the business. He has direct responsibility to his employers. That responsibility is to conduct the business in accordance with their desires, which generally will be to make as much money as possible while conforming to the basic rules of the society, both those embodied in law and those embodied in ethical custom. Of course, in some cases his employers may have a different objective. A group of persons might establish a corporation for an eleemosynary [charitable] purpose—for example, a hospital or a school. The manager of such a corporation will not have money profit as his objective but the rendering of certain services.

In either case, the key point is that, in his capacity as a corporate executive, the manager is the agent of the individuals who own the corporation or establish the eleemosynary institution, and his primary responsibility is to them.

Needless to say, this does not mean that it is easy to judge how well he is performing his task. But at least the criterion of performance is straightforward, and the persons among whom a voluntary contractual arrangement exists are clearly defined.

Of course, the corporate executive is also a person in his own right. As a person, he may have many other responsibilities that he recognizes or assumes voluntarily—to his family, his conscience, his feelings of charity, his church, his clubs, his city, his country. He may feel impelled by these responsibilities to devote part of his income to causes he regards as worthy, to refuse to work for particular corporations, even to leave his job, for example, to join his coun-

From *New York Times Magazine*, September 13, 1970, 32–33, 122–126. Copyright © 1970 by The New York Times Company. Reprinted by permission.

try's armed forces. If we wish, we may refer to some of these responsibilities as "social responsibilities." But in these respects he is acting as a principal, not an agent; he is spending his own money or time or energy, not the money of his employers or the time or energy he has contracted to devote to their purposes. If these are "social responsibilities," they are the social responsibilities of individuals, not of business.

What does it mean to say that the corporate executive has a "social responsibility" in his capacity as businessman? If this statement is not pure rhetoric, it must mean that he is to act in some way that is not in the interest of his employers. For example, that he is to refrain from increasing the price of the product in order to contribute to the social objective of preventing inflation, even though a price increase would be in the best interests of the corporation. Or that he is to make expenditures on reducing pollution beyond the amount that is in the best interests of the corporation or that is required by law in order to contribute to the social objective of improving the environment. Or that, at the expense of corporate profits, he is to hire "hard-core" unemployed instead of better-qualified workmen to contribute to the social objective of reducing poverty.

In each of these cases, the corporate executive would be spending someone else's money for a general social interest. Insofar as his actions in accord with his "social responsibility" reduce returns to stockholders, he is spending their money. Insofar as his actions raise the price to customers, he is spending the customers' money. Insofar as his actions lower the wages of some employees, he is spending their money.

The stockholders or the customers or the employees could separately spend their own money on the particular action if they wished to do so. The executive is exercising a distinct "social responsibility," rather than serving as an agent of the stockholders or the customers or the employees, only if he spends the money in a different way than they would have spent it.

But if he does this, he is in effect imposing taxes, on the one hand, and deciding how the tax proceeds shall be spent, on the other.

This process raises political questions on two levels: principle and consequences. On the level of political principle, the imposition of taxes and the expenditure of tax proceeds are governmental functions. We have established elaborate constitutional, parliamentary and judicial provisions to control these functions, to assure that taxes are imposed so far as possible in accordance with the preferences and desires of the public—after all, "taxation without representation" was one of the battle cries of the American Revolution. We have a system of checks and balances to separate the legislative function of imposing taxes and enacting expenditures from the executive function of collecting taxes and administering expenditure programs and from the judicial function of mediating disputes and interpreting the law.

Here the businessman—self-selected or appointed directly or indirectly by stockholders—is to be simultaneously legislator, executive and jurist. He is to decide whom to tax by how much and for what purpose, and he is to spend the proceeds—all this guided only by general exhortations from on high to restrain inflation, improve the environment, fight poverty and so on and on.

The whole justification for permitting the corporate executive to be selected by the stockholders is that the executive is an agent serving the interests of his principal. This justification disappears when the corporate executive imposes taxes and spends the proceeds for "social" purposes. He becomes in effect a public employee, a civil servant, even though he remains in name an employee of a private enterprise. On grounds of political principle, it is intolerable that such civil servants—insofar as their actions in the name of social responsibility are real and not just window-dressing—should be selected as they are now. If they are to be civil servants, then they must be selected through a political process. If they are to impose taxes and make expenditures to foster "social" objectives, then political machinery must be set up to guide the assessment of taxes and to determine through a political process the objectives to be served.

This is the basic reason why the doctrine of "social responsibility" involves the acceptance of the socialist view that political mechanisms, not market mechanisms, are the appropriate way to determine the allocation of scarce resources to alternative uses.

On the grounds of consequences, can the corporate executive in fact discharge his alleged "social responsibilities"? On the one hand, suppose he could get away with spending the stockholders' or customers' or employees' money. How is he to know how to spend it? He is told that he must contribute to fighting inflation. How is he to know what action of his will contribute to that end? He is presumably an expert in running his company—in producing a product or selling it or financing it. But nothing about his selection makes him an expert on inflation. Will his holding down the price of his product reduce inflationary pressure? Or, by leaving more spending power in the hands of his customers, simply divert it elsewhere? Or, by forcing him to produce less because of the lower price, will it simply contribute to shortages? Even if he could answer these questions, how much cost is he justified in imposing on his stockholders, customers and employees for this social purpose? What is his appropriate share and what is the appropriate share of others?

And, whether he wants to or not, can he get away with spending his stockholders', customers' or employees' money? Will not the stockholders fire him? (Either the present ones or those who take over when his actions in the name of social responsibility have reduced the corporation's profits and the price of its stock.) His customers and his employees can desert him for other producers and employers less scrupulous in exercising their social responsibilities.

This fact of "social responsibility" doctrine is brought into sharp relief when the doctrine is used to justify wage restraint by trade unions. The conflict of interest is naked and clear when union officials are asked to subordinate the interest of their members to some more general social purpose. If the union officials try to enforce wage restraint, the consequence is likely to be wildcat strikes, rank-and-file revolts and the emergence of strong competitors for their jobs. We thus have the ironic phenomenon that union leaders—at least in the U.S.—have objected to Government interference with the market far more consistently and courageously than have business leaders.

The difficulty of exercising "social responsibility" illustrates, of course, the great virtue of private competitive enterprise—it forces people to be responsible for their own actions and makes it difficult for them to "exploit" other people for either selfish or unselfish purposes. They can do good—but only at their own expense.

Many a reader who has followed the argument this far may be tempted to remonstrate that it is all well and good to speak of government's having the responsibility to impose taxes and determine expenditures for such "social" purposes as controlling pollution or training the hard-core unemployed, but that the problems are too urgent to wait on the slow course of political processes, that the exercise of social responsibility by businessmen is a quicker and surer way to solve pressing current problems.

Aside from the question of fact—I share Adam Smith's skepticism about the benefits that can be expected from "those who affected to trade for the public good"—this argument must be rejected on grounds of principle. What it amounts to is an assertion that those who favor the taxes and expenditures in question have failed to persuade a majority of their fellow citizens to be of like mind and that they are seeking to attain by undemocratic procedures what they cannot attain by democratic procedures. In a free society, it is hard for "good" people to do "good," but that is a small price to pay for making it hard for "evil" people to do "evil," especially since one man's good is another's evil.

I have, for simplicity, concentrated on the special case of the corporate executive, except only for the brief digression on trade unions. But precisely the same argument applies to the newer phenomenon of calling upon stockholders to require corporations to exercise social responsibility (the recent G.M. crusade, for example). In most of these cases, what is in effect involved is some stockholders trying to get other stockholders (or customers or employees) to contribute against their will to "social" causes favored by the activists. Insofar as they succeed, they are again imposing taxes and spending the proceeds.

The situation of the individual proprietor is somewhat different. If he acts to reduce the returns of his enterprise in order to exercise his "social responsibility," he is spending his own money, not someone else's. If he wishes to spend his money on such purposes, that is his right, and I cannot see that there is any objection to his doing so. In the process, he, too, may impose costs on employees and customers. However, because he is far less likely than a large corporation or union to have monopolistic power, any such side effects will tend to be minor.

Of course, in practice the doctrine of social responsibility is frequently a cloak for actions that are justified on other grounds rather than a reason for those actions.

To illustrate, it may well be in the long-run interest of a corporation that is a major employer in a small community to devote resources to providing amenities to that community or to improving its government. That may make it easier to attract desirable employees, it may reduce the wage bill or lessen losses from pilferage and sabotage or have other worthwhile effects. Or it may be that, given the laws about the deductibility of corporate charitable contributions, the stockholders can contribute more to charities they favor by having the corporation make the gift than by doing it themselves, since they can in that way contribute an amount that would otherwise have been paid as corporate taxes.

In each of these—and many similar—cases, there is a strong temptation to rationalize these actions as an exercise of "social responsibility." In the present climate of opinion, with its widespread aversion to "capitalism," "profits," the "soulless corporation" and so on, this is one way for a corporation to generate goodwill as a by-product of expenditures that are entirely justified in its own self-interest.

It would be inconsistent of me to call on corporate executives to refrain from this hypocritical window-dressing because it harms the foundations of a free society. That would be to call on them to exercise a "social responsibility"! If our institutions, and the attitudes of the public make it in their self-interest to cloak their actions in this way, I cannot summon much indignation to denounce them. At the same time, I can express admiration for those

individual proprietors or owners of closely held corporations or stockholders of more broadly held corporations who disdain such tactics as approaching fraud.

Whether blameworthy or not, the use of the cloak of social responsibility, and the nonsense spoken in its name by influential and prestigious businessmen, does clearly harm the foundations of a free society. I have been impressed time and again by the schizophrenic character of many businessmen. They are capable of being extremely far-sighted and clear-headed in matters that are internal to their businesses. They are incredibly short-sighted and muddle-headed in matters that are outside their businesses but affect the possible survival of business in general. This short-sightedness is strikingly exemplified in the calls from many businessmen for wage and price guidelines or controls or incomes policies. There is nothing that could do more in a brief period to destroy a market system and replace it by a centrally controlled system than effective governmental control of prices and wages.

The short-sightedness is also exemplified in speeches by businessmen on social responsibility. This may gain them kudos in the short run. But it helps to strengthen the already too prevalent view that the pursuit of profits is wicked and immoral and must be curbed and controlled by external forces. Once this view is adopted, the external forces that curb the market will not be the social consciences, however highly developed, of the pontificating executives; it will be the iron fist of Government bureaucrats. Here, as with price and wage controls, businessmen seem to me to reveal a suicidal impulse.

The political principle that underlies the market mechanism is unanimity. In an ideal free market resting on private property, no individual can coerce any other, all cooperation is voluntary, all parties to such cooperation benefit or they need not participate. There are no "social" values, no "social" responsibilities in any sense other than the shared values and responsibilities of individuals. Society is a collection of individuals and of the various groups they voluntarily form.

The political principle that underlies the political mechanism is conformity. The individual must serve a more general social interest—whether that be determined by a church or a dictator or a majority. The individual may have a vote and a say in what is to be done, but if he is overruled, he must conform. It is appropriate for some to require others to contribute to a general social purpose whether they wish to or not.

Unfortunately, unanimity is not always feasible. There are some respects in which conformity appears unavoidable, so I do not see how one can avoid the use of the political mechanism altogether.

But the doctrine of "social responsibility" taken seriously would extend the scope of the political mechanism to every human activity. It does not differ in philosophy from the most explicitly collectivist doctrine. It differs only by professing to believe that collectivist ends can be attained without collectivist means. That is why, in my book *Capitalism and Freedom*, I have called it a "fundamentally subversive doctrine" in a free society, and have said that in such a society, "there is one and only one social responsibility of business—to use its resources and engage in activities designed to increase its profits so long as it stays within the rules of the game, which is to say, engages in open and free competition without deception or fraud."

Robert L. Lippke

Setting the Terms of the Business Responsibility Debate

There are two approaches to determining the limits of business moral responsibility that are quite prevalent in the literature of business ethics. One of these approaches, initially suggested by Milton Friedman, and recently rejuvenated by Douglas J. Den Uyl, involves conceiving of business people as constrained to deliberate and act in ways that are only minimally demanding.[1] So long as business people avoid harming others in certain traditional and obvious ways, and live up to their agreements, nothing else is (morally) required of them. The second approach, advocated by Thomas Donaldson and Norman Bowie, shares certain basic tenets both historically and logically with

From Robert L. Lippke, "Setting the Terms of the Business Responsibility Debate," *Social Theory and Practice*, Vol. 11, No. 3 (Fall 1985). Reprinted with modifications by permission of the author and *Social Theory and Practice*.

the first approach.[2] However, utilizing the device of a social contract, the second approach adds responsibilities commensurate with the economic, social, and political power of business people. Hence, on the second approach, the responsibilities of business people are held to exceed those of moral agents in other contexts.

After sketching the logic of these two approaches, I will argue that the first approach is more defensible than the second. Then, I will contend that the real debate over the limits of business moral responsibility is between the first approach and a third approach, the outlines of which I will also sketch. While retaining the normative moral principles of the first approach, this third approach builds in a concern for the considerable power and influence of some agents (for example, business people) that the second approach acknowledges, but fails to incorporate adequately. In addition to indicating the plausibility of this third approach as a model for the analysis of business moral responsibility, I will show why the debate between it and the first approach turns on a solution to issues like the moral status of property rights and the nature of economic justice. While I will not try to address these difficult ethical issues in this paper, I do hope to show that they cannot be sidestepped in determining the limits of business moral responsibility.

The first and second approaches both have their origins in the writings of classic liberals like Hobbes, Locke, and Mill. Both approaches are predicated on what might be termed an "abstract individuals" conception of moral agency. This involves initially conceiving of moral agents independently of the more concrete social, economic, and political relations they have to one another. Put another way, agents are conceived of independently of the specific causal chains they are in a position to initiate. So conceived, agents are seen as rough equals in terms of their abilities to affect one another. This conception is then combined with some traditional liberal ethical assumptions:

... individuals are in an important sense "ends in themselves." On this theory, to be an "end in oneself" means that no one's purposes are subservient to or a means to the purposes of other individuals or groups. Each person is free to pursue his or her own ends provided those ends do not prevent others from being able to formulate purposes of their own.[3]

An emphasis on freedom and autonomy is at the heart of both general approaches. This emphasis, along with the commitment to the equal moral worth of persons, yields a familiar set of moral constraints on action. The constraints prohibit killing, violence, coercion, fraud, and deception, and thereby secure persons from the sorts of harms and interferences that might defeat their freedom (understood in terms of the range and quality of options effectively open to them) and their autonomy (understood in terms of their ability to form and execute a rational life-plan).

Importantly, these constraints, if generally observed, can be seen as making possible a free enterprise system where persons engage in only those business transactions they freely and rationally choose to engage in. Often, those in the classic liberal tradition wrap individuals in moral rights that are seen as the basis or ground of these moral constraints. Hence, depending on the author, one will find an emphasis on rights to freedom and autonomy rather than on obli-gations to not interfere with freedom and autonomy. Little seems to turn on these differences in emphasis, though as we will see, some might wish to argue otherwise.

Further moral constraints on action derive from the voluntary agreements of persons. The operative notion is that of *consent*. Persons are the rightful possessors of their time, energy, and efforts. As such, these resources can only be construed as under moral constraint where persons themselves have placed them under constraint by consent.[4] Putting all of this together, we get the first approach to the limits of business moral responsibility, as neatly summarized by DeGeorge:

Providing its actions do not harm anyone, and providing its transactions are fair, the corporation is a morally acceptable kind of entity. . . .[5]

The transactions of business people will be fair so long as they are reached through "free and open competition, without deception or fraud."[6]

Additionally, those attracted to this first approach revolt at the suggestion of any responsibility on the part of business people to serve non-contracted-to noneconomic ends. Friedman is famous for thumbing his nose at such proposals, stressing the fiduciary role of management vis-á-vis the property rights of the stockholders.[7] In keeping with the logic of this first approach, Narveson sweepingly rejects the idea of corporate responsibility to aid the less fortunate in society by citing the lack of any agreement "struck on terms of mutual self-interest" between business people and the less fortunate.[8]

Up to this point, the moral responsibilities of business people supported by the first approach, though not insignificant, are nonetheless quite modest. Let us call this approach the "Abstract Individuals Approach" (*AIA*). Aware that the effects of business activity often outstrip those wrought by ordinary agents, some writers have sought to utilize the notion of a *social contract* to add responsibility beyond those the *AIA* supports. The "Social Contract Approach" (*SCA*) initially conceives of individual moral agents abstractly, but employs the time-honored notion of *consent* to add constraints on business activity commensurate with the social and economic power and influence of business. Donaldson and Bowie both contend that the *ground* of these further responsibilities (for example, minimizing pollution and the depletion of natural resources) is a social contract between business and society.[9]

The *SCA* is an extension of the logic of the *AIA*. This extension immediately runs into serious problems when the nature of this contract is queried, as one supporter of the *AIA* has pointed out.[10] Is this contract supposed to be an actual or explicit contract? Bowie cites the existence of the corporate charter as evidence of the reality of this contract. Ostensibly, the claim is that by obtaining a charter, those who form a corporation agree to do more than simply avoid malfeasance and honor their business contracts. Yet, as Hessen shows, the articles of incorporation require no such promise or agreement on the part of those who form a corporation.[11] In the main, certain kinds of factual information are all that is required, and Hessen claims that where that information is given, the relevant state official has little or no discretionary power:

He cannot demand any additional information; he cannot extract any oath of corporate allegiance to the public interest; he cannot even refuse to certify the corporate charter.[12]

If these claims are correct any argument that relies on the existence of the corporate charter to expand the responsibilities of business people beyond those implied by the *AIA* seems most unpromising.

Moreover, the move to an *implied* contract is laden with difficulties.[13] A thorough investigation of the conditions under which an individual can properly be said to *imply* her agreement to something would take us well beyond the scope of this article. This much is clear, however. In order to an agreement to be implied by a set of circumstances, the agents involved must be in a position to have a fairly determinate idea of what the provisions of the agreement are. It is primarily on this point that the implied *SCA* surely flounders. Are those who apply for a corporate charter supposed to be aware that they are to serve the "public interest," whatever that is? Or, are they supposed to recognize (and how, exactly?) that their responsibilities do not end with those supported by the *AIA*, or by existing norms and practices? Are these matters we could hold any normal business person knows (or has reason to know) the forms and limits of?[14] I think not.

In the political-legal domain, the notion of implied consent has often been used to ground obligation to the law on the part of citizens. However, even if we grant the cogency of such an argument in that domain, carrying it over to the business domain is no easy matter.[15] At least in the political-legal domain, citizens can pretty straightforwardly find out what they have "agreed" to, by consulting constitutions, positive law, and case law. But there seem to be no comparable sources for business people to rely on in order for them to apprise themselves of the provisions of their implied agreement. Indeed, debate about what the "public interest" consists in, or about what business people have implied their agreement to, is likely to be protracted, and for that reason, the implied *SCA* seems unattractive.

Donaldson is not averse to employing the notion of an "abstract" contract between society and what he calls "productive organizations."[16] The difficulty with such a move has been forcefully pressed by Dworkin.[17] While an actual or implied agreement might bind agents (if made under certain conditions), it is not clear what independent obligatory force an abstract or hypothetical agreement has. At best, the notion of an abstract agreement seems a device to call attention to an independent argument of some kind. What is that argument in this case? It cannot involve the existence of the corporate charter for the reasons already cited. Neither will it do to cite corporate use of society's infrastructure. Corporations pay taxes to cover that use, so why should their responsibilities extend beyond those of other taxpayers? Nor will it suffice to simply invoke the idea that property is "society's" to divide up, dole out, and determine the legitimate uses of. For one thing, there is a long, venerable tradition against this interpretation of property rights. But even if there were not, it is far from clear how such a premise can aid in establishing the conclusions of those who opt for the *SCA*.[18]

My suggestion is that the use of *consent* in attempting to ground responsibilities should be kept within strict limits. Actual or implied consent may establish specific responsibilities for agents, or may release agents from responsibilities that would otherwise be binding on them. Once one starts to invoke consent to ground more open ended or vague responsibilities (for example, to serve the public interest), the argument becomes problematic. Fairness requires that agents have some determinate idea of what they have or have not consented to. When this is not the case, consent becomes a device for adding (or subtracting) responsibilities on the whims of those who can offer no substantial argument as to why such an addition (or subtraction) is justified.

Though I have sided with supporters of the *AIA* against supporters of the *SCA*, I think the latter are onto something of considerable importance. Those who favor the *SCA* are aware that many business people (especially those situated in large corporate power structures) have access to resources, technology, and labor power on a scale that no adequate accounting of their responsibilities should ignore. Yet, if the *SCA* is defective, what is to replace it?

In its place I want to offer a model for analyzing the responsibilities of business people that I will call the "Social Niche Approach" (*SNA*). According to the *SNA*, it is usually a mistake to conceive of persons abstractly in attempting to delineate their moral responsibilities. Persons always have a social niche, that is, a set of concrete social, economic, political, and historical relations to other persons. In a variety of ways, and with varying magnitudes, these relations determine persons' abilities to affect others' lives and interests. As we have seen, on the *AIA*, violence, deception, and fraud are taken to pretty much exhaust wrongful interference. This, I think, ignores many of the more subtle ways in which positions of power and influence are used to initiate causal chains that affect the freedom and autonomy of others. The *SNA* fastens on relevant differentials in power, influence, and ability, and tailors an agent's moral responsibilites accordingly.[19]

In other words, the *SNA* spells out the theoretical underpinnings of the notion that increased power brings with it increased responsibility, but without grounding that increased responsibility in *consent*. Building on the normative moral principles of the *AIA* (namely, principles requiring respect for the freedom and autonomy of individuals), the *SNA* draws attention to the real world of concretized agents that the *AIA* ignores. Of course, these moral principles could be challenged as well, but doing so would take me beyond the scope of the paper. My aim is to propose the *SNA* as a plausible alternative model for analyzing the responsibilities of business people. Thus, the *SNA*, like the *SCA*, can be seen as a development of the *AIA*.

The idea behind the *SNA* is the following: if the function of moral constraints on action is to secure the freedom and autonomy of persons, then the *SNA* can be understood as requiring that we consider the social niche of agents in determining what constraints are applicable to their decisions and actions. Attention to the social niche of agents prevents moral responsibility from being reduced to lowest common denominator terms—that is, to the ways in which abstract individuals are constrained to act toward others. According to the *SNA*, it is inappropriate to characterize an agent's responsibilities independently of an empirical investigation of that agent's social niche.[20]

The implications of the *SNA* can best be illustrated by considering some examples of the ways in which the social niche of some agents determines their ability to affect others in morally significant ways: (1) Some business people routinely make decisions about what natural resources to develop and at what rates. Obviously, these decisions may affect the range and quality of options open to both present and future persons, as well as their ability to execute rational life-plans. In the case of future persons, the limitations of the *AIA* are especially apparent. Conceived abstractly, agents are not likely to be seen as able to significantly affect the life-prospects of many future persons. To object here that the ramifications of any single decision by a business person in this area are slight and perhaps unforeseeable no doubt raises an important point. In some cases (though not all), it is the aggregate effects of many decisions that are significant. But this may only show that what is needed is a framework of public policy to funnel these decisions in a direction conducive to minimizing the adverse effects of decisions made on the basis of a business's self-interest. In such cases, the responsibility of business persons is to support (or at least not resist) the implementation of such a public policy, and to abide by it once it is implemented. (2) Decisions about what technology to use in the production of goods and services may have significant adverse implications for the freedom and autonomy of employees. The concerns expressed by Donaldson and others about the dulling or stifling of initiative and creativity, and the loss of a sense of responsibility or of a sense of self-worth, can all be accommodated by the SNA. The ability to form and execute a rational life-plan is surely threatened by the atrophy of abilities brought about by some working conditions. It is also threatened by an agent's loss of the sense that it is important to control his own destiny, or by his loss of the sense that he is able to do so. Also, exposing employees to hazardous chemicals, or to noise and pollution whose effects take years to manifest themselves threatens their freedom, if we assume that being diseased or disabled limits the range and quality of options open to them. All of these more subtle effects are less likely to be seen as morally significant if the AIA is uncritically adhered to. (3) The use of sophisticated advertising techniques, and what Braybrooke refers to as the "aggregate and cumulative effects" of advertisements, raise serious questions about the ability of persons to resist the self-serving and in many cases arguably harmful messages promulgated.[21] The sorts of nonrational persuasion used by advertisers would likely be seen as objectionable if used by political regimes out to promote their interests—especially in the absence of countervailing information. Yet, why not raise the same objections to the increasing use of corporate resources to affect the thought-processes and emotional responses of consumers? Again, the access to resources and the sheer volume of advertisments this makes possible seem to outstrip the confines of the AIA. (4) Relevant here also are decisions about plant closings or the automation

of jobs long held by persons. It can be argued that in making decisions about these matters, business people have an obligation to take into account the effects of their actions on the range and quality of options left open to employees.[22] The SNA brings this argument into sharper focus. That business people may find such moral requirements unusual may only show their allegiance to existing moral standards, or to the AIA. Also, that an agent's social niche has historical dimensions serves to reinforce the contention that the symbiotic relationship that develops between a plant and a community is morally relevant to closing decisions. The unilateral termination of such a relationship, especially when this occurs without warning and without efforts to ameliorate its effects, seems a type of ingratitude that is condemnable. The sense that employees and other members of the community *deserve* better than this can be accounted for in terms of the idea that those who make plant closing decisions in this manner fail to return the sort of treatment that has been the reciprocal *status quo*.

While the preceding examples illustrate some of the implications of adopting the SNA, much needs to be said by way of further elaborating on and defending it. Let me undertake these tasks by considering several counterarguments to the SNA.

One likely response by supporters of the AIA will be predicated on the notion that the adverse effects of business activity that the SNA calls attention to are not ones that persons have moral rights protecting them from. Or, supporters of the AIA might concede that persons have moral rights in these areas, but insist that the property rights of stockholders outweigh such rights. Neither of these objections is conclusive in the absence of solutions to some more fundamental normative ethical problems.

The first objection leads us to consider the *basis* or *ground* of moral rights. On this, a variety of normative ethical approaches is available. Regardless of which one is chosen, it is hard to imagine how the kinds of effects mentioned in the preceding examples can be in principle distinguished from the effects of more traditional harmful actions (for example, violence, deception, fraud). It will not do for supporters of the *AIA* to maintain that because such affects are unusual (especially if one conceives of matters via the *AIA*) they are not right-protected. For why should their unusualness matter?[23]

The second objection admits the moral relevance of these adverse effects, and perhaps their overridingness in other contexts, but throws up property rights as a trump card to sweep all such considerations aside. As Den Uyl rightly points out, critics of business cannot simply assume that the property rights of stockholders must yield to demands for greater corporate responsibility.[24] However, supporters of the *AIA* equally cannot assume that property rights inevitably outweigh other rights. One notorious difficulty with rights-talk is that many who resort to it offer little guidance as to how moral rights are to be ranked—or if one prefers—qualified in ways that render them congruent with one another. This is something that it seems an adequate ethical theory must do, and given the enormity of the undertaking, something supporters of the *AIA* might be excused for having failed to do. Nonetheless, the point remains that invoking property rights at this juncture is, at best, the beginning of an argument against the implications of the *SNA*, nothing more. Whatever considerations may be offered in support of property rights will have to be systematically examined and weighed against the considerations supporting other rights.[25]

Once all of these considerations are taken into account, it is far from clear that property rights will prevail over the other rights the *SNA* calls attention to. This is especially true in the case of stockholders' property rights. In some cases, the money they invest is arguably surplus property—that is, property over and above what they require to meet their basic needs or promote their most vital interests. Also, it is part of the commonly accepted ideology of the stockmarket that there is risk involved. Presumably, those who invest often have other (perhaps less lucrative) options open to them that are less risky, and in this way they differ from employees or other members of the community who may be harmed by business activities.[26]

However, leaving the two preceding points aside, there are other reasons why it is surely not inevitable that the stockholders' rights will prevail. The adverse effects the *SNA* focuses attention on are far from insignificant. The loss of a sense of self-worth, damage to one's health, interference with one's capacity to make rational, autonomous choices, and so on, all seem more significant, morally speaking, than what may only amount to a decline in the value of one's investments. Why this is so is not hard to discover. The former sorts of effects undercut the capacity to work at all, and thus acquire property. Or, they injure a person's ability to use and enjoy whatever property he or she has managed to acquire. Even where a sizeable portion of stockholder investments are of things like pension funds, which do affect investors' most vital interests, it is important to not exaggerate the conflict that must be theoretically resolved. It will generally not be the case that accommodating the rights of employees and members of the public will require that stockholders' investments be wholly jeopardized. Rather, stockholders may simply have to accept somewhat less in earnings if the rights of others are to be respected.

It will also not do for supporters of the *AIA* to contend that most persons have consented to suffering the sorts of adverse effects not prohibited by the *AIA*. For one thing, this contention has the familiar ring of open-ended (and therefore indeterminate) consent, and thus suffers from the defects noted earlier. Second, while we cannot embark here on an examination of the difficult matter of stating the conditions under which persons can be said to freely undertake risks, the following points are pertinent: (1) Those to be adversely affected must know of the dangers or it must be reasonable to say they should have known. It seems likely that there will be (and have been) many cases of harmful business activity of the sort the *SNA* calls attention to where this epistemic condition is not satisfied. (2) Those to be adversely affected must have other options open to them that it is reasonable for them to choose so as to avoid suffering the effects. Notice that with respect to the agreements or contracts of business people, the contrast between the *AIA* and the *SNA* is informative. Because of the sometimes enormous differences in power that exist between business persons and those they deal with, the former are able to gain agreements on terms highly favorable to their interests at the expense of others' interests. Where all agents are conceived abstractly, they appear as rough equals, with none in a position to force or hold out for extremely favorable terms. The differentials in power that the SNA calls attention to raise questions about the voluntariness of certain exchanges. In cases where business people are in a position to determine the range and quality of options open to those they deal with, the issue whether an agreement is made under duress must be considered. For instance, if a firm threatens to close a plant unless concessions on working conditions are made by the employees' union, it is relevant to assessing the voluntariness of such an agreement to consider the other options open to the employees. Suppose that short of unemployment and its attendant hardships, there are none, and that the concessions on working conditions render the work significantly more dangerous. Can we say simply that the employees have "consented" to suffering such adverse effects if they make the concessions? It seems we cannot. After all, if the adverse effects are ones that persons have a right not to suffer, then an "agreement" forged under such conditions is surely morally suspect. Perhaps the firm cannot fairly be held responsible for the lack of other viable options open to the employees. This may be a matter on which collective social action is necessary and appropriate. But, it does seem plausible to say that the situation is one that the firm is not morally at liberty to exploit.[27] (3) Related to the preceding, the inability to prevent the suffering of adverse effects should not be taken as equivalent to consenting to them. Employees or members of the general public may know that industries hire lobbyists to promote exclusively industry interests, but lack the resources to effectively counter such activities on the part of business persons.

A third objection to the potentially demanding responsibilities of the SNA receives impetus from an alleged crucial difference between types of moral requirements. The constraints supported by the AIA might be seen as defensible ones because they are largely negative in character, requiring agents simply to refrain from harming or interfering with others (plus honoring their agreements). The constraints do not require agents to invest their time, energy, or other resources in efforts to aid others. As we have seen, Friedman and others will insist that it is not appropriate for management to use corporate resources to pursue social causes of management's (perhaps idiosyncratic, or worse, objectionable) choosing. Better, so the argument goes, that business people refrain from harming others and attend to safeguarding the property rights of the stockholders.

This line of reasoning involves a number of confusions and unargued for assumptions. First, it tries to draw a distinction between what some have called "negative injunctions" and "affirmative duties," and then suggest that the former can be satisfied by doing nothing.[28] However, the inaction/action distinction is not the same as the negative injunction/affirmative duty distinction. In reality, adherence to even the negative injunctions will require agents to do things—to allocate time, energy, and resources in some ways rather than others. For instance, treating employees with only minimal respect will require business people to pay them adequately, deal with unsafe working conditions, institute fair evaluation procedures, and the like. Similarly, avoiding fraud or deception may require business persons to advertise and sell their products in some (perhaps more costly) ways than others.

The negative injunction/affirmative duty distinction is actually aimed at capturing the difference between adverse effects that an agent himself causes (or might cause) and ones that are caused in other ways, but regarding which an agent could do something to help lessen or alleviate. It may be that any plausible ethical theory will seek to restrict the range of affirmative duties agents have lest they do overburdened by moral demands on their time, energy, and resources.[29] But that is different from requiring agents to concern themselves with effects that they themselves cause. In essence, the SNA calls attention to the unusual and varied range of causal chains that some agents are in a position to initiate.[30]

Also, though management's fiduciary role poses serious obstacles to attempts to apply the concept of affirmative duties to business people, it is important to note the larger issue that lurks just beneath the surface. We might admit that if the property rights of stockholders always withstand moral scrutiny, then Friedman's argument is compelling. However, that is certainly a problematic "if." It seems clear that property holdings are greatly influenced by factors that are largely beyond any given individual's control. Factors such as a person's native talents, socioeconomic starting point, and the occurrence of past injustices may all have a significant effect on property acquisitions. Also, it is apparent that collective efforts can be undertaken to modify the influence of these factors. The question then is whether justice requires such collective efforts, and to what extent, or are we simply to allow such factors to have their full impact on property holdings? Property holdings determine both the range and quality of options open to persons, and influence their ability to execute effectively rational life-plans. These effects on freedom and autonomy, combined with the seeming moral arbitrariness of allowing such factors to determine life-prospects, makes it plausible to contend that some collective efforts are warranted.

Of course, any such changes in public policy, or in the structuring of the basic institutions in society, are matters that go well beyond the responsibilities of business people. On this point, Friedman is certainly correct when he warns against asking business people to be the agents of social change. Still, there will be one very important responsibility of business people if justice requires some modification of property holdings—namely, to refrain from using their considerable power (perhaps at the stockholders' behest) to undermine or obstruct such collective efforts. Admittedly, it is hard to be optimistic that such a responsibility is one that will be fondly embraced by business people.

There is one further counterargument that I will only briefly deal with. It might be alleged that by requiring business people to observe only the constraints of the AIA, greater benefits will accrue to all persons over the long term. This rather crude teleological argument suffers from a number of defects. Chief among them is that there is no attempt to demonstrate that

those who suffer is some way because only minimal constraints are adhered to are the ones who subsequently receive some of the allegedly greater benefits. It is reasonable in some cases to ask an individual to accept a loss in the short term if that loss will be outweighed by a future benefit. Yet, where there is no such linkage of short-term losses with long-term benefits, the imposition of a loss seems unjustifiable. By contrast, the SNA secures all individuals from losses in a more certain and equal fashion.

In conclusion, I have tried to establish the SNA as a legitimate contender with the AIA in the debate over the limits of business moral responsibility. I have also suggested that resolution of that debate will force us to focus squarely on a variety of fundamental issues in ethics and social philosophy. It seems to me that supports of the AIA and the SCA have tried in different ways to sidestep those difficult issues. If the arguments I have offered are sound, then it is precisely to issues like the ground of moral rights and the nature of economic justice that the business responsibility debate must turn.[31]

Notes

1. Milton Friedman, *Capitalism and Freedom* (Chicago: The University of Chicago Press, 1962), see especially the Introduction and Chapter 1. Douglas J. Den Uyl, *The New Crusaders: The Corporate Social Responsibility Debate* (Bowling Green State University: The Social Philosophy and Policy Center, 1984), pp. 24–26.
2. Thomas Donaldson, *Corporations and Morality* (Englewood Cliffs, NJ: Prentice-Hall, Inc., 1982), pp. 18–57. Norman Bowie, "Changing the Rules," in Tom L. Beauchamp and Norman E. Bowie, (eds.), *Ethical Theory and Business* (Englewood Cliffs, NJ: Prentice-Hall, Inc., 1983), pp. 103–106.
3. Den Uyl, *New Crusaders*, p. 24.
4. Ibid., pp. 24–25.
5. Richard T. DeGeorge, *Business Ethics* (New York: Macmillan Publishing Co., Inc., 1982), p. 133.
6. Friedman, *Capitalism and Freedom*, p. 133.
7. Ibid., p. 135.
8. Jan Narveson, "Justice and the Business Society," in Beauchamp and Bowie, *Ethical Theory and Business*, 613–21, p. 617.
9. Donaldson, *Corporations and Morality*, pp. 41–49, Bowie "Changing the Rules," p. 103.
10. Den Uyl, *New Crusaders*, pp. 12–19. Den Uyl makes further damaging criticisms of the SCA.
11. Robert Hessen, *In Defense of the Corporation* (Stanford, CA: Hoover Institution Press, 1979) pp. 25–26.
12. Ibid., p. 25.
13. Bowie, "Changing the Rules," p. 105.

14. For instance, if at one time it was common practice, as it likely was, to expose employees to unsafe working conditions, would an implied contract oblige employers to act in a way that was contrary to such an established practice?

15. Even in the political-legal sphere, the presence of factors like poverty, language-barriers, etc., raises questions about whether one who has continued to live under a political-legal system can unproblematically be said to have implied her consent to abide by its laws and institutions.

16. Donaldson, *Corporations and Morality,* pp. 41–42.

17. Ronald Dworkin, *Taking Rights Seriously* (Cambridge, MA: Harvard University Press, 1977) p. 151.

18. It is also not at all clear how the privileges gained by incorporation (namely, entity status, perpetual duration, and limited tort liability for stockholders) establish any sort of obligation to serve wider interests.

19. The *SNA* has certain affinities to the approach to business moral responsibility articulated by David Braybrooke in *Ethics in the World of Business* (Totowa, NJ: Rowman and Allanheld, 1983), see especially pp. 145–46.

20. Instead of attributing responsibilities to organizations like corporations, I prefer to attribute them to individuals *within* such organizations. It is within the context of such an organization that agents have access to resources, technology, and labor power. That agents within an organization must often share responsibilities with superiors and subordinates complicates attributions of responsibility a bit. It seems reasonable to say that one of the responsibilities of business people will be to ensure that procedures and mechanisms necessary to fulfill their shared responsibilities are established and maintained within a corporation. On this, see Kenneth E. Goodpaster. "The Concept of Corporate Responsibility," *Journal of Business Ethics* Vol. 2 (1983): 1–22.

21. Braybrooke, *Ethics,* pp. 327–28.

22. John P. Kavanagh, "Ethical Issues in Plant Relocation," in Beauchamp and Bowie, *Ethical Theory and Business,* pp. 106–14.

23. See William T. Blackstone, "Ethics and Ecology," in Beauchamp and Bowie, *Ethical Theory and Business,* pp. 411–18. Blackstone argues that the right to a livable environment emerged with an awareness of the impact of potentially damaging technology.

24. Den Uyl, *New Crusaders,* p. 33.

25. If one conceives of property only in terms of individuals' personal effects (for example, houses, automobiles, clothes), the moral constraints of the *AIA* may appear sufficient. However, the employment of property as means of production has consequences that outstrip the confines of the *AIA*.

26. Admittedly, some assumptions made by investors would have to be changed under the *SNA* because of the greater constraints on business activity the approach supports. However, I see no reason to believe that people would refuse to invest where such constraints are taken seriously.

27. Even where duress is not present, and so the issue of consent is not directly relevant, a further question about the fairness of contracts can be raised. Courts have held that a contract may be "unconscionable." The reasoning behind such cases seems in part to be that the terms of an agreement may be so substantively unfair to one of the parties that the agreement should be considered void. Such agreements seem more likely to occur between parties of unequal economic (or other) power. Though relevant to my discussion, the philosophical problems unconscionability raises are too complex to attempt an analysis of here. For a discussion that is somewhat critical of the courts' decisions, see Charles Fried, *Contract as Promise* (Cambridge, MA: Harvard University Press, 1981) pp. 103–109.

28. On this, see John G. Simon, Charles W. Powers, Jon P. Gunneman, "The Responsibilities of Corporations and Their Owners," in Beauchamp and Bowie, *Ethical Theory and Business,* pp. 86–93.

29. Simon, Powers, Gunneman "Responsibilities of Corporations," pp. 88–90.

30. Importantly, my acceptance of the distinction between negative injunctions and affirmative duties indicates one reason why the SNA does *not* rely on a "can implies ought" inference. Also, I admit that where those who suffer adverse effects on their freedom and autonomy have consented to risk such effects, agents responsible for initiating the relevant causal chains have no obligation to refrain from doing so, though they can refrain from doing so.

31. I am grateful to the referees who read this paper for making some valuable suggestions about how to improve it.

George G. Brenkert

Private Corporations and Public Welfare

I

The doctrine of corporate social responsibility comes in many varieties.[1] Its most developed version demands that corporations help alleviate "public welfare deficiencies," by which is understood problems of the inner city, drug problems, poverty, crime, illiteracy, lack of sufficient funding for educational institutions, inadequate health care delivery systems, chronic unemployment, etc.

In short, social responsibility, it is contended, requires that corporations assume part of the responsibility for the basic prerequisites of individual and social life within a community or society. Social responsibility demands this even though, it is claimed, corporations are not causally responsible for these conditions and doing so may not enhance their profits.

In response, corporations today provide job training for the hardcore unemployed, help renovate parks, sponsor clean-up programs, establish manufacturing plants in ghetto areas, offer seminars to high school students on how effectively to seek employment, support minority business adventures, provide educational films as well as additional instructors and tutors to public schools (i.e. "adopt" schools), etc.[2]

Such projects have, seemingly, met with a great deal of approval. Indeed, during a time when the welfare of many is deficient, one wonders how anyone could object to such activities. It might seem that any objections to such corporate behavior would stem not from their participating in these activities, but from their not participating even more.

From George G. Brenkert, "Private Corporations and Public Welfare," *Public Affairs Quarterly*, Vol. 6, No. 2, (April 1992). Reprinted by permission.

Nevertheless, a number of objections to corporations engaging in such activities have been raised and are well-known. Many of these criticisms are not very good and will not be reviewed here. There is however, one objection that is much more interesting, even if it is rarely developed. The essence of this objection is that corporate social responsibility to produce directly the public welfare involves the illegitimate encroachment of private organizations into the public realm. There is much greater merit to it than might appear at first glance.

II

This objection takes various forms. Theodore Levitt, for example, claims that the essence of free enterprise is the production of high-level profits. Private business corporations tend to impose this narrowly materialistic view on whatever they touch. Accordingly, corporate responsibility for welfare threatens to reduce pluralism and to create a monolithic society.[3] George C. Lodge similarly maintains that "the demand that business apply itself to problems which government is finding it increasingly difficult to comprehend or affect ... is ... absurd. Corporations, whatever else they may be, are not purveyors of social assistance."[4] Unelected businessmen, he claims, have "neither the right nor the competence" to define or establish the goals and the criteria by which society should repair or remake itself.[5] Finally, Richard DeGeorge claims that

there is great danger in expecting corporations to take upon themselves the production of public welfare, because they already have enormous power and are not answerable for its use to the general public. Politicians are elected by the public and are expected to have the common good as their end. We should not expect corporations to do what they are neither competent nor organized to do ...[6]

These criticisms question the right as well as the competence of corporations to contribute directly to the public welfare. Further, they challenge the influence which corporations in so acting may gain over society. Both increased corporate power and a decrease of social pluralism are feared results.[7]

Unfortunately, these criticisms are, more often than not, simply noted, rather than elaborated upon. In particular, the suggestion implicit within them that the provision of public welfare by private corporations runs afoul of an important distinction between what is public and what is private has not been discussed in recent literature. It is this point which requires greater attention.

The argument offered here is that corporate responsibility for public welfare threatens to reduce, transform, and in some cases eliminate important public dimensions of social life. For this reason we must be wary of it and reluctant to accept it in its present forms. Several characteristics of this argument should be noted at the outset. First, it does not pretend to show that all corporate measures that address public welfare deficiencies are (by themselves or individually) wrong, mischievous, or mistaken. Still, we must not be overly impressed by particular instances and thereby miss the systematic and general implications that are thereby promoted. It is not uncommon for individually rational actions to lead to collectively irrational or morally problematic results.

Second, this argument does not address corporate social responsibilities with regard to damages that corporations may themselves directly cause to the environment, employees, members of society, etc. For all these harms it is reasonable to believe that corporations do have responsibilities. The question this paper addresses concerns the implications of demanding that corporations go beyond correcting the damages they have brought about and assume responsibility for public welfare deficiencies for which they are not causally responsible.

Finally, if we could identify the harms that corporations directly *and* indirectly cause, then the arena of responsibilities that corporations have to society might significantly increase and the deficiencies in public welfare (assuming corporations fulfilled their responsibilities) might correspondingly decrease. This paper presupposes that, even in such a situation, there would remain public welfare deficiencies for which corporations are said to be socially responsible and for which they are neither directly nor indirectly causally responsible.[8]

The present argument has four parts. To begin with, it is important to highlight the different relation that exists between an individual (or group) who is aided by a private corporation, and the relation between such an individual (or group) and public attempts to aid their welfare. The differences in these relations will, in practice, often be insignificant—especially when things go well. However, when problems arise theoretical and practical differences can be important. Surely cases could be identified in which corporations have successfully enhanced the public welfare. However, it is not to be expected that corporations will always act so successfully or so clearly in accord with public needs.

The point here is not that corporations may act in misguided ways so much as what happens in those instances where there are problems. Obviously appeals and complaints can be made to the corporation. However, the fact remains that appeals to the corporation tend to be appeals from external constituencies. Inasmuch as those aided by the corporation are not members of the corporation, they have no standing, as it were, within the corporation other than the one the corporation decides to give them. They have no "constitutional" rights against corporations as they do against public endeavors. They are not "citizens" of the corporation. Thus, they have, in principle, no internal access to the corporation's decision-making processes. They are part of that process only if the corporation allows it. Those who make the decisions to undertake various programs cannot be voted out of office—there is no political, and little legal control, over them. Accordingly, to advocate corporate provision of, and responsibility for, public welfare is to advocate that the basic requisites for human well-being are to be provided by institutions whose deliberations, at least at present, do not in principle include representation of those whose interests are affected. Those deficient in welfare lack formal control or power over those agencies from whom they obtain their welfare. Further, since those deficient in welfare tend to be those who are (in general) powerless, the advocacy of corporate responsibility for welfare tends to continue their powerlessness. Corporate social responsibility, in excluding any formal relation between those who are recipients of corporate aid and the corporation, maintains a division between the powerless and the powerful. A democratic society, one would suppose, would seek to moderate, rather than increase, the inequality presupposed in this division.

This situation contrasts with the state or other public bodies which provide, as part of their nature, various forms of administrative, legal and political redress.[9] The state's activities on behalf of its citizenry are hemmed in (at least in principle) by safeguards and guarantees (voting, representation, public hearings, sunshine laws, etc.) which are not imposed on corporations. Indeed, such public forms of access and standing are generally said to be contrary to the corporation's private status. Accordingly, whenever people outside the private corporation are granted such access it is simply due to the benevolence of the corporation.

Now this different relation between individuals and the agencies (private or public) which provide support for them is particularly crucial when that support concerns their basic welfare, i.e. items to which one might reasonably claim a right: e.g., minimal health care, educational opportunities, physical security, shelter, and food. Surely various private institutions such as corporations, churches, etc. may appropriately give aid to those who are deficient in such welfare, when this occurs on an occasional or special basis. Accordingly, private institutions may aid the welfare of their members (those who have access and voice within the organization) as well as non-members (those who do not have such access and voice).

However, those who advocate that this become the normal situation are (implicitly at least) also advocating a condition that places the recipients in a tenuous position vis-á-vis the granting agencies. Though recipients may receive various goods and/or services they need from private corporations, not only are such individuals dependent on those agencies for the aid they receive, but they also lose any formal or "constitutional" voice in the agency which pur-

ports to aid them. In effect, any right they have to such welfare is degraded to an act of benevolence on the part of the contributing organization. They can no longer insist or demand that they be treated in various ways, but must play the role of supplicants.

It is in this kind of situation that the view attributed to Andrew Carnegie can arise unchecked by formal mechanisms to control it: "In the exercise of his trust he was responsible only to his own conscience and judgment of what was best for the community."[10] Recipients of such aid lack means of redress which, in matters of basic importance such as welfare, are terribly significant.

Furthermore, when the institutions (i.e. large business corporations) involved in providing welfare are not themselves dedicated to the welfare of others but primarily focused on their own self-interested economic ends, and when these organizations are extremely large and powerful, then we must reflect on the implications of the lack of membership, and hence the lack of redress and voice, within those organizations. Specifically, we need to consider whether these needs ought not to be met by organizations which will grant those receiving such aid the voice and access which has traditionally protected people who are dependent upon others.

In short, when corporations are asked to undertake public welfare on an ongoing basis, the welfare they give is privatized in a manner that eliminates an important relation for those receiving such welfare. To the extent that it formalizes a relation between the powerful and the powerless, it exposes the recipients of such aid to abuses of power. At the same time, the equality that democracy implies is also jeopardized.[11]

Second, a variation on the preceding point concerns the standards by which decisions on the nature and means of implementing corporate welfare measures are made. Again, this might not appear to be a significant problem with regard to the construction or reconstruction of an inner-city park, a neighborhood clean-up campaign, or reading tutors in the schools.[12] Surely corporations will, by and large, consult with the people involved to get their ideas and approval. On other occasions, the people involved will seek out a corporation to aid them. But this does not lay the issue to rest since the standards the corporation seeks to follow may be primarily private in nature, rather than public or general.[13]

Suppose, for instance, that the welfare measures which the corporation seeks to provide (and to which their recipients agree) are of questionable constitutionality. They agree, perhaps, on educational films with a religious or a racist message for the public schools. Or, suppose they agree on an educational program but the corporation liberally sprinkles the presentation with its corporate logo, mascot, jingo, and the like. Suppose that in training of the hard-core unemployed they aim at white, rather than black or Hispanic, populations. The point at issue concerns the legitimacy of these decisions.

The standards according to which the public welfare is fulfilled must be a matter for the public (through its representatives) to determine, not the private corporation.[14] Two reasons lie behind this claim. Such welfare concerns what is common among the citizens, what holds the members of a society together, and what is the nature of their basic prerequisites. It constitutes a statement about how we, as a community or society, believe that we should live. Fulfillment of welfare deficiencies for some that manifests prejudice against other groups, or works to their disadvantage, requires special justification and close public scrutiny, if it is allowed to stand.

In addition, to the extent that corporate contributions to public welfare are tax deductible, the foregone tax revenues constitute a public contribution to itself, through the agency of the corporation. Since public monies are committed through such contributions, the public has a right to assure itself that the standards according to which such monies are expended meet its (minimal) standards.[15]

Accordingly, the legitimacy of the decisions the private corporation makes regarding public welfare cannot be judged simply according to its own private standards. Thus, if the corporation tries to impose its own view and standards, it is crossing an important line between the private and the public. It is naive, then, simply to argue

that people's welfare is the responsibility of corporations, without providing for social determination and direction of the activities which corporations undertake.[16]

In those instances in which corporate contributions are of a charitable (or prudential) nature *and* the objects of their actions are wholly private, it would seem that corporations might legitimately give to those individuals or organizations which promote their own values and ideas. In this way, their gifts may reflect their own idiosyncratic standards. Accordingly, some object to business giving to private universities whose faculty advocate ideas opposed to capitalism.[17] However, in contrast, the direction and satisfaction of public welfare according to private standards is not appropriate, since the public welfare is not to be determined simply by this or that individual corporation's ideas and values, but by a political process and, ideally a community dialogue, on what those values should be.[18]

Finally, if corporations are said to be responsible for remedying certain deficient levels of public welfare, but are not given control (both in terms of applicable standards and practical direction) over how such remedies are to be emplaced, then when these measures fail the corporation can hardly be held accountable. Nevertheless, since they will be associated with such efforts, they will often be faulted for their lack of success. Hence, if corporations are required to engage in social responsibility efforts, there will be an understandable tendency for them to seek control over the situations in which they participate. This means, however, supplanting (or reducing) public control and substituting their own judgments and standards for those of the public. Consequently, the demand for corporate social responsibility is a demand that encourages the substitution of private standards, authority and control for those of the public.

III

Third, the demand for corporate social responsibility arises, it has been assumed, due to deficient public welfare, which stems, at least in part, from inadequate public funding. Corporate opposition to higher taxes has played a contributing role to this situation, since taxes are viewed as coercive takings of corporate property.[19] The lower the taxes the greater the return on investment corporations make and the greater the flexibility corporations have to use their resources as they choose. Part of the appeal of corporate social responsibility for public welfare is that the aid that is given is voluntary. Provision of such aid heads off higher taxes, government regulation and hence coercion. In short, behind the demand for corporate social responsibility is a view that holds that the public realm and the state constitute a sphere of coercion, while the private realm and the actions it takes are voluntary.[20]

This is illustrated in Friedman's comment that "the political principle that underlies the political mechanism is conformity.... It is appropriate for some to require others to contribute to a general social purpose whether they wish to or not."[21] Corporate social responsibility, then, explicitly seeks to reduce the realm of the public, by reducing the area within which coercion and force might be used.

Now if the public were simply a realm of coercion, such a view would seem unexceptionable. On the contrary, however, such a view arguably distorts the realm of the public. Corporate social responsibility implies that the public is simply an area within which individual prudential interests are worked out and coercion imposed by the state. Both eliminate an important sense of the public.

The public is also the area within which general and common interests are articulated. It is what binds people together, in contrast to the private realm within which people are separated from each other and view each other as limitations upon their freedom.[22] Accordingly, it is the realm of the "we," rather than the "you" or "I." It is what is done in all our names, and not just yours or mine. It is the area, some have even held, within which freedom is only possible.[23] There is (or can be) a different sense of accomplishment when the community builds or creates something rather than simply this or that private organization. Conversely, there is a different sense of loss when a public figure, a

President or Prime Minister dies, rather than the head of a private corporation.

Now charity is an extension of the private into this public realm. It is personal, self-given, and can't be demanded in particular cases. It need not be based on political discussion or compromise so much as on one's own willingness to aid others. Those who receive do not have grounds upon which they can demand or negotiate beyond which the charitable organization allows. Charity does not necessarily involve any political or public process by which recipient and contributor are bound together. Thus, Hannah Arendt comments, "The bond of charity between people ... is incapable of founding a public realm of its own ..."[24] In short, charity cannot be the basis of a public or political dimension between people.

As such, corporate social responsibility drives out the political and the public. The appeal to corporate responsibility is a confession that the public or political realm has broken (or is breaking) down. It is an unwitting manifestation of liberal individualism extending the realm of the private to encompass the public.

Consequently, Friedman is quite wrong when he complains that the doctrine of social responsibility "taken seriously would extend the scope of the political mechanism to every human activity."[25] This is plausible only in that case when the corporation and its executives both engage in social responsibility activities *and*, as a result, become subject to political election procedures since they are viewed as "civil servants."[26] On the other hand, if this does not happen (and there is little present evidence that it will), then the doctrine of social responsibility extends the nature of private activities to many activities in the public or political realm. In short, quite the opposite of what Friedman contends, it extends the scope of the private "to every human activity."

The problem with this approach is that it is implausible to treat society as simply an example of an ideal market situation. This is implied by the above comments on the nature of the public. Not all public (or private) values can be produced or sustained by market exchanges. Friedman slips from discussion of market activities to talk of society without argument. Thus, after he portrays the voluntary nature of the ideal free market, he immediately goes on (without argument) to equate such exchanges with society itself.[27] However, it does not follow (and it is not plausible) to think of society as itself simply an ideal free market. Once again, then, corporate social responsibility involves views and demands which question legitimate distinctions between the private and the public.

IV

Finally, though the relation of the public and the private is a shifting relation, we must guard against collapsing one—either one—term of this relation into the other. The view that the public is simply the arena in which individual actions affect others without their voluntary approval impoverishes the notion of the public.[28] As noted above, the public is more and different than this. The public is what binds a people together and relates them to each other.[29] It is what is done in their common name; it is what makes them a people, rather than simply a random collection of individuals. It embodies the values, norms and ideals we strive towards even if we fail fully to achieve them. It is the responsibility of public agencies (the state or its government) to foster (at least) the minimal conditions under which the public may exist. To be a citizen is to owe allegiance to the government as it works to realize these principles and values.

Now suppose that the government does not fulfill its responsibilities to individuals for basic welfare. The demand that private corporations—rather than the government—dispense public welfare is a step in the privatization of the public realm. The benefits that individuals receive from the government have long been thought to play an important role in their obligations to the state and, hence, their citizenship within the state.[30] If these benefits come from private groups, rather than the state, then one would expect loyalties and obligations to be modified accordingly.

Consequently, if a corporation provides training for the hard-core unemployed, renovates the local park, or provides the house which shelters the sick, it is to the corporation that those aided will be grateful and indebted, not to the community or society of which they are members.[31] It is the corporation to which one's loyalties will be turned, and not to the city or state of which one is a citizen. Indeed, the very notion of citizenship thereby becomes impoverished. The grounds upon which the state has been said to acquire the obligations of its citizenry have been narrowed. In its place develop isolated (groups of) individuals beholden to private institutions of which they are not members (or citizens) and over which they have no formal control.

Surely in these days of popular advertising, the corporation may seem more personal, less abstract, than the community or the state. Through logos, jingoes and mascots corporations seek to get people to identify with them and their products. And through corporate measures to aid their welfare, individuals would have concrete reason to be indebted to them, even if not members or citizens of them. But to accept or promote this situation, and the view of the individual's relations to private and public institutions which it involves, merely reveals the state of poverty to which our notions of the public and citizenship have come. Such corporations encourage us to seek a common identity, rather than to foster our common (public) interests.[32] We are invited to replace the realm of the public which unavoidably involves impersonality with a personal and privatized realm. We transform a realm laden with political meanings into a private and psychologized realm.[33]

However, the danger here does not simply stem from the implications of the altered identifications and loyalties that characterize citizens. The increasing privatization of the public realm that we see in shopping malls, corporate housing developments, the suburban environment, and corporate attempts to establish their own identity and role models within the schools carry other consequences to which we must be keenly sensitive. For example, in private shopping malls people may be prevented from political speech; in corporate housing developments, they may be prohibited from having children and remaining in their home; and cultural exhibits may be skewed to suit corporate purposes.[34] Rights which all citizens share may be wittingly or unwittingly, foregone through private efforts uninformed by public reflection and participation. In short, the public values and interests of a society can be threatened not simply by an authoritarian government but also by self-interested, though well-meaning, private groups and institutions which lack a sense of the significance of the public realm and the meaning of citizenship.

V

In conclusion, several comments are appropriate. First, it may be allowed that many objections which can be brought against corporate attempts to secure public welfare can also be brought against government or public attempts. Thus, both government and corporations may be inflexible, insensitive, impersonal, non-innovative, as well as hard to move or get through to. They may produce programs which are misconceived, uncoordinated, and/or precipitously stopped, leaving people in the lurch. The production of such programs may increase their power, size and influence; they may also deal paternalistically with those they seek to aid. One would be tempted to abandon all attempts to aid those deficient in welfare were it not for the fact that many people continue to suffer grievously from inadequate welfare. Thus, the question is a complex and messy one. There is no easy and neat answer.

Second, large corporations, however, will continue to be part of our social and political landscape. Their significant economic and political power are obvious. In this situation, the thrust of the public/private argument is two-sided. It can be taken to urge the separation of private corporations and public institutions. This is fraught with all the problems of bureaucratization, distant government, powerful but indifferent corporations, and failed efforts to satisfy public welfare needs. This is not to say that these problems could not be overcome within a fairly strict separation of the private and the public.[35] Still, this would involve a recommitment (and rediscovery!) of the public realm that might be difficult in countries such as the U.S.

On the other hand, the above argument can also be taken to recommend that we require such large corporations be made more fully public, social organizations. Indeed, many argue that large corporations are no longer simply private organizations. George C. Lodge, for example, comments that "it is now obvious that our large public corporations are not private property at all... The best we can say," he continues, "is that the corporation is a sort of collective, floating in philosophic limbo, dangerously vulnerable to the charge of illegitimacy and to the charge that it is not amenable to community control."[36] Thus, that corporations increasingly are called to participate in the production of public welfare is not so surprising given their present, quasi-public nature. The further claim that has been made is that this quasi-public nature needs to be institutionalized so as to make it amenable to greater public control and direction. This direction, however, is one that others violently oppose.

Thus, we stand at a crossroads. This juncture is part and parcel of that "tension between self-reliant competitive enterprise and a sense of public solidarity espoused by civic republicans" that some have identified as "the most important unresolved problem in American history."[37] If one rejects the view that corporations must more fully take on the character of public institutions, then demands for corporate social responsibility for public welfare should be seriously curtailed.

The preceding arguments do not show conclusively that corporations ought never to aid public welfare. They are one set of considerations which might, in some circumstances, be overridden. However, they do indicate important reasons why we should be more reluctant to proceed down the path that many have been encouraging us to take. When we are repeatedly told that the sight of corporate social responsibility is so lovely, and that the prospects of corporate responsibility for public welfare are so rosy, one may rightfully come to suspect that we are being led down the garden path.[38]

Notes

1. "Private corporation" will be used to refer exclusively to private corporations engaged in the production of goods and services for profit.
2. Sandra L. Holmes reports in a study of how executives perceive social responsibility that 78% of the execu-

tives surveyed either strongly agreed or agreed more than they disagreed with the statement that "Business possesses the ability and means to be a *major* force in the alleviation of social problems" (pp. 39–40). It is clear from the context that by "social problems" is meant the kinds of problems listed in the text under "public welfare." Cf. Sandra L. Holmes, "Executive Perceptions of Corporate Social Responsibility," *Business Horizons* (June, 1976).

3. Theodore Levitt, "The Dangers of Social Responsibility," *Harvard Business Review*, vol. 36 (September–October, 1958), pp. 44–47.

4. George C. Lodge, *The New American Ideology* (New York: Alfred A. Knopf, 1975), p. 189.

5. Ibid., p. 190. Cf., also p. 218.

6. DeGeorge, *Business Ethics*, 3rd ed. (New York: Macmillan Publishing Co., 1986), p. 171.

7. Cf. Levitt, "The Dangers of Social Responsibility."

8. The importance of indirect causal factors and the resulting responsibility of corporations has been defended by Larry May in his comments, "Corporate Philanthropy and Social Responsibility," given on an earlier version of this paper, before the Society for Business Ethics meeting in Boston, MA, on December 28, 1990. How we might determine for which harms corporations are directly or indirectly causally responsible is not addressed in this paper. Both topics, but especially the latter, raise significant problems.

9. Even if this is not true in any particular case, it is still appropriate to demand such access and forms of redress of present (i.e., democratic or republican) forms of government.

10. Robert H. Bremner, *American Philanthropy* (2nd ed.; Chicago: The University of Chicago Press, 1988), p. 101.

11. This argument allows that other private organizations, such as churches, etc., may legitimately contribute to individuals' welfare needs. The smaller the organization, the more individual the contribution, and the greater the identity of the organization is bound up with promoting the public good, the less there is a problem. On the other hand, some organizations, such as churches, run into problems (e.g., First Amendment issues and attempts to convert others rather than simply aid them) that other private groups do not.

12. Even the park example is not all that simple. There are questions that need to be asked before the park can be built or renovated: what will be the nature and form of the park? Who will maintain it (will anyone?)? Will trash containers be put out and regularly emptied (by whom?)? Is the construction of this park likely to require increased police patrols? Are additional burdens being placed on the city recreational department, trash department, police department? If so, who decides and upon what basis? Admittedly, these questions must be faced whether the city *or* a corporation builds the park. However, the important point is that when corporations aid public welfare many important questions remain to be answered. The city or the public is not suddenly let off the hook.

13. The problem is even more complex since those individuals the corporation addresses in the public forum may themselves primarily hold private values. That is, their vision of themselves and society may have lost any sense of the public. Bellah et al document the degree to which "Americans . . . are genuinely ambivalent about public life" (Bellah et al, *Habits of the Heart* [Berkeley: University of California Press, 1985], p. 250).

14. Similarly for a host of other projects there are questions which demand social or public decision, which only the public through the government can legitimately give. For example, it might be asked whether it is really so bad for corporations to provide tutors for secondary schools to help with basic reading skills. But are these tutors trained in teaching? Do they serve to justify inadequate teaching staffs? Do they undercut the demands of teachers for adequate social commitment for education? What programs are they trained to teach? Do they constitute an influx of business oriented courses rather than humanity courses, or science courses? These are serious issues which need to be addressed on the social and public level, not simply on the private corporation level.

Likewise, it might be asked whether it is wrong for corporations (e.g., McDonald's) to start drives for houses for relatives of the seriously ill to stay in while at the hospital. But again, supposing that the rest of the community contributes the preponderant amount, why should the community not get the credit for the house? Why doesn't the name of the house reflect public values or ideals?

We need not assume that public answers to all these questions may be easily arrived at. However, if corporations (or other private groups) simply operate on their own standards, the public discussion which may lead to public standards and agreement will be short-circuited. As a result, the public will be impoverished.

15. This claim applies to similar contributions that come from other private groups, e.g., churches, the Audubon Society, etc. When such contributions come from small and numerous groups, there is less reason for concern since they may counterbalance each other. It is reasonable for a society to encourage such contributions. Nevertheless, society may legitimately review the nature of their contributions, given that their contributions are tax deductible and they enjoy (where applicable) tax-exempt status.

This issue is particularly of concern, however, when such contributions come from large corporations which can bring significant power and resources to bear. Similarly, when churches or other private groups become large and their powers significant, the consideration raised in the text applies as well. In short, when the contributions of private groups are supported by the public through tax deductions and when those contributions may in particular cases have a significant effect on the public, the public may legitimately review the standards according to which the contributions are made.

16. For example, Control Data's program, called "City Venture," which sought to write blueprints for economic rebirth of down-and-out city neighborhoods had to be withdrawn: "A bossy, 'we know what's best' attitude offended prickly independent community groups in Minneapolis and Miami, forcing City Venture to be withdrawn" (Neil R. Peirce, "To Corporate Social Involvement," *The Knoxville Journal*, 1982, p. A4).

17. Robert H. Malott, "Corporate Support of Education: Some Strings Attached," *Harvard Business Review*, vol. 56 (1978), pp. 133–38.

18. This is not to say that corporations, or anyone, must (or should) give to causes they believe to be wrong-headed. Rather, if corporations (or other organizations) are given responsibility for public welfare, they may not simply apply their own idiosyncratic standards. This allows, of course, that they could choose, from a range of public welfare needs, to support those compatible with their own views. Since the issue concerns basic deficiencies from which people suffer, this should not be impossible.

19. Similarly Levitt argues: "American capitalism also creates, fosters, and acquiesces in enormous social and economic cancers. Indeed, it fights against the achievement of certain forms of economic and social progress, pouring millions into campaigns against things which people have a right to expect from their government. . ." (Levitt, "The Dangers of Social Responsibility," p. 48).

20. Since corporate social responsibility is, usually, viewed either as charitable or as prudential in nature, corporations can make their own, voluntary choices as to when, what and how much they will do. The alternative is to have the public (the state or the government) take more from them in order to fulfill the public welfare needs. Because this restricts their choices—their freedom (as they would see it)—they argue against state action here. In short, corporate social responsibility is an expression of the liberal view of society. It is also an expression of an individualistic view: "utilitarian individualism" and "expressive individualism" (Bellah et al, Habits of the Heart, p. 27ff). These views contrast with what they call "civic republicanism."

21. Milton Friedman, "The Social Responsibility of Business is to Increase its Profits, in Milton Snoeyenbos, Robert Almeder, James Humber (eds.), *Business Ethics* (Buffalo, New York: Prometheus Books, 1983), p. 78.

22. Ibid., pp. 245, 248.

23. Nancy L. Schwartz, "Distinction Between Public and Private Life," *Political Theory*, vol. 7 (1979), p. 245.

24. Hannah Arendt, *The Human Condition* (Chicago: The University of Chicago Press, 1958), p. 53.

25. Milton Friedman, "The Social Responsibility of Business is to Increase its Profits," in Milton Snoeyenbos, Robert Almeder, James Humber (eds.), *Business Ethics* (Buffalo, New York: Prometheus Books, 1983), p. 79.

26. Friedman, "The Social Responsibility of Business is to Increase its Profits, p. 75.

27. Ibid.

28. Cf. John Dewey, *The Public and its Problems* (Chicago: Gateway Books, 1946).

29. Cf. Hannah Arendt, "The public realm, as the common world, gathers us together and yet prevents our falling over each other, so to speak"; *The Human Condition* (Chicago: The University of Chicago Press, 1958), p. 52.

30. Cf. A. John Simmons, *Moral Principles and Political Obligations* (Princeton: Princeton University Press, 1979), pp. 157–90.

31. The following comes from a letter to an editor from a mother of a child in a school adopted by IBM. She was responding to objections that others had raised because children in the school were preparing posters and having assemblies to thank IBM for adopting their school. She argues: "to say that this is taking away from the children's learning time is not true. What better learning experience is there than to teach our children what's going on in their schools and to have them have a special program to thank these companies? . . . I believe it is very important that these adopting companies realize, by way of parents and children, that we are honored and grateful that they are willing to help 'our' children with their education" (Letters to the Editor," *The Knoxville News-Sentinel*, November 28, 1986).

32. Cf. Richard Sennett who complains that as part of the end of public culture "the pursuit of common interests is destroyed in the search for a common identity" (p. 261); *The Fall of Public Man* (New York: Vintage Books, 1976).

33. Cf. Sennett, Ibid.

34. IBM, for example, "barred the display of computer-art works designed for the equipment of a major business competitor, Macintosh, in the company's heretofore prestigious IBM Gallery of Science and Art in midtown Manahattan"; Susan Davis, "IBM Nixes Macintosh," *Art in America*, vol. 76 (1990), p. 47. The works barred were part of a touring show organized by the Walker Art Center. IBM, which finances its namesake galleries, "bars its competition 'as a matter of policy'" (Ibid., p. 47).

35. It would not, for example, prohibit linking education and business in various ways. Various courses of study in schools might be coordinated with job opportunities in private business, without corporations providing for those courses or other educational needs. Public and government welfare measures would have to be tied much more closely to local needs and allowed much greater flexibility in resolving those needs.

36. Lodge, *The New American Ideology*, p. 18.

37. Bellah et al, *Habits of the Heart*, p. 256.

38. I am indebted to John Hardwig, W. Michael Hoffman, Larry May, Richard Nunan, and an anonymous referee for their perceptive and helpful comments on earlier versions of this paper.

1. What does Friedman mean when he says that "in a free society, it is hard for 'good' people to do 'good,' but that is a small price to pay for making it hard for 'evil' people to do 'evil' "? Do you agree or disagree and why?
2. Many commentators feel that Friedman's position implies ethical egoism. Do you agree? Why or why not?
3. Why does Lippke characterize Friedman's approach as the "Abstract Individuals Approach" (*AIA*)? How does it differ from what he calls the "Social Contract Approach" (*SCA*)?
4. Could Friedman accept Lippke's "Social Niche Approach" (*SNA*)? If not, what criticisms do you think he would make of it?

5. Brenkert claims that "the appeal to corporate responsibility is a confession that the public or political realm has broken (or is breaking) down?" Do you agree? Why or why not?
6. Does Brenkert's argument demonstrate that corporations should not act philanthropically? How would Brenkert respond to the suggestion that businesses have an obligation to act philanthropically, but that the standards that govern their actions should be set politically?

CASE 16:1 SOCIALLY RESPONSIBLE LOANS

It is well known that major banks are wary of making loans in low-income neighborhoods. Loans are available from second-mortgage companies, but at a much higher rate of interest. Federal and state governments have shown little interest in regulating these companies, and as a consequence, there are few limits on what interest rates they can charge. Rates of 20 or 30 percent are not uncommon and service fees often further inflate the cost of borrowing. In many instances, elderly homeowners in low-income neighborhoods are actively targeted. Such homeowners frequently receive phone calls from mortgage brokers wishing to lend them money. Recipients of such phone calls are well advised to think very carefully before borrowing, since the number of people who have lost their homes through such second mortgages is remarkably high. For example, a study by a Boston community group revealed that over 80 percent of the homeowners who took out mortgages with the second mortgage lender Resource Financial Group lost their homes or were facing foreclosure. Even more revealing was the fact that 90 percent of Resource's loans were in low-income minority neighborhoods where the mainstream banks are reluctant to make loans.[1]

What is less well known is that many banks lend second mortgage companies money for operating expenses and frequently purchase home equity loan contracts from these companies. From 1990 until 1991, the number of big banks buying home equity loans on the secondary market grew from 12.5 percent to 20.9 percent.[2]

The banks disclaim any responsibility for the sometimes shady practices of mortgage brokers on the basis that these companies are entirely separate businesses and that the banks have no way of knowing when abuses have taken place. Critics urge that banks are at least partially responsible for the problem inasmuch as they have denied low-income communities mainstream credit.

CASE STUDY QUESTIONS

1. Do banks have any responsibility to lend money in low-income communities?
2. Should the amount of interest that can be charged on a loan be regulated? If it should, then by whom?

CASE 16:2 BUSINESS AND PUBLIC EDUCATION

In a time when there is increasing concern over the ability of government to provide adequate funding of the public school system, many are suggesting

that corporate sponsors play a role in schools. In Toronto, Ontario the school board recently signed an agreement with Pepsi-Cola. Under the agreement, Pepsi gets exclusive sales access to vending machines selling pop and juice to the student population. The agreement also includes the distribution of promotional videos featuring celebrities speaking on topics such as drug abuse and "Pepsi student of the month awards," in which students win Pepsi clothing and have their names inscribed on plaques donated by Pepsi.[3] This is not an isolated practice in public schools. In return for television news and advertising packages involving the loan of a satellite dish and television sets for each classroom, many school boards in the United States require their students to watch advertising provided by corporate sponsors. One popular contract stipulates that 90 percent of the children in a school must watch the program 90 percent of the time it is shown, and that each program must be watched in its entirety, i.e., the show cannot be interrupted and the teacher does not have the right to turn it off.[4] Inasmuch as students are required by law to be in school and the schools are obliged to honor the contract, advertisers are assured of an audience. An even bigger role for business may be forthcoming. Burger King has opened a number of accredited high schools and many other corporations are considering opening profit-making schools as alternatives to publicly funded institutions.

CASE STUDY QUESTIONS

1. Some shareholders have expressed concern that they pay taxes to support education and that corporate donations to education constitute a second tax they ought not to have to pay. Do you agree or disagree and why?
2. Critics of corporate sponsorship have expressed concern that corporate donations are heavily tied to advertising. Should corporate sponsors be allowed to tie their donations to advertising? Why or why not?
3. Are corporately backed alternative for-profit schools a good idea? Defend your answer.

Notes
1. Michael Hudson, "Loan Scams That Prey on the Poor," *Business and Society Review*, No. 84, Winter 1993, pp. 11–15, p. 12.
2. Hudson, p. 13.
3. Naomi Klein, "Only Pepsi To Be Sold in Schools," *Toronto Globe and Mail*, Jan 15th, 1994 A1.
4. Jonathan Kozol, "Kids as Commodities: The Folly of For-Profit Schools," *Business and Society Review*, No. 84, Winter 1993, pp. 16–20, p. 16.

FOR FURTHER READING

1. Thomas Donaldson, "Constructing a Social Contract for Business," in *Corporations and Morality* (Englewood Cliffs, NJ: Prentice Hall, 1982) pp. 18–35.

2. John Kultgen, "Donaldson's Social Contract for Business," *Business & Professional Ethics Journal*, Vol. 5, No. 1, 1985, pp. 28–50.

3. Theodore Levitt, "The Dangers of Social Responsibility," *Harvard Business Review*, Vol. 36, September/October, 1958, pp. 41–50.

4. Fred D. Miller, Jr. and John Ahrens, "The Social Responsibility of Corporations" in *Commerce and Morality*, edited by Tibor R. Machan (Totowa, NJ: Rowman & Littlefield, 1988), pp. 140–160.

5. Thomas Mulligan, "A Critique of Milton Friedman's Essay 'The Social Responsibility of Business Is to Increase Its Profits,'" *Journal of Business Ethics*, Vol. 5, 1986, pp. 265–269.

Chapter Seventeen

Business and the International Community

Introduction

In Chapter Seventeen we consider some of the many ethical issues that arise in the course of doing business internationally. In considering this topic, we do well to remember that most, if not all of the ethical issues discussed in this text can be raised not only in a domestic but also in an international context. In most instances, doing business in foreign markets does not so much present us with new issues, but rather with familiar problems that must be addressed in an unfamiliar context. Ethical issues introduced earlier in the text are met again here in an international setting. What is true is that the international context generally makes these already very complicated issues concerning intellectual property, pollution, gender equality, and marketing even more difficult.

In his article "The Moral Legitimacy of Intellectual Property Claims: American Business and Developing Country Perspectives," Paul Steidlmeier comments on the increasing tension between developed and developing countries over the issue of intellectual property claims. Developed countries with strong business cultures view intellectual property as private property and argue that it deserves strong protection in the interests of encouraging research and development. Less developed countries tend to view intellectual property as a form of common property which should be accessible to all. There exists a debate over whether the monopoly claims of patents and copyrights asserted by the businesses of developed countries are legitimate. Steidlmeier goes on to note several factors that complicate the debate. Among these factors are the fact that property is understood differently at different times and in different cultures, and tension exists between individual and social values. Although he avoids drawing firm conclusions concerning how the debate should be resolved, Steidlmeier seems unconvinced that intellectual property rights can be justified in their present form. He appears open to viewing intellectual property as primarily a form of common property which may take limited private forms.

Jang B. Singh and V. C. Lakhan discuss the growing tendency of industrialized countries to export hazardous wastes to third-world countries in their article "Business Ethics and the International Trade in Hazardous Wastes." They argue that to export wastes to countries which do not benefit from the industrial processes which produce these wastes and whose citizens do not maintain lifestyles which lead to the production of such wastes, is unethical. They also argue that decisions to import hazardous wastes are often made by governments which hold power by force and have no democratic mandate to expose their populations to the risks involved.

In "Ethics and the Gender Equality Dilemma for U.S. Multinationals," Don Mayer and Anita Cava explore the difficulties of applying American views on gender and racial equality in foreign markets. They attempt to avoid both cultural relativism and ethnocentrism, suggesting there are minimum universal principles that can be legitimately broadened to include gender and racial equality. It is useful to compare their treatment of this issue with Mary Midgley's general treatment of cultural relativism ("Trying Out One's New Sword") in Chapter Two.

James C. Baker's article "The International Infant Formula Controversy: A Dilemma in Corporate Social Responsibility" explores the decision of Nestlé and other producers of infant formula to market infant formula in less-developed countries and the international boycott that emerged in response to that decision. Baker's article illustrates the complexity that is often characteristic of ethical issues. An analysis of the controversy reveals that empirical data to support assertions made by those opposed to marketing infant formula in lesser-developed countries was scarce, and in many instances ambiguous. It also becomes clear that Nestlé, although certainly not beyond criticism, was not the corporate villain it was often portrayed as. Nevertheless, the boycott led to an improvement in marketing practices and better research on issues of formula usage and breastfeeding.

Paul Steidlmeier

The Moral Legitimacy of Intellectual Property Claims: American Business and Developing Country Perspectives

I. THE GROWING DEBATE OVER INTELLECTUAL PROPERTY

In international trade and development circles a battle is raging over intellectual property. The term intellectual property generally covers, patents, copyrights, trademarks and trade secrets. The essence of the current debate is whether such items should be protected by governments on a global scale and, if so, to what extent.

The theoretical positions on intellectual property rights vary widely as do the practical prospects for actually protecting anything at all in particular regions. Nowhere is the difference more sharp than between the developed and developing countries. The developed countries argue that strong protection of intellectual property is essential to provide incentives for future innovations and to ensure the competitive profitability of companies that spend on research. The developing countries are more interested in the diffusion of technology and generally support only very weak protection of intellectual property. This paper reviews the positions adopted by each side in deciding whether intellectual property rights are really rights rather

From Paul Steidlmeier, "The Moral Legitimacy of Intellectual Property Claims: American Business and Developing Country Perspectives," *Journal of Business Ethics*, Vol. 12, 1993. Reprinted by permission of Kluwer Academic Publishers.

than privileges and outlines the conditions to be met by an international intellectual property regime if it is to possess moral validity. In what follows I first clarify the notion of property and then review the claims put forth by developed and developing countries to legitimate their views.

II. INTELLECTUAL PROPERTY AND PRIVATE, COMMON AND PUBLIC FORMS OF PROPERTY

Ownership of property is

1. a *right* that people have regarding
2. a (commercial) *resource*
3. over *time* (Munzer, 1990; Reeve, 1986).

The modern Western notion of property (derived principally from John Locke and Adam Smith) recognizes the property owner as the one having the *greatest possible interest* in a thing (consistent with a fair legal system). That is, from the start the property owner is recognized as the *principal stakeholder* but not the only stakeholder in the product or process which is denominated as property. The rights of owners over such assets consist in the power to use, obtain income from and exchange the assets, while denying such determinative power to other parties. At the same time, property owners must be mindful of the legitimate rights of third parties. Third parties have a stake in another's private property rights if they are affected by the consequences of the owner's property decisions (Freeman, 1984). Legal examples are provided by zoning regulations and the granting of rights of way. The rights of these other stakeholders are defined in terms of the property owner's *duties*. The moral question is this: with respect to a particular asset what constitutes a fair set of reciprocal rights and duties between all stakeholders, defined as those with a legitimate interest in a resource or asset denominated as property?

Even when something is recognized as property, however, there are different approaches to specifying its nature in terms of

1. *private* individual,
2. *common* and
3. *public* (government) forms of property.

Common property differs from private individual property in that under common property access is granted to all, although some individuals may enjoy specific use-rights. For example, in most of Sub-Saharan African agriculture land is considered *common property* while clans, families and individuals are granted use-rights. Also, in the United States, most sources of water are common property which are publicly administered through the grant of use-rights. Public property differs from common property in that the government is the owner (of forest land in the U.S., for example) and the decision-making authority regarding the property is vested in government acting in a fiduciary capacity on behalf of all the people. The people themselves, however, hardly exercise any property rights as such (in terms of allocation and exchange of property).

Western business increasingly views "not yet specifically applied" technology as

1. a commodity with commercial value— expressed in direct sales, licensing, and contracts for technical, management and engineering assistance—and
2. as private property.

Developing countries tend to view such technology as non-commercial scientific knowledge and, therefore, as a sort of a "common property" transferable to them without payment to the discoverer(s). In the intellectual property debate, therefore, U.S. business interests are claiming private property rights while developing countries assert that such property—if indeed it can be "property"—is common or public property.

The principal questions for ethical research which emerge from this discussion are

1. what counts as property, and
2. to what extent may owners establish exclusive claims over it.

The debate is complicated by the fact that the words "ownership" and "property" have different meanings in various social and historical settings. "Property" in Aristotle, the Bible, Aquinas, Kant, Locke or Marx does not represent an univocal concept. This for two reasons. First, what counts as property changes historically. In many areas two hundred years ago, for example, slaves and even women represented socially legitimate property. In the twentieth century Western world they do not. Even the defense of something like land as private property is not unambiguous. For example, land as private property in the middle ages meant feudal institutions of property; in much of Latin America today it may mean institutions of landed estates (*latifundiae*). It emerges that "property" is a tremendously dynamic and fluid reality both in *concept* and *historical sociological form*. It is inseparable from cultural values and legal traditions.

While an asset such as land has almost universally counted as property, an intellectual discovery generally has not. Something resembling patents existed in sixteenth century Italy and in seventeenth century England. The first set of completely formalized procedures only appeared in 1790 [in the United States] (Congressional Quarterly, 1990). In the rest of Western Europe patent law was very much a nineteenth century development which has been subject to almost continual modification of conditions. To patent scientific ideas and information as property is a very new development in human history indeed. Traditionally, intellectual ideas have been treated as part of the public domain—much like the alphabet or nuclear physics. While applications, such as a particular keyboard or a nuclear plant design, might be patented or copyrighted the idea itself could not be.

This scenario is further complicated when one adds the dimensions of the *exclusion of others* and *time*. Time not only raises the issues of inheritance but of the limits of monopoly power associated with patents and copyrights. One point put forward by developing countries in the intellectual property debate calls for restricting the period of patent monopoly, rather than granting patent holders generous monopolies of seventeen years or more. Exclusion of others is especially called into question when the property owner does little or nothing with the property for the public good. The alleged failure to productively exploit patents has led Brazil and India to adopt the policy of compulsory licensing and even the loss of patent rights (Gadbaw and Richards, 1988, pp. 4, 167, 203).

In what follows I discuss in turn the approaches to intellectual property rights put forth by American business interests and the counter position articulated by the Government of India (1989) in the context of the current Uruguay round of the General Agreement on Tariffs and Trade (GATT) negotiations. India has emerged as the principal voice of the developing countries.

III. LEGITIMATING WHAT COUNTS AS PROPERTY AND PROVIDING FOR EXCLUSION

Property rights are a deeply philosophical issue—the thorniest point being the legitimation of a set of property claims. Claims to property are rationalized in a variety of ways. The most absolute legitimation is theological where God's will, providence and "manifest destiny" are appealed to as having conferred these rights upon the chosen. Such arguments have been brought to bear to justify colonialism; they are also put forth by parties who wish to settle land in the Middle East. In today's pluralistic world, however, theological reasoning does not find widespread acceptance across creeds and cultures and people are seeking a more secular philosophical rationale. It is not all that clear that intellectual property rights are really "rights." In the intellectual property debate it is often forgotten that the property rights advocated by American companies are primarily based upon modern Western values and culture. I say modern, because many contemporary capitalists have forgotten the way Adam Smith linked property rights to distributive justice, not just to self interest (Johnson, 1989). Furthermore, Islamic cultures, which stretch from Morocco to Indonesia and account for almost a quarter of the world's population, articulate a coherent, sophisticated and distinctively non-

Western view of property rights (Behdad, 1989). Buddhism (Pryor, 1990; 1991) also possesses a long and nuanced tradition regarding economics and property rights. Hinduism (Uppal, 1986), which forms the backdrop for the Indian position, has definite implications for patterns of economic development. The end result is that while intellectual property rights are a global issue, it is notoriously difficult to establish a global basis for their legitimation.

Granting this complexity and the meta-ethical issues it raises, in what follows I confine myself to three general sets of philosophical arguments which are often cited to legitimate a set of property rights:

1. liberty and self-realization;
2. rights to livelihood; and
3. rights to the fruit of one's labor and effort.

All of these rights are associated with efficiency, social benefits and the common good. In what follows I examine in turn the U.S. Business and developing country positions.

The Business Arguments

The arguments put forth by U.S. companies in favor of tightening up international intellectual property law and enforcement reflect the legal position set forth in Article I, Section 8, of the U.S. Constitution which granted to Congress the power:

To promote the progress of science and useful arts, by securing for limited times to authors and inventors, the exclusive right to their respective writing and discoveries.

This Constitutional orientation has spawned six different regimes of U.S. intellectual property law, including copyright, patent, semiconductor chip and trademark protection at the Federal level and trade secret and misappropriation of other information at State levels (Besen and Raskind, 1991).

Incentives and rewards form the centerpiece of the American heritage regarding the purpose of an intellectual property protection system. Yet the rationale of intellectual property protection is based on more fundamental principles that lead proponents to argue that intellectual property claims are based on rights, not mere privileges.

A moral right identifies an interest which any individual should be free to pursue as s/he chooses. Furthermore, the free pursuit of such interests cannot be subordinated to the interests of others. In discussing whether intellectual property is such a fundamental interest a number of reasons come to the fore.

The first major argument advanced for private property in general is tied to the right of liberty and a correlative view of the creative self-fulfillment of the person. According to this philosophical position the possession of property confers a degree of freedom and self-determination upon the possessor. Rather than being subjected to others for their sustenance, property confers upon people the possibility of being subjects of their own destiny. Property ownership enables people to decide some of the details of their lives for themselves. In this context, property rights are an expression of liberty and linked to the innovative process in terms of creative liberation of human potential. The free creative process is cumulative. In general business wants the inventive process to be as free as possible. Business interests have been very active in trying to get the government to remove anti-trust regulations which might affect cooperative research and exchange of information.

The second general argument put forth by business for the protection of intellectual property advances from reflections upon the free, creative processes of property creation to rights to the fruit of one's labor. Intuitively, people have argued for centuries that those who work and make an effort have a right to the fruits of their labor. This argument was formalized by John Locke in his famed example of the hunter going into the forest to hunt a deer (Locke, 1965). Locke's argument assumes plentiful natural resources as well as conditions of fair access—assumptions of questionable realism. The point is that labor creates assets and the value of those assets accrues to the laborer.

U.S. business presents the "fruits of labor" argument collectively in terms of the enterprise. The pharmaceutical industry, for example, claims that on average it costs over $100 million

to develop a new drug and bring it to market (Pfizer, 1989). Pharmaceuticals are easily cloned and the industry is one of the more seriously affected by pirating (U.S. International Trade Commission, 1989). Cloning, it is asserted, unjustly robs the company of the fruit of its labor.

The third principal argument of U.S. business is based upon incentives to innovate. Many American businesses spend on average 5% to 10% on their sales on research (U.S. Patent and Trademark Office, 1990). Business leaders argue that if the fruits of their expenditures on research and development are not effectively protected, then incentives to innovate will perish. In the long-run, a decline in innovation will lead to stagnation of the economy and significant social harm in terms of lost jobs, the erosion of community tax-bases, and the decline in general well-being which continued innovation proffers. This argument is more utilitarian in nature and claims that strong protection of intellectual property rights will lead to the most beneficial social consequences. The point is set in the context of efficient use of property and the overall social benefits generated thereby. The future welfare of humanity sorely depends upon technological innovation. It will not be forthcoming at the desired rate unless it is protected. This position reflects a view of human motivation suggested by Adam Smith when he argues that people will manage best when they have a personal stake in the outcome. This view of human psychology and economic activity led to his belief in the greatest social utility being produced by the invisible hand of property owners and entrepreneurs interacting in a climate of fair competition. Transposed to the modern context, the argument is that protecting intellectual property rights creates incentives which, in turn, will induce greater overall efficiency and welfare in the economy.

Developing Country Arguments

Developing countries have generally taken a different approach to property claims (Deardorff, 1990). The fact that property is so linked to liberty and self-actualization is an argument developing countries employ for destroying rather than bolstering monopoly powers in property. At issue here are points such as negotiating the time of patent protection (with reference to a fair return on investment), compulsory licensing, the removal of trade barriers, access to credit, and measures to create new instruments of technology transfer.

In discussing the pressure exerted by the United States on South Korea regarding intellectual property, the (then) Ambassador to the United States, Mr. Kyung-Won Kim (1986) wrote:

Historically, Koreans have not viewed intellectual discoveries or scientific inventions as the private property of their discoverers or inventors. New ideas or technologies were "public goods" for everybody to share freely. Cultural esteem rather than material gain was the incentive for creativity.

Mr. Kim raised the question of whether intellectual property is not, after all, common property. Mr. Kim criticized the exercise of monopoly power with reference to intellectual property rights. In essence he was suggesting that the set of intellectual property rights proposed by the Untied States and other OECD countries was illegitimate. In this he found lots of company of the likes of Brazil, India, Taiwan, Singapore, Mexico, China and others. His argument counters the individualist argument by placing liberty and creativity in a more communitarian framework. The emphasis is upon the liberty and creativity of a people not just an individual. As Joseph Needham (1981) has shown in his exhaustive studies of China, such cultural frameworks can provide the basis for tremendous innovation.

If, indeed, intellectual property is a right, it is one conferred by society and is a secondary right. The Government of India (1989, p. 1) makes the case that intellectual property rights are necessarily relative:

The essence of the [intellectual property protection] system is its monopolistic and restrictive character; its purpose is not to "liberalise," but to confer exclusive rights on their owners. Recognising the extraordinary implications of the system, international conventions on this subject incorporate, as a central philosophy, the freedom of the member states to

attune their intellectual property protection system to their own needs and conditions. This fundamental principle should inform and guide all of the discussions in the Negotiating Group on the intellectual property protection system.

The reason India argues for the freedom of member states to set the fundamental conditions for intellectual property rights is that it believes that any principles or standards which govern intellectual property should be true to the socio-economic, developmental, technological and public interest priorities and needs of developing countries. Very specific concrete policies follow from the Indian position: patents must be fully worked (or exploited) in the host country, licensing of rights may be made compulsory, and certain areas (such as food, pharmaceuticals, agricultural chemicals, and biogenetic innovations) may be excluded from patentability altogether. India's position finds great sympathy in developing countries on both developmental and moral (fairness) grounds (Lepp, 1990; Rapp and Rozek, 1990; Siebeck, 1990).

In essence, therefore, developing countries argue that individual claims on intellectual property are subordinated to more fundamental claims of social well-being. Unlike inalienable rights, intellectual property rights can be subordinated to greater interests; in this case the right of a people to livelihood. In this view, intellectual property is primarily a form of common property which may take some limited private forms.

The developing country position regarding rights to livelihood follow from the above. Attention must be paid to the logic of the development position. For people to be able to live they must be able to either produce what they need or be able to purchase it. In agrarian societies having some land is directly linked to livelihood. This point assumes importance in terms of setting forth a comprehensive set of property rights for all *peoples and persons*. Developing countries implicitly reject the "trickle down theory" of development and limited technology transfer linked to private intellectual property rights. They shift priorities and define property rights first in a social and, then, in a private way. The argument contends that the "right to livelihood" (read development) takes precedence over other claims upon which property rights are based. In essence, therefore, such a position presents essentially the same arguments which would be put forth in arguing for radical land reform: the present system of intellectual property rights violates the (cultural) norms of distributive justice. The needs of the poor take priority over the wants of the rich. To this end the Government of India (1989, pp. 7) argues:

It is relevant to note that the food, pharmaceutical and chemical sectors have been accorded a different treatment in the patent laws of developing countries because of the critical nature of these sectors to their socioeconomic and public interests.

Developing countries are arguing that the rights of people to development take a certain priority over private property claims (Government of India, 1989). The statement goes on to link patent monopolies to predatory pricing in pharmaceutical and agro-chemical sectors and concludes (p. 8):

Every country should therefore be free to determine both the general categories as well as the specific products or sectors that it wishes to exclude from patentability . . .

The argument of developing countries is that while people may have a right to the fruit of their labor, they have a duty to reward society which practically made the very fruitfulness of labor possible. The historical patterns of interdependence (if not dependence) between peoples evokes a concern for the equitable sharing of benefits and bearing of costs. Some Third World countries voice the argument that the R&D infrastructure enjoyed in the first world was built off the labor of the poor and extracted by the Monroe doctrine, European colonialism and other rationalizations of "manifest destiny." That is, the historical conditions which have given rise to the opportunity set enjoyed by first world intellectual labor is not a moot point. For the private fruits of innovative labor were only made possible by the common property of research and development (R&D)

infrastructure. To the extent that this infrastructure was historically built from developing country resources, developing countries have a claim on the results. The costs which developing countries have borne may be measured not only by riches taken out but also by policies and practices which internally disrupted their proper development if not creating their underdevelopment. To put it bluntly, they claim that Third World labor has not always been equitably rewarded by First World business concerns. There are residual claims to be taken into account.

Regarding economic efficiency, developing countries argue that the marginal productivity of new technologies, when employed in the Third World, is far greater than in the first. The marginal argument means that the developed countries are already saturated in new technologies. While concentration of technologies in the developed world will continue to lead to productive growth, that growth is far smaller than the level of growth which would be unleashed if these technologies were introduced to the developing world where they are absent. To take an example from agriculture, Japan applies over 380 kilograms (kg) of fertilizer to a hectare (ha) of farmland. Additional applications of fertilizer will not significantly increase farm output at the margin. But that same fertilizer applied to farmland in a developing country where less than 20 kg/ha are now used, would dramatically increase output (Steidlmeier, 1987). It is for such a reason that India will not grant patents in agricultural technologies. This point suggests a utilitarian theme: that global redistribution of property rights would most benefit the majority, especially the world's poor who are struggling to meet basic needs.

IV. DILEMMAS

Most observers agree that new international institutions of intellectual property are needed to tap the innovative creativity of peoples and persons and to adequately diffuse the fruits of such innovation. New arrangements are needed both in terms of building up R&D infrastructures as well as in terms of enterprise policies.

This argument is important not so much for dividing up existing technologies as for generating new ones and diffusing them around the globe. There are a number of ethical problems related to prospective intellectual property regimes. I discuss three points: utilitarianism, rights and distributive justice.

Intellectual property rights restrict the diffusion of a particular technology for 17 to 20 years. Business frequently advances the position that intellectual property rights spur innovation, the production of greater wealth and improved well-being. Frequently, however, the utilitarian argument of business is based upon a narrow set of stakeholders—those within national boundaries and with direct ties to the company in question. Developing countries also use an utilitarian argument but with a very significant change: the world's poor become the principal stakeholders. The greatest utilitarian benefits are seen in an intellectual property regime which makes for the development of entire peoples. The greatest happiness of the greatest number is demographically weighted by the masses of the world's poor. In essence they argue that the greatest happiness of the greatest number would ensue if there were far greater diffusion of technology rather than greater protection of private property rights. Precisely for this reason both India and Brazil demand that a patent be fully worked and that, in many cases, licensing be made compulsory. Business people are suspect of the rhetoric. They point to local elites within developing countries who argue redistribution of property on the international level but give little attention to distributive justice within their own borders. In effect, business contends, these people are just out for themselves.

Secondly, almost without exception business argues intellectual property rights in collective terms. The important issue of the property rights of individual researchers working for the firm is passed over (Anawalt, 1988). The structure of modern science has been transformed dramatically over the past century. The Edisons of the world have been largely supplanted by Bell Labs and other research laboratories. Researchers engaged in such labs are contractually forced to cede all personal property claims to their discoveries. While management does deserve some return for the provision of a research infrastructure—without which many scientists would not be able to function—it is questionable whether it is legitimate to make the ceding of property claims a condition of employment. What happens in practice is that the fruits of scientific labor are passed to management and to owners. The rights of inventors have not been delineated; indeed, they are forced to forego them.

Aside from the comparative rights of inventors versus a company's rights, the rights of a people versus a company must be considered. In this context, developing countries consistently assert that the priority of the right of a people to their livelihood and development takes precedence over rights of private property. For this reason India restricts pharmaceuticals and agricultural chemicals from patents altogether. Furthermore, when patents are granted for items which are of crucial importance for people to meet their basic needs, many restrictive conditions are imposed.

Social rules which govern intellectual property raise many questions of distribution. The first area of distribution regards what is owed society for the bountiful research infrastructure which is supplied from *both* domestic and international sources. The right of property carries with it duties toward those who make the enjoyment of that right possible. If the labs make it possible for the scientist to function, it is the social infrastructure which makes it possible for the labs to function. Even granting Locke's assumptions about the hunter, labor does not confer absolute property rights; for labor takes place within a social milieu, whether the natural bounty of creation or the public infrastructure of knowledge, which serves as the basis for creative labor. The argument of what is owed society also surfaces in the discussion of compulsory licensing and the full working of patents. Both measures emphasize the distributive rights of society to a stream of benefits for the bountiful infrastructure it provides.

The structure of international research also raises the issue of the distributive fairness of initial conditions. In the intellectual property arena, people's access to education and R&D is widely uneven across countries and is further complicated by the brain drain. Thus, the ability to innovate is itself impaired.

The distributive issues are by far the most difficult to handle in the intellectual property debate. On an utilitarian basis, the developing countries would prevail unless business interests could show that strict protection of private intellectual property rights would lead to greater overall productivity. To date, historical evidence does not support such a contention (World Bank, 1991). An argument based on rights is even more difficult. If need has priority over effort or merit (in this context, what one is owed for innovativeness and brilliance), then the developing country argument prevails. If that order is reversed, then business interests would prevail.

If disputes over intellectual property are to be resolved, change must take place in three areas: the socio-ethical legitimation of the property rules which govern action, transformation of management towards a global stakeholder model, and the building up of a coherent international public policy process. This will be a long historical process, if for no other reason than that technology continually outpaces arrangements set up to manage it.

References

1. Anawalt, H. C.: 1988, *Ideas In The Workplace: Planning for Protection* (Carolina Academic Press, Durham, NC).
2. Behdad, S.: 1989, "Property Rights in Contemporary Islamic Economic Thought: A Critical Perspective," *Review of Social Economy* Vol. 47(2), pp. 185–211.
3. Besen, S. M. and L. J. Raskind: 1991, "An Introduction to the Law and Economics of Intellectual Property," *Journal of Economic Perspectives* Vol. 5(1), pp. 3–27.
4. Brown, C. G. and F. W. Rushing: 1990, "Intellectual Property Rights in the 1990s: Problems and Solutions," in F. W. Rushing and C. G. Brown (eds.), *Intellectual Property Rights in Science, Technology and Economic Performance* (Boulder, CO, Westview Special Studies in Science, Technology and Public Policy).
5. Congressional Quarterly: 1990, "Is the U.S. Patent System Out of date?," *Editorial Research Reports* Vol. 1(19), May 18.
6. Deardorff, A. V.: 1990, "Should Patent Protection Be Extended to All Developing Countries?," *The World Economy* Vol. 13(4), pp. 497–506.
7. Freeman, R. E.: 1984, *Strategic Management: A Stakeholder Approach* (Pitman Publishing Co., Boston, MA).
8. Gadbaw, R. M. G. and T. J. Richards: 1988, *Intellectual Property Rights—Global Consensus, Global Conflict?* (Westview Press, Boulder, CO).
9. Government of India: 1989, "Paper Presented By India In Uruguay Round Multilateral Talks" (Indian Embassy, Washington, D.C.) (xerox).
10. Hazarika, S.: 1989, "India and U.S. Disagree on Patents," *New York Times*, April 17, p. D-10.
11. Hoffman, G. M.: 1990, "Piracy of Intellectual Property—A Report of the International Piracy Project," *Bulletin of the American Society for Information Science*, pp. 9–11.
12. Johnson, R. D.: 1989, "Adam Smith's Radical Views on Property, Distributive Justice and the Market," *Review of Social Economy* Vol. 47(3), pp. 247–271.
13. Kim K. W.: 1986, "A High Cost to Developing Countries," *New York Times*, October 5, p. D2.
14. Lepp, A. W.: 1990, "Intellectual Property Rights Regimes in Southeast Asia," *Journal of Southeast Asia Business*, Vol. 6(11), pp. 28–40.
15. Locke, J.: 1965, *Two Treatises On Civil Government* (Mentor Books, New York).
16. Munzer, S. R.: 1990, *A Theory of Property* (Cambridge University Press, New York, NY).
17. Needham, J.: 1981, *Science in Traditional China: A Comparative Perspective* (Harvard University Press, Cambridge, MA).
18. Pfizer, Inc.: 1989, Interview with General Patent Counsel.
19. Pryor, F. L.: 1991, "A Buddhist Economic System—In Practice," *American Journal of Economic and Sociology* Vol. 50(1), pp. 17–32.
20. Pryor, F. L.: 1990, "A Buddhist Economic System—In Principle," *American Journal of Economic and Sociology* Vol. 49(3), pp. 339–349.
21. Rapp, R. J. and R. P. Rozek: 1990, "Benefits and Costs of Intellectual Property Protection in Developing Countries," *Journal of World Trade* Vol. 24 pp. 75–102.
22. Reeve, A.: 1986, *Property* (Humanities Press International, Atlantic Highlands, NJ).
23. Siebeck, W., R. E. Evenson, W. Lesser, and C. A. Primo Braga: 1990, *Strengthening Protection of Intellectual Property in Developing Countries. A Survey of the Literature* (World Bank, Washington, DC).
24. Steidlmeier, P.: 1992, "China's Most Favored Nation Trading Status: Activists' Attempts to Reform China and U.S. Business Prospects" (State University of New York, School of Management Working Paper, Binghamton, NY).
25. Steidlmeier, P.: 1987, *The Paradox of Poverty: A Reappraisal of Economic Development Policy* (Ballinger Publishing Co., Lexington, MA).
26. U.S. Patent and Trademark Office, National Technical Information Service: 1990, "Industrial Patent Activity In The United States" (Washington, D.C.).
27. U.S. International Trade Commission: 1989, *Foreign Protection of Intellectual Property Rights and the Effect on U.S. Industry and Trade* (USITC Publication 2065, Washington, D.C.).
28. Uppal, J. S.: 1986, "Hinduism and Economic Development in South Asia," *International Review of Economics and Ethics* Vol. 1(1), pp. 20–33.
29. World Bank: 1991, *World Development Report, 1990* (Washington, D.C.).

Jang B. Singh
V. C. Lakhan

Business Ethics and the International Trade in Hazardous Wastes

The export of hazardous wastes by the more developed countries to the lesser developed nations is escalating beyond control. The ethical implications and environmental consequences of this trade in hazardous wastes highlight the need for international controls and regulations in the conduct of business by corporations in the more developed countries. In the late 1970s, the Love Canal environmental tragedy awakened the world to the effects of ill conceived and irresponsible disposal of hazardous by-products of industries. Today, the media focuses its attention on the alleged illegal dumping of hazardous wastes in the lesser developed countries (see Barthos, 1988, and Harden, 1988). The most recent dramatic case so far is that of Koko, Nigeria where more than eight thousand drums of hazardous wastes were dumped, some of which contained polychlorinated biphenyl (PCB), a highly carcinogenic compound and one of the world's most toxic wastes (Tifft, 1988). The government of Nigeria has detained a number of Nigerians in connection with the incident and President Babangida has indicated that they may face a firing squad if found guilty of illegal dumping. Previous to this was the media documentation in the spring of 1987 of an American barge laden with 3000 tonnes of garbage being turned back to the United States

From Jang B. Singh and V. C. Lakhan, "Business Ethics and the International Trade in Hazardous Wastes," *Journal of Business Ethics*, Vol. 8, No. 8, 1989. Reprinted by permission of Kluwer Academic Publishers.

by the Mexican navy. The barge had already tried, unsuccessfully, to dump its noxious cargo in North Carolina, Alabama, Mississippi and Louisiana. The Mexican navy action was aimed at preventing the barge from dumping its cargo in Mexico.

The three cases cited above serve as disturbing examples of the international trade in hazardous wastes. Not all of the activities involved in this trade are illegal. In fact, governments are often directly involved in the business of hazardous wastes. This paper examines various characteristics of the international trade in hazardous waste and discusses the ethical implications of such business activity.

The International Trade in Hazardous Wastes and Attendant Problems

Miller (1988) defined hazardous waste as any material that may pose a substantial threat or potential hazard to human health or the environment when managed improperly. These wastes may be in solid, liquid or gaseous form and include a variety of toxic, ignitable, corrosive, or dangerously reactive substances. Examples include acids, cyanides, pesticides, solvents, compounds of lead, mercury, arsenic, cadmium, and zinc, PCB's and dioxins, fly ash from power plants, infectious waste from hospitals, and research laboratories, obsolete explosives, herbicides, nerve gas, radioactive materials, sewage sludge, and other materials which contain toxic and carcinogenic organic compounds.

Since World War II, the amount of toxic by-products created by the manufacturers of pharmaceuticals, petroleum, nuclear devices, pesticides, chemicals, and other allied products has increased almost exponentially. From an annual production of less than 10 million metric tonnes in the 1940s, the world now produces more than 320 million metric tonnes of extremely hazardous wastes per year. The United States is by far the biggest producer, with "over

275 million metric tonnes of hazardous waste produced each year" (Goldfarb, 1987). The total is well over one tonne per person. But the Untied States is not alone. European countries also produce millions of tonnes of hazardous wastes each year (Chiras, 1988). Recent figures reported by Tifft (1988) indicate that the twelve countries of the European Community produce about 35 million tonnes of hazardous wastes annually.

The problems associated with hazardous wastes started to gain world-wide attention after 1977 when it was discovered that hazardous chemicals leaking from an abandoned waste dump had contaminated homes in a suburban development known as Love Canal, located in Niagara Falls, New York. This event triggered a frantic search for new ways and places to store hazardous wastes, and an introduction of new environmental regulations to store, handle, and dispose of hazardous wastes. With the "not in my backyard" (NIMBY) syndrome in the developed societies, the manufacturers and creators of hazardous wastes began to escalate the practice of dumping their wastes in the lesser developed countries.

Table 1 mainly provides an extensive list of companies which are exporting various toxic wastes to the lesser developed countries. The United States and certain European countries are now turning to areas in Africa, Latin America, and the Caribbean to dump their wastes. Historically, the trade in wastes has been conducted among the industrialized nations: A major route involving industrialized nations is that between Canada and the Untied States. The movement of wastes from the Untied States into Canada is governed by the Canada-U.S.A. Agreement on the Transboundary Movement of Hazardous Waste which came into effect on November 8, 1986 (Environment Canada). In 1988, the United States exported 145,000 tonnes. Of this amount, only one third was recyclable, leaving approximately 96,667 tonnes of hazardous organic and inorganic wastes such as petroleum by-products, pesticides, heavy metals, and organic solvents and residues for disposal in the Canadian environment. Of interest is the fact that Canada restricts the import of nuclear waste, but not toxic, flammable, corrosive, reactive, and medical wastes from the United States.

Most of the United States hazardous wastes are shipped from the New England states, New York and Michigan and enter Ontario and Quebec which in 1988 received approximately 81,899 and 62,200 tonnes respectively. The neutralization and disposal of the imported hazardous wastes are done by several Canadian companies, with the two largest being Tricil and Stablex Canada Inc. Tricil with several locations in Ontario, imports wastes from more than 85 known American companies which it incinerates and treats in lagoons and landfill sites. Stablex Canada imports a wide variety of hazardous wastes from more than 300 U.S. companies. It uses various disposal methods, including landfills and cement kilns which burn not only the components needed for cement but also hazardous waste products. With the established Canada-U.S. Agreement on the Transboundary Movement of Hazardous Waste companies like Tricil and Stablex may increase their importation of hazardous wastes generated in the United States. As it stands, the Untied States Environmental Protection Agency estimates that over 75% of the wastes exported from the U.S. is disposed of in Canada (Vallette, 1989). This estimate will likely have to be raised in the near future. Canada-United States trade in hazardous wastes is not a one-way route. It is believed that all of the hazardous wastes imported by the Untied States (estimated at 65000 tonnes in 1988) is generated in Canada (Ibid).

An especially controversial trend in the international trade in hazardous wastes is the development of routes between industrialized and "lesser developed countries." For example, according to the United States Environmental Protection Agency there have been more proposals to ship hazardous wastes from the United States to Africa during 1988, than in the previous four years (Klatte et al., 1988).

African nations have recently joined together to try to completely ban the dumping of toxic wastes on their continent. They have referred to the practice as "toxic terrorism" performed by Western "merchants of death." Some African government officials are so disturbed by the newly exposed practices that they have threatened to execute guilty individuals by firing squad. Recently, Lagos officials, seized an Italian

Importing Country	Name of Firm	Point of Export	Type of Waste
1. Argentina	American Security International	Florida, U.S.A.	Solvents/Chemical Sludge
2. Benin	Sesco Ltd.	Gibralter	Non-Nuclear Toxic Waste
3. Benin	Government of France	France	Radioactive Wastes
4. Brazil	Applied Technologies	U.S.A.	Unspecified Toxic Wastes
5. Brazil	Ashland Metal Co.	Pennsylvania, U.S.A.	N/A
6. Brazil	Delatte Metals Inc.	California, U.S.A.	N/A
7. Brazil	Astur Metals Inc.	Puerto Rico, U.S.A.	N/A
8. Canada	Over 400 Firms	Mainly points in New England, New York and Michigan	Petroleum by-products, Pesticides, Heavy Metals and organic solvents and residues
9. Dominican Republic	Arbuckle Machinery	Texas, U.S.A.	PCB Wastes
10. Dominican Republic	Franklin Energy Resource	New York, U.S.A.	Refuse
11. Dominican Republic	World Technology Co.	Italy	Toxic Liquid Wastes
12. Equatorial Guinea	Unspecified British	U.K.	Chemical Wastes
13. Gabon	Denison Mining	Colorado, U.S.A.	Uranium Tailing Wastes
14. Guinea	Bulkhandling Inc.	Philadelphia, U.S.A.	Toxic Incinerator Ash
15. Guinea-Bissau	Hamilton Resources	U.K.	N/A
16. Guinea-Bissau	B/S Import-Export Ltd.	U.K.	Pharmaceutical Industrial Wastes
17. Guinea-Bissau	Hobday Ltd.	U.K.	Pharmaceutical Industrial Wastes
18. Guinea-Bissau	Intercontrat S.A.	Switzerland	Pharmaceutical Industrial Wastes
19. Guinea-Bissau	Lindaco Ltd.	Michigan, U.S.A.	Pharmaceutical Industrial Wastes
20. Guyana	Pott Industries	California, U.S.A.	Industrial Oil Wastes
21. Guyana	Teixeria Farms International	California, U.S.A.	Paint Sludge
22. Haiti	Palino and Sons	Philadelphia, U.S.A.	Toxic Incinerator Ash
23. India	Jack & Charles Colbert	U.S.A.	Lead Tainted Hazardous Wastes
24. Mexico	Arm Co. Steel	Missouri, U.S.A.	N/A
25. Mexico	Border Steel Mills	Texas, U.S.A.	N/A
26. Mexico	Chapparral Steel	Texas, U.S.A.	N/A
27. Mexico	Nucor Steel, Nebraska	Nebraska, U.S.A.	N/A
28. Mexico	Nucor Steel, Texas	Texas, U.S.A.	Furnace Dust
29. Mexico	Nucor Steel, Utah	Utah, U.S.A.	Furnace Dust
30. Mexico	Razorback Steel	Arkansas, U.S.A.	N/A
31. Mexico	Sheffield Steel Corp.	Oklahoma, U.S.A.	N/A
32. Mexico	Federated Metal	New Jersey, U.S.A.	Lead Wastes
33. Mexico	B.F. Goodrich	Texas, U.S.A.	PCB's, Mercury Cinders
34. Mexico	Diamond Shamrock	Texas, U.S.A.	PCB Wastes
35. Mexico	Bayou Steel Corp.	Louisiana, U.S.A.	Furnace Dust
36. Nigeria	Jack & Charles Colbert	U.S.A.	Lead Tainted Hazardous Wastes
37. Paraguay	American Securities Int.	Florida, U.S.A.	Solvents/Chemical Sludge
38. Peru	American Securities Int.	Florida, U.S.A.	Solvents/Chemical Sludge
39. Senegal	Intercontrat, S.A.	Switzerland	N/A
40. South Africa	American Cyanimid	New Jersey, U.S.A.	Mercury-Laced Sludge
41. South Africa	Quanex	Texas, U.S.A.	PCB Wastes
42. South Korea	Jack & Charles Colbert	U.S.A.	Lead Tainted Hazardous Wastes
43. Surinam	Mine Tech International	Netherlands	PCB Wastes
44. Tonga	Omega Recovery	California, U.S.A.	Hazardous Wastes
45. Uruguay	American Security Int.	Florida, U.S.A.	Solvents/Chemical Sludge
46. Zimbabwe	Jack & Charles Colbert	U.S.A.	Lead Tainted Hazardous Wastes

This table includes information mainly on actual waste shipments and active proposals for shipments from Europe and the United States to less developed countries.
SOURCE: Klatte *et al.*, 1988.

and a Danish ship along with fifteen people who were associated with transporting toxic wastes in the swampy Niger River delta, into Nigeria. This occurred shortly after the discovery of 3800 tonnes of hazardous toxic wastes, which had originated in Italy. Local residents immediately became ill from inhaling the fumes from the leaking drums and containers which were filled with the highly carcinogenic compound PCB, and also radioactive material.

Companies in the United States have been responsible for sending large quantities of hazardous wastes to Mexico. Although Mexico only accepts hazardous wastes for recycling, which is referred to as "sham re-cycling," there are numerous reports of illegal dumping incidents. Two Californian companies have proposed the shipping of 62000 tonnes of hazardous wastes each year to Guyana for incineration. They are also close to concluding a deal with the Guyana Government "to build a giant toxic waste incinerator in that country." The companies have suggested that "the incinerator ash be sold as fertilizer and building materials" (Morrison, 1988, p. 8). Guyana is one of a large number of developing countries whose economic plight makes it willing to accept proposals such as this, despite the long term human and environmental costs (Ibid., p. 9).

Given the fact that hazardous wastes are:

1. toxic;
2. highly reactive when exposed to air, water, or other substances that they can cause explosions and generate toxic fumes;
3. ignitable that they can undergo spontaneous combustion at relatively low temperatures;
4. highly corrosive that they can eat away materials and living tissues;
5. infectious, and
6. radioactive;

Miller (1988) has, therefore, emphasized correctly that the proper transportation, disposal, deactivation, or storage of hazardous wastes is a grave environmental problem which is second only to nuclear war.

The practice of transporting and dumping hazardous wastes in lesser developed nations, where knowledge of environmental issues is limited is causing, and will pose, major problems to both human health and the environment. Several comprehensive studies have outlined the detrimental impacts which hazardous waste can have on humans and natural ecosystems. Epstein *et al.*, (1982) have provided a thorough and dramatic coverage of the impacts of hazardous wastes, while Regenstein (1982), in his book *"America the Poisoned,"* gives a good overview of the implications of hazardous wastes. Essentially, hazardous wastes not only contaminate ground water, destroy habitats, cause human disease, contaminate the soil, but also enter the food chain at all levels, and eventually damage genetic material of all living things. For instance, when hazardous wastes enter water bodies, they are taken up by Zoo plankton, which single cell fish ingest while feeding. Other higher-level organisms also accumulate these substances, so that tissue concentrations become higher at higher levels of the food chain. The accumulation and biological magnification which occurs exposes organisms high on the food chain to highly dangerous levels of many chemicals. Understanding toxic chemical repercussions is still barely out of the dark ages, but it is known that metals present in water are toxic for fish. The metals irritate their gills and cause a mucus to build up on them, which eventually causes the fish to suffocate (Chiras, 1988). When hazardous wastes are deposited in the soil they are taken up by food crops, which eventually affect livestock as well as humans. When the ash enters the air, it also has the ability to cause pollution. Even though air is a finite resource capable of cleansing itself, it cannot entirely get rid of all pollutants. Besides causing respiratory problems in the local inhabitants, air pollution will damage the crops and reduce the yields. The rate of photosynthesis will be decreased with harmful effects on animal respiratory and central nervous systems (Miller, 1988.)

The hazardous wastes can also directly threaten human health through seeping into the ground and causing the direct pollution of aquifers, which supply "pure" drinking water. Today, in the United States, a long list of health related problems are caused by hazardous chemicals from "leaking underground storage tanks" (LUST). Investigations now show that human exposure to hazardous wastes from dumpsites, water bodies, and processing and storage areas can cause the disposed synthetic compounds to interact with particular enzymes or other chemicals in the body, and result in altered functions. Altered functions have been shown to include mutagenic (mutation-causing), carcinogenic (cancer-causing), and teratogenic (birth-defect causing) effects. In addition, they may cause serious liver and kidney dysfunction, sterility and numerous lesser physiological and neurological problems (see Nebel, 1987).

The Ethical Implications

The very notion of dumping one's wastes in someone else's territory is repulsive. When the Mexican navy turned back an American barge laden with garbage one Mexican newspaper columnist commented that "the incident serves to illustrate once again the scorn that certain sectors of U.S. society feel toward Mexico in particular and Latin America in general" (Mexico Sends Back, April 27, 1987, p. F9). Others have pointed to the export of wastes as an example of neo-colonialist behaviour. An official of an environmental organization expressed this view in the following manner: "I am concerned that if U.S. people think of us as their backyard, they can also think of us as their outhouse" (Porterfield and Weir, 1987, p. 343). In addition to arousing emotions such as those described above, the international trade in hazardous wastes raises a number of ethical issues. The rest of this paper examines some of these.

The Right to a Livable Environment

The desire for a clean, safe and ecologically balanced environment is an often expressed sentiment. This is especially so in industrialized countries where an awareness of environmental issues is relatively high—a fact that is gaining recognition in political campaigns. However, expression of the desire for a clean, safe environment is not the same as stating that a clean, safe environment is the right of every human being. But the right of an individual to a livable environment is easily established at the theoretical level. Blackstone (1983) examines the right to a livable environment from two angles—as a human right and as a legal right. The right to a clean, safe environment is seen as a human right since the absence of such a condition would prevent one from fulfilling one's human capacities.

Each person has this right qua being human and because a livable environment is essential for one to fulfill his human capacities. And given the danger to our environment today and hence the danger to the very possibility of human existence, access to a livable environment must be conceived as a right which imposes upon everyone a correlative moral obligation to respect.

(Blackstone, 1983, p. 413)

Guerrette (1986) illustrates this argument by reference to the Constitution of the United States. He proposes that people cannot live in a chemically toxic area, they cannot experience freedom in an industrially polluted environment and they cannot be happy worrying about the quality of air they breathe or the carcinogenic effects of the water they drink (Guerrete, 1986, p. 409). Some even argue (e.g., Feinberg, 1983) that the right to a livable environment extends to future generations and that it is the duty of the present generation to pass on a clean, safe environment to them.

Establishing the right to a livable environment as a human right is not the same as establishing it as a legal right. This requires the passing of appropriate legislation and the provision of a legal framework that may be used to seek a remedy if necessary. Such provisions are more prevalent in the industrialized countries and this is one of the push factors in the export of hazardous wastes to the lesser developed countries. This points to the need for a provision in international law of the right to a decent environment which with accompanying policies to save and preserve our environmental resources would be an even more effective tool than such a framework at the national level (Blackstone, 1983, p. 414). As ecologists suggest, serious harm done to one element in an ecosystem will invariably lead to the damage or even destruction of other elements in that and other ecosystems (Law Reform Commission of Canada, 1987, p. 262) and ecosystems transcend national boundaries. The need for international law in this area has not led to the formulation of the same. However, there have been campaigns to stop the flow of hazardous wastes across national boundaries. In a current campaign, the international environmental group, Greenpeace, is calling for a global ban on the transboundary movement of wastes. Greenpeace is basing its appeal on Principle 21 of the 1972 Declaration of the United Nations Conference on the Human Environment which declares that each state is responsible for ensuring that activities within their jurisdiction or control do not cause damage to the environment of other states or of areas beyond the limits of their own national jurisdiction (Klatte et al., 1988, p. 3).

A more direct harmful effect of the international trade in hazardous wastes is the damage to the health of workers involved in the transportation and disposal of these toxic substances. For example, prolonged exposure to wastes originating in Italy and transported by a ship called Zanoobia is suspected of causing the death of a crew person and the hospitalization of nine others (Klatte et al. 1983, p. 12). Whereas worker rights in work-place health and safety are gaining wider recognition in many industrialized nations this is not so in the "less developed" countries which are increasingly becoming the recipients of hazardous wastes. Widespread violation of workers right to a clean, safe work environment should therefore be expected to be a feature of the international trade in hazardous wastes.

Racist Implications

The recent trend of sending more shipments of hazardous wastes to Third World countries has led to charges of racism. West Africa, a weekly magazine, referred to the dumping of toxic wastes as the latest in a series of historical traumas for Africa. The other traumas cited by the magazine were slavery, colonialism and unpayable foreign debts. An article in another African magazine viewed the dumping of wastes in Koko, Nigeria as follows:

That Italy did not contemplate Australia or South Africa or some other place for industrial waste re-echoes what Europe has always thought of Africa: A wasteland. And the people who are there, waste beings.

(Brooke, 1988, p. A10)

Charges of racism in the disposal of wastes have been made before at the national level in the United States. A study of waste disposal sites found that race was the most significant among variables tested in association with the location of commercial hazardous wastes facilities. The findings of this national study which were found to be statistically significant at the 0.0001 level showed that communities with the greatest number of commercial hazardous wastes facilities had the highest concentration of racial minorities (Lee, 1987, pp. 45–46). The study found that although socio-economic status appeared to play a role in the location of commercial hazardous wastes facilities, race was a more significant factor.

In the United States, one of the arguments often advanced for locating commercial waste facilities in lower income areas is that these facilities create jobs. This is also one of the arguments being advanced for sending wastes to poor lesser developed countries. An examination of Table 1 would reveal that nearly all the countries receiving hazardous wastes have predominantly coloured populations. This is the reason why charges of racism are being made against exporters of wastes. However, it must be noted that even though the trend of sending wastes to countries such as those listed in Table 1 has recently gained strength, the bulk of the international trade in hazardous wastes is still within industrialized Europe and North America which have predominantly noncoloured populations.

For example, the United States Environmental Protection Agency estimates that as much as 75% of the wastes exported from the U.S. is disposed of in Canada (Klatte et al., 1988, p. 9). Another striking example is that a dump outside Schonberg, East Germany, is the home of well over 500000 tonnes of waste a year from Western Europe (Rubbish Between Germans, March 1, 1986, p. 46). Thus, while charges of racism in the export of hazardous wastes are being made by some Third World leaders, figures on the international trade in such substances do not substantiate these claims.

Corporate Responsibility

The international trade in hazardous wastes basically involves three types of corporations—the generators of wastes, the exporters of wastes and the importers of wastes. These entities, if they are to act in a responsible manner, should be accountable to the public for their behaviour.

> Having a corporate conscience means that a company takes responsibility for its actions, just as any conscientious individual would be expected to do. In corporate terms, this means that a company is accountable to the public for its behaviour not only in the complex organizational environment but in the natural physical environment as well. A company is thus responsible for its product and for its effects on the public.
>
> (Guerrette, 1986, p. 410)

Using Guerrette's definition of corporate responsibility, it seems clear that a corporation involved in the international trade in hazardous wastes is not likely to be a responsible firm. The importer of hazardous wastes is clearly engaged in activities that will damage the environment while the exporter being aware that this is a possibility, nevertheless, sends these wastes to the importer. However, it is the generator of hazardous wastes that is the most culpable in this matter. If the wastes are not produced then obviously their disposal would not be necessary. Therefore, in view of the fact that virtually no safe method of disposing hazardous wastes exists, a case of corporate irresponsibility could easily be formulated against any corporation involved in the international trade in these substances.

Government Responsibility

Why do countries export wastes? A major reason is that many of them are finding it difficult to build disposal facilities in their own countries because of the NIMBY syndrome mentioned earlier. Other reasons are that better technologies may be available in another country, facili-

ties of a neighboring country may be closer to a generator of waste than a site on national territory and economies of scale may also be a factor. However, to these reasons must be added the fact that corporations may be motivated to dispose of waste in another country where less stringent regulations apply (Transfrontier Movements, March 1984, p. 40). It is the responsibility of governments to establish regulations governing the disposal of wastes. In some countries these regulations are stringent while in others they are lax or non-existent. Moreover, some countries have regulations governing disposal of wastes within national boundaries as well as regulations relating to the export of hazardous wastes. For example, companies in the United States that intend to export hazardous wastes are requested to submit notices to the Environmental Protection Agency (EPA) and to demonstrate that they have the permission of the receiving country (Porterfield and Weir, 1987, p. 341). However, the effectiveness of these controls is in question. The General Accounting Office has found that "the E.P.A. does not know whether it is controlling 90 percent of the existing waste or 10 percent. Likewise it does not know if it is controlling the wastes that are most hazardous" (Ibid.). Moreover, there is evidence indicating that other U.S. government agencies are encouraging the export of hazardous wastes. The Navy, the Army, the Defence Department, the Agriculture Department and the Treasury Department are some government agencies that have provided hazardous wastes to known exporters. Also, major U.S. cities, sometimes with the approval of the State Department, have been suppliers to the international trade in hazardous wastes (Porterfield and Weir, 1987, p. 342).

While more stringent regulations, higher disposal costs, and heightened environmental awareness are pushing many companies in industrial countries to export hazardous wastes, it must be, nevertheless, realized that the governments of lesser developed countries are allowing such imports into their countries because of the need for foreign exchange. These governments are willing to damage the environment in return for hard currency or the creation of jobs. One must assume that on the basis of cost-benefit analysis these governments foresee more benefits than harm resulting from the importation of hazardous wastes. However, these benefits go mainly to a few waste brokers while the health of large numbers of people is put at risk. In some cases decisions to import wastes are made by governments which hold power by force and fraud. For example, Haiti which has imported wastes (see Table 1) is ruled by a military dictatorship and Guyana which is actively considering the importation of industrial oil wastes and paint sludge is ruled by a minority party which has rigged all elections held in that country since 1964. The ethical dilemma posed by this situation is that of whether or not an unrepresentative government of a country could be trusted to make decisions affecting the life and health of its citizens. In fact, a larger question is whether or not any government has the right to permit business activity that poses a high risk to human life and health.

Generally, governments of waste generating countries, in reaction to political pressure, have imposed stringent regulations on domestic disposal and some restrictions on the export of hazardous wastes. However, as the examples above illustrate, the latter restrictions are not strictly enforced, hence, indicating a duplicitous stance on the part of the generating countries. The governments of importing countries, in allowing into their countries, wastes that will disrupt ecosystems and damage human health, deny their citizens the right to a livable environment.

CONCLUSION

Hazardous wastes are, in the main, by-products of industrial processes that have contributed significantly to the economic development of many countries. Economic development, in turn, has led to lifestyles which also generate hazardous wastes. To export these wastes to countries which do not benefit from waste generating industrial processes or whose citizens do not have lifestyles that generate such wastes is unethical. It is especially unjust to send hazardous wastes to lesser developed countries which lack the technology to minimize the deleterious effects of these substances. Nevertheless, these countries are increasingly becoming recipients of such cargoes. The need for stringent international regulation to govern the trade in hazardous wastes is now stronger than ever before. However, this alone will not significantly curb the international trade in hazardous wastes. International regulation must be coupled with a revolutionary reorganization of waste-generating processes and change in consumption patterns. Until this is achieved the international trade in hazardous wastes will continue and with it a plethora of unethical activities.

Bibliography

Barthos, G.: 1988, "Third World Outraged at Receiving Toxic Trash," *Toronto Star* June 26, pp. 1, 4.

Blackstone, W. T.: 1983, "Ethics and Ecology" in Beauchamp, T. L. and Bowie, N. E. (Eds), *Ethical Theory and Business* 2nd. edition (Prentice-Hall, Inc., Englewood Cliffs, New Jersey) pp. 411–424.

Barthos, G.: 1988, "Third World Outraged at Receiving Toxic Trash," *Toronto Star* June 26, pp. 1, 4.

Brooke, J.: 1988, "Africa Fights Tide of Western Wastes," *Globe and Mail,* July 18, p. A10.

Chiras, D. D.: 1988, *Environmental Science* (Benjamin Commings Publishing Co. Inc., Denver).

Environment Canada: 1986, *Canada-U.S.A. Agreement on the Transboundary Movement of Hazardous Waste* (Environment Canada, Ottawa).

Epstein, S. S., Brown, L. O., and Pope, C.: 1982, *Hazardous Waste in America* (Sierra Club Books, San Francisco).

Feinberg, J.: 1983, "The Rights of Animals and Unborn Generation," in Beauchamp, F. L. and Bowie, N. E., (Eds), *Ethical Theory and Business,* 2nd. edition, (Prentice-Hall Inc, Englewood Cliffs, New Jersey) pp. 428–436.

Goldfarb, T. D.: 1987, *Taking Sides: Clashing Views on Controversial Environmental Issues.* (Dushkin Publishing Co. Inc., Connecticut).

Guerrette, R. H.: 1986, "Environmental Integrity and Corporate Responsibility," *Journal of Business Ethics* Vol. 5, pp. 409–415.

Harden, B.: 1988, "Africa Refuses to Become Waste Dump for the West," *Windsor Star,* July 9, p. A–6.

Klatte, E., Palacio, F., Rapaport, D., and Vallette, J.: 1988, *International Trade in Toxic Wastes: Policy and Data Analysis* (Greenpeace International, Washington, D.C.)

Law Reform Commission of Canada: 1987, "Crimes Against the Environment" in Poff, D. and Waluchow, W., *Business Ethics in Canada,* (Prentice-Hall Canada Inc., Scarborough), pp. 261–264.

Lee, C.: Summer 1987, "The Racist Disposal of Toxic Wastes," *Business and Society Review* Vol. 62, pp. 43–46.

Miller, T.: 1988, *Living in The Environment,* (Wadsworth Publishing Co., California).

Montreal Gazette: April 27 1987, "Mexico Sends Back U.S. Barge Filled With Tonnes of Garbage," p. F9.

Morrison, A.: 1988, "Dead Flowers to U.S. Firms that Plan to Send Waste to Guyana," *Catholic Standard,* Sunday, May 8.

Nebel, B. J.: 1987, *Environmental Science,* (Prentice-Hall, Inc., New Jersey).

OECD Observer: March 1984, "Transfrontier Movements of Hazardous Wastes: Getting to Grips with the Problem," pp. 39–41.

Porterfield, A. and Weir, D.: 1987, "The Export of U.S. Toxic Wastes," *The Nation,* Vol. 245, Iss. 10 (Oct. 3), pp. 341–344.

Regenstein, L.: 1982, *America the Poisoned* (Acropolis Books, Washington, D.C.).

The Economist: March 1 1986, "Rubbish Between Germans," p. 46.

Tifft, S.: 1988, "Who Gets the Garbage," *Time* July 4, pp. 42–43.

Vallette, J.: 1989, *The International Trade in Wastes: A Greenpeace Inventory (Fourth Edition).* (Greenpeace International, Luxembourg).

Don Mayer
Anita Cava

Ethics and the Gender Equality Dilemma for U.S. Multinationals

We hold these truths to be self-evident: that all men are created equal, and endowed by their creator with certain rights—life, liberty, and the pursuit of happiness.

> *U.S. Declaration of Independence, 1776*

All human beings are born free and equal in dignity and rights.

> *United Nations Universal Declaration of Human Rights, 1948*

Judging from the U.S. Declaration of Independence, gender equality was not self-evident in 1776. By 1948, however, the Universal Declaration of Human Rights took care not to exclude women from the ambit of declared rights. Since then, while gender equality has come a long way in the United States, many difficult and divisive issues remain unresolved. After completing a global inventory of attitudes on gender equality, Rhoodie (1989) concluded that many

nations give only "lip service" to the goals of gender equality articulated in international conventions and declarations such as the U.N. Declaration of Human Rights (1948). Given the uneven progress of gender and racial equality in the world, it is inevitable that multinational enterprises (MNEs) encounter uneven ethical terrain.

Recently, the U.S. Congress and the Supreme Court have differed markedly over how the principles of non-discrimination in Title VII of the Civil Rights Act of 1964 (Title VII) should be applied by U.S. MNEs in their overseas activities. Both Congress and the Court recognized that U.S. non-discrimination laws may create difficulties for U.S. companies doing business in host countries where racial and/or gender discrimination is a way of life. But Congress, having the last word, decided in the Civil Rights Act of 1991 that Title VII protects U.S. citizens from employment discrimination by U.S. MNEs in their overseas operations.[1]

In so doing, Congress effectively reversed the Supreme Court, which only a few months earlier had decided that Title VII did not apply "extraterritorially" (*E.E.O.C. v. Aramco,* 1991).[2] According to the Court, to apply U.S. laws abroad might cause "unintended clashes between our laws and those of other nations which could result in international discord." The majority of the Court wanted Congress to be entirely clear about its intent before imposing the ethical values inherent in Title VII on the activities of a U.S. company in a foreign country.

From Don Mayer and Anita Cava, "Ethics and the Gender Equality Dilemma for U.S. Multinationals," *Journal of Business Ethics,* Vol. 12, No. 9, 1993. Printed by permission of Kluwer Academic Publishers.

This reluctance is understandable. It seems logical to assume that companies would prefer not to have two personnel policies, one for U.S. citizens and one for host country nationals and others. Human resource directors indicate a preference for following the laws and customs of the host country while doing business there, but a concern for furthering human rights values in the U.S.[3] Such a preference corresponds to other observed realities, since the recent history of law and business ethics shows that a number of U.S. MNEs would engage in bribery in foreign countries, if that should be the custom, in order to remain "competitive." Similarly, many U.S. MNEs were willing to acquiesce to *apartheid* in South Africa, despite the fact that such behavior would not be tolerated in the United States.

The multinational that adopts such a policy of moral neutrality follows what Bowie (1977) has identified as moral relativism. The approach of a moral relativism is characterized as—"When in Rome, do as the Romans do." This prescription has its arresting aspects. If Rome existed today as a commercial power, would U.S. corporate executives entertain one another by watching slaves battle to the death, attending Bacchanalian orgies, or cheering while faithful but hapless Christians were being mauled by lions? While such practices do not have overt current counterparts, there are nonetheless substantial differences among cultures in matters of gender equality (Rhoodie, 1989).

How does the MNE deal ethically with such contrasts? Bowie suggests that while ethical relativism cannot support business ethics in the global economy, neither can we afford to be "ethnocentric" and assume that "our" way is the one "right way." Bowie uses the term "ethnocentric" to describe a view that "when in Rome, or anywhere else, do as you would at home," (Bowie, 1988; Wicks, 1990). Essentially, it was this concern that animated the Supreme Court's decision in *Aramco*, which explicitly worried about "unintended clashes" between U.S. law and Saudi Arabian law. Further, it is this concern about "ethnocentrism" that fuels speculation that applying Title VII's equal opportunity provisions in countries like Japan is a recipe for corporate non-competitiveness and perhaps even a form of cultural imperialism.

This article explores some of the difficulties faced by U.S. multinationals in complying with Title VII as applied abroad and examines the ethical arguments surrounding achieving the goal of gender equality. Part I discusses the current dilemma for international human resource managers and their employees, as well for citizens of host countries. We focus on Japan as a model of a country in transition and consider the extreme situation of the Islamic countries as a counterpoint in the analysis. The emphasis is on practical and legal considerations. Part II returns to the issues of ethical relativism and cultural imperialism, and suggests that U.S. multinationals should not opt for moral relativism by deferring entirely to cultural traditions in countries such as Japan, traditions that may be contrary to declared international standards for gender and racial equality and contrary to apparent global trends.

I. Perspectives on the Current Dilemma

Human resource managers, employees, and host country nationals will have varying perspectives on the application of U.S. civil rights statutes for the promotion of gender equality in the foreign workplace. Each merits consideration in order to understand the framework within which an ethical analysis can be applied.

A. The MNE Managerial Perspective

For a MNE whose operations cover the U.S., Europe, Asia, and the Middle East, the differing cultural norms with respect to equal opportunity in the workplace are a bit unreal. Despite strong movements for gender equality in the Scandinavian countries and, to a lesser extent, in the U.S. and Europe, the basic condition of women worldwide is largely "poor, pregnant, and powerless" (Rhoodie, 1989). The differences among various nations span a continuum from cultures with a strong commitment to gender equality in the workplace to those with strong commitments to keeping women out of the workplace entirely (Mayer, 1991).

For the MNE trying to "do the right thing," the situation suggests a kind of ethical surrealism, where reality retreats before an unreal mix of elements—social, cultural, legal, and philosophical. It seems natural that companies doing business abroad would want to follow host country laws and customs. Obviously, following U.S. law only for U.S. employees poses a dual dilemma. First, assuming that gender discrimination is culturally accepted and legally tolerated in many foreign countries, what should be the MNE personnel policy? The MNE has the option of designing a single non-discriminatory policy for all workers or creating a two-track system, protecting the legal rights of U.S. nationals while accommodating the host country's norms for their nationals and others. Second, where the MNE has adopted a Code of Ethics for global application and the Code specifically refers to equal opportunity, can the MNE honor its commitment in a principled way?

Strict compliance with an ethical position would suggest a simple solution to this conundrum: Adopt an equal opportunity program, educate all employees, and enforce it consistent with Title VII's mandates across the board. Admittedly, however, following U.S. law worldwide, for all employees, is surely "ethnocentric" and may also be unworkable. In some host countries, such as Saudi Arabia, the legal conflicts may be pronounced. In others, such as Japan, the cultural conflicts may undermine consistent enforcement of Title VII-oriented policies throughout the workforce.

Taking Japan as an example, the U.S. MNE doing business in Tokyo is confronted with a patriarchal society in which women are expected to manage household work while men dominate the other forms of work (Lebra, 1984). Although men and women receive comparable educations through the high school level, women are expected to marry by age 25. Employment after that age is generally discouraged (Prater, 1981). There is seldom, if ever, a managerial track for Japanese women: if employed by a major Japanese company, they are often given positions largely designed to make the office environment more comfortable (such as by serving tea and appearing "decorative"), and are not taken seriously as career office workers (Seymour, 1991).

For a U.S. MNE to announce a policy of equal opportunity for Japanese operations, tie that policy to Title VII enforcement, and expect no negative results would require a supposition that the overwhelmingly male population of Japanese customers, suppliers, and government officials would treat U.S. women and Japanese women equally. But, in fact, the sensitivity of Japanese males to sexual harassment issues is only dawning (Ford, 1992; Lan, 1991), and some other forms of overt discrimination are likely. Assuming, as seems warranted, that the MNEs female employees will be adversely affected to some degree by prevailing male attitudes in Japan, how would the company find that balanced approach that yields the least friction and the best results?

Such a question suggests that a utilitarian analysis, or some pragmatism, may be entirely appropriate here. It is well beyond the scope of this paper to suggest how absolute adherence to Title VII and equal opportunity principles should be tempered to achieve greater harmony with the host country culture, but a few observations are in order. First, Title VII's dictates may need to be culturally adjusted. An "appropriate" response to repeated incidents of Japanese males looking up female employees' skirts may be more educational than admonitory, at least for the first transgressions. Second, companies should be wary of any utilitarian or pragmatic approaches that predict a "non-competitive" result unless business hews to some perceived cultural norms. This point needs further elaboration.

In a country such as Saudi Arabia, the cultural norms and the sacred law, or Shari'a, are fairly congruent. The winds of change are not, seemingly, as strong as in other parts of the world. Japan, on the other hand, has demonstrated its willingness to adopt some "Western ways" in order to be part of the global economy, and there is considerable evidence that Japanese pragmatism has already created some new opportunities for women in the workplace (Prater, 1991). Moreover, legislation exists which purports to promote gender equality in the workplace, though some critics have questioned its efficacy (Edwards, 1988). In short, the "downside" of promoting equal opportunity in Japan because of cultural norms may easily be overstated; while Japanese males are not as sensitive to sexual harassment issues, for example, there are signs that they are becoming so (Lan, 1991).

For a host country culture that is less in flux, and whose culture and laws present a unified force against social change, the ethical issues change somewhat. This is because Title VII expressly allows discrimination in certain instances through the *bona fide* occupational qualification (BFOQ)[4] exception. The BFOQ exception provides that it will not be illegal to discriminate "on the basis of . . . religion, sex, or national origin in those certain instances where religion, sex, or national origin is a *bona fide* occupational qualification reasonably necessary to the normal operation of that particular business or enterprise."

In *Kern v. Dynalectron,*[5] for example, a company in the business of flying planes into the holy city of Mecca advised potential employees that Saudi Arabian law prohibited the entry of non-Moslems into the holy area under penalty of death. One pilot took instruction in the Moslem religion, but was Baptist at heart, and rescinded his "conversion." Returning to the U.S., he sued under Title VII for employment discrimination based on religion. The federal appeals court ultimately determined that Title VII applied but that being Moslem was, in this situation, a "*bona fide* occupational qualification" and not discriminatory.

It remains to be seen how gender qualifications may be raised and litigated for alleged discrimination overseas. But if those qualifications have the force of law, and are not the result of cultural preferences only, the most serious ethical dilemma is whether or not to do business in that country at all. To take an example based on racial classification, if South African law prohibited blacks from being hired by MNEs, the MNEs' only ethical choices would be to

1. do business in South Africa and comply with the law,
2. refuse to do business in South Africa, or
3. do business there and hire blacks anyway.

How are these three options analyzed from a perspective of ethics and the law? Option (3) may certainly be seen as an ethical policy, though probably of the "ethnocentric" variety, yet few ethicists and even fewer business executives would counsel such a course. Option (1) is well within the mainstream of ethical relativism, and, we would argue, is less ethical than choosing option (2). But again, *cultural* conflicts do not create such choices; legal mandates do. And countries whose cultural values are colliding with the values of "outsiders" may choose, at least temporarily, to preserve their culture through legal mandates. Saudi Arabia has laws which prohibit women from travelling alone, working with men, working with non-Muslim foreigners, and these laws apply to foreign women as well as host country women (Moghadam, 1988).

Even without such explicit laws of prohibition, MNEs and their human resource managers may hesitate to violate unwritten or cultural laws, and taking moral relativism's approach to the problem of gender equality in other countries may seem prudent. But such an approach seems to depend on a rather sketchy kind of utilitarian analysis: Engaging in overt equal opportunity policies will result in cultural condemnation, loss of customer and client contacts, and eventual unprofitability of the entire overseas enterprise. But in host countries whose culture is tied to the mainstream of world business, long-held attitudes will be difficult to maintain, and the negative impact of "doing things differently" should not be overestimated, nor should the definite benefits and opportunities of pursuing gender quality be overlooked (Lansing and Ready, 1988).

In this context, a comment about the employee's perspective seems appropriate. It might be difficult to generalize here because individual perspective often differs, depending upon personal ideology, situation, and career opportunities. However, from the viewpoint of a female manager in a U.S. MNE, we will assume that the greatest good would be a business world safe for gender equality and supportive of same. Adler and others have noted the difficulty of persuading MNEs that women managers can succeed in many countries whose cultures actively promote gender inequality (Adler, 1984). Certainly, a U.S. female manager's inability to obtain first-hand experience in dealing with Japanese businesses comes close to being a career handicap, and for Japanese women, the existence of opportunities outside the home may safely be regarded as benefits.

Ultimately, most American citizen employees of MNEs will test any policy by asking whether or not they are personally adversely affected. Companies that take care to structure career advancement opportunities such that experience in countries hostile to a protected class may find themselves with few employee complaints. However, MNEs not able to finesse the mandate of Title VII and the reality of certain foreign cultures will find themselves facing a similar set of choices described above with respect to apartheid. Now, however, a decision to accommodate host country norms must be accompanied by a fund out of which to pay judgments in Title VII litigation.

B. The Host Country's Perspective

From the overall Japanese societal perspective, the changes contemplated by a mandate of gender equality may indeed be troubling. The social structure that has built up over centuries, which has "worked" to achieve stability and a degree of consensus and comfort, could crumble if more and more women leave household work to obtain work in the "business world." Who will do the careful packing of lunches, the guidance for "cram courses" after school, tending to the children and dinner and bedtime while spouse is engaged in the obligatory socializing with office mates after hours? While Japanese men may now be undertaking more domestic duties, the differences are still staggering. One recent estimate suggested that Japanese women put in four to five hours of domestic work daily, while their husbands put in eight minutes (Watanabe, 1992).

Any change in the prescribed social order is bound to seem disruptive, and, therefore, negative. As one Islamic man declared to a National Public Radio correspondent during the Persian Gulf war, if women are allowed in the workplace, the forces of social decay would soon send the divorce and crime rates skyrocketing. This argument, a kind of utilitarian "parade of horribles,"[6] overtly trades on fear of change, is not empirically rigorous, and assumes that changes in the U.S. over a fifty year period represent the ultimate result of mindless social tampering. For the Islamic, this particular proponent of gender inequality in the workplace has a back-up argument, the *Qur'an*.

By appeal to divine, or infinite wisdom, we find an argument more akin to natural law or universalism. The argument may even suppose that not only Islamic society, but all other societies, would be well advised to follow this divinely decreed social ordering. What is manifest to the Islamic mind is contrary, it would seem, to "Western" notions of gender equality. This conflict pits two "objective" or "universal" truths against one another: the "truth" of the *Qur'an* and the "truth" of the Universal Declaration of Human Rights. Is the moral relativist right, after all?

II. ETHICAL RELATIVISM AND ETHICAL ETHNOCENTRISM: A SYNTHESIS FOR OVERSEAS GENDER DISCRIMINATION ISSUES

In general terms, the theory of moral relativism holds that different moral standards are "equally valid or equally invalid," and there are no "objective standards of right and wrong or good and evil that transcend the opinions of different individuals or different societies."[7] At the opposite extreme of the continuum is the objective approach, which is premised on the notion that there are "transcultural" norms that are universally valid.

Bowie (1988) suggests that the proper view is a point closer to the latter position. Although he stops short of embracing universalism, Bowie believes there are minimum ethical principles that are universally evident such as "do not commit murder" and "do not torture." These principles, clearly, can be enforced without imposing ethnocentric (or imperialistic) views upon a host country. To these minimum universal principles, Bowie adds the "morals of the marketplace," which are required to support transactions in the business world. These include honesty and trust. The combination of these two strands of quasi-universalism is as far as Bowie will go in staking his claim on the continuum.

Consider again the dilemmas faced by a U.S. MNE doing business in Japan, trying to integrate a tradition and practice of equal opportunity into a tradition and practice of unequal opportunity. One strategy for "blending in" with the Japanese market might be to adopt a thoroughly Japanese outlook and approach. That would include differing pay scales for men and women, actively discouraging women past the age of 25 from working with the company, and pointedly not inviting women employees to the after-five work/social functions that seem to play such an important part in an employee's successful corporate bonding.

Other than outright moral relativism, the social contract approach would appear to be the most likely proponent of such assimilation. Social contract theory examines the ethical foundations of societies by the relationships that exist within and between people, organizations, and groups. In an article on "extant social contracts," Dunfee (1991) explains and defends this communitarian approach to ethics, which appears grounded in relativism, but he also appears to offer an escape clause by way of a "filtering" device using utilitarian or deontological approaches. Dunfee would apparently recognize that racial discrimination is more widely condemned, and that gender discrimination is more widely tolerated, and conclude that perpetuating gender discrimination is less unethical than perpetuating racial discrimination. In a subsequent article, Dunfee and Donaldson (1991) retreat somewhat from the relativism approach and appear to suggest some dimensions of gender equality qualify as a "hypernorm," that is, a norm "recognized as core or foundational by most humans, regardless of culture." The example they give, however, is that of Saudi Arabia prohibiting women from driving, a rule that violates hypernorms of freedom of movement and rights of self-realization. Obviously, this issue does not approach the complexity posed by the international application of gender equality in the workplace.

In essence, what seems problematic for social contract theory is the substantial variance between the almost universally professed ideals of gender equality and the globally pervasive policies of gender inequality. If one looks to social practice for guidance as to what is ethical, gender inequality becomes relatively more ethical; yet if one looks to professed ideals and principles of equality, many existing forms of gender inequality (dowry deaths, female infanticide, widow-burning, and abortion based on male preference) (Howe, 1991) seem inexcusable. Ethical guidelines, apart from legal obligations, seem to require more explicit direction.

Bowie rejects relativism and argues for recognition of minimum universal principles and morals of the marketplace, an essentially deontological approach. He suggests that the latter may even control over the former where completely foreign agents meet to do business. Bowie draws upon democratic theory, torture and genocide, and examples based on bribery, apartheid, and political-economic values to make his point. He is, however, silent on gender discrimination. One wonders whether Bowie would view this issue as primarily social or as a political-economic priority on a plane with his other examples.

We take the position that neither relativism nor extant social contract theory are much help to MNEs in a host country whose values run counter to the company's ethical code or the laws and traditions of its country of origin. Instead, the concepts of minimum universal principles and morals of the marketplace legitimately can be broadened to embrace gender equality. Support for this position is evident in the increasingly international consensus on this point.

For example, as Frederick (1991) has pointed out, the United Nations Universal Declaration of Human Rights, the OECD Guidelines for Multinational Enterprises, and the International Labor Office Tripartite Declaration all give support to "nondiscriminatory employment policies" and the concept of "equal pay for equal work." Note that neither of these policies is widespread in Japan. In The United Nations Convention on the Elimination of All Forms of Discrimination Against Women (1979) was ratified by a large number of nations, both industrialized and developing. The European Community has passed a number of Council directives aimed at promoting gender equality in employment (Weiner, 1990).

We believe that by following policies which generally promote gender equality, without slavish adherence to all U.S. judicial opinions on Title VII and with good faith adjustments where cultural conditions require, a U.S. MNE in Japan can maintain its own code of ethics without the "inevitable" loss of "competitiveness." Moreover, it can do so without being "ethnocentric" or "imperialist," and by doing so it can avoid a kind of ethical balkanization that adherence to moral relativism would require. After all, a dozen different cultural traditions might require a dozen different HRM policies, each geared to the host country's dominant yet often changing traditions.

. . . In going to a traditional culture where gender inequality is the norm, the MNE must be aware that there is another community emerging, one whose shape is as yet dimly perceived, but a community where goods, services, and information are traded with ever-increasing speed. Included in the information exchange is the communication of different values, and while these values are not being passed along in traditional ways, their transmission is inevitable. In this exchange of values and ideas, the ideals of equality are manifest in many ways. Any MNE, whatever the cultural norms it confronts in a particular country, would be wise to pay attention.

Notes

1. Civil Rights Restoration Act of 1991, P. L. 102–166, Nov. 21, 1991, 105 Stat. 1071. For the purposes of this discussion, a U.S. MNE is an enterprise with operations in one or more foreign countries.
2. E.E.O.C. v. Aramco, Boureslan v. Aramco, 111 S. Ct. 1227 (1991).
3. The authors mailed a survey entitled "Use of U.S. Employment Discrimination Law Abroad" to human resource directors of 120 companies identified as multinational enterprises. In part, the questionnaire solicited information about whether or not the company felt it wise to apply Title VII abroad. The eight responses that were received provide anecdotal, as opposed to statistically significant, information. Six respondents indicated it would be "unwise" to attempt to apply Title VII to U.S. citizens working abroad. The reasons given appear predictable: it would be "difficult"; it is the "local manager's responsibility"; we "do not attempt" to impose our norms on others. Two respondents believed it would be wise to implement such a policy despite the obstacles

discussed in this paper. Nonetheless, all respondents indicated that the policy is appropriately enforced in the U.S. and two believed it would be wise to do so abroad as well.
4. 42 U.S.C. §2000e-1 (1988).
5. 577 F. Supp. 1196, affirmed 746 F.2d 810 (1984).
6. George Christie, of Duke University Law School, coined this phrase in reference to attorneys, who learn to see the dark possibilities issuing from any proposed action and are prone to recite a "parade of horribles" to their clients.
7. Van Wyk, Introduction to Ethics, St. Martin's Press, New York (1990), p. 15.

References

Adachi, K.: 1989, "Problems and Prospects of Management Development of Female Employees in Japan," Journal of Management Development Vol. 8(4), 32–40.

Adler, N.: 1984, "Women in International Management: Where are They?," California Management Review Vol. 26, 78–89.

Bassiry, G. R.: 1990, "Business Ethics and the United Nations: A Code of Conduct," SAM Advanced Management Journal (Autumn), pp. 38–41.

Bellace, J.: 1991, "The International Dimension of Title VII," Cornell International Law Journal 24, 1–24.

Bowie, N.: 1988, "The Moral Obligations of Multinational Corporations," in Luper-Fay (ed.), Problems of International Justice (Westview Press, New York), pp. 97–113.

Bowie, N.: 1977, "A Taxonomy for Discussing the Conflicting Responsibilities of a Multinational Corporation," in Responsibilities of Multinational Corporations to Society (Arlington, Va.: Council of Better Business Bureau), pp. 21–43.

Carney, L. and O'Kelly: 1987, "Barriers and Constraints to the Recruitment and Mobility of Female Managers in the Japanese Labor Force," Human Resource Management Vol. 26(2), 193–216.

Daimon, S.: 1991, " 'Karoshi' Phenomenon Spreading to Female Workforce," Japan Times Weekly (Intl. Ed.), Sept. 30–Oct. 6, p. 7.

Donaldson, T. and T. Dunfee: 1991, "Social Contracts in Economic Life: A Theory," No. 91–156 (revised) Working Paper Series, Department of Legal Studies, The Wharton School, University of Pennsylvania, pp. 27–32.

Dunfee, T.: 1991, "Extant Social Contracts," Business Ethics Quarterly Vol. 1, 22–37.

Edwards, L.: 1988, "Equal Employment Opportunity in Japan: A View from the West," Industrial and Labor Relations Review 41(2), 240–250.

Ford, J.: 1992, "Sexual Harassment Taken for Granted," Japan Times Weekly (Intl. Ed.), Feb. 10–16, p. 4.

Frederick, W.: 1991, "The Moral Authority of Transnational Corporate Codes," Journal of Business Ethics Vol. 10, 165–177.

Gundling, E.: 1991, "Ethics and Working with the Japanese: The Entrepreneur and the Elite Course," California Management Review Vol. 33(3), 25–39.

Howe M.: 1991, "Sex Discrimination Persists, According to a U.N. Study," New York Times June 16, p. A4, col. 1.

Lan, S.: 1991, "Japanese Businessman Produces Video to Prevent Lawsuits," *Japan Times Weekly* (Intl. Ed.), Nov. 11–17, p. 8.

Lansing, P. and K Ready: 1988, "Hiring Women Managers in Japan: An Alternative for Foreign Employers," *California Management Review* 30(3), 112–121.

Lebra, D.: 1984, *Japanese Women: Constraint and Fulfillment* (University of Hawaii Press, Honolulu).

Mayer, D.: 1991, "Sex Discrimination Policies for U.S. Companies Abroad," in Sanders, W. (ed), *Proceedings of the Council on Employee Responsibilities and Rights* (forthcoming).

Moghadam, V.: 1988, "Women, Work, and Ideology in the Islamic Republic," *International Journal of Middle East Studies* Vol. 20, 221–243.

Neff, R.: 1991, "When in Japan, Recruit as the Japanese Do-Aggressively," *Business Week* June 24, p. 58.

Prater, C.: 1991, "Women Try on New Roles; But Hopes Can Still Collide With Tradition," *Detroit Free Press* November 27, p. 1 (5th in a series, later published in the *New York Times*).

Rhoodie, E.: 1989, *Discrimination Against Women: A Global Survey of the Economic, Educational, Social and Political Status of Women* (London, U.K., McFarland and Company).

Seymour, C.: 1991, "The Ad-business: Talented Women Need Not Apply," *Japan Times Weekly* (Intl. Ed.), Dec. 9–15, p. 7.

Simon, H. and F. Brown: 1990/91, "International Enforcement of Title VII: A Small World After All?," *Employee Relations Law Journal* Vol. 16(3), 281–300.

United Nations: 1979, *Convention of the Elimination of All Forms of Discrimination Against Women*, U.N. Doc. A/34/36 (Dec. 18, 1979).

Watanabe, T.: 1992, "In Japan, a 'Goat Man' or No Man; Women are Gaining More Clout in Relationships," *Los Angeles Times* Jan. 6, A1, col. 1.

Weiner, M.: 1990, "Fundamental Misconceptions About Fundamental Rights: The Changing Nature of Women's Rights in the EEC and Their Application in the United Kingdom," *Harvard International Law Journal* Vol. 31(2), 565–574.

Wicks, A.: 1990, "Norman Bowie and Richard Rorty on Multinationals: Does Business Ethics Need 'Metaphysical Comfort'?," *Journal of Business Ethics* Vol. 9, 191–200.

James C. Baker

The International Infant Formula Controversy: A Dilemma in Corporate Social Responsibility

INTRODUCTION

More than a decade ago, a worldwide controversy began whose cast of characters has included some of the world's leading multinational companies (MNCs), international organizations, leading nutritionists, political figures from both industrialized nations and less-developed coun-

tries (LDCs), church activists, anti-corporate demogogues, and consumer advocates. This controversy is the infant formula issue and its relationship to the Nestlé boycott. It is an issue which has not been totally solved and still continues to emerge in some form from time to time.

The objective of this paper is to discuss the issue in depth and to analyze the way in which the controversy changed industry or corporate strategy with regard to the marketing of breast-food substitutes, especially in LDCs, and how it posed an international dilemma in marketing such products. The paper will attempt to provide analysis of both sides of the issue, as well as industry and corporate reactions. The international implications of the issue will be discussed.

THE ISSUE

The food and drug industries developed infant formula food in the 1920s as a substitute for breast-feeding. Sales grew during the succeeding three decades until declining birth rates in the industrialized countries resulted in a sharp drop

From James C. Baker, "The International Infant Formula Controversy: A Dilemma in Corporate Social Responsibility," *Journal of Business Ethics*, Vol. 4, 1985. Reprinted by permission of Kluwer Academic Publishers.

in such sales. The major producers then began to expand in the LDCs where population growth rates were high. Subsequent competition reached its zenith when as many as 17 companies were selling formula at one time.

Major consumer markets in developed countries were middle and upper income segments. Such consumers were very much fewer in LDCs; thus, infant formula began to be marketed to broad segments of the LDCs populations. These consumers were, at the best, only marginally able to afford the higher cost of infant formula foods. The literacy of these consumers was sufficiently low to present the possibility of misuse of these products. Thus, infant mortality and morbidity increased because of malnutrition and illness, spawning the infant formula controversy.

This controversy has resulted in: a libel suit filed by a MNC against the publisher of an adverse report; the birth of a non-profit group to finance action against infant disease caused by improper bottle-feeding; an international code to regulate sale of infant formula; a boycott of the products and services sold by leading MNC; U.S. Congressional hearings on the subject; corporate response of a significant magnitude by the producers of infant formula; formation of church groups to support the above-mentioned boycott; and a plethora of articles about every conceivable facet of the issue. The activity which produced the controversy may have caused the illness and death of millions of infants.

This paper will focus on the principal corporate responses to this issue. These will include those of Nestlé S.A.; Wyeth, a subsidiary of American Home Products; Ross, a subsidiary of Abbot Laboratories; Mead Johnson, a Bristol-Myers subsidiary; and Unigate, a British producer of an infant formula. The response of Nestlé will be the principal one analyzed. In addition, the response of the industry trade association, the International Council of Infant Food Industries (ICIFI) will be discussed.

The non-corporate response will be discussed and analyzed. Among the factors included in this section are the World Health Organization (WHO), the United Nations Children's Economic Fund (UNICEF), the International Pediatric Association, the Caribbean Food and Nu-

trition Institute, a British non-profit organization known as War on Want, and the World Council of Churches, the Infant Formula Action Coalition (INFACT), the International Baby Food Action Network (IBFAN), the Human Lactation Center, the Ethics and Public Policy Center, as well as the United Methodist Church and the Episcopal Church, national legislative bodies in the United States and West Europe and numerous influential individuals in these countries.

From the health standpoint, all parties to this issue have agreed that mother's milk is better than formula, at least for the infant less than one year of age. For example, it contains antibodies which help fight infection. Nursing, itself, acts as a contraceptive in delaying the menstrual cycle after pregnancy. The psychological bond between mother and infant is strengthened by nursing. Breastmilk is relatively much less expensive than formula. In fact, one might say it is costless.[1]

Dr. Derick Jelliffe, then director of the Caribbean Food and Nutrition Institute, initiated a 1970 attack on bottle feeding of infants. He argued that bottle-feeding resulted in nonlactation. In addition, powdered formula could be mixed with contaminated water or diluted to stretch out an expensive supply. The result was disease, illness, malnutrition, and, as Jelliffe termed it, "commerciogenic malnutrition."[2]

The controversy was then elevated to an international forum. A 1970 WHO-UNICEF conference was held in Bogota, Columbia, in which allegations of bad marketing practices by leading formula producers were made. The Protein Calorie Advisory Group then issued a 1972 statement outlining its concerns about infant formula, with a revision in 1973. In 1974, the World Health Assembly issued a resolution urging nations to regulate infant formula sales. The reason given was that misleading sales promotion had caused a decline in breastfeeding.[3] And in 1975, the International Pediatric Association passed a resolution requesting controls on promotion of infant formula by producers.[4]

The unfortunate part of the entire controversy is that little or no solid scientific research has been done to determine whether a relationship exists between use of infant formula and death and disease of infants in LDCs. One major study was conducted by WHO of 23,000 mothers in nine countries.[5] This study found that commercial influences had no significant effects on the method of infant feeding. WHO has estimated that as many as ten million serious cases of malnutrition or illness annually may be a result of *improper* use of infant formula or bottles. About 10%, of these babies die. And WHO studies show that infants breast-fed for less than six months or not at all are five to ten times more likely to die in their second six months than those which are breast-fed for longer periods.[6] Other estimates of the usage in LDCs seem to refute the WHO estimates. Only six million infants in LDCs are estimated to use infant formula.[7] And it has been estimated that infant formula accounts for only about five percent of weaning-food consumption in LDCs.[8]

The Corporate Actors

Worldwide sales of infant formula are dominated by Nestlé S.A., a MNC headquartered in Vevey, Switzerland, and three American companies: Wyeth, a subsidiary of American Home Products, with 15% world sales; Ross, a subsidiary of Abbot Laboratories, whose *Similac* sells very well in Canada and Europe, and Mead Johnson, a Bristol-Meyers subsidiary, whose principal sales are in the Caribbean. Nestlé's share of the market is estimated at 33–50%, depending on whose data is correct. Unigate of Great Britain is another marketer of an infant formula. Abbot has 55% of the U.S. market while Mead Johnson has 35% of the domestic market. In addition, Milupa of Germany also produces infant formula.

Thus, Nestlé became the focus of an international boycott because of at least two facts: the company has as much as 50% of the world market for infant formula with almost none of this in the United States, and its headquarters is a short distance from the Geneva headquarters of the World Council of Churches, a major character in the drama. The latter organization would become a major supporter of the anticorporate response to the sale of infant formula. Some also believed that Nestlé was singled out because it is a company run for profit whereas state-owned milk and formula cooperatives operated not-for-profit in the LDCs compete

against Nestlé, and are generally supported closely by their host governments.

Other companies did dispense free samples of formula. Salesmen for these companies sometimes posed as medical officials in order to convince mothers that bottle feeding was the modern, better way to feed their infants.[9]

The Public Action Groups

In 1974, a pamphlet entitled *The Baby Killer* was published by War on Want, a British nonprofit organization. This report was extremely critical of Nestlé's operations in Africa.[10] A Swiss group published a German-language version entitled *Nestlé Kills Babies*. As a result, Nestlé sued for libel. The trial held that the pamphlet was defamatory but the adverse publicity led to an American response in the form of shareholder demonstrations against the three leading U.S. producers of infant formula. This movement was supported by the Interfaith Center on Corporate Responsibility, a group sponsored by the National Council of Churches. Shareholder resolutions were aimed at the three U.S. producers during their annual meetings.

The next organization spawned by the issue appeared in 1977 in the form of INFACT, The Infant Formula Action Coalition, headquartered in Minneapolis. Its fund-raising campaign designed to support the attack on infant formula manufacturers included a four-page letter sent to various mailing lists showed several pictures of babies suffering from malnutrition as a result of not being breast-fed. The letter specifically attacked Nestlé and stated "how crucial INFACT is in stopping what may become a global Jonestown where instead of Kool-Aid, formula milk is the agent of death." INFACT has been the major force behind the boycott of Nestlé products.

Further Actions

In the meantime, Nestlé and the major formula producers formed the International Council of Infant Food Industries (ICIFI) as a response to the adverse shareholder reaction. ICIFI adopted a code in 1975 aimed at restraining the marketing of infant formula in LDCs. In 1978, Senator Edward Kennedy held hearings of the U.S. Senate Subcommittee on Health and Scientific

Research designed to investigate the infant formula issue.

In 1979, WHO and UNICEF held a joint meeting on Infant and Young Child Feeding. One of the issues addressed was the marketing of infant formula. The emphasis of this meeting was placed on the agreement that infant formula marketing should not discourage breastfeeding. A WHO-UNICEF movement toward an International Code of Marketing of Breastmilk Substitutes began to take shape.

Before such a code was drafted in 1981, the International Baby Food Action Network (IB-FAN) published a document alleging 202 violations of the 1979 WHO-UNICEF meeting recommendations, including 117 violations by ICIFI company members during the January to April, 1980, period. According to a document published by Nestlé, of these, 102 were found to be untrue, misleading, based on wrong information, or too vague to investigate. IBFAN was a worldwide cluster of some 90 activist groups in 40 countries with three main offices in Geneva, Minneapolis, and Penang, Malaysia. In 1981, IB-FAN alleged 682 violations by ICIFI members during 1980. Nestlé again investigated these and reported the vast majority to be unfounded.[11]

Results of the Controversy

In addition to the libel suit brought by Nestlé, the emergence of several protest groups, and a boycott against Nestlé products, primarily in the United States, the most significant result was the adoption by the World Health Assembly of the international code on breastmilk substitutes. The research basis for this code seemed to be the results of the one major study by WHO discussed earlier. In fact, the code is premised on commercial influences having an effect on breastfeeding practices.

Other studies have, for example, contributed to the issue. For example, one more recent study found that the distribution of free samples of infant formula to Canadian mothers who had elected to nurse their babies had little or no effect on the duration of breastfeeding.[12]

The issue of infant feeding and use of formula is a complex and emotional issue. Several points are usually ignored when the issue is discussed. Among these are:

1. breastfeeding is not always successful and infant formula may be the best substitute,
2. a health care professional should recommend infant formula when needed,
3. breastfeeding is declining in many centrally-planned economies where infant formula promotion is prohibited,
4. breastfeeding is sound practice until the infant is six months old, at which time his diet should be supplemented, and
5. there are many socio-economic reasons for the decline of breastfeeding in even the LDCs.

Among the latter reasons are: nutritional and health status of the mother, new pregnancy or desire not to become pregnant, infant health, maternal tension or anxiety, fear of damaging the breasts or figure, embarrassment about exposing the breast, husband's attitude, and work patterns and the availability of time for child care.[13]

However, a paucity of strong research support has been presented to clear the issue. Only the nine-country WHO study seems to be as comprehensive as such studies should be and its findings refute the breastfeeding advocates. Lack of reason in the entire agreement over this issue seems to have triumphed.[14]

Another organization which has studied this issue is the Human Lactation Center. This Connecticut-based research center believes the infant formula industry has heavy economic clout but is not the sole reason for the problem of breastfeeding and weaning among the poor. They believe, furthermore, that poverty's effects—lack of food and safe drinking water, absence of sanitation, and political indifference to poor mothers—are the prime determinants of infant disease and death in LDCs. These conclusions seem to be based on field research concerning the life situation, workload, and feeding practices of mothers.[15]

Furthermore, most LDC mothers believe that breast milk is better for their children than infant formula. The majority of these mothers who do not breastfeed make such a decision because they cannot breastfeed for various reasons. In addition, some LDC infants show poor growth rates when fed no food supplemental to breast milk. And, as mentioned previously, no evidence has been found to generally support a contention that infant formula manufacturers have influenced infant-feeding choices of LDC mothers with their advertising. Such findings are from WHO itself.[16] In short, there is a paucity of scientific research on infant formula and its effects. Most recommendations concerning this issue are based, therefore, on "clinical" evidence, i.e., health workers' observations from all over the world.[17]

The WHO Code

This debate led to the draft of an International Code of Marketing of Breastmilk Substitutes, passed by the World Health Assembly as recommendatory legislation. The code was to be a model for minimum national guidelines. Several countries have already drafted their own codes on infant formula, some stronger than the WHO Code. For example, the European Economic Community has adopted strict enforcement of the WHO Code by a 103–14 vote of its European Parliament.[18]

The Code, however, contains provisions which may be difficult to implement by infant formula producers, especially since the Code will be made a frame of reference for national expectations.[19] For example, the WHO Code requires that a statement concerning the negative impact of bottle-feeding on lactation be included in any educational literature made available to pregnant women and new mothers. Real-life experience worldwide does not seem to support this conclusion nor does in-depth research reported on bottle-feeding.

Second, a physician is precluded from providing a mother with samples of infant formula, even though she may have decided to use supplements at home. The result of this provision may be the use of an improper product purchased by the mother on the retail market.

Third, the Code restricts severely the amount of information which may be disseminated to mothers or mothers-to-be about selection, preparation, and use of supplemental or weaning foods. Since all infants need supplemental foods by their sixth or seventh month of life, this limitation may be dangerous to the health

of infants in LDCs. In fact, the Code places control over all these aspects of supplemental feeding with the national governments on the presumption that governments know best what information needs to be disseminated.

In addition, several specific points of information are required to be given to mothers. Many of these are not based on scientific data. These include statements about: the benefits of breast-feeding, the negative effect on breastfeeding from partial bottle-feeding, and the difficulty of reversing a mother's decision not to breastfeed.

Only one country, the United States, voted against the WHO Code. The negative U.S. vote was presumably based on the principle of a free market economic system as well as the fear of some-type international Federal Trade Commission and the enactment of a series of codes aimed at marketing of specific products.[20] Nevertheless, the lone dissenting vote was severely criticized.[21] U.S. formula producers and the Grocery Manufacturers of America lobbied heavily against the Code causing an interagency task force to recommend a U.S. abstention. However, the Reagan Administration, for the reasons stated earlier, decided to oppose the Code.[22] Both U.S. Houses of Congress have since passed resolutions censuring the U.S. vote in the World Health Assembly, asking that the Code be adopted in the United States.

GLOBAL ACTIVISM

How did the WHO Code come to the point of being considered at all? Global activism by many different groups opposed major MNCs. The boycott against Nestlé products was the focal point which moved the issue into an international organization.

With regard to an issue such as the infant formula controversy, a manufacturer has, perhaps, three alternatives. First, the company can continue to market these products in the same manner as it always has, unless prohibited by national law. The WHO Code, although in the realm of international law, has only public opinion as its enforcement powers. National codes may also be difficult to enforce unless they are legislated into law. Previous research has shown that solutions to social responsibility issues occur only through governmental efforts, meaning in this case national governments.[23]

Second, an infant formula producer could resort to a strategy of demarketing the product. Demarketing involves restraints and, in the case of infant formula, is only possible if industry, critics, and LDC governments become involved. Demarketing of a product is the result of a company's decisions to reduce or stop completely efforts to sell the product because of health and safety risks to the consumer.[24] The decision may be the result of management viewpoint, public pressure, or government regulation. In the case of infant formula, the product is not basically unsafe but it may be misused by the consumer, because of any of the reasons previously discussed, leading to harm to an unsuspecting infant. The product, thus, became hazardous in LDCs even though no thorough research has directly connected the hazardous nature of the product with its promotion by manufacturers. The weight of U.S. product liability law does not exist for the most part in the LDCs where the infant formula issue has arisen.

The third type of corporate strategy which may be implemented consists of adapting to the pressures which arise from the public while attempting to maintain some semblance of a viable market. With regard to the infant formula issue, public pressures involved shareholder resolutions at annual meetings of the leading American companies and a boycott of Nestlé products initiated by the INFACT group.

The American companies, fearing that their domestic markets might be jeopardized by the public's connection of their activities with the Nestlé boycott impetus, drafted codes of their own. These codes were held to be at least as far-reaching as the WHO Code. However, the companies kept their marketing policies in a middle-road position vis-à-vis demarketing or maintaining the status quo.[25]

THE NESTLÉ RESPONSE

The INFACT-led boycott against Nestlé products has become very pervasive. Several large church denominations had sections of their constituencies join the boycott. Several areas, for example, of the United Methodist Church and the Episcopal Church participated in the boycott, as well as the Church of the Brethren.

The boycott extended to areas of Nestlé operations which had nothing to do with infant formula. For example, the booking of a national convention of the American Public Health Association to be held in a Cleveland, Ohio, hotel was cancelled because the hotel was owned by Stouffers Company, a Nestlé subsidiary. The loss of this conference cost the Cleveland area 6,000 conventioneer room rentals. In fact, the effects of combatting the boycott reportedly may have cost Nestlé significant profits in 1980 and 1981.[26]

At first, Nestlé bitterly opposed both the WHO Code and the boycott. This, of course, widened the support of INFACT's boycott movement as groups such as the General Council of Ministries of the United Methodist Church threatened to bring the entire world congregation of the Methodist Church into the boycott.

One of Nestlé's first actions was to engage Hill & Knowlton Inc., a public relations firm, to assist the company in preparing a marketing strategy to combat the boycott. Next, the company formed a staff of 15 U.S.-based people, including five full-time officials, to work on boycott issues. The company mailed letters discussing the Nestlé viewpoint to 300,000 U.S. clergymen. The U.S.-based staff on boycott matters was formalized by the establishment of the Nestlé Coordination Center for Nutrition (NCCN), Inc., located in Washington D.C. Several publications were then issued by this organization. The publications issued by NCCN contain viewpoints which advocate breastfeeding where possible while at the same time they point out the need for supplemented feeding and allude to studies which seem to refute many of Nestlé's critics.[27] In short, these published statements seemed to be quite conciliatory. Nestlé and other members of the industry reviewed their strategies and modified them to reduce misunderstanding. As a result of these changes, the General Council of Ministries of the United Methodist Church took no action on the Nestlé boycott.

Nestlé had already sharply curtailed its worldwide consumer advertising for formula in 1978. Mass media advertising of formula began to be phased out of certain markets that year although marketing practices including advertising had not been linked to infant feeding patterns.[28]

A Nestlé official testified before hearings of the House Subcommittee on International Economic Policy and Trade in 1981 and outlined the official Nestlé strategy as follows:[29]

1. Nestlé fully supports the aim of the WHO Code;
2. Nestlé will continue to promote breastfeeding and insure that this will not be discouraged anywhere by Nestlé marketing practices;
3. Nestlé will work with nutrition professionals and health and nutrition of mothers and infants;
4. Nestlé will abide by national codes on infant formula wherever enacted.

This strategy was designed to recognize the infant formula issues while avoiding demarketing of the product. It was designed, in effect, to cut potential losses while insuring goodwill among the various interested publics. In short, Nestlé's second major strategy, to formally support the WHO Code, finally evolved by March, 1982. Once the issue reached the stage where remedy and relief were required and non-users of the product had entered the controversy, management's alternatives became limited.[30]

With nearly 50% of a $2billion market at stake, Nestlé was forced by several activist groups and an international agency to correct the mistakes that resulted from overly-aggressive competition caused by the growth of an industry from a handful of companies to some 17 competitors. Several questionable sales tactics had been practiced by all companies involved.

In fact, not all parties agreed that Nestlé's response was an above-board design. INFACT remained highly critical, especially of the role played in the Nestlé strategy by Herman Nickel, Washington editor of *Fortune Magazine* whose article, "The Corporation Haters," was labeled by INFACT as a treatise alleging a conspiracy by

"INFACT, the National Council of Churches, the Interfaith Center on Corporate Responsibility, and others against the defenseless giant, Nestlé."[31]

Johnson questioned the fee arrangement made by Ernest Lefever, head of the Ethics and Public Policy Center (EPPC) to Nickel for the draft of a study of the infant formula controversy which Johnson states was never written. Johnson, furthermore, discussed a documented contribution by Nestlé to the EPPC for an amount equal to the fee agreed to be paid to Nickels. Nestlé then, according to Johnson, mailed out reprints of the *Fortune Magazine* article, as did other industry members.[32]

Nestlé also sent packets of materials including the *Fortune* piece to community leaders whose addresses were on mailing lists purchased by Nestlé. Nestlé then made a $20,000 contribution to the EPPC. Nestlé, according to Johnson, became nervous about possible public reaction to this kind of "manipulation" and use of Nestlé funds to support the EPPC. But the Washington, D.C. attorney for the company said in a company memorandum that the situation could be handled.

Lefever, the EPPC head, then wrote an editorial piece in the *Wall Street Journal* attacking industry critics. This article was used by Nestlé to lobby against the proposed WHO Code.[33] However, during 1981, the boycott pressures caused Nestlé management to approve the WHO Code.

Nestlé made a final strategic move which, perhaps, was its best. The company formed an Infant Formula Audit Commission for the purpose of reviewing allegations that Nestlé had violated WHO or national codes. The Commission is chaired by former U.S. Senator Edmund Muskie, well-respected in diplomatic circles, and its other members are prominent health and church officials.

The first quarterly report[34] issued by this Commission noted that Nestlé had formulated a comprehensive plan as follows:

1. discouragement of retailers from promoting infant formula at any point of sale;
2. application of the WHO Code to infant formula products for use by children of any age;

3. preclusion of the use of 'mothercraft' nurses;
4. provision of free or reduced-cost supplies of infant formula only to children who cannot breastfeed;
5. discontinuation of the practice of routinely providing samples of infant formula to health workers for use with their own children;
6. cessation of advertising or promotion, directly or indirectly, of infant formula to mothers, pregnant women or the general public.

In October, 1983, the Muskie Commission made what appears to be its final report. Although the Commission reported that Nestlé had not fully complied with the WHO Code, it characterized the latter as a frustrating "imperfect compromise"[35] Nestlé agreed to change its infant formula labels to eliminate words to the effect that formula is ideal for infants and to cease giving free samples to institutions except for professional evaluation.

However, the Commission stressed in its report that these changes would not cure the central problem in LDCs, that of poverty and its consequences. In fact, it has been argued that a contradiction exists between the attempt by some organizations, such as UNICEF, to stop infant formulas and bottle-feeding on the one hand and data, on the other hand, which shows compatibility between increased use of formulas and bottle-feeding with declines in infant mortality.[36]

Finally, a result of the Muskie Commission audits and other reports, the boycott has been ended. Church groups such as the United Methodists and Church of the Brethren began pulling out of the boycott in late 1983. And the three major U.S. producers of the formula fully complied with the WHO Code.[37] In early 1984, leaders of the boycott reported Nestlé to be in general compliance of the WHO Code.[38] The boycott was effectively ended in February 1984.

by MNCs. They may not have intentionally violated any laws but their acts may have resulted in adverse social consequences. In the case of Nestlé, the second order effects of marketing infant formula in LDCs brought non-users into the fray. These non-users were comprised of WHO and other U.N. agencies, several large religious organizations, activist groups, and ultimately, national governments themselves.

The infant formula controversy has joined an issue between several large MNCs and a variety of international and national activist groups and governmental agencies. It included an international boycott against Nestlé products resulting in an international code, several national codes and laws, and corporate responses which drastically changed corporate policy toward the worldwide marketing of a specific product. In short, an international dilemma evolved.

This dilemma took its form in several areas. The population growth problem in LDCs creates food shortage problems. Infant formula, if properly used, is a necessary supplement to breastfeeding. The profit motive and severe competition among producers, however, resulted in bad marketing practices and incorrect utilization of a needed product in LDCs, thus further resulting in illness and infant death.

The business function of advertising has been severely limited, especially in LDCs where formula promotion has been banned. Any educational activities designed to assist mothers in using the formula properly will be considered violations of the WHO Code.[39]

Protest groups based their actions on shallow research but have succeeded in getting the problem recognized and, regardless of the tactics, alleviated. They have combined to solve the problems of mothers and infants in LDCs who did not have the ability to mobilize themselves. In short, the protest groups, led by INFACT, neutralized or turned the producers' power to the formula industry's disadvantage.

CONCLUSIONS AND IMPLICATIONS

The infant formula controversy, as analyzed in this paper, demonstrates the effects on an industry and, specifically, a major company in the industry, Nestlé S.A., of the pursuit of self-interest

Implications

The international protest movement against infant formula will probably go further than merely changing the marketing policies of an industry. Its interaction with industry may result in complex social system change in LDCs which could lead to better sanitary conditions.

The controversy will result in more research of better quality on matters such as infant formula usage and decline in breastfeeding. The corporate response, especially that of Nestlé, has already insured this will happen.

The controversy made significant inroads for consumerism. One can compare the case of Johnson & Johnson, maker of Tylenol, and its handling of the Tylenol poisoning case with the Nestlé *et al.* handling of the infant formula controversy. Johnson & Johnson publicized the worst aspects of the case immediately and acted before government forced it to act. The company was not evasive, did not mislead, did not attempt to place blame, did not make light of the case, and, apparently, had a contingency plan to follow. Profits were lost but the market loss has been recouped and public relations analysts believe the Johnson & Johnson response was the best policy for good consumer relations. Nestlé, on the other hand, seemed to muddle through the formula issue for years before a correct response was implemented.

Finally, the infant formula controversy should bring an indictment against the international community for the seeming hypocrisy or, at least, inconsistency with its handling of unhealthful products. Two major products areas can be identified. First, pharmaceuticals such as antibiotics are used by farmers to produce healthier livestock. Medical proof exists that these antibiotics are passed to humans through meat and milk consumption and that several dangerous strains of bacteria have become immune to these drugs because of too frequent usage. The result has been many documented cases of illness or death as a result.

The international inconsistency with regard to antibiotics arises from the fact that several leading agricultural countries have banned the use of certain antibiotics in the feedgrains of livestock. These bans have not been completely enforced and the practice continues. Furthermore, the last active research on this subject by WHO was in 1969.

The second area of inconsistency concerns tobacco products. Medical proof exists that these products are hazardous to human health.

Yet nations subsidize tobacco production and the United States exports large amounts of tobacco to other countries, especially the LDCs. The tobacco industry is also an important cash crop in some LDCs.

These two areas certainly merit more research and action by international agencies. However, large MNCs are again involved in their production. The international activist groups do not seem to be as vocal in these areas as they have been with infant formula. Yet medical research exists to show that these two products are certainly as hazardous as infant formula. International codes would seem to be merited in the case of both feedgrain antibiotics and tobacco products.

Finally, the role of the major element of the boycott is a prime candidate for research by sociologists and political scientists. INFACT began in 1977 with 20 people and a budget of $500. By the end of the controversy, it had led a boycott in nine countries and was spearheading as many as 85 national organizations in the United States alone. It had used a public issue to further its growth as well as to eliminate a possible worldwide problem concerning the dangerous use of a consumer product. Its role, however, does not seem to have found a solution to the fundamental causes of malnutrition and infant mortality in the Third World.

Notes

1. Tom Mathews, "The Breast vs. the Bottle," *Newsweek* (June 1, 1981), p. 54.
2. Derick B. Jelliffe, "Commerciogenic Malnutrition?," *Food Technology* Vol. 25 (1971), 153–154.
3. WHO, "Statement of the 27th World Health Assembly," May 23, 1974.
4. International Pediatrics Association, "Recommendations for Action Programs to Encourage Breastfeeding," *Bulletin of International Pediatrics Association* Vol. 4 (1975), 18–22.
5. *WHO Collaborative Study on Breast Feeding* (Preliminary Report). World Health Organization MCH/79.3, Geneva, 1979.
6. Mathews, "The Breast vs. The Bottle," *Newsweek,* op. cit., p. 55.
7. André McNiccol, "Different Ideologies; Different Diagnoses," *Maclean's* (Fall 16/81), p. 20.
8. James Grant, "Nestlé Crunch: The Campaign Against Instant Formula Reeks of Sophistry'," *Barron's* (July 16, 1979), p. 7.
9. Ellen Brown, "A Boycott Works-It Better," *The Humanist* Vol. 40 (1980), 50.

10. Mike Muller, *The Baby Killer* (London, War on Want, 1974).
11. "How Nestlé has Followed the WHO/UNICEF," October, 1979, Recommendations," published by Nestlé S.A., Vevey, Switzerland, April, 1981.
12. Y. Bergevin, M. Kramer, and C. Dougherty, "Do Infant Formula Samples Affect the Duration of Breast Feeding?," presented to the Ambulatory Pediatric Association, April 30, 1981.
13. Robert C. Gelardi, "The Infant Formula Issue: A Story in Simplification and Escalation," *Nutrition Today* (September/October, 1981), pp. 26, 29.
14. Charles D. May, "The 'Infant Formula Controversy': A Notorious Threat to Reason in Matters of Health," *Pediatrics* Vol. 68 (September 1981).
15. "Breastfeeding and Weaning Among the Poor," *The Lactation Review* Vol. 3 (1978), 1–6.
16. James Hickel, "Infant Formula: WHO Mixes It Up," *Reason* (December 1981), p. 41.
17. "In Dubious Bottle," *Commonweal* Vol. 108 (1981), 325.
18. Bruce Vandewort, "EEC Unit OKs Formula Code," *Advertising Age* Vol. 52 (October 26, 1981), p. 78.
19. See "Excerpts from Code," *World Health* (August 1981), p. 31, for major sections of the Code.
20. Elinor Constable, "WHO Infant Formula Code," *Department of State Bulletin* Vol. 81 (1981), 34–36, a statement before the Subcommittee on International Economic Policy and Trade of the House Foreign Affairs Committee on June 16, 1981.
21. See, for example, "Mother's Milk," *America* (June 6, 1981), p. 456, as typical of many editorials.
22. Kurt Andersen, "The Battle of the Bottle," *Time* (June 1, 1981), p. 26.
23. James C. Baker, Donald R. Domm, Herbert J. Roth, and John K. Ryans, Jr., "Institutional Investor Attitudes Toward Corporate Social Responsibility," *Arkansas Business and Economic Review* Vol. 7 (Summer 1974), p. 19.
24. James E. Post and Edward Baer, "Demarketing Infant Formula: Consumer Products in the Developing World," *Journal of Contemporary Business* (1978), 17–35.
25. Barbara A. Reynolds, "Breast or Bottle: The Right to Choose," *Essence* Vol. 13 (1982), p. 113.
26. Judy Grande, "Cleveland Convention Axed in Nestlé Boycott," *Cleveland Plain Dealer* (December 2, 1981), p. 1, 18-A.
27. Richard L. Barovick, "Activism on a Global Scale," *Public Relations Journal* Vol. 38 (June 1982), 31.
28. Leah Rozen, "Nestlé Curtails Worldwide Consumer Ads for Formula," *Advertising Age* Vol. 50 (April 23, 1979), 24, 28.
29. Prepared Statement of Dr. Thad M. Jackson, Vice President for Nutrition Research and Development, Nestlé Coordination Center for Nutrition, Inc., before the Subcommittee on International Economic Policy and Trade, Committee on Foreign Affairs, U.S. House of Representatives, Washington, D.C., June 16, 1981.
30. S. Prakash Sethi and James E. Post, "Public Consequences of Private Action: The Marketing of Infant Formula in Less Developed Countries," *California Management Review* Vol. 21 (Summer 1979), 48.
31. Douglas Johnson, "A Glimpse at Nestlé's Anti-Boycott Strategy," *Business and Society Review,* No. 37 (Spring 1980–81), pp. 65–67.
32. Herman Nickel, "The Corporation Haters," *Fortune* Vol. 101 (1980), 126–136, and reprinted as "Crusade Against the Corporation: Churches and the Nestlé Boycott," by the Ethics and Public Policy Center in Washington, D.C., 1980.
33. Ernest W. Lefever, "Politics and Baby Formula in the Third World," *The Wall Street Journal* (January 14, 1981), p. 22.
34. See "More on Nestlé," *The Christian Century* (November 10, 1982), p. 1128; Richard L. Barovick, "One Upmanship in Infant-formula Controversy," *Public Relations Journal* Vol. 38 (December 1982), 6; and "The Formula Crisis Cools," *Fortune* Vol. 106 (1982), 106.
35. Jeffrey L. Fox, "Nestlé Complying with WHO Code for Infant Formulas," *Science* Vol. 222 (1983), 400.
36. Harry Schwartz, "The State of the World's Children 1984," *The Wall Street Journal* (January 12, 1984), p. 24.
37. Randy France, "At Last, Nestlé Satisfies Some of Its Church Critics," *Christianity Today* Vol. 28 (1984), 54, 56.
38. "Boycott Against Nestlé Over Infant Formula to End Next Month," *The Wall Street Journal* (January 27, 1984), p. 18.
39. Stanley E. Cohen, "WHO Vote is a Disaster for Advertising," *Advertising Age* Vol. 52 (June 1, 1981), 24.

QUESTIONS

1. On what basis does Steidlmeier distinguish between common and public property?
2. How do you think Steidlmeier would respond to Paine's [Chapter Nine] defense of trade secrets?
3. What do Singh and Lakhan mean when they note that "expression of the desire for a clean, safe environment is not the same as stating that a clean safe environment is the right of every human being"?
4. Suppose a country with high unemployment and few natural resources decides to build a state-of-the-art disposal facility for processing hazardous wastes. If such a facility is economically viable and environmentally responsible, can it still be argued that to export "wastes to countries which do not benefit from waste generating industrial processes or whose citizens do not have lifestyles that generate such wastes is unethical"? In

such an instance would it be true that the importer was not benefitting from the waste generating industrial processes?

5. Does the view that there are transcultural moral truths imply ethnocentrism, i.e., that the moral views of one's own society are those transcultural truths? Explain.

6. Cava and Mayer suggest that with regards to gender equality, American multinationals should not slavishly adhere to all U.S. judicial opinions and should be prepared to make good faith adjustments where cultural conditions require. Is this too great a concession to ethical relativism? How does this advice differ in essence from the cultural relativist's advice "when in Rome do as the Romans"?

7. What are some of the reasons mentioned by Baker for Nestlé being singled out for boycott?

8. Was the boycott against Nestlé morally justified? Why or why not?

Case 17:1 Discrimination or Job Requirement[1]

Wade Kern, a helicopter pilot, was hired by Dynalectron Corporation on August 17, 1978. Through a subcontract, Dynalectron provided Kawasaki Heavy Industries Ltd. with pilots to work in Saudi Arabia. The duties of these pilots involved flying helicopters over crowds of Muslim pilgrims retracing Muhammad's path to Mecca. These flights were designed to protect pilgrims against any violent outbreaks and to help fight the fires that frequently resulted from cooking fires too close to pilgrims' tents.

The pilots were stationed at three bases: Jeddah, Dhahran, and Riyadh. Due to the fact that the pilots stationed at Jeddah were required to fly into Mecca and that Saudi Arabian law, in accordance with Islamic religion, forbids non-Muslims to enter Mecca on pain of beheading, Kern, who was to be stationed in Jeddah, was required by Kawasaki to convert to Islam.

Kern, a Baptist Christian, initially agreed to convert. He attended a course on the Islamic faith held in Tokyo, chose his new Islamic name, and signed a certificate of conversion. At this point he changed his mind, returned to Fort Worth at his own expense, and informed Dynalectron of his decision. Dynalectron offered him a job as a member of the air crew, a position which would not require his conversion, but Kern declined. Kern subsequently sued Dynalectron on the basis that he had been discriminated against on the basis of his religious beliefs.

Case Study Questions

1. Do you agree that in these circumstances, being Muslim is a legitimate occupational qualification?

2. Suppose the Saudis were to insist not only that the pilots be Muslim, but also male. Would it be legitimate for Dynalectron to hire only male pilots in such circumstances?

3. Would there have been anything wrong in Kern taking the course on Islamism and signing a certificate of conversion, but only pretending that his conversion was genuine?

Case 17:2 Conflicting Rights?[2]

In 1981 female secretarial employees of Sumitomo Shoji America Inc. brought a class action suit against their employer, claiming that its policy of hiring only male Japanese nationals for management positions was in violation of Title VII of the Civil Rights Act of 1964, which forbids discrimination on the basis of age, nationality, race or sex. In reply, their employer argued that under the provisions of the Treaty of Friendship, Commerce and Navigation between Japan and the Untied States, it is permitted to engage executive personnel of its choice and hence should be considered exempt from the requirements of Title VII of the Civil Rights Act.

Case Study Questions

1. Sumitomo Shoji further argued that there should be no difference in treatment between a parent Japanese company operating in the United States and a U.S. incorporated subsidiary such as Sumitomo Shoji. Do you agree? Why or why not?

2. How would you respond to the argument that Sumitomo Shoji is not discriminating on the basis of sex, and thus violating Title VII of the Civil Rights Act, but is simply exercising its acknowledged treaty right to appoint Japanese citizens in executive roles?

3. Is Title VII of the Civil Rights Act consistent with the provisions of treaties which allow foreign companies operating in the United States to hire personnel of their choice? Why or why not?

Notes

1. Based on *Kern v. Dynalectron Corp.* as found in 577 Federal Supplement 1196 (1983).
2. Based on *Avigliano v. Sumitomo Shoji America, Inc.* as found in 638 Federal Reporter 2nd series, 552 (1981).

For Further Reading

1. Thomas Donaldson, "Multinational Decision-Making: Reconciling International Norms," *Journal of Business Ethics*, Vol. 4, (1985) pp. 357–366.

2. Michael Hoffman, Ann Lange and David Fedo (editors), *Ethics and the Multinational Enterprise* (New York: University Press of America, 1986).

3. John Kline, *International Codes and Multinational Business* (Westport: Quorum Books, 1985)

4. Louis Turner, *Multinational Companies and the Third World* (New York: Hill & Wang, 1973)

Chapter Eighteen

BUSINESS AND THE ENVIRONMENT

Introduction

In the last few decades Western societies have become increasingly aware of environmental concerns. While most ethicists would agree that we need to take environmental issues more seriously, there is disagreement over whether this implies reform or revolution. Some insist that we must abandon the anthropocentrism characteristic of traditional ethical thinking, others maintain that we can satisfactorily address environmental concerns without abandoning the view that humans are preeminently valuable in the natural order.

In our first selection, "The Ethics of Respect for Nature," Paul W. Taylor argues that we must abandon the anthropocentrism of traditional ethical thinking in favor of an approach which recognizes the intrinsic value of all living things. Such an approach suggests that human interests have value but no more or less so than the interests of any other living thing. We must adopt, therefore, not an anthropocentric view, but a *biocentric* view which recognizes that humans have no greater inherent worth than any other species.

Tibor R. Machan's article "Environmentalism Humanized," provides a sharp contrast to Taylor's article. Machan argues that human beings are of the highest value in the known universe and an anthropocentric ethic is therefore appropriate. He denies, however, that an anthropocentric approach implies plants and animals have no value apart from their relationship to human beings. He suggests that many theorists reject an anthropocentric ethics on the basis of the mistaken view that recognizing a hierarchy in nature with man at the top of that hierarchy, commits one to accepting there are no moral constraints on how nonhumans may be treated.

573

Our final selection is the article "Ecological Marketing Strategy for Toni Yogurts in Switzerland." Thomas Dyllick describes a successful attempt by Toni, a Swiss firm producing yogurt, to combine environmental concerns and effective marketing. Dyllick suggests that economic goals do not necessarily collide with environmental responsibility, and attempts to distil some of the lessons that can be learned from Toni's successful venture.

Paul W. Taylor

The Ethics of Respect for Nature

I. Human-centered and Life-Centered Systems of Environmental Ethics

In this paper I show how the taking of a certain ultimate moral attitude toward nature, which I call "respect for nature," has a central place in the foundations of a life-centered system of environmental ethics. . . .

In designating the theory to be set forth as life-centered, I intend to contrast it with all anthropocentric views. According to the latter, human actions affecting the natural environment and its nonhuman inhabitants are right (or wrong) by either of two criteria: they have consequences which are favorable (or unfavorable) to human well-being, or they are consistent (or inconsistent) with the system of norms that protect and implement human rights. From this human-centered standpoint it is to humans and only to humans that all duties are ultimately owed. We may have responsibilities *with regard to* the natural ecosystems and biotic communities of our planet, but these responsibilities are in every case based on the contingent fact that our treatment of those ecosystems and communities of life can further the realization of human values and/or human rights. We have no obligation to promote or protect the good of nonhuman living things, independently of this contingent fact.

A life-centered system of environmental ethics is opposed to human-centered ones precisely on this point. From the perspective of a life-centered theory, we have *prima facie* moral obligations that are owed to wild plants and animals themselves as members of the Earth's biotic community. We are morally bound (other things being equal) to protect or promote their good for *their* sake. Our duties to respect the integrity of natural ecosystems, to preserve endangered species, and to avoid environmental pollution stem from the fact that these are ways in which we can help make it possible for wild species populations to achieve and maintain a healthy existence in a natural state. Such obligations are due those living things out of recognition of their inherent worth. They are entirely additional to and independent of the obligations we owe to our fellow humans. Although many of the actions that fulfill one set of obligations will also fulfill the other, two different grounds of obligation are involved. Their well-being, as well as human well-being, is something to be realized *as an end in itself.*

If we were to accept a life-centered theory of environmental ethics, a profound reordering of our moral universe would take place. We would begin to look at the whole of the Earth's biosphere in a new light. Our duties with respect to the "world" of nature would be seen as making *prima facie* claims upon us to be balanced against our duties with respect to the "world" of human civilization. We could no longer simply take the human point of view and consider the effects of our actions exclusively from the perspective of our own good.

II. The Good of a Being and the Concept of Inherent Worth

What would justify acceptance of a life-centered system of ethical principles? In order to answer

From Paul W. Taylor, "The Ethics of Respect for Nature," *Environmental Ethics*, Vol. 3, 1981. Reprinted by permission.

this it is first necessary to make clear the fundamental moral attitude that underlies and makes intelligible the commitment to live by such a system. It is then necessary to examine the considerations that would justify any rational agent's adopting that moral attitude.

Two concepts are essential to the taking of a moral attitude of the sort in question. A being which does not "have" these concepts, that is, which is unable to grasp their meaning and conditions of applicability, cannot be said to have the attitude as part of its moral outlook. These concepts are, first, that of the good (well-being, welfare) of a living thing, and second, the idea of an entity possessing inherent worth. I examine each concept in turn.

(1) Every organism, species population, and community of life has a good of its own which moral agents can intentionally further or damage by their actions. To say that an entity has a good of its own is simply to say that, without reference to any *other* entity, it can be benefited or harmed. One can act in its overall interest or contrary to its overall interest, and environmental conditions can be good for it (advantageous to it) or bad for it (disadvantageous to it). What is good for an entity is what "does it good" in the sense of enhancing or preserving its life and well-being. What is bad for an entity is something that is detrimental to its life and well-being.[1]

We can think of the good of an individual nonhuman organism as consisting in the full development of its biological powers. Its good is realized to the extent that it is strong and healthy. It possesses whatever capacities it needs for successfully coping with its environment and so preserving its existence throughout the various stages of the normal life cycle of its species. The good of a population or community of such individuals consists in the population or community maintaining itself from generation to generation as a coherent system of genetically and ecologically related organisms whose average good is at an optimum level for the given environment. (Here *average good* means that the degree of realization of the good of *individual organisms* in the population or community is, on average, greater than would be the case under any other ecologically func-

tioning order of interrelations among those species populations in the given ecosystem.)

The idea of a being having a good of its own, as I understand it, does not entail that the being must have interests or take an interest in what affects its life for better or for worse. We can act in a being's interest or contrary to its interest without its being interested in what we are doing to it in the sense of wanting or not wanting us to do it. It may, indeed, be wholly unaware that favorable and unfavorable events are taking place in its life. I take it that trees, for example, have no knowledge or desires or feelings. Yet it is undoubtedly the case that trees can be harmed or benefited by our actions. We can crush their roots by running a bulldozer too close to them. We can see to it that they get adequate nourishment and moisture by fertilizing and watering the soil around them. Thus we can help or hinder them in the realization of their good. It is the good of trees themselves that is thereby affected. We can similarly act so as to further the good of an entire tree population of a certain species (say, all the redwood trees in a California valley) or the good of a whole community of plant life in a given wilderness area, just as we can do harm to such a population or community.

When construed in this way, the concept of a being's good is not coextensive with sentience or the capacity for feeling pain. William Frankena has argued for a general theory of environmental ethics in which the ground of a creature's being worthy of moral consideration is its sentience. I have offered some criticisms of this view elsewhere, but the full refutation of such a position, it seems to me, finally depends on the positive reasons for accepting a life-centered theory of the kind I am defending in this essay.[2] . . .

(2) The second concept essential to the moral attitude of respect for nature is the idea of inherent worth. We take that attitude toward wild living things (individuals, species populations, or whole biotic communities) when and only when we regard them as entities possessing inherent worth. Indeed, it is only because they are conceived in this way that moral agents can think of themselves as having validly binding duties, obligations, and responsibilities that are

owed to them as their *due*. I am not at this juncture arguing why they *should* be so regarded; I consider it at length below. But so regarding them is a presupposition of our taking the attitude of respect toward them and accordingly understanding ourselves as bearing certain moral relations to them. This can be shown as follows:

What does it mean to regard an entity that has a good of its own as possessing inherent worth? Two general principles are involved: the principle of moral consideration and the principle of intrinsic value.

According to the principle of moral consideration, wild living things are deserving of the concern and consideration of all moral agents simply in virtue of their being members of the Earth's community of life. From the moral point of view their good must be taken into account whenever it is affected for better or worse by the conduct of rational agents. This holds no matter what species the creature belongs to. The good of each is to be accorded some value and so acknowledged as having some weight in the deliberations of all rational agents. Of course, it may be necessary for such agents to act in ways contrary to the good of this or that particular organism or group of organisms in order to further the good of others, including the good of humans. But the principle of moral consideration prescribes that, with respect to each being an entity having its own good, every individual is deserving of consideration.

The principle of intrinsic value states that, regardless of what kind of entity it is in other respects, if it is a member of the Earth's community of life, the realization of its good is something *intrinsically* valuable. This means that its good is *prima facie* worthy of being preserved or promoted as an end in itself and for the sake of the entity whose good it is. Insofar as we regard any organism, species population, or life community as an entity having inherent worth, we believe that it must never be treated as if it were a mere object or thing whose entire value lies in being instrumental to the good of some other entity. The well-being of each is judged to have value in and of itself.

Combining these two principles, we can now define what it means for a living thing or group of living things to possess inherent worth. To say that it possesses inherent worth is to say that its good is deserving of the concern and consideration of all moral agents, and that the realization of its good has intrinsic value, to be pursued as an end in itself and for the sake of the entity whose good it is.

The duties owed to wild organisms, species populations, and communities of life in the Earth's natural ecosystems are grounded on their inherent worth. When rational, autonomous agents regard such entities as possessing inherent worth, they place intrinsic value on the realization of their good and so hold themselves responsible for performing actions that will have this effect and for refraining from actions having the contrary effect.

III. THE ATTITUDE OF RESPECT FOR NATURE

Why should moral agents regard wild living things in the natural world as possessing inherent worth? To answer this question we must first take into account the fact that, when rational, autonomous agents subscribe to the principles of moral consideration and intrinsic value and so conceive of wild living things as having that kind of worth, such agents are *adopting a certain ultimate moral attitude toward the natural world*. This is the attitude I call "respect for nature." It parallels the attitude of respect for persons in human ethics. When we adopt the attitude of respect for persons as the proper (fitting, appropriate) attitude to take toward all persons as persons, we consider the fulfillment of the basic interests of each individual to have intrinsic value. We thereby make a moral commitment to live a certain kind of life in relation to other persons. We place ourselves under the direction of a system of standards and rules that we consider validly binding on all moral agents as such.[3]

Similarly, when we adopt the attitude of respect for nature as an ultimate moral attitude we make a commitment to live by certain normative principles. These principles constitute the rules of conduct and standards of character that are to govern our treatment of the natural world. This is, first, an *ultimate* commitment because it is not derived from any higher norm. The attitude of respect for nature is not grounded on some other, more general, or more fundamental attitude. It sets the total framework for our responsibilities toward the natural world. It can be justified, as I show below, but its justification cannot consist in referring to a more general attitude or a more basic normative principle.

Second, the commitment is a *moral* one because it is understood to be a disinterested matter of principle. It is this feature that distinguishes the attitude of respect for nature from the set of feelings and dispositions that comprise the love of nature. The latter stems from one's personal interest in and response to the natural world. Like the affectionate feelings we have toward certain individual human beings, one's love of nature is nothing more than the particular way one feels about the natural environment and its wild inhabitants. And just as our love for an individual person differs from our respect for all persons as such (whether we happen to love them or not), so love of nature differs from respect for nature. Respect for nature is an attitude we believe all moral agents ought to have simply as moral agents, regardless of whether or not they also love nature. Indeed, we have not truly taken the attitude of respect for nature ourselves unless we believe this. To put it in a Kantian way, to adopt the attitude or respect for nature is to take a stance that one wills it to be a universal law for all rational beings. It is to hold that stance categorically, as being validly applicable to every moral agent without exception, irrespective of whatever personal feelings toward nature such an agent might have or might lack.

Although the attitude of respect for nature is in this sense a disinterested and universalizable attitude, anyone who does adopt it has certain steady, more or less permanent dispositions. . . . We may accordingly analyze the attitude of respect for nature into the following components. (a) The disposition to aim at, and to take steps to bring about, as final and disinterested ends, the promoting and protecting of the good of organisms, species populations, and life communities in natural ecosystems. (These ends are

"final" in not being pursued as means to further ends. They are "disinterested" in being independent of the self-interest of the agent.) (b) The disposition to consider actions that tend to realize those ends to be *prima facie* obligatory *because* they have that tendency. (c) The disposition to experience positive and negative feelings toward states of affairs in the world *because* they are favorable or unfavorable to the good of organisms, species populations, and life communities in natural ecosystems.

The logical connection between the attitude of respect for nature and the duties of a life-centered system of environmental ethics can now be made clear. Insofar as one sincerely takes that attitude and so has the three sets of dispositions, one will at the same time be disposed to comply with certain rules of duty (such as nonmaleficence and noninterference) and with standards of character (such as fairness and benevolence) that determine the obligations and virtues of moral agents with regard to the Earth's wild living things. We can say that the actions one performs and the character traits one develops in fulfilling these moral requirements are the way one *expresses* or *embodies* the attitude in one's conduct and character. In his famous essay, "Justice as Fairness," John Rawls describes the rules of the duties of human morality (such as fidelity, gratitude, honesty, and justice) as "forms of conduct in which recognition of others as persons is manifested."[4] I hold that the rules of duty governing our treatment of the natural world and its inhabitants are forms of conduct in which the attitude of respect for nature is manifested.

IV. The Justifiability of the Attitude of Respect for Nature

I return to the question posed earlier, which has not yet been answered: why *should* moral agents regard wild living things as possessing inherent worth? I now argue that the only way we can answer this question is by showing how adopting the attitude of respect for nature is justified for all moral agents. Let us suppose that we were able to establish that there are good reasons for adopting the attitude, reasons which are intersubjectively valid for every rational agent. If there are such reasons, they would justify anyone's having the three sets of dispositions mentioned above as constituting what it means to have the attitude. Since these include the disposition to promote or protect the good of wild living things as a disinterested and ultimate end, as well as the disposition to perform actions for the reason that they tend to realize that end, we see that such dispositions commit a person to the principles of moral consideration and intrinsic value. To be disposed to further, as an end in itself, the good of any entity in nature just because it is that kind of entity, is to be disposed to give consideration to *every* such entity and to place intrinsic value on the realization of its good. Insofar as we subscribe to these two principles we regard living things as possessing inherent worth. Subscribing to the principles is what it *means* to so regard them. To justify the attitude of respect for nature, then, is to justify commitment to these principles and thereby to justify regarding wild creatures as possessing inherent worth. . . .

The attitude we take toward living things in the natural world depends on the way we look at them, on what kind of beings we conceive them to be, and on how we understand the relations we bear to them. Underlying and supporting our attitude is a certain *belief system* that constitutes a particular world view or outlook on nature and the place of human life in it. To give good reasons for adopting the attitude of respect for nature, then, we must first articulate the belief system which underlies and supports that attitude. If it appears that the belief system is internally coherent and well-ordered, and if, as far as we can now tell, it is consistent with all known scientific truths relevant to our knowledge of the object of the attitude (which in this case includes the whole set of the Earth's natural ecosystems and their communities of life), then there remains the task of indicating why scientifically informed and rational thinkers with a developed capacity of reality awareness can find it acceptable as a way of conceiving of the natural world and our place in it. To the extent we can do this we provide at least a reasonable argument for accepting the belief system and the ultimate moral attitude it supports.

I do not hold that such a belief system can be *proven* to be true, either inductively or deductively. As we shall see, not all of its components can be stated in the form of empirically verifiable propositions. Nor is its internal order governed by purely logical relationships. But the system as a whole, I contend, constitutes a coherent, unified, and rationally acceptable "picture" or "map" of a total world. By examining each of its main components and seeing how they fit together, we obtain a scientifically informed and well-ordered conception of nature and the place of humans in it.

This belief system underlying the attitude of respect for nature I call (for want of a better name) "the biocentric outlook on nature." Since it is not wholly analyzable into empirically confirmable assertions, it should not be thought of as simply a compendium of the biological sciences concerning our planet's ecosystems. It might best be described as a philosophical world view, to distinguish it from a scientific theory or explanatory system. However, one of its major tenets is the great lesson we have learned from the science of ecology: the interdependence of all living things in an organically unified order whose balance and stability are necessary conditions for the realization of the good of its constituent biotic communities.

Before turning to an account of the main components of the biocentric outlook, it is convenient here to set forth the overall structure of my theory of environmental ethics as it has now emerged. The ethics of respect for nature is made up of three basic elements: a belief system, an ultimate moral attitude, and a set of rules of duty and standards of character. These elements are connected with each other in the following manner. The belief system provides a certain outlook on nature which supports and makes intelligible an autonomous agent's adopting, as an ultimate moral attitude, the attitude of respect for nature. It supports and makes intelligible the attitude in the sense that, when an autonomous agent understands its moral relations to the natural world in terms of this outlook, it recognizes the attitude of respect to be the only *suitable* or *fitting* attitude to take toward all wild forms of life in the Earth's biosphere. Living things are now viewed as *the appropriate objects of the attitude of respect* and are accordingly regarded as entities possessing inherent worth. One then places intrinsic value on the promotion and protection of their good. As a consequence of this, one makes a moral commitment to abide by a set of rules of duty and fulfill (as far as one can by one's own efforts) certain standards of good character. Given one's adoption of the attitude of respect, one makes that moral commitment because one considers those rules and standards to be validly binding on all moral agents. They are seen as embodying forms of conduct and character structures in which the attitude of respect for nature is manifested. . . .

V. The Biocentric Outlook on Nature

The biocentric outlook on nature has four main components. (1) Humans are thought of as members of the Earth's community of life, holding that membership of the same terms as apply to all the nonhuman members. (2) The Earth's natural ecosystems as a totality are seen as a complex web of interconnected elements, with the sound biological functioning of each being dependent on the sound biological functioning of the others. (This is the component referred to above as the great lesson that the science of ecology has taught us). (3) Each individual organism is conceived of as a teleological center of life, pursuing its own good in its own way. (4) Whether we are concerned with standards of merit or with the concept of inherent worth, the claim that humans by their very nature are superior to other species is a groundless claim and, in the light of elements (1), (2), and (3) above, must be rejected as nothing more than an irrational bias in our own favor.

The conjunction of these four ideas constitutes the biocentric outlook on nature. In the remainder of this paper I give a brief account of the first three components, followed by a more detailed analysis of the fourth. I then conclude by indicating how this outlook provides a way of justifying the attitude of respect for nature.

VI. Humans as Members of the Earth's Community of Life

We share with other species a common relationship to the Earth. In accepting the biocentric outlook we take the fact of our being an animal species to be a fundamental feature of our existence. We consider it an essential aspect of "the human condition." We do not deny the differences between ourselves and other species, but we keep in the forefront of our consciousness the fact that in relation to our planet's natural ecosystems we are but one species population among many. Thus we acknowledge our origin in the very same evolutionary process that gave rise to all other species and we recognize ourselves to be confronted with similar environmental challenges to those that confront them. The laws of genetics, of natural selection, and of adaptation apply equally to all of us as biological creatures. In this light we consider ourselves as one with them, not set apart from them. We, as well as they, must face certain basic conditions of existence that impose requirements on us for our survival and well-being. Each animal and plant is like us in having a good of its own. Although our human good (what is of true value in human life, including the exercise of individual autonomy in choosing our own particular value systems) is not like the good of a nonhuman animal or plant, it can no more be realized than their good can without the biological necessities for survival and physical health.

When we look at ourselves from the evolutionary point of view, we see that not only are we very recent arrivals on Earth, but that our emergence as a new species on the planet was originally an event of no particular importance to the entire scheme of things. The Earth was teeming with life long before we appeared. Putting the point metaphorically, we are relative newcomers, entering a home that has been the residence of others for hundreds of millions of years, a home that must now be shared by all of us together.

The comparative brevity of human life on Earth may be vividly depicted by imagining the geological time scale in spatial terms. Suppose we start with algae, which have been around for at least 600 million years. (The earliest protozoa actually predated this by several *billion* years.) If the time that algae have been here were represented by the length of a football field (300 feet), then the period during which sharks have been swimming in the world's oceans and spiders have been spinning their webs would occupy three quarters of the length of the field; reptiles would show up at about the center of the field; mammals would cover the last third of the field; hominids (mammals of the family *Hominidae*) the last two feet; and the species *Homo sapiens* the last six inches.

Whether this newcomer is able to survive as long as other species remains to be seen. But there is surely something presumptuous about the way humans look down on the "lower" animals, especially those that have become extinct. We consider the dinosaurs, for example, to be biological failures, though they existed on our planet for 65 million years. One writer has made the point with beautiful simplicity:

We sometime speak of the dinosaurs as failures; there will be time enough for that judgment when we have lasted even for one tenth as long. . . .[5]

The possibility of the extinction of the human species, a possibility which starkly confronts us in the contemporary world, makes us aware of another respect in which we should not consider ourselves privileged beings in relation to other species. This is the fact that the well-being of humans is dependent upon the ecological soundness and health of many plant and animal communities, while their soundness and health does not in the least depend upon human well-being. Indeed, from their standpoint the very existence of humans is quite unnecessary. Every last man, woman, and child could disappear from the face of the Earth without any significant detrimental consequences for the good of wild animals and plants. On the contrary, many of them would be greatly benefited. The destruction of their habitats by human "developments" would cease. The poisoning and polluting of their environment would come to an end. The Earth's land, air, and water would no longer be subject to the degradation they are now undergoing as the result of large-scale technology and uncontrolled population growth. Life communities in natural ecosystems would gradually return to their former healthy state. Tropical forests, for example, would again be able to make their full contribution to a life-sustaining atmosphere for the whole planet. The rivers, lakes, and oceans of the world would (perhaps) eventually become clean again. Spilled oil, plastic trash, and even radioactive waste might finally, after many centuries, cease doing their terrible work. Ecosystems would return to their proper balance, suffering only the disruptions of natural events such as volcanic eruptions and glaciation. From these the community of life could recover, as it has so often done in the past. But the ecological disasters now perpetrated on it by humans—disasters from which it might never recover—these it would no longer have to endure.

If, then, the total, final, absolute extermination of our species (by our own hands?) should take place and if we should not carry all the others with us into oblivion, not only would the Earth's community of life continue to exist, but in all probability its well-being would be enhanced. Our presence, in short, is not needed. If we were to take the standpoint of the community and give voice to its true interest, the ending of our six-inch epoch would most likely be greeted with a hearty "Good riddance!"

VII. THE NATURAL WORLD AS AN ORGANIC SYSTEM

To accept the biocentric outlook and regard ourselves and our place in the world from its perspective is to see the whole natural order of the Earth's biosphere as a complex but unified web of interconnected organisms, objects, and events. The ecological relationships between any community of living things and their environment form an organic whole of functionally interdependent parts. Each ecosystem is a small universe itself in which the interactions of its various species populations comprise an intricately woven network of cause-effect relations. Such dynamic but at the same time relatively stable structures as food chains, predator-prey relations, and plant succession in a forest are self-regulating, energy-recycling mechanisms that preserve the equilibrium of the whole.

As far as the well-being of wild animals and plants is concerned, this ecological equilibrium must not be destroyed. The same holds true of the well-being of humans. When one reviews the realm of nature from the perspective of the biocentric outlook, one never forgets that in the long run the integrity of the entire biosphere of our planet is essential to the realization of the good of its constituent communities of life, both human and nonhuman.

Although the importance of this idea cannot be overemphasized, it is by now so familiar and so widely acknowledged that I shall not further elaborate on it here. However, I do wish to point out that this "holistic" view of the Earth's ecological systems does not itself constitute a moral norm. It is a factual aspect of biological reality, to be understood as a set of casual connections in ordinary empirical terms. Its significance for humans is the same as its significance for nonhumans, namely, in setting basic conditions for the realization of the good of living things. Its ethical implications for our treatment of the natural environment lie entirely in the fact that our *knowledge* of these causal connections is an essential *means* to fulfilling the aims we set for ourselves in adopting the attitude of respect for nature. In addition, its theoretical implications for the ethics of respect for nature lie in the fact that it (along with the other elements of the biocentric outlook) makes the adopting of that attitude a rational and intelligible thing to do.

VIII. INDIVIDUAL ORGANISMS AS TELEOLOGICAL CENTERS OF LIFE

As our knowledge of living things increases, as we come to a deeper understanding of their life cycles, their interactions with other organisms, and the manifold ways in which they adjust to the environment, we become more fully aware of how each of them is carrying out its biological functions according to the laws of its species-specific nature. But besides this, our increasing knowledge and understanding also develop in us a sharpened awareness of the uniqueness of each individual organism. Scien-tists who have made careful studies of particular plants and animals, whether in the field or in laboratories, have often acquired a knowledge of their subjects as identifiable individuals. Close observation over extended periods of time has led them to an appreciation of the unique "personalities" of their subjects. Sometime a scientist may come to take a special interest in a particular animal or plant, all the while remaining strictly objective in the gathering and recording of data. Nonscientists may likewise experience this development of interest when, as amateur naturalists, they make accurate observations over sustained periods of close acquaintance with an individual organism. As one becomes more and more familiar with the organism and its behavior, one becomes fully sensitive to the particular way it is living out its life cycle. One may become fascinated by it and even experience some involvement with its good and bad fortunes (that is, with the occurrence of environmental conditions favorable or unfavorable to the realization of its good). The organism comes to mean something to one as a unique, irreplaceable individual. The final culmination of this process is the achievement of a genuine understanding of its point of view and, with that understanding, an ability to "take" that point of view. *Conceiving of it as a center of life, one is able to look at the world from its perspective.*

This development from objective knowledge to the recognition of individuality, and from the recognition of individuality to full awareness of an organism's standpoint, is a process of heightening our consciousness of what it means to be an individual living thing. We grasp the particularity of the organism as a teleological center of life, striving to preserve itself and to realize its own good in its own unique way.

It is to be noted that we need not be falsely anthropomorphizing when we conceive of individual plants and animals in this manner. Understanding them as teleological centers of life does not necessitate "reading into" them human characteristics. We need not, for example, consider them to have consciousness. Some of them may be aware of the world around them and others may not. Nor need we deny that different kinds and levels of awareness are exemplified when consciousness in some form is present.

But conscious or not, all are equally teleological centers of life in the sense that each is a unified system of goal-oriented activities directed toward their preservation and well-being.

When considered from an ethical point of view, a teleological center of life is an entity whose "world" can be viewed from the perspective of *its* life. In looking at the world from that perspective we recognize objects and events occurring in its life as being beneficent, maleficent, or indifferent. The first are occurrences which increase its powers to preserve its existence and realize its good. The second decrease or destroy those powers. The third have neither of these effects on the entity. With regard to our human role as moral agents, we can conceive of a teleological center of life as a being whose standpoint we can take in making judgments about what events in the world are good or evil, desirable or undesirable. In making those judgments it is what promotes or protects the being's own good, not what benefits moral agents themselves, that sets the standards of evaluation. Such judgments can be made about anything that happens to the entity which is favorable or unfavorable in relation to its good. As was pointed out earlier, the entity itself need not have any (conscious) *interest* in what is happening to it for such judgments to be meaningful and true.

It is precisely judgments of this sort that we are disposed to make when we take the attitude of respect for nature. In adopting that attitude those judgments are given weight as reasons for action in our practical deliberation. They become morally relevant facts in the guidance of our conduct.

IX. The Denial of Human Superiority

This fourth component of the biocentric outlook on nature is the single most important idea in establishing the justifiability of the attitude of respect for nature. Its central role is due to the special relationship it bears to the first three components of the outlook. This relationship will be brought out after the concept of human superiority is examined and analyzed.[6]

In what sense are humans alleged to be superior to other animals? We are different from them in having certain capacities that they lack. But why should these capacities be a mark of superiority? From what point of view are they judged to be signs of superiority and what sense of superiority is meant? After all, various nonhuman species have capacities that humans lack. There is the speed of a cheetah, the vision of an eagle, the agility of a monkey. Why should not these be taken as signs of *their* superiority over humans?

One answer that comes immediately to mind is that these capacities are not as *valuable* as the human capacities that are claimed to make us superior. Such uniquely human characteristics as rational thought, aesthetic creativity, autonomy and self-determination, and moral freedom, it might be held, have a higher value than the capacities found in other species. Yet we must ask: valuable to whom, and on what grounds?

The human characteristics mentioned are all valuable to humans. They are essential to the preservation and enrichment of our civilization and culture. Clearly it is from the human standpoint that they are being judged to be desirable and good. It is not difficult here to recognize a begging of the question. Humans are claiming human superiority from a strictly human point of view, that is, from a point of view in which the good of humans is taken as the standard of judgment. All we need to do is to look at the capacities of nonhuman animals (or plants, for that matter) from the standpoint of *their* good to find a contrary judgment of superiority. The speed of the cheetah, for example, is a sign of its superiority to humans when considered from the standpoint of the good of its species. If it were as slow a runner as a human, it would not be able to survive. And so for all the other abilities of nonhumans which further their good but which are lacking in humans. In each case the claim to human superiority would be rejected from a nonhuman standpoint.

When superiority assertions are interpreted in this way, they are based on judgments of *merit*. To judge the merits of a person or an organism one must apply grading or ranking standards to it. (As I show below, this distinguishes judgments of merit from judgments of inherent worth.) Empirical investigation then determines whether it has the "good-making properties" (merits) in virtue of which it fulfills the standards being applied. In the case of humans, merits may be either moral or nonmoral. We can judge one person to be better than (superior to) another from the moral point of view by applying certain standards to their character and conduct. Similarly, we can appeal to nonmoral criteria in judging someone to be an excellent piano player, a fair cook, a poor tennis player, and so on. Different social purposes and roles are implicit in the making of such judgments, providing the frame of reference for the choice of standards by which the nonmoral merits of people are determined. Ultimately such purposes and roles stem from a society's way of life as a whole. Now a society's way of life may be thought of as the cultural form given to the realization of human values. Whether moral or nonmoral standards are being applied, then, all judgments of people's merits finally depend on human values. All are made from an exclusively human standpoint.

The question that naturally arises at this juncture is: why should standards that are based on human values be assumed to be the only valid criteria of merit and hence the only true signs of superiority? This question is especially pressing when humans are being judged superior in merit to nonhumans. It is true that a human being may be a better mathematician than a monkey, but the monkey may be a better tree climber than a human being. If we humans value mathematics more than tree climbing, that is because our conception of civilized life makes the development of mathematical ability more desirable than the ability to climb trees. But is it not unreasonable to judge nonhumans by the values of human civilization, rather than by values connected with what it is for a member of *that* species to live a good life? If all living things have a good of their own, it at least makes sense to judge the merits of nonhumans by standards derived from *their* good. To use only standards based on human values is already to commit oneself to holding that humans are superior to nonhumans, which is the point in question.

A further logical flaw arises in connection with the widely held conviction that humans

are *morally* superior beings because they possess, while others lack, the capacities of a moral agent (free will, accountability, deliberation, judgment, practical reason). This view rests on a conceptual confusion. As far as moral standards are concerned, only beings that have the capacities of a moral agent can properly be judged to be *either* moral (morally good) *or* immoral (morally deficient). Moral standards are simply not applicable to beings that lack such capacities. Animals and plants cannot therefore be said to be morally inferior in merit to humans. Since the only beings that can have moral merits *or be deficient in such merits* are moral agents, it is conceptually incoherent to judge humans as superior to nonhumans on the ground that humans have moral capacities while nonhumans don't.

Up to this point I have been interpreting the claim that humans are superior to other living things as a grading or ranking judgment regarding their comparative merits. There is, however, another way of understanding the idea of human superiority. According to this interpretation, humans are superior to nonhumans not as regards their merits but as regards their inherent worth. Thus the claim of human superiority is to be understood as asserting that all humans, simply in virtue of their humanity, have *a greater inherent worth* than other living things.

The inherent worth of an entity does not depend on its merits.[7] To consider something as possessing inherent worth, we have seen, is to place intrinsic value on the realization of its good. This is done regardless of whatever particular merits it might have or might lack, as judged by a set of grading or ranking standards. In human affairs, we are all familiar with the principle that one's worth as a person does not vary with one's merits or lack of merits. The same can hold true of animals and plants. To regard such entities as possessing inherent worth entails disregarding their merits and deficiencies, whether they are being judged from a human standpoint or from the standpoint of their own species.

The idea of one entity having more merit than another, and so being superior to it in merit, makes perfectly good sense. Merit is a grading or ranking concept, and judgments of comparative merit are based on the different degrees to which things satisfy a given standard. But what can it mean to talk about one being superior to another in inherent worth? In order to get at what is being asserted in such a claim it is helpful first to look at the social origin of the concept of degrees of inherent worth.

The idea that humans can possess different degrees of inherent worth originated in societies having rigid class structures. Before the rise of modern democracies with their egalitarian outlook, one's membership in a hereditary class determined one's social status. People in the upper classes were looked up to, while those in the lower classes were looked down upon. In such a society one's social superiors and social inferiors were clearly defined and easily recognized.

Two aspects of these class-structured societies are especially relevant to the idea of degrees of inherent worth. First, those born into the upper classes were deemed more worthy of respect than those born into the lower orders. Second, the superior worth of upper class people had nothing to do with their merits nor did the inferior worth of those in the lower classes rest on their lack of merits. One's superiority or inferiority entirely derived from a social position one was born into. The modern concept of meritocracy simply did not apply. One could not advance into a higher class by sort of moral or nonmoral achievement. Similarly, an aristocrat held his title and all the privileges that went with it just because he was the eldest son of a titled nobleman. Unlike the bestowing of knighthood in contemporary Great Britain, one did not earn membership in the nobility by meritorious conduct.

We who live in modern democracies no longer believe in such hereditary social distinctions. Indeed, we would wholeheartedly condemn them on moral grounds as being fundamentally unjust. We have come to think of class systems as a paradigm of social injustice, it being a central principle of the democratic way of life that among humans there are no superiors and no inferiors. Thus we have rejected the whole conceptual framework in which people are judged to have different degrees of inherent worth. That idea is incompatible with our no-tion of human equality based on the doctrine that all humans, simply in virtue of their humanity, have the same inherent worth. (The belief in universal human rights is one form that this egalitarianism takes.)

The vast majority of people in modern democracies, however, do not maintain an egalitarian outlook when it comes to comparing human beings with other living things. Most people consider our own species to be superior to all other species and this superiority is understood to be a matter of inherent worth, not merit. There may exist thoroughly vicious and depraved humans who lack all merit. Yet because they are human they are thought to belong to a higher class of entities than any plant or animal. That one is born into the species *Homo sapiens* entitles one to have lordship over those who are one's inferiors, namely, those born into other species. The parallel with hereditary social classes is very close. Implicit in this view is a hierarchical conception of nature according to which an organism has a position of superiority or inferiority in the Earth's community of life simply on the basis of its genetic background. The "lower" orders of life are looked down upon and it is considered perfectly proper that they serve the interests of those belonging to the highest order, namely humans. The intrinsic value we place on the well-being of our fellow humans reflects our recognition of their rightful position as our equals. No such intrinsic value is to be placed on the good of other animals, unless we choose to do so out of fondness or affection for them. But their well-being imposes no moral requirements on us. In this respect there is an absolute difference in moral status between ourselves and them.

This is the structure of concepts and beliefs that people are committed to insofar as they regard humans to be superior in inherent worth to all other species. I now wish to argue that this structure of concepts and beliefs is completely groundless. If we accept the first three components of the biocentric outlook and from that perspective look at the major philosophical traditions which have supported that structure, we find it to be at bottom nothing more than the expression of an irrational bias in our own favor. The philosophical traditions themselves rest on very questionable assumptions or else simply beg the question. I briefly consider three of the main traditions to substantiate the point. These are classical Greek humanism, Cartesian dualism [Descartes (1596–1650) is sometimes described as the father of modern philosophy. In his treatment of the mind-body problem he held that mind and body are distinct substances that causally interact. He denied that non-human animals had minds.] and the Judeo-Christian concept of the Great Chain of Being.

The inherent superiority of humans over other species was implicit in the Greek definition of man as a rational animal. Our animal nature was identified with "brute" desires that need the order and restraint of reason to rule them (just as reason is the special virtue of those who rule in the ideal state). Rationality was then seen to be the key to our superiority over animals. It enables us to live on a higher plane and endows us with a nobility and worth that other creatures lack. This familiar way of comparing humans with other species is deeply ingrained in our Western philosophical outlook. The point to consider here is that this view does not actually provide an argument *for* human superiority but rather makes explicit the framework of thought that is implicitly used by those who think of humans as inherently superior to nonhumans. The Greeks who held that humans, in virtue of their rational capacities, have a kind of worth greater than that of any nonrational being, never looked at rationality as but one capacity of living things among many others. But when we consider rationality from the standpoint of the first three elements of the ecological outlook, we see that its value lies in its importance for *human* life. Other creatures achieve their species-specific good without the need of rationality, although they often make use of capacities that humans lack. So the humanistic outlook for classical Greek thought does not give us a neutral (nonquestion-begging) ground on which to construct a scale of degrees of inherent worth possessed by different species of living things.

The second tradition, centering on the Cartesian dualism of soul and body, also fails to justify the claim to human superiority. That superiority is supposed to derive from the fact that we have souls while animals do not. Animals are mere automata and lack the divine element that makes us spiritual beings. I won't go into the now familiar criticisms of this two-substance view. I only add the point that, even if humans are composed of an immaterial, unextended soul and a material, extended body, this in itself is not a reason to deem them of greater worth than entities that are only bodies. Why is a soul substance a thing that adds value to its possessor? Unless some theological reasoning is offered here (which many, including myself, would find unacceptable on epistemological ground), no logical connection is evident. An immaterial something which thinks is better than a material something which does not think only if thinking itself has value, either intrinsically or instrumentally. Now it is intrinsically valuable to humans alone, who value it as an end in itself, and it is instrumentally valuable to those who benefit from it, namely humans.

For animals that neither enjoy thinking for its own sake nor need it for living the kind of life for which they are best adapted, it has no value. Even if "thinking" is broadened to include all forms of consciousness, there are still many living things that can do without it and yet live what is for their species a good life. The anthropocentricity underlying the claim to human superiority runs throughout Cartesian dualism.

A third major source of the idea of human superiority is the Judeo-Christian concept of the Great Chain of Being. Humans are superior to animals and plants because their Creator has given them a higher place on the chain. It begins with God at the top, and then moves to the angels, who are lower than God but higher than humans, then to humans, positioned between the angels and the beasts (partaking of the nature of both), and then on down to the lower levels occupied by nonhuman animals, plants, and finally inanimate objects. Humans, being "made in God's image," are inherently superior to animals and plants by virtue of their being closer (in their essential nature) to God.

The metaphysical and epistemological difficulties with this conception of a hierarchy of entities are, in my mind, insuperable. Without entering into this matter here, I only point out that if we are unwilling to accept the metaphysics of traditional Judaism and Christianity, we are again left without good reasons for holding to the claim of inherent human superiority.

The foregoing considerations (and others like them) leave us with but one ground for the assertion that a human being, regardless of merit, is a higher kind of entity than any other living thing. This is the mere fact of the genetic makeup of the species *Homo sapiens*. But this is surely irrational and arbitrary. Why should the arrangement of genes of a certain type be a mark of superior value, especially when this fact about an organism is taken by itself, unrelated to any other aspect of its life? We might just as well refer to any other genetic makeup as a ground of superior value. Clearly we are confronted here with a wholly arbitrary claim that can only be explained as an irrational bias in our own favor.

That the claim is nothing more than a deep-seated prejudice is brought home to us when we look at our relation to other species in the light of the first three elements of the biocentric outlook. Those elements taken conjointly give us a certain overall view of the natural world and of the place of humans in it. When we take this view we come to understand other living things, their environmental conditions, and their ecological relationships in such a way as to awake in us a deep sense of our kinship with them as fellow members of the Earth's community of life. Humans and nonhumans alike are viewed together as integral parts of one unified whole in which all living things are functionally interrelated. Finally, when our awareness focuses on the individual lives of plants and animals, each is seen to share with us the characteristic of being a teleological center of life striving to realize its own good in its own unique way.

As this entire belief system becomes part of the conceptual framework through which we understand and perceive the world, we come to see ourselves as bearing a certain moral relation to nonhuman forms of life. Our ethical role in nature takes on a new significance. We begin to look at other species as we look at ourselves, seeing them as beings which have a good they are striving to realize just as we have a good we

are striving to realize. We accordingly develop the disposition to view the world from the standpoint of their good as well as from the standpoint of our own good. Now if the groundlessness of the claim that humans are inherently superior to other species were brought clearly before our minds, we would not remain intellectually neutral toward that claim but would reject it as being fundamentally at variance with our total world outlook. In the absence of any good reasons for holding it, the assertion of human superiority would then appear simply as the expression of an irrational and self-serving prejudice that favors one particular species over several million others.

Rejecting the notion of human superiority entails its positive counterpart: the doctrine of species impartiality. One who accepts that doctrine regards all living things as possessing inherent worth—the *same* inherent worth, since no one species has been shown to be either "higher" or "lower" than any other. Now we saw earlier that, insofar as one thinks of a living thing as possessing inherent worth, one considers it to be the appropriate object of the attitude of respect and believes that attitude to be the only fitting or suitable one for all moral agents to take toward it.

Here, then, is the key to understanding how the attitude of respect is rooted in the biocentric outlook on nature. The basic connection is made through the denial of human superiority. Once we reject the claim that humans are superior either in merit or in worth to other living things, we are ready to adopt the attitude of respect. The denial of human superiority is itself the result of taking the perspective on nature built into the first three elements of the biocentric outlook.

Now the first three elements of the biocentric outlook, it seems clear, would be found acceptable to any rational and scientifically informed thinker who is fully "open" to the reality of the lives of nonhuman organisms. Without denying our distinctively human characteristics, such a thinker can acknowledge the fundamental respects in which we are members of the Earth's community of life and in which the biological conditions necessary for the realization of our human values are inextricably linked with the whole system of nature. In addition, the conception of individual living things as teleological centers of life simply articulates how a scientifically informed thinker comes to understand them as the result of increasingly careful and detailed observations. Thus, the biocentric outlook recommends itself as an acceptable system of concepts and beliefs to anyone who is clearminded, unbiased, and factually enlightened, and who has a developed capacity of reality awareness with regard to the lives of individual organisms. This, I submit, is as good a reason for making the moral commitment involved in adopting the attitude of respect for nature as any theory of environmental ethics could possibly have.

X. Moral Rights and the Matter of Competing Claims

I have not asserted anywhere in the foregoing account that animals or plants have moral rights. This omission was deliberate. I do not think that the reference class of the concept, bearer of moral rights, should be extended to include nonhuman living things. My reasons for taking this position, however, go beyond the scope of this paper. I believe I have been able to accomplish many of the same ends which those who ascribe rights to animals or plants wish to accomplish. There is no reason, moreover, why plants and animals, including whole species populations and life communities, cannot be accorded *legal* rights under my theory. To grant them legal protection could be interpreted as giving them legal entitlement to be protected, and this, in fact, would be a means by which a society that subscribed to the ethics of respect for nature could give public recognition to their inherent worth.

There remains the problem of competing claims, even when wild plants and animals are not thought of as bearers of moral rights. If we accept the biocentric outlook and accordingly adopt the attitude of respect for nature as our ultimate moral attitude, how do we resolve conflicts that arise from our respect for persons in the domain of human ethics and our respect for nature in the domain of environmental ethics? This is a question that cannot adequately be dealt with here. My main purpose in this paper has been to try to establish a base point from which we can start working toward a solution to the problem. I have shown why we cannot just begin with an initial presumption in favor of the interests of our own species. It is after all within our power as moral beings to place limits on human population and technology with the deliberate intention of sharing the Earth's bounty with other species. That such sharing is an ideal difficult to realize even in an approximate way does not take away its claim to our deepest moral commitment.

Notes

1. The conceptual links between an entity *having* a good, something being good *for* it, and events doing good *to* it are examined by G. H. Von Wright in *The Varieties of Goodness* (New York: Humanities Press, 1963), chaps. 3 and 5.
2. See W. K. Frankena, "Ethics and the Environment," in K. E. Goodpaster and K. M. Sayre, eds., *Ethics and Problems of the 21st Century* (Notre Dame, University of Notre Dame Press, 1979), pp. 3–20. I critically examine Frankena's views in "Frankena on Environmental Ethics," *Monist*, forthcoming.
3. I have analyzed the nature of this commitment of human ethics in "On Taking the Moral Point of View," *Midwest Studies in Philosophy*, vol. 3, *Studies in Ethical Theory* (1978), pp. 35–61.
4. John Rawls, "Justice As Fairness," *Philosophical Review* 67 (1958): 183.
5. Stephen R. L. Clark, *The Moral Status of Animals* (Oxford: Clarendon Press, 1977), p. 112.
6. My criticisms of the dogma of human superiority gain independent support from a carefully reasoned essay by R. and V. Routley showing the many logical weaknesses in arguments for human-centered theories of environmental ethics. R. and V. Routley, "Against the Inevitability of Human Chauvinism," in K. E. Goodpaster and K. M. Sayre, eds., *Ethics and Problems of the 21st Century* (Notre Dame: University of Notre Dame Press, 1979), pp. 36–59.
7. For this way of distinguishing between merit and inherent worth, I am indebted to Gregory Vlastos, "Justice and Equality," in R. Brandt, ed., *Social Justice* (Englewood Cliffs, N.J.: Prentice-Hall, 1962), pp. 31–72.

Tibor R. Machan

Environmentalism Humanized

INTRODUCTION

I want to argue here the case of a certain type of anthropocentrism, the view that human beings are more important or valuable[1] than other aspects of nature, including plants and animals. I begin with some clarifications of terms I plan to use and then explore whether anything in my anthropocentric position contradicts the tenets of evolutionary biology. I also consider whether the ascription of a moral nature to human beings makes sense and how it squares with certain objections from those who would take animals, for example, to have nearly equal moral status to human beings. I consider, next, some political implications of what I have discussed, specifically as they bear on environmental public policy.

First, by anthropocentrism is not meant that human beings—as a collectivity—are the *telos* of existence, [i.e., goal or purpose] the ultimate aim or end or the central fact of the universe. All that is meant is that human beings are of the highest value in the known universe.

To construe human beings as the highest value in the known universe, they are identified thus as individuals of a given kind. There is no concrete universal "human being," only individual human beings.[2] The conception of humanity as a kind of collective whole entity—derived, in the main, from the legacy of Platonic metaphysics that regarded general abstract ideas or universals, at least in its standard rendition, as concrete albeit intellectual or spiritual beings—is not metaphysically sound. On the other hand, neither are individuals entirely unique. They are of a specific kind—e.g., human, feline, male, apple, etc. For anthropocentrism to be metaphysically cogent, *individual*

From Tibor R. Machan, "Environmentalism Humanized," *Public Affairs Quarterly*, Vol. 7, No. 2, 1993. Reprinted by permission.

human beings would have to be the most valuable entities in nature. . . .

The individualism or egoism discussed here—dubbed "classical," so as to distinguish it from the "atomic" or "radical" variety commonly criticized by those who wish to call attention to the social nature of human beings—recognizes that the human individual is so classified for good reasons, based on the rational recognition of kinds of beings in nature. This then renders justified not only personal but several social virtues—generosity, charity, compassion.[3] It is also recognized in this view that a virtue must be practiced by choice and cannot be coerced.

All in all, the position here considered is still a *bona fide* individualism since it identifies human nature as essentially individual, in contrast to, for example, Karl Marx who states that "The human essence is the true collectivity of man" or August Comte who argues that:

[The] social point of view . . . cannot tolerate the notion of rights, for such notion rests on individualism. We are born under a load of obligations of every kind, to our predecessors, to our successors, to our contemporaries. After our birth these obligations increase or accumulate, for it is some time before we can return any service. . . . This ["to live for others"], the definitive formula of human morality, gives a direct sanction exclusively to our instincts of benevolence, the common source of happiness and duty. [Man must serve] Humanity, whose we are entirely.[4]

If my argument is sound, it will establish in large measure that in discussing environmental ethics—whether at the level of principles or applied morality—the highest value must be attributed to measures that enhance the lives of individual human beings on earth. There will be no reliance here on supernaturalism to advance the argument. The aim is to defend the anthropocentric position from within a naturalistic framework—that is, by sticking to considerations based on our understanding of the natural world, including the nature of living beings such as plants, animals and human beings.[5]

However, neither is it the position here that human beings are "uniquely important [or valuable]," a view avidly ridiculed by Stephen R. L.

Clark, who claims that "there seems no decent ground in reason or revelation to suppose that man is uniquely important or significant."[6] If human beings were *uniquely* important, that would imply that one had no basis for assigning any value to plants or non-human animals apart from their relationship to human beings. That is not the position to be defended. What will be argued, instead, is that there is a scale of values in nature and among all the various kinds of beings, human beings are the most valuable—even while it is true that some members of the human species may indeed prove themselves to be the most vile and worthless, as well. This is all that anthropocentrism requires.

THE IMPORTANCE OF BEING HUMAN

How do we establish that something is most valuable? First we must consider whether the idea of lesser or greater value in nature makes clear sense and we must apply these considerations to an understanding of whether human beings or other animals are the most valuable. If it turns out that ranking things in nature as more or less valuable makes sense, and if we qualify as more valuable than other animals, there is at least the beginning of a reason why we may make use of other animals for our purposes. . . .

Quite independently of the implicit acknowledgment even by many environmentalists of the qualitatively hierarchical structure of nature, there is evidence throughout the natural world of the existence of beings of greater complexity as well as of higher value. For example, while it makes no sense to evaluate as good or bad such things as planets or rocks or pebbles—except as they may relate to goals or purposes of living things—when it comes to plants and animals the process of evaluation commences very naturally indeed. We can and most of us tend to speak of better or worse trees, oaks, redwoods, or zebras, foxes or chimps. Clearly, if we could not do this rationally, there would be little point to environmental ethics in the first place, a field that presupposes value differentiation through and through.

Now, while at this stage we confine our evaluations to the condition or behavior of living beings without any intimation of their responsibility for being better or worse, when we start discussing human beings our evaluation takes on an additional, namely, moral component. Indeed, none are more ready to testify to this than environmental ethicists who, after all, do not demand any change of behavior on the part of non-human beings but insist that human beings conform to certain moral edicts as a matter of their own choice, as what ought or oughtn't be done but might not or might be done. This means that environmental ethicists admit outright that to the best of our knowledge it is with human beings that the idea of at least active moral goodness and active moral responsibility arises in the universe. Human moral goodness depends on individual human initiative.

Does this show a hierarchical structure in nature? What we may note is that some things do not invite evaluations at all—it is a matter of no significance or of indifference whether some beings are or are not or what they are or how they behave. Some beings invite evaluation but without implying any active moral standing with reference to whether they do well or badly. And some things—namely, human beings or their conduct—invite moral evaluation.

Why is a being that invites moral ranking more valuable in nature than one that invites mere ranking? Why would the addition of the moral component—one that involves the choosing capacity of the agent—elevate the being with such a component in the scale of values in nature?

When evaluation—or value—involves beings that are not self-determined, the capacity to contribute creatively to the values in nature is lacking. What human beings have the capacity to do is to create value,[7] not just exhibit it. They can produce a culture of science, art, athletics, etc., the diverse features of which can themselves all exhibit value. So while nature's non-human living beings can have value, human beings can create value as a matter of their own initiative. This would enable human beings, for example, to replace some lost values in nature, if that turned out to be the right course for them to take. So the addition of choice—the moral component—to value clearly makes a valuable difference.

At this point one might object that simply because human beings are capable of moral responsibility, it does not follow that they are the only beings of moral worth. But we need to keep in mind what "moral worth" comes to. To ascribe moral worth or merit to something, or to deny that it has such worth or merit, amounts to relating it to human action from the start. A wonderful sunny day has no moral worth, a destructive earthquake does not lack it. Morality involves beings with the capacity to make choices. So something can have moral worth or lack it only if some human (or other rational choosing) agent produced or destroyed it. Thus the success of a symphony can have moral worth, just as the failure of a saving and loan association may lack it (or even have moral disvalue), because human agency was involved in making it happen.

Accordingly, the agents of moral worth can also have moral worth—thus we consider men and women who produce morally good actions and results as morally worthwhile. But we do not consider horses or tidal waves either morally good or evil. It all has to do with the fact that the concept "moral" or "ethical" arises from circumstances where actions and results come about through the initiative of the agent.

Does creating what has value come to the same thing as creating value? It would seem that this is the only sense we can make of "creating value"—since value is inherently relational (meaning value is the abstract category of the relationship of being of value to something). It is not confounding value with having value to say this, since value and having value differ only from the point of view of greater and lesser generality. X's having value is, more broadly characterized, the phenomena of value in nature. Nothing else works—things are not just values, all alone, without making contributions to something, being pleasing to or enhancing or supportive of something.

After this brief defense of the superior value of human life, we may note, also, that the level or degree of value moves from the inanimate to the animate world, culminating, as we now know, with human life. Normal human life involves moral and creative tasks, and that is why we are, as a species, more valuable than

other beings in nature—we are subject to moral appraisal regarding all our creative activities; it is largely a matter of our doing whether we succeed or fail in our lives.[8]

Now when it comes to our moral task, namely, to succeed as human beings, we are dependent upon reaching justified conclusions about what we should do and summoning the will to do it. What we will do, in turn, often involves the transformation and utilization of the natural world of which we are a part. We have the moral responsibility to engage in the needed transformation and utilization in a morally responsible fashion. We can fail to do this and do so too often. But we can also succeed. That, indeed, is once again implicit in the field of environmental ethics.

The process that leads to our success involves learning what nature contains with which we may achieve our highly varied tasks in life, tasks that share the one common feature to make us good at living our lives as our nature, including our individuality, requires. Among these highly varied tasks could be some that make judicious use of nature's varied living beings, such as plants, animals, even other people (under certain conditions)—for example, to discover whether some medicine may cure us of some illness, is safe for our use, we might wish to use animals and plants.

Why would it be morally proper for us to make such use of nature? Because we are unique in having to make choices for purposes of doing well at living. We know from our study of the rest of the living world that doing well at living is what it means, at least predominantly, to be good. Our evaluations in zoology, botany, biology, and medicine makes this clear—the good is what is conducive and the bad is what is destructive of living, mostly of the individual living being, even if at times only in a complex fashion that may make it appear that individuals as such do not count for much.[9] So when we come to human life, the same general standard remains in force, namely, pro-life versus anti-life; only given the specifics of human nature, this will involve now a moral dimension and whatever is requisite for that, including certain sociopolitical principles. There are those, of course, who claim that much if not all of what human beings invent so as to enhance their existence is a kind of intrusion or trampling upon nature—unnatural or artificial, in fact. But there is no good reason to suppose this. Human beings emerged in reality alongside all other living things, and their activities—such as playing football, bowling, holding philosophy conferences in pleasant surroundings, driving cars from the airport to these surroundings, building tunnels, burning fossil fuels, cutting down trees, etc.—could be just as natural as it is for the bee to make honey, the swallow to fly south in winter time, or the beaver to dam up creeks. Human life is a form of natural life. Whatever derives from its consistent development or realization will be in accordance with nature, whatever subverts or corrupts it will not.

The major difference is, of course, something already mentioned, namely, that human beings can mismanage their lives, can (choose to) subvert their nature. But what would amount to a subversion of human nature? It would be to conduct oneself irrationally, thoughtlessly, imprudently, and by evading what is most healthy and productive for one's life. That is what amounts to living a vicious rather than a virtuous life. It is to fail in exercising one's unique capacity for coping with one's life, a capacity that in the case of human beings must be exercised by choice. Thinking is not automatic—and, indeed, environmental ethicists appear to assume this, implicitly, when they criticize failed thinking and the resulting conduct in various areas of private behavior and public policy. Indeed, ethics itself rests on the view that human beings can choose—"ought implies can" embodies this point.

Within the parameters of these broad standards, a great deal of the diverse things that human beings do can be perfectly natural, even when it is destructive or—or rather transforms and utilizes—certain other aspects of nature. (Notice that the frequently used phrase "domination of nature" has something suspicious or pejorative about it—it suggests hostility and cruelty toward the rest of nature. Transformation and use do not have to involve dominance.)

The rational thing for us to do is to make the best use of nature for our success in living our lives. That does not mean there need be no guidelines involved in how we might make use of plants, animals, etc.—any more than there need be no guidelines involved in how we make use of objects of art, technology, etc. But it can easily involve managing nature so as to serve our own goals and aspirations, to make ourselves happy.

WHY INDIVIDUAL HUMAN RIGHTS?

At this point we need to make an excursion into the realm of politics and law. As already hinted, the peculiar value dimension of human life, involving as it does moral choices all individuals will need to make so as to succeed in living well, has socio-economic-political implications. This involves the emergence of a normative realm known as the domain of individual human rights.

Why do individual *human* rights come into this picture? The rights being talked of in connection with human beings have as their conceptual source the human capacity to make moral choices. For instance, if (as has been argued in other forums[10]), each of us has the right to life, liberty and property—as well as more specialized rights connected with politics, the press, religion—we do so because we have as our central task in life to act morally and this task needs to be shielded against intrusive actions from other moral agents. In order to be able to engage in responsible and sound moral judgment and conduct throughout the scope of our lives, we require a reasonably clear sphere of personal jurisdiction—a dominion where we are sovereign and can either succeed or fail to live well, to do right, to act properly.

If we did not have rights, we would not have such a sphere of personal jurisdiction and there could be no clear idea as to whether we are acting in our own behalf or those of other persons. A kind of *moral tragedy of the commons* would ensue, with an indeterminate measure of *moral dumping and sharing* without responsibility being assignable to anyone for either.[11] No one could be blamed or praised for we would not know clearly enough whether what the person is doing is in his or her authority to do or in someone else's. This is precisely the problem that arises in communal living and, especially, in totalitarian countries where everything is under forced collective governance. The reason moral distinctions are still possible to make under such circumstances is that in fact—as distinct from law—there is always some sphere of personal jurisdiction wherein people may exhibit courage, prudence, justice, honesty, and other virtues. But where collectivism has been successfully enforced, there is not individual responsibility at play and people's morality and immorality is submerged within the group.

Indeed the main reason for governments has for some time been recognized to be nothing other than that our individual human rights should be protected. . . .

Is There Room for Non-Human Rights?

A crucial implication of a non-anthropocentric environmental ethics is the view that at least animals, if not plants, are as valuable as human beings, possibly even to the extent that the law should acknowledge animal rights and the legal standing of plants.[12] There may be other grounds for rejecting anthropocentrism but this one is certainly a significant aspect of the anti-anthropocentrist position or ethos.

We have seen that the most sensible and influential doctrine of human rights rests on the purported fact that human beings are indeed members of a discernibly different species. Central to what distinguishes human beings from other animals is that they are moral agents and thus have as their central objective in life to live morally well, to uphold principles of right and wrong for them in their personal lives and in communities.

Quite uncontroversially, there is no valid intellectual place for rights in the non-human world, the world in which moral responsibility is for all practical purposes absent. . . .

Perhaps the central point in support of animal rights is the view that no fundamental differences may be identified between human beings and other animals. Yet, this is a mistake. Human individuals are indeed members of a distinct species of animals. Their *human* nature is a fact, not merely a nominal category.[13]

No doubt many environmental ethicists sincerely believe that they have found a justification for opposing anthropocentrism. They seem to hold that anthropocentrism means human beings exercising random, capricious control over the rest of nature—trampling on the rest of the world as they desire. Yet many environmentalists might change their perspective if they became convinced that anthropocentrism does not endorse rapaciousness and is by no means in any inherent conflict with the rational management of the environment.

Not only does a perspective that favors human life above all appear to be better justified, as indicated in this discussion; as it happens it also generates the most environmentally sound public policy. Let's turn to this in the final section of this discussion.

Environmentalism and Politics

Of late no one can deny that collectivist political economies have fallen into some disrepute. Theoretically there were hints of this as far back as the 4th century B.C. when in the *Politics* Aristotle observed that private ownership of property encourages responsible human behavior more readily than does collectivism as spelled out in Plato's *Republic*. Aristotle said, "That all persons call the same thing mine in the sense in which each does so may be a fine thing, but it is impracticable; or if the words are taken in the other sense, such a unity in no way conduces to harmony. And there is another objection to the proposal. For that which is common to the greatest number has the least care bestowed upon it. Everyone thinks chiefly of his own, hardly at all of the common interest; and only when he is himself concerned as an individual. For besides other considerations, everybody is more inclined to neglect the duty which he expects another to fulfill; as in families many attendants are often less useful than a few."[14]

In our time the same general observation was advanced in more technical and rigorous terms by Ludwig von Mises, in his 1922 (German edition) book *Socialism*,[15] although he was mainly concerned with economic problems of production and allocation of resources for satisfying individual preferences. More recently, however, Garrett Hardin argued[16] that the difficulties first noticed by Aristotle plague us in the context of our concerns with the quintessentially public realm, namely, the ecological environment.

These various indictments[17] of collectivism, coupled with the few moral arguments against it, didn't manage to dissuade many intellectuals from the task of attempting to implement the system. Our own century is filled with enthusiastic, stubborn, visionary, opportunistic but almost always bloody efforts to implement the collectivist dream. Not until the crumbling of the Soviet attempt, in the form of its Marxist-Leninist internationalist socialist revolution, did it dawn on most people that collectivism is simply not going to do the job of enabling people to live a decent human social life. Although most admit that in small units—convents, kibbutzes, the family—a limited, temporary collectivist arrangement may be feasible, they no longer look with much hope toward transforming entire societies into collectivist human organizations.

The most recent admission of the failure of economic collectivism—in the wake of the collapse of the Soviet bloc economy (something most enthusiasts would not expect based on the kind of predictions advanced by Mises and F. A. Hayek)—comes from Professor Robert Heilbroner, one of socialism's most intelligent and loyal champions for the last several decades. As he puts it in his recent essay, "After Communism:" ". . . Ludwig von Mises . . . had written of the "impossibility" of socialism, arguing that no Central Planning Board could ever gather the enormous amount of information needed to create a workable economic system. . . . It turns out, of course, that Mises was right. . . ."[18]

But, not unlike previous thinkers who have seen various examples of the failure of some kind of perfectionist, idealist normative moral or political scheme, Heilbroner cannot quite say good bye to his utopia. He notes that there are two ways it may remain something of a handy concept. First, it may leave us piecemeal social

objectives to strive for—but these have always come in the context of essentially capitalist economics systems. Secondly, it may reemerge as the adjunct of the ecological movement. As Heilbroner puts it,

[If] there is any single problem that will have to be faced by any socioeconomic order over the coming decades it is the problem of making our economic peace with the demands of the environment. Making that peace means insuring that the vital processes of material provisioning do not contaminate the green-blue film on which life itself depends. This imperative need not affect all social formations, but none so profoundly as capitalism.[19]

What is one to say about this new fear, a new problem allegedly too complicated for free men and women to handle? Has Heilbroner not heard of the "tragedy of the commons" so that he could imagine the environmental difficulties that face the collectivist social system? Here is how Heilbroner issues the "new" warning:

It is, perhaps, possible that some of the institutions of capitalism—markets, dual realms of power, even private ownership of some kind of production—may be adapted to that new state of ecological vigilance, but, if so, they must be monitored, regulated, and contained to such a degree that it would be difficult to call the final social order capitalism.[20]

This somewhat novel but essentially old fashioned skepticism about free market capitalism needs to be addressed.

My first response is that there is no justification for any of this distrust of "the market," as opposed to trusting some scientific bureaucracy that is to do the monitoring, regulating, and containing Heilbroner and so many other champions of regimentation are calling for. Such distrust tends to arise from comparing the market system to some ideal and static construct developed in the mind of a theorist. But since human community life is dynamic, the most we can hope for in improving it is the establishment of certain basic principles of law, or a constitution, that will keep the dynamics of the community within certain bounds.[21]

Accordingly, put plainly, if men and women acting in the market place, guided by the rule of law based on their natural individual rights to life, liberty and property, were incapable of standing up to the ecological challenges Heilbroner and many others in the environmentalist movement have in mind, there is no reasonable doubt that those could not be met better by some new statist means.[22] Why should ecologically minded bureaucrats be better motivated, more competent, and more virtuous than those motivated by a concern for the hungry, the unjustly treated, the poor, the artistically deprived, the uneducated masses or the workers of the world? There is no reason to attribute to the members of any ecological politburo or central committee more noble characteristics than to the rest of those individuals who have made a try at coercing people into good behavior throughout human history.

As already suggested, lamentations about capitalism tend to rest on a kind of idealism that is ill suited to the formation of pubic policy for a dynamic human community. One might be able to imagine—in a Platonic sort of fashion, vis-a-vis the ideal state—a perfectly functioning ecological order. It is doubtful that even this much is possible. It is another thing entirely to attempt to implement policies that will produce such an idealized order in the actual world. What we actually face in our various human communities is a choice between what we may call live options, e.g., capitalism, socialism, the welfare state, fascism, etc. No ideal system is a contender and it is folly to compare any of the live options to such an ideal. In the actual contest, in turn, it seems the capitalist alternative is superior for reasons already alluded to and discussed elsewhere.[23] Yet it will help to sketch some central aspects of that alternative.

In the first place, if human beings have the right to private property, not to mention their lives and liberty, a just legal system would prohibit any kind of dumping by one person on another, including all environmental assaults such as transmitting toxic substances unto unsuspecting victims, polluting public realms, seepage, etc. Beyond a harmless level of waste disposal, no pollution would be legal, no matter whether jobs or the achievement of any other laudable purpose depended on it. Just as slavery may not be practiced regardless of how it might

facilitate certain valued objectives, just as rape is impermissible no matter how desperate one may be, so too may pollution and other forms of environmental offenses not be carried out regardless of the various possible valued objectives the pursuit of which would generate it. To put the matter into the language of the economists, if one cannot internalize the negative externalities associated with some production or transportation process, one will simply have to stop it.

There are, of course, technical problems associated with measuring how much waste disposal constitutes reaching the threshold. But this is in principle no different from determining how much of some food substance or medicine constitutes poison. Just as the criminal law employs forensic science to determine who is guilty of what degree of homicide, so various branches of environmental science would be utilized so as to establish culpability in environmental crime.

The worry that industrial civilization would be slowed to a dead halt by the above approach is unfounded. Alternative technologies to those that involve environmental assault will certainly emerge and are already on the way. Past errors, of course, cannot be fully remedied, yet some of what has been wrought upon us by way of the highly subsidized internal combustion engine could be mitigated by imposing full cost on transportation, not permitting owners of vehicles to dump on those whose permission they do not have or cannot obtain.

In general, then, clearly the anthropocentric—i.e., individual rights—oriented environmental ethics and law is more radical and just than anything offered within standard environmental ethics literature.

If free men and women will not manage the environment, nor will anyone else. In any case, more optimism about the capacity of free citizens to deal with this issue is warranted when we examine just what are the sources of our ecological troubles. Given, especially, the fact of collectivism's far greater mismanagement of the environment than that of the mixed economies we loosely label capitalist, there is already some suggestion implicit here about what the problem comes to, namely, too little free market capitalism. Given the comparatively worse environmental situation evident in political economies that rely on collective ownership and management, and given the natural individualism of human life, free markets appear to be more suited to solving the tragedy of the commons. What Heilbroner and friends fail to realize is that the environmental problems most people are concerned about are due to the tragedy of the commons, not due to the privatization of resources and the implementation of the principles that prohibit dumping and other kinds of trespassing. With more attention to protecting individual rights to life, liberty, and property, solutions to our problems are more likely, period.

The best defense of the free market approach to environmentalism in matters of public policy beings with the realization that it is the nature of human beings to be essentially individual. This can be put alternatively by saying that the individual rights approach is most natural—it most readily accommodates nature and, therefore, ecology.

If there is a crisis here, it amounts to the history of human action that has been out of line with ecological well being, health, flourishing. But how do we know what kinds of human action might have been more or less conducive to ecological well-being? It will not be to speculate on some ideal configuration of the living world, apart from considering what is best for human individuals. There simply is no standard of a right pattern to which the world should be made to conform—it is a dynamic system of living entities, with no final pattern discernible in it to which the current configuration should be adjusted. Indeed, if there is something we have learned about environmental wisdom, it is that the environment's health, so to speak, emerges spontaneously, reflecting something of a chaotic development, one that is not predictable.[24]

We need first of all to know about human nature—what it is that human beings are and what this implies for their conduct within the natural world. If, as the natural rights (classical liberal) tradition invoked here would have it, human beings are individuals with basic rights to life, liberty and property, that also implies, very generally at first, that this is how they are best fitted within the natural world, within the

rest of nature. Environmentalism is most effectively promoted if we trust free men and women with the task of choosing the best policies bearing on the same, not relying on governments to determine the most suitable relationship various individuals and organizations should cultivate with the rest of nature. Not that this will serve to avoid all failings vis-a-vis this area of human concern—anymore than leaving human beings free to choose in other spheres creates utopia. Nevertheless, when we consider that governments are administered by persons with no greater claim to virtue and wisdom than others can make, and if we also consider that officials of the government make their mistakes, when they do, without the chance of full accountability and with the benefit of the legal use of force, it is not at all unreasonable to suppose that when problems need solutions, governments are not going to be the most useful for this purpose unless their particular means of dealing with persons, force, is required.

LAST REFLECTIONS

The fact is that with human nature a problem arose in nature that had not been there before— basic choices had to be confronted, which other animals do not have to confront. The question "How should I live?" faces each human being but not other living things, not to mention inanimate nature. And that is what makes it unavoidable for human beings to dwell on moral issues as well as to see other human beings as having the same problem to solve, the same question to dwell on. For this reason we are very different from other living beings, plants and animals—we also do terrible, horrible, awful things to each other as well as to the rest of nature, but we can also do much, much better and achieve incredible feats nothing else in nature can come close to.

Yet, merely because we do have a moral dimension in our lives, it does not follow that we must agonize about everything in nature, as if we had the moral capacity to remake the entire universe.

Indeed, then, the moral life is the exclusive province of human beings, so far as we can tell now. Other, lower—i.e., less important or valuable—animals simply cannot be accorded—because they have no requirement for—the kind of treatment that such a moral life demands, namely, respect for and protection of basic rights.

As such it is to human life we must, rationally considered, attribute the greatest value in the universe. And since human life is essentially individual, not collective—which does not preclude its vital social yet largely voluntary dimension—the individual rights approach, that protects each person as a moral agent and provides for him or her a sphere of privacy or exclusive jurisdiction, is the most sensible environmentalist public policy.

Notes

1. In this paper no distinction will be made between "important" and "valuable." In some other context the difference between the meanings of these two terms may be significant but it is not for present purposes. Both terms are used to mean taking a positive difference to something or someone—e.g., the sun is important for the plant or the house is one of John's valuable possessions.

2. "Individual" does not have to translate to "atomistic, isolated, anti-social, asocial." Such a translation begs the question as to what kind of individual we are faced with. For a detailed discussion of the type of individual a human being is, see Tibor R. Machan, *Capitalism and Individualism, Reframing the Argument for the Free Society* (New York: St. Martin's Press, 1990).

   A different sort of defense of anthropocentrism is advanced in Thomas Palmer, "The Case for Human Beings," *The Atlantic,* vol. 269 (1992), pp. 83–88. Palmer notes that "in fact Homo sapiens is the crown of creation, if by creation we mean the explosion of earthly vitality and particularity long ago ignited by a weak solution of amino acids mixing in sunlit waters" (p. 88). Unfortunately, Palmer does not emphasize enough this feature of particularity in his defense and, thus, ignores the bulk of the important political and policy issues that arise in environmentalism.

3. Here a point needs to be raised concerning the perfectly sensible Aristotelian understanding of human beings as essentially social animals. Ecologists tend to stress this point often when individualism is presented to them as a sociopolitical alternative to their widely embraced collectivism (whether in a socialist, welfare statist, or communitarian version).

   Being essentially an individual does not preclude having also an essential social dimension to one's life. Briefly, although one makes for oneself a given, particular but human life, given that such a life has much to benefit from social involvement, it could well be "in one's nature" to be social as well as a matter of one's

individual decision to embark on a rich social, community and political life. It may well be one's moral responsibility as an individual to connect with other human beings—unless, of course, the available others are real dangers to one's life, which in the case of human beings is a clear possibility.

4. The source of this remark has eluded me since originally located in one of Comte's works.

5. There are many who believe that when one construes human beings as essentially individual, this means that they are "individual through and through." Yet something that is essentially individual—that is, the nature of which is such that its individuality cannot be omitted from understanding it—can also be elaborately involved with community, society, family, and other groups of individuals. It is, furthermore, an exaggeration indeed to say that, to cite an anonymous commentator on an earlier version of this paper, "life as studied by the life sciences is thoroughly social in nature with individual organisms embedded in interconnected supporting webs on which they are entirely dependent." Apart from the fact that being dependent on "supporting webs" does not render some being "thoroughly social"—so that, for example, the mere dependence of a Rembrandt, List, Chekhov or Keats on innumerable social webs (economic, manufacturing, political, familiar, artistic, etc.) by no means deprives him of the capacity to inject into his art a decisive individuality. See, for more on this, Conway Zirkle, "Some Biological Aspects of Individualism," in F. Morley, ed., *Essays on Individualism* (Indianapolis, IN: Liberty Press, 1977), pp. 53–86. See, also, Theodosus Dobzhansky, *The Biological Basis of Human Freedom* (New York: Columbia University Press, 1956). If, as has been argued by Roger W. Sperry, *Science and Moral Priority* (New York: Columbia University Press, 1983), human beings have a naturally grounded capacity for self-determination—i.e., free will—it makes eminently good sense that they should become individuated depending on the extent and intensity of their choice to exercise their will. Their choices are then indeed their own, sovereign choices, not explainable without remainder by other aspects of their nature, including their social entanglements.

6. Stephen R. L. Clark, *The Moral Status of Animals* (Oxford, England: Clarendon Press, 1977), p. 13. "Uniquely important" means that the being in question is unique in its being important, whereas saying "most important or valuable" does not preclude the value of other beings not just in their relationship to what is uniquely important—i.e., derivatively—but to themselves, in terms of their own nature.

7. It might be argued that this point assumes anthropocentrism but it does not—we are not just talking about human beings creating values for themselves but values as such. For example, human beings breed animals and plants, they create provisions for the same, they protect or enhance the lives of non-human beings. They create values more abundantly than does anything else, although, of course, they also destroy values aplenty.

8. It might be objected here that this line of argumentation assumes away the troublesome "is/ought" gap, moving illegitimately from fact to value, etc. It isn't possible to deal with the matter here but see Tibor R. Machan, *Individuals and Their Rights* (LaSalle, IL: Open Court Publ., Co., Inc., 1989), Chapter 2. The central point is that value is a type of fact attending to living beings for whom the alternative between flourishing and perishing is natural. What has value contributes to flourishing and what disvalue contributes to perishing, to put it into very general terms. I draw here on an idea developed in Ayn Rand, "The Objectivist Ethics," *The Virtue of Selfishness, A New Concept of Egoism* (New York: New American Library, 1961). See also, Karl Popper, *Unending Quest* (Glasgow: Fontana/Collins, 1974), p. 194: "I think that values enter the world with life; and if there is life without consciousness; (as I think there may well be, even in animals and man, for there appears to be such a thing as dreamless sleep) then, I suggest, there will also be objective values, even without consciousness."

9. The case for "altruism" in the animal world is widely debated but by no means settled. I rest my own reflections on this on the view that whatever version of "altruism" may be accepted, in the last analysis it is individual living beings that would benefit from it, aside from their species. For more on this, see James G. Lennox, "Philosophy of Biology," in Members of the Department of History and Philosophy of Science, University of Pittsburgh, *Introduction to the Philosophy of Science* (Englewood Cliffs, NJ: Prentice-Hall, 1992), p. 295.

10. Tibor R. Machan, *Human Rights and Human Liberties* (Chicago, IL: Nelson-Hall Co., 1975) and *Individuals and Their Rights*. See also, Tibor R. Machan, "A Reconsideration of Natural Rights Theory," *American Philosophical Quarterly,* vol. 17 (1982), pp. 61–72, and "Towards a Theory of Natural Individual Human Rights," *New Scholasticism,* vol. 61 (Winter 1987), pp. 33–78, "Are Human Rights Real?" *Review Journal of Philosophy and Social Science,* vol. 13 (1988), pp. 1–22, and "Natural Rights Liberalism," *Philosophy and Theology,* vol. 4 (1990), pp. 253–65.

11. See, for more, Garrett Hardin, "Tragedy of the Commons," *Science,* vol. 162 (1968), pp. 1243–48. Hardin's point had been advanced, much earlier, by Aristotle, with more explicitly moral punch. The point is, of course, that unless some sphere of personal jurisdiction is identified, moral responsibility—in the case of Aristotle and Hardin, vis-a-vis the consumption of resources—will be obscured, leading to confusion and indeterminacy.

12. A good example of the view on plants is Christopher Stone's, *Should Trees Have Standing* (Palo Alto, CA: William Kaufmann, 1975). The animal rights case is presented most thoroughly by Tom Regan, *The Case for Animal Rights* (Berkeley, CA: University of California Press, 1984).

Not all anti-anthropocentrists are animal rights advocates but most probably because they eschew the concept of rights altogether, not because they would draw a fundamental (morally and politically significant) distinction between other animals and human beings.

Some of the points discussed in the next several paragraphs form portions of previously published essays in *Public Affairs Quarterly* and *Journal des Economists et des Estudes Humaines* concerned with whether animal rights exists and the handling of pollution under capitalism, respectively.

13. For more on this, see Mortimer Adler, *The Differences of Man and the Difference it Makes* (New York: World Publishing Co., 1968), and, *op. cit.,* Machan, *Individuals and their Rights.* The former work concerns the issue of whether the human species is fundamentally distinct, the latter whether talk about "the nature of X" can have an objective foundation or must be nominal.

14. Aristotle, *Politics,* Bk.II, Ch. 3; 1262a30–40.

15. Ludwig von Mises, *Socialism,* 2nd ed. (New Haven: Yale University Press, 1951).

16. *Op cit.,* Hardin, "The Tragedy of the Commons."

17. I should note here that some of these are still in dispute and it would be rash to treat them as proven. Nevertheless, it is also fair to say that arguments made against the possibility of rational allocation of economic resources, the prudent use of the commons, etc., are widely admitted to be telling. This is certainly not the place where we could decided the matter once and for all. I will assume, however, that enough trouble faces collectivist political systems, at least as far as fostering human productivity is concerned, that drastic revisions would need to be made in order for them to become feasible. For example, the recent effort to develop what is called a market socialism has run into serious theoretical difficulties. See, e.g., David Schweickard, *Capitalism or Worker Control* (New York: Preager, 1980), Julian Le Grand and Saul Estrin, eds., *Market Socialism* (New York: Clarendon Press, 1989); Ian Forbes, *Market Socialism* (London: Fabian Society, 1986); David Miller, Market, *State, and Community: Theoretical Foundations of Market Socialism* (New York: Oxford University Press, 1989); James A. Yunker, *Socialism Revised and Modernized: The Case for Pragmatic Market Socialism* (New York: Preager, 1992); Anders Aslund, *Market Socialism or the Restoration of Capitalism?* (New York: Cambridge University Press, 1992). See, however, Anthony De Jasay, *Market Socialism: A Scrutiny 'This Square Circle'* (London: Institute of Economic Affairs, 1990), N. Scott Arnold, *The Political Philosophy of Market Socialism* (London: Oxford University Press, forthcoming).

18. Robert Heilbroner, "After Communism," *The New Yorker,* September 10, 1990, p. 92.

19. Ibid., p. 99.

20. Ibid., p. 100.

21. In other words, a feasible political system must focus on prohibitions, enforced by officers of the law, rather than on outcomes. For a good discussion of this point—contrasting end-state and procedural features of a political order—see Robert Nozick, *Anarchy, State, and Utopia* (New York: Basic Books, 1974).

22. For a more detailed discussion of the natural rights libertarian approach to environmental problems, see Tibor R. Machan, "Pollution and Political Theory," in T. Regan, ed., *Earthbound* (New York: Random House, 1984). A more developed versions of the argument showing that the dumping of externalities is to be treated as a crime (assault, trespassing, etc.) may be found in Tibor R. Machan, *Private Rights, Public Illusions* (New Brunswick, NJ: Transaction Books. 1993).

The essence of this approach is that if one is unable to conduct one's activities—productive, recreational, etc.—in a fashion that does not impose uninvited burdens on third parties—i.e., to use the economist's jargon, if one is unable to internalize one's negative externalities—one simply may not carry forth with them. Full cost of such production must lie with the agent and no uninvited "free" rider may be taken.

In contrast to standard approaches to solving environmental problems caused by human beings, namely, via the establishment of government regulatory agencies (which are beset with all the "public choice" and "tragedy of the commons" problems, especially in democratic welfare states), here the issue is one of criminal law and dumpers, just as trespassers, assaulters, rapists, arsonists, and the like, would be prosecuted. If someone with AIDS negligently or intentionally infects another who has not had the chance to exercise free choice in the matter, the perpetrator is prosecuted under the criminal law. Anyone with a serious contagious disease exposing others to his or her illness would suffer the same fate. There is no government regulation—rationing involved here, only prohibition and conviction of violators.

No doubt, complexities attend all of this, yet there seems to be nothing extraordinarily difficult about determination of threshold levels and prosecution of those who dump once the threshold has been reached. The individual rights approach is simply stricter than the utilitarian, social (risk) cost-benefit approach, yet the same science and technology can be employed in administering both systems.

23. See *op. cit.*, Machan, *Individuals and Their Rights*. See, also, Tibor Machan, *Private Rights, Public Illusions* (New Brunswick, NJ: Transaction Books, forthcoming).

24. See, Stephen Jay Gould, *Wonderful Life* (New York: W. W. Norton, 1989).

Thomas Dyllick

Ecological Marketing Strategy for Toni Yogurts in Switzerland

I. Ecological Problems and Company Responsibility

It was the unsettling message of the first report to the Club of Rome, "The limits to growth," that exponential growth of the population and its consumption would inevitably lead to a depletion of natural resources and a degradation of the environment, that convinced Walter Regez, a practicing Christian who should become Toni's CEO a few years later, of his company's ecological responsibility. In 1972 he gave orders to look into ways in which his

From Thomas Dyllick, "Ecological Marketing Stategy for Toni Yogurts in Switzerland," *Journal of Business Ethics*, Vol. 8, No. 8, 1989. Reprinted by permission of Kluwer Academic Publishers.

organization, a milk producers' cooperative in the Zurich area, could contribute in its own domain to solve the ecological problems of the time. Their interest was soon focused on the question of packaging for their yogurt products. They had followed the general trend in the industry in the fifties, by substituting the formerly used heavy glass containers with the cheaper plastic cups, thereby contributing to the coming of a wasteful "throw-away-society". Towards the end of 1972, he demanded to prepare for the reintroduction of returnable glass containers for Toni's yogurt products. Looking back some years later, he summarized his motives for this decision in the following way:

We tried to accept our responsibilities in our own domain of action, where we actually could contribute on our part. Growing amounts of waste, the depletion of natural resources, the degradation of the environment and energy shortages were reason enough to change our views and to include the ecology in our company's philosophy and strategy.[1]

One of his ambitions was to show that economic goals did not have to collide necessarily with ecological constraints, moreover, that there was a way to combine the company's goals with the preservation of the environment. The strategy developed, therefore, had to be *economically acceptable* on the one hand, but it had to be *ecologically reasonable* at the same time. Three ecological goals were stated explicitly:

1. Reducing the amount of resources and energy needed
2. Involving actively a number of external groups, mainly the consumers, the retailers, and the packaging industry
3. Strengthening and developing ecological consciousness among the population in general

What Toni had to experience in implementing this strategy was the fact, that good ecological intentions alone are not a sufficiently reliable basis to build its strategy upon. The inclusion of ecological goals into its marketing strategy needed an effective implementation at an operative level as well to make it a success, finally.

II. THE TONI COOPERATIVE AND THE SWISS YOGURT MARKET

The Toni cooperative is the largest of 13 milk producers' cooperatives serving the different regions of Switzerland. Together they form the Swiss Milk Producers' Association (SMPA), a national self-help organization founded in 1907 to represent the interests of the many small milk producers. Although the SMPA is organized in the form of a private corporation, it has been charged with a number of public duties: organizing for an orderly and cost-effective distribution of milk in the whole country, assuring the income of the milk producers, controlling milk production, assuring a high level of product quality by training the producers and providing them with technical assistance. Over and above these political functions, the SMPA plays a central role in the marketing of all milk products as well. They engage in market research, product development, product design, advertisement, sales promotion, and partly distribution as well. As one of their functions, they are offering to their members a national yogurt brand, Cristallina, to allow for a successful marketing of a nationally distributed brand. While product design, product development, and advertisement is done centrally by the SMPA, the actual production and distribution of the yogurt is done by the regional cooperatives. The national brand, offered by the SMPA, had come under increasing internal competition by private label brands, however, sold by some of the larger regional cooperatives, Toni being one of them. In general, the regional cooperatives are held not to intrude into the others' area, even though enforcement mechanisms are weak.

Toni, seated in Winterthur near Zurich, is the largest milk producers' cooperative within the SMPA. It operates in the central and eastern region of Switzerland, encompassing the Zurich metropolitan area, the most densely populated area of Switzerland. Its members include some 800 local milk and cheese cooperatives, adding up to some 11,000 individual milk producers, whose milk it is obliged to take. It operates 6 dairies in different locations and runs 120 local shops and milk businesses. It employs 1100 people, and processes 15% of the total Swiss milk production. Its total sales in 1986/87 reached 675 Million Swiss Franks. Yogurt amounts to somewhat more than 10% of total sales.

The sales of the swiss *yogurt market* in 1986 amount to 10% or 440 Million Franks, being the fifth largest segment within the total milk products market. At the same time it is a particular interesting segment within a stagnant and heavily regulated industry, showing the highest growth rate and above average returns. For this reason most competitors concentrate on the yogurt segment of the market. The market is heavily concentrated, typical of the Swiss food retail market in general. The leading brand, a private label yogurt of gigantic Migros, had 45% of the market in 1974 by itself, when Toni started its returnable glass project. The two leading brands had 65%, while Toni didn't have more than 1.8% of the market. Concentration is even heavier looking at the retail market. The two dominating food retailing chains in Switzerland, Migros and Coop, both being a cooperative themselves, captured more than 70% of the market. The yogurt market was characterized by very little product differentiation. Competition was focused on the price of the product alone.

III. THE ECOLOGICAL CONTEXT

Problems of resource scarcity, energy shortage, and deterioration of the natural environment have been on top of the political agendas since the mid seventies in most industrial nations. In particular this has been true for Switzerland. While the Swiss population has grown by 19% within the past 20 years, household waste has tripled within this period. The tremendous increase in per capita waste production is reflected in the corresponding figures: 150 kg p.c. in 1960 jumped to 375 kg p.c. in 1983. While this growth seemed to level off in the mid seventies, it resumed its continued growth and will be reaching 400 kg p.c. soon. Household waste makes up for some 30% of total waste production in Switzerland, a considerable part of it, around 40%, coming from packaging materials alone.

The use of plastic materials has been increasing enormously since the 1950s, thanks to its useful features and its wide applicability. Per capita plastic consumption increased from 47 to 75 kg between 1971 and 1983. Roughly one quarter is used for packaging purposes alone. Plastic materials are based on non-renewable oil and gas as their primary resources, and two thirds end up in the household waste. The recycling of plastic materials is only just beginning in Switzerland. Not more than 5% of total plastics consumption is being reused today, compared to more than 70% of total glass production. The rate of per capita glass recycling in Switzerland has reached more than 20 kg recently, a figure not reached anywhere else in the world.

IV. YOGURT PACKAGING

Four criteria are mainly used in evaluating different ways of yogurt packaging: protection (product safety, safety of the user and the environment, quality preservation, hygiene, durability), favorability (for transportation, storage,

handling, rationing), ecology (energy usage, resource usage, pollution, waste production), and cost (packaging material, packaging, transport, storage, recycling). These criteria demand very different qualities from any concrete form of packaging. Any single form of packaging will be better with respect to some criteria, and worse with respect to others. The mix of advantages on the one hand, and cost on the other hand is very different in the case of different forms of yogurt packaging, too.

Since the 1950s plastic cups sealed with aluminum foil have been introduced successively to become quickly the dominant form of yogurt packaging. Its advantages are economical: low price, little weight, and efficiency in transport because the empty cups can be stacked. Its disadvantages are mainly ecological: use of non-renewable fossil fuels and waste production. Glass packaging, on the contrary, has some ecological advantages: no waste, provided it is returned and reused, resource and energy savings, but it has qualitative advantages, as well. It preserves the quality of the contents better than any other form of packaging. Its disadvantages are mainly economical: price, cost of transportation, and storage of empty glasses. The difference in cost of packaging was at nearly 5 Rappen per piece, constituting some 7% of its retail price. The rate of glasses returned plays a critical role, reducing the difference in cost. But cost parity is impossible to be reached, even if 100% of glasses are returned. Plastic cups were used for nearly all yogurts sold in 1974, when Toni started its recyclable glass project. Only some yogurts were sold in non-recyclable glasses, accounting probably for as little as 1% of the market.

V. REALIZING THE PROJECT AND CRISIS IN 1981

The realization of Toni's project, named "Take care of the environment," started early in 1974 with a test run among Zürich's consumers. Toni proposed to them to decide themselves on the reintroduction. It announced to introduce Toni yogurt in a recyclable glass container and to invest half a million Franks for a washing machine, if the consumers would return more than 30% of the glasses sold within a 6-month-period. 30% was considered to be the economically justifiable lower boundary for the project. The experts polled were very negative about the outcome of this test. They estimated that no more than 5—10% of the glass containers would be returned, mainly due to the fact that they were to be sold without a deposit. When Toni announced that 40.2% of the glasses had been returned, the surprise was considerable. The press hailed the company for taking a bold step in the right direction, giving them free public relations. The consumer organizations and the ecologists supported the project as well. Toni subsequently installed a washing machine in its new Zürich dairy, where all the recycled glass containers were washed before being reused.

In the beginning, the Toni yogurt "in the glass" was sold mainly in the Zürich metropolitan area, while Toni's other dairies decided not to switch to the glass packaging right away. It was a high quality yogurt, sold at a premium price primarily by the small milk shops, the traditional retail outlet of the milk producers' cooperatives. The quality aspect of the yogurt dominated the sparsely used market communication, while the ecological aspect of the packaging was part of Toni's PR-campaign.

After modest initial increases, Toni's yogurt sales were stagnant the following years. In the beginning of 1981 the whole project was in a deep *crisis*. The signs of this crisis were:

- decreasing market share, while the total market was expanding.
- decreasing rates of glasses recycled: while they had reached 50% in the mid-seventies, by 1980 they were down to 35%, less than in 1974 when the project was started.
- increasing uneasiness on the part of the retailers, because of the cost of handling the returned glass containers.
- it was still mainly distributed by the small milk shops, while the dominating retail chains did not carry Toni because of the handling problems.
- a competitor, Emmi, another regional milk producers cooperative, had introduced a glass

container for their yogurts as well, although it was not recycled.
- the aluminum cap showed some leaking problems, as aluminum technically could not be fastened close enough to a glass surface.

But Toni was challenged on ecological grounds as well: a study on the comparative ecological advantage of the glass packaging, commissioned by Toni's competitors, came to the conclusion that the plastic cup was ecologically equivalent to the glass container, if not better, looking at the total energy balance over the whole life cycle of the packaging material. Although the study was criticized for looking at energy usage alone, not taking into consideration resource usage and waste production, it was a blow to Toni's ecological marketing strategy.

VI. MARKETING ACTIONS TAKEN TO COUNTER THE CRISIS AND SUCCESS IN THE MARKET

Toni was not willing to give up on the recyclable glass packaging. They studied the situation and came up with a number of *marketing actions* that were implemented after 1981. They included the following:

- the substitution of the aluminum cap by a reclosable plastic cap, that could be recycled and reused (for a different purpose) as well, improving the ecological motive of the packaging.
- development of a special crate for depositing the empty glass containers in front of the retailers' by the consumers themselves, freeing the retailers from any handling of the empty containers, while being a highly visible promotional device at the same time.
- a fresh and very original advertising campaign, based on a new corporate identity, that was to become a classic. It was based on the quality image of the yogurt, using the slogan: "Toni Yogurt in the glass, because for quality nothing is too good." The more valuable packaging material was suggested as tangible proof of the higher quality of the product.
- promotional discounts were offered to support the marketing offensive.

Sales took off rapidly beginning in 1982, after these actions had been implemented. The *economic results* are clearly demonstrating the great success of the actions taken. They consisted of:

- a tripling of sales within a three year period (1982-1985).
- a tripling of market share within a four year period (1981-1985), bringing Toni up to third place from fifth place.
- an expansion of the total market by 13%, 80% of which went to Toni.
- a number of retail chains was forced to include Toni in their assortments, due to consumer demand, allowing for a better national distribution.
- awards for their original and effective advertising campaign, which has become a classic. Its best pieces are sold today as a collector's item.
- a massive good will on part of the consumers in favor of the Toni brand and the whole organization.

VII. RESULTS CONCERNING THE ECOLOGY

But what are the results of Toni's marketing strategy concerning the ecology? With Toni's success in the market, its competitors were forced to react. What started then can be best characterized as an *ecological head-on race*, with Toni's competitors trying to match its ecological strategy. Hirz, the No. 4 in the market, that suffered from Toni's success, switched to a newly developed more ecological packaging, using 50% recycled paper. Emmi and Christallina were forced to introduce a recyclable glass packaging as well. Migros, the market leader, evaluated the decision to switch to a recyclable glass packaging, but decided negatively. Instead, it had improved on its plastic packaging steadily, reducing the amount of energy, resources, and waste by more than 40% between 1972 and 1982.

Toni reacted to this ecological head-on race with an increased ecological activity. It commissioned a new study in 1983, which pointed to the weight of the glass container and the rate of recycling as the critical factors in improving the

ecology of its glass packaging. Its *ecological actions,* implemented in 1985, therefore included:

- the development and introduction of a new glass container with 25% less weight, to save resources and energy.
- the foundation of a Toni foundation named "Take care of the environment" to spur recycling of their glass containers and ecological activity in society in general. They organized yearly glass returning campaigns, and promised to pay 1 Rappen to the foundation for every glass container returned. The foundation in turn financed a "Toni prize", which is awarded yearly to the organization found to have contributed most significantly to the betterment of the ecology. The board of the foundation includes, among other publicly known personalities, a former minister as its chairman.

The *ecological results* of these activities are considerable as well. They consist of:

- a more than doubling of the rate of recycled glasses, from 32% in 1981 up to an incredible 70% in 1985.
- a tripling the share of glass packaging in the whole 180 g market, bringing it to 17% in 1985 up from 6% in 1980.
- two awards for their recycling idea.
- the successful introduction of an ecological focus in marketing yogurts in Switzerland forced *all* competitors to improve on the ecology of their packaging as well, thereby reducing the amount of resources and energy wasted.
- the enhancement of the ecologic consciousness of the Swiss public in general, while offering a practical option to contribute personally to improving the ecological condition.

As a consequence of the ecological improvements of its glass packaging, Toni announced at a press conference in early 1985, without any doubt its packaging now could be considered the most ecological packaging available, even when looking at its energy balance alone. But as ecological performance, being a multi-dimensional construct, cannot be measured and judged un-ambiguously and as all its competitors are improving their ecological performance constantly as well, what has been aptly termed as a "war of beliefs" over the most ecological yogurt packaging will go on without any definite result. Trying to evaluate the ecological success of Toni's strategy, therefore, it will not be sufficient to judge Toni's comparative success on its own. Its real success has to be seen in the *collective ecological improvements* by the whole industry, brought about by Toni's bold move to integrate the ecology into its marketing strategy. By pushing ecologically ahead, it succeeded in shifting the main competitive focus of the industry from price to ecology. Toni, being only a minor competitor with some 2% market share in the mid-seventies, was able to change the strategic rules of the game to its own advantage, thereby causing all competitors to improve on the ecology of their packaging as well. This has to be considered the true ecological success of Toni's strategy.

LESSONS TO BE LEARNED

The *lessons* learned from the Toni case are telling in five respects, at least:

1. Value changes in society-at-large have changed the shape of consumer demand and created a new market for ecological goods and ecological arguments. This market offers new opportunities for active and creative competitors, that is only beginning to be realized. Within this domain of ecological values and demand it has become possible to reach economic objectives in terms of market share and ecological goals of society-at-large at the same time.
2. The Toni case, however, demonstrates the difficulties encountered in making an ecological marketing strategy work as well. Good ecological intentions alone are not sufficient. It takes stamina and all the marketing expertise used for any other commercial good as well to make it a successful innovation. In the Toni case it needed 8 years of collective learning and adaptation before sales finally took off.
3. Toni developed a new type of strategy particularly adequate for its ecological focus: a *collective* marketing strategy that includes external groups like consumers, retailers, packaging manufacturers, consumer organizations, ecological organizations, and the media.
4. It shows, too, how the competitive focus of a consumer product can be shifted successfully to ecology without any state intervention, if a committed competitor should decide to go ahead. The result may be, as in the Toni case, ecological improvements of all competitors, to the benefit of society.
5. Marketing thinking alone may be too weak as a motivation for embarking on an ecological strategy, although in the Toni case the strategy followed could be explained *ex post facto* as nothing else but good long term marketing thinking. What it needs to develop an ecological marketing strategy early enough, and what it needs to pull it through all the difficulties in realizing and adapting the strategy over time is a commitment to ecological goals as well. And this is where economic thinking does not reach far enough. For this it needs an ethical commitment as well.[2]

Notes

1. Walter Regez, Die Rolle unternehmerischen Handelns beim Schutz der Umwelt, Speach given at Toni's press conference on February 5, 1985, in Zürich, mim., p. 3.
2. For more cases and a thorough conceptual treatment of the topic "Managing the corporate external environment" see: Thomas Dyllick, Management der Umweltbeziehungen. Öffentliche Auseinandersetzungen als Herausforderung, Gabler Verlag, Wiesbaden 1989.

1. Taylor suggests that all living things have inherent value and that we should not elevate human interests above the interests of non-humans. Does a Human Immune Deficiency virus have inherent value? If so, is a doctor wrong in attempting to destroy it?
2. If a deer has inherent value, do we have any obligation to help it escape its predators? Why or why not? Suppose a deer will suffer less in dying from a hunter's well-placed bullet than from being pulled down by a hungry wolf. Is it more moral for the hunter to allow the deer to be killed by the wolf than to kill it himself?
3. Do you agree with Machan's claim that an anthropocentric ethics does not imply that non-human life has no value? Why or why not?
4. On what basis does Machan argue that human beings are the most valuable known things in nature?
5. Why does Dyllick suggest that marketing thinking alone may be too weak a motivation for embarking on an ecological strategy?
6. What does Dyllick mean when he suggests that to evaluate the ecological success of Toni's strategy is not sufficient to judge Toni's comparative success on its own?

CASE STUDY 18:1 SKI PANTS AND THE ENVIRONMENT[1]

Patagonia Ltd. is a successful outdoor-wear company with aspirations to conduct business in an environmentally responsible way. It recently undertook an environmental audit to investigate its impact on the environment. Among the concerns raised by the audit are that the use of polyester contributes to the depletion of petroleum, a non-renewable resource, that the use of cotton contributes to the use of highly toxic pesticides, and that the use of wool involves the destruction of fragile ecosystems by large flocks of sheep. As a preliminary response, Patagonia has decided to drop approximately one-third of its product line and seek out suppliers that grow only "organic" cotton. In the catalogue describing product lines, company president Yvon Chouinard tells potential customers that "Last fall, you had a choice of five ski pants, now you may choose between two. This is, of course, un-American, but two styles of ski pants are all that anyone needs." He goes on to state that his ultimate goal is to halt further growth of Patagonia.[2]

Reactions to Patagonia's policy vary widely. Many commentators praise Chouinard's decision. Tom Turner, a staff writer for the Sierra Club Legal Defense Fund, calls Chouinard's message glorious and sees the policy adopted by Patagonia as an important step in the voluntary restraint producers and consumers must adopt if we are to move towards environmentally benign technologies.[3] Hazel Henderson, an advisor to the Calvert Social Investment Fund, calls Chouinard a rare combination of clever entrepreneur and informed social conscience. In her view, he has anticipated the inevitable move to a more sustainable economy and is ahead of competitors in adapting Patagonia to the marketplace of the future. She suggests that "He may well end up with a jackpot: awards from social and environmental groups, a more desirable, higher-markup product line, plus a more manageable and highly valued company."[4] In a similar vein, J. H. Foegen, a professor of business, Frank Tsai, a financial consultant, and Alan Parker, director of shareholder relations and special projects at Ben & Jerry's Homemade Inc., suggest that Chouinard has anticipated the future in his emphasis on the limits to growth and applying environmentally benign technology.[5]

There are many other commentators, however, who feel that Patagonia's policy is misguided. Doug Bandow, a senior fellow at the Cato Institute, agrees with Chouinard's claim that consumers should not be spending simply for the sake of spending, but suggests that Chouinard errs in viewing pollution as a moral evil, rather than an unfortunate cost to be limited as far as possible. He suggests what is important is that we ensure that the benefits of processes that causes pollution, outweigh the costs of pollution they generate. He argues that in order for this to occur, it is important that a commodity, e.g., cotton, be priced to reflect its full costs of production. In his view, the problem is not economic growth, but political processes that skew the marketplace by artificially encouraging destructive and uneconomic growth.[6]

Jonathan Adler, an environmental policy analyst at the Competitive Enterprise Institute, comments that Chouinard confuses environmental impact with environmental damage. He notes, for example, that pesticide use has had environmental benefits as well as disadvantages. He argues that human action invariably impacts the environment, but that to equate environmental impact and environmental damage leads to the conclusion that primitive societies are preferable, even though they have dramatically shorter life expectancies and, in many respects, lower qualities of life. He raises the question of whether Chouinard's views imply not simply that we should limit the different styles of ski pants produced, but that we should not manufacture ski pants at all.[7]

Michael Silverstein, a writer and commentator on environmental economics, criticizes Chouinard on the basis that he tends to foster the view that we must choose between the environment and economic growth. This, Silverstein argues, has the consequence not of creating an ecologically sound marketplace, but of condemning underdeveloped nations to poverty in the name of saving nature. What is required, Silverstein suggests, is not that we attempt to restore nature to some pristine purity untouched by human intervention, but that we meld prolific consumption and economic well-being with environmental health.[8]

CASE STUDY QUESTIONS

1. Amongst other criticisms of Patagonia's policies, Bandow suggests that it is the quantity produced rather than the variety offered, that is the basic cause of pollution. On this basis, he suggests that Patagonia should be concentrating not on reducing the variety of styles offered, but on reducing sales? Do you agree? What would be the implications of taking such an approach?

2. What definition would you give of the term "pollution"? Adler wants to distinguish between environmental damage and environmental impact. Is this distinction a valid one? If so, how would you go about making it?

3. Chouinard suggests that "Third World resources are close to exhaustion." Is this consistent with the fact that the price of these resources has declined on world markets? Why or why not?

CASE 18:2 BANKRUPTCY, POLLUTION AND SOCIAL OBLIGATION[9]

William Kovacs was the chief executive officer and stockholder of Chem-Dyne Corporation which operated an industrial and hazardous waste disposal site in Hamilton, Ohio. In 1976 the state of Ohio sued Kovacs for maintaining a nuisance, polluting public waters, and causing fish kills. In 1979 Kovac settled the lawsuit by agreeing to pay $75,000 dollars to compensate the State for injury to wildlife, to remove specified wastes from the property, to bring no additional industrial wastes to the site, and to cause no further pollution of the air or public waters.

When Kovacs failed to comply with this agreement, the State obtained permission for a receiver to take possession of Kovacs' property and implement a clean-up of the Chem-Dyne site. The receiver took possession of the site, but had not completed a clean-up, when Kovacs filed a personal bankruptcy petition. In his petition he argued that since clean-up costs arose from a statutory violation rather than a contractual breach, these costs were dischargeable in bankruptcy and he had no obligation to pay them.

The State took the position that the costs of the clean-up were not dischargeable in bankruptcy and filed a complaint in Bankruptcy Court.

CASE STUDY QUESTIONS

1. Would Kovacs, even in the absence of a legal obligation to pay for the costs of a clean-up, nevertheless have a moral obligation to pay those costs?

2. Should the company which produces a pollution problem always be solely responsible for the costs of clean-up?

3. Suppose a problem of pollution is not detected, indeed could not have been detected or anticipated, until some years after the site has changed hands. Who should have the responsibility of paying for clean-up costs?

NOTES

1. This case study is based on J. Adler, D. Bandow, P. Barnes, J. Foegen, J. Frech, H. Henderson, S. Lydenberg, A. Parker, M. Silverstein, F. Tsai, T. Turner, D. Vogel, "Can Slower Growth Save the World," *Business and Society Review,* Spring 1993, No. 85, pp. 10–20.
2. Ibid. p. 10.
3. Ibid. p. 12.
4. Ibid. pp. 16, 17.
5. Ibid. pp. 17–19.
6. Ibid. pp. 14, 15.
7. Ibid. p. 15.
8. Ibid. p. 16.
9. Based on *Ohio v. Kovacs* as found in 105 Supreme Court Reporter 705 (1985)

FOR FURTHER READING

1. Terry Anderson and Donald Leal, *Free Market Environmentalism* (San Francisco: Westview Press, 1991).

2. W. Michael Hoffman, Robert Frederick and Edward S. Petry, Jr., (editors) *Business, Ethics and the Environment* (New York: Quorum Books, 1990).

3. Lisa Newton and Catherine Dillingham, *Watersheds* (Belmont, California: Wadsworth, 1994).

4. Tom Regan, editor, *Earthbound: New Introductory Essays in Environmental Ethics* (New York: Random House, 1984).

APPENDIX ONE
WRITING ARTICLE SUMMARIES AND CRITICAL ESSAYS

Writing Article Summaries

The aim of this text is not simply to introduce a body of material, but to engage the student and provoke critical analysis. The skills needed to detect, analyze, and respond to arguments are especially important for philosophers, but they will benefit all of us in our day-to-day activities. I have provided, therefore, some practical hints that will help beginners develop these skills.

One of the first things to keep in mind is to distinguish your own view from the view of the person you are reading. Put a little differently, it is very important to get clear what a person is saying before you begin to respond to her. Otherwise, you run the risk not only of misrepresenting her argument, but of responding to something quite different from what was actually said.

This seems straightforward, but it is easier said than done, even for professional philosophers. All of us read or listen with certain opinions and views already in place, and these often make it hard for us to be clear on what is actually said. Just as you might mistake a piece of cardboard on the highway for a dead rabbit if you were expecting to see a dead rabbit rather than a piece of cardboard, so it is easy to misconstrue a person's argument if you were expecting him to say something else.

It is essential, therefore, to examine a person's argument carefully, before you respond to it. A great aid to doing this is to construct an article summary. There are many ways in which this may be done, but all good summaries will have certain essential elements in common.

Most importantly, the summary should make clear the main claim or claims of the article. This is, in effect, the bottom line, the conclusion the writer wishes you to accept. Usually it can be stated very briefly in a sentence or two. This is especially true of well-written articles.

The summary should also make clear what arguments the author uses to support her main claim. It is important to discern the number and structure of the arguments given for accepting the conclusion, i.e., the main claim. This is not always easy, but it is essential. Remember that critical analysis cannot take place until we first become clear what the arguments we are critically analyzing are. As in the case of understanding the main claim, you will find that the more well-written an article is, the easier it is to discern the arguments used to establish its conclusion.

If an author has done his job well, he will also consider counter-arguments to his position and indicate how he answers or would go about answering these counter-arguments. You should include in your summary any objections the author considers and the replies he makes to them.

These are the essential elements of an article summary. It is sometimes useful to include a brief synopsis of the problem the author is considering or to provide some background information to set the context, but these are generally optional. I suggest, therefore, that the beginning student consider organizing her article summaries under four headings:

1. Main Claim (Thesis),
2. Supporting Arguments,
3. Objections Considered and
4. Author's Reply to Objections.

This is a suggestion only. It is often possible, for example, to consider an author's supporting arguments and replies to objections under one heading, since a successful counterargument is frequently also a supporting argument. The important thing to grasp is that you should seek to discern these four characteristic activities of stating a main claim, defending it by supporting arguments, considering objections, and replying to objections, in the articles you examine. To give some idea of how this works in practice, I have provided two sample summaries at the end of this appendix.

Writing Critical Essays

The same headings which provide a framework upon which to construct a summary can guide the writing of a critical essay. Although these headings will usually not appear in the essay, it is essential to state clearly your main claim, the arguments in support it, the objections to it, and your reply to objections. The essential difference between writing an article summary and a critical essay is that, whereas in an article summary you are simply aiming to be as accurate as possible in describing someone else's argument, in a critical essay you are formulating and developing an argument of your own. In practice, of course, the two processes intermingle, since in formulating and defending your own position you will generally find it necessary to respond to the views of others.

Several pitfalls need to be avoided by those beginning to write critical essays. One of the most common is making the main claim too broad. In a short paper where it is not possible to discuss all facets of a complex moral problem, it is usually better to focus on a specific claim than a very general one. For example, a student writing on the topic of abortion will probably write a better paper if she focuses on a specific issue such as whether abortion is justified in instances of rape, than if she tries to address all the problems associated with the issue of abortion. It is better to do a good job of discussing one issue than a mediocre job of discussing several. This is not to suggest that it is not important to develop a broad perspective and to examine whether what you say on one issue is consistent with what you say on another. Rather, it is to be realistic about what can and cannot be accomplished in a short essay.

Another pitfall to be avoided is underestimating the strength of the arguments of those with whom we disagree. It is important that you be fair in your treatment of objections to your position. Do not misrepresent counterarguments and do not select for discussion only the weakest arguments against your view. Your goal should be to refute the strongest arguments against your position, since if you can accomplish this you have nothing to worry about. Refuting only weak objections accomplishes little, since it is always open to your critic to reply that much bigger artillery can be brought to bear.

A useful way of accomplishing this is to think of yourself as possessing two hats: one is labelled "thesis," the other "antithesis." When wearing the "thesis" hat, you formulate and defend your main claim. When wearing the "antithesis" hat, you consider the ways in which an intelligent critic might attack your main claim and its supporting arguments. If, when you are writing a critical essay, you take time to exchange hats, it will prove a great aid to not underestimating the strength of objections to your position.

Another trap to be avoided is that of reinventing the wheel. Taking the time to do some reading on a topic to see what has already been said will help not only to clarify your position, but to avoid mistakes and dead-ends previously detected by others. It is also an aid to not underestimating objections to your position, since you become aware of some of the common arguments against your point of view. Do not, however, make the mistake of thinking that you must read everything that has ever been written on a topic before you can write a critical essay. All that is required is that you begin to get a grasp of the important arguments pro and con against the position you wish to defend.

It is important in this regard to give credit where credit is due. It is one thing to put into your own words an argument that has been used by another writer; it is quite another to appropriate it with little or no changes and characterize it as your own. It is important when you are using another author's words to indicate this to the reader. Failure to do so is called plagiarism and has very serious academic penalties if detected. A further reason why it is important to indicate when you are making use of another author's words is that it then becomes possible for our readers to determine whether you have quoted accurately and in context.

We learn by doing. You will find that as you write article summaries and critical essays their quality improves and that they are not so hard to produce. Writing them can never be a purely mechanical process, but it is a skill that can be fairly easily mastered if you pay attention to the basics I have described.

Sample Summaries

Article Summary:
Is Business Bluffing Ethical?
Albert Carr

Main Claim

The ethics of business are impersonal game ethics. No one should condemn business because its standards of right and wrong differ from the prevailing traditions of morality in society.

Arguments in Support of Main Claim

1. Just as the ethics of ordinary morality are suspended in games, so they are suspended in business. A business person is not, therefore, immoral if she does not follow ordinary morality in the course of doing business.

2. It is impossible to be successful in business if one applies the ethical standards of private life. Therefore, business people are entitled to conduct business on a different standard of morality.

Objection Considered

1. A person might have serious qualms about some of the seemingly immoral activities associated with business and not be able to reconcile the activities that take place in business with his personal beliefs.

Reply To Objection

1. The morality of business practices cannot be judged on the standards of private morality.

So long as a business practice is legal and produces a profit it is morally acceptable.

Article Summary:
Is There "No Such Thing As Business Ethics"?
Eric Beversluis

Main Claim

"If we define business ethics as the effort to decide how one should act, there necessarily is such a thing as business ethics."

Arguments in Support of Main Claim

1. One cannot escape the necessity of business ethics unless one opts for scepticism or egoism. Neither of these options seems defensible. We are left, therefore, with the necessity of business ethics. This means that we must recognize that one's right to well-being in business, as in other areas of life, must be limited by the recognition of others' right to well-being.

Objections Considered

1. Business is like a game and hence is not governed by moral concerns.

2. It is impossible to survive in business if one is ethical.

Replies To Objections

1. In response to objection #1, Beversluis argues that: (a) there are moral constraints operating even in the context of a game, (b) that business is in important ways disanalogous to a game, and (c) that if business is to be modelled on a game analogy it must fit the game as it is really played, not as it is ideally modelled in economists' abstractions.

2. In response to objection #2 Beversluis argues that a "right to economic survival" does not rule out business ethics. he does this by clarifying the notion of a right to survive in business and an examination of the implied premise that everyone survives by immoral behaviour.

Appendix Two
Latin Phrases and Their Meanings

a posteriori   behind, after

a priori   in advance, before

ad hoc   this specific thing (in context it often refers to an argument that is not well justified)

ab initio   from the beginning

amici curiae   friends of the court

bona fide   genuine

caveat emptor   let the buyer beware

ceteris paribus   everything else being equal

de jure   of justice, by law

de minimus   minimum

et cetera   and the rest

ex ante   from before (prior)

ex hypothesi   by hypothesis

ex nihilo   out of nothing

in foro interno   an internal forum or debate

ipso facto   therefore

iura fictus   derivative rights

mens rea   guilty mind (criminal purpose)

modus operandi   method of operation

per se   essentially

persona ficta   fictious (artificial) person

prima facie   initial presumption

qua   as

quid pro quo   something in return for something

res gestae   accomplishments or results

status quo   present order or standing

sub rosa   in secret; literally, "under the rose" (the rose was an emblem of secrecy)

suppressio veri   suppression of the truth

via media   middle way

vice versa   ton invert an order or relation